THE new London Property Guide '99/00

MITCHELL BEAZLEY

THE new London Property Guide '99/00

The **ONLY** guide you need to **buying** and **selling, renting** and **letting** homes in London

CARRIE SEGRAVE

The New London Property Guide '99/00

First published in 1999 by Mitchell Beazley,
an imprint of Octopus Publishing Group Ltd
2–4 Heron Quays, London, E14 4JP

ISBN 1 840 001 844

A CIP catalogue copy of this book is available from the British Library.

At Mitchell Beazley
Executive Editor: Rachael Stock
Executive Art Editor: Emma Boys
Project Editors: Claire Musters and Anna Nicholas
Editor: Kathy Steer
Designer: Russell Miller
Production: Paul Hammond
Cover design: Lisa Pettibone

Advertising sales: Logie Bradshaw Media Ltd, Strathallan House, Fernville Lane,
Midland Road, Hemel Hempstead, Herts, HP2 4Ls

Set in MetaPlus
Produced by Bath Press
Printed in Great Britain

This book is for Christopher Foulkes; for Eleanor, a Londoner; and in memory of John Brennan

Carrie Segrave

Carrie Segrave began writing on London's residential property scene in the early 1980s. She was founder-editor of the capital's first property newspaper and from 1988 wrote and edited the annual editions of the *London Property Guide*. During the 1980s and early 1990s she wrote on property for *The Financial Times*, *The Sunday Times Magazine* and *The Illustrated London News* among others and was UK Property Editor for a Japanese investment magazine.

Specialist writers

David Spittles is Property and Personal Finance writer for *The London Evening Standard* and *The Observer*. Liz Lightfoot is Education Correspondent for *The Daily Telegraph*. Susan Ware is an architect with a special interest in London homes and is a partner in a chartered practice. She teaches at the Bartlett, University College London.

Contributors

Elaine Allen, Mike Baess, Ken Ball, Victoria Barlow, Ebba Brooks, Sian Campbell, Nadia Cohen, Steve Cook, Diana Durant, Cara Frost, Kenny Grant, Simon Gwynn, Nick and Cynthia Hancock, Jermaine Ivey, Isabel Kay, Nicola Lampert, Matthew Lewin, Peter Lucas, Anna Macarthur, Andrew McGhie, Andy Mckee, Joyce McKimm, Wyn Middleton, Kate Morris, Richard Morris, Julia North, Tara Neill, Robert Parker, Donna Payne, Michelle Pickering, Gabrielle Shaw, Sean Sheehan, Barbara Sieverts, Caroline Simpson, Alex Smith, Nigel Spalding, Emmeline Stacey, Victoria Stagg-Eliott, Kathy Steer, Michèle Stevens, Rachael Stock, Nicola Tester, Carina Trimingham, Samantha Ward-Dutton, Helen Wilding, Chirs Wood, Eljay Yildirim.

Acknowledgments and thanks . . .

This book would in no way be possible without the enormous contribution made by a small army of London fanatics, prepared to tramp the streets (literally) on its behalf, and cross-examine town halls and the like: their names are above. In the course of their, and our, research well over 300 estate agents and other property people also gave up their time to help; for their local and professional expertise we are, as ever, deeply grateful. Too many, alas, to thank individually; but among those whose assistance was invaluable are Simon Agace, Linda Beaney, Tom Dennes, Diana Durant, Suzanne Goldklang, Howard Elston, Stefan Miles-Brown, Diana Rawell, Kevin Ryan, Jane Sandars, Sarah Shelley, Caroline Simpson, Jonathan Vandermolen, John Vaughan, Peter Wetherall, Hilary Wade, Seamus Wylie, Eljay Yildirim. It would not do to forget, either, the contributors to earlier editions of this Guide whose foot-slogging provided the foundations upon which this year's is built. Thanks, again, to the team at Mitchell Beazley, this year headed by Rachael Stock, with Claire Musters and Kathy Steer bearing up nobly under the whirling load of 600 closely-packed pages as they whizzed between us. Deepest thanks go once again to Anna Nicholas, last year's editor, who took up the reins once more for the vital closing stages. As I have said teamwork is everything on this book and it doesn't stop when editors, designers and proofreaders have done their bit. At the very end is a fast and expert indexer, Ann Parry, and last of all a brilliant production team who have the worst job of the lot – getting it over the out-of-house hurdles of printing, binding and distributing in a timespan that makes other UK publishers blink.   CS

Contents

Introduction

This book is an annual report on the progress of London as a place to live. It is also, if you like, a shareholders' report on the biggest investment most Londoners will ever make: their homes, their stake in the city.

The heart of the book is an area-by-area description of London's residential districts, from 'A' for Acton to 'W' for Wimbledon. These pages describe the streets and the types of homes of each neighbourhood. Each chapter has details of prices, transport, journey times, schools, boroughs . . . the facts you need to know to decide where in London you'd like to live.

The first part of the book gives you the analysis and the background information on how the market is working, and why. Here you will find major sections on matters that affect people's choice of where to live – transport plans, London's schools. You'll also find information on renting a home, buying and selling, mortgages, choosing and instructing an estate agent, planning and building regulations, and more. Cross-London guide charts show average buying prices and average rent levels.

So what is going to drive decisions in 1999? The steady climb back to favour of renting – as a way to pay for the roof over your head – and investing in homes let to others, is an even bigger theme this year than last. Will the impending flood of City money prove destabilizing? See *Renting and Investing* chapter.

This renewed investment is in part caused by the low-interest-rate environment we are (at time of writing) enjoying. But will it be all pleasure? London has spent 30 years getting used to high inflation and expensive loans. Nil inflation and cheap loans spell . . . no-one is quite sure what. Will prices rocket because we can afford to borrow more? Will they stagnate because, with nil inflation, if you take on an enormous mortgage it stays enormous? Inflation down-sizes debt. See *The Property Market in 1999*.

To make money from property, it matters all the more this year that you look in the right places. The key factor is transport. London's transport scene keeps changing – and with it the relationships of areas to the centre, and each other. This is the year to re-think your preconceptions. Take the north–south divide: which has (or will have) the quicker tube to the West End: north-bank Fulham or south-bank Surrey Docks? And which lies, in truth, north of the other? Which has the fastest rail route to Heathrow: Kilburn or Stamford Brook?

London used to have two hubs, the City and the West End. Now it has at least half a dozen more, with Canary Wharf (soon to have 40,000 workers) and Heathrow (twice that) heading the new list. Yet most transport, and most roads, point in to the old hubs. If you travel a lot, there are five airports to be got to, never mind Waterloo for the Eurostar. No working person can be sure where he or she might have to reach next. The options are there, with cunning use of maps and timetables, and more are coming: see our *London in 1999* chapter. My tip this year: buy on the Jubilee Line.

Do homes always make money? It may seem so in the light of the last three or four years. Many London homes are, of course, worth much more than in the height of the '80s boom, and it is those that make the headlines. But as we researched this edition, word came in of flats in Neasden still selling at their 1989 prices, of terraced houses in East and SE London that have yet to reward their owner's patience with that untaxed capital gain we all promised ourselves. A decade of mortgage interest payments have eroded the 'profits' of many another householder whose home may look, at a glance, to be worth more than he or she paid, but which in practice has been a poor investment.

That said, a home has this advantage over bonds and shares: you can live in it. And it will still be there after a slump, unlike many a company. Homes are not inevitably a wonderful investment, but – taking the very long view –they've been a steady one.

Some people have made magical sums investing in London homes, of course. But we seem to have forgotten, in the lingering afterglow of the 1980s boom, that this requires skill and cunning and hard work. People made money in the '80s – and in places in the '90s too – just by being lucky. In earlier decades the recipe was careful scouting of dodgy-looking neighbourhoods, cultivation of informants in estate agents' offices and other hot-beds of gossip, a keen eye for architecture, and hard work in an atmosphere of plaster dust and abuse from the neighbours. That way you got your hands on a Georgian cottage in Islington for £9,000, or a Chelsea mews house for not much more, or a warehouse in Wapping which you kept intact while the bulldozers moved in on the rest. Without inflation to give you a ride up the escalator, it's those prepared to put in the work, and do the research, who will (if their timing is right) come out ahead of the averages.

Alternatively, should you wish to avoid the plaster-dust and buy a sparkling new home, the brochures have never been so inviting. So, as you stand on your Juliet balcony (same size as her cap) of your skyline (penthouse, but they're thinking of shoving another on top) duplex (maisonette) or loft (at least a sticky-out galleried bit) in a vibrant, exciting area (close to a railway viaduct in Streatham) raise a glass to London, 1,956 years old this year – and to the ever-vivid imaginations of those spiritual heirs of Chaucer and Dickens, the developers' marketing departments.

CARRIE SEGRAVE
LONDON, FEBRUARY 1999

Note

How to use this book

The first part of the book contains the analysis and reference chapters: a guide to London's property market, how it works and the factors that will shape it in the coming year. Look here for information on the transport plans and their effects, the procedures of buying and selling property, the ins and outs of mortgages on offer today, the latest factors influencing the education system and the secondary schools performance tables . . . everything you need to know about moving house in London.

The core of this book is an alphabetical directory of London's main residential areas, from A for Acton to W for Wimbledon. Each area is profiled with descriptions of the neighbourhoods it is made up of.

To find out about an area look for it in the A–Z section, which starts on page 100. The initial letter of the area is printed in the margin of each page to help you find your way around. A list of the areas covered appears in the contents and on page 103.

There is also a full index of streets and neighbourhoods at the back of the book.

Maps

An overall area map of London is on page 12. Maps of individual areas are at the beginning of each area profile. A key to the symbols used in these is on page 100. See opposite for how to make best use of the maps and the information that accompanies them. These pages are for quick reference to the key facts about an area.

Prices

As it is an annual, this book is not intended to be used as a price guide. It does, however, gather together average prices for different sizes of property in each of the areas and provides a 'freeze-frame' picture taken at the start of the 1999 selling season. This gives you a basis for comparison throughout the year. For prices in a given area see the relevant area information section at the end of each chapter. See also the main price charts on pages 40–43, where you can search across London by price or by flat/house size.

Postal districts

These are listed on pages 14–17, each with a description of the areas it covers. Start with this list if you know only the postcode you are looking for. The postal districts are also listed in the information box alongside the maps at the start of each area profile.

Boroughs

Details about each of the Inner and Outer London boroughs are on pages 76–8. A map on page 77 shows where their boundaries fall, as does the area map on page 12.

Council tax

Detailed at the start of each area profile are the council tax rates of band D properties in the area. There can be a big difference from borough to borough. See pages 76–8 for a list of each borough's rate of council tax.

Future editions

This book is as accurate as the combined efforts of a large number of people could make it. We would be grateful to receive news from readers about changes to any areas and any other comments and (constructive!) criticism.

Area information

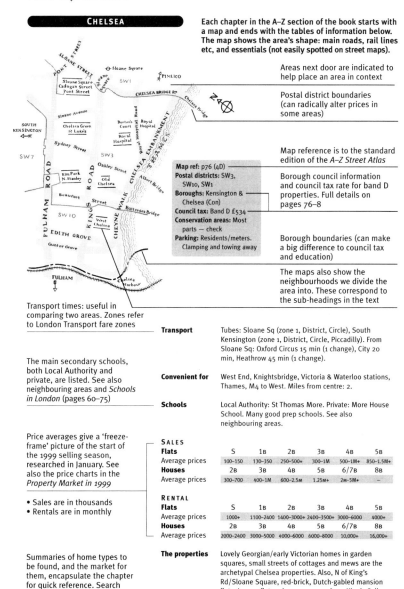

Each chapter in the A–Z section of the book starts with a map and ends with the tables of information below. The map shows the area's shape: main roads, rail lines etc, and essentials (not easily spotted on street maps).

Areas next door are indicated to help place an area in context

Postal district boundaries (can radically alter prices in some areas)

Map reference is to the standard edition of the *A–Z Street Atlas*

Borough council information and council tax rate for band D properties. Full details on pages 76–8

Borough boundaries (can make a big difference to council tax and education)

The maps also show the neighbourhoods we divide the area into. These correspond to the sub-headings in the text

Map ref: p76 (4D)
Postal districts: SW3, SW10, SW1
Boroughs: Kensington & Chelsea (Con)
Council tax: Band D £534
Conservation areas: Most parts — check
Parking: Residents/meters. Clamping and towing away

Transport times: useful in comparing two areas. Zones refer to London Transport fare zones

The main secondary schools, both Local Authority and private, are listed. See also neighbouring areas and *Schools in London* (pages 60–75)

Price averages give a 'freeze-frame' picture of the start of the 1999 selling season, researched in January. See also the price charts in the *Property Market in 1999*

- Sales are in thousands
- Rentals are in monthly

Summaries of home types to be found, and the market for them, encapsulate the chapter for quick reference. Search times can vary from days to months between boroughs – often the downfall of a sale

Transport   Tubes: Sloane Sq (zone 1, District, Circle), South Kensington (zone 1, District, Circle, Piccadilly). From Sloane Sq: Oxford Circus 15 min (1 change), City 20 min, Heathrow 45 min (1 change).

Convenient for   West End, Knightsbridge, Victoria & Waterloo stations, Thames, M4 to West. Miles from centre: 2.

Schools   Local Authority: St Thomas More. Private: More House School. Many good prep schools. See also neighbouring areas.

SALES						
Flats	S	1B	2B	3B	4B	5B
Average prices	100–150	130–350	250–500+	300–1M	500–1M+	850–1.5M+
Houses	2B	3B	4B	5B	6/7B	8B
Average prices	300–700	400–1M	600–2.5M	1.25M+	2M–5M+	–

RENTAL						
Flats	S	1B	2B	3B	4B	5B
Average prices	1000+	1100–2400	1400–3000+	2400–3500+	3000–6000	4000+
Houses	2B	3B	4B	5B	6/7B	8B
Average prices	2000–2400	3000–5000	4000–6000	6000–8000	10,000+	16,000+

The properties   Lovely Georgian/early Victorian homes in garden squares, small streets of cottages and mews are the archetypal Chelsea properties. Also, N of King's Rd/Sloane Square, red-brick, Dutch-gabled mansion flats. Luxury flats schemes may replace King's College, Duke of York's HQ and Barracks.

The market   Buyers are now mostly City-based and prosperous: the arty, up-market locals increasingly displaced by international bankers. Foreign buyers are Europeans and Americans rather than Far East. Chelsea's status and image ensure a lively market even in recessions, agents aver. Exceptional properties go well over the mainstream averages above. Local searches: 5–6 days.

Map of areas covered

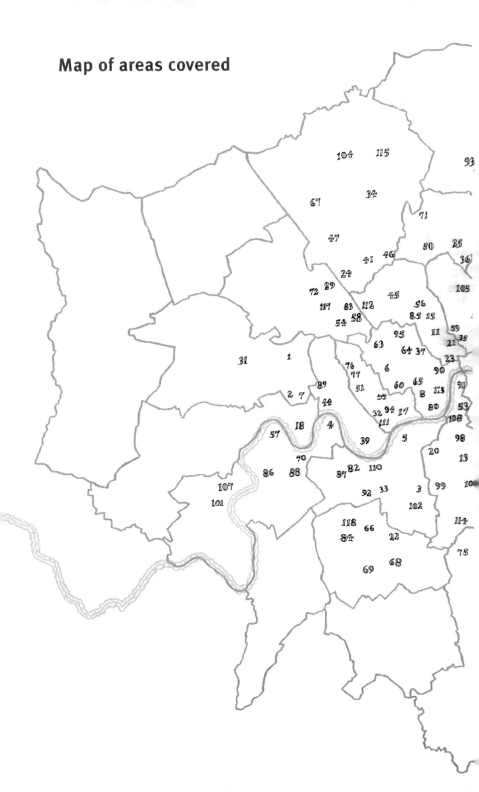

Key to areas

1	Acton	60	Knightsbridge
2	Acton Green	61	Lewisham
3	Balham	62	Leyton
4	Barnes	63	Maida Vale
5	Battersea	64	Marylebone
6	Bayswater	65	Mayfair
7	Bedford Park	66	Merton Park
8	Belgravia	67	Mill Hill
9	Bethnal Green	68	Mitcham
10	Blackheath	69	Morden
11	Bloomsbury	70	Mortlake
12	Bow	71	Muswell Hill
13	Brixton,	72	Neasden
14	Camberwell	73	New Cross
15	Camden Town	74	Newham
16	Catford	75	Norbury
17	Chelsea	76	North Kensington
18	Chiswick	77	Notting Hill
19	City and Fringes	78	Palmers Green
20	Clapham	79	Peckham
21	Clerkenwell	80	Pimlico
22	Colliers Wood	81	Poplar
23	Covent Garden	82	Putney
24	Cricklewood	83	Queen's Park
25	Crouch End	84	Raynes Park
26	Crystal Palace	85	Regents Park
27	Deptford	86	Richmond
28	Docklands	87	Roehampton
29	Dollis Hill	88	Sheen
30	Dulwich	89	Shepherd's Bush
31	Ealing	90	Soho
32	Earls Court	91	The South Bank
33	Earlsfield	92	Southfields
34	Finchley	93	Southgate
35	Finsbury	94	South Kensington
36	Finsbury Park	95	St John's Wood
37	Fitzrovia	96	Stepney
38	Forest Hill	97	Stoke Newington
39	Fulham	98	Stockwell
40	Gipsy Hill	99	Streatham
41	Golders Green	100	Stroud Green
42	Greenwich	101	Teddington
43	Hackney	102	Tooting
44	Hammersmith	103	Tottenham
45	Hampstead	104	Totteridge
46	Hampstead Garden Suburb	105	Tufnell Park
47	Hendon	106	Tulse Hill
48	Herne Hill	107	Twickenham
49	Highbury	108	Vauxhall
50	Highgate	109	Walthamstow
51	Holland Park	110	Wandsworth
52	Islington	111	West Brompton
53	Kennington	112	West Hampstead
54	Kensal Rise	113	Westminster
55	Kensington	114	West Norwood
56	Kentish Town	115	Whetstone
57	Kew	116	Whitechapel
58	Kilburn	117	Willesden
59	King's Cross	118	Wimbledon

Decoding the postcodes

London's postal districts are a matter first and foremost of Post Office convenience: they act as collection and delivery zones and are based around the location of sorting offices and the ease of routes. But those few letters and numbers also convey a powerful emotional and financial message. The difference between SW1 and SW2 is more than a digit: it is all of the gap between Belgravia and Brixton. Londoners absorb these subtleties with their mother's milk. But few natives appreciate quite how remote SE2 is, or that E4 is in Epping Forest while E14 is the upwardly mobile Isle of Dogs. And the borders can be arbitrary: some of Brixton is SW2, agreed – but so are the solidly respectable mansion blocks of Streatham Hill. Some postal districts are more logical than others. The Post Office says the whole system is quite clear: it's alphabetical. It is, and it is not. Use this list to check which areas a zone includes, and to spot anomalies. Estate agents quite frequently quote just postal districts in advertisements and by using this list you can get an idea if the area is one you want to look at. Follow the area names into the main A–Z in this book for a map, which shows post boundaries, and a profile of the area.

E1 The East End heartland, from the City E through Whitechapel and Stepney to Mile End. Also includes the smart warehouse conversions of riverside Wapping (see Docklands) and City fringe areas like Spitalfields and Shoreditch.
E2 North from E1, Bethnal Green and council flat-dominated Haggerston. Also a chunk of City fringe in Shoreditch.
E3 Bow, either side of the Mile End Rd in the East End.
E4 The NE fringe of London on the edge of Essex beyond the North Circular, including the suburban streets of Chingford Green and Highams Hill.
E5 The N part of Hackney Borough, with Lower and Upper Clapton and a good chunk of the Hackney Marshes. Also fringes of Stoke Newington.
E6 London's eastern edge, on the way to Southend: East Ham and the Docklands suburb of Beckton.
E7 Forest Gate, the S part of Wanstead. East of Stratford East.
E8 The W side of Hackney, on the border with Islington, including the area around London Fields and the SE corner of Stoke Newington.
E9 The E part of Hackney, across the Lea Valley and the Hackney Marshes. Includes Victoria Park and Homerton.
E10 Most of Leyton, E of the Hackney Marshes from Hackney. Includes a corner of Walthamstow.

E11 Centres around Wanstead and Snaresbrook; residential suburbs where the M11 meets the North Circular.
E12 Manor Park and Little Ilford on the E fringe of the London postal district: E from here is Essex, Ilford in particular.
E13 West Ham and Plaistow on the Barking Rd E from the East End.
E14 Diverse area including the Isle of Dogs, centre of the Docklands and site of Canary Wharf and other office and homes schemes, and housing in Limehouse and Poplar and the Limehouse riverside.
E15 Stratford, the metropolis of East London, and surrounding areas E of the Lea Valley.
E16 Contains the vast Royal Docks area, next on the hit-list for Docklands regeneration, as well as old-established industry and housing in riverside Silvertown and Canning Town.
E17 Walthamstow and Higham Hill in NE London.
E18 South Woodford on the suburban fringes of Epping Forest.

EC1 All four City postcodes are ECs. EC1 is the biggest, covering the relatively less prosperous tract from St Paul's N to the City Rd, and including large parts of Finsbury and all of Clerkenwell.
EC2 The money heart of the City, from the Bank of England N to Broad St. Includes the Barbican.

EC3 The E side of the City, including the Tower and the Lloyds building.

EC4 The riverside slice, including Fleet St, the Temple, Cannon St and Blackfriars.

N1 The classic Islington postcode, extending S from Highbury and Islington tube to the Angel. Includes Hoxton and De Beauvoir to the E, Barnsbury and King's Cross to the W.

N2 By contrast, the leafy streets and semis of East Finchley and Fortis Green in London's North West. Also the 'Millionaire's Row', Bishops Avenue, and the 'new' part of Hampstead Garden Suburb.

N3 Further out still, the next suburb NW covering most of Finchley.

N4 Crouch End, Stroud Green, Finsbury Park and Harringay, a widely contrasting chunk of North London.

N5 A small district covering Highbury, to the N of Islington. In Islington borough, so estate agents like to call it so.

N6 The centre of Highgate, Dartmouth Park to its S, some woods and a few streets of Fortis Green to the N.

N7 Where the Seven Sisters Rd crosses the Holloway Rd is the centre, with parts of Tufnell Park and a corner of Highbury.

N8 Hornsey, most of the 'ladder' district of Harringay, the N side of Crouch End.

N9 The N slice of Edmonton, especially Lower Edmonton.

N10 Most of Muswell Hill.

N11 Friern Barnet, New Southgate and Bounds Green: residential districts straddling the North Circular Rd.

N12 North Finchley and Woodside Park.

N13 Palmers Green, where the North Circular crosses Green Lanes due N of London.

N14 Southgate, on the northern edge of London on the Hertfordshire border.

N15 The southern part of Tottenham, at the NE end of the Seven Sisters Rd.

N16 Stoke Newington and the S part of Stamford Hill.

N17 Most of Tottenham.

N18 A slice along the North Circular N of Tottenham, including Edmonton and Upper Edmonton.

N19 Archway, from the fringes of Highgate and Crouch End in the N down to Tufnell Park.

N20 The semi-rural, prosperous and pony-infested Totteridge, Oakleigh Park and Whetstone, N of Finchley and S of Barnet.

N21 Winchmore Hill and Grange Park, suburbia plus a lot of golf courses on the fringe of North London.

N22 Wood Green, Alexandra Palace, the E side of Muswell Hill, Noel Park and the W edge of Tottenham.

NW1 One of London's most diverse districts, with the Nash villas of Regent's Park and the near-slums of Camden Town sharing the same postcode. Starts in the S at the Marylebone Rd, takes in part of Lisson Grove in the W, the edge of Kentish Town in the NE, all of Camden Town and Primrose Hill.

NW2 One of the less helpful postcodes. Covers Cricklewood, Childs Hill, Dollis Hill, an arbitrary slice of Willesden and a bit of Brondesbury.

NW3 The Hampstead postcode, and one with hardly an undesirable corner. Includes Belsize Park, part of Primrose Hill, the Finchley Rd – but not West Hampstead, which is NW6.

NW4 Hendon, from Brent Cross up along the M1 to the edge of Mill Hill.

NW5 Kentish Town, Gospel Oak and Tufnell Park, on the SE fringes of Hampstead and Highgate.

NW6 Once thought of as the Kilburn postcode – which it still is – but now associated more with West Hampstead. Also spreads W to include Queen's Park and Brondesbury Park.

NW7 Mill Hill and assorted golf courses, detached houses and green belt countryside out along the M1.

NW8 Clearly defined as St John's Wood, with only a few acres of council housing around Lisson Grove to lower the tone.

NW9 West Hendon, Colindale and Kingsbury, suburban areas NW of the Welsh Harp.

NW10 A large area extending W from Kensal Rise to the North Circular, taking in Neasden, Harlesden and parts of Willesden.

NW11 Golders Green and the older, smarter side of Hampstead Garden Suburb.

SE1 A big tract in the bend of the river opposite the City and Westminster: The South Bank. It extends from Vauxhall in the W to the Old Kent Rd in the E. Very varied: from the National Theatre to the riverside Tower Bridge quarter.

SE2 In Kent, really, E of Woolwich and even Plumstead, it comprises Abbey Wood and part of Thamesmead.

SE3 Blackheath, Blackheath Park, East Greenwich and Kidbrooke.

SE4 A small district S of New Cross and W of Lewisham, centred around Brockley.

SE5 Essentially Camberwell, though the SW end of Coldharbour Lane is better described as Brixton, the NW corner is in Kennington and the NE in Walworth.

SE6 Catford, and Bellingham to the S.

SE7 Charlton, on the river E of the Blackwall Tunnel and W of Woolwich.

SE8 Deptford, extending along the riverside opposite the Isle of Dogs and S of the Surrey Docks. Not part of the Docklands area, though similar to it. A corner of SE8 sticks down towards Lewisham, taking in St John's.

SE9 Far, suburban SE London, including Eltham and Mottingham.

SE10 Greenwich, except for East Greenwhich which is SE3. SE10 also includes the Millenium Dome peninsula to the NE beneath which the Blackwall Tunnel motorway passes.

SE11 Most of Kennington, from the Oval N to the Elephant & Castle and W to the river at Vauxhall. More SW than SE.

SE12 Lee and Grove Park, SE of Catford.

SE13 Lewisham, plus Ladywell and Hither Green to the S.

SE14 New Cross and a slice of the inland side of Deptford.

SE15 Peckham, though part of Peckham Rye falls into SE22, and Nunhead.

SE16 Bermondsey and Rotherhithe, including the entire Surrey Docks district of Docklands. Away from the river. SE16 includes streets on the edge of North Peckham. The NW corner, along the river, has some big new riverside developments.

SE17 Walworth, from the Elephant & Castle southwards. Includes part of Kennington in the W.

SE18 Woolwich, Plumstead and Plumstead Common.

SE19 Centres around the Crystal Palace hilltop, including Norwood New Town and the fringes of Penge.

SE20 Penge and Anerley, to the SE of Crystal Palace.

SE21 Dulwich, and the fringes of Tulse Hill. Most of East Dulwich is in SE22.

SE22 East Dulwich, part of Peckham Rye and a bit of Honor Oak.

SE23 Forest Hill, to the E of Dulwich. Also Honor Oak.

SE24 Herne Hill, also extending N towards Brixton's Loughborough Junction and NW to Brockwell Park and the Poets' Estate. Some streets in the SE corner are really in Dulwich.

SE25 South Norwood.

SE26 Sydenham, from Crystal Palace E to Bell Green and S to the edge of Penge.

SE27 West Norwood and the S half of Tulse Hill.

SE28 Thamesmead, the new town on the Plumstead Marshes E down the Thames.

SW1 Perhaps the smartest code of all, the postal address of Buckingham Palace and 10 Downing St, never mind the whole of Westminster, St James's, Belgravia, Victoria and part of Knightsbridge including Harrods, squeezed in by a dramatic jink in the frontier, forming an enclave in SW3. Pimlico is SW1 and now that has 'come up' there is hardly a scruffy corner left. Sloane Square is SW1 too.

SW2 Part of Brixton, the southern slice, and also Streatham Hill, the edge of Clapham Park and part of Tulse Hill.

SW3 Chelsea, though the HQ of Chelseadom, Peter Jones, is in SW1. Also a good part of Knightsbridge and some of South Ken – see the area map for the quirks of the boundaries here. SW3 stops at Beaufort St in the W and large tracts of Chelsea are in SW10.

SW4 Clapham, plus a portion of Stockwell W of Clapham Rd and a corner of W Brixton.

SW5 A small zone, essentially Earl's Court.

SW6 By contrast, the entire island cut off by the river and the railway, which is Fulham. Only in the N, where the boundary runs along Lillie Rd, is there any doubt. Some streets N of here are really in Fulham though they have W6 and W14 codes.

SW7 South Kensington, Knightsbridge (though see also SW3) and the Museums.

SW8 A mixed area, much crossed by railways, between the river and Stockwell. Includes parts of Stockwell, the Oval, Vauxhall, the E part of Battersea's Queenstown neighbourhood, and the industrial zone of Nine Elms.

SW9 The northern half of Brixton, the E side of Stockwell and a corner in the N that is really the Oval.

SW10 The western end of Chelsea, plus a patch to the N which is really West Brompton and, by sheer good luck for the developers, the big new Chelsea Harbour development which physical, if not postal, geography places across the creek in Fulham.

SW11 A big slice of smart and not-so-smart South London, from Battersea Park, through Central Battersea to Wandsworth Common.

SW12 Balham, including the streets in the 'Nightingale Triangle' where people say they're in Clapham South, and the lower tier of the 'Between the Commons' neighbourhood of Battersea.

SW13 Barnes, well-defined by common, river and White Hart Lane, which forms the boundary with SW14 and Mortlake.

SW14 Mortlake by the river and the suburban streets of East Sheen on the edge of Richmond Park.

SW15 Putney, plus Roehampton in the W and some streets that are virtually Wandsworth to the E.

SW16 Streatham, plus Streatham Vale and Norbury in the S.

SW17 Tooting.

SW18 Wandsworth, part of Wandsworth Common, Southfields and Earlsfield.

SW19 A large area including Wimbledon, Wimbledon Park, Merton and Colliers Wood.

SW20 The further reaches of Wimbledon towards the Kingston bypass, including Raynes Park.

W1 Grandeur and commerce, including Mayfair, Oxford St, Regent St . . . Essentially, the West End, plus homes in Soho and Marylebone.

W2 Bayswater and Paddington, plus Little Venice S of the canal.

W3 Acton, though not Acton Green in the S or the industry of North Acton.

W4 Chiswick, including Bedford Park and Acton Green.

W5 The centre of Ealing, including South Ealing. Ealing has three postcodes: see area map.

W6 Hammersmith and the northern fringes of Fulham.

W7 The western slice of Ealing Borough, including Hanwell and part of West Ealing.

W8 The heart of Kensington, around the High St and Church St.

W9 Maida Vale and Little Venice N of the canal, plus a sharply contrasting area to the W of Waterton Rd stretching up to Queen's Park.

W10 North Kensington N of the fly-over, plus Kensal as far N as Queen's Park.

W11 Notting Hill S of the fly-over and N of Notting Hill Gate. Includes the N part of Holland Park.

W12 Shepherd's Bush, plus East Acton and White City.

W13 The middle slice of Ealing, W of Ealing centre and E of Hanwell.

W14 A slice squeezed between Kensington and Hammersmith, including some of the smartest parts of Holland Park, Olympia, West Kensington and the NE quadrant of Hammersmith.

WC1 Bloomsbury, St Pancras and the W part of Finsbury.

WC2 Covent Garden, the Strand, part of Holborn.

London in 1999

The property market in 1999

Mid-1998 saw the end of the brisk upturn in prices that had spread Londonwide by 1996. It was still going strong in the spring, but by June the weather was bad, world finances looked dicey and the World Cup was on TV. After June came a half-year in which the homes market was like stirring lumpy porridge. Over-inflated prime central London prices fell back a bit; everywhere else plateaud. But the first weeks of January 1999 saw many parts of town get off to a roaring start again: months of dire headlines had failed to result in the end-of-the-world scenario widely predicted by the Far East problems, and mortgages were getting ever cheaper and were in good supply. First-time buyers, in particular, leapt out – but so too did investors. And there were rumbles that big institutions are also considering putting big money into London rented homes.

The double seesaw . . .

This news adds to the difficulties in forecasting how the homes market will perform from the point of view of London-dwellers. Where once it was a straightforward case of supply and demand – did enough people feel they could afford to buy, and were enough willing to move on and let them – supply is increasingly unpredictable.

We used to look for a Micawberishly simple equation: supply plus affordability plus buyer confidence equals a good market. Supply came from sellers eager to move to a bigger home or another district. And buyers were looking, by and large, for a home to occupy. If this seesaw was in balance, all was well.

Now there are two distinct but overlapping markets: occupying and investing. And the investing market – ie, owning rental property – has its own seesaw. The rent that tenants are prepared to pay must equate to an acceptable yield on the capital invested, and the supply of tenants must balance the supply of property to let.

So now, would-be owner-occupiers can find themselves in competition with would-be investors, who see bricks-and-mortar as a more tangible asset than shares, say, or a pension fund and liable to yield better that the building society anyway. So, does this lack of properties mean that prices will be forced up? Well, not necessarily.

If the world financial jitters have not caused collapse, they have certainly resulted in massive job losses in the City, with more to come. Result: a lot of internationals working over here have gone home – lots of tenancies given up. Thus rents are falling as supply of renters dries up, or at least lessens. So some property investors decide to take the profits of the hike in values of the last couple of years – and sell instead.

Homegrown City types are not counting on their jobs, and are stashing their bonuses if any under the mattress instead of, as in recent years, buying an investment property. Result: shortage of buyers, for some kinds of homes at least.

Meanwhile, in another corner of town, the downturn in market confidence came just as a welter of new homes developments were coming on stream. Result: oversupply, then? Well . . . not necessarily. Developers consider becoming investors, renting out their homes rather than trying to sell them in a quiet market.

And since, long term, the idea of owning London property now that there is an established rental sector is attractive, we have merchant banks rumoured to be close to launching the UK's first residential property unit-trust. Several more such are reported to be under way. Schroders, property insiders believe, are looking to spend some £500 million on acquiring low-maintenance blocks of flats 'on the edge of major conurbations', which could certainly have quite an impact.

So that's all right, then?

Well . . . IF the concerted efforts of our jealous EU partners to move Europe's financial hub away from London fail (which jealousy is likely to prove a bigger factor than our espousal or not of the Euro), and IF world financial markets stabilize, and IF King Hussein dying and Saddam Hussein living do not cause more flare-ups, and IF . . . .

Anybody got a crystal ball?

If this sounds gloomy – well, not necessarily. What it translates as is this: the market is unusually difficult to call, not least because the emergent rentals scene and the explosion of recent development has yet to be absorbed into the permanent picture. So this year, buy with care. Buy what you want to live in, not what you are assured will make a vast profit by next year. Do not listen to those offering to lend you 95% of the purchase price unless you are very, very sure you can't let this home go and you can, for sure, afford those repayments. There are those still in negative equity from the last recession. (If you don't know what that is, don't buy until you do.)

Don't buy as an investment to let unless you have really researched the area, the property, the likely yield – not forgetting to take into account the possibility of it standing unlet from time to time. Don't make the mistake of thinking of gross yield as money in the bank.

Don't buy for the short term. Long term, London has always come good. That's not to say that things must go on as they always have – and heaven knows the short-term ups and downs can be ferocious – but this is a unique city. If you are really worried that Frankfurt might steal London's financial crown, go and spend a week there.

The big shake-up

This could be the year the home-buying pattern really gets shaken up. Not where or what you buy, but how. Two things are happening, and interacting. The government is trying to speed up, and tidy up, the process. And information technology is working its magic on the dusty world of deeds and searches. The government's ideas – not proposals, so far – are outlined in the next chapter. They centre round making the seller do, in advance, a lot of the work that the buyer does now in a last-minute hurry.

Wholesale reform is far from easy, but speeding up the process is surely achievable – if only by enshrining the various simple measures we outline under the headings *Buying* and *Selling*, in the next chapter. We believe – and so does the government's working party – that to make the sale binding as soon as an offer is accepted would be neither workable nor desirable. But why not a sum lodged by both sides at that point, forfeitable should the deal fall through and calculated to cover the frustrated party for wasted legal and surveying fees? The prospect of giving up, say, £1000 would at least halt frivolous or cynical time-wasters. This would be more effective than insisting, as the working party suggests, on a survey before marketing even begins. This in itself would slow homes from coming onto the market and put off some people even starting.

Technology may bypass the present system anyway, whatever the government eventually decides to do. On-line searches are being trialled, conveyancing 'factories' are in business, mortgages are to be had via phone or Internet. Solicitor and agents – and their clients – are begining to realize that the whole buy–sell operation could be bundled into one package, with plenty of commissions to be earned on the way. We may look back on our High Street estate agents with the nostalgia accorded to the local baker. And watch out: if the compulsory Sell Packs the government is thinking about look like coming in, there will be a panic to sell before the rules come into force.

The Londonwide picture

London is about to gain a Mayor and a Greater London Authority – the GLA. The last time London had a city-wide council, the GLC, it ended in a row with the government. Mrs Thatcher won. What will the GLA and Mayor do? It is becoming clear that most peoples' perception of a mayor as an impotent figurehead will be uncomfortably short of the truth. Transport and planning are the headline tasks. Transport's knotty problems are dealt with below, but there are concerns about planning. The Mayor will be able to interfere in any planning application for a building over 50 metres high – which means 80 per cent of new space in the City. The City fathers are uneasy: perhaps the first of many rows between the Mayor and the domain of the Lord Mayor. More optimistic observers hope that the Mayor will be able to take a Londonwide view, avoiding parochial planning decisions.

The Mayor and GLA will also have a role in planning London's long-term development by creating a Spatial Development Strategy (SDS). It's widely accepted that there is a vacuum here, but the last attempt was not promising. The GLC's Greater London Plan of 1969 was devised, observed London planning guru Professor Peter Hall, 'by a cast of thousands – and achieved almost nothing'. Its 1940s predecessor, the Abercrombie plan, which by contrast 'changed the face of London irreversibly for the better' had a staff of just 16. The blueprint for the GLA and Mayor speaks of a small staff. One hopes that their efforts will be closer to Abercrombie than the GLC.

Planning experts are worried that the GLA could prove to be a bottle-neck clogged up with planning applications. 'Major developments in the boroughs should fit in with the Mayor's overall scheme', says the government, which seems to presage some epic rows with the boroughs – just as in GLC days, when, commented Prof Hall, 'it seemed that most of [the GLC and borough planners'] energies were thus spent'.

Given the remit to work out an overall transport strategy, and the problem of paying for it, one of the Mayor's key powers may be to raise money from road use charges, or at least to propose this, the veto being left with Whitehall. No-one can quite see how to set up toll-booths – you would have to block off a thousand side-streets. So the likely option is a set of zones and permits. This means drawing borders. If you draw a line, someone is going to be on the wrong side: there is no such thing as an uncontentious border. Suppose the car permit that allows you to drive in the Inner London zone is free to residents, and £100 a year to others? Inevitably, there will be streets where either end, or either side, are in different zones.

The guess is that the Greater London boundary – the edge of the old GLC, and new GLA – would be one border. Perhaps the ring of the M25 would be more logical and easier to police, for it, at least, exists, while the Greater London border is just a line on a map. But what about Inner London, assuming that there must be an inner zone to discourage journeys into and across the centre? Some have suggested the old Inner London area – the 12 boroughs, plus the City, that comprised the Inner London Education Authority. But examine these borders again: Kilburn, Barnes, Chiswick, Stratford, West Ham are in Outer; Putney Heath, Streatham, Gipsy Hill, Bellingham, New Eltham and even Thamesmead are in Inner. Can you imagine the scenes in Barnes when they find that the school-run into Putney is going to cost another £100 a year? Another, and clearer, border would be the line of the North and South Circular Roads. Or you could leave out Greenwich, and include Newham. And perhaps Haringey. Or not. We would not like the job of deciding.

Or will we have a sophisticated,electronic 'black box' system, which charges for the use of congested or scarce road space on a much more detailed basis? The last time the Department of Transport looked at such schemes, in 1997, it concluded that they were not feasible yet. So permits it will probably be.

Transport

Before you move this year, look carefully at London's changing transport patterns. London will enter the third millennium with a new public transport authority, and a new tube line – the extended Jubilee. It will also gain its first trams for 40 years – the Croydon–Wimbledon Tramlink – and a revived river-bus service. The Jubilee is already set to transform links to some of the capital's most inaccessible homes, those of South-East London – this area also gains a direct link to the jobs and offices of Canary Wharf as the Docklands Light Railway (DLR) reaches out across the river.

New trains

The new rail services previewed in last year's Guide should all be running during 1999 – though the Jubilee Extension (JLE) is proving to be a real cliff-hanger. The DLR is racing to get its southern branch to Greenwich and Lewisham finished before the magic 1/1/2000 deadline. Tube managers suspect this is to cock a snook at the JLE, which at time of writing is scheduled to be opened in three stages. Phase one will be from Stratford to North Greenwich: this is pencilled in for 'late spring'. The second phase, opening 'in late summer', sees the line extended west through the new Canada Water station and London Bridge to Waterloo. The final phase, promised 'by autumn', will complete the line by linking Waterloo with Green Park through the new station at Westminster. We will see.

The DLR Extension means that 500,000 more people will be within a sensible commute (ie, with connections, less than 45 minutes) from the Isle of Dogs. It links SE London – Lewisham, Deptford and Greenwich – to Canary Wharf and the City, and via interchanges, provides a range of new travel options, including links to the Waterloo, Westminster and the West End by the JLE and (via the DLR) the City Airport.

The third line, the Heathrow Express, whisks airport-bound travellers from Paddington to Heathrow in 15 minutes. It is a year old, and has already affected the property pattern in a big segment of NW London. Not new, but closed for so long it might as well be, is the re-opened East London Line, which will connect with the Jubilee at the new Canada Water station and offer SE London another range of links.

Effects of the new transport links

The Jubilee Line stations at Southwark, London Bridge and Bermondsey put these places right between the West End and Docklands. The new line will have a train every two minutes at busy times. It will call at Green Park, Westminster and Waterloo, and on eastwards via Southwark (new station at Blackfriars Road/The Cut), London Bridge, Bermondsey (new, Jamaica Road/Keeton's Rd), Canada Water (new, Surrey Docks), Canary Wharf, North Greenwich (new, The Dome), Canning Town (new) and Stratford. Key interchanges are at London Bridge for the City (via Northern line) and King's Cross (via Thameslink), Canary Wharf for the DLR to the rest of Docklands and Green Park for the Victoria and Piccadilly lines.

Areas that benefit are: the whole South Bank from Waterloo to the Surrey Docks, the Isle of Dogs, the Royal Docks/City Airport – and most of SE London via connections. Other areas to benefit include Westminster, with a clutch of new homes and now a direct link to Waterloo (Eurostar) and Docklands, Mayfair with two Jubilee stations – Bond St and Green Park – and the St John's Wood–West Hampstead strip with links as above plus the proximity of Paddington.

The line bypasses the City, meaning much faster journeys from the W side of Central London to Docklands, and to the South Bank and its rail terminii – which of course also opens up new links for commuters from the rail lines to the S and W. And as a property expert pointed out, the prosperous denizens of Canary Wharf will be able to get to the Ritz in 16 minutes.

The SW and NW commuter suburbs will also benefit. Developers have been touting the Jubilee Line as a plus as far out as Kingston. The Northern Line will interchange with the Jubilee at London Bridge, offering a Docklands link to the good City and West End connections that South London areas such as Clapham already enjoy.

The Docklands Light Rail (DLR) Extension has stations at the Cutty Sark, Greenwich rail station, Deptford Bridge, Elverson Rd and Lewisham. Lewisham is a busy shopping centre and an interchange for rail and bus routes, which between them serve much of SE London. Blackheath and Lewisham property prices saw some of the fastest rises in London during 1997, though they settled down in 1998.

Deptford also benefits, with a DLR station at the crossing of the A2 over Deptford Creek: the waterfront is seeing much redevelopment as a consequence. Further S, Lee has good houses but a poor train service: a bus to Lewisham DLR will expand its horizons. Catford and Sydenham to the S, and Eltham to the E all gain new travel options.

Other parts of SE London do well via interchanges. The **East London Line**, orphan of tube lines in its cut-off corner, will have an interchange with the JLE at the new Canada Water station. This will give New Cross, and points S on train and bus links, fast travel to Westminster and the West End for the first time.

The Heathrow Express, now open, makes Paddington and the Bayswater, Notting Hill and Maida Vale areas very sensible places to live if you travel far afield. Paddington has rather odd tube connections, but anywhere on the Circle Line, plus places in Mid-town – Clerkenwell, Fitzrovia, Bloomsbury – will be able to get to Paddington via the Hammersmith & City.

Getting to the airports

Even the most hardened car-user balks at the nightmare road journey to Heathrow, and the car park charges when you get there. So an enormous plus, in property value terms, is swift public transport access to Europe's major airport as well as to the centre of town. A nearby route to any of the other airports does no harm, either. Since mid-1998 the Paddington–Heathrow train has been running every 15 minutes, taking 15 minutes. It is a success despite its £10 fare, with 6 million passengers in its first full year. This summer, a rank of airline-style desks will be in operation at Paddington, allowing check-in with nine airlines. Already passengers with carry-on baggage can report there for BA, British Midland and American Airlines. Heathrow's other rail link is on the Piccadilly Line, which takes 50 minutes to the West End, but is cheaper.

To get to **Gatwick**, look out for homes within reach of Thameslink trains, which call at London Bridge, Blackfriars, City Thameslink and Farringdon plus a range of N London stations. The airport is also served by trains from Victoria (including the non-stop, 30-minute Gatwick Express) and Clapham Junction (close to Battersea, Clapham and Wandsworth). East Croydon takes on new importance as the hub where Gatwick trains intersect with the new Tramlink service, starting in 2000, which connects with Wimbledon, Mitcham and Beckenham (see below).

Stansted's rail link is from Liverpool St, with a stop at Tottenham Hale (Victoria Line connects here) and a 41-minute journey time. For **Luton**, use Thameslink (see Gatwick above) with a 50-minute service. The **City Airport** in Docklands can be reached via the DLR (Prince Regent station and 473 bus) and Silverlink Metro (North London Line), which takes approximately 30 minutes from Highbury & Islington.

Future airport links

Thus all five London airports can now be reached by rail, which is a step forward, but a lot more needs to be done before most London areas have sensible rail–air routes.

The most important, and well-advanced, plan is for the **St Pancras–Heathrow** express. This will benefit Mid-town, the West End and the City. It will have stops at Ealing Broadway and West Hampstead (Cricklewood was a contender, but almost certainly seems to have missed out) and is set to open in 2002 (it's already slipped a year), with a journey time of 35 minutes and two trains an hour. This will do for West Hampstead and its environs what the Paddington link has done for Maida Vale.

That takes care of access from Central London. But so many travellers start their trek to the airport in SW and NW London. The St Pancras trains will call at West Hampstead and Ealing, which will help, but studies have identified the annoying fact that none of the Waterloo trains connect with the airport, though there is a line only a couple of miles away from the terminals. To remedy this, Feltham station is being promoted as 'Heathrow South Gateway'. This links Waterloo and Clapham Junction trains to the airport via a 20-minute coach service. On the other (N) side of the airport Hayes & Harlington station, on the Paddington–Reading line, is identified as 'Heathrow North Gateway' or 'Hayes Hub'. The plan is for trains on the St Pancras service, due in 2002, to stop here to connect with the Great Western main line.

BAA are also talking to the Eurostar operators about running Paris trains into Heathrow via the Express tunnel. The timeframe is 2001–2. Even further in the future are thoughts of Airtrack: a direct line into the terminals from the South West line around Staines/Ashford. This would require serious tunnelling and depends on Terminal 5 going ahead. Trains from Richmond/Waterloo could use this link.

Cross-London, North–South

Thameslink 2000 is the decidedly optimistic name for a major revamp of the train service that runs North–South through Farringdon, City Thameslink and Blackfriars. Thameslink has been in operation for several years, and brings South London areas such as Elephant & Castle, Tulse Hill and Herne Hill within minutes of the City. Trains run deep into North London and beyond: West Hampstead, Kentish Town, on up to Cricklewood and Hendon. There are trains down to Gatwick, up to Luton.

But bottlenecks around London Bridge and at King's Cross restrict the number of trains Thameslink can run. The 2000 project will ease these pinch-points, allowing trains of 12 rather than eight carriages and extending the service to 166 stations in place of the existing 50. The £580 million plan aims to triple the number of trains through Central London. It will link into the burgeoning St Pancras interchange.

It will certainly be 2001 and beyond before any work actually starts. We won't know until December this year if there is to be a public inquiry – though it seems almost certain. Objections to the 1997 plan concern, among other things, the effects of the works on services to and from Blackfriars Station and the impacts on the Borough market conservation area.

Cross-London, East–West

Down in Croydon, **Tramlink 2000** seems likely to meet its start date. The network uses a lot of redundant rail lines but also runs through the streets of central Croydon. The trams are made in Vienna and they are just like their continental cousins, holding 200 people, travelling at 50 mph (though not through the streets . . .) and running every 10 minutes. If it is a success the tram system could be replicated in other parts of London. A London Transport study has spotlighted several possible places, from Kingston to Thamesmead. Thinking East–West, will this year see the announcement of the long-awaited Crossrail which would link Paddington to the City? See below.

London to Europe

The Channel Tunnel Rail Link, or the lack of it, has been a recurrent theme of this Guide since 1987. Early in 1998, the latest of several plans collapsed and the project had to be rescued – again. The ensuing year has seen more action than expected. Work has actually started: digging has begun. Not at the London end, but down in Kent. In order to get it re-started the scheme was split into two: phase one is the line from the Tunnel through Kent, under the Thames Estuary and into the Essex Marshes. This should be finished by 2003, but the trains will divert from it onto the existing track into Waterloo – until (and if) phase two is finished. This is the expensive bit, mostly in tunnels under East and North London to Stratford and into a new underground station beneath St Pancras. The betting is on 2010 for that.

Boats on the river?

Cinema-goers will have noted that in Shakespeare's time a Thames rowing boat was the equivalent of a taxi. For centuries the river was London's highway. Not in the 20th century, though, with attempt after attempt at a river-bus service ending up in failure. The Millennium Dome has prompted yet another try. £15 million has been spent on new or rebuilt piers at Westminster, Embankment, Waterloo, Bankside, Blackfriars, Tower and at the Dome in Greenwich. Further piers are proposed at Battersea Park and other locations up-river – though nothing definite yet. Docklanders of 1980s vintage will recall that there are lots of piers on both banks, most paid for by public money and all unused, for regular services at least. No word on what will happen to these.

The new piers programme is driven by the Millennium Dome, which is planned to be virtually car-free. It is hoped, though, that the river will go on being used after 2000. During the year of the Millennium Experience two companies, City Cruises and White Horse Ferries, will respectively operate river passenger services between Central London and the Dome, and a local service running between Cutty Sark and the Dome. White Horse will also provide a 'Hopper' service in Central London linking up to 10 piers at key attractions and transport interchanges along the river. City Cruises will also provide an express 'legacy' service after the Millennium Experience, linking upstream and downstream piers.

London Transport has set up a new subsidiary company, London River Services Limited, which will eventually take over and manage the piers currently owned by the Port of London Authority. As part of the new transport authority in the capital, London River Services is expected to play a vital role in securing the future of passenger services on the Thames, beyond the Millennium. We can only hope.

As ever this depends on cash subsidies: no amount of new piers and ministerial exhortations will get commuters onto boats unless they (the boats, that is) are cheap, reliable and predictable. Those who bought homes close to the Docklands piers a decade ago are still smarting from the experience.

Who owns the tubes?

All change and mind the gap is the motto of London Transport this year. The trouble is that the change is unpredictable and the gap is the financial one between the government's ideas about what needs to be spent and the private sector's willingness to invest. Private money is going to come into London's tube system, the question is how it will be arranged. A part-privatized route has been chosen, but the timetable, rather like that of the Jubilee Line, has already been abandoned. A list of 100 firms showed signs of interest in taking on some or all of the Tube lines – the idea is that they will get a 20-year lease on the lines, invest to upgrade them, and charge London Transport – or Transport for London (TfL), its successor – to run trains. The short-list of 20 firms came down in the spring to six consortia. But the wrangling was so intense that the takeover date – Spring 2000 – has been scrapped.

The campaign for the London Mayor election will no doubt focus on who owns, and runs, the Tube as a big issue. In the end it comes down to how much public money is available, for the private 'leaseholders' are going to charge the tube operator (TfL) the costs of improving the network – plus their profit. TfL will need a subsidy or fares will rocket. How big a subsidy will be decided by central government – not by the mayor, however much he or she may wish it were otherwise.

Transport: the future

What gets done depends so much now on how the system is managed: the politics are discussed above. What we can hope for is more joined-up thinking about joining up separate bits of London's infrastructure. The LT network and the 'overground' rail lines exist in different worlds. This was not always so: much of what is now called 'Underground' route is not beneath ground at all, or only just, and was built as ordinary railway: the Barnet and Edgware branches of the Northern Line, the Ruislip branch of the Central, the Hammersmith & City. Since 1940, the two systems have developed in their own ways and their bosses have shown little sign of talking to each other.

Several studies, carried out inside LT, within London authorities, and by outside pressure groups, have looked at London's rail infrastructure as a whole and found useful possible links. This exercise has been duplicated in Paris, Frankfurt, Hamburg and other continental cities – with the difference being that there they have done something about it. Visit Paris and try the RER; Germany and use the S-Bahns.

One attempt at a link-up has just resurfaced: the creation of an east–west line joining the Heathrow and Reading to Paddington services with the Essex to Liverpool Street ones. The missing link exists: the old Metropolitan Line from Edgware Road to Liverpool St. This route largely parallels the Crossrail scheme for a deep-level Paris-style 'regional rail' line across London. The Crossrail plans got a long way forward in the late 1980s, but were dropped in the early-'90s recession. The City Corporation has recently been talking to a French bank consortium about starting Crossrail up again. But cannot the existing lines be adapted? This too is being discussed. Many a promise has been made, and nothing happens except that residents of Mayfair get periodically agitated about the idea of Crossrail shaking their expensive foundations.

London Transport's list of other 'might happen' improvements is headed by a northward extension of the East London Line, which could provide stations at Dalston and Hoxton – see the Hackney chapter. This is inching its way along the planning process, but was held up again this year by the uncertainty about the new London authority. On hold for elections, like so much else.

Buying and selling in London

Buying or selling a London home brings the hapless householder, or would-be householder, into contact with a whole raft of archaic systems, a vocabulary of strange terms and half a dozen professions ranging from council officials to surveyors. This chapter examines the home-selling process and the government's thoughts on it, the question of leasehold and freehold and then moves on to how to buy and sell.

Speeding up the process: government gets involved

Buying or selling a home is, as a government report has just concluded, usually slow and undoubtedly stressful. The main culprit is surely our elephantine system, which allows too much time between the (non-binding) verbal agreement, the signing of the contract (still only committing the buyer to 10 per cent of the purchase price) and completion. Plenty of room for sellers to accept a higher, later offer, or for buyers to try to force the price down for some trumped-up reason at the eleventh hour, hoping that the seller will be too committed to the move to stand firm.

Labour, then in opposition, promised in early 1997 to stamp out gazumping and gazundering if and when it got into power. It proposed that buyers and sellers who backed out of deals without good reason would have to pay any costs already incurred by the other side. But when the new housing minister Hilary Armstrong got her feet under the desk, she was persuaded that this was just one symptom of a much bigger problem – the whole house-buying process was so slow and inefficient that it positively invited practices like gazumping. Everyone involved in the process wholeheartedly agreed – then promptly laid the blame at the door of one or more of the other participants. Estate agents blamed lenders and solicitors, lenders blamed borrowers and surveyors and so it went on.

The government has just finished consulting with the property industry on 'taking the stress out of home buying and selling'. A year-long research study tracked 800 buyers and sellers though their negotiations. A working party, which included estate agents, lawyers and other bodies and professions involved in the process (and one person from the Consumers' Association), came up with a set of proposals. All and sundry were next invited to comment direct to the ministry during the consultation period to the end of March 1999.

Due to this protracted process what we report here is only an interim stage. Anything, or nothing, may come of it.

The seller's information pack

The working party's main proposal is that a 'seller's information pack' should be available immediately a home goes on the market. Sellers could be encouraged to provide the pack voluntarily – or the law could be changed to make it compulsory. Potential buyers would be able to look at this pack (presumably at the estate agent's office). It would have a standard set of information and paperwork, giving would-be buyers most of what they need – deeds, local authority searches, draft contract – to decide if they want to proceed, and get on with the purchase if they do. So far, so sensible.

More controversial (unless you are a chartered surveyor) is the suggestion that a surveyor's report on the property should be included. This will cost sellers several hundred pounds, go out of date if the home fails to sell speedily – and, instead of saving time, will lose it, possibly crucially, by delaying the putting of the home onto the market. This goes, too, for another seller's-pack item: service charge and management accounts for leasehold homes. On top of all the rest, the seller will have to get his landlord or management to come up with these, and quickly, when he wants to sell. Then – since these will be both bulky and impenetrable – lawyers have come up with the idea that perhaps it would be advisable (at an extra cost, of course, in both money and time) for them not only to provide a draft contract but also a summary 'in plain English' of the pack's contents . . . Strangely, there doesn't seem to be much in the government's draft proposals on how we are to convince solicitors – frequently the worst culprits – to speed up *their* act.

So now we have lawyers (draft contract), surveyors, lenders (for the deeds), local authorities and then lawyers (summary) again who could all be required to do their stuff (and collect their fees). Then the whole pack has to be collated and copied before you instruct an estate agent . . . This seems to take little account of the cyclical nature of the selling market: by the time you've achieved all that – even if you don't pause for a furious row with the surveyor over his doleful findings – it will be quietening down for the summer hols.

True, there are exhortations from the government to various laggards and slow-coaches to try harder. Lenders are urged to make faster mortgage offers; local councils to speed up searches, buyers to get their finances sorted out before making an offer. But the actual work and expense falls to the would-be seller.

Should this come to pass, it will certainly mean that the decision to sell your home would have to be a serious one, not something sidled into on the 'let's put it on the market to see what happens' principle. It will cost you money, time and trouble. First conclusion: quite a lot of homes will simply not come to the market after all.

What the working party seems to have forgotten is that many deals are chivvied, jollied, worried along by estate agents. The vendor is a little half-hearted (and very often one half of a couple will be more enthusiastic than the other). A generous offer is extracted from a rather carried-away buyer, who has not been forced up against too much reality in the form of surveys, deeds and service charge accounts. The offer is accepted – and then the vendor is forced to rush about to get the paperwork together, something no amount of persuasion would have got him started on otherwise.

The clear conclusion is that first, *no-one* is going to do all this voluntarily. Second, that while some of this will indeed help speed things up and can easily be adopted by any keen seller (see Selling, below), it has one other great flaw. All the onus seems to be on the seller, not the buyer. For every gazump-accepting seller, there is also a gazundering buyer. While the pack would undoubtedly help to bring him (or her) more swiftly up to the mark, there is no financial compulsion to prevent him stalling, keeping the seller (or several sellers, unbeknown to each other) dangling while he sees who he can tie down to the best deal. He, meanwhile, does not even have the cost of a survey to lose.

But why not a sum lodged by both sides at offer, forfeitable should the deal fall through, to cover the frustrated party for wasted legal and surveying fees? The government seem to have lost sight of this idea. The prospect of giving up, say, £1000 would at least halt frivolous or cynical time-wasters.

The next step: technology?

Reaction to the seller's pack idea has ranged from the cynical (plenty of extra paid work for surveyors and solicitors) to the enthusiastic. The best way forward, should the government decide that this one will fly, would be to phase in the requirements gradually. That way, time will also allow the technology to catch up. The Land Registry is now computerized and its response speed is now an issue. On-line conveyancing is now possible. But lenders who hold deeds can be slow at producing them, and local authority searches are also often tardy. A pointer to the future is the on-line database of planning permissions and other documents compiled by Wandsworth Council. This can be searched via the Internet. A pilot scheme in Bristol provides on-line access to standard search material which takes about two weeks to collect by current methods. This on-line system is used in Sweden, Denmark and other countries.

Warming to its technological theme, the report discusses a major change to the property business. 'Work is already under way to prepare the ground for a national land information service (NLIS). The aim is to bring together land and property information held on computer databases by HM Land Registry, Ordnance Survey, the Valuation Office and other public and private bodies, and to provide easy, efficient and affordable access. This would help to speed up and simplify property transactions as well as to promote security for buyers and sellers. It would make details of all land ownership public.'

While the government deliberates, some sections of the house-buying industry are taking matters into their own hands and inching their way into the jealously guarded territory of others in a bid to speed up the process. Solicitors are setting themselves up as a 'one-stop-shop' offering estate agency, conveyancing and financial services under one roof. Meanwhile, the National Association of Estate Agents wants to see agents taking over some of the legal work now done by solicitors. Conveyancing 'factories', mortgages by phone, home-hunting on the Internet are all beginning to make their appearance.

Estate agents

Everyone knows that anyone can currently set up stall as an estate agent: there are no mandatory qualifications. There are three professional bodies to which most good agents belong: the Royal Institution of Chartered Surveyors (RICS), the Incorporated Society of Valuers and Auctioneers (ISVA) and the National Association of Estate Agents (NAEA) – all useful sources of information. Members will have undergone courses and passed professional exams (the NAEA's members are not necessarily qualified; with the other two it's a condition). The bodies also guarantee deposits held by their members and can be approached if you have a dispute with a member agent. (See Selling, below, for the business of choosing and instructing an agent.)

But there are some encouraging moves, not least the expansion last year of the previously limited ombudsman scheme to all members of these three professional bodies. The ombudsman has powers to award dissatisfied customers up to £50,000 compensation. Members of the scheme are expected to subscribe to a code of practice, and must ensure all published material is accurate, that they do not discriminate against any prospective buyer or property, and that they keep buyers informed of any other offers on the property for sale. Although membership is voluntary, most reputable firms are likely to have joined.

Of course, although the ombudsman scheme is voluntary and there is no licensing of estate agents, there are laws by which they must abide. The Estate Agents Act 1979 was tightened up in 1991 to clamp down on a number of nefarious practices including failure to pass on all offers and omitting to tell sellers about potential conflicts of interest. In 1997 the Director General of Fair Trading warned agencies to clean up their act after press reports that some were blatantly flouting the law. He has the power to ban agencies from practising, or to remove consumer credit licenses – and since 1991 has caused around 150 to cease trading. The Property Misdescriptions Act, implemented in 1993, outlaws the florid exaggeration, which passed for marketing in the 1980s. No longer can an agent describe a property as being in Blackheath if it's definitively in Lewisham, or rave on about the original Victorian cornicing in the spacious recep, unless he has checked that it isn't Homebase's best. Fear of being caught out under this Act may make estate agents' particulars duller reading, but at least they should be more accurate. So far less than 100 have been prosecuted.

One problem, highlighted by reputable agencies, is that since it is companies, not individuals, that are prosecuted, the usual result is that the employee concerned is sacked – only to resurface in another firm. Perhaps one day we will see more formal licensing requirements for entry into a profession that can, to say the least, have profound effects on the health, wealth and sanity of its clients, and equally some system for its practitioners to be 'struck off'.

The Misdescriptions Act is, by the way, supposed to cover developers' details too, though few seem to realize this: a big builder was fined last year for omitting the trees between his flats and the river on billboards and in brochures. Note that, while the Act does not directly cover home-owners, they are bound to answer all enquiries truthfully – and not just on the concrete facts. One couple landed up being sued for omitting to inform their buyers about the state of open warfare with the neighbours.

Freehold and leasehold

Londoners have got used to the idea, which seems extraordinary to foreigners, that you can buy slices of houses for a chunk of years. Leasehold, which is what this is, is still the norm for flats. (In large measure this goes right back to the basic assumption, built deep into the nation's psyche, that property ownership equates to possessing a physical piece of land. When flats arrived, the Brits couldn't conceive of owning property suspended in mid-air.)

In many parts of London the houses are leasehold too, which is what really surprises out-of-town buyers. In strict legal terms, you pay what can easily be a freehold price for a house but you don't own what you buy. You're just a tenant who pays the landlord a large one-off premium to live in his property for as long as the lease lasts, plus a small (usually) annual ground rent for the land it stands on.

Behind this anomaly is another one: the surviving ownership of many areas of London by ancient estates. These are relics of the days when the fields around London were private property. When they were built on, the landlords kept the ownership of the land, granting long leases to developers who built and sold the houses – again on leases. This continuous ownership has by and large been beneficial, safeguarding the character and appearance of areas such as Belgravia. Some of these estates belong to aristocratic families, some to charities, some to schools, some to the Church of England. The leading landlord, in size as well as status, is the Crown.

The development of the fields around London began in earnest in the late 17th century and continued until the 19th. Landlords granted leases to developers in return for an annual ground rent. The developers laid out the streets and built the houses, and then sold slightly shorter leases on the houses to the public at slightly higher ground rents. If a building lease was for 100 years, for instance, and the houses took a year to build, they'd be sold on 99-year leases. And if the ground rent the developer paid to the landlord worked out at £5 a building plot, the developer would ask a ground rent of say £15 from the house-buyers to provide himself with an income as well as capital. Finally when the 99-year leases ran out, the houses reverted to the freehold landlord, who could sell a new lease to a developer or new leases to the public.

Only now is this basic leasehold/freehold pattern being seriously challenged by recent changes in legislation giving leaseholders in flats, as well as houses, the right to buy the freehold of their block jointly. The estates of many of the vast landlords still remain more or less intact, but this is changing. The word 'freehold' is now to be found on sale details in Belgravia, for instance.

Leases can be for any length of time, and obviously the shorter they are, the lower the price. There are two exceptions to this. First, really short leases in good areas can be viewed as so many years' rent – paid, but therefore also fixed, in advance. This makes good sense to companies (who in any case don't have to worry about the difficulties of getting a mortgage for a short lease). Second, buying a short lease makes even more sense if you'll eventually qualify under the recent laws to buy the freehold from the landlord, or – a cheaper option – to extend your lease. Some great estates, including the Grosvenor and the Cadogan, have now started issuing leases of up to 99 years. Most landlords sell new or newly modernized properties on 99-year leases, but the purchasers can sell the leases whenever they want to move elsewhere. Furthermore, as with freehold they can usually sell for a good profit, because although the lease will be several years shorter, the chances are that property values will have risen during those years. This explains why a long leasehold can be more or less as expensive as an equivalent freehold property.

If you are a leaseholder, your landlord will not necessarily be the freeholder. When a freeholder originally granted a lease to a developer, the lease the developer sold to the public was a sub-lease, making him the sub-leaseholders' landlord. But today the chain of leaseholds can be even longer. In some cases freeholders sold long head-leases to companies that specialized in getting vacant possession, and as houses fell empty, these companies sold sub-leases to development companies which converted them into flats. Once the flats were finished, they were sold to owner-occupiers on sub-sub-leases . . . But although being a sub-sub-leaseholder sounds horrendously complicated, all it really means in practice is that the ground rent will have been bumped up a bit at every stage.

A final point: there are rare cases when a freehold does exist 'up in the air'. An example of what is known as a 'flying freehold' might be a large house, long ago split into two – not vertically, but in such a way that a bedroom in one half extends over a downstairs room in the other. This partial flying freehold may work perfectly well in practice, but is legally murky. Take advice before buying.

Service charges, low and high

To ensure a building divided into flats is well-maintained, each leaseholder, as a condition of his lease, has to pay a bi-annual or annual service charge. This generally covers their share of any outgoings on structural repairs: having the exterior painted; heating (if the central heating is communal); paying for the cleaning and lighting of common areas such as the hall and stairs; and seeing that the building is fully insured. The service charge is usually made by a managing agent who arranges for work to be done when needed, and includes his fee – usually 10–15 per cent of the money spent.

Buying a flat over-stretches many people financially, so they're often tempted to choose one where the service charge is low; but unless the flat was recently converted, it's probably low because maintenance has been neglected. As a result, they get hit with an astronomical service charge once the neglect becomes too serious to ignore. Sudden demands for £40,000 apiece to fund new lifts and roof are apt to come as a shock . . . Note, too, that such neglect of capital expenditure may by no means be apparent in the general appearance of the building. It is essential to check, before buying, that your regular payments contribute to an adequate sinking fund to budget for major expenses.

Abuse by landlords, with problems of poor management, shoddy repairs and high service charges in flats forced changes in the law recently. These are still bedding down, and only in January did the first case get decided (the landlord lost). London is still far from free of rogues.

The unscrupulous landlord uses a number of methods, usually beginning by issuing unsuspecting leaseholders with huge service-charge bills. Any repairs actually done are shoddy and carried out by cowboy builders – more often than not working for companies linked to the landlord. Protests from leaseholders are countered with threats that they would forfeit their leases and lose their homes unless they paid up. Existing laws including the Landlord and Tenant Acts of 1985 and 1987 (which in theory were meant to give leaseholders some protection against such abuses) were so poorly drafted that landlords could flout them with impunity, knowing that leaseholders would have to take them to court to stop them. Only a handful of leaseholders ever had the courage to do so, for fear that they would face huge legal bills if they lost the case.

The latest attempt to curb these practices was the 1996 Housing Act. Leaseholders protesting about poor management and high service charges were given the right to take landlords and their agents to Leasehold Valuation Tribunals (LVTs) rather than to county courts.

Taking a case to an LVT will cost leaseholders a maximum of £500 per block, and neither side will be forced to pay the costs of the other, thus removing the main obstacle for leaseholders trying to exercise their legal rights.

Leasehold Valuation Tribunals are the key to a number of important safeguards for leaseholders. Your landlord can no longer serve you with a notice forfeiting your lease because you refuse to pay high service charges, unless the charges have been accepted as 'reasonable' by an LVT. You can apply to the LVT for a new manager for your block if whoever is managing it (the landlord or his agent) is demonstrably incompetent, unscrupulous or both, and there's nothing to stop you and your neighbours forming yourselves into a company and applying to manage the block yourselves. But such an arrangement won't rid you of your landlord, who will still own the block unless you go the whole way and buy the freehold (see below).

Leasehold Valuation Tribunals started work in September 1997 but got off to a slow start – partly because the preliminary procedure of serving notices on the landlord is so lengthy and complex. Application forms for the LVT and free advice on how to fill them in are available from Lease, the government-funded advisory service, which has been one of the few beacons of hope for despairing leaseholders. In January 1999, in the first decision of its kind, an LVT appointed a new managing agent after eight years of rows and very high bills. It turned out that the landlord had faked some of the invoices for work done.

Like LVTs, Lease was initially set up to help leaseholders who wanted to buy their freeholds after they were given that right by the Leasehold Reform and Urban Development Act of 1993. But it became clear there was huge demand from leaseholders who either didn't qualify, or didn't want, to buy their freehold, but who needed help to fight their landlords.

In December 1998 the minister issued a consultation paper as a first step to yet another reform of leasehold. Proposals include:

- making it easier for leaseholders of flats to join together to buy the freehold
- options to cut down on arguments over the price of buying a freehold, avoiding the need for expensive professional advice
- a new 'right to manage' their block of flats for people who do not want to buy
- a range of options for improving management standards and controlling the activities of property managers
- options to tackle landlords who use the threat of forfeiture proceedings to intimidate leaseholders into paying unreasonable charges
- a thorough tidy-up of the existing law to help leaseholders of houses, as well as flats.

Finally, the government is looking once more at a new form of tenure for flats – commonhold – which enables individual flat owners in a block to own and manage the whole building collectively from the outset – as opposed to having to oust the developer as ground landlord. We can expect to hear more on this from the Lord Chancellor's Department.

Extending the lease, buying the freehold

As things currently stand, if you *do* qualify to buy your freehold and want to do so, there's nothing your landlord can do to stop you (although he can make things difficult). Under the 1993 Act, flat-owners have the right to join with their neighbours and buy the freehold of their blocks even if the landlord doesn't want to sell. Previously, they had only the right of first refusal if their landlord did sell up (a right that was almost universally flouted by landlords). Owners of leasehold houses that met certain conditions won the right to buy in 1967. To buy your block, two-thirds of the flats must be let to qualifying leaseholders and at least two-thirds of these must participate. At least half the participating leaseholders must have lived in their flats for more than 12 months. To qualify, your flat must have had a lease with an original term of more than 21 years at a low rent (less than two-thirds of the rateable value of the flat).

If you don't qualify you also have the right to extend your lease by up to 90 years, an important right because the shorter your lease gets, the less valuable your property and the trickier it is for any potential buyer to get a mortgage. Unlike buying the freehold, flat-owners can apply individually for a lease extension. Lease, the advisory service, offers free literature and advice on buying freeholds and extending leases. Leaflets are also available direct from the Department of the Environment (DETR).

Leases with less than 70 years to run anywhere except Central London should be extended if possible. But in Central and Inner London, on the great estates like the Grosvenor and Cadogan, short leases hold their value well because there's always demand (see above).

The big landlords have reluctantly accepted changes in legislation and started selling off freeholds to qualifying residents – although they admit they don't go out of their way to encourage it. And some residents who have bought their freeholds on great estates have been outraged to discover that the erstwhile freeholder can still compel them to comply with estate management schemes set up to protect the appearance of some of the grandest neighbourhoods of London including Belgravia, Mayfair and parts of Kensington. The great estates argue that they have a duty to make sure people don't paint their houses purple or replace Georgian iron railings with chain fencing.

The big landlords are found in Central London, and in one or two suburbs:

Crown Estate: Regent's Park, plus homes in Pimlico, in Kensington and at Victoria Park, Hackney.

Duchy of Cornwall Estate: now only directly controls around 50 homes in the Kennington lands that this royal estate has held since the Black Prince's days. The rest have been turned over to housing associations.

The Church of England: Hyde Park Estate (see Bayswater), a scattering of houses and flats in Kensington, Chelsea and Belsize Park, three properties in Maida Vale (they used to own it all, but have been selling to tenants).

Grosvenor Estate: Belgravia and much of the northern half of Mayfair.

Cadogan Estate: 90 acres including a large slice of Chelsea around Sloane St.

Portman Estate: 110 acres north of Oxford St and east of Edgware Rd.

Howard de Walden: the 'medical district' around Harley St.

Duke of Bedford: 20 acres of Bloomsbury.

Wellcome Trust: Now owns the former Henry Smith's Charity estate in South Kensington

Tonbridge School, Bedford School and **Rugby School** all own small pockets of WC1.

Eton College: 60 acres around Swiss Cottage.

Dulwich College: most of Dulwich.

Eyre Estate: Primrose Hill, Chalk Farm.

Buying

Buying your first home may seem an overwhelming step; in fact, once you have scraped up enough cash for a deposit and enough evidence of reliability to persuade a building society or equivalent to lend you three or three and a half times your salary, it will likely prove the most straightforward property deal you will ever make. You will find a wealth of advice, in print and in person, on this subject. Everyone smiles kindly on you and offers anything from free leaflets to better mortgage terms, special rates and money-off deals.

Estate agents in particular will be assiduous in their care, once you have convinced them that you have the money and the definite intention of buying. They'll escort you to view, ring afterwards to enquire politely as to your reactions, helpfully suggest alternatives. This is only partly tender solicitude on your behalf: you have, as a first-time buyer, one inestimable advantage: you are not encumbered with a home to sell before you can buy their client's. It is worth remembering this advantage that you have: it can clinch you a good deal if the seller is in a hurry to move. The other point to remember when looking for the first time is that an estate agent is just that – an agent. Not yours, but the seller's (or vendor's, as they are known). It is the agent's job to present the goods in the best light. He is bound not to lie; he is not bound to point out that the tube line passes underneath, shakes the foundations and rattles the windows. Nevertheless a good agent with a reputation to maintain is concerned to have satisfied customers on both sides. His clients will then often come from people to whom he has sold.

General pointers: London is luckily a very well-mapped city. Many people – and not just first-time buyers – will need to keep an open mind about their choice of areas. If you are free to live anywhere within reasonable lines of communication, it's worth bearing in mind that some areas have been altering well ahead of their reputation; the road you remember as the scruffy place where a friend had a bedsit may have changed out of all recognition. But journeying to far-flung corners can be frustrating if you find the place backs onto the rail line that carries the Channel Tunnel trains. A good look at a decent map alongside this book can fill in the gaps in the property details. (Note that alongside our sketch maps are cross-references to the relevant page of the standard *A–Z London Street Atlas* (Geographers' A–Z Map Co) map book. Look too at the section on transport changes in the *The Property Market in 1999* chapter.)

That being said, one man's drawback is another soul's way in to an area above his means. If you are hell-bent on a certain area, there are likely to be cheaper corners; the essential thing to remember, though, is that anything inexpensive for an unalterable reason – views over graveyards, for instance, seem to be a minus-point – will likely not just stay relatively cheaper but also take longer to sell. *Always look at a home with a view to having, one day, to sell it to somebody else – fast.* For inside information on whether an area is likely to be on the way up – apart from that in this book – a good clue can be had from watching for any interest being shown by developers, or the sudden appearance of 'for sale' boards belonging to the classier Central London estate agents. At the first signs, move quickly – it's almost too late.

The more estate agents' details (which are at least free) and newspaper ads you can wade through, the better idea you will get of what is going on in the market in a given area at a given time. The one golden rule when looking at a procession of properties is always to make brief notes at the time or immediately on leaving; three flats further on and you won't be able to recall which was the one that smelt damp, which overlooked a noisy playground. If you seriously consider a place is a strong contender, don't be afraid to ask if you can wander round again on your own. When you think you've found the one, visit the locality at different times of day. Many people who only have weekends for home-hunting can find on moving in that the street is a solid traffic jam on weekdays.

The anatomy of a purchase – until the government changes the rules – goes:

1. Budgeting for the move

Talk to a building society, bank or other lender as soon as you start looking, if not before. They will advise on how much you are likely to be able to borrow. (For further details, see the *Mortgages* chapter.) When looking, remember that you will be unlikely to be able to borrow the entire asking price and will therefore need money for a deposit. You may be able to borrow up to 95 per cent of the property valuation over 25 years, but the more money you can put down as a deposit the better. For one thing, lenders will offer you better rates with a larger deposit. For another, you run a greater risk of being trapped in negative equity (your mortgage is higher than the value of your property) if you borrow a large proportion of the property's value, and the market then slumps. For a third, you might, with some lenders, still be forced to take out expensive insurance (to cover your lender, not you!) if you borrow over 90 per cent (sometimes as low as 75 per cent) of the value. Then, remember that all the attendant fees – searches, stamp duty (tax on the transaction of buying a house), valuation, survey, solicitor – and the cost of moving will absorb another 2.5 per cent or more of the property's value. Stamp duty, in particular, has gone up a lot recently.

Price and value are not the same thing, as you may well discover when your mortgage-lender gets a valuer round. Try to get the lender to use the surveyor who you instruct for your own survey, especially if the house is not typical of the area. A surveyor not familiar with the area needs comparables to value the property. In a quiet market, with few if any recent sales, no such figures will exist, so the value will be lowered to be on the safe side. Some valuers are under pressure from lenders to do six surveys a day. How much can they discover in that amount of time?

2. Making an offer, and what happens next

Make an offer through the agent. If and when it's accepted, return to your lender with the details of the property and notify your solicitor who will start the searches and conveyancing process (see below).

Remind yourself that although your offer has been accepted, neither side is legally committed. Even if a 'Sold' sign goes up, it will be sure to say, in small letters, '*subject to contract*'.

From that point, there are two definite stages to acquiring the property: the first, up to exchanging contracts and putting down a deposit and the second, up to completion and paying the balance of the price. Until you've exchanged contracts neither side is bound to the deal and there's nothing to stop your seller accepting a higher offer.

The longer this period, the more danger of such 'gazumping' – which is why the government are trying to short-cut it (see above). In the run-up to exchange of contracts, your solicitor and the seller's solicitor will be juggling a number of papers between them:

(a) **Title deeds:** The seller's solicitor will retrieve the title deeds to the house and the Land Registry certificate (nearly all London homes are registered) to confirm the seller actually owns the property and has good title – ie, is free to sell it.

(b) **Drawing up the contract:** He or she will then draw up a contract containing information from the deeds and send it to your solicitor. At the same time, your solicitor sends a list of pre-contract enquiries to the seller to get basic information about the property. This should give you answers to such questions as who owns and is responsible for boundary fencing, whether the property is properly insured, who the managing agent or freeholder is (if the property is leasehold: see above) and whether service-charge bills are disputed or up-to-date. You should also find out if boilers have been serviced and get confirmation that the property is connected to all utilities (gas, electricity, water and telephone).

(c) **Local authority search:** Your solicitor will also arrange for a local search, which should tell you if there's a road planned at the back of your garden or a compulsory purchase order on the property. Search questions are set out on a standard printed form, but the answers will only relate to the area directly adjacent to your property so a road planned nearby but not directly next to you won't show up even though it could make your road a traffic nightmare. Check yourself with the town hall.

(d) **Surveys:** In the meantime, you're arranging your mortgage and getting a survey done. Lenders will insist on a valuation to make sure the property's worth the amount you want to borrow but this is to protect them, not you. Particularly if the house is old, you should arrange your own independent structural survey. This is expensive, but should highlight any major problems or areas of concern that need dealing with. The results may make you reconsider the deal as it stands: you might not have enough money left to renew the roof immediately (or even if you have, the cost of doing so, when added to the purchase price, may be too far above the house's value). You have not exchanged contracts; you are free to try to negotiate a lower price, or back out of buying altogether. (Note: surveys err on the pessimistic side and are hedged about with disclaimers, since you can sue if the surveyor misses some glaring fault; discuss the implications with someone experienced in reading them if this is your first.)

Surveyors who are members of the Royal Institution of Chartered Surveyors (RICS) have to accept a compulsory arbitration scheme to handle complaints from customers. For claims under £3000 each side pays a £200 registration fee. If the claim is successful, the surveyor has to pay the registration fee. If the claim fails, the complainant will forfeit his/her fee but won't have to pay the surveyor's fee. The RICS will pay the costs of the actual arbitration. For claims between £3000 and £50,000 each side pays a £200 registration fee with the surveyor paying the fee if the claim is successful. If the surveyor wins, the customer pays his fee but incurs no further cost.

3. Exchanging contracts

When all this is done, you exchange contracts and put down a 10 per cent deposit. If you back out now, you lose your money. You have bought a home; you must insure it immediately – even though you have not moved in, it is now your responsibility.

4. Completion

A month or so later (though it can be done in days if both sides are willing and able to move home fast) completion takes place, the balance of the purchase price is handed over and the deal is done. You are free to move in.

Buying a newly built home

The basic process is the same whether the house is Georgian or brand new. The main difference is that with a new home you will probably be dealing with the developer, via a sales office on site, rather than a private individual.

New homes in London are nearly always either conversions – of everything from riverside warehouses, Victorian schools, factories, lofts and depositories to long-despised 1960s office blocks – or on re-used land. Such sites tend to be former hospitals, water-works, power stations, sewage farms . . . This raises the question of what level of decontamination has been done to the land. The new Environment Act has a lot to say about this: quiz the builder and the local authority.

Hot competition for the best sites has opened up areas of London in which few Londoners would previously have thought of living, especially the City fringes (Clerkenwell, St Paul's, Ludgate, Blackfriars) and the less chic parts of Docklands south of the river (Rotherhithe and Bermondsey), which will be major beneficiaries of the new Jubilee Line. To the west, Battersea and Sands End (the unglamorous bit next to Chelsea Harbour) have large industrial sites being targeted by developers.

But remember that fringe sites could be the first to suffer if there's a downturn. Be cautious about schemes aimed at investors. If you plan to live in such a block yourself, neighbouring flats may stand empty while investors try to let them. It can be hard to sell, too, in any new homes scheme, until all the units have been sold by the developer – he can offer inducements and deals that a private seller can't match.

Whatever you buy there are certain steps you should take to check out the development and its builder. Check out the terms of any special financing deal carefully, particularly any scheme that relies on continuously rising house prices. Buyers of starter homes on some developments in the late 1980s tempted with an offer to buy half their property immediately and the rest in five years' time were badly hit: prices turned down, and they faced demands for a second payment based on the value of their property in the boom. By then many of them had negative equity and couldn't borrow the money they needed to complete the deal. Remember that any 'cheap' finance deal is almost certainly reflected in the price – there's no such thing as a free lunch.

For all new developments, a chat with existing dwellers as to the standards of after-care service can be informative. And ask the selling agents for names of schemes the developer has done before. Go and have a look to see how they are faring. Whoever you are buying from, check the specifications in the brochure carefully. Do not assume you will get the standard of fittings in a show flat unless they are specifically listed. Do not assume room sizes are accurate: they have been known to be a good bit smaller than the show flat.

In any newly built home, there are certain simple checks like, for example, jumping up and down in the centre of the floor. See if the pictures fall off the show-flat walls. Send your partner to the next room and upstairs and see if you can hear footsteps or conversation. New homes should carry a 10-year warranty from the National House Building Council (NHBC). But this isn't a guarantee, regardless of what the developer might tell you. It's an insurance policy, mainly intended to cover the builder. The cover is fairly basic and may not include what you might think are pretty glaring defects. The NHBC was forced to revise its warranty in 1997 to clarify its cover and is also extending it to conversions for the first time.

Ask searching questions about the future of the development. The model and plans may show a lovely new leisure complex, but when will it be built, and is there anything in your contract with the developer to say it must be? What is going up next door? Check, and don't believe bland assurances from the (often part-time) staff in the sales office. Most town halls have helpful planning enquiry offices these days. They will tell you what else is planned for the neighbourhood and let you see local development plans. This will avoid buying under the impression that the land across the road is going to be (as the sales lady put it) 'local shops' when it has outline permission for a 50,000-sq ft superstore and a 'leisure complex'. Yes, it happened.

Onto the housing ladder

If you're a first-time buyer, you'll be welcomed with open arms by estate agents delighted that you're not in a chain with something to sell. You should also be able to get a competitive mortgage deal (see also *Mortgages* chapter.)

Sharp falls in interest rates from their peak of 15 per cent in 1990 to around 6.9 per cent now have made mortgages vastly more affordable. First-time buyers are now spending less than a third of their take-home pay on mortgage costs – it was 81 per cent in 1990. Fixed-rate deals and discounts for the first two to five years help ease the pain, although coming to the end of the fixed-rate term can be a shock. Beware, too, of 'lock-in' clauses, again see *Mortgages*. But if you are struggling to put your first foot on the ladder, there are some schemes to help you:

• **Shared ownership** You can buy a share in a home, with the other share held by a housing association, council or other body. You pay this shareholder rent on the portion of the home it owns. You can buy extra shares when you can afford it at the price set on the home by the District Valuer. When you come to sell, the profit on the share you own is yours. It is best to go into shared purchase with at least a 50 per cent stake, otherwise the rent payable, and the small proportion of the profit gained on resale, make it uneconomic. Shared purchase is available in London, as is the related scheme allowing tenants of charitable housing associations to buy private homes at a discount. The Housing Corporation and your borough council (see *Boroughs* chapter) are the people to consult.

• **Council properties** There's now a significant market in ex-council flats bought by their tenants under the Right to Buy scheme. Flats can often appear very cheap, particularly if they're in well-established areas, and they can be spacious. But be warned: lenders may be reluctant to lend on properties in blocks more than six storeys high or built from non-traditional methods (system-built for example) or with a low proportion of home-owners on the estate. Even if you have the cash to buy, you may find it difficult to sell if a purchaser can't get a mortgage. The value of ex-council flats is also very vulnerable to downturns in the market.

There are some flats on the market for between £20,000 and £30,000, but almost the only takers are landlords wanting to rent them out. Purchasers of flats in some council blocks have also been faced with huge repair bills. Council blocks can be expensive to repair and many have been badly maintained for years due to council spending restraints. You will normally buy your home on a long lease with the council as freeholder, and will be bound to pay your share of any repair bill. Before you buy, check with the council that there are no outstanding repairs not paid for and get details of any works planned.

Some councils including Wandsworth and Westminster have been big supporters of Right to Buy and have made efforts to respond to purchasers' problems.

• **Joint mortgages** Until 1988, holders of joint mortgages could each claim tax relief on £30,000 of mortgage interest. A change to the rules restricting this to one set of relief per property was widely blamed for setting off a housing slump that led to deep recession. Today's sharers are not necessarily couples but two or more friends who buy a property jointly and split the costs. This needs careful drafting of a legal agreement setting out terms of ownership and making clear what happens if one participant wants to sell up.

Selling

There is always limitless advice available for the guidance of first-time buyers, from free leaflets from the building society to whole books on the subject. Strangely, there is almost nothing to help the seller – first-time or otherwise. This is surprising: selling a home is an activity even more likely to be carried out in conditions of stress, since in most cases you will also be trying to buy your next one, co-ordinate it with the sale, and arrange for the move. Yet, even before the promised reforms, there is much that can be done in order to get off to a good, fast start – and speed is generally all-important to one party or the other in a London property deal.

For example, a problem particularly peculiar to London is the length of time it takes to get the local authority searches carried out. Councils vary widely in the time they take to complete this bit of form-filling: the City of London, with only a few thousand private residents, has been known to reply in one day. Others drag their feet. With such councils, it's best if possible to do the searches in person: enquire at the town hall. You will find average search times listed in this book in each area's information summary at the end of the chapter – the official target date is 10 working days, which is what the councils tend to say they achieve, but this is not always true. These searches, by the way, are a task generally undertaken by the prospective buyer, but there's no reason why the seller shouldn't get a search carried out: a small extra expense that can save weeks. The results are valid for three months.

Your solicitor can of course arrange this for you – which is a second point. Alert your solicitor to the fact that a move is impending: people often forget to do this, assuming that there will be time enough when a buyer is in view. That is a bad point at which to discover that your solicitor is on holiday or even – as has been known – has died, retired or sold his firm since you needed him last. Once notified, he can also draw up a draft contract in readiness, and can retrieve the deeds to your property from bank, building society or other mortgagor (you by this time have probably forgotten that whoever lent you the money holds the deeds – and that they, too, can take their time about getting them out of the system).

The role of solicitors, whose busy offices (to put the kindest light on it) can hold things up to the point of jeopardizing the sale, is, like everything else, under review: see the start of this chapter. Whether you use a solicitor or a licensed conveyancer, keep ringing to ensure they're getting on with things.

A top London estate agent added the interesting rider that not only can such preparation hasten the conclusion of a sale, it helps the agent to test the true worth of the would-be buyer. If the seller's side isn't ready to proceed, it can be weeks before you discover that the apparently eager buyer's own home isn't, after all, quite sold, or that they haven't, after all, got access to quite enough money.

A good agent will point all this out to you, and in London there is no shortage of agents to choose from. Like the little girl in the old rhyme, when they are good they are very, very good, and when they are bad . . .

Choosing an agent

A lot hinges on the seller's ability to pick the right agent and then instruct them properly. You should see at least four. If you don't already have strong ideas on which are the most favoured locally, it can help to go window-shopping, checking for offices in a prominent position, with properties of the calibre of your own, well displayed, and run by welcoming staff. You can go in, describe your own place and ask for details of anything of that type on their books. This serves the dual purpose of finding what the competition is, and how much, and what their reception of your potential buyers is going to be like. You can get confirmation of your own feelings, and further recommendations, by asking people who come into contact with estate agents, such as building societies, banks, builders and solicitors – and local friends and neighbours.

Showing prospective agents your home is a good practice-run for showing potential buyers. Remember that agents are human too: they, like buyers, are seeing many different properties; they, too, can be put off by an untidy, uncleaned shambles smelling of last night's dinner. Light, warmth, flowers and furniture polish (the old-fashioned smelly sort) really can do wonders to underline a welcoming atmosphere. And tidy up – at least – outside: buyers can, and have, been put off before they've even got through the door. Clutter is a real turn-off.

Fixing a price

Having decided to sell and picked an agent, what do you need from them? First, of course, you want to know what price he (or she) suggests. A house is worth what someone is willing to pay: there is no absolute number. The agent needs to take into account not only what appears to be the going rate, but the state of the overall market and your personal circumstances, too. If you must sell by next week, both marketing and price will be different.

When you get your property valued, don't necessarily go for the agent predicting the highest price. They may be desperate to get instructions and inflate the price they say they can get just to impress you. (Their commission is also calculated on the price of the property.) It's no good putting your property on the market at an inflated price only to see it hang heavy for months. Ask the agent how he's arrived at that price and what evidence of other sales of similar properties there is to substantiate his view.

Conversely, there is the very low price that should in certain circumstances raise an eyebrow – perhaps suggested for the large, old, empty property you're selling on behalf of your dear departed aunty? Luckily it is, of course, illegal these days for agents to fail to disclose conflicts of interest – such as the developer who'd like him to look out for large, old, cheap properties . . .

Ask what the agent proposes to do to sell your home. Ask whether the agent has a regular contract with national or local magazines or newspapers. This can be a tangible benefit: contracts mean cheaper advertising rates and a saving to be passed on to you. It also indicates the level that the agency is working on, of course. Maybe expensive brochures will be appropriate. Some firms have press offices who will send out a release to papers and magazines about interesting homes. Does the firm have its own magazine? Or an Internet site? Will your home be included – and if so, how quickly and for how long? Will it have a photograph? Look at existing advertisements by the firm. Are the photographs clear? Is the wording precise and proof-read?

Fees come last. Some agents make a point of a lower percentage, but take this on the 'you get what you pay for' principle. A skilled agent's negotiating acumen can easily save you the half of a per cent extra he charges. What *will* vary the rate charged is whether you appoint one firm sole agent or, as you are perfectly entitled to do, instruct several at once. Agencies charge less if they get sole agency, and they work harder, because all the effort they put in will be rewarded if they get a sale. Appoint more than one, and only one will get a fee from the transaction; all of them will know this and it will be reflected in the intensity of their efforts.

You'll find that agents come in all shapes and sizes, from one-partner, one-office, old-established concerns, through brash, keen newcomers to big independent practices and the local offices of large chains. Each has its advantages. Weigh local knowledge against marketing skill, the personal touch against chain-breaking clout. With big firms, ensure that the people you deal with know your area and have not just been transferred from Sidcup. All this said, choosing an agent is a personal business. Whatever the firm, it is only as good as the staff in your local branch: choose the people who impress you most.

However expert the agent, you know your home best. He should therefore look to you to check draft particulars. They should be set out clearly and logically, and remember that items mentioned in them are generally understood to be included in the price unless otherwise specified. If you are going to be showing people around, he should brief you, because he can provide an objective list of selling points to mention. If you are not showing buyers round, who is? Can you meet them first, and are they both personable and intelligent (an elusive combination in junior staff in estate agents)? Who should you contact for progress reports – you should expect regular news, but remember that they have others places to sell too: don't ring them every day.

Selling tends to be fraught with excitements, and it's wise to keep cool. But what if you have appointed an agent and nothing seems to result? Give the agent a set number of weeks of sole agency, and if there is no action call him in for a progress report. There may be good reasons for the dearth of buyers. At this point decide whether to give him a longer period of sole agency, appoint a second agent as well, or even drop the first entirely. Good agents are loud in their encouragement of clients who are forthright: if there is a problem, let them hear about it.

Price charts: sales

The charts on the following pages consolidate the data in the Area Profiles in this book, showing broadly what certain kinds of homes cost in each of the areas covered. This gives you a freeze-frame picture across London at the start of the 1999 selling season: a basis for comparison thoughout the year.

The prices given are for typical examples of each type of home. Where a range of figures is shown, this reflects price variations within the area. Thus the range is also an indicator of the scope of the properties in the area: if the figures for, say, a 1-bed

FLATS — SALES   STARTING PRICES FOR 1999

65–75: range in £1000s   — too few for price average   → price carries over

	STUDIO	1 BEDROOM	2 BEDROOM	3 BEDROOM	4 BEDROOM	5 BEDROOM +
Acton	50–65	70–90	85–130	120–180	—	—
Balham and Tooting	45–60+	55–100	75–150	100–180	—	—
Barnes, Mortlake and Sheen	50–70+	75–150+	90–250+	120–300+	180–400	—
Battersea	60–90	70–150	90–230	175–300	400+	—
Bayswater	55–100	100–200	130–250	250–1M	350–1M	—
Bedford Park and Acton Green	60–100	90–170+	135–300+	150–300+	—	—
Belgravia	140–160	250–500+	400–1.25M	500+	1M+	›
Bethnal Green	55–63	65–100	75–160	85–165	—	—
Bloomsbury and King's Cross	60–80	95–200	130–300	175–250+	—	—
Bow	35–100	40–115	50–130+	75–180	—	—
Brixton, Herne Hill and Tulse Hill	35–50	35–100	60–140	70–160	—	—
Camberwell	35–55	50–95	70–150	80–170	100+	—
Camden Town and Primrose Hill	60–80	90–150	100–200	180–250+	—	—
Chelsea	100–150	130–350	250–500+	300–1M	500–1M+	850–1.5M+
Chiswick	60–80	85–125	100–180+	160–260+	—	—
City and Fringes	70–110	120–210+	130–350+	190–400	170–450+	—
Clapham	50–80	65–140	100–220	110–250	130–280	—
Clerkenwell and Finsbury	75–110	120–170+	150–350+	200–500	—	—
Cricklewood	45–55	55–80	80–100+	90–115	—	—
Crouch End and Stroud Green	55	85–110	100–130	150–200	—	—
Crystal Palace	23–30	35–65	60–115	70–130	100+	—
Dollis Hill and Neasden	45–50	60–70	80–90	90–95	—	—
Dulwich	35–60	45–110	65–160	80–200	—	—
Ealing	50–75	60–125	80–180	120–240	—	—
Finchley	35–60	60–105	75–130	100–150	—	—
Forest Hill	40–50	50–60	70–90	75–90	100+	—
Fulham	70–100	90–140	120–270	150–300+	200+	—
Golders Green	60–85	70–100	100–200+	120–250+	175+	—
Greenwich and Blackheath	40–60	65–130	80–180+	100–400	—	—
Hackney	30–45	40–80	55–120	70–140	100–130+	—
Hammersmith	60–100	75–170	130–250	›370	—	—
Hampstead	70–100	130–225	150–350+	200–450	300–1M+	300–2M
Hampstead Garden Suburb	—	85–120	100–280	140–350	—	—
Hendon and Mill Hill	45–50	65–75	85–130+	120–200+	—	—
Highgate	50–90	75–190	120–250+	150–350+	250–500	—
Holland Park	120–160	150–400	230–750+	3700–1M	›1M+	800–1.7M+
Islington and Highbury	70–90	80–130	130–250	250+	—	—
Kennington, Vauxhall and Stockwell	50–70	60–120	90–150	120–200	150–210	180–300

flat are 65–75, it is likely to be a fairly homogeneous area; £65–75,000 should give you a choice of flats here. If 65–115, it is clear that that there are some neighbourhoods that warrant a good premium, or perhaps there is a supply of recently developed, more luxurious flats. In all brackets, you will be likely to findcheaper homes and exceptional ones at the other end of the scale: a plus sign is used where we have not included the prices for a small number of unusual examples which would distort the averages.

HOUSES — SALES   STARTING PRICES FOR 1999

65–75: range in £1000s   — too few for price average   ⟩ price carries over

	2 BEDROOM	3 BEDROOM	4 BEDROOM	5 BEDROOM	6–7 BEDROOM	8+ BEDROOM
Acton	95–170	135–220	180–280+	250–350+	⟩	⟩
Balham and Tooting	95–150+	125–250	170–300+	240–350+	⟩750	400+
Barnes, Mortlake and Sheen	145–270	180–450+	250–800+	400–2M	450–3M	—
Battersea	150–250	200–400+	280–500+	500+	600+	—
Bayswater	200–700	275–800	350–1M	500–1M+	—	—
Bedford Park and Acton Green	175–300+	230–525	325–650+	450–1M+	⟩1.25M+	—
Belgravia	450+	600–900	825–1.8M	1M–5M	⟩	⟩12M+
Bethnal Green	85–190	110–180+	140–250	—	—	—
Bloomsbury and King's Cross	125–260+	150–300+	350+	—	—	—
Bow	100–160	115–250	125–320+	⟩	—	—
Brixton, Herne Hill and Tulse Hill	80–170	100–220	120–300	⟩450	200+	—
Camberwell	95–165	110–200	130–250	175–300+	400+	—
Camden Town and Primrose Hill	130–220	185–300+	275–500	350–550+	—	—
Chelsea	300–700	400–1M	600–2.5M	1.25M+	2M–5M+	—
Chiswick	190–260	210–330	260–500+	340–650+	400–1.5M+	—
City and Fringes	—	350–450	400–600+	575+	—	—
Clapham	135–270	180–370+	200–550+	300–750+	500+	800+
Clerkenwell and Finsbury	250+	350–500+	400–900+	—	—	—
Cricklewood	90–140	120–200+	150–425	220–695+	⟩	—
Crouch End and Stroud Green	130–200	160–300	250–350+	450–600	—	—
Crystal Palace	75–100	85–150	120–220	170–250+	235–500	300+
Dollis Hill and Neasden	85–95	130–165	150–190	—	—	—
Dulwich	100–230	120–350	150–600	175–800	225–1.3M	600–1.5M
Ealing	120–250	140–300	180–500	300–600	400–1M	⟩
Finchley	100–130	130–230	180–390	250–500	600–800+	—
Forest Hill	70–90	120–150	130–170	170–250	200–400	—
Fulham	200+	250–400+	280–500+	300–1M	400+	—
Golders Green	130–160	140–225	200–500	250–600	350–700	350–700+
Greenwich and Blackheath	100–200	140–400	200–500+	275–500+	600–1.6M	—
Hackney	80–160	95–220	145–300+	170–350+	—	—
Hammersmith	200–300	230–375+	330–500+	400–650+	⟩	—
Hampstead	250–450	300–900+	400–1M+	500–1.5M+	650–2.5M+	2M–15M
Hampstead Garden Suburb	120–300	200–350+	300–600+	400–1M	500–10M	⟩
Hendon and Mill Hill	100–130	140–260	180–350	300–360+	350–1M	1M+
Highgate	160–325+	270–425+	300–700+	400–5M	⟩	⟩
Holland Park	350–700	500–1M	750–2M	⟩3M+	⟩8M	⟩8M+
Islington and Highbury	170–300	200–400	260–600	450+	—	—
Kennington, Vauxhall and Stockwell	100–250+	160–350	200–500	200–600	400+	⟩

FLATS — SALES

65–75: range in £1000s   — too few for price average   → price carries over

	STUDIO	1 BEDROOM	2 BEDROOM	3 BEDROOM	4 BEDROOM	5 BEDROOM +
Kensington	90–140	140–300+	220–500+	300–600+	500–1M+	600–1.5M+
Kentish Town and Tufnell Park	60–85	75–120	100–200	130–220	—	—
Kilburn, Kensal Green and Queen's Park	55–65	75–110	100–150+	140–200	170–200+	—
Knightsbridge	85–200+	170–375+	250–700	340–1M+	500–1M+	750–1.5M+
Lewisham and Catford	25–40	40–70	50–75	55–80	75–130	—
Leyton and Walthamstow	25–40	35–70	50–90	60–110	—	—
Maida Vale and Little Venice	75–150+	100–300	150–450	250–700+	300–800+	—
Marylebone and Fitzrovia	85–125	120–275	150–400+	250–600	250–800+	380–1.4M
Mayfair and St James's	120–150	150–300+	275–850	450–1.3M	675–3.5M+	1M+
Morden, Mitcham and Colliers Wood	33–50	50–60	62–75	65–80	—	—
Muswell Hill	90+	100–200	150–175	180–200	—	—
New Cross and Deptford	35–50	50–60	55–90	75–120	—	—
Newham	28–40	35–50	35–60	45–65	—	—
Notting Hill and North Kensington	75–150+	110–300	160–400+	200–450+	350–750	—
Peckham	25–35	35–70	55–100	60–115	75–150	—
Pimlico and Westminster	85–165	110–250+	170–400+	200–400+	400–2M+	—
Poplar	50–60	60–90	70–90	70–100	—	—
Putney and Roehampton	60–85	100–135	130–250+	180–300	220–350+	—
Regent's Park	100–135	125–265+	220–800	300+	400+	'3M
Richmond and Kew	65–100	90–170+	135–300+	170–400+	250–420	—
Shepherd's Bush	50–80	70–125	110–180	120–220	150–250	—
Soho and Covent Garden	100–225+	140–330	200–525	250–750	—	—
The South Bank	50–150	60–200	65–300	175–400+	›	—
South Kensington, Earl's Court and West Brompton	85–160	140–300+	200–450	375–600	400–1M	—
Southfields and Earlsfield	45–75	60–110	80–150	90–160	—	—
Southgate and Palmers Green	35–45	50–80	70–100	100–130	—	—
St John's Wood	75–135	115–250	180–350+	300+	400–2M+	›
Stepney and Whitechapel	55–60	55–90	70–100	90–150	—	—
Stoke Newington	40–55	50–95+	70–150	95–150+	115–160+	—
Streatham	35–40	55–70	70–95	85–100+	120+	—
Tottenham and Finsbury Park	30–60	35–85	50–115	60–170	—	—
Totteridge and Whetstone	60–90	70–105	80–300+	1/5–325	—	—
Twickenham and Teddington	55–70	80–120	90–180	120–200+	—	—
Wandsworth	60–80	90–120	110–200+	150+	—	—
West Hampstead	55–80	80–130	110–190	150–300	200–350+	—
West Norwood, Norbury and Gipsy Hill	—	45–60	55–90	80–100	—	—
Willesden and Brondesbury Park	45–70	60–110	80–125+	90–200+		—
Wimbledon, Raynes Park and Merton Park	45–90	75–130	100–250	100–300+	—	—

HOUSES — SALES

65–75: range in £1000s   — too few for price average   ⇢ price carries over

	2 BEDROOM	3 BEDROOM	4 BEDROOM	5 BEDROOM	6–7 BEDROOM	8+ BEDROOM
Kensington	350–700	450–800+	600–1M+	800–2M+	1M–5M	2M+
Kentish Town and Tufnell Park	180–300	200–350	250–500	270–400+	—	—
Kilburn, Kensal Green and Queen's Park	130–160	150–300+	180–350+	220–350+	—	—
Knightsbridge	350–750+	500–1M+	800–1.4M+	1M+	2M+	4M+
Lewisham and Catford	70–90	80–150+	110–200	120–220	220+	—
Leyton and Walthamstow	60–90	70–180	100–250	⇢250+	—	—
Maida Vale and Little Venice	—	250–800	550–1M+	750–3M+	⇢3.5M+	⇢
Marylebone and Fitzrovia	250–500	350–700	350–1M	550–2M	⇢2.5M	—
Mayfair and St James's	450+	750+	850+	1.3M+	2.2M+	4.5M–10.5M+
Morden, Mitcham and Colliers Wood	75–85	90–150	110–150+	145+	—	—
Muswell Hill	170+	200–300	300–450	350–600	550+	—
New Cross and Deptford	60–120	85–140	110–250	⇢	⇢300	—
Newham	50–75	60–100	75–200	—	—	—
Notting Hill and North Kensington	220–650	250–750+	400–1M	600–2M+	⇢3.5M	⇢5.5M
Peckham	70–100	75–150	100–250	130–300	250–600	—
Pimlico and Westminster	—	380–700	450–750+	650–850+	800–2.75M	—
Poplar	90–125	100–200	120–250+	⇢	—	—
Putney and Roehampton	170–250	250–400	300–550	450–800	600–825	⇢1M
Regent's Park	350–650	450–800	520–1.1M+	⇢2M	1.75–6.5M	⇢20M
Richmond and Kew	160–280+	200–500	250–750+	300–900+	600–1.1M+	—
Shepherd's Bush	170–230	180–280	250–375	300–500	—	—
Soho and Covent Garden	350+	450+	650+	750+	—	—
The South Bank	125–300	160–500+	⇢	⇢	—	—
South Kensington, Earl's Court and West Brompton	85–160	140–300+	200–450	375–600	400–1M+	⇢8M
Southfields and Earlsfield	120–200	170–250	230–300	280–350		
Southgate and Palmers Green	90–120	110–140	150–200	250–350	—	—
St John's Wood	250–400+	350–800	525–1.5M	650–2M+	1M–2M+	3.5M–7.5M
Stepney and Whitechapel	80–115	110–150	180+	—	—	—
Stoke Newington	150–180	170–220	185–300+	220–320+	—	—
Streatham	90+	95–170+	160–250+	200–500	220–500	300+
Tottenham and Finsbury Park	65–90	90–160	100–200	120–200+	—	—
Totteridge and Whetstone	100–150	150–400	200–600	250–1M	600–1.5M	—
Twickenham and Teddington	130–200	150–300	200–450+	250–650+	500+–1M	800+
Wandsworth	140–250	210–400	250–500	400+	—	—
West Hampstead	220–350	250–375	300–450	300–500+	—	—
West Norwood, Norbury and Gipsy Hill	85–130	90–150+	130–350	200+	⇢	⇢
Willesden and Brondesbury Park	90–110	130–240	200–500	250–500+	—	—
Wimbledon, Raynes Park and Merton Park	125–250	150–350+	200–500+	250–1M+	400–2M+	—

Mortgages
by David Spittles

Decoding estate agents, hype and sweet-talking sellers into leaving the Designers Guild curtains are the easy bits of the house-buying process. The real anguish lies in finding the best way to fund the purchase. If you make the wrong decision now, you could be regretting it for the next 25 years.

There are dozens of mortgage lenders offering hundreds of loans. It can be extremely confusing, especially if you are a first-time buyer, and it is easy to get swayed, even misled.

In general, mortgage rates are low – about as cheap as they have been for 30 or so years – but many loans come with a sting in the tail. This usually takes the form of a redemption penalty if you later switch to another type of loan. Or you may be forced to take out insurance – life or household – that is not really suitable.

New deals

The mortgage market is cut-throat and even older and wise buyers preparing to move up-market can find themselves talked into unattractive remortgage deals.

One of the essential points to remember is not to over-complicate your mortgage finance. Most people have simple needs; all they require is a no-frills mortgage at a competitive rate of interest. Exotic loans like foreign currency mortgages have re-emerged, but the vast, vast majority of borrowers should not even consider them. Only if you are paid in a foreign currency are they worth considering.

The advent of the euro and the single currency has now complicated the issue of what type of mortgage you should choose because it has increased speculation about interest rates. Is it wise to opt for a fixed rate that is competitive now, but one which could become much higher than the going rate if Britain decides to sign up for the single currency?

Another factor is that low inflation is already having an impact on returns from endowment policies, which are still commonly used to back mortgages.

Basically, it is worth spending time now getting to know the various types of mortgages available. Assess your medium-to-long term plans and speak to several lenders. If the advice you get is fairly consistent, then check out the small print of the deals that are on offer.

'Don't look solely at the headline rate of interest. It is easy to be influenced by one particular lender dangling a seemingly unbeatable deal,' warns Patrick Bunton of Bath-based broker London & Country Mortgages.

Mortgage brokers can help if your circumstances are unusual or you just don't have time to shop around. Telephone mortgages have become a popular choice for borrowers in a hurry. It is possible to process an application and get a provisional quote within minutes. Lenders are also homing in on the Internet, but arranging a mortgage over the phone or on-line is only recommended for those people who know the ropes.

A mortgage of two halves

The first task is to get to know the various types of mortgage. Basically, a mortgage is two things: it is the interest rate charged and the repayment vehicle. The latter is the means by which you repay the amount you originally borrowed.

The standard variable rate quoted by lenders is used as a benchmark for the cost of a mortgage. Most lenders peg the rate at around the same figure, though mutual building societies like Nationwide tend to be lower than banks. Also, a lower variable rate may be charged if you take out a bigger-than-average mortgage.

Fewer and fewer people stick with the variable rate because lower special deals are pushed by lenders in the form of discount, fixed and capped loans.

Discount loans are where the variable rate is reduced by a set amount for a specified time. The downside is that you get a payment shock when the discount comes to an end and you are locked into the variable rate.

Fixed rates are attractive because they provide certainty when budgeting repayments. You can fix your mortgage for as little as one year or as long as 10 (though most experts currently advise against longer-term fixed rates because of falling inflation).

Capped rates are now popular because the amount you pay is guaranteed not to rise above the cap, but can drop if there is a reduction in interest rates. To an extent, this gives you the best of both worlds. But the cap is usually only for a short period.

Cashback mortgages appeal most to borrowers on a budget who need money for, say, a deposit or furniture. It is possible to get a cashback of more than £10,000, which is passed on when the loan is completed. The disadvantage, however, is that the interest rate is higher than average, and if you later switch loans, you may have to repay the cashback.

Paying it back

Lenders are quite flexible about the method of capital repayment. Indeed, if you are taking out a small proportion of the value of the property, you may not be required to put any repayment vehicle in place.

All repayment vehicles are savings plans, usually linked to the stock market. You make regular contributions which go into an investment fund that hopefully will grow sufficiently to pay off the mortgage. Often you can choose the investment area and balance out the risks.

One in three buyers takes out an endowment. A with-profits endowment pays annual bonuses that are added to the fund. At the end of the term, a maturity bonus is added that can be worth up to 50 per cent of the final amount.

Once added, the annual bonuses cannot be taken away. With a unit-linked endowment, the fund value can fluctuate. But you can increase your monthly endowment payments to counter any falls in value or to pay off the mortgage earlier than planned.

The problem with endowments is that, as with any growth-dependent investment, there is a risk that the lump sum at the end will not be large enough to pay off the loan. On the other hand, if equity markets rise, policy holders can expect a surplus. Life assurance is built-in and guarantees to repay the loan in the event of your death.

Pension mortgages work in much the same way, and are most suitable for the self-employed. There is an added advantage of marginal rate tax relief.

With a traditional repayment mortgage there is no pot of gold at the end of the term, but there is a cast-iron guarantee that the mortgage will be paid off. Under this method, if your fortunes improve, you can negotiate a shorter pay back time.

Basically you pay back interest and capital on a monthly basis. Life assurance has to be taken out separately.

Individual Savings Accounts superseded Personal Equity Plans and Tessas in April 1999. ISAs can be used to back mortgages. They are tax-efficient, but the investment ceiling may not be high enough for many borrowers.

There is nothing to stop you repaying your mortgage in a number of ways. For example, someone with a £90,000 loan could pay the first £30,000 on an interest-only basis (to maximize tax relief) and the rest on a conventional repayment basis.

Lenders are also introducing flexible mortgages that allow borrowers to top up payments to create a surplus, or reduce them if times are hard. These are handy schemes for people with an uncertain cashflow. But some critics say they encourage bad discipline. Regular mortgage repayments should be your priority.

There are lenders who will advance 100 per cent of the purchase price, though usually the loan is limited to a maximum of 95 per cent of value. A few innovative lenders, including Chelsea Building Society, take on buyers with bad credit ratings.

If you need to borrow a high proportion, look for those lenders that do not charge mortgage indemnity insurance. This is a back-up for lenders in case you default, but it can add hundreds of pounds to the loan.

Mortgage checkpoints

• It can pay dividends to use a financial adviser to guide you through the mortgage maze. Some brokers have exclusive access to superior deals. Some estate agents flaunt their independence, but beware: they may be tied to a life assurance company or a mortgage lender.

• Anyone can set up as a mortgage broker, whereas financial advisers are regulated. The latter earn commission from endowment and pension insurance, so if you do take out any of these, they are likely to waive fees. Reputable brokers comply with an industry code of conduct. Check the company is a member of the scheme. Most normally charge 1 per cent of the mortgage advance.

• Even if you go through a high-street lender, there are usually arrangement fees to pay on special discount and fixed mortgages.

• Lenders have a vested interest in getting you to pay off the mortgage over as long a period as possible, which is why the 25-year term is seen as standard. But if you have the extra income you can save a significant amount by agreeing to repay the loan over 10 or 15 years.

• Alternatively, you can chip away at the mortgage by paying extra each month. This can have a dramatic impact (see table below). It is important to study the lenders' rules on early repayments – to avoid redemption penalties and to ensure the extra money doesn't languish in your mortgage for up to a year.

• Should you use a lump sum – perhaps a bonus or surprise windfall – to pay off your mortgage? Tax relief is not the advantage it once was so really it depends on your attitude to debt. Some people like having money under the bed for an emergency, others can stand being in hock. Because a mortgage can be a lifeline to cheap credit, it is wise to keep the account open with a nominal sum – £100, for example. This will make life easier if you apply for a further advance sometime in the future.

How to reduce your mortgage
£50,000 repayment loan over 25 years at interest rate of 7.5 per cent
Current repayment: £340 a month*

Extra monthly payment	Reduced mortgage term
£25	21 years 9 months
£50	19 years
£75	16 years 11 months
£100	15 years 4 months
£150	12 years 11 months
£200	11 years

*Source: Halifax Building Society

David Spittles is the Property and Personal Finance writer for the London Evening Standard.

Renting and investing

In the booming 1980s, renting was second best. What every keen young couple wanted to do was buy and get their feet on the housing ladder before prices rose beyond them. But the last recession taught them and everyone else a sharp lesson – that prices could go down as well as up. Many people, seeing home-owners trapped in negative equity or forced to sell at a loss, decided to rent. National figures show that the average age of first-time buyers rose from 22 to 28 in the '90s.

At the same time, many 'reluctant' landlords, who couldn't sell their homes at a price they could afford to accept, rented out their properties. Mortgage lenders, traditionally wary of this, were mollified by changes in the law giving landlords more control. Ironically the early-'90s recession was a factor in bringing many good-quality properties onto the rental market (albeit temporarily). It is calculated that 50 per cent of the new supply of rental homes since 1989 came from 'reluctant' landlords.

The 1988 Housing Act made this rebirth of the private rented sector possible. For the first time, landlords could sign up tenants for just six months at a market rent, with no security of tenure after the initial period. Eviction of tenants for non-payment of rent or abusing properties was made simpler and, providing the right contract was signed, landlords were in no danger of creating a sitting tenancy.

The Act broke the vicious circle whereby landlords would not invest in new rental property or carry out repairs to existing stock because they couldn't be sure of getting possession of their property when they needed to, while private owners didn't dare let their homes at all – unless to a company, which would not become a sitting tenant. Even more importantly, it created a new climate in which renting became respectable. By vastly increasing choice and flexibility, the Act made renting a psychologically acceptable option for many middle-class Britons for the first time. Now there are almost as many agents letting and managing rented homes in London as there are selling them. For a guide to how much you have to pay for what where, see our London-wide charts on pages 56–59.

First, we look at the rental scene from the point of view of the tenant, then from the perspective of landlord/investor.

Renting

Landlords and tenants sign an assured shorthold tenancy agreement. This is for a minimum initial period of six months, after which the two sides can sign a further contract if everything is going well. To end the contract, the landlord or the tenant has to give two months' notice in writing. The landlord has the right to raise the rent at the end of any six-month period. The tenant can refer his rent to a rent assessment panel if he thinks it's excessive, but only during the first six months of the tenancy.

You shouldn't now be offered an assured tenancy. This was introduced in the 1988 Act alongside the assured shorthold tenancy, but landlords lobbied for its abolition because filling in the paperwork carelessly (or more likely leaving it to an agent ignorant of the law) could render landlords inadvertently open to creating a sitting tenancy. Under the Housing Act 1996 all agreements are assumed to be assured shorthold tenancies unless expressly stated otherwise.

Sharers should all sign the tenancy agreement so that they are jointly and severally responsible. The agreement should be drawn up by a solicitor or a reputable letting agency. The agency will also advise on matters, such as deposits and references.

Before you are granted a tenancy the landlord or their agent typically asks for three references, one of which must be from your bank and another from your employer. A deposit of four to six weeks' rent is needed, to cover breakages and unpaid bills, in addition to a month's rent in advance. This deposit is held by the landlord/agent and you should get a receipt for it. The landlord or agent should handle the transfer of utility and phone accounts into your name(s). Meters should be read on 'get-in'. Tenants are responsible for paying the council tax, and single occupiers can get a 25 per cent discount on applying to the local town hall. Tenants should insure their own possessions.

Rents are normally paid monthly, in advance. Note that some agents now quote rents in weekly amounts, though the tables in this book use monthly figures. There is no introductory fee payable by tenants, but there will be costs for leases and inventories. Lease costs will occur whenever a new lease is drawn up.

You should get, and check, the inventory of contents and a schedule of condition, setting out the state the place is in. Once you have signed these, they form the basis for any deductions for breakages and 'dilapidations'. When the tenancy ends and you are about to leave, the inventory should be checked by the landlord, the agent or a specialist inventory clerk working for them. After allowance for wear and tear, any breakages or damage will come out of your deposit.

Letting

As a landlord, you enter into a legal agreement with your tenants in the terms outlined above. Landlords should insist that sharers all sign the agreement so that they are jointly and severally liable. If a sharer leaves and a new one comes in, a new agreement should be drawn up. A good lettings agent, or your solicitor, will give advice on this. It is important to get the paperwork right as errors can create problems and expense. The agreement really ought to be specific to the property, though many agents use a standard one. Ensure that it covers the particular needs of the property, such as looking after gardens, exclusion of pets if necessary (and in come cases children), security such as alarms and locks and the precise number of people who will live in the home.

Some landlords find tenants themselves, and handle the paperwork for and management of their property (this should be with the help of a solicitor). Others use an agent. Agents will offer a range of services, from introducing tenants up to full management and rent collection. Landlords (not tenants) pay them a percentage of the rent, which varies according to the level of service.

Agents will, as their most basic service, find tenants, take up references, transfer utility accounts and arrange deposits. Be clear at the outset, before you sign anything, about how much you are contracted to pay to the agent. Will you have to go on paying the same percentage of the rent even if the tenants stay for years while the agents, who do not manage the property, do no more than renew the contract periodically (for which they may charge an additional fee)? Do the agents state that if the tenants buy the property from you they want a full estate-agency fee? If so, is there a cut-off date for this clause? Do the agents hold the tenant's deposit? Consult your solicitor if in doubt. If you opt for the basic 'introduction only' service, do not expect any more. Some agents are helpful and supportive of their landlords, working on the basis that a good relationship may lead to more business. Others, alas, are less than helpful.

Landlords need to insure the property, both structure and contents. You must also inform the insurer when it is let and check that cover continues if the property is vacant between lets. Insurance is also available to cover legal expenses and loss of rent due to damage such as a fire.

As a landlord you have to comply with the safety legislation designed to protect tenants. You must have all gas appliances (boilers, cookers and so on) inspected every year by a CORGI-registered gas fitter. You must also make sure all your soft furnishings, such as beds, chairs and sofas, comply with fire regulations, which outlaw furniture bought and installed before 1988. If you fail to comply and your tenants are injured as a result, you could be sued by your tenants. If you're prosecuted you could face a prison term of up to six months or a fine of £5,000.

If you're a landlord, you should, in theory, find it easier under recent legislation to repossess your property if the tenants are in arrears or are wrecking the place. In practice, it's not that simple. It takes months for the courts to handle repossession cases, even under the 'accelerated possessions procedure', and while the wheels of justice are grinding the tenants can stay on, leaving you powerless. You can use the accelerated procedure if the tenant is refusing to leave after the end of the agreement when you've served the correct notices. Otherwise there are two types of court proceedings for possession: discretionary and mandatory. Repossession for being at least two months in arrears with the rent is mandatory, while repossession for other reasons (eg having riotous parties or using the property as a business) are discretionary.

It should be stressed that existing 'fair rent' tenancies, established under the old law, continue without change. When a property falls vacant and is re-let it will, however, be subject to the new rules.

Agents

The rental market has grown: there are now plenty of specialist lettings agents competing for landlords' custom, and established sales agencies have set up lettings departments. As a result, fees have dropped. Fees are based on a percentage of the rent for the whole term of the agreement. Do not be afraid to negotiate, especially if you have, or intend to acquire, several properties. Agents like to be paid their fee as soon as the agreement is signed – and in advance. This can cause cashflow problems on a new tenancy; also, problems may arise if the tenant leaves before the term of the agreement is complete. For these reasons try to negotiate payment of fees either monthly or six-monthly in arrears. Some rental firms offer this from the outset, others will swear it is never done. Reputable firms are quoting fees in the region of 10 per cent for finding a tenant and collecting rent, with about 15 per cent for full management. Other firms charge 10 per cent for merely finding the tenant.

Check potential agents with care: membership of ARLA (Association of Residential Lettings Agents) and/or one of the three main estate agents' bodies, the RICS (Royal Institution of Chartered Surveyors), the ISVA (Incorporated Society of Valuers and Auctioneers) or the NAEA (National Association of Estate Agents), are good signs. The trade body, ARLA stipulates that its members have to have been in business for at least two years, hold professional indemnity insurance and run separate client accounts. From 2000, an ARLA member-firm must have an ARLA-qualified person in each office, be it main or branch. To find out names of ARLA members in a given area, phone 01923 896 555. For a copy of their leaflet *Trouble-Free Letting* send a SAE to ARLA Admin, Maple House, 53–55 Woodside Road, Amersham, Bucks. Other estate agents' bodies also supply useful information for both landlords and tenants. The RICS offers free leaflets to landlords and tenants: phone 0171 222 7000. The RICS also offers a £9.95 book entitled *Rent Only Residential Management Code*, which clarifies the law. In January the government announced the National Approved Lettings Scheme, which codifies the points outlined above and to which all the above bodies subscribe.

Investing in property

Buying a flat or house to let out is now widely discussed by individuals as an alternative to funding a pension scheme or building a share portfolio. And there is more than talk going on: looking across the country, 20 per cent of new homes produced between 1988 and 1996 were let.

The departure of most of the early-'90s batch of 'reluctant' landlords has been more than outweighed by the advent of a new breed of small landlords. At the same time companies and institutions are cautiously returning to residential property after an absence of 80 years. This investment is underpinned by the figures, as an important research study by FPDSavills points out. It calculates that returns on homes averaged 14 per cent per annum over the past 23 years. This is the sum of an average gross yield of 10 per cent plus capital gain. This long-term trend disguises some wild swings in capital values (selling prices). FPDSavills' research makes the point that rent levels track prices quite closely, but are generally far less volatile.

There are two ways of becoming a property investor. Short-term traders move in and out of individual properties, and the whole sector, buying and selling as the market changes. This route depends upon taking capital gains, including the profit made on developing (doing up) properties. Long-haul investors believe that rents and prices have a long-term, stable growth trend and look for a good rental income as their main return. They also hope property will at least keep pace with inflation. Such investors take comfort in FPDSavills' cautious comparison of the price of a semi-detached house compared to inflation since 1855: the house price is up by four times inflation, but has about kept in line with the growth of average earnings. There is evidence that most new small investors see themselves as long-term players, with residential property being considered as a viable alternative (or adjunct) to a pension plan.

Individual investors began to appear in strength in the mid-'90s, as City bonuses once again put flat-sized chunks of cash into bank accounts. Those lesser mortals needing to borrow to finance investment used to have a hard time, but an initiative from ARLA produced the Buy-to-Let scheme which offers mortgages at rates little different from those available to owner-occupiers. The total invested so far is more than £1.25 billion. To this figure add the (unknown) number of homes bought by institutions and companies and by individuals outside the ARLA scheme. There is little research yet on how many rental properties there are in total: the much-quoted national figure of 11 per cent probably includes tied properties, which are not in the open market. No-one knows exactly how many rented homes there are in London, though it naturally has a larger proportion than the country as a whole.

The figures are hard to compute because a rented home can quickly become an owner-occupied home, and vice versa. After all, a tenant is a home-seeker who decides to rent not buy.

The outlook for rents

Two months into 1999, interest rates are at a historical low, and fixed-rate loans for as long as ten years are available. This allows investors to tie down at least one of the many variables in the equation: financing costs. But how stable are rents?

Experts are convinced that in the short term rents will fall back. Several factors are reducing tenant demand, and the supply of homes to rent is increasing. But starry-eyed commentators (and of course feet-on-the-ground, keen-to-sell estate agents) were pointing out in January that London rented-property yields were averaging 10 per cent, while government bonds were yielding 4.5 per cent. 'The magic of buy-to-let' was one of the headlines. By the time the papers pick up on a good investment, the professionals are usually tiptoeing towards the exits.

True to form, we found reports of seasoned investors cashing in their property chips at the same time as new money was flooding into Docklands, Islington and Tooting. In some areas agents said that 30 per cent of flat-buyers were investors.

Will these new-wave investors find their sums adding up? The big factor is tenant demand. Many tenancies at all levels of the market are generated, directly or indirectly, by the City. On the one hand, last year saw many tenancies surrendered as redundancies and withdrawals of staff followed the dire financial forecasts and mergers. This led to over-supply of homes to let, particularly in prime central areas, and thus to rents weakening. But on the other hand, thanks to the same jobs' uncertainty, many other City workers postponed buying homes and decided to rent instead.

There again, looking at the wider market, low interest rates – and thus lower mortgage payments – may prompt other home-seekers to the opposite conclusion, to buy and not rent. Stock-market jitters can, on the one hand, prompt investment buying (bricks and mortar not erratic shares) and, on the other, lead (as with those City workers) to postponed owner-occupation purchases. If this balancing act leaves tenant numbers dropping this will drive rents – and thus yields – down, leading to investors getting out and the supply of homes to let contracting once more. No-one can predict exactly how this spider's web of variables is going to work out, but you should be aware of them this year.

London's international financial role adds further imponderables. Many tenants – and some investors – are foreign. Tenant numbers fluctuate as firms arrive, depart, merge, grow and shrink. Late 1998 saw relocation companies, which had been paying premiums to rent top-rank family homes, turn the tables and negotiate rent cuts.

The value of the pound influences foreign investors – but so does uncertainty in their own markets, which can provoke a 'flight to safety' with London property as the bolt-hole. The financial crashes in the Far East in late 1997 and early 1998 did not, as widely predicted, result in waves of panic-selling of residential investments in London. Agents found that most Far-East investors were not forced to sell up. They needed reassurance about the price they could get, should they need to sell (some worried phone calls came in at very odd hours, an agent recalls). Then they largely hung on, comforted by the income in Sterling that they were getting from rent, which many found useful to fund childrens' education in this country.

There has been an assumption among investors that rents will at least stay the same if not rise. FPDSavills, in the study mentioned above, observe that there are no data for long-term rent levels in London. FPDSavills can go as far back as 1985 and they reckon that rents rose steadily, in line with prices, though both fell ten years ago: prices fell from 1989 to 1992, and rents from 1990 to 1992, with a slight dip in 1994. Rents fell far less far than prices, however. A cautionary note is that London rents are quite a lot higher than in other European or American cities.

The outlook for supply

Last winter, landlords were meeting the new experience of having to lower rents, or at least not raise them, to get or keep tenants. This was patchy depending upon area. Not only classic central-London renting areas, but also those with a large supply of new homes to let, saw rents fall. Winkworth's lettings manager in Hammersmith, Andrew Johnson, observed in late January 'this year there are fewer people with budgets able to satisfy landlords' expectations, and our pricing is subsequently less aggressive'. He added that lower rents in neighbouring Kensington narrowed the price gap with Hammersmith – further lessening local demand.

Rents in Docklands, especially Canary Wharf, rose in late 1998, thanks to growing demand due to firms moving into the area. In Tooting, brisk demand pushed rents up 20 per cent in 1998, reported Winkworths, with overspill from Clapham and Battersea driving the market. Yet rents for one-bed flats in, for example, the Hampstead area (which had seen a lot of new developments) dropped by five per cent due to over-supply, said Knight Frank.

If house prices stagnate or fall, developers selling new homes adjust their prices faster than private vendors. The unsold units in some on-going schemes were being offered last winter with inducements and discounts of five to 10 per cent on early-'98 prices, and new developments are being priced cautiously. Lower prices mean investors can accept lower rents, and other homes in the area start to look overpriced.

Low and stable interest rates – a new experience to just about everyone in property – allows developers to turn investors. If the flats don't sell, reasoned Central

London developer Crown Dilmun in January, let's start our own rental agency and let them. Ten years ago this would have been a short-cut to receivership as the finance costs invariably exceeded the likely rental yield by at least 100 per cent. Now the equation is the other way round. Why not postpone the development profit, accept a gross yield (on your actual costs, not the marked-up selling prices) of about 12 per cent, pay the bank six per cent and wait for prices to rise? Some of these firms may well stay investors for the long term.

New developments can cause a glut of rental property in areas, points out Linda Beaney of Beaney Pearce. If 40 flats in a new block are sold (especially pre-sold) to investors, on completion they will all be seeking tenants at the same time.

No-one knows how much the predicted lower interest rate and inflation regime in the UK will influence investors' expectations. If they will accept yields from property that are lower than at present but are still higher than other investments, they may continue to hold property even if yields are forced down by lower rents. And the growth in supply of rented homes, as corporate, institutional, foreign and private investors discover the sector, would seem to point to lower rents, assuming that the number of tenants is broadly static. This is the view of Simon Agace, chairman of Winkworths, who in January found it odd that investors were expecting rental returns to rise at a time when interest rates were falling. He, however, believes that ultimately yields will recover.

Choosing an investment property
Buy with your head, not your heart: this is business, not nest-building. Look at a property through the eyes of potential tenants: is it very convenient or is the tube really close? Do your research: stick to areas you know, or can get to know. Read the relevant chapters in this Guide. Check the tube station's zone (see under Transport in the Guide's area chapters) and the time taken to get to the City and West End. Speak to several agents, asking specific advice on buying a rental property. Get hold of as many lists of homes for sale, and for rent, as you can, from agents' offices and the Internet. Once a likely prospect is found, pay for a survey and quiz the surveyor on the price compared to like properties: this is as important as dry rot in the basement.

Be sure about areas and neighbourhoods and postcodes: the information is all in this book. Some foreign investment buyers have been lured to areas neither they, nor most Londoners, are familiar with, but people coming to live in London for two or three years want to feel comfortable with an address. And it must be one that their friends, colleagues and bosses recognize as respectable. However lovely the living-room furnishings, the lure of the cheerfully scruffy up-and-coming area is lost on the average German banker. If your property is at banker level, be aware that relocation agents – valuable clients – will accept or reject a property with one look at the outside. Ensure before buying that the common parts and block management of flats are of good quality, and if you do invest in it keep it looking smart.

Out in the bread-and-butter, flat-share market, extra bathrooms are a plus, with the market being led by new developments which provide at least an additional shower-room. Universal advice from agents is that quality decoration makes a difference. Parking, especially secure parking, is a plus at every level and is expected in Docklands and other central new developments. Tenants want things to work: the central heating, the shower, the security. They do not want someone's ideas of daring decor, they prefer what agents call 'neutral' colour schemes. They want a garden (if any) that is small and easy to manage.

Within these generalizations there are fascinating sub-markets: landlords of Belgravia flats find it worth spending thousands on swagged curtains; homes on the US Embassy property list (a coveted status) must be packed with giant fridges and icemakers. Mayfair tenants these days want three bedrooms rather than two – the third for the office. One phone line seems antediluvian: ideally, four – to cope with the fax and the Internet. Kitchens must be ubiquitously marble, maple and stainless. Bathrooms are to be luxurious and above all efficient. In most prime areas over the last year, rents for larger flats and houses have gone up faster than for small ones.

At the other end of the market, tenants will rent a convenient, well-placed, well-maintained ex-council flat or house that they might hesitate to buy. The downside of ex-council flats is management. Unless you own the whole block, you can easily be a victim of uncontrollable service charges and (to put it politely) conflict of interest with the freeholder: the council. Successful investments in this sector are usually houses, preferably ones in small groups in otherwise privately-owned areas.

The best advice this year is to go for good-quality mainstream property, aimed at professional tenants, not to try to compete in the upper-level corporate-let market. Hedge your bets if possible by choosing areas with good access to the West End as well as the City, so if the bankers get jittery you can always hope for an art dealer or an advertising person. 'It's all common sense – but people don't use it' said an agent.

Upsides and downsides

There are some downsides – property is harder than shares to sell fast. It needs to be managed. Even if nothing goes wrong, there will be a steady trickle of maintenance bills. It also costs solid money to buy and to sell. The upside is that property diversifies your investments, is tangible (which helps some investors sleep at nights in uncertain times) and it offers the hope of capital gain as well as yield. There can be tax advantages, with relief on interest on borrowings, though capital gains tax must be considered: talk to an accountant. If your work takes you away for a period, say, then owning a home keeps you up with the London market. Otherwise, a big price jump can freeze you out.

Anyone investing in London property is banking on the long-term health of London as a financial world capital. If Frankfurt wins, you'd have been better off in Cardiff.

How much will your property earn?

To calculate net yield an investor must deduct agents' fees, service charges and ground rents (if any), insurance, repairs and maintenance. Some properties cost more to maintain: gardens, lavish common parts in blocks, lifts – all can run up bills. Make realistic provision for upgrading and refurbishing. And expect void periods (time when the property is unlet): even if replacement tenants are found straight away, it takes about 10 working days to take up references and process the paperwork. Finally, add in borrowing costs, or the cost in foregone interest of using your own capital. All these costs can soak up half your gross return.

Where are the institutions?

On paper, pension funds, insurance companies and others with long-term investment needs ought to be buying up homes to let. A handful of the Business Expansion Scheme rented housing projects, set up to exploit a tax break around 1989–92, are still trading, some as listed companies with Stock Exchange quotes. There is an active institutional market in buying and selling existing portfolios of residential rental properties.

Property unit trusts (PUTs) already exist in the commercial property sector. Early in 1999 there were reports that one of the big City firms was planning a residential property unit trust, aiming at a £500m portfolio, predominantly composed of modern flats, with perhaps 25 per cent invested in London. Two or three other institutions were working on similar schemes.

Of course, if this much money finds its way onto the London rented property scene, all those supply/demand equations will be straight in the waste-paper bin . . .

A NOTICE

PLEASE DO NOT BUY OR RENT
A LONDON PROPERTY BEFORE READING THIS:

Your alternative to calling hundreds of Agents is to
make just one call to 0171-491-8977
the **FREE PROPERTY LOCATOR SERVICE**
offered by RUMC Ltd, 21 Grafton Street, Mayfair, W1X 3LD.
E-mail:rumc@btinternet.com

How It Works

- ❑ A Property Locator Service Consultant will take the details of precisely what you want.
- ❑ An extensive search of Estate Agent databases, private vendors and Landlords is done.
- ❑ An initial short-list is compiled.
- ❑ Together with you, from that short list are selected the properties that most closely match your requirements.
- ❑ Arrangements are made for you to view this short-list at your convenience.
- ❑ Once you have made an offer on a property, you are guided and helped through all stages of renting or buying your property.

This unique service saves you hours of wasted time
and is **ENTIRELY FREE** to you

At the time of going to print
THIS SERVICE COVERS MAINLY:

MAYFAIR	KNIGHTSBRIDGE	KENSINGTON
CHELSEA	BELGRAVIA	FITZROVIA
HOLLAND PARK	ST JOHN'S WOOD	HAMPSTEAD
REGENT'S PARK	MAIDA VALE	COVENT GARDEN
NOTTING HILL GATE	SOHO	WESTMINSTER

Each month the service is being expanded until it covers the whole of London

Price charts: rentals

The charts on the following pages consolidate the data in the Area Profiles, showing broadly what certain kinds of homes cost to rent per calendar month in each of the areas covered. This gives you a freeze-frame picture across London at the start of 1999: a basis for comparison throughout the year.

The prices given are for typical examples of each type of home. Where a range of figures is shown, this reflects rent variations within the area. Thus the range is also

FLATS — RENTALS   STARTING PRICES FOR 1999

65–75: range in £1000s   — too few for price average   → price carries over

	STUDIO	1 BEDROOM	2 BEDROOM	3 BEDROOM	4 BEDROOM	5 BEDROOM +
Acton	500–650	600–900	850–1200	1000–1500	1300–2300	—
Balham and Tooting	430–550	450–750	650–1000	800–1200	—	—
Barnes, Mortlake and Sheen	600–700	700–1100	900–1200	1300–2000+	1600–2200+	—
Battersea	450–650	700–1500	800–1600	1300–3000	2000–3500	2500–3600
Bayswater	750–1200	850–2000	1300–2000	2000–3500	3000–4000	3600–6000+
Bedford Park and Acton Green	500–800+	700–1200	850–1700	1200–1900	1800+	—
Belgravia	1300	1500–2800	2400–3900	3000–5200+	4300–8700	—
Bethnal Green	400–600	560–780	600–1000	700–1500	—	—
Bloomsbury and King's Cross	500–865+	650–1400	950–2600	1750+	2000+	—
Bow	400–600	560–780	600–1000	700–1500	—	—
Brixton, Herne Hill and Tulse Hill	400–550	600–800	750–1000	1000–1500	1200–1800	—
Camberwell	350–500	450–600	550–800	750–1200	1000+	1100+
Camden Town and Primrose Hill	600+	800–900	900–1150	1400+	1750+	—
Chelsea	1000+	1100–2400	1400–3000+	2400–3500+	3000–6000	4000 ›
Chiswick	500–800+	700–1200	850–1700	1200–1900	1800+	—
City and Fringes	650–900	750–1500	950–2000	1300–3000	—	—
Clapham	500–1000	600–1200	800–2000	1300–2500	—	—
Clerkenwell and Finsbury	650–850	1000–1500	1200–2000	1500–3000	—	—
Cricklewood	400–700	500–900	700–1300	800–1700	—	—
Crouch End and Stroud Green	430–550	480–760	650–1000	800–1300	—	—
Crystal Palace	350–400	425–525	550–700	650–900	750+	—
Dollis Hill and Neasden	500–540	540–630	630–750	780–1000	—	—
Dulwich	380–500	500–800	600–1000	750–1500	1000+	—
Ealing	500–700	650–1000	750–1500	1000–1800	1200–2000	—
Finchley	350–550	540–750	600–1150	1200–1500	—	—
Forest Hill	320–400	400–550	500–700	600–800	800–1300	1300+
Fulham	600–800	800–1000	1200–1400	1600–1800	2000–2400	—
Golders Green	430–650	650–1000	780–1700	1000–2000	1500–2300	2000–3250
Greenwich and Blackheath	500–700	550–1000	800–1700	1000–2000	—	—
Hackney	370–430	500–690+	650–860	800–1150	1000–1500	—
Hammersmith	450–700	650–900	900–1300	1000–1500	1300–1800	1800–2500
Hampstead	690–850	850–1500	1300–3000	1700–4000	2600–6500	4300–8500
Hampstead Garden Suburb	780–1000	850–1200	1200–1700	—	—	—
Hendon and Mill Hill	520	700–860	780–1190	1120–1300	1500–2100	—
Highgate	520–1300	850–1700	1000–1950	1300–2600	1700–4000	2300+
Holland Park	700–1500	900–1700	1300–2800	1700–4300	2600–6500+	5200–10,000
Islington and Highbury	600–700+	700–1000	1000–1500+	1500+	—	—
Kennington, Vauxhall and Stockwell	400–650	600–900	750–1300	900–1500	1300–1800	1500–2200

an indicator of the scope of the properties: a small range indicates a fairly homogeneous area; a wide one either that there are some neighbourhoods that warrant a premium, or perhaps there is a good supply of recently developed, more luxurious flats. In all brackets, you are likely to find cheaper homes and exceptional ones at the other end of the scale: a plus sign is used where we have not included the rents for a small number of unusual examples, which would distort the averages.

HOUSES — RENTALS   STARTING PRICES FOR 1999

65–75: range in £1000s   — too few for price average   → price carries over

	2 BEDROOM	3 BEDROOM	4 BEDROOM	5 BEDROOM	6–7 BEDROOM	8+ BEDROOM
Acton	1000–1300	1100–1600	1300–2383	2000–3500	—	—
Balham and Tooting	800–1000	900–1500	1400–2000	1850–2200	2100–2400	—
Barnes, Mortlake and Sheen	1100–1700	1500–2400	2200–3800	4000+	5500+	—
Battersea	1000–1500	1500–2400	1600–2700	3000–3600	4000+	—
Bayswater	2000–3000	2500–3500	3500–6000	4000–7000	5000–8000+	—
Bedford Park and Acton Green	1000–1700	1200–2000	1800–3000+	2500–3500	—	—
Belgravia	3000–3900	3500–5200+	6000–10800	10800–15000+	›	22000
Bethnal Green	700–1200	750–1600	900–2000	2000–3000	2600+	—
Bloomsbury and King's Cross	1750+	2500+	4000	4500	—	—
Bow	700–1200	750–1600	900–2000	2000–3000	2600+	—
Brixton, Herne Hill and Tulse Hill	750+	1000–1500	1300–2000	1500–2100	1800–2500	—
Camberwell	600–900	800–1200	1100–1700	1400–2000	1700+	2000+
Camden Town and Primrose Hill	1250+	1500+	1950	2400–2600	—	—
Chelsea	2000–2400	3000–5000	4000–6000	6000–8000	10,000 ›+	16,000 ›+
Chiswick	1000–1700	1200–2000	1800–3000+	2500–3500	—	—
City and Fringes	—	—	—	—	—	—
Clapham	900–2000	1000–2000	1600–2600	2100–3000	3000+	6000+
Clerkenwell and Finsbury	1900+	—	—	—	—	—
Cricklewood	700–900	950–1700	1200–2000	1500–2600	—	—
Crouch End and Stroud Green	—	1200+	1300–2000	2000+	—	—
Crystal Palace	650–850	700–950	900–1000	1400+	2000+	2500+
Dollis Hill and Neasden	650–780	780–1000	1200–1500	—	—	—
Dulwich	750–1000	1000–1500+	1200 ›	1500 ›	2000 ›	—
Ealing	750–1600	1000–2000	1200–2500	2000–4000	3500–6000	—
Finchley	800–1100	860–1500	1100–2100	1400–3800	—	—
Forest Hill	550–750	600–1000	800–1000	1500+	—	—
Fulham	1200–1400	1600–2200	2000–2600	2600–3000	—	—
Golders Green	850–1300	1000–1700	1300–2600	1700–4300	2000–8000	4000–15,000
Greenwich and Blackheath	800–1000	1000–2500	1300–2500+	1500–2500+	2000+	—
Hackney	650–860	800–1100	900–1300	1000–1500	—	—
Hammersmith	1000–1200	1200–1700	1500–2000	1700–2500	—	—
Hampstead	850–3000	1700–6500	3000–8500	6500–10,000+	6500–13,000+	8500–17,000
Hampstead Garden Suburb	975–1500	1500–2100	1700–4300	2600–6500	4300–13,000	8600–21,000
Hendon and Mill Hill	850–1000	1000–1300	1200–1400	1500–1700	1500–2000	—
Highgate	1000–1300	1300–2600	1700–4300	2100–8500	8500+	—
Holland Park	1950–3000	2100–5200	3250–8000	4300–10,000+	13,000+	—
Islington and Highbury	1500–2000	2000+	2000–3000+	3000+	—	—
Kennington, Vauxhall and Stockwell	900–1100	1200–1600	1300–1950	1700–2600	—	—

FLATS — RENTALS

65–75: range in £1000s   — too few for price average   → price carries over

	STUDIO	1 BEDROOM	2 BEDROOM	3 BEDROOM	4 BEDROOM	5 BEDROOM +
Kensington	800–1000	1000–2000	1500–3000	2000–6000	4000+	6000+
Kentish Town and Tufnell Park	500–550	650–850	850–1300	1200–1400	—	—
Kilburn, Kensal Green and Queen's Park	450–560	600–1000	850–1300	1080–1500	—	—
Knightsbridge	1000–1500	1100–2000	1500–2500	2000–4000	3000–6000	4000+
Lewisham and Catford	300–500	450–600	500–750	600–950	750–1200	—
Leyton and Walthamstow	400–500	420–550	500–700	600–750	—	—
Maida Vale and Little Venice	650–1300	860–2000	1200–2100+	1700–4000+	2600+	—
Marylebone and Fitzrovia	780–1200	1000–1700	1500–2600	1700–4500	2600–5000+	—
Mayfair and St James's	1200	1500–2000	1950–3000	3000–3900	3900–5200	—
Morden, Mitcham and Colliers Wood	300–425	450–530	550–650	650–800	›1000	—
Muswell Hill	300–500	550–700	700–1000	800–1200	—	—
New Cross and Deptford	350–450	450–550	550–700	650–800	—	—
Newham	300–400	400–540	450–650	550–750	600–800	—
Notting Hill and North Kensington	600–1100	650–1700	900–2600+	1700+	2600+	—
Peckham	350–450	450–550	550–700	700–900	900–1200	—
Pimlico and Westminster	600–1000	850–1300	1100–2100	1700–2600+	—	—
Poplar	500–600	550–800	650–1000	900–1200	—	—
Putney and Roehampton	650–700	700–1000	1000–1200+	1200–2500	1800+	2500+
Regent's Park	650–1000	730–1700	1300–2400+	1800–6500	3000–13,000	5000+
Richmond and Kew	500–600	700–1200	850–1400+	1250–2000+	2000–3000+	—
Shepherd's Bush	565–700	750–950	950–1300	1150–1700	1450–2000	—
Soho and Covent Garden	800–1500	1000–2000	1300–3000+	1900–4500+	—	—
The South Bank	450–1000	550–1300	650–1500	750–1800	1000 ›	—
South Kensington, Earl's Court and West Brompton	700–1000	1000–1700	1200–2200	2000–3000	3000 ›	3200 ›
Southfields and Earlsfield	400–600	550–800	750–1000	1000–1200	1200+	—
Southgate and Palmers Green	400–550	600–700	650–750	800+	—	—
St John's Wood	700–900	1050–1500	1500–3000	2000–5000+	3500+	—
Stepney and Whitechapel	500–600	600–750	650–800	750–1200	—	—
Stoke Newington	350–520	475–600	610–780+	650–1200	—	—
Streatham	380–450	500–650	550–800	750–1000	—	—
Tottenham and Finsbury Park	400–500	480–900	600–1000	800–1100	1000–1600	—
Totteridge and Whetstone	—	600–780	750–850	1000 1300	1500–2100	—
Twickenham and Teddington	500–700+	600–800+	700–1500	900–1600+	—	—
Wandsworth	600–750	650–1200	900–1400	1000+	—	—
West Hampstead	550–800	730–1200	850–1300+	1000–1800+	1500–2500	—
West Norwood, Norbury and Gipsy Hill	400–450	450–600	600+	800–900	—	—
Willesden and Brondesbury Park	550–700	600–900	850–1000	1000–1500	—	—
Wimbledon, Raynes Park and Merton Park	500–800	650–1000	900–1800	1200–2200	1400–3000	—

HOUSES — RENTALS

65–75: range in £1000s   — too few for price average   → price carries over

	2 BEDROOM	3 BEDROOM	4 BEDROOM	5 BEDROOM	6–7 BEDROOM	8+ BEDROOM
Kensington	2000–2800	2400–3500	3500+	6000+	6000+	10 ›+
Kentish Town and Tufnell Park	1000–1300	1300–1500	1500–1950	1700–2000	1700–2000+	2300–3900
Kilburn, Kensal Green and Queen's Park	950–1050	1300–1600	1500–1800	1750–2800	—	
Knightsbridge	2400–3000	3000–5000	4000–7000	8000–10,000	12,000+	15,000+
Lewisham and Catford	600–1000	750–1000+	1000–1400	1000–1500+	—	—
Leyton and Walthamstow	500–700	600–800	800+	—	—	—
Maida Vale and Little Venice	—	2000–3500	3250+	6500+	›	›
Marylebone and Fitzrovia	2300–3900	2800–3900	3200–8000	6900–13000	—	—
Mayfair and St James's	2600–3500	3000–4300	4300–7350	6500–10800	17000	—
Morden, Mitcham and Colliers Wood	650–800	700–1100	800–1300	1400+	—	—
Muswell Hill	—	1200–2000	1200–2000	2200+	—	—
New Cross and Deptford	600–700	700–850	850–1200	1200–1500	—	—
Newham	550–700	650–800	700–950	—	—	—
Notting Hill and North Kensington	1100–2600	1300–4500	›8000	›	—	—
Peckham	550–750	750–1000	850–1200	1000–1300	1200–1500	—
Pimlico and Westminster	—	2100–3250	3000+	5000+	6000+	—
Poplar	700–1200	800–1600	800+	900+	—	—
Putney and Roehampton	1100–1600	1400–1900	1800–2100	2000–3000	—	—
Regent's Park	1500–3500	2300–5500+	3900–10,000+	8000+	›20000	—
Richmond and Kew	1000–1500	1500–3000	2000–3000+	3500–4500	5000+	—
Shepherd's Bush	1100–1300	1200–1800	1700–2300	2400+	2800+	—
Soho and Covent Garden	1400–2600	2500–3000	3500–5000+	—	—	—
The South Bank	750–1300	850–1500	1000 ›	1500+ ›	—	—
South Kensington, Earl's Court and West Brompton	2000+	2000–4000	3000–6000	5000–8000	6000+	—
Southfields and Earlsfield	800–1100	1100–1400	1400+	2000+	—	—
Southgate and Palmers Green	700–800	750–950	1000–1400	—	—	—
St John's Wood	2000+	2800–5000+	3500–8500+	6500+	—	—
Stepney and Whitechapel	700–1250	850–1400	1000–1800	—	—	—
Stoke Newington	650–1080+	820–1300	950–1500+	1200–1700	—	—
Streatham	700–850	750–1000	1000–2000	1300–2000	1800	—
Tottenham and Finsbury Park	550–770	700–1500	800–1800	1250+	—	—
Totteridge and Whetstone	550–850	1000+	1300–1400+	1500–2100+	—	—
Twickenham and Teddington	600–1500	1000–2000	1450–3000	1600–3200	—	—
Wandsworth	800–1600	1200–3000	1600–4000	3000+	—	—
West Hampstead	1000–1650	1300–1800+	1600–2500	2100–3000	—	—
West Norwood, Norbury and Gipsy Hill	700	900–1000	›1100	›1200	—	—
Willesden and Brondesbury Park	1000	1300–1500	1500–1700	2000	—	—
Wimbledon, Raynes Park and Merton Park	1000–1700	1250–2600	1500–4200	1700–4400+	—	—

Schools in London

by Liz Lightfoot

Be prepared to do your homework carefully if the quality of local schools is a factor in your home purchase. Estate agents are well aware that a sought-after school in an area can clinch the deal on a family property and will usually have details. If education is not something they mention, though your children are clambering all over their office, alarm bells should ring.

The quality of schools in London is mixed and the range of entry criteria and catchment areas can be bewildering. A good public transport system enables children to travel further, which widen options – and increases competition for places.

London contains some of the best independent day schools in the country and several state secondaries which regularly appear at or near the top of exam result league tables. However, it also has more than its fair share of schools which have been failed by Ofsted, the school inspectorate, and put on 'special measures' to improve them.

Competition for places at popular schools – whether fee-paying or state-funded – is fierce and where entry is largely dependent on the proximity of your home to the school it is important to monitor new developments that can change the map from year to year. Sudden gentrification of an area, a new housing scheme, a glowing Ofsted inspection report or outstanding test and exam results can quickly lead to a school being oversubscribed. Roads that previously nestled safely within the catchment area can suddenly be on the outskirts, so don't get carried away with a property until you have checked what is happening to schools in the area.

Who runs London's schools?

London has no uniform education system. Just as the capital is a collection of widely diverse neighbourhoods, so the range of state and independent schools varies according to the finer elements of your postcode, as can their quality.

Schools are run by 32 boroughs, plus the City of London Corporation, each with their own strengths and weaknesses. Generally, children transfer from primaries to secondary schools at 11 in the state sector and 11 or 13 in the private sector. Most secondary schools are comprehensives, but there are 15 grammar schools, mainly in Sutton, Kingston and Bromley, which are always vastly oversubscribed. Henrietta Barnett, a voluntary aided girls' grammar school in Barnet, gets some of the best GCSE and A level results of any state school in the country.

New government legislation has put the future of these grammars in jeopardy, however, by giving the opponents of selection the right to call local ballots on whether the schools should be effectively abolished by being forced to go comprehensive. It is still early days and there are hurdles in the way of the anti-grammar school campaigners who must provide a petition with the signatures of a fifth of the parents eligible to vote before they can even start the process.

Opinion polls have shown strong parental support for selection by ability, so the results are by no means certain and are made less so by the government's decision to give votes to parents with children at independent prep schools which sent five or more children to the grammar schools over the last three years.

So far only parents in Barnet have officially registered an interest in considering drawing up a petition for the future of its three grammars – Henrietta Barnett, Queen Elizabeth's, a boys' school, and St Michael's, a popular Roman Catholic girls' school – but grammars in other parts of London are also living in uncertain times.

The 191 grant-maintained schools in London will also be affected this year by the abolition of their special opt-out status from September. They can either revert to being local authority 'community' schools or voluntary aided church schools or they can choose the new 'foundation' status, which is a halfway house between the freedoms of grammar status and local authority control.

Some of the highest-achieving schools are voluntary aided and serve their own religious community, such as The London Oratory, a Roman Catholic boys' secondary school in Hammersmith and Fulham, and Cardinal Vaughan in Holland Park, which takes girls in the sixth form. Lady Margaret in Parson's Green is a popular Anglican girls' comprehensive and Hasmonean in Hendon serves the Jewish community.

Schools linked to the churches generally recruit from further afield than normal state schools, taking pupils from all over London who satisfy their entry requirements and are regular church attenders. Tony Blair, the Prime Minister, was able to escape the Islington comprehensives nearest his home and send his sons across the capital to the London Oratory School because of his family's affiliation to the Roman Catholic faith. Kathryn, his daughter, has got a place at the heavily oversubscribed Sacred Heart High School in Hammersmith, six miles from his Westminster home and nine miles from her present Islington junior school. The school puts more emphasis on the family's commitment to Roman Catholicism and parental support for the 'aims, values and expectations' of the school than the proximity of their address.

International schools such as the Lycée Français and the German School teach pupils whose parents come from abroad in their home languages, but are also used by Londoners who have ties with other countries and want their children to be bilingual. Londoners are very well served by the independent sector with a large and growing number of excellent preparatory schools and some of the finest day schools in the country. They do, however, tend to be pricey.

Single-sex girls' schools have become popular in recent years and there are several good ones in London. Competition for places is very strong and both Waltham Forest and Barnet are considering running girls-only classes in mixed schools to satisfy unfulfilled parental demand. A number of popular girls' schools in an area can cause problems for mixed schools which become heavily male-dominated.

Boroughs: the good, the bad and Hackney

The biggest divide in London education is between the inner and outer boroughs. Generally schools in the 13 Inner London authorities get worse results than those in the outer boroughs, but there are some very fine exceptions. Pupils in Inner London are typically poorer and more speak languages other than English at home, but the pupils are not always representative of local populations because the middle classes have deserted the state sector in droves and are paying for independent education. Pass through suburban railway stations at eight o'clock in the morning and you will see bleary-eyed children in school uniform from Central London getting off trains on one platform while business men and women board them heading for the City on the other.

The poor performance of pupils in the Inner London boroughs, with a few exceptions such as Camden which appears to have well-run schools, is a hotly debated issue. Boroughs such as Hackney, Tower Hamlets, Hammersmith & Fulham and Lambeth will tell you that they are beset by social problems and have high unemployment, families in poor housing and high numbers of pupils who are not fluent in English. High teacher turnover and the difficulty of recruiting sufficient well-qualified and experienced teachers in Inner London undoubtedly makes life difficult for headteachers.

A far higher proportions of pupils of Inner London are eligible for free school meals, a measure widely used in education to denote social and economic deprivation. Half of Inner London's pupils qualify for free school meals, compared with a quarter in Outer London. The highest proportions are found in Tower Hamlets (67.9

per cent), Lambeth (67.3), Southwark (63.5), Islington (58.6) and Hackney (58.4). The richest boroughs, on this indicator, are Kingston (8.3), Havering (14.3), Bexley (15.4), Merton (15.8) and Sutton (16.8).*

Half the pupils in Inner London local authority schools come from ethnic minority backgrounds and around a third in Outer London. A survey of 20 local authorities showed that around 1 in 10 pupils were not fluent in English.**

The fact that some schools in the poorer parts of London achieve very good test and exam results, however, points to other reasons for the majority's poor performance. Some blame the legacy of the Inner London Education Authority, a hotbed of progressive educational initiatives and teacher-union intransigence until shortly before it was abolished by the Thatcher government in 1990. Control over the schools passed to the 13 Inner London boroughs which assumed responsibility for those within their boundaries.

The so-called 'child centred' methods of teaching, where pupils are expected to find things out for themselves instead of being told, are still dominant in many Inner London primaries where children spend much of their time sitting in groups around tables filling in worksheets or working on projects rather than being taught directly. Ofsted reports have remarked on the low expectations teachers have of their pupils in some London schools, and the lack of rigour in the teaching of reading and arithmetic.

Again, there are exceptions – schools where standards are high and the teaching is excellent even within the worst London authorities. There are some good schools in Hackney, the East London authority which was failed by Ofsted and doesn't know how many pupils it educates. The government is threatening to contract its education services out to the private sector or other local authorities if it doesn't improve quickly.

Some of the worst schools in the deprived parts of the capital are joining together to become Education Action Zones run by partnerships of local authorities, private businesses and community groups. They will get more money and be freed to experiment with new initiatives, such as paying teachers more and opting out of the National Curriculum, but the results for pupils will take a time to come through. Generally, there are signs that things are going to get better as the government's literacy and numeracy hours, with their stress on direct instruction or 'interactive whole class teaching' are set to become compulsory for poor-performing primary schools in September. A return to more traditional phonic-based methods of teaching children to read by getting them to listen to the sounds and learn the letters that represent them is also being heavily pushed by the government and should bring improvements to the reading scores of Inner London pupils, a major problem for secondary schools which have to cope with the low literacy levels of many 11-year-olds when they come in.

Border skirmishes

The most confusing aspect of education in London is the way pupils move across borough boundaries to go to school. If you live in Haringey, for example, you may send your child across the border to Islington, while Islington's children gravitate westwards to Camden and Camden's to Westminster.

The latest figures available, for 1994, show that 13 per cent of the 11–16-year-old population attended schools outside the borough in which they lived – that is, 50,000 of the 384,930 in that age group.***

* Education in London: Key Facts 1997, London Research Centre
** Source: as above
*** Planning Secondary School Places in London: Funding Agency for Schools 1997

This cross-border drift between the boroughs means there is no guarantee that if you choose to move, to say Richmond upon Thames because it regularly tops the national table of primary school results, or Kingston which excels in the secondary school tables, that you will get the school of your choice, or even that nearest your home, if you happen to live near the borders with another authority.

Much though the boroughs hate it, and have tried to give their own residents precedence over outsiders, they are hamstrung by a judgement of the High Court called the 'Greenwich judgement'. The courts decided that it was unlawful under the legislation regulating parental choice and school admissions, for Greenwich Council to give a school place to a resident when a non-resident of the borough lived nearer to it.

The government has indicated it is not planning to change the law to give local authorities power to take residency into account, but Kingston says it is considering going to court to challenge the judgement. Meanwhile, beware, though it may well work in your favour. A large part of the drift is from Inner to Outer London.

Not surprisingly, anger about the right of non-residents to get school places at popular schools is greatest in the authorities which get the best test and exam results. Bromley, which has two popular grammar schools, imports many more pupils than it exports. In 1996, 23 per cent of the children entering its secondary schools came from outside the borough and the figure has increased since then. All but one of Bromley's secondary schools are grant-maintained and select a proportion of pupils, making finding places more complicated for parents.

Richmond upon Thames, which regularly tops the primary league tables, though its secondaries do not do so well, has a serious shortage of infant places, though the problem eases after seven because of the large number of parents who use its state infant classes but then go on to use private education. There is a shortage of infant places as schools reduce infant classes to the statutory 30 pupils. There is talk of at least one new school. Meanwhile some roads are slipping out of the catchment areas of the most oversubscribed infant and primaries.

Families are moving in and putting a premium on larger properties, because of Richmond's and Kingston's reputations, but can be disappointed if they live near the borders and have to travel further afield because their nearest school is oversubscribed. Parents near a popular school in East Sheen, for example, on the borders of Richmond and Wandsworth, have been pressing for the authority to give them priority over children coming in from the nearby Roehampton council estates, but failed because of the Greenwich judgement.

If you are planning to move into Kingston because of the reputation of its two Tiffin grammar schools then you may well be disappointed. Pupils travel a 10-mile radius across London to get to them, from Hounslow and Staines in the W, Clapham and Wandsworth in the E and from Epsom in the S. There is a roughly 50:50 split between Kingston residents and outsiders at the girls' grammar school and competition for places is fierce. 1,000 pupils sat the exam this year for 120 places. It is a similar story at the boys' grammar, in the centre of the town. A grant-maintained school, it is making dire predictions about budget cuts and having to make teachers redundant once it loses its grant-maintained status next year and has suggested parents might like to pledge £360 a year or more to plug the gap.

Camden is probably the most popular local authority in Inner London. It has several sought-after girls' and Roman Catholic schools and some creditable comprehensives including the Hampstead Comprehensive School run by Dame Tamsyn Imison which bucks the national trend because boys do as well as girls.

For many middle-class parents the choice is between costly independent education, buying an expensive home very close to a popular school, or state grammar schools further afield. Headteachers warn parents to think carefully about the toll lengthy travelling can put on their children. Mrs Pauline Cox, headteacher of the Tiffin Grammar School for Girls, says that while her pupils develop coping strategies, the hours spent travelling mean they are tired when they get home. 'Travelling to school also makes it harder for pupils to keep up their social lives and mix with friends out of school,' she says.

Admissions

Primary schools work on catchment areas unless they are voluntary aided and demand parental religious commitment. All are required to publish their admission criteria which can normally be obtained from the relevant local authority. They may differ in the importance attached to certain aspects, such as siblings, and some Roman Catholic schools put more emphasis on such things as accessibility to the school from home or parental support for their aims and expectations of pupils.

Secondaries are no longer allowed to select 15 per cent of their pupils by ability but they can still choose 10 per cent that way. The government has made clear its opposition to partial selection and is to allow parents or local admission authorities to challenge the practice by referring it to an adjudicator with the power to end it.

The criteria used by Roman Catholic secondaries vary. Though all require family religious commitment some give preference to pupils from named Roman Catholic primary schools. Some are more willing than others to take children with special needs or pupils who could benefit for pastoral reasons.

A growing number of comprehensives are becoming specialist schools able to select 10 per cent of pupils on the basis of their aptitude for technology, arts, sports or languages. They must attract sponsorship and get extra state funds to expand their facilities which are then shared with other local schools. There are nearly 400 on stream nationally and the early ones have improved their results significantly. It is well worth contacting the Technology Colleges Trust to find out where they are.

Private schools

Parents seeking private education for the children will find many excellent independent schools in London. Most of the secondary schools are single sex, at least up until the sixth forms. They are almost exclusively day schools and include Harrow, Westminster and St Paul's Girls and Boys.

Getting places at private nurseries, pre-preps and prep schools in Inner London is extremely difficult and most people register their children at birth. However, London has a very mobile population and places can often suddenly become available. If you are moving into London for the first time it may be worth asking the headteacher of your child's present school to ring up a school in which you are interested. But only if you are confident that he or she will give your child a good reference, of course! There are few independent schools in the E of London but plenty in the N, W and S, though competition to get into the best known is very strong. Generally, it is easier to find places in the Outer London independent schools.

Londoners, perhaps more than anywhere else in the country, need to check out the local situation and not rely on guide books and possibly out-of-date reputations. So, do all the usual things: read Good Schools Guides, scrutinize results and Ofsted inspection reports (available on the Internet), get hold of local authority information leaflets, talk to the schools about their results so they can put them in context (a number of pupils with special needs or several pupils absent on the day of the test, who are counted as if they were failures, can make a big difference).

But above all, keep you ear to the ground. Local people, play-group leaders, nursery teachers, school secretaries or parent governors can keep you up-to-date on catchment areas and other options available. Education in London will be in flux until into the next century as the government's changes shake down. Careful research may find a jewel in the crown.

For further information

Local education authority schools: contact the Education Department at your borough town hall – see the *Boroughs* chapter for town hall phone numbers.

Fee paying: ISIS (56 Buckingham Gate, SW1E 6AG. Tel: 0171 630 8795).

International: if you have come to London from abroad, you may wish to send your child to one of the international schools here. Some of the best known are listed below. Your embassy here will know of others.

Liz Lightfoot is the Education Correspondent of The Daily Telegraph.

American School in London
2/8 Loudoun Rd
NW8 0NP
Tel: 0171 449 1200

German School
Douglas House
Petersham Rd
Surrey
TW10 7AH
Tel: 0181 948 3410

Japanese School in London
87 Creffield Rd,
W3 9PU
Tel: 0181 993 7145

King Fahad Academy
Bromyard Avenue
W3 7HD
Tel: 0181 743 0131

Lycée Français
35 Cromwell Rd
SW7 2DG
Tel: 0171 584 6322

Norwegian School in London
28 Arteberry Rd
SW20 8AH
Tel: 0181 946 2058

Swedish School
Lonsdale Rd
SW13 9JS
Tel: 0181 741 1751

Secondary school performance tables

The following tables illustrate the performance of secondary schools throughout London, borough by borough. Published in November 1998, these are the second to be produced by the Blair government and the seventh overall. Although their introduction was clogged by controversy, they are now relied upon by parents choosing secondary schools.

Complete tables, containing previous results and the proportion of pupils with special educational needs, can be obtained from the Department of Education. They will be supplied free of charge on request (tel: 0800 242322) or by writing to School and College Performance Tables, Department of Education and Employment, FREEPOST (LON 102450), London SW1P 3YS.

Key

SCHOOL TYPE: C: County (ie state), GM: grant maintained, VC: voluntary controlled, VA: voluntary aided,
    SA: special agreement, CTC: city technology college, IND: independent school
ENTRY POLICY: COMP: comprehensive, SEL: selective, NONSEL: non-selective (independent school)
GCSE SUCCESS RATE: per cent of 15-year-olds who achieved five or more GCSEs grades A*–C
AVE. 'A' LEVEL SCORE: Average score per A-level /AS Exam

BARNET

	SCHOOL TYPE	ENTRY POLICY	GCSE SUCCESS RATE	AVE. 'A' LEVEL SCORE
The Henrietta	VA	Sel	98%	24.6
St Michael's Catholic Grammar	GM	Sel	97%	22.0
Pardes House Grammar	IND	Nonsel	96%	0.0
King Alfred	IND	Nonsel	88%	20.7
Queen Elizabeth's	GM	Sel	88%	28.7
The Mount	IND	Sel	84%	13.7
Menorah Grammar	IND	Sel	82%	16.3
Hasmonean High	GM	Comp	80%	20.1
Woodside Park	IND	Sel	80%	0.0
Beth Jacob Grammar for Girls	IND	Nonsel	79%	11.0
St Martha's Convent	IND	Sel	76%	16.8
Mill Hill Foundation	IND	Sel	74%	20.9
Copthall	C	Comp	70%	16.6
Mill Hill (GM) High	GM	Comp	67%	17.4
Ashmole	GM	Comp	66%	17.4
Queen Elizabeth's Girls'	C	Comp	61%	14.9
Christ's College	C	Comp	60%	15.0
Finchley RC High	GM	Comp	59%	14.7
St James' Catholic High	GM	Comp	59%	11.8
The Compton	C	Comp	59%	0.0
East Barnet	C	Comp	53%	15.9
The Albany College	IND	Sel	53%	15.5
Hendon	GM	Comp	52%	15.9
Tuition Centre	IND	Sel	50%	18.8
Bishop Douglass RC High	GM	Comp	45%	12.6
St Mary's CofE High	GM	Comp	45%	11.6
Friern Barnet County	C	Comp	37%	0.0
Christ Church CofE	VA	Comp	36%	0.0
Edgware, Edgware	C	Comp	28%	12.5
Ravenscroft	C	Comp	25%	11.8
Whitefield	C	Comp	14%	2.0
LEA average			**56.30%**	

BRENT

	SCHOOL TYPE	ENTRY POLICY	GCSE SUCCESS RATE	AVE. 'A' LEVEL SCORE
The Swaminarayan	IND	Sel	100%	20.0
Al-Sadiq and Al-Zharas	Ind	Nonsel	80%	0.0
Islamia Girls' High	IND	Sel	76%	0.0
Preston Manor High, Wembley	GM	Comp	59%	15.2
Convent of Jesus and Mary Language College	GM	Comp	58%	17.6
Claremont High, Harrow	GM	Comp	57%	15.8
Kingsbury High	GM	Comp	57%	16.1
St Gregory's RC High, Harrow	GM	Comp	53%	13.5
Copland Community and Technology Centre, Wembley	GM	Comp	45%	13.3
John Kelly Girls' Technology College	GM	Comp	42%	11.6
Alperton Community, Wembley	GM	Comp	40%	13.1
John Kelly Boy's Technology College	GM	Comp	40%	10.0
Queen's Park Community	GM	Comp	39%	9.3
Wembley High	C	Comp	35%	11.0
Cardinal Hinsley High	GM	Comp	30%	14.0
Willesden High	C	Comp	9%	5.5
LEA average			**44.80%**	

CAMDEN

	SCHOOL TYPE	ENTRY POLICY	GCSE SUCCESS RATE	AVE. 'A' LEVEL SCORE
South Hampstead High	IND	Sel	97%	26.8
North Bridge House	IND	Sel	95%	0.0
University College	IND	Sel	94%	24.9
St Margaret's	IND	Sel	89%	0.0
Royal School, Hampstead	IND	Sel	76%	7.3
JFS (Jews Free)	GM	Comp	73%	17.9
La Sainte Union Convent	GM	Comp	67%	14.8
Camden for Girls	VA	Comp	56%	18.3
Parliament Hill Girls'	C	Comp	50%	17.2
William Ellis	VA	Comp	50%	14.4
Hampstead	C	Comp	48%	15.8
Acland Burghley	C	Comp	43%	15.7
Maria Fidelis Convent (Upper)	VA	Comp	41%	14.5
Fine Arts College	IND	Nonsel	38%	19.0
Haverstock	C	Comp	21%	12.2
South Camden Community	C	Comp	14%	6.8
LEA average			**45.80%**	

EALING

	SCHOOL TYPE	ENTRY POLICY	GCSE SUCCESS RATE	AVE. 'A' LEVEL SCORE
Harvington	IND	Sel	100%	0.0
St Augustine's Priory	IND	Sel	100%	18.9
Notting Hill and Ealing High	IND	Sel	98%	25.0
St Benedict's	IND	Sel	95%	18.7
King Fahad Academy	IND	Nonsel	90%	14.5
Twyford CofE High	VA	Comp	64%	14.4
The Ellen Wilkinson for Girls	GM	Comp	60%	16.1
Ealing College Upper	IND	Nonsel	57%	2.5
Drayton Manor High	GM	Comp	55%	14.9
Greenford High, Greenford	GM	Comp	55%	13.3
Villiers High, Southall	C	Comp	52%	0.0
Cardinal Wiseman RC High, Greenford	VA	Comp	50%	14.2
Northolt High, Northolt	GM	Comp	41%	13.3
Featherstone High, Southall	C	Comp	40%	0.0
Acton High	C	Comp	36%	0.0
Dormers Wells High, Southall	C	Comp	32%	0.0
Walford High, Northolt	C	Comp	28%	0.0
Brentside High	GM	Comp	27%	12.1
Barbara Speake Stage	IND	Sel	13%	0.0
Greek of London	IND	Nonsel	0%	0.0
LEA average			**44.60%**	

ENFIELD

	SCHOOL TYPE	ENTRY POLICY	GCSE SUCCESS RATE	AVE. 'A' LEVEL SCORE
Palmers Green High	IND	Sel	100%	0.0
St John's Preparatory and Senior, Potters Bar	IND	Sel	100%	0.0
The Latymer	GM	Sel	98%	25.1
Enfield County, Enfield	C	Comp	66%	15.1
Southgate, Barnet	C	Comp	64%	16.7
St Ignatius College, Enfield	GM	Comp	57%	18.0
Enfield Grammar, Enfield	GM	Comp	47%	17.0
Edmonton County, Enfield	C	Comp	46%	16.2
St Anne's Catholic High for Girls	VA	Comp	45%	14.3
Bishop Stopford's, Enfield	VA	Comp	41%	10.2
Broomfield	GM	Comp	39%	8.3
Winchmore	C	Comp	37%	14.1
Chace Community, Enfield	C	Comp	29%	10.9
Kingsmead, Enfield	C	Comp	24%	9.9
Lea Valley High, Enfield	C	Comp	24%	11.1
Aylward	C	Comp	22%	12.5
Salisbury	C	Comp	19%	3.4
Albany, Enfield	GM	Comp	12%	10.6
LEA average			**41.50%**	

GREENWICH

	SCHOOL TYPE	ENTRY POLICY	GCSE SUCCESS RATE	AVE. 'A' LEVEL SCORE
Blackheath High	IND	Sel	94%	19.8
Colfes	IND	Sel	91%	19.8
Riverston	IND	Nonsel	71%	0.0
St Ursula's Convent	VA	Comp	71%	0.0
St Thomas More RC Comprehensive	VA	Comp	64%	0.0
St Paul's RC Comprehensive	VA	Comp	60%	0.0
Thomas Tallis	C	Comp	43%	16.8
Crown Woods	C	Comp	41%	15.7
Etham Hill	C	Comp	32%	9.8
Blackheath Bluecoat CofE	VA	Comp	31%	10.7
The John Roan	VC	Comp	30%	7.6
Plumstead Manor	C	Comp	29%	12.2
Woolwich Polytechnic Boys'	C	Comp	26%	11.6
Kidbrooke	C	Comp	24%	9.6
Eaglesfield	C	Comp	20%	10.9
Abbey Wood	C	Comp	18%	0.0
Eltham Green	C	Comp	12%	8.0
LEA average			**33.10%**	

HACKNEY

	SCHOOL TYPE	ENTRY POLICY	GCSE SUCCESS RATE	AVE. 'A' LEVEL SCORE
Yesodey Hatorah	IND	Sel	93%	0.0
Tayyibah Girls'	IND	Nonsel	77%	0.0
Our Lady's Convent High	VA	Comp	68%	12.4
Lubavitch House Senior	IND	Nonsel	59%	0.0
Cardinal Pole	VA	Comp	32%	6.0
Stoke Newington	C	Comp	32%	0.0
Haggerston	C	Comp	31%	0.0
Kingsland	C	Comp	25%	0.0
Clapton	C	Comp	22%	0.0
Homerton College of Technology	C	Comp	20%	0.0
The Skinners' Company's for Girls	VA	Comp	18%	15.3
Hackney Free and Parochial CofE Secondary	VA	Comp	16%	0.0
Beis Malka Girls'	IND	Nonsel	0%	0.0
Beis Rochel d'Satmar Girls'	IND	Sel	0%	0.0
Home of Stoke Newington	IND	Nonsel	0%	0.0
LEA average			**26.50%**	

HAMMERSMITH AND FULHAM

	SCHOOL TYPE	ENTRY POLICY	GCSE SUCCESS RATE	AVE. 'A' LEVEL SCORE
The Godophin and Latymer	IND	Sel	100%	26.1
Latymer Upper	IND	Sel	100%	23.7
St Paul's Girls'	IND	Sel	98%	29.3
The London Oratory	GM	Comp	88%	23.2
Lady Margaret	VA	Comp	87%	19.2
Sacred Heart High	VA	Comp	69%	0.0
Burlington Danes CofE	VA	Comp	40%	12.8
Fulham Cross Secondary	C	Comp	21%	14.0
Henry Compton	C	Comp	17%	16.1
Hurlingham and Chelsea	C	Comp	12%	14.6
Phoenix High	C	Comp	11%	11.9
Ravenscourt Theatre	IND	Sel	9%	0.0
LEA average			**43.50%**	

HARINGEY

	SCHOOL TYPE	ENTRY POLICY	GCSE SUCCESS RATE	AVE. 'A' LEVEL SCORE
Highgate	IND	Sel	99%	26.0
Channing	IND	Sel	93%	24.7
Fortismere	C	Comp	57%	17.4
Hornsey for Girls	C	Comp	43%	12.9
Highgate Wood	C	Comp	38%	13.0
St Thomas More RC	VA	Comp	31%	10.1
The John Loughborough	GM	Comp	25%	0.0
Gladesmore Community	C	Comp	19%	4.6
White Hart Lane	C	Comp	14%	13.5
Northumberland Park Community	C	Comp	13%	2.8
The Langham	C	Comp	13%	0.0
St David and St Katharine	VA	Comp	11%	7.9
LEA average			**26.60%**	

HOUNSLOW

	SCHOOL TYPE	ENTRY POLICY	GCSE SUCCESS RATE	AVE. 'A' LEVEL SCORE
Hounslow College, Feltham	IND	Sel	100%	0.0
The Arts Educational London, London	IND	Sel	74%	0.0
Gumley House Convent, Isleworth	GM	Comp	70%	15.7
The Green for Girls, Isleworth	VA	Comp	70%	14.6
The Heathland	C	Comp	60%	16.0
Heston Community	C	Comp	60%	14.4
St Mark's Catholic	SA	Comp	58%	17.4
Gunnersbury Catholic, Brentford	GM	Comp	55%	13.2
Isleworth and Syon Boys', Isleworth	VC	Comp	54%	14.0
Chiswick Community, London	C	Comp	48%	14.8
Lampton	C	Comp	44%	15.6
Cranford Community	C	Comp	40%	10.8
Longford Community, Feltham	C	Comp	34%	8.5
International of London, London	IND	Nonsel	30%	0.0
Brentford for Girls, Brentford	C	Comp	28%	11.0
Hounslow Manor	C	Comp	21%	11.3
Feltham Community, Feltham	C	Comp	20%	14.4
LEA average			**46.50%**	

ISLINGTON

	SCHOOL TYPE	ENTRY POLICY	GCSE SUCCESS RATE	AVE. 'A' LEVEL SCORE
Italia Conti Academy of Theatre Arts	IND	Sel	86%	0.0
Highbury Fields	C	Comp	43%	10.3
Central Foundation Boys'	VA	Comp	27%	8.3
Islington Green	C	Comp	27%	0.0
St Aloysius' College	VA	Comp	27%	6.9
Mount Carmel RC, Girls'	VA	Comp	24%	0.0
Elizabeth Garrett Anderson	C	Comp	21%	0.0
Holloway	C	Comp	19%	0.0
Highbury Grove	C	Comp	15%	10.7
George Orwell	C	Comp	10%	0.0
LEA average			**23.30%**	

KENSINGTON AND CHELSEA

	SCHOOL TYPE	ENTRY POLICY	GCSE SUCCESS RATE	AVE. 'A' LEVEL SCORE
Collingham	IND	Sel	100%	16.2
Lycée Français Charles de Gaulle (British Section)	IND	Sel	94%	24.5
Hellenic College of London	IND	Sel	92%	13.7
More House	IND	Sel	88%	16.7
Cardinal Vaughan Memorial	GM	Comp	83%	19.0
Queen's Gate	IND	Sel	80%	19.7
Duff Miller College	IND	Sel	73%	15.7
Mander Portman Woodward	IND	Sel	62%	17.8
Sion-Manning	SA	Comp	50%	0.0
St James Independent for Girls	IND	Nonsel	50%	21.2
Davies Laing and Dick College	IND	Sel	47%	15.0
St Thomas More's RC	VA	Comp	46%	0.0
Ashbourne Independent	IND	Nonsel	40%	15.1
Holland Park	C	Comp	29%	13.3
David Game Tutorial College	IND	Nonsel	0%	15.2
Lansdown College	IND	Nonsel	0%	16.6
LEA average			**45.40%**	

LAMBETH

	SCHOOL TYPE	ENTRY POLICY	GCSE SUCCESS RATE	AVE. 'A' LEVEL SCORE
Streatham Hill and Clapham High	IND	Sel	96%	21.5
La Retraite RC Girls	GM	Comp	48%	0.0
The London Nautical	GM	Comp	46%	15.0
Bishop Thomas Grant RC	GM	Comp	42%	0.0
Dunraven	GM	Comp	31%	0.0
St Martin in the Fields High for Girls'	GM	Comp	30%	0.0
Charles Edward Brooke	VC	Comp	27%	16.0
Archbishop Tenison's	GM	Comp	23%	0.0
Norwood	C	Comp	21%	0.0
Lilian Baylis	C	Comp	13%	0.0
Stockwell Park	C	Comp	13%	0.0
Bright Sparks Stage	IND	Nonsel	0%	0.0
LEA average			**28.80%**	

LEWISHAM

	SCHOOL TYPE	ENTRY POLICY	GCSE SUCCESS RATE	AVE. 'A' LEVEL SCORE
Sydenham High GDST	IND	Sel	94%	23.4
St Dunstan's College	IND	Sel	86%	22.0
Haberdashers' Aske's Hatcham College	CTC	Comp	70%	16.0
Bonus Pastor RC, Bromley	SA	Comp	63%	0.0
Prendergast	VA	Comp	59%	14.7
Sydenham	C	Comp	49%	12.8
Addey and Stanhope	VA	Comp	31%	8.4
Catford County Girls'	C	Comp	30%	4.0
Sedgehill	C	Comp	28%	10.9
Forest Hill	C	Comp	27%	13.7
Deptford Green	C	Comp	26%	12.2
Crofton	C	Comp	23%	16.1
Northbrook CofE	VA	Comp	17%	0.0
Hatcham Wood	C	Comp	14%	10.9
St Joseph's Academy	VA	Comp	12%	0.0
Malory, Bromley	C	Comp	11%	6.2
LEA average			**32.80%**	

MERTON

	SCHOOL TYPE	ENTRY POLICY	GCSE SUCCESS RATE	AVE. 'A' LEVEL SCORE
King's College	IND	Sel	100%	27.7
Wimbledon High	IND	Sel	97%	23.7
Hazelhurst for Girls	IND	Sel	89%	0.0
Ursuline Convent High	GM	Comp	60%	17.4
Ricards Lodge High	C	Comp	59%	0.0
Wimbledon College	VA	Comp	48%	16.2
Raynes Park High (Mixed)	C	Comp	40%	0.0
Rutlish	VC	Comp	35%	7.5
Rowan High	C	Comp	32%	0.0
Tamworth Manor High, Mitcham	C	Comp	20%	0.0
Watermeads High, Morden	C	Comp	18%	0.0
Eastfields High (Boys), Mitcham	C	Comp	18%	0.0
LEA average			**37.30%**	

NEWHAM

	SCHOOL TYPE	ENTRY POLICY	GCSE SUCCESS RATE	AVE. 'A' LEVEL SCORE
St Angela's Ursuline Convent	VA	Comp	58%	15.1
St Bonaventure's RC	VA	Comp	57%	11.8
Plashet	C	Comp	52%	0.0
Sarah Bonnell	C	Comp	44%	0.0
Langdon	C	Comp	42%	0.0
Stratford	GM	Comp	38%	0.0
Forest Gate Community	C	Comp	30%	0.0
Brampton Manor	C	Comp	28%	0.0
Lister Community	C	Comp	26%	0.0
Rokeby	C	Comp	25%	0.0

	SCHOOL TYPE	ENTRY POLICY	GCSE SUCCESS RATE	AVE. 'A' LEVEL SCORE
Woodside Community	C	Comp	20%	0.0
Little Ilford	C	Comp	16%	0.0
Cumberland	C	Comp	15%	0.0
Eastlea Community	C	Comp	13%	0.0
LEA average			**34.0%**	

RICHMOND UPON THAMES

	SCHOOL TYPE	ENTRY POLICY	GCSE SUCCESS RATE	AVE. 'A' LEVEL SCORE
St James Independent for Boys, Twickenham	IND	Nonsel	100%	18.8
The Lady Eleanor Holles, Hampton	IND	Sel	100%	34.6
The Royal Ballet, Richmond	IND	Sel	100%	11.7
Hampton School, Hampton	IND	Sel	99%	32.4
St Paul's	IND	Sel	99%	31.2
St Catherine's Catholic, Twickenham	IND	Sel	88%	0.0
Waldegrave for Girls, Twickenham	C	Comp	71%	0.0
Teddington, Teddington	C	Comp	64%	0.0
Grey Court, Richmond	C	Comp	62%	0.0
Shene	C	Comp	48%	0.0
Orleans Park, Twickenham	C	Comp	46%	0.0
Rectory, Hampton	C	Comp	42%	0.0
Whitton, Twickenham	C	Comp	34%	0.0
Christ's, Richmond	VA	Comp	20%	0.0
LEA average			**50.60%**	

SOUTHWARK

	SCHOOL TYPE	ENTRY POLICY	GCSE SUCCESS RATE	AVE. 'A' LEVEL SCORE
James Allen's Girls'	IND	Sel	100%	20.2
Dulwich College	IND	Sel	97%	24.8
Alleyn's	IND	Sel	94%	23.0
Notre Dame	GM	Comp	57%	0.0
Bacon's College	CTC	Comp	46%	13.1
The St Thomas the Apostle GM College	GM	Comp	44%	0.0
St Michael's RC	GM	Comp	41%	0.0
Sacred Heart RC	GM	Comp	41%	0.0
St Saviour's and St Olave's	VA	Comp	40%	0.0
Waverley	C	Comp	34%	0.0
Aylwin Girls'	C	Comp	27%	0.0
Geoffrey Chaucer	C	Comp	21%	0.0
Walworth	C	Comp	20%	0.0
Archbishop Michael Ramsey Technical College	VA	Comp	17%	7.0
Warwick Park	C	Comp	17%	0.0
Kingsdale	C	Comp	12%	0.0
Dulwich High for Boys	C	Comp	9%	0.0
LEA average			**29.10%**	

TOWER HAMLETS

	SCHOOL TYPE	ENTRY POLICY	GCSE SUCCESS RATE	AVE. 'A' LEVEL SCORE
Mulberry for Girls	C	Comp	50%	11.8
Raines Foundation	GM	Comp	44%	13.6
Bethnal Green Technology College	C	Comp	39%	0.0
Madni Girls' (London)	IND	Sel	33%	0.0
Bishop Challoner RC	VA	Comp	32%	6.7
Stepney Green	C	Comp	32%	0.0
Central Foundation Girls'	VC	Comp	31%	8.6
Morpeth	C	Comp	29%	0.0
St Paul's Way Community	C	Comp	27%	0.0
Oaklands	C	Comp	25%	0.0
George Green's	VC	Comp	23%	10.6
Swanlea Mixed County Secondary	C	Comp	23%	0.0
Sir John Cass Redcoat	VA	Comp	22%	6.0
Langdon Park	C	Comp	16%	0.0
The Blessed John Roche Catholic	VA	Comp	14%	5.6
Bow	C	Comp	6%	0.0
LEA average			**27.60%**	

WALTHAM FOREST

	SCHOOL TYPE	ENTRY POLICY	GCSE SUCCESS RATE	AVE. 'A' LEVEL SCORE
Forest	IND	Sel	92%	26.9
Highams Park	GM	Comp	59%	18.6
Connaught for Girls	C	Comp	58%	0.0
Walthamstow for Girls	C	Comp	57%	0.0
Normanhurst	IND	Nonsel	55%	0.0
Chingford	GM	Comp	44%	0.0
Aveling Park	C	Comp	41%	0.0
Leytonstone	C	Comp	39%	0.0
Willowfield	C	Comp	38%	0.0
The Holy Family College	VA	Comp	37%	11.9
Kelmscott	C	Comp	33%	0.0
Rush Croft	C	Comp	30%	0.0
Heathcote	C	Comp	27%	0.0
Norlington for Boys	C	Comp	27%	0.0
Tom Hood	C	Comp	27%	0.0
George Mitchell	C	Comp	23%	0.0
Warwick for Boys	C	Comp	21%	0.0
McEntee	C	Comp	16%	0.0
LEA average			**37.20%**	

WANDSWORTH

	SCHOOL TYPE	ENTRY POLICY	GCSE SUCCESS RATE	AVE. 'A' LEVEL SCORE
Putney High	IND	Sel	100%	24.0
Ibstock Place	IND	Sel	100%	0.0
Emanuel	IND	Sel	89%	15.7
Putney Park	IND	Sel	89%	0.0
ADT College	CTC	Comp	69%	15.8
Burntwood	GM	Comp	51%	17.9
Graveney	GM	Comp	51%	17.1
Upper Tooting Independent High	IND	Sel	50%	0.0
Elliott	GM	Comp	43%	18.1
John Paul II	GM	Comp	38%	0.0
Chestnut Grove	C	Comp	24%	6.2
Ernest Bevin	C	Comp	21%	10.5
Salesian College	GM	Comp	18%	0.0
Southfields Community College	GM	Comp	14%	10.6
Battersea Technology College	C	Comp	7%	0.0
LEA average			**34.70%**	

WESTMINSTER, CITY OF

	SCHOOL TYPE	ENTRY POLICY	GCSE SUCCESS RATE	AVE. 'A' LEVEL SCORE
Westminster	IND	Sel	99%	33.1
Francis Holland	IND	Sel	98%	22.8
Queen's College London	IND	Sel	96%	20.2
Francis Holland	IND	Sel	93%	20.1
The St Marylebone	VA	Comp	74%	12.5
The Grey Coat Hospital	VA	Comp	69%	17.8
Portland Place	IND	Sel	60%	10.3
The Urdang Academy of Ballet	IND	Sel	42%	11.3
International Community	IND	Nonsel	40%	11.5
Westminster City	VA	Comp	40%	12.4
Pimlico	C	Comp	37%	17.4
Sylvia Young Theatre	IND	Sel	36%	0.0
North Westminster	C	Comp	23%	13.1
Quintin Kynaston	C	Comp	21%	16.2
St George's Westminster	SA	Comp	19%	0.0
St Augustine's CofE	VA	Comp	15%	10.0
Centre Academy	IND	Sel	11%	0.0
Bales College	IND	Nonsel	0%	11.1
LEA average			**34.50%**	

The tables printed here are courtesy of The Daily Telegraph.

The Boroughs

Does it matter which of the 32 London boroughs you live in or move to? Under the unlamented poll tax, it certainly did: crossing the street from Wandsworth to Lambeth could cost a couple well over a thousand a year. Under the council tax, with its charge per dwelling, things have evened out – but not entirely. The list that follows gives the 'band D' council tax for each borough as an 'at-a-glance' comparison to show how charges differ. (Band D is the 'anchor' band: the other bands will differ in proportion.) The amounts change this spring.

Who governs London? No-one in particular until the Mayor gets elected, though lots of people tinker with bits of it. The most powerful is the Government Office for London, which is supposed to coordinate the actions of the various ministries. The boroughs work together to deal with things like Thames bridges, which mostly have different boroughs at each end. Each borough runs the schools in its area, and in this respect they differ greatly. Boroughs also have most planning powers, but the government will deal with any big development. The much-discussed Mayor of London, and the 25-member Greater London Authority (GLA) will be elected next year (2000). The Authority will have powers, so far rather ill-defined, over transport, planning and many other matters. The Mayor will be a figurehead – or more – for all of London. Together, he or she and the GLA will certainly be more powerful than the old GLC – but will only have a 'small staff'. The borders betwen the powers of the GLA and the boroughs are bound to be contentious – especially over planning matters.

Barnet
Controlling party: No Overall Control
Make-up: 26 Lab, 28 Con, 6 Lib Dem
Town Hall tel: 0181 359 2000
Search: 2–3 working days
Council tax, band D: £728

Brent
Controlling party: Labour
Make-up: 43 Lab, 19 Con, 4 Lib Dem
Town Hall tel: 0181 937 1234
Search: 10–12 working days
Council tax, band D: £589

Camden
Controlling party: Labour
Make-up: 43 Lab, 10 Con, 6 Lib Dem
Town Hall tel: 0171 278 4444
Search: 7–10 working days
Council tax, band D: £1074

Ealing
Controlling party: Labour
Make-up: 53 Lab, 15 Con, 3 Lib Dem
Town Hall tel: 0181 579 2424
Search: 7 days
Council tax, band D: £643

Enfield
Controlling party: Labour
Make-up: 43 Lab, 23 Con
Town Hall tel: 0181 366 6565
Search: 1 day
Council tax, band D: £680

Greenwich
Controlling party: Labour
Make-up: 52 Lab, 8 Con, 2 Lib Dem
Town Hall tel: 0181 854 8888
Search: 10 working days
Council tax, band D: £883

Hackney
Controlling party: Hung Council
Make-up: 28 Lab, 12 Con, 16 Lib Dem, 1 Green, 2 Ind
Town Hall tel: 0181 356 5000
Search: 5–10 working days
Council tax, band D: £789

Hammersmith & Fulham
Controlling party: Labour
Make-up: 36 Lab, 14 Con
Town Hall tel: 0181 748 3020
Search: 10 working days
Council tax, band D: £790

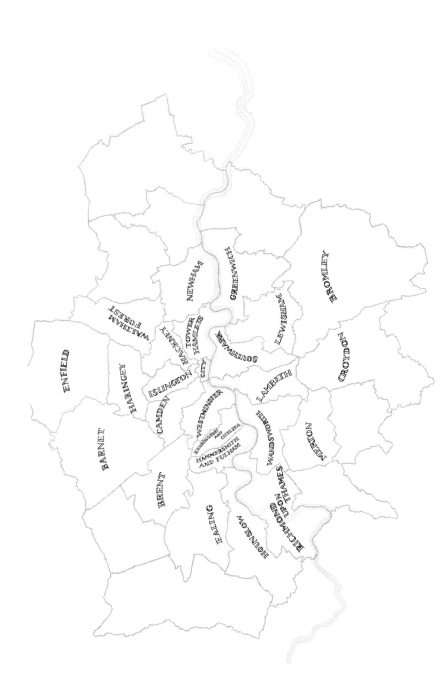

Haringey
Controlling party: Labour
Make-up: 50 Lab, 2 Con, 3 Lib Dem
Town Hall tel: 0181 975 9700
Search: 10 working days
Council tax, band D: £856

Islington
Controlling party: Joint Control
Make-up: 26 Lab, 26 Lib Dem
Town Hall tel: 0171 226 1234
Search: 10 working days
Council tax, band D: £912

Kensington & Chelsea
Controlling party: Conservative
Make-up: 15 Lab, 39 Con
Town Hall tel: 0171 937 5464
Search: 5–6 working days
Council tax, band D: £534

Hounslow
Controlling party: Labour
Make-up: 44 Lab, 11 Con, 4 Lib Dem, 1 Ind
Town Hall tel: 0181 570 7728
Search: 1 day
Council tax, band D: £730

Lambeth
Controlling party: Labour
Make-up: 41 Lab, 5 Con, 18 Lib Dem
Town Hall tel: 0171 926 1000
Search: 6–10 working days
Council tax, band D: £647

Lewisham
Controlling party: Labour
Make-up: 62 Lab, 2 Con, 3 Lib Dem
Town Hall tel: 0181 695 6000
Search: 10 working days
Council tax, band D: £683

Merton
Controlling party: Labour
Make-up: 39 Lab, 12 Con, 3 Lib Dem, 3 Ind
Town Hall tel: 0181 543 2222
Search: 5–10 working days
Council tax, band D: £747

Newham
Controlling party: Labour
Make-up: 60 Lab, 1 Ind Lab
Town Hall tel: 0181 472 1430
Search: 10 days
Council tax, band D: £679

Richmond
Controlling party: Liberal Democrat
Make-up: 4 Lab, 14 Con, 34 Lib Dem
Town Hall tel: 0181 891 1411
Search: 10 working days
Council tax, band D: £762

Southwark
Controlling party: Labour
Make-up: 33 Lab, 4 Con, 27 Lib Dem
Town Hall tel: 0171 525 5000
Search: 10 working days
Council tax, band D: £786

Tower Hamlets
Controlling party: Labour
Make-up: 43 Lab, 11 Lib Dem
Town Hall tel: 0171 364 5000
Search: 20 days
Council tax, band D: £658

Waltham Forest
Controlling party: Labour
Make-up: 30 Lab, 15 Con, 12 Lib Dem
Town Hall tel: 0181 527 5544
Search: 7–8 working days
Council tax, band D: £814

Wandsworth
Controlling party: Conservative
Make-up: 11 Lab, 50 Con
Town Hall tel: 0181 871 6000
Search: 7 days
Council tax, band D: £334

City of Westminster
Controlling party: Conservative
Make-up: 13 Lab, 47 Con
Town Hall tel: 0171 641 6000
Search: 2 working days
Council tax, band D: £325

Planning and building regulations

by Soo Ware

When buying a home, it is advisable to know something of the law that affects the development of residential property. There are, broadly, three building legislation acts that apply to domestic property: the Town and Country Planning Acts, the Building Regulations, and the Party Wall Act. If you are buying a property that has been modernized or converted – possibly over the course of a number of years – you will wish to reassure yourself and your building society that the conversion has been done with the full approval of the planning authorities, to the standards required by the Building Regulations and with the agreement of the adjoining owners. The searches for conveyancing purposes should reveal whether or not applications for planning permission and building regulation approval have been made. If not, you can visit the council offices and make your own enquiries, but finding out about Party Wall agreements with adjoining owners may be more difficult; the vendor should disclose this information if you ask.

However, once purchased, no matter how ideal the property appears to be, some alteration or extension to your new home may be necessary to adapt someone else's ideas to your own. This again brings you into contact with building law.

Planning permission

The Town and Country Planning Acts are complex and it may be necessary to obtain expert advice early on from architects, planning consultants or chartered surveyors. This chapter deals with controls on dwelling houses in terraces, semi-detached or detached houses. Blocks of flats are more complex and demand expert advice.

The Planning Acts are there to regulate development and protect the public interest in the development of land. Each application is looked at in context against the background of the development plan prepared by each London borough. Copies of the development plans can be obtained from town halls. Some areas within boroughs are designated conservation areas and usually the borough produces a separate, stricter policy document for such areas. Buildings that are listed are even more tightly controlled and you may need to obtain permission from English Heritage through the borough's Conservation Officer in the Planning department.

What might seem to you a very minor extension or alteration to a house can nevertheless have a far-reaching impact on the adjoining owners, the amenity and the appearance of a whole area. For example, motley roof conversions or new dormer windows on front elevations of terraces can change the appearance of a whole street. A planning application may be necessary for any of the following:

1. Extensions, alterations, garages, conservatories, roof gardens, balconies and loft conversions.

2. Garden fences, walls and the removal of trees (which are either the subject of preservation orders or in conservation areas). However, some garden sheds, greenhouses, swimming pools, sauna baths and summer houses may not require planning permission provided certain conditions are met.

3. Alterations to road access, drives and off-street parking. Additional consent from the highway authority (in London, the Department of Transport) may also be required.

4. Alterations to a previous planning consent or a change of use – for example, dividing a house into flats or flats back into a house.

5. The building is in a conservation area or covered by an Article 4 direction (an order placed on a whole street to maintain the integrity of its appearance). This can include changing doors, windows and roofs, painting brickwork, pebbledashing, sandblasting brickwork, etc.

6. If the building is listed (as of historical or architectural interest), a separate listed building consent will also be required. Make initial enquiries to the planning department of the appropriate borough council. A specialist Conservation Officer or Historic Buildings Officer will deal with your application and advise you as to whether or not you need to contact English Heritage. It is a criminal offence to make alterations (or even undertake some forms of maintenance) to a listed building without prior approval from English Heritage.

However, not all building work requires planning permission, and some quite modest extensions and alterations fall into the category of permitted development. Planning permission may not be required if you wish to extend your home by less than a certain volume, providing you can comply with certain conditions to do with height and location and (usually) make no changes to the front elevation.

The way in which the volume of a house is assessed is quite simple and relates to the 'original' house, that is as it was when first built or as it was on July 1, 1948 (if any extensions have taken place since then, the allowance may have been exceeded). The volume is based on the external dimensions of the house including the roof and the cellar. At present, the allowance for extensions to a terraced house is 1,765 cubic feet or 10 per cent of the original volume of the house up to 4,061 cubic feet; for a semi-detached or detached house, it is 2,472 cubic feet, or 15 per cent of the original volume of the house up to 4,061 cubic feet. However, there are no permitted development rights for flats. Planning permission for extensions or alterations will be necessary as will consent from the freeholder.

Even if the proposals fall within the volume for permitted development, it is advisable to consult the planning officer who deals with your area to confirm that no permission is necessary.

Planning permission may not be necessary but Building Regulation approval for the work will probably be required and a separate application should be made to the Building Control department. A Party Wall agreement or, at least, formal agreement by your neighbours may also be necessary. This is obtained through negotiation, and it is advisable to seek expert help.

How to apply

All boroughs have a planning enquiry office and most produce leaflets explaining their requirements for different types of development. Whenever possible, it is a good idea to have preliminary talks with the borough before making an application. It is, in theory, possible to contact the planning office to discuss your proposals before lodging a planning application. You should also talk to the Conservation Officer if appropriate. In some cases you may be able to arrange to meet an officer on site. However, the huge volume of planning applications and appeals made in London means that many boroughs are no longer able to offer these services until a formal application has been lodged.

Four sets of forms and a scale of fees can be obtained from the planning office. For the submission you will need to provide four sets of drawings. It is also useful to include photographs of both the property concerned and the surrounding buildings as well as a description of the proposed work. The drawings are very important and must be done well. A location plan showing the street and surrounding area on the Ordinance Survey map at a scale of 1:1250 is required together with the drawings of plans, elevations and sections differentiating between the proposed new work and existing buildings. For work to be carried out in conservation areas and on listed buildings additional detailed, large-scale drawings will also be required. There is a statutory fee payable on application which varies according to the type of alterations.

How long should it take?

In theory, planning applications should be processed within eight weeks; this is a statutory requirement. It is possible to check up on the progress of your application after four weeks from receipt of acknowledgement. Your application will normally be considered by a planning committee, though minor issues can be determined by the planning officer. The borough is obliged to consult with the immediate neighbours and, in certain circumstances, with more distant neighbours as well. Letters may be sent to adjacent properties and notice may be posted on the boundary of the property (a town hall euphemism for the front gate post or fence) so that local people are informed and can comment if they want to. Usually the council also puts notices in local newspapers about planning applications received. The procedures for public consultation vary from council to council. Once responses to consultations have been received it is possible to get some idea of the council's view of your application.

Many London boroughs are taking considerably longer than the eight weeks to process (technically called 'determine') applications – in some cases up to six months – before permission is granted or refused. The first hint of a possible delay over the eight weeks may come in the form of a letter from the council requesting a time extension. The eight weeks is counted from the time the authority acknowledges receipt of your application and many boroughs are taking a considerable number of weeks just to do this.

On receipt of the letter asking for a time extension, you can either accept the delay or appeal to the Secretary of State at the Department of the Environment on the basis that the authority has effectively refused the application because it has not issued a decision in time. If you are thinking of an appeal, it is certainly advisable to seek the assistance of a planning consultant, architect or surveyor with special planning expertise. There are three types of appeal: a written representation (which is called a written appeal), a hearing, where an inspector listens to the case presented by the parties involved, and an inquiry, which is like a court case and involves the appointment of a planning QC to act on your behalf.

Planning appeals are a lengthy and expensive business. It is usually quicker to negotiate with the borough to determine your application rather than appeal to the Secretary of State. However, if you are reasonably certain the borough is going to refuse your application and you feel you have a good case, you can refuse a time extension and appeal after the statutory eight weeks period. Once you have set the appeal in motion the borough will not process the application any further.

Where to get help and advice

Councils produce free leaflets available from their enquiry offices which explain the borough's own planning policies: Development plan, Conservation Area Policy documents, Borough Design Guides, and often a handbook explaining the procedures.

There are two useful Department of the Environment booklets: *Planning Permission – A Guide to the Householder* and *Planning Appeals – A Guide to Procedure*. These are often available from council offices or, if not, from the DoE, Tolgate House, Houltorn Street, Bristol BS2 9DJ.

The Royal Institute of British Architects provides leaflets describing services that architects offer in respect of planning applications and leaflets describing how drawings are prepared. These are available from the Clients Advisory Service, Royal Institute of British Architects, 66 Portland Place, London W1N 4AD. Tel: 0171 580 5533.

The Royal Town Planning Institute has leaflets about planning application procedure and appeals, lists of sources of planning advice in London, and can put people in touch with 'Planning Aid for Londoners' which is a free advice service manned by Chartered Town Planners, 26 Portland Place, London W1N 4BE. Tel: 0171 636 9107.

Lists of architects can be obtained from: Clients Advisory Service of the Royal Institute of British Architects (address previous page) which can give lists of local architects with special planning expertise.

The Royal Town Planning Institute (address previous page) can give lists of Planning Consultants who will help with applications.

The Royal Institution of Chartered Surveyors (12 Great George St, London SW1, Tel: 0171 222 7000) also produce lists of chartered surveyors and estate agents with expertise in planning matters.

Building regulations

To some extent, making an application for building regulation approval is more straightforward than making a planning application. There are two clearly defined procedures for obtaining approval: a building notice and full plans submission. It is also worth knowing a little about the background to the legislation and the kinds of work which need approval.

Background

The 1985 Building Regulations Acts introduced new regulations that now apply to both Inner and Outer London boroughs and are run by each borough council's Building Control Department. The new regulations have re-organized and superseded all previous legislation relating to those building works that were covered by the old building regulations and many separate local bylaws for Inner and Outer London. The 1985 regulations have been regularly updated with amendments and new regulations have been introduced covering matters such as sound and thermal insulation, control of condensation and energy, heat-producing appliances and provisions for the disabled.

What do you need building regulation approval for?

The procedures for obtaining building regulation approval are now the same whether you are building in a London borough or elsewhere in the country, and are administered through each borough Building Control Department. The kind of work for which approval is necessary includes:

1. The erection of a building.
2. The extension of a building (conversion into flats, loft conversions, some forms of conservatory).
3. The 'material' alterations to a building – alterations to structural walls (for example, knocking two rooms together, taking down a chimney breast), means of escape and fire resistance, particularly in relation to conversions into flats and loft extensions for individual houses.
4. Provision, extension or 'material' alteration to sanitary equipment (putting in a new bathroom or shower or extra WC), drainage, unvented water systems and putting in a stove, boiler or fire which runs on solid fuel, oil or gas.
5. Provision, extension or 'material' alteration of energy conservation, insulation (including cavity wall insulation systems) and ventilation in dwellings (particularly when installing an internal bathroom or WC or internal kitchen), ventilation of heating appliances.

The Party Wall Act 1997

Since the Great Fire of 1666, there has always been special legislation for the Inner London boroughs relating to the rights of adjoining owners and covering joint concerns such as party walls which provide support between dwellings and the prevention of the spread of fire between dwellings. Formal procedures were in place which worked very successfully in the prevention of neighbourly disputes. In 1997 a Party Wall Act was passed by Parliament to extend the procedures for party walls throughout the country. The procedures set out in the Act formalize agreements between owners when one building owner is undertaking building work to a party wall or fence or within certain distances of adjoining owners' foundations. The Act sets out the process for agreeing the condition of the buildings involved, the nature of the work proposed and the apportionment of costs. This involves serving notices on the adjoining owner and agreeing the appointment of architects or surveyors to act on behalf of the building owner and adjoining owner to ensure that the latter's property does not suffer as a result of the work. It is specialized and if you are considering any work which involves a Party Wall Award (meaning an agreement) you will need an architect or surveyor with the appropriate expertise.

Examples of work which would require a Party Wall Award include loft extensions, underpinning, extensions along the boundary or within certain distances of the boundary depending on the type of foundations proposed, works to the boundary walls, taking down chimney breasts, opening up between rooms where new beams are required bearing on the party wall and cellar/basement conversions.

How to set about it

You need to submit an application to your local council. Except in the case of very simple work, the services of an architect or chartered surveyor will be essential because detailed drawings are often required giving technical information on materials, insulation values, drainage and fire protection. You'll also need, in the case of any structural work, calculations.

It is possible to make an appointment with the building control officer, before putting in an application, to discuss the proposals and to find out if any particular information should be included (for example, specific calculations). Sometimes the officer (still called District Surveyors in some boroughs) will be happy to meet you on site if this is easier.

Building Notice route

Eighty per cent of building control applications involve a Building Notice. For buildings where it is not necessary to obtain a fire certificate before occupation – that is most homes – it is possible to serve a Building Notice. You should submit a completed application form (available from the Building Control Department), two sets of drawings and calculations, the appropriate fee and notice that you will commence work 48hrs later without waiting for approval. You should arrange a meeting immediately afterwards to establish whether or not there are any difficulties. As work progresses, the building control officer will pay regular visits to the site to ensure everything is done to his or her satisfaction.

A certain amount of confidence is needed to take this course, for if the regulations are not complied with, the local authority can enforce them up to a year after the work is completed, and this can prove to be extremely expensive for you. Less information needs to be shown on the drawings than on the Full Plan route, but the building control officer, during inspections, can (and does) insist on additional works being incorporated to ensure that the regulations are complied with as the work goes along. These people have very wide powers, and they use them.

There are other types of building work that may require additional applications. For example, some structures require a licence (a boundary wall more than 6 ft high or a steel balcony or external fire escape). These are regarded as temporary and special buildings. In the case of flats or maisonettes over shops, applications have also to be made to the fire brigade, but your building control officer will give you details of these.

Full Plan route

This is best used if you wish to have very tight control over the cost of the job and wish to have all details sewn up before the work starts to minimize the possibility of extra expenses. It's also necessary to have a reasonably long lead-in – at least five to eight weeks for the application to be processed.

Building regulation approval for the Full Plan route is in two stages: firstly, the drawings must be approved. A fee is payable and it should take between five and eight weeks. However, for complex submissions where a relaxation of the regulations is required, or where inadequate information is provided, building regulation approval can take considerably longer. Secondly, when work begins a Notice of Commencement should be submitted to the building control officer together with a further fee to cover the building control officer's inspection. The officer may need to be informed when certain work is taking place (for example, building foundations, damp-proof courses, laying new drains or covering up structural work), in which case further notices (but no fee) need to be served with one full working day's notice.

For the first stage, two sets of drawings and information should be submitted together with a letter or, in some boroughs, a form requesting that the proposals are considered for building regulation approval together with the appropriate fee. You can get details of the fees from the Building Control Department. During the five to eight week period before the Full Plan approval is given, a building control officer may ask for additional information or explanations and it is possible to have discussions with the officer about the best way to meet requirements.

Whichever route you select, when the works are completed, you or sometimes the solicitors doing searches will need to write to the Building Control Department requesting confirmation that the work was constructed in accordance with the regulations and a letter of confirmation will usually be sent to you.

What happens if you decide to go without Building Control approval? You could find it difficult to sell your property, as solicitors' searches may reveal that the work was done without the proper approval, licences, or Party Wall Awards. Or, you may be caught red-handed doing work for which approval has not been obtained, as building control officers take an eagle-eyed interest in the contents of skips. This may lead to the council taking legal action.

Soo Ware is an architect with a special interest in London property and is a partner in The Chartered Practice. She teaches Professional Practice at the Bartlett, University College, London.

Architectural styles

by Soo Ware

Foreigners coming to London have been known to express surprise that so many homes here are 'second-hand'. It is true that the majority of the city's houses are pre-1919. The only chance to buy a totally new house in Inner London comes with comparatively rare developments in odd corners.

The nearest most London buyers get to a 'new' home is a newly converted flat or a heavily modernized house. Even then, the façade will usually be carefully restored 'old' and many of the original features inside redesigned.

New homes have been built recently on a large scale along the riverside. From Greenwich to Richmond the riverside is being developed by the private sector to provide up-market flats and houses on previously industrial 'brown sites'. Away from the river, developers have been building on small infill sites and converting warehouses and offices to flats and 'loft' shells. At the very top of the market, there are also modern houses and new blocks of flats around Hampstead and near Regent's Park. Pockets of 'mews' type developments are taking place on infill sites in other areas. Some new estates of conventional family homes are being squeezed into surplus land beside railways in parts of South London. The architectural style of these new developers ranges from the high-tech avant-garde, through Post-modernism to Classical pastiche and bijou traditional.

A glance at London's skyline, with its many tower blocks of flats, shows that many homes have been built since the war. These homes have been built by London's local authorities, and until very recently were effectively outside the mainstream housing market as they were rented. Now, however, the 'Right to Buy' laws are bringing these flats, and the many council houses down at ground level, onto the market. This adds a new dimension to the choice of homes: modern properties (some simply convenient, some in fact excellent in both style and soundness) in central locations.

Most buyers, now and in the future, will be buying 'period' homes. This is a phrase widely used by estate agents who have no idea how old a house really is. It is often useful to know the vintage of a property, not just for interest but because different kinds of homes were built at different periods. Some are spacious, some cramped. Some were usually well-built, others a hurried response to fashion. Some kinds of architecture throw up more maintenance problems than others.

It should be said that there is some cause for sympathy with the agents' 'period' tag. First, some styles – eg 'Georgian' – were built, with little discernible evolution, for decades. Some were derived from earlier periods than when they were built – take the turn-of-the-century 'Queen Anne'. And this is still going on, with new London 'mews' popping up where none was there before. So the illustrations here are a starting point, a framework for reference. It can literally be impossible even for experts to date a London house by appearance only.

18th-century Georgian

These very elegant and much sought-after houses are found in small pockets. There are some in Mayfair, many of which were used as offices and are now being converted back into homes. Others are found in Islington, Hackney, Greenwich, Kennington, Kew, Clapham, Battersea, Richmond, Highgate and Hampstead. Detached or in terraces, each house is different. Flat-fronted, of Classical proportions, 2- or 3-storey with a slate mansard attic storey, usually three or five sash windows on each floor, often simple in appearance, soft yellow or red bricks, weathered in appearance. Often a fine front door with a carved wood door case with Classical details – pediments, columns and fan lights. Principal rooms on the first floor are reached by an elegant staircase. These buildings are invariably listed.

Georgian, late-18th and early 19th centuries

Built from the 1780s to the 1840s: often hard to date accurately without local knowledge. Found in Islington and Camden Town, Chelsea and Kensington, Bloomsbury, Kennington, Stockwell and parts of the West End. Usually in terraces, sometimes in squares and crescents, always in groups arranged as a whole. Three- or 4-storeys; sometimes an attic behind a parapet and a basement behind railings. Ground floor often stucco in an ashlar pattern. Other features: fanlight above front doors and ironwork balcony. Two sash windows per floor, brickwork usually soft London stocks, sometimes rendered with stucco and painted. Rooms are often modest-sized, main ones on first floor.

Regency villas and cottages

Built in the early 19th century, these pretty villas and terraces were intended to reflect a rural idyll in urban or suburban surroundings. Normally 2-storey, terraced or semi-detached, with ironwork canopies and wooden or cast-iron conservatories, trellises, sash windows and decorative railings. The front doors and porches often have delicate canopies. Slate roof, shallow-pitched with wide eaves. Rooms pretty but small. Found in pockets (Putney, Richmond, Kew or Twickenham), though a few survive in Chelsea, Mayfair and Regent's Park. A style much sought-after.

Regency terraces

In contrast to the picturesque Regency villas and cottages, there are also the more formal and magnificent terraces around Regent's Park and elsewhere in London and the river front at Richmond. These are buildings of Classical proportions, with 3, 4 or 5 storeys in sweeping crescents, terraces or lodges and substantial villas. Terraces are formed by a number of identical houses joined together, with the end of the terraces being defined separately like full stops. They are generally part of large estates, and are stucco – faced with identical decorations. Some are still single homes of truly magnificent proportions, others are converted into smart flats. Many are now used as offices or as company/diplomatic accommodation. Some have been rebuilt behind the original façade. Sometimes hard to distinguish from the early Victorian equivalent (see next page).

Early Victorian

Vast areas of London were built at this period, forming a ring stretching from Kensington and Chelsea through Camden and Islington, down through Hackney and to a lesser degree in South London: Blackheath, Camberwell, Kennington. They form part of the great estates of the time: Grosvenor, Gunter, Pimlico. Three-, 4- or 5-storey flat-fronted terraces or squares, usually with semi-basements, with Classical leanings: porticoes, Doric or Ionic columns, pediments and brackets. Almost always with a stucco, symbolic ashlar ground-floor storey, and sometimes painted above. Frequently whole areas are painted with the same colours. Now mostly flats, but planned as family homes for the burgeoning middle classes. Rooms often very large and well-proportioned, with attractive plasterwork, fireplaces and staircases.

Mews

Surviving mews date mostly from the 1830s to the 1890s. They were built to provide stabling and servants' housing, behind the terraces and squares in Belgravia, Knightsbridge, Mayfair, Marylebone and other parts. Today, they are converted to cottages in a hotchpotch of styles, with the coach house or stable used for garaging and the upper floor(s) forming 1 or 2 bedrooms. Some have been virtually rebuilt as larger houses. Usually brick, maybe painted or rendered or with a stucco finish. During conversion, they often gain features such as bay windows, shutters, ironwork, window boxes, hanging baskets. Some mews are still cobbled streets entered through an archway which once defined the estate.

Mid-Victorian

These large villas were typically built in pairs with the front door to the side, usually approached up some steps. They have a pitched roof with elaborate overhang or eaves. Detailing is 'Classical' stucco around windows and on the ground floor, with some being clad in stucco all over. Vestigal balconies, with ironwork, are found below sash windows. These are found in Chelsea, Kensington and other areas. Terraced houses in the same style, with similar Classical details, are widely seen. They are the result of a building boom in the 1850s and '60s and are found all round Inner London. Some, in less fashionable areas, fell into disrepair but many are now being restored. They are frequently turned into flats.

Late-Victorian

Houses of this period fall into three kinds: small, medium and large. Together, they are by far the most common type of house found in Inner London and many outer suburbs. It is difficult to imagine what London must have been like towards the end of the 19th century, with thousands of these houses being built all within 20 years. While the middle of the 19th century saw the construction of houses decorated with Classical 18th-century architectural details, the houses of this later period follow the Gothic fashion, with columns decorated with foliage, stained-glass windows, pointed arches and generally fussy detailing. They are usually built of yellow London stock brick or with stucco or red-brick dressing, mostly with slate roofs. Their front doors are set back in decorated porches. However, despite the Gothic detailing, most have sash windows. They are found particularly in a ring round London within the North and South Circular Rds.

The smallest houses (pictured on page 90) were working-class terraces, 2-storeys high, usually with white stucco bay windows on the ground floor to the front parlour with columns carrying foliage capitals, a narrow frontage and with rooms usually 2-up, 2-down.

The medium-sized house are the most common (pictured right), usually 2-storeys, sometimes with an extra room in the roof with dormer windows. These houses are found either in terraces or semi-detached. They often have stucco bay windows on both ground and first floors, with a small pointed·hip roof to the gable. These houses have wider frontages, extend far back and usually have 3 or 4 bedrooms. The main rooms have high, moulded ceilings and iron fireplaces with marble surrounds. Generally the small and middle-sized houses have small front gardens and modest back gardens or yards.

The large detached, semi-detached or terraced versions (pictured below) can be very grand, like the red-brick lion houses of Peterborough Estate, Fulham and the similar ones around Barnes Pond, Tooting Common, Highgate, Dulwich, Sydenham and Crystal Palace. They have 5 or 6 bedrooms, are usually 3 storeys high with very attractive

decorative mouldings both inside and out. Double-fronted or asymmetrical they are set back from the road with medium-to-large back gardens, square bay windows with gables, large rooms with high ceilings and attractive proportions. About half of all these three sizes of houses are still family homes, but many have been converted into flats – the large houses making excellent conversions into three flats.

Late-19th-century Dutch style

These tall, usually narrow-fronted soft terracotta-coloured brick houses, with elaborate moulded brick or faience decorations, are found in Knightsbridge and tucked away in Holland Park, South Kensington and Chelsea. Now softened with weathering, they were built at the end of the 19th century in a very free and eclectic style, usually in terraces (although sometimes semi-detached), but each house having varied features. Normally 4- or 5-storeys, with enormous chimneys and wiggly 2-storey gables (decorated with everything but the kitchen sink), and an elaborate porch up a few steps. The main rooms are on the first floor, very much following the plan of the mid-19th-century stucco estates. The windows have a different design on each floor, often with fiddly glazing patterns. The first floor sometimes has decorative ironwork, and rather fine railings separate the semi-basement from the street. Although some are still private houses, most are now flats or offices.

Mansion flats

These very large blocks of flats, usually 4, 5 or 6 storeys high, were built around the end of the 19th century and the beginning of this (1880–1910). Usually built of red bricks, with a horizontal stripy appearance formed by white stone banding and rows of windows picked out in white with white reveals. Façades are broken up with elaborate gable ends, bay windows, balconies and other features, giving an overall exuberant effect. They often have 'interesting' window designs, with glazing bars forming attractive patterns for both sash and casement windows. Arranged with two or four flats off a central staircase, often with well-proportioned rooms on the street frontage and secondary rooms facing rather dreary light wells. Mansion blocks range from very scruffy and poorly maintained to the extremely luxurious. Found all over London, examples include Prince of Wales Drive facing Battersea Park, around Baker St and behind the Royal Albert Hall in Kensington.

Early 20th century

These large detached and semi-detached houses were built for the wealthy middle classes who commuted from the healthy suburbs by train or tube. Many are found in such areas as Wimbledon, Putney, Hampstead, Dulwich, Greenwich and Streatham. They display the individuality of their original owners and a wide range of features were often used in one house.

Usually 2- or 3-storeys with 5 or 6 bedrooms, large reception rooms and entrance halls and generous staircases. Often double-fronted, built of brick or brick with render. Features include bay windows, steep gabled pitched tiled roofs, a variety of different types of casement window. Fewer Gothic touches than the late-Victorian buildings. More modest versions have a similar approach.

Nondescript 'Georgian'

Much loved by estate agents who call them 'period', which means they are unable to date them accurately or to define precisely the architectural style. Built early this century, in the '20s and '30s, and still being built. Very large, 2-storey, double-fronted houses, detached, with attic rooms in the steep pitched roof. Set back from the road,

with a sweeping drive, a full flight of steps and an imposing Classical front door. Many 'Georgian' features are incorporated: pediments, the Palladian window. Several large reception rooms, bedrooms with ensuite bathrooms as standard, staff quarters, large gardens. Found in Bishops Avenue in Hampstead, St John's Wood, Wimbledon Common, Bromley and Finchley.

Mock-Tudor

Built in large quantities around the perimeter of London mainly during the 1930s. More interesting examples occur nearer the centre of London and were built early in the century. And even now, still a popular style with the speculative developer. 1930s examples are found in ribbon development along arterial roads and on large estates. Detached, semi-detached or terraced, many with garages, and almost all family houses with 3 or 4 bedrooms and often substantial back gardens and smaller front gardens with off-street parking. Features: leaded lights in casement windows, steep pitched tiled gabled roofs, black and white timber decoration on white rendered walls, usually red brick on the ground floor and often with fussy brick decoration. Many now heavily altered with new windows etc.

1930s blocks of flats

These very large and rather anonymous blocks of flats, 5 to 7 storeys high, were widely built during the 1930s. Some were private developments (for example, those around Baker St, Maida Vale, Dolphin Square, Streatham). Others were built by the LCC or charitable trusts and are now coming on the market as individual flats. Built from yellow or red bricks with horizontal and vertical bands of render giving a stripy effect. Often they have balconies or bay windows. Windows sometimes are Georgian-type sash, but steel casement windows with very thin glazing bars also common. Blocks are set back a little from the street, with a landscaped area for parking or an entrance drive, and are often U-shaped or courtyard buildings with a central landscaped or paved area. Flats vary from 1- to 4-bedrooms.

Loft apartments

This is the new inner city domestic building form of the 1990s. Whether it will last into the next millennium depends on how easy it is to resell these flats when the original buyers move on. The location of these conversions, often on the riverside or in up-and-coming city locations, should ensure continuous interest. Converted from redundant industrial buildings, offices and schools, these highly individual flats were often sold as 'shells' to be fitted out by the purchaser with idiosyncratic results. Frequently these shells are double height allowing open plan, modern interiors. The structure, eg bare brickwork, roof construction and columns, is exposed to indicate the building's original use.

Modern private estates

Security and pastiche sum up the appearance of these modern developments. Prime sites in good locations, these estates are enclosed by a discrete security envelope and make no reference to any characteristic London vernacular. The developments, which include flats, maisonettes and houses feature electronic gates, security personnel, private roads with garages and parking, all in well-landscaped surroundings offering an anonymous secure environment. These new estates are located on land purchased from the Health Authorities, public utilities and educational bodies, freed up by privatization legislation. Many of the sites are located in prestigious areas including areas along the riverbank.

Glossary of architectural terms

Beetle infestation: timber in buildings can become infested with insect life. The most common is woodworm, which is often found in floor joists and roof timbers. The infected timber has numerous small holes, a little smaller than a pinhead in size. Depending on the amount of damage, the timber can be chemically treated or may need replacement. There are other wood boring beetles found in houses and causing damage usually identified by the size and shape of the flight holes in the timber left by the hatching insects.

Bricks: London stock bricks are the most common, made from yellowish clay in Kent. They weather down to greyish black but are often cleaned up and have a soft appearance. Red bricks are also widely used, often with London stocks as a decorative feature.

Casement window: a window with the opening part hinged on one side. Traditionally wood, but in the '20s they were made of steel and now also of aluminium or plastic.

Columns and capitals: vertical pillars with decorative tops. Can be either in Doric, a simple geometric style, or Ionic, a more elaborate style with curled motifs. Occasionally the third order, Corinthian, is seen and are elaborate designs decorated with leaves.

Doorcase: a wooden surround to a door opening, often very elaborate with carving or mouldings and Classical decorative features — eg, pediments or columns.

Dormer window: a vertical window (sash or casement) with upright sides coming through a sloping roof, having its own pitched or flat roof.

Dry rot: a fungus affecting timber in older houses. This is serious as all infected timber usually needs to be removed and destroyed and associated areas of brickwork chemically treated. Dry rot is often invisible and not detected until alterations reveal its existence, although the sensitive nose may detect a smell. The fungus spreads in hairline strands behind plasterwork and in brickwork courses. Timber becomes dry and powdery and loses its strength.

Faience: decorative moulded bricks, usually terracotta-coloured or yellowish, sometimes glazed; used in late-Victorian times for picking out features.

Frieze: a band of mouldings around a building usually at high level.

Gabled end or gable: a triangular end wall of a pitched roof, often becoming a decorative feature in its own right, for example, Dutch gables.

Glazing bars: the narrow strips of moulded timber or metal which hold the panes of glass together.

Leaded lights: small panes of diamond-shaped glass held together with narrow strips of lead.

Mansard roof: first rises steeply, almost vertically, with windows in it, and then has a flat top.

Moulding: continuous grove or ridge which forms a decorative feature with an original functional purpose, to throw water away from the face of a building. Can be in any material — brick, timber, stone, stucco. Internally, the term applies to decorative plasterwork or joinery, externally to many design features.

Palladian window: a composite window, designed to look like one big window but made up of three, of which the middle section has a semi-circular fanlight over.

Parapet: a small wall guarding the edge of a roof or, alternatively, the wall of the building extended above the roof line to conceal the gutters.

Pediment: triangular decorative motif usually found over doors and windows.

Render: a thick finish, usually sand and cement or pebbledash, which covers all the brickwork and can be painted as well. Popular on Edwardian or mock-Tudor houses with areas of brickwork or tile hanging.

Sash window: a window in which the opening parts slide up and down. They are usually balanced with ropes and weights concealed inside the frame. Traditionally wood, but replacement windows are now aluminium or plastic.

Slates: thin sheets of grey rock, once used extensively for roofing in London.

Stucco: similar to render, but popular in the 18th and 19th centuries as a smooth finish covering large areas of a building (often the whole wall), sometimes with Classical mouldings or details. Normally painted cream or white.

Tiles: made of clay, traditionally plain tiles, small rectangular rusty red and flat in shape, have been used in some areas for hundreds of years, and are seen on all periods of houses. They are used on roofs or can be hung vertically on walls as a decorative feature. In modern times, a wide variety of much larger profiled clay tiles have been used for replacement of old slate or tile roofs.

Velux window: a manufacturer's name for a window inserted into the sloping part of a roof, frequently used in loft conversions.

Wet rot: another fungus affecting timber in buildings. Usually more obvious than dry rot and found in areas where timber becomes wet, eg windowsills, the bottom of doors, the ends of joists in external walls, skirting boards on outside walls, in bathrooms and kitchens where there is condensation. The timber becomes wet and spongy and loses its strength. When the timber is painted the surface looks crazed if wet rot is present. Infected timber can be cut out and new pieces inserted. Generally not as serious as dry rot.

Soo Ware is an architect with a special interest in London property and is a partner in The Chartered Practice. She teaches at the Bartlett, University College, London.

Welcome home

Beckenham
2, 3, 4, 5, and 6 bedroom homes
● 0800 622 298

Mill Hill
2, 3 and 4 bedroom homes
● 0181 906 9736

Mill Hill
5 bedroom homes
● 0181 346 3790

Peckham
1 and 2 bedroom apartments
2 and 3 bedroom homes
● 0800 622 298

Romford
4 and 5 bedroom homes
● 01708 731986

Stanmore
5 bedroom homes
● 0181 954 8626

Teddington
1 and 2 bedroom apartments
3 and 4 bedroom homes
● 0800 622 298

Thames Ditton
2 bedroom apartments
3 bedroom homes
● 0181 398 0649

Wimbledon
1, 2 and 3 bedroom apartments
3, 4 and 5 bedroom townhouses
● 0181 947 3140

Coming soon

Ashtead, Balham, Battersea, Clapham, Horley, Putney, Stockwell.
For further information freephone
● 0800 622 298

Hackney, Hendon, Pinner, Spitalfields E1, Stanmore.
For further information telephone
● 0181 236 8810

Pictured is a typically grand Laing Homes entrance hall.

www.laing-homes.co.uk

London's Areas A–Z

How to use the A–Z section

This central section of the Guide is an alphabetically-organized guide to London's areas. The system is a two-tier one: each chapter covers an area of London, and each chapter is subdivided into the various neighbourhoods within the area. Parson's Green can thus be found under 'F' for Fulham, of which it is a part. This division, although less clear-cut than using the hard-and-fast boundaries of postal districts or boroughs, makes for more sense since, on the ground, areas refuse to stop at bureaucratic boundaries.

On page 103 is an *Index of Areas*, which lists the areas covered in this book for quick reference. Area and neighbourhood names are also found in the main street index at the end of the book.

If you only know the postal district of the place you are looking for, check the list that starts on page 14.

Maps

An outline map of London appears on pages 12–13. This shows the areas covered in the guide. The first page of each area chapter has a location map and a table of information. The map is designed to be a guide to the shape of the area, its main roads, railways and stations, the neighbourhoods it divides into, and which areas lie next door. Borough and postal district boundaries are also shown. These are rarely shown on street maps but can be important when house-hunting.

The maps are not designed to be street maps: to locate a particular street we refer you to the relevant page of the standard-sized *A–Z London Street Atlas* published by the Geographers' A–Z Map Company Ltd. The first line of information in the box beside each map in the book is a reference to the page and grid square of the *A–Z* that covers a central point of the area concerned. For example, the first page of the Acton section has 'Map ref p73 (1J)' indicating the page and grid square of Acton High Street. There is a key to these maps on page 100.

Boxed information

The map reference is to the standard-sized *A–Z London Street Atlas*. The postal district(s) of the area is given, and so is the borough(s) and controlling political party. Further details on both postcode (page 14) and borough (page 76) can be found in *London in 1999*.

Conservation areas are indicated where relevant. These are zones subject to special planning protection and where new building is generally not allowed unless it is in harmony with the existing architecture. Check with the local town hall (see *Boroughs*, page 76, for phone numbers) for exact boundaries.

Car parking restrictions are listed where information is available. The note on parking refers to residential, not commercial, streets. In most areas, there are restrictions on parking in shopping areas and on main through routes.

Area profiles

The text on each area consists of an area profile and sub-sections on neighbourhoods. These are the areas that people who live in the area divide it up into. Some have 'proper' names, others are defined as, for example, west or east of a certain point. See the area map for an indication of next-door areas. And note that the neighbourhoods are marked on the maps.

At the end of each area chapter there is a list of some of the main estate agents active in the area. This is neither an endorsement of the agents mentioned nor does it (or could it) mention all those you might encounter.

Each chapter ends with a summary of further useful information:

Transport

At the end of each area profile, you will find transport details giving the area's tube stations and local rail stations, and the fare zone the stations are in. The London Transport network is split into Zones 1, 2, 3 and 4, with 1 at the centre. Times are given from a central station in the area to three key points: the City (Bank station), Oxford Circus and Heathrow Airport. Where local rail lines are available, their main central destinations are given. Note that official journey times assume no hold-ups! Use the times given as a point of comparison with other areas. See the *Transport* section of the *Property Market in 1999* (page 23) for the latest news on new routes and improvements to existing ones.

The 'miles from centre' note under 'Convenient for' is the distance from the centre of the area to Charing Cross. The purpose of this figure is to give an immediate picture of an area's relationship to the centre of London, and as a quick point of comparison between areas.

Schools

At the end of each area profile we also list the main secondary schools and private secondary schools in the area. For more information see *Schools in London* (page 60) with the borough performance tables and *Boroughs* (page 76) to find out who to contact.

Prices

Average prices are given both sales and rentals of flats and houses of all sizes in the area. These prices give a 'freeze-frame' picture of where prices stood at the start of the 1999 selling season and are based on data collated in January. They indicate the price range into which each size of home mainly falls, not the price of the meanest slum or the grandest palace. Thus a narrow or a wide range for, say, a 2-bed flat is in itself an indication of the range of homes to be found in the area. See also *How to Use this Book* (page 10)

Below the price bands is a note on the kinds of homes to be found in the area and on the state of the property market there, and how long the local council takes over searches. This varies widely across London.

Finding a street

To find a particular street, refer to the main index, which lists the streets, areas and neighbourhoods mentioned in this book.

How to use the maps

Maps are not to scale and are intended for orientation and general reference. Check north point for orientation. Only main roads are shown. The neighbourhoods are those discussed in the accompanying text.

To locate a map, see arrows for surrounding areas and see the key map at the start of the A–Z section. For full details refer to the *A–Z London Street Atlas*. Each map has a cross-reference to the A–Z page and map square covering the centre of the mapped neighbourhood.

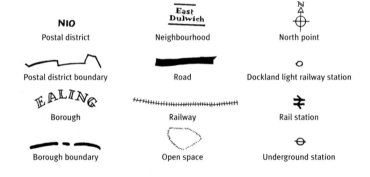

N10 Postal district	**East Dulwich** Neighbourhood	North point
Postal district boundary	Road	Dockland light railway station
Borough	Railway	Rail station
Borough boundary	Open space	Underground station

Index to areas

These are the areas and neighbourhoods covered in the following pages. For streets, see the main index at the back of the book.

ACTON

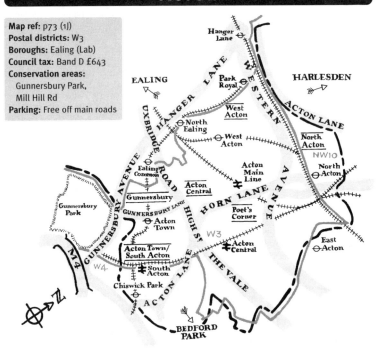

Map ref: p73 (1J)
Postal districts: W3
Boroughs: Ealing (Lab)
Council tax: Band D £643
Conservation areas:
  Gunnersbury Park,
  Mill Hill Rd
Parking: Free off main roads

The W3 postcode never carries the cachet of its neighbours W4, Chiswick, or W5, Ealing. This means that those who need a home more than they need status will do well here. In Acton, they get more for their money. They also get the benefits of Acton's many rail lines: fast communications. The rail lines, however, conspire with the main roads to carve the area into small, badly-linked pieces, eroding any sense of community the place might have. Again, contrast Ealing and Chiswick. But when you are struggling with a mortgage, a fast train to work and a few pounds less to pay each month compensate for a lot. The focus on value led to a good few of Acton's drabber corners being spruced up as old houses were converted into flats under the impetus of the BBC's move to their new White City headquarters.

Several grandiose schemes for Acton were shelved as the last recession hit – sometimes to residents' relief. A long-discussed widening of the A40 has been put on the back-burner indefinitely. The workaday **High St** did, however, gain a small-scale shopping centre, The Oaks, and **King St** was pedestrianized.

If the young buyers and renters who visit the good ethnic restaurants (and mutter of a fake-Irish theme pub too far) are not Islington or Battersea high-flyers, at the top end of the family homes market there's a different picture. Schools are the draw (Japanese School and King Fahad Academy) and have pushed the houses to very un-Acton prices.

Acton Central

Acton Central, between **Horn Lane**, **Hanger Lane**, **Uxbridge Rd** and the railway line, is nowhere near the train station so-named: a common problem around here. The

A

neighbourhood has some large family houses, although many fell to the Acton speciality – flat conversions. The people buying or renting the family homes in central Acton – particularly the 5-bed Victorian houses in leafy **Rosemont Rd** – may well be Japanese. Attracted by the school that moved here a few years ago from Camden Town, Japanese families moved into West London, served by their own estate agencies. Recent bad economic news has led to some families returning to Japan, but a nucleus remains. The area is also popular with families who want their daughters to go to Ealing Borough's only girls' comprehensive.

The general rule in central Acton, that prices rise the nearer you get to Ealing, means that flats in **Creffield Rd** and **Inglis Rd** are popular. Those in **Inglis** and some in **Creffield Rd** come with that dream of an Acton home-buyer . . . a W5 postcode. Further E, **Horn Lane** is a dirty, noisy main road; but **Pierrepoint Rd** and **Rosemont Rd** could be in another world – secluded, green and quiet. **Lynton Rd** is a mixture – a busy road with some '30s and '40s houses, some Edwardian, with an equal mix of flat conversions and houses. Prices for flats range from around £75,000 for 1-bed, £100,000 for 2-bed. A 3-bed house can command £190,000, with 4-bed ones on the market for £220–260,000. Check which side of the street it's on: the railway line lies to the N. Parking is slightly easier in this long, wide road than in most of Acton's jam-packed streets. Central Acton does suffer from being a long way from tube stations, and proximity to one of them adds to the price.

Acton Town/South Acton

The triangle S of **Acton High St**, E of **Gunnersbury Lane** and W of the railway line is dominated both physically and in reputation by the South Acton Estate. The council estate's ugly concrete towers loom above the pleasant Edwardian terraces around Acton Town tube station.

The main attraction for buyers of the terraced Edwardian houses and flat conversions in pleasant streets like **Avenue Rd** and **Mill Hill Rd** is the nearby tube station. The terraced houses are in good condition, the roads are tree-lined, and **Mill Hill Rd** is particularly pretty in the summer, with flowery front gardens. Three-bed houses in this conservation area cost around £190–220,000.

Poets' Corner

Estate agents wax lyrical about Poets' Corner – it is central, pleasant, full of converted flats and intensely gentrified. The area stretches N of the **High St**, between **Horn Lane** and **East Acton Lane**, S of the railway line and Acton rail station. The streets grouped (appropriately) around **Shakespeare Rd** give you a cultural choice which includes **Chaucer**, **Spencer**, **Milton** and **Cowper**. (Who, though, was **Myrtle**?) Home-buyers are mostly looking at terraces in tree-lined streets (3-bed houses c. £200,000). The houses in streets like **Cumberland Rd** and **Maldon Rd** were once grand family homes but are now almost all 2- or 3-bed flats (c. £120–125,000 for 2-bed garden flat).

Goldsmith Rd turns, northwards, into **Goldsmith Avenue** and an even more favoured corner: the Goldsmith estate's Edwardian homes. Some of the houses in surrounding streets are later, built about 1950. Across the railway to the E, **Shaa Rd** and around, N from Acton Park, are popular with Arab families, because of the road's exclusive school for Arab children – and there's the Barbara Speake Stage School nearby in **East Acton Lane**. A 5-bed house in **Shaa Rd** will command £320,000. Around **Beech Avenue**, across **East Acton Lane**, there are some modern developments, including one very popular estate by Barratt which includes a stylish block of retirement flats. **Beech Avenue** itself, however, is not yet 'up-and-come'. Among its mix of council and private homes you can find the odd large (perhaps 3-bed) flat for as little as £60,000. To the S, **Cowper Rd** and **Milton Rd** have small terraced houses that were once the homes of Victorian workers. They are too small to be turned into flats, and have tiny gardens, but a delightfully cottagey feel. They sell for £150–180,000 for 2-bed. **Shakespeare Rd** is a better bet for conversions, and some have big rooms and elegant façades. Be cautious in **Alfred Rd** and **Burlington Gardens**. The huge 3-storey Victorian terraces look imposing, but have been run down for years – although now many have been bought up by housing associations. A 2-bed flat may fetch £90,000 – but these streets link into the **High St** one-way system, so traffic is heavy.

West Acton

West Acton was the scene of a property buyer's dream in the early '80s – 3-bed semis were sold off for a fraction of the market prices, fetching just a few thousand pounds. These were the 'railway cottages': homes in and around **Saxon Drive**, built in the '30s for rail employees to rent, and sold to the tenants years later. Today these are very popular (and close to West Acton tube), and fetch around £150,000.

West Acton, which lies in the angle between **Horn Lane** and **Western Avenue**, is dominated by rail lines – the Piccadilly line to the N, the main line to the S, and the Central line which crosses it diagonally for good measure. But it is popular for more than its undeniably good access to public transport. It is greener than the rest of Acton, with a liberal scattering of sports grounds and playing-fields. And, to the W of West Acton station, is the Tudor estate – different from anything else in either Ealing or Acton, with black and white mock-Tudor homes built between the wars. Japanese and other families love this estate, with its 3-bed houses in roads such as **Queens Drive**, **Monks Drive** and **Princes Gardens**.

Acton stops here. Across the tracks the desirable curving roads that climb **Hanger Hill** to the **North Circular Rd** mark the start of W5 and Ealing.

North Acton

North Acton might be called Leamington Park by some estate agents, but don't let the up-market name blind you to the area's drawbacks. It has none of the Ealingesque atmosphere to which many in Acton are drawn. Much of the property in the triangle between **Old Oak Lane**, **Victoria Rd** and the **Western Avenue** is run-down, with a few unappealing purpose-built blocks of flats. £85,000 may buy you a 2-bed flat in **Leamington Park**, but the road of that name is on the one-way system onto the A40, and there is no parking in the street. But between Acton main line station and the North Acton tube, an area which straddles the A40 **Western Avenue** has seen some new developments. Westcott Park in **Cotton Avenue**, built in the late '80s, is a source of studios and 1- and 2-bed flats at reasonable prices.

Watch out for further transformation in this corner: there were plans for several hundreds of homes in the bullish '80s, variously dropped or delayed as recession struck and uncertainty over the road-widening scheme for the A40 **Western Avenue** reigned. The depressingly boarded-up houses that were blighted by this are appearing on the market at bargain prices, but the traffic pollution and noise would put off most.

Tucked into the corner between **Western Avenue** and the **North Circular** is the Park Royal neighbourhood, where a few streets of homes struggle on amid a vast industrial estate. Guinness, whose brewery is here, have plans for a major business and leisure development. This would include new housing, restaurants and even a new tube station. However, existing residents are unhappy about the impact on their homes. The plans have been altered in the last year to improve traffic flows and increase the amount of open space. You would never consider this area for peace, quiet and clean air, but get to understand the scale of the development if you're thinking of living here. The Park Royal scheme will have an impact on the wider area, of course, bring amenities where few exist and provide many new homes, but its effects on the already clogged **Hanger Lane** road junction can only be guessed at.

East Acton

East Acton is a small area in the midst of railway lines and bordered to the S by the busy A40 **Western Avenue**. The neighbourhood lies on the Hammersmith Borough boundary close to Wormwood Scrubs Prison and the common to the E. Nevertheless East Acton, a collection of two dozen or so roads, has a pleasant villagy feel – a mixture of council-built and private homes.

Running N from the **Western Avenue, St Andrews Rd** has '30s red-brick terraces with square bays extending from the ground to first floor. Council-built properties dominate **The Fairway** running W-E between the main line and **Old Oak Common Lane**. The majority are stone-clad semis and terraces – but some are of a warmer brown brick. Nearby on the pleasant green the homes – 1930s once again – are privately owned and arranged in both terraces and semis. Moving N through **The Bye** to **Long Drive**, clusters of 12 semis (prices around £130,000) are grouped around small greens in closes – creating a friendly atmosphere. Further down **Long Drive** towards the **Western Avenue** are one or two larger detached houses, some with gables, some with bays. However, these types are rare in East Acton.

Turning left into the heart of the neighbourhood once more, **Brassie Avenue** offers a mixture of council and private semis. The main shopping area is in nearby **Old Oak Common Lane** to the E near the A40 intersection. All the essentials are there.

Borders: Gunnersbury

A no-man's-land between Ealing and Acton, trapped in the triangle of **Gunnersbury Lane**, **Uxbridge Rd** and **Gunnersbury Avenue**, Gunnersbury is a pleasant area, with some roads of detached family homes that fetch high prices. **Lillian Avenue**, **Gunnersbury Gardens** and **Gunnersbury Crescent** are good for family homes, with large gardens. And the area is very convenient for the huge Gunnersbury Park, with its stately home-turned-museum. The 4-bed mock-Tudor homes of refined **Carbery Avenue** can fetch £300,000. For Acton Green – the neighbourhood SE of South Acton station – see the Bedford Park chapter.

Transport	Tubes: Acton Town (zone 3, Piccadilly, District), North Acton (zone 2/3, Central), others see map. From Acton Town: Oxford Circus 30 min (1 change), City 45 min, Heathrow 20 min. Trains: Acton main line (Paddington 15 min), Acton Central and South Acton on N London line, Silverlink. Miles from centre: 6.5.
Convenient for	Heathrow, routes to Oxford and the West, BBC in Shepherd's Bush.
Schools	Ealing Education Authority: Acton School, Ellen Wilkinson (g), Twyford C of E. Private: Japanese School, King Fahad Academy.

SALES

Flats	S	1B	2B	3B	4B	5B
Average prices	50–65	70–90	85–130	120–180	—	—
Houses	2B	3B	4B	5B	6/7B	8B
Average prices	95–70	135–220+	180–280+	250–350+	—	—

RENTAL

Flats	S	1B	2B	3B	4B	5B
Average prices	500–650	600–900	850–1200	1000–1500	1300–2300	–

Houses	2B	3B	4B	5B	6/7B	8B
Average prices	1000–1300	1100–1600	1300–2383	2000–3500	–	–

The properties Mix of late-Victorian and Edwardian terraces and inter-war suburbia. Few large houses. Ample 1- and 2-bed flat conversions. Recently some new-build including several big schemes. Best streets include those of Poets' Corner.

The market First-time buyers' stepping-stone, and family homes. Best parts of Acton can approach Ealing prices. These are bought by BBC types, or rented to families who move here for the Japanese School or King Fahad Academy. Local searches: 1 week.

Among those estate agents active in this area are:
- Bushells
- Rolfe East
- Churchill
- Barnard Marcus
- Hart
- Landsdowne
- Winkworth *

further details: see advertisers index on p633

BALHAM AND TOOTING

Map ref: p108 (2E)
Postal districts: SW12, SW17
Boroughs: Wandsworth (Con),
   Lambeth (Lab)
Council tax: Band D
   Wandsworth £334,
   Lambeth £647
Conservation areas: Include
   Heaver, Totterdown Fields,
   Trinity Rd
Parking: Free away from main
   routes and stations

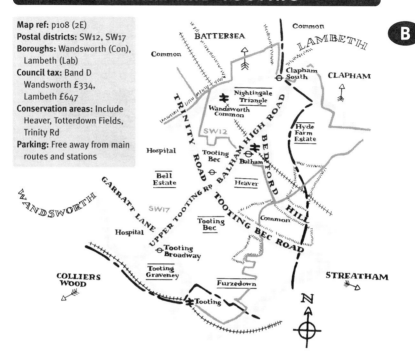

These days bits of Balham are deeply desirable, while the solid family homes of Tooting's Heaver Estate heave with bankers and lawyers. Like a lot of South London, Balham and Tooting spent much of the 20th century asleep in seedy respectability; it was only in the '80s that they began to be of interest to any but strictly local buyers. In some parts, the market is very local still, and there is a thriving Asian community. In the late-19th century Balham and Tooting were merely small hamlets on the main road into London. Their popularity grew with the advent of the railway, and the extension of the Northern line underground in 1926 was the final stage of metamorphosis from genteel settlement to inner city.

   'Balham, Gateway to the South', as it was immortalized by the late Peter Sellers, was favoured as the ideal area for a country residence by the professional classes of the 19th century, and this accounts for the impressive houses near to the commons still standing today. The later terraces crowd around the spine of the area, running S-E from the bottom tip of Clapham Common and called, successively, **Balham Hill/ Balham High Rd/Upper Tooting Rd/Tooting High St** (A24). 'Gateway' is right, in the sense of constriction. But the area is fringed with greenery: Tooting Bec, Tooting Graveney, Wandsworth and Clapham Commons, plus a golf course – and couple of large cemeteries. There is also a major teaching hospital, St George's, which moved here from Hyde Park Corner in the '80s. Today's incomers are attracted by easy transport by tube and train into and out of town, and the good supply of period properties still at a discount on Clapham and Battersea prices. There are relatively cheap buys around – particularly in Tooting Broadway and areas further from tubes: note that a car is not an alternative for commuters who want to arrive on time.

Most homes in Balham are Victorian, whereas Tooting ranges from the 1800s to the present day – the bulk, though, are mainly Victorian, Edwardian and '30s. Although the '80s contributed, first, widespread flats conversions and then small pockets of new homes – mainly in Balham – the late '90s have seen further development: it is Tooting Bec that is seeing the area's first really large-scale development: the site of the old Tooting Bec Hospital is adding a tract of more than 600 new flats and houses to the area. Homes are springing up here – see below – but as 1999 dawned the Stage Two plans were called in: the Minister will now decide . . .

Conversions of houses into small flats fell rapidly from favour as pressure on parking spaces and family-sized homes mounted. Wandsworth's planning policies are strict; anything less than 120 sq m is deemed too small to convert (excludes many 2-storey terraces) – and there are now 'house conversion restraint areas' across the borough where the minimum is 150 sq m. Split-ups *must* include a flat big enough for a family of four, unless you can show very good reason why not. Planning permission is also unlikely in areas with parking problems: no off-street parking, no conversions. Parking black spots include around **Bedford Hill**, S of **Elmfield Rd** in Tooting and around tube stations. Streets around the tube station in Balham are a busy shopping area, so parking is particularly difficult, and there is periodic talk of a permit scheme around Clapham South tube, at the northern extent of **Balham Hill**. A fiercely contested plan to add a Tesco Metro across from the tube, on the site of the old Women's Hospital, has gone to appeal. At least Tesco's latest plans keep the façade.

Balham has seen several new pubs and wine bars open in the last couple of years catering for a typically up-market, young professional crowd, mainly around the bustling **High Rd** which, though small, provides a real focus to town life in the area. Civic services are restricted to Central Balham Library, adjacent to Safeway on **Ramsden Rd**. However, neighbouring areas supply the cinemas (Clapham, Streatham), theatres and pub theatres (Wimbledon, Battersea), and village **Bellevue Rd**, at the foot of Wandsworth Common, has the fashionably smart shops, pubs and restaurants. Indeed Wandsworth Council's policy is now to try to restrict the increasing number of new bars and cafés in several 'hot spots' across the borough – **Bellevue** and **Balham High Rd** among them.

Traffic flow is always congested along the A24, and the many railway lines – with few road bridges – make car journeys tortuous and bus travel erratic at best (at least there is a large car park behind the smart, revamped Sainsbury's). Homes prices are thus with reason higher near tube and train stations, and also opposite commons;

lower on main roads and (say local agents) near the graveyards . . . The further S you go, the less you pay – Balham and Tooting Bec are more desirable than Tooting Broadway.

Balham

B

Some time around 1985 a local estate agent confided 'it's all right to talk about Balham now'. The combined efforts of Peter Sellers and Nikolaus Pevsner ('nothing of interest on **Balham Hill** except the Odeon') had damned the place into a sort of property limbo. Half-hearted attempts were made to shift it into 'south South Wandsworth'. Clapham South tube station gave its name to a swathe of what is really Balham. The quiet and pleasant streets between **Nightingale Lane** and **Balham High Rd** migrated upwards to become the Nightingale Triangle and, again, honorary Clapham, but are covered here.

Balham has all the attributes of a real place: a **High Rd**, a station (main line and Northern line tube), a parish church (St Mary, 1805) and a library. The rail line to Croydon, running W-E on its embankment, divides Balham in half and contributes largely to traffic congestion: there are only three bridges beneath it.

Nightingale Triangle

This is the most exclusive area in Balham: quiet, attractive and convenient for transport, and bordering Clapham and Battersea. It is bounded by **Nightingale Lane**, **Balham High Rd** and the railway. Roads running between **Ravenslea Rd** and **Chestnut Grove** contain neat Victorian terraced 3/4-bed houses, popular but smaller than some properties in the triangle. There are larger gardens in **Calbourne Rd** and **Mayford Rd**. **Nightingale Lane** starts on the brow of the Wandsworth Common railway bridge and contains very large and distinctive semi-detached 5/6/7-bed houses including some by T E Collcutt (1879) opposite **Endlesham Rd**. Then come '30s 4-bed houses leading to mansion flats near Clapham South tube, including Clapham Mansions (2/3/4-bed flats, mix of owner-occupied and tenants) and Hightrees House (Art Deco) overlooking the cricket ground. Service charges are quite high – but this includes insurance, porterage and use of gym and pool. **Western Lane**, leading S from the popular Nightingale pub, is a leafy alley with mid-19th-century cottages, newly and attractively paved, with Victorian-style lamp-posts. Through to **Linnet Mews** – built 1983 – are smart 1/2-bed red-brick houses and flats. South is the picturesque **Nightingale Square** – coveted large Victorian houses (winter '98, c. £640,000) that surround a garden for residents. Despite the bustle of two schools and a church at the far end, the square remains a popular corner. Nearby in **Oldridge Rd**, there's planning permission for eight loft-style houses on three floors with balconies and courtyard in an ex-industrial building marketed at £1.5 million in January.

Chestnut Grove, running on to the S, has pleasant cottage terraces and a large school on the W side. It gets less popular as it nears busy **Balham High Rd** and the tube. **Ramsden Rd**, cutting through the middle of the triangle, has a variety of red-brick and flat-fronted Victorian houses and terraces, some large and some small.

The houses are generally larger at the two ends of the road, but the **High Rd** end does get congested with Safeway's car park entrance on the E side. Two-bed cottages (once workmen's quarters) feature in **Bellamy St**, **Pickets St**, **Balham Grove** and **Temperley Rd**. **Bracken Avenue** is leafy and pleasant. **Badminton Rd** has period red-brick homes on the E side, early 20th-century unusual double-fronted maisonettes on the W. Front gardens on the E side are smaller (Nos 1–54). **Balham Grove** has a Safeway supermarket's goods entrance at the southern end but then a couple of lovely Georgian houses – one of which is now apartments.

Large Victorian houses follow with a small recent estate in **Ainslie Walk**. The Lochinvar Estate ('60s, concrete, low-rise) is an affordable, if uninspiring, first-time

Even the most ordinary corners provide quirky details for those who look. This unusual window, above the front door of a Balham home, shows its late-Victorian date with Gothic-style carving and decoration and the pattern of the glazing bars in the sash windows. Attractive as they may be, such bays need careful maintenance if damp is not to be a problem.

buy. A mews development off **Malwood St** at the apex of the triangle and just around the corner from the tube, is indicative of the popularity of this Clapham-borders corner. **Liberty Mews**, built in the '80s, was marketed as a good investment opportunity as well as for straightforward owner-occupation, and a number of the units are rented out. At 18–20 **Balham Hill** a 1990 mews has cottages and flats opening out around a courtyard, behind some small office units developed last year.

Hyde Farm Estate

A rectangle bounded by **Hydethorpe Rd**, **Emmanuel Rd** and **Radbourne Rd** in the eastern part of Balham and in Lambeth, not Wandsworth, borough. This network of streets consists of red-brick Victorian 3/4-bed terraces and maisonettes, with only slight variations in style from road to road (more 'bell-fronted' in **Haverhill Rd** than in **Scholars Rd**, for example). **Emmanuel Rd** is popular – it overlooks Tooting Bec Common, the railway line nearby being screened by trees. Two schools – Henry Cavendish and Telferscot (both Junior Mixed and Infants). Building of the Hyde Farm estate was begun in 1901 by speculative developers led by Ernest Hayes-Dashwood on land leased from Cambridge's Emmanuel College. Today, parts of **Radbourne Rd** and **Telferscot Rd** are set aside as rent-free accommodation for retired servicemen and war veterans.

The area N of Hyde Farm is more mixed, with an industrial estate in **Zennor Rd**. **Weir Rd** is industrial on the W side but soon calms down to Victorian terraces on the right and **Molly Huggins Close** on the left, and a recent development of 40 flats and houses for rent on an old hospital site. **Belthorn Crescent** has the smart Weir Estate. **Atkins Rd** has pleasant 20th-century semi-detached and terraced houses on the right – mainly in good repair, some mock-Tudor. There is a school on the left – St Bernadette Catholic Primary School (girls).

The roads running E from the **High Rd** to **Cavendish Rd**, between **Englewood Rd** to the N (really in Clapham) and **Rossiter Rd** (S), are almost entirely period terraces of 3/4/5-bed houses. Exceptions include gated, cobbled **Anchor Mews** off **Hazelbourne Rd** (around corner from tube and Clapham Common), where a fashionable loft-style flat with garage cost £305,000 last winter. There are also recent flats in **Hanson Close**, but it's back to period in **Ravenswood Rd**. **Old Devonshire Rd** has a mosque and some industrial buildings giving way to a mix of period and recent properties. **Laitwood Rd**, **Ormeley Rd** and **Ranmere St** form a quiet, pretty enclave. On either side of the railway line, **Fernlea Rd** and **Byrne Rd** have attractive flat-fronted upper façades, early Victorian in style, leading to Victorian terraces.

Byrne Rd, to the S of the railway, and E of **Bedford Hill**, curves into the leafy **Culverden Rd** with its impressive 6/7-bed period semi-detached houses – some converted, some needing repair. Those on the E side overlook Tooting Bec Common.

Neat terraces in **Dornton Rd** (some purpose-built flats with balconies) and **Fontenoy Rd**. Smart new maisonettes on the E of **Brierley Rd** are opposite period terraces. The Ryde Vale Estate (entrance **Ryde Vale Rd**) has a mix of styles – small blocks of terraced flats, low-rise concrete blocks and bungalows.

B

Bedford Hill's once notorious 'red-light' reputation is now largely unmerited, kerb-crawlers having been discouraged by blocking off the E end of **Elmfield Rd** and making **Carminia Rd**, **Childebert Rd** and **Cloudesdale Rd** one-way. The hill has large period properties – some very grand with ornamental brickwork. Recent schemes include 14 new 1- and 2-bed flats on the corner of **Culverden Rd**, and 12 flats in the shadow of the railway bridge for the Wandle Housing Association. The Priory, on the edge of Tooting Bec Common, dates from 1822 and is now flats.

Marius Rd, W of the **High Rd**, has attractive period houses and Marius Mansions – impressive Victorian flats, recently renovated – at the far end. More mansion flats are at the S ends of **Nevis Rd** (Cecil Mansions) and **Wontner Rd** (Stanley Mansions). There are many period terraces and some recent developments – notably the pleasant brick houses in **Ashdown Way** and the not-so-pretty yellow Flowersmead council estate ('40s) opposite (now nearly half private ownership).

The N end of **St James's Drive** boasts large covetable homes overlooking Wandsworth Common – popular because close to the train station and the amenities of **Bellevue Rd**, but pricey. **St James's Close** is an attractive new development of houses and flats around a central garden. **Balham Park Rd**, leading E from **St James's Drive** back to the **High Rd**, has half-million pound houses by the common, Victorian terraces, and towards the E end more modern flats and houses. Ducane Court on the main road – once the largest block in Europe – is a '30s block of 650 studio and 1/3-bed flats.

Balham Borders

West of **St James's Rd**, at the foot of the common in the triangle between it, deeply fashionable **Bellevue Rd** and **Trinity Rd**, are tucked some neat, prosperous, pricey, grey-brick terraced cottages. In SW17 rather than SW12, and emotionally Wandsworth Common (see Wandsworth chapter) rather than Balham.

The roads N of **Nightingale Lane** and S of **Thurleigh Rd**, while still in SW12, have been annexed into the area known these days as 'Between the Commons' in Battersea – see Battersea chapter.

The area E of Hyde Farm, and S of the **South Circular** with the wide **Kings Avenue** running N-S, has generally large, pleasant inter-wars and post-war housing with some flats scattered around. **Thornton Rd** is semi-detached mock-Tudor; **Thornton Gardens** is a small estate. There is also a late-'80s development off **Thornton Rd**: St Stephens **Mews** is 1- and 2-bed flats. The flats at the S of **Kings Avenue** give way to large modern houses with garages. More 20th-century houses in **Copthorne Avenue** and **Parkthorne Rd**. This area has aspirations to be Clapham Park, or perhaps Streatham Hill.

On the Tooting borders, the roads directly N of the Heaver Estate, from **Ritherdon Rd** up to **Elmfield Rd**, are neat period terraces apart from some '60s flats at the N ends of **Carminia Rd** and **Childebert Rd**. At the W end of **Elmfield Rd** there are mansion flats of impressive red-brick, some needing repair. Ravenstone School opposite (primary) and Balham Leisure Centre (pool, gym, solarium, etc) are the other features of the road. **Cheriton Square** is opposite the leisure complex: its curving terraces always enjoy top billing in estate agents' ads.

Tooting

The name Tooting excites a certain amusement, but the place has more history than nearby Balham and can boast a past back to Domesday. Little remains of the villages of upper Tooting (Tooting Bec) and lower Tooting (Tooting Graveney). The place stayed small and rural well into the last century, and the big development of houses happened relatively late. The result is a district of orderly grids of late-19th-century homes, some spacious, some small, all well served by the Northern line tube.

B

Tooting's two commons, Rec and Graveney, boast lido, sports and tennis facilities but are sadly cut up by rail and roads. They do, however, give Tooting a clear boundary to the E. To the N is Balham; W, beyond the sprawl of Springfield University Hospital and the (perhaps unfortunately placed) Streatham Cemetery, is Earlsfield. To the S, the rail line between Wimbledon and Streatham forms the boundary. Beyond is Colliers Wood. Tooting rail station is right on the (SE) edge of the district it is named after.

Tooting Broadway more closely resembles a typical South London inner-city neighbourhood, albeit with better shopping (including the underrated indoor Tooting market), than say nearby Streatham, which was more superior (and up-market) 20 years ago. The shopping and commercial hub of the area is centred on **Upper Tooting Rd/Tooting High St**, particularly concentrated around the junction with **Mitcham Lane**, around Tooting Broadway tube station. The two Northern line stations at either end of **Upper Tooting Rd**, the A24, provide useful, if somewhat beleaguered, access to the City and West End. Now, with the redevelopment of the Tooting Bec Hospital site, located on the south-western edge of Tooting Bec Common – see below – Tooting's main public landmark has become the enormous, sprawling complex of St George's Hospital, sitting quietly behind the bustling Tooting Broadway streets, on the edge of the Wandsworth/Merton border. Wandsworth Council has also introduced a scheme offering refurbishment grants for commercial property in a bid to revitalize the shopping area and secure its prosperity, especially around the **High Rd** in Tooting.

Heaver

By far the grandest and priciest neighbourhood in Tooting and Balham. The main conservation area lies between **Balham High Rd**, **Tooting Bec Rd**, the Common and **Ritherdon Rd**; with the neat terraces between **Ritherdon** and **Elmfield Rds** claimed by agents as outliers. This turn-of-the-century estate was built by the Heaver brothers, and consists of distinguished double- and single-fronted 3-storey houses and some maisonettes, all in red-brick with white detail. Approximately half have been converted, and these make for frequently very generous-sized flats. The unconverted houses are enormous – typical interior for an intact property would have 6 to 8 bedrooms, 2 bathrooms, kitchen plus three other reception rooms and a huge garden. Many original features remain inside and out – note the ornate front doors with stained-glass insets. Largely untouched by modern developments, the main exceptions being infill maisonettes in **Manville Gardens** and **Carnie Hall**, and smart flats at N end of **Hillbury Rd**, which also boasts some modern 3-bed town-houses and some 4/5-bed 'mock-Heaver' houses, built in 1989. Families wishing to escape cramped modern housing find havens in these popular, individually distinctive streets – for example, **Elmbourne Rd** (ornate brickwork framing door arches and windows) overlooking Tooting Graveney Common, and the wide, tree-lined **Streathbourne Rd** (each house name inlaid in decorative plaques). Average prices for intact houses are high: even unmodernized examples are likely to be c. £400,000, and the best price to date is believed to have been £750,000 – a considerable appreciation, even allowing for different houses, over the £450,000 sale that was a talking-point in 1988, at the end of the great boom.

Tooting Bec

The stretch enclosed by **Tooting Bec Rd** (N) to **Mitcham Rd** (S), **Upper Tooting Rd** (E) and **Rectory Lane** (W), this includes the area's main talking-point, the Tooting Bec Hospital site. The largest development site by far, Fairview has re-christened this swathe between **Tooting Bec Rd**, **Franciscan Rd**, **Mantilla Rd** and **Church Lane**

'Heritage Park': now half complete, it contains a mix of everything from studio flatlets to 4/5-bed houses, beginning with a handsome crescent. Prices at the end of '98 were: studios from £70,000, 1-bed from £75,000, 2-bed £95–123,000 (£130,000 with second bath), 3-bed, £145,000. Houses ranged from c. £130–158,000 for 3-bed 4/5-bed town-houses at £205,000, with those in the crescent from £235,000. Plans for Phase II, at the Common end, have been called in for Ministerial scrutiny, however.

This corner also holds an earlier, innovative, development – the delightfully named Totterdown Fields (streets between **Derinton Rd** and **Cowick Rd**), which has the distinction of being the first cottage council estate in the world – started 1903. A pity, some say, councils didn't stick to this style: now a conservation area, the houses are an 'olde-worlde' mixture of red-brick and grey stucco. Above this, close to Tooting Bec tube, the roads N of **Foulser Rd** are lined with charming Victorian terraces in red-brick, Edwardian and '30s in **Lynwood Rd**; more cottage-council in **Topsham Rd**. An ex-army building in **Brudenell Rd** was converted into 10 2-bed flats.

South of the Totterdown Fields comes more Victoriana. **Vant Rd** has modern maisonettes at the S end. **Franciscan Rd**, running S through the entire neighbourhood from **Tooting Bec Rd** to **Mitcham Rd**, is mainly period with a few modern 'pockets' – the latest at the Common end. **Barringer Square** is yellow 7-storey flats surrounded by smaller, pleasant, brown-brick blocks, with a communal garden for residents. **Bruce Hall Mews** is a small, smart development of 20 houses and flats based around a courtyard and **Groomfield Close** is '80s maisonettes opposite the church.

St Benedict's, in the triangle between **Mitcham Rd**, **Rectory Lane** and **Church Lane**, is a pleasant and popular estate; built mainly by Laing in 1984, it's made particularly nice by trees and landscaping, and has off-street parking. It has 1-, 2- and 3-bed houses and flats, with big lounges and relatively modest service charges.

Tooting Bec also includes some good-sized period family houses: in **Dafforne Rd**, just round the corner from the tube, a double-fronted, 5-bed, 3-reception rooms example was on the market for £325,000 last autumn.

Furzedown

Running between **Links Rd** to the S, **Rectory Lane**, **Thrale Rd** and **Mitcham Lane**, Furzedown is filled with Edwardian/Victorian properties popular with families, plus some students' halls of residence for the London Institute. No tube line nearby, so prices tend to be lower than elsewhere in Tooting. Approximately half is counted as Tooting – the area S of **Southcroft Rd** plus **Crowborough Rd**, **Idlecombe Rd**, **Salterford Rd** and **Freshwater Rd**. The remainder is thought of as Streatham. The borough boundary runs E-W between **Southcroft Rd** and **Seely Rd**. **Seely Rd** and **Links Rd** running parallel have identical terraces of solid, deep-porched turn-of-the-century houses. East of the junction with **Eastbourne Rd**, however, **Seely Rd** changes to less appealing, and often badly modernized, 20th-century terraces and then to bay-windowed, gabled homes. Crossing between **Seely Rd** and **Links Rd** are orderly rows of uniform terraces. Their regimentation is reflected in the road names, which run alphabetically from 'A' to 'J'. The only breaks in the regularity are the striking Links Primary School and the modern orange-brick flats of St Andrews Hall at S end of **Hailsham Rd** – horribly inappropriate amongst such general order. **Vectis Gardens** surrounds a small rectangle of fenced-off grass. The whole section has an air of well-cared-for, quiet suburbia. The side of **Links Rd** backs onto the railway.

Southcroft Rd has at its E end older terraces, giving way as you go W to post-war rows on the right and a series of pleasant 2-storey ex-council red-brick flats on the left. On the corner of **Nimrod Rd** is a low-rise block of modern flats. Both sides of **Southcroft Rd** are now brick flats. Ditto **Freshwater Rd** and roads off; these are similar buildings, but in less attractive orange-brick with stucco top halves. We regain

Victorian terraces at the western end of **Southcroft Rd** and adjoining roads running to the N, parallel with **Mitcham Rd.**

B

Tooting Graveney

West of Furzedown is Tooting Graveney, named after the Graveney family who owned the manor in the 12th and 13th centuries. The area, which is bounded by the Wimbledon–Streatham railway line to the S, **Tooting High St** to the W and **Mitcham Rd** to the N, is the cheaper end of Tooting. Good first-time buys in this area. At E end of **Longley Rd** there is a small block of red-brick flats/houses on the right – Kilmarnock Court – with a play-area for the kids. Opposite is Tooting Baptist Church and the intriguingly ugly Jubilee Villa (1887) – a pale yellow house with white trim and mosaic work insets. Handsome Victorian terraces continue left and right. Some later houses on the right. The railway runs behind S side of **Longley Rd.** Area to N of **Longley Rd** is a maze of period terraces and maisonettes with modern infills. **Bickersteth Rd,** leading N from **Longley Rd,** contains a veritable cocktail of architecture in places, and thus looks a little ragged. Prices vary as much as: a 2-bed – but double-fronted – house ('a true original', said the particulars) was for sale in January for just £92,500. **Otterburn St** (off **Byton Rd**) has well-cared-for large mock-Tudor houses opposite Edwardian maisonettes. The school in **Selincourt Rd** (Infants and Junior) stands among terraced houses each divided into two maisonettes (generally 2/3-bed). These provide a popular source of often rented homes; also found in **Trevelyan Rd.**

Across the A24, (here **Tooting High St**) **Garratt Lane** leading W from Tooting Broadway tube is lined with large, flat-fronted period semi-detached houses (first few with front gardens) and smaller terraces. Parking is a problem on this main road and larger properties have the usual uneasy mixture of garden and parking space. Smaller terraces without gardens on the left side have garages behind in **Garratt Terrace.** Opposite these garages is a long row of Victorian 2-storey houses, curving round to **Tooting High St** (resembling a pale imitation of the Royal Crescent, Bath). These include some conversions and are good first-time buys. A few smart modern houses stand at the top on the left. Roads to the S of **Garratt Terrace** have similar rows of period housing, but modern maisonettes appear in **Recovery St** and smart-looking '30s flats in **Tooting Grove.** Quaint cottage terraces line **Aldis St** and **Carwell St.** There is a recent development to be found in **Aldis Mews.**

Blackshaw Rd, SW of St George's Hospital, has smart 2/3-bed Edwardian terraces – these tend to be cheap as they're next to Lambeth Cemetery. Anderson House (1931) on the corner of **Fountain Rd** is a handsome-looking 3-storey block of red- and cream-brick flats with, as they say, scope for improvement inside. An archway in the block leads through to a public recreation ground. More Victorian terraces left and right in **Fountain Rd,** undone-up as yet – which also goes for some earlier flat-fronted 2-storey stucco houses. **Cranmer Terrace,** off **Fountain Rd,** leads down to Tooting Gardens – a small park with swings, etc – not quite Regent's Park, but quite a surprise among such intensive housing. Period terraces lie W of **Fountain Rd,** some quite quaint: for instance the cottage rows of **Bertal Rd.** Alston Rd's Edwardian terraces seem in better repair on left. At the junction with **Hazelhurst Rd** on opposite corner is a school (Smallwood Junior and Infants) and on the left is the imposing grey concrete of the Hazelhurst council estate. **Greaves Place,** E of **Fountain Rd,** holds the striking 'geometrics' of Tooting Leisure Centre (swimming, gym, etc).

The Bell Estate

The Bell Estate, to the W of **Upper Tooting Rd,** belonged to an old family trust which was developed during the '30s and '40s by the Bell in question. Comprising **Fishponds Rd, Ansell Rd, Hebdon Rd** and **Lingwell Rd,** its neat purpose-built 3/4-bedroom terraced houses are now very popular with families and convenient for Tooting Bec tube station. Houses in **Ansell Rd** have small roof extensions. **Lingwell Rd** and **Hebdon Rd** tend to be slightly cheaper as they back onto Springfield Hospital (built as Surrey County Lunatic Asylum, 1840s) and Streatham Cemetery respectively. Off **Hebdon Rd**, at the E end, is **Herlwyn Gardens** – a few pleasant brick bungalows and maisonettes. Parking here is a mystery as the road stops short of the buildings. **Holmbury Court**, at the N end of **Fishponds Rd**, has uninspiring maisonettes. **Fishponds Rd** itself has the occasional Edwardian property alongside.

The roads between **Broadwater Rd** and **Garratt Lane** have Victorian terraces, most of which have been painted, giving a multi-coloured effect to the streets. Endearing cottage terraces at E end of **Graveney Rd** and modern maisonettes opposite the junction with **Selkirk Rd**. Ungainly semi-detached maisonettes line **Rogers Rd** and the top of **Broadwater Rd** as it turns E to the A24. On the corner of **Rogers Rd** and **Garratt Lane** stands Bellamy House: council flats, stylish in red-brick and white detail.

Glenburnie Rd on the other (N) side of the Bell Estate has mainly smart Edwardian properties, but on S side of **Beechcroft Rd** there are some attractive large mock-Tudor detached houses. These are now joined, in the angle of the two roads, by Barratt's gated 'Trinity Square': handsome, pedimented Georgian-style houses around a garden complete with fountain; 3-bed/3-bath town-houses and 4-bed/3-bath houses were marketed at £260–410,000 last winter. **Beeches Rd** has pleasant red-brick terraces (Victorian), both sides giving way to less attractive small beige-brick maisonettes on the right (c. '83). To the left is **Parkhill Court** – an impressive '30s block of large 2/3-bed flats, although not much to look at from behind.

The roads between **Trinity Rd** and **Beechcroft Rd**, to the N of the Bell Estate, are part of a conservation area filled with large, appealing Victorian properties lining leafy streets. Red-brick dominates, although **Brodrick Rd** has some lovely Georgian-style 3-storey stucco houses. **Crockerton Rd** and **Dalebury Rd** have stately red-brick courtesy of the Heaver brothers. Modern flats at S end of **Crockerton Rd**. Ernest Bevan School is opposite in **Beechcroft Rd**. To the N of the school is the College Gardens Estate, built 1983, an attractive development of 1/2-bedroom houses and flats similar to Balham's **Ashdown Way** but slightly cheaper as further from the Northern line tube.

At the N end of **Trinity Rd**, where it crosses into Wandsworth, are shops and restaurants facing a playing-field. Then, going S, come impressive mid-19th-century flat-fronted stucco terraces and houses. Note No 172 – once home of Thomas Hardy. Victorian red-brick continues. Tooting Bec fire station and police station are close to the junction with **Trinity Crescent**, one of the most expensive roads in the area with magnificent mid-19th-century stucco houses of 7/8-bedrooms and large gardens. Impressive mansion flats on the right-hand side (St Nicholas). **Holderness Rd** has mock-Tudor houses, terraced and semi-detached, and the faithful Victorian terrace reappears in **Chetwode Rd**.

Transport	Tubes: Balham, Tooting Bec, Tooting Broadway (zone 3, Northern) direct to City, Charing Cross, Waterloo. From Tooting Bec: Oxford Circus 30 min (1 change), City 30 min, Heathrow 1 hr 30 min (1 change). Trains: Balham to Victoria 15 min; Tooting to London Bridge, Blackfriars.
Convenient for	South Coast routes and transport into town. Miles from centre: 5.
Schools	Local Authority: Graveney, Ernest Bevin (b), Burntwood (g). Private: Upper Tooting High.

SALES

Flats	S	1B	2B	3B	4B	5B
Average prices	45–60+	55–100	75–150	100–180	—	—
Houses	2B	3B	4B	5B	6/7B	8B
Average prices	95–150+	125–250	175–300+	240–350+	→750	400+

RENTAL

Flats	S	1B	2B	3B	4B	5B
Average prices	430–550	450–750	650–1000	800–1200	—	—
Houses	2B	3B	4B	5B	6/7B	8B
Average prices	800–1000	900–1500	1400–2000	1850–2200	2100–2400	—

The properties   Balham is Victorian, Tooting Edwardian/'30s, with a (very) few older homes in both. Terraced houses of all sizes (including very large), plus conversions and some p/b flats. Inter-war suburban homes, too, plus conversions and some p/b flats — and, of course, pockets of '80s and '90s developments.

The market   Buyers have traditionally been first-timers plus families seeking big, more affordable homes. Balham (especially the N end, which is now called 'Clapham South' and 'The Nightingale Triangle') and Tooting Bec (especially the Heaver Estate, and now a swathe of new homes) are popular as overspill from posher neighbouring areas. Tooting Broadway is cheaper, more cosmopolitan: a much more local market. Local searches: Wandsworth 1 week, Lambeth 2 weeks.

Among those estate agents active in this area are:
- Douglas & Gordon *
- Barnard Marcus
- Hooper & Jackson
- Heaver
- Winkworth *
- Woolwich *
- Halifax Property
- Bells

further details: see advertisers' index on p633

BARNES, MORTLAKE AND SHEEN

Map ref: p90 (2B)
Postal districts: SW13, SW14
Boroughs: Richmond upon Thames (Lib Dem)
Council tax: Band D £762
Conservation areas: Include Barnes Pond, Green and Common; Mortlake Green
Parking: Mostly still free, controlled zone in North Barnes, meters on High St

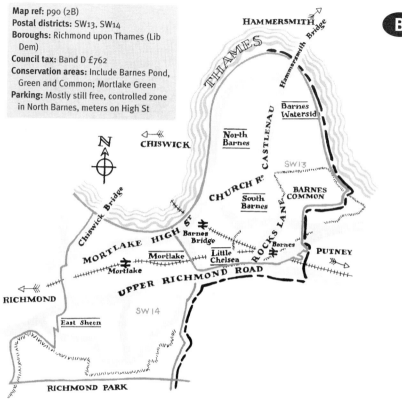

The meandering Thames on one side, parks and commons on two others: were it not for the road congestion, this would be the ideal London location. Barnes occupies a peninsula bounded by the River Thames to east, north and west. Much of the land is open, including playing-fields and the enormous wetlands nature reserve that once used to be Barn Elms Reservoir. Mortlake is more built-up, an ex-village lining the river bank. Sheen is situated inland, bordering Richmond Park and its associated enormous commons, the great green tract that defines the whole area to the south.

Barnes

Here, a stone's throw or two across the bridge from grubby, noisy Hammersmith, we are in a bourgeois heaven: river, green spaces, pretty houses with gardens, interesting shops and atmospheric pubs . . . Barnes, some feel, goes just a little over the top, even for this idyll, with its village duck pond.

Barnes thrived on market gardening throughout the 18th century. London merchants and nobility built their weekend retreats here. Some survive – **The Terrace** – others are remembered in local street names, such as **St Anne's, Elm Grove** and **Ranelagh**.

Only 5½ miles from Hyde Park Corner, Barnes has a rural atmosphere: locals say this is because it has no tube station (Barnes and Barnes Bridge rail stations – the latter with a limited service – make up for it). Once S of Hammersmith Bridge, urban grime gives way to Surrey village charm, with a village green, natural duck pond and the Sun Inn (crux of **Church Rd** and **Station Rd**).

Leafy riverside walks, more than 100 acres of pretty common, Leg of Mutton Reservoir (NW) where swans breed, Barn Elms Wetland Reserve (NE) for all kinds of aquatic wildlife, make Barnes a family favourite. Good local schools include St Paul's public school (boys) in **Lonsdale Rd**; Godolphin and Latymer (girls) and St Paul's (girls) are in nearby Hammersmith. The Swedish School (also in **Lonsdale Rd**) draws in expatriate and diplomatic families. The Harrodian School (independent, 11–18 years) is just along the road. Richmond Borough's schools achieve good ratings in the league tables, especially at primary level.

Large well-maintained houses, many of architectural merit, mean it is not an area for buyers on a tight budget. There are a few black spots. One penalty of living 30 minutes' drive from Heathrow is some aircraft noise. An effective pressure group, supported by a local MP, monitors problems. Alternative use of the north and south runways at Heathrow ensures occasional noise relief, but inhabitants pray for an east wind which removes the planes entirely. The planned Terminal 5 expansion of Heathrow is raising the temperature of this debate. Locals predict yet more planes.

There is a sprinkling of council property throughout Barnes; all spruce and no graffiti and many now in private hands. A 2-bed ex-council flat can approach £100,000. Some blocks are now mostly tenanted – but the owners are private landlords. This is a sector of the market to watch as relative bargains can be had. 1997 saw 'a dramatic turnaround', to quote a local agent: 3-bed houses rocketed from around £115,000 to £150–190,000, prices which still apply. But agents say such homes are hardest to sell when the market is quiet.

Barnes has a good range of 5- to 8-bed houses but coveted locations near the river or common mean prices can start at half a million. These sell very fast, often without involving agents or appearing on the open market. Smaller family houses form the bulk of the market. Expect to pay £220–400,000. There is a limited supply of 2-bed converted flats. Larger flats will be found in purpose-built blocks and those with prime locations like Riverview Gardens and Elm Bank Mansions have prices over £300,000.

The predominant home in Barnes is a Victorian or Edwardian terraced house. Houses greatly outnumber flats or maisonettes – though new developments are increasing supply. Great difficulty is experienced in finding flats and detached 3- or 4-bedroomed houses. Conversion into flats is rare as most houses have been well-maintained and are in demand as family homes.

The most sought-after streets are **Castelnau**, **Lonsdale Rd**, **Woodlands**, **The Crescent**, **Vine Rd** and **Station Rd**. Values fall where properties are near the railway line. The most expensive homes in Barnes are in the £1.5 million bracket, and there are whole streets with 'nothing under a million'. To the frustration of local estate agents these houses only change hands every 10–20 years. The Waterside development on the old filter beds site (see below) has added several dozen detached villas to the top end of the market, plus town-houses and apartments, and the Harrods Village scheme (also detailed below) is boosting the supply of flats.

The whole area benefits from an abnormally active and well-supported community association, which moniters schemes like that for the reservoir land at Barn Elms.

After a fairly frantic 1997, the market in Barnes has settled down. The influx of City money has slowed, and locals trading around the area are in the majority. Actors and writers of the more successful sort find Barnes congenial, and the new developments in the N of the area attract an international clientele. Newcomers join long-serving locals in defending Barnes' 'village' status. The typical newcomer starts in a mansion flat or Little Chelsea cottage and trades up to a family home. Once the bonuses stack up there are million-plus early Victorian houses in **Castelnau** to aspire to.

North Barnes

Castelnau – a boulevard named after the French lands of the Boilieu family – forms the spine of Barnes leading S from Hammersmith Bridge, via **Rocks Lane** down to the **Upper Richmond Rd**. Since the (allegedly temporary) closure of the bridge to cars, values in the road have rocketed. Despite a fierce battle to keep it closed, the bridge looks set to re-open in September 1999. **Castelnau** is a prime location with large 1840s semi-detached villas set well back; driveways and trees mask them from the road. Early Victorian styles near the bridge lead to later double-fronted houses towards the Red Lion pub (junction of **Rocks Lane**/**Church Rd**). Prices are £1.5 million-plus for good examples, with about £800,000 being asked for smaller (5-bed) houses.

Lonsdale Rd peels off W from **Castelnau** at the N end. Another area for Victorian villas, some with stunning white exteriors and Italianate towers (next to St Paul's playing-fields). Some are still rather seedy looking flats. Close to St Paul's School **St Hilda's Rd** leads to a few streets of terraced cottages. As **Lonsdale Rd** follows the river's curve, there is open land on the riverside and a range of property on the left (some flats, '30s and Edwardian houses) down to the Bull's Head pub and **The Terrace**.

Lonsdale Rd and **Castelnau** are linked by a lattice of streets – **Suffolk Rd**, **Nassau Rd**, **Lowther Rd**, **Westermoreland Rd** and **Baronsmead Rd** – with a range of 3- to 5-bed family houses; a mix of Edwardian/'30s/Victorian. Around **Verdun Rd**/**Barnes Avenue**/**Stillingfleet Rd** there is a council estate. Some houses have come into the market and can fetch £140–165,000.

The Barnes Waterside Estate is a new complex of 320 homes on a 34-acre site, adjoining a nature reserve. There are terraces, a crescent (Regency in style, as far as the ironwork goes) and enviably large sub-Palladian villas. The water lies to the S, jutting into the site as reed-lined ponds. On one pond stands 'Pipistrelle Pavilion', an edifice raised by the Prince of Wales' architecture school as a home for bats. Unfortunately the London pigeons can only read as far as P and have taken over. The last phase of the Waterside, two blocks of flats overlooking the Thames, was sold last year. Examples of resales include 5-bed houses at around £1.5 million and 2-bed flats at £200,000. Adjoining is 'Harrods Village', a 250-homes scheme involving new flats and houses and the conversion of the giant, looming, faience-decorated warehouse that recalls the parent store, only marooned amid trees. The first flats were finished last year, with more on offer this year: flats from £235,000; town-houses from £495,000. There will be leisure and business centres.

South Barnes

South of **Church Rd** (with shops, art galleries and restaurants) are more 3- to 5-bed houses. Roads off **Glebe Rd** are popular; their solid red-brick 'Lion' houses (also found in Fulham's Peterborough Estate) are among the most requested local homes. **Ranelagh Avenue** (some double-fronted Victorian property) faces the common. **Bellevue Rd**, **Rectory Rd** and **Elm Grove Rd** spill onto the common and have a touch of Little Venice as Beverley Brook passes beneath them. To the W **Laurel Rd** and **The Crescent** branch onto the green, bringing prices up to £650–750,000-plus.

Opposite Barnes Green is **Station Rd**, off **Barnes High St** leading to Barnes station; houses include 17th-century Milbourne House where Henry Fielding lived, a mix of small bow-windowed Victorian terraces; workers' flat-fronted cottages; pretty 18th-century cottages leading to the inevitable large Victorian houses close to the common. The former postal sorting office in **Station Rd** is being converted into shops, offices and 12 flats. Beverley Rd has 2-bed flats and houses: 2-bed flats are around £750,000.

Behind **Station Rd** and Barnes Bridge railway line is an area worth exploring. It was traditionally the 'wrong' side of the village but is now firmly OK, due (say locals) to an influx of 'new money' squeezing out the humbler inhabitants. Architecturally it is confused – small 2-bed cottages give way to flat-fronted 3-storey houses in **Cleveland Rd** with an outcrop of eight 'Lion' houses marooned at the corner of **Cleveland Gardens**. Terraced houses around here can fetch up to £350,000.

North of **Station Rd** is **Barnes High St** (with a good range of family-run shops and restaurants) which runs down to the river. Turn left into the riverside **Terrace** and a sweep of pastel coloured 18th-century houses – wisteria wrapped around wrought-iron balconies – gives a whiff of Brighton. These fetch from £400,000 to £1 million, but rarely change hands. Those closer to the bridge go for lower sums. Past Barnes Bridge (said by the unkind to be the ugliest to span the Thames) and the rail station are **Elm Bank Gardens** (large 5-bed houses), Elm Bank Mansions (red-brick blocks of flats) and more ivy-clad Georgian houses. **The Terrace** ends at the White Hart pub; **White Hart Lane** cuts S, marking the boundary between Mortlake and Barnes. Barnes continues beyond the railway crossing down to the **Upper Richmond Rd**.

Little Chelsea

East of **White Hart Lane** and W of the railway lie **Charles St**, **Thorne St**, **Archway St** and **Westfields Avenue**. The vogue for renovating these 2-bed cottages (some have three) was apparently started by a Polish builder in the '60s. His wife saw the potential of the area, comparing the brewery workers' home with their mews counterparts in Chelsea. An irregular style – they were added to as the Victorian workforce grew – make them less stately then their namesakes but prettier. Extensive renovation means some have an extra bedroom or conservatory and can fetch up to £300,000. Typical prices start around £170,000 for 2-bed, £250,000 for 3-bed cottages. Skirting the area are **Thorne Passage** and **Beverley Path** (reached on foot); cottages here are smaller or have the Hounslow loop rail line running behind their garden, factors which may give a discount. The same drawback applies to the **Railwayside** cottages, though their line is the busier: a 2-bed cottage here was £192,000 last winter.

Mortlake

Best known as the end of the Oxford and Cambridge Boat Race (rowed upstream from Putney), Mortlake is historically more important than Barnes. In medieval times the

Archbishop of Canterbury built his palace here (long gone); brewing has been a local industry since the 15th century and the large modern brewery dominates the river bank towards Chiswick Bridge. There is an active community association. The boundary with Barnes to the E is the postal district, with Barnes in SW13 and Mortlake in SW14. **White Hart Lane** marks the border. The railway line hems Mortlake in to the S: some of its prettier homes are unfortunately closest to the busy line.

The most popular type of home in Mortlake is the 2-bed flat or maisonette. Large detached houses are scarce, but there are plenty of houses in terraces and some pretty cottages. The more expensive streets are considered to be **Cowley** and **Ashleigh Rds,** with **First Avenue** and **Victoria Rd** also popular. Riverside houses when available rate the highest prices. Prices generally fall away with proximity to the railway line and the brewery.

There's little space for new housing here, but the occasional up-market scheme appears. A riverside site on the **High St,** formerly a garage, has been cleared and river-view flats are planned by developers Michael Shanley.

Property is cheaper than in Barnes: a 3/4-bed family house costs about what it did at the start of 1998 – around £290–300,000. There are some gems for those who care to look; **Victoria Rd** and **Wrights Walk** have large cottages with unusually large gardens. **Rosemary Cottages** (a row of pretty almshouses) is sandwiched between recently tidied-up blocks of flats and overlooks Mortlake station. They continue to sell for around £180–200,000 leasehold. **Cowley, Ashleigh** and **Avondale Rds** are mostly Edwardian terraces with 2-bed flats (£150–160,000). It's worth noting that property along **North Worple Way** overlooks the railway.

The green and the area to E and W surrounding it are a conservation area. **Tideway Yard**, near the White Hart (The Times/RICS award winner 1989), is a refurbished refuse depot and power station. There is a busy wine bar (with fittings from Aintree race course) which has stunning riverside views. The site was extended to include 18 riverside flats, built in Victorian warehouse style to blend in with existing buildings. Prices for these sybaritic apartments are around £300,000 for 3-bed.

Cowley Mansions has a range of flats from 1- to 3-bed: one of the latter was sold for £195,000 in December. One-bed flats start at around £125,000. Overlooking Mortlake Green, some Victorian shops have been refurbished into a small development of flats (2-bed around £95,000; £110,000 for 3-bed). And on the W side, a large Victorian building looks out across the green and holds 2-, 3- and 4-bedroom flats. An old warehouse here has become flats.

Sheen

East Sheen lies either side of the **Upper Richmond Rd West**, (the local name for the ever-busy, now Red Route, South Circular). To the E are Mortlake and Barnes; to the W Richmond. Its S

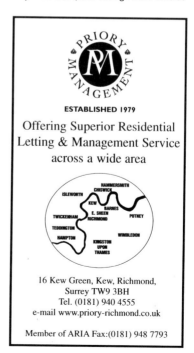

boundaries are Sheen and Palewell Commons. In the W, the streets around **Clifford Avenue** and **Derby Rd** blend into Richmond.

B

Richmond was once called Shene until Henry VII built a palace there and named it after his Yorkshire estates. East Sheen – a hamlet until the turn of the century – hangs on to the name. There is nothing rural about the **Upper Richmond Rd West**. It comprises a sprawl of '30s shops, with excellent supermarkets and plenty of restaurants attracting people from both Richmond and Barnes. **Sheen Lane** has developed recently into a useful street of specialist shops. However, there are stunning houses to the S on the fringes of Richmond Park (with prices to match) and bargain surprises on the N, Mortlake, side. Sheen may not be as fashionable an address as Barnes or Richmond, but it attracts young families and first-time buyers who enjoy much the same facilities and at much lower prices. The 1990s have seen a further shift in the area's character as older people have moved away to be replaced by professional families. Once dug in, schools and other ties mean they stay.

Between **South Worple Way** and **Upper Richmond Rd West** lie **Trehern Rd, Lewin Rd, Kings Rd, Princes Rd** and **Queens Rd** (sometimes referred to as The Royals). These are 2-bed cottages which mirror those found in Little Chelsea, Barnes. At around £160–190,000, they are slightly cheaper and some seem a little larger. A pretty 2-bed cottage along **South Worple Way** may cost less, but all the houses face a main Southern Region railway line which runs along the N side. Further W where **Vernon Rd** joins **Portman Avenue** and **Thornton Rd** is an area of 3/4-bed Edwardian property. Across **Sheen Lane** (small shops) is **St Leonard's Rd** which parallels the **Upper Richmond Rd West** and finally swings into a curve before meeting **Clifford Avenue** (another pseudonym for the South Circular). At the **Sheen Lane** end there are some lovely 3-storey, flat-fronted houses painted in pastel shades.

Behind **St Leonard's Rd** and **Elm Rd** there is a pathway called **Model Cottages**. These semi-detached cottages were built for poor labourers in the 1850s and have pretty front gardens with fruit trees and lavender bushes. Many have been extended to provide garages or extra rooms. Expect to pay around £390,000. A recently tarmacked road provides car access which makes them more desirable still.

The western curve of **St Leonard's Rd** is tree-lined and has large semi-detached Edwardian houses. Despite the railway it is surprisingly quiet.

In the angle formed by the South Circular and **St Leonard's Rd** is a grid of interesting Edwardian homes. **Graemsdyke Avenue** has quite plain terraced houses made pretty by tiny bay windows. **Holmesdale Avenue** has unusual cottages, with Dutch-style gables, and facing doorways slightly at a slant. **Ormonde Rd** and **Carlton Rd** have grey houses with white wooden fences. A 3-bed house here can cost around £295,000. Converted flats are scattered throughout this area but particularly along **Elm Rd** and **St Leonard's Rd**. There are some 1930s blocks on the main road, where 2-bed flats cost £110–120,000, but on the whole flats are scarce.

Parkside

South of the **Upper Richmond Rd**, between **Stanley Rd** (with pretty cottages at the bottom and the common end) and **Hertford Avenue**, a number of roads snake up to the common. **Stanley Rd** and **Derby Rd** begin with terraced cottages, '30s blocks and terraces. These cottages are popular with young buyers at around £180,000 despite being further from the station than those N of the main road. **Deanhill Rd** has Edwardian semis with good-sized gardens; **Coval Rd** has more of the same, plus some terraced houses. Coval Passage has a conversion of an old warehouse into live/work units with 2-bedrooms on three floors at £195,000.

Prices range from £260–310,000 in lower Parkside for 3/4-bed houses with a garden, but climb as the houses grow in size towards the common. The roads are wide and curving and houses are semi-detached or detached with driveways. Altogether an enviable corner, though one which lacks convenient shops and public transport. Around **Vicarage Rd**, **Stonehill Rd** and **Hood Avenue** large post-war family houses enjoy the kind of space associated with the Surrey suburbs and yet East Sheen is less than 7 miles from London. A detached house in **Vicarage Drive** was on the market for £575,000 in December. The most prestigious houses are found along **Fife Rd** (from £1 million to £2.5 million) and **Christ Church Rd**. There's a mix of Victorian/'30s/post-war mansions in the kind of individual architecture that money can buy.

B

Transport	Trains: From Barnes, Barnes Bridge, Mortlake to Waterloo 16–20 min. Tube at Hammersmith.
Convenient for	Richmond Park, River Thames, Kew Gardens. Richmond shopping. Hammersmith Bridge closed to cars, not buses or bikes, until September 1999. Miles from centre: 6.
Schools	Richmond Education Authority: Shene School, Richmond C of E High School. Private: Swedish School, St Paul's School (b). See also Hammersmith and Richmond.

SALES

Flats	S	1B	2B	3B	4B	5B
Average prices	50–70+	75–150+	90–250+	120–300+	180–400	–
Houses	2B	3B	4B	5B	6/7B	8B
Average prices	145–270	180–450+	250–800+	400–2M+	450–3M	–

RENTAL

Flats	S	1B	2B	3B	4B	5B
Average prices	600–700	700–1100	900–1200	1300–2000+	1600–2200+	–
Houses	2B	3B	4B	5B	6/7B	8B
Average prices	1100–1700	1500–2400	2200–3800	4000+	5500+	–

The properties	Charming cottages and 3/4-bed terraces; some large early Victoriana in Barnes, also splendid 18th-century and modern riverside homes. Mortlake is more Victorian; some excellent flat conversions here. Sheen has Edwardian and other 20th-century; cottages to mini-mansions.
The market	Barnes is the more expensive area, but neither is cheap. Ex-council property can offer bargains. The media, sporting and political people living here are diluted by European (especially Scandinavians) and US businessmen/diplomats, who find the area conforms to their idea of Englishness. Sheen is seeing an influx of professional families. Local searches: 10 working days.

Among those estate agents active in this area are:
- Barnard Marcus
- Allen Briegel
- FPDSavills
- Friend & Falcke
- Michael Gregory
- Priory Management *
- Gascoigne Pees
- James Anderson
- Boileau & Braxton
- Geoffrey Jardine

further details: see advertisers' index on p633

BATTERSEA

Map ref: p92 (1D)
Postal districts: SW11, SW8
Boroughs: Wandsworth (Con)
Council tax: Band D £334
Conservation areas:
   Numerous – check with
   town hall
Parking: Residents/meters
   in much of area. Red Route
   on Battersea Park Rd

The steady rise of Montevetro, the Richard Rogers-designed tower of expensive flats inexorably dwarfing the riverside St Mary's Church, is a sure sign of the times. Battersea has joined fashionable London with a vengeance. Now it has a 'statement' building from Lord Rogers, who has done the same for the City and Paris. A mountain of glass it certainly is: a wedge-shaped finger looming over the Thames in reply to Chelsea Harbour's tower.

Battersea has come a long way from the seedy Sixties days of Up the Junction. Redundant Victorian schools offer £1-million-plus 'loft' apartments (office-block conversions providing the poor(er) man's version), and the bemused original Batterseans (who watched the '80s property market crash just as they exercised their 'Right to Buy' in one of the tower blocks) are hoping that the remaining council properties will tidy up quickly to justify their investment at last.

Today publishers park their families in the grid of Victorian streets between Wandsworth and Clapham Commons; their staff rent flats above shops round the Junction. **Northcote Rd**, a mere dozen years ago a cheery South London street market, now has bars, bars and more bars, wine merchants, bespoke tailors and wall-to-wall estate agents. Masters of Wine muster round villagy **Battersea Square**; top chefs open restaurants in **Queenstown Rd**. Refugees from Chelsea prices bagged the roomy mansion flats round leafy Battersea Park decades ago; the '80s economic migrants found the streets off **Lavender Hill** and, misled by the name of the common and the railway station, believed they had moved to Clapham (this includes estate agents).

No matter; Battersea is now so trendy, they'll be glad they joined. The sons of royalty, the daughters of celebrities roost in Battersea's latest lofts or smartest

Thames-side schemes, along with all the City's baby bankers and their sisters with plum PR jobs in the West End. Mummy lives in Fulham; Dad has a pad in Chelsea Harbour . . . 'Minutes King's Rd' is a phrase that still crops up in property details.

Just so: at four in the morning. The rest of the time, driving through or from the area is bad for the blood pressure – and there is no tube, though if you are within reach of it the main line Clapham Junction more than compensates. Battersea's traffic tangle, hemmed in by river and (largely bridgeless) rail lines, is further enhanced by the South Circular, otherwise known as **Battersea Rise** and **Clapham Common North Side**. If the old Power Station ever gets redeveloped, gridlock could be total. **Battersea Park Rd** is now a Red Route, though traffic has been made even busier by traffic calming on parallel **Prince of Wales Drive**. Locals use buses: Vauxhall tube is a tolerable 15 min away.

Central Battersea and the River

From Clapham Junction shopping centre **Falcon Rd** leads N into the heartland of Battersea. To the right is the enclave of 'Little India', so-called after its road names – **Cabul Rd**, **Afghan Rd**, **Khyber Rd** and **Candahar Rd**: a 3-bed house fetches around £200,000. Houses on the N side of **Rowena Crescent** are nearest the tracks. The council sold the old allotments behind **Candahar Rd**: one house is being built here.

Off **Falcon Rd**, with a fine view of Clapham Junction railway station, is The Falcons, a '60s council estate bought from Wandsworth Council by Regalian in the '80s. The flats are quite spacious and facilities include a swimming pool, sauna and gym (included in the service charge). Although the awnings and ornate railings do not disguise the estate's municipal origins, the place makes a transitory roost for young City workers and the like, for whom the adjacent trains-to-everywhere Junction is a draw. Eminently unsuitable for families, which is why the council sold it. A 2-bed flat goes for £110,000.

Frere St, off **Battersea Park Rd**, has some pleasant 2-bedroom 3-storey semi-basement houses and a small terrace of town-houses (with garages). **Abercrombie St** – small late-Victorian terraces – is another Battersea road embraced by a railway. A development of town-houses here, **Ambrose Mews**, includes four 4-bed, 4-bath homes in close proximity to the Channel Tunnel freight line.

To the N of traffic-plagued, restaurant-ridden, Red-Routed **Battersea Park Rd** lies the oldest part of Battersea, a sometimes uneasy mixture of high-rise council estates and conservation areas. At the heart is café- and restaurant-surrounded **Battersea Square** – the charming but traffic-ridden junction of **Battersea High St** (almost entirely residential at this point), **Vicarage Crescent** and **Westbridge Rd**. The brick flat-fronted 3- and 4-bedroom houses may look early Victorian but looks are misleading. Virtually all have been reconstructed by a sympathetic developer. The dutch-gabled pub is extremely old, though. Work was under way last winter converting space above some High St shops into nine 1-bed flats.

Valiant House on **Vicarage Crescent** is a popular development of early '70s brick-built flats overlooking the Thames and Chelsea Harbour development. On the other side of **Vicarage Crescent**, still overlooking the river, are some of the oldest buildings in the area, including the early 18th-century Devonshire House and Old Battersea House which dates from 1699.

'Battersea Village', at the junction of **Vicarage Crescent** and **Lombard Rd** (heavy traffic at rush hours), is a pre-war estate of brick-built flats, set around courtyards, sold in the 1980s by Wandsworth Council to Regalian. Across the road, Groveside Court is a block of 1-, 2- and 3-bed flats and maisonettes. Nice spacious flats – but open access walkways (to tie in with the 'Village's' ex-council style?). Prices here for a 2-bed flat remain as in '98 from £170–250,000 – depending on its closeness to the adjacent Channel Tunnel freight line. Inland, Windsor Court is a charming conversion of an old school, with gated parking behind. The Fred Wells Garden is an asset to this corner:

children's playground, tennis court. Across the **High St**, off **Shuttleworth Rd**, is a grid of five streets running S from **Orbel St**, among the most popular locations in Battersea but hidden in an impenetrable road system. Agents dub these roads 'The Sisters': if you don't fancy **Edna**, take your pick from **Octavia** and **Ursula**. They offer 3- and 4-bedroom late-Victorian semi-detached houses with creamy gold brickwork. A 3-bed one was £335,000 in December. In **Shuttleworth Rd** some smaller terraced houses are around £230,000. A housing association is building eight flats in **Gwynne Rd**. Round on **Bridge Lane**, one of the Victorian school conversions, 'The Lanterns', offers huge flats: 4,000 sq ft and an 18-ft ceiling height in the main bedroom for £1.3 million.

Westbridge Rd, another conservation area, has some attractive early Victorian villas and the late-18th-century Battersea Laundry (close to the junction with **Battersea High St**), nowadays flats with a (small) outdoor swimming pool. It fronts the high-rise Surrey Lane Estate.

The Battersea riverside, from Wandsworth Bridge to Albert Bridge, is alive with increasingly more luxurious homes developments replacing the old industrial wasteland. One of the first was the vast Plantation Wharf, built in the late '80s halfway between Wandsworth Bridge and the heliport: an attractive scheme mixing business and residential to create, in effect, an entire new village, with Thames-side flats and 4-bed 'atelier' work-homes. Further S, Riverside Plaza has 74 flats, with maybe more to come. To the E, the Price's Candles factory, reprieved by the recession, has finally succumbed to redevelopment by Fairview: flats and penthouses ready this year.

Past the heliport and railway bridge, and the existing homes of Groveside Court and Valiant House (see above), **Battersea Church St** swings down to the river and one of the gems of the area, the Grade I listed parish church of St Mary's, built in 1777 but dating back to Domesday. Its fate is now to be flanked by modern developments: Old Swan Wharf to the W – and to the E, where once the great manor house stood, Lord Rogers' 'statement' glass tower, Montevetro, rears its wedge-shaped head, stepping down to the church from its 18-storey high point. Prices here start at £375,000 for a 1,082 sq ft balconied flat at the bottom to £1,710,000 for 1,951 sq ft on the 17th floor. The penthouses (with roof terrace and winter garden) have yet to be released. There is talk of a jetty and a resurgence of river buses from Montevetro – but nothing definite.

A return to a more family, domestic scale can be found in earlier schemes like the flats and houses of Morgan's Walk next to Battersea Bridge. (Street names in this gated estate include riverside **Thorney Crescent** and **Whistler's Avenue**.) Stanton Gate on **Battersea Church Rd** has 5-bed modern houses that continue to fetch £425–450,000.

Across **Battersea Bridge Rd** to the E, Thames Walk is a plate-glass office block with flats alongside the river. The Battersea Bus Garage site next door, also known as Albion Wharf, is subject to a planning row: a scheme for a 16-storey tower has been called in by the Ministry after local planners had approved it. Next door, developers are reported to have eyes on Majestic Wine's riverside site. A hideous block appeared beside it at the head of **Ransome's Dock**: designed (unbelievably) by Norman Foster, prices for flats in this plate-glass palace are only topped by those of Montevetro. Sir Norman wants to add two more floors on too: the planners disagree. On the other side of the dock, Waterside Plaza runs up to the bridge with houses inland; flats including vast penthouses (own pools) on the river. Another block better to look out of than at. And lastly, Albert Bridge House adds another 30 luxury flats and penthouses to Battersea's tally: in January the choice was down to a couple of penthouses at £1.5 million-plus and a 3-bed flat at £495,000.

Battersea Park

Difficult to guess, now, looking at the leafy riverside park ringed by staid, respectable mansion blocks, that here was the favourite haunt of Regency London's low-life. The

B

park swept away the notorious dens and taverns in 1853, and peace reigned – at least, until the 1890s, when the scandalous sight of lady bicyclists, banned from Hyde Park, shocked residents. The favoured **Prince of Wales Drive** late-Victorian mansion flats run the entire length of Battersea Park. Service charges can be high, and there have been problems in the past with maintenance charges, so leaseholders got together as the law changed, and bought out their landlords. Today, virtually all flats are sold with a share in the freehold of the block. The best is York Mansions (the only one with a lift), followed by Overstrand. Behind are more such blocks in **Lurline Gardens** and **Warriner Gardens**. Roads leading off, like **Soudan** and **Kassala**, feature 3-storey 4- and 5-bedroom red-brick houses.

The **Prince of Wales Drive** area is not just popular for being close to the 200 acres of Battersea Park, complete with art gallery, children's zoo, lake (the café has been smartened up), running track, tennis courts and the splendid Peace Pagoda, gift of Japanese Buddhists. Even given Battersea's notorious traffic problems, Sloane Square and Knightsbridge are not far away. The mansion flats often have balconies from which to enjoy the leafy park views; best of all are those flats with sweeping windows in the corner turrets.

On the other side of traffic-plagued **Battersea Park Rd** lie the high-rise Doddington and Rollo council-built estates. The '80s saw energetic work by the council to eradicate the notorious reputation of this corner. The hated exterior walkways were removed; one tower block was sold off to developers and renamed Park South and another, Park Court, was comprehensively refitted by the council, who sold the flats as starter homes: 500 buyers chased the 96 flats. This brings the number of owner-occupiers on the 1,000-home Doddington Estate to at least 500. Work continues: Turpin House, on the corner of **Queenstown Rd**, has just been smartened up.

The mansion flats which run most of the length of **Albert Bridge Rd** face E, thus benefiting from more light than **Prince of Wales Drive**, and also overlook Battersea Park. Best blocks are probably Albert and Albany, but all are popular. The mansion blocks are interspersed with some fine, large, mid-Victorian semi- and detached houses. Council-built blocks lie just to the rear. **Parkgate Rd** runs between **Albert** and **Battersea Bridge Rds**, with large plain 3-storey houses, mainly converted to flats. On the corner of **Anhalt Rd** and **Albert Bridge Rd** Prince Regent House is 5 new flats ranging from £225–650,000.

The grand plan to transform Battersea Power Station into a massive fantasy-land leisure centre turned out itself to be a fantasy. It's hard not to believe this site is jinxed. Serious money problems hit the first owners to try, and the landmark remains sadly open to the elements more than a decade after they backed away. Confusion – and much recrimination – abounded. Now Hong Kong-based Parkview International have outline permission for a comprehensive scheme to include two hotels, 500–750 flats, a multiplex cinema plus one or two theatres, a post-production film studio, smart shops . . . but this January, just as last, there is no further news of progress.

Queenstown

Busy **Queenstown Rd** leads from Chelsea Bridge past Battersea Park and Queenstown train stations to **Lavender Hill**. Much changed from its grimy past, these days it boasts a good parade of shops and smart restaurants from **St Philip Square** to **Lavender Hill**. The mainly flat-fronted Victorian houses and flats along the road have now mostly been renovated and improved for sale: they are popular with young buyers, who might pay £135,000 for a 2-bed flat – down 10 per cent on 1998. Between busy **Silverthorne Rd** and **Queenstown Rd** is the Park Town Estate, now a conservation area, much of which is still owned by the Peabody Trust. At the **Silverthorne Rd** end of **Tennyson St** the houses are 3-storey flat-fronted. Most of the Estate has Victorian cottage-style houses;

some are purpose-built flats with roof terraces for the first-floor-flats. Seven new 3-bed houses on the corner of **Tennyson** and **Thackerey Sts** should be ready this July. The larger houses with ornate carved balconies overlooking **St Philip Square** and the church have been modernized and converted. The flat-fronted cottages with their distinctive high chimneys in **St Philip St** remain very rarely available.

On the other side of **Queenstown Rd** lie the perfect Gothic cottages of the Shaftesbury Estate (built in the 1870s by the Artisans, Labourers and General Dwellings Co), which runs across to the traffic-snarled **Latchmere Rd**. The Peabody Trust were also the main landlords in the area: they sold off many of the 2- and 3-bedroom terraced cottages, previously let, as they became vacant. Popular with buyers seeking small, manageable houses – so small as to be better described as vertical flats – they have nevertheless recently been fetching £200–230,000. A traffic scheme stops rat-running in **Eversleigh Rd**, which has the railway line on its northern side. **Eland Rd**, leading down into the Shaftesbury Estate from **Lavender Hill**, has some of the larger houses in the area, up to 4-bed and holding at £350–450,000.

Separated from the Shaftesbury Estate by the railway line behind **Eversleigh Rd** lies a triangle made up of **Poyntz Rd, Knowsley Rd** and **Shellwood Rd**. Approached from **Latchmere Rd** and cut off by railway sidings on three sides are small 2- and occasionally 3-bedroom mainly flat-fronted cottages. The area is useful for access to the excellent (council-owned) Latchmere Leisure Centre off **Sheepcote Lane**. Prices are lower than in the Shaftesbury Estate, thanks to the train lines.

Busy **Latchmere Rd** features flats (3-storey blocks) at the upper (**Lavender Hill**) end, Victorian one side, modern on the W, and the usual flat-fronted cottages, normally reasonably priced because of traffic noise.

However, the roar of the road and the constant trains have proved no bar to the success of two schemes featuring that hottest of trends, the loft apartment. Victorian school buildings have proved fertile ground for Sapcote Real Lofts, who have created The Village (in **Amies St**) and Southside Quarter here. The Village is considered seriously posh, with security, parking, convenience for the Junction and above all large, light-flooded spaces. The Southside Quarter, near the leisure centre in **Burns Rd**, added some purpose-built 'loft houses' to the school conversion: conventional from the front, galleried and with floor-to-rafters glass at the back. A recent price for a 2-bed loft was £280,000. A very smart, very large one in The Village was £900,000.

Clapham Common North Side

South of **Lavender Hill** and bordered by **Cedars Rd, Lavender Sweep** and **Clapham Common North Side** is the grid of late-Victorian terraced houses known by local estate agents as the North Side Square. **Lavender Hill** has sprouted shops, wine bars and restaurants, with a good parade close to the junction with **Cedars Rd/Queenstown Rd**. Between Battersea Arts Centre and the library, estate agencies are almost wall-to-wall: easier to buy a house than a loaf of bread here.

Virtually the entire area consists of terraced 2- and 3-storey houses – although a fair number have been converted into flats. The exception is **Wix's Lane** (where both the SW4 and the borough boundaries run) which offers spacious purpose-built Victorian flats (backing onto a school playground) and some new mews houses (c. £270,000). **Nansen Rd** and **Gowrie Rd**, running parallel to the common, offer 3-storey 4-bedroom houses, as does **Garfield Rd**, where there is a thriving community centre. The E side of this area is within reach of Clapham Common tube. On **Cedars Rd**, Bellway are building some flats: no prices yet.

Roads running between Clapham Common and **Lavender Hill** such as **Stormont Rd, Sugden Rd** and **Taybridge Rd** suffer slightly from rat-running, but **Elspeth Rd** is a through-route for traffic from the South Circular heading for Battersea Bridge. **Sugden**

Rd is unusual for its semi-detached houses: £400,000 for 4-bed. **Parma Crescent** and **Eccles Rd** – more early Edwardian terraces – are also popular for their easy access to Clapham Junction station. Residents' parking schemes are almost universal now in the streets off North Side, giving the locals room to park their Mercedes and frustrating commuters who used to park here to be close to the station.

Larger houses, mainly converted into flats, are found in wide **Sisters Avenue**, **Mysore Rd**, **Lavender Gardens** (once home to the Duchess of York) and **Altenburg Gardens**. Properties in **Lavender Gardens** near the junction with **Lavender Hill** could experience late-night excitement from Jongleurs, a fringe cabaret venue. This does not prevent asking prices of £750,000 for a 6-bed house. On **Lavender Hill**, the old Battersea Town Hall is now the home of the Battersea Arts Centre.

The flats in Avenue Mansions, **Sisters Avenue** are unusually spacious, and the top flats offer good (N-facing) views across London. At the top of **Lavender Gardens** is The Shrubbery, a stunning late-Georgian mansion, complete with ballroom, converted to 16 flats under the watchful eye of conservationists.

The Junction

Clapham Junction's busy station and shops form a local centre: Railtrack has plans to rebuild the station at enormous expense, with the inevitable shopping and office development to pay for it. Watch this space. Leading off **Lavender Sweep**, roads like **Barnard Rd** and **Eckstein Rd** offer spacious purpose-built early Edwardian 2- and 3-storey red-brick flats and maisonettes, the upper-floor flats with large roof terraces. **Ilminster Gardens** and **Beauchamp Rd** feature plain 3-storey Victorian houses, virtually all converted to flats. Both suffer somewhat from their proximity to Arding & Hobbs, the area's very own department store, which has been expensively re-vamped to keep up with the Junction's new image.

In this area especially there are still some good buys possible, with the triangle between **Boutflower Rd**, **St John's Hill** and **St John's Rd** a fertile hunting-ground.

Off **St John's Hill**, past **Plough Rd**, are **Louvaine Rd**, **Cologne Rd** and **Oberstein Rd**, which feature some imposing early Edwardian and late-Victorian terraced houses – some, notably in **Louvaine**, ornate 3-storey-plus basement with porticoes. Virtually all of these are flat conversions. Houses in the northern leg of **Harbut Rd** (smaller 3- and 4-bedroom Edwardian – and mostly still family homes) will hear the passing trains from the Clapham Junction line. Prettiest – and most popular – road in the area is tree-lined **St John's Hill Grove** with a number of charming Regency and early Victorian cottages, some semi-detached. The road is a conservation area and the older houses command a premium.

This handsome Gothic tower stands somewhat incongruously above a shop on the Shaftesbury Estate. One of a pair, it marks the entrance to the estate of little cottages built a century ago as low-rent housing for the working classes. Today, the neat little homes are fashionable with young buyers. Pointed gables and other cottage details set these terraces apart from the norm.

B

Strathblaine Rd, **Vardens Rd** and **Sangora Rd**, running between **St John's Hill** and the railway line, are quite smart now and still improving. More large 3-storey Victorian houses here. Some, notably in **Vardens Rd**, are exceptionally large semi-detached 3-storey semi-basement houses, some of which have converted into very pleasant flats. This road gains from having been cut off from the traffic at the S end. Houses to the S side of **Strathblaine Rd** back onto the railway.

At the top of **St John's Hill** and running down alongside **Trinity Rd** is the East Hill Estate. The low-rise flats and houses were built by Wandsworth Council in the late 1970s. When the Conservatives took power in 1978, the estate was designated for a low-cost home ownership initiative, and it is entirely owner-occupied.

Between the Commons

Northcote Rd is the centre of the residential area, properly called Northcote and now known as 'Between the Commons', which runs from **Battersea Rise** to **Thurleigh Rd** and is bordered to E and W by Clapham and Wandsworth Commons. These protect the area from through traffic, and the leafy, peaceful streets are favourites with families. Most of this tract is in SW11, though the southernmost roads tip into SW12.

The mainly late-Victorian/early Edwardian terraced houses sweep down from the Commons to **Northcote Rd** which, from **Battersea Rise** to **Salcott Rd**, features a fruit and vegetable street market on Fridays and Saturdays. The once humdrum shops have transformed into cafés, delis, restaurants (which are coining it in two converted banks), excellent butchers (original), a serious cheese shop . . . The S end is the smarter.

The majority of houses are 2-storey, 3-bed Edwardian homes, some of considerable charm inside, and remain in single-family occupation. There are pockets of larger, 3-storey mainly flat-fronted houses (some with semi-basement) notably in **Mallinson Rd**, **Bennerly Rd** and **Salcott Rd**. Many of the houses in these three roads have been converted to flats. **Broomwood Rd** (some 5-bed houses here: £585,000) and **Thurleigh Rd** are the through roads between Clapham and Wandsworth Commons, and **Webbs Rd** where there are local shops has traffic running N-S between **Battersea Rise** and **Broomwood Rd**.

Chatham Rd boasts a row of attractive Victoriana: Hyde's Cottages, 1863 (facing a small, low-rise council estate) and one of the oldest pubs in the area, The Eagle. The private **Stonell's Rd**, (cul-de-sac off **Chatham Rd**) offers tiny flat-fronted early Victorian cottages facing a school playground. **Hillier Rd**, **Devereux Rd** and **Montholme St** are popular because of easy access to Clapham South tube (direct if not always speedy Northern line), as are **Kyrle Rd**, **Broxash Rd** and **Manchuria Rd**.

On **Clapham Common West Side**, and running back to form a continuation of **Roseneath Rd**, Rialto's latest scheme is adding 30 new houses on the old Walsingham School site. All have parking and internal garages, and are holding their opening prices of £370–450,000 – except for the grandest, which face out over the common.

There are virtually no private purpose-built flats in the area with the exception of Broomwood Chambers off **Broomwood Rd**, but former council flats are increasingly coming available. Council property in the area tends to be flats and small houses. Most have been bought under 'Right to Buy'.

The largest houses in the area are on and just off **Bolingbroke Grove** which runs along the length of Wandsworth Common. Most are late-Victorian semi-detached and terraced. Those on **Bolingbroke Grove** itself balance road noise with open views over the common. Here Bolingbroke House has become seven flats (£185,000 for 2-bed). The large 3-storey red-brick terraced or semi-detached Victorian houses of **Gorst Rd** and **Dents Rd** are quieter – and more expensive. Smaller mid-Victorian houses on **Bolingbroke Grove** are close to the junction with **Battersea Rise**. Separated from the road by a stretch of grassland, the mid-Victorian cottages overlook a cemetery.

Off **Chivalry Rd**, which forms an L-shape between **Battersea Rise** and **Bolingbroke Grove**, is Commonside, a small private estate of houses and flats. A number of the houses and flats back directly onto the railway to Waterloo/Victoria. A traffic scheme has eased rat-running in **Chivalry Rd**, which has attractive late-Victorian houses.

South of **Thurleigh Rd** is SW12, but the streets between **Thurleigh** and **Nightingale Lane** belong to 'Between the Commons'. These have the shops and services of Balham to call on, and the advantage of nearby Clapham South tube.

Transport   No tubes; nearest are Clapham Common, Clapham South. Trains: Clapham Junction to Victoria 9 min, Waterloo 7 min; Queenstown Rd to Waterloo 7 min; Battersea Park to Victoria 5 min.

Convenient for   Victoria and Waterloo, Gatwick Airport (28 min), Sloane Square, Thames, Clapham Common, Battersea Park. Miles from centre: 3.

Schools   Local Authority: Battersea Technical, Salesian College RC (b). Private: Emanuel School, St Francis Xavier RC.

SALES

Flats

	S	1B	2B	3B	4B	5B
Average prices	60–90	70–150	90–230	175–300	400+	–

Houses

	2B	3B	4B	5B	6/7B	8B
Average prices	150–250	200–400+	280–500+	500+	600+	–

RENTAL

Flats

	S	1B	2B	3B	4B	5B
Average prices	450–650	700–1500	800–1600	1300–3000	2000–3500	2500–3600

Houses

	2B	3B	4B	5B	6/7B	8B
Average prices	1000–1500	1500–2400	1600–2700	3000–3600	4000+–	–

The properties   Terraced late-Victorian houses, flat conversions and smart new town-house/flat developments. Five-bed-plus houses and larger flats are scarce (try round the park for bigger mansion flats). Smartest new homes are the new riverside developments and loft-style conversions of old Victorian schools.

The market   Ultra-luxury developments attract 'buy-to-rent' investors as much as well-heeled owner-occupiers, so the range and numbers of homes to rent (from ex-council to sub-Manhattan) increasing here. Clapham Junction (despite the name) is in Battersea: this draws City types who compete with Fulham's children for the smarter homes. Good, cheap ex-council to be had. Local searches: 1 week.

Among those estate agents active in this area are:
- Foxtons
- John Hollingsworth
- Bairstow Eves
- Winkworth *
- Barnard Marcus
- John D Wood
- John Thorogood
- Edwin Evans
- Bishop Beamish
- Douglas & Gordon *
- Thresher Owen
- Andrew Kent & Ptnrs

further details: see advertisers' index on p633

BAYSWATER

B

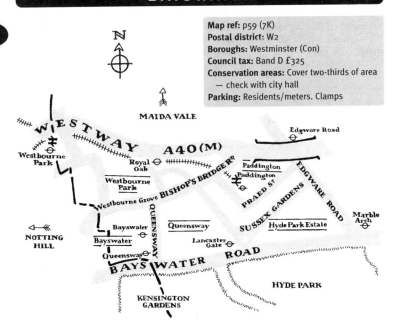

Map ref: p59 (7K)
Postal district: W2
Boroughs: Westminster (Con)
Council tax: Band D £325
Conservation areas: Cover two-thirds of area
    — check with city hall
Parking: Residents/meters. Clamps

Bayswater, traditionally stigmatized as 'the wrong side of the park' by the upper-crust inhabitants of Knightsbridge and Belgravia, is today more cheerfully schizophrenic than ever. Some of the West End's most luxurious homes are here, fronting Hyde Park and hidden behind in the area's best-kept secret, the Hyde Park Estate. But this ends at **Sussex Gardens**: N of the estate are the cheap hotels and dubious corners that crowd round any main terminus – in this case, Paddington – while westwards from **Lancaster Gate** to the borders of now-so-fashionable Notting Hill, there spreads, away from the park, a lively and very mixed web of streets (including, amid the bustle, prettier corners and occasional quiet, tucked-away mews). This has at its heart **Queensway**, a cosmopolitan shopping street that never closes. Shops in the Whiteley's Centre, which also holds a multiplex cinema, tend to trade until about 10pm most evenings, while the cafés, restaurants and bars operate into the small hours.

By the end of the '80s the huge decaying houses, split up into scores of seedy bed-sits, were beginning to be tidied up, and pockets of smart flats to appear. The N of the area, especially, attracted grants from the council to promote housing improvements. Now, given not only its well-heeled neighbours, but also the new, fast Paddington–Heathrow rail link, opened last year, its future has never looked brighter.

To define Bayswater: its southern boundary is the broad sweep of Hyde Park and Kensington Gardens. To the E the **Edgware Rd** is the frontier with the Marylebone area. To the N, beyond the elevated M40, the railway and the canal, is Maida Vale. To the W Bayswater blends into Notting Hill. The entire area is within Westminster City Council's jurisdiction, and the W2 postcode boundary also neatly encompasses it.

Its residents are as varied as its homes. The area, being close to the railway station and to the West End, has always catered for a large section of London's transient population and for low-income workers and students. At the same time it is

B

surprisingly parochial: the established home for many long-term residents – in council-built homes, as well as those who can afford the Monopoly-money prices commanded by the better properties. There are many tiny – but vociferous – residents' associations, covering single streets. They care passionately about every road hump here.

Renting is the other dimension to the Bayswater scene: thanks to the changes in the letting laws of the '80s, and its splendidly central position, there has been an explosion of homes to rent. For those buying – particularly flats – this is an area where it pays to check the age and quality of the conversion. Standards have risen considerably over the years, as developers realized the need for more spacious and higher-quality flats. Because there is such a huge variety of properties and such a variation in the quality of the conversions, prices, taken in isolation, can often be misleading.

Bayswater is also set to get its own mini-Docklands – sometime . . . The Paddington area holds not only the railway station but a canal basin, too: between them, the Paddington Goods Yards site, N of the station, and the Paddington Basin area to the E, behind St Mary's Hospital, add up to 40 acres, ripe for redevelopment. To be exact, it has been poised to become 'the alternative West End', with offices dominating, and smart homes on the waterfront sites, since the '80s; things stopped dead in 1990 as the recession bit, revived 18 months back, and have now quietened once more. However, Westminster council is working with the Paddington Regeneration Partnership, and ultimately this could result in some 700 new flats (including some housing association), 'millions of square feet of offices, shops and water-based facilities', improved transport, open spaces, 'a package of community benefits' and what is claimed will be the largest convention hotel in Europe. Planning applications are in from a clutch of homes developers, while Chelsfield have consent for 4 acres of homes and offices – 150,000 sq ft of which Associated Newspapers may (or may not) take. Don't count on living here before the next market upturn, however.

Traffic and parking are contentious issues here, as the number of flats and hotels put intolerable pressure on the available road space. However, much has been achieved by no-through roads and one-way streets, as any outsider trying to navigate through by car discovers. The best advice is to go by public transport – or take a taxi.

Bayswater – Westbourne Grove

Bounded by **Westbourne Grove** (N), **Queensway** (E), the borough boundary (W) and **Bayswater Rd**, this, with its once-gracious 5-storey stucco terraces, was the heart of Bayswater's traditional bed-sit land. The neighbourhood, especially in the S close to

Hyde Park and convenient for the West End, then saw 'For Sale' signs proliferate in the '80s as the larger houses were split and sold off as flats. Now those that are still single homes can command very high prices – in the right street: **Orme Square** opens onto the busy **Bayswater Rd**, thus gaining views over Kensington Gardens. One of its large Regency houses, in less than immaculate condition, still commands around a million. Most Bayswater houses, though, tend to be 3-bedroomed (ie, too small to be worth splitting); you are more likely to find a 6/7-bed apartment than a house. Or how about a bank? While most ex-banks seem to be becoming wine bars or restaurants, one on the **Bayswater Rd** is now 4,000 sq ft, no less, of upside-down home (sleep in the vaults . . .), with immensely stylish, sweeping spaces and a million-pound price tag.

Three very much larger squares dominate the N part of the neighbourhood – **Leinster Square**, **Princes Square** and **Kensington Gardens Square**. For many years very down-at-heel, with improvement slow and patchy; now, though **Kensington Gardens Square** still holds some busy hotels, most are filled with smart flats rented at high prices to young professionals who commute to West End or City. Each square has a large communal garden to which neighbouring residents have access – an oasis of peaceful green space in a noisy area (much of it emitting from foreign students at the area's many language schools). Nearby, in **Redan Place** behind Whiteley's, Barratt's grandly-named Kensington Gardens Lodge was 75 per cent sold off-plan by end '98; prices from £310,000 for the final 2- and 3-bed flats, and there's basement parking.

Moscow Rd, the tube at its Queensway end, holds the Orthodox Cathedral, which serves the large Greek community. Alexandra Court here is a smart 1989 development. Some larger mansion flats in this road: a whopping 6-bed one was on the market for £650,000 last winter. **St Petersburg Place**, running S, contains an attractive brick terrace of period maisonettes. A 2-bed flat here comes with the use of another communal garden. Further W is **Hereford Rd**, which contains a mixture of properties. There are smaller, less ornate, brick houses with wrought-iron balconies; the road is serviced by a few small local shops and restaurants. Evesham House is a development of 26 1/3-bed flats, with car park; **Hereford Mews** also has new homes.

Westbourne Grove itself has become positively chi-chi in parts. New bars and restaurants join those supplying Chinese, Malaysian, Indian, Greek or Lebanese food. Dotted about this gastronomic mecca are specialist shops for cooks or collectors of Oriental furnishings, an Arabic bookshop and more. The western end of the Grove becomes part of the smart Notting Hill antiques district. With Queensway, this is an ideal part of town for the nocturnal, rivalling Earl's Court in its ability to stay up late.

Queensway – Lancaster Gate

The neighbourhood bounded by **Queensway** in the W, **Bayswater Rd** to the S, **Gloucester Terrace** (E) and **Bishop's Bridge Rd** (N) reflects the tremendous social mix that is characteristic of this part of town. In the N of this area is the council-owned Hallfield Estate with its strong community feeling, its own health centre and school. The estate is bordered by **Inverness Terrace** and **Gloucester Terrace**. In the S, **Lancaster Gate** sports some of the neighbourhood's most luxurious developments, facing Kensington Gardens.

Gloucester Terrace is a wide, sweeping road which brings much traffic off the A40 motorway and into Central London. S from the Hallfield Estate the road features large, well-kept stucco houses, most already divided up into luxury flats (around £95,000 for a 1-bed one). These are broken by terraced brick houses. Where the road meets **Craven Rd**, another small 'village' begins. Going W along **Craven Rd**, a cluster of little shops provide local services as well as fresh fruit and flowers. And on either side are two sets of mews with steeply sloping entrances (**Gloucester Mews**, **Smallbrook Mews**, **Upbrook Mews** and **Craven Hill Mews**, whose little houses, once stables, are now capable of leaving scant change out of half a million). In **Westbourne Terrace** some of the enormous houses, long hotels, are reverting to homes. A new conversion here is yielding nine 1-, 2- and 3-bed flats with parking, £99,950–395,000. A luxury block appeared in the '80s on the site of Holy Trinity Church in **Bishop's Bridge Rd**. In the same road distinctive Bishop's Court, handsomely clad in stock brick above stucco, is 49 flats on seven floors: 2-bed, 2-bath cost £220,000 last winter, with prices escalating all the way to penthouse-level.

Around the corner off **Leinster Gardens**, **Craven Hill Gardens** and **Queens Gardens** contain more large, 5-storey multi-occupieds; **Cleveland Square** and **Devonshire Terrace** generally have smaller 3-storey houses, emerging from their B&B/holiday-lets image. Two larger **Cleveland Square** houses have become 14 small flats, for sale or rent; 1-bed for £145,000, 2-bed £220,000, 3-bed £285,000. The most desirable homes in Bayswater, beside those on the Hyde Park Estate, are to be found in the **Lancaster Gate** and **Porchester Terrace** areas. **Porchester**, which runs N from the park, contains an intriguing mixture of period town-houses with well-maintained gardens, interspersed with the occasional modern one with off-street parking. Many of the cars along this road bear diplomatic plates, and anti-burglar bars are evident on many a ground floor window. Dotted among the detached houses are some flat-fronted brick apartment blocks. The modern Hyde Park Towers apartment block affords wide views across Kensington Gardens. In **Inverness Terrace** is Park Gate, a major recent development of 37 flats. No 1 **Porchester Gate** is a block of 27 flats completed in 1988.

Lancaster Gate is a street of surprises. Here the large hotels have solid, respectable frontages. The square itself surrounds an eye-catching development of luxury flats created from a former church. On the corner, another luxury-level development produced 24 flats carved out of several 5-storey, colonnaded terraced houses. This sort of scheme allowed for Tardis-like lateral conversions – one boasted 4/5-bedrooms and a 43-ft living room.

In contrast to the atmosphere and scale of **Lancaster Gate**, neighbouring **Lancaster Mews** is like a small country village. Its sloping entrance is topped by the Mitre pub. Cottages here are beautifully maintained and colour-washed in attractive pastels. Mediterranean blue paintwork and abundant window boxes complete the picture of the busy light industrial/residential 'village'. The twin mews across **Craven Terrace** is smaller but equally well-maintained. There are rarely signs of sales.

Back on **Queensway** itself, at the W end of the neighbourhood, the traditional night life continues with restaurants pulling in tourists and visitors, and small shops catering for local residents. Thirties brick apartments, served by walkways, top the shopping arcades at the lower end of **Queensway** (£85–90,000 will buy you a studio flat here; c. £165,000 for a 2-bed). The famous Whiteley's department store – London's first, opened in 1863 – was reborn in 1989 as a shopping complex, harbouring a Marks & Spencer food hall as well as dozens of smaller shops, plus a multiplex cinema. This modern combination of shopping, eating and entertainment under one roof, open late and with parking, provided a much-needed and popular focus for this side of town.

Westbourne Park

Porchester Rd takes you N from the **Queensway** neighbourhood and up towards the motorway and **Harrow Rd**. Leaving **Bishop's Bridge Rd**, go N into **Porchester** and you are heading towards Royal Oak tube station. Pass by the local landmark of Porchester Hall, council-owned (you can hire this splendid venue) and always busy. Behind this is the Porchester Baths (public and private), with a luxurious health club.

To the E this end of **Gloucester Terrace** is the motorway access route: large 4-storey houses form what was once an elegant terrace; now the **Westway** overshadows them. The buildings have attractive wrought-iron balconies. **Porchester**

Square to the S has another busy communal gardens with playground for local residents (c. £185,000 for a 2-bed flat in a modern block here). In **Orsett Terrace** 90 flats were converted from the houses in the late '80s.

To the W of **Porchester Rd**, **Westbourne Park Rd** has a curious mixture of properties ranging from the flat-fronted brick apartment blocks to detached villa-style houses with ornate, oriental-inspired decorations and colonnaded entrances. Heron Homes built eight new houses and some offices in **Celbridge Mews** off **Porchester Rd** in the '80s; a balconied 3-bed mews house here was for sale last winter for £320,000.

West of the triangle bounding the church, **St Stephens Crescent** has an attractive terrace of stucco 5-storey properties with steps up to front entrances guarded by columns. St Stephens Gardens have recently been improved by the council. Around the corner, just off **Talbot Rd**, and E of **Chepstow Rd**, lies **Bridstow Place**, a tiny row of colour-washed Victorian cottages: these have been known to reach £400,000. Climbing roses and trailing plants splash colour over the pastel brickwork from their little gardens. Small-scale homes again in **Shrewsbury Mews**, where cottages, tiny, modern, but with garage, will cost some £275,000. But turn the corner, and you're back with **Chepstow Rd's** tall, 5-storey houses, scene of many a conversion scheme.

Talbot Rd itself has seen homes expensively renovated in recent years – after which, as whole houses, they can fetch c. £400,000 upwards (one was priced at three-quarters of a million). This corner, in fact, has been a hotbed of improvement and is now distinctly fashionable, numbering musicians and the odd pop star among its residents. Running between Talbot and tree-lined **Artesian Rd**, **Courtnell St** has more attractive colour-washed, brick-fronted homes, overlooked by copper beeches. W of here is the boundary of the W2 district and of Westminster borough: across it lies Notting Hill.

Paddington

Paddington station is the hub of the neighbourhood bounded by **Eastbourne Terrace**, **Harrow Rd**, **Edgware Rd** and **Sussex Gardens**. Like the surroundings of most major stations, the area contains a mixture of expensive homes, services and run-down property catering to the transient population. One day, though, this corner will be transformed: see introduction.

South of bustling **Praed St**, in **Sale Place**, **St Michael St** and **Star St** are little Victorian cottages, most once owned by St Mary's Hospital or by the railway companies for their workers. Over time these fell into disrepair; housing associations acquired some, but many benefited from the declaration of a Housing Action Area, which helped owners to improve their homes. Now their charm and location can command high prices. Tiny, 2-bed houses in **Spring St** can command some £300,000.

Five new houses in **Praed Mews** added to the air of revival. More new homes appeared around a courtyard off **Star St**. But **Praed St**, next to the station, reflects the dominant trend of the area: exchange bureaux, instant photos, heel bars and dealers in gold, silver and second-hand goods abound. **Norfolk Square** lies S of **Praed St** and contains mostly small hotels surrounding a communal garden. Westminster Council took over and renovated the neglected square gardens. South again, **Sussex Gardens** is a major road connecting **Lancaster Gate** and the **Edgware Rd**, its once-grand 4-storey terraces now flats (3-bed, £275,000) and bed-and-breakfast hotels. Three-bed flats rise to half a million or so in a private apartment block, Sussex Lodge, round the corner in **Sussex Place**. Across **Sussex Gardens**, in the triangle it thus makes between the park and the **Edgware Rd**, lies the exclusive Hyde Park Estate.

Hyde Park Estate

The Estate owes its character to its long-time landlords, the Church Commissioners. Once, the Bishop of London owned nearly all of Paddington. At the start of the 19th century the Bishop's architect built an elegant estate of squares and crescents – and called it, rather inauspiciously, Tyburnia. The Church Commissioners, heirs of the bishops, sold off all their Paddington land except this Hyde Park triangle in the 1950s. Much of ecclesiastical Paddington had sunk into a slum, populated largely by prostitutes (one corner, W of the station, was known as 'Sin Triangle'). Concentrating on the Hyde Park Estate, the Commissioners started widespread rebuilding. The result is a neighbourhood mixing lovely Regency stucco terraces, quiet little mews, handsome (some, anyway) modern houses and flats and – most notably forming a protective rampart along **Edgware Rd** – tower block apartments. The key is the Regency street-plan, which has survived the redevelopment. The Estate's lack of through-routes, and its clearly defined borders, keep it quiet and pleasant. It is a tribute to the Commissioners, or more especially to their agents and architects, that the Estate is still a desirable place to live.

Prices on the Estate are governed by whether they are for a (still less common than elsewhere) freehold – or, if leasehold, the length of the remaining lease. Also by period: the modern homes amid the stucco may be less attractive to the Brits, but more so to the international set; they often have a key advantage in this crowded corner: a garage. Thanks to the rebuilding and later conversions, there are flats, flats, flats of every size, period and lease length, at a commensurately wide span of prices: generalizations are difficult here. Note that, although the Leasehold Reform Acts have seen some at least of the residents able to buy their freeholds, the Church Commissioners still hold sway here: even freehold houses are liable to come under an estate management scheme.

From Marble Arch (originally built as an entrance to Buckingham Palace, but today standing at the western end of **Oxford St** as an entrance to nowhere), walk up busy **Edgware Rd**, turn left into cheap-hotel-lined **Sussex Gardens**, left again at the towering Royal Lancaster Hotel onto **Bayswater Rd**, and back along the Park to Marble Arch. You have thus circumnavigated the Hyde Park Estate. Better, branch to your left and penetrate the Estate's peace and quiet. It is like an island: hard to believe, once inside, how close is Oxford St. Leaving **Edgware Rd** is like going from a weekday to a Sunday.

The centre of life on the Estate is the Connaught 'village', with its mix of small shops, offices and homes; **Connaught St** is the 'high street'. It's a varied corner: for example **Connaught Place**, a mix of hi-tech offices and homes reconstructed behind the original stucco façade which faces out over Marble Arch and Hyde Park, houses the headquarters of a large multinational. And quietly camouflaged into the white stucco front of **Hyde Park Gardens** is the Sri Lankan embassy. The corner of **Sussex Place** and **Hyde Park Gardens Mews** is another picturesque hive of activity for eating, meeting and drinking, where on warm summer evenings people sit out at tables on the pavement – in (almost) Parisian style.

The centrepiece of the Hyde Park Estate is **Hyde Park Crescent**, and the lovely old church of St John's, which can be seen as a long-distance vista from as far as **Sussex Square**. The Crescent adds space and dignity to the church. Mirroring it to the E is **Norfolk Crescent**. The two form an elongated circle embracing the church, two squares (**Oxford** and **Cambridge**) and two high-rise blocks. **Norfolk Crescent**, a post-war rebuild of tall thin family houses, feels slightly crammed in contrast to **Hyde Park Crescent**.

Garden squares are a feature of the Estate, each with a character and atmosphere of its own. **Oxford Square** and **Cambridge Square**, for example, are bordered by '60s town-houses (a 5-bed, 4-bath, 43-year lease one asked £435,000 in January) and tall blocks of flats with underground garages. **Hyde Park Square** on the other hand is larger and has a range of styles surrounding it, from grandiose 5-storey stucco houses yielding conversions to spacious modern family homes to blocks of flats. **Sussex Square** has an even more spacious feel about it, with a circular green at the centre. One of the handsomest is **Connaught Square**, enclosed by classic Regency terraces.

B

While being just a stone's throw from the Marble Arch madness, it manages to retain its dignity and leafy peacefulness. Its houses are large; most are now flats, but not all: the freehold of 4,084 sq ft in this square cost £1,300,000 last winter. But the jewel in the crown is probably **Gloucester Square**. One can walk around the perimeter and not always be aware that it *is* a square: some of the (highly priced) houses have the luxury of backing directly onto the central green, concealing the communal central garden from the untutored eye. A recent block of de-luxe flats added onto the end of a cream stucco terrace were all eagerly snapped up. Some large 5-storey homes here, too.

Many of the Estate's big town-houses, once occupied by the wealthy families from the pages of history books and by the merchant classes and empire builders, have now been converted into ultra-luxurious flats. Some of the most exclusive are the stucco-fronted Regency buildings in **Hyde Park Gardens**, having their own huge communal garden opposite Hyde Park. Grand apartments here (some vast), with their high ceilings, huge windows and Park views come up both for buying and renting: a house-sized 5-bedroomed maisonette here currently costs £2,800 pw to rent.

In contrast to this quiet elegance and opulence, there is a variety of purpose-built modern blocks on the Estate, ranging from the workaday Park West in **Kendal St** on the E fringe, to the fountain-laden Water Gardens and the Quadrangle, both bordering on **Sussex Gardens**. The Water Gardens estate is a complex of towers and smaller blocks, with a '60s split-level feel and a profusion of pools and fountains.

Mews houses are ever more popular, here as elsewhere in London. They were originally built behind the big houses of the gentry as accommodation for horses, coaches and coachmen. It is only since the last war that they have been converted into homes, providing compact, easily manageable houses in villagy cobbled streets, retaining their period frontage and last-century atmosphere – helped, in most cases, by being cul-de-sacs. Some of the most charming and coveted mews on the Hyde Park Estate are **Hyde Park Gardens Mews**, off **Hyde Park Square**, and two smaller mews off **Albion St**: **Albion Mews** and **Albion Close**. The Estate is lucky to have a mews that is still used for its original purpose: **Bathurst Mews** houses a riding school, where you can hire horses and go riding in Hyde Park. Apart from the charm, mews houses often have their own garages, thus solving the main drawback to such central living. Nearly all the post-war flats and houses also have underground garages. But parking meters and parking permits put considerable pressure on movement, space and life in general.

The atmosphere on the Estate, once intimate, slow-moving and village-like, has become rather more cosmopolitan and anonymous with the years. The variety of languages that you can hear within a few paces ranges from Filipino to Swahili: many diplomats live here. Wealthy Arabs, many of whom only come for the summer months, also have their London bases here. The estate agents, banks, clothes shops, cinemas and restaurants at the top end of **Edgware Rd** all reflect this diversity. Nevertheless, the estate remains a prized oasis.

The Hyde Park Estate stops at **Sussex Gardens**, lined on either side by hotels and bed-and-breakfast houses filled with young travellers – as somewhere cheap and central to stay, you can't beat it. (**Sussex Gardens**' other claim to fame was traditionally that of being a red-light district – obviously encouraged by its proximity to both Paddington and Marylebone stations.) The Hyde Park Estate, however, feels genteel and safe, with **Sussex Gardens** acting like a divide. On the other side of the road, you're no longer on the Estate – there is a different atmosphere, the pace is faster and more commercial and the streets dingier as you near Paddington station. However, from there it is now a mere 17 min by express train to the airport, and the massive redevelopment long planned for the Paddington area will one day transform that corner, too.

Transport	Tubes, zone 1: Bayswater (District, Circle); Lancaster Gate, Queensway (Central); Paddington (District, Circle, Bakerloo, Metropolitan). From Lancaster Gate: Oxford Circus 6 min, Bank 20 min, Heathrow 55 min (2 changes). Trains: Paddington to Heathrow Express 17 min.
Convenient for	Hyde Park, West End, City, M40 to West. Miles from centre: 2.5.
Schools	Local Authority: Westminster North Secondary. Private: Pembridge Hall School (g).

B

SALES

Flats	S	1B	2B	3B	4B	5B
Average prices	55–100	100–200	130–250	250–1M	350–1M	–
Houses	2B	3B	4B	5B	6/7B	8B
Average prices	200–700	275–800	350–1M	500–1M	–	–

RENTAL

Flats	S	1B	2B	3B	4B	5B
Average prices	750–1200	850–2000	1300–2000	2000–3500+	3000–4000	3600–6000+
Houses	2B	3B	4B	5B	6/7B	8B
Average prices	2000–3000	2500–3500	3500–6000	4000–7000	5000–8000+	–

The properties	Bayswater's traditional image of seediness (fast altering) means its prettier, well-hidden corners and occasional quiet mews come as a shock to many. White terraces were once grand; currently a total mix: everything from pristine millionaires' squares (Hyde Park Estate) to hostels. Ramparts of flats along Edgware Rd. Flats most common. Houses either small or very expensive: the rest were converted to flats.
The market	The 17 min rail link to Heathrow has set the seal on this fast-changing area. Its excellence as a London base attracts the international set. Grand plans to regenerate Paddington will complete the transformation – one day . . . Local searches: 2 days.

Among those estate agents active in this area are:
- Chestertons
- Lurot Brand
- The London Mews Co
- FPDSavills
- Marsh & Parsons
- Winkworth *
- Kinleigh, Folkard & Hayward
- Foxtons
- Plaza Estates
- John D Wood
- Cluttons Daniel Smith
- Keith Cardale Groves
- Jackson-Stops & Staff
- Harrods Estates
- Sterling
- Anscombe & Ringland *
- Beaney Pearce *

further details: see advertisers' index on p633

BEDFORD PARK AND ACTON GREEN

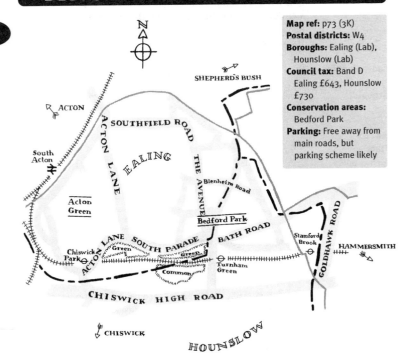

Map ref: p73 (3K)
Postal districts: W4
Boroughs: Ealing (Lab),
    Hounslow (Lab)
Council tax: Band D
    Ealing £643, Hounslow
    £730
Conservation areas:
    Bedford Park
Parking: Free away from
    main roads, but
    parking scheme likely

It is, of course, quite possible to live in Bedford Park without being keen on architecture, but it would be rather a waste. For this was London's first purpose-built suburb – laid out, and the houses designed, in the 1870s to high artistic standards for those of aesthetic (*the* in-word of the day) tendencies. It has survived virtually intact, an island in the less creative sprawl of West London. And a good number of the inhabitants spend a good part of their time protecting their neighbourhood against philistine encroachment.

Convenient position (it lies just N of Chiswick), a distinctive charm and family-sized – some outsized – houses are the solid attractions of this corner. Corner it is: Bedford Park is not very big, and its cachet leads to an extension of the name into Acton Green. 'Bedford Park Borders' or 'West Bedford Park' are terms to beware of if you have set your heart on the homes of the conservation area. Some roads outside the original estate belong in spirit, but to the true Park residents, the world immediately outside their conserved streets is, and will remain, forever Acton.

True Bedford Park consists of a mere dozen streets, contained by **Esmond**, **Blenheim** and **Abinger Rds**. Acton Green, the L-shaped area to the N and W of the conservation area, may hold more everyday homes, but these bordering streets are themselves a well-defined enclave: only **Acton Lane** crosses the tracks to Acton proper, and only **Bath Rd** connects through to Hammersmith. You would think the W4 postcode was a solid wall. Popular family homes here – ever more so, as Chiswick prices escalate – particularly the corner to the W, which has the tube.

Confusion is to a certain extent understandable: the tube station that serves Acton Green is called Chiswick Park, so agents naturally tend to adopt this name for

B

the surrounding streets. Then the open space of Acton Green Common itself lies S of **South Parade**, leading up to Bedford Park's tube – which is called Turnham Green. In its turn, the once thriving hamlet of Turnham Green seems to have been subsumed entirely into Chiswick, its name only commemorated, sadly, by the tube station, a Civil War battle, its green (which lies away to the S of **Chiswick High Rd**) and **Turnham Green Terrace** – which forms the gateway to Bedford Park.

Bedford Park

Founded in 1875 by Jonathan Carr, a cloth merchant with a taste for speculation and art, Bedford Park was the prototype garden suburb. Carr employed such well-known architects as (principally) Norman Shaw, plus E J May, E W Godwin and Maurice B Adams to design houses in the Queen Anne Revival style – all red-brick, dormer windows, Dutch gables, hanging tiles, balconies and pretty porches. Some 400 buildings, mostly Grade II listed, now make up the conservation area. Despite the odd bit of war damage and modern infilling, the estate remains remarkably homogeneous; the most obtrusive new building is St Catherine's Court, a 1930s block built on the site of Carr's own magnificent home, the Tower House.

There is great variety in homes, from little 2-storey 3-bedroom cottages to 6/7-bedroom detached houses, semis and terraces of up to 4 storeys. There are a couple of large mansion blocks, and some of the bigger houses have been converted into owner-occupied flats – only a few are rented accommodation. Despite its sobriquet of garden suburb many of the gardens are disappointingly small ('though not for Central London, which for practical purposes we are!' objected one resident), and prices reflect garden as much as house size and position. Garden flats also fetch proportionately more. Houses on street corners, often set at an angle to the road, have enviable extra garden space and beautiful detailing: perhaps a conservatory or pleasing gables or balconies. Because there is such a good size mix, residents often move within the area and many properties are sold through the grapevine – which is why some people move to Bedford Park's borders before working their way in.

The whole estate with its irregular layout (designed by Norman Shaw to preserve existing trees) was modelled on the ideal of a village complete with shops, pub, church of St Michaels and All Angels, church hall and club. The village atmosphere remains, which means lots of social and cultural activities plus a friendly atmosphere where everyone seems to know everyone else's business. The community spirit is fostered by the Bedford Park Society, which protects the area's architectural heritage.

B

Just about every house in Bedford Park is listed, and the whole place is a conservation area. So splendid details like this assemblage of gable, balcony and bay will survive. The wooden railings, close-set glazing bars in the square bay, heavy gable and tiled roof are typical. The houses are late-Victorian, but they hark back to Queen Anne.

Originally built as homes at modest rents for the aesthetic middle classes, Bedford Park from the first attracted many artists (the occasional purpose-built artist's studio can be seen) and personalities of the day. Nowadays it is more likely to house media folk, professionals such as architects, and others who can afford the considerably less-than-modest buying prices.

Carr chose the spot because of its proximity to the newly opened Turnham Green station; these excellent links to the West End and City remain, with the added advantage of being 20 minutes' drive on a good day from Heathrow down the M4. The area is, too, within walking distance of the shops and restaurants on **Chiswick High Rd**, as well as other W4 facilities. Acton Green Common, abutting the tube line, is the nearest open space, but the river, Kew Gardens and Richmond Park are only a few minutes' drive away. **Bath Rd, The Avenue** and **South Parade** are main roads with bus routes, while the latter, along with **Flanders Rd**, are close to the tube line. Streets around the station suffer commuter daytime parking but there are plans for a parking scheme to favour residents. **Abinger Rd, Blenheim Rd, Bedford Rd** and streets off **South Parade** become rat-runs during rush hour, though there are tentative proposals for a traffic scheme. It follows that roads in the heart of the conservation area, such as **Queen Anne's Gardens**, are quiet, but all roads have covetable houses.

Prices vary considerably with the desirability of the roads and the purity of the architecture, but you can count on spending around £500,000 for an 'ordinary' 4/5-bed family house here. It goes up from there, with classic Norman Shaw houses rarely on the market and priced accordingly. Last winter's stock for sale included a cottage 3-bedroom detached in **Marlborough Crescent** at £525,000, a detached 5/6-bed house in **The Avenue** (with coveted off-street parking) was £950,000 while two very large houses in **Bedford Rd** were £995,000 and £1.25 million respectively.

Bedford Park Borders; Acton Green

Non-listed houses, such as those in streets off **Flanders Rd** to the SE, along with mansion blocks and houses just outside the conservation area in **Blandford Rd, Fielding Rd** and **Vanbrugh Rd** to the N, and **Esmond Rd, Ramilles Rd, Rusthall Avenue** and **St Albans Avenue** – 'West Bedford Park' in estate-agentese – were built later than Bedford Park proper, with some inter-war additions (though note that the E side of **Esmond Rd** is still in the conservation area, and has some substantial houses – in size and price – at its S end). Homes here are cheaper in design and price, but still above the more humdrum homes of the surrounding 'borders' streets further N and W, which form the lower brackets of our price chart.

West of **St Albans Avenue** are the first streets of Acton Green, a neighbourhood still considered Chiswick for estate agents' purposes: since this corner is still in the

W4 postcode and uses Chiswick Park tube, perhaps they have a point. The homes are more ordinary than Bedford Park's, but some are of much the same date, with a good sprinkling of Edwardian and some mid-20th-century. It is here, and to the N of the area, that any new homes can be found, and there is also activity from developers splitting terraced homes into flats. These streets run off **Acton Lane**, but are kept distinct from Acton proper by the railway line that curls protectingly round to the NW. There is a difference between the streets to the W, which are wider and have some good-sized houses amid the terraces, and those just E of Acton Lane, which tend to be narrower with smaller homes.

To the W of **Acton Lane**, **Church Path** winds through the area; at one point **Cleveland Rd** joins it to run parallel behind a paved and tree'd strip: a pleasant villagy spot. At the head of this is a pretty corner house at the end of opulent-sounding and certainly pleasant **Rothschild Rd**. **Kingswood Rd** and **Cunnington St** cut through: wide roads with better architecture than average. **Bridgeman** and **Weston Rds** running beside the (not very busy) railway are popular. **Antrobus Rd** is also well-regarded. **Ivy Crescent**, which backs onto the railway, is a fertile field for flat conversions. This road, and **Weston Rd**, may be affected by the big office scheme planned for the other side of the tracks on the Gunnerbsury London Transport depot. However, this development, which would involve a new rail/tube station, is in abeyance at the moment. If it does happen, it would add Piccadilly line tubes to the District ones which stop at Chiswick Park.

Acton Green is seeing a fashionable warehouse conversion, too: 18 1-, 2-, and 3-bed flats on the corner of **Acton Lane** and **Fletcher Rd**, close to the rail line in the N of the area. Prices are aiming higher than those for conversions in this more humdrum, northern corner: 1-bed start at £165,000 with 3-bed up to £275,000. Off **Steele Rd**, a refurbished/rebuilt mews is tucked in behind smart and firmly shut gates. Round the corner off **Church Path**, a 3-bed modern mews in **Chapter Close** was £230,000 last December. Converted flats are a staple around here: prices start around £90,000 for 1-bed in busy **Acton Lane** (less for ex-council homes) while a garden flat in a road like **Kingswood Rd** can command £122,500. Two-bedroom flats in **Bollo Lane**, close to the tube, range around the £140,000 mark. In **Rothschild Rd** a terraced house, extended to give 5 bedrooms, was £335,000 last winter, while round the corner in **Temple Rd** an Edwardian 3-bed terraced house needing work was £260,000. Busy **Acton Lane** had a 2-bed terraced house last December at £190,000, while a modern 2-bed, 2-bath flat in the same road was £210,000.

The northern borderlands centre around **Southfield Rd**, a continuation of **The Avenue**, which leads on round to **Acton Lane**. **Southfield Rd** has standard square-bayed 1914 terraces; **Fielding Rd** the same; while **Speldhurst Rd** and the N end of **St Alban's Avenue** have homes from a slightly earlier period. There is a recreation ground and a school on **Southfield Rd**, as well as some 1980s houses and flats. A cache of 3-bed, 2-bath mews houses appeared off **Southfield Rd** in 1990. Houses in **Fielding Rd** have 3- and 4-bed and the ones that were for sale last winter ranged from £315–370,000.

A final point: unlike neighbouring Chiswick, Bedford Park is far enough from the flight paths to escape aircraft noise being a nuisance.

| **Transport** | Tube stations: Turnham Green, Stamford Brook, Chiswick Park (zone 2, District). From Turnham Green: Oxford Circus 25 min (1 change), City 40 min, Heathrow 25 min (1 change). Trains: South Acton on N London line/Silverlink. |

Convenient for   Heathrow and M4. Miles from centre: 4.

Schools   Ealing and Hounslow Education Authorities: Chiswick School, Acton School. Private: Latymer (b), Godolphin & Latymer (g), St Paul's (g).

SALES

Flats	S	1B	2B	3B	4B	5B
Average prices	60–100	90–170+	135–300+	150–300+	—	—
Houses	2B	3B	4B	5B	6/7B	8B
Average prices	175–300+	230–525	325–650+	450–1M+	→1.25M+	—

RENTAL

Flats	S	1B	2B	3B	4B	5B
Average prices	500–800+	700–1200	850–1700	1200–1900	1800+	—
Houses	2B	3B	4B	5B	6/7B	8B
Average prices	1000–1700	1200–2000	1800–3000	2500–3500	—	—

The properties   Distinctive enclave of late-19th-century Queen Anne-style houses, from 3-bed cottages up to large houses. Bordering streets are more everyday Victorian/Edwardian.

The market   Always fierce competition for the small number of genuine, conservation-area homes. Surrounding streets are also popular family homes — increasingly so, as Chiswick prices rise. These are at cheaper end of above prices. Local searches: Ealing 1 week, Hounslow 1 day.

Among those estate agents active in this area are:
- Barnard Marcus
- Knight Frank
- Foxtons *
- Winkworth *
- Quintons
- Bushells
- Whitman & Co

further details: see advertisers' index on p633

BELGRAVIA

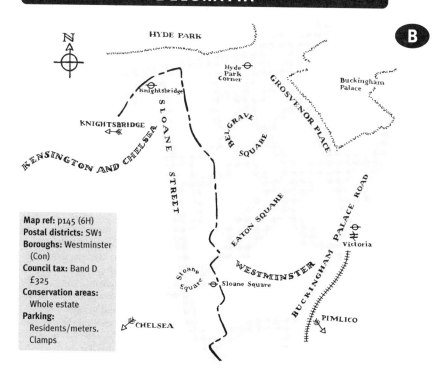

Map ref: p145 (6H)
Postal districts: SW1
Boroughs: Westminster
(Con)
Council tax: Band D
£325
Conservation areas:
Whole estate
Parking:
Residents/meters.
Clamps

To live in Belgravia is to be seriously rich – or at least to have someone else (like your company or embassy) paying the rent. For your money you get unrivalled ambience, discreetly excellent management of the overall estate, plus a position mid-way between Harrods and Buckingham Palace – and a short taxi ride from everywhere you would ever want to be. The key to Belgravia's charm is its changes of scale, from minute and charming mews homes in their cobbled cul-de-sacs, through low-storeyed terraces to the gleaming grandeur of the set-pieces of **Eaton Square**, **Belgrave Square** and **Chester Square**.

This pristine part of London, which fills the angle between Hyde Park, Green Park and **Sloane St**, must rank among the best property investments of all time. The sole proprietor of the whole of this patch of enviable real estate since its building, the enjoyer of its rents and revenues, has been the Grosvenor Estate, personified by a youngish man called Gerald Grosvenor, sixth Duke of Westminster. His family has owned the land for generations and in Regency times developed it with the help of builder and architect Thomas Cubitt. Much of London was built up at this time or a little later, but no other district has kept its character in quite the same way. The credit goes partly to Cubitt, whose building standards were, if not exactly high, then better than those of Nash. But the main upholder of the Belgravian character has been the Grosvenor Estate, and the snowy sweep of stuccoed terraces and squares stand seemingly unchanged. That said, the Duke's inheritance has been nibbled at of late by tenants exercising their rights under the Leasehold Reform Acts. The Estate contested the buy-outs and took the case to the European Court of Human Rights

B

under the complaint that the Acts infringed the Duke's right to freely enjoy his property. But the Estate now accepts the inevitability of people's right to buy and, while it doesn't go out of its way to offer freeholds, it negotiates with those leaseholders who approach it on this – or on extending their leases by up to 90 years. The Grosvenor Estate also changed its leasing policy last year, and will now offer new leases of 99 years outside **Eaton Square** (previously, the maximum was 75).

So, for the first time in two centuries, the word 'freehold' appears occasionally in Belgravia. The Estate office is still very much in charge, however: controlling tenancies, developing its own properties and stipulating just how the inhabitants – even the new freeholders – behave (try drinking on the pavement outside one of the Belgravia pubs). The control of the Estate office may be discreet but it is firm. Whatever their personal tastes, householders must paint their façades cream, and not just any old cream but the precise British Standard shade of magnolia that is the official Estate colour.

Central Belgravia is almost wholly residential. The Estate's policy is to use the fringes for offices and shops and hotels, but to keep the heartland free of commerce – unless you count embassies. Shops are to be found in a few streets: **Elizabeth St** and **Motcomb St** have the majority – and of course you can commission your furniture from Viscount Linley's shop among the galleries and antique shops on Belgravia's southern borders, the **Pimlico Rd**. There are a few discreetly hidden pubs in mews. But the rest is houses and flats. The properties within this enclave vary considerably in size. The grandest homes, those in **Belgrave Square**, have virtually all become embassies or institutes. Nearly all of the only slightly more modest **Eaton Square** mansions are now flats. Smaller-scale houses often survive as single homes, as do many of the mews cottages which were originally the stables for the grand streets and squares.

There are more freeholds available now, particularly of houses – but the standard commodity on sale here is the lease, either direct from the Estate or a sub-lease. Some leases can be very short, but those expecting a 15-year lease to be one-fifth the cost of a 75-year one are doomed to disappointment. For one thing, a short lease may qualify you to buy the freehold in due course. Then there are those buyers of short leases, usually companies, who view the sums demanded by these enviable London bases as so many years' rent paid upfront, rather than as a purchase. (Companies, though, do not have the right to enfranchise.) On the third hand, private foreign buyers hate leasehold, so prices for the still fairly rare freehold houses have rocketed. Understandably, all these considerations make price comparisons a tricky sport in Belgravia. Leasehold means paying ground rent, which can be noticeable: £3,000 a year on an Eaton Square flat, to add to a service charge of £8,000 – double that in a year when the Estate decides the façade needs painting.

The area is very popular with foreign diplomats and business people. Due to the positive ghetto of embassies in and around **Belgrave Square** there is a plethora of police, including the always-armed Diplomatic Protection Group. This presence reassures foreigners, say estate agents. There was a time, not more than a couple of decades ago, when Belgravia's grand houses were considered too big to inhabit. And by modern standards so they are; they were designed with the assumption of dozens of servants. What has happened is the great improvement in the art of conversion. The splendid old buildings are sometimes just façades, concealing flats which are in some cases vast and equally grand. Sometimes the conversions are lateral, running behind two or even three house façades to give house-sized apartments on one floor.

Southern Belgravia

Once, the Grosvenor family also owned the whole tract S from Victoria station down to the Thames: the Pimlico area was developed at the same time, and was once considered part of Belgravia. The railway cut Pimlico off, and it never achieved the same exalted status as its senior neighbour. The Grosvenor Estate eventually sold Pimlico, known as the 'southern estate', 50 years ago to fund international expansion.

Belgravia thus starts at busy, slightly seedy **Buckingham Palace Rd**, which runs alongside the station. The strip between this road and **Ebury St**, another busy through-route, contains little of the Belgravia character. The occasional mews, and some flats in **Ebury Square**, compete for space with the Victoria Coach Station. In this southern corner, off **Pimlico Rd**, are also The Peabody Buildings.

Ebury St has small (for Belgravia) early terraced houses, many of which are hotels. Until recently it was quite run-down, but now it is improving – and paradoxically these homes have some of the area's largest gardens. The houses are mostly brick, not stucco. To the W **Bunhouse Place**, tucked behind **Bourne St**, has a row of '70s neo-Georgian town-houses: quiet and popular.

Between **Ebury St** and **Eaton Square** is the first slice of Belgravia proper. And how proper it is, with quiet, pretty **Chester Square** as its showpiece. These houses were built as 'second rank' homes (second, that is, to the monster ones of **Belgrave** and **Eaton Squares**) but are today considered to be some of the best in the area. Nearly all are still single houses: in excess of £5 million apiece. **Chester Row** is similar, but the houses are on a smaller scale, and vary in size.

Eccleston St, which bisects **Chester Square**, is a busy one-way road taking traffic up to **Hyde Park Corner**. Some of the big houses here are still 5-plus bedroom homes: a longish (68 years) lease on one was £1 million in January. This is where the mews begin: the Belgravia 'back streets' where the little cottages, built to house the gentry's horses, now house the gentry. These, often cul-de-sacs boasting arched entrances and cobbles, can have enormous charm. **Ebury Mews**, running through from **Eccleston St** to **Elizabeth St**, is typical, although not a cul-de-sac. It has a mix of converted mews cottages of greater and lesser degrees of opulence, plus some new-build homes in mews style. Quite a few of these homes have garages where the stable once was. Mews houses may be smaller, but that does not mean they are cheap: one in **Eaton Mews West** was £500,000 for a 29-year lease last autumn. It does have two garages, though.

Lower Belgrave St is another busy road, southbound this time, with plain but handsome brick houses. An unmodernized freehold one was on offer for £1.25 million in January, while another split into two flats was £1.5 million. **Elizabeth St** has a selection of very up-market shops (including some serving quite everyday needs) and, increasingly, some good restaurants. Its homes include a very beautiful, low-built house – its style more reminiscent of the Nash villas of Regent's Park than of the usual lofty Belgravia terraces. Chantry House is similarly low-built, complete with garage in nearby **South Eaton Place**.

To the W, **Eaton Terrace** and splendidly appropriate **Caroline Terrace** have more handsome houses – most still single homes, not flats: typically 3- to 4-bedroomed, with gardens and a few with garages, which sell at around £900,000 (a few larger ones fetch in the region of £1.35–1.8 million). **South Eaton Place** has one or two freehold houses: one was on the market in late 1998 for £2.65 million. The far SW corner of the area has some smaller homes. **Bourne St's** 2-storey and semi-basement houses have 2 or 3 bedrooms. **Graham Terrace,** too, has more modest sizes. **Grosvenor Cottages** is tucked away off **Eaton Terrace**, a gated mews with a row of idiosyncratic 2-bed cottages, some double-fronted, and at the far end an elaborate 3-bed house which really defines the hoary old description 'convenient Sloane Square'. The house was on the market last autumn for £1.15 million for a 42-year lease; the cottages command half a million for a longish lease.

Eaton Square is the centrepiece on which the area turns. It has, to say the least, considerable presence. The buildings, in long, dignified terraces entered from large and pillared porches, are enormous. It could more properly be called 'Eaton Squares': it is on so large a scale that inhabitants hardly seem to notice the slight disadvantage of the main **King's Rd** running down the middle towards Chelsea. And two smaller roads cross at right angles, thus dividing the central garden into six – all of good size. Only a handful of houses here (some say five, some seven) are still single homes; the rest of these towering terraces have yielded some 350 flats. Penthouses top most of them, and prices are in the 'if you have to ask . . .' bracket. The Grosvenor Estate has itself recently developed Nos 1–5 **Eaton Square**, which has added a further 13 2- to 5-bed flats. Some of these were on the market last winter: 20-year leases could be had for £395–575,000, or alternatively 75-year leases from £1.25–2.65 million. Elsewhere in the Square, flats on long leases start at around £500,000 for 1-bed, while a 17 year lease on a large, smart 2-bed one was £1.15 million last winter. As for the whole houses, one recent sale was for over £12 million – including mews cottage in need of modernization. **Eaton Place**, on the way northwards towards the centre of the Estate, runs parallel to **Eaton Square**, its large houses, divided into grand flats, second only in scale to those of the Square.

Central Belgravia

Belgrave Square was planned as homes but is now mostly embassies and institutions. This is principally due to restrictive leases which state that each of the buildings can only be used for diplomatic or charitable purposes. Hence, the Red Cross are to be found occupy one of the most enviable plots on **Grosvenor Crescent**. However, in the last couple of years a few of the institutional buildings have reverted to homes. The three enormous corner mansions, set slant-wise across the Square's corners, are as big as any in London and are occupied by the likes of the Portuguese Ambassador.

Nevertheless, **Belgrave Square** is unlikely to figure on your shortlist unless you are the envoy of a new and very rich country. It is such embassies which saved the square from decline: since the Second World War, several dozen 'new' countries have now set up shop in London – and all, to the relief of the Grosvenor Estate, needed rather imposing buildings.

North of **Belgrave Square** are more mews – on a grander scale this time – with the stucco continuing behind the scenes. The arched entrances cut the mews off from the busy main streets. **Wilton Crescent** is the queen of this corner, its Regency sweep re-faced with stone at the turn of the century. The N end of **Wilton Place** has some rare early, pre-Cubitt brick houses: freehold, these fetch around £1.75 million. Little, villagy **Kinnerton St**, leading off, has concealed surprises: it is the entrance to an unusual warren of old and new cottages in mews and courtyards. To the S are some big blocks of purpose-built flats with car parking, then **Motcomb St** with more shops. The succession of mews and terraces continues on past **West Halkin St** back to **Eaton Square**, passing gems like **Grosvenor Cottages**.

The E corner of Belgravia has a cut-off collection of mews and little streets with a villagy feel, a couple of good pubs and even a general store. Streets like **Groom Place** and **Wilton Mews** have all the Belgravia assets plus a little more atmosphere. The NE corner is dominated by the Lanesborough Hotel, on **Hyde Park Corner**. A nest of little mews cottages behind it offers more charming and very desirable homes: these, in **Grosvenor Crescent Mews**, are deceptive – the Estate created 17 new homes behind the original façades three years ago, with more sybaritically sized rooms. Some really small 1-bed £300,000-plus cottages can be found in charming **Old Barrack Yard**, a pathway through to **Knightsbridge** from **Wilton Row**. To the W, the borough boundary running down **Lowndes St** and **Chesham St** marks, more or less, the end of the Duke's remit. **Lowndes Square**, often referred to as Belgravia, is more properly Knightsbridge. The end of the Estate's control is marked.

Transport	Tubes, all zone 1: Knightsbridge (Piccadilly), Sloane Sq (District, Circle), Victoria (District, Circle, Victoria). From Sloane Square to Oxford Circus 15 min (1 change), City 20 min, Heathrow 55 min (1 change).
Convenient for	West End, Hyde Park, Gatwick Airport. Miles from centre: 1.5.
Schools	Local Authority: Pimlico School, Greycoat Hospital C of E (g). Private: Francis Holland (g), The American International School, Westminster School (b), More House School (g).

SALES

Flats	S	1B	2B	3B	4B	5B
Average prices	140–160	250–500+	400–1.25M	500+	1M+	→
Houses	2B	3B	4B	5B	6/7B	8B
Average prices	450+	600–900	825–1.8M	1.5M–5M	→	→12M+

RENTAL

Flats	S	1B	2B	3B	4B	5B
Average prices	1300	1500–2800	2400–3900	3000–5200+	4300–8700	–
Houses	2B	3B	4B	5B	6/7B	8B
Average prices	3000–3900	3500–5200+	6000–10,800	10,800–15,000+	→	22,000

(B)

The properties   Mainly owned by the Grosvenor Estate; longer leases and freeholds now, thanks to Leasehold Reform Acts. Grand Regency homes provide equally grand converted apartments. Also houses of all sizes from mews cottage to embassy.

The market   'Average' prices here are a very general guide: all depends on length of lease and location. Discounting embassy-sized houses, Eaton Square commands highest prices. Short leases, c. 9–20 years, equate to rental, rather than sale, prices: those above are for reasonable leases. Small proportion of freeholds of (relatively) smaller houses. Local searches: 2 working days

Among those estate agents active in this area are:
- Best Gapp & Cassells
- DTZ Debenham Thorpe
- De Groot Collis
- Chesterfields
- Knight Frank
- Friend & Falcke
- FPDSavills *
- W A Ellis *
- George Trollope
- Aylesford
- Hamptons
- Cluttons Daniel Smith
- Beaney Pearce *
- Strutt & Parker *
- Beauchamp Estates
- Lane Fox
- Douglas Lyons & Lyons
- John D Wood
- Lord Francis Russell & Co
- Foxtons

further details: see advertisers' index on p633

BETHNAL GREEN

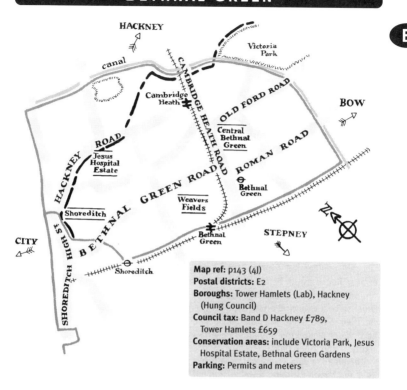

B

Map ref: p143 (4J)
Postal districts: E2
Boroughs: Tower Hamlets (Lab), Hackney
(Hung Council)
Council tax: Band D Hackney £789,
Tower Hamlets £659
Conservation areas: include Victoria Park, Jesus
Hospital Estate, Bethnal Green Gardens
Parking: Permits and meters

Bethnal Green is the spiritual heart of the East End, with a vivid past of gangsters, boxing and poverty. It is still poor, but its proximity to the wealth of the City and the new developments of Docklands, and the comparative cheapness of the property, is leading to its upwards ascent.

Docklands, with its mushrooming developments, is a mere mile or so to the SE but Bethnal Green's rows of 2-storey 1840–60s terraces, interspersed with the Model Dwellings of the Victorian philanthropists and later council-build, remain down to earth in character and price. The late '80s, in the wake of Docklands developments, spawned new flats and dual-purpose work-homes with names like City View, London Terrace, Lion Mills, Bowbrook, Twig Folly Wharf, The Minstrels. The City is just one stop away; City souls even cycle to work. At the same time locals started getting involved in self-build and housing co-operatives, and housing associations are at work on several sites. The local Tower Hamlets Council is keen to help local people stay in the area.

Recently there has been an influx of buyers from places like Islington as flat-dwellers trade up to houses – but the lack of night life can put some people off. The incomers are those working in the City or Docklands, and the market was buoyant during 1997 and 1998 until uncertainties about City jobs slowed things down last autumn. The new inhabitants are mainly couples without children: Tower Hamlets' schools have a poor reputation and an improvement here would boost house prices, say local estate agents.

Bethnal Green lies alongside the City: Hackney is to the N, Bow to the E, and Stepney to the S. **Cambridge Heath Rd**, **Hackney Rd** and **Bethnal Green Rd** are the three main thoroughfares. Busy **Cambridge Heath Rd** runs from Stepney through to Hackney and includes Bethnal Green Gardens, one of four conservation areas, and the Bethnal Green Museum of Childhood. The green is the centre of the old village.

Shoreditch, to the W of Bethnal Green, forms the boundary with the City. An indication for Bethnal Green is that this area was mainly commercial, but is seeing an influx of loft developments and is becoming positively fashionable: see City chapter. There are council-built flats in the Boundary Estate conservation area to the E of **Shoreditch High St**, which includes **Arnold Circus** with its bandstand. The imposing landmark of Shoreditch Church, which houses the impressive St Leonard's Gardens in its grounds, stands on the corner of **Shoreditch High St** which runs S to **Bishopsgate** and Liverpool St station. Sunday morning markets are a treat: try the wonderful **Columbia Rd** for flowers, **Brick Lane** for Europe's biggest flea-market. There is no real shopping centre, though.

Bethnal Green

The Victoria Park conservation area forms part of Bethnal Green's NE boundary; it is edged, on the Bethnal Green side, by the Grand Union Canal: homes in the conservation area with views over canal and park command a premium. **Sewardstone Rd** and **Approach Rd**, where 3- and 4-storey Victorian houses have been converted into flats, are popular but **Cyprus St** is more sought-after. Some of these neat 2-bed terraced houses, built before World War I, are Grade II listed, with original shuttered windows adding to their tidy appearance. The well-kept Victorian terraces have immense character and a plaque, dedicated to the memory of the men of **Cyprus St** who died in two world wars, hangs between Nos 76–78. The terrace is continued by the Duke of Wellington pub and further S is the Cranbrook Estate of council homes, largely 2- and 3-bed flats.

Roman Rd, a busy thoroughfare which runs E into Bow, has more council homes to the S and Meath Gardens, a welcome relief from the blocks of flats. Before the canal bridge in the corner of the Cranbrook Estate is the new Twig Folly development of 40 2-bed canalside flats. These proved a success and a second tranche was being built this spring. Next to this is Bow Brook, a converted school with interesting loft-style flats. The area W to Bethnal Green tube is known as Globe Town: with the London Buddhist Centre, a Thai restaurant on **Burnham St** and art and photography galleries on the **Roman Rd** itself, it has a very different atmosphere. Off **Globe Rd** to the S of **Roman Rd** is a new development, Sceptre Court, with 16 1-, 2- and 3-bed flats.

At the junction of **Roman Rd** with **Cambridge Heath Rd**, the tube station is situated in the splendour of Bethnal Green Gardens, another conservation area. **Victoria Park Square**, behind Bethnal Green Museum, leads to **Sugar Loaf Walk** and then a cluster of close-knit red-brick terrace houses in **Moravian St**, **Gawber St**, **Welwyn St** and **Globe Rd**. Opposite York Hall Baths in **Old Ford Rd** is an imposing Georgian house, called The Terraces, part of which has been converted into flats. Terraced houses, many refurbished, are on either side. Further E down **Old Ford Rd** is **Bonner Rd**, with a row of impressive council-built houses.

North along **Cambridge Heath Rd** is **Millennium Place**, a new flats block, and more council-built homes in **Patriot Square**, opposite the town hall. These command good prices and quick sales when they come onto the market. At the junction with **Hackney Rd** is Cambridge Heath station (trains to Liverpool St) and to the NW is a large refurbished council estate which takes in **Pritchard's Rd**, **Coate St**, **Teale St** and **Emma St**. Close by, **Wharf Place** has a canalside warehouse conversion of 2-bed flats, London Wharf. Next door, Regent's Wharf is a recent apartment block. Both are very popular.

To the W, the Jesus Hospital Estate is on the S side of **Hackney Rd** and includes **Columbia Rd**, **Baxendale St**, **Quilter St**, **Elwin St**, **Durant St**, **Ezra St**, **Wimbolt St** and **Wellington Row**. These two-up, two-down Victorian terraced houses are very popular and sell fast: £190,000 is a typical price. Many have hanging baskets of flowers outside in summer, in keeping with the area which has the famous flower market in **Columbia Rd** on Sunday mornings. **Columbia Rd** has seen some new and much sought-after developments: it is becoming positively desirable.

Bustling **Bethnal Green Rd** has a street market, a fantastic Italian café and a Tesco Metro, but a short stroll to the S is another contrast in **Derbyshire St** where delightful 2- and 3-storey Victorian terraced houses fringe the green space of Weavers Fields. In **Wilmot St**, opposite Hague Primary School, is the Waterlow estate, a 1980s Barratt development of a large Victorian terrace converted to studio, 1- and 2-bedroom flats. This has around 400 homes including some sheltered homes. At the bottom of **Wilmot St**, in **Three Colts Lane**, is Bethnal Green station (one stop to Liverpool St).

East along **Bethnal Green Rd**, at the junction with **Punderson's Gardens** and almost opposite the old Bethnal Green police station, is the City View development. This converted bakery now holds 110 flats, while the old police station is currently being redeveloped into 2- and 3-bed flats. **Paradise Row**, where **Bethnal Green Rd** meets **Cambridge Heath Rd**, lives up to its name, with 3- and 4-storey Georgian terraced houses. At the end of **Birkbeck St** off **Cambridge Heath Rd**, a converted factory is one of the newest developments in the area: Sunlight Square now holds 1-, 2- and 3-bed flats.

Shoreditch

Across the busy **Kingsland Rd**, the old Roman road due N out of the City, Shoreditch has reinvented itself as 'The Ditch', replete with trendy bars, the new Lux cinema and new-media companies. Most of the action takes place W of **Shoreditch High St** and the **Kingsland Rd**: see City chapter. On the E side of Shoreditch, much of the residential property is council-owned and situated around the Boundary Estate conservation area, which is the oldest council-built housing in London. It includes **Palissy St**, **Rochelle St**, **Navarre St**, **Calvert Avenue** and **Montclare St**. These streets, containing mostly flats, surround **Arnold Circus** with its bandstand. **Calvert Avenue** leads W to **Shoreditch High St** and Shoreditch Church, surrounded by the picturesque St Leonard's Gardens. North of the Circus is the Mildmay Mission Hospital while **Sclater St**, which has an animal market every Sunday morning, is to the S.

Shoreditch is bordered to the E by the Bethnal Green part of **Brick Lane**, now billed as 'the Portobello of the East': the Truman brewery conversion into artists' and designers' workspaces, together with the rebranding of this Asian community area as 'Bangla Town', is changing the character of the district. The erstwhile run-down tenement flats are being improved steadily. This area is the heart of the Asian garment industry. **Brick Lane** has been home to successive waves of immigrants: a chapel built for protestant Huguenots in the 1740s has been used in succession by Methodists, Jews and now Muslims. Some houses in the street date back to the first decade of the 18th century. Today, it has a thriving restaurant scene attracting City lunchers. Much renovation of council property has taken place recently. The Spitalfields scheme (see City chapter) will clearly have an impact on the neighbourhood.

B

Transport	Tube: Bethnal Green (zone 2, Central), Shoreditch (zone 2, East London line). From Bethnal Green: Oxford Circus 15 min, City 5 min, Heathrow 1 hr 20 min (1 change). Trains: Cambridge Heath, Bethnal Green – trains to Liverpool St, Essex and Herts.
Convenient for	The City, Docklands. Miles from centre: 3.
Schools	Local Authority: Daneford School C of E, Morpeth Secondary School C of E, St Bernards Secondary School RC.

SALES

Flats	S	1B	2B	3B	4B	5B
Average prices	55–63	65–100	75–160	85–165	–	–
Houses	2B	3B	4B	5B	6/7B	8B
Average prices	85–190	110–180+	140–250	–	–	–

RENTAL

Flats	S	1B	2B	3B	4B	5B
Average prices	400–600	560–780	600–1000	700–1500	–	–
Houses	2B	3B	4B	5B	6/7B	8B
Average prices	700–1200	750–1600	900–2000	2000–3000	2600+	–

The properties	Two- and 3-bed terraced houses increasingly available, plus new and ex-council flats. Large houses rare. Increasing: smaller flats and smart, Docklands-style warehouse conversions.
The market	Buy the best as you'll have plenty of competition when selling from all the new developments here and in Docklands. Lack of good schools deters families. Local searches: Tower Hamlets 4 weeks, Hackney 2 weeks.

Among those estate agents active in this area are:
- Land & Co
- Meade
- Alex Neil
- Mitchelson McCarthy
- Winkworth *
- Hamilton Fox
- Keatons

* further details: see advertisers' index on p633

BLOOMSBURY AND KING'S CROSS

Map ref: p140 (3C)
Postal districts: WC1, N1
Boroughs: Camden (Lab), Islington
  (Lab/Lib Dem)
Council tax: Band D Camden £1074,
  Islington £912
Conservation areas: Most of area
Parking: Residents/meters. Clamps

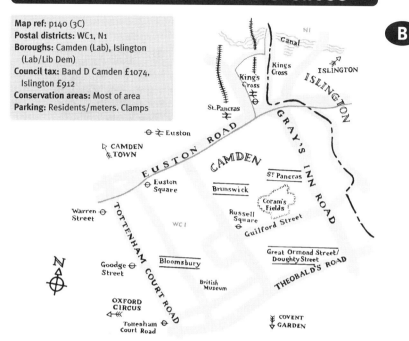

B

In the very heart of London, and once renowned as the home of the literary *beau monde* of the early 20th century, Bloomsbury is the capital's forgotten quarter. The City lies to the E, the West End and theatreland to the SW, all the big rail stations are within a walk or a cab ride, and the British Musuem, London University, British Library and dozens of academic institutions lie scattered around an area with Georgian bone structure and, for so central a location, green and peaceful corners.

But this mixture of academia and offices heavily dilutes the residential component, which is why the area is not well-known as an OK London address. One of Bloomsbury's most striking groups of houses – **Bedford Square**, built in the late-18th century and combining creamy classical stucco façades, Coade stone keystones and other delightful Georgian detailing – is now almost solely used for commercial purposes. If, that is, 'commercial' is the correct term for the polite trades like publishing, lawyering and running think-tanks.

Bloomsbury does not appeal to those international home-buyers who have been programmed only to look at W1, SW1 or SW3 because everywhere else in London is nowhere. (Indeed, such buyers will find the absence of designer dress shops and glossy restaurants unsettling.) For anyone not so concerned with fashionable addresses, and lucky enough to find a home here, it is a great place to live. One big boon is transport links. Bloomsbury is already central; with the St Pancras-Heathrow rail link (target date 2001: see St Pancras, below) it will become still better.

As a glance at its street names shows, Bloomsbury owes its existence to the nobility: the Southampton and Bedford families, to be exact, who developed the area as one of London's first planned suburbs. **Bloomsbury Square**, originally named after

the Earl of Southampton, was laid out in the 1660s, after the restoration of Charles II: alas, none of the houses from that era remain. The Southampton family estates were joined by marriage to those of the Russells, the Dukes of Bedford. Add in the Gower who married the fourth Duke and you have a complete gazetteer of Bloomsbury names.

As well as the British Museum, here since 1755, the University of London now takes up large tracts, and there are several hospitals. The university's buildings form an almost solid block between the **Euston Rd** in the N, **Gower St** in the W, **Woburn Place** in the E and **Russell Square/Montague Place** in the S. Many of the surviving Georgian buildings are still used as offices. Despite the incursions, much of Bloomsbury retains a pre-19th-century air of somewhat dowdy graciousness.

But now, would-be denizens – and developers – are taking a second look. Bloomsbury has received a boost from the revival of Clerkenwell, to the E, and from the inexorable price rises in Mayfair and other Central London residential neighbourhoods. Another boost has been a change of policy by the Bedford Estate, still Bloomsbury's largest landowner. They are starting to return buildings to use as homes after decades as offices. The other big owner of homes here is Camden council, which steadily built up its stock of homes, both new-built and existing, during the years when parts of Bloomsbury were declining in status and a few corners were virtual slums.

King's Cross, Bloomsbury's northern neighbour, could be the site of London's biggest single redevelopment scheme, or it could be left to moulder on. Meanwhile, it has some enviable houses in rather edgy surroundings.

The most common dwelling in Bloomsbury is the flat, with houses an almost impossible luxury. Studios, 1- and 2-bed are easily obtainable either in purpose-built blocks (mostly from the 1930s) or as new conversions, and 3-bed flats are becoming more common in new developments.

The area, for our purposes, is bounded by **Tottenham Court Rd** in the W, the **Farringdon Rd** in the E, **Theobalds Rd** and **New Oxford St** in the S and the **Euston Rd** to the N. This is a larger area than 'traditional' Bloomsbury, taking in streets which are allied to, but not quite part of, the old estate.

Bloomsbury can be divided into four distinct neighbourhoods: St Pancras in the NE, Great Ormond St/Doughty St to the SE, and Brunswick and Bloomsbury to the W. These four neighbourhoods radiate out from Brunswick Square and Russell Square, which lie together in the middle of the area. The SW quadrant, towards Bedford Square, is the most expensive, with the NE, towards King's Cross, the cheapest.

Great Ormond St/Doughty St

Sheltering between the busy main routes of **Southampton Row, Guildford St, Theobalds Rd** and the **Gray's Inn Rd** is a lovely quiet part of London with wide pedestrian-only streets and an abundance of patisseries, cafés and small shops. **Guildford St** is only partly Georgian: 1960s hospital and college buildings replace some of the originals, with an abundance of small hotels at the E end. **Doughty St**, which runs S from **Guildford St**, is most famous for once housing Dickens at No 48. But now the street has few private residents – although the lucky ones have 3- and 4-storey Georgian buildings with attics, mosaic steps and large portals for porches: they pay upwards of £1 million for a house. **John St** is a continuation of **Doughty St** to the S with similar houses, though many are offices.

Also running S, to the W of **Doughty St**, is **Doughty Mews**, which has a number of small houses with roof gardens above garages and a cobbled road. There is also a '30s block of flats at the junction with **Roger St** called Mytre Court, which is in very good condition and overlooking a primary school. There are a number of other mews in the neighbourhood, but they are used mostly for commercial purposes.

Millman St runs S from **Guildford St**, and has a row of modern maisonettes opposite some converted flats in Victorian 3-storey houses. This runs into **Rugby St** which combines shops and offices with very ornate, terraced 4-storey Victorian houses converted into flats. **Lambs Conduit St**, which is partly pedestrianized, is the centrepiece of the area with some good pubs and restaurants. There is a new block of flats above the shops at the N end. This links with a conversion of several houses on the corner into flats. In 1997 14 new flats were marketed here. Last winter a 3-bed, 2-bath flat was £300,000, while a 1-bed in a 1930s block was £105,000. The remaining property is shops with often spacious flats above. **Dombey St** leads W off **Lambs Conduit St** with houses built in 1884 and quiet courtyards at the back.

Orde Hall St, running N from **Dombey St**, again has 19th-century 3/4-storey sand-coloured houses decorated with red-brick. These have now been converted into flats. **Orde Hall** runs into **Great Ormond St**, which splits the area roughly in half. The W part of this has the hospital, but there are still some 18th-century houses scattered either side, with flats at the E end.

Holborn

South of **Theobalds Rd** and E of Kingsway, the Holborn district has a few homes dotted among the shops, offices and lawyers' chambers. Holborn was once a borough in its own right, London's smallest. **Red Lion Square** has some surviving 17th-century houses. They were built when the square was laid out in 1684, despite the violent opposition of the Gray's Inn lawyers, who resented the loss of their view. After a pitched battle, won by the builders, work went ahead. A careful look S and E from here, towards **High Holborn**, will reveal some superbly central homes, mostly flats above shops. The beautiful Georgian houses of **Bedford Row** are nearly all offices. There are signs of life in this neighbourhood, with a dozen new flats in **Red Lion St** to add to the 1930s mansion blocks.

St Pancras

Like Holborn, St Pancras was once a borough, and its town hall stands in **Judd St**. It is best known for its station, and for the new British Library building next door to it. The astonishing architecture of the hotel attached to the station could come into its own again if Manhattan Lofts proceed with their plans to convert the upper floors to homes. These could be some of the best-placed flats in Central London if (another if) the fast rail link to Heathrow opens as planned in 2001. The new service could in the future be extended to link up with Thameslink 2000 (see Transport chapter).

B

Judd St forms the border of St Pancras in the W, and **Guildford St** in the S. A lot of the N part, around **Cromer St** and **Argyle Walk**, has old council-built housing from the turn-of-the-century, but with wide open courtyards often decorated with small trees, plants and bright wall paintings.

Judd St runs S from **Euston Rd**, and has some flats above shops and three large blocks of private flats (studios around £80,000). Continuing S into **Hunter St** there is another large block of 63 apartments (1930s). The best homes in this corner are in the S and W: there are some lovely 3-storey houses on quiet, tree-lined **Mecklenburgh Square**. A Georgian house in the square was on the market for £825,000 last winter. However, a few have been converted into flats (including a 10-flat scheme in late 1997) and there is a purpose-built block, also on the square, facing the open space of Coram's Fields. Coram was a philanthropist who left the land to charity: the Fields are now a playground with animals, including sheep, for the delight of local children. Just to the N of **Mecklenburg Square** in **Heathcote St** there are also some pleasant neo-Georgian flats.

Crossing the **Gray's Inn Rd** E into **Calthorpe St,** there are flats in large 4-storey Georgian houses. The street was almost entirely scruffy a few years back but the number of derelict and poorly kept properties is now much smaller. Flats in some newly revived buildings went on the market last winter at prices from £255,000 for 2-bed. The adjacent **Wren St** has a number of smaller 2-storey houses with white façades and basements.

To the S **Gough St** has some new flats; and in Green Yard Mews some smartly designed new flats in that very 1999 colour turquoise. On the mostly commercial **Gray's Inn Rd** is an 8-storey purpose-built Mediterranean-looking block of flats, which lies incongruously in its surroundings.

Brunswick

The Brunswick neighbourhood, to the W of St Pancras, is arranged around the busy crossroads at **Tavistock Place** and **Marchmont St**, which run W-E and N-S respectively. There are a number of small bookshops, an art gallery, grocers, barbers and so on at this junction and on down **Marchmont St**, with flats above the shops: a characterful corner with a community feel.

Leigh St runs W-E out of **Marchmont St** and again has a number of converted flats in 3-storey buildings above bookshops, hardware stores and restaurants, with a modern development of flats and shops on the corner. **Thanet St** and **Sandwich St**, which run N from **Leigh St**, have some small 2-bed houses, and there is a large block of flats on the corner of **Hastings St** and **Thanet St**. **Leigh St** leads into the elegant crescent of **Cartwright Gardens** which features tennis courts surrounded by (mostly rented) flats and hotels.

In the S the Brunswick Centre dominates; built around 1970 in a striking stepped pattern around a square, this enterprise encompasses flats, shops (including supermarket), offices, a cinema and pubs. It is being refurbished at the moment. There are flats to rent here.

The hotel district is centred here around **Bernard St** and Russell Square tube station, which is served by lifts and gets incredibly busy in the tourist season. There is very little private housing from here S, except occasional flats above shops. However, **Russell Square** itself has seen a series of developments along the southern side – for example, a 1989 refurbishment of Nos 54–56 as a mix of offices and flats. Recently the square has gained further homes with the conversion of an office building at Nos 13–16 into Bloomsbury Mansions: 58 1- to 3-bed flats plus nine low-cost homes. Most have been sold to ex-pats and Asian investors. A mansion flat in **Russell Square** might cost £350,000-plus for 3-bed.

Bloomsbury

Bloomsbury covers the rest of the area, W to **Tottenham Court Rd**. Many of the streets in Bloomsbury have purpose-built blocks consisting of studios, 1-, 2- and 3-bedroom flats. Typical of these blocks, which normally charge service fees ranging from £500–1,000 per annum, are Endsleigh Court on **Woburn Place** (60 per cent studios, 30 per cent 1-bedroom and 10 per cent 2-bedroom flats) and Russell Court (95 per cent studios, 5 per cent 1-bedroom).

But there are a number of flats in converted houses in many of the area's quiet backstreets. Running N off **Store St** is **Ridgmount St**, which has a number of recent flats above garages. These are a development of the Bedford Estate, which is still the ground landlord in this area. Further N, the entire block between **Ridgmount St** and **Huntley St** is a vast mansion block. N again, several of the mansion blocks are council-owned: Gordon Mansions to the E and W of **Huntley St** for example. **Chenies St** also has Camden Council-owned mansion flats. **Store St** has flats over shops. **Chenies Mews** is part residential with a mansion block and the back gardens of **Gower St**. The N end of the mews is light industrial, with hospital and college premises. At the N end of **Huntley St** a row of flat-fronted 3-storey houses have been converted into flats.

Chenies St runs E into **Gower St**. The buildings in this busy road are mostly early 19th-century and are now used as hotels or for commercial or university purposes, with a few rather run-down flats. One of the quieter streets in the neighbourhood is **Gower Mews**, with Gower Mews Mansions, small '30s flats above garages. And to the S of here is **Bedford Square**, which is nearly all commercial – though 19 new flats were created behind an original façade in 1987. **Adeline Place** and **Bedford Avenue**, which run directly off it, have Bedford Court: blocks of well-appointed 1900-vintage flats. Penthouses have been added to these in recent years.

At the S end of the neighbourhood, close to the British Museum, a large mews, Gilbert Place between **Great Russell St** and **Little Russell St** is being converted. Homes will result. In **Coptic St**, just S of the Museum, a 5-bed, 5-storey freehold house was on the market last winter at £730,000.

King's Cross

The vast area of under-used and partly derelict land to the N of King's Cross and St Pancras stations is one of London's great lost opportunities. With the great new British Library open at last, and prosperity on every side, it is waiting in its weed-overgrown siding to join modern London. Instead, the astonishing and ongoing saga of the Channel Tunnel rail link has blighted these 200 acres for a dozen years.

In early 1998, another about turn stopped work on the Channel Tunnel rail link, a line to join London to the European high-speed rail network, and which was to terminate at St Pancras. During the year, the government latched up a deal whereby the line will be built – but in two stages. Stage Two involves the section into London. So yet again the King's Cross area is in limbo: see Transport chapter for more details.

The rail scheme will unlock the whole area for development – if it happens. As it is, we must wait to see what will happen to a tract of land that reaches in the N right up to Camden Town. Don't hold your breath, or trust your searches.

King's Cross, as it stands at the moment, is a blend of commercial and small business premises, with a scattering of residential property to the E of **York Way**. It has its problems with crime, but a new police station and video surveillance have had a positive impact.

There are some delightful roads in the neighbourhood, including **Swinton St** in the S and quiet backwaters like **Keystone Crescent** and **Balfe St** off the **Caledonian Rd**. Their greatest advantage is of course their extraordinary convenience. Apart from King's Cross, St Pancras is next door, Euston station down the road. You can stroll to the City. King's Cross also runs Oxford Circus a close second as the single most useful tube station on the entire network: the Northern, the splendid Victoria, the Circle, the Piccadilly (direct to Heathrow) and even the Hammersmith & City lines pass through here. The new King's Cross Thameslink station provides further options: S to the City and Gatwick, N to Luton and Bedford.

Across the Grand Union Canal which acts as the northern boundary lie the select realms of Barnsbury and Islington. The other boundaries are formed by **St Pancras Rd** to the W and **Calshot St** to the E. The southernmost part infringes the Borough of Camden ending at **Argyle St** and **Swinton St**.

Beware of the rail plans, which have on several occasions blighted whole streets in this district, with homes bought up by the developers, only for the plans to be abandoned and the homes resold. Both the Channel Tunnel link and Thameslink 2000 converge here, so careful searches are vital if planning a purchase.

Because the council is reluctant (unlike Hackney) to stop developers from splitting up houses into 2-bedroom units, anything like a 3-bedroom flat or 4-bedroom house is now extremely rare and hard to find. But 2-bedroom houses and small flats predominate with new conversions constantly under way. To spot them in time, though, requires a careful watching brief. Not many estate agents at any given time have properties on their books in King's Cross because of the shortage of private houses and flats. However, ex-council homes are sold at significant discounts to comparable 'private' prices.

The best houses tend to be in small, secluded groups and can surprise with the quality of their architecture. **Northdown St** has little flat-fronted Victorian houses and modern replicas. **Balfe St's** 3-storey houses have been well converted into 1-bed flats behind the early Victorian façade. This street also has some modern homes. **Keystone Crescent's** curve is echoed in the rounded windows of its pretty 2-storey houses: one was on the market for £450,000 last winter. These streets apart, most of the King's Cross station hinterland combines flats above shops, commercial property and council flats like the Derby Lodge estate on **Britannia St**.

The **Caledonian Rd** runs SW to King's Cross and splits the area into two, with most of the residential property on the SE side. The road has a number of converted flats and flats above shops – almost exclusively studios and 1-bed – with many in a poor state of repair. However, there are signs of revival with new businesses appearing.

The southern part of **Northdown Rd** runs S from the **Caledonian Rd** and features a major development of mostly 1-bed flats with original façade intact. And the northern part over the **Caledonian Rd** has 2-bed houses dating from 1845. This is probably one of the nicest streets in the area. **Balfe St** runs S from **Wharfdale Rd** and is similar to **Northdown Rd** with modernized flats and some small houses.

Other areas of small 2-bed houses include those of **Southern St**. There is a recent 14-flat conversion on the **King's Cross Rd** by Tilbury and a number of 3-storey Victorian houses clustered at the bottom end of **Wicklow St**, which look to be in good condition. Nearby **Swinton St** has some 5-bed houses: one was on the market for £375,000 last winter. **Leeke St** in this corner has some new bars.

There is also a new mixed commercial and residential development across the canal at **Thornhill Bridge Wharf** (see also Islington chapter) which epitomizes the new breed moving into the area – young couples without children. **New Wharf Rd** is dominated by the recently built Ice Wharf, which has nearly 100 1- to 4-bed flats due for completion this spring. Look along **All Saints Rd** for other similar schemes. Other schemes are under way or planned along the canal, including the re-use of some canal buildings such as a pumping station. The northern part of the **Gray's Inn Rd** is mostly commercial with a few flats above offices. But the area bounded by **Argyle St, Gray's Inn Rd** and **Euston Rd** is dominated by the Birkenhead Estate which is a complex of seven 1960s blocks. The remaining property is a mixture of private 3-storey Victorian houses (some split into flats), bed-and-breakfast establishments and private hotels. This is the place for lower prices. In **Penton Rise**, on the E edge of the area, there are plans to convert some old college buildings into homes and a hotel.

B

Transport	Tubes, all zone 1: King's Cross (Victoria, Piccadilly, Northern, Hammersmith & City, Circle), Russell Square (Piccadilly), others see map. From King's Cross: Oxford Circus 8 min, City 15 min, Heathrow 1 hr 10 min. Rail: King's Cross, St Pancras, Euston. To come: a fast link from St Pancras to Heathrow, due 2001.
Convenient for	Everywhere: British Museum, British Library, City, West End. Miles from centre: 1.5.
Schools	Camden School for Girls, Jewish Free School, University College School.

SALES

Flats	S	1B	2B	3B	4B	5B
Average prices	60–80	95–200	130–300	175–250+	—	—

Houses	2B	3B	4B	5B	6/7B	8B
Average prices	125–260+	150–300+	350+	—	—	—

RENTAL

Flats	S	1B	2B	3B	4B	5B
Average prices	500–865+	650–1400	950–2600	1750+	2000+	—

Houses	2B	3B	4B	5B	6/7B	8B
Average prices	1750+	2500+	4000	4500	—	—

The properties	Many of Bloomsbury's Georgian and early Victorian houses have now been converted into offices. Flats, however, abound in mansion, '30s or more recent blocks. King's Cross has some surprising corners of handsome Victoriana. King's Cross/St Pancras redevelopment will boost the area as a whole if it happens, but can blight nearest streets.
The market	Young, single people, couples without children and business-men find homes here to buy or rent from student-poor to quiet luxury. King's Cross is the cheaper end of the scale, and scene of much development. Local searches: Islington 2 weeks, Camden 2 weeks.

Among those estate agents active in this area are:
- Copping Joyce
- Winkworth *
- Barnard Marcus
- Property Bureau
- Banbury & Ball
- Frank Harris & Co
- Hurford Salvi Carr

further details: see advertisers' index on p633

BOW

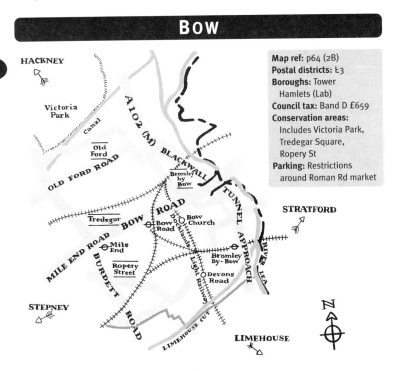

HACKNEY

Victoria Park

canal

A 102 (M)

Old Ford

OLD FORD ROAD

BLACKWALL

Bromley by Bow

TREDEGAR

BOW ROAD

Bow Church

Bow Road

Mile End

MILE END ROAD

BURDETT ROAD

Ropery Street

TUNNEL APPROACH

STRATFORD

Bromley By-Bow

Devons Road

Light Railway

RIVER LEA

STEPNEY

ROAD

LIMEHOUSE CUT

LIMEHOUSE

N

Map ref: p64 (2B)
Postal districts: E3
Boroughs: Tower Hamlets (Lab)
Council tax: Band D £659
Conservation areas: Includes Victoria Park, Tredegar Square, Ropery St
Parking: Restrictions around Roman Rd market

Bow's Victoria Park and Tredegar Square have been well-known for some years as places where fine houses can be bought for a lot less than their counterparts in smarter corners of London. Worries about job security in the City slowed price rises last winter after an upward move averaging 40 per cent since 1996.

The last dozen years have seen a veritable boom in the provision of new homes at the cheaper end of the scale, cementing this East End heartland's status as a residential area attracting locals to owner-occupation as well as 'refugees' from other, pricier, areas of London. The Bow Quarter, the grand re-naming and redeveloping of the giant Victorian Bryant & May match factory, has added 700 homes to the local stock. Hundreds of existing council-owned homes have been renovated and quite a few are for sale: £50–65,000 buys a 2-bed flat. The new developments have included homes with workspace attached, and a good sprinkling of their '90s cousins, the loft apartment.

The demolition of slums – artist Rachel Whiteread's 'house' sculpture was the cast of an old terraced house, the last in its row to be pulled down – is a good symbol of the modern East End. The artistic/professional classes are infiltrating previously working-class space. The Chisenhale Gallery and the new Bow Wharf development, including bars and comedy club, are symptomatic. The attitude to living here has changed from feeling proud and different to its being a sensible investment option. Bow has moved onto the conventional property ladder.

Bow has always been the tidier end of the East End, but is still a widely varying mixture of gaunt council towers, ostentatious Victorian terraces, industry, railway tracks and street markets. Residential property in Bow is not grouped in tidy neighbourhoods, it is scattered in pockets between all the other things jostling for space in this crowded corner. Typical Inner London, in fact. However, green space has been brought into the area with the new linear Mile End Park running down from Victoria Park along the canal. Lottery money to the tune of £25 million is being spent here, which could put Mile End on the map at last. Transport is fairly good, with Central, District and Hammersmith & City line tubes and the DLR for the rapidly growing north-south traffic: Bow, like much of the rest of Tower Hamlets, is benefiting from its new role as hinterland to Docklands.

Bow, as described here, is essentially the E3 postal district, but the name is used rather sporadically. People who live in the Tredegar conservation area are proud to say so, others nearby talk of living in Mile End. Victoria Park is a prestigious name attached to streets in the N of the area and it adds a premium to house prices, while in the S, along Limehouse Cut, new canalside developments annex the name Limehouse, made smart by Docklands. Of the old village of Bow, a crossing place over the River Lea, virtually nothing survives except the name. Just to confuse, there is a corner called Bromley-by-Bow, complete with tube station and High St.

The Lea Valley, to the E of Bow, is a sprawling flood-plain covered by industry, derelict and extant; gasworks ditto; railways and sundry waterways. This 650-acre tract features in sporadic plans as a place for big new developments. If the Stratford International rail station goes ahead (see Transport chapter) plans could be realized.

Mile End & Tredegar Square

Tredegar Square, N of the busy **Bow Rd** and within a stone's throw of Mile End tube station, is the pride of the East London property market. This delightful Georgian garden square is a conservation area and boasts the area's most impressive – and expensive – houses, some of which have 5- or 6-bedrooms. These can command £300,000-plus. It also boasts seven modern houses. But these, tucked on the corner, don't disrupt the unbroken Georgiana overlooking the central gardens. For one of the smaller, 3-bed originals with all its features intact, a more typical price would be £180,000. Modern 4/5-bed houses come on the market at £320,000.

The square is the centrepiece of a conservation area which includes **Lichfield Rd**, **Alloway Rd**, **Aberavon Rd**, **Rhondda Grove**, **Tredegar Terrace**, **College Terrace** and **Coburn Rd**. Sometimes referred to by estate agents as Mile End village, the area is made even more distinctive by its blue lamp-posts in keeping with the period. In **Coburn St**, Tredegar Villas, a recent development of 2-bed terraced houses, and flats built around a central courtyard, were carefully built in a similar style to neighbouring houses. **Morgan St**, too, has new houses appearing; particularly **Pembroke Mews**, a neo-Georgian development built around a cobbled courtyard with 2- and 3-bed houses. On **Bow Rd** and within the conservation area is Tredegar House, a fine 19th-century brick building that was first a shipbuilder's mansion, then a college and this spring became 20 flats: two 1-bed, 17 2-bed and a penthouse.

At the S end of **Aberavon Rd**, almost opposite the tube, is **Eaton Terrace**, a row of 1980s luxury 4-storey houses with ornamental pillars at each entrance. **Ropery St**, another conservation area, lies S of **Bow Rd** and E of **Burdett Rd**, and has Victorian terraced houses as do **Mossford St**, **Maritime St** and Lockhart St. **Bow Common Lane** leads on down to the Limehouse canal and Poplar. Between the Lane and **Ropery St** a development of terraced houses is under construction by Furlong Homes.

South of Victoria Park

Over the railway line, N of the **Tredegar Square** conservation area, are the popular 2-storey bay-fronted Victorian houses of **Antill Rd**, **Strahan Rd**, **Lyal Rd** and **Medway Rd**. In nearby **Arbery Rd** is the award-winning 1980s development of **School Bell Mews**, a converted school that provides a perfect setting for new flats and houses. A 2-bed galleried flat was for sale here at £150,000 in December. Three-storey Victorian

B

properties, some of which have been converted into flats, in **Old Ford Rd** and **Chisenhale Rd** are made more appealing by backing onto the canal. Nightingale Mews is a recent development of 12 3- and 4-bed houses in **Kenilworth Rd**. In nearby **Haverfield Rd** is one section of Mile End Park which runs beside the canal.

Victoria Park, which divides Bow and Hackney, is one of the largest parks in London. It was laid out in the 1840s and has several lakes as well as the Hertford Union Canal, which runs along the S side. It has a very good lakeside café, and is used for concerts, etc, in the summer. On the S side of the canal is a large, 4-acre site, from **Parnell Rd** in the E to **Gunmakers Lane** in the W. This involved the refurbishing of close on 400 existing council tower block and low-build homes and the building of nearly 500 new housing association homes. **Royal Victor Place** is a 1990 development in **Old Ford Rd**: 1-bed flats command around £90,000. Bow Wharf is a new canalside development which holds both a bar and a branch of Jongleurs comedy club – proof of the changing nature of the area. Off **Parnell Rd** is the optimistically named **Hampstead Walk**, with 3-bed 1994-vintage terrace houses. Empire Wharf is another new flat block with park and canal views: 2-bed flats are priced £125–135,000.

The canal runs along Victoria Park's S border to **Cadogan Terrace**. Three-storey Victorian properties in **Cadogan Terrace**, overlooking the park, command a premium (4-bed houses c. £320,000) although parking can be a problem. The busy A102M motorway is just behind. **Morville St**, off **Tredegar Rd**, is the site for 69 new flats for rent, being developed by Wimpey and the Tower Hamlets Action Trust. The Hermitage, a 1989 development of flats and houses in **Wrexham Rd**, is appealing despite being near the motorway which leads to Blackwall Tunnel to the S. **Brymay Close**, one of the Hermitage streets, is named after the old Bryant & May match factory nearby.

The factory itself, now known as the Bow Quarter, has been cleverly converted and extended into 730 flats around landscaped, fountain-filled squares. It boasts swimming pools and a sports complex, The Powerhouse has a bar, shop, video library and a laundry. This extraordinary old factory is vast, stretching back over 6 acres from **Fairfield Rd**. It has created its own environment, and given a considerable boost to the area. About half the homes are rented, often through the on-site agency owned by the leaseholders. Sale prices vary with size and position: a 2-bed flat was on the market for £115,000 this spring. Also in **Fairfield Rd** is a 1980s development of 12 2/4-bedroom houses. Red-brick bay-fronted houses in **Baldock St**, **Ridgdale St** and **Jebb St** lead to Grove Hall Park with its children's playground and football pitch. Alongside the park, a new development of flats is appearing in **Baldock St**.

Along **Bow Rd**, which is part of the main route E to Stratford, there are some handsome early Victorian and Georgian houses. A conversion of an existing building has produced 200 flats close to the town hall – and opposite the Bow Bells pub.

Bow Church

Bow police station, which has stables for horses, is on the opposite side of **Bow Rd** to the **Tomlin's Grove** conservation area where steps lead up to the 2-storey Victorian houses, some with attic rooms. The DLR station of Bow Church stands on the corner of **Campbell Rd**, part of which falls within the conservation area.

South of the railway line is the Lincoln Estate which includes council-built flats and houses in **Rounton Rd**, part of **Campbell Rd**, **Devons Rd**, **Blackthorne St**, **Whitethorn St**, **Tidey St**, **Bow Common Lane**, **Fern St** and **Swaton**, **Spanby**, **Fairfoot** and **Knapp Rds**. These are some of Bow's less desirable properties, as well as the Coventry Cross council estate. This estate includes **Devas St**, **Brickfield Rd**, **Empson St** and **St Leonard's St**. A large tract of land beside the DLR between the Limehouse Cut and **Devons Rd** is designated for Housing Association homes. There have been some good conversions of Victorian homes in **Devons Rd** among others. The canal is the focus for several work-home schemes, including Enterprise Works, in **Hawgood St**, a scheme where houses and flats include their own workspaces. Off **Hawgood St** is **Alphabet Square**, a development of industrial-looking flats.

Between the Blackwall Tunnel approach road and River Lea is Bow's fifth conservation area, situated in **Three Mills Lane** behind the Tesco's supermarket. Here there are facilities for weight training, floodlight football and fishing on the River Lea towpaths.

B

Transport	Tubes: Mile End (zone 2, Central, Hammersmith & City, District); Bow Rd, Bromley-by-Bow (zone 3, Hammersmith & City, District). From Mile End: Oxford Circus 20 min, City 10 min, Heathrow 75 min (1 change). DLR: links to Stratford, Tower, Isle of Dogs, Bank – and Greenwich & Lewisham by 2000.
Convenient for	City, Docklands, East Cross Route and Blackwall Tunnel. Miles from centre: 4.5.
Schools	Local Authority: Central Foundation Girls, St Paul's Way, Bow Boys.

SALES

Flats	S	1B	2B	3B	4B	5B
Average prices	35–100	40–115	50–130+	75–180	–	–
Houses	2B	3B	4B	5B	6/7B	8B
Average prices	100–160	115–250	125–300+	→	–	–

RENTAL

Flats	S	1B	2B	3B	4B	5B
Average prices	400–600	560–780	600–1000	700–1500	–	–
Houses	2B	3B	4B	5B	6/7B	8B
Average prices	700–1200	750–1600	900–2000	2000–3000	2600+	–

The properties	Bow's Georgian glories, among the many 2/3-bed terraced houses, have long since been rediscovered. Tredegar, Coborn, Rhondda, Chisenhale, Campbell are names to watch for. Old housing stock is now much improved and untouched property harder to find. Several new and recent developments; the 700-home Bow Quarter is an example of conversion at its best.
The market	Owner-occupation is higher than other parts of Tower Hamlets, and rising in this increasingly popular East End heartland. Best properties are mainly N of Bow Rd, especially the Roman Rd to Victoria Park stretch and new-build. Local searches: 4 weeks.

Among those estate agents active in this area are:
- Alex Neil
- Land & Co
- Mitchelson McCarthy
- Winkworth *
- W J Meade
- LMD
- Look Property Services
- Keatons
- Strutt and Parkers *

* *further details: see advertisers' index on p633*

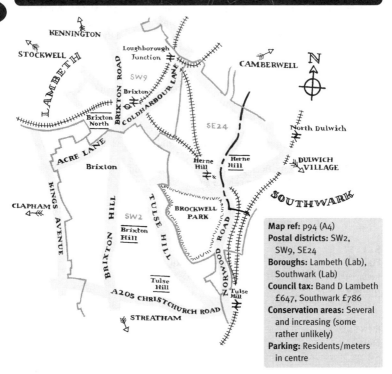

BRIXTON, HERNE HILL AND TULSE HILL

Map ref: p94 (A4)
Postal districts: SW2,
  SW9, SE24
Boroughs: Lambeth (Lab),
  Southwark (Lab)
Council tax: Band D Lambeth
  £647, Southwark £786
Conservation areas: Several
  and increasing (some
  rather unlikely)
Parking: Residents/meters
  in centre

Brixton is shaping up to be the nearest thing London has to the downtown districts of an American city – with all that implies. Fast-changing, a crucible of new ideas and a magnet for the young and unconventional, its social mix strikes the staid as explosive. But for others it works: for a lot of people, Brixton is liberated London.

At some unnoticed point in the last three years the media began thinking first of Brixton's vibrant social scene and good-value homes and only second of its erstwhile bad character. Brixton spent the 1980s as one of London's most notorious, and misunderstood, neighbourhoods. Everyone had heard of it, usually for the same reason: trouble. Few who judged it had been there. And you do need to visit Brixton, to spend time there, get to know it, before you buy or rent. Fascinating it may be, but – some fringe neighbourhoods apart – polite it ain't. Not everyone is a Brixton person.

Brixton today is on the upswing, with a new generation of young home-buyers adding to the cosmopolitan mix, and a born-again local council which is making a real difference. It remains wholly urban, sometimes abrasive, in places grimy, in a few places threatening. It offers an endlessly imaginative street scene, which even during its current night-life renaissance still manages to be busier at midday than midnight (no mean feat in Brixton), the integration of several strong, self-contained communities at street level, and the feeling that, even after the last 20 years of rapid change, it remains an oasis of essential difference in a grey, sprawling, patchily gentrified South London.

Brixton has always led a melodramatic, larger-than-life existence. Not content to be a workaday South London suburb, like its neighbours Clapham and Camberwell, it has undergone a series of booms and busts, a succession of rags-to-riches-and-rags-again swings of fortune. It is restless, transient, yet a real community. Indeed a truly urban place, Brixton. Here, no-one pretends they are living in the country.

At the start of the 20th century Brixton was a fashionable place to live and to shop. Its department stores and markets drew people from all over South London. Many large houses had been built in the 19th century, though few survived the pincer attacks of the German bombers and the 1960s council planners. Between the wars Brixton began to decline, becoming an area of seedy flats and lodging houses. It had, and still has, its streets of little Victorian terraces as well as the grander – some are Georgian – homes. But the big houses suffered as the City commuters, who had once favoured Brixton for its transport links, moved out to the green new suburbs. Their place was taken by a transient population; the latest and most permanent (and noticeable) wave being the West Indian immigrants of the '50s and '60s. Melodrama reasserted itself in Brixton once more as street life, local politics and rhetoric took on a distinctly Caribbean tone. Many of the West Indian families settled down in Brixton, and the third generation of black Londoners is now raising the fourth.

Things got pretty low in the early '80s, with well-publicized riots, a theatrically entertaining, well-meaning but inept council and heated words (and deeds) between locals and the police. Lambeth Town Hall has seen more rows over the last 20 years than Brixton's inhabitants could muster, singularly or collectively. All too often, the council showed the kind of local government and leadership which has caused its citizens varying degrees of hardship. In such unhappy times, not even the lure of the Victoria line tube, which had once more made Brixton a good commute from the centre, did much to help.

If the story of the '80s was of bristling confrontation, then in the '90s the typical Brixton renaissance has followed closely behind. While the council urged that more money must be spent, with a typical twist of irony it was the movement of young people into the area, not Whitehall mega-bucks, that really made the difference. The government-led £187 million Brixton Challenge ran from 1993 to 1998. All too soon the grand plans faltered. Delays both inside and outside Lambeth Council got the project off to a late start, and while some of the flagship schemes were eventually completed, albeit late, many quietly dropped off the end of the schedule never to be heard of again; as deadlines were missed, part of the money was forfeited and had to be returned.

Meanwhile, clubs and bars were opening, young and clever people were remaking Brixton the way they wanted it. The area is now a key point on the London music and fashion circuits. While

Brixton's most prosperous period was the mid-Victorian, when houses of all sizes were built, many with interesting detailing such as this elaborate porch and balcony. The carved leaves are typical. Stone or brick in contrasting colours was used for details, with stock brick and/or stucco for the walls themselves, the whole under a slate roof behind, in this street, a large gable.

bold plans like that to redevelop Brixton tube station into a shopping mall have resolutely failed to materialize, successes include the new, improved 5-screen Ritzy cinema and venues like The Fridge bar and nightclub, the Brixton Academy and the Loughborough Hotel.

The current council administration is a big change for the better, showing great zeal in pursuing those who dodge paying rent or council tax, ignore their parking fines, defraud the council or drop crisp packets. It is determined to improve life in Lambeth, and could bring the first effective leadership Brixton has had in a generation.

But a crucial component in the Brixton revival is its steady discovery by home-buyers. The 1970s saw a wave of young, radical squatters. Many stayed – some even bought their squats. In the 1980s, Brixton was found to be one of the last areas of relatively cheap, unconverted housing in Inner London. The seductive charms of a proper house, with room to move, are not lost on cramped flat-dwellers in more fashionable but less convenient areas. The 1990s saw a new wave of incomers, attracted by lifestyle and the lure of a young, lively population. School and factory conversions added lofts to the local choice. The new Brixtonians find Clapham 'mumsy' and Battersea far too Sloaney (and both too expensive). They dither between Brixton and Hoxton, and aspire to Notting Hill Gate or a Clerkenwell loft.

Despite the collapse of the grand plans to rebuild the shopping centre, Brixton retains the atmosphere of a town. It has a proper centre – not, as with so much of South London, a shapeless grey sprawl. The imposing town hall looks out from the corner of **Acre Lane** and **Brixton Hill** over a wide green triangle, with St Matthews (church turned arts centre/nightclub/restaurant) as its focal point. A new park has been laid out here, linking the centre to the green strip of Rush Common, which runs beside **Brixton Hill**. The triangle's apex points N, to the high street shops of **Brixton Rd** and the famous market. By the station is the leisure centre; there are lots of good sports facilities in the area. And there's the pleasant expanse of Brockwell Park with its outdoor swimming pool, tennis courts and a walled garden.

While plenty of people live in Brixton by choice, it's worth remembering that plenty more do so by necessity, stuck in grim council flats. True, it is a lively and entertaining place: some say that it has become the Left Bank of London. Others fear it is doomed to be forever peripheral, a place for people who can't afford to escape elsewhere.

The image of Brixton as the centre of London's Afro-Caribbean life is true enough, but that is only one side of Brixton's personality. Black people make up less than a third of the residents. Whites are the biggest single group, and there is a growing gay community, but these broad figures conceal a place where everyone is a minority, where there are communities of Chileans and Chinese, City workers and anarchist squatters, artists and – well, every other kind of -ist and -ian.

The Post Office confuses the geography of Brixton. It is often thought that Brixton equals SW2, but a glance at the map shows that Brixton station, and most of the town centre, lies in SW9, while SW2 takes in the positively suburban streets of Streatham Hill as well as grimy **Acre Lane**. Much of **Railton Rd**, the melodramatically named 'Front Line' street where police/black tension was highest a decade ago, is in SE24 – a district known more for the solid respectability of Herne Hill, rubbing shoulders with desirable Dulwich. And chunks of West Brixton stray into SW4, home of the Claphamites.

There are several conservation areas in Brixton protecting districts of outstanding architectural quality, and the number is growing. Properties in these streets command a premium. Examples are Angell Town, Loughborough Park and **Trinity Gardens**. Lambeth is putting great stress on tidying up the town centre, with some success.

Two Lambeth policies have helped boost the residential side of the area. One is residents' parking: many of Brixton streets have long attracted commuter parking. The second is a ban on flat conversions – or rather the insistence on off-street parking if there are to be more than two homes, which is much the same thing. However, residents claim that these two schemes have only partly alleviated parking problems.

The property market became brisk in 1996–97, with a new emphasis on the Clapham side of the area, though it has quietened down since. People move from Clapham, or look here as an alternative, for bigger and better buys. Two-bed flats and 2-, 3- and 4-bed houses, preferably with period features, are popular. The most desirable homes lie just off either side of **Brixton Hill**, handy for the frequent bus services to the town centre, the tube and Central London. There are, however, pockets of interesting houses all over Brixton, though their surroundings can sometimes be on the grim side.

Acre Lane

Acre Lane is a broad, busy street linking the centre of Brixton with Clapham. The neighbourhood to the N, bounded by **Bedford Rd** to the W, **Ferndale Rd** to the N and **Brixton Rd** to the E consists of small 3- and 4-bed houses and larger 3- and 4-storey Victorian ones, many converted into flats. The W side of the neighbourhood, including the W half of **Ferndale Rd**, is in SW4 and used to harbour aspirations to be Clapham until Brixton got more trendy. Indeed, many of these streets are closer to Clapham North tube than they are to Brixton. **Ferndale Rd** is wide and busy; to the N it backs onto a railway line taking the Dover trains into Victoria (and the Eurostar ones to Waterloo) and carrying a lot of freight traffic. Good-sized 3-storey Victorian terraces predominate, getting bigger at the W end, as they do on the parallel **Sandmere Rd**. Prices in **Sandmere Rd** in November last year were around £210,000 for a 5-bed house. Two- and 3-bed flats in a newly refurbished building started at £127,000. The old college building on **Ferndale Rd** has been bought by developer Charles Church for conversion to 1/3-bed flats, due on the market in 1999. **Tintern St** is small 3-bed flat-fronted Victorian terraces, as are **Ducie St**, **Medwin St** and **Allardyce St**. **Ducie St** has Gothic-style houses with pointed-arched doorways and decorative brickwork. The names of **Plato Rd** and **Solon Rd** (not the architecture . . .) have gained this area the tag of Philosophers' Corner. Many houses have been split into two or more flats.

Off **Acre Lane**, the old Victorian Santley Primary School in **Santley St** is being split into lofts, due on the market this April. Alongside, Rialto are to build flats and 3-bed town-houses. Just next door is the showpiece of the neighbourhood, **Trinity Gardens**, a Regency square of 3-bed cottages tucked away behind **Acre Lane** and close to Brixton centre. One sold for £300,000 in 1998. At the Clapham end of **Acre Lane** well-placed former council offices have now been refurbished into smart flats. It's a short step from here to Clapham's answer to Fulham, the well-heeled Abbeville Village . . .

South West Brixton

South of **Acre Lane**, across to **Lyham Rd** in the W, **Brixton Hill** in E and Windmill Gardens to the S lies a mixed area of large Victorian houses, Edwardian maisonettes and inter-war semis. The land rises towards the S, where a preserved windmill stands in a park. Beyond again is Brixton Prison. All this is SW2. It is one of the quietest parts of Brixton. To its W is Clapham Park, and some estate agents have taken to using this name for the **Lyham Rd** corner. **Lyham Rd** branches off **Kings Avenue**. Streets of small Victorian terraces – **Kildoran Rd**, **Margate Rd**, **Mauleverer Rd** – run off to E. Clapham agents have been boosting this area recently. Going S, **Lyham Rd** has council homes on both sides, with the spreading low-rise **Ramilles Close** estate running up to the windmill. **Lyham Rd** then has some pretty flat-fronted brick cottages, followed by the back wall of Brixton Prison, which is less overwhelming than some prisons one could mention. Two-bed cottages here have for the last two years fetched £120–130,000.

South of the prison, **Dumbarton Rd** has 1914-ish purpose-built flats, 2-storey terraces with gables and fancy porches. Some of those in the N side of the road back onto the prison. **Doverfield Rd** has similar flats, while **Felsberg Rd** has more – this time with an arts-and-crafts air. Dumbarton Court, a big block of inter-war flats, runs round onto **Brixton Hill**. **New Park Rd** has a neat parade of shops. This district is quite high up, and some homes in these peaceful, hilly streets have good views across London to the N and W. It is convenient for the buses that run down **Brixton Hill** to the tube station, and for Streatham's shops.

East of **Kings Avenue** in the furthest SW corner of the neighbourhood lie more streets of small 3-bed Victorian terraced houses. **Rosebery Rd**, **Thornbury Rd**, **Wingford Rd** and **Kingswood Rd** are typical of this area of clean, narrow streets full of family housing. There are relatively few conversions here. Nearby Windmill Gardens and the sportsground provide a welcome bit of greenery.

Back down the hill to the N, in the angle between **Brixton Hill** and **Acre Lane**, another grid of streets is almost cut off from those of **Lyham Rd** described above. **Hayter Rd** is typical, with large 3-storey double-fronted Victorian houses, many converted to flats, and eight very large 6-bed-plus 4-storey detached Victorian houses. **Bonham Rd**, **Lambert Rd** and the tree-lined **Haycroft Rd** follow a similar pattern. **Sudbourne Rd** has as its focus one of London's most successful primary schools. This has brought families to the area. **Baytree Rd** in the N is a good example of suburban-type inter-war semi-detached housing, a quiet leafy street yet close to Brixton centre. The Tesco store on **Acre Lane** backs onto some of these houses.

Brixton Hill

The biggest concentration of desirable properties in Brixton lies to the E of **Brixton Hill** around the **Brixton Water Lane** conservation area. In **Josephine Avenue** and **Helix Gardens** (new conservation area), some of the large, handsome, 3-storey Victorian terraced houses have 75-ft of garden frontage. These grandly curving, leafy streets were spaciously planned by the Victorian builders, and they have been the subject of a highly successful community architecture scheme. The long front gardens were reclaimed from the dumped-car-dotted wastelands they had become. New reproduction railings, improved street lighting, car parking spaces – it's all been done and has made a dramatic difference. The houses are 3-storey and quite wide. They make spacious family homes but many are flats. **Josephine Avenue** is known world-wide for No 7, a gay and lesbian guest house.

The nearby loop of **Appach Rd** is made up of small 3-bed Victorian terraces, which sell for around £225,000, with some charming 2-storey double-fronted houses on one side. Many houses in this area have retained their original period features such as marble fireplaces and ornate ceilings and picture rails.

Brixton Water Lane itself is busy, but has some of the area's most charming homes. They include a Georgian farmhouse, a few similar-period cottages – and all with Brockwell Park close by. The enclave of **Brailsford** and **Arlingford Rds** has big Victorian houses, some converted to flats. A quiet corner, and the homes on the E of **Brailsford Rd** back onto the Park.

The area further S, between **Brixton Hill** to the W and **Tulse Hill** to the E, is disputed between the neighbourhoods named for both those roads. **Holmewood Rd**, which runs E from **Brixton Hill**, is a wide road of rather ordinary Victorian terraced brick and stucco houses. But it leads into surprising **Holmewood Gardens**, where the same terraces suddenly open out to surround an irregular green. The road is wide, the effect spacious and cut off. A 4-bed house here sold for £180,000 last winter, while a 3-bed flat would be around £110,000. **Maplestead Rd**, to the E, has similar houses. East of here is covered under Tulse Hill next page.

Upper Tulse Hill winds across these slopes, with its E end in Tulse Hill, while to the W are a mixture of big mid-Victorian detached houses (now flats), 1920s terraced homes and council blocks. Tree-lined **Athlone Rd**, which runs off to the E, has '20s terraced homes, square-bayed. The neat, cared for atmosphere is maintained in **Elm Park** where topiary features in one front garden. **Claverdale Rd** is more Edwardian. Further down **Elm Park** is a mix of Victorian homes of varying sizes, some flat-fronted ones being quite attractive. **Elm Park** meets **Brixton Hill** opposite the prison entrance. On the Hill here is Tudor Close, a large block of '30s flats. Some inter-war houses, such as those in **Mackie Rd**, punctuate the Victoriana. There are several mansion blocks along the length of the Hill, varying in price and status.

B

Somers Rd leads, somewhat unpromisingly, into the unexpected, hidden corner of **Archbishop's Place** with its pretty little early Victorian semi-detached 2-bed cottages. The Place is a cul-de-sac, with a few of the cottages tucked down paths at the end. They sell for around £150,000. **Brading Rd** has more ordinary Victorian houses. **Upper Tulse Hill** nearby, at the junction with **Ostade Rd**, has pairs of pretty early Victorian villas facing mock-Tudor inter-war terraced homes.

Central Brixton

Central Brixton is mostly shops, offices, railways and council-built flats. There are pockets of private housing, though. South of **Coldharbour Lane** to **Morval Rd** and between **Effra Rd** W and **Railton Rd** E are streets of 2- and 3-storey Victorian housing. North of the railway that divides Brixton in two are some streets of 3- to 4-storey Victorian housing between **Dalyell Rd** and busy **Stockwell Rd**. Between **Stockwell Rd** and **Brixton Rd** is a triangle of council homes, with Stockwell to the N. **Brixton Rd** was once lined with solid early Victorian houses, and some still survive, though many are in commercial use. Converted flats in the old houses go for £85–90,000 for 1-bed.

East Brixton

East of the centre are neighbourhoods that have been changed most by Brixton's unruly past. Railways, the Blitz and the council between them have destroyed what were once two smart Victorian suburbs, Loughborough Park and Angell Town. **Loughborough Park**, the road, survives in part, wide and leafy, with pairs of Victorian villas of varying sizes. There is a small park, then a modern low-rise council estate off **Moorland Rd**. Here, too, there are some cream stucco Victorian villas that would be worth a couple of million each in St John's Wood. The giant reversed ziggurat council slab of **Clarewood Walk**, S of **Coldharbour Lane**, makes sense when you realize it was designed to turn its back on an eight-lane highway, planned but never built.

North of the railway, the street pattern is that of the mid-19th-century Angell Town Estate, but most of the buildings are '60s council flats. An exception is the rather grand 1880s complex on **Barrington Rd** that is now the loft apartments of College Green, though it was built as the Brixton Orphanage for Fatherless Girls. Being a Brixton loft development, there is a shared bicycle store. A few Victorian homes survive in **Villa Rd**: a tall, rather run-down terrace. Lambeth Council has restored some more original Angell Town detached double-fronted houses in **St John's Crescent**. **Vassall Rd** in the extreme N of the area has some handsome and expensive early Victorian terraced homes: see Kennington chapter.

Many houses in this part of Brixton are owned by, even if not built by, the council. Lambeth used to hang onto these tenaciously, 'Right to Buy' laws notwithstanding, but recently they have become keen sellers, with vacant homes selling by auction.

Brixton/Herne Hill Borders

Railton Rd had one of the worst reputations in Brixton. At the N end, where it runs into **Atlantic Rd**, it to a large extent deserved it. But further S there is a grid of pleasant streets between **Railton** and **Dulwich Rds**. With the inevitability of estate agents, these roads, each named after a literary giant, have been dubbed the Poets' estate (London has several others such).

Despite its position, Poets' Corner, as the area between **Dulwich Rd** S and **Railton Rd** N is alternatively known, is highly desirable, residents seemingly ignoring its proximity to the once riotous 'front line' of **Railton Rd**. Indeed one could be miles away from trouble of any sort in these tree-lined, well-cared for streets. It is a short walk from the town centre and borders on to Brockwell Park in the S. The Victorian houses were built on spec for letting. They are much sought-after for each one is largely unique – they were purpose-built and architecturally designed – most are detached 3-, 4- and 5-bed houses. A 3-bed one will cost you around £175,000, with 4-bed going for £200,000-plus. **Railton Rd** (3-bed around £130,000) and **Mayall Rd** are 'coming up' according to local agents, but bear in mind that houses on the E side of the latter back onto the railway.

Most of the streets are short and homogeneous, but **Shakespeare** runs on E beyond **Railton Rd** and the railway. This eastern section is scruffier than the traditional 'poet' area but, interestingly, a new series of council-built cul-de-sacs have appeared named after contemporary writers such as **Derek Walcott Close, James Joyce Walk** and **Alice Walker Close**.

Herne Hill and Tulse Hill

South of Brixton are two more areas with subtly different personalities. Their boundaries with Brixton are hard to define, but once in the centres of either Herne Hill or Tulse Hill you will know you are in another place. The bustle of Brixton is lacking, and some streets, especially in Herne Hill, have a solidly suburban feel. Another difference is the lack of a tube. Both places have rail stations on the Thameslink line, with trains to Blackfriars, City Thameslink and King's Cross, and to Victoria. As family areas, they benefit from the clutch of schools, state and private, in nearby Dulwich.

House prices are similar to those in Brixton, though Tulse Hill is less desirable than Herne Hill because of the latter's border with expensive and fashionable Dulwich. Both districts are convenient for Brockwell Park. Large 3-storey Victorian houses are very common, though most are being converted into flats. They are popular because they are spacious and full of character. Two-bed flats find ready first-time buyers, while the young couples who inhabit the smaller 2- and 3-bed houses move on to the roomy 4- and 5-bed houses when the children come along.

The smaller 2- and 3-bed Victorian houses and Edwardian maisonettes are largely concentrated in Tulse Hill, while the larger family housing of 4- and 5-bed-plus is more characteristic of Herne Hill – particularly along **Norwood Rd** facing Brockwell Park and in the streets running directly off **Herne Hill** and **Half Moon Lane**.

Tulse Hill

Along **Tulse Hill**, S from **Brixton Water Lane**, council-built housing gives way to private properties on the E side at **Craignair Rd** and the W side at **Trinity Rise**. Homes are a mixture of inter-war semis, some with mock-Tudor fronts, and smaller 3-bed Victorian houses. The former Dick Shepherd girls' school – it was closed down by Lambeth – has been bought by a developer. The site backs onto Brockwell Park and homes are planned, but in January the council had yet to approve a scheme.

Inter-war semis, selling for £135–150,000, line **Craignair Rd** and **Claverdale Rd**, giving way to small 3-bed Victorian houses at the W end. **Trinity Rise** comprises 4-bed Edwardian houses and inter-war semis, leading to the very desirable **Brockwell Park Gardens**, £175,000 3-bed Victorian terraces overlooking the park. **Deronda Rd, Deerbrook Rd** and **Romola Rd** contain semi-detached Victorian houses with 4-, 5- and 6-bed. Many of these have been converted into flats. Going W, **Upper Tulse Hill** is mostly council-built housing – some of the more attractive in this part of London. Some of these homes, and some on nearby **Tulse Hill**, are starting to come onto the open markets as former tenants sell. Downhill to the S is Tulse Hill station, with a collection of small shops. Opposite runs **Perran Rd** with small 3-bed Victorian terraces; to the W lies West Norwood. The A205/South Circular runs around this southern boundary.

Tulse Hill provides properties with better-sized gardens and a far more suburban feel than further N. It is a good place to look for the distinctive Art Deco-style houses that are seeing an up-turn in their desirability.

Herne Hill

Brockwell Park, a wide sweep of grassy hill surrounding a Victorian mansion, edges Herne Hill to the W. To the NW is the 'poets' district on the borders with Brixton (see Dulwich chapter). A railway line from Herne Hill station N to Loughborough Junction forms a barrier against Brixton. The ground rises to the E of this line, forming a pleasant, hilly quarter of solid red-brick houses between **Herne Hill** and **Milkwood Rd** and the railway. The area consists of predominantly Victorian and Edwardian 3- and 4-bed houses as in **Kestrel Avenue**, **Gubyon Avenue**, **Shardcroft Avenue** and **Woodquest Avenue** and larger double-fronted Victorian and Edwardian houses as in **Rollscourt Avenue** and **Fawnbrake Avenue**. Some are handsome examples of their period, some – thanks to the quite steep hill slopes – have sweeping views, and all are well-placed for the station and shops.

There is a mixture of homes strung along **Herne Hill**, from very large Victorian or Edwardian detached and semi-detached houses, plus some inter-war housing, to mansion blocks. To the N, the area between **Herne Hill Rd** and **Milkwood Rd** has smaller Victorian houses, and merges into Brixton around the multiple railway bridges of Loughborough Junction.

To the E of Herne Hill's central parades of shops around the station, the atmosphere becomes strongly suburban. Off **Half Moon Lane,** on the Dulwich borders and much sought-after, lie **Stradella Rd, Winterbrook Rd** and **Burbage Rd**. They are wide, tree-lined and quiet, predominantly late-Victorian/Edwardian terraced and semi-detached houses with small front gardens and 60-ft back gardens. **Burbage Rd** holds many surprises, with several large period-style detached houses with large gardens and driveways. It is a very popular road because it forms a direct link through to Dulwich Village.

There is a determined attempt on the part of estate agents to disinvent Herne Hill: the area bounded by **Half Moon Lane** to the S, **Herne Hill** to the N and **Red Post Hill** to the E has now been dubbed the 'North Dulwich Triangle', and those searching for a home here should look out for the term in property details. It contains many delightful streets of family housing – a mixture of Victorian, Edwardian and more modern terraced, detached and semi-detached homes. **Holmdene** is a good example, with its wide roadway, trees and hedges and 3-storey Victorian houses, with some modern semi-detacheds at the **Herne Hill** end. The solid Edwardian 3-bed terraced houses in streets like **Elfindale Rd** are popular. Dulwich Mead, off **Half Moon Lane**, is a development of smart 1-, 2- and 3-bed retirement homes.

Beckwith Rd, **Ardbeg Rd** and **Elmwood Rd** are more exclusive and expensive. These streets are even quieter, and stand on the Dulwich border. They have very popular 3-bed Edwardian terraced houses with small garden frontage. They are close to a charming, well-kept public park, Sunray Gardens, with its duck pond, tennis courts and children's play-area.

Back N of **Herne Hill**, on the slopes which lead to the Ruskin Park neighbourhood of Dulwich, **Brantwood Rd** and **Dorchester Drive** are quiet and could be anywhere in suburban London with their '30s-built semis and rose gardens. Becoming increasingly popular are the '20s purpose-built architecturally designed blocks in Dorchester Court. **Milkwood Rd's** southern end is convenient for the station and has small 3-bed Victorian terraces.

To the S of the station, **Norwood Rd** runs down towards Tulse Hill, with Brockwell Park on the W side. Just off **Norwood Rd,** but still well placed for Herne Hill station, lie **Guernsey Grove** and **Harwarden Grove**, next to a small estate of Peabody Trust housing. Mainly small houses and flats on **Guernsey**, 4- to 5-bed houses on **Harwarden**. Both back onto the railway which can be noisy. Facing Brockwell Park along **Norwood Rd** lie large 3-storey double-fronted Victorian houses, some detached, some semi-detached, turning into smaller 3-storey and 2-storey houses nearer to Herne Hill.

Tulse Hill Borders

The area bounded by, but cut off from, **Christchurch Rd** – the busy South Circular – to the N, and **Palace Rd** and its side streets to the S, is very pleasant. The roads stand on the Streatham/Norwood borders and are spacious, tidy and tree-lined. **Palace Rd** is by far the most expensive road in the area, with conversions becoming more widely available in these huge Victorian and Edwardian properties. As single homes, these have 5- or 6-beds: a 6-bed one sold for £365,000 in 1998. **Christchurch Rd** is mainly lined with large 3-storey and 5-storey Victorian houses of 5-bed-plus, most split into flats, though there are some double-fronted 2-storey, 5-bed houses available, and a large council estate in **Coburg Crescent**. The shorter roads between, like **Probyn Rd** and **Perran Rd**, are predominantly smallish 3-bed Victorian terraces. **Lanercost Rd** is the exception to this, having larger 5-bed Victorian houses, many that retain their original internal features.

Transport	Tubes: Brixton (zone 2, Victoria), to Oxford Circus 15 min, City 15 min (1 change), Heathrow 1 hr 10 min (1 change). Trains: Brixton to Victoria 10 min; Herne Hill to Victoria, Blackfriars, Tulse Hill to London Bridge, Blackfriars. Both on Thameslink.
Convenient for	Victoria and West End, City, South Circular, A23/M23 for Gatwick Airport and Brighton. Miles from centre: 3.5.
Schools	Local Authority: St Martins-in-the-Fields (g). Private: Streatham Hill & Clapham High School (g). See also Dulwich chapter.

SALES

Flats	S	1B	2B	3B	4B	5B
Average prices	35–50	35–100	60–140	70–160	—	—
Houses	2B	3B	4B	5B	6/7B	8B
Average prices	80–170	100–220	120–300	→450	200+	—

RENTAL

Flats	S	1B	2B	3B	4B	5B
Average prices	400–550	600–800	750–1000	100–1500	1200–1800	–
Houses	2B	3B	4B	5B	6/7B	8B
Average prices	750+	1000–1500	1300–2000	1500–2100	1800–2500	—

The properties   Wide range in Brixton: rows of Victorian houses, some of real quality. Also lots of council-build – ditto. Flats are mostly conversions; some '30s blocks. Tulse and Herne Hills have Victorian/'30s family homes, often in quiet streets. Three-bed flats converted from roomy Edwardian houses can have larger rooms than p/b 3-bed houses. Lot of council-owned homes have been sold recently.

The market   Fashion and good transport links drive a market in which younger buyers predominate. They also move here to swap flats in pricier areas for roomy houses. Brixton prices are cheaper; gap widens as size increases. Herne/Tulse Hill houses range higher, especially for big houses and near stations, but Clapham overspill has driven Brixton prices up. Local searches: Lambeth 2 weeks, Southwark 3 weeks.

Among those estate agents active in this area are:
- Burnet Ware & Graves
- Galloways
- Halifax Property
- Winkworth *
- Woolwich
- Morgan Berry
- Martin Barry
- Wates
- Creary's
- BWG
- Martin Barry
- Charles Sinclair
- Barnard Marcus

* further details: see advertisers' index on p633

CAMBERWELL

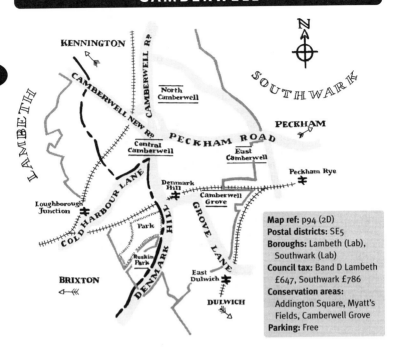

Map ref: p94 (2D)
Postal districts: SE5
Boroughs: Lambeth (Lab),
  Southwark (Lab)
Council tax: Band D Lambeth
  £647, Southwark £786
Conservation areas:
  Addington Square, Myatt's
  Fields, Camberwell Grove
Parking: Free

In a rather crowded corner of South East London you suddenly come across Camberwell Green, clearly a former village centre but now rather more of a traffic island, surrounded by shops. It takes time to get one's bearings around here as every street seems to be called 'Camberwell Something-or-other', but persistence is rewarded with the discovery of some fine and interesting residential corners – some with splendid Georgian houses – tucked amongst the drab streets and dire council buildings. Camberwell is very much a place of enclaves.

Camberwell is where the ground starts to slope up from the flat ground of Walworth and Bermondsey towards the southern heights of Dulwich. This means streets with unexpected views of London. What Camberwell still lacks is a tube. Hopes rise periodically, but there is nothing on the horizon. For now locals make do with traffic jams, the copious buses and Loughborough Junction and Denmark Hill rail stations. The old Denmark Hill ticket office, lovingly restored after fire, now houses the Phoenix & Firkin pub to tempt weary travellers.

The main shopping area is **Denmark Hill** (with **Walworth Rd** not far away). There is a large Safeway supermarket with car park and a Sainsbury's on **Dog Kennel Hill**. A number of lively and colourful bars have appeared in the area; restaurants are few but varied. Parking in Camberwell is restricted to side streets off the main roads and is especially difficult around **Denmark Hill**: a lot of the spaces are taken up by people visiting the local hospitals, King's College and the Maudsley. Because of the teaching hospitals and Camberwell Art School the area is rich in student-rented property.

The contrast between **Camberwell Grove** and **Champion Hill** half a mile to the S of the Green, and the streets to the N, is marked. **Camberwell Grove** has a good number of some of the handsomest Georgian houses S of the Thames. There are

C

leafy, quiet streets of villas of every period from Regency to '30s. And there are some of the nastiest of ex-GLC flats interspersed with some very ordinary late-Victorian terraces of the ubiquitous South London sort.

Camberwell Green, the centre of the area, sits at the junction of **Camberwell Church St**, **Camberwell Rd**, **Denmark Hill** and **Camberwell New Rd**. These busy roads define the various neighbourhoods of Camberwell, which is further divided by two railway lines. The boundary with Brixton to the W is ill-defined, and Camberwell fades into Walworth to the N. On the whole, the SE5 postcode equals Camberwell.

The area's price range is wide. Ex-council flats in walk-up blocks can be £45,000, while a conversion of a Victorian home can yield 2-bed flats around £70,000. A Victorian terraced house in a decent corner can be £170,000-plus, with the Georgian gems rising above half a million. Prices rise when within reach of Oval tube.

Camberwell Grove

The area S and E of the green, on the gentle slopes up towards Herne Hill and Dulwich, was the first to be developed as Camberwell began its expansion from village to suburb. **Camberwell Grove** survives virtually intact as a street of late-Georgian houses. Some, at the N end, date from the 1770s; others further up the street, such as **Grove Crescent**, are early 19th century. Sixteen houses in two stucco terraces at the S end were beautifully restored by Shorham Properties in 1997. Those on the E side, dating from 1845, were split into 35 flats, while the 1830 terrace on the W side became 10 houses, offered at shell finish from £250,000 and complete from £350,000. Flats surface as resales at around £125,000 for a 2-bed flat but house resales have been non-existent. A restored 5-bed Georgian house further N along the Grove was on the market at £545,000 in November. **Letsome St** runs E off the Grove with 1970s council-built flats.

The Georgian atmosphere continues on E into **Grove Park** (a few original homes, but largely lined with particularly peaceful Edwardian houses) and **Grove Lane**. Grove Lane is not as grand as Camberwell Grove, but it does have some lovely early 19th-century houses mixed with just about every 20th-century period. North of **Grove Park,** alongside the railway, Rialto have built 137 homes in **Lynwood Close**, while **Grovelands Close**, off the Grove and also beside the railway, has modern mews-style houses including some 1-bed ones which sell for £75,000.

West of **Grove Lane**, **Champion Hill** and surrounding streets were developed in the 1840s. Some of these elegant villas still survive. The style continues N of the railway and the Maudsley Hospital in **De Crespigny Park**. Back to the S, the Langford Green estate of 1968 is built in a Regency style, and has large town-houses in pleasant stock brick: highly desirable. Off **Champion Hill** itself is Ruskin Park House, a pair of large blocks of '20s mansion flats where a 3 bed flat can be around £90,000.

Ruskin Park

The bulk of King's College Hospital and the E-W railway line form a frontier cutting off the Ruskin Park corner in South Camberwell. The park is the centre of an enclave of 20th-century streets with a strongly but pleasingly suburban feel. A 2-bed flat in good condition above a shop can cost £60–70,000. **Denmark Hill** itself is a busy but pleasant road. To the E are large brick council blocks and further on the **Sunray Avenue** estate of 1920s homes on the borders of Herne Hill, built by the government as part of the post-First World War 'homes fit for heroes' campaign. West of **Denmark Hill**, roads like **Deepdene** and **Sunset**, with their '30s semis not to mention a green-roofed, Spanish-style bungalow slope peacefully down to Ruskin Park. **Ferndene Rd** lines the E side of the park, its 1920s gabled and bay-windowed villas having fine views across it and the rooftops towards Central London.

West of the park, **Finsen Rd** has handsome (c. 1914) terraces looking out over the green park from particularly pretty square-bayed windows. To the N, **Kemerton Rd** and surrounding streets have neat little Victorian cottages.

East Camberwell

Between **Peckham Rd** and the railway line to the S, there are several streets of late-19th-century terraces such as **Bushey Hill Rd**, **Vestry Rd**, **Crofton Rd** and **Shenley Rd**. The 4-bed Victorian houses in this sought-after corner command about £225,000, while some 1990s 4-bed houses in Crofton Rd are around £155,000. **Vestry Mews** has gained some new homes and a number of old houses have been converted into flats. These flats are popular but rarely on the market: when they do come up a 2-bed flat can reach £200,000.

North Camberwell

Most of the area E of **Camberwell Rd** is taken up by large council developments. A few older streets survive, notably around **Addington Square**. The square itself is early 19th- century, its irregular houses of the classic, tall, late-Georgian style plus a pair of low, Regency villas. It is, of course, a conservation area. Nearby is **Rust Square**, a pleasant Victorian corner.

Hopewell St has gained a distinctive new development: where once omnibuses and horses were stabled, Hopewell Yard is now an enclosed corner of flats, maisonettes and offices with central courtyard and basement parking. **Vicarage Grove** has some large Victorian houses. Other streets where private housing remains include **Havil St** and **Ada Rd** with its little flat-fronted cottages. The tower belonging to an old workhouse in Ada Rd was converted into flats in the late 1980s. The old Victorian St Giles Hospital off **St Giles Rd** and **Peckham Rd** is being split into 17 flats, most 2-bed. These will be ready this April at prices around £125,000, though the penthouses are already sold. The developer is Londonwide Properties; the building will be called Peacock House. **Vicarage Grove** has some large Victorian houses.

Georgian houses, some intact (some recently restored) and used as single homes with others flats, line long stretches of both **Camberwell Rd** and **Camberwell New Rd**. The latter leads directly to Vauxhall Bridge, passing the Oval and Vauxhall tubes: Camberwell is very close to Central London. Both roads are busy, however: **Camberwell New Rd** is the route E to Peckham and the A2/Dover Rd. Tucked in the angle of **Langton Rd**, **Vassall Rd** and **Camberwell New Rd** is Salisbury Square, a

1989 mewsy development. Flats in this pleasant and popular enclave command around £155,000. Expect to pay around £260,000 for one of the Georgian houses. South of **Camberwell New Rd**, Camberwell merges with Brixton. There are big council estates but also the conservation area around Myatt's Fields. The houses of the 1890s Minet Estate, in roads such as **Knatchbull Rd**, are attracting interest. A splendid one-off coach house went for £600,000 in 1998, but £300,000 is a more normal price for a 4-bed house. An 1890 semi with 6 bedrooms (and 3 cellars) was £500,000 last November. St Gabriel's Manor, off **Calais St**, is a conversion of an 1899 college into 50 homes. Towards Coldharbour Lane there are cheaper homes in streets such as **Lilford Rd**: a 4-bed Victorian house would be in the region of £225,000, well up on start-of-1998 prices.

Central Camberwell

You could drive through the area's traffic-filled heart every day without discovering Camberwell's most surprising corner. Off **Denmark Hill**, a tiny turning called **Love Walk** is, indeed, a no-through road for cars. At this end traffic can only penetrate, alongside a short terrace, as far as the entrance to a tucked-away group of 3- and 4-storey brick blocks of flats, owned by the Orbit Housing Association. Walk on, and **Love Walk** reveals its surprise. Surprising prices, too: a small 2-storey building went recently for £460,000. On the left is Selbourne Village, a 1982 Wates estate of small cottage houses built with great attention to materials and detailing in the highest flight of village vernacular. It is undoubtedly pleasant, peaceful and a successfully human-scale, well-hidden corner – but an extraordinary stylistic jolt in so urban an environment. Cars can enter from the E end: garages are hidden in groups between the houses. On the other side of the **Love Walk** are older, but equally unlikely homes. First comes a little row of earlier versions of the country cottage, tile-hung, gabled and hidden behind an older wall, reached only through two arched gateways. And further on are splendid, double-fronted small Regency detached houses with garages, which lead out onto **Grove Lane** where some dignified larger Georgian terraces still stand.

Transport	Trains: Loughborough Junction to City Thameslink 12 min; East Dulwich/Denmark Hill to Blackfriars, London Bridge, Charing Cross and Victoria. Nearest tube Oval.
Convenient for	City, Westminster, Dulwich. Miles from centre: 3.
Schools	Local Authority: Archbishop Michael Ramsey C of E, Sacred Heart RC. Close Dulwich (see chapter).

SALES

Flats	S	1B	2B	3B	4B	5B
Average prices	35–55	50–90	70–150	80–170	100+	—
Houses	2B	3B	4B	5B	6/7B	8B
Average prices	95–165	110–200	130–250	175–300+	400+	—

RENTAL

Flats	S	1B	2B	3B	4B	5B
Average prices	350–500	450–600	550–800	750–1200	1000+	1100+
Houses	2B	3B	4B	5B	6/7B	8B
Average prices	600–900	800–1200	1100–1200+	1400–2000	1700+	2000+

The properties
Scruffy main roads conceal pockets of fine Georgiana. Also ordinary terraces and converted flats. New developments appearing, adding town-houses and flats to an area which mixes some of the best and some of the worst of London homes.

The market
Not as well-known as it ought to be, the area has less bustle than Brixton, but nicer houses: unconverted Georgian coveted. Price range dependent on location and architecture as much as size. Local searches: Lambeth 2 weeks, Southwark 2 weeks.

Among those estate agents active in this area are:
- Andrews & Robertson
- Roy Brooks
- Winkworth*
- Hindwoods & White Dent
- Acorn
- Wilson Rogers
- Halifax
- Kinleigh Folkard & Hayward

* further details: see advertisers' index on p633

CAMDEN TOWN AND PRIMROSE HILL

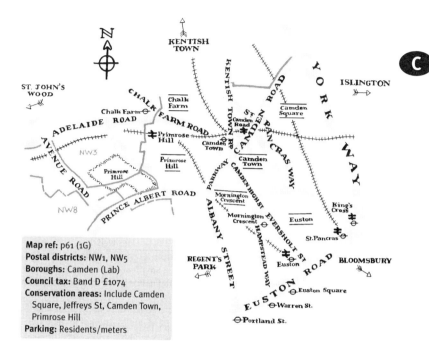

Map ref: p61 (1G)
Postal districts: NW1, NW5
Boroughs: Camden (Lab)
Council tax: Band D £1074
Conservation areas: Include Camden
  Square, Jeffreys St, Camden Town,
  Primrose Hill
Parking: Residents/meters

Camden Town is deliberate: it is not an overwhelmed rural village, like so many London areas, but an attempt at a planned suburb. Sadly for Earl Camden, the freeholder who in 1791 granted leases to build homes on the ancestral cow pastures, the land was in the wrong place. It was successively crossed and split up by the Grand Union Canal and the main railways from the N. These, and linked industry, lowered the tone. In the mid-19th century, though it had some claim to be a professional persons' suburb, it was never a smart one.

Primrose Hill, on the other hand, did establish itself, an enclave of handsome streets with Regent's Park to the S and the 110-acre open space of the Hill to the W. The railway forms a boundary to the N and E. Primrose Hill has been known for handsome houses and spacious converted flats for several decades and is an established alternative to its neighbour to the W, St John's Wood.

Camden Town is still bracketed by railway lines – but this means that it will eventually border not a desolate hinterland of derelict goods yards but the brave new world of the King's Cross (see chapter) development, set to create a virtual new town – eventually. As yet, however, Camden is a highly mixed area. Remnants of its industrial past jostle homes which range from council-build (a high proportion, especially in the S), sturdy Victoriana and modern flats to some award-winning ultra-high tech. This inner-city muddle inspires fierce loyalties among its equally colourful array of inhabitants, who have Regent's Park for a playground.

Camden Town is flanked by its satellite areas of Chalk Farm, Mornington Crescent, Primrose Hill and, to the S, what little housing there is in Euston. Camden residents

C

often have to put up with noisy main roads or the sound of tube or trains; as a result, each road commands a different price. What attracts them to the area, apart from the central location, is the high availability of popular Victorian properties and conversions – new purpose-built flats and maisonettes sell less well here. The narrow-fronted Victorian houses give no more than 1-, possibly 2-bedroomed flats; larger flats tend, therefore, to be maisonettes. The largest and smartest homes are in Primrose Hill, which is (as its prices show) among London's top residential districts, **Gloucester Crescent** and in the Camden Square neighbourhood.

One of the main advantages of the area is that it is so central. Young professionals, and quite a few celebrities, have been moving in, and the traditional inhabitants – Greek and Irish families mainly, and some Italians – moving out. Nevertheless, Camden retains its cosmopolitan atmosphere, with lots of excellent restaurants and specialist food shops. Clubs, pubs and other venues ensure a consistently high proportion of young people. The canalside markets at Camden Lock have been smartened up, as has the **High St**. Camden manages to entice a special kind of tourist: young people from all over the world arrive at the major rail terminals.

Note that Camden the borough covers a much larger area than Camden Town. The present borough adminstration has a strongly anti-car attitude and hopes to cut car use – especially school runs and commuting – by restricting parking spaces and refusing street parking permits to residents who have their own parking spaces.

Buyers should scrutinize searches carefully if they are near the main railway into Euston, which runs between Camden Town and Regent's Park/Primrose Hill, as there are big plans to modernize the line. These could lead to disruption. Look out also for the plans for the St Pancras–Channel Tunnel line, which may never happen (see Transport chapter) but could cause blight.

Camden Town

The heart of Camden Town is a busy road junction with the tube station on its busiest corner. **Camden High St**, running N from **Mornington Crescent**, is Camden's main shopping street, lively and always busy. The best residential area of Camden Town is – perhaps suprisingly – in the narrow strip W of the High St. On the map it looks hemmed in by roads and railways, but the houses are good-period early Victorian and the streets both handsome and interesting. Plans to pedestrianize the **High St** will boost the area.

On **Camden High St** there are flats and maisonettes above the shops in flat-fronted Victorian terraced buildings at the S end, and red-brick mansion blocks near the tube station. **Delancey St**, also busy and wide, is one-way going W towards Regent's Park, and has youthful cafés and shops at the **High St** end, with flats above; thereafter terraces on either side. The narrow, flat-fronted Victorian buildings provide flats, maisonettes and houses, some with gardens. The W end overlooks the main railway line into Euston.

Parkway is a colourful, crowded three-lane street going W towards Regent's Park; a good range of shops and restaurants on either side, the redeveloped Camden Odeon cinema and some terrific bookshops; 1- and 2-bed flats and studios above. **Jamestown Rd**, used as cut-through by traffic, has a recent development of period-style properties and older terraces opposite commercial buildings, providing flats and maisonettes.

Albert St, one of Camden's most attractive and expensive roads, is wide and has elegant and beautifully maintained terraces on both sides, providing large 4-, 5- and 6-bed family houses. In some, basements have been sold off separately. A house here would command around £625,000: more if really smart. **Arlington Rd**, parallel, has a similar middle section with terraced houses (smaller than in Albert) along either side, though prices are lower in this slightly less attractive street. On the corner with **Jamestown Rd**, 16 new flats to a Piers Gough design were mostly sold before completion last winter. There is a large bingo hall and some terraced housing opposite. An office development in **Carlow St** is crowned with 14 penthouse flats, ultra-smart, ultra-modern, with roof terraces. Twelve new houses appeared in **Beatty St** early in the 1990s. At the N end of **Arlington Rd**, after **Delancey St** junction, is council housing on the E side, more large terraced Victorian homes opposite.

Inverness St leads W off **Arlington St** to **Gloucester Crescent**, today reckoned the best address in Camden Town. Some of these big 1840s semi-detached houses are flats, some are enviable whole houses, and there is some later infill. Like the rest of Camden Town, the Crescent failed to cling to the status intended for it, and by the 1960s many of the big villas were split into seedy lodging houses. Playwright Alan Bennett has amusingly described how he and other young people, the first wave of 'gentrifiers', began to buy these houses in the '60s and return them to single homes. You need to be a lot more prosperous than the average young playwright to live there today. Prices in this area have increased quite sharply over the last year, and are now comparable to those of Primrose Hill.

Mornington Terrace is council in the S part; the N part has housing in Victorian terraces on E side only; the W side overlooks the main railway line into Euston. Most are still single houses, both modernized and unmodernized. **Mornington Place** ditto.

In the triangle formed by **Camden High St**, **Hawley Crescent** and **Kentish Town Rd**, small new developments of town-houses and purpose-built flats rub shoulders with the vast GMTV complex and large, ugly commercial and office buildings. In the triangle on the other side of **Kentish Town Rd**, bounded by **Camden St**, is a large Sainsbury's supermarket. On the canal edge of the Sainsbury's site is a real surprise: 10 high-tech houses by architect Nicholas Grimshaw, metal-clad pads with lofty galleried rooms behind vast, electrically operated windows. These award-winning (naturally) homes sold speedily for £260,000 in 1989, but the one on the market last winter was £210,000.

Camden St, the main southbound highway into the West End, has period terracing at the N end providing converted flats and maisonettes; plus mix of old and new council housing. The Greek Orthodox church is on the E side, and the London International School at the end of the W side. **Bayham St** is similar, with heavy traffic southbound, and has small light industrial factories and council housing on E side; shops with flats above in period terracing opposite, and Victorian terraces.

East of **Bayham St** is a relatively quiet, conveniently placed group of streets which form the best place to live in central Camden (**Gloucester Crescent/Albert St** excepted). **Greenland Rd** is a quiet tree-lined street with yellowish-grey brick flat-fronted Victorian terraced houses; these are 3-storeyed, with gardens both front and back, providing 3-bed houses. Some are privately owned, some housing association and some council-assisted, resulting in varying conditions of housing and a good mix of residents. **Carol St**, **St Martin's Close** and **Georgiana St** ditto. **Lyme St** has a pleasant row of early Victorian terraces on the E side overlooking the canal: the S part is best. Both **Lyme** and **Georgiana Sts** are blocked off to traffic which pushes prices up slightly. **Pratt St** only has private housing between **Bayham St** and the **High St**, in flats and maisonettes over shops, and some individual houses. **Plender St**, with a small fruit-and-veg market at its W end is similar, though it also has housing in some purpose-built blocks of flats.

The roads S of **Pratt St** to **Crowndale Rd** are mainly council with the exception of **College Place**, which has large Victorian terraced houses in the northern section only – a mix of modernized and unmodernized family houses, interspersed with owned properties. **Royal College St** (main through road, northbound only) has council housing at its S end; then terraces on both sides, some still single properties, most converted into flats and rooms.

On **Baynes St** a development of mews houses and flats, Reachview, occupies the S side overlooking the canal. Built in 1985, it attracted a lot of interest when new. **Rossendale Way** has conversions in period terrace to right, new mews houses beyond; it overlooks the canal at the rear. At the bottom of **Rossendale Way** is Elm Village, a development of town-houses, flats and maisonettes built in the mid-'80s, where some of the cheaper homes in Camden are to be found. **Rousden St**, a narrow street running up to Camden Rd station (the tracks run on the S side), has a run-down aspect but also some terraces of new town-houses, purpose-built flats, maisonettes and conversions in period houses. **St Pancras Way**, which runs S from **Camden Rd**, is a through road with industrial and commercial buildings.

Camden Town has many houses of mid-Victorian date, which feature sash windows such as this, often with vestigial 'balconies' in wrought iron. The window surrounds, of Classically detailed stucco, form a pleasing contrast to the earlier Georgian small ones, which staged a reappearance late in the century.

Tall Victorian terraced houses reappear on the northern part of **St Pancras Way** and **Royal College St**. **Jeffreys St**, through to **St Pancras Way**, has 3- and 4-storey Victorian terraces on either side with basements, black railings in front and small balconies on first floor. **Prowse Place**, closer to the railway line, has four brick-fronted cottages to the right, and is cobbled. **Ivor St** is a quiet, tree-lined street with brightly painted 2- and 3-storey houses, most in single occupancy, and many recently done up or being renovated. **Bonny St** is very mixed; some period houses offer conversions. A development of town-houses has recently been built, and there is railway-owned housing next to the bridge. In **Jeffreys Place** there are a dozen substantial new town-houses with garages.

To the NE of **St Pancras Way** lie 'the Rochesters', a group of streets tucked in beneath the borders of NW5 and Kentish

Town, which rank next in desirability and price to **Gloucester Crescent/Albert St** and **Camden Square**. **Rochester Rd** is part of an environmental area and a no-through road. It overlooks a small playground area, which lies between **Rochester Rd** and **Rochester Terrace**. Here prices are slightly higher, thanks to S-facing gardens and larger, grander houses. **Rochester Place** is a very narrow street in which are council blocks, small workshops and a school. To the W, **Reed's Place** is a tiny, hidden-away street, blocked off to traffic at both ends. Square, stucco-fronted Victorian houses, most still in single occupation, set the tone; most have pretty front gardens. **Wilmot Place** has substantial pairs of brick and stucco-fronted houses and terrace. **Rochester Mews** has several little, white-painted mews houses in its E section. **Whitcher Place** is low brick-built halls of residence for London University. The remaining 'Rochester' – **Camden Square** – lies across the **Rochester Rd**: see below.

Camden Square

The area on the Kentish borders, bounded by **York Way** to the E, **Camden Rd** to the W and **Agar Grove** to the S, has some good houses in spacious streets and squares, and has become popular as a consequence. It offers prices lower than those of Dartmouth Park (see Kentish Town) or Islington – Barnsbury is not far away across the Caledonian Rd – and agents say it is being considered as a location by those who also look in **Gloucester Crescent/Albert St** and **Primrose Hill.** The bigger 4-storey houses here command around £450,000, while a 1-bed garden flat might be £110–120,000.

Camden Square, where substantial 1850s houses, good-sized flats and maisonettes are to be had in a quiet attractive garden-square setting, establishes the tone. **Camden Rd** is a main road, but the Victorian properties on E side, almost all converted into flats, are well-shaded by trees and set well back. Some garden flats available. **Camden Park Rd**, **Cliff Rd** and **Cliff Villas** are a mix of council blocks, Victorian terraces mostly converted into flats, and mid-Victorian semi-detached cottages, sold as single houses.

North Villas and **South Villas** run N from **Camden Square** and have huge grey-brick villas on both sides. Garden flats are available in deep basements. All these villas are now conversions, providing 1-, 2- and 3-bedroomed flats and maisonettes, **Camden Terrace** likewise. **St Augustines Rd** – pleasant, wide, tree-lined and quiet – has large pairs of villas to either side in varying conditions of repair. Unmodernized examples are still sometimes available; conversions yield garden flats, flats and maisonettes. **Marquis Rd**, **Cantelowes Rd** and **St Paul's Crescent** ditto. **Camden Mews** runs parallel to the square on the NW side: a group of seven new mews houses were added in 1998 to an eclectic mix of styles and sizes (and thus prices). 'It's had every architect you could name playing with them,' observes a local estate agent. The same can be said of **Murray Mews**.

Camden Square itself – an elegant, leafy, subdued square – provides large family houses, especially on the S side, and flats and maisonettes in conversions. **Murray St** has a period terrace at its N end, modern parade of shops on W side with flats above. The narrow 6-ft wide entrance to **Agar Grove** restricts heavy traffic. Stratford Villas, council at S end, thereafter has tall grey-brick and stucco-fronted terraces, up to 5- storeys high, on both sides.

Rochester Square has private homes on two sides; some in pairs of Edwardian-style villas, 2-storey villas with raised ground floors plus semi-basements below, some in Victorian terraces, many also in the process of renovation. **Agar Grove** is a thoroughfare and prices here are 20–25 per cent cheaper than in **Camden Square**: noise from the road is augmented by noise from the railway lines. There is a mix of old and new council blocks on S side particularly, interspersed with modern town-houses and tall Victorian terraces which yield lots of converted flats and maisonettes. **St**

Paul's Crescent, a crescent no longer, leads to a low-level white-painted council estate. On either side are terraces of grey-brick houses, 2-storeys with basements. **St Paul's Mews**, 25 town-houses, dates from 1990. Council housing S of **Agar Grove**.

Chalk Farm

Going N, **Camden High St** holds a lively fruit-and-veg market from Monday to Saturday in **Inverness St** to the left and Saturday market stalls to the right. This one-way street becomes **Chalk Farm Rd** as it reaches the canal and Camden Lock – across which the famous (but rather touristy) weekend market takes place. To the W is The Roundhouse, a remarkable building used as a music/theatre venue. Beyond, on former railway land, is a Safeway food store and housing association flats.

The canalside building known as Gilbey House started life as a distillery and is now 76 flats. Regalian were the developers: they have remodelled the Grade II listed 1890s building and carved a huge, canopied courtyard out of the middle. The actual address is **Jamestown Rd**. **Hartland Rd's** 2-storey brick and stucco-fronted brightly painted late-Georgian terraces provided 3-bedroomed houses on three floors, with small gardens. The railway line runs overhead at the end of the street. No private housing beyond the junction with **Clarence Way**. Similar terraces are found in the N part of **Clarence Way**.

Hadley Street, to the E of the railway line, runs up to the borders of NW5 and Kentish Town. The street is divided in two by road block; the end is a peaceful cul-de-sac of narrow-fronted terraced houses, some Victorian, some built six years ago in original style. The railway line passes overhead on N side; council housing surrounds. The N section of street is pretty, tree-lined and not used by traffic; rows of brick and stucco-fronted 2-storey houses on both sides. Trains using Kentish Town West station pass behind; the street has a prosperous air. **Healing St** likewise, though houses here are slightly grander and taller.

Grafton Crescent, tucked in behind the main road, has large grey-brick and stucco-fronted terraced houses on both sides; many are recently modernized, though original ones can still be found. Homes here are mostly 3-bedroomed, some with gardens. The E end of **Prince of Wales Rd** is a busy, noisy road, but grey-brick and stucco houses, mostly conversions, are set well back. Homes in flats over the shops on **Kentish Town Rd** going N. **Hawley Rd** is a mix of old properties restored into spacious houses and new purpose-built flats, with more being built. Prices are lower here because of extremely heavy traffic.

Chalk Farm 'proper' lies W of **Harmood St**, taking in the area around the tube station. It is a small and highly convenient corner with a good deal of council housing intermingled with homes which borrow some of the aura of Belsize Park and some of the trendiness of Kentish Town.

Most of the homes here are in the huge blocks of mansion flats in **Eton College Rd**, or in small Edwardian villa-type houses in roads off the **Chalk Farm Rd**. The area has seen some modern redevelopment, with new blocks on the **Chalk Farm Rd** and on the corner of **Adelaide Rd**.

The S part of **Queen's Crescent** is worth a look, with pleasant little streets of cottages (3-bed c. £360,000) on the W side, but E of **Malden Rd** the Crescent goes down-hill as a place to live. This part is in NW5 and is debated with Kentish Town. **Prince of Wales Rd**: the N side has large blocks of red-brick council flats; on the S side are terraces of period houses, some in good condition, others run-down. Best terrace of the three is Nos 131–151. A converted school offers loft-style flats at loft-style prices. **Crogsland Rd**, likewise, is council on one side; on the W side, a short terrace of 4-storey houses have been laterally converted into flats. Further along the **Prince of Wales Rd** going E there are terraces of period properties on both sides of the street; some single houses, some maisonettes, some flats. **Harmood St**: rows of low 2-storey Edwardian terraced houses here, very mixed; some done up, some run-down. Chalk Farm bus garage and more council housing towards S part of street. **Clarence Way**, a pretty street, has rows of brick terraced houses similar to **Harmood St**, though the railway bridge for the North London line passes over the middle of the street. **Chalk Farm Rd**, the busy main road, has new developments of purpose-built flats and offices; flats over shops on E side.

Just to the W of the Chalk Farm tube station is **Eton College Rd**, a very pleasant, quiet road which has three huge mansion blocks known as The Etons. Flats in these blocks change hands regularly. A major refurbishment programme went on through the 1990s and is still under way, so service charges are high – but prices, correspondingly, lower than normal. Two-bedroomed flats are selling for around £160–170,000, 1-bedroomed £100,000-plus. A service charge figure of around £2,000 is normal. Some of these flats have problems with short leases and lease extensions.

This end of **Adelaide Rd** is also regarded as part of Chalk Farm. The houses here are large, stucco-fronted terraces, converted into flats, usually geared for first-time buyers. **Adelaide Rd** is busy, and these houses overlook the railway. Flats in modern blocks such as Kings College Court command prices around £145–160,000 for 2-bed.

Primrose Hill

Tucked away between St John's Wood, Regent's Park, Camden Town and Chalk Farm lies a small public park with soaring hilltop views over London. On its eastern slopes is a picturesque and prosperous enclave whose residents – many of whom are writers, photographers, actors and musicians – take great pride in the area. This is more of a family area than the rest of Camden Town.

The 'village' of Primrose Hill is tucked in between the main line railway to the E and the hill to the W. Quiet and secluded (due mainly to traffic controls on through roads), it commands high prices. This is the most coveted part of the neighbourhood, being composed mainly of wide, tree-lined streets and elegant stucco-fronted houses. It boasts a quaint shopping street with a good selection of increasingly smart shops. There are very few small houses to be had: the majority of Primrose Hill housing is 1-and 2-bed flats in converted period houses, and surviving 3/4-bed houses. There is strong demand for property here.

Regent's Park Rd, curving round past the Hill and back to Chalk Farm, forms the W boundary of the 'village' and at its bottom end is a busy thoroughfare for cars and infrequent buses, though its substantial semi-detached stucco homes, some with views over Primrose Hill, many still family houses, are still highly popular. A garden flat with 3 bedrooms was £365,000 last winter.

Gloucester Avenue forms an eastern boundary to the area: a wide, tree-lined street with the main line railway (Euston-bound) behind the homes on the E side – this can lower prices on some houses by as much as 40 per cent, say agents, though the W side of the avenue is as smart as anywhere in the neighbourhood. The period terraces on both sides have for the most part been converted into flats. There are also some modern blocks of flats. Unlike many Primrose Hill homes, these come on the market fairly frequently as young couples move on to bigger and better things. Expect to pay up to £350,000 for good 3-bed flats in a modern block, around £172,000 for a more modest modern 2-bed and between £250,000 and £300,000 for a 2-bed garden flat in a period conversion.

The 'village' to the W is a maze of quiet streets, secluded and sleepy. **Rothwell St**, **Chalcot Crescent** and **St Mark's Crescent** are among the most prestigious addresses: 4-storey stucco-fronted houses. Even bigger and better are the enviable mid-1850s houses of **Chalcot Square**. House prices in Chalcot Square and Crescent range up to

£900,000, though one – extra-wide and with a big garden – was on the market last year for £1.2 million and sold for £1.7 million. **Chalcot Rd**, **Fitzroy Rd** and **Princess Rd** have rows of tall period terraces, now mostly flats. The canal, running between **St Mark's Crescent** and **Princess Rd**, makes for attractive back gardens.

Off the N end of **Regent's Park Rd**, where prices are (slightly) lower, **Ainger Rd**, **Oppidans Rd** and **Meadowbank** form a quiet triangle. **Oppidans Rd** and **Ainger Rd** have large grey-brick terraces and semis divided into flats; in addition, **Meadowbank** has Primrose Hill Court (council), a well-maintained block, and some large modern town-houses. **Primrose Hill Rd** has two big modern blocks overlooking the hill, and the highly desirable period **St George's Terrace** at the bottom.

The E end of **King Henry's Rd** has strong links with Eton College and much of the land is still owned by the college: leasehold only here. Most of the elegant, tall grey-brick houses have been split into flats with well-proportioned rooms; garden flats available here. On the N side, and in the roads leading up to **Adelaide Rd**, are groups of small, modern, 2-storey, white-painted houses.

Mornington Crescent and Euston

To the S of Camden Town lies another area centred on a convenient tube station – finally open again after years of work. Mornington Crescent (the tube stop) is actually on the junction of busy **Hampstead Rd** and **Eversholt St**. **Mornington Crescent** (the street), once a grand, semi-circular terrace of tall stucco-fronted Victorian houses, is gradually being renovated and converted into flats. Prices here are lower than in central Camden.

Crowndale Rd, E of **Eversholt St**, has tall brick and cream stucco terraces on either side, mostly conversions: thereafter there is council housing and a small parade of shops. The N end of **Eversholt St** also has 4-storey high terraces.

Oakley Square's S side is council; the N side is a pleasant terrace of Victorian houses, brick and stucco-fronted with elaborate detail on doors and window frames, black railings in front, and deep basements. In keeping with the rest of the area, this is gradually being restored and renovated. At the N end a purpose-built block of luxury flats, St Matthews Lodge, has apartments of all sizes including studios. A 3-bed flat here was £210,000 last December. Both flats and houses face onto the leafy, green, small public garden. **Harrington Square** has a terrace of Victorian houses, most new conversions, on section running N-S only; in front runs a busy one-way street carrying traffic into the West End. Hurdwick Place, off **Hampstead Rd**, provides flat conversions in period terraces, and garden flats in some basements.

The Euston area, bounded by **Euston Rd** to the S, **St Pancras Way** to the E, **Hampstead Rd** to the W and **Oakley Square** to the N, is virtually all council-owned, except for some privately owned flats and maisonettes over shops on **Churchway** and **Chalton St**, which have the benefit of this very central location. Many of the council homes are handsomely restored period houses. Similar housing, too, on the S part of **Eversholt St**, in **Starcross St**, **North Gower St** and **Drummond St** to the W, where there is privately owned housing in Victorian terraces, well-sheltered from the main road and centrally located.

This southern part of Camden will one day benefit from all the amenities – and disruption – of the vast King's Cross/St Pancras redevelopment.

Borders

Over to the E there is a debatable land without a clear district name. **Agar Grove**, which runs S of the Camden Square neighbourhood, leads to **York Way** and the King's Cross/Islington borderlands. There is a large council-built estate here, interspersed with some private homes and commercial properties. In **St Paul's Mews**, a gated cobbled mews with some smart modern properties, a 4-floor mews house was £345,000 last winter. There are some Victorian terraced 2-storey cottages in nearby **Malden Lane** and **Malden Cresent**.

Transport	Tubes: Camden Town, Chalk Farm, Mornington Crescent, Euston (zone 1/2, Northern). From Camden Town: Oxford Circus 15 min (1 change), City 15 min, Heathrow 1 hr (1 change). Trains: Camden Rd to Liverpool St 20 min.
Convienient for	City & West End, Euston & King's Cross stations, Euston Rd to M40, M11 to Cambridge, Regent's Park. Miles from centre: 2.5.
Schools	Local Authority: Williams Ellis (b), Camden School for Girls. Private: London International School, Jewish Free School. See also Hampstead.

SALES

Flats

	S	1B	2B	3B	4B	5B
Average prices	60–80	90–150	100–200	180–250+	—	—

Houses

	2B	3B	4B	5B	6/7B	8B
Average prices	130–220	185–300+	275–500	350–550+	—	—

RENTAL

Flats

	S	1B	2B	3B	4B	5B
Average prices	600+	800–900	900–1150	1400+	1750+	—

Houses

	2B	3B	4B	5B	6/7B	8B
Average prices	1250+	1500+	1950	2400–2600	—	—

The properties	Victorian housing of all shapes and sizes, with wide variations in status and condition. Lots of converted flats. Quite a few modern homes and more on the way: flats and mews-style houses. Lots of council-built homes – some quite desirable.
The market	Influx of prosperous new buyers 'discovering' good period homes. General flats market, centres on conversions. The few family homes are in demand: once here, people stay. Primrose Hill and Gloucester Crescent are the smartest neighbourhoods. Local searches: 2 weeks.

Among those estate agents active in this area are:
- Bairstow Eves
- Stickley & Kent
- Camden Bus
- Hotblack Desiato
- Keith Cardale Groves
- Winkworth *
- Anscombe & Ringland *
- Benham & Reeves
- McHugh & Co
- John D Wood
- Tatlers
- Dennis & Hayes
- Hetheringtons
- Goldschmidt & Howland
- Compton Reeback

further details: see advertisers' index on p633

CHELSEA

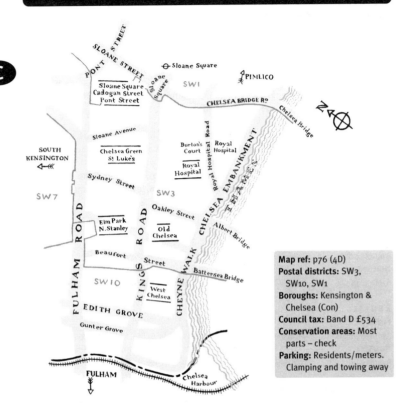

Map ref: p76 (4D)
Postal districts: SW3,
   SW10, SW1
Boroughs: Kensington &
   Chelsea (Con)
Council tax: Band D £534
Conservation areas: Most
   parts – check
Parking: Residents/meters.
   Clamping and towing away

Chelsea is more than a place, it is a byword, a symbol for a rather special kind of urban living: smart yet artistic, prosperous yet individual, expensive yet free-wheeling. In recent years the stress has moved to the expensive and away from the arty. Bohemian Chelsea, home of artists and their models, site of studio parties, has not survived the rise in property prices. The painters and sculptors have moved out, and their studios are owned by the usual mix of international residents found in any rich London area. Now, a buyer of a £1 million-plus studio house will find that the neighbours are merchant bankers not Royal Academicians.

All this said, the special Chelsea flavour lives on in the little pastel-painted streets, the elaborate mansion blocks, the occasional superb Georgian house. There is nowhere else in London quite like it.

It is easy to forget that until around 1980 quite a few of Chelsea's people were very ordinary, even poor, living in tenanted homes. Gentrification has done its work here too, with West Chelsea, spurred on by Chelsea Harbour and adjacent developments, the last enclave to be 'improved'.

Chelsea, strung along the **King's Rd** and the river, has a self-contained air. It has its own department store (Peter Jones in **Sloane Square**), a shop which is a way of life as much as a source of supply. You need not leave the area to be fed or entertained: restaurants abound, it has its own theatre, the Royal Court (currently being

C

expensively rebuilt). Shops sell most things, especially if they are ephemeral or expensive. The **King's Rd** fortunes wax and wane with fashion: it is still a key destination for every visitor to London, especially the young and well-heeled. The arrival of big supermarkets and Marks & Spencer added to its attractions. You will search in vain, though, for the butcher, the baker or the other 'village' shops. The last of these went in the early '80s.

The **King's Rd** may be busy, even tawdry at times, but a street away all is quiet: you are in a Georgian village, or a Victorian square. Chelsea keeps the villagy air which Fulham and such places somehow never quite attained.

The area was first made popular by Sir Thomas More, who went to live there in the 16th century. The aristocracy followed, building large country houses. They stayed and, over the years, their rural retreats have been replaced by their town-houses. To reach his country estate, Sir Thomas travelled by boat: the all-important road, genuinely as royal as its name implies, came later when King Charles II had a farm track cleared so he could journey to Putney to catch a boat to Hampton Court and, presumably, visit Nell Gwynn in Fulham en route.

The track became, literally, the **King's Rd**, later famous throughout the world as a symbol of the Swinging Sixties. **King's Rd** remains the main thoroughfare. It runs the entire length of Chelsea, W-E, 'playing every note in the social scale', as one of the area's most famous former inhabitants, writer/wit Quentin Crisp, observed. As it wends its way from fashionable **Sloane Square** in the E to World's End in the W, the restaurants, pubs, bars, boutiques, galleries and smart shops make way for handsome squares of traditional terraced houses.

Some may moan that Chelsea lacks a tube station apart from Sloane Square, and (off the map to the N) South Kensington. But there is the No 11 bus, used by everyone (knightly actors and ancient peers jostle on the stairs with German punk tourists and American bankers in Burberries) and the almost equally useful 19 and 22. And we have the testimony from 1834 of Thomas Carlyle that it took 'thirty-two minutes of my walking to Buckingham Gate' (just beside the palace). Carlyle lived in a house in **Cheyne Row**, for which he paid rent of £35 a year.

Chelsea's added bonus is the River Thames, which flows along its southern border. Once an inspiration for the likes of Turner, Whistler and the Greaves brothers, it now excites estate agents, who are well aware that anything with a view of the river commands a premium. Large parts of Chelsea, including a big chunk of the eastern, **Sloane St**, side, are owned by the Cadogan Estate. The Cadogan, Sloane and Stanley families, all linked by marriage, gave their names to many streets and squares, and the estate is still a big factor in the property scene in Chelsea.

Sloane Square, Cadogans and Pont St

This is the neighbourhood bounded by **Pont St** and **Walton St** in the N, **King's Rd** and **Sloane Square** to the S, **Sloane Avenue** to the W, and the borough border in the E.

Unlike the rest of Chelsea's squares, **Sloane Square** is a busy shopping area/traffic junction with traffic converging from **Knightsbridge**, the **King's Rd** and Pimlico. The paved square has plane trees and a fountain.

Lining the square are hotels, pubs, Peter Jones department store, the Royal Court Theatre and Sloane Square tube station. Both store and theatre are undergoing expensive refits. Peter Jones is soaking up £50 million: it should be quite a shop. The Royal Court has been virtually rebuilt at a cost of £28 million and will gain an underground restaurant. Many of the commercial uses occupy lower floors of the 19th-century residential blocks overlooking the square. These flats are convenient, if noisy. **Lower Sloane St** and **Sloane Gardens** to the S are dominated by the tall red-brick and stone-gabled mansion blocks found in most of the E chunk of the neighbourhood. They tend to be on leases of 40–50 years. Prices for such leases start at £250,000 for a 1-bed and range up to £750,000 for a 3-bed maisonette with garden access.

Heading N, **Sloane St** is the main thoroughfare to **Knightsbridge**. It is lined by a jumble of modern and period buildings, mainly flats, with concentrations of fashion shops and some embassies. This is the area of what was once called Hans Town, a complete estate built in the 1780s–90s. The developer was the architect Henry Holland. Some of his houses survive in **Sloane St** and **Cadogan Place**, though the name Hans Town has died out. It refers to Sir Hans Sloane, Lord of the Manor of Chelsea in the 18th century: his heiress granddaughter married Lord Cadogan.

The private square gardens of **Cadogan Place** (car parking beneath), spread along most of the E side of **Sloane St**, are overlooked by terraces of mixed-style period houses. An exclusive and opulent late-'80s development, Royal Court House, takes up the S side of the square (24 flats and maisonettes, from 1-bed to house-sized, sell for £800,000 to £2 million).

Tucked away behind **Cadogan Place** on the borders with Belgravia is quiet **Cadogan Lane** with its appealing mix of mews-type cottages and small houses.

West of **Sloane St**, in **Pont St**, are classic examples of the late-19th-century red-brick style which Osbert Lancaster dubbed 'Pont St Dutch'. These tall houses with stone detailing and splendid gables were derived from 17th-century Flemish and Dutch architecture. They form the predominant style in most of the area from **Cadogan Square** (a select address overlooking leafy gardens) W to Lennox Gardens, which curves round central gardens. Most of the houses have been split into flats and many are on short leases. Some leaseholders are exercising their right to extend their leases but many are not able to do so as the flats are not their main home. When the Cadogan Estate grants new leases these can be for 125 years, but 20–25 years is more usual. Prices reflect leases: a 1-bed flat on a 17-year lease in **Pont St** was £200,000 last winter while a 2-bed, 2-bath flat on a long lease was £600,000. There has been a lot of renovating of 2- and 3-bed flats in **Cadogan Place** in the last few years. Houses are still eagerly sought: a modernized 5-bed one with a garage recently sold for £4 million. Hidden behind these tall buildings are occasional quiet mews (**Shafto Mews, Clabon Mews**).

West of Lennox Gardens between **Walton St** and **Cadogan St** lies an enclave of much sought-after smaller houses – some freehold, some leasehold. **Ovington St, Hasker St, First St** – the most popular group – and **Moore St, Halsey St** and **Rawlings St** all have similar terraces of attractive 2/3-storey plus basement period brick and stucco houses. Unmodernized houses here go for between £750,000 and £1 million.

Running between the two groups is **Milner St** with its ornate 5-storey stucco terraces. **Walton St**, a narrow, busy little thoroughfare between South Kensington and Knightsbridge, is a mix of up-market shops/restaurants and stretches of pretty terraced houses. West of the cottage terraces are the Marlborough Buildings flats, the tall backs of which create a cul-de-sac in **Donne Place**, which has charming little mews-type houses. A London Underground line runs beneath some homes here which lowers prices: such a 2/3-bed flat would be around £550,000. To the S, **Cadogan St** is a mix of late-Georgian terraced properties on the N side, with St Mary's Church, St Thomas More Secondary School, St Joseph's Catholic Primary School and the Guinness Trust Estate to the S. A house in this street might be £800,000.

More red-bricks and a pocket of 2/3-storey terraced Victoriana (**Coulson St, Lincoln St, Anderson St**) lie between **Cadogan St, King's Rd** and **Sloane Avenue**.

Royal Hospital

This area stretches between the **King's Rd** and the river, W of **Lower Sloane St**/**Chelsea Bridge Rd** and E of **Smith St**/**Tedworth Square**/**Tite St**.

The most coveted address in this neighbourhood is **St Leonard's Terrace**, which boasts some of the oldest houses in Chelsea (18th and early 19th century) which fetch £2 million-plus (up from under £1 million in 1993). Most are listed, with leafy front gardens. But their main attraction, along with the grand mansions in **Durham Place**, is their view over Burton's Court (sportsground) and Wren's famous Royal Hospital. This imposing home for old soldiers forms the centrepiece of the area, with its extensive grounds (public tennis courts, handicapped children's adventure playground) and the neighbouring Ranelagh Gardens, stretching towards the river. Residents of **Embankment Gardens** have the best of both worlds with views of both the Royal Hospital and the Thames – the latter over the embankment traffic. A housing association is active here.

Dividing the neighbourhood in two is **Royal Hospital Rd**, lined at its W end by a mix of period and modern houses, flats, restaurants and shops. At its W end stands the National Army Museum and the drab modern concrete St Wilfrid's Convent. **Tite St**, running down to the river, boasts studio houses (ie homes with artists' studios, not today's 1-room flats) which recall Chelsea's bohemian past. Now their 2-storey windows stare glumly at the side of the convent. Nearer the river there are plans to replace two houses with a single vast house. Across **Royal Hospital Rd**, the 1930s mock-Tudor houses in **Ormonde Gate** (which sell for £1 million-plus) give way to tall red mansion blocks. The 1980s redevelopment of Cheyne House at the river end of **Royal Hospital Rd** resulted in 11 smart flats, most with splendid views along the river. Prices for these start at £1 million.

In **Tedworth Square** the new, ungainly brick development (1981) on the N side contrasts sharply with the traditional 4/5-storey terraces of brick and stucco/red-brick houses on the other three sides of the central gardens. Two houses here were sold recently for £1.65 and £1.85 million.

Head back along **St Leonard's Terrace** to reach **Royal Avenue**. This tree-lined, gravelled parade is flanked on both sides by gracious terraces of 19th-century houses, except for a post-war development at the **King's Rd** end. Its peace is guarded by the sensible barring of this end to traffic.

Just a few steps from the hustle and bustle of **King's Rd** stands **Wellington Square**, a fine group of 4-storey ornamental stucco Victorian houses. Despite its position, the terraces are set back from the road and the tall trees in the central garden give an air of seclusion and privacy. You can expect to pay £1.3 million for an unmodernized one, £1.85 million if done up. Beyond the brick and stucco terraces in **Walpole St** is the huge Whitelands House flats complex in **Cheltenham Terrace**, which dominates the terraces further along the W side of the street. Facing **Cheltenham Terrace** is the Duke of York's Headquarters, S of which lie blocks of flats and modern town-houses. The mansion flats in **Sloane Court** E and W share expanses of communal gardens: ground floor flats have direct access from graceful living-rooms. Negotiations are under way with the Ministry of Defence to sell off part of the Duke of York's Headquarters for development, but talks are at an early stage. A consortium involving the Cadogan Estate and a group of well-connected City-type territorial officers was negotiating as we went to press. The plan is to use the historic buildings at least in part for homes.

Just round the corner in **Chelsea Bridge Rd**, the sprawling Chelsea Barracks is up for sale. There are a number of listed buildings on the site, and local conservationists are keeping a beady eye on plans. Nothing has emerged yet.

Old Chelsea

As its name suggests, this area takes in the oldest parts of Chelsea and contains the most expensive properties. It is bounded on the N by **King's Rd**, by **Cheyne Walk/Chelsea Embankment** in the S, **Beaufort St** to the W, and **Smith St/Tedworth Square/Tite St** to the E.

Beaufort St is a main road N-S leading to Battersea Bridge. Most of the W side is lined by the red-brick and stone-gabled blocks of Beaufort Mansions, where a 3-bed flat leasehold can cost £250,000. More than 60 of the 242 tenants on the council's Thomas More Estate opposite have bought their flats: resales do come up. More mansion block with shops beneath front the **King's Rd**.

Neighbouring **Paultons Square** is one of the best-preserved of its type in the borough. Here handsome terraces of the 1840s with decorative black iron balconies and railings are arranged on three sides of an elongated central garden square. Houses go for £1.5–2 million depending on size. Terraces of a later date continue down **Danvers St**. Crosby Hall, on the corner of **Danvers St** and **Cheyne Walk**, is a Chelsea curiosity. It is a late-medieval building which once stood in the City and was moved, stone by stone, to Chelsea in 1910. It became a student hall of residence, but is now the centrepiece of a vast neo-Tudor mansion, built by businessman Christopher Moran after years of planning battles.

Turn E along riverside **Cheyne Walk**, which is one of the most sought-after addresses in London with its fine 18th-century town-houses. Two of these sold last year for astonishing sums. On the market now is a complex of flats and two houses, one of which is a genuine 1686-built, but totally modernized, gem: £1.6 million. Its neighbours are flats behind a river-facing Victorian façade, and modern flats behind it on the corner with **Lawrence St**. Flats in the development are from £480,000. **Cheyne Walk** continues past Chelsea Old Church (much of which is new: it was badly bombed in 1941) into **Old Church St**, the oldest in Chelsea. It now contains a hotchpotch of residential and commercial buildings in period and modern styles. Houses range from £500,000 to £2 million. It also holds the Old Rectory (1725) – with a 2¼-acre garden which sold in 1997 for £6 million. A builders' merchants' warehouse survived until 1997, but has now been replaced by Painters Yard: 19 flats and four houses which all sold between September and November last year at prices between £435,000 and £2.5 million.

Cut through the alleyway into **Justice Walk**, a delightful lane leading to the traditional heart and most exclusive part of Old Chelsea, **Lawrence St** and the **Cheynes**: quiet little streets with picturesque groups of houses and cottages, and fine brick and stucco terraces. Many houses here are dotted with blue plaques commemorating famous residents, from Rossetti and Isambard Kingdom Brunel to Thomas Carlyle. Rossetti left many memorials: one is the clause in local Cadogan Estate laws which bans the keeping of peacocks. These noisy fowl were among a domestic zoo assembled by the artist at Tudor House, where to quote a local 'he kept a lot of poets and other wild beasts'. Today's **Cheyne Walk** houses are among Chelsea's most expensive, and house few poets and no peacocks. The district has a real mix of houses of all sizes from cottages priced from £500,000 to the splendid Cheyne Walk house with studio and garden cottage on the market in January at £3.75 million.

The crossroads of **Cheyne Row/Upper Cheyne Row** and **Glebe Place** form one of the prettiest spots in the area. From here, **Glebe Place** follows a dog-leg course through to **King's Rd**. On the W side of the first leg is West House, a Queen Anne Revival studio house and one of the landmarks in the history of 19th-century British architecture. The W-E leg of the street has a mix of highly individual studio houses and the main N-S leg has purpose-built artists' studios (late 19th and early 20th century) facing a long terrace of 3-storey plus basement 19th-century terraced houses to the W (large rear gardens). Between **Lawrence St** and **Oakley St** lie more red-brick mansion blocks.

Oakley St is another major through-route N-S, leading to elegant Albert Bridge, Cadogan Pier and Battersea Park, Chelsea's adopted open space. On the W corner of the bridge stands Pier House, a vast modern red-brick development stretching well up **Oakley St** to merge with older red-brick blocks. The E side of the street is lined with tall formal terraces of stucco, or stucco and brick houses. Behind **Oakley St** lie smaller homes in **Margaretta Terrace** where house prices range from £750,000–1 million. Car parking is the main problem and a garage can sell for between £60–80,000, while a garage can add more than £100,000 to the value of a house. This leads to **Phene St** and horseshoe-shaped **Oakley Gardens**. Here 3-storey brick and stucco terraces in leafy streets with pretty gardens convey a village character.

At the top of **Chelsea Manor St** stands the Old Chelsea Town Hall, housing the library and sports centre (swimming baths, sports, sauna-solarium, multi-gym). Behind the town hall is the prestigious Swan Court apartment block, stretching through to **Flood St**: nine storeys built around a central courtyard. In **Flood St**, 3-storey brick houses with tall hedges and established front gardens lead to more brick and stone mansion blocks near the river and a striking top-of-the-market townhouse development in similar traditional style on the corner of **Alpha Place** (1986), which won a borough environmental award.

The scene changes again E of **Flood St** with a network of roads of smaller houses and cottages. Prettiest is **Christchurch St** with its 1830–50s artisan cottages, some with front gardens (prices: £750,000). Christ Church stands at the W end of the street near the infants' school. Between the gaily painted cottages in **Smith Terrace** and the **King's Rd**, 50 3/4-bed freehold houses are set around a cobbled courtyard: award-winning **Charles II Place** was finished in the early '90s. The homes sell for £600–900,000 (1990: £545–750,000).

The SE corner of the neighbourhood is covered by the famous Chelsea Physic Garden, founded 1673. **Swan Walk** with its glorious, and rare, detached Georgian houses (£3 million-plus on the rare occasions they change hands), and **Dilke St** with its rows of mews and studio houses, lead to **Paradise Walk**. The W side is lined by a terrace of brick 2-storey town-houses (Wates 1986). Phase II of the development is **Physic Place**, a mews behind the completed houses, through an arch off **Royal Hospital Rd**, next to the newly opened Ramsey's Restaurant.

West Chelsea

West Chelsea, until recently the area's poor relation, has now come up in the world. It is bounded by **Fulham Rd/King's Rd** to the N, the Thames (S), West London railway line (W), **Edith Grove/Beaufort St** (E).

The Chelsea Harbour development (see Fulham) has helped push up prices in a previously neglected part of Chelsea. But its timing could hardly have been worse – no sooner was it finished than the recession of the early 1990s set in. Some of the buildings, particularly the ones near the **Lots Rd** power station, are looking a bit tired. The inhabitants also lost their battle to have the borough boundary line moved so that they were within the coveted Royal Borough of Kensington and Chelsea. They still pay their council tax to Hammersmith and Fulham.

The power station, which supplies power to London Underground, is due to close in 2001. The council has released a planning brief stating what it would like to see there – houses, offices, shops and a museum – but so far no developer has come forward to work with London Transport. It is doubtful if anyone will be keen to engage in such a complex development until the economic climate is more certain. This is the second time closure of the power station has been announced: it was due to shut in 1990.

The old gasworks to the W (in Fulham) has just been bought by Berkeley and work is under way on 1,800 homes: see Fulham chapter. There is talk of building a tube station in Chelsea Harbour as part of the long-discussed Chelsea/Hackney line, which would also serve any development on the gasworks. But the line, which would involve extensive tunnelling, is a long way down London Transport's list of priorities. There is more chance of a station on the West London line (Clapham Junction – Olympia). Without a tube link, the **Lots Rd** area is poorly served by public transport. Minibuses run from Chelsea Harbour to Earl's Court and Kensington.

L-shaped **Lots Rd** comprises mainly light industrial/commercial uses ranging from Bonhams auction rooms to a scrap metal yard in the W leg. The exception is a modern town-house development, **Poole's Lane**, walled off from the street on the E side.

Turning the corner, the S leg is dominated by the power station, with its tall chimneys and vast wall of arched glass windows. Next to it stands a refuse transfer station, water-pumping station and Chelsea Wharf – a complex of small businesses and light industrial studios. The residential part lies along the extreme E end of the leg. Most of the brick and painted houses overlook the public Cremorne Gardens fronting the Thames. This corner is well-known for its villagy feel.

Lying inside the L-shape is a network of small streets lined with terraces of predominantly brick and stucco houses in varying styles and conditions. Many have been converted into flats/maisonettes. **Burnaby St** is typical: a 3/4-bed Victorian terraced house might cost £400,000. Many homes are owned by the council and Notting Hill Housing Trust. A park, West Field, cuts across the northern corner of the neighbourhood behind the World's End Health Centre in **King's Rd**. South of the park in **Uverdale Rd** is the Ashburnham Community Centre, which also houses the Heatherley School of Fine Art. A handful of red-brick/stone mansion blocks are found in **Ashburnham Rd**. The N end of the street merges with **Cremorne Rd** to form the S end of the West London one-way traffic system, a constantly busy road. The heavy traffic runs N up **Gunter Grove**, S down **Edith Grove**. A mixed commercial and residential development stands on the old Chelsea College site between **Gunter Grove** and **Hortensia Rd**. There is planning permission to develop the 20-acre main college site, between **King's Rd** and **Fulham Rd**, as apartments with some social housing. Nothing has yet happened on this site: the 1996 permission is for 291 homes and 23 affordable housing units, plus a public open space.

The one-way system creates a dividing line between the **Lots Rd** area and World's End, dominated by the dramatic World's End council estate with its handsome, angular red-brick towers. More than 100 tenants out of the 700-plus on the estate have bought their homes. World's End Place, a landscaped piazza facing **King's Rd**, leads into the estate. Standing within the piazza are the Chelsea Centre, a purpose-built community centre for the area (adult education classes), and Ashburnham Primary School. St John's Church is part of the flats complex. East of the estate, behind the 1950s Cremorne parade of shops, lie modern low-rise council flats, some now coming up for sale by former tenants who bought their homes.

Across **Milman's St** on the S-bend in **King's Rd** stands 355 King's Rd, an ex-council block which has been rehabilitated and converted into 50 luxury apartments. A 2-bed flat sells for around £260,000.

At the S end of the street, the houseboat colony moored on the river at **Cheyne Walk** comes into view. Houseboats offer a cheaper way of securing a smart Chelsea address, and are used as homes and business premises. Prices range from £50,000 up to £285,000 for a luxury boat with all mod cons. A recent price was £140,000.

Elm Park/North Stanley

This prime residential neighbourhood between the **Fulham Rd** and **King's Rd** to the W of **Sydney St** includes some of the choicest streets and best squares in Chelsea. It also boasts some of the world's top specialist hospitals, such as the Brompton and the Royal Marsden, as well as Chelsea's general hospital – the new Chelsea and Westminster. Part of the Brompton, on the N side of **Fulham Rd** at the corner of **Foulis Terrace**, is being converted into luxury flats (see South Kensington).

Sydney St, the broad N-S link between South Kensington and **King's Rd**, has dignified terraces, some listed, at its N end. Opposite St Luke's Church, the new National Heart and Chest Hospital has now been completed. South of **Britten St** sits the Chelsea Gardener gardening centre and Chelsea Farmers' Market – an off-street colony of smart food, arts and crafts shops and outdoor cafés.

Through the back of the market, fronting **King's Rd**, is **Dovehouse Green**. It backs on to the council's Thamesbrook home for the elderly, adjoining the Heart and Chest Hospital development. The Brompton Hospital and Royal Marsden cancer hospital stand each side of **Dovehouse St**, stretching through to **Fulham Rd** (main entrances).

Tucked in behind the Marsden is **Chelsea Square**, one of the area's most prestigious addresses, with 3-storey 1930s brick houses overlooking a tree-lined garden square. The E leg of the square becomes **Manresa Rd**, where houses have price tags up to £900,000. The buildings on the corner of **Manresa Rd** and **King's Rd** currently belong to King's College, but the college is due to move to the South Bank by 2000. A consortium headed by developer Godfrey Bradman has been talking about turning it into apartments, but nothing is concrete. The SW leg leads into **Carlyle Square**, the jewel in the neighbourhood's crown. The beautiful mid-19th-century brick and creamy stucco houses overlooking the square gardens change hands for £1.5–2 million. The square is unique in that it is blocked off from the traffic in the **King's Rd** by a barrier of railings, trees and shrubs.

Turn W into **Old Church St**, a main through-route between **Fulham Rd** and the **King's Rd**, and head N to **Queen's Elm Square**, where a group of mock-Tudor houses sit in a semi-circle off the street. The famous Queen's Elm pub, on the corner with

Fulham Rd, haunt of writers and artists, is no more. Their surviving watering hole, the Chelsea Arts Club, is a short walk S along **Old Church St**.

Between here and **Beaufort St** many of the big houses have been converted into flats. **Beaufort St** and **Elm Park Rd** are the main areas of multi-occupation. The more desirable **Vale**, **Mulberry Walk** and **Mallord St** form a uniform colony of houses and purpose-built flats, developed in the early part of the 20th century for artists, architects, musicians and writers of modest means.

At the S end of **Beaufort St** are the two parts of **Chelsea Park Gardens**, a development of 1920/30s 3-storey brick suburban villas. These much sought-after houses stand well back from the road on the E side behind a screen of trees and gardens. West side ones have leafy front gardens and the central section backs on to a communal garden. Some were once artists' studios: blue commemorative plaques dot the brick walls. The houses are worth as much as their owners' paintings: £1.75 million was asked for Sir Alfred Munnings' former home last winter.

Park Walk is dominated by the huge **Elm Park Mansions**, unique in the area in that the freehold is owned by the residents. The mansions have undergone major repairs and renovation in the last few years: current prices are from £190,000 for a 1-bed to £260,000 for a 2-bed. At the bottom of **Park Walk** is Park Walk Primary School, opposite the Man in the Moon pub on the **King's Rd** S-bend.

Between **Park Walk** and **Edith Grove** can be found a popular residential area of big mid-Victorian family houses with gardens (**Limerston St**, **Gertrude St**, **Hobury St**, **Shalcomb St** and **Langton St**). Surprisingly uniform terraces of mostly 4-storey brick and stucco houses: prices £700–900,000 for 3/5-bed. Distance from the underground used to be a disadvantage, but today estate agents say this does not matter. Presumably residents drive everywhere.

Chelsea Green/St Luke's

From **Sydney St** eastwards to **Sloane Avenue**, this largely residential neighbourhood N of **King's Rd** is characterized by big 1890s flats blocks to the N and a mix of bijou 'dolls house' cottages and '30s brick houses S of **Cale St**/**Elystan Place**.

Sloane Avenue, a main N-S through-route between Chelsea and South Kensington, is lined by sprawling flats blocks like Nell Gwynn House (E), Cranmer Court and Chelsea Cloisters (W). The latter has been refurbished and converted into luxury pied-à-terre apartments with back-up business services. **Draycott Avenue**, which runs parallel to **Sloane Avenue**, is similar. The buildings are smaller and the street somewhat quieter. Many conversions are under way.

Around the corner in **Lucan Place** (across the road from Chelsea police station) stands a 1989 Regalian development, Crown Lodge, set in an acre of landscaped gardens with fountains, waterfalls and pergolas. The building was once housing for policemen: now 2-bed flats go for £450,000 and penthouses top a million. Covering the whole block, bounded on the other three sides by **Petyward**, **Elystan St** (the entrance) and **Ixworth Place**, it contains 130 1/3-bed flats with a Romanesque-style swimming pool and gymnasium in the basement. A further block of 24 flats in **Petyward** is called Bryon Court. Across **Elystan St**, the NW corner of the neighbourhood is dominated by rented flats: the Sutton Dwellings and Samuel Lewis Trust Buildings, with the exception of narrow lanes of houses in **Pond Place** and **Bury Walk**.

At the S end of **Elystan St** at its junction with **Elystan Place** and **Cale St** lies **Chelsea Green**, with a pleasant village green atmosphere. The tiny green is encircled by up-market food shops, restaurants, art galleries and a general store, among others. On the edge of the green between **Whiteheads Grove** and **Sprimont Place** is the ivy-clad **Gateways** – '30s brick houses, laid out cloister-style around fountain courtyards. They have covetable garages: a 4-bed house with one can approach a million.

South of the green lies a series of much-favoured small-scale streets – **Bywater St**, **Markham St** and **Godfrey St** in particular – with their colourfully painted 19th-century 3-storey houses, and around the corner **Burnsall St** is extremely striking with its painted, gabled houses.

Caught up between them is **Markham Square**, one of the six formal squares facing the **King's Rd**. It is laid out in terraces of 3-storey plus basement brick and stucco houses with black iron railings. The Square gardens have won awards; one of the 5-bed houses facing it was on the market in November for £1.5 million.

In contrast are the 1930s brick houses in **Astell St** and **Jubilee Place** with their leafy front gardens. Different again is **St Luke's St**, lined with tidy terraces of 2-storey plus basement brick and stucco houses. The terraces on the W side back on to the public **St Luke's Gardens**, the leafy 'lungs' of the area. They were once a graveyard for St Luke's Church, a 19th-century Grade I listed building fronting **Sydney St**. North of the church lies St Luke's public playground.

Transport	Tubes: Sloane Sq (zone 1, District, Circle), South Kensington (zone 1, District, Circle, Piccadilly). From Sloane Sq: Oxford Circus 15 min (1 change), City 20 min, Heathrow 45 min (1 change).
Convienient for	West End, Knightsbridge, Victoria & Waterloo stations, Thames, M4 to West. Miles from centre: 2.
Schools	Local Authority: St Thomas More. Private: More House School. Many good prep schools. See also neighbouring areas.

SALES

Flats	S	1B	2B	3B	4B	5B
Average prices	100–150	130–350	250–500+	300–1M	500–1M+	850–1.5M+
Houses	2B	3B	4B	5B	6/7B	8B
Average prices	300–700	400–1M	600–2.5M	1.25M+	2M–5M+	—

RENTAL

Flats	S	1B	2B	3B	4B	5B
Average prices	1000+	1100–2400	1400–3000+	2400–3500+	3000–6000	4000+
Houses	2B	3B	4B	5B	6/7B	8B
Average prices	2000–2400	3000–5000	4000–6000	6000–8000	10,000+	16,000+

The properties	Lovely Georgian/early Victorian homes in garden squares, small streets of cottages and mews are the archetypal Chelsea properties. Also, N of King's Rd/Sloane Square, red-brick, Dutch-gabled mansion flats. Luxury flats schemes may replace King's College, Duke of York's HQ and Barracks.
The market	Buyers are now mostly City-based and prosperous: the arty, up-market locals increasingly displaced by international bankers. Foreign buyers are Europeans and Americans rather than Far East. Chelsea's status and image ensure a lively market even in recessions, agents aver. Exceptional properties go well over the mainstream averages above. Local searches: 5–6 days.

Among those estate agents active in this area are:

- Jackson-Stops & Staff
- Aylesfords
- John D Wood & Co
- Knight Frank
- Marsh & Parsons
- Farley & Co*
- Farrar & Co
- Foxtons*
- FPDSavills
- Friend & Falcke
- Winkworth *
- Hamptons
- Lane Fox

- Strutt & Parker*
- De Groot Collis
- Egerton
- Russell Simpson
- Hobart Slater
- Beaney Pearce *
- Humberts
- Douglas & Gordon
- W A Ellis *
- Gascoigne Pees
- Cluttons Daniel Smith
- Read Cunningham

further details: see advertisers' index on p633

CHISWICK

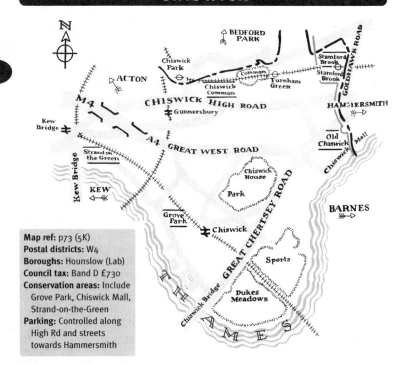

Map ref: p73 (5K)
Postal districts: W4
Boroughs: Hounslow (Lab)
Council tax: Band D £730
Conservation areas: Include
  Grove Park, Chiswick Mall,
  Strand-on-the-Green
Parking: Controlled along
  High Rd and streets
  towards Hammersmith

Leafy Chiswick, sitting snugly (and smugly) above its green open spaces in a protecting loop of the Thames, is nevertheless a community divided by the A4 **Great West Rd**. Although the twain meet frequently there is a slight difference of orientation between those who live between the A4 and the river and those who dwell on the other, northern, side. The riverside community uses South West Trains and looks as much towards Richmond and Sheen for its shopping, while the other half has easier access to District line tubes and to **Chiswick High Rd** – as its name suggests, the area's high street.

But the A4 is boon as much as bane. Lying on the most direct route out of London saves Chiswick from being a mere suburban backwater: dwellers here can live in its leafy, sleepy streets and yet get to Heathrow Airport in – theoretically – as little as 20 min.

Old Chiswick began as a riverside village whose traces can still be seen in **Church St**, where St Nicolas Parish Church has parts dating back to the 15th century. Glorious period homes front the Thames here, and at Strand-on-the-Green, the corresponding hamlet at the Kew end of the river loop. Today's Chiswick covers everything between the two, subsuming another old village site, Turnham Green, which lay along **Chiswick High Rd**. This name is less and less heard, though there is a tiny green still, and a tube station on the District line. Across the underground's tracks lie Acton Green and, alongside it, a different world: the splendid little enclave of London's first garden suburb, Bedford Park (see chapter).

Although a few earlier houses survive, Chiswick really began growing in the mid-19th century, the bulk of development happening between then and World War II. The result is a variety of choice from tiny early Victorian cottages to large turn-of-the-century properties, from inter-war semis and mansion blocks to the odd infill of modern town-houses. Generally, the more recent the property the tinier it is likely to be – even 1960s town-houses are positively roomy compared with the toy boxes of the '80s. Where this rule does not hold good (eg luxurious riverside developments), expect to pay dearly for the space.

Some of the larger houses, especially in the western half and N of the **High Rd**, have been converted to flats. Established locals prefer the spaciousness of older houses and mansion flats, for which they are prepared to put up with lack of garage and consequent parking problems – not helped by 'overspill' parking thanks to the new controlled parking zone (E from the Hammersmith border to **Turnham Green Terrace** and **Chiswick Lane North**, down to the A4), in addition to the pay-and-display zones around **Chiswick High Rd**.

Prices, high even by London standards, reflect the wide range as well as location. The biggest and most expensive houses are riverside ones – foremost among them those on **Chiswick Mall** (see p 208), but Grove Park conservation area, streets surrounding the Chiswick House conservation area, and roads between the **High Rd** and A4, all contain good-sized houses with generous gardens. Despite locals' preference for period homes, the most recent Thames-side developments are of a level of style and quality to command premium prices – very likely paid by 'outsiders'.

In the heart of Chiswick, just S of the **High Rd**, is the Glebe Estate (between **Duke** and **Devonshire Rds**), tiny 2- and 3-bed workmen's cottages now trendified into fashionable residences: prices, which start c. £180,000, can reach £280,000. Best to have a tiny car to match your tiny home here. There are other pockets of bijou homes, such as Chiswick Common, N of the **High Rd**, and many solid houses built just before and after World War I in neighbourhoods such as Stamford Brook on the Hammersmith borders. One of the top purpose-built flats blocks is the 1930s Watchfield Court, a complex S of Turnham Green that is large enough to show up on maps. New homes may well appear in **Stamford Brook Avenue**, on an old stores depot for the famous Queen Charlotte's maternity hospital in Hammersmith, which is due to move sites – see Hammersmith chapter for those already under way on the sites around the hospital.

South of Stamford Brook on the other side of the **High Rd**, **Netheravon Rd**, **Airedale Rd** and **Homefield Rd** are desirable streets with larger houses, close to transport and Hammersmith. Right on the Chiswick/Hammersmith borders, **British Grove** recently sprouted a clutch of 'executive homes' (these opened at £300,000 upwards). Westwards, down towards the Gunnersbury station end of the area, mansion blocks and houses of varying sizes, styles and periods are to be found.

Adding to the mix are conversions of industrial or commercial sites and buildings (a trend that caught on quite early here, where developers gaze in frustration at the rolling – and protected – green acres between A4 and river). Bovis Homes fashioned 'Devonhurst Place' from a splendid Victorian warehouse in the 1980s, and 51 flats surround a central atrium in what was the Army and Navy depot in **Heathfield Terrace**, S of Turnham Green. Another six penthouses perch above offices on the site.

On the Chiswick/Acton Green borders, near Chiswick Park tube, Chiswick Green Studios is an example of that most trendy style of homes development, industrial space turned into loft apartments – sold, even more trendily, as 'shell' units for you to fit out yourself, or part- or fully-fitted. Thus you could get in on the ground floor for a modest £175,000 (a ground floor loft?), while you can pay up to a top-lofty £750,000 for the best loft in the loft (sorry, penthouse). Last winter £495,000 sufficed for a blond wood floored, wall-of-glass, top-floor version under a gently curving roof, luxuriously fitted-out. Apart from high ceilings and galleries, you're buying basement parking, a porter and a 'gym facility'. These are also appearing on the rentals lists.

Still to come are rather more modest flats on **Chiswick High Rd** itself, where Barratt plan around 100 2- and 3-beds (underground parking; two penthouses), and another 100 flats behind Sainsbury's.

Chiswick has attracted artists of all types ever since Hogarth bought a house (delightful, still standing and open to the public) in 1749, along with leading businessmen. The current mixture remains much the same; it is popular with media people, City types, well-heeled executives, actors and professionals, especially architects. Young people try to gain a foothold near the tubes, marry and move southwards into a flat or small house then progress to a larger house with a garden. They contribute to various cultural and social activities and patronize the Riverside Studios and Lyric Theatre in Hammersmith, as well as Richmond Theatre, The Watermans Arts Centre, Brentford, local pub theatres or the almost professional Questors Theatre in Ealing. They play hard at the Hogarth Health Club or Riverside Club – both private – or Fountains Leisure Centre, Brentford, and rejoiced at the reopening of Chiswick's open-air swimming pool. It is a predominantly middle-class family district, where it still feels safe on the streets at night. Once people have found Chiswick, they tend to stay.

An immediate attraction is the greenery; apart from the river and open spaces of Dukes Meadows, many parts of Chiswick have their own little green, while the deer-filled acres of Richmond Park, and Kew's famous botanical gardens, are an easy drive away. Note, too, Ravenscourt Park on the Hammersmith borders: prized by mothers (1 o'clock club, adventure playground, etc). The resultant atmosphere is a combination of busy city and green suburb – even the **High Rd** is tree-lined and runs by Turnham Green. This is the main shopping street – although there are many little local parades of shops scattered all round the area – with a large Sainsbury's (enormous car park; open all hours) and token-sized multiples including a mainly food-purveying Marks & Spencer. **Turnham Green Terrace** and, increasingly, **Devonshire Rd**, have a range of up-market specialist shops, with many late hours to suit working customers. There are a growing number of bars and restaurants, from takeaway to moderately expensive. Good transport to the City or West End with Heathrow just down the M4 complete the list of pluses; the E side uses Stamford Brook and Turnham Green tube stations while the W has Chiswick Park and Gunnersbury, the latter being both tube and rail station. Those S of the A4 use Chiswick rail station.

No part of Chiswick could be described as unpleasant, but higher density housing – lots of flats, more conversions and rentals – are clustered round Turnham Green and Gunnersbury stations, along with the area by the Hogarth roundabout and flyover. Council-built estates are small, scattered and low-rise, with a high percentage of owner-occupiers – and thus occasional sales. The main industrial area is a small estate by Gunnersbury, but this is separated from the bulk of the residential sector by the railway and **High Rd**. Office development is confined to the **High Rd** environs, but controversial plans to turn the old Chiswick bus depot into a 1.5 million sq ft business park are going ahead after several years on the back burner during the early '90s recession. In general terms, any home too close to the railway, A4 or **Great Chertsey Rd** loses a little value because of noise and dirt from traffic. This is a growing problem as these roads suck more and more drivers from the West into London, increasing pressure on surrounding roads. Certain parts of Chiswick are also prone to aircraft noise (the local paper even lists flight-path schedules).

Grove Park

Grove Park is quintessentially Chiswick, with its wide, tree-lined roads (some specimens dating back to the original Grove House gardens) and range of properties. It takes its name from Grove House, in whose grounds the Duke of Devonshire built Chiswick's first large housing estate as a high-class area for wealthy merchants. The original estate was roughly bounded by the river, the **Great Chertsey Rd**, which leads up from Chiswick Bridge, the N London rail line, Silverlink, which marks the start of **Strand-on-the-Green**, and the Waterloo line. Estate agents today are insistent that Grove Park extends north of its railway and up to the A4. In terms of house style and price this is not unreasonable.

Some of the earliest houses are in **Grove Park Rd**; Grove House itself stood, until the 1920s, on the site of **Kinnaird Avenue**. Over the years further tracts were developed – and redeveloped in some cases, as war damage and demolition of bigger houses and gardens followed. Grove Park's leafy streets are particularly rich in Victorian architecture, from mid-19th-century terraces to Gothic, and from red-brick with hanging tiles to later brick and creamy stucco terraces. The last big chunk of the estate was developed between the wars with roomy semis, detached houses and the odd bungalow, while since the war there have been various small estates of townhouses and even the occasional striking example of modern brick and glass architecture. Flat-hunters can choose between the prestigious 1930s Hartington Court right on the river or modern small-scale blocks. There are virtually no conversions of bigger houses into smaller units.

Some of the best houses are in

Grove Park has long been popular for its solid, Gothic-looking late-Victorian villas. As this detail shows, they were designed as a piece, with even the front gate in style with the rest of the house. Note, too, the stone window surrounds, the stone detailing on the corners and the ecclesiastical tone conveyed by the perforation in the balcony over the bay window.

Hartington Rd, despite its busy rush hour traffic, with a few having huge gardens which sweep down to the river. Between **Hartington Rd** and the river, too, are three earlier examples of the modern Thames-side developments:

Chiswick Quay, a 1970s development of 3- to 6-bedroom town-houses round a marina, was designed to appeal to boat owners, although tidal variations do not allow for spur-of-the-moment sailings. A wide spread of prices, depending on size and whether it includes a river view (a 2-terraced, 3-bed one was £435,000 last winter). Despite their size these homes are unsuited to younger children since lack of garden and the sheer sides of the marina make playing near the water highly dangerous.

Chiswick Staithe: the word 'staithe' meant embankment, an appropriate name for these 69 3- and 4-bedroom houses, built in 1964 around a landscaped, traffic-free centre facing the Thames. These cost around £300,000 upwards, and come with stringent regulations concerning activities and development. The estate attracts couples (often both working), with older children, or retired couples.

Thames Village: the peace of this low-density estate is much appreciated by its mainly retired residents. Built in 1955, the 2-bed maisonettes (£150,000-plus) are set amidst immaculate lawns and flower beds. The residents' association holds the freehold, and strict covenants apply here.

Grove Park commuters use Chiswick station to reach Waterloo and the City; they may walk to Chiswick Park or Turnham Green tubes (District); some even commute outwards to satellite towns in the Thames Valley. Whatever their choice they need a car, or at least the local hoppa buses, to cross the A4 divide for school runs and shopping.

Streets around Chiswick House, once the home of the Dukes of Devonshire, are spacious turn-of-the-century dwellings, often with gardens to match. **Park Rd** is generally considered one of the best addresses in Chiswick, while **Staveley Rd** is famous for its avenue of flowering cherries (a house here will cost around £350,000). The site of a former school between **Staveley Rd** and **Burlington Lane** now holds flats and houses (all with parking space or garages, c. £345–375,000) built around courts and crescents named, rather tenuously, after former famous Chiswickites: **Fitzroy Crescent, Huntingdon Gardens, Crofton Avenue**.

The Duke began selling off this part of his estate in 1884, but the charming little neo-Palladian Chiswick House remains in its 66-acre garden, open to the public now and a haven for urban wildlife such as foxes, squirrels and 20 different types of bird. Extra green space in the form of school grounds, allotments and playing-fields makes it a particularly low-density neighbourhood. Much to the satisfaction of its predominantly owner-occupier residents the whole district N of the Waterloo line between **Sutton Court Rd**, the A4 and the **Great Chertsey Rd/Burlington Lane**, was declared a conservation area in 1977. This includes a little corner – **Paxton Rd, Sutherland Rd** and **Short Rd** – of early Victorian terraces once inhabited by Chiswick House gardeners and Reckitt & Coleman employees.

Chiswick Mall/Old Chiswick

This riverside corner, where Chiswick began, is a paradox: it has remained a hidden time capsule, cut off and somehow protected by the **Great West Rd**. Winding **Church St**, with its pretty houses and parish church, spans the centuries: the Hogarth roundabout is at one end, the glorious Georgiana of **Chiswick Mall** looks tranquilly out over the Thames at the other.

There is still very much a village feel to this tiny strip. Houses range from little add-on cottages to magnificent brick or stuccoed residences in a charming jumble of periods and styles facing on to the river. The façades indicate every century from the 17th to the 20th: some, however, are even older than they look, having been modernized 200 years or so ago.

Despite the apparent dangers of water – not to mention the greedy eyes of developers – this remains a predominantly family area where neighbours know each other and children play together. Several houses have vast gardens behind, while others have a garden patch across the road bordering the river. Virtually none of the houses have been converted into flats. They are usually owned by big families who sometimes even pass a house down to the next generation; these are plum properties and if they ever come onto the market they go, typically, at prices of £1.5–2 million for the large mansions. The list of residents, past and present, is a roll call of aristocratic, artistic and industrial names. Their community spirit is fostered by the shared fear of flooding; the river comes right over the road and there is a neighbourhood warning system so that cars are not marooned. Despite invasions from summer visitors strolling down the historic Mall, residents still love their pretty riverside pubs – not to mention the birds and other river life which pass their windows.

There have been three smallish modern developments, where houses with up to four bedrooms go for £390,000-plus. **Eyot Green**, built in 1960 round a green just off the Mall; **Millers Court**, a 1970s square leading directly to it; and **Chiswick Wharf**, 1980s brick town-houses facing the river on the W side of **Church St**.

Southwards from here, Chiswick's most concentrated (and smartest) clutch of 1990s developments have transformed the once industrial stretch of riverside along **Pumping Station Rd**. A peaceful corner: the road stops short of **Church St**, allowing access to the ancient village, but only by foot – and behind the inland side lies the church's cemetery.

Electric gates (albeit handsome ones) guard the landward privacy of Regency Quay, where McAlpine has confused its monarchs and named one road **Gwynne Close**. The riverside path is open to all, however. The long sweep of the Corney Reach scheme, by contrast, invites the public in, via its attractive central piazza, to a splendid bit of planning gain: a partnership with the developers, Persimmon, has resulted in a new pier that anyone is welcome to use. The Chiswick Pier Trust runs the pier from its offices here. Corney Reach also boasts a bar/restaurant, which has good views over the river.

Even smarter homes (sweeping crescents, distinctive gables, decorative ironwork) at Barratt's Royal Thames Crescent, mark the southern end of **Pumping Station Rd**.

A pleasing aspect of these Thames-side schemes is their mix of homes – from small flats to young mansions. A sample of last winter's prices include: 1-bed flat £160,000; 2-bed £220,000, with garden £250,000; 5-bed house on river c. £650,000.

The developers haven't finished with this corner yet, though: Bermac are contributing a small scheme of 13 flats, two houses. Alongside, McDonald Roofing declares that it is 'here to stay – we are NOT part of the redevelopment'.

Strand-on-the-Green

At the other, Kew, end of Chiswick is **Strand-on-the Green**, another ancient riverside village mirroring **Chiswick Mall** in the E. Where fishermen once caught eels and boatyards and breweries plied their trade, now tourists throng the popular towpath pubs. Strand-on-the-Green was a working riverside village up to 20 years ago, and there is still a bit of light industry to make this a deliberately unpretentious community. Here, too, many houses are older than they look; the village dates back to the 15th century. The medley of styles ranges from quite grand to a row of Arts and Crafts cottages, while little passages between the houses down to the towpath add to the informality. Artists (the most famous was Zoffany) were often attracted to the area and some houses have studios at the back. Many desirable residences have humble origins, having once been shops, pubs, a post office or tea house. Gardens tend to be small. It is now a conservation area, with many listed buildings along the river frontage. Flats are rare; the main inhabitants are families who stay for years, watching their children grow up messing around with boats on the river, which is the area's main hobby and focus. Anyone with less than 10 years' residence is considered a newcomer. This, however, is changing, as the odd well-off young couple discovers the cachet of a riverside address without quite the prices of **Chiswick Mall** – a 4-bedroom house might be found for under £400,000. That being said, Georgian gems come in the million-pound bracket.

There is the occasional modern development, including **Magnolia Wharf**, which offers 4-bedroom houses at prices that are upwards of £400,000. The roads behind were developed in late-Victorian red-brick; these were once occupied by the working classes, but now they have been taken over by young middle-class families who find around £250,000 good value for a 3-bedroom home. **Oliver Close** is a 1980s estate of tiny houses and flats. North of the railway, the McAlpine development in **Wellesley Rd** has 61 studio, 1- and 2-bedroom flats.

Residents use Kew Bridge Waterloo line or take a 10 min walk under the **Great West Rd** for **Chiswick High Rd** buses, or Gunnersbury on the District line tube and the N London line, Silverlink. Like other inhabitants on this side of Chiswick most find a car a necessity, though happily the bus service is good. Most houses have garaging at the back since unlike the Mall, which has a proper road running alongside the river, they only have a towpath. Flooding is, however, not a problem here since the advent of the Thames Barrage. Parking is difficult at the beginning and end of the school day as mothers sweep up in the car to collect their offspring from school (Strand-on-the-Green Primary has a reputation which extends beyond the immediate district), while **Thames Rd** is a dangerously busy rat-run. Unlike most of Chiswick they are free of aircraft noise (the threatened Terminal 5 might change this . . .), although Kew Bridge produces a background drone. The only other drawbacks seem to be bums and beermugs on their window sills during the summer tourist season.

Transport	Tubes: Turnham Green (zone 2, District, Piccadilly — restricted service); Stamford Brook (zone 2, District); Chiswick Park, Gunnersbury (zone 3, District). From Turnham Green: Oxford Circus 30 min (1 change), City 30 min, Heathrow 25 min (1 change). Trains: Chiswick station to Waterloo 20 min; Gunnersbury station for Silverlink/North London line.
Convenient for	Heathrow, M4 and routes to the West. Kew Gardens. Miles from centre: 6.

Schools	Hounslow Education Authority: Chiswick School. Private: St Paul's (g), Godolphin & Latymer (g), Latymer (b).

SALES

Flats	S	1B	2B	3B	4B	5B
Average prices	60–80	85–125	100–180+	160–260+	–	–
Houses	2B	3B	4B	5B	6/7B	8B
Average prices	190–260	210–330	260–500+	340–650+	400–1.5M+	–

RENTAL

Flats	S	1B	2B	3B	4B	5B
Average prices	500–800+	700–1200	850–1700	1200–1900	1800+	–
Houses	2B	3B	4B	5B	6/7B	8B
Average prices	1000–1700	1200–2000	1800–3000	2500–3500	–	–

The properties	Solid family homes, mainly Victorian/Edwardian (though larger ones scarce); some smaller terraces; also popular '30s mansion blocks. Riverside has superb Georgian buildings, plus cottages and new developments, some enviable.
The market	Riverside and Grove Park are smart, with high prices for family homes; best period riverside ones rarely for sale (and in the million-pound bracket). New developments too are pricey. The peaceful streets inland popular with young families. Younger people moving in: they cluster near underground. Local searches: 1 day.

Among those estate agents active in this area are:
- Barnard Marcus
- Foxtons
- Winkworth *
- Woolwich
- John Spencer
- Whitman & Co
- Quintons
- Chestertons
- Bushells
- Faron Sutaria & Co Ltd*
- Townsend Tyser Greenwood

further details: see advertisers' index on p633

CITY AND FRINGES

Map ref: p142 (6D)
Postal districts: EC1, EC2, EC3, EC4
Boroughs: City of London, Tower
    Hamlets (Lab)
Council tax: Band D £658
Conservation areas: Several – check
    with corporation/council
Parking: Residents/meters/clamps

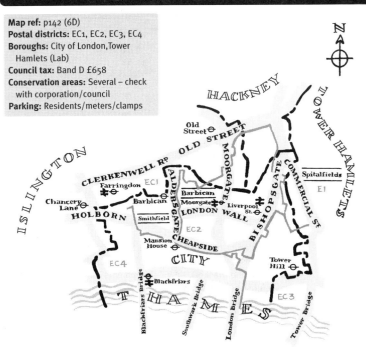

A map locating new homes in the City would have been pretty blank five years ago, but now it is worth the while of one agent specializing in the area to have one printed. It is dotted with solid City names like **Fleet St** and and **Cornhill** – and many more appear within the Clerkenwell area (which has its own chapter) and the area up round **Old St** now dubbed the 'Shoreditch Triangle'. (You know that an area has happened once the agents start inventing names for it.)

Once again, after a century, it is possible to live in the City. Most homes are in fringe areas such as Spitalfields and Smithfield, but quite a few are in the heart of the financial district. Despite the jostling presence of 500 foreign banks and myriad other companies and institutions, the urge to fill every corner with offices and dealing floors has gone. Docklands has taken some of the pressure, some sectors have moved out wholesale – the press, for instance, has deserted **Fleet St** – and there is space for homes as well as jobs.

The City's sleeping population reached a low in 1970 of about 4,500 people, compared to 30,000 at the start of the century. Around 1995 the numbers began to seriously increase. It is estimated that the figure is now 6,300, compared to a workforce of about 270,000. There could be 3,000 more homes in the City by 2006: most resulting from conversion of offices or industrial buildings, some new, and a few (as has already happened) old houses reverting after a century as offices. The only thing to slow this trend is the rise in office rents, which could choke off the supply of buildings for conversion to homes.

In 1997 233 new homes were completed in the City, half being conversions. At the start of 1998, over 400 new homes were being built, with planning permission for 460

C

more – and these figures do not include homes in other boroughs on the edge of the City. Just over half the City's homes are owner-occupied – and a surprising nine per cent is 'tied' to specific jobs – caretakers and the like.

The 'Square Mile' of the City of London is enclosed by **Commercial St** in the E, **Old St** in the N, **Chancery Lane** in the W and the River Thames. Here we deal with the Square Mile and its fringe areas to E, N and W. The City retains its place as one of the top three global finance centres, and the banks' towers loom over the narrow streets, unchanged in their alignment since medieval days. Despite its image, the City contains scruffy streets as well as rich ones. Until the 1980s, industries – printing and graphics, leather, metal-working, textiles – dominated tracts on the edge. These fringe areas still also house poorer, sometimes deprived, groups.

Living in the City is now possible. But is it pleasant? Go and see. If you have not visited the Square Mile for a few years it could surprise you. The 'ring of steel' street closures designed to ward off terrorists have cut traffic by 30 per cent (and air pollution by 15 per cent). Such was the popularity of this scheme that the 1997 extension to take in St Paul's, parts of Barbican, Smithfield and the Old Bailey has been made permanent. There are now plans to bring Broadgate within the 'ring'. Shops, restaurants and bars have opened – even multiples like Tesco Metro and Marks & Spencer, now developing their second City store on the corner of **Fenchurch St** and **Gracechurch St**. Lion Plaza, in **Old Broad St**, is an imminent scheme with shops and offices. There are rumours of a department store in **King St**, off **Cheapside**. Demand for retail space in the City has doubled over the past three years. And these days, amenities open at weekends – they used to close down at 5pm on Friday.

Transport is excellent during the week, and all other parts of London are within easy reach. Close by is the world-renowned Barbican Arts Centre, and the 'village' atmosphere of the City is prized by all its residents. The City is unique in that its local council, the City of London Corporation, is entirely independent and non-political – which contributes greatly to the area's feeling of detachment from the rest of London. There are a few downsides to living here: noise from traffic, lack of open space, few local services such as doctors and schools, cramped and overlooked homes, lack of daylight in some, limited parking space.

The swing back to City living began in the 1980s, but was hard to discern above the din of office building. It started when top firms insisted that key staff be close to their work places, with the change to virtual 24hr working as markets became global. One luxury block, Norfolk House, appeared on the riverside in **Trig Lane**, near the steps to

St Paul's in 1988, with prices of up to £1.5 million. Then came 140 new flats in **Little Britain** by St George's. Their parent Berkeley Homes knew a good idea when they saw it, and have followed up with schemes at **Ludgate Hill**, in various fringe locations (see below) and in the heart of the City at Monument. Now, it's possible to look in the City proper, in the Fleet St/Holborn area to the W, and in Barbican and its neighbours to the N. Then there is Smithfield just within the City boundary to the NW, and Shoreditch and Spitalfields outside the City walls to the NE.

The City Proper

Berkeley Homes currently offer the biggest range of City flats, and several of their earlier blocks provide resales. In **Monument St** their 37 flats at the start of 1999, ranged from £130–395,000. Lambert House in **Ludgate Hill** has flats from 1-bed to penthouses with views of St Paul's: prices from £265,000. At **Trinity Square**, 16 flats offer views across to the Tower of London: prices range from £210–430,000. The next Berkeley scheme is on the corner of **Ludgate Hill** and **Ludgate Square**.

Dotted around the heart of the City are smaller schemes: in a lovely corner near St Paul's, five flats have been created from a period building in **St Andrew's Hill**. **Ludgate Hill** has a scheme under way of flats intended to be let. On the river, **Queens Quay** has 1-bed flats. There is even a new conversion behind a listed façade in **Cornhill**: £90,000 studios a biscuit-toss from the Bank. And there are homes including a 2-floor, 4-bed penthouse in what must be the best street address in the City, **Crutched Friars**. Barratt has built 88 homes in **Aldersgate St** and **Pemberton Row**, and are now working on 136 at 'Globe View', Brooks Wharf, **Upper Thames St**. Not all the flats have river, or Globe Theatre, views. Prices are from £180,000, a 2-bed with a river view is £395,000. Goldcrest Homes' City Wall Apartments in **Wormwood St** are from £225,000. And there are more. For the first time in a hundred years.

Barbican and its Neighbours

For 20 years after the estate's completion in 1976, City living meant the Barbican. It had no competitors. With its 2,000 homes, it is still the largest residential district. The Barbican complex is bordered by **London Wall**, **Aldersgate St**, **Moorgate** and **Chiswell St**. It's described by the City Corporation, which controls it, as a 'city within a City' – and so it is. The fortress image is even more accurate: the whole thing turns inwards, looking down on the open space in front of the magnificent Barbican Arts Centre. Worryingly, there is no street level: walkways, stairs and lifts form a maze so cunning that yellow stripes had to be painted on the paving to guide bemused visitors to the arts centre. The three main towers – just some of the 21 residential blocks – dominate much of the Square Mile's skyline. To those expecting a world of penthouse flats and luxurious living, first impressions can disappoint. The complex looks rather drab, grey, concreted and uniform, and greenery on the balconies struggles to compete.

But the inside of many Barbican flats tells a different story – they belie their outward appearance and provide some of the most exciting homes in Central London. Biggest prices are paid for the luxury penthouses of Lauderdale, Cromwell and Shakespeare Towers. The latter is Britain's tallest residential building. The view from it reaches the hills surrounding London. The Barbican has a roughly 80/20 split between leasehold and rental. Leasehold is definitely the growing trend (it was 60/40 in 1990) and the estate's managers are keen to sell as many homes as possible. The turnover of properties has increased and local agents usually have a selection on their books. Homes range from studios right through to a small number of town-houses. The majority are 1- and 2-bedroomed flats. As would be expected, services such as estate cleaning and security are given a high priority and are of an excellent standard. The downsides are the under-floor heating, which is inflexible and expensive, and the service charges. The Barbican has a very strong and active residents' association which presents a powerful voice at local council meetings.

Near the Barbican is the well-regarded council-built **Golden Lane** estate, with 200 of the 550 homes now privately owned. Two-bed flats go for £120,000-plus and are very much in demand. Since 1994 this is actually in the City, though it has always been run by it. In adjacent **Fann St** 38 sheltered homes are being built. Just N of the Barbican **Bridgewater Sq** has newly converted 2-bed flats from £192,500. Also in this neighbourhood, Berkeley have just sold 10 flats in **Carthusian St** for £160–250,000. To the N, The Apex (formerly City Point) is another Berkeley conversion in **Bunhill Row**, on the fringes of the Old St area (see Clerkenwell). Here, the 34 flats start at £138,000. **Dufferin Avenue** has warehouse conversions. **Finsbury Square** has 10 2-bed flats and a penthouse from £245,000. In **Tabernacle St**, an old factory is becoming 23 lofts, some live/work units, others penthouses, priced from £160–445,000.

Spitalfields

Spitalfields is where the City merges with the East End. **Commercial St**, **Middlesex St** and **Bishopsgate** form the boundaries of this unique part of London, which is mostly in Tower Hamlets Borough. The big wholesale fruit and vegetable market between **Lamb St** and **Brushfield St** has now gone. Part of its site was intended for an enormous new complex for the LIFFE futures exchange, but things move fast in finance and it's no longer needed. Less ambitious office schemes will replace it, according to current plans. The market site will also include homes, some for Tower Hamlets Council. St George have a few flats left unsold at **Bishops Court** opposite the market site. Just to the W, the multi-million pound Broadgate office development now dominates the whole neighbourhood. There are, however, older buildings in Spitalfields: some beautiful early Georgian houses, built by Huguenot silk merchants, with interiors to make a Classicist swoon. Some have been lovingly restored, and will of course be retained in the area's redevelopment. These are found in **Fournier St**, **Folgate St**, **Elder St** and **Princelet St**. They command prices of around £450,000.

Conversions of old buildings provide nearly all the other homes. An early example was Pennybank Chambers, **Great Eastern St**, which has 65 small flats. The Cloisters, **Commercial St**, a purpose-built portered block, has 1-bed flats. Opposite, a new conversion called The Xchange offers smart lofts: the remaining ones were from £250,000 last November. In what they reckon is called 'The Silk Quarter', St George have 16 1- and 2-bed flats in **Lamb St** behind a Georgian-style façade overlooking Elder Gardens: from £149,000, 2-bed from £203,000. **Middlesex St** has a few developments: The Wexner Building is a 1901 cigar warehouse, now fitted (as opposed to shell-finish) flats: only three left in November, including a 4-bed duplex with roof terrace at £330,000. Rialto's Grade II listed Victorian pub opposite Broadgate is now 10 flats, from £149,000. Just off **Middlesex St**, in **Strype St**, 1-bed flats are £130,000, though a 2,200 sq ft penthouse can be had for £625,000.

Further S, the **Leman St** area on the W edge of Whitechapel has a few homes. Leybourne House is a modern block with swimming pool and that ever more vital City amenity, an underground car park. The Rialto scheme in **Prescott St** of fully-fitted 'loft-style' flats is 90 per cent sold. There is Guinness Trust housing in **Mansell St**. Developer Willow Acre's Prospero House in **The Minories**, once a bank, will be 14 flats above a restaurant. All flats will have air conditioning and prices will start at £150,000. For more developments see the Stepney and Whitechapel chapter.

Smithfield

Smithfield, at the NW edge of the City, is dominated by the splendid Victorian wholesale meat market. It is rather under the influence of Clerkenwell (see chapter) as that successful neighbourhood expands its borders. The meat market, however, is prospering and has been expensively modernized: the City Corporation is keen for it to stay. And, to the delight of the whole of London, Bart's Hospital has been at least in part reprieved. Smithfield is a good place for restaurants, and of course the well-known pubs which serve carnivorous breakfasts from 4am. Contained by **Charterhouse St**, **Aldersgate St** and **Newgate St**, Smithfield has an increasing if still small clutch of homes amid the commercial buildings. This is definitely one of the City's up-and-coming areas, a trend strongly backed by the Corporation. Its policy is 'to encourage an increase of residential accommodation in suitable locations within Smithfield' – though they reckon flats overlooking the market itself might be a bad idea. One popular development is Florin Court in **Charterhouse Square**: 2-bed flats go for £190,000, studios for £90,000. Regalian refurbished the 9-storey 1936 building to provide over 100 luxury flats. A smart hotel is also planned for the square, which also has Georgian houses dating from 1700–1775. In **Long Lane**, nine new flats have appeared in the last year and there are two schemes in **Carthusian St** on the Barbican borders. A parade of 10 mews-style homes in the side street of **Cloth Fair** dates from the late '80s, as do 10 flats in **Charterhouse St**. See also Barbican.

Fleet St and Holborn

It seems an age, not just a decade, since **Fleet St** meant national newspapers. They have all gone, leaving the Street of Shame for the shiny new world of Docklands. It has, though, taken the best part of a decade for the area to find a new identity, as a place to work (but on a modest scale, no big blocks of offices) and to live. It is very popular with lawyers and City firms wanting company flats – Goldman Sachs recently rented an entire block. Big developers Barratt and Berkeley are active. The latter were responsible for the sought-after Gallery in nearby **Ludgate Hill**, and a refurbishment in **Fleet St** itself: six flats from £205,000. Sovereign House, in **Poppin's Court**, off the street, has 14 flats, all sold at prices from £125–285,000. Barratt's Pemberton House, just off **Fleet St**, has 39 flats: 1-bed from £140,000. The Whitefriars Estate, **Carmelite St**, is to gain 52 homes in an offices/flats plan: St George again. Just to the S the Temples, Inner and Middle, house lawyers and a few favoured others in a very select live/work estate: London's oldest. **Wine Office Court** off **Fleet St** – an enviable address, and a charming paved courtyard – has six flats from £250,000 converted from a Victorian newspaper building.

The Holborn area to the N has surprisingly few homes. **Red Lion Square** has some handsome houses, and there are a few small modern blocks. There is plenty of semi-redundant commercial space here so, like Smithfield, it could be an area to watch. (See also Bloomsbury chapter.) Such is the pressure of all this development that agents have yet to invent a name for the riverside strip between **The Strand** and **The Embankment**. There are homes here: Berkeley has just finished Blythe House, with 4- bed, 4-bath: sold at £895,000. There are others – and where is more central?

Hoxton and Shoreditch

Those who have not been following the City Fringe closely may blink at eulogies about 'the many bars and restaurants of **Rivington St** and **Charlotte Rd**' – these streets are in EC2, not W11 or N1. But here we are in the 'Shoreditch Triangle', no less, between **Old St**, **Great Eastern St** and **Curtain Rd**. An influx of computer and new media firms is taking advantage of the cheap office space. More customers for the new bars come from the loft apartments such as those in **New Inn Yard**: 1,500 sq ft for upwards of £240,000, and **Curtain Rd**: 950 sq ft for around £200,000.

Another newly fashionable loft-living area is Hoxton, lying due N of the City and W of the **Kingsland Rd**. Blighted by well-intentioned post-war council monstrosities (would you believe a block of flats called Caliban Tower?), it yet manages to cling to the remnants of its vigorous past: the music hall in **Hoxton St** still stands as a thriving theatre/community centre. It has been joined by a highly fashionable cinema, The Lux. **Hoxton Square**, once a very dangerous place to enter without an entrée, now has a name as an artists' hangout.

The canal which runs W to Islington is the focus of several factory conversions: Manhattan Lofts have completed The Factory in **Shepherdess Walk**, and in the same street is Millennium Lofts' Canal Building: 74 lofts and live/work units all pre-sold at their launch in September. Close by on Welbeck Basin an old print works called the Royle Building has 82 fitted loft-style flats from £150,000 for 2-bed plus 10 new penthouses at £250,000.

Transport	Tubes & main line, all zone 1, in profusion: see map. From Bank: Oxford Circus 10 min, Heathrow 1 hr 15 min (1 change).
Convenient for	West End, Docklands & City Airport. Miles from centre: 1.5.
Schools	Local Authority: no secondary schools in City, see neighbouring areas. Private: City of London School (b) (g).

SALES

Flats	S	1B	2B	3B	4B	5B
Average prices	70–110	120–210+	130–350+	190–400	170–450+	–
Houses	2B	3B	4B	5B	6/7B	8B
Average prices	–	350–450	400–600+	575+	–	–

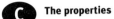

RENTAL						
Flats	S	1B	2B	3B	4B	5B
Average prices	650–900	750–1500	950–2000	1300–3000	—	—
Houses	2B	3B	4B	5B	6/7B	8B
Average prices	—	—	—	—	—	—

The properties   Homes at last re-appearing both on fringes, including Fleet St and Holborn, and among the offices. Barbican has modern flats and houses. A very few period homes in fringe areas like Spitalfields and Smithfield, plus company flats, a few ex-council homes – and a clutch of new flats and loft conversions.

The market   Barbican homes, originally rented, are now bought and sold. Prices can be good value compared with West End — but watch service charges. Rare period homes joined by a rash of new developments and conversions. Local searches: City of London 1–2 weeks, Tower Hamlets 4 weeks.

Among those estate agents active in this area are:
- Hurford Salvi Carr
- Frank Harris
- Hamptons
- Stirling Ackroyd
- Barbican Estate Office
- Jarvis Keller
- Daniel Watney *
- Phillips Residential Sales and

further details: see advertisers' index on p633

trinity square

LONDON   EC 3

Exceptional apartments possessing an outstanding City location overlooking Trinity Gardens and the Tower of London.

The fine building of Fourteen Trinity Square comprises thirteen elegant new apartments, just a short stroll from the City of London. These superb apartments offer the very best of city living -an exquisite combination of modern style, within a vibrant historical setting.

These apartments are available now
— be one of the first in line —

To receive further information and to request a brochure, contact David Prole at **FPD**Savills.

0171 824 9011

A DEVELOPMENT BY
DENCORA HOMES LTD
Telephone: 01638 663433

CLAPHAM

Map ref: p93 (4G)
Postal districts: SW4, SW9
Boroughs: Lambeth (Lab),
    Wandsworth (Con)
Council tax: Band D Lambeth
    £647, Wandsworth £334
Conservation areas: Old Town,
    High St, Common and others
Parking: High St imminent
    Red Route, residents' in
    many areas

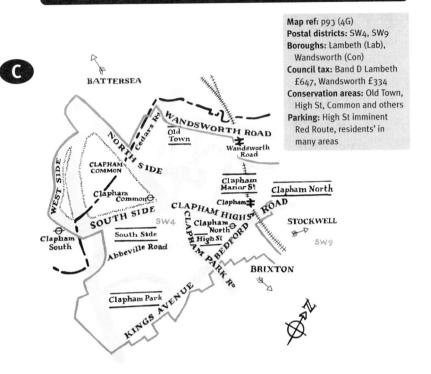

'Clapham,' observed a fashionable young thing just setting up home in Brixton, 'is mumsy.' By which she meant that the tract around **Abbeville Rd** and South Side is so blessed with offspring that the nursery schools can be counted in dozens, and that the domesticity was a trifle stifling. Clapham is indeed now a solid, family area – with home prices to suit. Its key assets are tube, common and plenty of 3- and 4-bed houses. The hyper-modern designer Sainsbury's in the **High St** and the restaurants in **Old Town** set the seal on an area that had been 'up-and-coming' for 15 years. Judging by the prices, it has 'up-and-come'.

Clapham was once a little hamlet surrounded by big houses, where prosperous Londoners kept country retreats. Pepys, for instance, lived and died here. In early Victorian times more grand houses appeared as the ubiquitous Thomas Cubitt built a whole suburb of them and called it Clapham Park. But as the century went on, and trams and later tubes made Clapham cheap and easy to get to, the houses got smaller and smaller. By the turn of the century, Clapham was a byword for ordinariness. 'The man on the Clapham omnibus' became a judicial simile for all that was everyday and reasonable.

The tube, the arrival of which abetted the demolition (begun with the railways) of so many grand houses and their replacement with modest terraces, has more recently been Clapham's salvation. For thanks to the Northern line, Clapham, unlike most parts of South London, has a direct link to the West End and the City. In the '80s, house-buyers began to discover that Clapham is as close to Sloane Square as Fulham

is, and that the journey to Oxford Circus or the City is a lot quicker. Clapham was re-established, after spending most of the 20th century in genteel, steady decline.

Clapham began as a village at the N end of the wide common. The old village is still there, with a pleasant mix of buildings that includes a row of fine Queen Anne houses. From here the houses spread out W and E, beginning with a handsome 1820s row and going on to Cubitt's 250 acres of 'capacious detached villas' in Clapham Park. Later Victorian times saw the growth of **Clapham High St** and a shift in Clapham's commercial centre of gravity from the **Old Town** eastwards. Today, the Old Town and the **High St** have blossomed with smart restaurants and bars (though the council is not keen on the burgeoning pavement terraces), and Clapham at last has a night life.

Clapham divides into several distinct neighbourhoods radiating out from the **Old Town** – both a street name and the heart of the old village. The area W of the common is Battersea (see chapter), or now 'Between the Commons'. The flat, low-lying streets N of **Wandsworth Rd** are thought of as Battersea too: Clapham is proud of being on a low but distinct hill. To the S the roads around Clapham South tube are now called 'Clapham South' but were Balham (see chapter): it would have been less confusing if the tube people had stuck to their original name for the station, Nightingale Lane. East, beyond Clapham Park, is a zone debated with Brixton. Clapham Junction, by the way, is in Battersea: a source of confusion for over a century.

The Common survived the Victorians, and is now a valuable green lung and backdrop – and the source of some fine, open views from the handsome houses and flats which gaze out over it.

Old Town

Strictly speaking, **Old Town** is a street, but the core of old Clapham has annexed the name. As with all such desirable tags, estate agents try to stretch it as far as possible. It is usually reckoned to run N as far as **Larkhall Rise** and **Wandsworth Rd**. **Old Town** proper has Clapham's oldest and handsomest houses, a row of three dating from 1705. These rare Queen Anne survivals go for around £600,000. To the E is **Grafton Square**, a pleasant garden square surrounded on three sides by tall, handsome, white stucco 1850s houses, which often have attractive semi-basement flats. There are three pretty 2-storey stucco houses, plus some new-build in the road off the square. The site SW of the square is owned by the Home Office; plans for a new police headquarters caused a local fuss in 1997, but things have gone quiet since. North of **Grafton Square** are several streets of solid, 3/4-storey Victorian houses: **Offerton Rd** (particularly nice), **Liston Rd** and **Fitzwilliam Rd**: a 5-bed house here was on the market for £590,000 last winter. On the **Liston Rd** corner of the square is a 1990s scheme of four flats.

Rectory Grove runs N from the **Old Town** to pass the old parish church and link with **Larkhall Rise**. This is normally a busy traffic route, but the closure for two years of the railway bridge at its E end has lessened the flow. The Rise has some attractive houses of varying periods: a pretty double-fronted 4-bed one was £460,000 last autumn. **Rectory Gardens** is a row of tiny, restored mews cottages. Between **Rectory Grove** and **North St** is the large site of an old factory, where plans for a mixed homes and commercial development – and possibly a Holmes Place health club – are being prepared. **Turret Grove**, named after a feature of the Elizabethan manor which once stood here, has some pretty cottages as well as the Victorian terraces it shares with **Rozel Rd** and **Iveley Rd**, the latter peacefully tucked away by the old church. Prices for 3/4-bed houses here hover around £300,000.

West of **Old Town** and its continuation **North St** is a quiet network of streets. **Macaulay Rd** was built in late-Victorian times with very large gabled detached and semi-detached houses, many of which survive. Most are flats but some are still vast single homes which, when very smart, can command around £1 million. **Macaulay Square** is a small council estate. Macaulay Court is a block of '30s flats, nicely positioned in the angle of **Macauley Rd** and **Lillieshall Rd**, always with some for sale. **Lillieshall Rd** has some substantial Victorian terraces plus some pretty, very small cottages at the E end. Parallel **Broadhinton Rd** has some attractive early Victorian cottages. **Orlando Rd** has large 3-storey Victorian houses, many flats. Off **Hannington Rd**, **Redwood Mews** has nine new 1- and 2-bed houses around a courtyard, and **Sycamore Mews**, on the site of the old royal laundry between **North St** and **Orlando Rd**, is a new mews scheme of flats and houses. One-bed flats go for around £130,000.

Across **Macaulay Rd** to the E, **The Chase**, a parallel grand avenue, has similarly vast Victorian houses: where possible, the large houses of this corner of Clapham are being re-converted back to single homes. Some of the enormous double-fronted houses boast 6 or 7 bedrooms, and 120-ft gardens – and prices have reached up to £1.75 million. A third avenue, **Victoria Rise**, has gaunter and less kempt, but still huge, grey-brick and stucco houses; next comes **Cedars Rd**, a main bus and traffic artery.

The **North Side** of Clapham Common has a succession of terraces of various periods, from 1695 through early Georgian and mid-Victorian to 1930s flats. The two commanding blocks on either side of **Cedars Rd** are remarkable examples of 1860s grandiose. Enviable flats come up for sale occasionally in the E block. Several of the enormous houses are also now flats, which have fine views across London to the N and the common to the S. If you fancy a whole house, a Georgian 5-bed one was for sale in the winter for £950,000. **Cedars Rd** itself, once lined with villas, is now mostly council-built housing: resales are common. Tiny **Wix's Lane**, to the W of **Cedars Rd**, marks the border both of Lambeth Borough and SW4 (for the SW11 streets that run down from **North Side** to **Lavender Hill**, see the Battersea chapter). Three new mews houses have appeared here: one was on the market for £260,000 last winter.

Back now towards the Old Town, where next to the library at the E end of **Clapham Common North Side**, a big computer company has just done up an old factory as offices for its 300 staff. **North Side**, **Old Town** and **The Pavement** meet to form a triangle that has an irresistible village-green feel; a curve of increasingly tidy shops face Holy Trinity Church on the common. There are some flats above shops (with three smart 3-bed ones coming soon), and two popular inter-war blocks of flats.

Across the common, **West Side** scrapes into the SW4 postcode though its hinterland is SW11 (see Battersea). The tall, popular houses stand in their quiet road facing the common: traffic is deflected down **The Avenue**, part of the South Circular.

Clapham Manor St

The Old Town area is bounded to the E by a tract of council-built housing around **Cubitt Terrace**. These are nicely designed, brick-built, mainly 2-storey, and arranged in pleasant closes and green squares. Some are appearing on the resale market, competing with the original 2-bed early Victorian cottages (which are priced at around £275,000). To the N of **Larkhall Rise** are some sloping streets of terraced houses: **Brayburne Avenue**, with 4-bedroom houses, has become quieter since access to **Wandsworth Rd** was cut off at the northern end. **Hesewall Close**, completed in 1995, is a street of 12 3-bed family houses on land which was once allotments. **Netherford Rd** and, E of the railway, **Killyon Rd** are Victorian terraces. The little Wandsworth Rd station runs to Victoria and London Bridge. The line is used by Channel Tunnel trains.

  Clapham Manor St, especially at its N end, is handsome with 2- and 3-storey Cubitt terraces, much in demand as family homes. The S end, towards the **High St**, is more mixed. The little roads off to the E like **Navy St** and **Voltaire Rd** have later Victorian terraces, and **Edgeley Rd** has rather looming 3-storey Victorian ones, most flats. The E side backs onto the railway. Twelve new mews houses have been inserted behind a Victorian façade. Elmhurst Mansions is a purpose-built block. A 2-bed flat around here might go for £130–150,000. The corner between **Old Town** and **Clapham Manor St** has some 3-storey purpose-built Victorian flats in **Bromells Rd** and some flats in smaller terraces in **Venn St**, 2 min from Clapham Common tube station.

High St

Clapham High St has been transformed by the advent of a new Sainsbury's on the site of the old bus garage. It has a large and fairly cheap (2hr max) car park. Another important plus is the Clapham Picture House, in **Venn St**. Its bar has added to a rash of new drinking holes: seedy shops are being replaced by tapas bars, an Egyptian pizza joint patronized by supermodels, and smart cafés. The **High St's** biggest undeveloped site is a row of seedy shops between **Venn St** and **Stonehouse St** once owned by the Church Commissioners, but now sold on. At last plans are in for three new shops and 22 1/3-bed flats. Rumours abound about which chain will take the shops. Further E, Budgens has given up and gone away, leaving another vacant site. Note that the **High St** and **South Side** are due to be a Red Route, and that the ever-growing controlled parking zone, while popular with residents, hampers shoppers.

  South of the **High St** is a mixed area of Victorian terraces and council housing. It is very close to tubes (Claphams North and Common), shops and common, and offers better value than the more 'tidy' areas of Clapham. **Nelson's Row** with its dozen flat-fronted Victorian cottages leads on down to a much-tidied-up '30s red-brick council estate, then to the attractive modern council houses of **Haselrigge Rd**. St Luke's **Avenue** and the roads to the E (**Tremadoc Rd**, **Kenwyn Rd**, **Cato Rd**) are mostly 3-storey Victorian, many now flats, which are cheaper here than in other Clapham neighbourhoods: 1-bed flats start at around £125,000. On the corner of **Aristotle Rd** and **Bedford Rd** is **Aristotle Mews**: this is 17 houses by Fairview, just sold for £210–260,000. **Lion Yard** is a development of business units, built in mews style, in **Tremadoc Rd**.

  The streets off the south side of **Clapham Park Rd**, down as far as the corner with **Abbeville Rd**, are largely council-built homes. There is a large and smart new mews of 'business units' in **Clapham Park Rd**. **St Alphonsus Rd** has some Victorian terraces and 14 new flats are planned by Goldhawk. **Northbourne Rd** has some well-preserved detached and semi-detached mid-Victorian houses on a handsome scale. These are some of the nicest houses in Clapham, but are tucked away in rather drab surroundings. Substantial 5-bedroomed houses here can fetch around £750,000. A once-derelict 19th-century building here has recently been restored as four flats. A rather sad office block on **Clapham Park Rd** has gained a new floor and façade and become St Paul's View ('wiv a ladder and some glasses'). These 1- to 3-bedroomed flats by Barratt help to tidy up what was a scruffy corner: a 2-bed one has just changed hands for £150,000. **Park Hill** runs up as far as Clapham Park. It contains some '20s gabled terraces, some modern flats and a few large early 19th-century detached houses: a pair has been split into eight flats ('The White House') from £110–250,000.

Clapham North

East of the tube station and N of the railway (which is used by Channel Tunnel trains), and in the SW9 postcode, is a rather cut-off corner of Victorian terraces and council housing. The Southwestern Hospital forms the border with Brixton. Housing in this district was until recently cheaper than in other parts of Clapham: it is further from the common and some streets were distinctly down-at-heel. However, the little network of roads N of **Landor Rd** – **Atherfold Rd**, **Hemberton Rd** and **Prideaux Rd** – is becoming a popular area now that neighbouring Brixton is downright fashionable. Three-bed Clapham North houses which were £80,000 five years ago now reach £190,000 smartened up, while a 6-bed one was on the market at £205,000 late last autumn. **Landor Rd** itself is busy and unreconstructed. Along **Clapham Rd** towards Stockwell are some fine Georgian houses, most used as offices, but some reverting to homes.

West of **Clapham Rd**, **Gauden Rd**, **Bromfelde Rd**, **Sibella Rd** and **Chelsham Rd** have some big Victorian houses. Good flat conversions can be found, including one in **Gauden Rd** where several houses have been split into flats. Each of these flats share the large communal garden and a swimming pool. Some houses are still single homes: they are large (some 6-bed) with big gardens and can be spectacular – and £500,000 or more.

Clapham Park

Cubitt's elegant suburb of detached mansions has vanished, leaving as its legacy large trees and the occasional surviving square early 19th-century house, now flats. This area, centred on **King's Avenue**, is furthest from tubes or trains – though the South Circular marks the southern borders with Balham. **King's Avenue** has several blocks of flats – Queenswood Court includes one of the Victorian houses – Robins, Oakfield and Thorncliffe Courts are '30s blocks; Peters Court is '60s. Prices for a 2-bed in these blocks are from £95–130,000. Inter-war suburban-style detached houses punctuate the flats. **King's Mews** is a modern group of houses that is tucked behind an old house. East of **King's Avenue** is in SW2 and is a border zone between Brixton and Clapham Park. There are several quiet streets of Victorian terraces. Brixton Prison dominates the eastern end of **Thornbury Rd**. **Kingswood Rd** has some larger, 3-storey houses. These streets are fairly evenly split between single houses and flat conversions. A typical price is £125,000 for a 2-bedroom garden flat. The S end of **King's Avenue** and west to **Clarence Avenue** is all council-built housing, houses and low blocks set in a pleasant green space. Some resales: a pleasant 3-bed semi was £150,000 last November. The northern end of **Clarence Avenue** has some 1930s semi-detached houses.

Continuing N, the streets leading E off **Lyham Rd** are SW2, and have received a boost from the renaissance of Brixton (see chapter).

South Side/Abbeville

This is the largest residential neighbourhood in Clapham and the most uniform, consisting almost entirely of Victorian terraced housing. The grid of streets runs down a gentle slope from **Clapham Common South Side** to **Abbeville Rd** then on up again towards Clapham Park. The parade of shops at the junction of **Abbeville Rd** and

Narbonne Avenue was dignified in the '80s by estate agents with the name 'Abbeville Village'. Here life has followed art, and what was a humdrum little suburban parade is now truly a neighbourhood, with its own night life, designer shops – and even a village fair. It is a family area undergoing a positive baby boom: nursery schools abound, with an Anglo-Spanish one the latest to open.

There is no way through from **Clarence Avenue** in Clapham Park to the next road W, **Rodenhurst Rd**, which belongs to the Abbeville neighbourhood. This divide is architectural as well as physical: much of **Rodenhurst Rd** (except the S end) is large, popular Edwardian semi-detached double-fronted houses set well back from the wide road; these now command prices of £450–500,000, though really big and/or good ones can go up to £700,000. **Poynders Rd** forms the S boundary of Clapham – and is also the **South Circular Rd**. It has some rather depressed-looking inter-war flats, some modern town-houses and some Edwardian ones. Its equally busy continuation, **Cavendish Rd**, has big turn-of-the-century houses.

West from **Rodenhurst Rd** is **Elms Crescent,** which is lined with late-19th-century bay-windowed terraced houses. It and the roads off it to the W are very uniform: exceptions to the 2-storey terraced rule include **Elms Rd**, which has some handsome tall-gabled, wider than average houses on the N side. A 6-bed semi can command £600–800,000. The W end of **Elms Rd** runs up towards the common and has some large 1880s houses, some detached and double-fronted. Five large square Victorian houses at the W end are flats. The parallel streets such as **Leppoc Rd** and **Narbonne Avenue** have mostly 4-bed houses. The number of trees, width of the road (and thus ease of parking) and distance from the tube and shops are the variables around here. The 4-bed houses, typical of the area, were selling in the winter for around £300–350,000. **Hambalt** and **Mandalay Rds** are mostly terraced housing with quite a few purpose-built flats, which can be spotted by their pairs of front doors under a single arch. These are popular, and go for £170–185,000. The streets S of **Narbonne Avenue** are mostly Victorian terraces, but with some post-war 3-storey flats.

Abbeville Rd, which carries a fair amount of traffic, has some bigger than usual houses, many divided into flats. There are also flats above the shops in the parade and a few nice big purpose-built flats in Edwardian blocks.

The common, at the junction with **Elms Rd**, is lined with big mid-Victorian terraces set back behind a strip of grass. These are South Kensington-like houses with pillared porches, all flats. A splendid low-built detached villa, now offices, is on the market if you want a truly grand Clapham home. **St Gerards Close** is a little estate of 4-storey flats built within the last 10 years. On **Clapham Common South Side**, next to **Elms Rd,** is Brook House, a development of 11 luxury apartments. Also on **South Side**, former halls of residence have become a new-build scheme of flats and houses for a housing association. Opposite, on the common, is the popular Windmill pub with a few tall houses behind it in **Windmill Drive**. Most are splendid flats, their turret roofs partially glazed to form big rooms with wide views. Several newly converted flats were on the market in the winter at prices up to £340,000.

South Side continues with the hideous Notre Dame estate. But past **Crescent Lane**, which meanders through to **Abbeville Rd** and on to **King's Avenue**, lies Clapham's premier street, **Crescent Grove**. This is a fine Regency crescent facing a row of grand semi-detached villas of the same period, the whole forming a private road entered through a gateway. These enviable houses command prices of £750,000 upwards. The coachhouses which link the big villas have themselves become sought-after small homes: a 3-bed was £320,000 leasehold last winter.

The old women's hospital at the S end of **South Side**, across from Clapham South tube, is under seige from Tesco who plan a Metro store. The result of a planning appeal is awaited.

Transport	Tubes: Clapham South, Clapham Common, Clapham North (zones 2/3, Northern); Oxford Circus 20 min (1 change), City 25 min, Heathrow 1 hr 10 min (2 changes). Trains: Wandsworth Rd, Clapham High St, to Victoria and London Bridge.
Convenient for	City, West End, Sloane Square. Miles from centre: 3.
Schools	Local Authority: No local authority secondary schools in area. See Battersea, Dulwich and Streatham chapters.

SALES

Flats	S	1B	2B	3B	4B	5B
Average prices	50–80	65–140	90–220	100–220	110–250	130–280
Houses	2B	3B	4B	5B	6/7B	8B
Average prices	135–270	180–370+	200–550+	300–750+	500+	800+

RENTAL

Flats	S	1B	2B	3B	4B	5B
Average prices	500–1000	600–1200	800–2000	1300–2500	–	–
Houses	2B	3B	4B	5B	6/7B	8B
Average prices	900–2000	1000–2000	1600–2600	2100–3000	3000+	6000+

The properties	Many Victorian terraces; some splendid Queen Anne, Georgian and Regency around the Clapham Common, Old Town and Crescent Grove, lots of converted flats (including good large ones) and some 20th-century flats blocks. Large houses in The Chase, Macaulay Rd, Rodenhurst Avenue; typical house is 3/4-bed terraced, 4/5-bed around Abbeville.
The market	South Side, Abbeville 'village' and Old Town are well 'discovered'; former pair attract families wanting space, latter has older, more character properties. High St improving fast in wake of new Sainsbury's. Prices drop in N and E, though catching up fast due to 'Brixton effect'.

Among those estate agents active in this area are:
- Halifax Property
- Barnard Marcus
- Bells
- Winkworth *
- Hamptons
- Price & Co
- Kinleigh Folkard & Hayward
- Bushells
- Hugh Henry
- Friend & Falcke
- Woolwich
- Richard Oakey
- John Hollingsworth
- Douglas & Gordon*
- Foxtons*

further details: see advertisers' index on p633

- We have many thousands of flats and houses available across the capital.

- We have the local information and up-to-date knowledge on availability.

- We would be delighted to help you find your home.

Winkworth
The London Property Specialists

CLERKENWELL AND FINSBURY

C

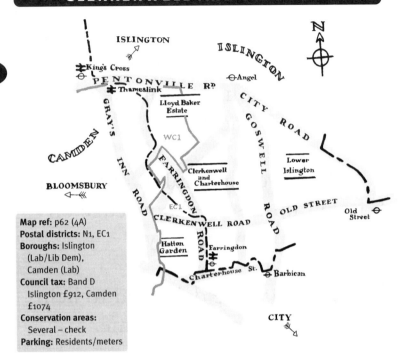

ISLINGTON

ISLINGTON

King's Cross

Angel

PENTONVILLE RD

Thameslink

Lloyd Baker
Estate

WC1

CITY

GOSWELL

ROAD

GRAY'S

Clerkenwell
and
Charterhouse

Lower
Islington

CAMDEN

INN

FARRINGDON

BLOOMSBURY

ROAD

EC1

ROAD

OLD STREET

Old
Street

CLERKENWELL ROAD

CLERKENWELL

ROAD

Hatton
Garden

Farringdon

Charterhouse St.

Barbican

CITY

Map ref: p62 (4A)
Postal districts: N1, EC1
Boroughs: Islington
  (Lab/Lib Dem),
  Camden (Lab)
Council tax: Band D
  Islington £912, Camden
  £1074
Conservation areas:
  Several – check
Parking: Residents/meters

The Clerkenwell loft has become a byword for smart urban living, the successor to the mews houses (redundant stables) and church conversions of earlier generations of achievers. 'Loft living' is an established London sub-culture, and it is apparently blossoming as far away as Leeds and Glasgow (wherever they may be). Back in 1988 this book commented 'Clerkenwell and Finsbury have at first sight enormous potential as a residential area: ideally situated [just N of the City], with a high proportion of Georgian buildings . . .' Any homes that did appear were snapped up; the problem was, very few did.

How things have changed: there are now around 1,000 homes more than a decade ago, and 2,000 more are in the pipeline. The catalyst was a switch in planning policy. Islington Council finally acknowledged that the commercial space in the area was largely redundant. The light industries that had grown up over the previous two centuries – printing, metalwork, wines and spirits – departed suddenly as technology changed. The City offices expanded eastwards, into Docklands, not north as had been expected. Only the media business stayed put.

The planners at last relaxed the usage conditions early in the 1990s; pioneer developers bought empty warehouses, offices and factories and started to convert them to homes around 1994. The precedent was the Docklands warehouse boom of a decade before; but since the Docks had caught a bad cold when the market crashed before the infrastructure was well in place, these new conversions looked to Manhattan for a new gloss, and the term 'loft apartments' became the '90s buzzword.

Today, Clerkenwell has risen in status and price to overtake the Finsbury neighbourhoods to the N. As a result Clerkenwell 'proper' is extremely expensive so would-be loft-dwellers are now looking E to the area around **Old St** and **City Rd**. The live/work concept, so slow to mature elsewhere in London, has caught on here. Photographers, designers, artists all find it an attractive way of life. But they have to be successful ones. The majority of homes are 1- to 2-bed flats (lofts or otherwise); large houses and studios are rare. Such 2-, 3- and 4-bed houses that exist are mostly in the N of the area: finding them is like pulling plums out of the pudding.

The property framework here is a curious mixture: there's Georgian, converted commercial, modern. The swathes of Victorian housing – the staple for so much of London – was either bombed or has been demolished since the war. Post-war, it has been the council that has provided almost the only opportunity for living in this historic corner of London: most tenants have lived there all their lives, often working in the printing trade; this contributes a continuity in the population now missing from other corners of town. Streets are a rich mixture of architectural styles and periods, and residential and commercial uses: this is what gives the area its distinctive flavour.

The first wave of lofts, essentially ex-industrial space, were airy, galleried affairs; these have been joined by smaller, much more cramped versions and by new-build blocks. There's a feeling that saturation has been reached: the new homes are harder to sell outside the core, though 'real' lofts are much in demand as existing residents trade up within the area and newcomers arrive. Renting is on the rise as City people discover the area, joining the artistic pioneers (the academic, publishing, design, media and fashion worlds are well-represented, both in workplaces and inhabitants).

To define the area: it lies N of the City and **Fleet St**, E of the **Gray's Inn Rd**, St Pancras and Bloomsbury, S of **City Rd** and the Angel – close to the West and East Ends, 5–10 min from the City, and close to major stations, it's convenient for just about everywhere. Despite a large number of squares and parks, it remains essentially urban. This is the place for restaurants, bars and general buzz . . . the people who work here tend to party rather than go home to the family, and the loft-dwellers join them.

It divides into four neighbourhoods: Clerkenwell and Charterhouse; Lower Islington; Hatton Garden; the Finsbury district centred around the Lloyd Baker estate. These are all approximations; there are no definitive boundaries, and no clear consensus among either inhabitants or estate agents as to what to call neighbourhoods. Finsbury, once the accepted local name, is easily confused with Finsbury Park, a couple of miles to the N. Finsbury was a separate borough from 1900 to 1965, when Islington took over. (There is, too, a confusing tendency among agents and developers to use the name 'Islington' for everything in the borough . . .)

The real point about Clerkenwell is its history. It has been urban since the Middle Ages. Monasteries, mansions, churches, almshouses, sober Georgian homes, Victorian slums and distilleries succeeded one another. Some roads retain their medieval flavour still, twisting and turning like snakes and ladders on a board. Clerkenwell and its sub-zones Farringdon and Charterhouse are districts of narrow, dense streets, with concealed alleys and arches and mixtures of architectural styles and residential and commercial uses. There is a high percentage of Georgian; many other buildings have been given post-modern spruce-ups. Clerkenwell has shot in a decade from cheapest to priciest neighbourhood, overtaking the Smithfield and Barbican borders and the Lloyd Baker estate. In the last category, prices are still below those in Islington. If you want to buy more cheaply try the King's Cross (see chapter) borders – especially in the streets with dense traffic such as **King's Cross Rd** or those near railway lines – for example **Britannia St**. Or near densely populated housing estates such as **Wynyatt St** or **Exmouth Market**. Shoreditch (see City chapter) is another area to try.

Lower Islington, between the **City Rd** and **Goswell Rd**, is almost exclusively council-built housing, with a large number of very high '60s-style tower blocks with

20-plus floors. Some lower-rise housing occurs towards the Clerkenwell border and in the N towards the Angel, and there is a lot of commercial property, some of which is being converted to residential.

On the W edge of the area lies the late-Georgian Lloyd Baker estate, the New River Estate and a swathe to the E of **Rosebery Avenue** and W of Lower Islington which has no accepted name, but is sometimes referred to as North Clerkenwell. The architecture is mainly Georgian mixed with some modern high-rises, a little commercial and a high proportion of council housing. This neighbourhood has a higher percentage of home ownership than most of the area, but still not a majority. Still not as select as Islington proper, but getting there. This area still has enormous potential and is the place to look for a family home. The cultured find it to be conveniently close to Sadler's Wells Theatre (open again this year after a massive lottery-financed rebuild).

Hatton Garden is traditionally the centre of London's jewellery trade, especially diamonds. It's next door to Holborn, and so has a distinctly up-market, big-business feel; streets are wider and less medieval in appearance. The surviving Georgian houses are being joined by a rash of new-build and converted apartments.

Clerkenwell and Charterhouse

The wider Clerkenwell area has seen the biggest boom in development: around 50 schemes have been built or are in the process of being built, with about 30 planned. Most of the existing ones are conversions, with new-build predominating among the planned schemes: the supply of suitable buildings for conversion has dried up – partly because office rents are rising and homes are no longer the only profitable use for the space.

Clerkenwell centres around **Clerkenwell Green** and the surrounding small streets. The very overcrowded **Clerkenwell Rd** cuts through the neighbourhood from W-E, and **Farringdon Rd** runs N-S. To begin from the N, from the crossroads of **Rosebery Avenue** and **Farringdon Rd**, the area up to **Calthorpe St** is on the NW boundary of central Clerkenwell and houses a variety of commercial buildings, including the old Times newspaper building in **Coley St** and **Gough St**, and the vast Mount Pleasant Post Office, which dominates **Farringdon Rd** and the top of **Mount Pleasant**. Continuing S down **Rosebery Avenue** there are a number of Victorian commercial buildings with shops beneath, followed by Rosebery Square Buildings, a large Victorian workmen's flats development that dominates both sides of the street as it goes to join the **Clerkenwell Rd**. It has been refurbished by the St Pancras Housing Association to provide 100 flats.

Clerkenwell Rd runs W-E, with **Rosebery Avenue** forking off to form a triangle. The area between the two is typical Clerkenwell, with a warren of narrow, densely packed streets running higgledy piggledy, their names betraying their medieval origins: **Herbal Hill, Vine Hill, Baker's Row**. The architecture is mainly Georgian or early Victorian, and uses have traditionally been mainly commercial – though now four modern blocks in **Topham St** and **Warner St** provide some flats as well as shops and offices. The Herbal Hill apartments, 1–10 **Summers St** and the Warner Building were among the early conversions and provide some of the most expensive flats in the district: £385,000 for a 1/2-bed unit. The Ziggurat Building in **Saffron Hill** has 'true' lofts. Prices in these buildings range from £160–600,000. This part of Clerkenwell ends at **Farringdon Rd**, which completes the triangle in the E. Just E of the **Farringdon Rd** and the railway in its deep cutting is **Clerkenwell Green**. This is the centre of old Clerkenwell, gathering place for the Peasants' Revolt and now home to the Karl Marx Library. The heart of the area is a jumble of Victorian, Georgian and modern architecture, with its bars, up-market restaurants, pubs and posh design studios . . . a decidedly prosperous atmosphere.

The two main streets of central Clerkenwell are **Clerkenwell Close**, running NW from the Green, and **Sekforde St** running NE. **Clerkenwell Close** retains a number of small Georgian terraced homes. To the left is a new commercial and residential development by Islington Council, with shops below and 28 flats above. To the right is the imposing St James's Church, with its clock tower spire and surrounding small garden. At the end of the Close are the distinctive yellow-and-white-brick Peabody flats, which go on round into **Pear Tree Court**. To the E, **Clerkenwell Close** twists round to meet **Bowling Green Lane** and **Corporation Row**, with their mainly commercial buildings of mixed periods; after this **Clerkenwell Close** becomes **Rosoman St**. Past **Northampton Row** is an adventure playground, followed by the gardens of **Rosoman Place** on the left; opposite is a high tower block. Continuing along **Rosoman St**, the turning to the left is **Exmouth Market**, a pedestrian street which is smartening up with restaurants and cafés – even a designer jewellers.

Sekforde St, one of Clerkenwell's finest streets, runs NE from **Clerkenwell Green**. It is made up of 2- and 3-storey Regency terraces, the middle portion of which have balconies. Residential and commercial uses mingle, with a former bank now stylishly changed into a single, 7,000 sq ft house, on the market in the winter for £1.85 million. Towards **St John St**, **Woodbridge St** to the N has 3-storey Georgian terraces overlooking a school. Between **Sekforde St** and **St John St** is Bellway's St Paul's Square: a big complex of flats behind a listed façade (of an old debtors' prison, actually). Forking to the N from **Sekforde St** is **St James's Walk**: on one side a mixture of Georgian homes and Victorian commercial buildings; on the other a children's playground and the garden surrounding St James's Church. The originally fine network of medieval streets that made up the middle of this area has now been obliterated, and the area is bordered by **Sans Walk** in the N and **Clerkenwell Close** in the W.

East of **St John St** across to the **Goswell Rd**, bounded on the S by **Clerkenwell Rd**, is an 8-acre block of property called the Clerkenwell Estate. This was owned by the Governors of Sutton Hospital for 350 years until 1995, when they sold to Bee Bee Developments. The new landlords, working closely with Islington Council, have drawn up a long-term plan to improve and develop the estate: 75 homes have so far resulted. Due in 1999 are three developments: 14 clever modern-style flats next to the smart Gee St Studios, from £150,000; 17 fully fitted flats in **Goswell Rd**, from £160,000; and 21 in **Great Sutton St**, available as shells or fitted, from £140–600,000.

The area S of **Clerkenwell Rd** down to **Charterhouse St** and W to **Farringdon St** is also Clerkenwell, although the streets to the E of **St John St** up to **Aldersgate** are more commonly termed Charterhouse. Anything in this area or along the Smithfield border is at a premium because of its proximity to the City. There are virtually no houses here, what homes there are being predominantly small flats used as pieds-à-terre and commercial conversions. The Charterhouse, which gives this corner its name, was a medieval Carthusian monastery. The site is located on the corner of **St John St** and **Charterhouse St**, and stretches back to the **Clerkenwell Rd**. Used since the war by St Bart's Medical School, it is still a special corner which mixes the Elizabethan with the utilitarian around a central park with plane trees, with tall commercial property in the W and down **Charterhouse Mews**. In **Charterhouse Square** – one of London's last private, gated squares – are peaceful Georgian homes, plus a '30s Art Deco block refurbished a decade ago to provide nine floors of pieds-à-terre for City folk, complete with its own pool, gym and roof garden. A 2-bed flat was £190,000 in November. To the E, **Charterhouse Square** becomes **Carthusian St**, which sees the occasional small flats development. Roads to the N off Aldersgate are solidly commercial.

To the W, off **St John St**, roads continue in a familiar Clerkenwell pattern, though a little more orderly. The lower end of **St John St** used to be largely commercial with many tall Victorian and Georgian buildings, some adapted in a post-modern style to provide posh office space close to the City, some concealing flats. At the moment, large chunks of the street are being converted into homes, and quite a few of the ground floors have become restaurants. The site of the old gin distillery, derelict for years, has just got planning consent for new shops – Sainsbury's and Boots – offices and flats, and there's talk of a cinema. Parallel to **St John St** is **St John's Lane**, which terminates in the N at St John's Gate, a stone arch dating from 1504 and the original entrance to the Grand Priory of St John of Jerusalem.

Britton St to the W runs parallel to **St John's Lane**, with mainly 4-storey Georgian and Victorian commercial. No 1 Britton St was mostly sold off-plan in late 1997 at prices up to £800,000 for the penthouse. Next door and building over the winter is Persimmon's Clerkenwell Central: 20 warehouse apartments (£170–425,000), 5 houses (£400,000-plus) and 28 new-build flats (£160–200,000) on the **Turnmill St** frontage (facing the railway cutting). Continuing down **Britton St** to the junction with **Brisset St**, there is a modern 5-storey office/home with intriguing post-modern exterior, built for a well-known showbiz client. Between **Benjamin St** and **Cowcross St** Exchange Place, a hotel/offices/100 flats scheme, is imminent. Further down, at the corner of **Benjamin St** is tiny **St John's Garden**; to the S is **Eagle Court** which joins **Britton St** to **St John's Lane**. It is mainly modern commercial, but has one 3-storey Georgian mews house. Down **Benjamin St** and left into **Turnmill St** is Farringdon station, the tube and train link for the area. It has been expanded, being on the north-south Thameslink rail line. Nearby, on **Farringdon Rd**, is a Berkeley Homes scheme of 1- to 3-bed flats, all sold. More are being built above the Post Office. **Charterhouse St** runs E-W, forming the southernmost boundary of the area, passing behind Smithfield Market and across the **Farringdon Rd** divide on its way to Holborn Circus.

Hatton Garden

The area to the N of **Holborn** and W of **Farringdon Rd** is Hatton Garden, traditionally the home of the diamond business. Its streets are wider, less densely packed and more logical in layout than Clerkenwell's. **Hatton Garden** itself leads N from **Holborn Circus**, and is a mixture of modern office blocks, including the sumptuous New Garden House, and smaller Georgian and Victorian terraces. It houses the best and most expensive jewellers of the area. The district to the E is acquiring some smart new flats, such as the Ziggurat and Da Vinci buildings in **Saffron Hill**. **Viaduct Buildings**, a cul-de-sac (entrance at the corner of **Charterhouse St** and **Saffron Hill**), has a 4-storey flats block refurbished in a post-modern style. At the turn of the year Camden Council, whose patch this is, said it would resist further change of use. At time of writing there are five new blocks in the neighbourhood with between 10 and 44 flats each. One is the conversion of old jewellery workshops leading through to **Hatton Place**. Local prices typically are £80,000 for studios, £140,000 for 1-bed, £200,000 for 2-bed.

To the W of **Leather Lane, Dorrington** and **Beauchamp Sts** form a quiet square with plane trees: mainly commercial with a row of modern maisonettes at the end. **Leather Lane** itself is the site of the famous market, which runs down the length of the street between Georgian terraces with shops below. In **Baldwins Gardens** the Beeching Building is now lofts, and St Alban's Church Hall has been bought recently for conversion into 20–25 homes. Further W, off the **Gray's Inn Rd**, is **Brookes Court**, a new 3-storey maisonette development by Ideal Homes in dark brown-brick, facing gardens.

The streets between **Verulam St** and **Clerkenwell Rd** surround the council's Bourne Estate – quiet, '30s-style 5-storey flats entered by arches from the surrounding roads.

Old Street/Lower Islington

The **Old St** roundabout is the most easterly point of the area; from it **City Rd** runs NW and **Old St** SW. The area between the fork is sometimes dubbed 'Lower Islington':

almost exclusively modern council-built housing, mixed with some commercial property. Developers have been finding that this commercial space is as unwanted as Clerkenwell's. **Bath St** runs N-S: at the **Old St** end, modern low-rise maisonettes extend W towards **Lizard St**. Continuing N, you enter the high-rise estates, tower blocks of between 16 and 20 storeys, including roads to the E and W: **Peerless St**, **Galway St**, **Radnor St**, **Mora St** and the lower portion of **Lever St**. At the **City Rd/Bath St** junction, City Approach is a new flats scheme. Ten years ago the Old St fire station was turned into studios and 1-bed flats. It also houses a restaurant. Turning W along **Lever St**, roads to the N are mainly commercial. To the E of **Macclesfield Rd**, a successful development of derelict land has brought a business centre and several conversions, including the £245,000-plus loft apartments of No 1 **Dingley Place** carved out of a former coffee warehouse. The new Barbican Hotel is off **Dingley Rd**. Further W, **King Square** has 4- and 6-storey blocks, with a shopping precinct and a large rose garden.

To the S of **Lever St** is commercial property in **Ironmonger Row**, followed by the Turkish baths and swimming pools and more offices in **Europa Place**, at the back of which is a 5-storey tenement building. Further S past **Norman St** is a park and the Finsbury Leisure Centre; this is bordered by **Mitchell St** which, together with **Bartholomew Square**, runs W-E. Both are commercial, although the streets at right angles to them off to **Old St** are residential, including the refurbished tenement block in **Anchor Yard** and the 3-storey Georgian terraces in **Helmet Row** (partly offices). St Luke's View in **Bartholomew Square** has seven new flats: from £130,000.

Goswell Rd, to the W, has seen little action so far but this is about to change. Several schemes are starting in 1999, including Dallington Lofts (corner **Dallington St**), 32 loft-style flats by Berkeley; a new-build block from Western Homes and 14 modern-style flats at 93–99 **Goswell Rd**. Existing homes include the Triangle development, 5-storeys on the corner of **Percival St**. The rest of the housing is mainly scruffy Victorian and Georgian terraces with a multitude of small shops beneath.

To the E of **Goswell Rd**, running like the rungs of a ladder, are **Seward St**, **Pear Tree Court**, **Bastwick St**, **Ludlow St** and **Gee St**, all of which have commercial developments of between 3 and 5 storeys: homes are planned for several buildings here. **Gee St** also has a 12-floor tower block, Parmoor Court, and a large City University hall of residence.

To the W of **Goswell Rd**, street patterns are a little more diverse. **Compton St** has a row of low Georgian terraces to the S, and an 8-storey tower block to the N. Running at a diagonal to **Compton St** is **Cyrus St**, which has low '30s-style tenement blocks at the **Compton St** end. The Percival Estate continues on the other side of **Percival St** with Harold Laski House, and tower blocks continue on both sides ending at College Heights on the corner of **St John St**.

The end of **Goswell Rd** forms an acute angle with **City Rd**. Several big commercial users have left this corner, to be slowly replaced by homes and small office schemes. **Gard St** and **Masons Place** to the S, and **Pickard St** to the N, have large '60s tower blocks to flamboyant heights. Continuing N, **Hall St** has the 25-storey Peregrine House. The area to the W up to the Angel is mostly commercial. **City Rd** is mainly 3- and 4-storey Georgian terraces, set back from the road on both sides with shops and offices down to **Nelsons Terrace**; from here the height drops dramatically, the standard becomes more uneven, and begins to include modern developments. Some of the **City Rd** terraces are being redeveloped as homes.

Finsbury, the Lloyd Baker estate and North Clerkenwell

South across the **Pentonville Rd** from Islington, this neighbourhood is bounded by **St John St** and **Rosebery Avenue** to the E and S, and **King's Cross Rd** and **Penton Rise** in the W. It includes two distinctive enclaves of early 19th-century houses, the Lloyd

Baker and New River estates. From the Angel tube, **St John St** runs N-S along the E edge of the neighbourhood. At the top on the W side stands the large smoked-glass British Telecom building; on the E an untidy array of late-Victorian commercial properties with ornate gables; soon these give way to flat-fronted Georgian terraces on both sides. Past the **Chadwell St** junction is a row of little shops, early gentrified. More Georgiana in tiny **Owens Row**, where gracious houses have been painstakingly restored. **Rosebery Avenue** has the newly rebuilt Sadler's Wells Theatre on the N side and some fine Georgian terraces on the S, which also command good prices when they come up for sale. Further down, past the theatre, is the imposing New River Head Building. This important (indeed, historic) building has now become flats. The splendid boardroom makes a superb dining room – available to all the flats. St James Homes have sold all the first phase and are now marketing 'the Lab Building', an Art Deco block converted to 35 1- and 2-bed flats, from £133,000. **Rosebery Avenue** continues in a mixture of predominantly industrial Victorian buildings and Victorian workmen's flats; at the intersection with **Rosoman St** is the old Finsbury Town Hall with its distinctive stained-glass and wrought-iron porch. Near the **Farringdon Rd** junction, a large mixed development known as Rosebery Court has light industrial workshop space, offices and a new block of 27 flats at the corner of **Rosebery Avenue** and **Coldbath Square**.

Chadwell St runs from **St John St** into the centre of the New River Estate, built in the 1820s. The street has a modern Georgian-style mews development through an arch on the right; the rest is Georgian terraces which open out into the vast **Myddleton Square** with its central garden and church, surrounded on all sides by tall Georgian homes – one of the finest squares in the area. The roads running off to the W – **River St**, **Inglebert St** and **Mylne St** – have fine, wide streets and terraces of large houses. **Claremont Square**, which completes a right-angle with **Amwell St**, is particularly

imposing. It runs N-S to join **St John St**, and has Georgian terraces of varying sizes and states of repair, and a number of small shops.

Amwell St marks the boundary between the New River and Lloyd Baker estates. The Lloyd Baker estate was originally built by the eponymous family in 1819, and was partly sold to Islington Council on the death of Miss Lloyd Baker in 1975. It consists mainly of Georgian flat-fronted brick terraced houses, retaining an old charm with its fine squares with central gardens. Streets are wider here and houses larger, generally 3/4-bed houses and 2-bed flats. Three roads parallel each other W from **Amwell St**. First is **Great Percy St**: tall Georgian terraces, 4 storeys with first-floor balconies. The road is steep and drops sharply just before **Percy Circus**, giving a superb view to the W over London. **Percy Circus** is a fine square with a park in the centre, two-thirds encircled by a long crescent of terraces. But it is sadly marred by the last third, which is a low-level flats block and car park. Parallel to **Great Percy St**, **Wharton St** and **Lloyd Baker St** converge at **Lloyd Square**. This is the heart of the estate, with a railed garden in the centre, a fine view across to the Post Office Tower and spacious double-fronted Georgian houses. The style continues down **Wharton St** (both sides) and **Lloyd Baker St**; NW of **Rosebery Avenue** is composed of large Victorian and Edwardian tenements and modern commercial and residential blocks, until **Wilmington Square** and **Tysoe St** which border on **Rosebery Avenue** and mark the limit of the area. **Wilmington** is the last fine period square, with tall Georgian terraces and a large central garden. **Tysoe St** has smaller and slightly scruffier terraces but is now up-and-coming. A new block in **Margery St** offers 2-bed flats from £162,500.

The area E of **Rosebery Avenue** up to **Goswell Rd** and N of **Skinner St** and **Percival St** is not part of the Lloyd Baker estate but has some similar features. It is composed of two approximate triangles, the first formed by **St John St** and **Rosebery Avenue** as they diverge S from the Angel, and completed by **Skinner St** which runs W-E along the bottom. The area enclosed is predominantly council tower blocks: **Gloucester Way** has the 23-storey Michael Cliffe House on stilts. **Myddleton St**, which forms a cross with **Gloucester Way**, is the only period street, with neat Georgian houses and a handful of tidy shops at the bottom. Lloyd's Row has another large tower block. The point where it joins **St John St** also marks the end of the Georgian terraces there, which are replaced to the S by more modern commercial and academic buildings. An airline office building here is now 14 flats called St John's Point: 2-bed £180–325,000.

The last part of North Clerkenwell is enclosed by **St John St** and **Goswell Rd** as they diverge away from the Angel, making another triangle bounded by **Percival St** in the S, which is a continuation of **Skinner St** to the E. The whole of this area is very mixed. In the S, on the corner of **St John St** and **Percival St**, is the 4-storey College Heights development. Originally an old warehouse, it was stylishly refurbished in the late '80s into a 24-flat complex with gym and car park, adorned with royal-blue awnings. More recent schemes include Pattern House, which is known as the Ingersoll Building. Two-bed flats fetch around £260,000.

To the N, forming a circle with roads radiating off it, is **Northampton Square** and the central core of the City University. The quiet square, with a garden and folly in the centre, is bounded on the N by the 7-storey university complex and on the other side by a crescent of 4-storey Georgian terraces with first-floor balconies. The streets leading off to the E, **Ashby St** and **Sebastian St**, are also mainly Georgian terraces. Where **Sebastian St** meets **Northampton Square**, an ex-factory/warehouse has been converted into four 2-bed, 2-bath flats. They go for around £225,000. Recently, a well-known TV actor bought two. **Spencer St** to the N has anonymous university buildings on one side and **Earlstoke St** council estate on the other. Among the best ways of buying into the area cheaply are either to pick up ex-council property or to find property which overlooks modern council estates. This is possible in North Cleveland since there are many small clusters of Georgian houses dotted about. **Rawstorne St** up to **Friend St** is a mixture of low modern mews developments, ex-council homes and small period terraces. One-bed ex-council flats go for £135,000 and houses start at £275,000. The last remaining streets up to the Angel are mostly commercial.

Transport	Tubes: Angel (zone 1, Northern), Farringdon (zone 1, Circle, Metropolitan). From Angel: Oxford Circus 10 min (1 change), City 6 min, Heathrow 1 hr 10 min (1 change). Trains: Farringdon (Moorgate 10 min and Thameslink).
Convenient for	The City and West End, stations. Miles from centre: 1.5.
Schools	Local Authority: Central Foundation (b).

SALES

Flats	S	1B	2B	3B	4B	5B
Average price	75–110	120–170+	150–350+	200–500	—	—
Houses	2B	3B	4B	5B	6/7B	8B
Average prices	250+	350–500+	400–900+	—	—	—

RENTAL

Flats	S	1B	2B	3B	4B	5B
Average prices	650–850	1000–1500	1200–2000	1500–3000	—	—
Houses	2B	3B	4B	5B	6/7B	8B
Average prices	1900+	—	—	—	—	—

The properties	In Finsbury, handsome Regency and Victorian houses; everywhere, loft conversions of commercial/warehouses, and council- and housing trust-built flats.
The market	Waiting lists for the biggest (earliest) lofts, and for new-build schemes. Newer developments have less space for the money. The market has been rising since 1993 but slowed in late '98. Local searches: Islington 2 weeks, Camden 2 weeks.

Among those estate agents active in this area are:
- Hurford Salvi Carr
- Urban Spaces
- Hamptons
- Kerr Gilchrist
- Stirling Ackroyd
- Jarvis Keller
- Daniel Watney *
- Winkworth *

further details: see advertisers' index on p633

CRICKLEWOOD

Map ref: p43 (4G)
Postal districts: NW2
Boroughs: Barnet (No Overall Control), Brent (Lab)
Council tax: Band D Barnet £728, Brent £589
Conservation areas: – none
Parking: Free

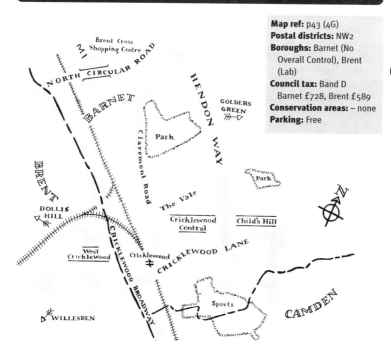

It's good news/bad news time for Cricklewood. Four large 'ifs' loom in the area until now unkindly dismissed as 'rather a no-man's-land' by estate agents, who like to upgrade it to 'Hampstead borders', 'West Heath estate', even solidly respectable Golders Green or Willesden Green. And yet . . . might the railway, whose spread began the blurring of London's original hamlets, yet reinstate the name of Cricklewood?

First, *if* a multi-million pound Railtrack scheme gets the go-ahead it will create a new complex of homes, plus leisure, retail and entertainment facilities, out of the disused railway sidings along **Claremont Rd**. Also planned are new roads, pedestrian and cycle access routes and a footbridge across the railway.

The bad news is that these are not the only plans for the vast stretch of old railway land. BNFL intend to use the siding to store (wait for it) spent nuclear fuel for 'a few hours' each week – *if* they are not stopped by existing residents who, it hardly needs saying, are up in (non-nuclear) arms.

Then, *if* they get permission, Brent Cross shopping centre on the other side of the **North Circular Rd** will create yet another department store, several new shops and a bus terminal – not to mention hundreds of new job opportunities for the locals.

And Barnet is still pushing hard for a major staging-post here on the Heathrow Express rail link that will join the airport and St Pancras. Eventually. *If* (the biggest *if*) it doesn't get to stop in West Hampstead instead. This would certainly provide a splendid boost to an area whose main claim to fame is the ease at which you can get out of it to almost anywhere else.

Road access in and out of town is good: as well as the North Circular, Junction 1 of the M1 is a couple of streets away. But once again the railways, thanks to Thameslink, is the key. Nowadays you can wheel your suitcase up to the platform and, when your train arrives, get to King's Cross, or Moorgate for the City, in 15–16 min. You can even travel direct, unimpeded by road traffic, N to Luton Airport or S to South London, Gatwick Airport, Brighton and the whole of the South East Network.

Cricklewood does, though, lack one form of transport: the Underground. Nearest stations are Golders Green or Willesden Green, both a brisk walk or bus-ride away.

One man, at least, firmly believes Cricklewood to be the next boom town. He has bought its biggest and oldest pub, the run-down Crown, which he intends to transform into a magnificent 4-star hotel, creating 250 new jobs into the bargain. And the area is to gain that most '90s of status symbols, an up-market private gym on the site of Production Village, a small entertainment complex in **Cricklewood Lane**.

But for now prices sag in the centre of Cricklewood, rise towards its borders with E, West Hampstead on the SE, Gladstone Park on the W, Golders Green to the N. Child's Hill, now part of the same postal district, is on the Hampstead side. Both are ancient places compared to the nouveau London boroughs in which they lie.

The grip of the past lingers perceptibly in the main roads – **Cricklewood Lane**, (formerly Child's Hill Lane) and **Cricklewood Broadway**, part of Roman Watling St – and along ancient rights of way, still here but now secluded footpaths between the houses. People have lived here, worked here (often catering for their more prosperous neighbours in Hampstead or Central London), for centuries: running laundries, storing furniture, carriages, repairing cars. There's still a fair amount of open space, not only in gardens but in local parks, playing-fields, sportsgrounds, municipal playgrounds, offering opportunities for relaxation and exercise.

Development of the area has come in recognizable spurts. The opening of Cricklewood station in 1868 resulted in a rash of Victorian brick villas in **Claremont Rd** and **Cricklewood Lane** alongside, also in streets opposite called misleadingly after the trees of the forest (to fit into the Wood of the Crickles?): **Oak**, **Ash**, **Elm** and **Yew Groves**. Roads named respectively **Olive**, **Larch**, **Pine**, **Cedar**, **Ivy**, etc, are further to the W on the other side of **Cricklewood Broadway**.

Hendon Way to the E followed in the years between the wars; a bypass, precursor to the roads leading northwards, now the M1. Ribbon development spread alongside: semi-detached houses with garages for the new mobile motor age. Council housing from those years, and post-1945, began to appear on the market as tenants cashed in on their 'Right to Buy' in the late '80s, broadening the spread of homes available. (Some are now downright desirable, others well-nigh unmortgageable.)

Child's Hill and more particularly Cricklewood are mixed areas: predominantly, though not exclusively, residential. Infilling in such a long-established area has produced some apparently unselfconscious mixes of homes cheek-by-jowl with industrial property. There is a great deal of shopping – and some historic pubs – available (including antique shops, pine furniture emporiums, restaurants), but local shops along the main road arteries are mostly specialist and mini-markets: Brent Cross, conveniently a mile or so up the road, throws a large shadow. A new shopping centre opened in **Cricklewood Lane** in 1991, which added a little more convenience, and a little more employment, beyond the shops, factories and workshops which already enable many local residents to walk to their work. This retention of neighbourhood facilities also enables elderly and relatively immobile residents to find many of their requirements locally, though sadly market stalls outside the Crown pub in the Broadway look set to be moved on when work starts on the new hotel.

Churches of various denominations include St Agnes' Catholic Church and Primary School in **Cricklewood Lane**, and a Mosque and Islamic Centre stretching from **Chichele Rd** to **Howard Rd**. There are two local libraries, half a dozen primary schools, and Hampstead (comprehensive) School in **Westbere Rd**. The disadvantages include lack of access to London's tube network, to local hospitals and fee-paying schools, all outside the area. When and if the various schemes for the ex-railway land take place, however, an area within 3.5 miles of Marble Arch with homes available at so many levels is going to be increasingly worth looking at – especially if access to the City is important.

Child's Hill

On the electoral map, Child's Hill is a Barnet ward extending well into NW11. Not so in estate agents' descriptions, where it's usually defined as the NW2 area of Hampstead.

Semantics apart, the select Hocroft estate certainly includes some very prestigious and expensive houses, and residents to match. Broadcaster and writer Alan Coren, whose Pooterish 'Despatches from Cricklewood' brought fame to the area, now has to come clean: his own detached house here was on the market in January for £1.25 million. Hocroft houses are one-off brick-built neo-Georgian, detached in **Ranulf Rd** (which leads down towards Fortune Green), detached and semis in **Hocroft Rd**, **Hocroft Avenue**, **Farm Avenue**, **Harman Drive**. Even the semis here have 5-bed, usually 2-bath and car ports for the second car. **Harman Close** is a surprise: it has some half-dozen architect-designed 1970s houses, all individual, young and smart.

Most of the area's blocks of flats are in Child's Hill; Vernon Court at the corner of **Finchley Rd** and **Hendon Way**, Wendover and Moreland Courts about 30 yards further on at the top of **Lyndale Avenue**. All three were built in the 1930s: mock-Tudor red-brick with 1/2/3-bed flats. Ground-floor flats have access to the garden. As original tenants slowly give up the ghost and their protected tenancies, flats have been modernized and come on the market with regularity. They're popular with the newly retired (some of whom may always have lived nearby, or have children living there), and with young professionals whose pockets don't run to West Hampstead prices. **Finchley Rd** dwellers also have the option of a longer bus-ride down to Finchley Rd tube. It's further away than Golders Green, but reckoned worth it for Jubilee line (half the stops to Charing Cross) – and the large Waitrose for shopping on the way home.

Further along the **Finchley Rd**, Orchard Mead, a former police barracks, was spruced up by Regalian in the late '80s with all the latest mod cons – porters, sauna, small garden to sit out in, parking . . . though that yuppie icon, the gym, appears to have been replaced by a snooker room. Owners have a share of the freehold; it is at least partly let for investment. Heathway, at the corner with **West Heath Rd,** has 54 flats, some of which have come on the market unmodernized.

In 1989, the 20 new luxury 1/2/3-bedroom flats of Portman Heights opposite appeared at £200–340,000 for a 125-year lease. Popular at least partly because of their NW3 postcode, they have now regained their pre-slump values. Note that the outgoings in purpose-built blocks include service charges which also cover elements of maintenance and can run well into four figures.

The former Child's Hill House, near the junction of **Hermitage Lane** and **Pattison Rd**, is still in single occupation, but most of the Victorian 3-floor houses in the latter street have been converted into flats and/or maisonettes. There's an intermingling of older houses with others built pre-1914, between the wars, and since, in these sought-after roads which lead up to Hampstead Heath. Often, as in **Hermitage Lane**, there has been a deliberate attempt to adapt to existing spacious pre-war houses with latticed windows and mock-antique touches, but there are also two terraces of newer, more frankly functional, houses for people who prefer equipping their homes to looking after them full-time. More enthusiastic gardeners live in the bungalows of **Hermitage Terrace**, a secluded place where children and/or grandchildren can play in safety.

Back across the **Finchley Rd**, there's concrete-jungle Sunnyside House above shops and motor car showrooms. Opposite, **Crewys Rd** – sometimes known as Little Sicily – has small turn-of-the-century houses, mostly terraced with gardens and lovingly spruced up by owners, apparently oblivious of industrial premises nearby.

More light industry, and less space for housing, in **Granville Rd** though this includes Granville Nurseries at its junction with **The Vale**. Nurseries are useful in areas with so many individual gardens, and locals with space and taste for keeping their gardens looking better than the Jones' next door.

There are also ex-council properties on the market here. In the '80s Barnet encouraged tenants to exercise their enterprise this way, and sold off close to a third of its housing stock. The range of these homes is, to say the least, wide: buyers have difficulties getting a mortgage on some ex-authority homes . . . But others are very popular: look for 2/3-bed houses, terraced, in **Garth** and **Cloister Rds** off **Hendon Way**, 2/3-bedroom flats in **Longberrys, Cricklewood Lane** (a 2-bed here can now sell for c. £80,000) and 2-bed flats in Hermitage Court where about half the flats are now in private hands.

Cricklewood Central

This area covers a broad band each side of **Cricklewood Lane**, starting from **Hendon Way** to the NE, the **Farm Avenue** sportsground on its S side, and with its other two sides bordered by **Cricklewood Broadway** and the **North Circular Rd**. The railway runs right through the middle. It includes large areas of council-built housing in the **Claremont Rd** area, also the Westcroft Estate in **Lichfield Rd** which is Camden Council housing on land leased from Barnet. Main kinds of property to look for: pre-1914 housing near the railway station (as already mentioned) and the semis built between the wars the time the **Hendon Way** was being developed.

Often the two mix and mingle, 1930s 3-bedroom semis alongside and opposite Victorian villas in **Cricklewood Lane**, solid residential semis with gabled entrance lobbies and steep-sided roofs, sometimes joined up in terraces of four and six as in **Somerton** and **Gillingham Rds**. Then there are stretches of widely spaced semis in **Greenfield Gardens, Purley** and **Sanderstead Avenues**, roads which are incongruously wider than the main thoroughfares. Most of the semis are owner-occupied, although there's also a certain amount of letting. Some former bungalows in **The Vale** and nearby have had their roofs opened up and extended and indeed, much individual attention, money and ingenuity has gone into changing and adapting these houses and gardens.

But building land is scarce here now. Developers manage to find patches of land to build on, though: sandwiched in the angle between **Brent Terrace** and **Claremont Rd, Romney Row**, a smart terrace of 2-bed houses, was completed in the early '90s next to 32 new flats at **Dover Close** and **Rye Close**.

Behind the other side of **Brent Terrace**, however, is the aforementioned vast wasteland of redundant railway sidings and depots. Will the terrace back onto the new swathe of housing, offices, shops – even parks – that figure in the ambitious regeneration plan? Or will BNFL get its way? (see introduction). Whatever, 3-bed semis here cost the gambling man, or woman, c. £114,000 at present . . .

An expensive, inward-looking 1990s Shakespearean fantasy development lies between **The Vale** and **Somerton Rd**. Boasting over 150 flats and houses, **Elsinore Gardens, Hamlet Square** and **Ophelia Gardens** attract prices above the average for the area (c. £175,000 for 3-bed houses).

Next door, on the corner of **The Vale** and **Claremont Rd**, Wimpey Homes have completed Compton Place, 21 3-storey, 3-bed town-houses. Prices for the remaining ones last December were around £180,000. Further S on **Claremont Rd**, on the site of Express Dairies, Fairview Homes squeezed Somerton Gardens, a development of 99 studio, 1- and 2-bed flats. Phase II was selling at the start of the year; prices c. £81,000 for 1-bed, £101,000 for 2-bed flats (again good for this area), location definitely convenient: views over Cricklewood station. Quite a lot of industry remains in these residential streets, but rubs shoulders fairly unobtrusively with placid suburban semis in **Somerton Rd** and **The Vale**, less so in **Dersingham Rd**.

Most of the houses in these streets are well-maintained, often on a do-it-yourself basis. Many of the older houses in the **Cricklewood Lane** end of **Claremont Rd** are subdivided for letting, but when they come up for sale are attracting 'Hampstead overspill' young professionals.

It's a different, more crowded world on the other side of the railway bridge. It is more cosmopolitan: shops near and in **Cricklewood Broadway** include Halal butchers, sari shops, jewellery and Oriental greengrocers, grocers and bakers.

'The Groves' – **Yew Grove, Ash Grove, Elm Grove, Oak Grove** – are all turn-of-the-century 2-storey houses which seem to have been rebuilt, converted, improved and adapted as if to show just how many variations on the original could be achieved: dormer windows, balconies, teak and glass doors, cladding. They must be among the most economically priced 2-bed conversions within 3 miles of Marble Arch.

But there's simply not enough pavement and kerbside space for residents, shoppers and railway users to park their cars. They try, which helps to explain why the council sweepers don't seem to be able to keep these streets litter-free. There's not much they can do to sweep behind and under parked cars.

So far, so predictable. But the former railway cottages (know locally as just 'the Cottages') some 300 yards up **Cricklewood Broadway** on the E, Barnet, side are a surprise. Sold off to the then residents some 25 years ago, these are five parallel terraces of 2- and 3-bedroom houses, some boasting pretty gardens, sometimes one large communal lawn on one side, individual private patches on the other. Access by car is limited, but it's a cosy spot (if close to the tracks, it's also close to the station) where residents have shrugged off the original railway grime and coal dust. It attracts a mixed bunch – including actors and magicians. Many get to love it and stick, and even start families in accommodation where it might not be easy to swing a cat or a baby. Prices here have shot up. A 2-bed cottage in **Johnson Terrace** that would have fetched around £80,000 in 1996 was on the market in December 1997 for £129,950, and prices for these have risen by another £10,000 over the year; one was listed at £160,000 last winter. Four-bed, which are also tiny, could sell for as much as £175,000. Still, Victoriana is in, and these houses are collectors' pieces.

West Cricklewood

Streets named after trees to the E of **Cricklewood Broadway** are 'the Groves'; here, on the W (Brent) side, are 'the Roads'. Most of them contain 2-storey houses built at the turn of the century, so there has been plenty of time for **Pine, Larch, Cedar, Olive, Ivy, Oaklands** etc, **Rds** to have developed leafy mature trees (not of appropriate species) and for conversions into flats, maisonettes, garden flats. More conversions still being carried out, often by landlords who continue to live on the premises.

Multi-occupation usually means parking problems, especially in streets built before cars – or indeed bathrooms – were considered necessary, so it's worth considering the width of any road before deciding to live in it (there have been arguments at the kerbside in streets like **Ashford Rd** between residents and 'outside' parkers). Ashford Court is the only really large blocks of flats, with 180 1/2/3-bedroom flats at quite moderate prices. An active Lessees' Association operates here.

Between **Sheldon Rd** and **Cricklewood Broadway**, **Sylvan Grove**, a clutch of 33 flats and 21 houses, appeared in 1992 on the site of an old aircraft factory. The whole development has now been taken over by a housing association.

Purpose-built flats, two to each house, were built pre-1914 in **Wotton, Temple** and **Langton Rds**. Note the double front doors: one leads to the staircase for upstairs. Usually several for sale; check these streets for sale boards. There are also late-'80s Liang flats and houses, in and off **Langton Rd**; again now mainly housing association.

More conventionally up-market are the wide leafy roads near **Gladstone Park** with comfortable 4/5-bed houses, some of them detached in **Anson Rd**, **Oman Avenue** and many of the roads running into the former. Some, ie **Oman Avenue**, also have blocks of flats where elderly parents of local residents can live near, but not with, their children.

These are sights for the eyes for anyone who thinks that civilization stops at the boundary with Brent (which includes at least one Child's Hill estate agent). It's true that this area contains a larger percentage of industrial buildings, also garages, workshops and even itinerant sellers of produce and textiles. **Hassop Rd** is totally industrial. But what seems to be happening to the better roads is that they're renamed Willesden Green. (Indeed, see also the Willesden and Dollis Hill chapters.) No wonder Cricklewood is said to be shrinking.

Transport	Trains: Cricklewood, direct to King's Cross/Moorgate (16 min).
Convenient for	Gatwick and Luton Airports by train. Routes both into and out of town: M1 (Junction 1), Golders Green, Willesden Green, Kilburn tubes and roads to the West End. Ikea and Tesco superstores. Hampstead Heath. Miles from centre: 4.5.
Schools	Barnet and Brent Education Authorities: Hampstead School. See also Hampstead.

SALES

Flats	S	1B	2B	3B	4B	5B
Average prices	45–55	55–80	80–100+	90–115	—	—
Houses	2B	3B	4B	5B	6/7B	8B
Average prices	90–140	120–200+	150–425	220–695+	—	—

RENTAL

Flats	S	1B	2B	3B	4B	5B
Average prices	400–700	500–900	700–1300	800–1700	—	—
Houses	2B	3B	4B	5B	6/7B	8B
Average prices	700–900	9500–1700	1200–2000	150–2600	—	—

The properties	Wide range, from prestige Hampstead-fringe detached houses and mansion flats, via '30s semis, to Victorian and Edwardian terraces, semis, cottages and converted flats. Prices for individual houses can rise over a million towards Hampstead. Pockets of new-build; more to come.
The market	Good prospects for area with good links to everywhere else. The smarter corners gained from Hampstead spillover as prices rose. Local searches: Barnet 2–3 days, Brent 2 weeks.

Among those estate agents active in this area are:
- Albert & Co
- Kay & Co Estates*
- Chattin Estates
- Callaway & Co
- Gammell & Co
- Nelhams William
- Kinleigh, Folkard & Hayward
- Winkworth *
- Ellis & Co
- Gladstones
- Bairstow Eves

*further details: see advertisers' index on p633

CROUCH END AND STROUD GREEN

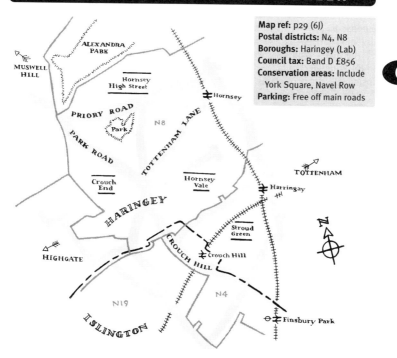

Map ref: p29 (6J)
Postal districts: N4, N8
Boroughs: Haringey (Lab)
Council tax: Band D £856
Conservation areas: Include York Square, Navel Row
Parking: Free off main roads

Is Crouch End now downright fashionable or is it still waiting for its moment of fame? The debate continues, but many locals aver that the area has at last arrived. The largely residential north London districts of Crouch End, Stroud Green and Hornsey, like so many others, began to change rapidly in the heady days of the '80s, as landlords of neglected old houses sold out to developers – both companies and owner-occupiers – and those priced out of its neighbours began to search the streets here. Now chic health clubs and arty shops have sprung up, a testament to – well, gentrification is perhaps the wrong word, but certainly modish bohemianization.

The area is indeed strategically placed: to the N it is bounded by lovely, hilly Alexandra Park, to the W by up-market, Georgian Highgate, to the S by the residential streets of Finsbury Park and to the E by the Great Northern railway line. It became a respectable suburb in the second half of the 19th century, but spent most of the 20th in unassuming obscurity. It is now a solid 15 years into a revival, and is lively both by night and day. Home prices stabilized late last year, but the market did not see the nervousness that hit more central areas. This is perhaps because the new inhabitants are more media than City.

The inward flow of young professionals renting or buying here highlights this area's convenience for both City and West End – although it lacks a tube station. There are, however, four within a 1-mile radius (Finsbury Park, Highgate, Archway and Turnpike Lane), and three buses to get you to Finsbury Park tube and train station (Nos W2, W3, W7). Some say that a tube would change the ambience: they like the feeling of apartness. Prices for Crouch End's better houses are now much more on a par with those of genteel, prosperous Muswell Hill: it is no longer the poor relation.

The houses were largely designed with Victorian or Edwardian families in mind. In the '80s it became popular for Hampstead flat-dwellers to seek a whole house here; however, these solid houses also convert into good, roomy flats (more common than purpose-built blocks), and now families, with schools catchment areas in mind, tend to climb the heights to Muswell Hill.

The villagy Broadway, with its newly restored clock tower (the clock is wrong, but who's counting?) mingles smart clothes shops – for kids, too – with a great cosmopolitan mix of shops and restaurants, thanks to the wider area's Greek, Afro-Caribbean and Asian communities.

The other plus of this swathe of London is its topography. The land climbs steadily northwards towards Highgate and Muswell Hill, and a high ridge along the line of Hornsey Lane and the understandably named **Ridge Rd** and **Mount View Rd** makes for long, open views. Then there's the greenery: even in the meaner streets, open parkland, woods, playing-fields, etc, are never far away – and the route of an old railway is now the Parkland Walk, which runs all the way from Highgate to Finsbury Park. Greenery and postcodes are the keys to prices: the more street trees, the better. As for postcodes, N8 carries a premium.

Crouch End

The Broadway, at the heart of this part of the old borough of Hornsey, eventually eclipsed Hornsey's **High St**, away to the N at the end of **Middle Lane**, as the area's centre. The many tree-lined streets and green spaces away from the main roads lend Crouch End an almost rural feel, but there has been a sea change in the population. The first wave of young singles and the dual-income-no-kids-yet brigade are being joined by more and more families. As in Muswell Hill, this is arts-and-media land – but more rock than opera here. Indeed, Crouch Hill boasts a recording studios in an old church, and everyone hangs out at the World Café opposite. Lots of new shops (arty, funky furniture – that sort of thing), and loads more cafés, bars, nice coffee houses, eclectic eateries from Thai to West Indian, have appeared for the largely kid-free and carefree to chill out in. The latest news is 'yet another health club' (as an observer put it) in **Topsfield Parade**. Alas, the old-fashioned corset shop has closed.

Highgate Borders

The most expensive homes in Crouch End are found to the W of **Park Rd**, **The Broadway** and **Crouch End Hill** because of their proximity to Highgate. Roads such as **Glasslyn Rd**, **Wolseley Rd**, **Coolhurst Rd** and **Clifton Rd** going down to **Coleridge Rd** and **Crescent Rd**, are tree-lined and mainly contain large Victorian Gothic and Edwardian 3-storey terraces or semi-detached houses. Many of these have been converted into roomy flats: whole houses command prices up to £600,000.

The 1980s contributed smart modern flats and maisonettes to **Crescent Rd** and **Coolhurst Rd**, and more new homes off **Wolsely Rd** and **Stanhope Rd**. Some of the best streets have gardens bordering the Parkland Walk nature reserve along the former railway line – though this patch considers itself Highgate. This area is particularly well off for open spaces, which include Crouch End playing-fields off **Park Rd**. There's an up-market tennis club, too.

Similar Victorian/Edwardian houses occur in the streets between **Crouch End Hill** and **Crouch Hill**, in for example **Christchurch Rd** and **Haslemere Rd**. They sometimes belie their staid exteriors, though: one quietly unassuming house in **Haslemere Rd** has a Moorish-inspired interior designed for an eccentric Russian banker in 1911.

Further S, in the N19 district, roads between **Crouch Hill** and **Hornsey Rise** such as **Warltersville Rd**, **Heathville Rd**, **Ashley Rd** (the best) and **Shaftesbury Rd** have some mansion flats, council-built blocks and 3-storey Victorian houses, mostly reborn as flats: the postcode lowers the prices here, though these streets are closer to tubes. There are a few roads W of **Hornsey Rise** and S of **Hornsey Lane**, such as **Sunnyside Rd** and **Beaumont Rise**, which are on the borders of Crouch End and Archway. This corner also holds the Whitehall Park conservation area. See also the Highgate and Kentish Town chapters.

Middle Lane

The triangle of roads N of **Tottenham Lane** and **Park Rd**, which is bisected by **Middle Lane**, is a less expensive hotchpotch of different types of houses which reflect the different stages of growth and function of Crouch End. There are the large Victorian and Edwardian houses, which yield many flats, such as in **Hillfield Avenue, Harold Rd** and some in **Middle Lane**, and the more modern ones like those found in **Rokesly Avenue** and **Elmfield Avenue** – which are more likely to remain intact. There are also some original cottage houses to be found in **New Rd**. Houses get grander, and sprout gables and spires, as you go north: £300,000-plus near Priory Park. The bus route to Finsbury Park tube goes down **Middle Lane** from **Priory Rd** and then turns up **Rokesly Avenue**, where a 3-bed house costs £230–240,000.

Hornsey

The Hornsey High St neighbourhood lies N of **Priory Rd** and **High St Hornsey**, and S of Alexandra Park. **Nightingale Lane** divides the district in two: to the E are mainly council-built properties and to the W mainly private. **Linzee Rd** is popular, **Redston Rd** has good, bigger villas, **North View Rd** has a good number of purpose-built Edwardian maisonettes. Some have beautiful views of Alexandra Park, where 'Ally Pally' limped back to life after fire almost destroyed it. Exhibitions and concerts are held there once more, and there's an ice rink and the famous Palm Court: the best place in North London on November 5th! **High St Hornsey** is looking up a little as a shopping centre: the ubiquitous interior shops are moving in.

The old waterworks site between Alexandra Park and the **High St** looks set to become a vast Sainsbury's superstore plus 129 new houses. Agents opine that this will boost the area – but there has been strong local opposition to the superstore.

Hornsey Vale

Agents are trying to rename this neighbourhood, S of **Tottenham Lane** and E of **The Broadway** and **Crouch Hill**, 'Crouch End Heights' – a sure sign of rising fashionability. From **Weston Park** there is a steep incline up to **Mount View Rd**, which forms the border with Stroud Green. **Mount View Rd** has huge, double-fronted houses. The very high prices asked (and on occasion achieved) do not seem to have stuck. Good family houses can be had in the £270–350,000 bracket. The roads either side of **Weston Park** contain mainly 2- (but some 3-) storey terraced houses, often converted into flats. **Ferme Park Rd** is on the bus route to Finsbury Park tube, so proximity to this road may be useful. The streets between **Ferme Park Rd** and **Crouch Hill** hold a mixture of good-quality homes of varying sizes, mostly now smart or being improved. Look out for those with spacious, convertible basements. Good roads here include spring blossom-lined **Cecile Park, Tregaron Avenue** and **Weston Park**.

Stroud Green

This neighbourhood forms a triangle which lies to the S of **Mount View Rd** and is bordered by **Stroud Green Rd** to the W and the railway line to the E. It used to have large areas of sub-standard housing but this area is slowly improving. Hopeful talk about 'Stroud Green Village', however, has yet to bring about mass gentrification. Residents think the volume of traffic in the area may be to blame for this. In some roads, prices are close to Crouch End's, but other parts are both scruffier and cheaper. At the N end of Stroud Green **Mount View Rd** has some expensive houses which overlook a green space atop a covered reservoir and – as they are at the top of Crouch Hill – the rest of Stroud Green. The streets coming down off **Mount View Rd** are wide and tree-lined: roads like **Mount Pleasant Villas, Granville Rd** and **Oakfield Rd** contain large 3-storey terraced houses which are almost all converted into flats. Again, those at the top get splendid views.

At the bottom, towards the tracks, **Mount Pleasant Villas** contains pretty little early Victorian villas. A good harbinger for this corner is the transformation of the old dairy (once a car repair shop) into a smart wine bar/restaurant, one of a clutch of new arrivals. **Stapleton Hall Rd**, which snakes across both the railway and the Parkland Walk, is a long street of substantial Victoriana, currently reckoned to be good value for money: £300,000 will buy you a 5-bed example, £400,000 a double-fronted one. Crouch Hill rail station, with trains into St Pancras, serves this area.

The roads to the E of **Lancaster Rd**, like **Cornwall Rd** and **Connaught Rd**, contain 3-storey houses decorated with white stucco – again, good flat-hunting territory. Intact houses command £250,000-plus. Moving down towards Finsbury Park tube, the roads and the houses in them are not in such good order, with noisier, more crowded streets and more of an inner-city feel: lots of local shops, clothing manufacturers, ironmongers, launderettes, garages intersperse the houses. Look for cheap, convenient homes here. **Upper Tollington Place** has big houses in a busy road; **Florence Rd** and **Victoria Rd** have nice early Victorian homes; **Osbourne Rd** and **Marquis Rd** are mostly council blocks.

Borders

East of Hornsey, across the railway line, is the Harringey 'ladder' – so-called because its streets march parallel to each other like rungs between the busy through-routes of **Wightman Rd** and **Green Lanes/Grand Parade**. The houses here are cheaper than those further W: nice suburban terraces of 3/4-bed houses, but a little too close to Wood Green for high prices. However, popular with young couples; local shops in **Green Lanes** are open all hours (Greek and Turkish food in abundance) and inexpensive eateries here. The northern 'ladder' roads have the coveted N8 postcode. The W ends of the roads, away from crowded **Green Lanes**, are most popular.

West of **Stroud Green Rd** Stroud Green merges with Finsbury Park. In streets such as **Evershot Rd** and **Marriot Rd** you'll find 2- and 3-storey terraced houses, many of which have been converted into flats. The N4 postal boundary runs along the **Hornsey Rd**. N and W of here is in the N19 zone.

Between **Hornsey Rd** and **Holloway Rd**, there is a tract which does not really belong to Crouch End but is not quite Tufnell Park either. Once it was Holloway, but this is a name that today seems less used, perhaps because of the prison (though Brixton survives a similar stigma). Perhaps the name is due for a renaissance: agents are tipping this area for bargain-hunters looking for a corner that should improve. The houses are spacious and away from the **Holloway Rd** the streets are fairly quiet. North of the railway there are flat-fronted Victorian houses in **Fairbridge Rd**. The rather mixed area round about is said to be coming up. South of the railway the houses are smaller. Housing associations are active here.

The streets with **Tollington** in their names form a fairly distinct district: wide roads with big churches and solid houses. In **Tollington Way**, Bellway are building on a fairly large scale: 2- and 3-bed flats and 3-bed town-houses round a quad. Prices from £135,000 for 2-bed, £138,000 for 3-bed. Off **Sussex Way**, 23 flats and houses have been carved out of a mews: some are converted stables, some new-build, from £90,000; 2-bed ex-stables from £190,000.

Transport	Tubes: Finsbury Park (zone 2, Victoria, Piccadilly); to Oxford Circus 11 min, City 30 min (1 change), Heathrow 1 hr. Trains: Hornsey, Harringay, Finsbury Park (Moorgate 13 min, Kings Cross 8 min). Crouch Hill (Silverlink/North London line).
Convenient for	Wood Green Shopping City, Alexandra Park. Miles from centre: 5.
Schools	Haringey Education Authority: Hornsey School, St David & St Katherine. Private: Highgate Boys School.

C

SALES

Flats	S	1B	2B	3B	4B	5B
Average prices	55	85–110	100–130	150–200	–	–
Houses	2B	3B	4B	5B	6/7B	8B
Average prices	130–200	160–300	250–350+	450–600	–	–

RENTAL

Flats	S	1B	2B	3B	4B	5B
Average prices	430–550	480–760	650–1000	800–1300	–	–
Houses	2B	3B	4B	5B	6/7B	8B
Average prices	–	1200+	1300–2000	2000+	–	–

The properties	19th-century suburban houses, many now converted to flats. Largest and smartest close to Highgate, smaller ones elsewhere. Some p/b flats. Also ex-council bargains.
The market	Crouch End's status has risen: now very popular with young professionals commuting to City or West End – though pressure on school places has lessened its appeal to families. More impecunious home-hunters head away from the pleasant (and pricey) hilly streets of Crouch End and parts of Hornsey; meaner, cheaper streets, though even more convenient, towards Finsbury Park. Local searches: 2 weeks.

Among those estate agents active in this area are:
- Dennells
- Martyn Gerrard
- Paul Simon
- Prickett & Ellis
- Tatlers
- Davies & Davies
- Winkworth*

further details: see advertisers' index on p633

CRYSTAL PALACE

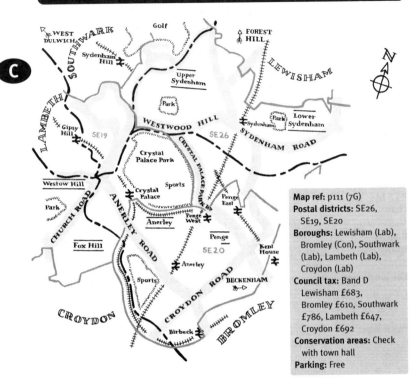

Map ref: p111 (7G)
Postal districts: SE26,
SE19, SE20
Boroughs: Lewisham (Lab),
Bromley (Con), Southwark
(Lab), Lambeth (Lab),
Croydon (Lab)
Council tax: Band D
Lewisham £683,
Bromley £610, Southwark
£786, Lambeth £647,
Croydon £692
Conservation areas: Check
with town hall
Parking: Free

The wooded heights of South London offer long prospects, cleanish air and solace for those who get claustrophobia in the former marshlands closer to the heart of town. Sydenham Hill rises greenly and abruptly from Dulwich and forms a distinct boundary between inner London to the NW and the essentially suburban borough of Bromley which meanders off SE into Kent. Indeed, the London postal districts stop on the hill's SE slopes, and the inhabitants of Beckenham put 'Kent' on their notepaper.

Crystal Palace – which took its name from Paxton's vast glasshouse, moved to the hilltop from Hyde Park after the Great Exhibition of 1851 – is the name of a park and a landmark (the soaring TV masts), rather than a place: Anerley and Penge slope away to the SE, Sydenham is to the E, Upper Sydenham to the N, Gipsy Hill to the W and Upper Norwood along the ridge to the SW. Five boroughs meet at the hilltop, so it's more than usually necessary to enquire who gets, and spends, your council tax.

The hills and valley of this interesting landscape give character to the area, define the neighbourhoods and influence the type of property. Large houses and mansions (the popularity of the Palace persuaded wealthy Victorians to build here) occupy lofty vantage points with compelling views; modest terraces cluster the lower reaches. Property is predominantly owner-occupied.

With dramatic irony, a century and a half later the major talking-point – or rather, bitter row – is *still* the Crystal Palace. The building itself is long gone: burnt down spectacularly in 1936. The site has remained empty, but the 1960s construction of the National Sports Centre and Bromley Council's current ambitious plans to modernize

C

that, restore the park and regenerate the area contributed to an up-turn in fortunes. To cap it all, the Palace looked set to rise again, phoenix-like, from the long-cold ashes.

However, the sight of the architect's drawings of the proposed 'leisure complex', with its 18-screen multiplex cinema, its nine restaurants 'carefully selected to avoid conflict with existing outlets' and its 'cultural space' for local groups to use, sparked a major protest campaign. The 1990 Crystal Palace Act says that any new building on the site should reflect the style of the original. Bromley Council says it does. The Campaign disagrees. So do eco-warriors, camped out in the trees, though they're likely to be ejected soon (the cost to council tax payers of removing a similar group in Kingston last year was £600,000). Anyone considering buying in the area this year would be well advised to judge the plans, and their effects, for themselves . . . At present, it's 1–0 to the Campaign, which won the right to a full judicial review when they took the matter to the Court of Appeal in September. Watch this space.

At the summit of the Crystal Palace Hill is the area known locally as the 'Triangle', bordered by **Westow Hill** to the N, **Westow St** to the W and **Church Rd** to the E. It's part of Croydon but abutted by Lambeth, Southwark and Bromley Boroughs. **Fox Hill** and **Belvedere Rd** make an elegant descent from **Church Rd** parallel to the busy **Anerley Hill** and houses here are much sought-after. North of Anerley Hill, beyond Crystal Palace rail station, Crystal Palace Park acts as a barrier with Penge.

Sydenham, to the N of Penge, is an elegant suburb which enjoys a good community spirit – the Sydenham Society is very active. Upper Sydenham historically had more lavish properties – surviving examples on **Westwood Hill** and **Sydenham Hill**. Other hill-climbers here are **Wells Park Rd** and **Longton Avenue**. Historic **Jews Walk** enjoys repute. Sydenham today still has the atmosphere, which it shares with the other slopes of the hill, of having strayed from an Edwardian novel. A character from H G Wells, perhaps, or even Sherlock Holmes himself, seems likely to emerge from the pillared drives lined with laurels. Houses of that period were lavishly spacious, and even flats made from them are as big as any in London.

Lower Sydenham has the sought-after, turn-of-the-century Thorpe Estate but ends modestly round **Bell Green**. To the S of **Westwood Hill**, the roads starting with the name **Lawrie Park** are popular.

The even spread of rail stations across the area makes for convenient commuting. Gypsy Hill station between **Westow Hill** and **Crystal Palace Parade** to the N has a quarter-hourly service into Victoria station and is in zone 3, which is popular with commuters: the other rail stations are in zone 4. There are also good bus routes, many ending at **Crystal Palace Parade**. Escaping to the country is quick (the M25 is 10 miles away) although the vast Crystal Palace Park offers respite from city hassles. Parking can be extremely difficult, and grid-locking is frequent.

Westow Hill

Westow Hill, Victorian and villagy in character, has a good selection of shops and many new better-than-average restaurants – some quite chic. To the N, the bay-fronted Victorian semis of **Farquhar Rd** are bed-sit and flat-land. Further down are large detached Tudor-timber-style houses in **Dulwich Wood Avenue**. **Jasper Rd** has large Victorian terraces. **Westow St** to the S has small shops and a new supermarket and community centre complex. There are luxury 1- and 2-bed retirement apartments here; also a rather pedestrian new development of flats squeezed in behind the shops between **Westow Hill** and **Church Rd**. Up-and-coming **Church Rd** (which runs S towards Croydon) has Nesbitt Square, an award-winning small development of eight 5-bed homes; also Nightingale Court, luxury sheltered retirement apartments. In the 'Triangle' between **Westow Hill** and **Church Rd, St Aubyn's Rd** has recent bay-window-style houses and modern terraced houses in **Brunel Close**. A deconsecrated church tower re-emerged as a £1.2 million 5-bed des res in 1997.

Fox Hill

This leafy district slopes down from the hilltop between **Church Rd** and **Anerley Hill**. **Fox Hill Rd** starts with small cottages and a modern development. It's steep (20 per cent gradient) and offers a truly panoramic view. Large Victorian houses, semis and detached, as well as '60s town-houses, complete the road. A low terrace of stuccoed watermen's cottages which used to back on to the canal starts **Belvedere Rd**. Composition of the road is similar to **Fox Hill** – No 73, Tower House, is a striking property. Many of **Hamlet Rd's** large Victorian homes have been split into flats. Modern town-houses (3-bed, with garage) off **Stambourne Way** in **Fitzroy Gardens** go for £120,000. This tree-lined neighbourhood is further enhanced by small greens. Trees shield the large houses in **Auckland Rd**. Some of these have been converted into flats. There is an elegant new development here of a coach house plus six new 5-bed houses by Sunley Estates. The road continues with private flats, Victorian detached and semis, and travels down past playing-fields and South Norwood. **Sylvan Rd** has modern terraces as well as Victorian – also Sylvan High School and Sports Centre.

Anerley

Busy **Anerley Hill** starts loftily at the roundabout with **Westow Hill** – commanding views of South London and beyond. Victorian detached and terraced properties – many converted into flats – and '60s town-houses make the descent. Midway, there are a number of council estates. Shops near Anerley station provide for basic needs. **Thicket Rd's** large detached houses follow the S edge of Crystal Palace Park. Here, Orchard Park is a 'village-style' scheme on a 5-acre former goods yard. Its studios, 1- and 2-bed flats fetch from around £40–70,000. **Anerley Park's** large Victorian semis yield many a flat. Terraced, cottage homes are found in **Trenholme Rd**.

Penge

Modern shopping facilities in **Penge High St** contrast with the quiet dignity of the King William IV Naval Asylum and the almshouses of **Watermen's Square**. The focal point of the four low-built rows is the chapel, now the area's most unusual home, twin-towered and standing loftily above its neighbours. More almshouses are found in **King William IV Gardens** – sadly fronted by a council block. **Wordsworth Rd** has bay-fronted Victorian terraces, while **Parish Lane** is cottage terraces. Swallows Court is a recent development of 2-bed flats in **Morland Rd**. Larger houses are found in **Lennard Rd** (Victorian and mock-Tudor semis), **Cator Rd** (Victorian detached) and **Woodbastwick Rd** ('30s semis).

Running parallel to the A213 **Croydon Rd**, **Maple Rd** has a street market at the **High St** end. To the E, **Kenilworth Rd's** bay-fronted 1930s terraces have wooden porches. **Clevedon Rd** is similar. Quiet and popular roads are **Chesham Crescent** and **Chesham Rd** – '30s semis. **Ravenscroft Rd** and **Birkbeck Rd** have more Victoriana.

Sydenham

The N-S railway line divides Sydenham Park from Lower Sydenham to the E. Quiet and leafy **Sydenham Park** starts with Victorian but also has some council blocks. **Sydenham Park** crosses it, mixing '30s bay-fronted and large Victorian terraces with some cottages and large semis. **Wells Park Rd** runs W from **Kirkdale**, starting modestly with Victorian terraces – most with small ground-floor shops. Off on the right, narrow **Halifax St** comes as a surprise – variously bright-painted terraced cottages with white wooden fences. Council-house building and estates occupy the lower part of the hill. Further up on the left is the hilly **Sydenham Wells Park** (Sydenham was a minor 19th-century spa). Half-way up the hill, modern private flats start to appear – they have balconies, and raised gardens protected by fences and hedges. **Canonbury Mews** is a modern estate with neatly tended lawns. Right at the top is the large, modern St Clement's Heights estate.

Sydenham Hill skirts the NW edge of the neighbourhood. From **Kirkdale**, the wide, busy road continues SW with a private modern block on the left and detached houses on the right. Here some woodland appears; there is a walled-off, modern Corporation of the City of London estate. Lammas Green council estate has some stuccoed terraces. Imposing Sydenham Hill House has an entrance tower and Jacobean roofline, while The Cedars boasts a bay-front, with balustrades and stained glass. Council estates appear – including high-rise blocks. Victoriana mingles with '30s detached, modern terraces and town-houses; also the occasional, almost enchanted, wooded cul-de-sac. Impressive, sweeping views of London are a major plus. Near the roundabout with **Westwood Hill**, back on the hilltop by the park, there's the recent **Wavel Place** development. The television mast soars into view.

Westwood Hill descends to the E towards central Sydenham with modern town-houses on the left and mansions on the right. Torrington Court is a '30s mansion block. Sydenham High School is here. Off **Westwood Hill** is popular **Jews Walk**. Some modern town-houses are followed by retirement flats on the corner with **Kirkdale**.

Sheltered from main traffic is **Beaulieu Avenue** – '60s town-houses with neat handkerchief-size front lawns around a small fenced-off green. Wide **Longton Avenue**, beside the Wells Park, has large 19th-century bay-fronted semis and modern terrace house infills. Further up are '30s semis with sloping front gardens; higher still these become larger, with the occasional detached house. Delightful views of the park.

South of **Westwood Hill**, **Lawrie Park Rd**, wide, tree-lined and gently undulating, is a variety of Victoriana: mansions, detached, semis, bay-fronted terraces with upper balconies and some balustrades. Many flat conversions and also modern terraces and flats. There are luxury 1/2-bed apartments in a development diametrically opposite **Lawrie Park Crescent**. On the corner with **Lawrie Park Rd** is Sydenham Tennis & Croquet Club. Facing is St Christopher's Hospice. Nearby is a site being developed by Aspen Homes as 1- and 2-bed luxury flats. Off **Sydenham Avenue** Bewley have just built eight 3-bed, 3-bath town-houses, from £200,000. **Lawrie Park Rd** ends by **Crystal Palace Park Rd** with mansion blocks – '30s Park Court and the more modern Ashley Court.

On **Crystal Palace Park Rd,** now a conservation area, large Victorian red-brick mansions were built overlooking the park – many are now flats. Also large detached

'30s infills. **Sydenham Avenue** (mock-Georgian and big Victorian semis) has a bucolic air – there's a bench beneath the protective branches of a tree on the green, and it looks towards St Bartholomew Church in **Westwood Hill**. It continues as **Lawrie Park Avenue** – Victorian mansions and 1930s detached, while **Lawrie Park Gardens** adds some modern flats to the mixture.

Sydenham Rd leads past the station into Lower Sydenham. This Victorian red-brick street has a useful range of shops in the upper part. Behind lies the popular Thorpe Estate (every street name ends in '-thorpe') of turn-of-the-century terraces. On this side of the tracks, too, Portland Homes have turned a warehouse in **Silverdale Rd**, near the station, into an imaginative conversion of 24 flats.

Sunnydene St climbs a gentle hill, boasting Victorian/turn-of-the-century terraced cottages but also an unappealing council block. **Highclere St** is similarly terraced.

Transport	Trains: Crystal Palace to Victoria; Penge West, Sydenham to London Bridge and Charing Cross; Sydenham Hill, fast line to Victoria.
Convenient for	Crystal Palace Park. Miles from centre: 7.
Schools	Local Authority: Westwood Secondary School (g), Harris Technology College.

SALES

Flats	S	1B	2B	3B	4B	5B
Average prices	23–30	35–65	60–115	70–130	100+	–
Houses	2B	3B	4B	5B	6/7B	8B
Average prices	75–100	85–150	120–220	170–250+	235–500	300+

RENTAL

Flats	S	1B	2B	3B	4B	5B
Average prices	350–400	425–525	550–700	650–900	750+	–
Houses	2B	3B	4B	5B	6/7B	8B
Average prices	650–850	700–950	900–1000	1400+	2000+	2500+

The properties	Grand Victorian villas, many now flats; smaller terraced Victorian, flats blocks and inter-war homes. Quite a few modern houses and flats. Gardens and long, long views.
The market	Substantial growth in rental market. Larger houses popular with families particularly in the conservation area of Fox Hill, Belvedere Rd. Few very large houses left: most now flats. 1- and 2-bed flats are plentiful. Agents have high hopes for 'up-and-coming' Sydenham. Local searches: Lewisham 2 weeks, Bromley 2 weeks, Lambeth 10 working days, Southwark 2 weeks, Croydon 2 weeks.

Among those estate agents active in this area are:
- Woolwich Property
- Halifax Property
- Park Regent
- General Accident Properties
- Wates
- Conrad Fox
- Cooper Giles

DOCKLANDS

Docklands is growing up. It is nearly 20, in its post-modern, non-functional, ex-seaport reincarnation. It is no longer the mood-swing teenager, it has survived a sickly infancy and a childhood in which it outgrew its strength. The rest of London accepts its new neighbour: no-one now predicts the demise of Docklands. In property terms, there are two sides to this maturity: the market for homes, both owning and letting, is now not that different from other leading London areas. And the workplaces – offices, in large part – are built and full of busy and well-paid people.

This Guide is about homes, not offices. But the maturity of the Docklands commercial property market underpins the whole area as a place to live. When you have 25,000 people from 30 companies working in Canary Wharf alone, and a shortage of office space on the Isle of Dogs as a whole, then the Docklands phenomenon has something solid to it. Docklands is now an established business location. It will not go away, any more than the towers of Broadgate or London Wall will stand empty. The early '90s recession prompted talk (though not from this Guide) of Docklands staying forever a depressed, half-empty, third-best location. Now, blue-chip companies are taking Canary Wharf space at rents higher than on the fringes of the City, and international banks are building their own towers alongside.

The droves of people in smart suits (it's very much that sort of place) are attracting a good range of shops, restaurants and other amenities which benefit the residents as well as the workers. Interestingly, these two groups are often one and the same, with proximity to the office towers a big selling point in residential schemes. This in part reflects the transport picture: the new tube line is still not open (promised 'during 1998' a year ago, it now looks like a cliffhanger to get it ready for January 1 2000 . . .). Will Isle of Dogs homes become paradoxically less attractive when it is easier to commute to the Wharf by tube? Or will people buy into Docklands because they can more speedily get to their work/leisure in the West End?

Whatever the answer, no-one with an eye on the homes market expects dramatic change. This is another sign of maturity. The market has been through extraordinarily turbulent waters, but the current mix of renters and owner-occupiers has a stable air for the first time, despite the withdrawal of a large tranche of the investment buyers following the Far East economic downturn. The fears of job losses in the City had much more effect on Docklands property: another sign that this is now a mature homes market that responds to real economic news, not the froth of speculation.

Twenty years ago there was no homes market here at all. . .

The what, where and when of Docklands

I once stood in a warehouse flat in Wapping with a Japanese visitor and gazed out across the deserted Thames. He was puzzled: where were the ships? Why was the river not used? Why was the warehouse no longer a warehouse? What had happened? It was hard to explain to him; indeed it is hard to convey to anyone how sudden the change, how total the death of London's docks. Ships still unload way down the river at Tilbury, but the 6 miles from the Tower eastwards is no longer a trading port. That is Docklands. From being the busiest port in the world in the 1950s it is now . . . read on, and you will see.

So what is Docklands, and how did it get this way? A map helps a lot, first to make the point that Docklands is big. If a home in Docklands appeals, the first thing to know is that some bits of it are a stroll from the City, while others are more or less in Essex. It is 6 miles long – it's as far from the Hogarth roundabout on the A4 in Chiswick to London Bridge, as from London Bridge to the eastern edge of Docklands.

Match Docklands against some other world cities: from our City it is 6.3 miles in a straight line to the E end of the Royal Docks. Drive the same distance in New York, and you cover most of Manhattan from Battery Park to somewhere in the middle of Central Park. In Paris, you cross the whole city inside the ring of the *Périphérique*.

Second, Docklands is not one place but a confederation of areas: Wapping, Limehouse, Shad Thames – about a dozen definable districts. Some, like Rotherhithe, are ancient villages; others, like the Surrey Quays and most of the Isle of Dogs, did not exist as residential neighbourhoods before about 1982. Now, Docklands is the biggest single source of new homes in London, perhaps the UK. From 660 new homes built in 1984 the annual crop has fluctuated, yielding in total some 25,000 homes, with 3,300 under construction in the second half of 1998.

No ships on the river: the sudden death of London's docks

The history would be a book in itself, beginning on the Roman quays of Londinium. The legacies of that history are the great sheets of water, the surviving warehouses, the beleaguered communities of little houses built for dock workers. Another legacy is a virtually empty river. Up to the late 1960s all these docks were lined with ocean-going ships. The river was packed with freighters, barges and tugs. The tideway from the Tower to the sea was a highway for vessels of all sizes. Then, from 1967 to 1981, the docks closed one by one; the ships vanished. Suddenly, the London docks were out-of-date. New methods of cargo handling had made them unworkable: a freighter took up to a fortnight to unload using traditional methods, but a container ship could be turned round in 24hrs. Equally important was the change from rail to road for transport to and from the docks. Much of the cargo that used to be shipped through London transferred to roll-on roll-off truck ferries scuttling to and from Europe.

The Docklands dilemma

London was faced with a problem on an epic scale: what to do with 700 acres of water, 5,000 acres of land, 20 miles of river bank and hundreds of buildings that suddenly had no function. By the 1970s, the docks, from the City to Woolwich, had one thing in common: decline. The response was indecision, wrangling, piecemeal demolition as the docks closed, one by one. The Port of London Authority (PLA) had, and still has, the job of running the port. The rest of the area was split between four boroughs and a myriad private owners, each with different powers and priorities. The City fathers looked on the docks as potential opposition, not opportunity. London has never been a place for grand strategic plans, but the docks certainly needed one.

So after much talking and several abortive attempts at co-operation, in 1981 Mrs Thatcher's government imposed a new kind of body, a development corporation, on a great swathe of riverside London. Fierce rows arose, with the established communities, and more especially their politicians, opposing the centralized, undemocratic London Docklands Development Corporation (LDDC). The Greater London Council (GLC), in particular, was a sworn enemy.

Lest we forget, let's recall the words of George Nicholson, Chairman of the GLC's Planning Committee in 1985: 'Anyone who regards as a success story the systematic attacks by the LDDC on local and strategic planning, and on local accountability . . . the madcap schemes for an airport, luxury housing and huge office developments, cannot be said to have the interests of the residents of Docklands at heart. The truth is that Docklands is for sale to the highest bidder.'

Mr George Nicholson was, happily, wrong about much of this, as this chapter shows; but he was right on his last point, right to bemoan the fate of the residents. Despite much well-intentioned effort by the LDDC and others, the traditional communities of Millwall and Poplar were late and reluctant converts to the Docklands dream. There is still an uneasy air of two cultures, with the gleaming office towers rising above some pretty mean streets.

The LDDC is now wound up. While it ruled, it wielded great power. It decided planning applications, compulsorily bought and then sold derelict sites and also planned the infrastructure. While it could not force private firms to build what they did not see as profitable, it was able to steer and direct in a way no local council has ever managed. One key achievement by the LDDC has been to get the rest of London to think of 'Docklands' as an entity. This is valid: it is a new place overlaying a clutch of old ones, and newness and the attitudes it engenders are common to places well apart, in geography as well as character. But from the Docklands collective the local neighbourhoods are happily re-emerging.

The first dock to re-emerge from decline was St Katharine's, next door to Tower Bridge. In 1828 it cost £1,700,000 to build; in 1969 the PLA sold it for £200,000 less. By the mid-'70s a large new hotel had been built (opening to a noisy 'homes before hotels' protest) and the marina, shops and homes complex now in being, had taken its basic shape. Most of the London Docks, a little to the E, were filled in as if they had never existed. Shadwell Basin is all the water that survived, though some of the housing schemes surround ornamental canals: sort of watery memorials.

The Surrey Docks closed in 1969 and by 1974 their deserted, overgrown acres were the home of 90 species of birds. Within 10 years several thousand new homes in park-like surroundings had arisen. The West India and Millwall Docks on the Isle of Dogs survived until 1980, and the last ship to unload in the the Royals, the great down-river complex, steamed away in October 1981. The same year, the LDDC took over.

The transformation begins

The 1980s were the most remarkable decade in the docks' long history. No-one at the LDDC in 1981 knew they were starting a new business city; they thought they might with luck achieve a business park and some new homes. In 1982, land in Wapping sold for £60,000 an acre and by 1987 the going rate was £4 million. In early 1988 this Guide described the completion of the Docklands Light Railway (DLR), listed literally thousands of new and converted homes and reported on the first stages of Canary Wharf. The 1988 Guide also recorded that the warehouse buildings constructed only six or seven years beforehand, in the first days of the Enterprize Zone (EZ), were being torn down and replaced as they no longer earned their keep on the rapidly appreciating sites.

The real, untold story of 1980s Docklands is the rapid rise in the area's expectations. After decades in which many hopeful plans dissolved on contact with reality, this time the reason was due to the plans being far too timid. The growing pains – awful traffic congestion, lack of services – were the product of totally unpredicted success. The Docklands Light Railway was only five years old when Canary Wharf came along: the DLR had to be virtually rebuilt to allow more people to use it than had ever been foreseen. Even the much-derided City Airport has survived and is now a big success.

Then came the 1990 recession. Wiseacres across London bored fellow guests at innumerable dinner parties with how they knew Docklands would never work. For quite a few people, the disaster was real. Developers went bust, owners of smart new flats found their blocks filled up with council tenants as despairing landlords struck discount deals at Tower Hamlets Town Hall. Even Canary Wharf went bust. It would have taken a brave speculator to buy into Docklands around 1992. But they would have been wise: Shad Thames and Bermondsey came second to Kensington on a survey of property price growth from December 1992 to March 1997. Investment buyers reappeared: see next page for the rentals/investment market in more detail.

The years 1997 and 1998 saw the Docklands market return to a steady state: price increases were seen, but no mad queues of buyers before a new block was 'released'. It must be stressed that prices have not returned to their 1988 levels in quite a few places. The price for a 1-bed flat in a well-located Wapping block is the same now as the sum paid for studios in the same block in 1988. Factor in inflation and interest costs and you are well out of pocket. Anyone with stars in their eyes about Docklands prices is referred to the 1988 edition of this Guide.

However, investors who bought between 1991 and 1993 will have seen some dramatic returns – in some cases over 200 per cent and on average over 75 per cent. This has been possible because Docklands fell more than probably anywhere else in London. The difference between today and 1989 is that, while property may be nominally a similar price, the transport and services infrastructures have greatly improved; and so they should have – more public money has been spent here than anywhere else in the UK in the same period. Price growth has been built on solid foundations – the West End will only be 15 min away when the long-delayed Jubilee line extension opens.

The homes

Mention Docklands in Hampstead or Hammersmith and people will think of smart riverside flats. Perhaps warehouse conversions come to mind. Once, that was about all you could find. Today, the choice is much wider. There are whole districts of modern 3- and 4-bed houses with gardens, some of just above council standard and others as good as anything you'll find in London. There are fairly ordinary 'inland' flats, there are indeed riverside ones, and dockside ones. Some blocks are serviced and have every luxury, and compete in style with the grand apartment buildings of Regent's Park or Mayfair. Others are very ordinary indeed.

There are warehouse conversions, and these range from vast airy spaces full of river-reflected light to cramped little dens looking out on stagnant, sunless docks or back streets. Even the bigger warehouse flats can have a lot of floor space relative to the window area. Check you get some sun. And, of course, there are new, shiny, straight-from-the developer properties and others that go back 15 or 20 years. If you look really hard, you might find a flat or (even rarer) a house that pre-dates the Docklands boom of the 1980s. People have been living round here since Shakespeare was a lad.

The Docklands property market

Some estimates reckon that one in five new Docklands homes sold in 1997 went to Far East buyers. When things started to go wrong at home – that autumn saw the Thai bubble burst – the buyers went on strike. However, the feared completion crisis – failure by investors to honour deals they'd paid deposits on – has not emerged. The Far East buyers may be reluctant landlords, and some are selling, but at least they have a rental yield to console them. Despite their absence Docklands prices increased by about 15 per cent over 1998, with most of the action in the first six months. The word in January 1999 from the more established areas – Wapping, Shad Thames, the Canary Wharf quarter – is that European and US buyers are active but that they are outnumbered by the British, with owner-occupiers joined by a new wave of investors. City sentiment remained the dominant influence, however.

The investment and rental market

In the 1990 recession renting was the desperate remedy for investors or developers who had got stuck holding a block of new flats no-one wanted to buy. As a result, the tenants tended to be supplied by the DHSS. Now, renting in Docklands is a normal, uncontroversial transaction. In the areas closest to the City and Canary Wharf the number of rented homes equals that in owner-occupation, though the proportion fluctuates with yields and prices.

Docklands is overwhelmingly a British market, both for investors and tenants. Agents Knight Frank chart a decline in the proportion of Americans renting via their Canary Wharf office, down to 5 per cent by the end of 1998. Other groups renting via this office were Europeans at 31 per cent, Far East at 7 per cent with British tenants making up the 57 per cent balance. Turn to investors, and a thumping 88 per cent are British, with 11 per cent Far East and 1 per cent European. In Wapping the figures are even more strongly British on both sides of the equation: 64 per cent of tenants, with 12 per cent USA and 22 per cent European; while an overwhelming 94 per cent of investors are British, with Europeans and Far East splitting the remainder equally. Comparing these figures with Kensington, we find the tenants 38 per cent USA, 32 per cent European, with a remarkable 50 per cent of investors from the Far East and 41 per cent British.

D

Investment buying is still a mainspring of the Docklands market with many developments marketed primarily for their rental yield. Knight Frank's figures show a 10 per cent yield on Canary Wharf neighbourhood properties at the start of 1999 – up 2 per cent on the figure for mid-1998. This increase reflects the success of Canary Wharf and consequent increased demand from tenants. The uncertainties in the financial sector also led people to postpone buying decisions and rent instead, Knight Frank reckon.

Progress report

If you want to depress office workers elsewhere in London, start a rumour that the management are planning a move to Docklands. Visit a relocated office and you'll probably find the workforce a lot more cheerful: Docklands (and in office terms this means the Isle of Dogs) is a lot better than they expected.

As noted above, the health of the Docklands's homes market is linked to that of its office market. In the gloomy days of the early 1990s recession everyone (including most of the media) was talking down the Canary Office complex as over-ambitious – its future usage was being speculated about and it was also being compared to the cheap and dowdy banking and insurance back offices of Croydon and Brighton. Now, it is a clear success – and the story of Canary Wharf is the story of the whole of the Docklands.

Let's look at the best index of success: what tenants actually pay for offices. Prime City rents are around £50–52 per sq ft. Big developers reckon that £40 per sq ft is a base level: rents may drop that far in tough times. Move out to the City fringes and you might be expected to pay £20–25 per sq ft. You can find space of comparable quality on the Isle of Dogs for £15 per sq ft, but choose Canary Wharf and the going rate is £35 per sq ft.

For those with a long term vision, the success of Canary Wharf was never in doubt – but that didn't stop some of those visionaries going bust on a scale to match the project. The tower was completed in November 1990; Olympia & York, the developers, went into receivership in May 1992 and re-emerged (owned by the banks) in October 1993; in December 1995 it was sold to a consortium led by Paul Reichman (other investors include Saudi and US/Canadian interests). Mr Reichman was one of the three Canadian brothers who, as Olympia & York, rescued the scheme the first time round after the original backers got cold feet. There is now talk of Canary Wharf being floated on the Stock Exchange.

Canary Wharf now has 4.5 million sq ft of extremely high quality offices (the 36-ft lobby of the Tower has 90,000 sq ft of Italian and Guatemalan marble) and retail space in 10 buildings. The working population has grown to 25,000 and Canary Wharf is over 99 per cent let with only the top (50th) floor of the tower available. There are now firm plans to complete the complex as planned in the '80s. Speculative building has re-started with a 200,000 sq ft Terry Farrell-designed block. A further 2.3 million sq ft of space is either under construction or due to start during 1999.

Big banks continue to dominate the occupiers' lists, with HSBC the latest to confirm a move: its Norman Foster tower will rise almost as high as the existing one, will have 1.1 million sq ft of space and room for 8,000 staff. Newspapers also cluster at Canary Wharf, which has led to quite a few 'as I gaze out of my window at the shining Thames below' features (and to a sharp decline in articles knocking Docklands). On current predictions, the workforce will rise to 43,000 by 2002, and by 2005 or thereabouts office space will have tripled to 10 million sq ft and spread out on to the 15 acres of Heron Quays (also owned by Canary Wharf after Regalian sold out their 50 per cent stake). The existing Heron Quay offices will go.

Not all the news is good: nervous banks scaled down their plans in autumn 1998, and the Euro is an unknown factor. Within a month of the currency's launch Bank of America pulled out of plans to relocate its European HQ at Canary Wharf, saying it preferred to wait until the effects of the Euro became clear.

There are now over 60 shops and restaurants open in Canary Wharf including Boots, Pret a Manger, Café Rouge and the crucial Tesco Metro that provides a community focus for the whole N side of the Docklands. There are also 20 bars, cafés, pubs and restaurants – and now they stay open in the evenings. Back in 1992 the few bars used to shut at 8pm.

Canary Riverside began construction in June 1997. This is a 750,000 sq ft development to the W of the main complex, beside Westferry Circus. The four residential blocks will have 322 flats and there's a luxury Four Seasons hotel, leisure club (swimming pool and two tennis courts) and restaurants; all due to open in autumn 1999. Singapore investors, with Canary Wharf Ltd in a minority role, own the Riverside complex.

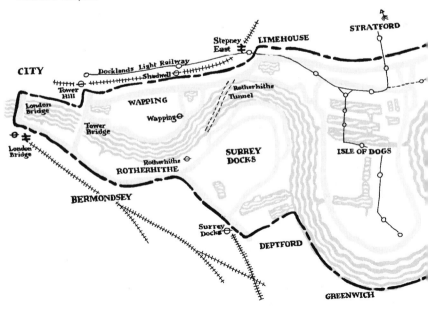

The Jubilee line tube station at Canary Wharf is a beautiful but at present purposeless structure. When the line eventually opens, it will connect the Docklands to the West End in 15 min. The Limehouse Link, a 4-lane underground highway, was completed in May 1993 and links Tower Hill to Canary Wharf; it and a big network of fast (most of the time) roads now provide access to City, West End and City Airport.

A new riverbus service is planned to start this June, primarily to serve the Millenium Dome but with stops at Canary Wharf and other Docklands piers. However, riverbus services have come and gone before and it would be a fool who bets his property investment on river connections until the service has survived at least one recession. The Docklands Light Railway should be running to Greenwich and Lewisham by the end of 1999. Those other elements of an infrastructure, entertainment and shopping, are now coming. Surrey Quays has a big shopping development around a Tesco hypermarket, opened in 1988 and a major success. An 8-screen UCI cinema is now open next to the shopping centre. On the Isle of Dogs, Virgin's 10-screen cinema forms part of the West India Quay complex.

The shape of Docklands

First time visitors start here for a whistle-stop tour. The most central Docklands areas are N and S of the Thames within view of Tower Bridge. Downstream on the N bank is Wapping; facing it on the S side, Bermondsey and Shad Thames/Tower Bridge. Wapping has the restored St Katharine's Dock, a mature, successful business/tourist/homes centre. The Wapping waterfront has the best warehouse conversions,

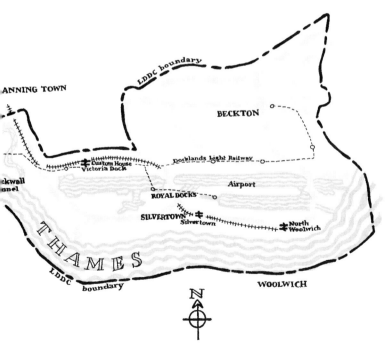

with sunny river views and large spaces, plus a large choice of new-build flats. Inland are new streets of small, well-placed houses and flats.

The S bank, around Shad Thames and Butler's Wharf, has a wealth of new and converted flats in a classy new neighbourhood with shops, restaurants and museum.

Further E on the N bank comes Limehouse: a riverside strip between Wapping and Canary Wharf with more converted warehouses, new flats and the continuing, large-scale Limehouse Basin development. And here begins the great bend of the river that wraps around the Isle of Dogs, Docklands' heart. This was the most depressed and derelict corner, virtually cut off by water, and is now a vibrant mix of giant office schemes – including Canary Wharf – and homes. Look here for riverside homes of varying views and quality, inland houses and apartments at good prices.

Across the river, the Isle's mirror image is the Surrey Docks peninsula. Riverside homes are backed by many new-build schemes of family homes and the giant Surrey Quays shopping complex. The new tube will call here. The SE corner of the area has the dock- and marina-side homes. Surrey Quays and Rotherhithe already has an established community feel to it which has just expanded with new development.

East from the Isle of Dogs, the Docklands is future not present. The Leamouth sites have been cleared for development which is now beginning. East again, the vast Royal Docks has a small airport, plenty of new roads – and several mega-schemes on paper or tentatively starting (and in some cases stopping again). In five years time, all being well, there will be shopping areas, industry, an exhibition centre, a new university as well as homes.

Wapping

Wapping is the oldest established of the Dockland neighbourhoods – perhaps because it is the closest neighbourhood N of the river to the City. The W parts are a pleasant walk from city offices, further E people use the DLR at Shadwell. Going E to Canary Wharf is just as important to many, and the DLR and the Limehouse road tunnel provide that link. Shopping facilities have improved with the Safeway store on **St Thomas More St**, but most people shop at Canary Wharf.

Wapping starts, in the shadow of the Tower, with **St Katharine's Dock**. This is only just Docklands; more City-with-scenery: the two dock basins shelter yachts and provide an attractive outlook for homes and a hotel just a step from the City. Development of this quarter has been under way since the mid-'70s. There are 300 local authority homes – some bought by tenants. **Mews St** has 10 small cottages; **Marble Quay** has four flats in an office development. **The Ivory House**, a fine old converted warehouse, has 2-bed apartments to let from £600 a week. Spread over two sides of St Katharine's Dock, Taylor Woodrows' **City Quay** is an impressive new addition: the last phase of this long-running scheme (see 1990's Guide . . .) will be complete by the end of this year. It offers 209 1-, 2- and 3-bed flats and 3- and 4-bed penthouses; prices from £460,000 (2-bed) to £1.38 million. At the entrance to the dock is **Harrison's Wharf**, a crescent of seven 4/5-bed 'Nash' style stucco £1 million houses amid a large commercial scheme. Barratt are active in the area with **Hermitage Waterside** E of the dock. This features 1/2-bed flats and 3-bed houses. A detached Georgian house on the edge of the dock now reckoned to be worth over £2,000,000.

Back on the river, **President's Quay** is a particularly stylish development; the twin glass-roofed pyramids of its penthouses a riverside landmark: 1-bed flats: £165,000. Quality is high. Next door, **Miller's Wharf** has 22 pricey homes in a Terry Farrell-designed, handsome warehouse conversion. On **St Katharine's Way** and next to the Berkeley Homes **Hermitage Wharf** block is **Riviera Court** which has a dozen 'spectacular new-build 2- and 3-bed flats overhanging the Thames': priced from £250,000. **Tower Bridge Wharf** is a 64-home new-build (1990) development. One end

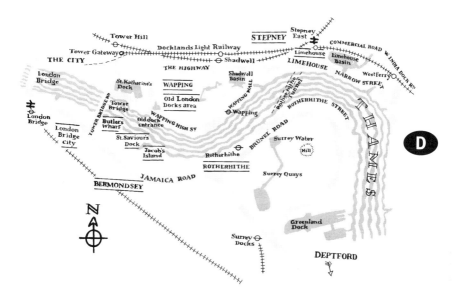

is semi-circular, with a courtyard, which gives the opportunity for some unusual shapes and two differing but enviable penthouses at either end of the crescent.

As the river flows on E the next large development which backs onto **Wapping High St** is Berkeley Homes' Capital Wharf, 85 riverside flats from £330,000 to £695,000: a handful left last winter. **Hermitage Wharf**, a big (2+ acre) Berkeley site yet to be developed, will have 93 flats, a restaurant and a new public park.

On the inland side of **Wapping High St** is **Hermitage Court**: 97 homes (1-bed flats: £140,000) over shops and offices. Next comes the glorious **Wapping Pierhead**: the area's one remaining enclave of Georgian houses. These change hands for well over £600,000. Extending inland, new local authority houses match the Pierhead style exactly. **Pierhead Wharf** has a cheerful, typical brick and red paint look.

Back on the riverside, **Oliver's Wharf** has some of the most coveted flats in Docklands: it was converted in 1973 by a group of architects and artists, some of whom still live there. This is the one that started the whole warehouse conversion fever off. The group each paid some £14,000 for their industrial space. Today they remain some of the largest of Docklands (or, indeed, London) flats – a typical one has a 54 x 38 ft galleried living room. Expect to pay over £500,000 for a riverside one, over £400,000 on the inland side.

Orient Wharf is let by a housing association. On the inland side of the High St, **Dundee Court** has 48 1- to 3-bed flats dating from 1986 and now priced at around £390,000 for a 2,000 sq ft 3-bed. **The Sanctuary** is inland, but with some good river views. It boasts rooftop pool and gym and basement parking. Also inland on **Brewhouse Lane** is warehouse-style **Chimney Court**, with 41 studios plus 1- and 2-bed flats: £275,000 for a large duplex. 78 **Wapping High St** was once a wine warehouse; now 16 homes. **Aberdeen Wharf** is probably the last warehouse conversions on the Wapping riverside. It has 17 flats on the southern tip of the Wapping bend: ready this spring. The '60s apparition nearby covered with abstract glass-fibre heiroglyphs and bound to be listed one day is the river police's boathouse.

St John's Wharf was turned into 22 large (some are nearly 3,000 sq ft) flats in 1984. Resales are sought-after. **King Henry's Wharves** are next door.

Barratt's **Gun Wharf** conversion provided 68 flats in 1985. The adjoining **Gun House**, by the same developer, eight flats plus a penthouse, is new-build. **Gun Place** is on the inland side of the High St and has 73 flats in a conversion. Alongside, **Bridewell Place** is also Barratt: this one is a mews-style scheme with 52 homes completed in 1988. Also on the inland side – and close to Wapping tube station – is The Carronade, 42 flats, some double-height and galleried, by Broadwell. Towerside, by Wates, straddles **Wapping High St**; the waterside part is new; the rest – **Prusom's Island** – award-winning refurbished warehouses. A total of 97 flats and new-build houses were built. Although not the most sophisticated of Wapping schemes, it does provide among the least expensive riverside flats: a 1-bed riverside flat might be £145,000, a 2-bed: £230,000. **St Hilda's Wharf** is a late-1980s riverside scheme of 39 large, especially for new-build flats. A 4-bed penthouse was on the market last winter for £795,000.

New Crane Wharf is a warehouse conversion with a courtyard, around which are grouped 143 homes plus some offices, shops and also restaurants. This is a very popular development and of good quality, too; 1-bed non-river view flats are priced around £130,000.

Great Jubilee Wharf, refurbished in 1996 by Galliard, created 30 flats. Further along, in a development that straddles **Wapping High St**, Persimmon have just completed **Thorpe's Yard**, a group of three buildings; riverside warehouse conversion and new-build, with 2-bed flats from £185,000; river view flats from £285,000; penthouses from £390,000.

Pelican Wharf, next door to the Prospect of Whitby, has 13 large 2,000 sq ft apartments – each bigger than a normal family house. Walkways round an atrium and a whole floor penthouse with three roof gardens are among its attractions. The painstaking Roger Malcolm had problems with this tricky site (taking due care of the historic pub not least among them).

On the other side of the pub **Prospect Wharf** is in a rather ungainly, gabled roof 1980s warehouse style, built by Trafalgar House in an enviable position between the river and Shadwell Basin. Great views, therefore, on both sides, though some eccentrically-shaped rooms. Another plus is the open courtyard between the river and the curve of the buildings: a rare commodity in crowded Wapping. The flats are 1- and 2-bed, with 2-bed priced around £200,000. **Prospect Place**, N of **Wapping Wall**, has 70 houses and flats in a successful layout next to a Regalian refurb of a block of council flats, **Riverside Mansions**, **Milk Yard**, which were sold to waiting-list locals at a discount. These are 750 sq ft 2-bed maisonettes (many with views over Shadwell Basin) and are reckoned good value at £120,000.

Shadwell Basin consists of 172 flats and houses, some with 5 bedrooms, grouped round the dock, home to a youth watersports club. The gabled brick buildings with their distinctive semi-circular windows and red detailing are popular: not surprising, given their attractive dockside position. **Peartree Lane** has 4-bed dockside houses (c. £340,000); **Newlands Quay** has 3-bed duplex flats at around £135,000. Heading W, Tobacco Dock, a listed warehouse, started out as a shopping centre around 1990 but has never really taken off: recent rumours have spread mentioning part of it may be becoming a hotel. The conversion is glorious, though.

Wapping's inland quarter is mostly built on the site of the old London Docks, but only Shadwell Basin and a few shallow, ornamental canals remain to remind us. The tree-lined canals do provide an attractive environment for some good-value homes in developments now mature after 10–12 years. Industry such as News International's giant printworks come rather close to some homes, though. Among several 'inland' schemes, award-winning **East Quay** and **Waterman Quay** have 170 houses and flats grouped around the new canal. **Portland Square** is a 1986 Barratt development with some (rare) large 3-storey houses (c. £180,000) grouped around a private square with fountain, and a range of other homes. Also on the old site of the London Docks are **South Quay** – 182 low-cost (originally) homes by Broseley (some houses are shared-ownership through a housing association) and Quay 430, a 300-home Regalian scheme. Sample prices: in **Waterman Way**, a 2-bed canalside flat might be £108,000; another such in **Welland Mews** £137,000. Also 'inland' are some ex-council homes which can sell at lower prices.

On **The Highway**, Wapping's main road, **Telford's Yard** has 68 particularly spacious flats in a warehouse conversion. Next door **Breezers Court** was divided, in 1985, into 30 flats. Further along **The Highway**, Barratt's **Pennington Court** is a 1987 scheme. Finally on the fringes and going towards Limehouse is Regalian's rather gaunt riverside **Atlantic Wharf**, which has 213 1-, 2- and 3-bed flats – most with river views. A 1-bed penthouse flat with river view was £185,000 last December, the general run of 1-bed around £145,000.

Limehouse

Limehouse is a hugely popular area, being between the City and Canary Wharf and is much quieter than the Isle of Dogs. Villagy **Narrow St** has shaken off the dust of development and is now most attractive. Limehouse Basin, also badly affected by the road tunnel beneath it which finally opened in 1993, is at last emerging as another marina-style development.

A number of major developers built landmark river developments in the late 1990s, although the area still retains a sense of history. The launch (against the trend of the times) by Galliard Homes of the **Papermill Wharf** development in 1992, which sold out within hours, is credited with having kick-started the entire Docklands property market in the last recession.

Regalian's orange ziggurat landmark **Free Trade Wharf** stands sentinel at the end of Wapping which is the beginning of Limehouse. This is a large scheme of 171 new, and six luxurious converted warehouse apartments. The scheme includes its own gym and swimming pool, but the shops never found tenants and they are to be converted into flats. Part of the Wharf dates from 1795 – an old salt-petre store. **Keepier Wharf**, a re-clad warehouse with 24 spacious flats completed in 1987, stands at the beginning of Limehouse's best-known corner, **Narrow St**. Narrow St is a warehouse-lined road running the length of the Limehouse waterfront. It is also famous for its short surviving run of riverside Georgian houses as well as for the venerable Grapes public house.

A number of new riverside developments have been built on Narrow St: **Papermill Wharf**; Barratt's **Victoria Wharf**, 67 2-bed flats completed last winter at sensible prices; **Chinnocks Wharf** by St George's (2- and 3-bed flats); **Old Sun Wharf**, a joint venture by Galliard Homes and Frogmore Estates of 36 2- and 3-bed duplex apartments all with river views. Opposite **Victoria Wharf** is Fairclough's **Victoria Lock** – a mixed development of 1-, 2- and 3-bed apartments and 3- and 4-bed houses.

On the inland side, between **Narrow St** and **The Highway**, is **St George's Square**, a remarkable mixture of architectural styles from Docklands vernacular to mock-Tudor, executed in red-brick. 41 houses and flats surround a small courtyard.

Along the riverside are several smaller new buildings and conversions: **Ratcliffe Wharf**, which is new, and **London** and **Commercial Wharves**, both conversions. Both **Ratcliffe** and **Commercial** are by the hand of the unquenchable Mrs Rae Hoffenburg, a Docklands pioneer who started converting warehouses (and living in them) in the 1970s, and has just started a Narrow St residents' association.

Sun Wharf is just one home: it changed hands about four years ago for nearly £3 million; it used to belong to the film director David Lean. It is unique in Docklands in having a complete waterside garden – lawns, trees and all – with a 124-ft frontage to the river. The whole place was carved out of four old warehouses in 1985. The living space totals more than 11,000 sq ft.

Across the road from **Victoria Wharf** sits the Limehouse Basin, a 25-acre site and the entrance to the country's canal system. The Basin's development was held up not just by the 1990 recession but by the digging of the giant road tunnel which runs beneath it. Now, several developers are busy with St George being one of the first developers to restart building with Quayside – a modern but classical-looking development being carried out in several phases of 1-, 2- and 3-bed apartments and duplexes which are arranged around a courtyard. **Commercial Wharf** (yes, another one) is Barratt's scheme of low, brick terraces just back from the E side of the Basin: 1- to 3-bed flats from £118,000; 3-bed town-houses from £205,000; 4-bed from £250,000. Bellway are busy on the W side of the Basin with **Limehouse Marina**: six rather dramatic blocks and a smart steel tower: 300 homes in all, with the first phase priced at £130–330,000. There's more to come around Limehouse Basin, an area that will please anyone with a nautical bent.

Back on the river, **Blyth's Wharf** is a terrace of 16 2,000 sq ft-plus 4-bed houses, all with river views. It boasts an extensive pier, giving a promenade now open to the public. Opposite Blyth's Wharf inland is The Watergardens, a stylish refurbishment of former council property by Ballymore with 1- and 2-bed flats. Past these two are the real thing: the Georgian waterside homes and the Grapes pub. **Duke Shore Wharf** is next, a successful new-build development in a horseshoe shape.

Inland, opposite the Grapes pub on Ropemaker Fields, is a terrace of large modern 4-bed houses attached to a pub on the end of the terrace called 'The House They Left Behind' (which refers to a former terrace of Victorian houses that were demolished). Between this and the Watergardens is **Sovereign Place**, by Persimmon: 51 homes ranging from 1- and 2-bed flats (from £145,000) to 3-bed town-houses (£320,000).

Narrow St curves on round the N side of Limekiln Dock, an inlet off the main river which survived the Limehouse Link tunnelling – at one time it was going to be filled in, but it was reprieved. The N side of the dock is lined by Fairbriar's **Dunbar Wharf**, part converted warehouse and part new. The third and last phase has 107 homes, most sold off-plan but with a few left unsold last winter at £235,000 for 2-bed. A big penthouse in the block on the river corner is £950,000. **Limehouse Wharf** is a small 1840 warehouse, an early conversion into flats/working studios: large with unusually high ceilings. **Limekiln Wharf** at the head of the inlet has six flats in a renovated building, and 23 new ones being built in an L-shaped block.

Just inland on **Three Colts St** is **Dundee Wharf**, a 10-storey block variously described as 'futuristic' and 'imposing', with spidery balconies and a tower that looks like a post-funtional crane. There are 112 flats, 21 penthouses and five houses. Most have splendid views up river to the City or across to Canary Wharf. The 2-bed flats start at £200,000, with a penthouse at £900,000.

London Bridge

The westernmost tongue of Docklands intrudes right into the heart of London, facing the City, between London and Tower Bridges. **London Bridge City** has a million sq ft of offices, plus shops and restaurants in the handsome Hays Galleria with its soaring atrium, flats to rent, health club and a private hospital. The 13-acre vacant site to the E, stretching to Tower Bridge, was planned as London Bridge City Phases II and III. It went quiet in the early '90s but was bought by CIT in 1998, and they appointed Stanhope (the people behind Broadgate) to develop it. They plan 1.5 million sq ft of offices including a futuristic 'pod' for the Mayor of London. Leisure space will be involved but no homes are envisaged. The area S of London Bridge, discussed in the South Bank chapter, is a good hunting-ground for warehouse conversions and new-build homes. There is a lot of activity, including the £9 million conversion into a hotel of a former factory on **Tanner St**.

Shad Thames/Tower Bridge and Bermondsey

Not so long ago, **Shad Thames** was of interest only to TV companies looking for seedy, derelict locations. The dripping brickwork of the abandoned warehouses, the sinister iron walkways spanning the narrow streets, the weed-grown cobbles . . . it's a bit different now. This is the most successful, established and expensive Docklands neighbourhood, known both for its flats (few houses here) and its restaurants. It could be said to have moved out of Docklands and into Central London, except for its concentration on warehouse conversions and modern copies of them. In price terms it is up with, and probably ahead of, longer-established Wapping.

Shad Thames is the name of the atmospheric, narrow street which runs behind the riverside wall of warehouses, and it has given its name to the neighbourhood, though some prefer the classier-sounding Tower Bridge, and Butler's Wharf, the biggest single warehouse complex, also lends its name to the district.

This area, which stretches on the southside downstream from Tower Bridge, starts with one of the river's most splendid buildings. Not another warehouse, but an old Courage brewery. The **Anchor Brewhouse** is a 10-storey edifice rising sheer from the river right next to the bridge. The interior has been totally rebuilt: the shell of the old Boilerhouse, with its towering landmark chimney, has 35 flats including the spectacular treble-decker penthouse. This changed hands in 1997 for around £1.5 million. Its opening price (1988) was £2 million – though it's unclear if this was ever reached. Certainly the flat saw more use as a film-set than a home: Docklands-addicts spotted it again and again whenever a flash pad was called for.

The Malt Mill, nearest the bridge, has more large flats, all with river views. Here too, is an amazing penthouse: this time on four floors, and boasting the original cupola and belvedere galley. Where the first was glass-walled modern, its main room like the deck of a '30s liner, this one will be more like owning a Georgian house – set high in the air. It even has a garden: a double-height conservatory. It was on the market last winter – for £3.95 million, if you can take the silly name 'High Command'. On a more mundane level, there are 1-bed and 2-bed flats. From here you see the Tower of London framed within Tower Bridge.

Directly behind the brewery lies **Horsleydown Square**, where unlovely 1950/60s buildings were cleared to be replaced by shops, offices, workshops et al, around an open landscaped square. 178 homes, some conversion, some new-build, have been built. Names to look out for in this corner are: **Eagle Wharf**, **The Cooperage**, **Crown Court** and **Horsleydown Court. Tower Bridge Square**, on **Gainsford St**, was built for sale by the Nationwide Housing Trust: 1- and 2-bedroomed flats and town-houses. **The Cardomom Building** is a smart warehouse conversion fronting Shad Thames.

Next along the river from the brewery is **Butler's Wharf West**, a vast converted complex of five blocks of flats, including 80 or so which are let. Prices are similar to the Anchor Brewhouse. On the ground floor three out of the four local Terence Conran restaurants are housed: The Chop House, Pont de la Tour and Cantina del Ponto; it is to the long-term vision of Conran that the Shad Thames area owes a lot of its fortunes. This 'gastrodome' complex revived Conran's own fortunes after Butlers Wharf Development Company (in which he had a large interest) went into receivership in the early '90s.

Also beside the river is **Spice Quay**, a new block being built by Galliard Homes, with 92 1- and 2-bed flats and penthouses from £433,500 (for 2-bed) upwards. Completion is due during 1999. Next to this is the Design Museum, in which is the Blue Print Café (the fourth local Conran restaurant – but first to open).

East of the Design Museum is the still-derelict original Butlers Wharf Building. This is owned by Galliard, who plan to develop it – but timing is unknown. It has a superb site on the corner of **St Saviour's Dock**, a river inlet, now bridged. Many warehouse conversions and new-build schemes crowd together along the narrow waterway. It is north-facing, so lack of light can be a drawback especially on lower floors. On the W side of St. Saviour's Dock is **Cinnamon Wharf** – a stylish late-'80s conversion of a former 1950s block into 66 flats. **Saffron Wharf** followed – an '80s office converted into 13 units by Berkeley Homes (priced £280,000–540,000).

Christian's Warehouse is a 1989 conversion and new-build scheme, with 87 flats overlooking St Saviour's Dock. Next door is **Java Wharf**. Behind Spice Quay and stretching to **Gainsford St** is **Tamarind Court** – a warehouse carved into 62 flats by Galliard; prices for a 2-bed flat are from £230,000. On the other side of **Gainsford St** on the corner with **Shad Thames**, Nicholson Estates are creating a complex of homes located around a gated courtyard. The splendidly-named Butler's Grinders & Operators buildings are being reborn as **Butlers and Colonial Wharf** (why wharf?), with some new town-houses and flats – and some live/work units – completing the quadrangle. Fairview are planning 123 1- to 3-bed flats for mid-1999 on a site next to **Tamarind Wharf**.

Straddling **Queen Elizabeth St** is **The Circle**, with its fluid lines and blue-brick fascias. Further along on the same side of the street and at 16–19 **Lafone St** is **Raven Wharf** – 21 new-build 2- and 3-bed flats and two live/work units by Gleeson Homes. **Boss House** on **Boss St** is a conversion of a 20th century warehouse where spacious 2-bed flats command £300,000.

The footbridge at the mouth of St Saviour's Dock links the Shad Thames quarter to the Bermondsey riverside. On the E side of the creek is **Scott's Sufferance Wharf**: a courtyard of shops, offices and 93 flats of various sizes. **Lloyd's Wharf** has 24 flats sold as shells in 1985 for £30–60,000. Now worth around £160,000–200,000-plus. **Unity Wharf** has four gloriously large work/liveflats. **Vogan's Mill** is the conversion of an old flour mill; providing 64 2/4-bed flats and a penthouse in six buildings. Thanks to the existence of the mill's tall silo, the developer got the chance to replace the structure with a new 18-storey high-tech tower – prices in this quality development range from £230,000 to £1,500,000 for the penthouse in the tower.

St Saviour's Wharf, back on the Dock, is a refurbishment which provided 47 flats and offices. And downstream, at the creek's mouth, is the award-winning **New Concordia Wharf**, discovered on the point of demolition by young developer Andrew Wadsworth; his 1985 conversion sparked the revival of the entire Bermondsey bank. The development is still the benchmark for Bermondsey quality, and is much requested by home-seekers. Next to New Concordia Wharf is the new-build **China Wharf**: smaller rooms, glorious views, architecture (more awards) loved by some, not by others. **Reeds Wharf**, adjoining, has flats and offices. Next to Reeds Wharf a single 5-storey house is being built on a riverside plot. **Springalls Wharf** is a handsome new flats block.

Jacob's Island – a new-build scheme by Berkeley Homes – has eight contemporary blocks of 1- and 2-bed flats and penthouses on the E side of **Mill St**: the last three blocks have just been released, with prices from £140,000 (635 sq ft) to £310,000 (1044 sq ft). Next to Jacob Island is **River View Heights** (formerly **Tower View Wharf**) – 62 1-, 2- and 3-bed flats on eight floors. Just 2-beds are left at £450,000 – apart from the penthouse, which if it sells at the asking price of £1.5 million will set a new record for SE16.

The future of the large **Chambers Wharf** site downstream is still unclear. Next comes **Cherry Garden Pier**, with 64 riverside council houses (new and rehab) and five terraces of flats and town-houses built in the 1980s. **Corbetts Wharf** was converted to flats back in 1984; **Angel Wharf** on the other side of the road in 1995; 2-bed flats are around £300,000 and 4-bed around £425,000. Next to Corbetts Wharf and on the river is **National Terrace**, 10 4-storey, 4-bedroom houses with garages.

Rotherhithe

The surviving waterside hamlet of Rotherhithe boasts a glorious 1715 parish church, St Mary's, whose internal pillars are not stone but old ships' masts, plastered over. Surrounding the church, the old school, rectory and some of the warehouses – not to mention the Mayflower pub – also date at least from Georgian days. As a plaque on the 16th-century inn (formerly named the Spread Eagle) states, this is where the Pilgrim Fathers set off from in 1620 on their way to America. On the W edge of the village **Elephant Lane/Mayflower Court** has 76 houses and flats, plus offices, built in 1984 in an avenue running away from the river to the Rotherhithe Tunnel roundabout. Around the old village are several blocks of pre-war council flats.

At the very beginning of **Rotherhithe St** at King's Stairs Close stands an imposing 1930s-inspired white block of apartments known as **Princes Tower**. This has 1-, 2- and 3-bed flats. The historic, award-winning **Thames Tunnel Mills** is a riverside warehouse converted into fair-rent flats, while **Ronald Buckingham Court** is sheltered housing. The conversion of two warehouses and also the building of a new block at **Hope Wharf** between the river, Rotherhithe St and Mary Church St has created 32 homes: flats and stylish 2-bed glasshouses (10 houses left unsold in January). **Isambard Place**, whose name recalls the tunnel's builder, has 94 2- to 4-bed flats plus 44 for a housing association. Across the road, the **Atlas Reach** scheme adds a further 100 flats.

Surrey Quays

The river bends like the shape of an upside down horseshoe as we travel downstream from Rotherhithe to Surrey Quays. This area is uninterrupted by the traffic and general mayhem that one would normally expect so close to the City; there are no main roads so there is no through traffic. It is quiet beyond belief.

From Rotherhithe on E, round the great bend of the river, is the frontage of the old Surrey Docks. Nearly all the docks were filled in, and over the last 15 years large areas of new housing have been built. These houses differ markedly in character, if not in style, from the river-front schemes: houses with gardens predominate, rather than warehouse flats. Prices are also lower here. The Surrey Quays shopping centre has been joined by Surrey Quays Phase II and includes an 8-screen cinema, bingo and bowling. To the N, on **Surrey Quays Rd**, the new Canada Water tube station is where the Jubilee line and East London line intersect. The Jubilee line has been the spur for a new leap in development: the long river frontage has changed beyond recognition since the dead days after the docks' closure, and now derelict and vacant tranches of river front land have now been bought up and built on; old empty warehouses have been refurbished.

Rotherhithe St runs right round the peninsula. On from Isambard Place and to the E of **Brunel Rd**, Bellway Homes have built **Brunel Point:** 2- and 3-bed flats, some with river views, and town-houses on the other side of **Rotherhithe St**. The pier on the river was refurbished by Bellway and is now open to the public. This part of **Rotherhithe St** has been permanently closed off to traffic. An inlet leads through a disused lock to Surrey Water, an ornamental lake surrounded by homes. From Surrey Water a canal (again, just to look at) winds through various housing developments to Canada Water, the site of the new Jubilee line station. Along the canal are various pleasant developments which vary from social housing flats, to **Wolfe Crescent** built by Lovell (includes 1-, 2- and 3-bed flats and 4-bed houses) in a red-brick semi-circle curled around four pale-coloured strikingly designed octagonal blocks. **Hithe Point** was built by Barratt (includes 1-, 2- and 3-bed flats and 2- and 3-bed houses). Opposite **Wolfe Crescent** and bordering **Surrey Quays Rd** is **Canada Waters** (includes 2- and 3-bed flats as well as 3- and 4-bed houses, 75 per cent sold). These homes are very close to the new tube station.

At Island Yard, by the lock, a large pub called Spice Island has been built by one of the major breweries. Adjacent to Island Yard and on the corner of **Rotherhithe St** and the YMCA a new block of 18 flats is to be known as **Tradewinds**: prices start at £90,000. Next to this on **Rotherhithe St**, and before **King & Queen Wharf**, is **Prince's Riverside** – a large development (184 units) of 1- and 2-bed river view flats and 2- and 3-bed houses completed at the end of 1997. **King & Queen Wharf** is nicely detailed new-build by Fairclough which was first marketed in 1990: 140 flats with porterage, swimming pool/leisure complex.

Next to **King & Queen Wharf** is Berkeley's **Globe Wharf**, a sensitive restoration of this former flour warehouse, 95 per cent sold. **Sovereign View** – a large neo-Georgian development (including the refurbishment of the old fire station on Rotherhithe St) – was built by Barratt between 1991–93; units vary from 1- and 2-bed flats (700–900 sq ft) to 2- and 3-bed houses with garages built round six squares, most with river views. Also facing the river is **Pageant Steps**, built by Barratt in 1996. This consists of three blocks of 1-, 2- and 3-bed flats, some with river views and 3- and 4- bed houses (from £300,000) with conservatories and gardens and direct river views. Opposite **Pageant Steps**, and inland, is the 141-home **Lavender Dock**.

Canada Wharf is the glitzy refurbishment of a former flour mill by Metropolis Developments. Homes are 1- to 3-bed flats (from 500–1,600 sq ft), several with high ceilings and bed decks. Next to Canada Wharf on the riverside is the Holiday Inn Hotel (622-bed) – formerly the Crown Scandic Hotel. The original warehouse Columbia Wharf, and Nelson Dock and Lawrence Wharf were all part of Port Nelson, a scheme developed by Islef. Columbia Wharf and Nelson Dock now form part of the hotel while the original Lawrence Wharf apartments have been turned into timeshare apartments. This old ship repair dock at one stage had a marina, but this did not survive the last recession. Opposite, on the inland side, the **Amos Estate** has 131 housing association flats. Next comes **Lavender Dock North**, 51 1985 Wimpey houses, inland. Alongside is Lavender Pond nature park. **Lavender Green**, inland across **Salter Rd**, is 1981 low-cost housing by Lovell.

Opposite **Lawrence Wharf** is Silver Walk, a local authority refurbishment of flats and 21 large stylish 3- and 4-bed houses and some new-build units (Patina Walk). Patina Walk was sold to the LSE for student housing in the early '90s. In the midst of the scheme Nelson House is a rare and charming Georgian survival.

A tiny, peaceful park (**Durands Wharf**) gives access to the riverside plus views to the Isle of Dogs and the Canary Wharf towers. Next to the park is **Trinity Wharf**, where Bellway have sold the first phase of 42 homes and plan to release the next batch this spring: 1-, 2- and 3-bed flats from £120,000. **Barnard's Wharf** and **Commercial Pier Wharf**, next to the splendid Surrey Docks Farm, have 139 homes built by housing associations. This is Downtown, for years a very depressed corner of council flats, now a thriving area after a £55 million rehabilitation of the flats blocks by a group of housing associations. Further down is the riverside **New Caledonian Wharf** which is 104 luxurious flats and includes swimming pool and sports centre, extensively sold off-plan in 1987. Next door is **Custom House Reach**, a 1970s 9-storey block of undistinguished flats.

Greenland Dock in the SE corner of the Surrey Docks area is the only surviving, unfilled-in dock. It, plus adjoining South Dock, has provided sites for a variety of builders for 15 years now. It is also a thriving marina. **Greenland Passage** at the dock's mouth has 152 homes, many of family size. Next inland is **Rainbow Quay**, just built with 144 1-, 2- and 3-bed flats, most having dock views.

Just N of Greenland Dock is **The Lakes**, built on **Plover Way** on the site of Norway Dock (177 houses and flats grouped around a lake, with the largest villas actually on pontoons, by Ideal Homes). It was finally completed in 1995 after a long pause during the recession. This is a very popular development with flats and large 4-bed semi-detached villa-style houses. Back on Greenland Dock, **Finland Quay** has 1- 2- and 3-bed flats and duplexes and are priced from £142,500 for 2-bed (Lovell). **Russia Court East** juts into the dock, with a circular 7-storey tower of flats on the point; the scheme includes further homes, shops, offices and a pub.

Finland Yard is a new block with 1- to 3-bed flats priced: £100–179,000. **Greenland Quay** uses open courtyard layouts to give everyone water views. **Swedish Quays** sits between **Greenland** and **South Docks**: 96 flats and houses (some very large) completed in 1990. **Brunswick Quay** and **Russia Court West** are close to Surrey Quays shopping centre and the new cinema complex.

Baltic Quay, in **Sweden Gate**, is on the S side of South Dock. A 12-storey tower has 24 flats and a 5-storey block another 133, on the market last winter for £150–250,000 for 2-bed. The scheme dates back to the '80s and was blue and yellow (Swedish national colours) but current owners Pathfinder toned it down to white and grey.

The Surrey Quays Marina, London's biggest working marina, opened in South Dock in 1989. On the S side of the dock, Fairview completed a range of flats and houses in 1996. These flats have fantastic views of the marina and Canary Wharf. The marina has prompted a marine workshops building, and there are offices overlooking the water. At the tip of Greenland Dock on a corner of the dock near the shopping centre and **Lower Rd** two blocks of flats sit next to each other – **Howland Quay** (Fairclough, 1996) and **Lock Keepers Gate** (Redrow, 1997).

The interior of the Surrey Docks has large areas of 'normal' housing: put up by large builders, the wide open expanse giving them more familiar greenfield sites, and the result has a strong flavour of Milton Keynes. No new town, however, has the dramatic view of the City towers offered by Stave Hill, the artificial hill at the centre of the area. A tree-lined walk, flanked by new houses, leads from the hill to Surrey Water, an artificial lake with a tall fountain. The walkway is cleverly aligned to point straight at the City skyscape across the river: a view which contains more of London's landmarks than almost any other. This is the affordable side of Docklands, with 4-bed houses still available for the sort of money which would barely buy you a studio in some of the top-flight Docklands developments. If the close-packed terraced streets of South and West London give you and your family claustrophobia, this is the place to look. And note that some time soon, the Canada Water tube station will take you to Waterloo and Westminster – or one stop under the river to Canary Wharf.

The Isle of Dogs

The Isle of Dogs is indeed an island, cut off by a great bend of the Thames and with its isthmus severed by the West India Docks. Unlike the Surrey Docks it has kept its water, providing vast lengths of quayside. The Isle is special in two other ways: it has the most cut-off indigenous community, for decades hardly part of London at all and only tenuously involved in the rest of Docklands, and it has Canary Wharf, described in detail under Progress Report above.

Now, 18 years after the start in 1981, the Isle renaissance is old enough to have a history. The hesitant days of light industry, timidly built on land almost given away by the LDDC with no rates to pay thanks to the Enterprize Zone (EZ), were succeeded by homes and then by taller, smarter, more self-confident commercial. By the time the DLR arrived, early 1980s buildings were being torn down: they no longer earned their keep on the rapidly appreciating sites. Then the recession came and everything halted. Now the property world is eyeing the low-rise office buildings in the S half of the Isle and wondering if it is worth replacing them with proper towers. The Isle of Dogs is now a city-centre location, not a business park, say the experts.

Not all the building sites are new office blocks: homes are appearing at a brisk pace. The Isle's riverside has a wide and varying range of residential developments, from modern social housing to glitzy apartment blocks with state of the art features. The first thing to watch for is the date of the development, since nobody could at first believe quite how smart the Isle was going to get and so things built after 1985 tend to be a lot better quality.

Most Isle housing is new-build: there were no old riverside warehouses to convert. The exception to this are the listed buildings of **Burrell's Wharf** and the flats in the West India Quay scheme. The second point is that the homes are around the 'coast' of the Isle: the centre, much of which was in the EZ, is nearly all commercial – and is becoming more so as Canary Wharf restarts building.

Coming onto the Isle from the NW, **Canary Wharf** dominates. This enormous 'city within a city' spreads from the river across the Isle between two of the surviving West India Docks – one dock, the old middle section, has been built over. The Canary Wharf complex will soon expand across the Heron Quays site just to the S.

West India Quay, to the N of Canary Wharf, has some of the last warehouses left unconverted – and some of the finest to survive the last war as well as the developers. These warehouses date from 1802 and are Grade I listed, so the builders working on them have had to number every one of the 6,000 paving slabs from the York stone floors – and put them back in the right order. Flats in the warehouse conversions are priced from £175,000 (studio) to £550,000 (3-bed). There are also shops, restaurants, a 10-screen Virgin cinema and the Museum of Docklands – and a hotel in a futuristic 34-storey tower.

GREENWICH

In **Garford St**, in the shadow of Canary Wharf and close to Westferry DLR stop, is Regalians' **Premier Place**, a development of 1-, 2- and 3-bed flats. On the river front is **Canary Riverside**, with a Four Seasons hotel designed by Philippe Starck, a health club, several restaurants, 322 1-, 2-, 3- and 4-bed flats and double-height penthouses (ranging from 625 sq ft to 2,400 sq ft) and gardens. Prices for the homes range from £335,000 to £2.6 million – and a third of the first release was sold by January.

Cascades, completed in 1988, is also close-by: a landmark, a stepped, 21-storey riverside tower of 171 flats. Equally placed is **The Anchorage**, on **Sufference Wharf**, which is next door, beside the former (and once again?) Riverbus pier on **Cuba St**. Built out of light-coloured brick it is understated chic and expensive; there are 123 homes in this block ranging from 1- to 3-bed flats to eight houses.

Next to the Anchorage on **Westferry Rd** is Millennium Harbour with 276 flats new this year, ranging from 1- to 3-bed. Seacon seems likely to keep their riverside site industrial, as they have throughout the Isle's booms and busts. To the S, **Hutchings Wharf** and **Ocean Wharf** are riverside flats being built now. A welcome open riverside space, Sir John McDougal Gardens, will remain a park. Opposite, **Glengall Place** is an early inland estate by Barratt with 79 houses. **Arnhem Wharf** is 62 1989/90 1- and 2-bed flats and 2-bed penthouses (2-bed from £155,000). Next to this and opposite the Docklands Sailing Club is **Old Bell Gate** by Galliard Homes – 61 1- and 2-bed flats; prices for 2-bed from £170,000.

Cyclops Wharf is a new-build late-'80s development with 176 waterfront flats and 24 houses, inland, grouped around a square. Atlas Wharf is Persimmon's riverside 150-flats scheme 'coming soon'. Inland along **Spindrift Avenue** Fairview Homes are building **Mill Quay** – 390 homes, the phase released in October had 2-bed, 2-bath flats from £130,000 with the last 11 flats to be ready this July.

Other inland sites are **Island Square**, **Cahir St**, which has 31 homes – 1-bed flats to 3-bed town-houses – by Laing. **Cahir St** also has a few Edwardian terraced cottages. **Clipper's Quay** is 256 homes around an old dock. **Quay West** comprises 127 homes including 4-bed town-houses by Wimpey in a surprisingly undistinguished style.

One of the few remaining historic sites in the Isle is **Burrell's Wharf**. Here the Great Eastern, the largest ship of its time, was built in the 1850s. The piles of its launching slipway can be seen, and remain on public view. The development combines old with new-build. At **Napier Avenue**, next door to Burrells Wharf, is **Maritime Quay** by Redrow Homes; 60 2-, 3- and 4-bed houses; prices from £120,000–200,000 (700 sq ft to 2,000 sq ft) currently under way (a third sold off plan). There are plans to build a further 99 2-bed flats.

Machonochie's Wharf next door is the site of a self-build project, where local people have created their own houses. **Clyde Wharf** and **Langbourne Wharf** (the British Steel site) are

superbly placed at the very tip of the Island. Fairview Homes plan 1- and 2-bed flats and penthouses, due for release this spring. On the southernmost site on the Isle, 7-acre **Lockes Wharf**, St George are building 466 homes (including 4-storey houses, some with top floor studio room onto roof terrace from £240,000) and a leisure centre. **Felstead Wharf**, a 1984 Wates scheme of 28 homes in an open square onto the river, has great views across to Greenwich. Next to it is the 14-house **De Bruin Court**. **Horseshoe Court** has 80 homes, mostly flats, on an inland site very close to the Island Gardens DLR station. Inland are terraces of pre-war cottage council houses, with large gardens. Some occasionally come up for sale. Back on the river, Barratt's **Luralda Gardens** scheme of 48 flats, their first Docklands venture, also shares views of the Cutty Sark and Greenwich.

D

Cumberland Mills is architecturally one of the most pleasing new-build developments anywhere in Docklands. Its tiers of roof gardens step courteously down to the riverside from the high point of its four quarters without looming over its surroundings, which include a fine church.

It is worth noting that riverside homes past **Cumberland Mills** on eastwards have views of the Millennium site at East Greenwich. The award-winning **Caledonian Wharf** comes next; an earlier 104-home scheme by the same developer as Cumberland Mills, Bates. Inland is Tower Hamlets' Cubitt Town Estate; on the riverside is **Plymouth Wharf**, a 2-acre site with 62 homes around a square. Going N from Mariners Mews, Redrow Homes are building **Millennium Wharf** – a selection of 160 1- and 2-bedroom flats including some warehouse conversions which are spread over 10 blocks (prices start at £110,000).

Compass Point by Costain has 134 houses and some flats, stretching inland across the road. Unusually, the riverside has 5-bedroom town-houses rather than flats. Two rows of houses reminiscent of early Victorian brick villas run inland, facing each other across a central garden; across the road the square is completed by a white-rendered crescent of flats. **London Yard**, one of the earlier schemes on the eastern bank, consists of very large orangey brick buildings grouped around ornamental water. Inland from this is **Friars Mead**, 72 houses built in 1986. The attractive 'pagoda' blocks of four houses are also unusual in having gardens: the developers went to the trouble of treating the toxic, ex-industrial land.

From **London Yard** north for a long stretch is council housing. Barratt's **Pierhead Lock** at **Stewart St** is one of the more ambitious current schemes designed to capitalize on the Isle of Dogs views of the Millennium site. This white high-tech development is crowned by a 14-storey tower. There is a total of 91, 2- and 3-bed flats; prices: 1-bed from £145,000, 2-bed from £165,000 and 3 bed from £260,000. Nearby on **Preston's Rd**, Wates are building **Vantage 2000**, 79 1- and 2-bed apartments, duplexes and town-houses – prices range from £84,000 (580 sq ft) to £136,000 (870 sq ft). On the water front at Marsh Wall is Cor-Dor Group's **Meridian Place**, a development of 32 1-bed and 80 2-bed flats; prices from £120,000 and £160,000. On the water front at Millwall Dock, Epsom Homes' 6-storey glass and brick **City Harbour** has 2-bed with balconies and dock views from £183,700, 3-bed from £249,000.

At the entrance to and around Blackwall Basin is **Jamestown Harbour**, by Wates; its latest phase, known as **Cotton's Landing**, has 101 homes. A picturesque site, making good use of the water – which offers private mooring as well as watersports. It gets fine views of the towers of **Canary Wharf**. So does Bellway's **The Boardwalk** on Poplar Dock: over 300 homes including houses: from £110–440,000.

By now we are at the top NE corner of the Isle of Dogs. This corner is one to watch, with enormous empty sites and potentially good communications. Going on round to Blackwall, one of those enormous sites, once a power station, has been lying empty for a decade. But its fallow years are over for it lies bang on the Greenwich Meridian and thus will have a good case for being the place to live come the Millennium. Barratt are building 600 homes.

The Royals and Beckton

Get as far E as the Greenwich Meridian, longitude of the Millennium Dome, and you are only half-way in your journey from the Tower to the far frontier of Docklands at Gallions Reach. The Royal Docks, graveyard of grand plans in the 1980s, are still to come. Very slowly, plans are becoming reality – as the chapter on Newham reveals.

D

- Carleton Smith & Partners
- Knight Frank
- Lincoln Radley
- Michael Kalmas & Co
- Kinleigh Folkard & Hayward
- Duncan Allen
- Burwood Marsh

- McDowells
- Cluttons Daniel Smith
- FPDSavills *
- Alex Neil
- Oliver Jaques
- Tower Property Services
- Winkworth *
- Chestertons
- Hamptons

- Chandlers
- Phoenix
- Cityscope
- Roger Lewis
- John D Wood
- Burnet Ware & Graves
- Phillips Residential Sales and Estates

* further details: see advertisers' index on p633

DOLLIS HILL AND NEASDEN

Map ref: p42 (3D)
Postal districts:
   NW2, NW10
Boroughs: Brent (Lab)
Council tax: Band D £589
Conservation areas:
   Neasden village
Parking: Free, but £50
   charge under discussion

You might be forgiven for thinking that North West London road planners intended to prevent people from going to either Dollis Hill or Neasden. The **North Circular** and **Edgware Rd** will carry you along, past these suburban enclaves, leaving you blissfully unaware of their existence. But people do live here. Very happily. According to one estate agent, every community of the globe has a representative somewhere among the local population . . .

It is mostly families that live in the area – the conversion bug hasn't really bitten – and there is a strong family feel to the area. Property here is largely in the form of 3-bed semis and flats in purpose-built blocks. Schools, churches and little parades of shops proliferate to serve the local inhabitants. Unfortunately, the tube stations of Dollis Hill and Neasden lie away towards the S of the area, but there are good bus services and the **North Circular** and **Edgware Rd** (A5) are nearby, providing good links into the centre of town. There are numerous local amenities: the Brent Reservoir, known as the Welsh Harp (see also Hendon), where you can indulge in all kinds of watery pursuits; Gladstone Park in Dollis Hill for weekend walks, the tiny Stables Art Gallery on **Dollis Hill Lane** for a touch of culture, and the Grange Museum, marooned on its island at the junction of **Neasden Lane/Dollis Hill Lane/Dudden Hill Lane** – although there's talk of moving it to somewhere more accessible.

Dollis Hill

Charmingly named Dolly's Hill after an ancient local resident, Dollis Hill lies on two sides of Gladstone Park, partly in NW2 and partly in NW10. 'Hill' is right: from this high spot you get fine views over Harrow and Ealing. The view to the S is almost as good as that from Hampstead; on a clear day the North Downs are visible. The NW10 neighbourhood – streets such as **Fleetwood Rd**, **Ellesmere Rd**, **Dewsbury Rd** and **Burnley Rd** – has been named the 'Dollis Hill estate' by estate agents. This enclave of older, Edwardian houses commands a premium; typically 3-bed, they sell for up to £180,000. (Don't confuse the agents' 'estate' with the Dollis Hill Estate on **Brook Rd**, which is council-owned and on the other side of the park.) Neighbouring Willesden, particularly Willesden Green, is relatively up-and-coming: those who can't afford property there are prepared to look N of the tube line in Dollis Hill. Here, say agents, they get more for their money, and first-time buyers can find 1-bed flats in the £65–70,000 bracket. **Cornmow Drive**, off **Aberdeen Rd**, is one source of recent flats in this corner, but is tucked away by the railway line.

Dollis Hill Avenue and **Gladstone Park Gardens** – small neat semis, around £150,000 – lead off the busy **Edgware Rd** towards the park where Prime Minister Gladstone often stayed with Lord and Lady Aberdeen in the late 19th century. Sadly their Regency mansion, Dollis Hill House, by now owned by the council, suffered a great fire in 1995. In the same year, residents were startled to learn that accommodation for 200, hitherto unsuspected, lay in the grounds, beneath the park's putting green. The 'Paddock' bunker would, if the last war had gone differently, have been the secret headquarters for Churchill and the War Cabinet. Might the last action of World War II have been fought on these green suburban slopes? Now at last the mansion's future is assured, courtesy of some lottery money and the Network Housing Association, who have acquired the lease on the buildings. Flats and houses for rent, sale (from £70,000; available September '99) and/or shared ownership will appear here. Developers have promised not to disturb the design of the existing building, and those underground bunkers will be kept open for visitors. Gladstone Park itself has also won lottery funding for restoration work and sports facilities.

Dollis Hill Lane, the busy thoroughfare linking Dollis Hill and Neasden, skirts the top of Gladstone Park. As well as houses and bungalows, this is the place to look for purpose-built blocks of flats. In particular, look at Dollis Heights and Neville's Court where some flats will have views overlooking the park and, in Neville's Court, command prices of up to £115,000. Off **Parkside**, the E side of the park, the site of William Gladstone School was converted into Campbell Gordon Way in 1995 – a Wimpey development of 1- and 2-bed flats. These now sell for around £70–85,000.

Neasden

'Everyone makes fun of Neasden,' complain residents and local estate agents – which is rather unfair. Neasden boasts one of Tesco's largest superstores (24 hours, six days a week) at Brent Park, the Ikea home furnishings warehouse on the **North Circular** and a drive-in McDonalds on **Blackbird Hill**. Now **Neasden Lane** even has its own Internet café. What more could you possibly want? More spectacularly, the largest Hindu temple outside India, hand-carved from white marble, now rises above the rooftops of the semis on **Brentfield Rd**.

The first homes in Neasden were 2-bed cottages built for workers on the Metropolitan Railway in 1876, and there was further development in the late 1920s and '30s when the **North Circular Rd**, which bisects the area, arrived.

The majority of homes in Neasden are 3-bed terraced and semi-detached houses in roads such as **Tanfield Avenue** and **Cairnfield Avenue**, though there are also some purpose-built blocks. In the heady days of the late '80s eager developers somewhat over-estimated the need for 1-bed flats in this family-semi land. While generally prices have recouped the ground lost in the recession, agents reckoned in January that flats were *still* not back up to the prices realized in the 1988 boom and that there is still some negative equity. Take, for example, **Hawarden Hill** in **Brook Rd**, right down on the Neasden/Dollis Hill border. Built by Barratt, it is a red-brick block of 1- and 2-bed flats very near to Gladstone Park, but also to the large Dollis Hill council estate. A 1-bed here will cost around £65,000, compared to £67,000 in 1990; 2-bed flats, at £80,000, have increased slightly. At nearby **Shepherds Walk** – 1- and 2-bed flats and 2- and 3-bed houses – homes start from £65,000 – just as they did nine years ago.

The first 2-bed flats (no 1-bed here) were completed by winter 1997 in a new development by Beverley Homes on **Dog Lane** (called, would you believe, Baskerville Court), handy for the **North Circular**. Priced from £83,000, they were joined last summer by 2-, 3- and 4-bedroom houses, all of which sold at prices up to £162,000. These replaced – sign of the times – the 200-year-old Spotted Dog pub. We await the building of a replacement Spotted Dog, for which they have permission . . .

Across **Neasden Lane** (which leads to Neasden tube), lies **Prout Grove**, whose 4-bed Victorian houses are accounted Neasden's top homes. Agents also talk about the Brent Water estate to the N of Neasden which includes roads such as **Review Rd**, **Dawpool Rd** and **Warren Rds** – but transport here is not as good as other parts of the area. Shopping, however, is not a problem. What Neasden lacks in charm it makes up for with shops. Not only is there Ikea and the Tesco superstore (markers along the **Edgware Rd** tell motorists how far they are from the store) but also the huge stores at Staples Corner, the **North Circular/Edgware Rd** junction. Staples' bed shop has long gone and in its place are all manner of furniture superstores, electrical, computer and office suppliers; also a huge multiplex cinema. To the E, over the junction, lies Brent Cross shopping centre.

More new homes are found (to navigate by superstores) across the **North Circular** from Ikea, in the southernmost reaches of Neasden. Here **Brentfield Rd** leads towards Harlesden, and the old Neasden Hospital site gave way in the late '80s to developments such as the flats and studios of Mitchell Brook Gardens.

Coles Green Rd runs all the way from the stores at Staples Corner to **Dollis Hill Lane**. Here there are purpose-built blocks such as Coles Green Court and, to the E, smaller terraced houses scattered amid the little industrial pockets: 3-bed are available for around the £115,000 mark. Along what was a country lane is the Ox and Gate pub by **Oxgate Lane**, and a delightful surprise, a little ivy-covered cottage called Oxgate Farm, last remnant of a more rural Neasden.

Transport	Tubes: Dollis Hill, Neasden (zone 3, Jubilee). From Dollis Hill: Oxford Circus 25 min, City 30 min, Heathrow 1 hr 15 min.
Convenient for	North Circular Rd, Brent Cross shopping centre, Ikea, Edgware Rd. Miles from centre: 6.
Schools	Brent Education Authority: John Kelly Technical College (b), John Kelly Technical College (g).

SALES

Flats	S	1B	2B	3B	4B	5B
Average prices	45–50	60–70	80–90	90–95	–	–
Houses	2B	3B	4B	5B	6/7B	8B
Average prices	85–95	130–165	150–190	–	–	–

RENTAL

Flats	S	1B	2B	3B	4B	5B
Average prices	500–540	540–630	630–750	780–1000	–	–
Houses	2B	3B	4B	5B	6/7B	8B
Average prices	650–780	780–1000	1200–1500	–	–	–

The properties   Thirties semis dominate in Neasden, plus smaller blocks of flats, private, council and housing association. Dollis Hill is more spacious: similar to Neasden plus some older, turn-of-the-century properties to the south. Some early 20th-century terraces. Some expensive new-build and larger period houses.

The market   Families and DIY enthusiasts dominate this self-contained area. Flat-buyers moving in on recent conversions if they can't find what they want in Willesden Green. One-bed flats in purpose-built blocks are only just recovering from the early '90s price slump. Families on restricted budgets buy here for gardens and open space. Local searches: 2 weeks.

Among those estate agents active in this area are:
- Hoopers
- K Estates
- Rainbow Reid
- Gladstones
- Camerons Stiff
- Woolwich
- Chattin Estates

DULWICH

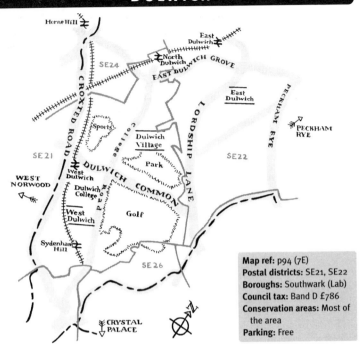

Map ref: p94 (7E)
Postal districts: SE21, SE22
Boroughs: Southwark (Lab)
Council tax: Band D £786
Conservation areas: Most of
the area
Parking: Free

Dulwich is unique: a country village with its mill pond and cottages, finger-post road signs, its tollgate and its wide sweep of green space – an island in the South London sprawl. The village gains its character, and its history, from the charitable foundation set up by Edward Alleyn, an actor-contemporary of Shakespeare who prospered in the reign of James I. Alleyn was a successful businessman, a partner in the Rose Theatre, where Shakespeare also acted, around the corner from the Globe. He spent his money on the manor of Dulwich, leaving the 1,500-acre estate as an endowment for a school. Dulwich College still exists, and its playing-fields are among several extensive green expanses which surround the village. The College (in the person of the Estate Governors) is a major landowner still: many Dulwich homes are on long Estate leases, and it owns all the freeholds to purpose-built flats.

There is more to Dulwich than the village. East Dulwich – really NE of the old centre – is straightforward 1880s suburbia. There are fringe areas to the W and S too. Everything within the Estate boundary has a certain leafy unity, though the ages of the houses vary. The Estate has sold off various of its acres for development over the last century, and in consequence Dulwich has houses from the Victorian, Edwardian, inter-war and modern periods. Despite the Village's ancient air, there are not many truly old houses. It was not a very big place, Dulwich, until the railways came. Even the College is 19th-century, the foundation having fallen into positively Trollopian corruption and disrepute until it was reformed.

As with any reputable area, bits of surrounding neighbourhoods try to edge into Dulwich. All of Dulwich proper is in SE21, with East Dulwich spreading into SE22 (and

D

what is rapidly becoming known as the North Dulwich Triangle spilling into SE24). The whole area relies on trains for commuting, with stations all around, but not in, the area (the Estate Governors were reluctant to let the railways near the place at all; when forced to concede, they stipulated that all railway bridges should be to their own architect's design).

A (very) tiny glimmer this year for East Dulwich's long-held hopes for a tube: an extension of the East London line down from Surrey Quays. The plan is not in the current programme, but John Prescott has at least given a green light to London Underground 'to apply for legal powers' to build two extensions southwards. Don't, however, hold your breath . . .

The Estate Governors maintain a strong interest in their 1,500 acres, be it built-on or open space. Leaseholders have to adhere to strict conditions. About half of the 6,000 houses on land owned by the Estate have been bought by leaseholders under the Leasehold Reform Acts – but even then the Estate keeps control: it has retained powers over the appearance of houses and (a major concern of the Estate, this) the trees in their gardens. Touch a tree in Dulwich and the Estate Governors will have something to say about it.

So between **Croxted Rd** in the W and **Lordship Lane** in the E, the heights of Crystal Palace to the S and Denmark Hill to the N, you are in Dulwich Estate country. Owning a home here means playing by their rules – but you get to live in one of the tidiest, and most charming, corners of London.

Agents here report that 95 per cent of buyers are families, and/or professional people. First-time buyers and singles may look at fringe areas – which have better rail links – but the village is family country. People come here from Clapham or Battersea for more greenery and more space – but they sacrifice good travel links, for the **South Circular** is a nightmare, and as yet there are no tubes for miles. Meanwhile the (private) schools in Dulwich extend their catchment areas with a (private) school bus service, which brings in pupils from as far away as Clapham.

Dulwich Village

First, outsiders should note that the main street in Dulwich Village is called . . . **Dulwich Village**, and that **Dulwich Common** is not an open space, but a stretch of the **South Circular**. The Village (the neighbourhood) starts abruptly; a busy W–E suburban road, starting in Herne Hill as **Half Moon Lane**, becomes **Village Way**, then **East Dulwich Grove**, and skirts the village centre. Turn S into **Dulwich Village** (the road) and you are instantly in the old village. Houses are Georgian (or well-built 20th-century Georgian pastiche) and highly desirable.

Noteworthy roads within Dulwich are **Dulwich Village** (possibly the most coveted street) and **College Rd**. **Pickwick Rd** and **Aysgarth Rd** are about the only smaller terraced houses in the area and **Roseway** features picturesque 1920s semi-detached overlooking the sportsground. On the edge of the Village, just off **Half Moon Lane**, a 3-bed Edwardian terraced house might cost a quarter-million. Close to the Village, expect to pay another £60,000 or so. Some new mansions called Dulwich Oaks were added to **College Rd** in the '80s; last winter Osborne were marketing Chapel Walk: 10 new 3- and 4- bed houses (plus one 3-bed flat) priced from £345,000. **Turney Rd** has open ground to the rear of the houses on both sides, a fairly common feature in Dulwich. Desirability continues S and W past the Picture Gallery and the College (Reynolds and Latin). **Alleyn Park** runs close to the College and on down into West Dulwich near the station. **College Rd** runs S across the **South Circular** (a regrettable intrusion) with the modern 5/6-bedroom homes of **Frank Dixon Way** in the angle. South, on the slopes of Sydenham Hill, you find a mixture of a few older properties and big inter-war and modern detached homes. Hereabouts, views across much of London are an extra bonus.

To the E of the Village, roads of large, smart inter-war semis and detached houses run as far as **Lordship Lane**. On the W side of **Court Lane** they overlook Dulwich Park. There is so much green space in Dulwich that many houses back onto parks, sports grounds or golf courses. This includes Barratt's Dulwich Gate, which once won Prime Ministerial approval, until she discovered Belgravia. It is now known by its street address, Hambledon Place; *her* old home was on the market last October for £675,000.

East Dulwich

To the E and NE of the old centre there is **Lordship Lane** and East Dulwich. **Lordship Lane** is the main shopping area; it has most shops necessary for everyday existence, a fantastic variety of restaurants and a small pub/comedy theatre. The Lane itself meets at the S with the A205, which is of course the **South Circular**.

East Dulwich really describes the area that flanks **Lordship Lane**. Properties are mainly early Victorian terraced or semi-detached houses. At the N end the properties are smaller 2- or 3-bedroom terraces. To the S (in for example **Friern Rd** and **Upland Rd**) the houses are larger 4-bedroom family style; many of these have been converted to flats. High up in **Overhill Rd** are some late-'80s 1- and 2-bed flats. All the above streets with the exception of **Lordship Lane** have unrestricted, on-street parking and many have speed bumps. An old hospital site close to East Dulwich station provided room for St Francis Place: 185 2- and 3-bed Wimpey houses in **Abbots Wood Rd**, **Burrow Rd**, **Shaw Rd** and **Talbot Rd**. Access is from **Dog Kennel Hill**; prices from just under £100,000. A new Sainsbury's superstore is next door. Behind this, and accessed from **Dulwich Grove**, is a new development by Buxton Homes called St Barnabus Gate: 3- and 4-bedroomed houses, starting from £174,995.

Goose Green, a small wedge-shaped park, forms the borders of East Dulwich. The neighbourhood stretches a good way E towards Peckham Rye Common. North of **Goose Green** and **East Dulwich Rd** are streets of turn-of-the-century terraces. These streets are considered to be Peckham Rye, not Dulwich, but prices on the fringes of Dulwich have soared: large Victorian houses in **The Gardens** will make over half a million pounds here.

West Dulwich

West Dulwich is the SW tip of the area, running down to Sydenham. There are fewer properties here: the land is largely taken up by the golf course, allotments and the sportsground belonging to the College. **Alleyn Park** and **College Rd** lead from the Village southwards off Dulwich Common, the South Circular; there are some popular Edwardian houses and '60s flats at the top end of **College Rd**. Choice **Alleyn Park** is joined by **Alleyn Rd** as it crosses the tracks below West Dulwich station; between **Alleyn Park** and the rail line Rialto has contributed five new detached houses 'in linear style', prices from £220,000. As Dulwich meets Sydenham there are blocks of purpose-built maisonettes and flats on the borders: these can command superb views.

Dulwich Borders

The allure of Dulwich leads to a slow spread of the name into neighbouring areas. One border district that has a good claim to the revered name is the neighbourhood W of **Croxted Rd** and centring around **Rosendale Rd**. This road runs down from Brockwell Park and Herne Hill, and the railway bridge which crosses it perhaps marks the true Dulwich frontier. There is a street of local shops with a growing number of trendy (and good) stores and cafés, a sportsground with tennis courts, and attractive streets of mixed terraced houses. The neighbourhood is equidistant from West Dulwich and Herne Hill stations. Recent homes here include a cobbled mews of 14 traditional-style houses with garages in the angle of **Croxted Rd** and **Thurlow Park Rd**. Also in **Thurlow Park Rd** is Thurlow Mews, again in period style, but with a mix of new flats, maisonettes and bungalows, plus a conversion of the original Victorian house.

In the N of the area, the two railway stations of North and East Dulwich confuse geography: they lie a mere few hundred yards apart – and East Dulwich station is N of North Dulwich station. Many now call the streets off **Half Moon Lane** North Dulwich. Those E of **Beckwith Rd** perhaps qualify, but the other pleasant streets further W, such as **Stradella Rd**, **Winterbrook Rd** and **Burbage Rd** with their spacious family homes, are Herne Hill borders, and are dealt with under that area. **Burbage Rd**, after crossing S of the railway, does indeed run down to Dulwich. The houses have green sports grounds (which hold Herne Hill stadium) behind them.

There is a determined effort to disinvent Herne Hill; the tract bounded by **Half Moon Lane**, **Herne Hill** and **Red Post Hill** has been branded, in estate-agent-speak, the 'North Dulwich Triangle'; whether the people who live here think of their homes as Dulwich or Herne Hill (see chapter) probably depends on which station they use: Herne Hill for Victoria, North Dulwich for London Bridge. The latest move is to lay claim to the area on across **Herne Hill** (the road) as far as **Milkwood Rd**: this is definitively Herne Hill; beyond **Milkwood Rd** is Brixton.

Transport	Trains: East Dulwich, North Dulwich (to London Bridge); West Dulwich, Sydenham Hill (to Victoria, some to Blackfriars), Herne Hill (Thameslink to Kings Cross, Blackfriars, Cannon St). Average times to London termini: 15–20 min.
Convenient for	Parks and golf courses, Dulwich schools, South Circular. Miles from centre: 5.
Schools	Local Authority: William Penn School (b), Kingsdale School, Waverley School (g). Private: Dulwich College (b), Alleyn's School, James Allen's Girls School.

SALES

Flats	S	1B	2B	3B	4B	5B
Average prices	35–60	45–110	65–160	80–200	–	–

Houses	2B	3B	4B	5B	6/7B	8B
Average prices	100–230	120–350	150–600	175–800	225–1.3M	600–1.5M

RENTAL

Flats	S	1B	2B	3B	4B	5B
Average prices	380–500	500–800	600–1000	750–1500	1000+	–
Houses	2B	3B	4B	5B	6/7B	8B
Average prices	750–1000	1000–1500+	1200	1500	2000	–

D

The properties   Centuries-old Dulwich Village has carefully tended family homes from 18th to 20th centuries. Some 'country' cottages. Very few flats. Fringe areas were developed later, and have late-Victorian terraces, converted flats and some new property.

The market   Family homes within Dulwich College Estate always popular: large gardens, lots of open space, close to schools. East Dulwich attracts flat-dwellers and buyers of Victorian terraces. Lower prices above are East Dulwich but also some very large, very expensive houses which range from modern mansions to glorious Georgiana which can exceed a million.
Local searches: 2 weeks.

Among those estate agents active in this area are:
- Burnet Ware & Graves
- Winkworth*
- Harvey & Wheeler
- Acorn
- Ludlow Thompson
- Spencer Kennedy
- Wates

further details: see advertisers' index on p633

EALING

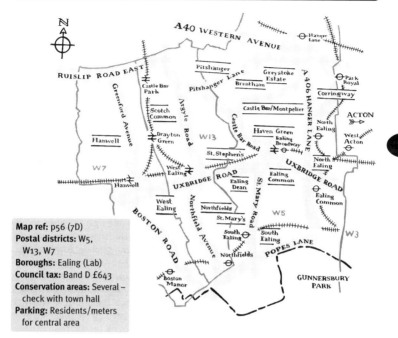

Map ref: p56 (7D)
Postal districts: W5,
 W13, W7
Boroughs: Ealing (Lab)
Council tax: Band D £643
Conservation areas: Several –
 check with town hall
Parking: Residents/meters
 for central area

Ealing – pretty, leafy, genteel Ealing, the 'Queen of Suburbs'. The ghost of this soubriquet, earned in the 1880s when a determined local authority only allowed the building of solid, middle-class homes, hangs over Ealing still. 'In short,' explained a local agent, 'the sort of place you'd expect Agatha Christie's grandmother to live in – as, of course, she did.'

The post-war years brought a whiff of greasepaint: the area famous for being Britain's film centre is now often used as the backdrop for TV dramas and documentaries by the BBC film unit based near Ealing Green. It's the right side of town, too, for the enormous new headquarters of the BBC at White City (see the Shepherd's Bush chapter).

Oases like Walpole Park, Lammas Park and Brent Lodge Park, as well as Hanwell's canalside walks, draw summer crowds from neighbouring boroughs.

Ealing's old guard of middle-class inhabitants are still holding strong – particularly in the Castlebar/Montpelier area. They are joined by young couples who cannot afford to be closer into town, or who like Ealing's pretty streets and good facilities – 'lecturers and advertising executives', according to estate agents, and workers from Heathrow Airport who want a London base. The Japanese happily bought up family homes with gardens following the Japanese School's move across town to Acton. They add to a rich cultural mix here which includes Irish and Asian families – and Ealing is also the centre of London's large Polish community.

A fast new rail link to Heathrow from St Pancras is planned to call at Ealing Broadway. Timescale: 2001.

The self-confidence of Ealing and its populace is reflected in its shopping scene. It remains buoyant in the face of the domineering presence of the massive Brent Cross centre in the N and of Kingston to the not-too-distant S. The usual malls are complemented by interesting and individual chocolatiers, interiors shops and designer hair salons. Central Ealing now also has many good restaurants, pubs and wine bars.

What Ealing also has plenty of is traffic trying to use the major arteries. The main roads in and out of the borough (Uxbridge Rd, the M40 and the North Circular) star frequently on the radio bulletins of traffic holdups.

Ealing Common

A room with a view comes at a price on the common. Ealing Common's outlook is so popular with house-buyers that they are prepared to pay through the nose for it.

The common is convenient – for the shopping centre, for the North Circular and the Hanger Lane junction with the A40 (not quite so much of a nightmare now it has traffic lights) and for the Ealing Common tube station which is on the District and Piccadilly lines, and the station at Ealing Broadway (District, Central tubes and trains to Paddington).

Around the common there's a good mix of properties, from flat conversions small and large to huge Victorian houses. To the NE **Creffield Rd** snakes off towards Acton: a good hunting-ground for small flats, interspersed with some elegant 4/5-bed semis. To the SE lies **Tring Avenue**, which has some very large Victorian houses at one end, followed by a greater number of 1920s and '30s detached and semi-detached houses, while the enclave of the **Delamere Rd** estate has 3- and 4-bed Art Deco semis.

The biggest and most impressive houses are found looking directly out over the common from all four sides; among the best are the six individual, detached houses of **Warwick Dene**, which sits close to the up-market local pub, the Grange in **Warwick Rd**. Next to the Grange are a few tiny streets of cottages located off the common. Built originally for workmen, these are popular with small families and young couples.

Greystoke/Brentham

Popular schools are a draw on this estate of semis in the N of the area, which is home for many young families. Homes on the Art Deco Greystoke estate, S of the **Western Avenue** and just W of **Hanger Lane** junction, are snapped up by parents who want their children to go to Montpelier First and Middle Schools. The '30s 3/4-bed semis are not as imposing as the older homes further S. But they are spacious, with large gardens and easy access to major roads, Ealing Golf Club, Helena Park and the pretty Hanger Hill park. The atmosphere is rather 'villagy' and very family orientated. Importantly, parking is no problem. A 3-bedroom semi in **Kingfield Rd** or **Brookfield Avenue** will set the upwardly mobile couple back between £180,000 and £220,000.

The Brentham estate around **Brentham Way** is for anyone who has the money to spend on a romantic rose-covered cottage. Prices are high for these little houses, with young professional couples ready to spend perhaps £165,000 on a small cottage or £199,950 on a 3-bed house. They know they will have little problem reselling, as the estate is one of the most coveted in Ealing. The whole Brentham estate is a conservation area. The Brentham cottages are very popular and attractive, but some are truly tiny. Particularly at a premium are the small Victorian cottages in **Woodfield Rd**. Two-bedrooms here cost £165–170,000 and three-bedrooms £220,000.

Hanwell

Canalside walks and the cutely nicknamed 'Bunny Park' give a real village atmosphere (if you ignore the run-down Broadway) to Hanwell, the district which borders the River Brent in the W of the borough. It has its up-market enclaves but is the cheaper compromise for those young professionals who cannot quite afford Ealing proper – yet.

Hanwell is bounded on the SW by the Grand Union Canal. 'Old Hanwell' in the S (SW of **Boston Rd**) is a bit of estate agents' jargon, but the turn-of-the-century cottages around **St Marks Rd** and **St Margarets Rd** are charming, with prices from £120–170,000 for 2- to 3-bed. Old Hanwell has an excellent country-style pub, The Fox, and over towards Northfields is the popular Fielding First School. The St Marks canalside neighbourhood is a conservation area. A new development of red-brick houses and flats called Billets Hart Close has taken up wasteground down by the canal and, say agents, raised the general popularity of the area. Two-bedroom houses there may fetch £140,000 with 2-bedroom flats at around £110,000.

Further S the area around Boston Manor tube station is popular with commuters. There are '30s semis in the roads off **Clitherow Avenue** which boast that prized commodity to Londoners – a garage. Three-bedroom/2-reception room houses there are around £150–200,000. Properties in **Haslemere Avenue** may be older – turn-of-the-century, but the road is a locals' cut-through from Boston Manor to **Northfield Avenue** and is therefore less popular. The area is convenient for two Piccadilly line stations at Boston Manor and Northfields, and for shops in West Ealing and **Northfields Avenue**.

Close to **Hanwell Broadway**, the area's main thoroughfare, there is a mixture of homes around the tightly parked streets in the **Montague Rd** area: neighbours here report a friendly atmosphere where popular 4-bedroom Edwardian semis are priced £280–300,000. **Hanwell Broadway** itself is, alas, currently a drab witness to the phenomenon of the struggling high street, and its most bustling business would seem to be the large off-licence. There are a few pubs of varying quality, and one has a weekend comedy club which pulls in a young crowd.

North of the **Broadway** are some streets with terraced turn-of-the-century homes – **Laurel Gardens**, **Myrtle Gardens**, **Conolly Rd** and **Lawn Gardens** where the Edwardian terraced houses can sell for £140,000 for 3-bed to £190,000 for those with a loft conversion. These houses have roomy receptions and bedrooms but often tiny kitchens and cramped gardens. These homes are close to one of Ealing's most popular beauty spots – the Brent Lodge Park bunny park, full of frolicking pets, adored by children and parents.

Backing onto the park, N of the railway, is the aptly named Golden Manor estate – the jewel in Hanwell's crown, and the Park Lane of the village. The estate includes Hanwell rail station, with a direct line to Paddington. The gardens are beautiful and the houses large and well-maintained. Among the most desirable streets in Golden Manor is probably **Manor Court Rd** by virtue of its location, but also because of the individual architectural styles. A 3-bedroom Victorian house may sell

Ealing is unashamedly suburban. Even the tennis club, hallmark of the Thirties, has reappeared in a modern development with an attractive clubhouse. This building has many of the features now fashionable on new housing: the deep eaves, round 'porthole' window. The overall result owes something to the mid-Victorian villa, something to the stable yard.

for £220,000, but prices for the larger homes can nudge up to £400,000. In the less popular **Campbell Rd** you may find a 5-bedroom house for £250–300,000. The side nearer the railway line tends to fetch cheaper prices.

To the N of Hanwell station is a 'Poets' Corner' – **Shakespeare**, **Milton**, **Cowper**, **Tennyson** and **Drayton Rds**, where 3- and 4-bed semis are sought-after (not to be confused with the similarly named enclave in Acton). These command a premium over the streets. Further N, around **Framfield Rd**, £90–120,000 will buy 2- to 3-bedrooms. Nearby are the large **Copley Close** council-built estates. The Cuckoo estate is mostly private now: these 'suntrap'-style homes sell for £120,000. The High Lane council estate lies to the W near the Brent Valley Golf Course. Homes in **Studland Rd** near **Greenford Avenue** are 3-bedroom semis (£215,000).

West Ealing

The run-down streets of the poor-relation neighbourhood of Ealing are hunting-grounds for a bargain. North of the **Uxbridge Rd** the area is dominated by the Green Man council estate, an area lacking in facilities. There are a few streets of owner-occupied homes, backing onto West Ealing Broadway – **Ecclestone Rd**, **Endsleigh Rd** and **Felix Rd**, where flats are the norm. A 1-bedroom flat can be yours for £75,000.

South of the **Broadway**, West Ealing is more up-and-coming – particularly in the streets nearest **Northfields Avenue** in the E. The terraced houses that line the parallel streets E of **Grosvenor Rd** have a more suburban feel. The pebbledashers have done their worst here and in many cases the Victorian and Edwardian character has been smothered by faddish renovation. Here a 2-bed house may cost you £162,000. The whole scene changes as you venture N away from the busy **Uxbridge Rd**. By the time you hit the **Waldock Rd** area you will be expecting to pay £600,000 for a double-fronted Victorian home with 6 bedrooms.

Flats here go for upwards of £85,000 for a 1-bed conversion, £115,000 for 2-bed ones. West Ealing **Broadway** is not too exciting as a shopping area. Marks & Spencer, British Homes Stores and Sainsbury's are the main attractions; the rest is cheap and (not very) cheerful. An up-market Waitrose supermarket was, however, built on **Alexander Rd**, near West Ealing station – despite controversy with neighbours about traffic problems. **Coldershaw Rd** has 3-bed houses selling for £190,000.

Northfields

Northfields boasts an old-style shopping high street, and a major draw, particularly to young couples and families, are the numerous small cottages and turn-of-the-century houses. There are also roads on either side of **Northfield Avenue** such as **Midhurst Rd**, **Camborne Avenue** and **Elers Rd**, where you will find larger 3-bed terraced homes right up to 4/5-bed Edwardian houses with prices starting at £150,000. **Elers Rd** is especially popular because it backs on to parkland. A 4-bedroom Edwardian semi will cost up to £400,000 here.

Shops line the whole of **Northfield Avenue**, and at the S end there is the particularly pretty Lammas Park and the Piccadilly line station. The general rule of thumb here is, the further E you go off **Northfield Avenue**, the more you can expect to pay.

Home-buyers concentrate on houses – there are not many flat conversions because the houses are so small. The roads – **Altenburg Avenue** is typical – have rows of 2- and 3-bedroomed terraced houses, all very similar. Parking is a problem – and so is rat-running. But the shops are a definite plus – with a traditional butcher, fruiterers and fishmonger. **Churchfield Rd** and **Culmington Rd**, near **Walpole Park**, have large town-houses, divided into flats: elegant, spacious and pricey. Two-bedroom flats are selling for £125,000. There are some houses with price tags of £170–250,000.

Haven Green/Castlebar/Montpelier

Some would call this Ealing's best area – it is certainly the home of the 'old guard' of middle-class Ealing residents, whose families have often lived in the borough for generations. Haven Green is a pretty parkland patch just N of the **Broadway**, and the Castlebar/Montpelier area lies N of the green, leading up the hill to Hanger Hill Park. Haven Green, where a 1-bedroom flat will cost £120,000, 2-bedroom up to £160,000, is the home of Ealing Broadway station and tube, and Ealing's taxi rank. Homes on the green are mostly in luxury purpose-built blocks or, to the E along **Madeley Rd**, in large red-brick detached houses – mostly converted into flats. **Madeley Rd** is very busy, a cut-through to Hanger Lane. Prices for flats here start at £110,000 for 1-bedroom to £190,000 for 3-bed.

Haven Lane, leading N from the green, is a charming street of terraced cottage-style homes, each with pretty flower gardens. The lane is tight for parking, but also has two nice pubs: it is one of Ealing's most popular roads.

In **Eaton Rise**, **Montpelier Rd** and **Helena Rd** the houses are large, Edwardian and detached, with many conversions and a few purpose-built blocks. Prices are high, as befits the most popular area in Ealing. Generously proportioned Victorian double-fronted houses in **Helena Rd** have commanded asking prices of up to £850,000 – and maybe that's just with 4 bedrooms. Converted flats can range in price from between £180,000 for 2-bedrooms to £220,000 for 3-bed. Four-bedroom houses in the 10-year-old **Goldcrest Mews** may fetch £350,000. Six-bedrooms in the equally new **Magnolia Place** cost £450,000. Houses such as those in **Corfton Rd**, probably the biggest in Ealing, can sell for £750–900,000. The status of Castlebar was confirmed by the late-'80s Courtfield encampment of luxury-level houses on **Castlebar Hill**.

The area is particularly popular with the parents of young children, thanks to the excellent reputation of the state primary school, Montpelier, in **Helena Rd**. The Greystoke estate of '30s semis to the N of the Montpelier area, and the conservation area around the highly priced cottage-style Brentham estate area (for both see p 284) are also in the school catchment zone.

St Mary's

St Mary's is real village Ealing, the oldest part of the area. The roads around the parish church on **St Mary's Rd** are Victorian terraces and detached homes. The area is close to the **Broadway**, and to all the facilities of central Ealing. The Grange schools are popular. The homes nearest Lammas Park top the bill, but all the streets are pretty, tree-lined and very expensive. This favoured little spot offers a mish-mash of styles from Victorian to Art Deco. There are some small 3-bedroom flats here for around £150,000. Four-bedroom houses can fetch £250,000. **Clovelly Rd** is particularly popular with families anxious for spacious detached homes. Four-bedroom red-brick homes with Victorian/Edwardian features are on the market for £350,000.

Further S, South Ealing around the tube station is less rarefied, but still popular and expensive to buy.

Pitshanger and Scotch Common

The northernmost area of Ealing, S of the A40, is a lively neighbourhood with a village atmosphere – indeed, you'll find estate agents have dubbed it 'Pitshanger Village'. Centred on the bustling **Pitshanger Lane**, the streets leading down to Pitshanger Park are nearly all Edwardian 3-bed terraced homes in the £180,000 range. Pitshanger is good for access to the A40, though the nearest station is the one at Castle Bar Park. It is close to the popular Ealing Golf Course and Brentham Country Club and Lawn Tennis where Fred Perry was once a member.

To the western end of the area is Scotch Common, where a large modern development built in the early 1970s provides a variety of homes from small studios through to 4/5-bed town-houses. Among the purpose-built blocks in this part of town, called the Cleveland Estate, some are decidedly better built than others. Check surveys. Two-bedroom flats here cost £125–135,000; 4-bedroom houses £250,000. West of the common, there are '30s-style houses in the £200,000 bracket for 3-bed.

St Stephens and Drayton Green

South from Scotch Common, this is a large area forming the bulk of middle-class Ealing. In the centre is St Stephen's Church – a landmark converted into plush and expensive flats which caused quite a stir when they appeared on the property market in 1987. Take with you £400,000 and you can buy a lovely 5-bed detached Victorian house in the leafy **St Stephen's Avenue. Bradley Gardens** has enjoyed a boom in recent years, where a 4-bedroom Edwardian house will fetch up to £350,000. To the SW is Drayton Green and a group of roads each with 'Drayton' in their title. This is a good hunting-ground for conversion flats in the £60–70,000 price range. West Ealing station is close by.

Hanger Hill/Corringway

For those who live on Hanger Hill it is '*the* Estate of Ealing' – large houses, with spacious gardens and garages. This select enclave lies just E of **Hanger Lane**, and its concentric rings of roads include **Corringway, Audley Rd, Beaufort Rd, Chatsworth Rd, The Ridings** and **Ashbourne Rd**. For those who do not live on the estate, Hanger Hill is sneered at slightly for a certain ostentation: a place of stone lions roaring on pillars. The Haymills homes built in the late '30s are quite varied in their styles and generally fetch £300–600,000 (though over £800,000 was achieved for a sumptuous home at the height of the' 80s boom). **Corringway** and **Ashbourne Rds** have the area's only drawback – they are a bit of a rat-run.

Park Royal and North Ealing tubes bracket this corner; near the latter Anglia Secure Homes have just added smart 1- and 2-bed retirement flats to the area's homes tally.

Be careful of flats in the Tudor-style Hanger Hill area. There are, in some cases, very short leases and service charges can be high.

Borders: Brentford

Although strictly speaking Hounslow, Brentford just lies to the S of Ealing. It is divided in two by the M4 motorway: New Brentford, the part nearest Ealing and N of the motorway, has areas of suburban housing. The corner people get excited about is **The Butts**, a square in the old town, of which little else remains.

The Butts lies S of motorway and railway, and is close to the Thames. It has several late-17th- and early 18th-century houses: look here for genuine Queen Anne, with 4/5-bedrooms and huge gardens. Posh Central London agents solemnly make the journey to Brentford for these.

The other bit of Brentford that matters is the waterside. It has plenty: two rivers (Thames and Brent), and a canal. British Waterways are offering a big canalside site N of the **High St** for development: new homes should feature as part of this.

What exists, just across the **High St** on the riverside, is Brentford Dock – a 21-acre complex of flats and houses that is one of W London's best-kept secrets. Reached via **Augustus Close**, its equally classically named blocks of typical 1970s-vintage architecture have worn well, and the trees and gardens have filled out. Here is a very active community: all owners share the freehold of estate, which is grouped around a marina and forms a triangular island. On one side is the Thames, another is the Brent and the mouth of the Grand Union Canal – and the third is the boundary wall of Syon Park. The on-site management office have details of homes for sale here: houses (4-bed) come at around £250,000; flats for £87,000-plus. Service charges are quite high but they do include heating.

East of the Brent confluence, towards the bridge, Barratt are building a development called Kew Bridge Wharf; next comes the new flats of Regatta Point, then the site destined to hold classy offices under the umberella name of Kew HQ . . . They certainly offer fine views across to Kew (see chapter).

Transport
Tubes: Ealing Broadway (zone 3, Central, District), Ealing Common (zone 3, District, Piccadilly). From Ealing Common: Oxford Circus 40 min (1 change), City 1 hr 10 min (1 change), Heathrow 25 min. Trains: Ealing Broadway to Paddington 10 min.

E

Convenient for
A40 fast route to West End, Heathrow, M4/M40 and roads to the West, North Circular Rd. Miles from centre: 8.

Schools
Ealing Education Authority: Brentside School, Drayton Manor, Ellen Wilkinson (g). Private: St Benedict's School (b), St Augustines Priory (g), Notting & Ealing High School (g), Elthorne Park.

SALES

Flats	S	1B	2B	3B	4B	5B
Average prices	50–75	60–125	80–180	120–240	–	–
Houses	2B	3B	4B	5B	6/7B	8B
Average prices	120–250	140–300	180–500	300–600	400–1M	–

RENTAL

Flats	S	1B	2B	3B	4B	5B
Average prices	500–700	650–1000	750–1500	1000–1800	1200–2000	–
Houses	2B	3B	4B	5B	6/7B	8B
Average prices	750–1600	1000–2000	1200–2500	2000–4000	35000–6000	–

The properties
Late-Victorian and turn-of-the-century red-brick houses and terraces. Some '30s semis and modern blocks. Lots of conversions, a few mansion blocks. Hanger Hill, Castlebar and Montpelier are the most favoured areas.

The market
People with young children move here thanks to family houses and good schools including Japanese and Arabs, who both have schools in Acton. Hanwell's canalside terraces are becoming popular with young couples. Local searches: 1 week.

Among those estate agents active in this area are:
- Sinton Andrews
- Raymond Bushell
- Bairstow Eves
- Barnard Marcus
- Grimshaw & Co
- Brendons
- Faron Sutaria & Co Ltd*
- Winkworth*

further details: see advertisers' index on p633

FINCHLEY

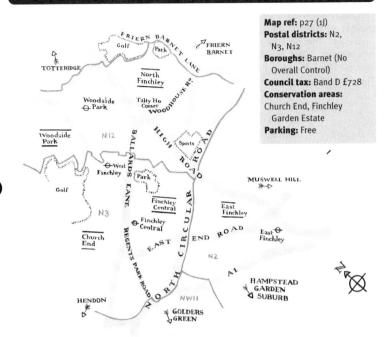

Map ref: p27 (1J)
Postal districts: N2, N3, N12
Boroughs: Barnet (No Overall Control)
Council tax: Band D £728
Conservation areas: Church End, Finchley Garden Estate
Parking: Free

Londoners once headed for Finchley Common to escape the Great Plague. Three hundred and forty years later the exodus starts at 5.30pm as commuters leave the City concrete and make their way north-westwards to the quiet, dignified, leafy suburb of Finchley.

Originally part of the forest of Middlesex, the woods that are echoed in names like Woodside Park and Finchley ('a wood frequented by finches') slowly disappeared when the manor belonged to the Bishop of London, who found sheep raising more profitable. Finchley was once a busy coaching stop, placed as it is on the old main road to the North, and a favourite haunt of highwaymen – but these days vehicular travellers are more likely to be held up in streets lined with parked cars, a result of the age of flat conversions. Finchley, originally defined as East End, Church End and North End, grew naturally as hamlets sprang up along the main **Great North Rd** (which still doubles as the area's **High Rd**) from London. But today the **North Circular Rd**, with its long-running saga of fiercely opposed road-widening proposals and junction improvements, effectively cuts off East Finchley to the south.

With the 19th-century train whistle that heralded the arrival of the Great Northern Railway, the suburb began to blossom; soon most of the large houses, estates and meadow land gave way to mainly middle-class housing. The first big villas of the 1860s are still in evidence to the E of the **High Rd** in North Finchley. Later, the Northern line tube opened up further tracts for development.

But developers were careful to retain the green open spaces, and residents can enjoy the untethered Dollis Brook which cuts N-S and separates Finchley from Hendon, as well as the cultivated Victoria Park in Finchley Central, Friary Park on the

Friern Barnet borders of North Finchley, and Cherry Tree Wood in East Finchley. (This latter was called Dirt House Woods in a less sensitive era.) There is even, in the midst of suburban splendour, a working farm.

Much conservation work took place in the last decade to improve a huge green area sandwiched between **Summers Lane** and **North Circular Rd**. On the Glebe Land a mixed civic and private sports complex offers football, bowling, tennis and open-air swimming. Between this and the North Circular lie a nature reserve, allotments and, to the E, Coppetts Wood, which masks the 24hr Tesco superstore at the **North Circular/Colney Hatch Lane** junction. The 'lungs' of the area are also provided by the two large cemeteries serving Central London parishes (St Marylebone, St Pancras & Islington), a golf course and numerous playing-fields.

Finchley boasts some fine surviving Georgiana – including the original manor house off **East End Rd**, a listed building dating back to 1793. Renamed the Sternberg Centre, it is now used as a private Jewish teaching centre, museum and school. Further along **East End Rd** stands Avenue House, once the home of 'Inky' Stephens, the philanthropist MP and pioneering ink manufacturer. Almost opposite, its remaining grounds – now public – hold a collection of rare trees.

There is an abundance of 3-bedroomed semi-detached property throughout Finchley. Houses are larger and more spacious in Woodside Park; terraced and more cosy in the 'county' roads of East Finchley.

Otherwise the area is bursting with flats. Many of the old suburban villas have been converted and more and more luxurious – and expensive – blocks have sprung up wherever developers can get planning permission. There are still examples of 1930s blocks between Finchley Central and Tally Ho Corner shopping areas, and beyond North Finchley along the **High Rd** to Whetstone. Plenty of homes, but still plenty of demand, too – especially for flats, either for occupation or rented out as an investment.

The area was given a boost in 1996 with the opening of the Finchley Lido development at the junction of the **High Rd** and the **North Circular Rd**. This has a bowling alley, restaurants, a multiplex cinema, a swimming pool and a leisure complex. Local shopping is concentrated along Finchley's spine, the **High Rd**, and on **Ballards Lane**, which meet at Tally Ho Corner; this, though, has been affected by the huge, and growing, Brent Cross shopping centre, just 10 min away by car or by the regular bus services. The area has a large and powerful watchdog in the guise of the Finchley Society.

Finchley suburban style makes constant references to rural models in its streets and buildings and, thanks to generous gardens and plentiful trees, goes a good way towards achieving the idyll. Mock-Tudor touches such as half-timbering, leaded light windows and tile hanging add to the charm. Such houses are more appreciated today than they were, and purists deplore the excesses of DIY improvers.

East Finchley

Row upon row of terraced houses give a distinct flavour to what was traditionally called East End (and changed by sensitive residents lest they be confused with the Cockneys). Today the area is wider than the site of the original hamlet, with its weekly hog market, within the triangle made by **East End Rd**, the **North Circular** and **East Finchley High Rd**, and is fertile hunting-ground for flats, too. Recently, Barnet Council have erected a sign welcoming you to 'East Finchley Village' – not entirely without justification: it does indeed have that feel, with local shops that still include a butcher, baker, fishmonger and greengrocer, and a cinema that's old, atmospheric and single-screened.

This is home to those who balk at Highgate prices, and (unlike Muswell Hill to the E) it has the tube. It also has its own red-brick 'university' by the tube station – the hamburger training centre which forms part of McDonald's British HQ. Behind this academy, and a common sight elsewhere to the W of the **High Rd**, are purpose-built maisonettes and blocks of flats. Popular streets include pleasant **Leslie Rd**; 2-bed flats here fetch around £120,000.

On the E side of the **High Rd**, **Fortis Green** is busy but picturesque: here large houses accompanied by their attached cottages (originally staff quarters), lie along a tree-lined route to Muswell Hill (see chapter). There are firemen's cottages and Grade III listed farmworkers' cottages from the early part of the century, an '80s mews and, near the tube station, modern flats. Nearby, at the end of **Southern Rd**, a clutch of new houses appeared by the archery club in 1996, in their own private, gated road.

North of **Fortis Green** are the so-called 'county' roads – **Hertford**, **Bedford**, **Huntingdon**, **Leicester**, **Lincoln**, **Durham Rds** – ever popular with 30-something professionals and minor soap celebrities who can afford prices that have approached £300,000 for the best terraces. The 'county' roads are fairly quiet, although they are used as a shortcut around the traffic lights at the Bald Faced Stag junction. Typical Victorian/Edwardian terraces of 2- and 3-bed cottages, these were not built to accommodate cars, as evidenced by the heavily parked streets. The further away from the **High Rd** (and the nearer to Muswell Hill) in roads like **Creighton Avenue** to the N of the 'county' roads, the larger and more detached the houses, with the luxury of their own drives and garages and prices to match.

South of **Fortis Green** homes in the roads that run down to pleasant Cherry Tree Wood, one of East Finchley's few open spaces, have the benefit of being close to the tube as well. Here **Summerlee Avenue's** terraces of 3-bed white-painted 1930s homes fetch around £210,000. Neighbouring streets such as Park Hall Rd have older and more varied terraces: expect to pay c. £265–270,000 for a 1900s 4-bed house.

South of **East End Rd**, and W of the tube station, is a different ball game: this is the Hampstead Garden Suburb and Highgate borders, with prices as large as the houses in **Abbots Gardens**, the top end of **Deans Way**, **Bancroft Avenue**, and the northern stretch of 'Millionaire's Row', the **Bishop's Avenue**.

Returning northwards, the North Circular end of the **High Rd** is flanked by two strongly contrasting council-built estates: Barnet's own Grange Estate, an older-style modest complex, runs well back from the **High Rd** in small tree-surrounded blocks. Almost opposite is the Strawberry Vale Estate, a Camden Council-controlled estate on Barnet land, sandwiched between the **North Circular Rd** and the St Pancras & Islington Cemetery. Outside, this Estate looks like a prison, with its semi-circular wall shielding the noise of the North Circular traffic from the '70s mix of flats and houses inside.

North Finchley

Beyond the complex fly-over system of the **North Circular**, the terraces begin to disappear and the suburban 3-bedroom semis spring up in roads like **Squires Lane** and **Queens Avenue**. This is far more family homes territory (hence, no doubt, Sainsbury's decision to open a new Homebase in **Woodberry Grove**, near the junction of **Ballards Lane** and the **High Rd**). New flats appear where there's space, and **Bow**

Lane is home to a housing association development built on the site of the old school kitchens. Across on the E side of the **High Rd**, **Summers Lane** skirts the sports complex, football, bowling, tennis and open-air swimming alongside the Glebe Lands and the nature reserve. (This green corner near Coppetts Wood no longer houses Barnet's refuse disposal and recycling facilities, leaving at present an empty site.)

The shopping area around Tally Ho Corner and N up the **High Rd** is heavily traffic congested; parking is difficult, and side-streets suffer as a result. A trial period of pedestrianization is taking place in **Nether St** to assess the consequences of a more widespread scheme. No signs as yet of the hoped-for lottery-funded arts centre manifesting at the southern base of the Tally Ho triangle.

To the E of the **High Rd**, streets of terraces mix with avenues of late-19th-century suburban villas; grass verges appear on roads such as **Ravensdale Avenue**, which may start by Sainsbury's superstore, but ends down the road from the golf course. On towards Friern Barnet, in the tract bordered by **Woodhouse Rd** to the S and **Friern Barnet Lane** to the E the '30s suburbia is in full blossom, with many mock-Tudor and modern town-houses overlooking Friary Park. **Torrington Park** and **Friern Park** also include blocks of flats; Friar's Place, a development of 17 1- and 2-bed flats on **Friern Park**, was on the market in late '98, with prices for luxury 2-beds at £130–140,000.

To the W of the **High Rd** the picture is more of the large villas, converted into attractive and spacious mansion flats. **Lodge Lane** is particularly pretty (although busy – thanks in the main to lorries from the bakery and the Post Office sorting office), with rows of tiny cottages all beautifully modernized and spruced up.

North, pleasant streets between the **High Rd** and the tube line, lead across to Woodside Park – many have 'Woodside' in their names.

Woodside Park

These 'Woodside' streets, near the Woodside Park underground, reflect the popularity of this side of Finchley as a place to settle into a comfortable and convenient flat – perhaps after the children have left home. Here large houses mingle with modern schemes both basic and (the more recent developments) sybaritic. Above all, flats. The latest, Sycamore Court, adds another 30, completed at the end of '98, to **Woodside Lane**. These ranged from £90–100,000 for 1-bed flats, £135–145,000 for 2-bed.

Across on the W side of the tube tracks, there is an air of affluence to Woodside Park proper. Houses are larger, the cars are BMWs and Mercedes, the roads are wider. **Holden Rd** itself has changed its character in the last 20 years: what was once an avenue of enormous houses with gardens tumbling down the banks to Dollis Brook has been transformed. A section of the road is devoted to a mid-'70s development of square town-houses facing late-'80s flats and the remaining original houses. More luxury-level flats to come in this road, regularly combed by developers; a block of 28 2-bedroomed and four 1-bed flats will be completed this year.

Next door is another outbreak of rows of early '70s houses – entirely council-built, but nicely developed on the corner of **Holden Rd** and **Laurel View** – which was held up by an illustrious resident who refused to sell until almost the last bricks were laid all around his house and garden. There have been problems with a few of the units built too near the brook, but otherwise they are pleasant.

Across Dollis Brook, in the angle between it and the delightfully named Folly Brook, **Southover** and **Northiam** are posh houses with pseudo-column additions and roof extensions. Below Folly Brook, the streets with South Downs names – **Lullington Garth, Walmington Fold, Chanctonbury Way, Cissbury Ring North** and **South**, etc – are ideal for families whose purse strings are a little more tied. The prices can dip further away from the tube stations and the shops – but not far, thanks to the green, open aspect and the peace and quiet. A 3-bed semi here costs around £190–200,000.

Church End

The home of Finchley's largest houses, most picturesque avenues and most historic buildings: the Christ's College building, St Mary's school house and, on **East End Rd**, Avenue House and the original manor house. This is the area most often depicted in paintings and sketches representing old Finchley.

Church End itself surrounds St Mary's Church in **Hendon Lane**; this is the heart of the old village, and the site of the turnpike on the old road from Marylebone. At the apex of **Hendon Lane** and **Regents Park Rd**, it is Finchley's most visible and congested conservation area, lying close to the shops and Finchley Central tube.

To the W down prestigious (million-plus) **Hendon Avenue** is a more peaceful idyll, and another conservation area. **Village Rd** is the core of Finchley Garden Village, 54 semi-detached houses built around a rectangular green in the early 1900s. It was the brainwave of architect Frank Stratton who lived there himself. Equally attractive, and with its own 'village green', is **Crooked Usage**, where a 7-bedroomed property was on the market recently for £695,000.

But the immediate triangle of Old England at Church End, around the cottages of **College Terrace**, has become a virtual island – surrounded by tasteful, luxury flat developments down **Hendon Lane**, and an enormous development of red-brick flats and office blocks in **Regent's Park Rd**. One-bed flats here are c. £95,000. 1980s-built retirement homes face them across the road.

The luxury developments continue down this road, punctuated by the fields of the picturesque College Farm, once the Express Dairies showhouse farm, to the **North Circular Rd**, the famous Naked Lady statue and Henly's Corner.

Around the side-streets like **Tillingbourne Gardens** the houses are impressive, detached and dear. Kinloss Gardens Synagogue is at the corner of the ambitious but popular Chessington Estate. The homes of **Allandale Avenue** and **Fitzalan Rd** have the amazing bonus of overlooking what is still a working farm, with an emphasis on rare breeds. Cars flock to the regular Sunday open days, but they are reckoned a small price to pay for this slice of the country.

Road experts at Barnet Council have turned the streets to the east of **Regents Park Rd** – **Mountfield Rd, Stanhope Avenue, Cavendish Avenue, Holly Park** and **Holly Park Gardens** – into a maze of one-ways and no-through roads to stop rat-running. The older houses here have gradually been converted into flats. St Luke's Court, a 1980s development in **Mountfield Rd**, however, went for exclusivity with a private courtyard behind remote-control gates. It has as its star the refurbished 6-bed old vicarage (the developers built the vicar a new one), sold in 1988 for half a million. Two new houses, flats and penthouses with 'cathedral-proportion living rooms' completed the scheme.

Finchley Central

What's in a name? Finchley Central is really just the name of the tube and belt of shops along **Ballards Lane**, but estate agents seized on it in the '80s to describe the area N of the railway line on either side of **Ballards Lane** before you come to the postal district of N12 and Woodside Park. Now Barnet Council have attempted to reverse this trend with a sign near the tube station firmly labelling this end of Ballards Lane as 'Church End Town Centre'. Further N is the equally nebulous West Finchley which, again, covers the few streets around the tube station of the same name.

The overwhelming appearance in the residential streets on either side of **Ballards Lane** is of overcrowding – largely due to commuters' cars. Again there are lots of flat conversions, although the further away from **Ballards Lane** you go, the more the 3-bedroomed semi dominates.

Victoria Park, N of **Long Lane**, is the outstanding feature of Finchley Central – a small but pretty park with tennis courts and bowling green, it is an oasis in suburbia's sprawl of large detached houses and purpose-built flats such as those of **Etchingham Park Rd**. The park is also home to the annual Finchley Carnival. Houses here have large gardens – but no garages. Almost opposite the park are the flats of Finchley Court. A spacious, well-maintained '30s development, this is still one of Finchley's most attractive; a 2-bed flat here will cost £100–110,000.

West of **Ballards Lane**, **Alexandra Grove** covers the whole spectrum of property styles – from larger, detached mock-Tudor homes through medium-sized semis and a few '70s town-houses, to purpose-built flats of all ages: dull, everyday but sturdy '30s blocks to far more appealing recent luxury schemes. It ends with a curious yellow purpose-built block at the junction with **Nether St**. **Moss Hall Crescent**, just off **Ballards Lane**, is a parade of attractive mansions reclaimed from the ravages of post-war use as bed-sits.

Nether St joins Finchley Central to North Finchley and runs beside West Finchley tube station. In the past it has been used as a parallel short-cut to the **High Rd** and road planners have tried to stop this with a complicated junction at **Dollis Rd**/**Crescent Rd**. Traffic has always been a problem here, particularly on weekdays, by Moss Hall Junior and Infants Schools (junction with **Moss Hall Grove**) and by the West Finchley tube station which has no car park. Now the N end, which leads to the shops at Tally Ho Corner, is a pilot pedestrianization scheme. At this end, **Nether St** begins with terraces of neat houses which transform naturally to larger semis and, where these have been pulled down, blocks of 1/3-bed flats. Some of the very large villas beyond the junction with **Argyle Rd** have been converted into old people's nursing homes or new blocks of luxury flats.

Transport	Tubes: East Finchley (zone 3, Northern); Finchley Central, West Finchley, Woodside Park (zone 4, Northern). From Finchley Central: Oxford Circus 32 min (1 change), City 40 min, Heathrow 1 hr 30 min (1 change).
Convenient for	Brent Cross shopping centre, Wembley Stadium. M1 to the North, M25, North Circular Rd. Miles from centre: 7.
Schools	Barnet Education Authority: Christchurch C of E, Woodhouse 6th-form College, Christ's College (b), Compton School, Finchley Catholic High School, St Michael's Convent Grammar (g).

SALES

Flats	S	1B	2B	3B	4B	5B
Average prices	35–60	60–105	75–130	100–150	–	–
Houses	2B	3B	4B	5B	6/7B	8B
Average prices	100–130	130–230	180–390	250–500	600–800+	–

RENTAL

Flats	S	1B	2B	3B	4B	5B
Average prices	350–550	540–750	600–1150	1200–1500	–	–
Houses	2B	3B	4B	5B	6/7B	8B
Average prices	800–1100	860–1500	1100–2100	1400–3800	–	–

The properties   Quintessential suburbia: typical home is the 3-bed inter-war semi. Also Victorian/Edwardian terraced and larger homes, and modern flats in smart blocks, plus large houses in select streets. Higher flat prices in recent luxury blocks. £1 million mansions in best streets.

The market   A settled family community, strong but changing as newcomers move in. Popular with young singles and professional couples who rent or buy; older couples swap family-sized homes for luxury flats here after the kids move out. Strong Jewish and Asian communities. Local searches: 3 working days.

F

Among those estate agents active in this area are:
- Anscombe & Ringland*
- Arthur Benabo
- Ellis & Co
- Jeremy Leaf & Co
- Copping Joyce
- Stevens & Son
- Addisons
- Winkworth*
- Bernard Tomkins
- Martyn Gerrard
- Bairstow Eves
- Capital Estates
- JAC Strattons
- Spicer McColl

further details: see advertisers' index on p633

FOREST HILL

NUNHEAD

One Tree Hill

Honor Oak Park

HONOR OAK PARK

DULWICH

Hornimans

Honor Oak Road

Park

BROCKLEY RISE

CATFORD

A205 STANSTEAD ROAD

A205

LONDON ROAD

N

Forest Hill

Forest Hill East

PERRY VALE

SYDENHAM

PERRY HILL

F

Map ref: p111 (2K)
Postal districts: SE23
Boroughs: Lewisham (Lab)
Council tax: Band D £683
Conservation areas: Check with town hall
Parking: Free off main roads

This South London eminence rises to the east of Dulwich, north of Sydenham, and west of Catford and Lewisham. The 'forest on the hill' of ages past is long gone, but wooded areas and quiet, tree-lined roads continue to give the name meaning. Like Sydenham, the area owes its development to the railway, which reached here in 1836. Some impressive 19th-century villas have survived the depredations of developers.

The hilly land gives Forest Hill its character, but – if you discount tenuous royal connections with Elizabeth I, in whose honour Honor Oak is said to have been named – its hero is a tea merchant, who gave it a 21-acre park and a museum. F J Horniman amassed an extensive anthropological and natural history collection from his world travels. This he made a gift to the people, along with the museum he had built (1897–1901). Next to the Horniman Museum are the delightful gardens with interesting views. The area's best homes are in this corner.

The **South Circular** runs through Forest Hill in the guise of **London Rd**, **Waldram Park Rd** and **Stanstead Rd**, and is now a Red Route. A local traffic management scheme, introduced last year, uses traffic lights, road closures and sleeping policemen to deter rat-runners trying to skirt round the congested town centre. As always, the changes will bring both winners and losers.

The area, which is essentially the SE23 postal district, divides roughly into two parts – the hilly ground in the W (between **Honor Oak Park** to N, the railway line to the E, **Thorpewood Avenue** to S, **Wood Vale/Sydenham Hill** to W), and the lower-lying ground to the E of the railway line. The centre and principal area for shops, restaurants, etc, **London Rd/Dartmouth Rd** meets basic needs but lacks the attractive character of, say, Blackheath Village – it is, however, being tidied up, and recently old commercial buildings have been turned into bistros and even new pubs. Some of the modern council flats in this corner would not look out of place in a private development. Off **Dartmouth Rd** are some tucked-away homes in little unmade-up roads. The major shopping centre for the area is at Lewisham, a direct bus ride or short car trip away.

In terms of homes, the most sought-after neighbourhood and most elevated – in price and geography – is Hornimans, the estate agent shorthand for the roads N of the Horniman Museum and Gardens.

The south-eastern quarter between **Waldram Park Rd**, **Stanstead Rd** and **Perry Vale/Perry Rise** is generally flatter and has a mixture of property – detached and semis, terraced, Victorian/turn-of-the-century and '30s/modern as well as council blocks. Streets off **Honor Oak Park** near Honor Oak rail station have modest terraces.

The largest properties are usually found on the high ground but few roads are homogeneous – you'll find Victorian houses next to bay-fronted '30s semis. Victorian properties predominate, though, and top the popularity list.

Forest Hill is still an affordable area both for first-time buyers and those seeking a larger home. The stock of these diminished slightly in the '80s, when larger properties became the target for conversion to flats; now, however, the tide has swung back the other way. **Wood Vale**, with its road humps, has seen some recent conversions, with names like Woodlands Court and Beech Court; also some new-build, but in traditional brick-and-white-stucco style. A redundant pub, too, has been turned into flats (closing-time never comes . . .). Nearby, however, other large and hitherto neglected Victorian houses have been lovingly restored and sold as grand, £300,000-plus family homes, with views out over the Hornimans nature trail. In other parts of this long road a 2-bed flat can be had for c. £79,000. **Langton Rise**, which crosses Wood Vale, has a new development of flats and four modern houses.

Forest Hill's leafiness and quiet tend to belie its inner-suburban location. It has a good share of gardens and parks, and Dulwich and Sydenham Hill golf course is nearby. There are no real pockets of deprivation. London Bridge is 12 min by train and connections to Gatwick are possible from East Croydon on the same line. There is also a new (though slower) service to Victoria, and a link to Croydon (change for Gatwick Airport). The steepness of the hills demands fitness (some have 18 per cent gradients) and in winter heavy snow leaves cars immobilized in the hilly parts.

Hornimans

One approach to Hornimans is up popular **Honor Oak Rd** at the **London Rd** entrance. **Honor Oak Rd** has surviving Italianate villas which have largely become roomy flats. The road is a mixture but not jarringly so – modern box developments, a council estate, Victorian homes and '30s semis. A block of flats, Angela Court, is being joined by a twin, to be built in keeping with the original. Dainty Ashberry Cottage was once home to William Duke of Clarence, later King William IV, and his actress-mistress Mrs Jordan. The Regency cottage dates from 1809.

Trailing hillward off **Honor Oak Rd** are **Westwood Park** and **Horniman Drive**. Desirable **Horniman Drive** has '30s detached homes with pretty front gardens, some recent low, 3-storey flats, and ends, by an entrance to Hornimans Gardens, with modern town-house cul-de-sacs. It also has enviable views over London. Large, detached '30s also in demand in **Ringmore Rise**. The Drive and the Rise meet at a quaint, triangular communal garden, with **Liphook** and **Rocombe Crescents** curving round the other sides. (At the top of **Ringmore Rise**, a '40s-style house, unexpected and out of keeping, adds a sense of light relief to this very proper corner.) **Westwood Park**, which now boasts speed humps, starts with some large Victorian semis and later follows round the hillside with '30s bay-fronted detached and semis. Smaller

'30s properties in **Tewkesbury Avenue**. For spectacular views of the City and a mixture of Victorian, turn-of-the-century, '30s semis there's **Canonbie Rd**. Canary Wharf, the Houses of Parliament, St Paul's, Battersea Power Station, the Telecom Tower . . . all the capital's landmarks are there – even if the gradient is 18 per cent, difficult for the elderly and impossible in snow. **Netherby Rd** (bay-fronted semis and occasional large Victorian ones) looks to the wooded One Tree Hill.

Worth investigation is **Devonshire Rd**, running parallel to the railway line – and thus with a station at either end. Victorian semis, detached, turn-of-the-century, 1930s. Plenty of renovation has gone on here, and speed humps slow those rushing for a train. A small nature reserve comes as a pleasant surprise; in short, a very central corner, with train stations at both ends. Several small blocks of flats have appeared here in the last 10 years, replacing rambling Victorian properties. These are not always harmonious: Leyton Court's garish yellow brick, for instance. But then the '30s Postmens' Office (red-brick, sculptures on roof) is not exactly retiring, either . . .

Busy **London Rd** (it's part of the South Circular) in its western stages near the museum has council blocks, but also brightly painted Classical terraces – now flats – further down. On the N side is Horniman Grange, a 1988 redevelopment of some previously wrecked Victorian houses. Now there are studios, 1- and 2-bed flats. Off to the S is **Taymount Rise** (mansion flats, Victorian detached, '60s town-houses, '80s flats), ending with renovated, but dull, '30s mansion blocks, Taymount Grange and Forestcroft. **Thorpewood Avenue** – here '30s semis outnumber the occasional Victorian houses – marks the southern boundary of this side of Forest Hill.

Forest Hill East

East of Honor Oak Park station the more illustrious properties are left behind. Shops line both sides – there is a small gallery, and a good music shop. Small roads such as **Ballina St** and **Gabriel St** have stolid, uniform turn-of-the-century terraces – also some '60s town-houses in **Grierson Rd**. (The streets in the right-angle between **Honor Oak Park** and **Brockley Rise** have a fiendishly confusing traffic system to stop access from **Honor Oak**.) In Blythe Hill Place, **Brockley Park**, a new development of 2-bedroomed 'cottages', sold fast last year for £80,000 upwards.

Large Victorian houses on **Waldram Park Rd** have made for excellent flat conversions, close to Forest Hill rail station and buses into town. **Stanstead Rd** is notoriously busy (it's part of the South Circular), but has large Victorian semis and cottage-style dwellings. The roads leading off both sides of **Vancouver Rd** are quieter and have terraced homes – Victorian and turn-of-the-century. Also some 1930s and modern infills. A 5-bed terraced house sold for £170,000 here last winter.

Perry Vale, which runs SE from Forest Hill rail station, starts with Christchurch C of E Primary School, and a concentration of unattractive council estates. Older-type constructions with walkways, their impact is lessened by the surrounding trees. Large turn-of-the-century semis follow, with a parade of shops in the curve. Running S from Perry Vale, a council estate, Forest Hill School and a town-house development make up **Dacres Rd** until the right turn. Then come detached Victorian houses, leaf-obscured modern town-houses and a modern mansion building. Off **Mayow Rd**, which leads back up to Perry Vale, **Acorn Way** is a small cul-de-sac of 2-storey homes, built 2–3 years ago, where children play in the street. Herons Court is a new development of red-brick flats. There is a real mixture of house styles in this corner: **Wynell Rd**, for example, contains council-built estates and 3-storey red-brick houses; but by the time it joins Perry Vale these have given way to larger, brick-and-stucco houses, with fittingly large gardens, that would not look out of place in Notting Hill.

Across on the N side of Perry Vale, **Sunderland Rd** has large Victorian, turn-of-the-century detached, and '30s semis. Some of the big Victorian mansions remain as single homes: one vast house boasts eight bedrooms (the smallest one 11 sq ft). **Woolstone Rd** starts with bay-fronted Victorian, turn-of-the-century terraces, and neat 1930s semis; tree-lined, the leaves brush together in the middle of the road. Also some large Victorian detached houses towards St George's Church.

Off **Perry Rise**, **Allenby Rd** is quiet and leafy: large Victorian detached; neighbouring **Garlies Rd** is less uniform – it mixes in some 1930s semis. **Paxton Rd** now boasts one of the area's biggest redevelopments: more than 150 flats made pretty by balconies and gardens, in 3-storey blocks. More are being built, 4-storey and in the same red-brick, behind. **Queenswood Rd** is terraced – Victorian, turn-of-the-century and '30s semis. Tucked away on the site of the old Forest Hill sports club is a small development of 3-bed houses. **Perry Rise** itself offers bay-fronted Victorian semis before giving way to small terraced houses near **Bell Green**, on the Lower Sydenham borders, with its gasworks – where 6 acres of freehold land is up for sale. This is next to the new hypermarket which at weekends offers 24hr shopping.

Transport	Train: Forest Hill to London Bridge 12 min, Victoria 30 min. Also to Croydon (for Gatwick). Buses to West End.
Convenient for	Dulwich golf course, Crystal Palace Park and National Sports Centre, Lewisham shops. South Circular Rd. Miles from centre: 6.
Schools	Local Authority: Forest Hill School (b), Sydenham School (g). Private: Sydenham High (see Dulwich, Catford).

SALES

Flats	S	1B	2B	3B	4B	5B
Average prices	40–50	50–60	70–90	75–90	100+	—
Houses	2B	3B	4B	5B	6/7B	8B
Average prices	70–90	120–150	130–170	170–250	200–400	—

RENTAL

Flats	S	1B	2B	3B	4B	5B
Average prices	320–400	400–550	500–700	600–800	800–1300	1300+
Houses	2B	3B	4B	5B	6/7B	8B
Average prices	550–750	600–1000	800–1000	1500+	—	—

The properties	Respectable Victoriana, larger homes in the W of the area, smaller terraces to the E. Three-bed houses most common; larger houses have often been converted into flats; some now being converted back.
The market	First-time buyers after 1/2-bed flats join families seeking space and greenery. They, and agents, reckon area is still good value. Local searches: 2 weeks.

Among those estate agents active in this area are:
- Woolwich Property Services *
- Scotchbrooks
- Robert Stanford
- Acorn
- Halifax Property
- Oak Estates*

further details: see advertisers' index on p633

FULHAM

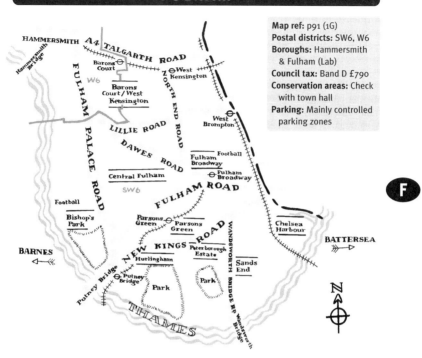

Map ref: p91 (1G)
Postal districts: SW6, W6
Boroughs: Hammersmith
 & Fulham (Lab)
Council tax: Band D £790
Conservation areas: Check
 with town hall
Parking: Mainly controlled
 parking zones

Are there 1,300 people who want to buy a luxury flat in Sand's End? We, and developers St George, will soon find out, for the largest new homes scheme in London is about to be unleashed on the old gasworks on **Imperial Rd**. And will the residents ever be able to get out of Fulham, a notoriously gridlocked corner?

If it comes off, this ambitious plan will put the seal on Fulham's transformation from humble suburb to the heartland of middle-class London. Until 1880 almost all of Fulham was market gardens. With the completion of the District line tube an enormous development took place – the bulk between 1880 and 1900, but extending up to World War I in various small areas. These houses – almost entirely terraced, with only a few detached and semi-detached in areas such as Hurlingham and Bishop's Park – cover most of Fulham. There still exist a very few 18th-century buildings, mainly associated with the original villages of Walham Green (now **Fulham Broadway**) and Fulham (sited by what is now Putney Bridge) and extending along the **New King's Rd**.

After the pre-1914 building boom, Fulham relapsed into a condition of quiet respectability. Much of the housing was let unfurnished: as late as 1971, more than 40 per cent of the homes in most of Fulham were privately let. In that year over 20 per cent of Fulham homes lacked an inside WC.

Fulham was a stable community, with strong local loyalties and a tendency to stay put: three generations of the same family would live in the same group of streets. This pattern was shattered by the closure of many industrial firms which provided employment for the local people and by the property boom of the early '70s. Demand from would-be owner-occupiers spilt over from Chelsea and Kensington, and the first quiet streets of Fulham were 'discovered'. Landlords, beset by the Rent Acts then in force, hastened to sell their tenanted homes as soon as the residents could be persuaded to leave. The early '80s cemented the trend, which spread across the whole area. In came the young professionals (yuppies had not quite been invented then), out went the skilled workers and their families to new estates on the fringes of London. In a few frantic years, the face of Fulham changed . . .

Fulham has a fair sprinkling of council estates, though they have been affected by the 'Right to Buy' legislation. The biggest estate is Clem Attlee Court in the N of the area, off **Lillie Rd**. These big blocks, named after Socialist luminaries of the 1940s, form a community of their own and provide a source of good-value housing. Two have been demolished to make room for low-rise housing association homes. In the SE corner of Fulham, Sand's End has more council blocks in a fast-changing area. Smaller clusters of council-built and housing association homes occur across the borough. Some, such as those by the river off **Stevenage Rd**, are very attractive.

The old Fulham turned its back on the river which curves around it on three sides. Or to be more precise, it used the river rather than looked at it. The banks were lined with wharves and with industry, and barges delivered materials to many a riverside works. Few of these remain, and many of the industrial sites have been, or are being, replaced by housing. A by-product is the opening up of the riverside: public paths now follow much of the western bank.

The wide sweep of the Thames forms Fulham's southern and western boundaries. The river is crossed at two points to the S at Putney (the oldest and lowest fording point on the River Thames, and used by the Romans) and Wandsworth Bridges. The eastern boundary is the main N-S railway line which runs from Kensington Olympia to cross the river to Battersea: three roads cross the line. The northern barrier which separates Fulham from Hammersmith is the A4/Hammersmith Flyover and **Cromwell Rd Extension/Talgarth Rd** which leads westwards to the M4 motorway. Three roads cross this. There are thus only eight roads into or out of Fulham, something which often becomes painfully obvious.

The E-W roads define neighbourhoods. From S-N, they are **New King's Rd**, **Fulham Rd**, **Dawes Rd**, **Lillie Rd**. There are two main N-S routes: **Fulham Palace Rd**, leading to Putney Bridge; and **North End Rd/Wandsworth Bridge Rd**, leading to Wandsworth Bridge. Again these routes are neighbourhood demarcation lines.

New King's Rd and **Fulham Rd** have changed a lot in the last 15 years, acquiring fashionable shops selling antique furniture, clothing and specialist delicatessen, plus restaurants and bars. **Lillie Rd** and **Dawes Rd** still maintain many of the old-style small local shops, selling a wide range of goods, but they are changing fast. To the amazement of those who knew it a few years back, **Munster Rd** boasts street bars and restaurants. **Fulham Palace Rd**, especially S of **Lillie Rd**, is predominantly residential. **North End Rd** has a colourful street fruit-and-vegetable market operating side-by-side with a Safeway supermarket, while **Wandsworth Bridge Rd** is a mix of residential and trendy shopping – it has been the stripped-pine capital of West London for years. The Sainsbury's on **Townmead Rd** is a hub of life for the southern end of the area.

Fulham has a number of open spaces and parks. In the S is Hurlingham Park with its sportsground. The Hurlingham Club, which adjoins it and has all the river frontage, is (very) private. It has a swimming pool and tennis courts and is centred around the 18th-century Hurlingham House. South Park, also in the S, has children's play-areas, cricket pitch and tennis courts. Parson's Green and Eel Brook Common are tree-lined open spaces overlooked by many attractive homes. To the W, Bishop's Park borders the river above Putney Bridge: this was originally the gardens of the 16th-century Bishop's Palace. To the N is the Queens Club private tennis club and Normand Park, which houses a modern swimming pool complex. Assiduous tree-planting along the streets has also helped to mitigate the main difference between Fulham and neighbouring Chelsea: the lack of the general leafy impression provided by Chelsea's square gardens. Fulham, built later, has rows of streets, not squares.

Fulham also boasts two football grounds. To the W is Fulham's riverside ground, while on the Kensington/Chelsea borders is Stamford Bridge, home of Chelsea. Both grounds have for years been the focus of plans, rows and more plans. Chelsea's ground, now called 'Chelsea Village', has seen the biggest changes. It has acquired a hotel, a 9-storey block of flats, three restaurants and other facilities. The stadium will grow in size from a capacity of 28,000 to 43,000, and will be in use all year, not twice a week in winter as now. Craven Cottage, Fulham's ground, is due to close some time in the next five years for rebuilding. A 26,000-seat stadium will emerge. Both grounds attract a great deal of traffic, which looks set to grow.

There are three tube stations, with good connections into Central London. Just outside the area, the two Piccadilly line stations at Baron's Court and West Kensington also have direct links to Heathrow. However, large tracts are quite a distance from a tube station. There are hopes of a river bus service as part of the millennium revival of the Thames.

There are good road connections out of London to the W along the M4 to Heathrow and the M25, to the S over Putney or Wandsworth Bridges to join the South Circular or A3, and to the N through Shepherd's Bush. However, the snag with the road system is that it is saturated with traffic, which affects the bus services and main routes out of London. Putney and Wandsworth in particular are choke-points on the routes S and W. The long-term closure of Hammersmith Bridge has resulted in virtual gridlock at certain times of day.

The West London rail line runs along the area's E edge – but does not stop, as there are no stations S of Olympia. There are plans (hopes would be a better word) for new stations at West Brompton (the District line already has a station there) and either/both Chelsea Village and Chelsea Harbour/Imperial Wharf (see p305).

Parking in the residential streets is an ever more desperate problem, as many owners of the narrow-fronted terraced houses now have at least two cars. Overnight double parking is a common feature of many streets. Most of the residential roads are now in controlled parking zones. If a house has a parking space, it is the first asset an estate agent will mention.

As far as most estate agents and inhabitants are concerned, Fulham tends to end at **Lillie Rd**, the SW6 border. The W14 area to the N between **Lillie Rd** and **Talgarth Rd** has a very different character, centred around Barons Court and West Kensington tube stations. It is largely composed of big, late-Victorian houses and mansion blocks, and until recently rental property was dominant. (See Hammersmith.)

The neighbourhoods of Fulham can be divided into the expensive, the established and the up-and-coming, and are dealt with here in that order.

Peterborough Estate

Perhaps the best-known neighbourhood in Fulham is the ever-popular but ever-so-pricey Peterborough Estate, a conservation area between **New King's Rd** and South Park bounded by **Peterborough Rd** to the W and **Bagleys Lane** to the E. Incoming owner-occupiers started buying these houses in the early 1970s and called the neighbourhood Hurlingham: no-one in Chelsea had heard of Fulham in those days. By the end of the decade these houses, smartened up, were the first in Fulham to break the £100,000 barrier. Now the Peterborough Estate is a well-known name.

The most sought-after roads are those to the W of **Wandsworth Bridge Rd**, with a series of N-S streets off the Parson's Green stretch of **New King's Rd**: **Perrymead St**, **Chipstead St**, **Quarrendon St**, **Chiddingstone St**, **Bradbourne St** and **Coniger St**.

These are matching rows of substantial terraced houses. Red-brick, gabled, flat-fronted late Victoriana, of 3-, 4- or 5-bedrooms, many with additional space from loft and cellar conversions, extensions and conservatories. They have small back gardens. These are very distinctive houses, with attractive mullioned windows and terracotta lions (the trademark of J Nicholls, the builder) decorating the party walls at roof level. The majority are still single-family houses. A variety of internal layouts can be found as many have been virtually rebuilt. A good one costs £650,000-plus. A slightly less smart location, such as **Peterborough Rd**, can mean a price nearer £400,000. A 4-bed house might rent for £650 a week. Prices here ended 1998 where they began.

Hurlingham/High St

Hurlingham, also S of **New King's Rd**, is a much smaller conservation area, consisting of **Napier Avenue**, **Ranelagh Avenue**, **Ranelagh Gardens**, **Edenhurst Avenue** and **Hurlingham Gardens**, bounded to the N by **Hurlingham Rd**. Predominantly, there are imposing late-19th-century detached and semi-detached 5- or 6-bed houses, each with its own character and architectural style, set back from the tree-lined streets, with drives and off-street parking. In **Ranelagh Gardens,** there are two '60s apartment blocks – also much sought-after – and a new riverside development, **Carrara Wharf**, a private enclave of 20 houses and 69 flats. Two-bed flats here are £300,000, 4-bed ones double that. Along the river on Hurlingham Gardens is a large inter-war luxury apartment block. The appeal of this corner is also enhanced by the nearby Putney Bridge tube and the proximity of Bishop's Park. On **Hurlingham Rd**, **Melbray Mews** is a new group of live/work units priced from £265,000.

Fulham High St is a bit of a misnomer. It has a few shops, but is mostly mansion flats on the W side and a mix of uses on the E. On the High St, 'Parkview Court' has 112 flats backing onto the grounds of Fulham Palace with planning permission for another 12 on the roof. A 2-bed flat might be £190,000. **Steeple Close** is tucked in W of the High St and backing onto the Bishop's Park: 4-bed modern town-houses with garages are priced at around £395,000.

On the far side of Hurlingham Park with its club, Barratt recently added a new square to the area. **Hurlingham Square**, in the angle of **Peterborough** and **Sullivan Rds**, has 50 4/5-bed homes in an enclave reached via electronic entry gates. A 4-bed house sells for around £550,000, or £500 pw to rent. Further N off **Peterborough Rd** the neat, pleasant Sullivan Court estate of council-built homes runs through to **Broomhouse Lane**. These crop up for sale at around £145,000 for a 3-bed flat, with 2-bed houses renting at £240 a week. The riverside **Carnwath Rd** has seen big changes as industry and commerce are replaced by homes. A 1950s office block, the former British Gas research HQ, has been sold as 'The

Fulham, at first sight a district of uniform terraces, has some unusual domestic buildings such as this splendidly ornate turret house near Hurlingham. The slate-capped turret, the Romanesque detailing around its eaves, the handsome sash windows and the iron railings make up an attractive whole.

Piper Building' (artist John Piper was commissioned by the Gas people to provide an abstract mural on the building). Most of the shell-finish 'loft' apartments were sold in 1997; last November a handful were available from £285,000 to over £400,000.

Bishop's Park

Another small conservation area, bounded on the E by **Fulham Palace Rd** and on the W by **Stevenage Rd** facing Bishop's Park, stretching from **Fulham Palace Gardens** and **Bishop's Park Rd** to the S, into the pleasant first few of a grid of tree-lined roads – **Cloncurry St, Doneraile St, Ellerby St** and **Finlay St**. Here you'll find terraced or semi-detached houses which were built at the end of the 19th century or later and have 4/5 bedrooms. Many have been extended upwards (not always sympathetically), with loft extensions, and to the rear with back extensions and conservatories. Most have substantial gardens. A good one can go for upwards of £700,000. The later date of these houses reflects the stubborn hold-out of the last major market gardener. The road names continue to follow the alphabet past Fulham FC (at the W end of **Finlay St**) up to **Inglethorpe St**. Here you will find more flat conversions: 2-bed flats go for £165–175,000. A typical extended house with 4-bed would be £375,000.

Extending north of Fulham FC along the river are a string of apartment blocks built in the '70s, with fine views across the river to the old Barnes water meadows, now a wildlife sanctuary and (the N part) the expensive Barnes Waterside housing. River Gardens, which has pool and sauna, has 2/3-bedroom flats with spectacular terracing and balconies; Rosebank is a conventional high-rise block with 2/3-bed flats. Service charges must be considered in these blocks. The further N you go here, the more distant from a tube.

Chelsea Harbour

The biggest clutch of modern apartments and houses can be found on the Fulham/Chelsea borders. Many more will be added near here if the Imperial Wharf scheme happens: see Sand's End p 307. Chelsea Harbour is a parable of the times. Only in the 1980s could a developer take a triangular site bounded by a railway and a muddy creek and present these as advantages – even if the third side, as here, is river frontage. But this cut-off corner can offer that goal of every really top-flight development: complete security. Chelsea Harbour is the W side of town's answer to Docklands, a total of 310 homes in blocks, terraces, crescents and the landmark tower. Not to mention the apart-hotel, and shops and offices and other commercial buildings on the railway side.

Chelsea Harbour is far from public transport – a hoppa bus supplies the missing link to Earl's Court tube, High St Kensington and Putney – though the hoped-for rail station (see area profile) would help. But, the argument goes, it is alongside Chelsea, not the Isle of Dogs. The flats vary widely in size and price. Check position, condition and sound insulation: some back onto the increasingly busy rail line.

The centrepiece is the reopened harbour. This provides the neighbourhood with a much-needed tranquil spot to relax by the river (a public walkway runs along the Thames) – not, of course, possible along the Chelsea embankment, nor yet the Sand's End stretch.

The **Lots Rd** power station, which is owned by London Transport, was due to close in 1990. To the annoyance of Chelsea Harbour residents it has stayed open, though it is now planned to close it this year. Or in 2001: it depends who you talk to. Kensington and Chelsea Council, whose writ runs here, has drawn up a planning brief for 150 flats, offices, art gallery and museum (of Delayed Developments perhaps?). No developer has yet taken the bait. More is happening here on old gasworks site to the W, across the railway: see Sand's End.

Moore Park Rd

A pocket of large mid-Victorian stucco terraced houses and later Victorian detached and semi-detached houses on the Fulham/Chelsea borders, between **Fulham Rd** and **King's Rd**. Some houses have been converted into flats. This was the first bit of Fulham to become respectable, almost Chelsea actually, and it is a stable, established corner. The proximity to busy Chelsea football ground is mitigated because the roads – **Moore Park Rd**, **Britannia Rd**, **Maxwell Rd**, **Holmead Rd** and **Rumbold Rd** – are barricaded off to through traffic. However as 'Chelsea Village' grows, so does the pressure on these streets, where the shops already close on football Saturdays. A 4-bed house here can command £500,000.

Parson's Green

In estate agents' terms, this covers an ever-larger area, bounded by streets either side of **Fulham Rd** to the N (up as far as **Bishop's Rd**) and either side of **New King's Rd** to the S, extending as far as Eel Brook Common to the E and **Munster Road** to the W. This neighbourhood is regarded as being that which is within easy walking distance of pretty, triangular Parson's Green and its nearby tube station. The big 3-storey houses overlooking the actual green are coveted and priced accordingly: £875,000 was being asked for one last winter. There are a few Georgian houses, but mostly the streets are lined with 1890s bay-windowed terraced houses, many of which have been extended upwards with loft conversions to provide a fourth bedroom. Popular streets include **Delvino Rd, Linver Rd, Guion Rd, Crondace Rd, Felden St**. There are more substantial houses of a different architectural style of 5/6 bedrooms in **Whittingstall Rd, St Maur Rd, Winchendon Rd, Lillyville Rd, Clonmel Rd**. In this latter area many of the houses have been converted into 1/2-bed flats or 2/3-bed maisonettes, but the trend now is to convert them back into family homes. Prices over half a million are routine for these 4/5-bed houses. **Mustow Place**, homes in attractive mews style, has been squeezed in between the railway and **Munster Rd**. Another new mews, Claridge Court, has 10 town-houses and two flats. And 35 homes have appeared on the Courtaulds site, also in **Munster Rd**: the Coda Centre.

On the fringes of Parson's Green are two small neighbourhoods. To the E is Eel Brook Common with large late-19th-century terraced houses overlooking a pretty park with tennis courts: **Musgrave Crescent** and **Favart Rd** being particularly popular. Five new 2- and 3-bed houses are being squeezed in on a corner site, priced from £365-415,000 secure parking is a big plus. To the W, **Fulham Park Gardens** is a small conservation area of very distinctive substantial red-brick houses of 5/6 bedrooms and considerable character. The tube line from Parson's Green into town is one of most crowded on the network, according to London Transport.

Fulham Broadway

This old but now submerged village was known as Walham Green until London Transport renamed the station in 1948. Conservation areas include **Walham Grove**, which is a street of 1840s semi-detached villas, and **Barclay Rd**, mid-Victorian terraced houses. The area has been subject to a major redevelopment plan – the Fulham Centre Plan – for many years, but progress has been limited to the paving of part of the shopping area to form 'Fulham Piazza', intended to be a mini Covent Garden. Big plans for the **Broadway** were turned down by the council in the winter – the fifth plan to founder in the last 10 years. The latest scheme includes a health club and a 12-screen cinema. Homes exist in the gaps between roads and shops: there are some new town-houses in **Harwood Terrace**. Pleasantly named **Farm Lane** curves round behind the big Samuel Lewis Trust housing estate N of the **Broadway**. **North End Rd** is scene of a thriving street market.

Central Fulham

Extending N from **Bishop's Rd**, bounded by the river to the W (across **Fulham Palace Rd**), **North End Rd** to the E and up towards Charing Cross Hospital to the N are many streets of similar 3/4-bedroom terraced houses, all built between 1890 and 1910. Many of these have been converted into flats and there are several pockets of pretty roads (**Marville St, Brookville St, Rosaville St, Parkville St**) with occasional streets of unusual mansion blocks in yellow London brick (**St Olafs Rd, Orbain Rd**). This area is attracting more interest as it offers better value than the southern neighbourhoods of Fulham. Even **Dawes Rd**, once a byword for dowdiness, is cheering up. Shops and restaurants are joining the immemorial dirty-windowed bike shop, the pet shop and the gents' barbers. An attempt to boost the area is the use of the term 'Dawes Village' – though whoever thought that up must have quite an imagination. There are some big, older-style flats, though many of the flats around here are above shops.

A number of interesting streets lead from **Fulham Palace Rd** down towards the river: **Kenyon St, Lisia St, Niton St**. These continue the Bishop's Park neighbourhood but their status is lower. Further N, north of **Crabtree Lane**, the 1911 Crabtree estate is an up-and-coming corner. A mews has been built by Barratt off **Hartismere Rd**.

Sand's End/Riverside

Sandy End, Addison called it, when he stayed here in 1708. The house survives as Sandford Manor, but its surroundings went downhill from then on, attracting a monster gasworks in 1824 and gaining a name for slums and later for dodgy council estates. Meanwhile, the riverside was lined with factories, warehouses and (in 1936) a coal-fired power station. Sand's End became a pretty grim place.

Its revival began when it was declared a Housing Action Area in the '70s. Owner-occupiers dipped tentative toes into the little terraces in the '80s, reasoning that the Peterborough Estate was not that far away. The Chelsea Harbour development and a large Sainsbury's in **Townmead Rd** put the seal on Sand's End's rehabilitation.

Along the S river frontage, on the site of the former Fulham power station, is a new complex of 250 flats all with a river view. They range from 1-bed to 4-bed penthouses, and the name has changed from Sand's Wharf to 'Regent on the River' and 'Sailmakers Court'. A 2-bed flat in the former was £375,000 last winter. Another part is called Ferrymans Quay. A leisure centre (the Harbour Club) has been built in the power station's old turbine rooms with squash, tennis and a swimming pool. Residents get a free minibus ride to the tube at peak hours. Barratt have built two developments off **Harwood Terrace** in the N corner of Sand's End. Chelsea Walk and Chelsea Lodge – named to stress proximity to the borough border – have a total of 20 4-bed houses.

There are small pockets of council housing and a large area of typical Fulham-style late-Victorian terraces not yet completely smartened up: many are still occupied by aboriginal Fulhamites: **Stephendale Rd, Broughton Rd, Lindrop St, Glenrosa St, Byam St**. The exception is a small area of **Wandsworth Bridge Rd**, where **Rosebury Rd, Oakbury Rd, Cranbury Rd, Haslebury Rd** are smaller Peterborough Estate-type houses, many of which have been converted to flats and maisonettes and have 'come up' to make a very attractive corner. They even have an estate agent name: 'the Bury Triangle' (as in 'don't bury me in Fulham'?). You pay £400,000 for a 4-bed house here.

The big news here is the future of the land along **Imperial Rd** down to the river. For a decade British Gas has been trying, on and off, to develop this site, which it inherited from the Imperial Gas Company. Now, St George proposes 1,800 homes, 500 of them for the council, plus other goodies like a 10-acre riverside park and a station on the West London line. Tucked behind the still-standing (but for how long?) gasometer is delightful, restored **Imperial Square**: Victorian cottages. And Sandford Manor is in there somewhere, used as the gasworks manager's house for decades.

Borders

For Barons Court and West Kensington see the Hammersmith chapter. To the E of
Fulham, off **Seagrave Rd**, is 'Brompton Park': flats and houses, complete with pool and
health club. This area is affected by the growth of 'Chelsea Village' – the Stamford Bridge
stadium, where far more than football goes on these days. Locals were embroiled in a
row with the owner last winter over the 900-person raves that went on until 6am.

Transport	Tubes: Parsons Green, Fulham Broadway, Putney Bridge (zone 2, District). From Fulham Broadway: Oxford Circus 30 min (1 change), City 45 min (1 change), Heathrow 45 min (1 change).
Convenient for	A4, M4, Sloane Square and King's Rd shops. Miles from centre: 4.
Schools	Local Authority: Fulham Cross (g), Hurlingham & Chelsea, London Oratory RC (b), St Edmunds RC, St Marks C of E, Lady Margaret C of E.

SALES

Flats	S	1B	2B	3B	4B	5B
Average prices	70–100	90–140	120–270	150–300+	200+	–

Houses	2B	3B	4B	5B	6/7B	8B
Average prices	200+	250–400+	280–500+	300–1M	400+	–

RENTAL

Flats	S	1B	2B	3B	4B	5B
Average prices	600–800	800–1000	1200–1400	1600–1800	2000–2400	–

Houses	2B	3B	4B	5B	6/7B	8B
Average prices	1200–1400	1600–2200	2000–2600	2600–3000	–	–

The properties	Row after row of solid, late-19th-century family houses. Also some Victorian/Edwardian/'30s p/b flats and many, many conversions. After two decades of energetic renovation, many houses boast top-flight interiors. Much new-build and conversions on infill and river sites, including Chelsea Harbour.
The market	Fulham, with its overgeared, school-fee'd families, was hit hard by the last recession. But aided by City money (lots of bankers money here) it was one of the first areas to bounce back to well above '88 prices. Local searches: 2 weeks.

Among those estate agents active in this area are:

- Hamptons
- Douglas & Gordon*
- Winkworth*
- John D Wood
- Friend & Falcke
- Lawsons & Daughters
- Chesterfields
- FPDSavills
- Sebastian Estates
- Foxtons*
- Faron Sutaria & Co Ltd*

further details: see advertisers' index on p633

GOLDERS GREEN

Map ref: p27 (7H)
Postal districts: NW11
Boroughs: Barnet(No
Overall Control)
Council tax: Band D £728
Conservation areas: Check
with town hall
Parking: Free off main roads

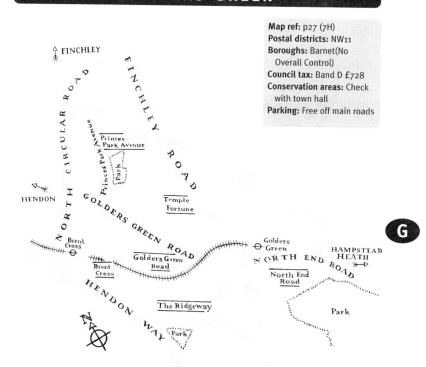

'Tis pleasant, through the loopholes of retreat, to peep at such a world . . .'
Thus 'Sanctuary', the famous 1908 Underground poster, exhorted people to hear the
roar of the 'great Babel' at a safe distance – from a bright new, turn-of-the-century,
stockbroker-Tudory, Arts-and-Craftsery, Golders Green home. The tube had bored its
way through from beneath Hampstead Heath three years earlier, to virgin farmland.
Cowper's words, and the allure of the new homes, worked: today, if no longer quite
so tranquil a sanctuary, this remains one of NW London's best-known suburbs and a
major rallying-point for Northern line commuters. Anonymous it is not: by and large
people live here because they've chosen to live here. They are in Golders Green – not
just some convenient corner of North London.

The bustling **Golders Green Rd**, which runs through the centre from the tube up to
the **North Circular Rd** and Hendon, boasts some of North London's best shops. Today
these are staying open later, and a bit of a café society is developing. People swear by
Carmelli's Bakery, get fit at the new gym, head for Blooms, an off-shoot of the famous
East End restaurant. For this is home for many of London's Jews; it is awash with
delicatessens, kosher bakeries and take-aways. At festival times you'll see people in
their holiday clothes strolling the streets, and during Chanukah (December's festival
of lights) the tube station houses a huge candelabra which is lit every evening. There
are also Asian and Far Eastern communities (though recent influxes from Hong Kong,
Singapore and Russia have lessened perceptibly due to the problems of the eastern
economies). These too are reflected in the area's shops and restaurants.

One of the big talking-points in Golders Green is still – after several years' heated argument – the issue of the proposed North London 'eruv'. The eruv is an area within which Sabbath laws would be relaxed for Orthodox Jews. The largely notional boundary follows existing features, but wires strung between poles would bridge 'gateways'. Planning approval was finally granted for these last October, and the eruv is likely to become a reality this year. Homes within the proposed area are naturally attracting much interest among Orthodox families; see also the Hendon and Hampstead Garden Suburb chapters.

Unlike other areas which have merged into an amorphous suburban sprawl, Golders Green's boundaries are well-defined. Its limits are the **Finchley Rd** to the E, the **North Circular Rd** to the N, the **Hendon Way** to the W as far as **The Vale**, and S to the NW11 border, which runs along **Dunstan Rd, Hodford Rd** and **Golders Hill Park**. Property-wise, Golders Green is, still, primarily an area of family houses: 3/4/5-bed homes which are large if not grand, and speak of comfortable, semi-detached family life. These are Edwardian villas, the area having been developed too late for the usual tide of Victorian terraces – though there are some patches of '20s and '30s ones. There are also many purpose-bullt blocks (along **Golders Green** and **Finchley Rds** and in the area around **Woodlands**) and the '80s saw a lot of conversions around Temple Fortune. Here, too, is a fair amount of rented accommodation, so there are lots of young single people: Golders Green is very convenient for several of the London University colleges.

Golders Green is blessed with churches of every denomination, and synagogues, official and unofficial, of every shade of orthodoxy. Estate agents know the synagogues in detail, since purchasers will often only consider properties in roads near to a particular one. There's plenty of open space too, if you'd rather commune with the Almighty in less formal surroundings; and the Hampstead Heath extension is nearby.

If godliness is its first name, convenience in the form of transport is its second. The Northern line provides great links to West End and City; direct to Tottenham Court Rd, Leicester Square and Bank. Buses are very good, too.

The Ridgeway

Some of the best houses in Golders Green are found in the area to the W of the **Golders Green Rd**, off **The Ridgeway**. In roads such as **Ridge Hill, Gresham Gardens, Armitage Rd, Basing Hill, Hodford Rd** and **Dunstan Rd** you'll find 4- and 5-bedroom houses, detached and semi-detached, with large gardens. Little Basing Hill Park, the nearby tube station, cinema and shops are all attractions, though parking can be a problem in **Rodborough Rd** and **Helenslea Avenue**. Jewish residents have often chosen to live here because of the proximity to synagogues in **Dunstan Rd** and **The Riding**. The busy **Hendon Way** runs past the bottom of **Wessex Gardens** and **Ridge Hill**, so prices may be lower at that end. Cheaper, too, S towards Cricklewood.

Brent Cross

Brent Cross does not really constitute a neighbourhood by itself, though it houses the famous shopping centre and has a tube station (the two aren't as near to each other as you might think). Smaller, 3-bed terraces can be found for £160–170,000; but **Highfield Avenue**, with the tube station, is one of the nicest roads in Golders Green and **Highfield Gardens** is where you'll find one of Golders Green's most popular purpose-built blocks, Windsor Court. In **Hamilton Rd** prices may be more modest since the street runs parallel to the **Hendon Way**; houses on the **Sandringham Rd** side won't suffer from noise as much as those right by the main road, but will still be relatively inexpensive for the area. Also look out among the 3-bed terraced houses and semis in **Woodville Rd** and **Elmcroft Crescent** for properties at the lower end of the price scale.

Golders Green Rd

This runs northwards like a main artery through the area from the station and the Hippodrome – first a music hall, then a theatre, now a BBC studio. Shopping, much of it seven days a week, causes parking problems; triple-parking in Golders Green is legendary. Busy residents can buy a suit on Sunday and toiletries until midnight every day, but the local shopping centre has suffered from the competition from Brent Cross. Heading towards Hendon, the flats above the shops give way to large family houses around **Ravenscroft Avenue**; some towards the **North Circular** are run-down.

Golders Green isn't usually noted for exceptionally pretty houses, but there are some surprises in **Brookside Rd**. You'll find conversions and family houses in streets off the **Golders Green Rd**, **Gainsborough** and **Powis Gardens** to the left and **Beechcroft** and **Elmcroft Avenues** to the right, where there are also a couple of blocks of flats and small hotels. There are larger purpose-built blocks along the main road – Gloucester Court and Eagle Lodge, for example. The 1930s block in **Golders Green Rd**, Riverside Drive, holds its value well. A 3-bed flat there sold recently for £320,000.

Princes Park Avenue

As with the streets around **The Ridgeway**, there are some very large houses to be found in the vicinity of Princes Park, to the N of **Brookside Rd** between the **Finchley** and **Golders Green Rds**. Look for them in the **Princes Park Avenue/Leeside Crescent/Bridge Lane** triangle. Princes Park in the centre makes houses here particularly desirable; on Saturday afternoons the little park is full of children. Again, agents mention the synagogue factor; Jewish people who live here have often chosen the neighbourhood specifically. Coveted bungalows, some with extra rooms in the roof, are to be found in **Decoy Avenue** across **Bridge Lane**. Popular purpose-built blocks in the neighbourhood include Dolphin Court in **Woodlands** and the luxurious Riverside Drive on the **Golders Green Rd**. Not as convenient as the Ridgeway area, though buses to Golders Green are numerous and frequent on the main road.

Temple Fortune

This area brackets the **Finchley Rd** northwards from **Hoop Lane/Wentworth Rd** up to Henly's Corner, the junction with the **North Circular**. The neighbourhood takes its name from the **Temple Fortune Parade** of shops (among them the police station) which is slightly less frantic than the chic **Golders Green Rd**. There's also a tennis club for sporty types, and a major Marks & Spencer food hall. Roads between **Hoop Lane** and **Temple**

Fortune Lane have small houses and some conversions, cheaper even though they are nearer the prestigious Hampstead Garden Suburb because they back onto a cemetery. Further up on that side of the **Finchley Rd** you find purpose-built blocks like Belmont Court. Roads on the other (W) side of the **Finchley Rd** – **Templars Avenue**, **St Johns Rd**, **Portsdown Avenue**, **St George's Rd** and further up, also on the left, **Hallswelle Rd** and **Monkville Avenue** – have smaller family houses and some conversions. To the S, homes in **Corringham**, **Middleton** and **Rotherwick Rds** can fetch £500,000.

North End Rd

The neighbourhood to the S of the tube station, nestling in the angle between **North End Rd** and the **Finchley Rd**, sports Golders Hill Park (look out for the flamingos and wallabies in the zoo). Enviable roads like **West Heath Avenue** and **The Park** triangle have lovely views of the park, which merges into West Heath; half-million pound homes here. Flat conversions and blocks are gathered along **North End Rd** itself.

G

Transport	Tubes: Golders Green, Brent Cross (zone 3, Northern). From Golders Green: Oxford Circus 20 min (1 change), City 30 min, Heathrow 1 hr 25 min (1 change).
Convenient for	Brent Cross shopping centre, Hampstead Heath, North Circular Rd. Miles from centre: 6.
Schools	Barnet Education Authority: Hendon School, Whitefield School.

SALES

Flats	S	1B	2B	3B	4B	5B
Average prices	60–80	70–100	100–200+	120–250+	175+	—
Houses	2B	3B	4B	5B	6/7B	8B
Average prices	130–160	140–225	200–500	250–600	350–700	350–700+

RENTAL

Flats	S	1B	2B	3B	4B	5B
Average prices	430–650	650–1000	780–1700	1000–2000	1500–2300	2000–3250
Houses	2B	3B	4B	5B	6/7B	8B
Average prices	850–1300	1000–1700	1300–2600	1700–4300	2000–8000	4000–15,000

The properties	Mock-Tudor suburban homes, large and comfortable, mix with prosperous blocks of flats and some conversions. Less pricey suburbia towards Hendon Way and Brent Cross.
The market	Primarily family; long-established community (largely Jewish; also Japanese). Good transport links and solid, peaceful family homes ensure its position. These now supplemented by some pricey luxury flats schemes. Local searches: 2–3 working days.

Among those estate agents active in this area are:
- Winkworth *
- Ellis & Co
- Alexander Ross
- Glentree Estates
- Kinleight Folkard & Hayward
- Kingsleys

further details: see advertisers' index on p633

GREENWICH AND BLACKHEATH

Map ref: p80 (7E)
Postal districts: SE10, SE3
Boroughs: Greenwich (Lab),
    Lewisham (Lab)
Council tax: Band D
    Greenwich £883,
    Lewisham £683
Conservation areas: Several,
    check with town hall
Parking: Residents/meters

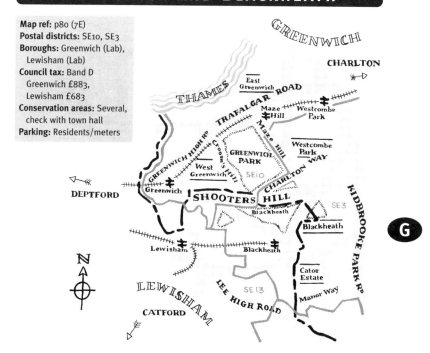

Greenwich is gaining new notoriety as the home of the biggest tent in Europe: The Dome. In truth the sorry structure is way out on a literal limb, the North Greenwich Pensinsula. You can forgive people who live in SE10 and SE3 their ignorance of this neighbourhood: it's long been an industrial wasteland, and the only time anyone went near it was to dive under it via the Blackwall Tunnel. Now the 200-plus acres of British Gas land has been cleaned up, and the Millennium has at least jolted London's transport planners into connecting Greenwich to the rest of London.

Riverside Greenwich has long suffered as well as gained from its position. Unrivalled views of the majestic Thames have to be traded against grossly overloaded roads, and rail lines stuck in the 1940s. Greenwich grew up as a royal favourite at a time when monarchs – and everyone else – used the Thames to get places. Now the only river users are tourists. There are no bridges closer than Tower Bridge one way and Dartford the other. The tunnels are notorious choke-points. There is (at the moment) no tube nearer than Surrey Quays. Greenwich is cut off from vibrant Docklands by the river, and from the West End by traffic-ridden Deptford and Peckham.

The solutions are two new rail lines – the Jubilee line tube and the extended Docklands Light Railway (DLR) – both just months away from completion. After a series of opening dates has come and gone, this Guide has given up publishing them: for the latest we can glean, see the London in 1999 chapter. The Jubilee line will be a little frustrating for Greenwich as it will only actually go to North Greenwich, AKA The Dome. The DLR will be a lot more use. Its stations at the Cutty Sark, Greenwich rail station, Deptford Creek and Lewisham will offer fast travel to Canary Wharf and on to the City. Once again, Greenwich will be easy to get to.

G   For now, the most impressive way to approach the area is to drive (or try to) across South London, through the congested, most workaday tide of Victorian expansionism. Suddenly you reach the hills and high heathland where Greenwich and Blackheath speak of an earlier, more gracious time. One must dispose of the history quickly: the whole place reeks of it, and any local will fill you in at length, beginning with Romans, Saxons and marauding Danes, via half the Kings and Queens of England (all the best died at/were born in/rebuilt the country palace beside the Thames) to romantic 18th-century highwaymen. As far as the streetscape goes, however, the period that has stuck is the Georgian/Regency one: glorious examples encouraged some of the better exponents of Victorian building in their wake.

Greenwich, gathered around the royal park by the Thames, has the bustle and air of a seaside, more than riverside, town. Trippers flock to the Cutty Sark, the Maritime Museum, the Observatory. It is a happily mixed area: here the property market can, and does, embrace everything from tiny 2-up, 2-down terraces to a wing of a red-brick, battlemented castle, built by Sir John Vanbrugh for himself in 1719. On the high plateau at the top of Shooter's Hill, Blackheath – at heart a country hamlet – considers itself a cut above. Those with money can choose Georgian restrained elegance or even, tucked away, Marbella-level opulence.

The bad news is the amount of traffic. A council scheme to ring-fence Greenwich centre, the 'lorry screen', was started in 1996. So far the result is that Greenwich is still choked, and the A2 across Blackheath is even busier. Pollution levels are well above official limits. A tortuous public enquiry is under way, but the outcome cannot please both Greenwich *and* Blackheath. Meanwhile, the Millennium will bring yet more tourists . . .

Greenwich divides neatly into two, the boundary being the superb sweep of park from hill to river. East Greenwich still retains a working identity through its riverside industry. Its cottages have been snapped up recently by young professional couples. Westcombe Park, sloping up the hill S of the railway, is grander though still affordable.

West Greenwich is steeped in history and boasts 17th-century masterpieces such as the former Royal Naval College (originally Greenwich Hospital for retired sailors, soon to be Greenwich University), National Maritime Museum and Royal Observatory. It also has street after street of superb 18th-century houses.

Blackheath, over the hill to the S, has long been regarded as a more sought-after area than Greenwich. Native SE Londoners cruelly regard it as a home for snobs; but Blackheathens say it attracts those who love elegance and culture.

Westcombe Park

This is the name for the rectangle of residential streets E of **Maze Hill**, S of the railway and W of the A102 motorway. Around Westcombe Park station is a cluster of tree-lined streets of small terraced family houses which are more reasonably priced than their near neighbours in East Greenwich. **Maze Hill**, with its large Victorian and turn-of-the-century houses, runs along the side of Greenwich Park. Climbing up the slopes away from the river are the larger 3- and 4-bed houses of peaceful **Mycenae Rd** and **Beaconsfield Rd** (Victorian Gothic and '30s, all with large gardens). A 6-bed house in need of work went for £360,000 last autumn – but such are rare. These streets adjoin **Westcombe Park Rd** with its delightful, ornate 2- and 3-storey Victorian mansions. **Vanbrugh Hill** has Victorian houses and flats: a 2-bed may be £125,000. **Westcombe Hill** is a busier road with smaller terraced houses at around £160,000. A truly unique collection of homes can be found in the converted flats of Vanbrugh's Castle.

East Greenwich

North of the railway (and thus in SE10, not Westcombe Park's SE3) and E of the Royal Naval College is East Greenwich. The riverside has some enviable homes: a dozen new houses by Berkeley on **Highbridge Wharf** (from £332,000 – one left as of October) have splendid views, as do the Georgian houses on charming **Ballast Quay**. To the S and N of **Trafalgar Rd** and around Greenwich District Hospital, typical East Greenwich homes – terraced workmen's cottages – quickly reassert themselves. Land to the N of the hospital is largely filled by well-kept, low-rise council homes. But to the S and W 3-bed terraces abound. The little houses lacked inside toilets and bathrooms until the 1980s, but have been converted by waves of young buyers. Today they go for around £140,000, less for 20th-century ex-council. Parking is the bugbear here.

Heading E along **Trafalgar Rd** the picture is largely the same, although there is some low-rise council housing. Most cottages are 2-bedroom, with tiled roofs and signs of recent renovation. Many were formerly rented from the Morden College estate, but owner-occupying young City types are increasingly common.

To the N, working and derelict wharves and factories line the river until the Millennium site. There will be homes here one day, but it is unclear who for and when.

West Greenwich

Heading W, Wren's Royal Hospital, until recently the Royal Naval College, is to become the home of Greenwich University. Past its grandeur, **Romney Rd** leads into the heart of West Greenwich with its generous mix of Georgian and Regency style. **Croom's Hill**, with its huge high-ceilinged Georgian and Victorian houses overlooking the park, is the most enviable address in Greenwich. One beautifully modernized 6-bed Regency home was on the market for £1.8 million last winter. Near the bottom of the hill lies one of the prettiest streets in South London – **Crooms Hill Grove**. Thousands pass by its tiny entrance, not realizing that a beautiful row of 2- and 3-storey terraced homes lies yards from the park's entrance.

Also off **Croom's Hill** and near to Greenwich Theatre lies the late-18th-century crescent of **Gloucester Circus**, with its 2-storey houses and fenced garden to the front. The perfect proportion of the Circus is, however, spoiled by the block of brick-built council flats which stands opposite. Nearby **Burney St** has handsome 1840 terraced houses, complete with wrought-iron balconies. They go for £500,000. **Luton Place** has early Victorian brick-faced semis which command around £380,000.

From the Circus you can cross over **Royal Hill** and **Circus St** to the **Brand St** area, where the grander mansions give way to 3-storey Victorian terraces. The Royal Hill council estate stands at the base of **Royal Hill**, but is medium-rise and not too intrusive. Travel up the hill and pass the marvellous **Hamilton Terrace**, 3-storey with garden flats. Six 1930s semis near the top of the hill make a sudden appearance. Going back down **Royal Hill** you arrive in **Greenwich South St**, a busy thoroughfare but with some lovely late-Georgian, early Victorian houses and a charming terrace of almshouses. Between **South St** and **Greenwich High Rd** is the Ashburnham Triangle conservation area: roads lined with 2/3-storey flat-fronted, early Victorian homes.

Some houses in this area can be quite small, but no-one seems to mind if the style is right. Style comes in all shapes and sizes. Heading W towards Deptford, the listed former West Greenwich Boys' School has undergone the loft treatment by Sapcote. More typical are the handsome 3-bed early Victorian semis of **Egerton Drive**: one was on the market last winter for £295,000.

To be at the heart of traditional, naval, Greenwich, what could beat a house in **King William Walk**, an 1830 terrace with the Cutty Sark's masts looming at the end of the street? Some are in less than pristine condition. A bay-fronted 3-bed house here went for £230,000 early in 1998; another, split into flats, was up for auction last winter.

Blackheath

Most of Blackheath is in the borough of Lewisham, not Greenwich. The busy A2, **Shooters Hill**, forms the boundary. It also carries the traffic from Central London to Dover, as it has done for two millennia. Blackheath grew up in Georgian times as a smart suburb and the heart of the neighbourhood so remains. Elegant terraces line the wind-blown heath, and the Village is a good facsimile of a rural one, only the shops are smarter. The wider area is defined to the N by the heath; by **Lewisham Rd** in the W; by **Lee High Rd** to the S; and by an upwardly curving arc which excludes the Ferrier council estate before joining with **Kidbrooke Park Rd** in the E.

The best way to approach Blackheath must be from the W up the steep **Blackheath Hill**. Taking a right turn into **Dartmouth Hill**, you are rewarded with a breathtaking view of the heath and the Village. In **Dartmouth Row**, many of the 18th-century houses are now smart flats: a 2-bed one cost £115,000 recently, while another in Dartmouth House itself is on the market at £169,000. Crossing the heath into **Hare and Billet Rd**, you first pass a small '60s development of box-shaped houses with flat roofs, and then some typical terraced 2- and 3-storey houses in a dip in the ground which appear from a distance to stand just a few feet tall. **Aberdeen Terrace** has grand mid-Victorian houses, one, a former student residence, just carved into four flats and a coach house, plus nine more homes in its 1960s extension. Other splendidly confident terraces and mansions – in roads like **The Pagoda, Eliot Hill, The Paragon, South Row** – gaze across the heath all the way to the Village and beyond. Many have been split into flats. Tucked behind the Georgiana in **Fulthorpe Rd** is one of the poshest council-built estates in Britain, dating from the 1950s. N of the heath the streets round **Vanbrugh Park** and **St John's Park** are Victorian and blend into Westcombe Park. Prices are lower here than in Blackheath proper and some modern flats add to the choice.

Blackheath Park

Go down **Pond Rd** and into Blackheath's surprise package – the exclusive Blackheath Park or Cator Estate. This incredible array of private housing was first built by a developer called John Cator at the start of the 19th century, and now has every conceivable architectural style. The estate spreads E from **Lee Rd** and S to **Manor Way**. Gates at the five entrances are closed during rush hours, though the lodge keepers have long gone There are Victorian and Edwardian mansions, mock-Tudor 1930s detached houses and a sprinkling of 14 small 1960s Span estates, highly praised by architects: one estate has just been listed. The Span houses seem good value: a smallish 3-bed one can be £175,000. Some smart modern houses have been squeezed in: a 4-bed one was sold for £460,000 a few months back. Many homes have swimming pools. Some are very opulent. In contrast, the SE corner has the ugly Ferriers Estate of brutal GLC public housing.

SW of Blackheath Village, **Lee Terrace** marks the N edge of a district of pleasant streets such as **Belmont Park** and **Dacre Park**, where a 4-storey Georgian house sold for £325,000 late in '98. The W edge of Blackheath, towards Lewisham, has excellent transport links. **Belmont Hill** has a dozen smart flats newly converted from The Cedars, a fine 1860s mansion.

Borders

Along **Lee High Rd**, properties are a jumble of council-built and terraced homes with the quality generally declining as you leave the heath behind. On the steep slopes just to the N there is a fair sprinkling of 1- and 2-bed conversion flats, where incomers are replacing fireplaces ripped out by over-zealous workmen in the '70s. Properties here are cheaper than those with a heath view.

For a cheaper alternative with Victorian charm, try Charlton Village, a mile to the E of Blackheath, or Brockley conservation area to the W (see Lewisham). Beware of estate agents selling Kidbrooke (or indeed places halfway to Dover) as Blackheath. The only thing they have in common is the SE3 postal address. Woolwich to the E is cheaper, but too industrial for most people's liking. However, this corner, and Plumstead and the 'new town' of Thamesmead beyond, offer some relative bargains. Hundreds of homes at Thamesmead are now under control of a private company, having been sold off after the demise of the GLC. New waterside homes at affordable prices get more numerous the closer you get to Thamesmead.

Transport	Trains: Greenwich to London Bridge 15 min, Charing Cross 20 min; Blackheath to London Bridge 12 min. DLR extension from Cutty Sark and Greenwich station will link to Docklands and City; Jubilee line will link North Greenwich to West End. See also map.
Convenient for	Docklands, A2 to Dover/Channel Tunnel, Millennium Dome. Miles from centre: 5.5.
Schools	Local Authority: St Ursulas' Convent RC (g), The John Roan School, Blackheath Bluecoat C of E, St Joseph's Academy RC (b), St Theresa's RC (g). Private: Blackheath High School (g), Thomas Tallis.

SALES

Flats	S	1B	2B	3B	4B	5B
Average prices	40–60	65–130	80–180+	100–400	—	—
Houses	2B	3B	4B	5B	6/7B	8B
Average prices	100–200	140–400	250–500	275–500+	600–1.6M	1M+

RENTAL

Flats	S	1B	2B	3B	4B	5B
Average prices	500–700	550–1000	800–1700	1000–2000	—	—
Houses	2B	3B	4B	5B	6/7B	8B
Average prices	800–1000	1000–2500	1300–2500+	1500–2500+	2000+	—

The properties Superb Georgian in Greenwich and Blackheath, mid-Victorian in Blackheath Park (prices to £1 million-plus here) and Westcombe Park, plus more ordinary period and modern homes in East Greenwich and other fringe areas.

The market Prices vary dramatically from East Greenwich (still cheap) to heath views and period homes in top roads, eg Croom's Hill. These are the nearest established residential areas to Docklands and will be linked by tube from the Greenwich Peninsula and the DLR extension. Local searches: 2 weeks.

Among those estate agents active in this area are:
- Halifax
- John Payne
- Winkworth *
- Woolwich Property
- Humphreys Skitt & Co
- GA Property Services
- Harrison Ingram
- Comber & Co

* further details: see advertisers' index on p633

G

HACKNEY

Map ref: p47 (5H)
Postal districts: E5, E8, E9
Boroughs: Hackney (Hung Council)
Council tax: Band D £789
Conservation areas: Include Victoria
Park, Albion Square, Sutton Place,
Clapton Square
Parking: Pay and display, residents',
some meters

Renewed confidence in Hackney as a place to live is shown by the brisk rise in home prices in 1998 and by the success the council is having in reviving council estates. There may even be a hint of hope in the long wait for a tube line – Hackney has not a single underground station.

The Chelsea Hackney tube is now certainly shelved (yet again – a re-run of the '70s and '80s). But a northward extension of the East London line to Dalston seems more possible. The new line would transform the accessibility of the W side of the area, bringing a direct link with Docklands and the City. Stations would be at Bishopsgate, Hoxton (Geffrye St), Haggerston (Stonebridge Park) and Dalston Junction. There are hopes of a further extension W to Highbury Corner. London Transport has been given the go-ahead to plan the line, but all still depends on money and that will (it now seems) depends on the new London Mayor and Assembly. 2002 looks like an optimistic opening date.

The borough of Hackney takes in Clapton, Homerton, Dalston, Stoke Newington and half a dozen other former hamlets. (See Stoke Newington chapter.) Hackney abuts on the City to the S, and ends in the E with the Hackney marshes in the broad Lea Valley.

Like most of North London, all was sylvan peace here once, interspersed with country seats and pleasure gardens. The late-Georgian era saw houses spread along the main roads – look above the shops and you'll see them still. Hackney became smart for a while, as its few surviving Georgian squares show. Then came the railways and the

Victorian housing boom. The underground missed Hackney, but the many thousands of City clerks and respectable working men who rented the terraced homes found their way to work by foot, by horse, bus or train into Liverpool St, and they formed the heart of Hackney. Outright slums and filthy factories intruded into the SE corner, around Hackney Wick, but the bulk of the place was a commuter suburb for the great army of London's ordinary people. And so it remains today.

Hackney has moved on from the days when rich and poor where polarized. Hackney today equals affordable homes for thousands of London's less well-paid young couples and families. Conflict between incoming owner-occupiers and council-flat-dwelling locals is yesterday's issue. Most newcomers find the place a happy mixture of inner-city scruffiness and enlivening bustle. That is because, perhaps, the typical incomer is a computer programmer, a social worker, a secretary or a teacher rather than a stockbroker, a millennial Blairite rather than yesterday's yuppy. And the council estates are being redeemed by enlightened town hall activity – those that have not been dynamited and replaced by better-planned homes.

The newcomers are rediscovering Hackney's proximity to the City and discovering some of the community spirit in a new form. They find that Hackney has surprisingly usable communications (buses and trains, not tubes – yet) and that local amenities are improving, especially on the cultural side.

On **Mare St** plans for a new library and arts centre have got the go-ahead but the Hackney Empire music hall has just missed out on a lottery grant (it will be re-applying). The new Technology and Learning Centre will house a library, museum and shops, and is due for completion in spring 2000. Opposite the town hall, the Ocean Music Venue is being built. Funded partly by the lottery and Hackney Council, it will house a large auditorium, training and rehearsal rooms, bars and cafés. It is due to open April 2000.

Hackney's young population, and cheap warehouse/living space, lends credence to the borough's claim to be home to the biggest concentration of working artists in Europe. They concentrate in the S of the area, in Hoxton and the City fringes (see City chapter). Agents in Hackney routinely list live/work units as well as flats and houses.

Hackney has a high percentage of parkland for inner London. Some areas stand out as attractive for home-buyers, usually because they are close to these parks but primarily because they have some surviving 19th-century homes. Properties around London Fields and Victoria Park are popular and, among the regulation terraces, some grander Victoriana and even some Georgian corners survive. The De Beauvoir area, W of the busy **Kingsland Rd**, carries a premium as it is near the border with fashionable Islington (see chapter) and has an N1 postal address.

Victoria Park, a conservation area, is divided between Hackney and the neighbouring borough of Tower Hamlets. The wide park forms part of Hackney's boundary while the River Lea provides the border with Waltham Forest to the E. Hackney Marshes is marshland no longer, but is another large area of welcoming greenery – its flat expanse makes for excellent football pitches. Look in this direction for cheaper homes. The Marshes are in the SE part of Clapton; further N is picturesque Springfield Park, a much more attractive hilly area with Springfield Marina and City Orient Rowing Club on the River Lea. The **Ridley Rd** market area of Dalston, leading to busy **Kingsland High St**, is less enticing, but does have the wonderful 24hr bagel shop - and a new multi-screen cinema is opening in spring 2000.

Hackney's house prices shot up by 17 per cent in 1998, according to Land Registry figures. This broad average hides wide local variations, though, and prices in some corners are static, hardly up on 1988. Ex-council homes offer a lot of space for a little money. Some estates remain unhappy places, but others have been transformed and are pleasant communities. The whole area offers prices to bring a smile to the faces of those frustrated by looking at parts further west.

Hackney Central

The central spine of Hackney is the N-S road variously named **Mare St** and **Lower Clapton Rd**. Here are the town hall, the famous Russian baths, now refurbished as the King's Hall Leisure Centre, and Hackney Central station. Hackney Downs station, with trains to **Liverpool St**, is close by. Off **Lower Clapton Rd** is **Clapton Square**, a conservation area and one of several garden squares in Hackney. It is surrounded by Georgian listed terraced houses, some 5-storeys. The square leads on to **Clarence Place** and **Clapton Passage**, which both have a charming villagy feel and desirable period homes, large impressive 3-storey and ivy-clad terraced Georgian houses graced with entrance steps, railings and tiny wrought-iron balconies. This whole network of streets forms a green oasis in the midst of Hackney. Prices here should be around £125,000 for a 2-bed cottage or the mid-'90s for a 2-bed flat. One of the **Clapton Square** houses changed hands late last year for £355,000.

On **Lower Clapton Rd**, an Art Deco factory has become The Strand Building: 1- and 2-bed flats starting at £69,000. West of the Duke of Clarence pub, at the junction with **Clarence Rd**, is the Pembury council estate which includes **Hindrey Rd**, **Shellness Rd**, **Bodney Rd**, **Pembury Rd**, **Dalston Lane** and **Downs Park Rd**. Ugly tower blocks which were once part of this estate have now been demolished.

From the southern edge of the estate **Amhurst Rd**, a busy bus route, leads back SE to the **Mare St** shopping centre. The Aspland council estate lies along part of **Amhurst Rd**. On the junction of **Dalston Lane** and **Amhurst Rd** is the 1998 conversion of an Edwardian college, now 57 flats. Prices were from £60,000 for a 1-bed, to £127,000 for a 2-bed with vaulted glass roof and £220,000 for a 4-bed galleried apartment.

To the S of the railway serving Hackney Central, **Graham Rd**, another busy main road, provides good business for estate agents with numerous decent 3-storey terraced houses, some with basements, on both sides. A good number have been converted into flats. On the E side of **Lower Clapton Rd**, opposite **Clapton Passage**, more 2- and 3-storey Victoriana can be found in **Powerscroft Rd** and **Glenarm Rd**, near Hackney police station.

Another street worth a second glance in central Hackney is **Sutton Place**, backing onto the grounds of St John's Church, S of **Lower Clapton Rd**. Sutton House in **Homerton High St** here is the oldest brick-built house in East London. Owned by the National Trust, it can be used for receptions, concerts . . . even weddings. This is another conservation area, with big listed Georgian terraced houses with steps, railings and basements. Several were bought from 1990 by intrepid DIY converters and turned into superb homes. One 5-bed house, still requiring a lot of work, was £320,000 in November. The land behind these houses, once the old Metal Box factory, has been developed as **Sutton Square**, an up-market development built around central gardens, with a courtyard and illuminated fountains. Other attractive streets S of **Sutton Place** include **Mehetabel Rd** and **Isabella Rd**. The former has well-preserved flat-fronted cottages, while the houses in the latter are grander in scale.

Other changes in this busy area include a new Tesco superstore on previously derelict land in **Morning Lane**, close to **Mare Street** and S of **Sutton Place**; and a school conversion in **Chelmer Rd**, next to Homerton Hospital: 30 flats will be available when the development comes onto the market this spring. **Dalston Lane** saw another of the ubiquitous inner London school conversions in 1998, with loft-style flats in 'Eastside Academy' which were priced at launch from £77,000.

Victoria Park

The park, laid out in 1845 conveniently in time for the Chartist rallies of 1848, is one of London's largest. It gives its name to a neighbourhood containing some of the biggest and most expensive houses in Hackney. Much of the housing is on land owned by the

Crown Estate, so residents can claim to have Crown leases just like their grander counterparts in Regent's Park. There are homes of all kinds, both Victorian and modern. These houses have a tendency to change hands privately. Purpose-built flats in roads such as **Pennethorne Close**, near the park, offer good value. Conversions of the big old houses provide flats with far more space than in higher-priced areas, and quite a number have lovely views of the park and its several lakes. Another green space, Well Street Common, adjoins the park and provides open views for the Victorian and 1930s mock-Tudor houses of **Meynell Rd** and **Meynell Crescent**. Some of the priciest homes in Hackney are here: a 5-bed house overlooking the Common goes for £275–320,000. In **Victoria Park Rd**, Ideal Homes refurbished six Victorian houses as 6-bed homes rather than flats, and tucked in the 'Sovereign Mews': 2- and 3-bed town-houses and 1-bed flats. The same street has a new pub conversion: 2-bed flats for between £120,000 and £160,000.

On **Cassland Rd**, St George have built 'Victoria Park Crescent', a terrace of flats and a single 3-storey house. **Cassland Crescent** is the real thing, a beautiful Georgian terrace with walled gardens. Some of its early Victorian neighbours are almost as fine. The disadvantage here is lack of communications. Bethnal Green tube is a mile or so to the S and Cambridge Heath and London Fields stations gives access to Liverpool St.

Gore Rd, overlooking the N side of Victoria Park, has some of Hackney's most desirable properties. Imposing 3- and 4-storey terraced houses with steps to their front doors present a dignified front to the large and pleasant park. **Gore Rd** leads W into **Victoria Park Rd** and, at the junction with **Mare St**, boasts a new development in **Earlston Grove** and **Northam St**. Flats and houses here are blessed with private garages – an important plus in such a busy area. A little to the N, the conservation area of **Fremont St** and **Warneford St** provides fine 2- and 3-storey mid-19th-century terraced houses with basements. By contrast, nearby **Sharon Gardens** (said to have been built by Jewish immigrants) offers some of the few 1930s semis in the area. **Beck Rd** is also popular. In nearby **King Edward Rd** is a new development of live/work units in a converted 1930s industrial building: a galleried loft was £90,000 in December.

London Fields

The 26 acres of London Fields, successively sheep pasture and cricket pitch, are the centre of a neighbourhood W of **Mare St** and N of the canal which is beginning to shadow De Beauvoir to the W in popularity. Here are streets of solid, readily modernized houses that are popular with young couples. Impressive 4-storey Victorian terraced houses, some converted into flats, are found in **Lansdowne Drive**, W of London Fields. On the corner of **Lansdowne Drive** and **Gayhurst Rd** is a converted pub, now 1/3-bed flats. A 2-bed sold not long ago for £100,000. **Mapledene Rd** and **Lavender Grove** have smaller but attractive homes.

To the N, **Navarino Grove** has neat flat-fronted terraced cottages. The Old Vicarage, a conversion of a Victorian Gothic parsonage beside the Fields, has added lavish flats with period features.

The E side of London Fields is less attractive with industrial units and London Fields rail station. Even here, new homes are being built: 2-bed flats from £95,000 will be available this June. **Middleton Rd**, **Albion Drive** and **Shrubland Rd** border the Fields council estate. The council-built homes are in a good location and they are popular buys. These roads, too, have pleasant 2/3-storey flat-fronted Victorian houses, some with 120-ft gardens. To the W, **Albion Square** is one of the finest garden squares in Hackney. Early 19th-century semi-detached houses with pretty gardens lie away from the main traffic route: expect to pay £400,000. To the N of London Fields two new 3-bed houses in **St Phillip's Rd** are £185,000. In the area generally are many lofts and live/work units which range from £75–250,000.

Clapton

Clapton is an area to the N and E of Hackney on ground rising up from the Lea Valley. One of the cheapest parts of the borough in which to buy a home, and undergoing gradual gentrification, it holds more streets of Victorian and Edwardian housing, modern council estates and, in the far N of the area, attractive Springfield Park. Agents report a price divide between Lower and Upper Clapton, which is to the N. The latter is still more expensive, but the former saw a large jump in prices during 1998. A 3-bed terraced house typically costs £125,000 in Lower Clapton, £40,000 more in Upper Clapton.

Near the junction of **Lea Bridge Rd** and **Lower Clapton Rd**, two of the area's busiest thoroughfares, are **Thistlewaite Rd**, **Thornby Rd**, **Newick Rd** and **Fletching Rd**: a cache of large 2- and 3-storey Victorian terraced houses in tree-lined streets. Among other corners worth noting is attractive **Ashenden Rd** in the SE of the district. This street includes Tower Mews, a warehouse conversion of flats that have kept some of the original features. Parking space is provided in a tidy courtyard.

Homes in the hilly Springfield Park area of Upper Clapton, E of the Clapton Common conservation area, have the added attraction of the nearby River Lea and the open spaces of the Walthamstow Marshes. North of the park is **Watermint Quay**, on the river and reached via **Craven Walk**. This is a facing pair of 1980s terraces set end-on to the river towpath, with 77 houses and 18 flats at the river end. The houses have 33-ft basements running the full length of the house, which can be used as play-areas, storage or cellarage. Four-bed houses sell for around £140,000 – about the same as in 1990. Just to the S, rows of 2-storey Victorian terraced houses in **Spring Hill** lead down directly to the Lea with its Springfield Marina and City Orient Rowing Club. Similar homes are in **Lingwood Rd** and **Overlea Rd**. In **Theydon Rd**, a 1930s factory is now 'The deHavilland Building' with loft apartments at around £90,000.

Overlooking Clapton Common is **Clapton Terrace**, where large Georgian terraced houses with basements and gardens give respite from the prevailing 19th-century rows. By contrast, some of Clapton's cheaper (and smaller) properties are found to the S beside Hackney Marshes which also border the River Lea. **Riverside Walk**, a recent development by Wimpey in **Mount Pleasant Hill**, has 1- and 2-bed flats. Close by is the massive Kingsmead council estate, encircled by **Kingsmead Way**. This has seen a remarkable turn-round, with tenants now in charge of the estate, the worst system-built homes razed and replaced and crime plummeting. The final phase will see 277 homes built on the sites of four unloved and now demolished tower blocks. Seventy-four homes will be for open-market sale and 176 for low-cost/shared ownership.

The big builders have found sites in Hackney Wick for low-priced schemes. The trouble is, they have stayed low-priced. **Victoria Mews**, off **Swinnerton St**, is a 1980s scheme with 1- and 2-bed flats and 3- and 4-bed houses. A riverside factory site off **Berkshire Rd** has been redeveloped as **Leabank Square**: flats and houses. Its developer went bankrupt in 1989 due to over-exposure to Docklands, and the estate has become rather run-down with depressed prices.

Dalston

Dalston is N of the London Fields neighbourhood, W of Hackney central and on the borders with Stoke Newington and Islington. Despite its position, it is as yet the least promising Hackney neighbourhood. Stoke Newington police station is in **Kingsland Rd**. **Ridley Rd** market, where anything and everything can be bought, is one of Hackney's best-known landmarks. The bustling market leads to more shops in busy **Kingsland High St** and the surrounding streets reflect the area's cosmopolitan image. Dalston Kingsland rail station is also in **Kingsland High St**. Dalston Cross shopping centre, off **Dalston Lane** and **Kingsland Rd**, opened in 1989. A 14-screen cinema and shops are due to open in 2000 at the junction of **Kingsland High St** and **Dalston Lane**, next to the site for the proposed tube station (see introduction).

Downs Park Rd, Cecilia Rd, Ferncliff Rd and **Sandringham Rd** are part of the Mountford council estate. Large 3- and 4-storey Victorian terraced houses with steps can be found in sought-after **Sandringham Rd** and **Montague Rd**. **Colvestone Crescent**, another of the streets around St Mark's Church, has more massive 4-storey Victorian houses. Chester Gate, a new development off **Ridley Rd**, provides some relief. Impressive 2- and 3-bed 3-storey houses are sited away from through traffic. Off **Wilton Way**, new homes have been built in **Walkers Court**. Independent Place is a work-homes development off **Shacklewell Lane** and opposite is **Gateway Mews** – a complex of flats in a converted warehouse and listed buildings. In nearby **Dunn St** three new 'loft-style' flats were on the market last winter from £75,000.

Transport	Trains: Hackney Central, Hackney Wick, Homerton (N London line/Silverlink); London Fields, Hackney Downs (Liverpool St).

Convenient for	Victoria Park, the City, Docklands, Blackwall Tunnel. Miles from centre: 4.

Schools	Local Authority: Cardinal Pole School, Homerton House School, Hackney Free & Parochial School.

H

SALES

Flats	S	1B	2B	3B	4B	5B
Average prices	30–45	40–80	55–120	70–140	100–130+	–
Houses	2B	3B	4B	5B	6/7B	8B
Average prices	80–160	95–220	145–300+	170–350+	→	–

RENTAL

Flats	S	1B	2B	3B	4B	5B
Average prices	370–430	500–690+	650–860	800–1150	1000–1500	–
Houses	2B	3B	4B	5B	6/7B	8B
Average prices	650–860	800–1100	900–1300	1000–1500	–	–

The properties	Many Victorian houses, some early and desirable, a few Georgian. De Beauvoir and Victoria Park now established residential zones, other parts more mixed with widespread council housing and 'gentrified' pockets.

The market	Owner-occupation rising: people who cannot afford Islington take advantage of Hackney's lower prices. Smart new developments and converted schools/factories among the Victorian rows. Local searches: 2 weeks.

Among those estate agents active in this area are:
- Winkworth *
- Strettons
- Shaw & Co
- Douglas Allen Spiro
- Bunch & Duke
- Castles
- Bennett-Walden
- Foxtons*

further details: see advertisers' index on p633

HAMMERSMITH

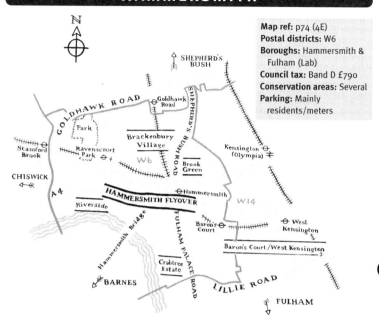

Map ref: p74 (4E)
Postal districts: W6
Boroughs: Hammersmith &
   Fulham (Lab)
Council tax: Band D £790
Conservation areas: Several
Parking: Mainly
   residents/meters

Hammersmith would be a large square on the map if it were not for the curving Thames, which bites off the south-western corner. As it is, the boundaries are the protective arm of the **Goldhawk Rd** to the W and N, the river and **Lillie Rd** to the S, and to the E the borough boundary — reinforced by the much more physical barrier of the railway, which runs N-S. Within this square lies Hammersmith proper (essentially the W6 postal district), Baron's Court and West Kensington – which, with Kensington's name but in Hammersmith's borough, is always good for confusing outsiders.

The most outstanding thing about Hammersmith is how everyday it is. The whole area is average apart from the presence of the prestigious Lyric Theatre, the vast Labbats Apollo and the Riverside Studios, whose stage productions and art-house and European film screenings receive a lot of national media attention. In Hammersmith, the luxury properties (with a few well-known exceptions) are not that luxurious; and the down-market bits are not slums. There are some nice, well-established residential corners, such as Brook Green, Ravenscourt Park and the Brackenbury 'village'. For the rest, by and large, the streets are too narrow, the houses are too tall and the ways through too confined. A built-up borough – but, largely thanks to the river, not that claustrophobic.

Its main asset is its position: in West London, on the way to Heathrow – and close to the BBC's vast White City HQ in next-door Shepherd's Bush. The area attracts media workers: apart from the BBC, there's EMI in Brook Green, Disney in Hammersmith. The direct route to the airport reinforces the area's attractions for such people. It also, of course, means heavy traffic, but public transport is good.

Now, just over its borders, comes the plans for the vast, futuristic White City shopping mall (see Shepherd's Bush chapter), Will this be an asset? Or will it presage the final clogging of routes in and out of Hammersmith? Certainly more shops would be welcome, although at last Hammersmith Broadway – which should be the heart of the area, but which had long been part of a vast, dreary traffic island – has been transformed. The Broadway was for a decade the focus of a classic local government conflict, following a change of power on the council, which it took the Secretary of State to resolve. The final product – £100 million worth of offices, shops, restaurants, bus terminal, community centre – has been much welcomed. The offices are Coca-Cola's European HQ, the tube and bus stations are gleaming and usable, the shops are smart.

The most common homes in the Hammersmith area are small 1- and 2-bedroomed flats; most in demand, overall, are flats with two large rooms. Enclaves of family houses include some rare, riverside Georgian splendour, some unexpected delights in Brook Green, plus the popular terraces of Brackenbury and Ravenscourt. Office developments are dotted over the entire borough: neighbourhoods with the fewest are most in demand. But it is a general (very general) rule that those who want access to Central London will opt for the east side of Hammersmith, while those who focus on the airport opt for the area W of **Fulham Palace/Shepherd's Bush Rds**.

Hammersmith has a low-key cosmopolitan character; all social classes and most races are represented here, with small, well-established Irish, Polish and Afro-Caribbean communities; but there are no high concentrations of individual groups. Hammersmith divides fairly neatly into districts.

Barons Court/West Kensington

H

Fulham Palace Rd is the boundary to the W; **Hammersmith Rd** to the N; **Lillie Rd** to the S; the railway line to the E. The whole district is bisected by the A4 **Talgarth Rd**.

Most properties in this neatly defined square are those tall Victorian houses that convert well to flats – and flat-land it is: it's estimated that they outnumber houses by 10:1. These streets are truly a hotchpotch: on almost every road there's one building that won't please the aesthetically inclined, though council-build not sprawling. The nearest open space is Holland Park; otherwise greenery is in very short supply. With little room for new developments, it's not an area prone to change. Convenience is its watchword; a middle-market, middle-of-the-road, middle-of-everywhere neighbourhood: within a taxi-ride of West End or airport; on both District and Piccadilly lines.

So flats prevail. But floorspace is limited and little 2-bed apartments are the norm: usually one large bedroom and a much smaller one – fine if you only need a spare room; less so for sharing renters (and thus investors). Three-bedroomed flats are rare, but occasionally they can be constructed out of the top two floors since, in these tall, thin houses (pity the Victorian servants), one floor more often than not simply won't accommodate more than one or two rooms. North of **Talgarth Rd/A4**, in streets such as **Gunterstone Rd**, lined with roomier mid/late-19th century houses, the 2-bed flats get more spacious, but 3-bedroomed places are still scarce.

A particularly popular segment of Barons Court/West Kensington is the grid bordered by **Gledstanes Rd**, **North End Rd**, **Barons Court Rd** and **Star Rd**. This corner is close to both Barons Court (District and Piccadilly) and West Kensington tube stations. The Barons Court station area is now a residents' parking zone, which has alleviated problems caused by commuter parking. Prices start around £130,000 (1-bed) and £170,000 (2-bed). Young, as yet childless, couples in their 20s and 30s discovered the Gledstanes grid in a big way a decade ago – along with investors on the lookout for high rent yields, and developers on the lookout for yet more properties to convert . . . Note, as you drive westwards along the **Talgarth Rd** highway past this corner, the splendid, soaring, idiosyncratic windows of a row of High Victorian artists' studios: it's a sad irony that such windows should have inherited such a view.

The most sought-after properties in Barons Court are the red-brick Victorian houses in **Queen's Club Gardens**, just south of the famous tennis club itself. **Queen's**

Club Gardens, a conservation area, has a small central park; its aura of affluence and gentility makes it an oasis in an area not renowned for exclusive residences. **Fitzgeorge** and **Fitzjames Avenues** and **Queen's Club Gardens** contain examples of the few mansion blocks available in this district, built around 1910. Prices in these varies widely to reflect their differing ages and conditions: some still lack central heating and rejoice in original kitchen and bathroom fittings . . . last winter a 1-bed flat 'needing attention' was £169,000; a modernized 2-bed flat was £250,000.

The pastel-coloured 1930s villas on and around **Palliser Rd** are in great demand. The triangle enclosed by **Palliser**, **Barons Court** and **Barton Rds** consists of about three-quarters of an acre of communal greenery. These villas are rarely sold – well, they have something rarer than hens' teeth: their own garages.

There are a lot of council properties – on **North End Rd** itself as well as in the less popular part of this neighbourhood, the roads leading E off **Fulham Palace Rd** such as **Greyhound Rd**. This mixed street has cheaper flats above shops (from about £70,000) as well as conversions (1-bed from c. £97,000). **Greyhound Rd** is close to the big Charing Cross Hospital, with sports facilities including a gym and swimming pool.

Riverside

The thin strip of river bank bounded – and protected – by the roaring traffic of the **Great West Rd**/A4 to the N, **Hammersmith Bridge Rd** to the E and the borough boundary to the W is an eastward continuation of **Chiswick Mall**. The river, here suddenly smaller-looking and more rural than in Central London, runs to the S. In summer, the small patches of grass and trees fill with locals enjoying the rowing on the river. Their wants are supplied by a couple of pubs, among them one of the nicest, oldest riverside pubs in London: The Dove, originally a Georgian coffee-house.

This slice of Hammersmith is the exception that proves the rule: as with next-door **Chiswick Mall**, some of London's rarer surviving Georgian homes are here, strung along **Hammersmith Terrace** (which dates from the 1750s) and **Upper** and **Lower Malls**. The homes on **Hammersmith Terrace** have no road separating them from the river, but the two Malls are a little more public than the corresponding Chiswick stretch. Still, this most affluent and desirable corner of Hammersmith has estate agents reaching for words such as 'ambassadorial'. When the riverside houses do come onto the market (which is hardly ever), expect to pay in the millions. Some modern homes here, too: King Henry's Reach, a 1996 block of 70 flats, yields a wide range of sizes and prices, from c. £135–450,000 and upwards for a penthouse. **Lord Napier Place** is a peaceful enclave of town-houses just off **Upper Mall**. Recent prices included a 3-bed one at £320,000; a 4-bed with riverside garden, £710,000.

North from the riverside and **Great West Rd**/A4, just S of **King St** (Hammersmith's high street, with stores and small shopping mall), is **St Peter's Square**, a conservation area full of unusually large (for Hammersmith), handsome, 5/6-bedroomed stucco-fronted houses. These were built around 1825–30 in sub-Belgravia mode, and the surrounding streets of more modest houses are plainly of the same date. One of these, in **Black Lion Lane**, was £480,000 last winter, and a 2-bed cottage was £340,000.

Brackenbury Village

North of Hammersmith's shopping centre, this neighbourhood is bounded by **Paddenswick Rd**, **Hammersmith Grove**, **Glenthorne Rd** and **Goldhawk Rd**. Over the past 10 years it has moved from newly discovered, through up-and-coming, to firmly established. It still has a delightful village atmosphere: little shops, pretty, unspoilt Victorian street-corner pubs with hanging baskets, pavement seating or gardens. Buyers who moved in from Notting Hill and Kensington in search of affordable family homes have spent money on their houses and tidied the neighbourhood up. To serve them, smart restaurants have joined (sometimes replaced) the pubs. There is very little through traffic, but a 24hr parking problem in these streets – commuters by day, residents by night – is being solved by the growing residential parking zones. Generally the homes are small 2- and 3-bed early Victorian terraced cottages (from c. £220,000) and small villas, especially on the W side of the area (for example **Carthew Rd**, **Cardross St** and **Dalling Rd**), while some larger houses can be found towards the E in the streets leading to **Hammersmith Grove**. In the NW, **Wingate Rd**, **Wellesley Avenue** and **Dorville Crescent** fringe the Ravenscourt Park conservation area and are seen by their residents as being part of Ravenscourt Park. These very pretty streets contain early Victorian terraced houses or villas with many a desirable feature. And buyers, especially young couples, are still willing to pay for an address. Two-bedroom cottage houses can reach £300,000 (they were £165–175,000 a decade ago) – and larger houses and those in the conservation area go for considerably more. **Brackenbury Rd**'s 3-storey-plus-basement houses fetch c. £320–350,000. Demand from the BBC in Shepherd's Bush – more prosperous BBC persons are moving out from Central London – seems certain to maintain the popularity of this area.

Ravenscourt Park

To the west of Brackenbury, on the Chiswick border, this neighbourhood is bounded by **Goldhawk Rd**, **King St** and **Paddenswick Rd**. Most of it falls within a conservation area centred around Ravenscourt Park itself, formerly the grounds of a fine 18th-century house which was bombed during the war. All that is left now are delightful gardens and formal lake, a pretty coach house (used as a tea house) and rather splendid gates. There are also a number of leisure facilities (including tennis courts) available for the locals to use.

Look for property backing onto the park, for example along **Goldhawk Rd** and **Ravenscourt Rd** – with a price tag of £795,000 for a 4-bed detached house. There are pockets of pretty 18th- and 19th-century villas and terraces (**Ravenscourt Park**, **Ravenscourt Gardens**, **Hamlet Gardens**) and a rather pretty square (**Ravenscourt Park Square**) which has some lovely houses on three sides – the fourth side opens to the park. There are not that many homes in this area – but this is likely to change, since much land is taken up for the Queen Charlotte's Hospital complex. The park itself is geared to children, which is not surprising: Queen Charlotte's is one of London's foremost maternity hospitals; it is, however, scheduled to move over the next couple of years to a new site in Du Cane Rd in Shepherd's Bush. The vast Royal Masonic Hospital site, which stands between the park and Queen Charlotte's, has already re-emerged as a clutch of 870 sq ft, 2-bed, 2-bath flats, completed last year and marketed at £245–277,000.

On the fringes of Ravenscourt Park, it is worth looking at **Wingate Rd**, **Dorvill Crescent** (where a 5-bed home can fetch £450–500,000) and **Wellesley Avenue**; and to the N, on the other side of the **Goldhawk Rd** (but still in the conservation area), **Ashchurch Park Villas**, **Rylett Rd** and **Ashchurch Grove**, **Minden Rd** and **Ashchurch Terrace** (see also Shepherd's Bush chapter).

Ravenscourt Park has a very suburban feel to it, more reminiscent of Chiswick's wide open spaces across the borough border than of densely packed Hammersmith. This area and Brook Green (see below) are neck and neck in the desirability stakes, but Ravenscourt Park has a definite edge thanks to houses that include some more substantial in size, and detached.

Brook Green

Strictly speaking 'Brook Green' consists only of **Brook Green** itself (a conservation area), plus the small handful of roads leading immediately off it – **Blythe Rd** is the obvious divide. But the term is often used to describe an entire area that stretches as far N as **Minford Gardens/Sinclair Gardens** and as far E as **Sinclair Rd**, which continues alongside the railway line down to Olympia. It is one of the biggest residential parking zones in the borough, covering the streets to the N of **Hammersmith Rd** to Shepherd's Bush Green, from the Hammersmith & City line to the W and the railway line to the E.

Needless to say, homes on the E side of **Sinclair Rd**, which back onto the tracks, are not so popular with insomniac buyers. But, apart from properties which are bang next to the railway, the Olympia corner is not significantly less in demand than any other part of Hammersmith. This Brook Green borders area between **Sinclair** and **Blythe Rds** (I seem to remember 'Blythe village' being touted as a name for it in the '80s!) is a great hunting-ground for BBC workers: it contains many larger terraced houses, frequently converted into 1- and 2-bed flats. They often have semi-basement or garden-level flats which have the advantage of Victorian-sized back gardens, often with mature trees. In some cases, semi-basement and ground floors combine to make good maisonettes. High-ceilinged rooms with ornate plasterwork on the ground floors are attractive features. Look out for property in **Addison Gardens**, **Bolingbroke Rd**, **Lakeside Rd**, **Irving Rd**, **Hofland Rd** and **Milson Rd** (price for a 'rare, unmodernized' but good-sized 1-bed in the latter, £117,000 last winter). **Ceylon Rd** has some modern town-houses: 4-bed, 2-bath, garage and half a million pounds, thank you.

Blythe Rd, which curls through from **Shepherd's Bush Rd** to **Hammersmith Rd** to enclose the Brook Green enclave, has a mix of Victorian and later houses (a 1980s terrace of 4-bed houses boast 3 baths plus garages, but also gables in a graceful nod to 19th-century neighbours). Other, older homes have been refurbished or extended; houses here can thus cost £370–700,000.

At the **Hammersmith Rd** end of **Blythe Rd** stands Kensington West, an 8-storey, luxury 1989 apartment block with its own sports complex. Lots of flat to rent in the 1- to 4-bed homes of the big Latymer Court mansion block (complete with porter and ornate cage lift) on **Hammersmith Rd**: £200–400 pw includes heating and hot water. Just off the start of **Brook Green** (the road), **Windsor Way** is an enclave of 200 top-of-the-market houses and flats.

Brook Green proper, despite its smaller houses and location just off the less than salubrious **Shepherd's Bush Rd**, is every bit as popular with house- and apartment-hunters as Ravenscourt Park. The scattered family houses overlooking the green itself are splendid, often leafily secluded and highly prized (and priced). They also get access to the green's tennis courts. Look also at the peaceful network of little streets tucked into the triangle between the green, **Shepherd's Bush Rd** and **Hammersmith Rd**: the homes in streets like **Rowan Rd** and **Bute Gardens** can be deceptively big, wider than average and particularly pleasant. A 4-bed house in **Bute Gardens** was £395,000 last winter. **Rowan Terrace** is a tiny close of cottages.

Crabtree Estate

This neighbourhood, built between 1910 and 1930, used to be predominantly industrial, but more and more homes – some luxurious by Hammersmith standards – are becoming available as Crabtree changes its image (signs of former industrial use are disappearing). The neighbourhood runs from **Hammersmith Bridge Rd** beside the river to **Crabtree Lane**, with **Fulham Palace Rd** as the E boundary. Leading the new developments is the Richard Rogers-designed Thames Reach complex, whose living rooms have floor-to-ceiling glass on the riverside, giving them wide, uninterrupted views across to Barnes Waterside, the nature reserve and up-market housing estate, and the picturesque Harrods Depository building, now becoming flats as 'Harrods Village'. Balconied flats here fetch £400–600,000.

Another Thames-side scheme is Chancellor's Wharf, next to the Riverside Studios: a £10 million 1990 vintage development of eight 5-storey town-houses and 32 flats in **Crisp Rd** just downstream from the bridge and the Riverside Studios. These, in the words of the developers, boast 'dramatic brick-clad elevations, slightly nautical in appearance, with large porthole windows'.

Transport	Tubes: Hammersmith (zone 2, Piccadilly, Hammersmith & City, District), West Kensington (zone 2, District), Barons Court (zone 2, Piccadilly, District). See also map. From Hammersmith: Oxford Circus 25 min (1 change), City 35 min (1 change), Heathrow 40 min.
Convenient for	Heathrow via M4, roads to the West. Miles from centre: 4.
Schools	Local Authority: Phoenix High, St Edmund's, Sacred Heart (g). Private: St Paul's (g), Godolphin & Latymer (g), Latymer (b).

H

SALES

Flats	S	1B	2B	3B	4B	5B
Average prices	60–100	75–170	130–250	·370	–	–

Houses	2B	3B	4B	5B	6/7B	8B
Average prices	200–300	230–375+	330–500+	400–650+	–	–

RENTAL

Flats	S	1B	2B	3B	4B	5B
Average prices	450–700	650–900	900–1300	1000–1500	1300–1800	1800–2500

Houses	2B	3B	4B	5B	6/7B	8B
Average prices	1000–1200	1200–1700	1500–2000	1700–2500	–	–

The properties	Very mixed but Victorian terraces predominate. Beautiful old riverside homes, modern flats, some new flats and houses. Many converted flats. Thames-side industrial swept away by luxury new developments towards Fulham border.
The market	BBC workforce and City commuters look for homes here. Riverside houses scarce and expensive. Good location (tubes, M4 to airport) and BBC relocation to nearby Shepherd's Bush make this a good hunting-ground for both flats and family houses. Local searches: 2 weeks.

Among those estate agents active in this area are:
- Barnard Marcus
- Bushells
- Marsh & Parsons
- Foxtons*
- Lawsons and Daughters
- Winkworth *
- FPDSavills
- Priory Management*
- Wilmotts

further details: see advertisers' index on p633

HAMPSTEAD

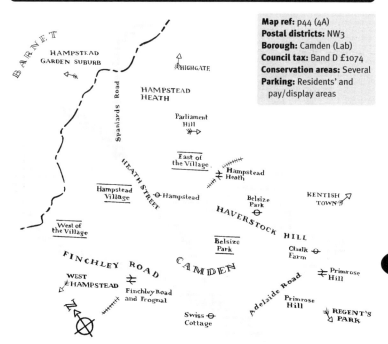

Map ref: p44 (4A)
Postal districts: NW3
Borough: Camden (Lab)
Council tax: Band D £1074
Conservation areas: Several
Parking: Residents' and
pay/display areas

Since around 1985 Hampstead has gained more than its fair share of London's lavish new flats and security-conscious, multi-bathroomed houses. Their inhabitants add to a community that deserves its reputation for prosperous intellectualism. Hardly a writer of note is published who does not live here, or on its shores – though the pressure on the intelligentsia's pockets has become intense as the merely wealthy have come after a share of the Hampstead charm. There is, nevertheless, still a strong community feeling about the way Hampstead looks. Residents resisted the advent of a McDonalds by means of a heavily supported campaign, although the burger chain finally won – after a 12-year battle. And any attempt to touch as much as a sapling on Hampstead Heath is fiercely resisted. Equally any planning issue, from a conservatory to a block of flats, faces scrutiny from an informed and vocal public. Once roused, the Hampstead intellectuals are a force to be reckoned with.

Hampstead dates back a thousand years to 986 AD, when King Ethelred the Unready gave the old Saxon 'homestead' to the monks of Westminster. Later, the village was to become a fashionable spa resort in the 17th and 18th centuries, a popular retreat in the 19th century, and today a prime residential area, the main attractions of this essentially Georgian village being its elevation above the smog of the city, and its proximity to the famous 800 acres of Hampstead Heath.

If Hampstead has a drawback it is traffic congestion and parking. Nearly every corner of Camden Borough has or soon will have residents' parking schemes, and the council is keen to discourage school-run traffic and other car movements it deems unnecessary. Two-car families (probably the majority) face the threat of being denied street parking permits if their home has off-road parking.

Hampstead today is up in the top handful of London residential areas: as an agent put it, quizzed on where was best, 'Hampstead is good roads surrounded by better roads.' Recent years have seen Hampstead very much a sellers' market with demand far outstripping supply, and this resulted in property price rises probably not matched in any but the most exclusive areas of Central London. Values nearly trebled in five years in the 1980s, and the area was one of the first to recover from the 1989/90 slump. This has meant, inevitably, that the population has changed, as more traditional inhabitants are squeezed (or tempted) out by the high prices, and the proportion of high income professionals, business people and foreign investors increases. The market slowed in 1998, with expensive new flats in particular proving harder to shift, but seasoned locals view this as a pause, not a dip: if the supply of would-be Hampstead residents dries up, there is something very much amiss with the world economy.

It is a popular area to rent in, with 70 per cent of the tenants – and quite a few of the landlords – foreign. The American School down the hill in St John's Wood generates a regular flow of families – there are never enough family homes to let, say agents – and international business people fill up the 2-bed flats.

Hampstead Village

Few visit Hampstead Village without wanting to live there, the only constraint being the failure of the lottery numbers to come up. The choice ranges from wide, leafy avenues with imposing detached mansions to picturesque, almost medieval lanes, squares and cul-de-sacs. The place is packed with a fascinating variety of homes dating back 300 years and more – many with historical and literary connections.

The population still contains a remarkably high proportion of artists, writers, actors, musicians, diplomats and professionals, and the shopping centre reflects the cosmopolitan flavour of the area with many fashion boutiques, specialist food shops, bookshops, restaurants of all descriptions and some celebrated pubs, like the Flask and the Hollybush. Difficult to buy a needle and thread here, though.

From **Hampstead High St**, streets like **Gayton Rd** and **Flask Walk** lead to the old spa area where roads named **Well Rd** and **Well Walk** reflect the history. Here, too, is Burgh House, the Grade I listed mansion built in 1702, now a community centre, art gallery and local history museum. The Everyman cinema is in **Holly Bush Vale**; it is due to reopen this February. Houses in this area are mainly Georgian, Edwardian and Victorian terraces, the majority of which have been converted into flats. But there are still the occasional large and medium-sized detached and semi-detached houses in secluded streets like **New End**, **Cannon Place** and **Christchurch Hill**, where you'll find the New End Theatre. All the prices, however, reflect the area's proximity (across **East Heath Rd**) to Hampstead Heath. You will be asked £750,000 for a 3-bed cottage in the best streets. Particularly attractive is the **Gainsborough Gardens** private estate, off **Well Walk**, a ring of houses on its own circular access road. Mansion block flats in The Pryors and Bell Moor, literally overlooking the heath, are also reckoned an excellent investment.

The other main road through the village is **Heath St** leading, on the N side, to the upper part of the old town, with beautiful houses in tightly packed squares such as **Golden Yard** and **The Mount Square**, and delightful secluded streets including **Windmill Hill**, **Hampstead Grove** and **Admiral's Walk**, with its unusually shaped houses with naval names.

The potential for new homes schemes of any size is limited by the extreme scarcity of available land, with nearly all the new homes of the last decade resulting from the conversion or replacement of redundant public buildings like hospitals and colleges. The old New End Hospital in **Heath St** became flats in 1998; this year sees the further marketing of the Mount Vernon Hospital conversion. This adds 62 flats to **Frognal Rise**, in the heart of the Village. They were launched on the market in late 1997 at prices up to £2.85 million: there were still several available in January.

Heath St leads, on the S side, to the splendid terraces (some Queen Anne) in **Church Row**, past the ancient St John's Parish Church and Frognal Gardens, to **Frognal** – one of the oldest roads in Hampstead, and the site of University College School. There are some magnificent hidden properties in this area. Further S are the very large houses in **Fitzjohns Avenue**, many of which have been converted into schools, hotels and clinics. **Maresfield Gardens** also has large houses, the Freud Museum in the house where Sigmund Freud died in 1939, and UCS's sister school South Hampstead High. Some of these homes are now luxury flats. Look out, too, for terraced houses and flats in the **Vale of Health**, an exclusive enclave on the heath itself. Once known as Hatche's Bottom, the land was drained in 1777 and a few houses are Georgian.

West of the Village

These are the quiet, tree-lined avenues, bounded by **West Heath Rd**, **Platts Lane**, **Finchley Rd** and **Arkwright Rd**, which have attracted so much attention from developers as it becomes more and more difficult for individual families to maintain large Victorian mansions. Luxury flat conversions have been flowing in a steady stream in this area since the mid-'80s, and quite a few new homes – houses and flats – have either replaced, or been squeezed in between, the surviving mansions.

At the top of the heath on **North End Way**, the enormous Inverforth House, built as a single mansion, will now be lived in once more after a career as a hospital. Three of the seven vast homes into which it's been split – flats is the wrong word – were on the market last winter at prices between £2 million and £4.5 million.

Examples of the upper-tier blocks include Heath Park Gardens, 13 flats overlooking the heath on the corner of **Templewood Avenue** and **West Heath Rd**. Living rooms resemble football pitches, averaging around 45 x 30 ft, and all the flats share a private swimming pool – except for the 6,000 sq ft duplex apartment which has its own. Similarly luxurious is Summit Lodge in **Upper Terrace** next to Whitestone Pond which, at 440 ft above sea level, is the highest point in London. There are 12 large flats (some around 2,800 sq ft), also sharing a swimming pool complex. The top flats have unbeatable 360-degree views of the capital from the roof.

The big new Westfield scheme in 4 acres of land on **Kidderpore Avenue** will have 145 flats: the first should be ready in the first half of this year. They are from 1- to 4-beds, priced up to £830,000.

The biggest houses – some positively ambassadorial – are in **West Heath Rd**, directly opposite the West Heath, all with price tags well in excess of £1 million. Most remarkable, near the junction with **Platts Lane**, is 'Sarum Chase', which Pevsner described as 'unashamed Hollywood Tudor'. These are being joined this year by eight new houses in **Eden Terrace**, just off **West Heath Rd**, from £1.75 million to £3.5 million.

But there are also houses of all sizes and in all conditions in roads such as **Redington Gardens, Heath Drive, Hollycroft Avenue, Ferncroft Avenue, Templewood Avenue** and **Greenaway Gardens**, some with very large gardens. **Chesterford Gardens** has a particularly fine terrace of houses, as does **Redington Rd**, an extremely graceful curving street which links **West Heath Rd** with **Frognal**. Flats in **Redington Rd** range around the £500,000 mark; quite a bit more for large ones with gardens. The award-winning Firecrest development, between **West Heath Rd** and **Templewood Avenue**, has exciting modern houses and flats on a beautiful, wooded site. The two largest houses have their own basement pools. New homes are not the only ones to be had: existing flats offer opportunities to those who prefer a more traditional style. A large 2-bed ground-floor flat in need of work was £795,000 last winter.

These roads also have easy access to **Finchley Rd** which runs N to connect with the M1 and A1, and S through St John's Wood and Regent's Park to the West End. Bus services along the **Finchley Rd** are good and it's a short hop to Golders Green or Finchley Rd tubes – and to the new O2 shopping/cinema complex on the **Finchley Rd**.

H *East of the Village*

South of **Willow Rd** is a district of pleasant Victorian terraced roads, now almost exclusively converted into flats and maisonettes, though the odd entire house does come onto the market: £1 million was being asked for a 5-bed in **Carlingford Rd** in the autumn. Down the hill is what is sometimes known as the Downshire Hill triangle, comprising **Downshire Hill, Keats Grove** and **South End Rd**. This is one of the most elegant (and sought-after) areas in Hampstead. **Downshire Hill** has a pleasing number of stuccoed brick houses dating from the early 19th century, the majority of which have remained as single-family houses. They are nearly all listed, and as a group they are listed Grade II as being of 'considerable merit'. **Keats Grove** contains lovely Keats House, now a public library and museum.

Further down the hill is villagy **South End Green**, with its shops and cafés, Hampstead Heath rail station (N London line, Silverlink) and a three-screen cinema. Here, too, is **Pond St** and the giant, modern, Royal Free Hospital.

Also off **South End Green** is the attractive enclave of streets, reached only via **South Hill Park**, which juts out into the heath at the foot of Parliament Hill. It holds a mixture of family houses and flat conversions, as well as a few post-war blocks of flats in **Parliament Hill** (the road). Two new 4-bed houses in **Tanza Rd** were on sale for £595,000 each in December. The great attraction here is the lack of through traffic and the instant access to the heath and hill. Most popular are the houses on the N side of **South Hill Park** which overlook the Hampstead Ponds.

There is a very attractive group of streets around **Fleet Rd, Constantine Rd** and **Savernake Rd**, including **Rona Rd, Estelle Rd, Courthorpe Rd** and **Shirlock Rd**. They are surrounded by busy roads but are themselves virtually free of traffic. This is the cheaper end of Hampstead: it runs across to Gospel Oak and borders Kentish Town. They still have the coveted NW3 postcode, though gracious 4-storey Victorian houses can be found here at a fraction of the price of similar houses a quarter mile up the hill. Lots of homes have been converted into flats, so parking is at a premium. A residents' parking scheme has just been introduced.

Also interesting, although not as reasonably priced, are **Parkhill Rd, Upper Park Rd** and **Lawn Rd**, which have a mixture of flat conversions, family houses and some modern council estates. The architecturally famous 1930s Isokon Flats block is in **Lawn Rd**; built in the Bauhaus style it was originally designed for artists and musicians and is now owned by Camden Council – though they are considering a sale to a developer as we go to press. Some very interesting homes could thus come onto the open market.

Belsize Park

Originally from the French 'Bel Assis' ('beautifully situated'), Belsize Park was once regarded as the less desirable end of Hampstead, but now has a character and atmosphere all its own. It has two shopping centres, around the Belsize Park underground station in **Haverstock Hill**, and in what has become known as 'Belsize Village' in **Belsize Lane** – which also has some attractive mews developments and the arty Screen on the Hill cinema. The population density is high, and the streets can become very congested, but the architecture is charming and the typical Belsize Park flat will have generous-sized rooms and gloriously high ceilings. But like everywhere else in Hampstead, family-sized houses are now very scarce indeed.

The dominant road is **Belsize Avenue**, which runs from **Haverstock Hill** all the way to the Swiss Cottage end of the suburb. On the N side are the roads that lead up to the graceful, tree-lined **Lyndhurst Gardens** and **Wedderburn Rd**. On the S side, **Belsize Park**, **Belsize Park Gardens** and **Belsize Square**. Also interesting are 'The Glens' – **Glenloch Rd**, **Glenilla Rd** and **Glenmore Rd**, only a minute or two's walk from the tube.

Englands Lane has a very useful shopping centre, very convenient to the large houses in **Steeles Rd** (home of several film stars), where homes regularly sell for more than £1 million, interesting terraces in secluded **Primrose Gardens**, and some new town-houses in **Antrim Rd**. **Haverstock Hill** itself has a good selection of purpose-built blocks of flats, some of which are quite modern.

Swiss Cottage

Long-standing Central European residents wistfully remember the days when Swiss Cottage was known as Schweizerhof, and they whiled away the hours drinking coffee and eating pastries in Viennese cafés like Louis. But the street market disappeared, they built a business complex, and the area lost most of its student party atmosphere and became a sharply contrasting area between those who use the community centre and City/estate agent types. Conservation area status has enhanced the appeal.

Swiss Cottage took its name from the original Regency chalet-style tavern: this architectural oddity has been perpetuated by a more recent pub and restaurant complex opposite the tube station (Jubilee line). It also has a large sports complex, one of the finest libraries in the country, a hotel, a six-screen cinema and close proximity to the thriving **Finchley Rd** shopping centre – and the new O2 complex (see West Hampstead chapter).

Much of the area – some 243 acres – was once owned by Eton College which was also responsible for a great deal of the housing development. The estate still owns a great deal of property in the area, particularly in roads like **Eton Avenue**, **Fellows Rd**, **Provost Rd** and **King Henry's Rd**. There are still large detached Victorian houses here, but most are subdivided into flats. The area gained over 100 modern flats and town-houses in the Quadrangles development, between **Adelaide** and **Fellows Rds**.

The district is also characterized by a number of council estates and tower block developments, as well as a number of large privately owned mansion blocks, including Regency Lodge in **Avenue Rd**, and Northways in **College Crescent**. There are some beautiful houses in the broad sweep of **Elsworthy Rd**, but the street does suffer a little from being an unofficial traffic through-route from Primrose Hill to St John's Wood. Some of the houses on the N side share a magnificent common garden with houses in **Wadham Gardens**.

Transport	Tubes: Hampstead (zone 2/3), Belsize Park (zone 2), both Northern line. From Hampstead: Oxford Circus 20 min (1 change), Bank 25 min, Heathrow 1 hr 10 min (1 change). Trains: Hampstead Heath, Primrose Hill, both North London line/Silverlink. To Liverpool St: 20 min.

Convenient for   Hampstead Heath; M1, A1 to North. Miles from centre: 4.

Schools   Local Authority: Hampstead School, Haverstock School. Private: University College School (b), South Hampstead High School (g), The Hall School (b).

SALES

Flats	S	1B	2B	3B	4B	5B
Average prices	70–100	130–225	150–350+	200–450	300–1M+	300–2M
Houses	2B	3B	4B	5B	6/7B	8B
Average prices	250–450	300–900+	400–1M+	500–1.5M+	650–2.5M+	2M–15M

RENTAL

Flats	S	1B	2B	3B	4B	5B
Average prices	690–850	850–1500	1300–3000	1700–4000	2600–6500	4300–8500
Houses	2B	3B	4B	5B	6/7B	8B
Average prices	850–3000	1700–6500	3000–8500	6500–10,000+	6500–13,000+	8500–17,000

The properties   Georgian gems in heart of Village and scattered among the surrounding gracious streets. New developments, generally towards the heath, are luxury-level: some innovative, some merely opulent. Victoriana reasserts itself down the hill towards Belsize Park.

The market   Everyone wants to live here. Prices rise, with the hill, to ultra-luxury level homes around the heath: figures above reflect the wide spread of quality. Houses (and even flats) inclined to sprout swimming pools etc. Local searches: 2 weeks.

Among those estate agents active in this area are:
- Anscombe & Ringland*
- Knight Frank
- Foxtons*
- Behr & Butchoff
- Naylius McKenzie
- Goldschmidt & Howland
- Benham & Reeves
- Talisman Wayne
- Faron Sutaria & Co Ltd*
- Keith Cardale Groves
- FPDSavills
- Hamptons
- Parkheath
- Alan Charles

further details: see advertisers' index on p633

HAMPSTEAD GARDEN SUBURB

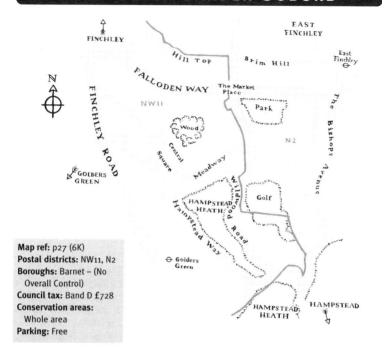

Map ref: p27 (6K)
Postal districts: NW11, N2
Boroughs: Barnet – (No
    Overall Control)
Council tax: Band D £728
Conservation areas:
    Whole area
Parking: Free

At the birth of the 20th century, a woman had a philanthropic dream. The result was a model village — known across North West London simply as 'The Suburb' — gathered at the head of its own extension of Hampstead Heath.

Leafy Hampstead Garden Suburb is still a place apart, though the farmland which once surrounded it has long since vanished under a sea of brick. It remains that way in large part thanks to the ministrations of the HGS Trust, which keeps a strong regulatory eye on things. It lies just to the north of the Hampstead golf course and the Hampstead Heath extension, across the **Finchley Rd** from Golders Green. The Trust provides a map with the boundaries of the area clearly marked, though less punctilious estate agents claim swathes of Golders Green and East Finchley as 'HGS borders'.

Hampstead Garden Suburb was built at the beginning of the 20th century; it was carefully designed by architects Parker, Unwin and Lutyens but the inspiration was Dame Henrietta Barnett's. Her dream was for it to be an area where people of all classes, conditions and ages would co-exist happily in beautiful tree-lined streets, with woods and open spaces available to all.

Consequently you find a great variety of type and style of housing in the area, from the terraced cottages around **Erskine Hill** and **Hampstead Way** (where 'artisans' were to live) to the double-fronted mansions of **Winnington Rd**, built later for those who didn't need to work quite so hard. Baillie Scott's purpose-built block, Waterlow Court in **Heath Close**, was originally intended for that then strange phenomenon, the working woman.

Alas, Dame Henrietta would find that few indeed of the deserving poor dwell here today, though the fabric of her model suburb remains virtually unchanged.

The Suburb was once viewed as being inhabited largely by eccentrics – 'crazy, freakish people', observed *The Times*, not mincing matters. It is very different from Hampstead across the heath, and it was designed to be. When a careless journalist accorded government Minister Peter Mandelson a Hampstead childhood, his old teacher from Hampstead Garden Suburb Infants' School was careful to set the record straight in a letter to the *Telegraph*. Today the Suburb's residents are much like those in the rest of North West London – though probably rather richer. There are many Jewish inhabitants, and also Americans and South Africans who love the feeling of space here. In the last few years the inhabitants have changed, with most of the old founding families now gone and a younger age-group moving in. Young or old, there are plenty of would-be Surburbites: local agents reckon they have 10 home-seekers for every property on their books.

The talking-point in the Suburb has been for several years and still is the controversial proposal for the formation of an Orthodox Jewish 'eruv' that will cover much of the Suburb as well as Golders Green and parts of Hendon. The eruv is likely to become a reality (depending upon how you view it) during 1999. It is a notional boundary within which Sabbath laws will be relaxed, allowing observant Jews to push wheelchairs and carry their children on Saturdays. Most of the eruv's boundaries will be existing features such as gardens, walls, the M1 motorway, etc, but there are some gaps or 'gateways' that will be spanned by thin wires strung between high poles. Planning permission for these poles and wires was finally granted by Barnet Council last autumn.

The debate – which has received national and, indeed, international attention – has raged for the last seven years. Proponents claim that the eruv would largely exist only in the minds of those who believe in it and would benefit from it. Opponents argue that it would mean new and unsightly poles and wires, and that it would turn the area into a 'ghetto'. Some of the most virulent opponents have been prominent Jews.

Market Place, along the **Falloden Way**, provides some (expensive) shopping and a welter of estate agents, but you have to drive down to Golders Green/Temple Fortune or up to East Finchley for most things. There's a well-concealed post office along **Lyttelton Rd**, a library, schools, churches, a synagogue and – the Suburb's pride and joy – the Institute on **Central Square**, which is as old as the Suburb itself. Founded in the spirit of self-improvement, it's where you can take courses in everything from photography to pottery and where your au pair (this is very much au pair country) can learn English.

Suburb residents tend to stay once they've lived in the area for a while, and there are always people looking to move in. It's an estate agent's dream. The houses, particularly those in the Old Suburb or NW11 area, really are 'full of character' and there's no need for agents to take advantage of artistic licence when composing details. The major roads are wide and tree-lined, and hedges rather than fences divide the plots. Little secluded closes suit those who prefer more privacy. Living in the Suburb means you're close to Kenwood House and the heath for summer walks and concerts, yet you are just five miles from the centre of London, combining the advantages of both town and country.

When it comes to disadvantages the major one, apart from the price of property, is transport. Neither Golders Green nor East Finchley stations are close by and those who don't drive or have access to a car are apt to feel stranded. There are no amenities for teenagers in the Suburb itself, though the area is great for small children. The Suburb mini-buses, the H2 and H3 'Hopper', run a circular tour from Golders Green station – prospective buyers might invest 50p on a round trip to see the area. Ask the driver to stop when you see a house you like the look of; he'll halt anywhere along his route.

Parking in the Old Suburb, which is full of closes and cul-de-sacs, can be problematic – particularly as few of the houses were built with garages. Residents in **Willifield Way** often have to resort to parking on the pavement, much to the fury of Barnet Council officials. Residents were not intended to have carriages or cars – especially the 'contented artisans' the founders hoped would populate the Suburb alongside the middle classes. A number of traffic calming measures have recently been introduced in busy **Meadway** among other roads.

Depending on which way you look at it, another possible disadvantage of the area is that it is a conservation area and you have to apply to the Trust (862 Finchley Rd, NW11 6AB) as well as to Barnet Borough before making any alterations to your property down to painting the front door – even if you own the freehold. Wily residents in need of extra living space have been known to develop very luxurious 'garages'.

On the other hand, you can be sure that the character of the area and the price of property in it won't be massacred by unscrupulous types or those with a penchant for modern, incongruous architecture. Indeed, a large number of the houses are listed Grade II as being of significant architectural and historical importance – and many of them are 'starred' listings. Two years ago there was a mass listing of a further batch of more than 500 houses in the Suburb that had not been listed before, and many already listed were given a star. This was the result of years of pressure by the Hampstead Garden Suburb Trust on English Heritage and the government's Heritage Department. Most residents were delighted by the decision.

NW11, the Old Suburb

The area around Big and Little Woods and around **Central Square** and **Meadway** is known as the Old Suburb, although it is actually not that much older than the New. Generally, it covers the NW11 part of the Suburb, where the houses were built between 1907 and 1914, are full of character and are more expensive.

Central Square, designed by Lutyens, is the heart of the suburb; a very green and peaceful centre, where you'll find neo-Georgian terraced houses and flats at prices guaranteed to give you sleepless nights. Here, too, you'll find the parish church of St Jude, the Free Church for Non-Conformist worshippers and the Institute which also accommodates the Henrietta Barnett School for Girls. In the corner of **North Square** is a Meeting House for the Society of Friends and in **South Square**, opposite St Jude's Church, is a purpose-built block where flats have only recently become available for sale. There's a memorial to Dame Henrietta on the fourth side of the square, and one of the Suburb's many passageways (the aim was to keep pedestrian and motor traffic separate) leads down to **Willifield Way**. This is possibly the most charming road in the area, with a village green which is overlooked by Fellowship House where the over-60s meet. Many of the Suburb's younger residents attend the Garden Suburb School which is also in **Willifield Way**. A 4-bed semi in this road was £500,000 last winter.

If your taste is for a cottage with roses round the door, then the roads around **Willifield Way** are where you should look. The first cottages to be built in the Suburb were at Nos 140 and 142 **Hampstead Way** in 1907. They were designed by Parker and Unwin who were strongly influenced by the Arts and Crafts movement, hence the traditional East Anglian cottages with medieval German vernacular gable, dormers and wood window frames. Particularly charming are **Erskine Hill** and **Asmuns Hill** where you'll find 2- and 3-bedroom cottages with pretty gardens. Some of the cottages in the Suburb are rented: a handful have yet to be modernized and if you find one of these, get in quick. But you must ask both the Trust and Barnet Borough for planning consents.

The cottages are favourites with the more affluent sort of young couple (a decade ago this Guide reckoned them suitable for first-time buyers . . .) and with older people. **The Orchard**, nearby, is still inhabited by elderly residents, just as Dame Henrietta intended – though the original homes have been rebuilt. **Addison Way**, where the cottages and purpose-built maisonettes have slightly less character, leads into **Falloden Way**, the busy A1, where prices are lower because of the noise. Still, if you're immune to traffic or want to save money, these houses have lovely views over **Northway Gardens** where there are tennis courts. **Market Place** has flats above the shops and some purpose-built maisonettes tucked away on the **Ossulton Way** side, but these can be noisy, too.

Cross over the **Falloden Way** and you're on the 'wrong' side of the Suburb, although the roads are just as pretty and cottages in **Westholm**, **Midholm** and **Eastholm** (the names indicate how carefully planned the Suburb was) and in **Brookland Rise** are decidedly desirable. **Hill Top**, **Maurice Walk** and **Midholm Close** all have purpose-built maisonettes, usually with their own gardens.

Back in the main part of the Suburb, **Oakwood Rd** links **Addison Way** with **Northway** and the New Suburb. The road used to be something of a rat-run until speed bumps were built to dissuade motorists from using it as a short-cut.

South of **Central Square** is **Meadway**, the Suburb's main thoroughfare which leads from **Hoop Lane** and Golders Green. Meadway Court, a mansion block around 60 years old, lies on the N side of the road, and leading off on the S side are the prestigious Closes, some of them private roads, where the 6- and 7-bedroom houses are the largest in this part of the Suburb. Unless you knew they were there, you'd never come across **Linnell**, **Turner** or **Meadway Closes**. The same applies to **Linnell** and **Turner Drives** which both have terrific views over the Hampstead Heath extension. For splendid views – and splendid 6-bedroomed houses – look in **Wildwood Rd**, where an outlook over the heath and Hampstead Golf Course commands high prices. **Heathgate**, just S of Central Square, has some 6-bed houses. On the other side of the heath extension runs **Hampstead Way** where you'll find Heathcroft, a popular block not far from Golders Green station, and some splendid 5-bed, close-to-a-million houses which share coveted access to the HGS Trust-run tennis courts.

N2, the New Suburb

Suburb snobs are rather patronizing about the 'New Suburb', the N2 area, which lies E of **Ossulton** and **Kingsley Ways**, plus **Northway**, **Southway** and **Middleway** back in NW11. It's true that the architecture is less interesting and the area is more densely constructed, but the houses are large (and expensive), with grand gardens and plenty of space. Parking – which is difficult in the Old Suburb – is not such a problem here. Cars were considered a normal adjunct to life when the New Suburb was laid out and were catered for (if not necessarily approved of) by the architects.

Holne Chase is the continuation of **Meadway** and off it run the elegant **Spencer Close** and **Neville Drive**. Houses on the 'right' side of **Neville Drive** have a splendid view of the golf course. **Linden Lea** and **Norrice Lea** (where you find the Suburb synagogue) both have large family houses, often detached, and are very much in demand.

North of the noisy **Lyttelton Rd** – where popular purpose-built blocks include Widecombe Court, set back from the road – are roads like **Gurney Drive**, **Widecombe Way** and **Edmund's Walk**: all quiet, pretty and with the advantage of being nearer East Finchley station. Westwards, at the top of **Ossulton Way**, **Neale Close** is a favourite with first-time buyers and has purpose-built 2-bedroomed maisonettes kept private by hedges. Across the road, **Denison Close** has a popular block set around a pretty garden square. This northern district is reckoned better for schools than the Surburb's heart.

Fanning out from **Central Square** and counted as the New Suburb despite their NW11 postcodes, are **Northway**, **Middleway** and **Southway** which are joined by **Thornton** and **Litchfield Ways**. Here you'll find large family houses with gardens to match in spacious hedge-lined roads.

The most expensive roads in the Suburb are **Ingram Avenue** and **Winnington Rd**, where prices resemble telephone numbers and the detached houses are huge and (particularly in **Winnington Rd**) rather ostentatious. Agents in the area also claim the famous **The Bishops Avenue**, known with reason as 'Millionaires' Row'. It is favoured by the ultra-rich international set as much for the privacy and security that the vast (for London) 2- and 3-acre plots afford as for the houses themselves, which are imposing but undistinguished 1950s mansions. There are more Middle Eastern royals here than in Marbella. 'In the Middle East,' observes a knowledgeable estate agent, 'the Bishop's Avenue is probably the best-known road in London.' In 1991 King Fahd bought five more homes opposite his family's existing mansion – to house his guests. Such are the Avenue's prices that developers often find it worthwhile buying one of the (relatively) modest homes in order to knock it down and build a really palatial one.

H

Transport	No trains or tube, but Golders Green and East Finchley tubes are nearby. H2 and H3 buses do circular routes via Golders Green.
Convenient for	Brent Cross shopping centre, Hampstead Heath, North Circular Rd. Miles from centre: 7.
Schools	Barnet Education Authority: Henrietta Barnett (g), Whitefield School.

SALES

Flats	S	1B	2B	3B	4B	5B
Average prices	–	85–120	100–280	140–350	–	–
Houses	2B	3B	4B	5B	6/7B	8B
Average prices	120–300	200–350+	300–600+	400–1M	500–10M	–

RENTAL

Flats	S	1B	2B	3B	4B	5B
Average prices	780–1000	850–1200	1200–1700	–	–	–
Houses	2B	3B	4B	5B	6/7B	8B
Average prices	975–1500	1500	1700–4300	2600–6500	4300–13,000	8600–21,000

The market	Inhabitants include international and Jewish families. Radical, doctrinaire past is now a memory. Million-pound properties found on fringes of area – principally in The Bishops Avenue. These attract princes, showbiz stars and tycoons.

The properties   Purpose-built turn-of-the-century suburb mixing picturesque cottages with houses of all sizes including mansion scale. A few flats. 'Old Suburb' is smaller-scale, distinguished English-picturesque. 'New' (most in N2) has less distinguished, more ostentatious larger, later houses. Local searches: 2–3 days.

Among those estate agents active in this area are:
- Glentree Estates
- Hotblack Dixon
- Godfrey & Barr
- Goldschmidt & Howland
- Benham & Reeves
- Foxtons*
- Chestertons
- Ellis & Co
- Kinleigh, Folkard & Hayward
- Litchfields
- Anscombe & Ringland *
- FPDSavills
- Knight Frank

further details: see advertisers' index on p633

H

HENDON AND MILL HILL

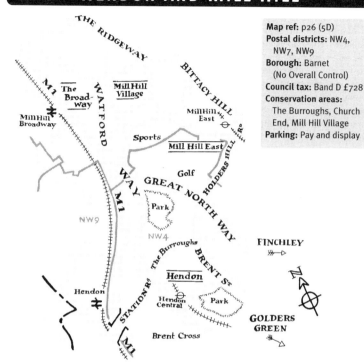

Map ref: p26 (5D)
Postal districts: NW4,
  NW7, NW9
Borough: Barnet
  (No Overall Control)
Council tax: Band D £728
Conservation areas:
  The Burroughs, Church
  End, Mill Hill Village
Parking: Pay and display

Somehow Hendon seems to be the crossroads for all roads that lead somewhere else. The area is dissected by the **Hendon/Watford Way**, the **Edgware Rd**, the A1 **Great North Way** and the M1 motorway . . . not to mention the **North Circular Rd** which forms an eastern boundary. Consequently, the North West London suburb of Hendon still divides into several old-style hamlets, each with their own identity. There is no real centre.

When Hendon Central tube station opened in 1923 it was surrounded by open fields – as witnessed by the 17th-century Church Farm House, today a museum. Hendon Hall in **Ashley Lane** still stands – complete with the famous, but incongruous, brick columns which the renowned actor David Garrick reputedly won in a card game. He became Lord of the Manor in 1796 and rebuilt the Hall, today a select hotel. Garrick Park is the remnant of his estate.

Such rural tranquillity is hard to imagine in the busy and congested suburb today; the '30s saw a rash of speculative development – one of the biggest architects of this suburban sprawl being John Laing, whose headquarters were in Mill Hill's **Pursley Rd**. (One of Laing's award-winning designs was first used to build the Sunnyfield site, off **Lawrence St** in **Mill Hill**). Nevertheless, the area today has a wide range of amenities to offer – among them the Brent Cross shopping centre, the Copthall sports stadium, the RAF Museum and all the water-sport activities associated with the Welsh Harp.

However, note that on the planning front there are no less than three public inquiries pending which concern the first two of these, plus a Mill Hill site; the outcomes will affect neighbouring homes. The Brent Cross shopping centre is looking to develop new shops and cafés out along the River Brent; the Copthall sports complex on **Pursley Rd** wants to extend to make room for a new 10,000-seater stadium, and there are plans for a new equestrian centre on **The Ridgeway**, Mill Hill.

Another reminder of a more spacious past has been the amount of land devoted to the forces; these days it pays to remember that Ministry of Defence land may well not stay that way: more and more sites are being sold off wholly or in part for housing. The famous Hendon aerodrome (actually one of two in Hendon; the other was in **Stag Lane**) is now in part the site of the council's Grahame Park Estate. The rest of the land is now a large and ongoing development site for new homes, and the same goes for the Inglis Barracks in Mill Hill. Only some street names and the RAF Museum commemorate the aerodrome that Claude Grahame White established in 1910: it saw the first British loop-the-loop, the first parachute descent and also the first British air mail delivery, a flight from Hendon to Windsor. The law likes this corner, too: residents sleep safely in their beds since the Metropolitan Police training school is here, just off **Aerodrome Rd** – and the new North West London Police HQ is up the road in Colindale.

A focal point in the area is the Victorian town hall in **The Burroughs**. Hendon is the oldest part of the Borough of Barnet, and it is fitting that it should be the political centre of the borough. Next door is a fine public library which also lends records, tapes, videos and CDs convenient for students at nearby Middlesex University (Hendon campus of a very split site).

The area's major talking-point of recent years, the proposed introduction of an Eruv, was finally given planning permission in October last year. This year should see the erection of the requisite poles and wires to span the gaps, or 'gateways', in this notional boundary line – within which strict Jewish Sabbath laws will be relaxed – which encompasses much of Hendon, Golders Green and Hampstead Garden Suburb. Controversial even among Jewish communities, it has nevertheless attracted many Orthodox families to buy or rent here, in anticipation of the freedom to push wheelchairs and carry their children on the Sabbath.

Mill Hill – contrastingly green and pleasant, with an abundance of wide open spaces – lies to the N of Hendon. Psychologically, too, Mill Hill is further out of town, and prices can be slightly cheaper. The original village stands on a hill, and close by is Mill Hill School, built in 1807 with a splendid Classical frontage. It was here that James Murray, a master at the school, edited much of the Oxford English Dictionary. Established for the sons of Protestant Dissenters, the school was originally known as 'an island of nonconformity in a sea of Roman Catholicism' – there are still several notable Roman Catholic institutions here, led by St Joseph's College in **Lawrence St**. Mill Hill is also home to the Medical Research Laboratory.

Cut off from the rest of Mill Hill by the roaring **Watford Way** is **The Broadway**, a busy shopping parade with bars, boutiques, health food shops and a Marks & Spencer. The train station, Mill Hill Broadway (26 min to Moorgate, 20 min to King's Cross), is located here too, and there are also buses to both local destinations and Central London.

Hendon

If you take a detour from the speeding roads, Hendon has homes to suit every taste, from large detached houses in **Brampton Grove, The Downage** and **Cedars Close**, to luxury retirement flats in **Church Rd**, rows of suburban terraces round **Montague Rd**, West Hendon, and quaint cottages which border the picturesque **The Burroughs**.

Turning into **The Burroughs** from the **Watford Way** is a surprise. Immediately the grey commercial buildings which match the busy road make way for cottages and larger old houses converted into luxurious modern flats. The old bus garage has now become a luxury office block, changing the appearance of the street. **Brampton Grove**, the first on the right, is probably Hendon's most exclusive road; a pair of new houses here fell effortlessly into the million-pound-plus bracket. Just along the road from the imposing town hall, flanked by a modern library and fire station, is the beautiful corner of Church End which has the Norman St Mary's Church in **Greyhound Hill** as a focal point. Next door, the old Church Farm House (dating back in parts to the 17th century) is home to the borough's museum. It twice escaped the post-war bulldozers. Between the museum and church stands the Greyhound Inn, originally the Church House and used for parish meetings. Opposite the museum, the back of the Middlesex University campus includes a fitness centre, which is open to residents. Further down **Greyhound Hill** the suburban semis are neat and tidy, just as the planners of the '30s imagined them: many with lovely green views, though the road is used as a cut-through from the **Watford Way** to **The Burroughs/Church Rd** and isn't as tranquil as it once was. A cache of new homes – flats and small houses – appeared behind **The Burroughs** on a large site, originally the back of school playing-fields, in the late '80s.

Heading down **Church Rd** (permanently congested) towards **The Quadrant**, **Sunningfields Rd** and **Sunningfields Crescent** are to your left, both pretty, both with plenty of conversions. Smart new flats developments (three last year alone) grace **Sunningfields Rd**; opening prices at CALA's pleasant King's Mount scheme were from £180,000 (2-bed). This corner leads up to Sunny Hill Park, and also houses a private hospital. **Florence St**, just off **The Quadrant**, is a real find: not as cut off as the Sunningfields roads, it has charming little houses set along a narrow street. The corner of **The Quadrant**, once the local cinema, is now sheltered housing. (The area is well supplied with homes and housing for the elderly.)

Turning left down **Parson St** brings you to some of the premier streets in Hendon: **Downage**, **Ashley Lane** and **Cedars Close** with its mock-Tudor houses set in a circle around little private gardens. **Tenterden Grove**, **Tenterden Close** and **Tenterden Gardens** are also nice but homes at either end of **Tenterden Drive** may suffer a little from noise from the **Great North Way**. **Westchester Drive**, at the junction of **Parson St** and the **Great North Way**, is surprisingly unaffected by its proximity to the main roads, and has small houses and Westchester Court flats. **Parson St** itself boasts Glebe Court, a new cache of 16 luxury flats by Berkeley Homes, marketed last winter at £275–450,000. Across the A1 divide, more such have sprouted in leafy **Holders Hill Rd**, which links Hendon with Mill Hill (see opposite).

If Hendon could be said to have a high street, then **Brent St** is probably it. Here you'll find the mini-shopping centre at **Sentinel Square**, with pay-and-display parking. There are also many kosher restaurants and take-aways – including one of only two kosher Chinese restaurants in the UK. **Bell Lane** leads down towards the **North Circular**; to the left roads like **Alexandra Rd** and **Albert Rd** have smaller semis and terraced houses. **Albert Rd** is the site of Jew's College with its fine library. To the right, **Green Lane** and the roads around have large family houses and a number of synagogues. The **Brent St** shops give way to a number of attractive '30s semis. South of **Brent St** lies the Shirehall Estate, where many of the detached and semi-detached 4/5-bed houses have delightful views over Hendon Park. **Shirehall Lane**, which runs through the middle, is however used as a short-cut by Hendon's shoppers on the Brent Cross trail. At the Golders Green end of **Brent St**, a recent block dubbed The Carltons by its developers has prices that rise, with the storeys, to half-million-pound penthouses.

Queen's Rd runs alongside the park down to Hendon Central tube station – not to mention that new health club. **Queen's Gardens** has the benefit of the park without the commuter-traffic drawback. **Queen's Rd** is very much the target for developers, both for new-build (two new flat blocks have recently been built) and for luxurious conversions: look in this street for spacious, bathroom-per-bedroom apartments, and expect to pay upwards of a quarter-million.

To the N of **Queen's Rd** lie more of Hendon's best streets. **Brampton Grove** (see page 344), **Wykeham Rd** and **Raleigh Close** have large family houses. They are particularly popular with Jewish residents due to the proximity of synagogues in **Egerton Gardens** (the Yakar centre) and in **Raleigh Close** itself.

Station Rd, where you'll find the popular Highmount block, runs down from **The Burroughs** to Hendon rail station and provides a link between the **Watford Way** and the **Edgware Rd**. The grid of roads off **Vivian Avenue** have 4-bed semis which get less expensive as you near the M1 motorway. To the S of them lies the Brent Cross shopping centre, which plans to expand yet further.

West Hendon, on the other side of the motorway, is the cheaper end of Hendon. Shopping facilities are not very good (the locals use Brent Cross) and the area, with its terraces and small semis, has a slightly run-down air. However, it is convenient for the **Edgware Rd,** leading all the way to Marble Arch, for the facilities of the Welsh Harp and for Wembley Stadium. Welsh Harp Village, in **Goldsmith Avenue** at the northern tip of the Welsh Harp Reservoir, is one of this area's most popular developments (you'll have seen it, if you remember the 'dancing milk bottles' TV ad). Its wide range of homes and prices – from studios to 3-bed, around £45–120,000 – attract first-time buyers.

Mill Hill

A trip to Mill Hill is in order for London house-hunters who would prefer to be in the country. It lies to the N of Hendon, from which it is cut off by the **Great North Way** (the A1) and a swathe of green open space that holds golf course, cemetery and playing-fields. The link between the two is **Holders Hill Rd**, a major hunting-ground for luxurious new homes – mainly flats, to take advantage of the views of the golf course. It sprouted four or five new blocks in the '80s, and several more last year: look not only in the **Rd**, but also in the **Crescent, Gardens** and **Drive**. As well as quarter-million-pound flats, this stretch holds modest 3-bed semis which go for c. £160–180,000.

The road leads up towards Mill Hill East. Mill Hill has a rail station, but the tube line (Mill Hill East; Northern Line) ends here, at the bottom of **Bittacy Hill**, definitely the cheaper end of Mill Hill: it doesn't venture up to the dizzy heights (in terms of altitude and price) of **Uphill Rd**. But the E edge of Mill Hill has a popular riding school at the N end of **Frith Lane**, which seems to take in every little North London girl.

Mill Hill East is an attractive belt of suburbia with a carefully planned grid of roads. Here the semis each have their own identity with a variety of modern windows and extensions. The main avenue, **Devonshire Rd/Sanders Lane**, radiates out from **Holders Hill Circus** and overlooks Hendon golf course and Copthall playing-fields – where a planning battle over the proposal to build a new 10,000-seater stadium has now gone to a public inquiry. The bottom end of **Devonshire Rd** is overshadowed by huge gasometers behind **Bittacy Hill** – another area about to see major redevelopment. The former Inglis barracks is another tranche of MoD land that has been sold off to be replaced by new homes – beginning with mainly 2-bed flats. The gasworks site is also earmarked: residents pray that any development here might remove the gasometers, which would really improve this corner.

Moving W, you come to **Pursley Rd**, **Page St** and **Wyse Lane**. The houses here are fairly ordinary semis but, surrounded by green open spaces, they are very pleasant (John Laing has added new 2- and 3-bed houses, from around £160,000 last year, on the site of its former headquarters). From there, climb **Milespit Hill** to **The Ridgeway**. Here, Mill Hill Village stands quiet and glorious, still with its village pond, overlooking the green fields. Not all the houses are old: a handful are 'modern architect-designed', as the estate agents say, but all are very 'des res'. The **High St** belies its name: the nearest main shops are in **Mill Hill Broadway**. At **The Ridgeway** end, **Wills Grove**, which branches off to the left just before Mill Hill School, is charming, with larger houses and plenty of trees. Across **The Ridgeway**, the Belmont Farm Riding School is fighting for permission for an Equestrian Centre: locals fear it would affect traffic, and views on footpaths along Totteridge Common and Folly Brook.

In the angle of **Daws Lane** and **Hammers Lane** lies Mill Hill's 'poets' corner'. This one is a surprise, with pleasant 4- and 5-bedroom houses in roads named after literary greats such as **Tennyson, Milton** and **Shakespeare**. Further along **The Ridgeway** at **Holcombe Hill**, where the Old Forge stands, lies **Lawrence St**, off which is Mill Hill's premier road, **Uphill Rd**. Home-owners in neighbouring **Sunnyfield**, **The Reddings**, **Uphill Grove** and the **Tretawn** roads have extended their houses in all directions. With spacious gardens and views over the grounds of St Joseph's College, they stand on gently undulating ground which enhances the feeling of space that they enjoy.

Back across **Watford Way** lies the area's high street: the shops and restaurants of **The Broadway**. A convenient corner, flanked by fast roads (A1, M1) and rail routes: **Flower Lane** has an estate of Georgian-style houses, and a new one, of 4-bed houses, completed last year (prices were from £375,000.) **Russell Grove** and **Weymouth Avenue** are both good roads with detached houses. **Newcombe Park** is popular, too.

Highwood Hill has larger-than-average old cottages along just one side – which therefore also have splendid views; off it, the very exclusive (and reputedly haunted) **Nan Clarke's Lane**: a home here can cost more than £2 million. Roads to the N of the picturesque **Marsh Lane** (which takes motorists down to the busy A1), such as **Hankins Lane** and **Glenwood Rd,** are equally pleasant up-market residential turnings.

Transport	Tubes: Mill Hill East, Hendon Central (zone 3, Northern). From Hendon Central: Oxford Circus 30 min (1 change), City 30 min, Heathrow 1 hr 30 min (1 change). Trains: Mill Hill Broadway (King's Cross 20 min, Moorgate 26 min).
Convenient for	Brent Cross shopping centre, Yoahan Plaza Japanese shopping centre, 24-hr superstores, Copthall Sports/Swimming Centre, Welsh Harp/Brent Reservoir. A1, M1, North Circular Rd. Miles from centre: 7.
Schools	Barnet Education Authority: Copthall (g), Hasmonean (Jewish) Schools (b) & (g), Mill Hill County High, St James' High RC, St Mary's C of E. Grant Maintained: Hendon. Private: Mill Hill (b), The Mount (g).

SALES

Flats	S	1B	2B	3B	4B	5B
Average prices	45–50	65–75	85–130+	120–200+	–	–
Houses	2B	3B	4B	5B	6/7B	8B
Average prices	100–130	140–260	180–350	300–360+	350–1M	1M+

RENTAL

Flats	S	1B	2B	3B	4B	5B
Average prices	520	700–860	780–1190	1120–1300	1500–2100	–
Houses	2B	3B	4B	5B	6/7B	8B
Average prices	850–1000	1000–1300	1200–1400	1500–1700	1500–2000	–

The properties   The 3-bed semi of inter-war vintage is most common. An increasing number of flat conversions, plus smaller houses, including some ex-council. Some larger prestige homes and new flats.

The market   Popular for family homes: sizeable Jewish and Indian communities. Also commuting flat-dwellers, students renting and first-time buyers. Homes backing on to the many main routes are cheapest. Local searches: 2–3 days.

Among those estate agents active in this area are:
- Alexander Jay
- Martyn Gerrard
- Anscombe & Ringland *
- Philip Phillips
- Ellis & Co
- Bairstow Eves
- Douglas Martin
- Barnard Marcus
- Shaw & Reeves
- Seymours
- Cosway
- Culwick Lerner
- Gerald Linke & Co
- Talbots
- Winkworth *

* further details: see advertisers' index on p633

H

HIGHGATE

Map ref: p29 (6F)
Postal districts: N6
Boroughs: Haringey (Lab),
Camden (Lab)
Council tax: Band D Camden
£1074, Haringey £856
Conservation areas:
Highgate Village
Parking: Free, but residents'
parking planned for
Highgate Hill. Congested
in village

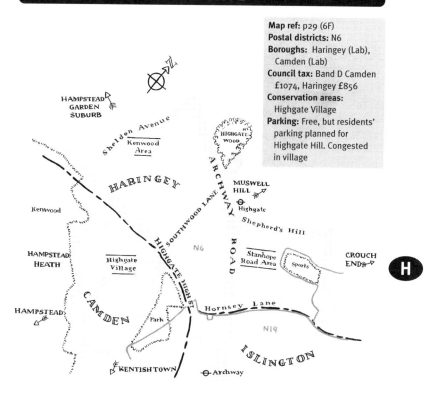

Highgate's residents claim that their village is just as nice as Hampstead –
but without the noise, congestion and over-inflated property prices. Those prices,
however, have been steadily catching up with NW3. Indeed, mansions with grounds
and security gates are becoming as much part of Highgate as gentlemanly Georgian
gems. Taking the wider area, Victorian and Edwardian homes are more common than
Georgian, which are found only in the heart of the village. The 20th century has added
blocks of flats and suburban houses of every level from modest to opulent.

One of the old villages that command the 'northern heights' around London,
Highgate has plenty of history, and considerable charm. It was on Highgate Hill that the
disillusioned young Dick Whittington heard the sound of Bow Bells and was persuaded
to 'turn again' to resume his progress towards becoming 'thrice Mayor of London'. The
alleged spot is marked with a stone and a statue of his famous cat.

Highgate is certainly not cheap. The overflow from Hampstead continued through
the '80s and '90s as the neighbouring 'village' became more and more expensive.
Furthermore, the increasing buying pressure in Highgate created its own overflow areas
in the rest of N6, Muswell Hill and Crouch End (see chapter) that, until the '80s, were
fairly sleepy enclaves with relatively stable property prices – especially the section E of
Archway Rd.

The population is well-heeled and traditional, with musicians and media folk among
the area's best-known residents. It is not quite as cosmopolitan as Hampstead but

there are pockets of wealthy Middle Eastern residents – the vast Witanhurst mansion at the top of **Highgate West Hill** (the largest house in London – if you exclude the royal palaces) is rumoured to be owned by King Hussein of Jordan, and the splendid Beechwood stately home in **Hampstead Lane** belongs to the Sultan of Oman. Witanhurst may, it's rumoured, be on the market – for £30 million.

As well as the international set Highgate has its own, settled, population: 'a huge base of local moneyed people who move within the area,' says one agent, probably through gritted teeth as private deals (no agent's commission) are not unknown. Traditionally these are actors, playwrights, top professionals – but recently there's been an influx of media, entertainment and City people. Local schools are good, which attracts and keeps families. The prosperous local market insulates the area from property price recessions. People pay up to £10 million to live in the mini-mansions of **Sheldon Avenue** and **Stormont Rd**.

Highgate shares with Hampstead the 800 acres of fields, woods and ponds of the heath, owned and managed by the City of London Corporation, plus the grounds of Kenwood where open-air concerts are held during the summer. Kenwood, a beautiful Adam mansion, houses the Iveagh Bequest, a notable collection of old masters.

Transport is less than ideal: Highgate tube is N of the village off **Archway Rd**. It suffered congestion last year when its escalators broke down: it is one of the deepest stations in London. There were fears that it would be closed, but funds have been found.

Highgate Village

This is what residents reckon is Highgate proper: the old village, still recognizable as such, with its accretion of lovely homes that have offered fresh air and sylvan views to prosperous Londoners from Elizabeth I's day onwards. It is bisected by **Highgate High St**, with its smart (though still useful) shops and restaurants. The **High St** is the boundary between Camden borough in the S and Haringey in the N. The main residential section of the village is on the Camden side, including the marvellous **Pond Square** with its 18th-century houses, late-Victorian mansion flats and the headquarters of the Highgate Society and the Highgate Literary and Scientific Institution, side by side in **South Grove** at one end of the square. South Grove House, opposite Witanhurst and the internationally famous Flask pub, is still one of the most desirable blocks in the village.

The premier address in the village is, however, **The Grove**; a row of houses, some of which date back to the 1680s, set back from the road behind an avenue of trees. Distinguished residents include violinist Yehudi Menuhin and pop icons such as Sting.

Houses in **The Grove** command £1–3 million. **North Grove**, just across **Hampstead Lane**, has some modern neo-Georgian houses.

Off **The Grove** is **Fitzroy Park**, an exclusive private road leading to a number of sumptuous and secluded homes – two new ones coming this spring – as well as to the 24 new luxury houses in **Highfields Grove** on the lower slopes of the grounds of Witanhurst. Also very popular is the 1970s development of houses and flats in **Highgate West Hill** called West Hill Park. Near the bottom of **Fitzroy Park** is a splendid 15th-century house called Fitzroy Farm, set in well over an acre of land adjoining Hampstead Heath, and with its own private access road. It was marketed at the end of the 1980s at a cool £7 million.

Back at the village, the terraced houses in **Bisham Gardens** are almost all converted into flats which, on the S side, have stunning views towards the City over Waterlow Park (one of London's most delightful parks), Lauderdale House (one-time home of Nell Gwynn) and the extraordinary Highgate Cemetery which, apart from being the last resting place of Karl Marx, is a major tourist attraction – guided tours are given.

Swain's Lane with its Victorian homes – a 3-bed one was for sale recently for £670,000 – leads down from the village to enclose, with **Highgate West Hill**, the celebrated cemetery and the Holly Lodge estate. This enormously popular residential area on the site of philanthropist Baroness Burdett-Coutts' estate comprises a mixture of houses and blocks of flats (the flats now council-owned) built between the wars in a mainly mock-Tudor style which is either smashing or vulgar, depending on your point of view. One of the houses sold last year to a showbiz buyer for £900,000 – a record for the estate, £650–700,000 is a more usual price. Next door is **Holly Village**, a group of 1865 Gothic houses around a 'village green', built for the estate servants: buyers now pay £360,000 for a 2-bed cottage. Also popular is **West Hill Park**, an award-winning private estate of flats and houses built in the 1970s in **Merton Lane**, overlooking the Highgate Ponds. South of **Swain's Lane** is NW5, and the popular streets of Dartmouth Park (see the Kentish Town chapter).

The Haringey side of the village, N of the **High St**, is slightly less dramatic, but attractive nevertheless, with some lovely leafy and secluded streets well-supplied with a mixture of semi-detached houses and conversions, and even a few large post-war purpose-built blocks of flats such as Southwood Hall, Cholmeley Lodge and Northwood Hall. Particularly popular are **Southwood Lawn Rd**, **Cholmeley Park**, **Cholmeley Crescent** and **Cromwell Avenue**, with a fascinating development of flats in a converted church. The spacious Victorian houses in these streets are popular: a 6-bed one can command up to £750,000.

This area did suffer somewhat in the late '80s when it seemed inevitable that the then government would insist on a dramatic widening of **Archway Rd** (which leads to the A1) as it went through Highgate, but fierce opposition by a coalition of local groups at a series of public inquiries (together with the opening of the M25 orbital motorway, which has reduced the amount of traffic using the road) managed to stop the plan.

Kenwood

Hampstead Lane leads from the village around the N end of Hampstead Heath to the grounds of Kenwood House. Directly opposite Kenwood are expensive roads like **Courtenay Avenue**, **Compton Avenue**, **Sheldon Avenue** and **Stormont Rd**, all a stone's throw from **The Bishops Avenue** (better known as Millionaires' Row) in the neighbouring borough of Barnet. These streets, almost exclusively with large detached houses, lead to Highgate Golf Club in **Denewood Rd**. Prices regularly top well over £10 million. Some are a little cheaper: two recent examples are a large house in **Stormont Rd** marketed at £2.5 million and another in **Sheldon Avenue** at £1,650,000. For more on **The Bishops Avenue** see the Hampstead Garden Suburb chapter.

Other roads in the area encircle the large grounds of Highgate School (which also owns a lot of property in the vicinity), such as **Bishopswood Rd**, **Broadlands Rd** and **View Rd**. Mostly traditional large houses, but a sprinkling of new properties as well.

North Rd and **North Hill** have some Georgian houses (one at the village end has just sold for £950,000) and a number of large mansion blocks, including the architecturally renowned 1938 Highpoint block, which has the distinction of having the highest rooftop in the whole of London. Also worth scrutiny are the well-mixed properties in **Talbot Rd**, **Bishops Rd**, **Bloomfield Rd** (some fine 5-bed mid-Victorian houses, around £800,000) and **The Park** – although the **Archway Rd** ends of these streets suffer noise and vibration from the heavy traffic.

Stanhope

East of **Archway Rd** is a clearly defined area of Highgate bounded in the N by **Shepherds Hill** and **Priory Gardens** (a sought-after cul-de-sac leading to Highgate tube station), in the E by **Coolhurst Rd**, and in the S by **Hornsey Lane**.

Shepherds Hill, with an increasing number of modern blocks of flats replacing the semis, has unparalleled views to the N over Muswell Hill and Alexandra Palace and Park for those properties whose outlook is not obscured, and dramatic views to the S for others. Blocks like Panorama Court and Highgate Heights are well-named.

The area is bisected N-S by **Stanhope Rd** which carries most of the traffic, leaving other streets relatively free. The prime road is **Hurst Avenue** which has very large £1 million houses overlooking the playing-fields of nearby St Aloysius Catholic Boys' High School. There is occasionally talk of the playing-fields being developed at some stage – which could bring prices down a little. **Avenue Rd**, at the bottom of the dip, now has a row of fairly new blocks of flats on the south side – much to the disgust of the house- and flat-owners across the road. The main drawback of this area is its distance from public transport – it's a stiff walk in either direction to Archway or Highgate tube stations, although there are buses along **Archway Rd** to the City and West End.

An important feature of this area is the Parkland Walk, formerly the route of the old railway which ran from Finsbury Park to Alexandra Palace, now turned by Haringey Council into a nature trail and wildlife reserve very popular with ramblers, walkers and joggers. Houses adjacent to or with access to the Parkland Walk are much in demand (despite the slightly increased security risk). Streets in this vicinity are **Avenue Rd**, **Stanhope Rd**, **Hornsey Lane**, **Milton Park**, **Orchard Rd** and **Claremont Rd**, all of which have increased in popularity in recent years. Parkgate Mews, a development of 16 flats and four houses in **Stanhope Rd**, was snapped up quickly in 1997. 'The Miltons': **Milton Park Avenue** and **Milton Park Rd** are popular with a good selection of smaller flats and houses which get less expensive the closer they are to **Archway Rd**. Lots of purpose-built flats in **Avenue Rd** and **Hornsey Lane**, including the huge Northwood Hall block.

Borders

South of Hornsey Lane is an attractive group of streets called the Whitehall Park Conservation Area (in Islington Borough) with beautifully preserved Victorian terraces in **Whitehall Park**, **Gladsmuir Rd** and **Harbetton Rd**. These have increased in value dramatically in the last decade. The district is sometimes called 'Highgate borders' and even 'Highgate slopes', but is really Archway (see Kentish Town chapter).

On the E side there are some pleasant streets more correctly called Crouch End, including **Crouch Hall Rd**, **Coleridge Rd** and **Birchington Rd**.

The boundary with Muswell Hill has some very interesting streets, including **Lanchester Rd** with its 5-bed houses and **Woodside Avenue** behind Highgate Wood, and the group of streets surrounding Haringey's Queen's Wood, including **Onslow Gardens**, **Connaught Gardens**, **Summersby Rd** and **Wood Lane**.

Transport	Tubes: Highgate, Archway (zones 2/3, Northern). From Highgate: Oxford Circus 25 min (1 change), City 18 min, Heathrow 1 hr (1 change).

Convenient for	Hampstead Heath, Kenwood. A1/M1 to North, City. Miles from centre: 5.

Schools	Local authority: William Ellis (b), Acland Burghley, Parliament Hill (g), Highgate Wood. Private: Highgate (b), Highfield, Channing (g), St Aloysius (b).

SALES

Flats	S	1B	2B	3B	4B	5B
Average prices	50–90	75–190	120–250+	150–350+	250–500	–
Houses	2B	3B	4B	5B	6/7B	8B
Average prices	160–325+	270–425+	300–700+	400–5M	→	1 →

RENTAL

Flats	S	1B	2B	3B	4B	5B
Average prices	520–1300	850–1700	1000–1950	1300–2600	1700–4000	2300+
Houses	2B	3B	4B	5B	6/7B	8B
Average prices	1000–1300	1300–2600	1700–4300	2100–8500	8500+	–

H

The properties	The roads around this ancient hill village hold not only 18th-century houses but some 1680s ones. Victorian terraces and converted and purpose-built flats have been added, plus large and ever-more-opulent mansions, town-houses and coveted private estates, from '30s to present day.

The market	Musicians, media folk and the professions buy here, joined by exalted foreign potentates for the large mansions in vast grounds. Flat-buyers get glorious views. Prices vary widely as does the range of homes. Local searches: Haringey 2 weeks, Camden 2 weeks.

Among those estate agents active in this area are:
- Anscombe & Ringland *
- Prickett & Ellis
- Winkworth *
- Sturt & Tivendale
- Stonebridge
- Keith Cardale Groves
- Benham & Reeves
- Godfrey & Barr
- Taylor Gibbs
- Fitzroys
- Knight Frank
- Goldschmidt Howland
- Hamptons
- Heathgate
- FPDSavills
- Foxtons *

further details: see advertisers' index on p633

HOLLAND PARK

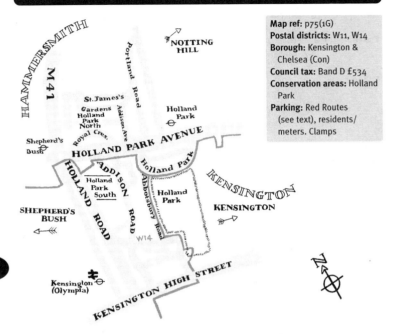

Map ref: p75(1G)
Postal districts: W11, W14
Borough: Kensington &
   Chelsea (Con)
Council tax: Band D £534
Conservation areas: Holland
   Park
Parking: Red Routes
   (see text), residents/
   meters. Clamps

The serene streets of Holland Park slope gently away from Kensington,
down the western flanks of Campden Hill. Leafy and spacious, the area known
as Holland Park boasts the biggest concentration of large houses in the Royal
Borough. 'The area known as' is said with care, since there's Holland Park (the park)
and also **Holland Park** (the road – which isn't: it's more a sort of square, in
the middle of which is sandwiched **Holland Park Mews**). The grandest, largest,
ambassadorial residences – some *are* embassies – are here. On the N side is
the park, on the S side, the busy **Holland Park Avenue**, which runs westwards to even
busier Shepherd's Bush roundabout. 'The area known as' fans leafily out on either
side of the broad, tree-lined avenue: southwards it runs between the park and
Holland Rd, down towards the W end of **Kensington High St**. Here there is further
confusion in the shape of **Holland Park Rd**, which is right at the S of the area.
Northwards the area has, over the years, pushed upwards into Notting Hill and
Notting Dale to take in the pleasant corners between **Portland Rd**, **St James's
Gardens** and **Royal Crescent**.

Holland Park, wherever its frontiers, is one of the luckier parts of London. Lucky to
have been in the right place at the wrong time.

Perhaps because Notting Hill, with its then raffish connotations, was a little close,
the area escaped the knock-down-and-build-flats boom of the '60s and '70s. Its early
Victorian elegance remained intact, if seedy. Now the grand old houses are once again
solidly fashionable, either as single homes or converted into unusually roomy flats.

Add to these a number of modern flats/town-house developments, usually set in
their own landscaped grounds, and also the small mews cottages with their garages
that are the legacy of the horse-drawn age in which the area grew up, and you have
a neighbourhood with a very good range of home sizes and styles – though not of

prices. Nothing is cheap. This has attracted families (schools, the park, communal square and crescent gardens), City people (the Central line goes straight there) and Hampstead-style politicians, actors and media-persons (the BBC mega-HQ is down the road at Shepherd's Bush). And now ambassadorial-level personages and international millionaires have completed the circle and re-inhabited the ambassadorial-sized homes, reclaimed after years as rented flats.

Today, the pleasant, community feel is added to by small, villagy shops and good restaurants. Thanks to the neighbouring areas' amenities, there's been no incentive to clutter up the place with sprawling supermarkets and the like. Most streets are within easy walking distance of either of the two main shopping/entertainment centres of **Kensington High St** and **Notting Hill Gate**. Between them these boast three cinemas, numerous clubs, pubs, restaurants and a wide range of shops. Several leading stores line **Kensington High St**. If as seems likely the White City development goes ahead (see Shepherd's Bush chapter) Holland Park will be a stroll away from a monster-Marks & Spencer.

Another of the area's attractions is the vast amount of public open space in the shape of Holland Park itself and in nearby Kensington Gardens. Holland Park covers 55 acres of woodlands and formal gardens, many sports, an adventure play park and an open-air theatre. Note though that **Holland Rd, Addison Crescent** and the southern part of **Addison Rd** form a major through-route. The controversial Red Route no-parking system is planned for these streets. Residents fear it will increase traffic flow – the council believes it will reduce congestion. As we go to press the campaigning residents are taking the council to the High Court in a last-ditch attempt to stop the Red Route.

Because much of the property reached a good international standard of finish some time back, and because of the embassies in the area, this has long been a favoured area for renting. The big blocks of flats in Holland Park South, and the converted mansions in the heart of the area, offer flats of varying sizes and characters. There is usually a choice of family houses with gardens and parking: plenty of these, too are being revamped and the quality on offer is rising.

Holland Park South

Tree-lined **Holland Park Avenue** sets the tone for this choice neighbourhood made up of large houses and leafy gardens. Vast stucco, or brick and stucco, mansions set back from the road behind sloping front gardens spread along the southern side of the busy avenue. Some have been converted into hotels. Pairs of large brick and stucco houses, split into flats, lie to the W, beyond the increasingly up-market shops and restaurants clustered around newly refurbished Holland Park underground station. A 2-bed flat on the Avenue recently sold for £350,000, but values vary as there is quite a mix of property on this long road.

The most coveted of imposing Victorian mansions are found in **Holland Park** (the road). Many of these double-fronted, detached, creamy stucco houses still have their decorative, highly ornate cast-iron and glass entrance canopies. (This delightfully idiosyncratic feature sits strangely, to be honest, on the dignified, pillared entrances: they look for all the world as if they were drawn in as an afterthought by Ronald Searle.) Many have been divided into flats, particularly popular with the diplomatic community. Small security video cameras are a regular feature of the area. Some are indeed used as embassies, but the council's Unitary Development Plan states that planning permission to convert houses into embassies will be given less readily in the future. Whole houses, backing onto the park, have been known to fetch up to £11 million, though not all prices are publicized. A whole-floor, and thus spacious, 3-bed flat in one of the big houses can cost £800,000. Cheaper (unmodernized) ones do exist. Size, individuality, condition and proximity to the park all affect the price.

Lying between the N and S arms of the street through a stone arch is **Holland Park Mews**, lined by 2-storey cottages with ground-floor garages. You can pay £600,000 for a 2-bed mews house here – and twice that was being asked last winter for a spectacular former stable-cum-folly. Note that **Holland Park** (the road) and its mews takes the W11 postcode together with the streets N of **Holland Park Avenue**.

Holland Park merges with **Abbotsbury Rd**, which runs southwards along the W side of the park itself: the postcode changes to W14. The road has road humps in a bid to slow traffic down but it is still a popular route from **Holland Park** to **Kensington High St**. Most of the homes on the W side of the street are from the second half of the 20th century, from the 10-storey flats block, Abbotsbury House, at the NW end to the series of select private cul-de-sacs, some with garages, which make up **Abbotsbury Close**. Immaculate 2/3-storey terraced brick houses stand in neatly landscaped enclaves set well back from **Abbotsbury Rd**. This is the deepest, most secluded part of Holland Park, select even for Kensington. Urban grime seems a world away.

The scene changes dramatically with the appearance of **Oakwood Court**, a development of 7-storey red-brick Victorian mansion blocks, which form the street of the same name. A strip of lawn, trees and shrubs divides the blocks on each side of the street. The mansions have recently been refurbished. On the corner is a new development of 3-storey red-brick homes and some mock-Tudor flats called Manderley. **Ilchester Place** opposite is leafy and salubrious. The big low-built houses, some with gardens backing on to Holland Park, command top prices.

Melbury Rd to the S is noted for its artist's-studio houses designed by the likes of Norman Shaw and Halsey Ricardo. An outstanding example is the eccentric red-brick Tower House, a copy of the Welsh Castell Coch. Built in the 1870s, it was renovated in the 1960s by actor Richard Harris. The houses are a legacy of the days when **Melbury Rd** and **Holland Park Rd** to the S formed a 19th-century artist's quarter. There are several more big red-brick detached studio houses, including Leighton House, once the home of painter Lord Leighton, now an art gallery and museum. The size of these Victorian mansions, built on the scale of country houses, makes for spectacular flats in those that are converted. These include the erstwhile home of pre-Raphaelite artist Holman ('Light of the World') Hunt, and a pair designed by architect Halsey Ricardo for his father-in-law and his patron respectively. They are now six huge apartments of which the smallest is a mere 1,723 sq ft (3-bed, 3-bath, 3-recep) and the most impressive the vast 4-bed/4-bath/3-reception room one of 3,036 sq ft – excluding its two terraces, conservatory and 76-ft private garden. Another spectacular conversion, of sculptor Sir Hamo Thorneycroft's 1870s studio, produced three flats. To the S of **Melbury Rd**, near the **Kensington High St** end, grand houses are punctuated by exclusive modern flats. Woodsford is a 5-storey red-brick development, Stavordale Lodge a 5-storey slate-coloured block with private parking and Park Close a 9-storey flat development overlooking the park and Commonwealth Institute grounds.

The S side of the street forms **St Mary Abbots Terrace**, a modern development of neo-Georgian town-houses. The 3-storey houses are set around a series of three cul-de-sacs. Some are turned sideways on to the street, their rear gardens adding to its leafy look. At the end of this terrace facing **Addison Rd** lies a 9-storey block of flats. Opposite this is the private road **Strangeway Terrace** with its water sculpture and attractive flats. It is closed to through traffic from **Holland Park** to **Melbury Rd**.

Addison Rd S of **Addison Crescent** forms part of the southbound one-way traffic system, which detracts from the character of this otherwise exclusive road. Detached and semi-detached stucco and brick/stucco villas, and a terrace of Gothic-style houses, sit on the W side. Opposite are two large modern flats blocks, 10-storey Monckton Court and 6-storey Farley Court. Both are set in landscaped grounds off the road.

The S curve of **Addison Crescent** forms the link in the one-way system between **Addison Rd** and **Holland Rd**. This short stretch of detached and paired villas consequently suffers from the heavy traffic and noise. Work is imminent to turn this stretch into a Red Route. The N curve with its big 2/3-storey detached brick and stucco villas and walled front gardens is noticeably quieter and more desirable. Traffic or not, these enormous villas make enviable homes.

Grander white stucco-fronted detached villas line the W side of the N stretch of **Addison Rd**. They are set back behind walled gardens and small sweeping driveways: as is normal, at least two were undergoing expensive rebuilds last winter. Security cameras are another feature of the street scene here. On the opposite side of the road is a group of detached and semi-detached houses, including the intriguing glazed brick and tile Richmond House, headquarters of the Richmond Fellowship. Selby Court, a 9-storey block of flats, lies between **Somerset Square**, a modern development of red-brick town-houses and flats, and **Woodsford Square**, a 1970s development of large town-houses. Both are set in landscaped grounds walled off from the road behind a shield of tall trees.

Homes at the N end of **Woodsford Square** overlook the Holland Park tennis club, tucked in behind **Holland Park Gardens**. Holland Park Mansions, a 4-storey red and white block on the E side of **Holland Park Gardens**, also overlooks the courts. A 3-bed flat here was £500,000 last December.

At the N end of **Addison Rd** next to Cardinal Vaughan School stands Addisland Court, an 8-storey brick and stone block, which stretches around the corner into exclusive **Holland Villas Rd**. Opposite this stands the 4-storey modern Parkland flats. The large brick and stucco detached villas in this quiet, leafy street fetch eye-watering prices: one, owned by the same family for a century, was for sale last winter for £3.35 million: well done, grandpa. Developers still find the occasional one in a tatty state: four were being worked on last winter. Off the NW end of **Holland Villas Rd** are **Upper** and **Lower Addison Gardens**, both tree-lined streets of 3-storey terraced houses. At the top end, near **Holland Park Rd**, a new development of 27 flats is called Fitzclarence House.

Holland Park North

On the N side of **Holland Park Avenue** stands **Royal Crescent**. Two curving terraces of white-painted, 5-storey homes sweep around a tree-lined semicircular garden with ornate iron railings, which were recently reintroduced after residents and the council raised the money. Each of the end houses has graceful circular pavilions to finish the row, and the whole crescent appears to have been transported from Regency Brighton. Alas, it gazes out on the Kensington Hilton rather than the English Channel. Two-bed flats in the Crescent go for around £280,000. Tucked in behind the W side is the curve of **Royal Crescent Mews**, a 1980s terrace of 2-storey brick and stucco cottages with their own garages.

St Ann's Villas, which leads off **Royal Crescent**, is a relatively busy local road, which used to suffer from severe congestion until the introduction of controlled parking. It has a mix of houses and flats – notably a group of Victorian Gothic detached brown-brick gabled houses. Cutting W-E through this street is **Queensdale Rd**, a pleasant and very popular street of Victorian terraced houses. Boundary changes have brought **Queensdale Crescent**, **Norland Rd** and **Kingsdale Gardens** into the Royal Borough rather than Hammersmith. At the end of **Norland Rd** stands a splendid mosque with a roof adorned with gold. **Norland Place** is made up of pink stucco and brick houses with railings and is closed to traffic: on foot, it leads to Holland Park roundabout. Opposite these homes a large Victorian stucco house has been converted into social housing and next to this is another new development of affordable housing. Norland House, set behind these homes, is a 22-storey council block. This still belongs to Hammersmith and Fulham Council which is busy modernizing the flats. The best stretch of **Queensdale Rd**, E of **St Ann's Villas**, has 3/4-storey and basement brick and pastel-painted stucco houses. One was on the market for £650,000 last winter. Off it, **Queensdale Place** is a pleasant little cul-de-sac of 2-storey stock-brick and stucco terraces, to which has been added a spectacular trio of homes, one of which has an indoor pool. **St Ann's Rd**, the northern continuation of **St Ann's Villas**, has some pleasant 4-storey houses, priced when in modern condition between £400,000 and £500,000 depending on size.

Addison Place, off the opposite side of **Queensdale Rd**, is lined by a variety of period and modern 2-storey mews cottages and ends in cobbles. It curves around behind the E parade of **Royal Crescent**, debouching into **Addison Avenue**, the showpiece of the area with handsome 2-storey houses. Opposite is **Taverners Close** with five red-brick detached houses. The best stretch of this wide tree-lined avenue with its splendid vista of St James Norlands Church lies N of **Queensdale Rd**: here homes can fetch more than £1 million. Elegant paired stucco houses painted in pastel shades line both sides. The smaller paired stucco houses S of **Queensdale Rd** give way to an attractive parade of shops, offices and the Norland Arms pub. Green Victorian street lamps add to the avenue's period character.

St James Church sits in the central garden of **St James's Gardens**, another of the neighbourhood's choicest addresses. Pairs of attractive semi-detached houses linked by paired entrances are set around the communal gardens. The lower floors of these handsome 3-storey plus basement brick and stucco houses are painted in pastel shades, adding to the distinctive character of this Victorian square.

Return down **Addison Avenue** to **Queensdale Rd** and turn S into **Queensdale Walk**, a tranquil cul-de-sac of 2-storey painted cottages, E, facing a long garden wall with overhanging trees. North into **Princess Place** are three 2-storey homes. One street away is **Norland Square** where three terraces of 4-storey with basement stucco-fronted houses stand around a large tree-filled private central garden with a tennis court. Off the square runs **Norland Place**, a cobbled mews of 2-storey painted cottages which stretches through to **Princedale Rd**. **Princedale Rd** has mainly Victorian terraces, a mix of houses and flats, plus speciality shops near the junction with **Penzance Place**. Here the homes are individually coloured. More brick and stucco terraces are found here, next to St Clements and St James Primary School.

Penzance Place with its flat-fronted Victorian terraced houses leads into **Portland Rd**, another popular street of Victorian terraced houses. Many of the 3-storey plus basement houses here have now been converted into flats. Properties on the E side are more expensive, being wider with larger gardens. The road is sealed off to traffic at Clarendon Cross, a smart villagy enclave of posh shops, galleries, antique shops, restaurants/wine bars.

Lying behind the NW side of **Portland Rd**, across the road from Avondale Park, is award-winning **Hippodrome Mews**. Two terraces of 3-storey brown-brick town-houses face each other across a narrow cobbled mews in this private cul-de-sac (1970s). The pleasingly bulbous shape of an old kiln, as high as the houses, is preserved among them, and no doubt accounts for the name of **Pottery Lane** which, running S from here, has an attractive group of 3-storey painted brick and stucco terraced houses at its junction with **Penzance Place**. **Clarendon Rd**, which parallels **Portland Rd** to the E, marks the start of the climb up Notting Hill (see chapter), where graceful crescents still echo the shape of the racecourse they replaced. Many of the big detached Victorian houses are split into flats – though one, complete with cottage/garage, was £2.5 million unmodernized in January. Close to the tube station, between **Holland Park Avenue** and **Lansdowne Mews**, 12 new houses were built in 1989.

Borders

Holland Rd (N-S), the area's western boundary, is a major traffic artery running down to **Kensington High St** from the M41, which ends at Shepherd's Bush roundabout. Its S end is one-way: the traffic flows northwards, while the southbound stream dives down the bottom half of **Addison Crescent** into **Addison Rd**. The Red Route will affect these streets. A series of small hotels cluster around the S end of **Holland Rd**. The rest is lined by mainly 4-storey and basement stucco, or brick and stucco, terraced houses of varying quality. In common with most properties in the neighbourhood, they are split into flats. Double glazing is cited in sales details: they need it. Despite the traffic, a big 2-bed flat was £225,000 last winter, though more ordinary ones are nearer £140,000.

More bed-and-breakfast hotels are found in **Russell Rd** to the W. They are mixed in with further flats in the 3-storey and basement brick and stucco terraces overlooking the increasingly busy West London railway line (which carries Channel Tunnel freight trains) and the glass façade of the Olympia Exhibition Centre. A thin strip of land along the railway which for years was home to a variety of small firms – and which was forever under threat from various road schemes – has become 'Kensington Park'. a development of 125 new homes by Barratt. Prices start from £215,000 for 1-bed flats. A footbridge over the tracks links **Russell Rd** with the Kensington Olympia station, just across the borough boundary with Hammersmith.

Russell Gardens is a short parade of small local shops and restaurants, plus a pub. **Russell Gardens Mews** has several working garages at its entrance S, giving way to 2-storey brick/painted cottages towards the rear. Properties at the NW end of tree-lined **Elsham Rd** also back on to the railway.

Transport	Tubes: Holland Park, Shepherd's Bush (zone 2, Central); Kensington Olympia. To Oxford Circus 12 min, City 22 min, Heathrow 50 min (2 changes). Trains: Kensington Olympia, trains to Clapham Junction and some long-distance services.
Convenient for	BBC TV Centre at Shepherd's Bush, M4/M40 to Heathrow and the West. Direct tube line to West End, City. Miles from centre: 3.5.

Schools   Local Authority/Grant Maintained: Holland Park School, Cardinal 6th-form College, Cardinal Vaughan School (b). Private: Norland Place School, Notting Hill & Ealing High (g).

SALES

Flats	S	1B	2B	3B	4B	5B
Average prices	120–160	150–400	230–750+	3700–1M	→1M+	800–1.7M+

Houses	2B	3B	4B	5B	6/7B	8B
Average prices	350–700	500–1M	750–2M	→3M+	→8M	→8M+

RENTAL

Flats	S	1B	2B	3B	4B	5B
Average prices	700–1500	900–1700	1300–2800	1700–4300	2600–6500+	5200–10,000

Houses	2B	3B	4B	5B	6/7B	8B
Average prices	1950–3000	2100–5200	3250–8000	4300–10,000+	13,000+	→

The properties   Vast, snowy-white villas and terraces, imposing Victorian red brick, smaller-scale squares, modern town-houses, all gather round Holland Park and Avenue. Rich source of family homes, flats converted and mansion, ambassador-level grandeur, in leafy streets. Some new conversions and mews houses to be found.

The market   Firmly in the top bracket: prices reflect that it is N of Kensington rather than next door to North Kensington. The embassy-sized houses have reverted to multi-million pound single occupancy after years as tatty flats. Local searches: 1 week.

Among those estate agents active in this area are:
- John Wilcox
- Aylesfords
- Marsh & Parsons
- Addison Properties
- John D Wood
- Berkeley International
- Beauchamp Estates
- Winkworth *
- FPDSavills
- Hamptons
- Anscome & Ringland *
- Foxtons
- Jackson-Stops & Staff
- De Groot Collis
- Scotts *
- Beaney Pearce *

* further details: see advertisers' index on p633

ISLINGTON AND HIGHBURY

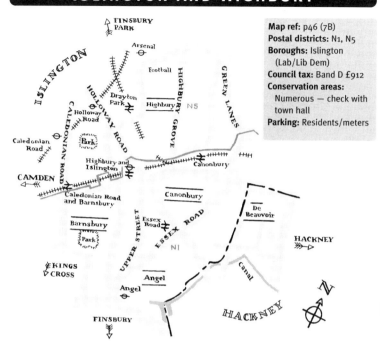

Map ref: p46 (7B)
Postal districts: N1, N5
Boroughs: Islington
(Lab/Lib Dem)
Council tax: Band D £912
Conservation areas:
Numerous — check with
town hall
Parking: Residents/meters

Islington, perched high above the City, has arrived. Recommended, a decade ago, as a good area to buy into – up-and-coming. The last couple of years of City bonuses (not to mention the Blair factor: New Labour, new Islington) saw the '90s complete what the '80s had begun.

During the 1990s the place moved up-market. **Upper St** smartened itself up considerably, led by the development of The Business Design Centre, which has proved a great success (and which spawned a new underground NCP car park and an adjoining hotel). The development of the Angel Square office complex has created a new entrance to the tube, with greatly improved access to the platforms.

More fundamentally, Islington's axis swung: it stopped lifting its eyes northwards unto to the hills, and saw itself no longer as sub-Hampstead, but rather as super-City. Fast transport to Docklands via the DLR from Bank, as well as easy access to City and West End, brought a new breed of well-heeled buyers.

However, many of these were looking for new apartments with security systems and state-of-the-art fittings. These dutifully began to appear – and sold, as well, to overseas buyers who bought them off-plan as an investment. It follows that there is also an increase in smart homes to rent.

The original, period homes are very British pleasures, and their inhabitants (wherever they may have hailed from originally) are somehow very British folk. The international jet-set do not appreciate, as do we, the inconvenience of the tucked-away, charming – but often narrow-gutted, many-staired – houses, however Georgian the terraces. ('The madness of King George is explained,' claimed one.)

But for all its inhabitants, old or new, city-slickers or middle-class radicals in 'the Arts', Islington, with Highbury to the N, is a most satisfactory place. It has a definite

shape, which starts from the southern base-line of **Pentonville Rd/City Rd**, unfurls on either side of the central spine of **Upper St**, and is neatly capped by Highbury with its green, open fields. Then, too, it is set on pleasantly hilly ground for variety; it boasts a village green to offset the commercialism of the S end, also theatres (the Almeida, for one), clubs, galleries, a canal – and real gems of residential corners which are made all the more pleasing by the fact that through traffic can dash along the main routes without suspecting their existence. After a hundred years of cheerful cheapness, **Upper St** is now one of London's smarter locations: wall-to-wall designer bars, restaurants, clothes and gift shops (and more to come) from the Angel up to Highbury Corner.

Due N from the City, the Highbury and Islington territory lies E of **Caledonian Rd** and King's Cross, W of **Green Lanes** and thus Hackney and Stoke Newington, and S of Finsbury Park (**Gillespie Rd**). Inhabited from Saxon times, what was 'Iseldone' developed rapidly in the 18th century as a spa resort, thanks to its many underground springs and rivers. It was also on the main routes to Smithfield and developed a reputation as a market garden, providing cattle and produce for the whole of London.

The area divides into four neighbourhoods; Canonbury, Barnsbury and the Angel in Islington with, to the N, Highbury around the green open spaces of its Fields. Follow **Essex Rd** as it forks off to the E side of the green to find Canonbury, Islington's heartland. A popular spot since the days of Elizabeth I, it thrived under the Georges and still has some fine terraces from this period set in its leafy roads. (The cost of these can be as much as 10–15 per cent higher than for a comparably sized home in the other neighbourhoods.) Mainly family houses here, but flats and some larger houses are available.

Barnsbury is a little later: a stock-brick and stucco land laid out by Cubitt (see Belgravia) in the 1820s. This is almost exclusively family housing, quieter (thanks to a fiendishly maze-like traffic scheme) and more completely residential in character, arranged in pretty streets around half a dozen garden squares. The Angel corner, aside from the commercial area, is predominantly composed of small flat-fronted Georgian/early Victorian terraces. Front gardens are rare, but some streets have central greenery; roads tend to be narrower, broadening towards the N, and the area S of **Essex Rd** has larger property and more flats.

By contrast, Highbury is virtually all Victorian, aside from roads bordering Highbury Fields. Generally you'll find ornate late-Victorian houses with broader avenues and gardens, split between flats and family homes. Some large properties in **Highbury New Park** and **Highbury Hill** – if you can find one that has not been transformed into flats.

In short, the area around the Angel and the southern end of **Upper St** is definitely a young singles corner; the family stamping-grounds remain Barnsbury, Highbury and Canonbury. Traditional buyers (from the media, the law) still look for period properties, while the incomers go for the new developments, one step away from the fashionable 'lofts' of Clerkenwell. These continue to come on-stream, though City jitters over the turmoil of the Far East finances slowed sales and calmed the property market here more quickly than most. Now over 50 per cent of buyers are people moving within the area.

The Angel

The Angel neighbourhood centres on the junction of **Upper St** and **City Rd**. **Islington High St**, **Upper St** and immediately adjacent streets are the main shopping areas in Islington. The area to the N of **Pentonville Rd**, from the **High St** W to **Penton Rd**, is mainly commercial property and offices. This has become an important office centre, though a flats development appeared a year back, running N from **Pentonville Rd** to **White Lion St**. Angel Square, a big office complex over the tube, has provided a new entrance to the underground with the longest escalators in London. Running W-E is **Chapel St**, which has a large, well-known fruit-and-veg market – supplemented by a big Sainsbury's and Marks & Spencer in **Liverpool Rd**. A new, pedestrianized scheme, with shops and the inevitable multiplex cinema, are planned for 2002 around **Parkfield St**, in the angle of **Liverpool Rd** and **Upper St**.

On the E side of **Upper St**, just before the green, is the distinctive Mall antiques arcade; behind this, and running parallel, are **Islington High St** (a surprise: it is more of a charming lane) and **Camden Passage** (an equally confusing name), a great centre for antiques. Antiques and small, old-fashioned shops continue down **Essex Rd**.

The area to the E of **Upper St** and **Essex Rd** is quiet and residential and almost exclusively glorious flat-fronted Georgian terraces. Streets are narrow and parking is restricted. **Colebrooke Row** has tall terraces set behind a strip of greenery, across which is **Duncan Terrace** and the imposing red-brick St John the Evangelist Church.

Turning into **Vincent Terrace**, fine Georgian houses give lovely views onto the Grand Union Canal; on the other side of it, **Noel Rd** houses turn their back on the water – and thus have raised gardens that stop at – or rather, above – the towpath: the Hanging Gardens of Islington. S of **Vincent Terrace** and W of **City Rd** basin, houses tend to be smaller, streets narrower. Some modern housing, particularly along the **City Rd** edge: **Elia St** has low Georgian terraces on one side and low council blocks on the other.

North of the canal, at the corner of **Packington St** and **Prebend St**, is the Packington Square Estate – modern '70s low-rise blocks (still one of the less-popular parts of Islington, despite a council clear-up scheme). E from here, across to the **Southgate Rd** and the borough boundary, are some fine period terraces (mainly family houses). Streets are wider, squares and trees more common, parking easier and prices higher. **Arlington Avenue** and **Square**, with the tucked-away Clock Tower Mews development (among the first, and best, of the modern mews re-creations), are typical. **Wilton Square** is also particularly quiet and fine.

Essex Rd

The streets that lie between the **New North Rd**, **Essex Rd** and **Southgate Rd** are more mixed, with different periods appearing in the same road. Streets are wider and parking a little less of a problem, despite the large houses and many flat conversions. **Elizabeth Avenue** contains an 8-storey tower block to the N of **Rotherfield St**. The roads in this neighbourhood have predominantly flat-fronted, substantial terraces and some houses are double-fronted. Other streets are later in period, such as **Elmore**

St and **Northchurch Rd**. Dover Court council estate is just beneath the **Essex Rd** and **Balls Pond Rd** junction. This corner is attracting developers, too: 'The Pinnacle', a new scheme of 19 1- and 2-bed flats priced from £104,950, is appearing at the **Balls Pond** end of **Essex Rd**, complete with rooftop terrace and Japanese garden. Nearby, off **Ockendon Rd**, Ockendon Mews is a cobbled courtyard redevelopment of ex-industrial buildings; this makes for roomy flats (some galleried), one house and a large live/work unit. A 1-bed flat was for sale here last winter for £135,000.

Canonbury

Upper St is the main artery of Islington, running N into its heart. At **Islington Green** the road forks: **Upper St** continues N and **Essex Rd** NE. The sharp angle now holds Grove Manor Homes' key site on the N side of the green, running up to between **Upper St** and **Gaskin St**. The 1- to 3-bed flats and penthouses at 'Angel on the Green', grouped round a central courtyard with angel sculpture, were completing by the end of last year with only six out of the 86 apartments (2- and 3-bed, £277–447,500) still to sell. Prices started at £147,500 for 1-bed flats and rose to a million for penthouses.

Overlooking the Green itself, and next door to the Slug & Lettuce pub, eight roomy 1- and 2-bed flats plus a 3-bed penthouse are appearing: completion is due in July; prices from £195,000.

Little passageways and courtyards continue N up to the period terraces of **Florence St** and **Cross St**. To the E of these are the red-brick mansion flats of **Halton Rd** and **Canonbury Villas**. Running NW and intersecting with the **Essex Rd** is **Canonbury Rd**, forming a triangle with **Upper St** at the top. Georgian flat-fronted terraces on either side of **Canonbury Rd** give way to modern council blocks just before **Canonbury Square**, a superb Regency square with tall, thin terraced houses and a garden in its centre (and at the heart of Canonbury). This is one of its most prized corners, but not as peaceful as you'd expect since **Canonbury Rd** which cuts across it.

Round the corner we rejoin the main **Upper St** where **Compton Terrace**, a fine, lofty Regency row, is sheltered from **Upper St** by a line of trees and a garden. New homes appeared in 1990 behind the S end of the terrace in **Compton Avenue**: 11 3- and 4-bed houses called The Cloisters. Just to the N, **Upper St** and **Canonbury Rd** meet at Highbury Corner, the vast roundabout beyond which Highbury begins. Eastwards from **Canonbury Square**, **Compton Rd** has tall Georgian terraces which give way to double-fronted period houses where it joins **Alwyne Villas**' broader-fronted rows. Here you'll find Canonbury Tower, a romantic 16th-century relic which now houses the famed Tower Theatre amateur company, which mounts ambitious rep seasons.

Continuing, **Canonbury Place** has the pleasant Canonbury Tavern and genteel little shops. To the N along **St Marys Grove** are a whole series of neo-Georgian developments, low flat-fronted terraces culminating in **John Spencer Square**. At the end of **Canonbury Place**, the road splits into **Grange Grove** and **Canonbury Park North** and **South**. The area is very mixed: modern semis nestle with mock-Georgian ones which rub shoulders with the real thing. Grove Manor Homes has squeezed nine houses and 25 flats into **Canonbury Park South** to such good effect that they received a 1998 Civic Trust award. At the corner of **Canonbury Park South** and **Willow Bridge Rd** is an imposing red-brick Victorian mansion which sets the tone for the rest of the street – spacious Victorian semis with quiet, unrestricted parking. This, along with **Alwyne Place**, forms the two Victorian streets in Canonbury.

Running S, **Willow Bridge Rd** crosses **Alwyne Rd** and **Canonbury Grove**, which together enclose the New River Walk and small, charming public gardens (quiet, covetable streets with superb period houses). To the NE, contained by **Essex Rd** and the **Balls Pond Rd**, is the quiet low-rise council estate with maisonettes and interconnected walkways called the Marquess Estate, which is centred around

Clephane Rd. You'll have to cross the **St Paul's Rd** highway to find Canonbury's little station, which links with the N London line, Silverlink, and has a handful of shops. **Wallace Rd**, which leads to it, has fine, tall flat-fronted terraces on the right, and on the left later ones with good front gardens. To the E are the fine terraces of **St Paul's Place** and **Northampton Park**. Much of the area towards Highbury to the W is large period houses, which are realistically priced especially along busy **St Paul's Rd**.

Back at the **Essex Rd/Canonbury Rd** junction is Essex Rd station, which has a service into Moorgate on weekdays. City Heights is at the junction, just opposite the railway station. Developers Grove Manor Homes sold all 66 flats, some off-plan, a third of them to singles.

Canonbury Riverside seems at first glance a contradictory address, being as Islington is a fair way from the Thames. But the New River, built in the 17th century as London's first proper water supply, used to flow through Canonbury. It now ends in Stoke Newington, but a replica channel runs through a linear park from **St Paul's Rd** down to **Canonbury Rd**, forming the New River Walk. This is presumably the excuse for the Canonbury Riverside address ascribed to 'Royal Canonbury Tower', a development in **Canonbury St** of 35 flats and four 3-bed houses. There's a communal gym and a rooftop terrace. Next door, the same firm built 'City View', where the 25 flats share a roof terrace with fine views to the S.

Barnsbury

Liverpool Rd running N from the Angel is the main avenue, and is typically composed of flat-fronted brick terraces. To the E the junction with **Upper St** forms a thin strip of land up to Highbury. This is not strictly Barnsbury, but may well be referred to as such by estate agents. **Barford St** marks the site of the newly restored Business Design Centre, with its glass arches. North is the fine **Gibson Square**, and above this **Milner Square**, an 1840s creation completely restored by the council in the 1970s. A modern private development around the corner mimics its rather eccentric, vertical style. East is **Almeida St**, home of the Almeida Theatre, and small period terraces continue up to Islington Park.

To the W of **Liverpool Rd** across to the **Caledonian Rd** is Barnsbury proper, whose homogeneous residential groves were laid out by Cubitt in the 1820s. In the best Islington traditions, it's a secretive corner. Its peace is unassailable, courtesy of an outsider-proof one-way system. Maps are issued to friends. To the S **Ritchie St** and **Bachelor St**, with their neat terraces and first-floor balconies, border on the Angel and end in Culpeper community garden. Continue W along **Tolpuddle** (**Culpeper St**), which intersects with **Barnsbury Rd** and **Penton St** running S-N. To the W **Copenhagen St** crosses **Barnsbury Rd** and curves round to meet the **Caledonian Rd**. S of here are Pentonville council estates.

Cloudesley Rd runs N from **Culpeper Gardens**, and to the W is Barnard Park – a rare open space for the Islington area, it boasts tennis courts. To the E is **Cloudesley St** with its wide avenues and dignified double-fronted houses, leading into the superb **Cloudesley Square** (1820s Regency with the Celestial Church of Christ at the centre). **Richmond Avenue** runs W from **Liverpool Rd**, and connects with the **Caledonian Rd**. To the N is the secluded **Lonsdale Square**, substantial terraces of – a sudden shock – heavily Gothic styling: the only Victorian square in the area.

North of this is the ivy-clad **Morland Mews**, one of the few modern developments. West is the delightful **Ripplevale Grove** – small, tidy terraces and gardens – and further W still **Thornhill Square**, a fine Regency square with substantial properties (a 3/4-bed house was priced at £650,000 last winter). Its curved end mirrors **Thornhill Crescent**. Off **Matilda St**, which runs S from Thornhill Square, is the 1995-built **Bramwell Mews**; a 2-bed cottage in this courtyard development was £295,950 last winter.

Barnsbury ends with the **Caledonian Rd**, predominantly small, old shops, cheerfully and irredeemably scruffy, though conversions are increasing. The junction with **Offord Rd** in the N marks the top limit of Barnsbury. **Offord Rd** is full of rather dishevelled Georgian houses; it travels E to join the **Liverpool Rd** at a junction marked by the Samuel Lewis red-brick flats.

Highbury

Highbury & Islington station (rail/Victoria line tube) is at Highbury Corner, at the start of the **Holloway Rd**. **Highbury Grove/Park** runs N from **St Paul's Rd**, bisecting the area. To the W of **Highbury Grove**, **Corsica Rd** and **Baalbec Rd** describe an area of late-(1889) Victorian terraces with elaborate façades. Parallel with this is **Highbury Place**, which marks the beginning of the green acres of Highbury Fields. Flat-fronted Georgian terraces overlooking the fields are the poshest part of Highbury. The lovely open expanse of the fields lives up to its name, a breath-of-fresh-air common with the civilized addition of a swimming pool at the S end, tennis courts in the N, and an award-winning adventure playground, staffed at times – but check. They are bounded on the W side by **Highbury Crescent** and **Terrace** (respectively vast detached mansions and tall period terrace, many now flats), which are Highbury's only Georgian streets. Just off Highbury Fields is **Ronalds Rd**, where the old central hall has been split into 10 flats.

Otherwise homes are exclusively Victorian terraces with bay windows, wide streets – though **Highbury Terrace Mews** is an exception. Tucked behind **Highbury Terrace**, this is a modern development, with one of the 3-bed houses recently on sale for £285,000. To the N of the Fields is **Highbury Hill**, a pretty corner with St John's Church to the E and a clock tower at the centre. Another coveted location, houses are large Victorian double-fronted, decreasing in size and becoming terraced towards Arsenal. A new mews, **De Barowe Mews**, appeared a few years back in **Leigh Rd**.

Roads to the N of **Highbury Hill** and W of **Highbury Park** are later Victorian terraces, again reducing in size and quality towards **Gillespie Rd** and Arsenal football ground. Some still unrenovated properties towards the bottom, and prices around the football stadium are naturally cheaper (but not much). Since last year plans to expand the Arsenal ground have been shelved, and some matches are now played at Wembley. The area is still best avoided on match days, though. Despite this, 100 **Drayton Park**, a vast office-block (or rather a whole square, around courtyard with 'water feature'), is becoming Art Deco-inspired flats. This will add 84 new 1-, 2-, and 3-bed homes, complete with maple doors, maple-floored living rooms, to the road to the footie ground – and yet another roof garden: 'the largest in Islington', we are told. The prices for Phase I, completed in January, start from £110,000, £150,000 and £215,000 respectively.

Victoriana continues NE of Highbury Park and **Riversdale Rd** to **Mountgrove Rd**. Off **Mountgrove Rd** is a development of 1- and 2-bed flats, 'Old Stable Mews', which is built round a cobbled courtyard. At the corner of **Highbury New Park** overlooking Clissold Park is the noted White Horse pub. The Highbury Quadrant estate covers the area from here down to **Green Lanes**: housing is low-level tower blocks. South from **Sotheby Rd** to **Highbury New Park** in the SE is late Victoriana: large terraces with ornate exteriors and quiet tree-lined streets. The exceptions are **Kelross Rd**, off Highbury Park, which has some modest 1930s semis, and **Fountain Mews** which opens onto **Highbury Grange**, an extensive development of post-modernist and tower blocks.

Across the road are a series of large mansion flats, **Taverner Square** and **Peckett Square**, with interconnecting courtyards. **Aberdeen Rd** runs S to **Aberdeen Park**, the most secluded corner in the district: prices are high and styles range from 1930s semis to spacious Victorian mansions. **Highbury New Park** skirts the area to the E, broad and long, with newer property on the right-hand side, Quadrant estate in the N and Spring Gardens estate in the S. On one side vast period mansions have mainly been converted into flats such as the sophisticated Belmont Court, on the corner of **Balfour Rd**. To the E, **Petherton Rd** runs N to **Green Lanes** with 4-storey Victorian terraces in a wide avenue with a grassy shoulder down the middle. A grid of roads crosses W-E to **Newington Green Rd**, made up of Victorian terraces decreasing in size from **Poets Rd** to **Green Lanes**.

Borders

Highbury and Islington have three main border areas. To the E of Islington lie 'the De Beauvoirs'. Still in the N1 postal district but just across the borough boundary (it runs along **Southgate St**), the pleasant cache of wide streets around **De Beauvoir Square/Rd** came up rapidly in the '80s, and its denizens look to Islington rather than Hackney. Its modest-sized, unfussy villas come in ones, twos and threes as well as the more usual rows, offering a rare chance to buy half a house rather than a slice of terrace. Even rarer is the size of garden these 2/3-bed homes enjoy: 75–100 ft or more is not uncommon – and some get garages. A fourth bedroom often betokens roof or back extensions. De Beauvoir lies to the N of **Downham Rd**, W of the **Kingsland Rd** and S of the **Balls Pond Rd**. Another sign of evolution is the way the place has changed its name: you'll find it labelled 'Kingsland' on maps, but that word seems to have dropped out of use. (The part to the S of **Downham Rd** labelled 'De Beauvoir Town' is now largely occupied by the high- and medium-rise tower blocks of the De Beauvoir council estate.) To the N of **Downham Rd**, the terraces resume. **De Beauvoir Square** is an 1840s Gothic square of smart pairs of 4-storey villas with bay windows and ornate gables, around a central garden (a 3-bed house here was on the market for £399,500 last winter). The square is the hub of a network of streets – similar homes can be found in streets like **Mortimer Rd**, **De Beauvoir Rd** (a busy thoroughfare), **Hertford Rd** and **Englefield Rd**. Those closest to **De Beauvoir Square** tend to be best; quality frays a little towards the edges, eg **Southgate Grove**. In **Culford Rd** a recent development, Eagle Court, added 30 flats and houses to the area. On **Kingsland Rd**, the E edge of the neighbourhood, 'De Beauvoir Place' is a conversion of listed Georgian terraces into 1- and 2-bed flats and 2- and 3-bed duplexes. Apart from being across the border in Hackney, two other factors hold De Beauvoir prices down: many houses are leasehold rather than freehold, and there is no tube.

Lower Holloway, to the N of Barnsbury, lies N of the railway line and W of the **Holloway Rd**. Property is almost totally council-built (modern) radiating off **Paradise Passage**. The exceptions include **Arundel Place** and **Arundel Square**: spacious flat-fronted terraces surrounding a central garden and playground, and **Ellington St**, which has lower-level Georgian terraces, rising to the substantial. Look, too, at **Furlong Rd** which, with **Orleston Rd**, runs E from **Liverpool Rd**: both have large semi-detached period houses. North along **Liverpool Rd** are a few small Victorian terraces, **Morgan Rd**, **Ringcroft St** and **Sheringham Rd**, quality uneven. **Liverpool Rd** itself has some handsome, flat-fronted early 19th-century houses.

Over on the **Caledonian Rd**, there's a Piccadilly line tube station. There are some recent developments around here, for example in Stock Orchard Crescent and Frederica St, and the old police station opposite the tube.

The area to the W of Islington, between the **Caledonian Rd** and **York Way**, N of **Wharfdale Rd**, is also mainly low-level council homes, of various periods. The main interest here is Thornhill Bridge Wharf, a recent development, post-modern in style, coral pink in colour, overlooking the canalside walk.

Transport Tubes: Highbury & Islington (zone 2, Victoria), Angel (zone 1, Northern). From Highbury & Islington: Oxford Circus 8 min, City 18 min (1 change), Heathrow 1 hr 10 min (1 change). Trains: Highbury & Islington (Liverpool St 10 min and N London line/Silverlink); Drayton Park, Essex Road, Caledonian Rd, Canonbury.

Convenient for City, Docklands and West End; King's Cross, St Pancras and Euston. Miles from centre: 2.5.

Schools Local Authority: Islington Green School, Highbury Fields (g), Highbury Grove (b), Elizabeth Garrett Anderson School (g), St Aloysius College.

SALES

Flats	S	1B	2B	3B	4B	5B
Average prices	70–90	80–130	130–250	250+	—	—
Houses	2B	3B	4B	5B	6/7B	8B
Average prices	170–300	200–400	260–600	450+	—	—

RENTAL

Flats	S	1B	2B	3B	4B	5B
Average prices	600–700+	700–1000	1000–1500+	1500+	–	–
Houses	2B	3B	4B	5B	6/7B	8B
Average prices	1500–2000	2000+	2000–3000+	3000+	—	—

The properties Good choice of early and mid-Victorian houses in attractive areas such as Barnsbury and Canonbury (latter also some stunning Georgian). Highbury has more small houses. Two-bed converted flats in good supply. New developments appear where space allows.

The market Character period homes in interesting area attract City workers and media types and lawyers. Highbury cheaper than Islington. Greatest demand is for 2-bed flats, family houses. Local searches: 2 weeks.

Among those estate agents active in this area are:
- Bairstow Eves
- Holden Matthews
- Evans Baker
- Hotblack & Co
- Brooks & Co
- Hugh Grover Associates
- Healey, Graham & Co
- The Property Bureau
- Kinleigh, Folkard & Hayward
- Stickley & Kent
- Hamptons
- Winkworth *
- Copping Joyce
- Thompson Currie
- Foxtons *

further details: see advertisers' index on p633

KENNINGTON, VAUXHALL AND STOCKWELL

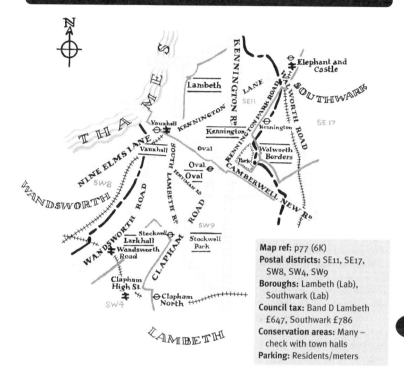

Map ref: p77 (6K)
Postal districts: SE11, SE17,
SW8, SW4, SW9
Boroughs: Lambeth (Lab),
Southwark (Lab)
Council tax: Band D Lambeth
£647, Southwark £786
Conservation areas: Many –
check with town halls
Parking: Residents/meters

K

Kennington ought to be – and perhaps soon will be – a great place to live.
It is the apex of a compact triangle whose other corners are the West End and the City.
It has quite large areas of Georgian and early Victorian housing, the river and all its
South Bank excitement, and plenty of tubes and buses. Yet until now Kennington has
stubbornly failed to gell as a vibrant London area. Partly this is due to busy roads,
partly to the blighting legacies of industry and wartime bombing and perhaps mostly,
until the early '90s to Lambeth Council's doctrinaire politics. Now all this is changing.
Lambeth is sending out all the right signals: it is determined to improve its patch,
proactive in developing long-empty sites, stern in combating fraud and mayhem on
its housing estates, proud of the area's many architectural gems. And Lambeth
dwellers now find really helpful people at the town hall.

The area lacks a 'high street', though several centres provide focal points for
neighbourhoods. Kennington's heart is at the crossroads where **Kennington Lane**
intersects with **Kennington Rd**. The tube station is on **Kennington Park Rd** to the E.
Vauxhall until 1859 the site of a famous pleasure gardens, has shrunk to be little
more than a giant traffic intersection – and the Victoria line tube station. However,
Vauxhall should soon see action as several schemes – including a modern pleasure
(we now call it leisure) centre – get under way. The Oval, to the E, centres round its
tube station at a busy crossroads and the world-famous cricket stadium. Stockwell,
to the S, is a mix of lovely houses and grim council-built estates, and lacks a focus apart

from its tube station and a rather down-rent parade of shops on busy **Clapham Road**. Stockwell received a boost 20 years ago when the Victoria line brought it within minutes of the West End; it has some enclaves of real character, but does not seem to have kept up the momentum of improvement begun in the 1970s. Over to the E, a few pockets of interesting housing are to be found on the borders with Walworth and Camberwell. There are no tubes here, so distance from Kennington station becomes an important factor. To the N, Waterloo and the Lambeth area (the site of the old village, not the sprawling borough) have moved into the residential frame: see the South Bank chapter. This renaissance may spill over into North Kennington, though predictions that Elephant & Castle will become fashionable seem optimistic.

The whole area is very mixed, with quiet squares that could hold their own in Chelsea only yards away from roaring, dirty through roads; with mews tucked into corners behind gasworks and with council tower blocks looming over the Georgian terraces. If you look hard and don't mind being part of the patchwork, a Georgian house can be had in a handsome square at a handsome discount to north-of-the-river prices.

People looking to buy here are mostly young, always busy and usually childless. Government ministers may base their families in Kennington's Georgian houses (though they try to keep their teenagers out of the pubs), but couples with kids tend to look at Clapham and points southwest. Much of Vauxhall and Kennington are in the Division Bell zone, and MPs favour the area as being about the closest place to Westminster where one can find a family house. (Partly because of the MPs, judges and other notables who live here, the area is considered part of Inner London by cabbies.)

Young families who want to find a house but stay in the area, or who cannot afford the move to Clapham or Wandsworth, look at the southern and eastern fringes, towards Clapham and Brixton. The neighbourhood served by Clapham North tube is 'moving from funky to family' to quote a local agent.

These areas are 'discovered' every time the London market gets busy. There was a veritable boom in Stockwell in the early '70s, following the first discovery of Kennington in the late '60s. The 1980s saw big increases in prices, but as the boom collapsed, buyers looked to safer areas such as Clapham and Battersea – or to more daring, and cheaper, ones like Brixton and the South Bank. Now local agents report that Kennington has been found once more, with the real bargains having been in 1996 or so. (Bargain-hunting pioneers should head south and east.) Of the three areas in this chapter, Kennington shows most optimism. The release of Duchy of Cornwall homes for sale has improved the choice of properties, as has the lofts movement.

As the young flat-buyers of the 1980s enter middle age, the market for houses is growing larger and more broadly based: hitherto only the Georgian gems excited much interest; the action was in flats. The rental market is busy, with landlords trawling the area for investments – even dipping toes into formerly grim council-built estates like Stockwell Gardens, which is but a step from a Victoria line tube. Despite this, selling by reluctant, negative-equity-hit landlords has cut the supply of rented homes, forcing up rents: 1-bed flats that were £150 pw last year now go for £200.

More than in most places this area demands careful use of the map when considering a move. There are two railway lines running through the area at high level. The W one, leading to Waterloo, takes Channel Tunnel trains. The main roads are choked with traffic more often than not. It remains to be seen how the new designation of Red Routes will affect traffic-flow, but schemes are now under way on a smaller scale to restrict rat-runs through residential areas. The E-W route past the Oval to Vauxhall Bridge is signposted as an 'inner ring road' and therefore attracts much heavy through traffic. There is also quite a bit of industry scattered around, though the premises of Sarson's Vinegar are now homes and several other factories (and old Victorian schools) have become 'lofts'.

Transport is good, with Northern and Victoria line tubes and Waterloo (Eurostar and the forthcoming tube to Docklands) just up the road. There is a big Sainsbury's at Vauxhall and there are plans for a Tesco in **Kennington Lane**. The area falls into no less than three boroughs – Wandsworth illogically sticks a finger into the W corner. Their council tax, education and other policies differ, so look hard at the map. There are also four postcodes, plus a bit of SW4. None carries much of a premium.

Kennington

The heart of the area, Kennington, gains much of its character from its historical association with the Duchy of Cornwall Estate. The Princes of Wales have owned land here since the Black Prince had his palace in Kennington. (Had he survived, would Kennington, rather than Kensington, have been the Royal Borough?) In the last decade, however, that influence has waned as most of the Duchy's homes have been passed on to housing associations or sold.

The road names around here are very confusing: it is hard to recall which is **Kennington Park Rd**, which is **Kennington Rd** and which is **Kennington Lane**. The first-named is the main road, following the line of the old Roman Stane St and linking the Elephant & Castle in the N with the Oval and Stockwell, passing Kennington and Oval tubes. **Kennington Rd** runs due N from near the Oval to the Imperial War Museum at Waterloo. The area called 'Kennington Cross', at the junction of **Kennington Rd** and **Kennington Lane**, is the nearest thing to a village bit, boasting tapas bars, deli, etc – not to mention a plethora of estate agents. A Pizza Express and a French restaurant are imminent in **Windmill Row**.

To the W of **Kennington Rd** is the old heart of the neighbourhood, the 45-acre Duchy of Cornwall Estate. A chunk stands NW of **Kennington Lane,** S of the site of the Black Prince's palace, which lay between **Black Prince Rd** and **Sandcroft St. Courtney Square, Cardigan St** and **Courtney St** are Duchy-built homes in neo-Georgian style: however authentic they look, they were built in 1913. Ex-Duchy cottages here cost around £250–275,000. **Woodstock Court** is an attractive enclosed square of homes which the Duchy rents to elderly tenants.

Kennington Rd owes its existence to the building of Westminster Bridge (1750) and its regular rows of Georgian terraced houses are still largely in place. Many are flats, some offices – but some remain as large, potentially grand, houses. Some have had their potential realized: agents, though, report them as being slow to shift (traffic may be the snag). Expect to pay £375–400,000. To the E of the road, in the angle formed by its intersection with **Kennington Lane**, is another part of the Duchy Estate. Pretty **Denny Crescent, Denny St** and **Chester Way** are all 20th-century Georgian. These, like other Duchy homes, have come onto the open market and are considered a good buy, although they may well be in need of total modernization. Unmodernized ones go for around £190,000; done up, a 2/3-bed cottage can command prices of £240,000. **Kennington Rd** has at its N end the park which surrounds the Imperial War Museum.

Just S of the museum, between it and the Lambeth Hospital, is very early Victorian **Walcot Square**, which dates from the 1830s. The charitable Walcot Estate occasionally sells unmodernized houses: prices are around £250,000; £325,000 for a modernized one. **West Square**, which is is in truth to the E, has houses from three decades earlier, as does **St George's Rd** on the N edge of the area – but this road carries heavy traffic from the Elephant. **West Square** and the surrounding streets are by contrast peaceful. These Georgian houses overlook a garden square; one was for sale last winter for £530,000. Those with smaller budgets look in streets such as nearby **Hayles St**, with its 2-bed flat-fronted cottages. **Brook Drive** offers plenty of flats, and some houses, all late-Victorian 3-storey. A 2-bed flat might be £120–130,000. Nearby **Oswin St** has solid 4-storey Victorian houses. Lovely Georgian houses in **Walnut Tree Walk** were offered unmodernized in 1989, and those who bought did well.

Much of the rest of the district E of **Kennington Rd** and W of **Kennington Park Rd** is council-built housing. One mid-'70s flats development is private, however: Vanbrugh Court on **Wincott St**. This popular complex has communal gardens and an underground garage. S of the hospital, a 1980s mews development has been slotted into the angle between **Gilbert Rd** and **Renfrew Rd**: **Heralds Place** has underground parking for its compact 3-bed houses. Round the corner is 'Parliament Terrace', off **Gilbert Rd**, 1997 houses in neo-Georgian style, now reselling from £240–280,000.

To the E of the **Kennington Lane**/**Kennington Rd** junction is **Cleaver Square**, one of the best places to live in the area and the first to be 'discovered' – allegedly by a '60s barrister trying to find his way back to civilization from a court hearing at Newington Causeway. This urban-feeling square has a mixture of houses, but all are extremely attractive. Those '60s barristers were scandalized when houses in the square reached £20,000 in 1971. Today, their sons and daughters might have to find £550,000 for the biggest ones, perhaps £250,000 for a 2-bed cottage. South from here, in the angle of **Kennington Rd** and **Kennington Park Rd**, is a neighbourhood of smaller terraced Victorian houses of an unusual design, with spacious semi-basements. **Stannary St's** name makes clear the connection with Cornwall and thus the Duchy. **Ravensdon St**, **Methley St** and **Radcot St** are similar. **Kennington Green**, a small widening of **Kennington Rd**, has a few pleasant old houses, some being restored last winter. **Montford Place** adjoins the site of the planned new Tesco. Flat-fronted Georgian 3-bed houses here go for around £220,000.

To the W, along **Black Prince Rd**, Lambeth Council have big plans for the 30-acre 1960s ex-GLC housing estate up to Lambeth Walk. Under the name 'Project Vauxhall' Lambeth, working with housing associations, plans demolition of bad council housing and relocation of the Lilian Baylis School to **Kennington Lane** as a flagship technology college. There will be homes to buy and rent, plus some for shared ownership.

The loft boom has had its effects on Kennington. The old college situated on **Kennington Rd**, close to **Stannary St**, is now 'The Lycée' loft apartments. Over towards the river in **Vauxhall Walk**, Spring Gardens Court has 1- to 3-bed flats. On **Albert Embankment**, the riverside office block long graced by Lord Archer's penthouse is now flats. In **Kennington Lane** Imperial Court, with its fine 1836 portico, has become flats. Prices for the current release from £120–300,000.

Kennington is best known for its Georgian terraces, but the area also has some interesting survivals from other periods including these almshouses with their Gothic porches and windows. Other interesting architecture can be found on the Duchy of Cornwall Estate, where small houses in Georgian style were built before World War I.

The Oval

Partly because of heavy traffic, and also owing to the depressing influence of some pre-war council estates, the Oval neighbourhood has less charm than

Kennington. Cricket fanatics might consider the period houses in the S side of the Oval itself, although the new stands will probably restrict their view of the pitch. The other sides of the Oval are lined with council blocks. South of the Oval, and sealed off from the traffic, **Ashmole St** and **Claylands Rd** have small terraced houses, rather overwhelmed by the huge amounts of council developments. **Meadow Rd** has flat-fronted terraces.

The prime street around here is **Fentiman Rd**, a long terrace of dignified mid-Victorian houses and a known address for MPs and the like. Most of the houses lack Kennington's Georgian charm, but are big and conveniently between Oval and Vauxhall tubes. Periods vary between Regency and mid-Victorian. Higher odd numbers overlook the park. One of the larger houses might go for £500,000. Off neighbouring **Rita Rd**, with its smaller terraced houses, is the gated entrance to **Regents's Bridge Gardens** – more popularly called 'the Vinegar Works'. This is an expensive 1986 conversion of the Regency/early Victorian Sarson's works, the manager's house and his splendid ballroom. Some homes are enormous, such as that carved from the former ballroom and the loft apartments in the works itself. There are flats and town-houses, too; some are conversions, some are skillfully matched new-build – it can be difficult to distinguish which is which. All have access to a large private swimming pool complex. Two-bed flats go for £150–160,000. Between **Fentiman Rd** and **Richbourne Terrace** is 1980s **Usborne Mews**. **Richbourne Terrace** has handsome early Victorian houses in a scruffy area.

Close to the tube, **Hanover Gardens** is a very popular pocket of early Victorian houses and cottages situated within a pretty cul-de-sac. East of the Oval tube, a few streets such as **Handforth Rd** have 3-storey Victorian houses which convert into pleasant flats that sell for £95,000 unmod; £130,000-plus for a smart one. A few survive as single homes.

K

To the E again, in **Langton Rd** off the **Camberwell New Rd**, is 1980s **Salisbury Place**. This successful scheme has 100 homes from studio flats to 4-bed houses. **Vassall Rd** has big Georgian houses that can command the area's top prices: £675,000 for a 5-bed detached.

Vauxhall

Roads, railways and the New Covent Garden Market take up much of the floorspace in Vauxhall, and council-built homes dominate the rest. The shadow of the vast (still as yet only planned) Battersea Power Station scheme falls over the S of the area. Change, though slow, is now on the way. The Effra site, on the river next to the bridge, is being built on at last. This 8.6-acre site has been subject to planning rows for 25 years, back as far as the proposed 'green giant' office tower. Secretary of State John Prescott gave the go-ahead in November for a scheme with 650,000 sq ft of offices and 206 homes in three towers. St George hopes to start Phase 1 of the residential plans this winter. On the opposite corner of the bridge approach is the Hollywood-Babylonian biscuit-coloured block that is the lair of MI6, forced out of Mayfair by rising rents.

Inland, Lambeth Council has big plans for its housing N of **Kennington Lane**: under Project Vauxhall, some homes will be knocked down, others refurbished. Spring Gardens, a little park on the site of the old pleaure gardens, may be halved in area under another major scheme, for a leisure centre/hotel/cinema. As yet, this is merely at the planning stage.

Back at Vauxhall Cross, **Vauxhall Grove** looks promising on the map: a square tucked in off the Vauxhall Cross junction. The Grove is, however, rather scruffy: 3-storey Victoriana looms over the narrow streets. Round in **Bonnington Square**, a housing association has improved some similar 3-storey flats buildings. Much of the square seems to be inhabited by young people in a sort of post-hippie timewarp; there's a community garden, a café, an annual street parade . . . At the junction of **Langley Lane** and **South Lambeth Rd** is a turn-of-the-century mansion block, Park Mansions, which has a steady turnover of flats for sale. At the end of **Lawn Lane** is a council estate around **Ebbisham Drive**: 2-storey houses and two tower blocks. To the S – in what used to be called 'South Lambeth', but is now a fringe area between Vauxhall and Lambeth – roads such as **Tradescant Rd** have a lot of flats carved out of 3-storey Victorian terraces. Some recent mews houses in **Dorset Rd**. From here S is considered Stockwell.

A tract to the W of **Wandsworth Rd**, towards Battersea, is attached to Vauxhall – mostly because railway lines shut it off from anywhere else. Most is the Patmore Estate, council-built homes of varying sizes. You can buy a 2-bed flat here for £55–65,000. North of the railway, off **Stewart's Rd**, is a 1980s development of studio and 2-bed flats with a fine view of the Eurostar trains as they curve round on their roof-level viaduct. Back up **Wandsworth Rd**, a complex entered from **Cowthorpe Rd** including **Crimsworth Rd** has rather scruffy late-Victorian cottages and some purpose-built flats. Round the corner in **Thorpatch Rd**, a development of town-houses and flats dates from 1988. A 3-bed house sold last winter for £160,000. Along the river towards the old Battersea Power Station are some new blocks of flats with good views of Pimlico (better views, in fact, than the other way round). The enormous riverside Regalian development of 'Elm Quay' in **Nine Elms Lane** includes a sports and leisure complex complete with heated swimming pool, gymnasium, sauna and whirlpool spa for the health conscious. It comprises 1-, 2- and 3-bedroomed flats and penthouses.

The tract sometimes called 'South Lambeth', on either side of **South Lambeth Rd**, has quite a big Portuguese community. There are some excellent local cafés and restaurants here.

Stockwell

Stockwell struck lucky in the early 19th century, with an expansive estate of Regency villas. Just enough survives to provide some gracious streets and architecturally interesting homes, but not enough to make Stockwell a fully-fledged gentrified suburb. The select streets have an air of being marooned in an ordinary patch of South London. West of **Clapham Rd** is **Albert Square** and its associated streets. The giant mid-Victorian houses in the square loom over the central gardens, and are in turn dominated by nearby tower blocks. A house here, needing a complete face-lift, was on the market for £375,000 in late 1997: it sold for less, and is now back on, done up, at £625,000. **Wilkinson St** and **Aldebert Terrace** have a more human scale. The former is the smarter. Just off **South Lambeth Rd** is 'Sadlers Mews', even recent 2-bed houses. Down the street, Wingfield House, a former masonic banqueting hall, is now flats. West of **South Lambeth Rd** is a mixed neighbourhood of pleasant new council houses and surviving Regency villas. Most of the period homes are clustered around **Landsdowne Gardens**, which opens up in the middle into a perfect circus. The 1840 houses are double-fronted, detached, with big pillared porches. One was for sale last winter for £525,000. **Guildford Rd** and linking roads are similar. **Landsdowne Way** is a busy E-W road with a mix of properties, some Georgian. **Thorne Rd's** handsome 1840s houses offer 4-bed for around £350,000. West of **Hartington Rd** is a big council-built estate.

East of **Clapham Rd** comes Stockwell Park, the surviving Regency suburb. Over the last few years it has become – to quote a local agent – 'dead posh'. Many of the houses are good-sized family homes, often inhabited by parents with young children. This encourages more sense of community, with the sharing of school runs etc. Beware, though, confusion with the Stockwell Park Estate, a concrete jungle as yet unredeemed by Lambeth's efforts. **Stockwell Terrace** overlooks the roundabout and tube station: tall early 19th-century houses. There are similar homes in adjoining **South Lambeth Rd** and **Clapham Rd**. **Stockwell Park Rd** runs E with a mix of homes from small Regency to '20s gabled villas. At the junction with **Groveway** and **Stockwell Park Crescent**, the road opens out. All these streets have a mix of 1830s villas and terraces, with lots of trees and gardens. A 4-bed detached villa was £460,000 last winter. **Durand Gardens**, hidden away to the N, is a surprise: a pear-shaped square with big Victorian houses, mostly semi- and detached. One 5-bed house was £565,000 last autumn. A little Gothic villa and an enormous detached house add variety. A few arts-and-craftsy 1898 gabled terraces stand on the way out to **Clapham Rd**. West of **Stockwell Park Crescent**, **St Michael's Rd** and **St Martin's Rd** have 3-storey mid-Victorian brick terraces. Flats converted from these start at c. £115,000 for 1-bed. A little to the east, **Hackford Rd** has some handsome flat-fronted early Victorian houses. New (1994) 3-storey houses here are around £165,000. South of Stockwell tube is a mixed district of council blocks and routine Victorian terraces. **Landor Rd** marks the border with Clapham North and Brixton. Agents point out that this side of Stockwell is close to Brixton. This used to be kept quiet, but Brixton is now buzzing – and Stockwellites frequent its bars, cinemas and night life. Thus little houses off **Landor Rd** that were £80,000 in 1994–95 are selling for £190,000.

Larkhall Lane becomes **Larkhall Rise** as it runs through to Clapham, carrying a lot of morning and evening traffic – though work on the railway bridge will keep it closed for two years or so. The housing off it is mostly council, though there are a few good corners. The Lane itself has some early Victorian houses, much interrupted by car sales yards and council blocks. West of the Lane, **Priory Grove**, overlooking the recently created Larkhall Park, has some pretty, small houses. From **Larkhall Lane** E to Stockwell tube is council. To the S of the area lies a grid of wide streets on the Clapham (see chapter) borders: **Chelsham Rd** and **Bromfelde Rd** have big houses, some with generous Victorian Gothic gables, and mostly now flats. One or two are large family homes: a Bromfelde 6-bed was £525,000 last winter. **Gauden Rd** is similar, with some extensive flat conversions, and 4-bed family houses at around £500,000.

Walworth Borders

East from Kennington tube is mostly council housing. **Sutherland Square**, though, has some handsome early Victorian houses: these are popular despite the proximity of the railway line just beyond the E side of the square. A 4-bed, 4-storey house here could fetch £240,000-plus. Nearby streets such as **Berryfield Rd** have Victorian terraced houses. **Lorrimore Square** has a mix of Victorian terraces and new houses. All the streets S of here are part of, or are dominated by, a vast council estate. The mostly post-war flats and houses are interspersed with restored Victorian terraces. A few handsome early Victorian houses survive to the W in **St Agnes Place**, by Kennington Park. This area also has several streets of rather run-down purpose-built Edwardian flats. **Surrey Square**, over towards the **Old Kent Rd**, has some Georgian houses.

This is a good hunting-ground for really cheap, mostly ex-council homes. A 2-bed flat in a tower block can be around £50,000 – but ask about the service charges.

Transport	Tubes: Kennington, Elephant & Castle, Oval, Clapham North (zones 1/2, Northern), Stockwell (zone 2, Victoria, Northern), Vauxhall (zones 1/2, Victoria). From Stockwell: Oxford Circus 10 min, City 20 min, Heathrow 1 hr 15 min (2 changes). Trains: Elephant & Castle (Thameslink), Vauxhall (to Waterloo), Clapham High St, Wandsworth Rd (both to Victoria & London Bridge).

Convenient for	City and Westminster. Miles from centre: 2.
Schools	Local Authority: Lilian Baylis, Stockwell Park, Archbishop Tenison's C of E (b).

SALES

Flats	S	1B	2B	3B	4B	5B
Average prices	50–70	60–120	90–150	120–200	150–210	180–300
Houses	2B	3B	4B	5B	6/7B	8B
Average prices	100–250+	160–350	200–500	200–600	400+	›

RENTAL

Flats	S	1B	2B	3B	4B	5B
Average prices	400–650	600–900	750–1300	900–1500	1300–1800	1500–2200
Houses	2B	3B	4B	5B	6/7B	8B
Average prices	900–1100	1200–1600	1300–1950	1700–2600	—	—

The properties	Enclaves of handsome Georgian amid Victorian houses; some modern mews and flats, pretty repro-Georgian on Duchy of Cornwall Estate. Widespread council-built housing. Old schools and factories fast becoming loft apartments.
The market	Good communications attract professionals, City people, MPs and doctors. Location matters a lot: select enclaves are close to run-down inner-city. Local searches: Lambeth 1–2 weeks, Southwark 2 weeks.

Among those estate agents active in this area are:

- Ludlow Thomson
- Barnard Marcus
- Murray Estates
- Daniel Cobb *
- Halifax
- Winkworth *
- Kinleigh Folkard & Hayward
- Foxtons*

further details: see advertisers' index on p633

K

KENSINGTON

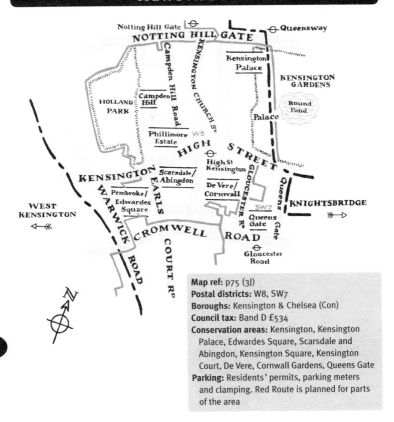

Map ref: p75 (3J)
Postal districts: W8, SW7
Boroughs: Kensington & Chelsea (Con)
Council tax: Band D £534
Conservation areas: Kensington, Kensington
Palace, Edwardes Square, Scarsdale and
Abingdon, Kensington Square, Kensington
Court, De Vere, Cornwall Gardens, Queens Gate
Parking: Residents' permits, parking meters
and clamping. Red Route is planned for parts
of the area

Kensington deserves its 'Royal Borough' title. It owed its origin as a
fashionable suburb to the presence of Kensington Palace, and the royal connection
continues. It is not many years since the nonagenarian Princess Alice, last surviving
granddaughter of Queen Victoria, used to potter around from the Palace to morning
service at St Mary Abbots. The Prince and Princess of Wales lived in the Palace during
their marriage and Princess Diana continued to live there after their divorce.
Following her death, part of Kensington Gardens is to become a memorial to her,
though plans have been scaled down following opposition from residents who feared
being overwhelmed by 'pilgrims'.

The favoured streets of this corner, closely thronged with some of London's most
enviable homes, seldom yield space for new ones. Perhaps the last large site was
that of the old St Mary Abbots Hospital in **Marloes Rd**. This is now the gated
'Kensington Green' complex. In **Wrights Lane** is 'Royal Gate Kensington': yet more
flats and penthouses due for completion this January. But the star, due to be ready
this spring, is **Earls Terrace**, an entire row of Grade II listed Regency – 23 houses, from
£3 million – with choice of swimming pool or cinema in the basements.

Kensington began as a roadside hamlet, but real development began after 1689
when King William III moved his court to Kensington Palace, drawing people of rank

to the area. However, the main building boom came during the second half of the 19th century, immediately after the Great Exhibition. The result is a rich mix of Georgian and Victorian terraces, grand stucco villas, attractive cobbled mews, tall red-brick mansion blocks and eccentric studio houses. It is very much a desirable place to live: estate agents estimated that house prices went up by 50 per cent between 1990 and 1997, though buyers became a lot more cautious during 1998.

Most streets are within easy walking distance of either of the two main shopping/entertainment centres of **Kensington High St** and **Notting Hill Gate**. Between them they boast three cinemas, clubs, pubs, high street stores and designer shops, and **Kensington High St** has a supermarket. **Kensington High St** has been the subject of a special study recently to make it more pedestrian-friendly and to ease the flow of traffic through the area. The shopping area has attracted big high street names and has become more popular than ever with tourists, but it retains its quaintness and the tiny lanes and roads off the **High St** and **Kensington Church St** are still quiet. Another of the area's attractions is the vast amount of public open space in the shape of Kensington Gardens (riding and swimming) and Holland Park.

This chapter deals with Kensington proper: Holland Park has its own chapter, as do North and South Kensington.

Campden Hill

Campden Hill Rd climbs sedately uphill from **Kensington High St** and down again to **Notting Hill Gate**. A through-route between the two main shopping streets, it is lined by a wide range of period and modern homes, merging with pubs, shops and restaurants at its N end. Off it are some of the most charming, private and unexpectedly peaceful places to live in inner London.

King's College's Kensington campus lies hidden away behind a tall brick wall and trees on the corner with **Duchess of Bedford's Walk**. Opposite stands Campden Hill Court, a red-brick and stone gabled mansion block with elaborate towers, turrets and domes. The Uruguayan Embassy and the securely walled South African ambassador's residence lie just beyond here, down the hill on the W side. A short distance away in **Airlie Gardens** is Holland Park Comprehensive School. A series of large modern flat blocks extend between **Airlie Gardens** and **Notting Hill Gate**. Many have superb views E across London.

Turn W into **Aubrey Walk**, a surprisingly quiet leafy backwater sitting on the hilltop. Brick and stucco terraces, 20th-century Dutch-gabled houses and some highly individual studio houses line the S side facing the waterworks opposite. Campden Hill Tennis Courts are in **Aubrey Walk** and are above an underground reservoir. There are plans for the site to be redeveloped with new covered and open courts and homes.

The large houses around the corner in **Aubrey Rd** slope downhill to **Holland Park Avenue**. Halfway down **Aubrey Rd** is the entrance to select **Campden Hill Square**. The main terrace of this three-sided Regency square perches near the brow of the hill above the private, tree-lined central gardens. The remaining two terraces are stepped down on either side. Street trees add to the summer canopy of greenery. The houses also have leafy front gardens.

The houses and painted cottages in **Hillsleigh Rd**, E of the square, slope down to **Holland Park Avenue**. This corner also hides two enormous mansions, which crown the Hill. One, Hill Lodge, a virtual country mansion, boasts 60 ft of reception rooms and has a separate cottage within its walled grounds. Another, Aubrey House, in **Aubrey Walk**, sold late last year for around £20 million.

East across **Campden Hill Rd** is Hillgate Village, an extremely popular enclave of pretty painted little 1850s cottages. The village is bounded by **Notting Hill Gate** (N), **Campden St** (S), **Campden Hill Rd** (W) and **Kensington Church St** (E). Best examples

Foxtons

Central London's largest estate agent, specialising in:

- Residential Sales
- Long Lets
- Short Lets
- Property Management
- Investments & Acquisitions
- New Homes
- Financial Services
- Worldwide Apartments

People, not property

of the gaily coloured all-cottage lanes are **Jameson St**, **Calcott St** and **Farmer St**, **Hillgate Place** and tree-lined **Farm Place**.

Kensington Place has terraces of attractive 2-storey and basement stucco/brick cottages N. On the opposite side is Fox Primary School and a 1970s red-brick development of 3-storey town-houses lying between two tall blocks of flats set back from the road. **Peel St** and **Campden St** are more mixed. The latter has terraces of 2/3-storey period/modern cottages and houses – and also Byam Shaw House, once the studio and art school of the famous Pre-Raphelite artist. The average price for a house in **Campden St** is £500–600,000. More painted/brick and stucco cottages are found in **Peel St**, where half of the N side is taken up by the tall red- and grey-brick blocks of Campden Houses. **Bedford Gardens** to the S is a leafy street with mainly 4-storey houses which usually just top £1 million, though one with a 2-bed cottage in the garden sold last year for £2.1 million.

Terraces of mainly 3-storey white stucco houses and some big villas stand on the N side of **Sheffield Terrace**. (Poet and novelist G K Chesterton lived at No 32.) By contrast, most of the S side is lined by a long row of matching tall red-brick gabled buildings with white stucco and striped entrances. Another 6-storey red-brick and stone block, Campden House, lies at the corner of **Hornton St**. Hidden away behind the S side of **Sheffield Terrace** is a 2½-acre private communal garden. Residents of properties in **Hornton St** and **Gloucester Walk** also have access. **Gloucester Walk** has a mix of modern flats and red-brick gabled mansions as well as 3/4-storey brick and stucco houses. Campden Grove has 5-bed houses which go for £800,000–1.1 million.

Tucked away off the NW end of **Hornton St** opposite **Gloucester Walk** is **Campden House Close**. A narrow lane leads to a group of 2-storey cottages set around a pleasant spacious courtyard. Varying styles of houses and flats stretch down **Hornton St**, including some large semi-detached stucco properties. An eye-catching terrace of brown-brick and white striped Victorian buildings with elaborate stucco decoration is stepped down the W side as far as **Holland St**. The style continues into **Observatory Gardens** with its red-brick and stone striped 3-storey houses. An attractive terrace of 20th-century Dutch-gabled houses extends down **Hornton St** opposite the town hall.

Cutting across **Horton St** is **Holland St**, a popular narrow road where detached stucco houses and Georgian-style terraces are interspersed with a handful of speciality shops and restaurants. An undistinguished terrace of 20th-century houses lies on the S side. Halfway along **Holland St** is **Gordon Place**. The S end forms a pretty, overgrown walkway, set back from the road and looking like a country lane. Hidden behind the trees and mature front gardens are two terraces of Georgian-style houses turned sideways on to **Holland St**. Just N of the E end of **Holland St**, through a gateway off **Kensington Church St**, is Bullingham Mansions. This yellow- and red-brick and stone Dutch-style block is built around a landscape fountain courtyard guarded by some impressive stone lions.

Dominating the SE corner of the neighbourhood is Kensington's parish church, St Mary Abbots, with its dramatic 250-ft spire, the tallest in London.

Kensington Palace

The focal point of the neighbourhood is the Renaissance-style palace, rebuilt in the late 17th century by Sir Christopher Wren, and set in beautiful Kensington Gardens.

The next most exclusive address in the neighbourhood is **Kensington Palace Gardens**, a long tree-lined avenue running N-S past the palace and gardens. Stately mansions with sweeping driveways and landscape grounds line this prestigious private road. Although known as 'Millionaires' Row', most of the once private residences have now been taken over by embassies. The road is guarded by gates and gatekeepers at both ends. Among home-owners is the Sultan of Brunei. At the SW end, overlooking Kensington Palace is 3A Palace Green. These very prestigous flats range from £1.5 million to £8 million. Some have servants' accommodation attached.

Alongside 3A Palace Green in **York House Place**, a narrow passageway leads to York House, a prestigious Victorian mansion block. The 7-storey red-brick and stone block with red-and-white striped gables stands in a relatively quiet cul-de-sac with an ornamental water garden in the middle, creating a courtyard.

The passageway continues into **Kensington Church St**. From here the streets wend their way gradually uphill to **Notting Hill Gate. Church Close**, opposite the Carmelite Church in **Kensington Church St,** is a 3-storey red-brick and stone Tudor-style complex, set around an inner garden courtyard.

The scale suddenly changes where **Vicarage Gate** branches off **Kensington Church St**. Two 8-storey 1930s flat blocks, Winchester Court (W) and Vicarage Court (E), spread along each side of the street. The side of the latter block also occupies most of the S side of the E arm of **Vicarage Gate**. A Victorian brick and stucco terrace with polished marble porch columns stands on the N side. The 3-bed flats here are around £325–450,000.

St Marys Abbot's modern vicarage is set in a private courtyard at the end of the street, forming a cul-de-sac. **Vicarage Gate** N contains a jumble of tall houses in varying styles. It leads to **Vicarage Gardens**, lined terraces of white stucco properties at the N end and brick and stuccos. A barrier of trees and shrubs separates **Vicarage Gate** from **Inverness Gardens**, a semi-circular sweep of 3-storey white stucco houses. More terraces of white stucco houses, some split into flats, are found in **Brunswick Gardens** and **Berkeley Gardens.**

The white paint continues in tree-lined **Palace Gardens Terrace** – 3-storey basement terraces on the E side and 4-storey basement houses with elaborate Greek-style columned porches on the W. **Strathmore Gardens**, lying off the W side of the street, is a short cul-de-sac of 4-storey and basement stucco terraces. Houses in these two streets fetch between £1.5 million and £2 million. Just beyond here, **Palace Gardens Terrace** becomes part of a district one-way traffic system linking **Notting Hill Gate** with **Kensington Church St. Church St,** a residential/shopping street lined by pubs, antique shops, galleries and jewellers among others, is a main N-S traffic route running between **Notting Hill Gate** and **Kensington High St.**

Queen's Gate

Queen's Gate is a busy boulevard lined by the grand stucco terraces which are a feature of this neighbourhood. The majority were built between 1850 and 1870 and have now been converted into vast, grand flats, hotels, embassies and ambassadorial homes. East of here is considered Knightsbridge.

More long stretches of 4/5-storey Victorian terraces, with columned porches, stand on both sides of **Queen's Gate Terrace** (white and cream stucco) and **Elvaston Place** (brick and stucco). Both are wide streets with extra parking space in the middle, as in **Queen's Gate**. In **Queens's Gate Gardens,** the imposing 5/6-storey stucco terraces are set around three sides of a large leafy central garden screened by trees. A 1960s flats block, Campbell Court, which fronts **Gloucester Rd,** backs on to the W side of the garden with its extensive lawns.

Dotted around this network of streets is a series of small-scale mews, which once served as stables and staff quarters for the large houses they lie behind. Most have mixtures of groups of 2-storey brick/painted cottages and working garages and car showrooms. **Queen's Gate Mews,** lying just off **Queen's Gate Terrace,** has the added attraction of its own pub, the Queen's Arms. Impressive Classical-style stone arches lead into **Elvaston Mews** and **Queen's Gate Place Mews.** The latter sits behind more 5-storey brick and stucco terraces in **Queen's Gate Place.** It is wider that the other mews, leaving room for cobbled forecourts in front of the varied modern and period 2-storey cottages.

The tall brick and stucco terraces reappear in **Gloucester Rd**, a busy district road and shopping centre. They have been turned into hotels, offices or flats, usually with shops on the ground floor. **Gloucester Rd** merges into **Palace Gate**, which is lined mainly by a collection of highly individual stone, or red-brick and stone, period buildings, occupied by embassies, offices and flats.

Exclusive **Kensington Gate** lies to the E at the point where **Palace Gate** and **Gloucester Rd** meet. Two grand terraces of richly ornamented 3/4-storey white stucco Victorian houses stretch along a narrow strip of garden with tall trees and well-kept flower beds. At each end of the terraces stand paired 'tower' houses, looking like iced 'wedding cakes'. **Kensington Gate** and **Hyde Park Gate** to the N still have high proportions of single-family houses.

The E leg of **Hyde Park Gate** contains a mix of period/modern houses and flats, plus some large 'one-off' houses such as No 28, where Sir Winston Churchill lived and died. Tall red-brick and stone mansions and 11-storey 1960s red-brick flats block, Broadwalk House, stand on either side of the entrance to the more exclusive W leg of the street. Beyond here, the street opens out into a circle with a central garden. A handful of elegant detached villas with their own large gardens sit around the circle. Halfway along the street off to the W is **Reston Place**, a charming little enclave of 2-storey white-painted cottages set around a secluded courtyard.

The **Kensington Rd** frontage of the neighbourhood is dominated by the huge modern 11-storey red-brick Thorney Court flats block, and Broadwalk House, which overlook Kensington Gardens. In common with the other period/modern properties lining the N boundary (flats, embassies and offices), they are set back from the road behind driveways and screens of trees. Facing out across to the park, the handsome, white stucco 58–59 **Hyde Park Gate** became 24 2- and 3-bedroom apartments in 1989.

It may look 18th century – but it is modern. A clever pastiche of the Kensington town-house style, with 'Georgian' fanlight, panelled door with windows either side – even the ivy is authentic. For the real thing in Kensington, visit Kensington Square, which grew up as homes for Palace courtiers and has some beautiful Queen Anne and early Georgian houses.

K

De Vere/Cornwall

West of **Gloucester Rd** is a neighbourhood that in many ways is the heart of Kensington. It runs southwards from the centuries-old **Kensington Square** in a series of quiet, leafy streets. **Gloucester Rd** is a busy road lined by a mix of residential and commercial properties and shops. It has a tube station. The main residential grouping is the 4/5-storey Edwardian red-brick and stone mansion block of St George's Court, which has a row of shops on the ground floor.

Behind St Stephen's Church at the SW end of **Gloucester Rd** is **Emperor's Gate**. This almost triangular-shaped street has a tiny triangle of green in the middle and a central block of painted stucco terraced properties sitting on a similarly shaped site.

A terrace of late-Victorian red-brick and stucco buildings with ornate columned porches stand on the W side and a terrace of 5-storey and basement on the E. Most are split into flats: £475,000 is an average price for a 3-bed. Concealed behind a red-brick and stone arch in the NE corner of the street is **Osten Mews**, a looped cobbled mews of 2-storey painted cottages.

The view here is dominated by the towering shape of Point West – an apartment block converted from the former West London Air Terminal fronting **Cromwell Rd**. This huge development was on hold for a decade after the former owners ran out of money in 1987, but in 1997 a consortium restarted the scheme. On completion during 1999 there will be over 300 flats from £250,000. Still to be completed are offices, a swimming pool, gym and shops.

On either side of **Grenville Place** (brick and stucco terraces) lies pretty **Cornwall Mews South** with a mix of 2-storey period/modern brick painted cottages. Just up the road, the scale changes dramatically in **Cornwall Gardens** with its tall cliffs of white stucco. Terraces of mid-19th-century Italianate houses with columned porches stretch along both sides of three large private gardens. The trees match the height of the 5-storey and basement houses, long ago divided into flats of various sizes and conditions.

Launceston Place to the N signals the beginning of an enclave of highly desirable, quiet streets lying in the heart of the neighbourhood. The group is bounded by **Launceston Place** itself and **Victoria Grove** E, **Stanford Rd** W, **Albert Place** N and **Kynance Mews** S.

Picturesque **Kynance Mews** must rate as the most attractive mews in the whole of the Kensington and Chelsea area. Divided in two by **Launceston Place**, the shorter E section is lined by 2/3-storey white/cream painted cottages and has a splendid view of Queen's Tower. The W and most delightful selection is full of charming vine-covered 2-storey cottages of different styles. A profusion of flowers and shrubs spread along the mews in tubs and urns. Part of the N side backs on to the walled gardens of houses in **Eldon Rd** and the prize-winning gardens of Christ Church in **Victoria Rd**, giving the mews a particularly leafy look at this point.

Halfway along the mews, a set of steps leads to **Victoria Rd**. Many a household name has been attracted to the elegant homes in this street known in former days as 'Love Walk'. Small groups of semi-detached stucco or brick-and-stucco villas with leafy front gardens line the most desirable stretch of the street S of **Cambridge Place**, where homes range from £1.75–3 million. North of here, the road is flanked by the backs of hotels fronting adjoining streets. **Victoria Rd** continues N to meet **Kensington Rd** and Kensington Gardens.

More 2-storey semi-detached Victorian villas are found in **Launceston Place**, running parallel. The black and white colour scheme is accentuated by the black window canopies remaining on the houses on the W side of the street. **Eldon Rd** is a particularly attractive street with terraces of pastel-painted 3-storey stucco houses adjoining Christ Church on the corner of **Victoria Rd**. Groups of highly individual brick/stucco houses stand on the N side. Tree-lined **Cottesmore Gardens** to the N has paired 3-storey stucco villas and more big individual houses.

The W end of the street runs into **Stanford Rd**, lined by detached brick and stucco villas, with some paired houses and simple brick and stucco terraces. Standing in their midst is Cottesmore Court, a tall 1930s brown-brick flats block, which spreads around into **Kelso Place**. The S arm of this T-shaped street has rows of 2/3-storey brick terraced houses backing onto the Kensington Green development on the W side (see below). The modern brown-brick town-house development lies in a private cul-de-sac at the end of the W arm of **Kelso Place**, which flanks the underground line (running above ground at this point).

Running across the N end of **Stanford Rd** is **St Alban's Grove**. More brick and stucco detached and paired houses can be found on the S side opposite Richmond College, the American international college of London. Next to it is the red-brick and stucco block of St Alban's Mansions. The W end of the street culminates in a small local shopping centre, a feature of which is the famous Leith School of Food and Wine. A bunch of grapes and a knife and fork have been wittily worked into the brickwork of the gabled building. Just around the corner to the S, hidden from the street, are the vine-covered St Alban's Studios, set around a neo-Tudor courtyard.

The E end of the street also forms a pleasant villagy centre at its junction with **Victoria Grove**. A terrace of 1840s stucco houses with a continuous black first-floor canopy and unusual decorative ironwork columns stretches along the N side. It joins up with more shops spilling around the corner from **Gloucester Rd**.

Canning Place just to the N is a pleasant, leafy street with pairs of linked stucco villas and a terrace of 2/3-storey and basement stucco houses. On the N side are the entrances to two converted mews developments, **De Vere Cottages** and **De Vere Mews**. **De Vere Gardens** off to the N is lined mainly by tall brick and stucco terraces converted into flats with hotels at its N end.

Canning Passage, a pedestrian walkway, runs through to **Victoria Rd**. Off this road is a series of three leafy cul-de-sacs – **Albert Place**, **Cambridge Place** and **Douro Place**. The first two have early Victorian stucco villas. Much of **Douro Place** was completely rebuilt following war damage, resulting in modern and period houses standing side by side. The cul-de-sac here is created by the rear of the flats in Kensington Court.

Kensington Court is both the name of the street and the red-brick Dutch-style development which dominates this 7-acre triangular site S of **Kensington High St**. A series of mansion blocks and terraces of gabled houses of differing heights and degrees of ornamentation make up the complex. Built 1880–1900, Kensington Court was the first group of buildings in London to be lighted by electricity. At the S end of **Kensington Court** is **Kensington Court Mews**, an unusual late-Victorian multi-storey stable block, which now has two tiers of flats above ground-floor garages. Another 5/6-storey red-brick block, Kensington Court Gardens, stands on the E side of **Kensington Court Place**, dwarfing the terrace of early 19th-century cottages opposite.

Beyond **Thackeray St** with its parade of shops is **Kensington Square**. This is one of London's oldest squares, dating back to 1685, when it was built to house Palace courtiers. Blue plaques dotted around the square with its large central gardens give a clue to its former distinguished residents, including Edward Burne-Jones, Mrs Patrick Campbell and John Stuart Mill. Some of the buildings, which range from Jacobean and Georgian to 1900s developments, remain as houses: expect to pay up to £3 million for the best. Others have been converted into offices.

K

Scarsdale/Abingdon

The Circle line in its deep cutting and the Kensington Green development divide this neighbourhood from **Kensington Square** to the E. **Wrights Lane** is the entry point from **Kensington High St**. A short way down **Wrights Lane** the Royal Gate development of 119 1-, 2- and 3-bed apartments and penthouses is nearly complete: underground parking, a fitness centre and prices from £275,000 to £2.7 million. **Wrights Lane** leads on to the big London Copthorne Tara and Kensington Close Hotels. On the W side of the street, not far from its junction with the **Kensington High St**, stand two of the late-Victorian mansions blocks which make up Iverna Court. Iverna Court is a set-piece development of 5/7/8-storey and basement red-brick and stone mansion blocks with elaborate entrances and black cast-iron balconies. The blocks spread around the corner into **Iverna Gardens**, stretching almost to its junction with **Abingdon Villas**. Flats in the square at the N end of the street overlook the unusual white marble St Sarkis Armenian Church, which sits in the middle, behind a strip of trees and shrubs.

More tall brick and stone mansions, including the popular Zetland House, line the E side of busy **Marloes Rd** as far as 'Kensington Green', a new complex of 1- to 4-bedroom houses and flats with prices ranging from £250,000 to more than £2 million. Access is via **St Mary's Gate**, with the main street called **St Mary's Place**. The rest of **Marloes Rd** has terraces of 3/4-storey and basement brick and stucco properties, some with shops and offices on the ground floors. The large grey concrete and blue glass building at the S junction with **Cromwell Rd** is the private Cromwell Hospital. **Pennant Mews** runs behind the hospital.

Lexham Gardens stretches across the neighbourhood, changing in character as it goes. The S crescent, which curves N from **Cromwell Rd**, contains mainly hotels, presumably remnants from the days when the West London Air Terminal stood behind the street. The rest of the brick and stucco terraced properties here have been converted into flats. Leading off the N end of the crescent is **Lexham Walk**, a pleasant

passageway lined by white 2-storey cottages. It crosses into the De Vere/Cornwall neighbourhood to the E. **Lexham Gardens** E of **Marloes Rd** is made up of 4/5-storey and basement brick and stucco terraced houses of varying quality set around narrow central gardens. The houses in the W arm across **Marloes Rd** are built in the same style but generally of better quality. As in the E arm, most have been split into flats.

Tucked away behind **Lexham Gardens** are **Lexham Mews** and **Radley Mews**, which join together at the S end of **Allen St**. The long cobbled mews has mostly 2-storey period/rebuilt brick/painted cottages with some garages and other light industrial uses. Emerge from the mews into **Stratford Rd** with its up-market village shopping centre and terraces of 3-storey and basement brick and stucco houses, some with small front gardens and forecourt parking.

Lying off the N side of **Stratford Rd** around the corner from the parade of shops is **Blithfield St**, an appealing tree-lined cul-de-sac of colourfully painted 3-storey terraced houses dating back to the 1860s. **Sunningdale Gardens** stands on the S side of **Stratford Rd** at the junction with **Abingdon Rd**. Here the terraces turn sideways on to form an attractive enclave of 3-storey and basement brick and stucco houses on two sides of a small central garden with trees in the middle.

Well-hidden behind the houses in the N side of **Stratford Rd** near its junction with **Earls Court Rd** is **Shaftesbury Mews**, a development of modern 4-storey brown-brick houses with garages. **Scarsdale Studios**, off **Stratford Rd**, is an enclave of nine artists' studios built in the 1890s around a private courtyard.

Tree-lined **Scarsdale Villas** has Victorian terraces of 3-storey and basement stucco, or brick and stucco houses up to **Allen St**. To the E they become paired 3-storey and basement stucco-fronted villas N and similar style in groups of four S. In tree-lined **Abingdon Villas**, a mix of 3-storey Victorian terraces stand alongside tall red-brick and stone mansion blocks. **Abingdon Court** N, which stretches from **Iverna Gardens** to **Allen St**, is a late-Victorian block, and **Abingdon Gardens** S is Edwardian.

Allen St and **Abingdon Rd**, which runs N-S from **Kensington High St** to **Stratford Rd**, combine a mix of residential and commercial uses. Shops and restaurants spill around the corner from the **High St** into both. A short distance S of the **High St** in **Allen St** is **Wynnstay Gardens**, a development of 4/5-storey red-brick and stucco flats blocks. One group fronts **Allen St** while further blocks are tucked away behind, lining a private road. Allen House, a red-brick gabled block of timeshare flats, stands on the opposite side of the street near the listed Kensington Chapel, built in 1855 and noted for its classical façade. More mansion flats and 3-storey brick and stucco terraces lie to the S.

Beside the chapel is one of two entrances to **Adam and Eve Mews**. (The other is in **Kensington High St**.) The mews contain 2/3-storey modern/period houses, some garages and offices. Houses command prices of between £400,000 and £1 million. **Eden Close** at the NW end is a new red-brick development where a mews has been created within a mews.

Abingdon Rd is lined with 2/3-storey terraced houses of varying styles. The brown-and red-brick late-Victorian flats in **Pater St** to the W spread around the corner into the N end of the street, merging with the shops and restaurants which lead to the **High St**.

Earls Court Rd on the W boundary of the neighbourhood is a two-way street as far as **Stratford Rd** where it joins the notorious West London one-way traffic system. The most attractive residential section – a terrace of 4-storey and basement stucco-fronted houses – lies between **Stratford Rd** and **Scarsdale Villas**. The unusual new cream- and brown-stone, brick and glass development at the junction of **Earls Court Rd** and **Kensington High St** is a flats and offices block, topped by a penthouse overlooking Holland Park. Monarch House has luxury flats to let, aimed at businessmen and expatriates, with hotel-style amenities.

K

Pembrokes/Edwardes Square

Although bounded by some of the busiest and noisiest roads in the borough this desirable neighbourhood contains some of the earliest and choicest properties in Kensington. The first surprise lies at the end of an unpromising lane off the N end of bustling **Earls Court Rd**, behind the Odeon Cinema. Turn the corner to find **Pembroke Place**, an oasis of pretty painted 3-storey Victorian houses set around a courtyard with trees in the middle. The 3-storey brick and stucco terrace on the E side is a modern rebuild. Plans for a multi-screen cinema, offices, 32 flats and car parking space on the site of the Odeon cinema on the corner of **Kensington High St** and **Pembroke Mews** have fallen through, though the cinema has been tidied up.

Tucked away behind Kensington police station immediately to the S is **Pembroke Mews**. The mostly 2-storey brick/painted brick and stucco cottages vary widely in quality and condition but rebuilding and renovation is under way. Two cottages were recently sold for development: £1 million for the pair.

Within yards of **Earls Court Rd** with its mix of residential/commercial properties is **Pembroke Square**. This Georgian square is neatly shielded from the main road by Rassells garden centre and the flower-bedecked Hansom Cab pub. Two terraces of 4-storey mellow brick terraced houses with stucco-faced ground floors line a long private central garden. The garden has its own tennis court and even a daily weather chart posted on the gate. The W end of the square becomes **Pembroke Villas** to the S, an attractive colony of 3-storey paired stucco or brick and stucco villas set in gardens with tall trees overhanging the street.

Pembroke Walk, an easily missed cul-de-sac tucked away off the E side of the street, is a narrow lane with unusual, nay eccentric, 2/3-storey period and modern houses/studios. North of **Pembroke Square**, past the pretty Scarsdale pub with its profusion of hanging baskets, stands **Edwardes Square**, the gem of the neighbourhood. This fine late-Georgian square was built 1811–20. Immaculate terraces of beautiful 3-storey and basement brick houses with stucco ground floor stretch along the W and E sides of mature central gardens. Front gardens, wisteria-covered houses, hedges and overhanging trees contribute to the leafy look of the square, only a short walk from the shops and restaurants which line **Kensington High St**. Green Victorian street lamps, original cast-iron fanlights and black cast-iron railings with unusual pineapple kingheads add to the period character of the area.

The N side of the square is bounded by a long brick wall and a mass of trees in the rear gardens of **Earls Terrace**, which fronts **Kensington High St**. Here a long uniform Regency terrace, set back from the main road behind a carriageway, is the talking-point of Kensington – its high-security, 6-bedroomed, £3–6 million houses are being renovated to superstar status. A matching terrace stands in nearby **Edwardes Place**, separated from the high street by a private passageway, iron gates and trees.

The S arm of **Edwardes Square** feels like a separate street, being a complete contrast to the Georgian terraces. It has mostly studio houses (Annigoni lived here) alongside 1930s Pembroke Court, a 5-storey brick and stone flats block. These buildings face the white 'Temple', a listed gardener's cottage in the square garden designed to look like a Grecian temple. Lying just to the S of the square at its W end is **Pembroke Gardens Close**, a private landscaped cul-de-sac of very desirable 2-storey brick houses. This exceptional enclave has the peaceful air of a village green.

Pembroke Gardens (the name derives from the Welsh estates of Lord Kensington's family) is split into two arms. A feature of the N arm is **Pembroke Studios**, 2-storey red- and brown-brick Victorian houses looking like a group of 19th-century almshouses. The studios are set around a central courtyard and the complex itself is separated from the street by a garden and cast-iron gates. The rest of the street has a mix of brick and stucco paired houses, 1920s Dutch-gabled houses, modern brick terraces and Victorian brick and stucco terraces. A 4/5-bed house in **Pembroke Gardens** sold last year for £2.5 million.

Pembroke Rd is cut in two by the heavily trafficked Earls Court one-way system, which runs southbound along the E stretch to join **Earls Court Rd**. Two large flats blocks – Chatsworth and Marlborough Courts – dominate the S side of the E arm. Painted brick, or stucco and brick, paired/detached stucco houses line the rest of the S and N sides.

A new red-brick apartment block, Huntsmore House (formerly called Pembroke Heights), stands at the junction of **Pembroke Rd** and **Cromwell Crescent**. The development of 79 1- to 3-bed flats stretches to the council's central works depot on the corner with **Warwick Rd** W. It encloses a large private garden and boasts a swimming pool as well as a gym.

Although **Warwick Gardens** forms the S-bound section of the Earls Court one-way system, it is a relatively pleasant tree-lined street. Pairs of large Victorian stucco houses with columned porches and terraces of 3-storey and basement brick and stucco houses predominate. St Mary Abbots Court is a group of three large 7-storey brick flats blocks which congregate at the NW end of **Warwick Gardens**.

Warwick Rd is a major route on the N-bound section of the one-way system. The council's central works depot with a modern housing estate perched on top dominates the E side of the road. On the W side, public car and lorry parks, a petrol station, a Sainsbury's Homebase DIY centre, a smart new Tesco superstore and the West Kensington telephone exchange lie between the road and railway line.

Phillimore Estate

Substantial Victorian houses and villas predominate in this leafy, salubrious neighbourhood where properties consis-tently change hands for £1 million-plus. The streets climb gently uphill and are remarkable peaceful considering their proximity to busy **Kensington High St**, just to the S. Most of the big white stucco detached villas and 4/5-storey stucco or brick-and-stucco terraced houses on the W side of **Phillimore Gardens** have the added advantage of rear gardens backing on to Holland Park. Leases are short at about 20 years. More large detached mansions are on the E side, alongside 4-storey semi-detached houses. Some have front gardens, others patios with flower-filled tubs.

A pedestrian passageway leads into Holland Park from the N side of the street where it joins **Duchess of Bedford's Walk** at the top of the hill. Plane Tree House, an award-winning 7-storey 1960s flats development, stands in the N corner overlooking the park. Three-bed flats here command prices around £800,000. A series of Edwardian flats blocks, including the prestigious Duchess of Bedford House, spread along the rest of this tree-lined street, adjoining the campus of King's College on the E corner. The 7-storey brown-brick and stone blocks stand in beautifully kept landscaped grounds, set back behind neatly clipped hedges.

They overlook the walled back gardens of houses in **Upper Phillimore Gardens**. This street is lined by large white stucco linked houses and smaller brick and stucco terraced homes, all front gardens, hedges and doorstep urns full of roses and shrubs and bushes. Tall trees add to the street's charm. **Phillimore Place**, a one-way street, and **Essex Villas** have mainly 3-storey and basement brick and stucco terraced houses. The exception is a group of Tudor Gothic houses in the former. Taller, more ornate, brick and stucco terraces are found in **Stafford Terrace**.

The scene changes completely in **Phillimore Walk**, which is overshadowed by the back of Stafford Court, a big early 20th-century brown-brick and stone flats block. It fronts **Kensington High St** and takes up the whole block between **Phillimore Gardens** and **Argyll Rd**. More large semi-detached houses and white stucco terraces with front gardens line **Argyll Rd**.

The S end of **Campden Hill Rd**, which forms the neighbourhood's E boundary, also has big white houses and brick and stucco terraces. They look across to the modern red-brick Kensington Town Hall in the E side of the street.

Transport	Tubes: Notting Hill Gate (zone 1/2, District, Circle, Central), Queensway (zone 1, Central), High St Kensington (zone 1, District, Circle), Gloucester Rd (zone 1, Piccadilly, District, Circle). From High St Kensington: Oxford Circus 15 min (1 change), City 25 min (1 change), Heathrow 40 min (1 change).
Convenient for	Hyde Park, West End, Heathrow and West. Miles from centre: 3.

Schools   Local Authority: Holland Park, Cardinal Manning RC (b), Cardinal Vaughan RC (b), St Thomas More RC, Sion Manning RC (g). Private: St James', Falkner House (g), Queens' Gate School (g).

SALES

Flats	S	1B	2B	3B	4B	5B
Average prices	90–140	140–300+	220–500+	300–600+	500–1M+	600–1.5M+

Houses	2B	3B	4B	5B	6/7B	8B
Average prices	350–700	450–800+	600–1M+	800–2M+	1M–5M	2M+

RENTAL

Flats	S	1B	2B	3B	4B	5B
Average prices	800–1000	1000–2000	1500–3000	2000–6000	4000+	6000+

Houses	2B	3B	4B	5B	6/7B	8B
Average prices	2000–2800	2400–3500	3500+	6000+	6000+	10 ·+

The properties   Heart of desirable, residential London: Victorian houses, some earlier; large numbers of flats, both mansion and converted; plus mews cottages and some new-build flats and houses in smart gated developments. Hardly a bad street in the place.

The market   Kensington has never been unfashionable. Today, the settled, prosperous population is joined by international buyers/renters. More domestic than Knightsbridge, more smart than South Ken, more respectable than Notting Hill. Some glorious multi-million homes. Local searches: 5 days.

K

Among those estate agents active in this area are:
- W A Ellis *
- Knight Frank*
- Chesterfield
- Marsh & Parsons*
- Aylesfords*
- Friend & Falcke*
- Jackson-Stops & Staff
- FPDSavills
- John D Wood
- Douglas & Gordon *
- Daniel Cobb *
- Foxtons *
- Winkworth *
- Lane Fox
- Strutt & Parker *
- Hamptons
- Beaney Pearce *
- Scotts *
- Berkeley International *
- Chestertons *

further details: see advertisers' index on p633

KENTISH TOWN AND TUFNELL PARK

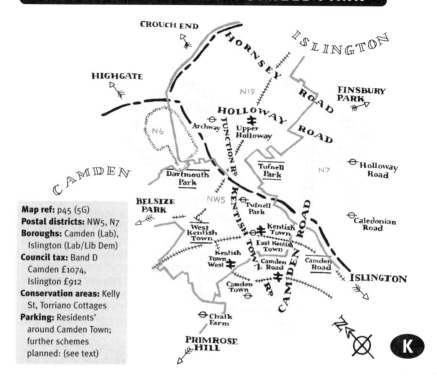

Map ref: p45 (5G)
Postal districts: NW5, N7
Boroughs: Camden (Lab),
   Islington (Lab/Lib Dem)
Council tax: Band D
   Camden £1074,
   Islington £912
Conservation areas: Kelly
   St, Torriano Cottages
Parking: Residents'
   around Camden Town;
   further schemes
   planned: (see text)

Kentish Town basks in the reflected glow from Hampstead and Highgate,
and its image continues to improve. Indeed, the grander, larger houses of Dartmouth
Park are cheap only in comparison to these lofty neighbours. For the rest, the
handsome early Victorian terraces that survive in a somewhat mixed area are now
'riddled with trendy property' according to local agents, who pray that, given its
neighbours and its convenience, it's only a matter of time before it catches up with
Camden. We draw your attention to the N London line, Silverlink, which goes direct to
the City Airport – thus making Gospel Oak rail station a mere 2 hours 10 minutes from
Paris. No need to wait, then, for the Eurostar to arrive at St Pancras . . .

   Transport is much in residents' minds just now – or rather parking. Those areas that
haven't got residents' parking now will certainly have them within a year or three.
Clampers are rampant, and the council is threatening not to give permits to inhabitants
of any new developments in the borough which have their own parking spaces.

   The first mentions of 'Kentystown', 'Kentisshton' and 'Kentissetone' appear in
documents dating from as early as the 13th century, when it probably started life as a
cluster of houses around an inn – a welcome refuge on what was one of the few roads
leading northwards from the City through the forbidding Forest of Middlesex. The
village grew as the area around became important farm land, but the real population
explosion came in the 1840s, when large-scale development began – catering for
middle-class families with servants, but not able to compete with its illustrious
northern neighbours, Hampstead and Highgate, for really wealthy inhabitants.

The area passed through ups and downs, becoming at first a rather pretty and fashionable place, but then (as the railways carved the area up) falling into a long and steady decline which lasted until the 1960s when two important things happened. The first was the dramatic acceleration of large council housing development schemes started by St Pancras Council and then, with more vigour, by the newly formed larger Borough of Camden, which changed the face of Kentish Town, particularly in the W.

The second was that Kentish Town – in particular, leafy Dartmouth Park – began to benefit as an overflow area into which trickled those who just couldn't quite afford to buy homes in Hampstead or Highgate. This factor is still the dominant feature of the property market in the area – only now people moving in are those who just can't quite afford Belsize Park or Camden . . . Here they find pockets of substantial family houses, a good supply of small- and medium-sized homes, and a good number of converted flats, particularly 1- and 2-bed ones – though the conversion frenzy of the '80s assumed nothing like the proportions here that it did in, for example, West Hampstead.

Dartmouth Park

This is the area where people first realized that Kentish Town had streets to offer that were every bit as nice as in Hampstead, *and* just as close to Hampstead Heath *and* with all the same advantages of good transport links (see above) *and* close to the West End . . . but where prices were, and still are – comparatively – lower.

Formerly owned by the Earl of Dartmouth and developed in the 1870s, the area lies between **Dartmouth Park Hill** in the E to **Highgate Rd** in the W, and from Highgate's Holly Lodge Estate and the famous cemetery down to busy **Chetwynd Rd**. Particularly popular (prices can approach a million) are **Dartmouth Park Rd** and **Dartmouth Park Avenue** with their grand terraced houses in blocks of three, many of which have been converted; as well as **Boscastle Rd**, which is literally a stone's throw from the heath across **Highgate Rd**.

Camden Council has brought in a number of measures to stop rush hour through traffic from using the area, but these streets can still get a bit choked in the morning rush hour as motorists desperately search for alternative ways through the Kentish Town bottleneck. However, myriad attractions (including four excellent state secondary schools virtually on the doorstep – William Ellis, Parliament Hill and Acland Burghley comprehensives, as well as La Sainte Union convent school) heavily outweigh the disadvantages.

There are also hidden delights, such as the sportsground, tennis courts and bowling club tucked away off **Croftdown Rd**, and the sudden views W and S from some of the houses in the higher streets. This is not the corner to look for glitzy new developments, though a cache of 11 houses appeared in 1989 in **St Albans Rd**.

Perhaps the most elegant (and pricey) homes in Kentish Town are the splendid row of deceptively large houses in **Grove Terrace** off **Highgate Rd** which significantly pre-date the rest of the area, having been built in the late 18th century.

West Kentish Town

This is the area of Kentish Town (W of the busy **Kentish Town Rd** shopping centre) dominated by huge council estates which have swallowed up dozens of Victorian streets. They range from some of the worst of municipal mistakes to shining showpieces of successful modern urban development. But, in among the large estates and tower blocks, there are still pleasant streets where bargain-hunters search for unmodernized homes in some handsome, early Victorian terraces (c. £250–325,000). There is also, of course, ex-council. There are interesting terraces in Maitland Park, on the W edge of the neighbourhood, in **St Leonard's Square**, and also at the SW end of **Queen's Crescent** (the NE end becomes a bustling street market on some days), with its set of little cul-de-sacs running off: **St Thomas's Gardens, Baptist Gardens, St Ann's Gardens** and **Modbury Gardens**. In the angle of **Gordon House Rd** and **Highgate Rd** little **Mortimer Terrace** has a dozen 3-bed houses, built in 1989. Watch for change in West Kentish Town as tenants' associations take control on council estates.

Pockets of good properties can also be found in the S, towards Chalk Farm, in streets around **Castle Rd** in the area S of **Prince of Wales Rd**. There is a positively delightful group of streets including **Healey St**, **Grafton Crescent** and the northern end of **Hadley St** containing cheerful and exquisitely preserved 2-storey terraces which are part of the Kelly St conservation area – the only one to be found in Kentish Town proper.

The former North London Polytechnic building at 1 **Prince of Wales Rd** has been transformed by Dorrington into 65 mainly 2-bed galleried loft apartments. The first phase sold rapidly off-plan in 1987, the bulk during last year at c. £180,000, and the remaining 10, with terraces, still available in December were £210–299,000. Planning permission awaited for a further 'exciting' (we are told) loft scheme in Kentish Town.

East Kentish Town

The triangle bounded by **Kentish Town Rd, Camden Rd** and **Brecknock Rd** contains the heartland of Kentish Town and is largely unvandalized by the council, with the exception of some crumbling pre-war estates in the **Islip St** area. Otherwise the area is awash with improving and improvable streets, with a good supply of (smaller) family houses and conversions. Residents are cheered by more and better shopping; a Pizza Express has arrived, other well-known names are eyeing the area and even Woolies has gone in for a million-pound refit . . .

There is also a great deal of charm and elegance, particularly in roads like **Patshull Rd, Bartholomew Rd, Lawford Rd** and **Bartholomew Villas** (which contains the well-known Kentish Town Community Health Centre), most of which have attractive 3-storey terraces, with pleasing architectural features such as cast-iron balconies. Closer to the tube lie **Gaisford St** and **Caversham, Holmes** and **Inkerman Rds**.

North of the narrow and busy **Leighton Rd** there are more rewards and surprises. The main surprise is **Lady Margaret Rd**, built in the early 1860s, which is almost twice as wide and gracious as any other street in the area. Leading off it are the rewards, traditionally narrow streets that are among the most intensively gentrified in London, including **Falkland Rd, Ascham St, Dunollie Rd, Leverton St, Ravely St, Countess Rd** and **Montpelier Grove**, all with 2- and 3-storey terraces and semi-detached rows.

Tufnell Park

Mainly in the Borough of Islington, this area, bounded by **Camden Rd, Brecknock Rd** and **Holloway Rd,** was almost completely ignored by buyers and even estate agents until the last couple of decades, and it is still more blighted by its rather down-market reputation – and association with the Holloway area – than it deserves. In reality it contains a nest of extremely pleasant streets which, although bordered by some polluted and juggernaut-dominated trunk roads, are themselves quiet, charming and relatively free of through traffic. Flat conversions proliferated throughout the area.

This is a friendly area, with a real community spirit – for example, new parents who move in find that local families have set up a support group to help with everything from advice to holiday playgroups.

There are some large council estates in the southern part (as well as the famous Holloway Prison for women), but closer to the tube station in the W there are popular streets: **Hugo Rd** and **Corinne Rd** with attractive 2-storey terraces; **Lady Somerset** and **Burghley Rds** on the Kentish Town side; **St Georges Avenue,** S of **Tufnell Park Rd,** where a 3-bed flat can make £200,000, houses around £350,000.

North of **Tufnell Park Rd** itself there is the very pleasant **Huddleston Rd** cul-de-sac, and the group of roads around **Tytherton Rd** which include **Mercers Rd** (convenient for open playing-fields), **Yerbury Rd**, **Beversbrook Rd**, **Campdale Rd** and **Foxham Rd** with its unusually pleasing development of modern council houses together with communal gardens and children's playground.

In Tufnell Park, the rule of thumb is: avoid **Holloway Rd**. But at the same time it is interesting to see just how close one can get to that road before it starts impinging on the neighbouring properties. Watch out also for rail lines – some may one day carry Eurostar trains if the St Pancras terminal gets built (see below).

King's Cross Borders

The southernmost part of Kentish Town is destined to benefit dramatically from plans to develop – eventually – the giant King's Cross railway lands site. This is linked to the Channel Tunnel Eurostar terminal, which will (one day) be at St Pancras. This vast scheme has been on/off since the early 1980s, and the whole Channel rail link, and thus the King's Cross scheme, has yet to get the final green light. Locals, remembering past false dawns, will believe it when they see it. Or, more likely, when they feel the vibration from the enormous Eurostar trains. Streets closest to the vast site will no doubt suffer the inconvenience of being near what will be the largest single development in Europe, but eventually proximity to it, with its envisaged housing, new park and huge commercial centre, can only have a beneficial effect on prices. Values in the immediate area of the site began to rise sharply in the late 1980s, and will doubtless be good long-term investments.

Camden Road Borders

Strictly speaking part of Camden Town (see chapter) and in the NW1 postal district, the Camden Square conservation area is in essence part of the eastern section of Kentish Town. The houses are larger here, though, and more splendid, particularly the terraced and semi-detached examples in **Camden Square** itself (with its children's playground), **Cantelowes Rd**, **St Augustine's Rd**, **North Villas**, **South Villas** and **Murray St**. There are also attractive houses in **Camden Mews** and smaller terraces in **Marquis Rd**. These roads are protected from traffic by a series of road closures.

Across **York Way** and NE of a large council estate, there are roads off **Hillmarton Rd** which have grand houses, now mostly flats. These streets, too, are well-blocked off to through traffic and are convenient for Caledonian Rd tube on the Piccadilly line. On the Islington borders, on old railway sidings off **Stock Orchard St**, **Heddington Grove** is a street of 134 flats and town-houses that appeared in the late '80s.

Archway Borders

On the Camden (W) side, this area is sometimes known as Highgate New Town because of its proximity to the rather superior examples of council housing built by Camden at the northern end. But between **Junction Rd** and **Dartmouth Park Hill** there are some streets full of character such as **Bickerton Rd** and **Tremlett Grove**, which also adjoin a little-known and unnamed park around a covered reservoir.

On the Islington side, and E of **Archway Rd**, which is virtually a motorway at this point, there is a surprisingly secluded set of roads which have become very popular in recent years. North of the huge GLC-built council estate blocks in **St John's Way**, these streets include the Whitehall Park conservation area, comprising **Whitehall Park**, **Gladsmuir Rd** and **Harberton Rd**, a relatively well-preserved Victorian estate ranging from grand semis to modest 2-storey terraces, but all with attractive architectural features. The land slopes quite steeply giving splendid views, up to a ridge along which runs **Hornsey Lane**, the N19 postcode boundary and the northern frontier of Islington

Borough. Beyond are N6 and Haringey. Other streets here well worth a long second look include **Gresley Rd**, **Dresden Rd**, **Cheverton Rd**, **Parolles Rd** and **Prospero Rd**.

Transport	Tubes: Kentish Town, Tufnell Park (zone 2, Northern). From Tufnell Park: Oxford Circus 20 min (1 change), City 15 min, Heathrow 55 min (1 change). Trains: Kentish Town (to St Pancras); Gospel Oak, Kentish Town West, Camden Rd (North London line/Silverlink).
Convenient for	Hampstead Heath, Islington, road links to North. Miles from centre: 3.
Schools	Local Authority: Acland Burghley, Parliament Hill, Jewish Free School, Camden School for Girls, William Ellis (b), La Sainte Union Convent (g).

SALES

Flats	S	1B	2B	3B	4B	5B
Average prices	60–85	75–120	100–200	130–220	–	–
Houses	2B	3B	4B	5B	6/7B	8B
Average prices	180–300	200–350	250–500	270–400+	–	–

RENTAL

Flats	S	1B	2B	3B	4B	5B
Average prices	500–550	650–850	850–1300	1200–1400	–	–
Houses	2B	3B	4B	5B	6/7B	8B
Average prices	1000–1300	1300–1500	1500–1950	1700–2000	1700–2000	2300–3900

K

The properties	Victorian terraces appeared early – 1840s onwards – so those remaining can be handsome; many houses now flats. Some streets of Hampstead quality, other parts disrupted by council building good and bad. Grander in Dartmouth Park and on Camden borders.
The market	The rental investment market has its eyes on this convenient if mixed area, where many homes have been spruced up or turned into flats. The closer to tubes and the further from main through-routes, the higher the price. An area growing in status. Local searches: Camden 2 weeks, Islington 2 weeks.

Among those estate agents active in this area are:
- Salter Rex
- Day Morris
- Benham & Reeves
- Captital Sales
- Barnard Marcus
- Dillons

KILBURN, KENSAL GREEN AND QUEEN'S PARK

Map ref: p59 (2J)
Postal districts: NW6, W10, W9
Boroughs: Brent (Lab), Westminster (Con)
Council tax: Band D Brent £589, Westminster £325
Conservation areas: Queen's Park, Kilburn, N Kilburn, S Kilburn
Parking: Free away from Kilburn High Rd

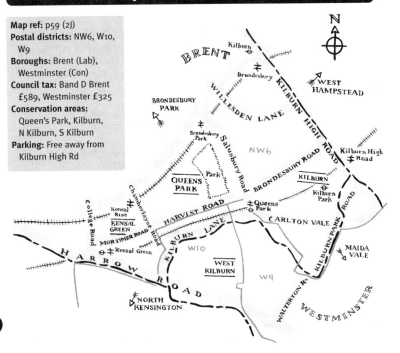

Caught between creeping West Hampstead to the E, expansionist Maida Vale to the S and a swollen Queen's Park to the W, Kilburn seems in danger of extinction. Confusion over tube station names and postal districts further erodes Kilburn as a residential area. Whatever this tract is called, it has several things in its favour, first being location. It is just as close to the centre of London as North Kensington – closer than Hammersmith, let alone Shepherd's Bush. The Bakerloo and Jubilee lines which serve it have useful connections, not least with Paddington and its Heathrow link. In addition, there is a good choice of (mostly converted) flats of a decent size, and a few family houses: both kinds of home at prices a good bit lower than in nearby areas. Even those sensitive to postcode subtleties need not miss out: Kilburn and Kensal share NW6 with West Hampstead and W10 with North Kensington, and there's even a corner with Maida Vale's postcode, W9.

Much of the present-day Kilburn was built between 1860 and 1890, as what was a vaguely defined village on the **Edgware Rd** became organized urban sprawl. The railway lines that dissect the area became punctuated with stations to meet the needs of the new inhabitants, and the **High Rd** grew into a flourishing shopping centre. Another wave of building spread up from Paddington along the canal, to add Kensal Town and Kensal Green to the area's neighbourhoods. Today, good transport and parking, and solid Victorian terraces, underpin Kilburn's growing popularity. It is no longer a down-market area (once you look beyond the modern council-built estates to the S), but the respectable and increasingly fashionable neighbour of West Hampstead and Maida Vale.

Up to 1890, most of the housing (and perhaps many of the residents) finished at Kensal Rise Cemetery. Next (1895–1905) and to the N came the larger houses and wider avenues of Queen's Park. There is much confusion over the name 'Queen's Park', because there are two of them: parks (or green spaces) as well as suburbs (streets around said spaces). The name was first used for the estate of terraced cottages which are to be found to the S of the railway line in W10 (hereafter referred to more properly as Queen's Park Estate). These were built by the Artisans, Labourers & General Dwellings Company in the 1870s. However, the 30-acre park N of **Harvist Rd**, laid out in 1886, was given the same name, and Queen's Park as a neighbourhood now signifies the streets around the park itself. The term carries a premium: be warned that estate agents have a tendency to use it freely and loosely.

Kensal Green, just across **Chamberlayne Rd** to the W, is less assuming. Built up in 1880–1900 and run-down by 1920, it is now reasserting itself on the market, increasingly popular because of its proximity to the Sainsbury's superstore and the top end of **Ladbroke Grove** (without that area's prices). Its high-density terraces, now mixed in with some dull council houses, are arranged (by means of barriers and no-entry signs) into curious little groups of roads that the casual house-hunting motorist may never happen across.

Another neighbourhood that must be treated separately is West Kilburn, S of **Kilburn Lane** – not least because it is in Westminster rather than in Brent, and in W9 not NW6. Apart from the unspoilt Queen's Park Estate (which is in W10 . . .), it is an area undergoing much change, with new flats fitted snugly in Victorian terraces.

Rail and tube station names seem designed to confuse the local geography. Kilburn tube (Jubilee line) is on **Shoot Up Hill** in the far N of the area, just in NW6 but outside Kilburn by most definitions. It serves the Mapesbury Estate neighbourhood, between Willesden Green and Brondesbury Park. Local zealots want the station name changed to Mapesbury. Kilburn Park tube (Bakerloo), to the S, is closer to the **High Rd**. Queen's Park and Kensal Green stations (also Bakerloo) are sensibly placed, as is Kensal Rise (N London/Silverlink) though Brondesbury station is on **Kilburn High Rd** – as is Kilburn High Rd station (trains to Euston). Confused? Blame the Victorians.

For the area as a whole the police consider the crime rate high but this only really applies to particular estates. Pubs, for all Kilburn's traditional reputation as an area much liked by hard-working, and hard-drinking, Irish immigrants, are cavernous rather than numerous and are concentrated in the main shopping streets. Estate agents assert that schools are not an issue, as it is largely first-time buyers and young couples who are moving in. Professional people with families continue to buy into leafy Queen's Park and are looking hard at the streets W of **Kilburn High Rd** and on the borders with Maida Vale. Prices have risen briskly since the mid-1990s, but are still attractive compared to neighbouring areas.

Kilburn

The **High Rd**, with its shops, chain stores, pubs and stations (from N to S Kilburn tube and Brondesbury and Kilburn High Rd rail stations), is the main artery rather than the heart of Kilburn. At its southernmost end, the Regents Plaza hotel was finished in 1995, complete with restaurants and health club – and, as well as the hotel rooms, serviced 1-, 2- and 3-bed flats. See Maida Vale chapter for details.

The junction of **Kilburn High Rd** and **Kilburn Priory** marks the centre of the old village, virtually nothing of which survives. A Baroque 4-storey terrace on **Kilburn Priory** and four Georgian town-houses on **Springfield Lane** stand out from their surroundings. Less distinguished corners include the Abbey Estate – council-built on the NW8 border towards **Abbey Rd** – and Kilburn Vale Estate S of **Quex Rd**. The latter includes 1980s mews-type homes over garages on **Mutrix Rd** and **Bransdale Close**.

Kilburn High Rd forms the border between Westminster and Camden. The latter, to the E, has stern views about car parking and residents' permits here may become expensive and scarce. Just about every residential street to the E of the **High Rd** is claimed by West Hampstead. **West End Lane** here has some purpose-built flats blocks, both private and council; **Birchington Rd** has 4-storey terraces with imposing porches. Off **Quex Rd**, in **Quex Mews**, 10 1- and 2-bed flats have been added to the existing five mews houses. North of here near the main Catholic church are the ornate terraces of **Mazenod Avenue**, while **Kingsgate Rd** has a mixture of terraces with basement flats, council blocks and flats over shops. The terraces of **Messina Avenue** stand opposite a school and little Kilburn Grange park, N of which is more council housing up to the railway line.

Across the **High Rd** to the W, and N of **Willesden Lane**, **Dyne Rd** has some large square-fronted houses, not all converted into flats, that look at a first glance like semis but which are linked at the back. Note that the N side of the road backs onto the railway. **Torbay Rd** has smaller terraces while **Plympton Rd** and **Buckley Rd** have 3-storey ones – all bright and cheerful houses on quiet streets. These roads were declared a conservation area in 1994. Houses in **Buckley Rd** command prices around £300,000 unmodernized, with £400,000 more typical for done-up ones with 5 bedrooms. **Willesden Lane**, with its small shops, mansion blocks and junior school, is the N border of a tract of more modest rows running S to **Glengall Rd**. Mansion flats on **Willesden Lane** might cost £135,000 for 2-bed, while a 3-bed conversion from a Victorian house might reach £150,000-plus. In the grid of streets to the S **Tennyson Rd** (for example) has an unbroken terrace along the W side incorporating a dozen minor variations on, and later amendments to, its Victorian artisan theme. These back onto Willesden Lane Cemetery, as do homes on the N side of **Lonsdale Rd**. The houses on **Donaldson Rd**, **Victoria Rd** and **Hartland Rd**, many of which have been converted into flats, display a touching homogeneity: nearly all highlight the decorative panels on the 2-storey bays. Buyers look here for 2-bed converted flats at £100,000-plus and 3-bed houses at c. £265,000.

Brondesbury Rd runs the gamut from council tower blocks at **Kilburn Square** in the E, through large red-brick 3-storey terraces – some ornate, some Italianate, but nearly all flats – to some very suburban semis near Queen's Park station in the W. Homes range from 1-bed flats, which can be spacious if in the enormous Victorian houses, through normal-sized 2-bed conversions to some large, elegant 2-bed, 2-recep garden flats. The latter can command £200,000-plus prices. **Brondesbury Villas**, which runs parallel to the S, echoes its namesake for much of its length, but has some particularly ornate houses, now mostly flats. The fact that it backs onto the railway line does little to lower prices; a sought-after address. Both roads, as well as **Honiton** and **Lynton Rds**, were made a conservation area in 1993.

South of the railway is largely sprawling council estates on either side of **Carlton Vale** and surrounding the 1860s James Bailey villas of **Cambridge Avenue**, **Chichester Rd**, **Cambridge Rd** and **Oxford Rd** near Kilburn Park (tube) station. These villas have been restored in a £12 million scheme by freeholder Paddington Churches Housing Association. Some are now coming onto the market. A 1-bed flat in **Princess Rd**, which also has some of these enormous Victorian houses, might be £85–90,000. **Malvern Rd** has some flats above shops: £100,000 for a 1-bed. Just off this street is Malvern Mews, a mixed residential (mostly) and commercial corner: a freehold mews house here was on the market for £225,000 in December.

The modest terraces of the **Fernhead Rd/Saltram Crescent** area are a less expensive corner in a mixed council/private area: see the Maida Vale chapter. Visible just to the S of **Kilburn Park Rd**, across Paddington Recreation Ground, are the mansion blocks of Maida Vale.

West Kilburn

West Kilburn is between **Harrow Rd** on the S and **Kilburn Lane** on the N. The E boundary with Maida Vale runs along **Fernhead Rd**, **Shirland Rd** and **Walterton Rds**, and former Westminster council tenants in these terraced streets – after epic battles with the authority and developers – banded together to form a housing association, buy their own homes and carry out a major programme of repairs. The late '80s added several new flat developments to this corner. A modern estate separates these streets from the terraces of **Bravington Rd**, **Portnall Rd** and **Ashmore Rds**: there are many rented flats here. Next is the Mozart Estate, a jumble of red-brick blocks, which boasts a sports centre on **Caird St**. Despite much work, the Mozart still has a poor reputation. **Beethoven St** has a few private houses, some light industry and schools.

South of **Kilburn Lane**, which has some shops and terraces, is the placid Queen's Park Estate of charming terraced brick cottages (1870s–80s), many with almost Gothic porches suggesting benign ecclesiastical origins, despite the rationalism of the **First Avenue** to **Sixth Avenue** names. Now a conservation area, the estate passed through council hands but today the houses are privately owned (just think: you could live on Fifth Avenue). A modernized 2-bed house was on the market for £175,000 last November. From the E, busy **Harrow Rd** has shops and pubs near its junction with **Great Western Rd**, then has modern council housing below Queen's Park Estate opposite the canal, up to the junction with **Ladbroke Grove**.

Housing associations are very active in this area, offering shared ownership deals and putting up new developments. Between the **Harrow Rd** and the canal, Paddington Churches Housing Association has built 80 2-bed flats on **Woodfield Rd**. Some shared ownership. The PCHA also owns the modern canalside homes of **John Collins Close**.

Further E on the **Harrow Rd** an unusual development for the area appeared in 1997. Eleven new loft 'shells' were created in space above offices.

Kensal Green

The small triangle bounded by **Chamberlayne Rd**, **Harrow Rd** and the North London rail line, is Kensal Green. **Harrow Rd** here has cemeteries to the S, offices etc on the N, behind which are 3-storey terraces giving way to smaller ones in the quiet area of **Wakemen Rd**, **Pember Rd** and **Rainham Rd**. **College Rd** passes Kensal Green station (rail station and tube), and divides larger terraces of **Ashburnam Rd** and **Mortimer Rd** from smaller homes (including some council) S of **Purves Rd**. The similar terraces of **Napier Rd** and **Victor Rds** are tucked away behind, and very easy to miss from, **Harrow Rd**, which here has shops and some flats above; note terraced cottages next to **Alma Place**. **Purves Rd**, running back E, leads to the shops of **Station Terrace** below Kensal Rise station, and a mansion block. Here are the shops of busy and steep **Chamberlayne Rd**. The pleasant name 'Kensal Rise' seems to have been eclipsed (save for the station) by that of Queen's Park.

Queen's Park

Across **Chamberlayne Rd** are the putative beginnings of desirable Queen's Park, marked by the monkey puzzle trees of **Chevening Rd**; this runs E with its huge semis, mostly flats (a 2-bed is c. £135,000), and large terraces – those above **Dunmore Rd** having garages at rear. But Queen's Park proper, the conservation area with its rich mixture of late-Victorian and Edwardian styles, begins only at **Peploe Rd** (and continues between the railway lines as far as **Salusbury Rd**). On roads that cross this W border, such as **Kempe Rd** and **Keslake Rd**, both house prices and flights of architectural fancy can soar as one nears the park. The most desirable road is reckoned to be **Kingswood Avenue**. The smaller houses of **Milman Rd** directly across the park are also sought-after. The smaller terraces of the streets behind **Kingswood**

Avenue are popular but **Montrose Avenue** and **Hopefield Avenue** are marred by some drab modern houses which detract from the essentially gracious tone of Queen's Park. **Harvist Rd** has a variety of 3-storey terraces (note the Dutch touches of Nos 10–16) running up parallel to the rail line to **Salisbury Rd**. This runs between Brondesbury Park and Queen's Park stations, and furnishes the locals with schools, shops, churches, constabulary and a library. On **Salisbury Rd**, Vicarage Place, a 30-flat development by Laing, went up in 1995. St Anne's Court, in the same street, is a new development of 2-bed flats – and a new church completed next door – that has been built on the site of St Anne's church.

Transport	Tubes: Kilburn (zone 2, Jubilee); Queen's Park, Kensal Green, Kilburn Park (zone 2, Bakerloo). From Kilburn: Oxford Circus 20 min (1 change), City 25 min (1 change), Heathrow 50 min (1 change). Trains: Brondesbury 35 min to Liverpool St; Kilburn High Rd 8 min to Euston, 30 min to Liverpool St. Others see map.
Convenient for	West End, M1, North Circular Rd. A40. Miles from centre: 4.
Schools	Local Authority: Queen's Park Community School, St Augustine's C of E, St George's RC.

SALES

Flats

	S	1B	2B	3B	4B	5B
Average prices	55–65	75–110	100–150+	140–200	170–200+	–

Houses

	2B	3B	4B	5B	6/7B	8B
Average prices	130–160	150–300	180–350+	220–350+	–	–

RENTAL

Flats

	S	1B	2B	3B	4B	5B
Average prices	450–560	600–1000	850–1300	1080–1500	–	–

Houses

	2B	3B	4B	5B	6/7B	8B
Average prices	950–1050	1300–1600	1500–1800	1750–2800	–	–

The properties	Terraces of small Victorian homes give way, round Queen's Park, to large Edwardian ones in broader streets.
The market	Continues to grow in popularity thanks to good transport links and this area's position next door to West Hampstead, Maida Vale and Ladbroke Grove. Good hunting-ground for first-time and investment buyers of flats and small houses; Queen's Park area's family homes command a premium. Local searches: Brent 2 weeks, Westminster 2 working days.

Among those estate agents active in this area are:

- Brondesbury Estates
- Greene & Co
- Harris & Co
- Queen's Park Partnership
- Westminster Property Services
- Homeview Estates
- Plaza Estates
- Westways
- Margo's
- Michel Pauls
- In London Properties
- Aladdin Property
- John Best & Co
- Direct Real Estate

KNIGHTSBRIDGE

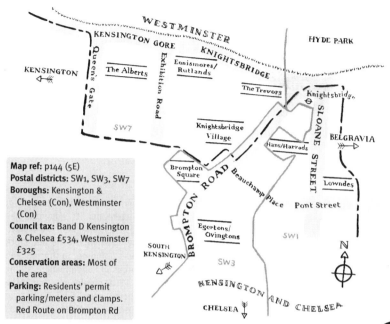

Map ref: p144 (5E)
Postal districts: SW1, SW3, SW7
Boroughs: Kensington &
  Chelsea (Con), Westminster
  (Con)
Council tax: Band D Kensington
  & Chelsea £534, Westminster
  £325
Conservation areas: Most of
  the area
Parking: Residents' permit
  parking/meters and clamps.
  Red Route on Brompton Rd

K

Knightsbridge is beyond doubt one of the most prestigious and traditional addresses in London. Here the wealthy in their grand apartment buildings, elegant terraced houses and pretty mews cottages cluster around one of the world's most famous shopping centres.

The area lies S of Hyde Park, which is fringed by the busy road variously named **Kensington Gore/Kensington Rd/Knightsbridge**. To the S the boundary is **Walton St/Pont St**. In the W, the museums and colleges cut Knightsbridge off from Kensington, while Belgravia is on the E. The old hamlet of Knightsbridge was originally part of a large forest around London, of which Hyde Park and Kensington Gardens are surviving open remnants. The parks are the area's biggest asset. They provide a 600-acre playground, and some fine views.

The other big draw is the cluster of shops and department stores, which may grow further if plans for a new store come to fruition. Harrods, the turn-of-the-century department store in **Brompton Rd**, with its distinctive green and gold canopies and royal warrants, sets the tone for the high-class shops in the area, where the 'by appointment' sign is a familiar sight. Gold-braided commissionaires, chauffeur-driven limousines and security cameras over the doorways are also essentials of the Knightsbridge streetscape. In recent years, Harvey Nichols and the stores in **Sloane St** have added a fashion dimension to Knightsbridge shopping.

The 4½-acre Knightsbridge Green development plans a new department store, on the **Brompton Rd** just across from Harrods, with 220 flats and a hotel facing the park, and a 19-storey office tower in the middle. Planners' reaction is awaited to both this and an alternative scheme for the same site: ownership is extremely tangled.

Like Harrods, the Royal Albert Hall and the other establishments within it, Knightsbridge is itself an institution. As one estate agent put it: 'You have the confidence that the market is never really going to collapse because there is too much to go down with it.' This is, of course, to take the long view: what's the odd stock market dive to the Old Money of Knightsbridge? This was borne out in the 1989–90 economic crash as Knightsbridge was one of the few areas in London where asking prices for properties were routinely achieved. Things are a little quieter now than in the bustle of 1997 and early 1998, when homes were being bought unviewed, but investment buying is still strong: this is seen as the best London area in which to invest.

The area is favoured by bankers, both British and international, businesses and diplomats. Several embassies and foreign cultural centres are located here.

Every urban taste in homes is created for, from the tall late-Victorian red-brick gabled apartment buildings in the **Hans Gardens/Egerton Gardens** neighbourhoods to the grand Portland stone blocks in **Ennismore Gardens**. Bijou mews cottages and 19th-century terraced houses, large and small, are spread throughout the area in some particularly pretty streets and cobbled mews.

Most homes are flats and leases are often short, though some longer leases are coming onto the market. Strict maintenance conditions are contained in many leases to keep up the tone of the area by preventing properties slipping into disrepair. Service charges can vary widely but you usually get what you pay for, according to local estate agents. Leasehold reform has changed the game in some streets, finally allowing leaseholders to buy the freeholds. Both the Cadogan and Wellcome Estates have property in this area – and both enforce estate management agreements even on homes they do not own.

A peculiarity of the area is that it falls within two boroughs. All of the area N of **Brompton Rd** (with the exception of **Brompton Square**, **Cottage Place**, the Oratory, Holy Trinity Church, **Cheval Place**, **Rutland St**, **Fairholt St** and **Rutland Mews South**) is in the City of Westminster. The rest is in Kensington. The confusion of the two boroughs within Knightsbridge leads to chaos with residents' parking. Where the boundaries run through the middle of the streets (as in **Lowndes St**) or squares (as in **Rutland Gate**) neighbourly co-existence can be strained.

Brompton Rd is the main shopping street, lined by a jumble of period and modern flats, blocks and offices with shops beneath. These range from fashion and shoe shops to jewellers, antique shops, galleries, banks, restaurants and bars. **Knightsbridge** and its continuation **Kensington Rd** is a busy main through-route running alongside the tracts of park in the W to Kensington and in the E to the West End. It is flanked by a combination of tall apartment buildings and various embassies and institutions – and by the enormous bulk of the Albert Hall.

Lowndes

Lowndes Square forms the heart of the neighbourhood, which is bounded to the W by **Sloane St**. It differs from other garden squares in Kensington and Chelsea in that it is dominated by huge 1900s flat blocks. The 6/7-storey brown-brick buildings spread along whole blocks of the square and loom over its narrow central garden. Some earlier properties remain, mostly 5-storey and basement stucco-fronted terraced houses, many split into flats. But overall, the atmosphere is of a square of hotels. This impression is heightened by the appearance at the N end of the Sheraton Park Tower Hotel, which fronts **Knightsbridge**. **Lowndes Square** is very popular, especially with foreign buyers. Lowndes Court is an ultra-luxurious 25-flat development dating from 1989 including two 6/7-bed penthouses. Last September a 4-bed flat sold for £1.9 million.

Lowndes St, a continuation of the square's E leg, contains more flats, shops, galleries and banks. Terraces of 4-storey stucco-fronted houses stand on both sides of the S end of the street. Another 1900s flat block, Chelsea House, provides visual interest as it curves around the corner of **Lowndes St** into **Cadogan Place**. A collection of period and modern houses and flats at the N end of **Cadogan Place** overlook its large tree-lined gardens. The prettily named **Harriet Walk** has gained seven 1990 mews houses and two studios. **Sloane St** on the neighbourhood's W boundary serves as both the main road to Chelsea and an increasingly smart shopping street.

Hans/Harrods

This neighbourhood is dominated by Harrods: the Baroque-style store with its ornate dome and turrets covers 4½ acres of one of the choicest parts of London. Harrods is surrounded by tall red-brick and stone gabled blocks of flats in **Hans Crescent**, **Hans Rd** and **Basil St**. The most ornate can be found in **Basil St** alongside a mix of hotels, restaurants, shops and Knightsbridge fire station. A big block on the corner of **Basil St** and **Hans Crescent** spent many years doing duty as one of London's crown courts, but is now becoming flats and offices in a big conversion scheme which will also provide underground parking. **Hans Crescent** is another shopping street. It links up with **Herbert Crescent**, where a group of large mock-Tudor houses stand out among the prevailing blocks of ornate red-brick mansions.

The crescent leads into **Hans Place**, a very popular garden square where largely red-brick Dutch-gabled buildings, converted into flats, encircle the private central gardens. Prince Charles' old prep school, Hill House, stands in the SE corner of this relatively quiet square.

Just beyond the NW entrance to the square, the red-bricks are replaced by terraces of mid-19th-century (around £1 million) white stucco houses in **Walton Place**. At the S end of this attractive street is the brick Gothic-style St Saviour's Church, providing a striking contrast to the white stucco. A drawback here is the amount of traffic taking short-cuts through the street. Queues of lorries also form at the junction with **Hans Rd** and **Basil St**, waiting their turn to make deliveries to Harrods – though the **Basil St/Hans Crescent** development may ease this. To the E of **Walton Place** through a pointed red-brick arch and an automatic barrier lies **Pont St Mews**, a collection of 2-bed gabled cottages. **Brompton Place** to the W is a narrow private road, choked in the daytime with cars waiting for a place in Harrods' car park at the end of the street.

Beaufort Gardens used to be lined by small hotels but many of the tall brick and stucco Victorian terraced buildings have been converted into luxury flats. An unusual feature of this wide street is the line of trees down the middle with car parking on each side. The street is closed off at its S end by a stucco balustrade and the backs of the houses in **Walton St**. **Beauchamp Place** at the W edge of the neighbourhood is a high-class shopping street, containing some of the area's top shops and restaurants.

Egertons/Ovingtons

This corner, enclosed by **Brompton Rd** to the N and W, contains several streets and squares of handsome houses. **Ovington Square** contains good examples of the 'Kensington Italianate' style – tall narrow white stucco terraced houses with rich detailing. The 4-storey and basement houses, built in the 1840/50s, are set around narrow private gardens. The **Square** and **Ovington Gardens** to the N are both relatively busy roads because they are used as a short-cut by through traffic from **Brompton Rd** and **Walton St**. **Ovington Gardens** has 3/4-storey stucco-fronted or brick and stucco terraced houses. Tucked away at right angles to the eastern side of the street is **Ovington Mews**. Pretty 2-storey painted cottages line this pleasant little backwater. Tubs of flowers and window boxes add extra colour. **Yeoman's Row**, situated just one street away, is different again. A short terrace of 2-storey Georgian cottages remain on the eastern side of this small-scale street. Further along the same side is an attractive group of paired brick houses with stucco entrances and leafy front gardens. A newly done-up house here sold for £1.4 million last autumn; a second, needing work, was a mere £1 million. Another handful of cottages is to be found in **Egerton Garden Mews** through a red-brick arch, which marks another sudden change of scene.

Rows of late-Victorian red-brick gabled buildings congregate around rear communal gardens in **Egerton Gardens** and the northern end of **Egerton Terrace**.

Knightsbridge has several enticing corners of mews cottages, which have evolved a long way from their earthy origins to become a style of home all their own. Many are in cul-de-sacs, tucked away from the busy streets. Mansard roof extensions are popular, as are shutters and flower tubs beside the doors. The most prized are those with a surviving garage: parking around here is impossible.

The blocks, built during the 1880s/90s, form the main concentration of flats. Leases are often short: 18 years on average. However, recently the Wellcome Trust has been granting 105-year leases. Cross the road to the two most exclusive streets in Knightsbridge – **Egerton Crescent** and the S end of **Egerton Terrace**. A curved terrace of elegant early Victorian white stucco houses sweeps around **Egerton Crescent**. The 3/4-storey houses are screened from the road by a semi-circular private garden. One house has two enormous gardens tucked behind the crescent. Victorian lamps line the crescent and tubs of trees and shrubs on the first-floor balconies emphasize the green and white colour scheme. In **Egerton Terrace**, pairs of mid-19th-century white stucco houses have large leafy front gardens. The street is closed off at its S end by a balustrade and trees.

Brompton Square

Brompton Square, to the N of **Brompton Rd**, is a very distinct neighbourhood to itself. Terraces of 3/4-storey early 19th-century houses stretch along narrow central gardens. Virtually all the houses in the square, built 824–39, are Grade II listed buildings. Houses here are very popular and have been known to sell for more than £2 million. A few have been converted into flats. The gardens are also listed as being of architectural or historic interest.

To the W is one of Knightsbridge's most important landmarks, the Oratory Catholic Church. This Renaissance-style church with its impressive white stone façade and dome is the focal point of this end of **Brompton Rd**. Behind the Oratory sits Holy Trinity Church. Its large tree-lined churchyard provides welcome fresh air and a leafy open space and outlook for adjoining properties in the Ennismores and a playground for inner-city squirrels. To the W the Victoria & Albert decorative arts museum ('V&A') forms the boundary with Kensington.

Ennismore/Rutlands

North of **Brompton Square** as far as Hyde Park stretches a quiet, cut-off neighbourhood of mews and squares. L-shaped **Ennismore Gardens Mews** is a delightful long cobbled mews lined by gaily coloured 2-storey cottages. Tubs of flowers and window boxes add a picturesque touch. The cottages in the S leg of the mews overlook the peaceful tree-lined graveyard of Holy Trinity Church. An imposing stone arch of Greek-style columns at the entrance to the mews is a hint of things to come in **Ennismore Gardens**. Here grand 5-storey Portland stone terraces with double-columned porches and ornate black iron balconies are set around a large private garden. The majority of properties are now divided into flats with only two houses remaining complete. Most of the sales are for short leases: a newly refurbished top-floor flat recently commanded £975,000 for a 28-year lease. Longer leases are sometimes available. The more traditional stucco-fronted terraces reappear in the eastern arm of the square, and further stucco terraces can be found in **Princess Gardens**.

Spreading along the W-E section of **Ennismore Gardens** is the highly rated Kingston House flats complex, which stretches right back to **Kensington Rd**. The apartments are very popular with foreign buyers including Americans, Italians and Spanish. Around the corner, on the western side of the N leg of **Ennismore Gardens**, is **Bolney Gate**, a development of modern 5-storey brick and stone town-houses. When they come on the market these are priced at more than £1.3 million. On the E side of the road stand, in quirky juxtaposition, the Russian Orthodox Church and the Omani Embassy. S of the church is **Ennismore Mews**, an exceptional example of its type with often large 2-storey painted/brick houses. Window boxes, flower tubs and Victorian street lamps abound. Another attractive feature is the Ennismore Arms pub at the corner with **Ennismore St**. **Ennismore St** leads into **Rutland Gate,** which is made up of two separate garden squares. Terraces of brick and stucco houses line the N square, just off **Knightsbridge,** and cream and white stucco-fronted houses are set around the more desirable southern square. The properties have mostly been converted into flats or house foreign cultural institutes and other organizations. One of the surviving houses, with 6 bedrooms, was bought by a French buyer last winter for £4.5 million. A large brick mansion block – Eresby House – stands at the point where the two squares meet.

Rutland Gardens and its tiny mews contain a mix of interesting houses, cottages and flats of very different sizes and styles, but the dominant view here is of the tower of Knightsbridge Barracks, consistently voted one of London's biggest eyesores in public opinion polls. S of **Rutland Gate** lie more small mews, including **Rutland Mews W**, no more than a tiny group of white stucco cottages clustered around a cobbled courtyard. **Rutland St** and **Fairholt St** are two more small-scale streets. They have mainly 2-storey stucco/brick and stucco/painted houses.

Knightsbridge Village

Exclusive **Montpelier Square** is the centrepiece of this neighbourhood of predominantly single family houses. The 19th-century brick and stucco/painted stucco houses in the square face on to mature private gardens. One smart 5-bed house sold in October for £2.75 million, while another needing £600,000 spending on it still commanded a price of £1.5 million.

Narrow **Montpelier Walk** is a mix of painted brick/stucco houses. It leads to **Cheval Place**, where the 2/3-storey painted cottages stand alongside modern flat blocks, smart shops, restaurants and the Aston Martin salesroom. **Montpelier Place** is a pleasant street of 3-storey brick and stucco/stucco-fronted houses with two flower-bedecked pubs, one right next to the German Evangelist Church. Houses range from £800–950,000 depending on size and condition. **Montpelier St** to the E is the main street of the village, lined with a mix of 3/4-storey brick and stucco terraced houses, pubs, restaurants, shops, galleries and auction rooms. There is no route for traffic W from the village to the adjoining **Rutland Gate**, thus traffic is relatively light. A footpath, leading through a gap in an old brick wall, allows pedestrians to cut through to **Rutland Mews** and on, under a grand archway, along **Ennismore Gardens Mews** to **Prince's Gate Mews** and the museum/university quarter of South Kensington; one of the most charming walks in London.

The Trevors

East of Knightsbridge Village come the streets around **Trevor Square**, dominated by 3/4-storey 19th-century terraced houses. In **Trevor Square**, they are set on two sides of a long narrow private garden.

A stretch of modern flats can be found at the NW end of **Trevor Place**, a quite busy road taking traffic to Harrods despatch depot S of **Trevor Square** and through to **Brompton Rd**. Harrods have permission to convert their depot into a 5-star hotel, but work has yet to start. In **Lancelot Place**, a row of 2-storey brick cottages stands opposite the post office.

Turn E into **Raphael St**, which links up with **Knightsbridge Green**, a pedestrian passageway lined with small shops, cafés and restaurants. Standing alongside the passageway is Park Mansions, a large red-brick and stone block fronting **Knightsbridge** and stretching to Scotch Corner. The Knight's Arcade of luxury shops runs beneath the mansions at ground-floor and basement level through to **Brompton Rd**. This whole quarter could be transformed if the Knightbridge Green redevelopment scheme (see introduction) goes ahead.

The Alberts

The Royal Albert Hall is being modernized with £40 million of lottery money. Benefits to its neighbours include a new underground service yard which will mean less disturbance when shows are getting in or out. The Hall is the focal point of the neighbourhood from which the main residential complexes take their names. They are Albert Hall Mansions – five large blocks of flats on the E side of the famous concert hall – and Albert Court to the rear in **Prince Consort Rd**. The tall red-brick and stone Norman Shaw blocks, the very first to be built in the Dutch style, contain 80 flats each, including some of the largest family apartments left in Knightsbridge. They were built in the 1880s/90s by the Commissioners for the Great Exhibition of 1851, who remain the freeholders to this day. The flats are popular with wealthy overseas, as well as established British, buyers. They are also used as a base for international companies and business people. Very few are let out. Some have been modernized, others still have the original panelled walls, staff quarters – even wine cellars. A 3-bed flat with a view of the Albert Memorial (you would never be bored) sold last autumn for £950,000 for a 64-year lease. Prices can go up to £2 million.

K

Transport	Tubes, both zone 1: Knightsbridge (Piccadilly), South Kensington (Piccadilly, Circle, District). From Knightsbridge: Oxford Circus 10 min (1 change), City 22 min (1 change), Heathrow 42 min.
Convenient for	Hyde Park, Harrods and Harvey Nichols, Sloane St, West End, Heathrow (via taxi, tube or Paddington). Miles from centre: 1.5.
Schools	Local Authority: Holland Park, Cardinal Manning RC (b), Cardinal Vaughan RC (b), St Thomas More RC, Sion Manning RC (g). Private: St James' Independent (b) (g), Falkner House (g), Queen's Gate (g), St Charles 6th-form College.

SALES

Flats	S	1B	2B	3B	4B	5B
Average prices	85–200+	170–375+	250–700	340–1M+	500–1M+	750–1M+
Houses	2B	3B	4B	5B	6/7B	8B
Average prices	350–750+	500–1M+	800–1.4M+	1M+	2M+	4M+

RENTAL

Flats	S	1B	2B	3B	4B	5B
Average prices	1000–1500	1100–2000	1500–2500	2000–4000	3000–6000	4000+
Houses	2B	3B	4B	5B	6/7B	8B
Average prices	2400–3000	3000–5000	4000–7000	8000–10,000	12,000+	15,000+

The properties   The scale ranges from tiny mews via elegant 18th/19th-century squares and terraces, to lofty apartment blocks in stone or the red-brick, gabled style widely known as 'Pont St Dutch'.

The market   The wealthy market for these coveted homes, whether true-blue British or international jet-set, are as one in considering this the hub of London. Large homes are scarce and at a premium. Flats reign, with companies buying the short-lease ones as London bases. Prices vary widely according to degree of luxury/lease length/views: a quiet square is more desirable than a park view, as this can mean traffic noice. Local searches: Kensington & Chelsea 6 days, Westminster 2 days.

Among those estate agents active in this area are:
- De Groot Collis
- Knight Frank
- Allsop & Co
- Winkworth*
- FPDSavills
- Foxtons*
- Keith Cardale Groves
- Hobart Slater
- Harrods Estates
- Hamptons
- W A Ellis *
- Beaney Pearce *
- Douglas & Gordon *
- Lane Fox
- Aylesfords
- Anscombe & Ringland*
- Strutt & Parker*

further details: see advertisers' index on p633

K

LEWISHAM AND CATFORD

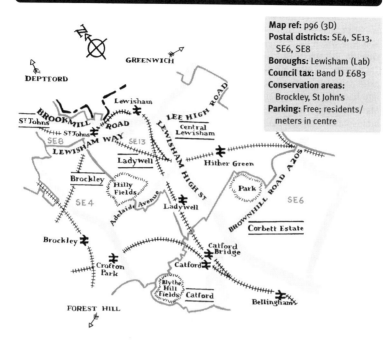

Map ref: p96 (3D)
Postal districts: SE4, SE13, SE6, SE8
Boroughs: Lewisham (Lab)
Council tax: Band D £683
Conservation areas:
   Brockley, St John's
Parking: Free; residents/meters in centre

Lewisham, lying to the south west of historic Greenwich, also has its roots in the past: a large village was already established there in Domesday times, but the area hardly grew until the 1840s, when the railway arrived and turned it into a new centre for commuting. By the start of the 20th century much of the available land had been built over. The area is ringed with convenient little stations – see map above – and criss-crossed with less-than-convenient railway lines, which carry fast through trains as well as local traffic. Those allergic to noise should check maps carefully before getting carried away when house-hunting.

Today, the prospects for Lewisham and surrounding areas are once again bound up with railways – this time the long-awaited southwards extension across the river of the Docklands Light Railway (DLR). Work is well under way, and causing a bit of congestion in the area – particularly around Lewisham station, where parking has had to make way for building contractors. If completed, as promised, in time for the Millennium it will provide a direct link with Canary Wharf and the like: the effect on this part of London will be galvanic.

At least the traffic congestion has been somewhat eased already, by the introduction of a Red Route down the main Lewisham–Bromley through-route. Away from the rail-tracks and the busy main roads, the area has a surprising number of parks and open spaces. Some, like Ladywell, have tennis courts, a running track and warming-up equipment. Fitness enthusiasts are well catered for: there are health clubs in most neighbourhoods. Lewisham has a bowling alley, but there are few good restaurants and the nearest cinemas and theatres are in Catford and Greenwich. There are plans, however, for a multi-screen cinema in Lewisham.

Central Lewisham

The best bits of Lewisham are those closest to the southern tip of Blackheath. From Blackheath Village turn W into **Lee Terrace** and explore the roads to your left bearing the SE13 postcode. Some of Lewisham's best buildings were destroyed by the heavy bombing which the borough suffered during World War II, but happily roads such as **Quentin Rd, Dacre Park, Eton Grove** and surrounding streets escaped untouched. These 4-storey mansions with their grand sash windows and huge back gardens are extremely well-kept and would not be out of place in Kensington. Most were converted into flats, but some remain as superb family homes. The nearby parish church of St Margarets and little backstreet pubs all add to the quiet, country feel – until the atmosphere is broken by modern low-rise council housing off busy **Lee High Rd**.

The biggest development in the area is on **Belmont Hill**, the continuation of **Lee Terrace**. The Cedars involves the restoration of a Grade II listed mansion to create 10 apartments. The site, in front of Our Lady of Lourdes School, is also seeing new-build flats, courtesy of a separate company: all were reserved before completion. Nearby, 4-storey flats have also appeared on the corner of **Brandram** and **Blessington Rds**. More new flats, too, N of the tracks in William Close off **Granville Park**, which curves from **Lewisham Rd** back up to Blackheath. Some homes in this area – on **Morden Hill**, for example – boast views right across London.

Lee High Rd joins **Lewisham High St**, recognized as the biggest shopping centre in SE London. It includes a massive indoor shopping complex and most well-known big-name stores. 'Lewisham 2000', a major redevelopment of **Lewisham High St**, has brought a welcome and well-managed pedestrianization (except for buses) of almost the entire **High St**, re-routing traffic around the back of the Riverdale shopping centre down **Molesworth St**, and adding a new road bridge over the river Ravensbourne, close to the forthcoming Docklands Light Railway. Although the town centre has lost Army & Navy, its main department store, pedestrianization has encouraged the wonderful (daily) market and shopping is an altogether more pleasant experience. The clock tower has been moved back to where it stood in Victorian times, and the town centre now also boasts three new pubs, a night club and a large new library reputed to be the finest of its type in London. Opposite, a new development of shops, restaurants and some homes between the **High St** and **Engate St** will complete this year.

Roads to the E mostly contain Victorian town-houses, many of which have undergone conversion work after years of neglect. **Limes Grove** with its 3-storey pitched roofs and sash windows is a prime example of this process, as are **Clarendon Rise** and **Gilmore Rd**, which sport terraces with steps to the front door and black wrought-iron balustrades. Opposite stands a 20-year-old development of red-brick terraces. Each home has its own garden and there's a small park at the centre. These were council-built, but not suprisingly tenants exercized their Right to Buy and these homes now appear on the open market. A good area for children: the streets are paved over and can be played in without fear of traffic; however, inside the houses are tight for space compared with their Victorian counterparts opposite.

To the N of Lewisham station (and impending DLR link), Fairview are just completing a development of studios, 1- and 2-bed flats in **Conington Rd** between **Lewisham Rd** and the river Ravensbourne. A corner to watch: the existing, 2-storey homes in this basically light-industrial corner (even the pub has closed) may look unloved now, but will soon be on a door-to-door link with Canary Wharf . . .

St John's

Next, explore St John's – which you'll find by following road signs for Deptford. St John's Village is bordered by **St John's Vale, Albyn Rd, Lewisham Way** and **Tanner's Hill**. There is a variety of housing here. **Tanner's Hill** has red-brick council blocks along its entirety, with small shops, pubs and restaurant at the top end. **St John's Vale** starts with 2-storey, 3-bed terraces, gains basements halfway up and ends with 3-storey, semi-detached and basemented houses past the station. (Lewisham College is also nearby, so parking is at a premium.) The homes in **Lucas St** have a park area for the kids to play in. The top end of **Friendly St** is made up of neatly kept, pretty little close-packed 2-bed workmen's cottages, many of which are listed. **Ashmead Rd**, by contrast, has enormous, 5-bed houses with semi-basements, some still whole family homes.

Some streets are sealed to traffic by ornamental bollards, and the rows of neat yellow-brick terraces and 'Coronation Street' style shops and pubs remain quiet. The area has its own station, and rail commuters are relieved to find that at last BR's successor is improving the erstwhile patchy service. The SE8 postal address is usually associated with Deptford, but this corner is well worth a look.

Leaving St John's, travel back along **Lewisham Way** uphill to **Loampit Vale** (MFI, Allied Carpets and other DIY sheds, here). The small 2-up, 2-downs are replaced by grander 4-storey homes, now converted into flats but still neatly kept with window boxes and many with new roofs. From here turn right into **Shell Rd**, which winds its way towards Hilly Fields and Brockley. **Shell Rd** and surrounding streets are dominated by 2- and 3-storey houses with exuberant Gothic-style turrets, ornate porches and high-pitched roofs. Cognoscenti of this period will find fine examples of decorative plaster mouldings – often a shell motif echoes the street name. **Algernon Rd**, however, boasts a modern development of 3-storey houses called Highland Terrace.

Brockley

On reaching the Hilly Fields park, where '30s-style semis are dotted among the Victorian conversions, turn back towards New Cross and the still improving – and charming – Brockley conservation area. By the end of the '80s these quiet tree-lined avenues had already been well-discovered by young, upwardly mobile commuters. The area's large spacious flats have become increasingly sought-after but buyers should beware: Brockley's charms are contained almost exclusively within its conservation area. Land to the W of **Brockley Rd** and the railway line is still widely regarded as being on the wrong side of the tracks, say estate agents. Instead, first check out the area boundary, marked by **Tyrwhitt Rd** to the E, **Lewisham Way** to the N, **Upper Brockley Rd** and **Brockley Rd** to the W, down to the **Adelaide Avenue** junction. These streets are largely filled with 3- and 4-storey houses, mostly – but not entirely – converted into flats (a 2-bed **Brockley Rd** example was £60,950 last winter). Some have huge 150-ft gardens and there are panoramic views across to St Paul's for people with attic bedrooms. Inside the grand-looking yellow-brick mansions the rooms are large with high ceilings. Flats in **Manor Avenue**, **Breakspears Rd** (a big 3-bed here was £135,000 last winter) and **Tressillian Rd** are particularly popular. The **Wickham Rd/Breakspears Rd** part of the conservation area have a cache of new homes. **Breakspears Mews** is a recent development of 3- and 5-storey homes (the 4-bed houses sold within weeks of the 1997 launch for £132–139,000; last year 3-bed houses, £120–126,000, and 2-bed flats, £80–82,000, followed. Look out, too, for some original mews and coach houses in this corner: for example the unreconstructed, un-tarmac'd **Wickham Mews**.

Ladywell

From Brockley travel on to the nearby Hilly Fields playing-area, mostly surrounded by post-war 2-storey family homes, some with balconies. From **Vicars Hill** look out for **Adelaide Avenue's** ornate terrace fronting the park. Next, head down the hill into Ladywell Village, perhaps more of an invention of local estate agents than a real village, but getting smarter. There is a good selection of shops in the 'Village' centre

on **Ladywell Rd** – and yet another station within a few minutes' walk. The impressive and huge Ladywell Leisure Centre and the bigger shops of **Lewisham High St** are also just round the corner. 'Village' properties are largely Victorian conversions of 2- and 3-storeys – some with huge gardens – although there are some '30s semis to provide a contrast, notably in **Veda Rd** and **Ermine Rd**.

Catford and the Corbett Estate

Catford will never be quaint, but its fast-improving centre, further shopping in Bromley and Lewisham – and, above all, the impending DLR at Lewisham – may well prove estate agents' assertions that the long-sighted may find they've bought a bargain . . . Like the rest of the area, Catford was rapidly developed towards the end of the 19th century, but unlike Lewisham owes much of its housing character to a single man – Archibald Corbett. This canny Scot bought nearly 300 acres of then virgin land and proceeded to build thousands of houses, laying out the roads in a strict grid pattern. Catford today has its own shopping centre, two rail stations and even its own dog track; but it is best known for the massive Corbett Estate and its distinct lack of pubs – Archibald Corbett was teetotal. Many of the street names have a Scottish flavour – **Arngask** and **Glenfarg Rds**, for example. The boundary roads are **Wellmeadow** to the E, **Hazelbank** to the S, **Brownhill** to the N and **Muirkirk** to the W.

Homes here are 3- to 6-bedroomed houses, all solidly built, with large spacious rooms. Many of the bigger properties have now been converted into flats, but the estate still retains its prim and proper identity. All the houses have their own front garden and most have 80-ft rear gardens. The smaller, single-fronted Corbett houses are almost exactly half the size of the double-fronted ones, which are slightly more ornate. The area remains very quiet, very respectable – and very desirable. Doctors, solicitors and the like head for these large family homes. Be warned though: visitors will need a map; every road really does look the same!

Another popular estate lies close by, this time made up of '30s-style semis and bounded by **Bellingham Rd** to the S, **Thornsbeach** to the E, **Bromley Rd** to the W and **Culverley Rd** to the N. Homes here boast extremely wide roads, 3 and 4 bedrooms and large gardens – one or two even have swimming pools. Look to **Culverly Rd** for flats: eight or nine big houses here were converted in the late '80s (a 2-bed maisonette can cost £78,000), and a new red-brick 4-storey block has appeared.

After years of running to seed, the shopping centre is now being redeveloped: 'Catford Island' is a retail/leisure complex in **Plassy Rd**, part of the one-way system in the town centre. New shops are appearing in **Bromley Rd**, and a huge Halfords nearby. Flats in **Bromley Rd** can be found at around £48–49,000 for 1-bed, up to c. £65,000 for 3-bed; housing associations and other developers are also busy in the road.

Some down-market streets surround the stations, but popular St Dunstan's College lies on **Stanstead Rd** backed by the open space of Blythe Hill Fields and attractive 3-storey Victorian family homes in roads such as **Ravensbourne Rd** and **Montem Rd**.

Look out, in this area, for offices being converted for residential use: one large building has already been bought from Lewisham Council to become flats.

Bordering Areas

Hither Green is a fertile hunting-ground for first-time buyers seeking inexpensive flat conversions or terraced cottages. The area is bordered by Lewisham, Lee Green and Blackheath; it has its own well-served station. To the W leafy Forest Hill (see chapter) has a mixture of Victoriana and '30s semis in peaceful roads, but also many flat conversions and a good cache of cheapish properties for first-time buyers. Crofton Park, sandwiched between Brockley and Catford, consists mainly of terraced streets which some will probably find too drab. Some new-build near Crofton Park station, however.

Transport	Trains: St John's, Lewisham (London Bridge 14 min, Charing Cross 18 min), Ladywell, Catford, Catford Bridge. Docklands Light Railway extension building now.
Convenient for	Docklands, West End, City, Greenwich, Kent. Miles from centre: 6.
Schools	Local Authority: Crofton, Prendergast (g), Addey & Stanhope. Private: Blackheath High School (g), St Dunstan's College (b).

SALES

Flats	S	1B	2B	3B	4B	5B
Average prices	25–40	40–70	50–75	55–80	75–130	—
Houses	2B	3B	4B	5B	6/7B	8B
Average prices	70–90	80–150+	110–200	120–220	220+	—

RENTAL

Flats	S	1B	2B	3B	4B	5B
Average prices	300–500	420–600	500–750	600–950	750–1200	—
Houses	2B	3B	4B	5B	6/7B	8B
Average prices	600–1000	750–1000+	1000–1400	1000–1500+	—	—

The properties	Mainly Victorian, from tiny workers' homes through larger terraces to grander villas with conservatories. '20s/'30s suburban houses interspersed and new-build. Catford has well-preserved and popular estate of 3/5-bed 1880s houses, many now flats, plus '30s semis in large gardens.
The market	The Lewisham area, once hardly considered London, is now on the Central London workers' list of possibles. Prices are still modest considering City/Docklands proximity — but set to alter fast as and when the DLR appears. Fertile first-home hunting-ground. Local searches: 2 weeks.

L

Among those estate agents active in this area are:
- Mann & Co
- Oak Estates *
- Winkworth *
- Rocodells
- Saxtons
- Quest Residential

further details: see advertisers' index on p633

LEYTON AND WALTHAMSTOW

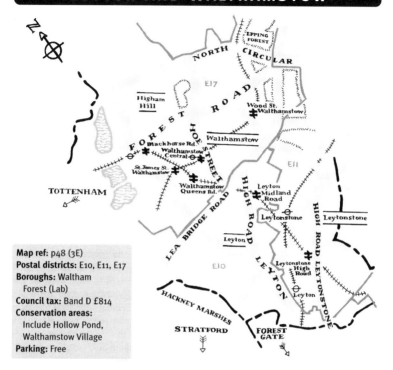

Map ref: p48 (3E)
Postal districts: E10, E11, E17
Boroughs: Waltham
   Forest (Lab)
Council tax: Band D £814
Conservation areas:
   Include Hollow Pond,
   Walthamstow Village
Parking: Free

Walthamstow is a place in waiting. Mention the name, and people will think either of greyhound racing at the track in **Chingford Rd**, or of the busy street market (proudly proclaimed to be Europe's longest) which brings the **High St** to life six days a week. But the area, with neighbouring Leyton and Leytonstone, has changed over the last decade. Many young people have found their first homes here, buying or (increasingly) renting the affordable flats and little houses in the neat rows of Victorian terraces, with their good transport links into town. In the past couple of years, residents looked on with satisfaction as the axis of London's 'up-and-coming' areas tilted eastwards, and hope this area will follow Hackney's lead. But many things have happened – or rather, not happened, to frustrate them. The controversial link to the M11 is not quite linked; Stratford, down the road, is not yet 'Stratford International'. Even the planned town centre redevelopment for Walthamstow, which would have included a multi-screen cinema/shops complex, more parking and leisure facilities, failed to get government funding approval.

However, when the plans have been re-drawn it is likely to turn the area into one of the biggest shopping centres in East London. A new swimming pool and athletics track by Lloyds Park has improved amenities there; and the Jubilee Line Extension *will* reach Stratford this year – so this is the one corner of town that *will* be able to get to the Dome . . .

Even though they are separated from Tottenham and Hackney by reservoirs and marshland, Walthamstow and Leyton are not cut off. These areas are eminently accessible and between them have no fewer than 11 stations (tube and rail) with fast, direct routes into the West End and City. Local bus services are excellent too. To the N, the top slice of the Borough of Waltham Forest is Chingford: what this corner lacks in convenience – it lies across the North Circular – it makes up for by its salubrious position on the edge of Epping Forest.

Road pressure should be eased by the Link Rd to the M11: completion is expected late this year (not all transport links are welcome: this was the subject of a decade of ferocious debate, with locals likening the proposal to the Berlin Wall before it was knocked down). This link from the Blackwall Tunnel approach motorway, the A102M, to the Redbridge roundabout on the North Circular and the M11, drives right through Leyton, Leytonstone and Wanstead. It is what the planners call a 'high standard road', not a motorway. One positive benefit will be an end to the appalling congestion of **Leytonstone High Rd**. This in its turn is expected to attract further improvements to the Leytonstone shopping centre, and the area expects to move considerably further up in the world (and closer to the rest of it).

Or at least to Europe: those with well-tuned crystal balls look forward to boarding a Channel Tunnel train on the fringes of Leyton, at Stratford. At time of writing, however, it is but a month or three since they began Section One of this (due 2002), and Section Two is dependent on a funding rescue package . . . One day. Maybe . . .

Walthamstow

A pleasant tradition says that the name comes from the Old English 'wilcumestou', meaning a welcoming place. It may not be one of London's most elegant corners, but it is probably one of its liveliest. It lies 6½ miles NE of the City of London, between the River Lea and Essex's beautiful Epping Forest. To the N is Chingford, to the E are Woodford and Wanstead and to the S Leyton. The town centre enjoys excellent transport links: it has a tube/overland rail link with good bus connections, close proximity to the M11 and North Circular, and the M11 Link Rd (almost linked). Most of the homes here are terraces built in late-Victorian and Edwardian times, but there are also purpose-built blocks of flats; small cottages behind the Vestry Museum in Walthamstow Village; large detached houses in the area to the E known as Upper Walthamstow.

Walthamstow is very popular with first-time buyers, and prices are still relatively cheap compared with price rises in other London boroughs. The **Higham Hill** area, in particular, has small homes ideal for first-time buyers. These include the Lloyd Park estate and the Markhouse Road estate. Lying W of the **Chingford Rd**, the area around **Lloyd Park** and **Higham Hill** holds a mixture of houses and purpose-built flats. It is a quiet area and contains a large number of 2- and 3-bedroomed houses. Here **William Morris Close** recalls Walthamstow's most famous resident, who lived in Water House on **Forest Rd**. There's a museum which is dedicated to his work. Prices here have stabilized during '98, and can still start from £45–50,000 for a 1-bed maisonette or £60,000 for a 1- to 2-bed maisonette. The Village is currently the most popular corner for buyers, but agents comment on the growth of the rentals market in the Lloyd Park area.

Other terraced houses tend to be found in the **St James St** corner of Walthamstow, and property here is often cheaper than elsewhere; it has, though, its own railway station and is convenient for the tube and rail station at **Blackhorse Rd**. There's a 1980s development of flats in **Markhouse St**. Heading E, there are also many reasonably priced 2- and 3-bed houses in the area off **Hoe St** near Walthamstow Central stations.

A little further E but still near the Central stations, Walthamstow holds a surprise for home-seekers – 'Walthamstow Village', a conservation area, where prices are high, homes for sale scarce and street names are ecclesiastical. A lot of conversions have taken place here of late. These few streets contain houses and nice little cottages which command higher than average prices when they come onto the market. Two of the best roads here are **Church Hall Rd** and **Church Lane**. Besides the bohemian atmosphere the major attraction is the closeness to Walthamstow Central tube station, good bus and rail connections and excellent shopping facilities. This has attracted more City workers into the area, who are able to travel into the City on the Chingford to Liverpool St line within 15 min.

This is not an area for massive new-build schemes at present, though there is the occasional pocket: the latest additions have been near the **High St** and off **Hale End Rd**. In **Willow Walk**, just off the **High St**, The Willows is a new Rialto scheme of 1- and 2-bed flats, from £54,000 and 65,000 respectively; another recent housing development appeared in **Westbury Rd**, also close to the market and behind the tube car park. But generally, all major developments are being given over to housing associations who are building low-rise homes for residents moving out of tower blocks that are being demolished.

Travelling eastwards again brings you to **Wood St** – a road with its own station. Upper Walthamstow leaves the tiny terraces behind. The tree-lined roads of big 1930s properties boast many large detached houses, often with five or more bedrooms.

Leyton and Leytonstone

Leyton and Leytonstone lie between Hackney Marsh and Wanstead Flats in E10 and E11. Well situated, it's on a direct line to the City and West End and, equally, is near Epping Forest heading out to Essex. Despite the rises of the last couple of years, here is still some of the cheapest property this close to Central London. Leytonstone in particular is an area of continual improvement. When the M11 Link Rd is fully up and running, house prices in Leytonstone are likely to escalate in the next up-turn of the London market. At the moment they are still relatively cheap.

The area features a good mix of high-quality turn-of-the-century houses and terraces with wide streets. Most of the homes here are in terraces built in the early 1900s, though some date back to the 1880s. Three-bedroom terraced houses are the most common and homes with more than 4, possibly 5, bedrooms are rare. Many conversions are available, and these can still be bought quite cheaply – though the council tightened up on the rash of new ones in an attempt to avert parking problems. Developers have been quietly adding to the so far small stock of purpose-built flats. There is also still scope to buy cheaper and unrepaired property. Look, too, for the terraces of little houses built as two flats. Sometimes these provide an interesting phenomenon: first floor flats with gardens.

One of the most sought-after areas in Leytonstone includes the Bushwood estate, while in Leyton the Barclay estate is very popular.

Prices in the area, which rose by an average of 10–15 per cent in 1997, went right on through the first half of '98 – another 12–13 per cent – before levelling off. Thus 3-bed houses in Leyton, which could be found for as little as £63,000 at the start of 1988, began 1999 at nearer the £70,000 mark. Top prices seem to have consolidated too: at the close of 1997 £170,000 for a 4-bed semi in **Chadwick Rd** was one of the highest prices in the area; a year later, on the day we walked in to research this edition, just such another in the same road had sold for the same price.

Upper Leytonstone, though split by the M11 Link Rd, contains some of the largest and most desirable properties and has the advantage of closeness to public transport. **Forest Drive East**, **Forest Drive West** and the surrounding areas have big, double-fronted houses in tree-lined streets. A new Tesco superstore is scheduled for Leytonstone, on the site of the old Langthorne Hospital. To open when the M11 Link Rd becomes fully operational, it lies alongside what was the Green Man roundabout. (The series of small roundabouts, installed while the Link Rd was under construction, will soon be replaced by a major junction connecting the M11 Link to the local roads.)

On the borders of Upper Leytonstone is the area known as the Barclay estate, which contains some of the best houses in Leyton. These lie at the back of Leyton Midland Rd station: the roads here are quieter and pleasanter in appearance, with more trees than is common in the area. A cache of good-value, and equally convenient, terraces include roads like **Colchester, Nottingham, Canterbury, Ely, Epsom, Cromer, Essex** and **Sandringham. Grove Green Rd** stretches from Leytonstone to Leyton, and the streets which lie off it are plentifully supplied with terraced houses and flat conversions, though there are also many run-down properties. The roads surrounding Leyton Orient football club also hold an abundance of terraced houses at reasonable prices, and are close to Leyton tube station.

There are few blocks of flats in the area, save for some council-build, and the majority of flats are conversions. However, there is a large purpose-built block on the corner of **Francis Rd**. This, and the homes near the station and football ground, are well served by the shops in **High Rd Leyton**. A 6-acre site in **Church Rd** has been developed partly as light industrial, partly as homes/workspaces.

The area along **High Rd Leyton** is residential, and purpose-built flats are a feature here; Leytonstone Court – 1- and 2-bedroom flats – is towards the Stratford end of the **High Rd. Buckland Rd**, which runs parallel, has 19 1990 1-bed flats; **Ruckholt Rd** too has sprouted smart 1- and 2-bed apartments.

South of **Leytonstone High Rd**, almost in Wanstead, lies the popular Bushwood estate. Here are some of the largest properties in the area. **Bushwood**, overlooking Wanstead Flats, is sought-after for its grand late-Victorian 4-bedroom terraced houses. **Browning Rd** is a pretty conservation area of tiny early Victorian cottages, refurbished in the '70s. **Barclay, Leybourne** and **Leyspring Rds** contain solidly built 3-bed terraced houses, most still unconverted to flats and many with original features. A well-planned one-way system leaves this estate free from all but residential traffic. It's attractive to renters, too; a 3/4-bed flat here was let for £1,000 a month last winter: top dollar, as they say in Hong Kong.

Chingford

The salubrious northern end of the borough holds the spacious streets of Chingford, its origins as a cluster of rural hamlets showing in the old village names like Chingford Green and Chingford Hatch. Airier streets and larger, roomier houses – though 5- bedrooms are quite hard to find – characterize this area, with the occasional older building still to be found amid the Victoriana.

Select North Chingford, based around the Ridgeway area, holds the premier streets. At Chingford Green the streets peter out on the edge of Epping Forest – all homes bordering the forest are much prized. **Connaught Avenue** is a typical plum location: its 3-bedroomed Victorian homes now go for £170–180,000 – though all will depend on the rate of survival of original features. No garages here, though.

Among the less expensive but equally spacious streets of South Chingford, the Palace View estate is considered to be one of the most desirable corners. Turn-of-the-century 3-bed semis average about £130,000 in this leafy corner, which lies close to beautiful Larkswood. Some of the best Victorian/Edwardian houses are in the Highams Park neighbourhood, which boasts its own park with boating lake.

Borders: Redbridge

At the old Green Man roundabout at the top of **Leytonstone High Rd**, you cross the borough boundary and enter Wanstead. Prices rise in this leafy corner, and larger homes can be found in roads running off **Overton Drive** near the golf course. There are also more flats to be found here for local first-time buyers, being cheaper than next-door Redbridge, but just as well placed for travel into town. Redbridge itself is a solidly middle-class area, with tidy blocks of flats and family houses of good appearance. Well served by Redbridge tube. Running alongside Wanstead are Snaresbrook and South Woodford. Here, too, are smart areas with a lot of quiet, tree-lined streets: all sizes of houses and some of the best roads in that part of Redbridge Borough. There are many blocks of purpose-built flats, all of which are quite expensive. South Woodford is well served by tube direct into London, and sited on the edge of Epping Forest.

Transport Tubes: Leyton, Leytonstone (zone 3, Central); Walthamstow Central, Blackhorse Rd (zone 3, Victoria). From Walthamstow Central: Oxford Circus 25 min, City 40 min (1 change), Heathrow 1 hr 20 min (1 change). Trains: Walthamstow Central to Liverpool St 15 min.

Convenient for Transport to City, West End, Epping Forest, Lea Valley, M11 to Cambridge, M25 City Airport, Stanstead Airport; tubes/trains into town. Miles to centre: 7.

Schools Waltham Forest Education Authority: Leytonstone School, Aveling Park School, McEntee Secondary School, Walthamstow Girls. Private: Forest School.

SALES

Flats	S	1B	2B	3B	4B	5B
Average prices	25–40	35–70	50–90	60–110	–	–
Houses	2B	3B	4B	5B	6/7B	8B
Average prices	60–90	70–180	100–250	250+	–	–

RENTAL

Flats	S	1B	2B	3B	4B	5B
Average prices	400–500	420–550	500–700	600–750	–	–
Houses	2B	3B	4B	5B	6/7B	8B
Average prices	500–700	600–800	800+	–	–	–

The properties Largely 1900s terraces of 2/3-bed homes and p/b flats. Upper Walthamstow boasts some large detached houses; bigger ones, too, in Leyton's Barclay estate. Flats, converted and p/b, abound.

The market Good transport links and cheap first homes provide a stepping-stone for buyers from a lot further afield than the East End. Watch, when buying, for the new link road from the Blackwall Tunnel to the M11. Local searches: 2 weeks.

Among those estate agents active in this area are:
- A Kennedy
- Central Estates
- Clarke Hillyer
- Douglas Allen Spiro
- Bairstow Eves
- Woolwich Property
- Spicer McColl
- Churchill
- W J Meade

MAIDA VALE AND LITTLE VENICE

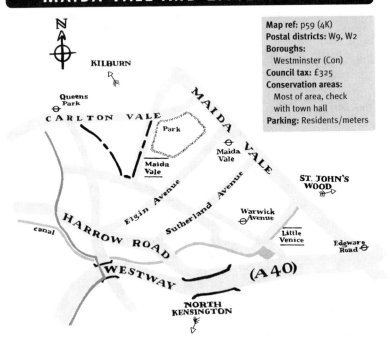

Map ref: p59 (4K)
Postal districts: W9, W2
Boroughs:
 Westminster (Con)
Council tax: £325
Conservation areas:
 Most of area, check
 with town hall
Parking: Residents/meters

Maida Vale is a wholly residential district, spacious, well-placed and decidedly popular. The area is N of the **Harrow Rd** and W of the **Edgware Rd** and its continuation to the N, **Maida Vale** (the road). Strategically placed for the main routes out of town to the W and N, its position was confirmed by the long-looked-for Paddington–Heathrow rail link, finally inaugurated in 1998. Next-door neighbour to St John's Wood, replete with the sort of creamy, dignified terraces that typify Belgravia, its slower rise to full-throttle desirability was only because, until some 15 years back, hardly any of its homes were for sale.

This Guide has been promoting Maida Vale for its location for rather a long time. It has at last fulfilled our hopes: nearby Paddington Station – one stop on the tube from Warwick Avenue – has got its 15 min train to Heathrow Airport, and check-in facilities at the station for nine airlines will open this summer. The equally long-awaited Paddington Basin development looks set to start this year. This involves a big tract of canalside land just across the motorway which forms Maida Vale's S boundary. The first phase, on **North Wharf Rd**, will include a big office schemes, 350 new homes and a new public-access leisure centre. Another 472 homes are planned for **South Wharf Rd**. Also planned are improvements to the tube and rail stations and a canalside tidy-up.

Maida Vale's character was largely determined by the district's long-time ownership by the Church Commissioners, who planned, built, maintained, laid down the rules for and also let the property. This meant very little buying and selling: nearly all homes were let. Only in the 1980s did this begin to change. Those tenants who could afford to bought their homes at preferential rates (20 per cent discount), some making large sums by reselling (often in 'back-to-back' deals). Developers moved in wholesale; the snowy terraces were converted, the hitherto run-down and decidedly

seedy area was transformed, prices soared. Many developers were however caught out by the early '90s slump, and flats were hastily let instead of sold.

Renting remains a staple of the area (a lot of buy-to-rent sales were made in 1995–7): flats, rather than houses, are the norm here, and their accessibility makes them favourites with multinational companies, embassies and the likes. The tidal wave of developers are moving on to other areas, although there is still some building.

It is now fairly common for flats to appear on the market with a share of the freehold. Many leaseholders have purchased the freehold to their properties since 1993, when the law changed to make this process easier. This accelerated in the mid-'90s when some leaseholders faced five-figure bills for major refurbishments in their mansion blocks. Take good advice, if buying, about the state of the block's sinking fund.

Warwick Avenue, running N from the **Harrow Rd** across the Grand Union Canal, set the tone for this extremely pleasant corner in the 1840s and '50s. The large cream stucco houses here and fronting the canal are still the area's biggest single homes, and the smartest. The pretty neighbourhood around the canal is known as Little Venice. Later building confirmed the spacious feel: wide avenues, large terraced houses and mansion flats behind whose ramparts are often concealed large (some vast) shared gardens – a secret unsuspected by passersby. These delightful 'inverted square' gardens are the area's hidden bonus: they can include tennis courts, and ground floor flats often have direct access through gates at the bottom of their own back gardens: a delight for those with kids.

Overall, Maida Vale is a rich mine of particularly nice flats, big and small, old and new. What you won't find here are the usual London rows of small terraced houses, although there is a scattering of new and refurbished mews houses. In this area the garden level maisonette replaces the house – and can be bigger and nicer than other areas' narrow Victorian terraces. The spacious layout of Maida Vale makes for exceptionally light and pleasant flats with leafy outlooks. Those with access to one of the 'hidden acres' mentioned above are the ones to watch for.

The most coveted homes, however, are those nearest to or overlooking the canal: truly a 'Little Venice' – though estate agents now use this more picturesque name for all the Vale's most desirable white stucco streets (which leads to Kilburn homes being described as 'borders Little Venice'). These snowy rows form the heart of the area, and are succeeded further N and W by streets of red-brick mansion flats: these can provide a lot of space for your money. The Church land ends in the W at **Shirland Rd**: next come smaller-scale Victorian terraces, fast improving.

Little Venice

Blomfield Rd and **Maida Avenue** residents have homes made magic (and even more expensive) by the presence of water. The canal runs between the two, widening by the **Warwick Rd** bridge – where it branches – into a young lake with willow-pattern islet and waterside public gardens and walk. The canal-ends of adjoining roads also get called Little Venice; non-natives can be startled by narrowboats apparently gliding across the top of the street. A charming, prized corner of London.

Starting from **Paddington Green** to the S of the canal (today marooned between the **Westway** and '60s college blocks and council towers) **St Mary's Terrace** runs up towards the canal: No 1, in classic double-fronted stucco, sets the tone for the left side. On the other side is Fleming Court (council-built), then the stately red-brick mansion blocks of Osborne House and **St Mary's Mansions**, which comprises several blocks around its own courtyard (unmodernized flats are very occasionally available). **Porteus Rd** opposite leads to **Hogan Mews**, an early '80s mews development close to the **Westway**. The opposite side has council-built flats. **St Mary's Terrace** becomes **Park Place Villas**, which runs to the canal – and Little Venice proper. On the corner with **Maida Avenue**, an enormous Italianate villa has a prime position. This 9-bed, 9-bath mansion with indoor swimming pool came up for sale for £4.5 million at the end of 1997. Both **Maida Avenue** and **Blomfield Rd** have large and covetable white stucco villas (strictly for multi-millionaires) facing over the water. These give way to later Victoriana towards the **Edgware Rd** end; mansion blocks can provide very large flats here, though. A 2-bed ground and garden floor flat just off **Maida Avenue** was on the market for £435,000 in December.

From Harrow Rd Bridge westwards, the S bank of the canal is Westminster City's Warwick Estate; pleasant '60s low-rise, now increasingly in private hands. Prices are low for their neighbourhood: a 3-bed flat overlooking the canal might be £140,000. The canal then dips below the **Harrow Rd**, and between the two on the site of St Mary's Hospital is Maida Vale's biggest new-build area: on **Admiral Walk**, Carlton Gate and neighbouring Swift and Swallow Courts were completed in 1995. These blocks of 1- and 2-bed flats are strategically placed to serve as a London base for country-hopping executives and the like – but note that those who opt for canalside flats here also get fine views of the elevated section of the Westway and the tower blocks of North Ken.

Behind **Blomfield Rd**, to the W of **Warwick Avenue** lies villagy **Warwick Place**, with the pleasant Warwick Castle pub, which overlooks Clifton Nurseries (entrance in **Clifton Villas**), one of London's first and best garden centres. More little shops in **Bristol Gardens**, off which **Bristol Mews** was reborn in 1995 as 15 smart new homes. Across **Formosa St**, the same year finally saw the complete refurbishment of the 44 mews homes of **Elnathan Mews** (a process which was rudely halted by the 1990 slump). These mews corners add a cache of small houses – otherwise a rarity in both Little Venice and Maida Vale – to the area. Even rarer, they have garages. In **Bristol Gardens**, an 1840s artist's studio, renovated in the 1980s and now a 4-bed house, was for sale last November for £550,000. East of **Warwick Way**, the streets that lie between the canal and **Clifton Gardens** also enjoy the Little Venice premium. An unmodernized (potentially 5-bed) freehold house in one of these streets was on the market for £1.5 million last winter.

Maida Vale Central

The name really applies to the old Church estate, from Little Venice northwards, with **Maida Vale** (the road) forming the E boundary. **Warwick Avenue**, which is the Vale's boulevard, runs NW from Little Venice into the heart of the district with the clean, striking lines of the modern St Saviour's Church (junction with **Clifton Gardens**) as its focal point. The church has matching flats, Manor House Court, behind. The Avenue is a delight – lined with classical white early 1850s mansions, many of which escaped being sub-divided and are still single homes, particularly on the E side.

Clifton Gardens, a wide and desirable street of 1860s stucco terraces, runs NE from St Saviour's (and the tube station) to **Maida Vale.** Top-class conversions into luxury flats back, on the N side, onto vast communal gardens. Cumberland House, on the junction with **Warwick Avenue,** is new (1987) despite its handsome 'period' appearance: top-of-the-market apartments. Another such is Europa House in **Randolph Avenue:** this has the handy anachronism of underground parking – very necessary, nowadays. Many flats here are rented out rather than sold. **Randolph Avenue** saw several more luxurious developments in 1988. **Clifton Gardens** becomes, at the E end, **Clifton Rd** – the Vale's 'high street'. Enviable **Warrington Crescent** curves N from **Clifton Gardens** to **Sutherland Avenue,** and is mostly more conversions with communal gardens both sides, reckoned to be some of the area's best. Flats in **Warrington Crescent** go for around £250,000 for 2-bed, rising to £800,000 for a 4-bed, garden level one. Ditto for style and price in **Randolph Crescent,** running parallel, though the 3-acre triangular gardens the E side shares with stretches of **Clifton Gardens** and **Randolph Avenue** are even more highly rated.

Castellain Rd, parallel to (and converging with) **Warwick Avenue** on the E, is a long road which crosses **Sutherland Avenue** to reach **Elgin Avenue.** Between these two avenues is Castellain Mansions, a large block of red- and grey-brick mansion flats. A 2-bed flat here on a long lease might be £220,000. Behind, to the E, are communal gardens; to the W, Paddington Bowling and Sports Club offering 'bowls, tennis, squash, social'. In the angle behind **Castellain** and **Sutherland,** the communal gardens boast tennis courts. An old garage site in **Castellain Rd** has become Katherine Court, whose style handsomely acknowledges its neighbours'. Across the road in **Warrington Gardens** more than 50 new flats, with parking, were built in 1995.

Sutherland Avenue is classic Maida Vale, wide, tree-lined, parking down the centre, its vista stopped to the E by the '60s Stuart Tower. At the western end (W of **Shirland Rd**), stand ornate stucco houses, with wrought-iron balustrades at the first floor. Then come slightly smaller models, then enormous Victorian red-bricks. Note 'The Sutherlands' – cream Italianate villa by the circus at the E end: now 10 flats, one with a first floor conservatory, plus a house. Most recent conversions in **Sutherland Avenue** offer 2-bed flats at £205–260,000, with one 4-bed garden level maisonette at £550,000. **Lauderdale Rd** runs from the E end of **Sutherland Rd** westwards to **Elgin Rd** with more mansion flats, with large gardens behind those of the S side.

Elgin Avenue starts in the E at Maida Vale tube, runs W to cross **Shirland Rd** and on into western Maida Vale (see below). Compared with **Sutherland Avenue** it is more anonymous, more of a through-way, lined with comfortable red-brick mansion blocks. Elgin Mansions is a big flats block with access to some recently re-landscaped communal gardens. Behind its lovingly restored façade, the flats of Westside Court are not the usual anonymous rooms: architect Stewart Moss put personality into them, though his rather less successful waterfalls in the foyer had to be removed because of damp. On the corner of **Elgin Avenue** and **Morshead Rd,** a traditional-style red-brick block of 2- and 3-bed flats was built in 1995. **Elgin Mews, North** and **South,** are tucked behind the shops around Maida Vale tube. **Mews North** has been rebuilt: smart town-houses. **Mews South** is still original: pretty, painted brick homes.

Grantully Rd runs beside Paddington Recreation Ground: hardly scenic, but at least green and open. Facing it are mansion flats; Leith Mansions then Ashworth Mansions – a quiet corner. **Ashworth Rd,** which crosses **Elgin Avenue,** has mansion flats at the N end. A surprise here: **Ashworth Rd,** S of **Elgin,** suddenly becomes Surrey: low-built between-the-wars pairs of houses joined by garages – the nearest semis to Marble Arch? Low eaves, deep porches, stockbroker-Tudor and £800,000. . .

Morshead Rd, **Wymering Rd** and **Widley Rd**, plus **Essendine Rd**, are red-brick mansions. Wymering Mansions has undergone £4.5 million in refurbishments over the last few years: 2-bed flats are around £215,000 with 3-bed around £230,000. Views from the **Morshead** ones (Nos 25 onwards) are across the recreation ground. There is a small school (junior mixed primary) in **Essendine Rd**.

Randolph Avenue and **Lanark Rd** run parallel to Maida Vale, with large houses (mostly recent flat conversions). The smart new villa-style blocks of flats in **Lanark** were built by Westminster Council in '83 as starter homes. These now appear on the open market. Other **Randolph Avenue** homes are flat conversions carved out of some very large Victorian semi-detached stock-brick and stucco houses, though a few do remain as single homes – with close-to-£2 million price tags. The S end of **Randolph Avenue** runs down to the canal and enters Little Venice. There are big stucco terraces here. The red-brick electricity sub-station in **Randolph Mews** was transformed into a house in 1988 – complete with a conservatory bathroom (one-way glass!). In 1996 it sold for £1.6 million. At the N end, Nos 171 onwards overlook the recreation ground. The N end of **Lanark** is a council estate with tower blocks.

Maida Vale, a major road, bounds the district. To the E is St John's Wood. At the far N end, almost in Kilburn (or St John's Wood borders if you're being kind) is Regent's Plaza, a big and smart hotel/flats complex with restaurants, 24 hr room service etc. Flats can be had here on 998 year leases from £250,000 for 2-bed to £350,000 for 3-bed. The W side of **Maida Vale** starts (from the N) with a Westminster Council estate; then past **Elgin Avenue's** '30s mansions, then more council, then Y-shaped Stuart Tower: private 1-bed flats, enjoying fine views from upper floors. South of **Sutherland Avenue** are big 1890s mansion blocks such as Blomfield Court and Sandringham Court. On the E side of the road are more of the same: these are still in W9. Look here for spacious flats, but without the garden access of those in the communal-gardens roads. Four-bed flats in these blocks command about £350,000. Going on S over the canal bridge, **Maida Vale** becomes **Edgware Rd**, a scruffy but lively shopping street.

Borders

Having converted everything in sight in Maida Vale proper, the developers moved W into a zone which is somewhat of a no man's land of council estates and small terraces, many of which have now been converted into flats. The southern part, N of **Harrow Rd** and up towards Queen's Park station, is in Westminster Council's patch. The NE corner is in Brent. Agents recall that at one time, people were reluctant to move W of **Shirland Rd**: the first question for an **Elgin** or **Sutherland Avenue** flat was which side of **Shirland** was it?

The N part of the borders district is largely sprawling council estates on either side of **Carlton Vale**. South of here, the modest terraces of the **Fernhead Rd** – **Saltram Crescent** area are a good-value corner in a mixed council/private area. **Saltram** was discovered early by converters. Here a 2-bed flat can sell for c. £130,000 – in 1998 this was £110,000, while back in 1996 it would have been worth £85,000. The Westminster frontier runs from the S end of **Kilburn Park Rd** up behind **Saltram Crescent**. The streets between **Walterton Rd** and **Fernhead Rd** became a bitter battleground between Westminster Council and local tenants in the late '80s. A group of residents eventually grouped together, formed a housing association, Walterton and Elgin Community Homes, and bought their homes *en masse* from Westminster (which had been set on selling the small Victorian terraces off to developers). They have since been carrying out major renovations. Some homes here are on the market: a 3-bed maisonette in **Warlock Rd** was £165,000 last November. A modern estate separates these streets from the private terraces of **Bravington Rd**, **Portnall Rd** and **Ashmore Rd**: a good hunting-ground for less expensive 2-bed flats (c. £115,000). Across the **Harrow**

Rd to the S, and just in W9 and Westminster Council's patch, are **Hormead Rd** and **Fermoy Rd**: Victorian terraces, close to the canal. Many are flats, with 2-bed at around £150,000. Next, and into W10 and (fast-eroding) Kensal, is the council's unreconstructed Mozart Estate: not an asset. West again, Maida Vale has its eye on annexing the placid Queen's Park Estate of charming terraced council cottages. . .

Transport	Tubes: Maida Vale, Warwick Avenue (zone 2, Bakerloo); Oxford Circus 15 min, City 25 min (1 change), Heathrow 1 hr (1 change).
Convenient for	Paddington, roads to W and N, West End. Miles from centre: 3.
Schools	Local Authority: St George's RC, North Westminster. Private: American.

SALES

Flats	S	1B	2B	3B	4B	5B
Average prices	80+	100–200	140–250	200+	350–600+	–
Houses	2B	3B	4B	5B	6/7B	8B
Average prices	150–275+	300–450+	450–800+	500–1M+	1M+	→

RENTAL

Flats	S	1B	2B	3B	4B	5B
Average prices	650+	850–1075+	950–1500+	1300–2150+	2000+	–
Houses	2B	3B	4B	5B	6/7B	8B
Average prices	2000	1700–3000	3250+	6500+	–	–

The properties	Gracious white stucco terraces and villas, rows of neat red-brick mansion flats, some modern mews/town-houses. Flats reign: mainly mansion or period conversions. These can be large. Small houses rare; the garden maisonette replaces, and can be lovely. Few houses: best canalside ones over £2 million.
The market	The range of flats, rather than houses attract buyers, renters or buy-to-rent investors. Red-brick mansion flats (watch the service charges), period conversions, loads of recent luxury conversions. Large flat sizes common here, also some small mews houses. The Vale's location makes it a good long-term bet. Area's 'hidden gardens' are its best asset. Local searches: 2 working days.

Among those estate agents active in this area are:
- Ashley Milton
- Greene & Co
- Hamilton Wood
- Vickers
- Pembertons
- Chestertons
- Marsh & Parsons
- Foxtons *
- Cohen & Pride
- In London Properties
- Brian Lack
- Gladstone Estates
- Central London Properties
- Clifton Residential
- Londonwide Estates
- Winkworth *
- Anscombe & Ringland *
- Howard Estates

further details: see advertisers' index on p633

MARYLEBONE AND FITZROVIA

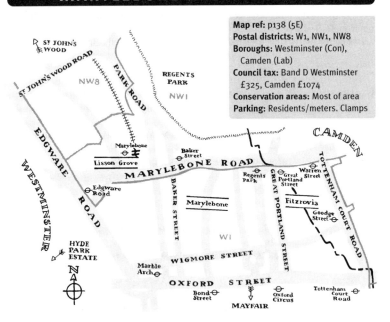

Map ref: p138 (5E)
Postal districts: W1, NW1, NW8
Boroughs: Westminster (Con),
Camden (Lab)
Council tax: Band D Westminster
£325, Camden £1074
Conservation areas: Most of area
Parking: Residents/meters. Clamps

Marylebone is starting to reappear as a neighbourhood name, after half a century of obscurity. Several big-name developers have smart flats for sale here, and at last some of the decaying Georgian homes are virtually being rebuilt to provide more flats and houses. **Marylebone High St** is becoming a fashionable retail and restaurant centre. Nearby Paddington now has a fast rail link to Heathrow, making the area still more convenient.

Marylebone is the name for most of the slice of London sandwiched between **Oxford St** and Regent's Park. It could hardly be more central. Homes here range from the 18th century to the present day, from tiny studio apartments through mews cottages to vast family mansions with dining rooms that seat 50. Blue plaques, commemorating famous residents of yesteryear, abound – sometimes more than one on each (very likely listed) building. Fringe neighbourhoods include the bustling Great Portland and Fitzrovia districts to the E and the rather mixed Lisson Grove/North Marylebone tract N across the roaring divide of the **Marylebone Rd**.

Despite the rediscovery of Marylebone, this is as yet not an area that springs instantly to the home-hunter's mind. Mayfair, Belgravia, Kensington – all those are, in fact, further from the hub. But this tract is a diverse one: many of its family homes have been appropriated for shops or offices, its through-routes are busy. People think first of its landmarks, and they are not domestic ones: the BBC's Broadcasting House, the Courtauld Institute, Middlesex Hospital, the University of Westminster . . . and of course **Harley St**, heart of the medical profession.

The continuing ownership by major landlords such as the de Walden and Portman Estates means few freeholds and, frequently, short leaseholds. The Estates are at last waking up to the area's potential, with interesting opportunities for investors.

Marylebone's orderly 18th-century grid of streets and squares is broken by the irrepressible wiggle of **Marylebone Lane** which, with the **High St** (straight for a while, but not for long), marks the centre of the original village of Marylebone. Across to the E the grid resumes its orderly progress to **Portland Place**, a giant boulevard more reminiscent of Paris than London, lined with many a luxurious apartment on its way up towards Regent's Park.

Parallel to the E is **Great Portland St**, and at **Cleveland St** the grid swings slightly on its axis to mark the borough boundary and the start of Fitzrovia. In the other direction, W of the still-village **Marylebone Lane**, the orderly pattern runs across to the diagonal of the **Edgware Rd**. To the N, over the **Marylebone Rd**, W1 gives way to NW1 and **Lisson Grove**, with the **Dorset Square** neighbourhood E of Marylebone station and abutting the margins of the Park: this is the scruffier but up-and-coming corner.

A few years back there were still real bargains, considering the location, among – particularly – the flats to be found above shops or in the less obvious of the mansion or more recent blocks. And it is still an area well worth a searching look. You have the advantage that a limited number of house-hunters even think of looking here; the disadvantage of competition from companies, or businessmen looking for pieds-à-terre. It best suits single people – no need (or parking space) for a car, the West End on your doorstep – and those unburdened with young children. Although many happy families live N of **Oxford St**, they are not typical. Proof of this is offered by estate agents in the area, many of whom say that they have never been asked by anxious parents for advice on local schools.

Recently, the competition for homes has increased, but so has the supply. For the first time in decades, it's possible to list several new homes schemes either under way or planned. And efforts to boost the attractiveness of the area are bearing fruit. Away from the bustle of Selfridges and John Lewis in **Oxford St** lie corners of surprising residential peace and tranquillity. This is an orderly and discreet part of town. Embassies signal this: Switzerland and Sweden enjoy the sober peace of the **Bryanston Square** neighbourhood.

The most common type of home here in the West End is the 3- or 4-bedroomed flat, but there is today less demand for these than for smaller apartments: more recent developments have recognized this, and produced small 1- and 2-bed flats. Only about 10 per cent of West End properties are houses; and nearly all are terraced. Despite leasehold reform, freeholds are still hard to come by. Leases, even new ones, can be short: 60 years is good. Quiz agents on leases when considering anything except a new flat – most of these have 999 years or share of freehold – or a freehold. Even freeholds may be subject to restrictive estate management agreements.

Marylebone

The name 'Marylebone' has always been synonymous with medical excellence, for it is here that the cream of the British medical profession is gathered, crammed into **Harley St** and its immediate environs (**Wimpole St**, for example). This district, which is bordered by the southern margins of Regent's Park, as well as **Edgware Rd** and **Great Portland St**, encompasses street-by-street variations in architecture, general character – and price.

Differences in property prices (one flat can cost double what a seemingly similar flat costs) depend not just upon the quality and location of the property itself, but upon the length of the lease. Private landowners such as the Howard de Walden Estate (which owns 120-acres worth of the freeholds in Marylebone, mostly around the medical area, between **Marylebone High St** and **Great Portland St**) do not often deal in long leases. A fair amount of this land is also owned by the Crown Estate (for example, parts of **Harley St** and **Park Crescent Mews West**). If landlords like the De Walden Estate mean few freeholds, they also make for continuity. Thus the unchanging nature of the medical groves. They are responsible for the lovely Georgian doorways, staircases and rooflines still so much in evidence. These older buildings are supplemented by the red-brick blocks built at the turn of the century and some modern apartments that replaced wartime damage (a purpose-built block in **Wimpole St** is one of the few buildings hereabouts which can offer underground parking). Doctors must still get permission from the estate in order to mount their brass plate on the door of one of their houses.

There is much to choose from in Marylebone. There is the almost rustic 'olde-worlde' charm of Marylebone Village, with its pretty little shops and restaurants (and also the fashionable American College). There is the cheerfully commercialized (busy but not unpleasant) **Baker St**, home of Sherlock Holmes, sleuth of legend. **Baker St** stretches from Regent's Park at one end to the up-market Selfridges department store at the other; and where it bisects **Marylebone Rd** are the waxworks of Madame Tussaud's and the London Planetarium, each a focus for sightseers and day-trippers. There is **Wigmore St**, with its world-renowned concert hall and smart shops, visited by a quite different clientele from the **Oxford St** crowds. A major refurbishment of a big former store on the corner with **Welbeck St** resulted in some very smart new flats. Welbeck House, a recently cleaned stone block on the corner of **Wigmore St**, has vast flats.

Then there is **Portland Place**, the grand, wide-avenued refuge for the BBC's Broadcasting House, the Royal Institute of British Architects and a clutch of embassies. **Portland Place** homes are likely to be luxurious (discreet luxury, or dripping-with-gilt-and-marble luxury – but decidedly luxury) apartments in conversions or – more likely – the modern buildings that have superceded Robert Adam's original elegance. This is company, or perhaps top BBC-executive, territory. Many blocks have uniformed porters; a large and elegant one in nearby **Mansfield St** runs to maid service and its own restaurant. At the N end of **Portland Place** is a delight: instead of debouching straight onto the roaring **Marylebone Rd**, the street divides into the two curving arms of Nash's **Park Crescent**, its lovely homes sheltering behind the protective half-moon of its gardens. The rare family home with garage is occasionally to be had in its mews.

Indeed, one of the area's special delights is the many and varied mews tucked away behind its main streets. These compact little homes – mainly modernized, but some unrefurbished – are dotted across the area, though many are concentrated in the **Harley St** environs. People pay up to £850,000 for mews houses. These, of course, are often the extremely proud possessors of garages, thanks to their original function as stables – some still have rings for tethering the horses. Though if you don't care for history look to **Richardson's Mews**, just off **Warren St**, and **Weymouth Mews** which have new houses, for the modern version.

There is the discreet elegance of the various squares, such as **Bryanston Square** and **Montagu Square**, with their communal gardens in the centre. These well-kept and railed patches of green are accessible only to residents and are not to be sniffed at in a district where private gardens are almost non-existent, or barely bigger than a suburban household's window box. Octagon, suppliers of mini-mansions to the Surrey golf course belt, have come into town to provide 25 new flats and three new houses at 16–18 **Bryanston Square**. Quality will be very high, it's promised: on the market in April 1999 at prices yet to be decided.

There is always a good supply of mansion flats, of every standard from scruffy to palatial, in this part of town. Turn-of-the-century buildings like Bickenhall Mansions, with their high ceilings and coved fireplaces, are particularly popular, with 4-bed long-lease flats. And there are occasional 9-bedroomed flats in mansion blocks like Orchard Court in **Portman Square**. These have been refurbished and now have, among other things, new lifts and – what seems to be becoming a fashion – 10/12 new penthouses built on top of the original block. **Harley St** is, as you might expect, another much-prized address, but is mostly medical consulting-rooms. A major 1980s scheme in **Marylebone St**, Maybury Court, has 80 1- to 3-bed flats.

Marylebone High St may be pedestrianized, which will increase its attractions. Already, smart shops and restaurants – books, fashion, Conran Shop – are making this one of the more expensive London 'villages'. Across the **High St** from the Conran Shop is Copperfield House, a 20-flat block on the site of a petrol station: half the flats were reserved by last Christmas, even though it will not be ready until late 1999. Prices start at £220,000. In **Devonshire Place**, 10 flats are being created in the conversion of two Georgian terraced houses and will be ready in April. Prices start at £365,000.

For those who appreciate 1960s commercial architecture and want a room with a view there is Marathon House, a converted office tower on **Marylebone Rd**. Nearly all the 107 flats were sold by last winter at prices up to £525,000.

Great Portland St

The area E of Portland Place has a style of its own. It has been, and to a large extent still is, the centre of the London fashion trade. However quite a few warehouses and offices are being converted into homes. Berkeley's West One House in **Wells St** has 1- to 3-bed flats and 3-bed town-houses, priced from £200–625,000: 10 of the 73 homes were left unsold last October. Nearby, enticingly named **Market Place** is at present just a wider bit of road, but landlords Great Portland Estates plan a piazza with shops and bars. The new flats join existing mansion blocks around **Mortimer St**, **Riding House St** and **Foley St**. There are mews, many still commercial, and odd corners like **Booths Place**, where a 2-bed flat with its own garage was priced at £295,000 last October. In **Mansfield St**, three unmodernized Grade II* Georgian houses built by the Adam brothers, and virtually untouched since, were being offered last November on new Howard de Walden leases of 150 years for £2.6–4 million each. The Estate is planning to redevelop the rest of the block with mews cottages, flats and a leisure centre.

Lisson Grove

The area around **Lisson Grove** (NWI) remains the least fashionable part of Marylebone. The Regent's Canal runs through the area, conveying hints of neighbouring Little Venice and Regent's Park. Despite these assets, **Lisson Grove** has resolutely refused to budge. The Lisson Green and **Church St** estates still have a bad reputation. Even here, new homes are appearing: Galliard plans Bourne House, a block of 1- to 3-bed flats in **Old Marylebone Rd** priced from £200,000. There are already some mansion blocks in the road: £130,000 buys a 1-bed flat.

The Georgian façades of **Bell St**, which runs from **Edgware Rd** to **Lisson St**, have attracted attention. Europe's largest permanent, undercover antiques market on the junction of **Cosway St** and **Bell St** has given the area a boost. Two 2-bed flats in a newly tidied-up block in **Lisson St** were on the market last autumn at £143,000 and £147,000. Barratt are planning 400 homes for sale on reclaimed railway land W of **Park Rd**: a NW8 postcode and proximity to Regent's Park should make them popular. In the same scheme are 97 homes for the Acton Housing Association. Portman Gate in **Lisson Grove** is a 1980s development of 114 houses, flats and penthouses. Today 1-bed flats go from £140,000, 2-bed from £200,000, houses from £400,000.

East of Marylebone station, faced by the superbly restored 1900 Landmark Hotel, is a quiet district of Georgian, mid-19th-century and modern houses. **Gloucester Place** is a roaring highway, but **Dorset Square** and **Balcombe St** are pleasant, low-key and mostly residential. Prices are lower than in Marylebone proper: 4-bed houses command from £350,000 up. There are plenty of flats in conversions from around £125,000 for 1-bed and £160,000 for 2-bed. **Glentworth St** has some period mansion blocks which are well-located for the Baker St tube and Regent's Park.

Fitzrovia

Fitzrovia is the rectangle enclosed by **Euston Rd** to the N, **Oxford St** to the S, **Great Portland St** to the W and **Tottenham Court Rd** to the E. Presiding over the northern end of the neighbourhood named after it is **Fitzroy Square**. This is a handsome, semi-pedestrianized conservation area, inhabited by offices and embassies, but also by private residents. Fitzrovia is a quiet, quirky London village with a bohemian flavour and history – William Blake lived in **Fitzroy Square** and the area as a whole has long attracted artists, writers and aesthetes. Fitzrovia has gained popularity over the last decade and is a well-known centre for advertising and TV companies. As a result, more new homes have appeared. Fitzrovia divides into three sections: there is the **Charlotte St/Tottenham Court Rd** slice – a 'fun' area with pedestrian walkways. There is the grandeur of **Fitzroy Square** and its surroundings. Then there are the streets to the W between **Great Portland** and **Great Titchfield Sts**, home of the wholesale fashion industry (described opposite under Great Portland St). The landmark that keeps reappearing – always, somehow, where you least expect it – is, of course, the soaring Telecom Tower.

Fitzrovia is packed with interesting period properties. Modernized blocks house hundreds of studio and 1-bedroom apartments. Old-style – and increasingly scarce – mansion blocks are being carved up to meet the demand for small, compact flats. Look for these on the western side of the neighbourhood. In **Charlotte Place**, interesting old houses have been done up by a housing association. Modern homes include a clutch of flats and mews houses in **Whitfield St** (1988) and new houses with garages in **Fitzroy Court**. New 3-bed and garage houses in **Whitfield St** were £279,000 in 1990 – now from £400,000.

Although Fitzrovia is more up-market than Lisson Grove, there are still relative bargains to be had. It is very popular with young couples and people who simply need a 'little place in town' now and then. Westminster Council is trying to ease the traffic problem and improve the area in general. Westminster controls the W half of Fitzrovia; Camden's patch spreads E from **Cleveland St** and includes **Fitzroy Square** itself. Camden have plans to boost businesses in the area with a 'Fitzrovia Business Initiative'. Some might say that the area, with its unique atmosphere, proximity to Regent's Park and first-class restaurants and bars, doesn't need much improving.

(M)

Transport	Tubes, all zone 1: Baker Street (Jubilee, Circle, Hammersmith & City, Bakerloo), Oxford Circus (Bakerloo, Victoria, Central), Marylebone (Bakerloo), Marble Arch (Central). Others see map. From Oxford Circus: City 15 min, Heathrow 52 min (1 change).
Convienient for	West End, Regent's Park, City. Miles from centre: 1.5.
Schools	Local Authority: St Marylebone C of E (g). Private: Queen's College (g), North Westminster School.

SALES

Flats	S	1B	2B	3B	4B	5B
Average prices	85–125	120–275	150–400+	250–600	250–800+	380–1.4M
Houses	2B	3B	4B	5B	6/7B	8B
Average prices	250–500	350–700+	350–1M	550–2M	→2.5M	–

RENTAL

Flats	S	1B	2B	3B	4B	5B
Average prices	780–1200	1000–1700	1500–2600	1700–4500+	2600–5000+	–
Houses	2B	3B	4B	5B	6/7B	8B
Average prices	2300–3900	2800–3900	3200–8000	6900–13000	–	–

The properties   The cry in the heart of the West End is for flats, from tiny studios to company luxury. Cheaper ones above shops, red-brick mansion blocks, conversions of the gracious period homes. Also mews, and a few surviving family homes. Parking atrocious, garages at a premium.

The market   Marylebone is long-established, especially the medical district. Fitzrovia is more bohemian but changing. Whole area is mixed residential/commercial, therefore cheaper than other central areas. Ideal for young buyers and businessmen's pieds-à-terre. Local searches: Camden 2 weeks, Westminster 1 week.

Among those estate agents active in this area are:
- Winkworth *
- Plaza Estates
- Chestertons
- York Estates
- Oakleys
- Hurford Salvi Carr
- Whitehouse Lews
- Hunter & Co
- Egertons
- Alexanders
- Park Estates
- James Anthony
- Executive Homes
- Kay and Co Ltd *
- Foxtons *

* *further details: see advertisers' index on p633*

MAYFAIR AND ST JAMES'S

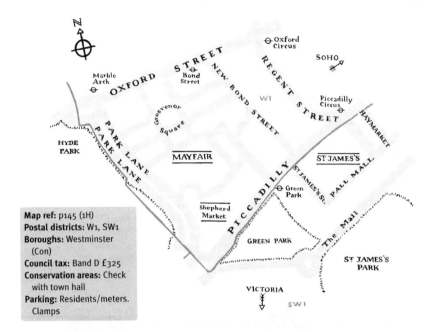

Map ref: p145 (1H)
Postal districts: W1, SW1
Boroughs: Westminster
(Con)
Council tax: Band D £325
Conservation areas: Check
with town hall
Parking: Residents/meters.
Clamps

M

Mayfair is the place to look if you need a mansion – and not just a mansion flat. It is the only part of Central London where the really rich can find a really large house, with servants' quarters and a grand suite of reception rooms and somewhere to garage the Rolls. Luckily for the rest of us, there are plenty of less opulent homes too, giving the lie to Mayfair's outdated reputation as an office district.

What Mayfair offers is street after street, square after mews, of homes of every period from 1700 to 1999. They have one thing in common: they were built for the rich, or at least their servants. Offices did indeed take over large tracts when commercial space was scarce in London following World War II bombing, but the tide of commerce has been turned back. Some lovely Georgian buildings on Park Lane once more have drawing rooms, rather than boardrooms, behind their elegant bow windows. Mayfair is reverting to type.

'Mayfair,' said a local estate agent 'has always been for the really rich.' And so you might think, if you set out to buy a whole house here (they do change hands occasionally: two £10 million houses were sold in 1998). Yet this is only part of the story. Mayfair, and St James's to the S, are still surprisingly residential. This may be the centre of town, crammed with coveted shops and offices, but there are plenty of people who live here, and not all are anonymous executives or country-hopping potentates. Mayfair even has a thriving residents' association, vigilant in defence of peace and amenity.

Top people have lived in Mayfair since early Georgian times. Never has it sunk from its position as a centre of fashionable London. Other places – Soho, Bloomsbury, Holland Park – have had their ups and downs but Mayfair has always been a correct address. Until within living memory it was dotted with the very grand houses (palaces really) of dukes and other noblemen. These have gone, to be replaced by great blocks of flats and hotels. Yet many of the smaller Georgian houses, and some large Victorian ones, survive, providing the slightly less ostentatious but no less luxurious London homes of today's magnates.

The less rich have a choice of flats of every degree of size and smartness up to the demi-royal, of mews cottages which range from tiny to surprisingly big, of serviced apartments, of purchase or rentals both short and long. Buying prices start at £120,000 and go on up. And up.

Mayfair is bounded to the N by the great shopping parade of **Oxford St**, in the E by **Regent St**, to the S by **Piccadilly** – across which royal St James's slopes gracefully down to its Park – and in the W by **Park Lane**, the 8-lane highway that separates Hyde Park from Mayfair's western rampart of hotels and car showrooms.

The NW part, about half the total, from Marble Arch down to **Berkeley Square**, belongs to the Grosvenor Estate, as does Belgravia. The rest is divided among several landlords, and until the advent of the Leasehold Reform Act, freeholds were rare.

Now this is changing, as residents exercise their right to buy. BP (British Petroleum), which owns an area of southern Mayfair, started to sell off its freeholds. A freehold house in **Charles St** was selling this spring for £4.5 million. Leaseholders in **Chesterfield Hill** are among those being offered the opportunity to buy their freehold. BP is keen to negotiate rather than having to go through the rigmarole of receiving tenants' notices under the enfranchisement legislation. The Grosvenor Estate, by contrast, is more reluctant to sell off freeholds without going through the legal procedures. However, it is now offering new leases of 99 years at an annual ground rent of 'one peppercorn'. The Estate maintains that its tenants are comfortable with the leasehold system and will still negotiate 20-year leases for reduced capital terms.

The other important change to this London heartland began at the end of 1990, when the 'temporary' planning permission granted for office use of many Mayfair sites – including houses – finally expired, allowing a small but significant increase in the number of people actually living here. Now around 30 per cent of the area is offices – though art galleries, restaurants, hotels, etc, account for another 40 per cent.

More than 40 office buildings have reverted to homes, about 20 of them to single houses – mansion is sometimes a better word: one in **Park St** was sold to developers for £4.6 million, and is being converted this spring. It totals 20,000 sq ft plus swimming pool. The local agents' grapevine has it that £20 million will be asked. Nor is this the largest Mayfair mansion: one is reckoned to be twice that size. Nearby, No. 51 **Green St** is emerging as five luxury flats. Even the many-storeyed ramparts of Park Lane are yielding apartments and penthouses that gaze (across the traffic) at Hyde Park.

Mayfair

Mayfair is big, and has its quiet corners and districts of bustle. As a broad generalization, the further W, the quieter and smarter. In general, the E and S are older than the N and W. The SW corner, Shepherd Market, has an air of its own and is dealt with below. A few controlled-rent and housing association flats apart, Mayfair is the province of the mansion block and expensively converted flat, with a slowly increasing supply of period houses – some mansion-sized – thanks to office reversions, and rather more mews cottages. No area is without homes, but in some parts (especially the E) they are hard to spot amid the shops, offices and banks. While nothing in Mayfair is cheap, the prices asked for properties can vary widely – based on the two variables of freehold/length of lease and degree of modernization/opulence.

The NE corner, around **Hanover Square**, is among the oldest parts of Mayfair – the Square dates from 1715 – but is today mostly commercial, with offices and shops spilling out from **Oxford St**. **New Bond St**, Mayfair's main shopping street (and light years away in style from **Oxford St's** tourists and department stores), divides this area from the fashion quarter centred around **South Molton St**, now pedestrianized. **Davies St**, running N-S and dead straight, as so many Mayfair streets are, forms the edge of a more residential district to the W. The crowds of **Oxford St** are a moment away, but here is a more peaceful world of mansion blocks and converted period houses. **Gilbert St, Binney St** and **Duke St**, running parallel N-S, contain some attractive red-brick mansion blocks with gabled skylines. Many apartments sit above shops. Whole houses are rare, though the (very) occasional large one does come up. Off **Duke St** is an unusual garden, raised on a plinth over an electricity station. This once neglected square with its pavilion is happily restored. Hereabouts are some early red-brick council homes, now run by the Peabody Trust, and also mansion blocks in what Pevsner calls 'typical Northwest-Mayfair style – red-brick and pink terracotta, gables, and much smaller Renaissance detail'.

This is Grosvenor Estate country. Few realize that the northern part of Mayfair includes not only grand houses and flats but also a wide area of low-rent housing. These flats are tucked away between **Grosvenor Square** and **Oxford St** and are owned by the Grosvenor Estate and run by it in partnership with housing associations. Off **Brook St** is **Avery Row**, a narrow lane with attractive 3-storey, stucco and brown-brick terraces of flats above shops. Behind Claridges in **Brook St** is **Brook's Mews**. Its flat-fronted brick cottages face an unattractive modern development providing 5 storeys of flats. These achieve high prices as pieds-à-terre.

To the S, in a tucked-away corner above **Berkeley Square**, **Bourdon St** has Bloomfield Court, a handsome modern interpretation of the traditional red-brick mansion block built in 1989 by the Grosvenor Estate. The 1- and 2-bed flats were sold with 75-year Estate leases. Prices here tend to be c. £300,000 for a 2-bed. The block boasts no garage, but there is an NCP car park in the street. Also in **Bourdon St** a cleverly converted 3-bed mews house (with double garage) is priced at £885,000 for a new long lease. Next to that, flats in the grey concrete Grosvenor Hill Court are popular London bases. **Mount St** boasts mansion flats above some of London's premier antique shops, and is considered to be Mayfair's 'High Street'. Here, the local bank is Coutt's, the local bed-and-breakfast the Connaught, and the local fish and chip shop is Scotts. A 2-bed flat in **Mount St** was on the market last winter at £845,000 for a 62 year lease. Rentals are common here. **Mount Row**, to the W of **Davies St**, has brown-brick homes with casement windows and leaded glass with mansard roofs. On the S side stand red-brick mewsy houses with shutters at their windows.

Mount St leads into **Carlos Place**, curving round into **Berkeley Square** with red-brick and terracotta Dutch-gabled blocks above galleries and restaurants. This enormous square has everything from beautiful early Georgiana, to '30s, to a modern block with stepped roof line and shops and bank below. There are handsome stucco and brick houses along the W side. Flats are rare here, though one penthouse with large roof terrace was on the market last winter at £1.2 million for a 36-year lease. On **Curzon St** is the Christian Science Church, behind which a courtyard of flats and offices was cunningly inserted. Smart modern blocks like Glendore House punctuate the houses of **Clarges St** and **Half Moon St**. In **Half Moon St** attractive red-brick gabled houses line the SW side. The former Naval and Military Club building runs through to Piccadilly: the club has moved to St James's Square and the old building, the famous 'In and Out' (from the signs on its gateposts) is for sale. Also in **Half Moon St** is the Green Park Hotel along with some attractive period properties.

Chesterfield Hill contains an attractive row of 5-storey stucco and brick period houses with handsome railings at the front, its decorative, cast-iron balconies bedecked with window boxes. This small area of **Hill St** and **Hays Mews** contains some of the most attractive mews and traditional homes, tucked away in relative peace and quiet. Approaching from **Charles St** (where grand period houses fetch around £3 million), you pass plaques commemorating the former residence of King William IV, the sailor king who lived there in 1826. **Hays Mews** is a wide sloping road with charming mews cottages of brick (some bare, some painted) with garages below. A pair of 5-year-old mews houses, with 2/3 bedrooms, were on the market in January with 70-year leases at £795,000 and £895,000. Curled around the top of the mews is **Red Lion Yard**, with a pretty pub giving it an 'out of London' atmosphere. Cobblestones lead to more 3-storey brick town-houses in the yard itself, and three just done-up mews houses (see **Audley Square** below). The E end of **Hay's Mews** on the opposite side of **Chesterfield Hill** is perhaps less attractive, but has the same wide roadway, a mixture of modern houses and little 2-storey brick cottages and a 5-storey block of modern brick-built flats, Rosebery Court (main entrance **Charles St**).

Farm St gained a pair of newly built houses (real rarities in Mayfair) in 1989: one was for sale this spring at £3.45 million freehold. Another two houses are due to make way for a single, large new mansion. Plans envisage eight bedrooms and an underground swimming pool. However, the scheme is currently held up. **South St** is residential, with red-brick conversions, a primary school and a number of attractive smaller houses, for which you will nevertheless need a million or two. **Audley Square** is a small enclave leading off **South Audley St**. Two houses have just been restored: one as a 6-bed mansion complete with garden, garage, staff flat and lift: £4.9 million for the freehold. The second house has become five flats, starting at £650,000, while the three adjoining mews houses in **Red Lion Yard** are also available from £375,000–£795,000.

Waverton St contains Mayfair House, and the imposing brick mansion Garden House, whose name is the only clue to the hidden garden shared (by the houses only) between **South St/South Audley St/ Waverton St** and **Hill St**. Travelling up **South Audley St** there are dignified cream stucco houses and gabled red-brick and terracotta mansion flats above pleasant shops. A freehold house was sold last year for more than £10 million. Purdey's, the famous gun shop, is on the corner of **Mount St** and **South Audley St**, with refurbished flats above on sale last winter at £850,000–1.2 million. Mayfair Library, built in 1894 in a cul-de-sac alongside the Grosvenor Chapel, sits next to the Mount St Gardens, a quiet public space. The garden, with rows of benches, is overlooked by more mansion blocks. To the W is **Balfour Mews**, where the red-brick continues, sometimes relieved by stone detailing and balustrades. Balfour Cottages are a pair of pretty, painted brick homes with tub trees outside. **Reeves Mews** has brown-brick and stone flats opposite its row of mews cottages.

Culross St behind the US Embassy has terraces of traditional town-houses.

They are of varying heights and materials, brick, painted brick and stucco fronts. A very smart modern house with garage and atrium was on the market this spring at £2.95 million. Some houses here are freehold. Shutters and tiny steps up to the front doors on some homes give this road a village feel. **Green St's** tall houses, many now flats, hide another concealed garden which is shared with **Park St** and **Dunraven St**. A 5-bed **Green St** house overlooking the gardens was on the market last winter at £4.5 million for a 98-year lease. One, currently split into flats, was £2.7 million this spring. **Green St** is a fertile source of flats from around £250,000 upwards.

Park St, the main spine of this NW corner of Mayfair, has some large red-brick and stone mansion blocks with colonnaded façades and balconies. It also has some splendid late-19th-century houses built as London mansions by those who had not had the luck to inherit a Park Lane palace, but who found tall, narrow Belgravia houses just too confining. Now they are returning to use as homes after 50 years as offices. Some of these buildings have become flats. The word 'flat' can sometimes be inadequate in Mayfair: in **North Row**, at the Marble Arch corner of Mayfair, a late '80s conversion yielded 15 house-sized apartments: the penthouses have 5 bedrooms, conservatory, roof terraces – and a summer house. One with 4-beds was on the market last winer for £1.3 million.

Certainly 'big is beautiful' is the motto (in terms of both money and square footage) in the far from aptly named **Park Lane**, with its eight roaring lines of traffic that separate Mayfair from Hyde Park. Only a handful of its grand original homes survive, having been replaced by monolithic hotels and car showrooms. One flat covering the first and second floors of a white stucco building, and with three reception rooms totalling 72 ft in length, went for £1.5 million last year. But this is one place where homes (or at least flats) are reappearing: the biggest recent such development is Brook House, on the site of the old MEPC offices. This was sold in its entirity to an Arab group. The flats are now re-selling at prices rumoured to work out at £1,000 per sq ft. Another office reversion will when converted yield a house-sized maisonette, two 2-bed flats and a duplex penthouse: as it stands, £4.5 million was being asked in January for the 76-year lease.

Then there are the new penthouses on the 9th and 10th floors of Fountain House. These two floors were added specially in 1997 to create the super-apartments: 4-bedroomed, double-garaged, lofty views over Hyde Park or Mayfair . . . The largest runs to 4,400 sq ft, plus roof terrace and 45-ft living room. All have been sold at prices from £3.5–4.5 million. On a more normal, but decidedly sybaritic, domestic scale, one of the two large blocks of the Grosvenor House Hotel is in fact flats, some available to rent long-term – with the bonus of all the hotel's facilities on hand, should you so desire. Next door to the Hilton, a big office/retail/homes scheme is planned on a site running back to **Curzon St**, with one listed house being kept and other buildings to be demolished. Watch this space.

Grosvenor Square, the largest square in the district at 6 acres, is best known as the site of the enormous American Embassy. The other sides have some smart flats, reckoned the most luxurious cache in Mayfair. Mostly owned, these days, by overseas buyers or companies, the majority are on short leases, the longest being 70 years. The odd longer lease is appearing, for example a huge flat here was on the market this spring at £3.5 million for 99 years. **Upper Brook St**, which runs W from the Square towards Hyde Park, saw the most expensive house sale in Mayfair last year at £10.5 million. For the money the buyer did get a 50-ft drawing room, a swimming pool and an adjoining mews house with parking for four cars. Other houses in this street have sold recently for £6.5 million and £4.75 million.

The SE corner of Mayfair, towards **Piccadilly Circus**, has fewer homes. **Albany**, the famous warren of prestige 'chambers' off **Piccadilly**, is very exclusive and inhabited by the great, the good and the long-term rich. There are flats above shops, a few mews, and some blocks in streets such as **Hay Hill**.

Shepherd Market

Shepherd Market is an unexpected village of narrow Georgian streets and small-scale buildings, incongruous amid Mayfair's grandeur. Once it was frowned upon as being seedy and the haunt of prostitutes. Today the area's image has greatly changed; more streets have been pedestrianized and it is seen as Mayfair's restaurant quarter. The pretty cottages to be found there are now being gradually done-up and are much sought-after. Nevertheless, there is a variety of property in the area ranging from modern luxury apartments through period mansion blocks to tiny town-houses and mews cottages.

Approaching from **Hertford St**, there are mansion flats in brick and stucco blocks and some handsome old houses. A massive 7-storey block, Carrington House, occupies the corner site of **Hertford St**, **Shepherd St** and **Carrington St**, where 1- and 2-bed flats come up for sale. Until recently the flats were rented on short lets and had a high turnover of residents. Turning into **Shepherd St** there are some attractive old cream-painted little 2-storey cottages. The brick and painted-brick homes over shops are now much in demand. On the other side of the street is a modern red-brick block, May Fayre House, whose flats are available to rent.

The Shepherds Tavern sports bow windows and a jaunty, flower-hung exterior which sets the tone for the pretty village that scatters down **Shepherd St** and round into **Shepherd Market**. On the left of **Shepherd St** is a terrace of flat-roofed homes over shops. In **Shepherd Place** are more small, 2-bedroomed houses. Larger 3-storey brick and stucco buildings line the continuation of **Hertford St**; cobblestones lead you on towards 3-storey mewsy houses. An unmodernized freehold Georgian house in **Trebeck St** was on the market last winter: £600,000 for a potential 3-bed, 3-reception home.

St James's

The best homes in St James's are palaces, and are unlikely to be for sale. Non-royals have to hunt hard for a flat, harder for a house. **Cleveland Row**, next-door to St James's Palace, is mostly offices though there is at least one house. **Little St James's St** has some old houses in mixed use, and there are some exclusive flats in **St James's Place** – the best with wonderful views over Green Park. This is the plushest address in St James's: a 2/3-bed flat recently went for £2 million. St James's is much favoured by English buyers (and increasingly by Italians), but spurned by some of the more serious shopping nations (notably the Middle East) because it's too far from the shops. More flats are found along the park itself, reached from **Arlington St**, which itself is a source of flats: the 1936-built Arlington House has some vast ambassadorial-sized ones.

Despite the scarcity of St James's homes, people buying here are choosy . . . One otherwise impeccable penthouse famously suffered a 6-figure reduction: the block's entrance was cramped, and there was no private lift.

St James's St itself has a mere handful of homes. Some flats are in a corner block next to **Little St James's St**. Further E is **St James's Square**, which was once a dignified assembly of town-houses, but by 1990 had only one residential building. However, Berkeley Homes have converted a house on the corner with **King St**: this adds 10 2- and 3-bed flats to the stock at prices starting at £1.25 million. **Bury St** has some flats in tall buildings, often above shops and offices, as does **Duke of York St**. **Duke St** and **Ryder St** both have some mansion blocks. The best source of flats is **Jermyn St**, where Nos 76 and 25 were both redeveloped to provide 23 and 35 flats respectively. The 2-bed flats at No 76 are typically £380–550,000.

Transport	Tubes, all zone 1: Marble Arch, Bond St (Central); Oxford Circus (Victoria, Bakerloo, Central); Piccadilly Circus (Bakerloo, Piccadilly); Green Park (Victoria, Piccadilly). From Green Park: Oxford Circus 2 min, City 10 min (1 change), Heathrow 1 hr.	
Convenient for	West End, City, Hyde Park. Miles from centre: 1.	
Schools	Local Authority: Westminster City C of E.	

SALES

Flats	S	1B	2B	3B	4B	5B
Average prices	120–150	150–300+	275–850	450–1.3M	675–3.5M+	1M+
Houses	2B	3B	4B	5B	6/7B	8B
Average prices	450+	750+	850+	1.3M+	2.2M+	4.5–10.5M+

RENTAL

Flats	S	1B	2B	3B	4B	5B
Average prices	1200	1500–2000	1950–3000	3000–3900	3900–5200	–
Houses	2B	3B	4B	5B	6/7B	8B
Average prices	2800–3500	3000–4300	4300–7350	6500–10,800	17,000	–

The properties	Mostly flats and mostly grand ones, in mansion blocks or conversions of period homes – and now also of office blocks. Some mews cottages and a few lovely Georgian and Victorian houses. Degree of luxury ranges from the ordinary mansion flat to the super-opulent. St James's has fewer homes, but some with lovely park views.
The market	Prices from £120,000 all the way to £10.5 million. Freeholds slowly becoming more common. Flat prices vary wildly, with length of lease and degree of opulence key price factors. Check service charges in big blocks. Inhabitants are highly international plus old-established or very rich British. Mayfair is enjoying something of a renaissance. Local searches: 2 working days.

M

Among those estate agents active in this area are:
- Wetherell
- Strutt & Parker *
- Keith Cardale Groves
- DTZ Debenham Thorpe
- Beauchamp Estates
- Knight Frank
- Egertons
- John D Wood
- FPDSavills
- Chestertons
- W A Ellis *
- Mercer Pasqua
- Beaney Pearce *
- Foxtons *
- Wetherell *

* further details: see advertisers' index on p633

MORDEN, MITCHAM AND COLLIERS WOOD

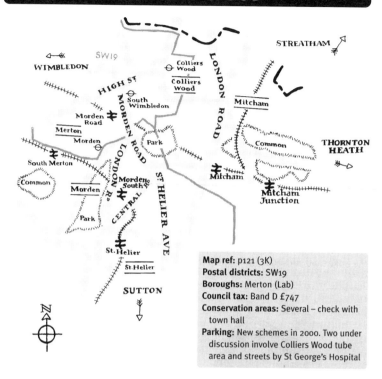

Map ref: p121 (3K)
Postal districts: SW19
Boroughs: Merton (Lab)
Council tax: Band D £747
Conservation areas: Several – check with town hall
Parking: New schemes in 2000. Two under discussion involve Colliers Wood tube area and streets by St George's Hospital

This is where Victorian London's southward sprawl came to a reluctant halt among the villages, fields and woodlands of Surrey. Here the ubiquitous London terrace dies out, to be succeeded by leafy suburban streets: urban expansion received a further boost in 1926, when the Northern line made it to Morden.

The Borough of Merton, which takes in all this area, shelters a wide spread of suburbia of every 20th-century vintage (wartime bombs made room for more) lapping around the remnants of the past. Wimbledon, on its hill, commands the W of the borough. To the SE is Croydon. The area between centres around the valley of the Wandle, which flows northwards from here through to the Thames at Wandsworth. Merton itself is ancient, but little survives except the parish church and a stretch of road called **Merton High St**. Merton Priory, which for some reason the borough decided to elevate to an abbey (it wasn't), was the medieval focus for the villages of Mordern, Mitcham and especially next-door Collier's Wood. Much of Merton has been annexed by South Wimbledon – the name of the tube station – and marooned across the rail tracks on that western side is the interesting turn-of-the-century enclave that still carries Merton's name, Merton Park (see Wimbledon etc, chapter).

Morden also clings onto what's left of the rural charm: there is a church dating from 1636, and behind the church a pub with 16th-century foundations. Morden Hall Park belongs to the National Trust; through it wanders the Wandle, dividing and rejoining to form lake and islands – but the Georgian buildings within the park such as the Hall itself and a 'gentleman's villa' have found interesting new occupations, such as Beefeater pub/restaurant, council offices . . . . The snuff mill and the stables are craft shops. Mitcham is an old place too, with a few survivals of its rural days – and one of the largest caches of recently built homes in South London. Of Colliers Wood the only notable landmark is the underground station – or was, until the advent at the Merton end of the vast flanks of the Sainsbury's Savacentre, more or less where Merton Priory once stood and the young Thomas-à-Becket was educated.

The **Merantun Way** relief road and the Savacentre improved **Merton High St**. The Savacentre is not quite the 'Crystal Palace lookalike the size of Brent Cross, with leisure complex, pubs and restaurants alongside the shops' we expected. 'More like a huge warehouse but nicer,' a local commented, kindly (it does, though, include travel agent, post office, playcentre, shoemender, etc, to supplement the super-Sainsbury's, BHS store and Mothercare, plus café, petrol and masses of free parking). It forms part of the River Wandle development area, behind **Merton High St** and alongside **Christchurch Rd**. The latest addition is a new shopping mall, the Tandem Centre, by the **Merantun Way/Christchurch Rd** roundabout.

Across **Merantun Way** lies something altogether more attractive, however: the Merton Abbey Mills complex, which has successfully revived some old Wandle-side buildings into a pleasant corner of craft shops, bookshops, pubs, restaurants and museum. Here Liberty's used to print their famous silks, and William Morris had his workshops: clothworking and dyeing had in fact been carried out on this spot since the Huguenots arrived in the reign of the first Elizabeth.

This Morden/Mitcham/Colliers Wood corner appeals strongly to those who need to get at a tube station yet prefer the charms of suburbia to more cramped living further in. The Northern line takes a good half-hour to get into the West End or the City, and the many rail stations offer faster progress. Yet the Morden tube does, in a definite way, tie the area into London. Now the Tramlink scheme, a light rail line (à la DLR) linking through to Wimbledon and Croydon (not to mention Ikea) and beyond will improve the area's E-W links when it opens this year. Homes for all here: a wide range of styles and prices, from ex-council to modern new-build (1-bed starter homes are a freehold alternative to flats); from city terraces to semi-detached suburbs.

Mitcham and Morden mushroomed in the 1920s and '30s, after the extension of the Northern line tube speeded commuting into the City. The result was wide areas of neat, semi-detached homes. Mock-Tudor detailing was popular — this is quite a restrained example. The tile-roofed porch-cum-bay is also typical. After a period of disdain, these houses are now fashionable.

Morden

Morden, until the mid-1920s, was a small agricultural community. The landscape was dramatically changed by a high concentration council house-building programme and today can be described as '1930s semi suburbia'.

Morden is at the southern end of the Northern Line tube. Atop the terminus is a large modern office complex, with Civic Centre and library. From here the tube reaches Waterloo in 30 min, the City in 40, while the new Tramlink (stations at Morden Rd, Phipps Bridge and Belgrave Walk) will link to East Croydon, and thus Gatwick and to Wimbledon train and tube connections. A 20/25 min drive away, the Reigate/Leatherhead M25 intersection gives access to both Heathrow and Gatwick Airports.

Generally, Morden is a green, leafy, residential area and includes three large open spaces: Morden Hall Park (more than 50 acres of National Trust parkland, with craft centre, city farm etc), Morden Park (swimming baths, playing-fields) and, to the W, Cannon Hill Common. Houses facing, or with views of, park areas are naturally the great favourites. Premier roads include the leafy **Lower Morden Lane** and **Hillcross Avenue** (mainly 1930s 3-bed solid semis, with front and rear gardens and garages). Flats and bungalows are scarce and so is building land, though Croudace Homes did manage to find room for 75 1- and 2-bed flats, some with bay windows, in landscaped gardens in **Bordesley Rd**.

The St Helier Estate, built by the LCC in the 1920s and '30s and considered advanced for its time, is a large area of wide, well-planned roads (**Blanchland Rd** is typical) of 2/3-bed red-brick semis and terraces with gardens fore and aft. These pre-war council-built houses are of high quality and popular with first-time buyers – they account for 25 per cent of all sales in the district. Many new owners have added imaginative (and sometimes misplaced) exterior features to their homes.

Mitcham

Mitcham, once renowned for its lavender fields and watercress beds, is an odd blend of bustling town, light industry and country village. Though it, like Morden, has a Surrey postal address, it comes under Merton Council.

Determined to retain its rural atmosphere, Mitcham resisted efforts to link it to London's underground. Consequently, it now presents commuters with a goodish walk or a bus ride to the nearest tube stations (Collliers Wood or Tooting Broadway). Mitcham Junction station (a mile from the centre of Mitcham) serves Victoria (18 min), though Mitcham and Mitcham Junction are stops on the new E-W Tramlink. There is good access to the M23 (Gatwick) and M25 (Heathrow), but the centre of town is busy and often congested with through traffic. A new road and pedestrianization from the bottom of **London Rd** to **Upper Green West** helped.

Georgian cottages, manor houses, 18th-century houses and Eagle House (a superb example of Queen Anne architecture) are reminders of Mitcham's rural past. **Commonside East**, looking out over Common and pond, has a row of pretty 2-bed Victorian terraced cottages. These, like homes facing Fair Green and Mitcham Park, are the streets people aspire to – a waiting list has been known to develop for the homes of the **Cricket Green** conservation area, for example. (The game in question is reputed to have been played there for over 300 years.) Other desirable streets include **Gorringe Park Avenue** and **The Close**.

The 1980s saw quite a few new schemes in Mitcham but the early '90s slump, and the lack of land, saw the pipeline dry up. Size and scope remain under wraps of one good-sized development awaiting the go-ahead this year; meanwhile buyers can expect plenty of choice from resales of the last rash of building. Examples are the 1- and 2-bed flats and 4-bed semis off **London Rd**; in **Church Rd**, Cannons Place has 2/3/4-bedroomed houses with private gardens and garages/parking. At **Lower Green West**, Mitcham Village Studios is a converted Georgian school house, now studios and apartments. **Chestnut Grove** has 20 Victorian-copy 1/2-bed flats and 2/3-bed houses. More new homes, too, have appeared in **Crossways Rd** on the edge of Streatham Park.

New developments also appeared in the **Western Rd** area, influenced no doubt by the new Savacentre near its Merton end. Laing's were busy here, building every size from studio flats to 3-bedroom houses. The biggest site by far for new homes is the old King's College playing-fields behind **Lavender Avenue**. A thousand homes have appeared here, as the street map (with its squiggly closes and little squares) clearly shows. This is a good source of 2- and 3-bed houses and 1- to 3-bed flats. For other new homes developments, look in the **Mount Rd**/**Lewis Rd** area, across **Western Rd.**

A point to watch here is that since new streets these days are usually blocked to through traffic from the outset, pinch-points occur when the deluge of residents try to leave for work . . . One such is the right-turn from **Lavender Avenue** into **Western Rd.**

Mitcham, like most of the capital's satellites, divides into the good, the bad and the definitely ugly – but strenuous efforts have been taking place to reduce the latter. This has included the removal of some hardly scenic tower blocks by **Phipps Bridge** and their replacement with attractive low-level housing, and much improvement to other such council-built estates. Privatized ex-council homes allow for a low start to the wide range of prices, and can provide a great deal of space for your money.

Colliers Wood

Colliers Wood is sandwiched between **Merton** and **Tooting High Sts.** Somewhat overshadowed by a large grey tower of offices, it was dismissed for years as a 'depressed' area. It perked up in the late '80s, and is showing signs of doing so again now that the neighbours are going up in the world. A good hunting-ground, especially for first-time home-owners, but still not a name to entice buyers. As a result, some bits get 'moved' to South Wimbledon or even Tooting by estate agents and developers. By way of revenge, Colliers Wood has annexed the eastern part of Merton, so counts the vast Savacentre and the Merton Abbey Mills (see page 441) as part of its patch. The car boot sale at the latter is its Saturday entertainment.

Nearby Wandle Park (part-owned by the National Trust) provides some welcome green space. With direct access to Central London from Colliers Wood tube station (Northern line: 25 min Waterloo, 35 the City), it's good commuter territory. Homes here are a pleasant mix of 1880s, 1930s and 1960s houses with pretty stucco/stock-brick Edwardian villas, many Victorian terraces (some with bay windows) and some conversion flats. Bargain-hunters search out the pockets of Victorian terraces which survived the last wave of improvers undisturbed.

 Few houses have off-street parking, but most have the bonus of long back gardens. The better roads are bordered by **Cavendish Rd** and include **Marlborough Rd**, **Clive Rd** and **Warren Rd**, **Daniel** and **Defoe Closes**, **Norfolk** and **Harewood Rds**. Some have bollards, preventing noisy through traffic.

The other side of **Colliers Wood High St**, the streets around **Boundary** and **Acre Rds** are very popular with those who work at St George's Hospital Tooting, just across the tracks, which can be reached by a footbridge at the end of **Boundary Rd**. Since patients have discovered this too, a residents' parking scheme is under consultation.

Mead Park, Wimpey's big development in the Wandle Valley NW of the **High St**, has provided this corner with 160 new homes, from studios to town-houses on ex-sewage-works land; a short walk away from both the tube and Haydons Rd Thameslink station.

Merton

See introduction. The Merton Park Estate is described in the Wimbledon chapter.

Transport   Tubes: Colliers Wood, Morden (zone 3, Northern). From Morden: Oxford Circus 35 min (1 change), City 40 min, Heathrow 1 hr 30 min (2 changes). Rail from Mitcham Junction and Mitcham. Tramlink to Croydon opens this year.

Convenient for   Tubes to Central London, routes South, Wimbledon.

Schools   Merton Education Authority. High Schools: Eastfields High (b), Raynes Park, Rutlish (b), Rickards Lodge (g), Rowan (g), Tamworth Manor, Ursuline Convent (g), Wimbledon College (b), Watermeads. Middle Schools: Cranmer, St Thomas of Canterbury.

SALES

Flats	S	1B	2B	3B	4B	5B
Average prices	33–50	50–60	62–75	65–80	—	—
Houses	2B	3B	4B	5B	6/7B	8B
Average prices	75–85	90–150	110–150+	145+	—	—

RENTAL

Flats	S	1B	2B	3B	4B	5B
Average prices	300–425	450–530	550–650	650–800	›1000	—
Houses	2B	3B	4B	5B	6/7B	8B
Average prices	650–800	700–1100	800–1300	1400+	—	—

The properties   Victoriana peters out after Colliers Wood. Behind the busy main roads, all three areas have large estates of 1930s terraces. These generally provide the most common source of converted flats or 2/3-bed homes: larger, 4+ bed are scarce. The top houses are found alongside Mitcham's parks. New homes are plentiful – including tiny 1-bed 'starter homes': freehold alternative to flats.

The market   First-time buyers find good-size, good-value flats here. Mitcham prices are held back by lack of a tube, except for the best family homes (see above). Inexpensive ex-council homes are now widely available. Three-bed flats and larger houses are rare: generally ex-council or above shops. Local searches: 2 weeks.

M

Among those estate agents active in this area are:
- Goodfellows
- Tarrant & Co
- Andrews & Partners
- Barnard Marcus
- Singletons
- Christopher & James
- Ellisons
- Drury & Cole
- Bairstow Eves

MUSWELL HILL

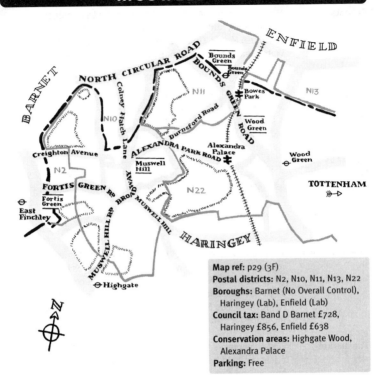

Map ref: p29 (3F)
Postal districts: N2, N10, N11, N13, N22
Boroughs: Barnet (No Overall Control),
   Haringey (Lab), Enfield (Lab)
Council tax: Band D Barnet £728,
   Haringey £856, Enfield £638
Conservation areas: Highgate Wood,
   Alexandra Palace
Parking: Free

The hilltop suburb of Muswell Hill is a place of pilgrimage once more, though St Mary's Well, with its miraculous healing waters, has long since disappeared beneath **Muswell Rd.** Today's pilgrims were drawn here by the schools, or by economics as prices in neighbouring Hampstead and Highgate moved beyond the reach of mere mortals' pockets. It has become re-established as a place in its own right – a prosperous, middle-class family area, where the pilgrimage vehicle of choice is a four-wheel drive.

Its bone structure is good. A pleasantly hilly, residential neighbourhood with its own distinctive and dignified character, it is not anonymous: a community, if not (as some would have it) a 'village'. The wider area can be defined to the N and E by a loop of the **North Circular Rd**, taking in the more industrial/commercial end of **Colney Hatch Lane** and **Bounds Green** plus its tube, across to **Wood Green**. To the S, it meets Hornsey/Crouch End at the southern tip of Alexandra Park, and reaches down to Highgate tube on the A1/**Archway Rd**.

The eccentric architecture of Muswell Hill sails red-bricked above the more polluted air of lower domains. Indeed, the air is purer (and some say colder) than that of its lower neighbours, not only thanks to physical height, but surely because of the Highgate Wood and Queen's Wood at the end of **Muswell Hill Rd** and the extensive parkland surrounding Alexandra Palace. There are, indeed, many other smaller pockets of parkland, complete with bowling greens and tennis courts, which invoke the leisurely Edwardian era of the suburb's flowering. The little town, with the

Broadway as its high street, is set in a splendid position on one of the highest hills in North London, giving long, long views over the City and West End: both St Paul's and Canary Wharf can be seen on clear days. There is that sense of being a place apart, a slight but definite distance from the main thrust of London . . .

Although the actual Muswell, with its early monastic links, dates back to medieval times, little was built here at all except the odd elegant country retreat until the mid-Victorian period. Most of the building was started in the early 1900s, however, and went on apace until the onset of World War I, in large estates of varying-sized houses, as well as many-storeyed mansion blocks of bachelor apartments (big by today's standards) on the **Broadway** itself, and those purpose-built flats above the shops.

Shopping in the **Broadway** is small and friendly, with everything you need for immediate purposes; delicatessens abound, there are several useful small, late-opening supermarkets and a Marks & Spencer food hall. There has been a flowering of cafés, art shops, coffee houses and other independent shops and restaurants. The necessary chain- and departmental-store shopping is supplied by the nearby Brent Cross shopping centre – London's first major edge-of-town complex – and also the more humdrum centre at Wood Green. Closer to home, a 24hr Tesco superstore on the **North Circular** (junction with **Colney Hatch Lane**), and Ikea. There's a cinema and swimming pool in the area, as well as the golf course and Alexandra Palace, restored for arts, leisure and other uses, but chronically under-funded and in debt. Interestingly, as the main estates were built on Methodist Church land there are few original pubs; this, however, has been rectified of late with several newcomers, plus bars and restaurants, on the **Broadway** drag. Muswell Hill night life has a distinctly youthful air: not as rock'n'roll as Crouch End, but certainly enough to keep the 18–30s happy. The chicest place to be seen, however, is the health club: *très* '90s, *très* full of celebs.

The greatest drawback (or blessing, according to some Muswellites) is the lack of a nearby tube. Highgate and Bounds Green are a 10 min bus ride away, and Finsbury Park's a good 15 min. There are several bus routes to the West End and to the City, which is also served by train from Alexandra Palace to Moorgate, and by an express bus in weekday rush hour.

Nevertheless, this is a car driver's area and a good number of households have two. Luckily, streets tend to be wide and parking is not the nightmare it is in denser-packed suburbs. But the number of people using their cars to get to work or schools is reflected at the frustrating bottleneck of the main Muswell Hill roundabout and junction of **Archway Rd**. (There are fears that the situation will worsen if the proposed pedestrianization of part of the **Broadway** goes ahead.)

So, on the whole, the sort of people buying and living in this area are families: middle-class, dual-income ones, many in the media-type industries or smart, *Guardian*-reading, high-income professionals who holiday in Bordeaux or Tuscany. ('In fact, typical New Labour – dream champagne socialists' was one summing up.) There is a very high density of au pair girls in Muswell Hill. Stemming from this, most local schools have a good reputation as they are well-supported by aware parent groups, who donate not only money but a great deal of time and energy to their children's education. There is thus an obvious requirement for houses/flats in the 'right' catchment area – and this reached frenzy point of late, as Fortismere's catchment area has been drastically reduced, effectively excluding those until now content to live in Crouch End. Stress levels, and prices for strategically placed homes, can be high.

Muswell Hill

Muswell Hill has always had a genteel air. Its homes are mostly ranged in grandiose Edwardian terraces or set in wide leafy roads (which have escaped parking restrictions so far – except for the weekend of the spectacular Guy Fawkes fireworks). They boast almost bizarre architectural features including spires and balconies, heavily ornamented gables, pillastered bays. After elderly people, whose families had often owned the larger homes since they were built, moved on, many houses were divided into flats or maisonettes. This trend has been reversed over the last decade, with many reconversions to splendid family homes of up to 6 bedrooms in some cases.

Haringey Council traditionally frowns on conversions, and is also against the building of small flats rather than family homes. (That said, it is now working with housing associations on new projects to provide both.)

There are three main, covetable enclaves that ring **Muswell Hill Broadway**: one to the E of the Broadway across to **The Avenue**, above the park; another, the grid of streets at the W end of the Broadway between **Fortis Green Rd**, **Grand Avenue** and **Midhurst Avenue**; a third in the angle of Highgate Wood and Queen's Wood, to the E of **Muswell Hill Rd**.

This last enclave holds some of Muswell Hill's choicest homes. These select streets to the S, in the angle of **Cranley Gardens** and **Wood Vale**, also have the advantage of lying nearest to Highgate tube. Prestigious **Onslow Gardens**, **Woodland Rise**, **Woodlands Gardens**, **Connaught Gardens**, **Wood Vale**, as well as the main **Muswell Hill Rd**, are lined with very large houses, sometimes with balconies and basement areas (easily converted to utility rooms) which are definite assets. Often set further back, or higher up, from the road, probably with a car port, these houses command high prices for the most luxurious – anything from £350–500,000-plus (the odd £700,000 one). Parking can be a problem: many homes have two or three cars apiece.

The popular Fortis Green conservation area has a grid of similar roads, more convenient for East Finchley tube, spreading out from the top of **Muswell Hill Rd** westwards to **Midhurst Rd**. **Grand Avenue** matches its name: one of the prime streets, it also has no through traffic – and homes easily reach £400–500,000. **Collingwood Avenue, Leaside Avenue, Fortismere Avenue** and **Birchwood Avenue** are popular – but expensive. Half-a-million houses again, though some '20s 3-bed go for c. £200,000.

Modern '80s developments here include the 4-bed town-houses of **Alexandra Mews**, and the 3-bed flats of 'The Copse', a refurbishment of ex-police flats – both on **Fortis Green**, both very nice. Cheaper but not so large and grand are the streets off nearby **East Finchley High Rd** itself – smaller-scale versions intermingled with 1930s semis; much more everyday roads, but highly convenient for the tube and only an extra 5 min tube journey (above ground at this point) to town. Look for the 'county' roads: pleasant, grey-brick Victorian terraces with names like **Lincoln Rd**, **Leicester Rd**, etc; with luck, a small home in one of these can be found for c. £175,000, though the best can approach £300,000. To the S across this end of **Fortis Green**, the streets down to Cherry Tree Wood get dearer again (and closer to East Finchley tube).

The third coveted enclave lies off **Dukes Avenue** behind **The Broadway**, stretching north-eastwards across to encircling **Alexandra Park Rd**. The peaceful streets are tree-lined and wide enough to take four cars abreast (no parking restrictions as yet). The houses are mostly large – anything from 3- to 6-bed, some double-fronted – with longish gardens and festoons of the 'original features' so beloved of estate agents.

There are other, somewhat plainer Edwardian estates stretching from the far side of **Alexandra Park Rd**: the 'lake' roads – **Windermere Rd**, **Grasmere Rd** (very popular, close to the golf course: c. £350,000) – across to **Sutton Rd**, **Wilton Rd** and **Greenham Rd** off the W side of **Colney Hatch Lane**: popular, but here the houses do not have quite the same dignified air. However, they still boast interiors which can command £250–300,000, plenty of space, are close to Coldfall Wood and still not far away from the main shopping area. Some developments have been squeezed into the area: **Kendalmere Close, Audley Close, Louis Mews** have appeared, and in '97 The Heights, glamorous and expensive apartments off **Alexandra Park Rd**.

Less sought-after areas, commensurately cheaper in price, lie to the N up towards the **North Circular Rd**. Between **Colney Hatch Lane**, the **North Circular, Alexandra** and **Wetherill Rds** the tenor gets decidely more commercial (small industrial outcrops, **Hampden Rd** bus terminus and even a tattoo shop are to be found here), but this corner, though mixed, is improving: prices, and new developments, have risen in recent years. Edwardian homes jostle with smaller Victoriana, '20s and '50s blocks with '80s and '90s schemes: detached modern 4-bed houses in **Pembroke Mews**, **Cambridge Gardens**, a cul-de-sac of new homes; retirement flats in **Wetherill Rd**.

Houses off **Coppetts Rd** to the W, although in leafy streets, are generally less popular, there being a '60s block of flats and a fairly large council-built estate of indifferent architectural value there. Here, however, new flats and houses will appear, both housing association and private, on land sold off by the Coppetts Wood Hospital. **Colney Hatch Lane** leads across the **North Circular**, where the Rialto development, a decade old, is neat and quiet. Beyond that, the old Victorian mental hospital is the centre of major redevelopment: see Totteridge and Whetstone chapter.

Newer parts of Muswell Hill regarded favourably are in the 1920s Collins-built private estate off the main Hill (the road which runs up to the **Broadway** from the S tip of Alexandra Park) itself. The Rookfield Estate has neat houses set in privately maintained roads – with five barriers to disallow through traffic. A decade later came the 1930s bay-fronted houses of **Creighton Avenue** and **Pages Lane**, as well as those lining **Alexandra Park Rd**, in a broad sweep across the area. These are typical of their kind; since they often have garages, they fetch high prices. So, too, do those in **Cranley Gardens** on the Muswell Hill/Hornsey borders. The Baptist Church Hall off **Creighton Avenue** has been interestingly converted into 13 new flats. Apart from the Rookfield Estate, these roads are all quite busy so more traffic noise is likely here.

Bounds Green and Wood Green

If you are not willing or able to invest the larger sum required for Muswell Hill proper, the surrounding areas may be the answer. Bounds Green to the E, perhaps the best investment now, has the same sort of houses – not such elegant roads, but close to the tube (Piccadilly line – a straight run to Heathrow), and therefore a good compromise for those requiring space and convenience. Retirement flats have been built just opposite the tube. Nearby, 3-bed 1920s houses can be had for less than £200,000. Neat semis with garages, set back from the quiet, more suburban roads, can be found between **Bounds Green Rd**, **Durnsford Rd** and Muswell Hill golf course.

Some smaller Victorian 'artisan dwellings' around Bowes Park are still affordable: agents tip this corner, with its villagy atmosphere, close to the tube and with its own rail station, as a good starting point for first-time buyers, with prices around £120–160,000. This also goes for the small but quiet roads near Alexandra Palace station, which hold purpose-built maisonettes as well as houses.

Back on the Muswell Hill side of the tracks, but N22, not N10, the triangle between **Durnsford/Albert Rds**, **Victoria Rd** and the railway line is leafy and popular: it is likely to figure in estate agents' details as 'Alexandra Park', though the continuation of **Alexandra Park Rd**, which skirts the park itself, considers itself a place apart from the hinterland. **Crescent Rd** and **Palace Gates Rd** are the best streets, and the W (ie, Muswell Hill) end of **Victoria Rd**. There are more flats here, and solid houses; terraced, 3-bed Edwardian with original features inside and out in **Clyde Rd** was £240,000 last winter; larger 4- to 5-bedroomed ones was £275,000. The E sides of **Crescent Rise** and **Dagmar Rd** back onto the tracks.

Over this line to Wood Green, the desirability lessens, but **Truro Rd** and **Nightingale Rd** are reckoned good value for first-time buyers. However, the small pocket between **Park Avenue** and **Station Rd**, N of Wood Green Common, has little

2-storey Victorian cottages in tree-lined streets. These are no-through roads, and thus peaceful despite the railway line nearby: popular with City workers, who can travel quickly from here. Two-bed cottages are c. £105–110,000. Just to the N lies a little cache of pretty railway cottages, between **Bridge Rd** and the station. Further afield, towards **White Hart Lane**, are busy rows of red-brick Edwardian houses, mostly flats and maisonettes. Wood Green has its Shopping City which has many amenities, but is less select – with a very much more urban, bustling, multi-cultured atmosphere – than the tranquil climes of Muswell Hill. However, the Shopping City and the **High Rd** is now to receive a £17 million renovation: as well as new shops, cinemas, bars and restaurants, a 25,000 sq ft market hall will be included.

Transport	Tubes: Bounds Green, Wood Green (zone 3, Piccadilly – direct to Heathrow); East Finchley, Highgate (zone 3, Northern). From Highgate: Oxford Circus 20 min (1 change), City 25 min, Heathrow 1 hr 15 min (1 change). Trains: Alexandra Palace to City.
Convenient for	Brent Cross shopping centre, Ikea, Wood Green Shopping City. North Circular Rd, A1/M1. Miles from centre: 6.
Schools	Barnet, Haringey and Enfield Education Authorities: Fortismere School. Private: Channing (g), Highgate School (b), Norfolk House.

SALES

Flats	S	1B	2B	3B	4B	5B
Average prices	90+	100–200	150–175	180–200	–	–

Houses	2B	3B	4B	5B	6/7B	8B
Average prices	170+	200–300	300–4500	350–600	550+	–

RENTAL

Flats	S	1B	2B	3B	4B	5B
Average prices	300–500	550–700	700–1000	800–1200	–	–

Houses	2B	3B	4B	5B	6/7B	8B
Average prices	–	1200–2000	1200–2000	2200+	–	–

The properties	Solid, superior Edwardian houses, some very large, providing roomy conversions as well as excellent family homes. Also some mansion flats. Smaller houses '20s/'30s, but smallest are modern or little Victorian terraces in fringe areas.
The market	Spacious houses attract families – many of media/professional/ liberal persuasion – who find value in this green, well-schooled area. Big jump in quality (and prices) from 3- to 4-bed homes. Local searches: Barnet 3 days, Haringey 2 weeks, Enfield 1 day.

Among those estate agents active in this area are:
- Sturt & Tivendale
- Keats
- Delemere
- Kinleigh Folkard & Hayward
- Prickett & Ellis
- Winkworth *
- Holden Matthews
- Bairstow Eves
- Barnard Marcus
- Stonebridge & Co
- Martyn Gerrard
- JHK
- Tatlers
- Anscombe & Ringland *

further details: see advertisers' index on p633

NEW CROSS AND DEPTFORD

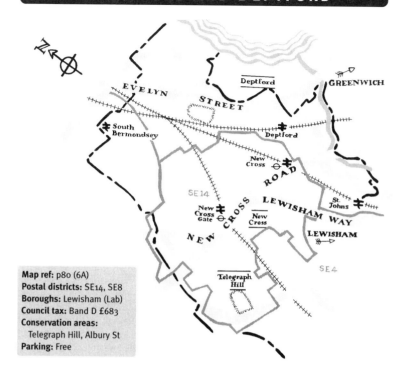

Map ref: p80 (6A)
Postal districts: SE14, SE8
Boroughs: Lewisham (Lab)
Council tax: Band D £683
Conservation areas:
Telegraph Hill, Albury St
Parking: Free

Back in Tudor times Deptford was to London what Heathrow is now: the launching pad for trade and adventure, and replete with bustle, business (and thieving) and well-paid work. Here the East India Company's ships were built. Drake, Frobisher and Raleigh set out from here, and this summer archaeologists are probing the Deptford Creek mud for the wreck of Drake's Golden Hind. Times change ... Henry VIII's Royal Naval Yard closed in 1961, and the Victualling Yard, which Pepys knew, was all but razed in the 1960s to make way for a council estate. The end of the nearby Surrey Docks in the '70s destroyed the rest of Deptford's economy.

Decline has been Deptford's insistent companion since the World War II, but at last the trend is moving upwards. Improving transport, a more enlightened approach to the surviving bits of local history, and the spillover from Docklands and Millennium-obsessed Greenwich are all playing their part. The more residential areas of New Cross and New Cross Gate, to the S and SW of Deptford, have been regaining some of the favour they found in Victorian times.

Transport is the real key: as in much of SE London roads and thus buses are appalling: the area relies on trains. These run into London Bridge, and New Cross's endless terraces were built to house City clerks. There's also a tube: the East London line, which has just reopened after a three-year upgrade. It used to get you to Wapping and Whitechapel and not much else, but a link with the Jubilee Line Extension at the new Canada Water station will at last make the West End a single change away. And now Deptford is getting a pair of stations on the southwards-extending Docklands Light Railway (DLR): a direct line to Canary Wharf and the City.

All the local stations are in zone 2. New Cross main line also has a useful link to Gatwick Airport. In response to these changes home-buyers have been moving in: agents cannot quite believe their good fortune. The 10,000 students of Goldsmith's College underpin rental values, boosting buyers' confidence. Prices in the area went up in 1998 when other areas were stagnating.

Many of Deptford's homes are council-built and (still) owned, but the stock of private houses still includes inexpensive, unmessed-about, unmodernized ones. New developments are appearing, and more and bigger ones are scheduled. Resales on these residential developments offer plenty of choice.

The larger, once-grand terraces of New Cross make for flat conversions. The Telegraph Hill area at the southern end is a pleasant and surprising corner (long discovered by property writers). It is one of several conservation areas: prices in these can be a good jump higher than elsewhere. A knowledgeable local agent reckons that a 2-bed flat in a conservation area costs the same as a 3-bed elsewhere.

These areas are among the few in London offering a decent choice of homes below £70,000. Ex-council homes, 1980s 'starter' homes (including that oddity the 1-bed house) and conversions of Victorian houses into flats offer plenty of choice. A decent-sized 3-bed Victorian house on Telegraph Hill might be £150,000-plus.

Deptford

'Deptford,' said an inhabitant, 'is *local*'. This was the closest she could get to explaining why this untidy, unkempt corner of town, cheerfully grimy in some parts, plain grim in others, nevertheless feels like a proper place – unlike many a politer but more faceless tract of South London. Deptford lies on the river, between Greenwich, New Cross and Surrey Docks. In Tudor and Stuart times, Deptford Strand was the scene of events as disparate as the knighting of Walter Raleigh and the murder of Christopher Marlowe in a riverside tavern. He is reputed to be buried in an unmarked grave in St Nicholas Churchyard. Deptford Creek, at present a wasteland, has figured in several ambitious development schemes. The Environment Agency, and local groups, are currently keen on a softer, low-density approach.

Deptford's industrial and sea-faring past is still in evidence, with streets such as **Mechanics Path**, **Shipwrights Rd**, **Frigate Mews** and **Bronze St**, not to mention the statues of famous admirals which adorn the top of Deptford Town Hall. The **High St** was long a byword for scruffiness. In 1550 it was 'so noisome and full of filth that the King's Majesty might not pass to and fro to see the building of His Majesty's ships'. The Navy paid for it to be repaved, and Whitehall money has helped a considerable tidy-up in the last few years. Over on **Griffin St/Deptford Church St** is the new Wavelength Leisure Centre, which includes a swimming pool, library, bar/café and fitness suite. St Paul's Church, another pointer to Deptford's past status, lies between the **High St** and **Church St**. This magnificent Baroque building was erected for the people of Deptford in the 1720s, after their request for a 'grand church' – they got it. Deptford market is fairly comprehensive (and very cheap), the best days being Wednesday and Saturday, when the **High St** is closed to traffic.

A scheme by Fairview is bringing flats and houses to the mouth of Deptford Creek off **Creek Rd**. At the head of the Creek, Mumford's Mill, a Grade II listed flour mill, is flats and business units. New flats have appeared on the **High St** near the station, and another recent development of houses in **Mary Ann Gardens**. **Albury St** is a cobbled Georgian street that escaped the bombing – but not years of decline while waiting for the GLC, who had emptied the houses, to restore them. However, its terraced 18th-century houses (some virtually untouched) have at last been renovated to English Heritage standards. One 2-bed flat here was on the market last winter for £123,000, a 1-bed for £60,000 on the **High St** itself. Around the back of **Albury St**, facing onto

Creek Rd, are some new houses and flats. Modern flats off **Watson's St**, W of the **High St**, go for £60,000 for a 2-bed.

Heading up towards Surrey Docks along **Evelyn St**, you pass large houses, many with semi-basements. These are nice when restored, but suffer from main-road noise. There are small Victorian terraces in **Gosterwood St** and **Etta St**, and 3-bed ones in **Alloa Rd, Trundleys Rd** – and in **Scawen Rd**, where the houses can look out over Deptford Park: these fetch around £100,000. At the other end of **Trundleys Rd**, near the one-way system leading to Surrey Docks, is 1990-vintage 'Chester Circus': 30 handsome homes ranging from studio to 3-bed houses. Opposite here, on the corner of **Evelyn St** and **Sayes Court**, is Sayes Hall Court: 55 flats and houses built in 1989 around a courtyard.

Between **Evelyn St** and the river lies the Pepys Estate, a '60s council scheme: multi-storey concrete towers and low-rise blocks built on the site of bombed Georgian merchants' terraces . . . but look in your A–Z map book for **Deptford Strand** and, at right angles to it, The Terrace, along **Longshore**. Here are the remains of that Georgian heritage: houses in The Terrace, and what were waterside warehouses now converted into flats – some private, some council. The Pepys was a model estate in the '60s (it won a clutch of design awards) and is now recovering from its former dangerous reputation. Aragon Tower, the largest, has stunning views, as estate agents would say, over the river and Central London (there being nothing very high in the Surrey Docks to get in the way). Inside the blocks are split-level flats with the sort of layout that costs serious money in the private sector.

The same cannot be said of the grimmer blocks of Milton Court, another council estate which runs between **Milton Court Rd** and **Sanford St**, in the angle between two railway lines. This is not the place for your evening stroll. Between **Sanford St** and the railway line is a 1980s Wimpey estate of houses built for sale: **Southern Gate Way** and **Sterling Gardens**. A 2-bed flat here might cost £60,000. The area to the NW, on the borders with Rotherhithe and the Surrey Docks, is fast improving due to the spillover effect from Docklands. Surrey Quays tube is on the same line as New Cross and New Cross Gate. There are vast areas of new housing in Surrey Docks: see Docklands.

New Cross

New Cross, apparently, used to be a pretty village until it started being used as a coaching stop to avoid taking tired horses over Blackheath – then a notorious haunt of highwaymen on the Dover Rd. This proved to be its eventual downfall, as its high street evolved into the main road which effectively sliced the place in half. New Cross thus has once-grand early (some very early) Victorian terraces (whose potential depends on distance from the road) which are extremely convenient for trains, tube and buses – but feels somewhat transient, compared to Deptford's far more villagy feel. However, from time to time a new restaurant or a new smarter shop appears: a general tidy-up seems to have begun. A major boost to the area was the arrival of a large Sainsbury's foodstore at the bottom of Telegraph Hill which opened in 1995. Much recent development is squeezed in close to busy rail lines.

Central New Cross is unlovely, but look around the evocatively named **Friendly St**, with its artisan cottages, and among the turn-of-the-century houses around **St John's Vale** and the mid-19th-century ones in **Florence Rd**. Houses get grander as they reach the tops of these roads . . . and that bit closer to Brockley. Many of the tall houses along **Lewisham Way** and **New Cross Rd** have been converted into flats; these 5-storey houses near Goldsmith's College are set comparatively far back from the road. There are also some 3-bed flats – mostly over shops. The college has been making big investments in new student housing, but flats to rent are still in demand. A surplus Lewisham College building nearby has just been converted into 66 homes.

But go S from the two stations, past the '30s terraces and the 4-bed purpose-built Victorian mansion flats on **New Cross Rd**, and you come to a neighbourhood with an identity all its own. These are the pleasant boulevards, lined by trees and flanked by roomy (and some huge) Victorian homes, which run up and around Telegraph Hill and its park. The telegraph station which gave the hill its name passed the news of Waterloo. This corner was developed by the Haberdashers' Company, and this quiet, pleasant area has become increasingly popular: the houses yield nice flat conversions or make good-size family homes. **Pepys Rd**, **Kitto Rd** and **Vesta Rd** also have magnificent, panoramic views over Central London. Lower down the hill, **Musgrove Rd** has 3-storey Victorian houses that convert well into flats. A 1-bed one might be £57,000 – 20 per cent up on a year ago. **Waller Rd** has 5-bed houses which top £200,000, **Jerningham Rd** has 2-bed flat conversions at around £90,000. Some of the houses at the bottom end of the streets leading to the hill suffered from subsidence following dry years, and may need underpinning. Watch your survey. Some council-built homes here offer a cheaper option: resales around £85,000 for 3-bed house, £70,000 for a 2-bed. S of the park, **Drakefell Rd** has Victorian terraces, some flats: a 2-bed one with a big garden (but a railway at the end of it) might be £67,000.

Almost directly N of Telegraph Hill, across **New Cross Rd**, is the Hatcham Park conservation area. There are still houses in need of refurbishment, though many have been tidied up. Streets include **Brocklehurst St** (3-bed cottages: around £95,000), **Billington Rd** (4/5-bed Victorian terraces with gardens), **Camplin St** (2-bed terraces), **Hundson Rd** (3-bed around £15,000) **Hatcham Park Rd** and **Hatcham Park Mews**. Many homes here were sold to tenants of the Haberdashers' estate. There is a good, well-regarded school in **Hunsdon Rd**. New-build flats in the same area sell for around £55,000. Off **Avonley Rd** is a Barratt-built estate of 1990 studios, flats and houses. All have garaging or parking-space.

Transport	Tubes: New Cross, New Cross Gate (zone 2); Oxford Circus 30 min (2 changes), City 20 min (2 changes), Heathrow 90 min (2 changes). Trains: New Cross, New Cross Gate, Deptford (London Br, Charing X, Cannon St). DLR from Deptford Creek due 'soon'.
Convenient for	Docklands, City, Greenwich. Miles from centre: 4.5.
Schools	Local Authority: Haberdashers' Aske's, Hatcham (b) (g), South East London Secondary School.

SALES

Flats	S	1B	2B	3B	4B	5B
Average prices	35–50	50–60	55–90	75–120	—	—
Houses	2B	3B	4B	5B	6/7B	8B
Average prices	60–120	85–140	110–250	→	→300	—

RENTAL

Flats	S	1B	2B	3B	4B	5B
Average prices	350–450	450–550	550–700	650–800	—	—
Houses	2B	3B	4B	5B	6/7B	8B
Average prices	600–700	700–850	850–1200	1200–1500	—	—

The properties   Deptford's small stock of homes for sale (most housing is council) include some unmodernized 3-bed Victorian terraces. New developments appearing. New Cross is full of 19th-century terraces, many converted into flats; they are stately in Telegraph Hill (flats or 4/5-bed houses), run-down on the main roads, cottage in conservation areas.

The market   Cheap, convenient (only tubes for miles) homes attract first-time buyers unable to aspire to nearby Surrey Docks or Greenwich. Lots of bargains to be had, some with river views. Families head for the enclave of Telegraph Hill. The DLR extension will link Deptford to Docklands. Local searches: 2 weeks.

Among those estate agents active in this area are:
- Burnet, Ware & Graves
- Oak Estates *
- Seigo Homes
- Trafalgar Property Services
- Quest Residential
- Wilson Rogers
- Halifax Property Services
- Meridian Estates

further details: see advertisers' index on p633

N

NEWHAM

Map ref: p49 (K7)
Postal districts: E6, E7, E12, E13,
 E15, E16
Boroughs: Newham (Lab)
Council tax: Band D £679
Conservation areas: Woodgrange,
 Three Mills
Parking: Controlled parking zones
 in East Ham and Stratford and
 more planned – but residents
 can park free in these zones

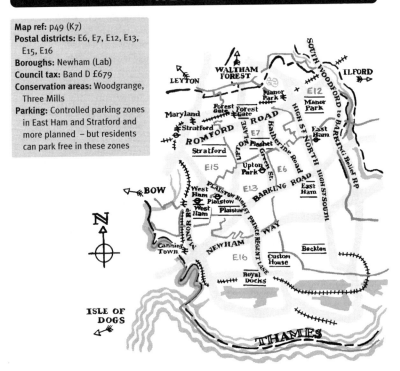

New transport links, London's first new university campus for half a century, thousands of new homes: these are among things actually happening in Newham. Add in the bright ideas, plans, proposals and sheer off-the-wall schemes and you have a pretty fast-changing part of London.

Newham takes in what might be called the outer East End. The old Boroughs of East Ham and West Ham, themselves successors to a dozen medieval hamlets, mushroomed in the second half of the 19th century. In 1965 they merged to become Newham (why not New Ham?). The '70s and '80s saw the final closure, and the start of redevelopment, of the giant Royal Docks which take up the southern swathe of the borough and were once its biggest employer. Now the Royals are finally showing up on the map as a place of real, brick-and-concrete buildings, not the spectral landscape of sketchy plans and architects' models that diverted us for so much of the 1980s. So many plans, so little built. The Royals would be the best location for the Museum of Unbuilt Developments. Now these great sheets of water sport, around their margins, a successful airport, a new university, a technology park, several hundred homes and some prestige offices. A large exhibition centre is being built.

Newham has seen more changes than any other London borough over the last 10 years, with more planned for the next decade. Once recognized as England's most deprived area, government money has been pumped into it to pull it out of decline. Stratford, once a town in its own right and today a shopping centre on the W side of the borough, still hopes for fame as the site of Stratford International station, an interchange on the London–Paris line. This is a decade in the future if it happens at all.

Turning from the planned to the actual, 1999 will see the Jubilee Line Extension to Stratford and a new interchange at nearby West Ham, plus the opening of the M11 Link Rd. London City Airport, in the docks, is doing well with 1.2 million passengers a year and flights to 21 cities in Europe.

Newham Council has taken over the Royals area from the London Docklands Development Corporation, though the English Partnerships quango has some powers. Among ongoing projects for the Royals is an exhibition centre on the N side of Royal Victoria Dock that will rival the biggest and best in London. Work has started: it's due to open in 2000. Even ELRIC (the East London River Crossing – a bridge to the rest of us) is back on the possible list after having been a certainty, and then scrapped, in the early '90s. A glance at the map shows that the approach from the N already exists – the A406/**North Circular Rd** comes to a sudden end at the A13 junction, and it was intended to go on S to join ELRIC. On the S side, environmentally sensitive Oxleas Wood scuppered ELRIC – or at least that was the excuse the government found for not spending the money. In the old scheme the road was to go right though to the A2 at Falconwood. The new scheme may well be less ambitious, routing the traffic further E along the A2106 towards Erith and Dartford. A new idea has surfaced for a rail tunnel under the river at Woolwich, which could link Newham's rail lines to those in South London. Here we enter the realm of the grandiose Thames Corridor plans – which make the various Docklands schemes sound like toy town.

Education is one of Newham's new priorities – it used to be considered something you put up with before getting a job in the docks. Now there's a university – the University of East London – with campuses at Stratford, Barking and (now building) alongside Royal Victoria Dock. The new campus will stress design and technology, and will be linked to a technology park, with two dozen 'business incubation units' for new hi-tech companies.

Recreation has gained from Docklands' water sports centres. And the S of the borough is already famous for the Beckton Alps dry ski slope – officially called 'Mountaintop'.

Up until 1996 Newham Council actively encouraged housing associations to develop land but now it wants more private developers to come into the borough. They believe that now there is more private than council housing. According to the late-1998 Land Registry figures, Newham is still the second-cheapest London borough to buy in after neighbouring Barking and Dagenham. Prices were still rising briskly in Newham in the summer of 1998 when other areas had slowed down: a 10 per cent rise was recorded in the year to September.

Turning to the area's homes, over a quarter of Newham's houses were destroyed in the Blitz. This, plus the borough's legacy of poor housing, led to a programme of slum clearance and regeneration: the result was 115 tower blocks (reduced now to less than 100 after the most notorious were blown up), post-war terraces, recent gentrification of the few remaining Victorian villas, and a general '70s cladded tattiness. But the 1980s saw a renewal of private new-build, with the stress on low-rise developments. Newham still has drab, seedy districts. Equally, most parts are affordable: house prices in six figures are rare.

Newham is crossed by main and trunk roads en route from Central London to Essex; ubiquitous tubes and train services provide good links to the City, West End and Essex suburbs. In the S the Woolwich ferry service crosses the Thames.

Stratford is the nerve centre, dominating the N of Newham. The shopping mall and the Theatre Royal, which found fame under the legendary Joan Littlewood, are huddled together on an island in the middle of a permanent carousel of traffic herding to and from the nearby City. Stratford could have a golden future if the Channel Tunnel rail link ever gets built (work has started on the line – but only on Phase I, out in Kent.

the London end is Phase II . . .). Stratford would be a major rail interchange between the Continent and all points N of London. The Jubilee line tube is a certainty (by end 1999? – the cliff-hanger still continues): links to the Millennium Dome, the South Bank and Westminster.

Dick Turpin lived in Plaistow and married a girl from East Ham. It's not too hard to imagine Black Bess galloping down the wide thoroughfare of the **Barking Rd**, now a monument to the congested 20th century. It can take nearly an hour to creep from Canning Town on the western tip of Newham to East Ham on a No 15 bus at rush hour, even though the A13 has off-loaded much of the City-bound traffic.

South of the A13 lies the Docklands. This diverse and crowded collection of communities includes the Royal Docks, the largest group of enclosed docks in the world and once the pride of the Port of London.

Follow Newham's eastern frontier, the River Roding, northwards and you eventually hit Little Ilford, sitting to the W of its larger namesake and perched on Newham's NE edge. The **Romford Rd** takes you back to town through cosmopolitan Manor Park and up-and-coming Forest Gate back to Stratford. To the SW lies West Ham – industrial, terraced and cheap. The map shows the differences between the two Hams: East is newer, with regular grids of terraced houses dating from 1880–1914; West Ham is older, less rigidly laid out, with a mix of homes, some very basic, and prices to match. Flat conversions are generally rare in Newham because the council does not allow properties under 1,184 sq ft to be converted – and most Newham homes are smaller than this.

Stratford

After the Royals, Stratford is the area facing the most change locally over the next 5–10 years. Its transport will be transformed by the Jubilee line and the new link road to the M11. The Safeway superstore in **The Grove** should open this year. This development includes a new parade of shops, a library, hotel and parking for 300 cars. In **Salway Rd** a performing arts centre is planned to complement the existing Theatre Royal which is presently being renovated. The road now also boasts a new 4-screen multiplex cinema, Stratford Picture House, that specializes in first-run and arthouse movies. On **Great Eastern Rd** work is about to start on a major office block next to the present bus station.

Stratford's young and optimistic atmosphere is attracting home-buyers who work in the City or Docklands yet who need cheap housing. You can spend as little as £35,000 and buy a studio flat, while £70,000 gets you a 2-bed house in a decent road. Maryland Point was a bustling agricultural village in the 17th century; today it marks Stratford's northern tip, on the outskirts of Leytonstone. This is where you'll find the real **Albert Square**: an anticlimax of a road that doesn't resemble a square or 'The Square'. Neatly anonymous terraces line this street – and, indeed, most of the area bounded by **Forest Lane** to the S and Forest Gate to the E. But don't knock it until you've had a look: new flats are to be found there and they are modestly priced. On the other side of **Leytonstone Rd** you can pick up a newish 2-bedroomed terrace for about £70,000 – a word of warning though: it's pretty isolated here. No tubes or shops. Closer in to Stratford centre, **Windmill Lane** and **Carolina Close** are popular for their purpose-built flats. These and nearby roads could be well-placed for the Stratford International station and associated developments on the goods yard to the W.

Move further S and the picture brightens – follow **West Ham Lane** past Queen Mary's Square, an enclave of 1980s 1- and 2-bedroomed flats. This Countryside development is part privately owned and part rented to East London Housing Association tenants. Prices were pocket-money, and flats were instantly snapped up when new because it's so convenient (and next to the police station).

The **Portway** is a pleasure, and opposite the surprisingly verdant West Ham Park. Don't stick to the road itself – slip down one of the side-streets. **Church St North** is definitely mewsy; walk through here and you'll catch a glimpse of what Stratford could be all about. Recently built town-houses stand elegant in the privacy of this quiet off-shoot. Across West Ham Park, **Mathews Park Avenue** is in the perhaps optimistically named 'Little Hampstead of Stratford'; bigger houses are situated here (3-bed, £90,000-plus), the location is excellent: 12 min walk from the station and close to the park. No restaurants, but the local pubs are good. This area is tipped as the best place to buy in Stratford – leafy **Ham Park Rd**, which skirts the park, especially: here the properties are large, Victorian and have lots of original features. Prices have gone up by £10,000 a house since late 1997. A 5-bed house could set you back £180–200,000.

Plashet

There has been some investment in the area's largest shopping centre, **Green St**, with the old Ace cinema being demolished to make way for much-needed car parking. The grubby parade of shops by the cinema are to be replaced by new shop units and also some housing. Plashet has some of Newham's more desirable homes and a highly regarded girls' school. Look in **Stopford Rd** for family homes: 3-bed and large pre-war houses at £70–85,000. The neighbourhood extends N and S along **Plashet Rd** to **Green St** and **High St North**, East Ham. The cluster of streets to the N of **Plashet Rd** is known as Upton: slightly smarter than Upton Park, and with the use of the latter's tube station.

Huge Edwardian mansions line the **Romford Rd**, heading towards Forest Gate: many have been converted into B&Bs, others remain run-down – definitely room for tidying-up and conversion here. But you'd better consider double glazing and a bus pass, for town-houses and terraces are set nearer the road, traffic charges through day and night, and double yellow lines extend to Ilford. For the more up-market (or un-handy) buyer, East Ham and parts of Forest Gate are a better starting point.

Forest Gate

'Up-and-coming' are the enthusiastic words which spring to estate agents' lips when they mention Forest Gate. The neighbourhood has long been considered the jewel of Newham's crown, with larger Victorian houses still very much sought-after by agents.

Capel Rd overlooks Wanstead Flats, the southernmost outpost of Epping Forest (hence 'Forest Gate'). Don't be surprised to see cows wandering off the flats onto this speed-humped and very popular street. Although it has an E7 postcode, **Capel Rd's** £135,000 family-sized terraces face desirable homes across the park in Redbridge.

'Woodgrange Village' isn't really a village, but an estate agent's term for the gentrified area bordering less-fashionable Manor Park. Great for home-buyers who prefer more salubrious surroundings and don't mind travelling by train. The conservation area of the Woodgrange estate instantly 'ups' the price of houses in this part of Forest Gate, and even the nearby run-down council blocks are undergoing a face-lift, so buying here could be a shrewd move. Council policy is to permit no more building here to preserve the area's character. Prices for a 2-bedroomed terrace are around the £72,000 mark near the pretty little station. The Woodgrange estate itself boasts handsome 1880s villas in orderly, leafy streets to the E of **Woodgrange Rd**. Wander down **Richmond Rd**, **Hampton Rd** or **Windsor Rd** to view these regal residences, which might cost anything from £130–160,000 depending on their condition. Some have front drives and distinctive, original glass porches extending across the width of the house, fringed with decorative wooden 'teeth'. Stratford is a mere two stops down the track and the City 15 min thereafter.

Manor Park

Manor Park is largely devoted to resting places. Lacquer-black horse-and-carriage Cockney funerals regularly plod to the huge City of London Cemetery and Manor Park's own smaller graveyard. But the area itself is far from dead; it's brash, bustling and cosmopolitan, especially in the area around the **Romford Rd** – indeed, one of the most important developments planned here is a block of around 100 homes on part of the site of the present Woodgrange Cemetery. **Romford Rd** lies just to the S of the railway track, a useful natural boundary. The South Woodford to Barking Relief Rd (A406) forms the E boundary, **High St North** the W, and East Ham's tube line cuts across to the S.

The neighbourhood of Little Ilford provides a quiet backwater, and the parks and playing-fields in the W of Manor Park form a welcome break from the row upon row of terraced housing. The heart of Manor Park is a comparatively sleepy area centring around poetic-sounding streets – **Browning Road, Coleridge Avenue, Shakespeare Crescent** and **Shelley Avenue** reside here. Three-bed terraces in these ever-popular streets fetch around £85,000 (for a large one). £65,000 is a reasonable price to pay for a 2-bed Victorian terrace. Flat conversions abound: £52,000 buys a large 2-bed flat and £45,000 is the going rate for a 1-bed period conversion. Popular homes for first-time buyers are 1-bed flats above shops in **Romford Rd**, which go for around £38,000. Yes, compared to the rest of London it's dirt cheap, but entertainment-wise there's not much to recommend it, unless you fancy a trip to nearby Ilford for a taste of night clubbing. But it is near East Ham tube station, Woodgrange Park and Manor Park stations, and the area boasts some marvellous Indian restaurants.

Capel Manor is the jewel in Manor Park's crown. A Grade II listed manor house was carefully converted 10 years ago into luxury flats, with town-houses neatly attached to its flanks. Resale prices: flats range from £72,000 and houses cost £135–160,000.

Plaistow and West Ham

Plaistow is deceptively large, running from the station along the **High St**, down **Greengate St** and **Prince Regent Lane** to the A13. To the E it extends to the Abbey Arms pub on the **Barking Rd**, continuing to **Green St** which marks the Boleyn neighbourhood of Upton Park. Scattered between the stock-brick terraces are new purpose-built flats. A Wimpey development of such flats lies tucked away behind the Memorial Recreation Ground (the birthplace of West Ham Football Club). Rowan Court in the **Broadway** and flats in **Plaistow Park Rd** offer a similar style. For something slightly cheaper, larger and older look in **Balaam St** (pronounced Bale-am).

Plaistow allegedly means a place where people gather to play, and if you are sports-mad a house near the roaring **Newham Way** (A13) could be ideal – a fantastic new leisure centre has just been built here. To the N of the road lies a spacious neighbourhood. Houses in **Holborn Rd**, **Botha Rd** and **Denmark St** have more breathing space – but they are treacherously near the busy A13. And you are a fair walk from the tube station here.

Local estate agents report a rise in the popularity of the New City estate in Plaistow, a triangular grid of around 15 roads of terraced 20th-century houses centring on **New City Rd**, with **Boundary Rd** marking the E edge, **Barking Rd** (the A124) the N and **Tunmarsh Lane** to the S. This district abuts the well-regarded Central Park estate in East Ham (see opposite).

One of the most important changes to West Ham will be the opening, probably late in 1999, of the new interchange for West Ham station connecting the Fenchurch to Tilbury line, the Jubilee Line Extension, and the District line. West Ham is still the cheapest end of the borough to live and, in terms of the capital, it is the innermost. Much of West Ham's housing is owned by Newham Council: the rest is small and terraced. West Ham can seem like an industrial wasteland to the uninitiated. Don't be fooled by the A–Z map – West Ham, to locals, is considered to be the area around the tube station, nowhere near West Ham Park, Stratford (see page 456). This confusion arises from the days before Newham when the borough existed as East Ham and West Ham. West Ham Town Hall, for example, is in the middle of Stratford.

West Ham itself is a small area roughly consisting of the streets off **Manor Rd**, where a 2-bed terrace can cost around £67,000. In the late 1980s Barratt beautifully modernized the old council estate – now retitled Woodlands, the flats are huge and very smart. To the W of **Manor Rd**, Gainsborough Park is a big, 1990-vintage development between West Ham and Canning Town.

Upton Park and East Ham

Upton Park is a fairly small neighbourhood, stretching from the tube station in **Green St** down to the Boleyn pub on the **Barking Rd** and extending eastward to **Katherine Rd**. Purpose-built flats and new terraces are scattered in the streets around the football ground. West Ham Football Club's Upton Park ground has undergone a huge rebuilding programme. There are plans to rebuild the West Stand to three tiers taking the capacity from its present 26,000 to 36,000. **Inniskilling Rd** typifies the older-style streets crammed with 2-bed terraces which go for around £67,000. East Ham's better for shopping, and Upton Park's Queens Market has recently had a council-financed facelift.

East Ham is considered to be the best part of Newham. House prices reflect this. Central Park is a popular inter-war terraced estate. **Cotswold Gardens** contains the only line of semis on the estate, which sell for £92,000 or so. **Lonsdale Rd**, **Henniker Gardens**, **Haldane Rd** and most of the other streets contain 2-bed '30s terraces – some with ground-floor bathrooms. All have neat gardens at the rear which are secluded and much cherished. £77,000 seems to be the current bench-mark set for such properties. **Central Park Rd** and its off-shoots contain larger, often pebbledashed, versions. Houses in this area boast 3 double bedrooms and go on the market for close to £90,000.

For convenience, investigate the streets on the E side of **High St North**. Streets like **Lathom Rd**, **Caulfield Rd**, **Clements Rd** and **Skeffington Rd** are within easy reach of the tube and close to the shops. Apart from the usual high street stores East Ham has the covered market, an Aladdin's cave of goodies at knock-down (possibly knocked-off?) prices. It's 'Onest East End round here; just go into one of the cafés and listen to the tales you overhear. And you won't have to pay West End prices for a dainty lunchtime sandwich here – bacon, eggs, sausages and fried slice are more the menu.

Burges Rd, **Leigh Rd** and **Watson Rd** are situated close to the new A406. But don't worry, these rat-runs have now been blocked off, leaving a quiet, respectable neighbourhood to clock up the house prices. £85–90,000 for a 3-bedroomed house hereabouts. Pockets of select 4-bedroomed dwellings can also be found in this corner of East Ham.

But there's a big difference between East Ham's **High St South** and **High St North**: look to the E of **High St South** and you'll see suburbs mirroring those in Central Park but a fraction cheaper. The huge minareted town hall divides the 'posher' south and the less-well-favoured north of East Ham.

According to local agents, East Ham has gone up in the world since part of **High St North** was pedestrianized. A new leisure centre here is due to open in 1999. An extension to the present East Ham shopping centre is on the cards: several retail firms have their eyes on it, say insiders.

Beckton and Custom House

As the Royals return to the Newham Council fold, the old names are being used more: Silvertown, S of the docks and N of the Thames, Custom House on the N side of the docks, Canning Town at the W end towards the Lea valley. The Royal Docks is one of the biggest urban development areas in Europe: see introduction, and Docklands chapter.

Canning Town was a slum as early as 1855, and the devastation caused by bombing in World War II gave the opportunity for the building of enormous municipal estates. But then the Docks closed, and the sprawling estates lost their economic mainspring. Five years ago cautious people from West Ham would avoid Canning Town after nightfall: today things are improving. Canning Town and Custom House very nearly died with the docks: the flood of '53 almost assured them a watery grave. The Thames Barrier takes away that risk, and the community soldiers on in mainly council tower blocks and terraces. The council has just begun a £21 million programme to revive Canning Town, and new housing is appearing.

The Docklands boom has at least meant this part is no longer cut off: the DLR rail link, and sundry new roads, have joined these districts onto London. By the end of 1999 a tube station at Canning Town will make it possible to get to the Millennium Dome as well as just gaze at it. Among homes with a view of the white blob across the river are those at Barrier Point and Britannia Village, both between the river and the S side of the Royal Victoria Dock. Barrier Point (by Barratt) is a big scheme with tower and other blocks, river views and a 23-acre park. The 1/2-bed flats are from £89,000 (543 sq ft) to £160,000 (895 sq ft, 2-bed with large terrace). As the economy slowed last winter Wimpey stopped work on Britannia Village, another 1,200-home site accessed via **Britannia Gate**, which was progressing at 300 homes a year. This still leaves plenty to buy: in January Wimpey had 2-bed flats from £108,000, from £142,000 with a dock view. More homes will be ready from March to July.

Further E, in the rather cut-off neighbourhood of North Woolwich, Fairview are building 900 homes at Gallions Reach overlooking the Thames: the first tranche will be released in 1999. Housing associations are active here with shared-ownership schemes like that in **Fernhill St**: £36,000 for a 60 per cent share in a new 2-bed house.

To the E, Beckton saw some early, and successful, Docklands-inspired housing. The new estates were Docklands' first concentration of cheap new homes and a runaway success. Beckton is now well-established with a brisk resale market in its modern homes (none over 15 years old), but less new-build. Local agents produce special Beckton property lists: 1-bed flats start below £40,000, while houses start at £65,000: under £100,000 buys you a 3-bed one with a garage and a good garden.

Transport	Tubes: Stratford, West Ham (Central & Jubilee); Plaistow, East Ham (District – and Hammersmith & City during peak hours). From Stratford: Oxford Circus 30 min, City 12 min, Heathrow 90 min (1 change). DLR: Stratford and Royals Docks to Tower, Isle of Dogs. Trains: Stratford (Liverpool St 8 min), others see map.
Convenient for	City, Docklands, City Airport; Epping Forest, M11; A12, A13 for M25. Miles from centre: 7.
Schools	Local Authority: Brampton Manor, Cumberland, Eastlea, Forest Gate, Langdon, Lister, Little Ilford, Plashet, Rokeby, Sarah Bonnell, Stratford, Trinity, Woodside, St Angela's RC, St Bonaventures RC, St John's RC. Private: Grangewood.

SALES

Flats	S	1B	2B	3B	4B	5B
Average prices	28–40	35–50	35–60	45–65	–	–
Houses	2B	3B	4B	5B	6/7B	8B
Average prices	50–75	60–100	75–200	–	–	–

RENTAL

Flats	S	1B	2B	3B	4B	5B
Average prices	300–400	400–540	450–650	550–750	600–800	–
Houses	2B	3B	4B	5B	6/7B	8B
Average prices	550–700	650–800	700–950	–	–	–

The properties   Largely 1900s terraces of 2/3-bed homes and p/b flats. Woodgrange Park boasts large period houses, now mostly flats. East Ham's Central Park estate has mainly inter-war family homes. Custom House and Beckton have wide tracts of new homes, as do Royal Docks.

The market   Prime hunting-ground for first-rung-of-the-ladder home-buyers with some very affordable homes. At the other end of the scale the handsome Woodgrange estate conservation area houses cost up to £160,000. Local searches: 2 weeks.

Among those estate agents active in this area are:
- Douglas Allen Spiro
- Bairstow Eves
- Guardian Estates
- Halifax
- Adam Kennedy
- Taylors
- Abbotts
- Chandler
- Spicer McColl
- J Webb
- A J Scott
- McDowalls
- Bryants
- Michael Steven
- Suttons

N

NOTTING HILL AND NORTH KENSINGTON

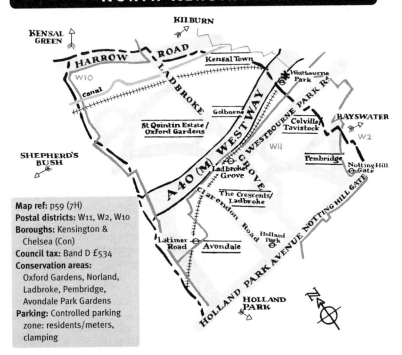

Map ref: p59 (7H)
Postal districts: W11, W2, W10
Boroughs: Kensington &
  Chelsea (Con)
Council tax: Band D £534
Conservation areas:
  Oxford Gardens, Norland,
  Ladbroke, Pembridge,
  Avondale Park Gardens
Parking: Controlled parking
  zone: residents/meters,
  clamping

Notting Hill's image has moved in a generation from seedy to svelte. The area has retained its arty, bohemian air and has added a solid note of respectability. North Kensington, ever the poorer relation, has made real gains in status. Both areas prospered during the early 1990s when other parts of London stagnated. Now, Notting Hill is a key point on the circuit of fashionable London: cosmopolitan, raffish, a bit daring – the antithesis of Fulham. However, this is still an area of striking contrast, where £1 million-plus houses can be found in the same street as council blocks. To generalize, the wealthy and respectable live on top of the hill in their big family houses backing on to acres of delightful communal gardens, and the poor and the unconventional at the bottom. The big houses have, in many cases, seen a revival in their status: until the 1970s the area was a warren of bed-sits and dilapidation.

Notting Hill is the area N of **Notting Hill Gate**, bounded on the E by the border between Kensington Borough and the City of Westminster, and on the W by Holland Park neighbourhood (see chapter). The N border with North Kensington is by some reckoned to be the elevated M40 motorway, the **Westway**; by others to be further S, at the foot of the quite distinct slope on which Notting Hill sits. Certainly the corner to the NW, in the angle of the M40 and the M41, is not Notting Hill. It used to be called Notting Dale, and was a notorious slum, but is now known as Avondale, and is a mix of private, housing association and council homes. Certainly, all of Notting Hill is in W11, but not all W11 is Notting Hill. All of W10 lying S of the **Harrow Rd** is North Kensington: a small part of W10 forms the Queen's Park neighbourhood of Kilburn and Kensal.

Over the years, the less well-off have been pushed further N by gentrification. This accounts for the high proportion of council and housing trust developments in the relatively deprived N of the borough, particularly in Golborne and Kensal Town. The mix of social classes and the multi-racial nature of the area, with its large West Indian, Moroccan and Filipino communities, make Notting Hill/North Kensington a cosmopolitan and lively place to live. The streets are busy at midnight, and there is a distinct inner-city feel to the place. This character in recent years has attracted first art galleries then cafés, bars and restaurants to the area, which now rivals Soho.

Whereas property prices in the rest of Kensington and Chelsea are beyond the means of all but the well-off, people on moderate incomes are still able to get a foothold on the property ladder in this area. This is partly thanks to the council's Right to Buy scheme which encouraged tenants to become leaseholders. Local housing associations also operate shared-ownership schemes which allow the tenant to part-own their home – the Rootes site development in North Kensington is one such place where this is happening.

At the same time, the well-off get better value for money here than in other parts of Kensington and Chelsea. Houses are generally cheaper, there are probably more communal gardens than anywhere else in London and the area is well-placed with direct underground links to the West End and City. However, the grandest parts of the Hill are now on a par, in reputation and price, with Holland Park. There is plenty of property to rent here: investors have been active for some time and there are lots of flats and a good sprinkling of houses. Flats to rent are especially plentiful in the SE corner of the area, towards **Notting Hill Gate** and **Queensway**, and around **Ladbroke Grove**, which has been boosted by the new BBC complex in nearby White City.

One unusual feature of the housing scene here is the domination by housing trusts. These own very large amounts of property – usually homes they have bought up and converted, though some are new-build. Unlike council properties, these homes are dotted around in otherwise owner-occupied streets. And once in housing association hands they stay that way, never being resold. This 'freezes' whole sections of streets and reduces the number of homes on the open market.

Two major street events also shape the character of the area – the internationally famous **Portobello Rd** market (Saturdays) and the annual Notting Hill Carnival, Europe's biggest street festival. It draws more than 2 million people to the area every August Bank Holiday weekend. The festivities are usually concentrated in the Colville/Tavistock and Golborne neighbourhoods. For two days, the streets are alive with pulsating rhythms and superbly colourful floats. Residents either love it or hate it. Carnival is notably more peaceful than in previous years, and is more organized, with sound systems now having to be registered and illegal systems banned. Despite this, many locals leave town for the Bank Holiday weekend: there are even plans to organize evacuation of groups of locals. A new event is the Portobello Festival which brings a week of music, literature and arts to the area.

Portobello Rd has had a market since the 1860s when it was known as The Lane. Antiques, bric-a-brac, fruit-and-vegetable and clothing stalls spread for two-thirds of a mile along the road from **Simon Close** to **Golborne Rd**, with the antiques concentrated at the S end. The market is a major tourist attraction, drawing thousands of visitors to the street every Saturday. Council proposals to tidy it up brought a flurry of protests from locals, who like it the way it is: scruffy and lively. Controlled parking came to North Kensington last year to the dismay of some stall holders, who find it restricts their access to the market.

The social N-S divide in the area is accentuated by the physical barrier of the **Westway** elevated motorway. Built in the mid-'60s, it runs S of **Cambridge Gardens**. The space under the **Westway** has been put to good use by the North Kensington

Amenity Trust. Small community groups, community transport groups, a fitness centre, centre for the elderly and an information point can be found in the archways. The latest occupant is a large new restaurant close to Ladbroke Grove tube. Long-term residents include the group of travellers whose caravans have been parked below the **Westway** near Shepherd's Bush since the early 1970s.

Ladbroke Grove is the area's main traffic artery, stretching from the desirable leafy S boundary of the neighbourhood to the scruffy N border. The main shopping centre for the area is **Notting Hill Gate** to the S, the eastward continuation of **Holland Park Avenue**. **Notting Hill Gate** also boasts two cinemas (at the moment) and a number of popular restaurants and pubs. The Electric Cinema in **Portobello Rd**, reckoned the only surviving purpose-built cinema in Europe, has been saved from development after a very typical North Ken campaign. It will be restored and will reopen with a restaurant attached. On a more prosaic level Sainsbury's store at the N end of **Ladbroke Grove** has brought superstore shopping to the area.

Rising property prices and general prosperity have led residents to spend money on their homes, and there has been a rash of painting, decorating and modernizing. However, the council's planners are tightening controls, making it harder to extend homes upwards (loss of light is feared) and downwards.

Notting Hill

This is the smarter half of the area, but even here the contrasts can be great: serene mansions to the south, stimulating street-life to the north.

Pembridge

Pembridge stretches N from Notting Hill Gate as far as **Westbourne Grove**, bounded by the W by **Kensington Park Rd** and on the E by **Chepstow Place** and **Ossington St**. The eastern part of the neighbourhood is in W2. **Pembridge Rd**, the S half of the main route between the Gate and **Westbourne Grove**, leads into the heart of this sedate and leafy neighbourhood. To the E lies **Pembridge Square**, the only one in the borough lined by large detached villas. The 4-storey ornamental stucco houses overlook a narrow private central garden. Some remain as family homes but many have been converted, a few into hotels and schools: scaffolding is a feature of the area as the tall buildings are painted and tidied. The E side of the square is across the borough boundary in Westminster.

South of the square, a short walk from bustling **Notting Hill Gate**, are the cul-de-sacs of **Linden** and **Clanricarde Gardens**. In **Linden Gardens** is The Limes, a 6-storey modern development with private parking. There is also the private, gated **Linden Mews** with its quaint brick houses and **Garden Mews** where four new houses can be found. Tall ornate stucco terraces characterize both streets. In **Clanricarde Gardens**, the large houses of bed-sits are gradually being converted into smart flats. A council school stands at the end of the street. The scale changes in **Ossington St** on the E edge of the neighbourhood. Here terraces of smaller stucco houses face the backs of buildings fronting **Palace Court**. At the end of the street is little **Victoria Grove Mews**. More large houses are found N of **Pembridge Square** in leafy **Pembridge Place** and **Dawson Place**. Both are lined by paired stucco villas with front gardens. **Dawson Place** also has detached villas, some with the same decorative cast-iron and glass entrance canopies as the imposing Victorian mansions in Holland Park. Prices are not dissimilar: to around £3 million if really smart. Groups and pairs of substantial houses curve around **Pembridge Villas**, the N half of the main route through the neighbourhood. Two houses here were £675,000 each in December: they needed total modernization having been multi-occupied. Leading off to the NW, **Pembridge Crescent** has more groups and pairs of stucco villas. These contrast with the 2-storey painted cottages in **Pembridge Mews**.

Chepstow Crescent, which has mainly 3/4-storey brick and stucco terraces with wrought-iron balconies and a couple of hideous post-war flats blocks, leads into tree-lined **Chepstow Villas**, considered the most prestigious address in the neighbourhood. About half of the elegant paired stucco or brick-and-stucco villas remain as family houses. Leading N from here into the Colville/Tavistock neighbourhood is **Ledbury Rd**, a pleasant and smart street of 3-storey stucco houses with antique and designer clothes shops, galleries and bars. (Only 25 years ago an architectural author warned his readers not to walk down this street alone.) A new addition is the 2-storey **Ledbury Mews East** development. Behind the much-improved Walmer Castle pub is a clutch of workshops, and Westbourne Grove Church hides tiny **St John's Mews** with more. **Denbigh Rd** has a mix of properties ranging from Longlands Court council estate to low-rise modern brick homes and painted stucco houses. **West Hill Court** is a new mews of 2/3-bed flats reached via an archway opposite the council estate. A winged stucco arch halfway along the E side leads through to **Pencombe Mews**, a group of 3-storey town-houses.

The W side of the neighbourhood is dominated by **Portobello Rd**, although only part of the famous market falls within its boundaries. S of **Chepstow Villas** stands a row of charming gaily painted 2-storey stucco cottages with front gardens. Street trees add to the leafy look. These face the backs of the big red-brick and stone 1890s flats blocks fronting **Kensington Park Rd**. Lying at the rear of the cottages is **Simon Close**, a small cul-de-sac of modern 2-storey town-houses.

Although this stretch of **Portobello Rd** is quiet during the week, on Saturdays it is invaded by thousands of tourists from all over the world heading for the market. Antique stalls spread along both sides of the street, spilling around into **Denbigh Close**, a pleasant cobbled cul-de-sac of mews cottages, some with roof terraces. **Denbigh Terrace**, one street away, has an attractive pastel-shaded stucco terrace of 2/3-storey and basement family houses on the southern side, looking across to Longlands Court council estate.

N

Stucco is the trademark of the Ladbroke area. The pillared porch, the rusticated stucco around the ground-floor window, the steps, the railings, the balcony, all are typical of these large houses. Many are now flats, which benefit from the lofty rooms. Many of the houses back onto communal gardens: the area was planned as one estate, though built over quite a long period.

The Crescents/Ladbroke

This is the most prosperous and elegant part of the area, set on the highest ground at the top of the hill, and benefiting from an expansive street-plan of crescents and gardens. The area dates from the mid-Victorian age and many large houses survive undivided. **Clarendon Rd** on the W edge of the neighbourhood sets the tone of this highly desirable area. The best stretch, between **Lansdowne Walk** and the smart Clarendon Cross shops, has big paired brick and stucco villas with front gardens. South of here are terraces of 3-storey and basement Victorian houses, modern town-houses and flats. North of the junction with **Elgin Crescent**, the street becomes more mixed and less attractive with the appearance of council blocks and a parade of shops. However, a terrace of 4-storey pastel houses on the E side has the advantage of backing on to the beautiful communal gardens between **Elgin Crescent** and **Blenheim Crescent**.

Terraces of 3-storey together with semi-basement houses line both sides of tree-lined **Blenheim Crescent**. Properties on the S side back on to the communal gardens. **Blenheim Crescent** is like a different street to the E across **Ladbroke Grove**, combining a mix of private (S), council and housing trust properties (N), which merge with the shops, pubs and cafés in the stretch between **Kensington Park Rd** and **Portobello Rd**. Tucked away here is **Codrington Mews**.

Leafy **Elgin Crescent**, more salubrious and sought-after than Blenheim, has terraces of mainly 3-storey painted stucco houses with basements and attic windows. Huge communal gardens lie at the rear on both sides of the street. As with **Blenheim Crescent**, many houses have been converted into flats.

South of **Elgin Crescent**, the streets climb uphill. **Arundel Gardens** has mainly 4-storey brick and stucco terraces with small ornate iron balconies on the first floor. **Ladbroke Gardens** is lined by ornate stucco terraces with attic windows. This street leads into **Stanley Crescent** with its huge 6-storey brick and stucco paired villas at the bottom of the hill, and a terrace of 4- and 5-storey ornate painted stucco houses at the top. Interesting gaps and intriguing arches between the houses give glimpses of the sky, trees and gardens at the rear. The houses overlook communal gardens between the Crescent and **Kensington Park Gardens**.

The summit of the hill was developed in the form of an oval cut in two by **Ladbroke Grove**. **Stanley Crescent** forms one half of the oval, and across the Grove to the W is the complementary **Lansdowne Crescent**. An elegant white 'iced wedding cake' terrace curves halfway round the semi-circle to the N. The richly decorated houses have distinctive rounded façades and Corinthian-columned entrance porches. Big paired brick and stucco villas, stone-gabled houses and some modern brick town-houses spread around the rest of the crescent.

More extensive communal gardens lie behind **Lansdowne Crescent** and **Lansdowne Rd**, another choice residential street, lined with trees taller than the buildings. Terraces of 3-storey and basement stucco painted houses, some gabled, wind around the hill, merging with pairs of villas where the street drops down again to **Holland Park Avenue**. South along **Lansdowne Rd**, at the junction of **St John's Gardens**, the road becomes 'No Entry'. You are now entering a complex series of one-way streets aimed at reducing traffic speed and flow: it can be very confusing. **Lansdowne Walk** has groups of handsome stucco and brick-and-stucco houses. On the NE corner of the street, set back from **Ladbroke Grove**, is Bartok House, considered one of the best blocks of flats in the Notting Hill area. The modern brown-brick development with its own communal gardens joins up with a terrace of brick and stucco houses (split into flats) and another modern flats block. These flats face **Ladbroke Grove** but are separated from the road by a private driveway and a screen of trees and lawns. Tall trees in the gardens surrounding St John's Church on the hilltop add to the leafy outlook. The church spire can be seen from miles around rising above the treetops. This stretch of **Ladbroke Grove** and the leg between **Ladbroke Square** and **Ladbroke Rd** (attractive 4-storey wide-fronted painted stucco houses) are the best sections of this long road.

Lying between the houses in **Kensington Park Gardens** and **Ladbroke Square** are the largest private gardens in the borough – indeed, at 7 acres, one of the largest in London. Despite its name **Ladbroke Square** is made up of a long terrace of 4- and 5-storey brick and stucco houses on one side of the street, facing the gardens. Most are divided into flats. The gardens are enclosed by tall trees and hedges, and street trees stretch along adjoining roads as far as the eye can see.

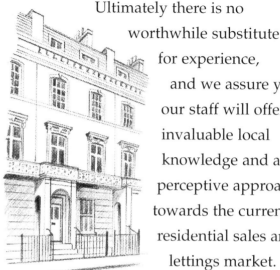

Ladbroke Rd, a relatively busy but pleasant local road, has a mix of smaller terraces: Bonham House, a 4-storey block of flats, big detached houses and a 5-storey 1900s flats block. Traffic has been slowed by a new roundabout at the junction with **Ladbroke Terrace**. Notting Hill police station stands on the corner with **Ladbroke Grove** and the Kensington Temple at the E junction with **Pembridge Rd**. Leading off here are a series of small streets and cobbled mews including **Wilby Mews**. The mews, tucked in behind the flower-bedecked Ladbroke Arms pub, has a mix of little 2- and 3-storey cottages and five new houses set around a wide inner courtyard. More low, painted Victorian cottages are found in **Horbury Mews**. **Horbury Crescent** has curving terraces of larger brick and stucco properties. Hidden away behind the houses at the SE end of **Ladbroke Rd** and the shops in **Pembridge Rd** and **Notting Hill Gate** is **Bulmer Mews**, a development of 2-storey brown-brick houses with garages (1987).

Forming the E border of the neighbourhood is **Kensington Park Rd**, a busy bus route. Terraces of 3-storey brick and stucco buildings with shops, restaurants and wine bars on the lower floors line the N end of the street. They give way to terraces on the W side, broken up by stretches of the area's splendid communal gardens and Kelvin Court, a 5-storey block of flats. Really grand houses in this road have sold for £3 million; some famous names have homes here. Last December a more everyday 4-bed one was on the market for £800,000.

Avondale

Newly created private squares and mews stand amid large council estates and housing association developments in this very mixed, rather confusingly laid out but increasingly fashionable neighbourhood in the W of the area. It is on the border with Hammersmith Borough, and is cut off to the W and N by motorways.

The W end of **Lancaster Rd**, a short walk from Ladbroke Grove station and the shops clustered around it, combines residential, education, health and light industrial uses. A terrace of 3-storey and basement brick and stucco houses, many split into flats, lines the NE arm of the street. Opposite stands the Royalty Studios, a complex of studios/workshops. Next door is the London Lighthouse HIV/AIDS hospice and support centre. Standing alongside is the City of Westminster College annex, empty while its future is debated. Thomas Jones Primary School is tucked in behind.

Ruston Mews, in the shadow of the **Westway**, is a recent development of mews houses. **St Mark's Rd** leads under the **Westway** into **St Quintin Avenue**, a busy bus route. **Barlte Rd** runs between **Lancaster Rd** and the **Westway**. Off it are **St Andrew's** **Square** and **Wesley Square** with their modern 3-storey brick houses with off-street parking and pleasant communal gardens. Properties are shielded from **Lancaster Rd** by a high brick wall, adding to the sense of enclosure and privacy. Opposite is part of the large Lancaster West estate.

Beyond Notting Hill Methodist Church, **Lancaster Rd** becomes **Silchester Rd** and you cross into W10. Where the road ends with the junction of **Bramley Rd** Arthurs Court has been built, a 3-storey development. Opposite is the new 4-storey Goodrich Court, sited on **Bramley Rd** at the junction of **Darfield Way**, a dead-end road which leads onto the Silchester West Estate and **Waynflete Square** and **Shalfleet Drive**. Eleven new flats make up **Charlotte Mews**. The estate with its tower blocks spreads through **Verity Close** where it becomes a cul-de-sac of modern 2/3-storey red-brick terraced houses with small gardens. Some council houses are now appearing on the market. The remainder of the estate stretches along the N side of **Cornwall Crescent**, where it joins up with more council flats. A Victorian terrace stands on the S side.

More Victorian terraces are found to the N in **Ladbroke Crescent** – 3-storey, basement and attic, painted stucco houses converted into flats. At the NW end of **Walmer Rd** is Kensington Sports Centre with swimming and many other sports. More brick council blocks extend S along the street, leading to the smart **Hippodrome Mews** development. Here 3-storey brown-brick town-houses line two private mews overlooking Avondale Park. Terraces of modern brick low-rise housing association properties are found in **Wilsham St** and **Kenley Walk** S of the park and **Runcorn Place** and **Hesketh Place** to the N. Beside **Kenley Walk** and at the top of **Wilsham St** lies a new development of 2/3-storey town-houses. There is no way through for cars but pedestrians can walk to **Walmer Rd**.

Private residential property in the SW corner of the neighbourhood is concentrated in **Avondale Park Rd**, **Mary Place**, **Sirdar Rd**, **Stoneleigh Place** and **Stoneleigh St**, **Treadgold St** and **Grenfell Rd**. **Avondale Park Rd** has been cut off to form a cul-de-sac. Many of the 2/3-storey terraced houses found here are split into flats. Tucked away in the middle of this group is **Avondale Park Gardens**, a pleasant square of 2-storey brick artisan cottages with walled front gardens set around a small central green with trees. Avondale Park Primary School is also found here. The cottages, which were built by the former LCC after the World War I, passed on to the council, which gradually sold them off. Bordering this chunk of private property is the big Henry Dickens council estate, fronting **St Ann's Villas**.

Boundary changes in 1996 extended the Borough of Kensington and Chelsea in this area, removing an anomaly so that both W11 postcode and borough border now follow the physical barrier of the M41 highway. A clutch of streets W of Henry Dickens Court on **Bramley Rd** that used to be in Hammersmith and Fulham are now in the Royal Borough. **Rifle Place** leading into **St Katherine's Walk** is a new square of 3-storey flats in light brown-brick set around gardens. This development continues along **Bramley Rd** until the junction with **Freston Rd**. **Mortimer Square** with its low stucco and brick homes is another new addition. The Designers Guild building in **Olaf St** houses a collection of media companies: five new houses have just been built in front of it. This is an area rich in media-related companies and small business units and the Royal Borough is encouraging more to locate here. At the top end are residential blocks and other small business units. Just off the square, near the junction is a cul-de-sac with a collection of motor workshops and stucco and brick houses converted into offices.

The Harrow School Community Centre, which is going to be revamped using lottery money, Notting Dale Technology Centre and the Latimer Education Centre can be found in this tatty-looking road along with new 6-storey offices of a record company. **Bramley Rd**, which eventually runs into **St Helen's Gardens**, is made up of 2-storey stucco and brick homes, council flats, schools, pubs, shops and the Latimer Rd tube station. You will search in vain for **Latimer Rd**. It used to be here, but was cut off by the looming elevated motorway intersection.

This neighbourhood will be close to the proposed, enormous White City development just W of the motorway (see Shepherd's Bush chapter).

Colville/Tavistock

This is the heart of the 'other' Notting Hill, down the slope and a world away from the snowy crescents of Ladbroke. Even here, things are changing fast. **Westbourne Grove** with its proliferation of increasingly smart antique shops, galleries and other ways of spending money is a main W-E route between Notting Hill and Bayswater. Where **Westbourne Grove** meets **Denbigh Rd** is a little group of shops, graced by a modernist public loo and flower stall, on an island in the road, which has won architectural prizes. On Saturdays antique and bric-a-brac stalls spill around the corner into the NW arm of the street from the famous **Portobello Rd** market. Stucco/brick terraces line this end of **Westbourne Grove**, many of which have shops on the ground floor. **Lambton Mews**, with its health club and business premises, is tucked away to the S.

Around the corner on the E side of **Kensington Park Rd** is an attractive terrace of 3-storey and basement painted houses with front gardens. More antique shops are found at the S end of **Ledbury Rd**, beneath the 3/4-storey brick and stucco properties which stretch along the W side. The E side is in Westminster.

Off to the W is tree-lined **Lonsdale Rd**, probably the nicest street in the neighbourhood together with the S end of **Colville Rd**. Hidden between the two are **Colville Mews** and **Lonsdale Mews**, with businesses and homes. Attractive terraces of 3-storey painted houses stand in **Lonsdale Rd**, E of the brown-brick Portobello Court council estate, which spreads back to **Westbourne Grove**. Taller stucco terraces line the E side of **Colville Rd** and 4-storey semi-detached villas the W. **Colville Terrace** has 4/5-storey painted stucco houses, mostly converted into flats. This neighbourhood is showing the fruits of a long programme of council improvements.

Powis Square to the N has a mix of private 4-storey stucco terraced houses to the W and a long modern terrace of 4-storey brick council flats to the E. They lie on either side of a public garden with a children's playground in the middle. This is a popular street for DIY co-ownership schemes. Standing at the N end of the square is the Tabernacle Community Centre, recently revamped with lottery money and now boasting a community café.

Another public garden and playground lies to the W in **Colville Square**. Backing on to the E side of the garden is the 5-storey and basement Pinehurst Court flats block (painted stucco – and recently cheered up using City Challenge cash), which actually fronts **Colville Gardens**. It is set back off the road behind railings, lawn and trees, and the buildings are newly painted in cream and yellow. A 2-bed flat in this improving corner will set you back around £280,000. Overlooking the W side of **Colville Square** are more 4-storey and basement terraces. Lining the W side of the square in **Talbot Rd** are a series of tall modern red-brick housing trust flats blocks, including Daley Thompson House. The former Olympic champion was brought up in the area.

Westbourne Park Rd, another busy W-E road, contains mainly brick and stucco terraces with clusters of shops on the ground floor. The council's Covent Gardens Estate and a modern housing trust development take up the S side of the street from **Ladbroke Grove** to **Kensington Park Rd**. Off to the N is **All Saint's Rd**, once notorious only for drug dealing and street robberies, but now home to fashionable restaurants and other attractions. If not as forbidding to outsiders as it used to be, **All Saint's** is still not the place to take your nervous granny. In 1997 the council, in partnership with the police and City Challenge, introduced closed-circuit television (CCTV) into **All Saint's** and surrounding areas. This has improved the streets but some displacement is being felt by residents who live in **Clydesdale Rd** and **Westbourne Park Rd**.

Few homes in **All Saint's Rd** and the immediate streets are available for purchase. Most properties are 3/4-storey brick and stucco buildings with shops below. Standing at the SE end of the street is the Mangrove Community Association and restaurant, a traditional focal point for the local West Indian community. **All Saint's Rd** also lies in the heart of Carnival territory. The two day Notting Hill Carnival is concentrated in the streets around here (see area profile). Crossing **All Saint's Rd** and running parallel to **Westbourne Park Rd** is **St Luke's Mews**, with one end housing an interesting blue building with small offices and some new mews houses. On the opposite side of **All Saint's Rd**, the Mews continues with older more characteristic homes.

McGregor Rd off the E side of **All Saint's Rd** is lined by 3-storey and basement Victorian terraces. It is a designated play street from 8am to sunset. Traffic is banned during these hours except for access.

Long stepped terraces of modern yellow-brick housing trust co-ownership flats stretch along **Tavistock Crescent**. It runs into **Tavistock Rd** (3-storey brick and stucco terraces), which is pedestrianized at its W junctions with **Portobello Rd. Basing St,**

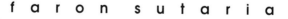

where cars are allowed, has 2-storey stucco and brick houses. This stretch of **Portobello Rd** takes in the heart of the market. Antique and bric-a-brac stalls line the section between **Westbourne Grove** and **Elgin Crescent** (Saturdays only). Fruit-and-veg stalls (Monday–Saturday) take over between here and the covered market under **Westway** – bric-a-brac, new and second-hand clothing (Saturdays). From **Acklam Rd** to **Golborne Rd** there is a junk market on Friday morning and Saturday.

Several small mews off the E side of **Portobello Rd** are used by market traders to store their barrows and stock. But **Alba Place**, a short cul-de-sac between **Lancaster** and **Westbourne Park Rds**, also has gaily painted 2/3-storey cottages, some with roofs terraces, at its E end. Opposite is **Hayden's Place**, a cobbled road with no homes but the Portobello Studios at the end. An up-market development of new red-brick cottages stands in **Dunworth Mews** between **Westbourne Park Rd** and **Talbot Rd**.

Lancaster Rd, which leads W to **Ladbroke Grove**, has mainly 3-storey terraces and paired villas in varying states of repair, divided into flats. The Serbian Orthodox Church and community centre stands on the S side nears the junction with the Grove across the road from the Lancaster Youth Club. The council library stands on the corner of **Ladbroke Grove** and **Lancaster Rd**. Next door to St Saviour's Church is the Campden Technical Institute (built and owned by Campden charities).

North Kensington

From here on we are N of the motorway, and into North Kensington and the W10 postcode. North Kensington has a fair amount of poverty, quite a lot of sub-standard housing and higher than average unemployment. This, plus the opportunities apparent in the area, helped in the winning of City Challenge government money in 1993. The agency has invested £35 million and attracted private finance for various economic, social and environmental projects.

Golborne

Golborne is tucked into the NE corner of the area, bounded by the railway line to the N and E and the **Westway** to the S. Most of the Golborne area is dominated by council and housing trust/association developments, mainly low-rise lookalike modern brick dwellings. They are concentrated in **Bevington Rd**, **Swinbrook Rd**, **Acklam Rd**, **Wornington Rd** and **St Ervan's Rd**.

Portobello Rd, **Golborne Rd** and **Ladbroke Grove** have some conversion flats, often above shops. These are the cheapest homes in the area – except for ex-local authority flats. The latter can start at £70,000 for a 1-bed flat, while a conversion will be at least £30,000 more. This stretch of **Portobello Rd** N of the Westway fly-over is on the fringe of the famous market. It is given over to stalls selling mainly second-hand clothing and household goods. More stalls spread along **Golborne Rd**, a bustling local shopping centre in its own right. **Wormington Rd** has council housing.

Kensal Town

In the far N of the area, and about as far in atmosphere from the lush Kensington heartlands, is Kensal Town. Crossing **Golborne Rd** railway bridge into Kensal Town is like entering another world. Grim concrete council blocks scar the landscape on the E side of this socially deprived neighbourhood lying between the railway line in the S and the Grand Union Canal in the N. Dominating the skyline at the gateway to Kensal Town is 30-storey Trellick Tower. This grey concrete 1970s council block is regularly singled out in opinion polls as one of the capital's biggest eyesores – but residents enjoy spacious flats and stunning views. Some flats are for sale: a 3-bed recently went for £130,000. However, most are still owned by the council or housing trusts.

The rest of Kensal is taken up by trading estates, workshops and industrial uses, mainly concentrated in **Kensal Rd**, with only a handful of private homes scattered about the neighbourhood. But this corner is home to two splendid community gardens: Meanwhile Gardens complete with wildlife section; and Emslie Horniman's Pleasance, a park which is being smartened up with lottery cash.

On the W side of **Ladbroke Grove** alongside the railway line is the 1930s Kensal House complex. A big Sainsbury's supermarket stands immediately to the N. Behind the supermarket site, between the railway line and the canal, is the 7-acre gasworks site, which stood vacant for 20 years until 1998. The Peabody Trust intends to build affordable housing, private homes and industrial units. On the other side of the canal in the NW corner of the neighbourhood is Kensal Green Cemetery, a favourite haunt of wildlife enthusiasts – and an official conservation area. A canal-side activity centre offers canoeing etc to young people.

St Quintin Estate/Oxford Gardens

This neighbourhood, cut off to the S by the **Westway**, is as distinct in its way as Golborne to the E. Immediately N of the motorway lies the main concentration of family homes. Hundreds of 2-storey, red-brick terraced houses, built between 1890 and 1925, dominate the SW corner, in **Oxford Gardens, Highlever Rd, Balliol Rd, Finstock Rd, Kingsbridge Rd, Kelfield Gardens, St Helen's Gardens, Wallingford Avenue** and the W end of **Barlby Rd**. Most have reasonably sized front and rear gardens and many of the streets are lined with trees. A mix of 3- and 4-bedroom houses, they are still cheap in Kensington terms, though a 3-bed house in **Wallingford Rd** was on the market in December for £375,000, and £425,000 was being asked for a **Highlever Rd** example. Properties are cheaper towards the less accessible north and at the W end of **Oxford Gardens**, where they back on to the fly-over.

Cutting through this enclave is **St Quintin Avenue**, a pleasant tree-lined street, popular despite being a main through-route between **Scrubs Lane** and **Ladbroke Grove**. Pairs of semi-detached brick and pebbledash and red-brick and stucco houses stretch along the avenue from the local shopping centre in **North Pole Rd**. Halfway along on the N side is St Quintin Health Centre and Princess Louise Hospital for the Elderly. Behind the hospital lies Kensington Memorial Park, 5 acres of public open space. **Oakworth Rd, Hill Farm Rd** and **Methwold Rd** N of the park are given over to inter-war council dwellings comprising 2-storey brick houses and flats.

Late-Victorian 3-storey and basement brick and stucco terraces, and 2-storey brick and painted pebbledash houses with timber porches, appear in the N end of tree-lined **Highlever Rd**. More 2-storey pebbledash houses stretch along the W end of **Barlby Rd** into **Dalgarno Gardens** and **Pangbourne Avenue**. At this junction is the new **Blakes Close** development of affordable homes with car parking. A small parade of local shops lies at the junction of **Dalgarno Gardens** and **Barlby Rd**. On the W edge of the area, close to the motorway, **Bracewell Rd** has 4-bed houses. An 11-acre former industrial site on the N side of **Barlby Rd** has just been transformed into a massive council and housing association estate with hundreds of people living in shared-ownership and rented 2/3-storey flats and houses. Near where **Barlby Rd** meets **Ladbroke Grove** is the Pall Mall depositary building which is offices. The Shaftesbury Centre and Barlby Hall, two recent additions, house community projects.

The NW corner of the neighbourhood is dominated by the Peabody Trust flat blocks in **Dalgarno Way** and Sutton Dwellings in **Sutton Way**. The latter flanks Little Wormwood Scrubs, a 22-acre recreation ground just over the borough border in Hammersmith. Also along the N boundary are warehouses/industrial uses and Barlby Rd railway sidings. At the NE end of **Barlby Rd** is **Barlby Gardens**, a small enclave of 2-storey brick and pebbledash houses set back off the road around a tiny green. On the S side of the road is Barlby Primary School. South of the school, between **Ladbroke Grove** and **Exmoor St,** are the council's Treverton and Balfour/Burleigh Estates, built to house returning servicemen from World War II. The estate is one of the most popular in North Kensington with a long-standing, close-knit community. **Exmoor St** and **Hewer St,** between the two estates, have 2-storey late-Victorian houses, mainly 3-bedroom. They go more cheaply because of the warehousing in the area and their proximity to St Charles Hospital, Kensington's general hospital.

The main entrance to the hospital is in **St Charles Square,** which is half made up of private homes and half housing association: 3-storey and basement brick and stucco semi-detached houses converted into flats. An ex-council 3-bed house with garden here was £215,000 in the winter – while a 'private' 1-bed conversion flat was £140,000. Clustered around the square is a Carmelite Monastery, the RC Sion-Manning Girls' School and St Charles 6th-form College plus St Pius X Church.

The most sought-after properties in the neighbourhood lie S of the square in **Chesterton Rd** W, **Bassett Rd** and **Oxford Gardens** (between **St Helen's Gardens** and **Ladbroke Grove**). These were designed for the first railway commuters when the Metropolitan Railway from the Hammersmith and City line opened up North Kensington in the 1860s, linking it to the City.

Both sides of **Chesterton Rd** are linked by 4-storey Victorian terraced houses. The more expensive, leafier **Bassett Rd** has big 4-storey paired and detached brick and stucco houses with front gardens. Many have been split into flats, some large. More large semi-detached houses, mostly split into flats and bed-sits, are found in **Oxford Gardens** and **Cambridge Gardens**. Properties here have front gardens and cherry trees line the former, bursting into a cascade of white blossom between April and May. This is the best stretch of **Oxford Gardens,** with big flats and whole houses on offer. The E arms of both streets across **Ladbroke Grove** are more mixed, with a number of council and housing trust properties. Off **Cambridge Gardens** is **Trinity Mews,** a 1988 development of live/work studios.

A handful of streets across to the E of **Ladbroke Grove** link architecturally with the neighbourhood but have little garden space. **Bonchurch St** and **St Michael's Gardens** S are both lined by 3-storey and basement brick and stucco houses converted into flats. The Romanesque-style St Michael of All Angels Church stretches along the N side of the latter, fronting **Ladbroke Grove**. **St Lawrence Terrace** features high Victorian rows, notably 3-storey and basement brick houses with bands of stucco to give a striped effect. Some properties are still unconverted.

N

Transport	Tubes, all zone 2: Notting Hill Gate (Central, District, Circle); Holland Park (Central); Latimer Road, Ladbroke Grove, Westbourne Park (Hammersmith & City). From Notting Hill Gate: Oxford Circus 10 min, City 20 min, Heathrow 42 min (1 change). Trains: Kensal Green to Liverpool St 30 min.
Convenient for	Kensington Gardens, West End, City, A40 to West, Bayswater (Whiteley's), Paddington Station. BBC Television Centre. Miles from centre: 3.5.
Schools	Local Authority: Sion Manning RC (g). Grant maintained: St Charles 6th-form College (b) (g).

SALES

Flats	S	1B	2B	3B	4B	5B
Average prices	75–150+	110–300	160–400+	200–450+	350–750	—
Houses	2B	3B	4B	5B	6/7B	8B
Average prices	220–650	250–750+	400–1M	600–2M+	›3.5M+	›5.5M

RENTAL

Flats	S	1B	2B	3B	4B	5B
Average prices	600–1100	650–1700	900–2600+	1700+	2600+	—
Houses	2B	3B	4B	5B	6/7B	8B
Average prices	1100–2600	1300–4500	›8000	›	—	—

The properties   Handsome Victorian terraces and paired villas characterize the area, from the grand white crescents and rows at the Hill's top, smaller brick/stucco streets, to the newly fashionable (and occasionally undone-up) roads down the Hill and in North Kensington, punctuated by council blocks.

The market   Inhabitants are as mixed as the area: young people (rich and not-so-rich) buying the profusion of small flats; Far East investors, media millionaires, the more raffish kind of banker. Flats, mainly converted, are the market staple. Cheapest homes at the North Kensington end. Local searches: 1 week.

Among those estate agents active in this area are:
- John Wilcox
- Marsh & Parsons
- John D Wood
- Foxtons *
- Winkworth *
- Chestertons
- Anscombe & Ringland *
- Jackson-Stops & Staff
- FPDSavills
- Leslie Marsh & Co
- Townsends
- Faron Sutaria and Co Ltd *
- Knight Frank
- Granvilles
- De Groot Collis

further details: see advertisers' index on p633

N

PECKHAM

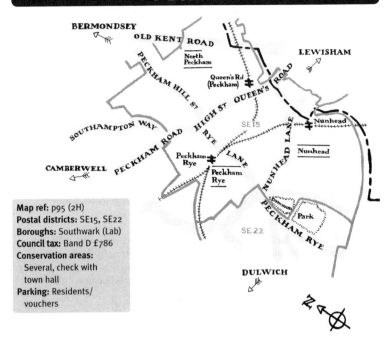

Map ref: p95 (2H)
Postal districts: SE15, SE22
Boroughs: Southwark (Lab)
Council tax: Band D £786
Conservation areas:
  Several, check with
  town hall
Parking: Residents/
  vouchers

Poor Peckham: sandwiched between Camberwell and New Cross, it was once known, if at all, to the majority of Londoners as the site of a traffic jam on the Dover Rd. Then it spent several years blighted by one of the proposed routes for Channel Tunnel trains. That threat at last removed, people are once more discovering some streets of surprisingly pretty and spacious houses by the tracks and the wider area: look S of the line to the pleasant streets of Peckham Rye for some enviable homes at bargain prices.

Behind the grime of the main road – **Peckham Rd/High St/Queen's Rd** – the area divides into two very different neighbourhoods, Peckham and Peckham Rye. Built as one of the original London suburbs for rail-commuting clerical workers, the area used to consist of many small streets of late-Georgian and Victorian terraced houses. Not any more. Much of the north of Peckham was rebuilt following war damage and slum clearance. This rebuilding is at the root of the sharp contrast between the north and south of Peckham: the southern bit, Peckham Rye, survived. The north did not.

Although there are several potentially desirable properties N of **Peckham High St** the area is mostly council housing – until recently mainly of the least-inspired period. Now, however, 3,000 flats in the vast and unenviable North Peckham housing estate are disappearing around **Sumner Rd** and are fast being replaced with a well-designed, well-laid out and pleasant new neighbourhood which will harbour 2,050 2-storey homes. This is a development being carried out under the banner of the Peckham Partnership, and although the properties are mainly housing association and council there are plans to have 600 for private sale. The first families moved in last year. This £260 million scheme is easily the largest single project of its kind in the country, and is rumoured to be Europe's biggest, too. The remaining couple of tower blocks are staying: their refurbishment has won a RIBA award.

Next, turn southwards: by contrast Peckham Rye, across the **High St** and S of the railway, is a surprise. A mature Victorian suburb opens up, sloping away round either side of a pleasant and picturesque park. Respectable streets of solid homes have more in common with Dulwich and Forest Hill, their neighbours to the S and E, than they ever do with Peckham proper on the other side of the tracks. That said, North Peckham is very close to Docklands and to Central London. It will require a major shift of social and financial geography before North Peckham becomes actively desirable, but respectability is creeping in at the edges . . .

Transport is a Peckham plus if you can clear your mind of the thought of tubes. Peckham Queen's Rd station has a fast and regular service into London Bridge (every 5 min at peak time, every 30 min off-peak), Halfway up **Rye Lane** there is Peckham Rye station. The trains run with the same frequency into London Bridge station as from Peckham Queen's Rd, and there is also a less frequent service into Victoria. There is, too, an excellent bus service to practically all areas. Better still, having given up waiting for its own – long-promised – tube, Peckham now has plans to run a bus speed link to the nearest useful interchange at Elephant & Castle.

The parking in central Peckham and Peckham Rye is operated on a voucher scheme and costs 60p an hour. Vouchers are available from newsagents. Car parks are reasonably plentiful (as are the wardens). Residents' parking permits cost about £72 per year. It should be mentioned that the one-way systems can be a nightmare for those attempting to navigate without detailed local knowledge . . .

Peckham North

The traffic grumbles along **Peckham High St** in a vain attempt to reach the Dover Rd (laughing at bemused foreign drivers is a local sport). On either side, the North Peckham area extends to the **Old Kent Rd** to the NE, the old canal to the N, **Pomeroy St** to the E and **Southampton Way** to the W. The railway line bridging **Rye Lane** forms the most widely accepted frontier with Peckham Rye to the S.

The N part of the neighbourhood has the unexpected amenity of Burgess Park, a large green space, complete with lake, carved out of the slum streets by Southwark Council over the last quarter of a century. A few 19th-century houses survive in the park. They were scheduled for demolition in sterner days, but now seem likely to remain.

South of the park, at long last the grim ramparts of the North Peckham estate no longer dominate the neighbourhood, and the brand-new houses, instead of being one vast estate, form ordinary streets with mixed public and private ownership – see above.

North Peckham also holds some areas that escaped the post-war slum clearance: N of **Queen's Rd** are some streets of small terraced houses such as **Asylum Rd**, which runs from the **Old Kent Rd** to the Queen's Rd station. This also includes some old almshouses, built for retired Licensed Victuallers (almshouses, especially with alcoholic connections, are a feature of Peckham). Very rarely, one appears for sale: tiny, 1-bed houses. The streets between **Asylum Rd** and **Meeting House Lane** are similar, with houses and converted flats. **Kings Grove** has some roomy 3-storey flat-fronted houses. Further W, **Friary Rd** boasts some surviving late-Georgian town-houses and to the N **Glengall Rd** too has handsome stucco flat-fronted, raised ground floor houses. To the S of the **Old Kent Rd**, a few streets have terraced homes which can be very good value. The E borders of Peckham, beyond Queen's Rd station, have some quiet if unexciting streets of Victorian terraces such as **Dayton Grove** and **Astbury Rd**. Useful properties, good value (houses from around £85,000) in a convenient and improving corner. The first developers are discovering this end of Peckham, too: in **Woods Rd**, off **Queen's Rd** to the S and close to Queen's Rd station, Fairclough have Maple Court, a pleasing scheme of 1- and 2-bed flats aimed at first-time buyers, priced at £66–80,000.

Peckham High St, at its junction with **Rye Lane**, holds the local shops. There's a mall, the Aylsham Centre, which includes a Safeway (with petrol station), car park, and sports centre. However, the brand-new 'Peckham Pulse' is just across the **High St** in **Melon Rd**: two swimming pools, a leisure/fitness centre with gym, hydrospa and café. Alongside, the new library in **Peckham Hill St** will open in the autumn.

To the W of the shops, a maze of streets makes up the most interesting residential corner in this district. There are Victorian terraces and some large detached houses in the conservation areas of **Chadwick Rd**, **Holly Grove**, **Elm Grove**, **Highshore Rd**, **Bellenden Rd** (handsome flat-fronted cottages) and **Lyndhurst Way**. **Lyndhurst Square** is an interesting 1840s cul-de-sac of gabled, large-gardened houses on the Camberwell borders. **Denman Rd**, to the W, shares the same leafy environment but has later-Victorian purpose-built maisonettes. Houses here can transcend their area; in **Holly Grove** last winter, a big-name agent was asking £325,000 for a splendid four-square detached house, Georgian in appearance, which stands behind its large walled garden. The station is at the end of the road; and across the tracks is Peckham Rye itself.

Peckham Rye

Choumert Square, tucked away W of **Rye Lane**, contains some of the smallest, but most desirable, houses in Peckham Rye: a tiny 2-bed one sold for £95,000 last autumn. The immaculately tended trellised rose gardens won a best-kept square award. Nearby **Choumert Rd** has yet more almshouses and an extremely vibrant street market, while **Blenheim Grove**, conveniently, if noisily, close to the station, has some recently converted 1-bed flats. Look, too, at the charming little 2-bed early Victorian cottages at this end of neighbouring **Chadwick Rd**.

Going S, **Rye Lane** suddenly widens and, there, for all the world like some small market town, is a little green surrounded by a cluster of shops. Across the **East Dulwich Rd**, Peckham Rye Common and Park open out in a sweep uphill to the S. Mile for mile, the areas of Peckham, Peckham Rye and Dulwich have more green spaces than many a more well-thought-of area of London. There is an attractive new development here on the site of the old Austins furniture depository: 1-, 2- and 3-bed houses and flats with private parking and entryphone systems facing the green. Two-bed flats were going for £70,000 and houses £115,000 earlier this year. Facing this on the other side of the green there is another pleasantly appointed recent development, again 1- and 2-bed flats. Apart from the park and common the green spaces include Warwick Gardens, behind **Lyndhurst Grove**, the gardens in **Holly Grove** and the gardens in **Elm Grove**.

The houses that flank Peckham Rye Common are large 3/4-storey family homes, many of which have been converted into flats. A noteworthy road is **Colyton Rd** which faces N over the park and has a big variety of properties varying from Victorian to 1920/30s. This is a road of impeccable suburban style.

Peckham Rye (the road) divides to run down either side of the common; the E side has some of the area's very few 1930s purpose-built flats (these can start from £50,000, with common views). Here, too, a little Georgiana has survived intact – with 100-ft gardens to supplement the sweeping expanse of common it overlooks. These fetch in the region of £280,000. Adjoining the common is Peckham Rye Park, which includes a water garden, rockeries, a beautiful trellised rose garden, a bowling green and duck pond.

West of **Peckham Rye** and N of **East Dulwich Rd** is a district of small terraced houses with streets including **Nutbrook St**, **Maxted Rd** and **Bellenden Rd**, **Amott St** and **Ady's Rd**. Some houses in the latter are bigger than they look, having 5 bedrooms, and at under £150,000 are good value.

The houses in **Fenwick Rd** are larger still, 3-storey with big bays. Many are flats. In this district it is worth watching out for new homes being built on the expanses of land that fringe the many railways. **Lynwood Close** is one of these: here a 1-bed house will sell for c. £60,000; 2-bed ones c. £70,000. To the W this district shades into East Dulwich (the cheaper end of that select suburb: see the Dulwich chapter and search here, too).

South of **East Dulwich Rd** and W of the common is the wide tract of respectable Victorian and Edwardian housing. The ground slopes up towards Dulwich, adding interest to the long straight such as **Barry Rd**. **Crystal Palace Rd**, misleadingly named because it is miles from the place, has flat-fronted cottages which make good small houses or pretty flat conversions. **Barry Rd** and **Upland Rd** have larger houses, many with good views as the land rises. The summit, at **Overhill Rd**, is crowned with a large block of council flats which must be nicer to look out of than at. Barratt have built some smart new flats here in a neighbourhood which is perhaps more East Dulwich than Peckham. The S end of this neighbourhood has spacious Dulwich Park as well as Rye Common to play with.

A mention here should be made of Goose Green. This is an area at the SW end of Peckham Rye where it meets with East Dulwich. It consists of a wide strip of grass with **East Dulwich Rd** on one side and large Victorian houses on the other. Many of these houses have been converted into flats. A new mews and some refurbished flats have joined the pleasant houses overlooking the green. Transport is good, being situated very close to East Dulwich station and car parking is unrestricted in most roads – though you can stay only 20 min in **Lordship Lane**.

East of the common there are neat flat-fronted terraced houses in streets such as **Somerton Rd**. Prices here are lower than on the W side of the common, which is closer to Dulwich.

Nunhead

Nunhead is the neighbourhood to the E of Peckham Rye. It is an area of small residential roads of little 2- and 3-bedroom houses that run southwards off **Nunhead Lane** and **Evelina Rd**, the latter providing the busy main shopping streets. It overlooks a small village green on the N side, a quiet, tucked-away corner which spreads around the hilly slopes of Nunhead Cemetery and Water Board land. A portion of the latter has been sold off, and now contains 'Water Mews': 22 new housing association homes.

As with Dulwich and Peckham, there is no tube; however Nunhead too has its own rail station. There is free parking off the main roads, and the main streets have all the shops necessary for day-to-day living including one of the best-known bakers in the area (Ayre's) and Sopers, a very good, very well-stocked wet fish stall.

The better properties are found S of **Evelina Rd**, in particular the houses on **Tresco Rd** and the Victorian square-bayed terraces of **Carden Rd** (houses c. £150,000). **Somerton Rd** and **Waveney Avenue** are similar. **St Mary's Rd** is another noteworthy road with early Victorian 3-bedroom houses on one side and larger Victoriana on the other. **Machell Rd** has tidy, flat-fronted, 19th-century cottages which fetch some £110,000. Nunhead also has a fair turnover of ex-council houses, as many former tenants have found it worth their while to buy. **Seldon Rd**, for instance, has unpretentious '60s terraced houses with the benefit of a parking space. Three-bed for £60,000. Like its neighbour Peckham, Nunhead has very few purpose-built flats. However, most of the larger period houses have been made into flats.

Three years ago an old hostel – formerly the Camberwell Workhouse (known locally as 'The Spike') off **Gordon Rd** – was converted into flats.

The Nunhead Estate of council flats (1930s brick blocks) overlooks the common. The Rye Estate further up the hill, on **Peckham Rye**, is similar. **Rye Hill Park** has '60s council towers, **Torridge Gardens** and adjoining **Limes Walk** have low-rise council-built houses. These are roomy and particularly well-designed, with large bedrooms, and now appear on the open market.

The expanse of Water Board land abuts the cemetery and the allotments which blanket the slopes of a considerable little hill. In **Stuart Rd** a block of six flats has been done up. The triangle of streets E from here towards Brockley has several peaceful corners: **Limesford Rd** and **Harlescott Rd** are late-Victorian cottages, **Lanbury Rd** has '30s cottage-style council homes. The **Ivydale Rd**/**Kelvington Rd** corner has more of these. Here, too, more waterworks and a golf course. **Brenchley Gardens** bounds the area, from One Tree Hill up towards Brockley with more council homes in a green setting. In a leafy corner at the end of **Brockley Way** behind Camberwell New Cemetery, and (well) above the railway, are 19 new mews houses by Whelan Homes.

A point of interest is Nunhead Cemetery. This large and overgrown Victorian cemetery is as renowned as the Highgate one and offers tours at certain times of the year.

Transport	Trains: Queen's Rd (Peckham), Peckham Rye, Nunhead to London Bridge, Victoria, Holborn Viaduct.
Convenient for	Dulwich, South Circular Rd and Elephant & Castle. Tubes at Kennington, Oval, Brixton, New Cross and Elephant & Castle. Miles from centre: 3.
Schools	Local Authority: Warwick Park, St Thomas the Apostle RC (b), Waverley (g), Private: Alleyn's (see also Dulwich chapter).

SALES

Flats	S	1B	2B	3B	4B	5B
Average prices	25–35	35–70	55–100	60–115	75–150	–
Houses	2B	3B	4B	5B	6/7B	8B
Average prices	70–100	75–150	100–250	130–300	250–600	–

RENTAL

Flats	S	1B	2B	3B	4B	5B
Average prices	350–450	450–550	550–700	700–900	900–1200	–
Houses	2B	3B	4B	5B	6/7B	8B
Average prices	550–750	750–1000	850–1200	1000–1300	1200–1500	–

The properties	Peckham Rye has pleasant Victorian/Edwardian (a few earlier) terraces and larger family homes, some Georgian, focused on the little green and the common. Flats are mainly conversions. North Peckham is more mixed: large council estate being rebuilt; some older terraces.
The market	Peckham, in common with other areas in London's SE sprawl, has surprising, nice corners of good homes at some of London's most reasonable prices. These include some pretty terraces. Local searches: 2 weeks.

Among those estate agents active in this area are:
- Roy Brooks
- Burnet Ware & Graves
- Kinleigh Folkard & Hayward
- Winkworth*
- Charterhouse
- Acorn
- Roberts
- Andrews

* *further details: see advertisers' index on p633*

PIMLICO AND WESTMINSTER

Map ref: p77 (5G)
Postal districts: SW1
Boroughs: Westminster (Con)
Council tax: Band D £325
Conservation areas: Several,
  check with town hall
Parking: Residents/meters

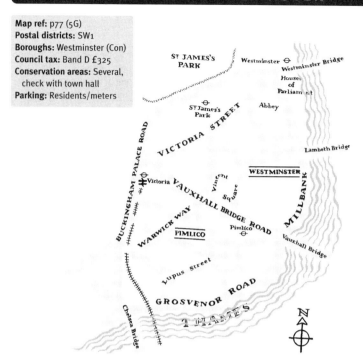

There has been more buzz on the homes scene in Westminster over the past year than at any time in the last century. The last time so many new homes were on the market was during the Edwardian mansion flats boom. Westminster is still known far more for its grand buildings than its homes, although the Georgian front door of its most famous residence, 10 Downing Street, gets more TV coverage than most. It is possible to live in Westminster without being Prime Minister, as many MPs and officials – and City workers – have discovered however, and new developments and cunning conversions are appearing at a brisk pace.

Pimlico, which shares the SW1 postcode, is already almost entirely residential; its long white terraces a hunting-ground for wonderfully central flats and pieds-à-terre either to rent or buy – though family-sized homes are scarce.

Both areas have their own individual presence and charm. While being very much at the centre of things (a main line terminus and major tourist attractions bring their own problems), they have the river and the Royal Parks to bring air and perspective into the city streets. And outside working hours the residential corners can be surprisingly peaceful. Both areas fall within the City of Westminster and are run from City Hall in **Victoria St** – or Oil St, as rude residents call it after the number of looming oil-company office tower blocks which line it. During the week **Victoria St** is a canyon of bustling commerce, yet but a few hundred yards away is the quiet of **Vincent Square**, with period houses overlooking a public school's cricket pitch. And a few streets away from Victoria station are the stucco terraces and squares of Pimlico, almost as handsome as Belgravia and a lot less expensive.

Pimlico

Bordered by plush Belgravia and august Westminster, Pimlico, tucked into a bend in the river, remained for a long time remarkably unknown. The social mix of the community changed as, throughout the '80s, a tenanted and rather run-down district became a place of converted flats and smart developments.

This is MP land, full of politicians' pieds-à-terre or main homes within the division bell boundary – the zone close enough to the House for them to rush from dinner, or whatever, to be counted through the lobbies. If you live in one of the streets known for a high political population, watch out for the strange stampede when there's a vote in the House. **Cambridge St** is a typical 'little Westminster': at one count, 25 MPs had homes there. They are joined by City people who love the central location and good transport links.

Pimlico used to be part of the Grosvenor Estate, like Belgravia. Thomas Cubitt, the Estate's architect and builder, laid out the straight streets and regular squares. The land was open, marshy and used for market gardens and pasture. In order to raise the level above the Thames floods, Cubitt with typical ingenuity brought thousands of tons of gravel and earth up by barge from St Katharine's Dock, which he happened to be excavating at the same time. If your Pimlico cellar is damp, remember that it's sitting at original marsh level.

Pimlico may look superficially like Belgravia – lots of Regency stucco, Classical detailing and regularity – but it has never been quite as smart. During most of the 20th century it was the province of the small hotel, the house clumsily divided into bed-sits, the shared bathroom. The Grosvenor Estate sold off the whole area in the 1950s, preferring to concentrate on Belgravia and Mayfair. It was only in the 1972/3 property boom, which coincided with the opening of Pimlico's Victoria line tube station, that Pimlico began to be 'discovered'. The big old houses began to be converted into smarter flats, the MPs and busy people of all sorts found out how close it is to everything, and Pimlico began to change. The process was helped (though some would claim hindered) by the council's pioneering scheme to ban through traffic. The place is a maze of one-way streets, blocked-off cul-de-sacs and residents' parking bays, and thus remains remarkably peaceful, a place apart, despite being so central.

An average Pimlico property today is a big Cubitt town-house split into flats. They are of varying sizes but a good number are small, aimed at single people or pied-à-terre owners. Family houses exist, but this is primarily flat-land. The network of streets at the heart of Pimlico ('The Grid') are predominantly Cubitt terraces: **Clarendon**, **Cambridge**, **Alderney** and **Sutherland Sts** for example, and **Gloucester**, **Winchester**, **Sussex**, the **Moretons** and the **Westmorelands**. But even here there are gaps in the stucco and brick, often caused by wartime bombing, which have been at various times filled by small and often ugly blocks of flats. These are less admired ('quite unpleasant' remarked one local agent) than the period conversions. Prices for 2-bed converted flats range between £175,000 and £265,000. Other exceptions are the mews cottages both behind the squares and terraces and, occasionally, on the main roads: **Clarendon St** has a few such. Look for the cobbled, sloping charm of **Warwick Square Mews**. **St George's Square** also has its mews, and **Moreton Terrace** boasts two: **North** and **South**. Modern mews houses in **Charlotte Place**, off **Wilton Rd**, go for around £375,000. Some houses have survived the mania for conversion: try **Cambridge** and **Alderney Sts** and **Westmoreland Terrace**. A 4-bed period house might cost £650,000. For new-build, turn to **Buckingham Palace Rd**, 'only 600 metres from Sloane Square', where Berkeley have 93 1- to 3-bed flats in a new block with gym, business centre and parking. Fourteen were left in December, priced from £315,000.

Pimlico is short of open space, though there's Ranelagh Gardens over on the Chelsea side and the splendid (if rather more public) St James's Park on the other. So the three large garden squares have long been its most desirable addresses – apart from the riverside flats. The big houses in the squares convert readily into spacious flats. **St George's Square** has some interesting recent conversions, and lots of tiny flats and maisonettes. Round the corner in **Aylesford St,** which backs onto **St George's Square Mews**, small 2-bed flats start at around £150,000 upwards.

The elegant stucco terraces surrounding the gardens make **Eccleston Square**, **Warwick Square** and **St George's Square** hugely attractive – in that order. With an eye to the lack of parks, while the first two have private gardens, those of **St George's** and **Bessborough Gardens** are both open to the public. Two stucco Grade II houses in **St George's Square** are being split into 11 1- to 3-bed flats, due for completion this summer at prices from £175–350,000.

The only new London square to be created since the war, **Bessborough Gardens** is part of the Crown's Millbank Estate. The gardens (locked at night) have a fountain in honour of the Queen Mother's 80th birthday. The L-shaped terrace surrounding the garden on two sides is classic Cubitt: the smooth stucco finish, decorative iron-work balconies, the mouldings of windows and pillared doorways . . . or so you might think: but these rows didn't exist until the late '80s! The Wimpey-built replacements of war- and flood-damaged terraces for the Crown Estate have provided a cache of new flats and penthouses, from studio to 3-bedroomed. The detailing inside matches the exterior, and on occasion the sales team had trouble convincing buyers that the apartments really were new. Much more development has followed on the Crown Estate: next door to **Bessborough Gardens** and sharing its entrance in **Drummond Gate**, is **Lindsay Square** which has 29 new town-houses. In **Balvaird Place**, just opposite Pimlico tube station, there are 40 2- to 4-bed town-houses with garages.

The main road along the riverside is **Grosvenor Rd**; it does not hug the embankment, however, and wherever it bends slightly inland a waterside development has been squeezed in. The most successful of these is Crown Reach, which lies just W of Vauxhall Bridge, past a former office block (see below) and an undistinguished earlier flats block. Its jutting, staggered riverside floors give the maximum light, privacy and unimpeded views to its apartments and their balconies, while the landward side's sweeping gull's-wing roofs have become a landmark. The 22-storey office tower at the corner by the bridge has become 'The Panoramic', which is accurate enough as a name. It has 88 flats (from £595,000 in Phase I), plus a yet-to-be-released 2-floor penthouse for which around £8 million is being mooted – in shell condition. Other plush and pricey waterfront blocks include River Lodge, parked on a narrow site almost in front of **Dolphin Square**, and St George's Wharf which appeared in 1990. These have been joined by the Riverside Belvederes, with 43 apartments and penthouses. Tyburn House, a 5-storey Georgian house right on the river with its own jetty, was on the market for £825,000 last autumn.

Lupus St runs E–W, a wide busy road paralleling **Warwick Way**, the other main cross-route to the N. On the S side the splendidly uncompromising modern lines of Pimlico School are reticent in one thing only: the mass of the 'glass school', as it is generally known, stands, amid its playground, considerably below the level of the surrounding streets. However, there is currently a plan to completely redevelop the school site including some housing. This was given the go-ahead last winter amid much wrangling.

Beyond the school rises the riverside, red-brick mass of **Dolphin Square**. A huge '30s flats development, it was at the time of its building the biggest in Europe. Its 1,200 flats surrounding a private courtyard are half rented, half privately owned (on fairly short leases). It is large enough to form a complete community, with its own shops, garage, pub and restaurant: the latter, open to non-residents, overlooks the indoor pool. Not surprisingly, there is a long waiting list for homes here.

South of **Lupus St** are some of the most enviably placed council-built homes in London, the riverside towers of the Churchill Gardens Estate. To the E along **Vauxhall Bridge Rd**, in contrast, is the red-brick of Lillington Gardens, with its roof gardens, third-storey trees and terraces: better-looking than many a private development. Many tenants on both estates bought their homes, which appear on the resale market far cheaper than other Pimlico properties. On **Peabody Avenue** and the wonderfully' named **Turpentine Lane**, and further E towards **Vauxhall Bridge Rd**, are two estates of red-brick rented flats run by the Peabody charitable trust. There are plans, still being considered by Westminster Council as we go to press, to convert 176–184 **Vauxhall Bridge Rd** into flats.

Behind **Lillington Gardens** the irregular meander taken by **Tachbrook St**, contrasting with Cubitt's orderly grid, betrays its earlier origins. This is Pimlico's village high street, complete with not only shops but a thriving, much-prized street market. There is also some council resale here. To the N it joins **Warwick Way** (once a track through the marshes), and to its W lies **Belgrave Rd**: largely unreconstructed Pimlico, this. It is a main through-route to Victoria and is still full of cheap hotels, although recent years have seen a quickening of the pace of change in **Belgrave Rd** as more of these are converted into flats.

Westminster

Westminster is once more climbing the scale of visibility as a place to own a home. Some big blocks have been done up, and new developments are under way. Indeed SW1, with more than 600 homes being built in mid-1998, is nearly as busy as the Clerkenwell/City fringe area. That said, it is still true that homes are a secondary matter here: Westminster is first and foremost the home of Parliament and the Civil Service. The nearest shopping facilities are either over in **Tachbrook St**, or in **Victoria St**, which boasts the Army and Navy store and Sainsbury's. Westminster shopping does have one saving grace, however: the excellent morning street market in **Strutton Ground**.

Tucked away in side roads there are homes that can be peaceful, considering their centre-hub position; the most plentiful are the mansion blocks whose brickwork echoes the Roman Catholic Cathedral. But there are also, by contrast, modern flats, a few neat terraced homes and a little cache of unsuspected Georgiana. The last year has seen Vincent Square re-emerge as a residential neighbourhood.

Westminster the place – as opposed to the borough – starts across the **Vauxhall Bridge Rd** from Pimlico and runs up to St James's Park in the N. The stretch between the park and the river is home mainly to the Ministries of this or that along Whitehall. **Downing St** boasts only temporary accommodation, sheltering, strictly for their terms of office, the Prime Minister and the Chancellor of the Exchequer. The riverside holds the only other exception: the fantastical turrets of **Whitehall Court**, where you can pay a small fortune for a very short lease: views of the river and the Changing of the Guard. Some of the flats are enormous – up to 5 bedrooms.

Mansion flats are the staple form of what homes there are between the main through road, **Victoria St**, and St James's Park. Vandon Court in **Petty France** for example offers a range from studios upwards. This corner has hidden delights, though: glorious **Queen Anne's Gate**, where the stately houses date from the reign of that monarch and are wasted as offices, even if one is the headquarters of the National Trust. One 10-room house was on the market last winter for £1.5 million. Near Victoria station lies tiny, hidden **Victoria Square**: its homes date from 1838.

But the bulk of Westminster's homes lie S of **Victoria St**. Again at the end nearest Victoria station, Edwardian mansion flats are the norm. A new block of ultra-smart flats appeared in the '80s in **Artillery Row**. **Morpeth Terrace** and **Carlisle Place** are typical of this corner, both lined with similar red-brick blocks. Inside, the apartments are impressive, with large rooms and high ceilings; their entrance halls have an olde-worlde feel, with shining wood panelling and crusty porters in traditional uniform. Nearby is a cache of new homes with that most covetable London asset, garaging: the Crown Estate has developed adjoining sites in **Old Pye St** and **Abbey Orchard St** – 1- and 2-bedroom flats and penthouses with basement garages. In **Ashley Gardens** off **Victoria St**, at the station end, 32 flats in a brick mansion block have been refurbished and are reported as selling well at prices from £165,000 to 'traditional British buyers' – perhaps the great-grandsons of the Empire types who bought these flats to be near 'The Stores' and their West End clubs.

The area's largest current development is appearing on the site of the old Westminster Hospital around **St John's Gardens** in the angle of **Marsham St** and **Horseferry Rd**. This is yielding 186 flats: from £160,000 to £2 million-plus. Another large scheme is planned for **Victoria St**: 187 flats (including 25 social homes).

Though tree-lined, street succeeds street until, crossing **Rochester Row**, the vast green rectangle of **Vincent Square** surprisingly opens up. Some houses are lucky enough to overlook this open space, larger than **Belgrave Square**, used as a playing-field by the boys of Westminster School. Watching the cricket this summer will be an increased population of Square-dwellers: at least three big developments are under way. At No 87, Berkeley have 24 1- to 3-bed flats plus duplexes and penthouses, prices TBA. Vincent House is a refurbished 'NY-style period building' with 39 flats and town-houses: 2-bed flats from £275,000; houses from £520,000. The Atrium is a 6-storey building, locally controversial for its height, with 2- and 3-bed flats from £330,000.

It is towards Westminster Abbey that the oldest buildings are found. These include the Georgian gems of **Smith Square** and surrounding streets. Some have been lost, some serve other purposes (such as the Conservative Central Office – though that is to be sold), but some are still enviable homes. One, in **Barton St**, was on the market last winter at £2.75 million 'suitable for refurbishment as a grand home' with 5 reception rooms and 6 bedrooms. In **Rochester Row**, 24 new 1- to 3-bed flats and duplexes were all sold before completion in 1998. Between **Vincent Square** and **Horseferry Rd** is **Maunsel St**, a pretty terrace of brick cottages with gardens. Rowan House and Stockton Court are two recent blocks of 2-bed flats in **Greycoat St**. A new development called Greycoat House added 30 more 2- and 3-bed flats.

Some of the Edwardian blocks in Westminster are being refurbished, and other blocks have moved from rental to sale. Gladstone Court in **Regency St** is four red-brick blocks surrounding a central inner courtyard. Regalian's 1988 conversion resulted in 52 luxury apartments sharing a fitness complex. Alice House in **Douglas St** was another block to get the 5-star treatment in 1987 from developers Great Gable. Back in **Regency St**, there is a modern 6-storey block with 19 flats, 2 penthouses and basement parking, and close by are three new mews houses in a courtyard, plus an office building with three penthouse flats. In the same street is a new courtyard with 10 flats and a single house, prices from £155,000. Artillery Mansions, on **Victoria St**, has been extensively done up to create 174 flats – studios to 3-bed – around two courtyards with fountains. Priced from £180,000 and due to be ready this April. A site between **Marsham St** and **Tufton St** has been redeveloped as Millicent Court, with 36 flats and three houses around a communal garden and with underground parking. Completion is due this March, with prices from £190–750,000.

The other source of Westminster homes can be found in the southernmost corner, towards Vauxhall Bridge. En route, in **John Islip St**, is Millbank Court convenient '60s flats: high ones get river views. The far end of **John Islip St**, and the streets surrounding it in the angle of the river and **Vauxhall Bridge Rd**, form the Westminster side of the Crown's Millbank Estate. There are neat terraced houses in **Ponsonby Place** and

Ponsonby Terrace, and beautiful converted apartments in the river-facing white stucco **Millbank** terraces (the stretch culminating in the Paolozzi leaping dancer statue was painstakingly restored and converted by Rosehaugh). The Crown's houses are a mixture of fair-rent homes and others available, when they come up, on long leases.

Transport	Tubes, all zone 1: Pimlico (Victoria); Victoria (Victoria, District, Circle); Westminster, St James's Park (Circle, District). From Victoria: Oxford Circus (5 min), City 20 min, Heathrow 1 hr (1 change).
Convenient for	West End and City; Gatwick Airport (express from Victoria). Tate Gallery. Miles from centre: 1.5.
Schools	Local Authority: Pimlico School, Grey Coat Hospital C of E (g). Private: Francis Holland (g), Westminster School (b), The American International School.

SALES

Flats	S	1B	2B	3B	4B	5B
Average prices	85–165	110–250+	170–400+	200–400+	400–2M+	—

Houses	2B	3B	4B	5B	6/7B	8B
Average prices	—	380–700	450–750+	650–850+	800–2.751M	—

RENTAL

Flats	S	1B	2B	3B	4B	5B
Average prices	600–1000	850–1300	1100–2100	1700–2600+	—	—

Houses	2B	3B	4B	5B	6/7B	8B
Average prices	—	2100–3250	3000+	5000+	6000+	—

The properties	Regency stucco terraces, now mainly flats; mews cottages; p/b flats in Dolphin Square; ultra-mod or repro schemes (the best repro indistinguishable from the outside), and council blocks. Westminster has mainly mansion flats (some very large), plus a few 19th-century and Georgian houses: look here for new schemes and conversions since Westminster, long overlooked as a place to live, is once more in the spotlight.
The market	Young professionals can buy or rent here; also MPs and pied-à-terre seekers; they find some imaginative conversions of Pimlico's stucco houses into flats. Quality, however, varies widely depending on vintage: Pimlico's rise from down-at-heel bed-sit land to high fashion began in the '70s. Local searches: 2 weeks.

Among those estate agents active in this area are:
- Foxtons *
- Downtons
- Barnard Marcus
- Silver & Silver
- Winkworth *
- Hamptons
- Chestertons
- FPDSavills
- Jackson Stops & Staff
- Cluttons Daniel Smith
- DTZ Debenham Thorpe
- Best Gapp & Cassells

further details: see advertisers' index on p633

POPLAR

Map ref: p64 (6D)
Postal districts: E14
Boroughs: Tower Hamlets (Lab)
Council tax: Band D £659
Conservation areas: Include
  York Square, Naval Row
Parking: Restricted

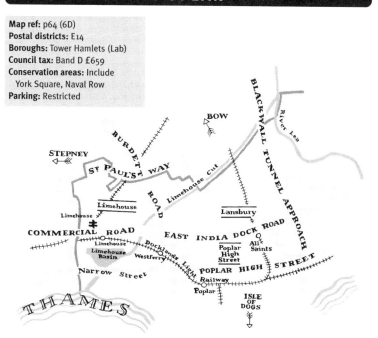

The Docklands revolution changed more than the economy and population of London's East End. It changed the names, too. Poplar, once a little village, grew in 1817 into a parish and took in the Isle of Dogs and Blackwall. The docks came, and with them tens of thousands of workers. From 1900 to 1964 Poplar blossomed as a proud if prickly borough. Its town hall ruled Bow until Tower Hamlets subsumed them both. Then came the London Docklands Development Corporation and the Isle of Dogs Enterprise Zone. Much of Poplar's territory was lost. Its name became little used as the new residents attracted by the Docklands boom said they lived on the Isle of Dogs or at Limehouse. As Docklands becomes an historical chapter rather than a place, the old neighbourhoods re-emerge, and Poplar is a place once more, back to its roots as a village around its inland **High St**. The West India Docks, which once formed a boundary to the S, have been replaced by the new highway of **Aspen Way**, which funnels traffic in and out of the City via the Limehouse Tunnel.

Before the Docklands takeover, Poplar's fortunes had already sunk, however: World War II and its savage bombings had left but half the population and few indeed of the buildings. Today the greater proportion of homes in Poplar and Limehouse are council-built. Quite a few were bought by their tenants and are now bought and sold, offering bargain alternatives to the increasing supply of smart flats aimed at workers in the City.

Limehouse, to the W, has seen a renaissance as the Limehouse Basin has been developed with waterside homes – and since the road tunnel beneath it has been finished. Limehouse has not only kept hold of its romantic name (though London's Chinatown has relocated to Leicester Square), but is indeed expanding somewhat:

P

the Limehouse Cut, the canal which runs from Limehouse up between Poplar and Bow to the River Lea, has seen several smart waterside developments following the Docklands example. These are thought of as Limehouse, but the original area lies largely to the W of **Burdett Rd**/**West India Dock Rd**.

The ultra-smart riverside developments that have sprung up since the '80s are dealt with fully in the Docklands chapter.

Poplar and Limehouse are within 2 miles of the City of London. With no tube station in the vicinity – Bromley-by-Bow and Mile End are the nearest – the opening of the Docklands Light Railway (DLR) has given the area a much-needed boost. Poplar and Limehouse stations now provide a regular service to Stratford (interchanges with trains and tube) and Bank, and Canning Town and the Royal Docks to the E. The DLR will also connect at Canary Wharf with the Jubilee line, due to open during 1999.

Poplar and Limehouse are bordered by the Isle of Dogs to the S, Bow to the N and Stepney to the W. To the E of Poplar is the Blackwall Tunnel Northern Approach motorway. **East India Dock Rd** is the area's main thoroughfare. The enormous (and expensive) road building programme linked to the Docklands regeneration has given the area several new roads: make sure your street map is a recent one. The main highway is an E-W dual carriageway from the City via Limehouse Tunnel, on across the S edge of Poplar, then over a new bridge across the River Lea to the Royal Docks. This lot has eased the chaos on the **East India Dock Rd**.

Many local men worked in the West India and East India Docks before their closure and unemployment in the area has stayed high. The docks are part of the fascinating history of Poplar and Limehouse and the area includes six conservation areas – **York Square** close to the border with Stepney, St Anne's Church, St Matthias Church, All Saints Church, **Naval Row** and **Narrow St**.

One of Poplar's attractions is lively **Chrisp St** market, which is part of the Lansbury Estate, named after Labour Party stalwart George Lansbury. It is one of the more appealing parts of Poplar, with a true small-town atmosphere. Sadly the restaurants of Chinatown are now for the most part a distant memory.

Poplar

The Lansbury Estate, which includes **Chrisp St** market, is one of Poplar's more attractive parts. The Estate, built in the early '50s, comprises much of the district to the N of the busy **East India Dock Rd**. **Duff St, Grundy St, Susannah St** and **Ida St** have much-improved terraced ex-council houses. Houses in **Bygrove St**, N of **Grundy St**, are split into maisonettes and flats with roof gardens. Some of the newer town-houses and terraced houses in **Brabazon St, Carmen St** and at the N end of **Chrisp St** have been purchased from the council by their owners and tastefully improved. So, too, have smart terraced houses in **Giraud St** and flats and maisonettes in **Hobday St** and **Cordelia St**, which has Poplar Boys Club on its corner next to the Young Prince pub and Susan Lawrence Primary School halfway down. Quite a lot is happening on the Lansbury Estate: 38 refurbished houses and flats in **Broomfield Rd** will be ready this summer, plus 24 more flats for rent. Busbridge House in **Brabazon St** is being modernized: Phase I is due to be finished this March.

To the W of the Lansbury Estate, the towering St Mary's and St Michael's Roman Catholic Church, opposite Mayflower Primary School, is flanked by more terraced ex-council houses in **Canton St** and **Pekin Close** which take their names from the nearby area once known as Chinatown. North of **Canton St**, with its neat gardens, is St Philip Howard Roman Catholic Mixed Comprehensive School and then Bartlett Park, a rare stretch of greenery. Opposite the S end of **Chrisp St**, on the S side of **East India Dock Rd**, is the DLR's All Saints station. The station sits between the two conservation areas of All Saints Church and St Matthias Church.

The grounds of All Saints Church are adjacent to some of Poplar's most desirable private homes, imposing 3- and 4-storey Victorian terraced houses in **Newby Place** and **Mountague Place**. Similar houses can be found to the W in **Woodstock Terrace** facing Poplar Recreation Ground which houses Poplar Bowls Club's green and the entrance to St Matthias Church. S of **Woodstock Terrace** and **Newby Place** is **Poplar High St** – council flats on each side – which leads eastwards to **Naval Row**, another conservation area.

The area along **Poplar High St** has gained from the road-building to the S. It is now quiet, and increasingly a desirable place to live. The refurbished council flats of the Will Crooks Estate and the new Tower Hamlets College (very high standards) are among local successes. Next to the college a sports centre is due to be finished this March. The Church Housing Association owns much of the S side, but there are 24 new flats in Stoneyard Lane, very convenient for Poplar DLR station. Caraway Heights, at 216–242 **Poplar High St**, is the latest flats development here.

Past The Steamship, yet another pub, pre-war flats in **Naval Row** have been modernized. New leases on the 2-bed flats were marketed after conversion. The old Poplar Power Station has gone to make way for part of **Aspen Way**, the new E-W highway. Blackwall Tunnel Northern Approach motorway is flanked to the W by the still run-down Teviot Estate although **Daniel Bolt Close**, with its '60s-built 3-storey terraced houses, is popular with buyers. **Bright St**, **Byron St**, **Burcham St** and **Hay Currie St** are dominated by Langdon Park School and a sports centre and social club. **Byron St** also includes The Germans pub (it used to called the Duke of Wellington). Near the tunnel entrance, Copthorne Homes are building flats and houses, and other schemes are under way or planned.

A redundant church in **St Leonard's Rd** has become St Michael's Court, a clutch of 34 smart flats including some verty desirable ones in the church tower. Opposite, on the edge of Langdon Park, are a dozen new houses. Further up **St Leonard's Rd** a pub has become six flats. These, together with the former church conversion and some shops, form a pleasant group.

East of the motorway are some of Poplar's worst properties. The area is improving, but is still rather out-of-the-way and run-down. The flats in Oban House, **Oban St**, have been refurbished, but the ones off **Blair St** still look run-down. Both streets also have terraced houses. Canning Town Bridge over Bow Creek provides Poplar's eastern boundary with Newham.

St Paul's Way is the northern boundary with Bow. The steady work on local council-built estates continues on the Burdett Estate, which stretches S to Limehouse Cut through **Wallwood St**, **Burgess St**, **Selsey St** and **Thomas Rd** where small industrial units can be found on the S side. Flats in **St Paul's Way**, **Thomas Rd** and **Wallwood St** are due to be ready during 1999.

P

Limehouse

Limehouse dates back to Elizabethan times and has always been a place closely linked to the river. Seamen and dockers were its inhabitants for centuries until the closure of the docks brought the tradition to an abrupt end. Road schemes and the looming presence of Canary Wharf have meant enormous changes over the last decade. The area is hardly recognizable.

The N end of **West India Dock Rd** is flanked by Barley Mow council estate and there is a stark contrast as the Estate sweeps down to very expensive **Narrow St**, whose riverside houses were among the first to be 'discovered' by West End artists and politicians. Now the Limehouse Link tunnel entrance affects the W end of the street. This is a conservation area and is covered in greater detail in the Docklands chapter. W leads to **The Highway** and Tower of London.

West India Dock Rd continues to the N across **East India Dock Rd** into **Burdett Rd** where some of the larger properties on either side have been converted into split-level flats. W of **Burdett Rd** are the council homes of **Turners Rd**, **Clemence St**, **Dora St** and **Norbiton Rd** which all lead into **Salmon Lane** where some delightful Victorian houses can be found on either side at the W end (Mercers Estate). A new Higgins development of 23 large flats is under way in **Salmon Lane**. Attractive Victorian properties are found S of **Salmon Lane** in **Barnes St** and **York Square**, a conservation area, as well as **Flamborough St** which includes the Queens Head pub. A 2-bed flat in **Flamborough Walk** was on the market for £125,000 last December. The Grade II listed houses in **Barnes St** command premium prices. In **Wakeling St** 11 new houses wll be on the market this spring. This is a favoured corner, with real character.

The southern end of **Barnes St** leads into busy **Commercial Rd**, almost opposite the Limehouse DLR station. Further E along **Commercial Rd** is St Anne's Church which is another conservation area. **Aston St** is Limehouse's western boundary with Stepney while the northern boundary with Bow is **Rhodeswell Rd**, which includes East London Stadium with its football pitch and athletics track and open-air concerts.

Where Limehouse Cut canal passes under **Burdett Rd** is Limehouse Court, a new canalside development (built in 1990) in **Dod St** with 50 homes and 50 commercial units. Further along the canal, Enterprise Works in **Hawgood St** uses the Limehouse name despite being in E3. The courtyard development consists of work-homes, ranging from 4-storey houses to 1-bedroom flats. And further E at the **Morris Rd** bridge, 'The Limehouse Cut', a big 4-phase conversion of warehouses into work-homes, sold in shell finish, proved successful in the late '80s.

Further S, there is lots happening around the Westferry DLR station on the edge of the Isle of Dogs. **Grenade St** has the Compass Point development, with flats to rent, and Compass Point West with 1- and 2-bed flats by Furlong Homes. In **West India Dock Rd** is a new Peabody Trust development; and in the same corner the old Limehouse Church Hall is now flats to let by the Quality Street Company. The Peabody Trust are working on 1- and 2-bed flats for rent on **West India Dock Rd/Gill St**.

Transport	Docklands Light Railway: Limehouse, Westferry, Poplar, All Saints. Trains: Limehouse.
Convenient for	Docklands, City, rail interchange at Stratford, Fenchurch St. Routes East. Blackwall Tunnel to South. Miles from centre: 4.5.
Schools	Local Authority: Langton Park, St Paul's Way, St Philip Howard RC.

SALES

Flats	S	1B	2B	3B	4B	5B
Average prices	50–60	60–90	70–90	70–100	—	—
Houses	2B	3B	4B	5B	6/7B	8B
Average prices	90–125	100–200	120–250+	·	—	—

RENTAL

Flats	S	1B	2B	3B	4B	5B
Average prices	500–600	550–800	650–1000	900–1200	—	—
Houses	2B	3B	4B	5B	6/7B	8B
Average prices	700–1200	800–1600	800+	900+	—	—

The properties   Docklands-style warehouse conversions and work-homes plus new flats schemes: prices below Docks, but well above local homes, which are largely 2/3-bedroom flats and maisonettes, many of them ex-council. Studios and big houses are scarce. Owner occupation: as yet still lower than average, though more council flats being sold.

The market   The lower end of the flats scale represents ex-council sales; other 2-bed flats will range c. £65–90,000. Exceptions at top end are the new canalside schemes, and the occasional listed home around Salmon St. Riverside Narrow St, annexed by Docklands (see chapter), is not included here. Local searches: 4 weeks.

Among those estate agents active in this area are:
- Alex Neil
- Chandler
- Stirling Ackroyd
- McDowalls
- Baker Allen
- Docklands Estates

P

PUTNEY AND ROEHAMPTON

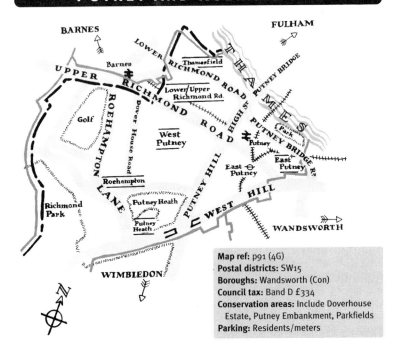

Map ref: p91 (4G)
Postal districts: SW15
Boroughs: Wandsworth (Con)
Council tax: Band D £334
Conservation areas: Include Doverhouse
   Estate, Putney Embankment, Parkfields
Parking: Residents/meters

With the Thames, Putney Heath, Putney and Wimbledon Commons and Richmond Park bordering the area, Putney offers much to the dog- and child-owning classes. Younger flat-dwellers find plenty of homes for sale and (increasingly) to rent, and find the **High St** useful for shopping and entertainment.

The majority of Putney houses are substantial late-Victorian and Edwardian properties built for the middle classes and those who aspired to that status. The social mix has not changed. Good schools, and a tube that calls at Sloane Square, make this a natural next step for Fulham and Battersea flat-dwellers setting up their family home.

The huge number of flat conversions in East and central Putney, plus the many mansion blocks and a sprinkling of new developments, attract younger buyers. Families look further south and west. Five- and 6-bedroom houses are, if not the norm, certainly not unusual, particularly in West Putney, which has one of the biggest concentrations in London.

Wandsworth Council was a pioneer of selling off council homes, and the large areas once owned by the council are now widely private. These ex-council homes, many near Putney Heath, offer a cheaper buy for newcomers to the area. You don't have to be someone in the City to afford a SW15 postcode. Indeed, the postcode takes in Roehampton, whose enormous blocks of council-built flats are now partly private.

Putney people are sworn enemies of property developers and people who cut down trees or build unsuitable extensions to their homes. As a result, the machinations of those trying to get onto committees of the astonishingly active Putney Society, an 'illegal' tree-felling, or the council's latest bid to solve the area's traffic problems are major topics of conversation. The problem of getting a daughter into Putney High School also provides a fruitful source of local debate. Most Putney residents pay a Commons Rate (seldom more than £10–15 a year) towards maintenance of Putney Common, Putney Heath and Wimbledon Common. Each of these commons has its own special character. Putney Heath is wild and much is heavily wooded while Putney Lower Common is old meadow land with a few spinneys and hosts the annual 'country' Putney Show each summer. Richmond Park, which marks the borough boundary, offers fine walking and horse-riding with livery and riding stables at Roehampton Gate and Robin Hood Gate.

At the heart of Putney is the traffic-choked **High St** which boasts some surprisingly good shopping, including multiples like Sainsbury's, BHS and Marks & Spencer. The Putney Exchange shopping mall has a Waitrose and several more chain stores. There is a cinema (ABC) at the junction of the **High St** and **Putney Bridge Rd**. An ever-increasing number of bars and restaurants line the **High St**, which is noticeably busy in the evenings.

The **High St** sweeps down the hill to Putney Bridge, with its handsome lamp-posts and the riverside parish church. St Mary's is sadly dwarfed by towering, slab-sided office blocks – but St George (the name on virtually every London riverside development) are hoping for permission for a scheme that would ameliorate the 16 floors of the ICL tower with a rounded, galleried extension: this would add 89 flats and a restaurant to this bleak waste of waterfront. A public inquiry into this and an adjoining scheme in **Brewhouse St** began in January, with no result as we went to press. West of the bridge on this corner of **Lower Richmond Rd** and the **Embankment**, a boat-shaped modernist restaurant (very non-Putney) gets spectacular river views.

Every area in London has it own special problem. In Putney, that problem is the motor car. **Putney Bridge** and **Upper Richmond Rd** seem to act as a magnet for commuters from across the whole of South and West London and the result is monumental traffic jams during rush hours. The closure of Hammersmith Bridge has not helped. Traffic jams mean rat-running. 'Traffic calming' measures and parking restrictions proliferate, with Wandsworth Council touring the area with a 'parking road show' to assess reaction to parking schemes.

Rail commuters are well catered for with the tube transport via Putney Bridge (District line) on the Fulham side of the river, or East Putney (**Upper Richmond Rd**); rail into Waterloo from Putney (**High St**) or from Barnes stations.

Anybody considering buying a house in Putney — especially in West Putney or Thamesfield — should first read Jilly Cooper's *The Common Years*. The book caused severe offence to a number of Putney notables (not to mention those who walked their dogs with Mrs Cooper) but it remains a remarkably accurate reflection on aspects of life in Putney . . . a sort of conservative Hampstead.

P

Thamesfield

This little wedge-shaped area lies between the river and the **Lower Richmond Rd** to the W of **Putney Bridge**, running westwards to Putney Hospital and the common. Generally, prices here are slightly less expensive than in West Putney, with smaller, cottage-style, late-Victorian terraces predominant. There are also pockets of older Regency and early Victorian houses — and a few exceptionally large houses around Putney Common.

Lower Richmond Rd runs from **Putney High St** along the length of Thamesfield to Putney Common where it meets **Queens Ride**. There are small parades of shops sufficient for day-to-day needs strung along it, as well as a number of smart restaurants and bars. Estate agents are keen to brand this the latest 'village'. They indeed cluster thickly here, avid for gossip no doubt. The road carries through traffic from Richmond and Barnes but does not suffer as severely as **Upper Richmond Rd** — which forms part of the South Circular. There are mainly terraced houses on **Lower Richmond Rd** although there are some Victorian detached and semi-detached villas set well back: notably attractive are Nos 139–144.

West from **Putney High St** are three large Victorian mansion blocks — Star and Garter Mansions, Kenilworth Court and University Mansions. Most but not all of the flats have river views although you may need to crane your neck. Some flats in Star and Garter Mansions and Kenilworth Court may suffer noise from the nearby pubs. A 3-bed flat in Kenilworth Court was £270,000 last winter.

The roads leading off **Lower Richmond Rd** towards the river tend, in the main, to be smaller mid- and late-Victorian terraced cottages, some purpose-built maisonettes and flats. **Ruvigny Gardens,** which forms a loop off **Lower Richmond Rd,** features larger 3-storey Victorian terraced houses; some now converted to flats, some backing on to the **Embankment,** with gates at the end of the garden for launching your boat. Don't skimp on surveys close to the river: problems with settlement have been reported among properties in Putney which stand very near the Thames.

Festing Rd is one of the most popular streets in this area, with 4-bed houses at about £375,000. Some of its houses are purpose-built Victorian flats and maisonettes. It runs down to **Putney Embankment** and its boathouses. By the junction is Leader's Gardens, a small, attractive park with tennis courts. Popular **Ashlone Rd**, a street of mid-Victorian terraces, also leads down to Leader's Gardens. Adjoining **Ashlone Rd** is **Stockhurst Close**, a small council development of flats, some with river views. **Pentlow St** features attractive Victorian houses, mainly 3-bed houses, some semi-detached. A 4-bed house in this street was on the market for £330,000 in December. **Sefton St** offers small Victorian terraces leading to **Horne Way**, inter-war blocks of council-built flats backing onto sportsgrounds. **Commondale**, overlooking Putney Hospital and Common, is a row of 2-bed cottages, some flat-fronted. The prettiest ones were built in the 1870s to house the 'deserving poor' with money provided by Putney Pest House and wealthy benefactors. In **Danemere St** an infill development, Waters Place, has added 16 3-bed town-houses, while the Victorian ones sell at about £330,000.

There are plenty of flats above shops on **Lower Richmond Rd. Putney Embankment** has few homes available — they are generally tied to the boathouses and rowing clubs which line the **Embankment**. Ruvigny Mansions, a small Victorian block, has spacious flats, most with river views. It is inadvisable to leave cars parked on the **Embankment** owing to the tide's unfortunate habit of rising above road level. This is, however, popular with local garages called upon to repair the damage.

Lower Richmond Rd to Upper Richmond Rd

On the other (S) side of **Lower Richmond Rd** from **Commondale** is **Putney Common**, a tiny no-through road used as a turn-around point for the No 22 bus, which terminates here. Past the pub on the corner of **Lower Richmond Rd** are cottages, then late '60s flats (Commonview) backed by a builders' merchant's yard, then a primary school and Victorian church. A path leads through into **Egliston Mews** and **Egliston Rd**.

Lower Common South is a road of huge detached houses, mainly 1870s–80s, mainly red-brick and wonderfully ornate, set well back from the road and overlooking Putney Common — this is one of the very rare 'common' views not to be spoiled by heavy traffic. Residents should stay away one weekend a year — during the Putney Show. These homes are very, very rarely for sale. **Chester Close** and **Sherwood Court**, off **Lower Common South**, have small, attractive, late-'70s 'traditional' 3-bed town-houses (style is half 'Georgian', half clever-architect).

Egliston Rd (Jilly Cooperland) has vast mid- and late-Victorian detached houses with a handful of almost-as-large semi-detached early Edwardian houses; virtually all have substantial off-street parking and very large gardens. **Egliston Mews**, at the junction of **Egliston Rd** and **Lower Common South**, is a smart development of flat-fronted 4-bedroom, 2-bathroom town-houses, in 'developers' Georgian' style. Red-brick Dryburgh Mansions occupies a larger corner site on **Dryburgh Rd** and **Egliston Rd**. Unfortunately, the lovely, big, roomy flats have short leases. A huge late-Victorian mansion, Dryburgh Court, is split into five flats. The main part of **Dryburgh Rd** runs parallel to the Barnes–Putney railway line and has late-Victorian/early Edwardian houses, mainly semi-detached, some detached. Odd numbers back onto the railway but have reasonable-sized gardens as barriers. Hidden at the end of the road is tiny **Beauchamp Terrace** with Victorian cottages. The low numbers are nearer the railway.

Erpingham Rd runs between **Dryburgh Rd** and **Lower Richmond Rd**, with 3-storey early Edwardian semi-detached and terraced houses and there are some unusually large conversion flats. Rat-running is still a problem

Elaborate Edwardian is the hallmark of suburban Putney. These homes, solid and spacious, are eclectic in style. This one has copious 'Tudor' detailing In the heavy gable, the stuck-on 'timbers' and the tall chimneys. Other styles to be found frequently in the same house are Queen Anne and Gothic. However mongrel their architecture, they find favour with families.

although **Dryburgh Rd** is closed to traffic at **Upper Richmond Rd** junction during the morning rush hour. **Felsham Rd**, with its late-Victorian terraced houses, and a few early Victorian and larger ones, runs from **Erpingham Rd** through to **Putney High St**. Traffic measures have helped to reduce problems. Roads running off are generally unexceptional South London late-Victorian/Edwardian terraces.

Stanbridge Rd, which crosses **Felsham Rd**, has some pleasant semi-basement flat-fronted mid-Victorian houses, while **Westhorpe Rd** attracts such exalted residents as MPs and the like. Houses in **Roskell Rd** are slightly larger 2- and 3-storey Victoriana, some semi-detached. By the mid-100s **Felsham Rd** houses are larger, mainly 3-storeys. In **Henry Jackson Rd** is a council-built infill development of low-rise homes. Thereafter more small council-built blocks and St Mary's Church of England Primary School with Putney St Mary's Youth Club (which has a good local reputation) opposite. **Bemish Rd** includes some flat-fronted Victorian cottages and larger Edwardian houses but suffers traffic using it as a short-cut from **Lower Richmond Rd** to **Putney High St**.

Charlwood Rd provides a welcome release from red-brick Edwardiana with Georgian/Regency semi-detached flat-fronted cottages and larger detached houses set well back from the lane running from **Felsham Rd** across **Hotham Rd** to **Clarendon Drive**. Perhaps the prettiest houses are between **Felsham Rd** and **Hotham Rd**: this is rightly a conservation area. **Redgrave Rd** also has pretty, smart mid-Victorian homes.

The E end of **Lacy Rd** is dominated by the Putney Exchange shopping centre. Putney Exchange includes some flats, up to 3 bedrooms, which are popular to rent as they have 24hr security and parking. Otherwise **Lacy Rd** includes 2- and 3-storey Victorian terraces, some small Victorian cottages, a public house and some council infill development. **Modder Place** has nice plain flat-fronted 2-bed cottages and looks directly onto unprepossessing '60s council-built flats, Crown Court Estate, which is why they can be less expensive than neighbouring roads — not because the estate agent made a mistake with the valuation. A group of cul-de-sacs — pedestrian-only **Quill Lane, Lifford St** and **Stratford Grove** — lie between the red-brick walls of the shopping centre and the 1960s estate. For all that, the flat-fronted 2-storey cottages retain their charm. West from **Lacy Rd, Hotham Rd** is mainly Edwardian 2- and 3-storey houses, most semi-detached (just) with an adult education centre and primary school at the junction with **Charlwood Rd**. Most houses here have four or more bedrooms.

Clarendon Drive features more 2- and 3-storey late-Edwardian and '20s semi-detached houses. Houses on the S side of the road back onto the railway line but have gardens of up to 100 ft to keep it at bay. **Norroy Rd**, and parallel **Chelverton Rd** with its good-sized late-Victorian family houses, are both convenient for Putney rail station. **Spencer Walk**, to the W off **Charlwood Rd**, has pretty, early Victorian, flat-fronted 3-storey houses with semi-basements and some modern infill town-houses. Some train noise is possible here, as is noise from the popular Quill pub, but crime problems are unlikely as it is the 'local' for detectives and senior officers from Putney police station in **Upper Richmond Rd**.

Upper Richmond Rd is a major trunk road carrying traffic not only from Richmond but also from the M3 and M25 and is busy at all times. However, the majority of houses on the road are set well back. From the junction with **Putney Hill** it becomes increasingly commercial. Thereafter are increasing numbers of '30s and more modern mansion blocks as the road heads E towards Wandsworth. Off-street parking is essential. Where **Upper Richmond Rd** meets **West Hill** there is a development of 14 flats and 26 houses with an indoor swimming pool. The W section of the road features many blocks of flats ranging from early '20s to fairly new. Brittany House has recently gained new penthouses in a total refurbishment. Maintenance charges on the older blocks are off-putting to some buyers. Among the best-known blocks close to **Putney High St** are old-style Ormonde Court and '30s-built Belvedere Court at the junction with **Dryburgh Rd**, overlooking Putney Leisure Centre and convenient for early morning swims. All properties on this side of **Upper Richmond Rd** back onto railway lines although the majority have large gardens to cut noise levels. Harwood Court (opposite **Colinette Rd**) is another '30s-style block while **Isis Close** is a modern '60s-built development. Wellwood Court is next, then **Breasley Close** a council-built infill of flats and houses; **Fairdale Gardens** is a small town-house development. Northumberland Row in **Dyers Lane** (a no-through road) is a small terrace of mid-Victorian cottages, some flat-fronted, overlooking modern council homes.

Probably the best-known houses in **Upper Richmond Rd** are the 'Nelson Houses', a row of half a dozen lovely late-Georgian/early Victorian detached

houses supposedly built for Nelson's sea captains. The houses are set well back from the road with gravel sweeps and Regency iron-work canopies.

East Putney

Popular with people moving into the area who cannot yet afford to live in Thamesfield or West Putney but choose not to live in Wandsworth or Earlsfield, and are determined to have SW15 on their headed writing paper. Prices for the late-Victorian/early Edwardian terraced houses are generally below those in Thamesfield, even though transport and shopping facilities are better, with the rail station in **Putney High St**, East Putney District line tube in **Upper Richmond Rd** and Putney Bridge tube just over the river.

Putney Bridge Rd runs parallel to the river from **Putney High St** to Wandsworth, meaning very heavy traffic at times. Wandsworth Park runs most of the length of **Putney Bridge Rd** so many of the late-Victorian terraces of 2- and 3-storey houses and purpose-built flats have views across the greenery to the river and Hurlingham beyond. Few of the houses are very special with the exception of Park Lodge at the junction with **Atney Rd**: an early Victorian detached house followed by the single-storey Sir Abraham Dawes Almshouses.

Fawe Park Rd, with its early Edwardian terraces, also suffers some rat-running, and even numbers back onto the railway line. A 4-bed house here can command £320,000, trains notwithstanding, and there are some sizeable converted flats. Terraced houses in **Skelgill Rd** overlook Brandlehow Primary School playground, while the 3-bed houses in **Brandlehow Rd** overlook the front of the school. **Bective Rd** is a popular mix of flat-fronted mid-Victorian cottages and bay-windowed late-Victorian terraces. Disraeli Gardens is a large Victorian mansion block on the corner of **Bective Rd** and **Fawe Park Rd**. **Wadham Rd** has a very popular mix of small, pretty, flat-fronted, late-Victorian cottages, many 2-bed, 2-storey, some 3-storey. But the tube line runs at roof level behind.

Oxford Rd runs between **Upper Richmond Rd** and **Putney Bridge Rd**. 'Sleeping Policemen' have reduced the speed of the rat-runners, but not the numbers. There are some large detached mid-Victorian houses with porticoed entrances (mainly odd numbers). The remainder are Edwardian semi-detached with some modern (council) infill. **Montserrat Rd**, **Werter Rd** and **Disraeli Rd** run from **Oxford Rd** to **Putney High St** with a range of large Victorian houses, most of which are now converted into flats. The roads are all one-way, either to or from **Putney High St**, and suffer from frustrated, hopelessly lost rat-runners.

Deodar Rd, off **Putney Bridge Rd,** is the most popular (and expensive) street in East Putney. It has large 3-storey semi-detached houses: odd numbers overlook the river and are the last houses before Central London to have private moorings at the end of their big gardens (although actual boats are scarce). There are drawbacks of course — the District Lline bisects **Deodar Rd** (at roof level). The Blades development gets river views and has three stucco-fronted houses and 3-bed flats, backed by a commercial development of workshops with studio accommodation above.

Oakhill Rd links **Upper Richmond Rd** (and the rat-runners) to **Putney Bridge Rd**. The street is first Victorian and more recent mansion flats, then detached double-fronted mid-Victorian, then smaller red-brick terraces. Streets running between **Oakhill Rd** and **West Hill** — **Schubert Rd**, **Galveston Rd**, **Mexfield Rd**, **Cromford Rd**, **Santos Rd** — are generally substantial Edwardian terraces, with an increasing number converted to flats, causing some parking problems, but all convenient for East Putney tube. Off **Upper Richmond Rd** is **Wood Close**, a modern development of small town-houses with garages. The least known corner is **Point Pleasant**, tiny terraced flat-fronted Victorian cottages hidden off **Putney Bridge Rd** with 'scope for improvement . . .' Railway at head of terrace, river at foot. This corner is hidden no longer with the completion of Prospect Quay, two new riverside blocks, an office/leisure block and a restaurant. A quay, houseboats and a 'drinks pontoon' add to the amenities; the neighbouring industry detracts somewhat – though there are plans for the big adjoining Shell site: see Wandsworth. It is also remote from public transport.

Putney Heath and Putney Heights

Putney Heath is wild and heavily wooded and walkers can get to the neighbouring Wimbledon Common by an underpass under the A3. A small neighbourhood at the junction of **Telegraph Rd** and **Portsmouth Rd** is isolated in the midst of the heath. It is approached via **Wildcroft Rd** and includes the Telegraph pub and unusual 1930s Wildecroft Manor mansion flats, built in mock-Tudor style with exposed beams, with large 3- and 4-bedroom flats. Many go to overseas buyers who are unworried by hefty service charges. Then comes Highlands Heath, also '30s mansion flats with slightly smaller homes, lower service charges and tennis and squash courts. Both blocks back onto the heath. Prices start at around £129,000 (1-bed, unmod). **Heathview Gardens** and **Bristol Gardens** have among the most popular — and pricey — houses in this enclave and indeed in the area: vast 6/7/8-bedroom Edwardian detached houses in quiet tree-lined roads with large gardens, some running onto the heath. Virtually all remain in single occupation. **Bensbury Close** has small flat-fronted mews cottages, 2- to 4-bed houses. **Portsmouth Rd**: small (in comparison with **Heathview Gardens**) detached houses overlooking the heath, including Bowling Green Cottage, a flat-fronted, white-washed country cottage thought to date back to the early 18th century. **Bowling Green Close** is a private development of extraordinary large 1930s Art Deco detached houses, very rarely on the market.

Lynden Gate is 1980s 'Developers' Regency': 3-storey semi-basement stuccoed town-houses, 2- and 3-bedroom in a high-security development surrounded on three sides by the heath and woodland. **Putney Heath** (the road) runs from Roehampton to **Putney Hill** and suffers from serious rat-running at rush hours with traffic out to beat the **Roehampton Lane**/A3 junction lights. It's mainly council-built developments (increasingly owner-occupied) along the heath, then Exeter House, a large 1930s mansion block development in its own large grounds. Many, but not all, the flats have magnificent views over the heath. Two-bed flats were recently fetching about £160,000. **Manorfields** is a huge 1930s mansion flat development of 9-plus acres on the corner site between **Putney Heath** and **Westleigh Avenue**. Prices for these flats start around £210,000. Newnham House, rebuilt in the 1980s after a gas blast levelled it, has superb 2-, 3- and 4-bed flats, all with good views of beautifully kept landscaped grounds with specimen trees and ponds. The service charges are high but full-time gardeners and porterage explain why.

The triangle bordered by **Putney Hill**, **West Hill** and **Upper Richmond Rd** offers the largest choice of modern purpose-built flats in Putney, although there is also a wide selection of older Victorian and Edwardian houses. **Putney Hill** is a busy through road but flats in the blocks on either side of the road remain popular. Properties include some substantial double-fronted mid-Victorian houses still in single occupation and some popular, mainly '30s and '50s, blocks of flats, while Fairhaven is a Victorian detached mansion now converted to flats. Putney High School for Girls (fee-paying) fronts onto **Putney Hill** between **Carlton Drive** and **Lytton Grove**. **Radcliffe Square**, between **Lytton Grove** and **Kersfield Rd**, is a '70s flats development. On **Carlton Drive**, 1999 will see a new block of 12 flats at No 38: £170–350,000 for 1- to 3-bed. At the top of Putney Hill is a no-through road spur of **Putney Heath Lane** with two mansion blocks including Ross Court, which is popular for its large flats with big rooms.

St John's Avenue is probably the best road for (well-heeled) flat buyers in Putney, with some of the best modern blocks in the area — Downside, Claremont, Marlin House, all well-maintained with indoor swimming pools and 5 min walk to East Putney tube. **Carlton Drive** is also lined with modern '60s blocks of flats but is slightly less popular. Neither road is, however, the prettiest in Putney.

Lytton Grove is a mixture of good-sized late-Victorian detached and semi-detached houses with some '30s and modern infill. Some of the houses are now converted to (fairly spacious) flats. The road suffers from bad rat-running, especially in peak hours. Houses on the S side of the road between the junctions with **Holmbush Rd** and **Rusholme Rd** back onto the tube line but sidings between rails and gardens cut noise.

Kersfield Estate by the junction with **Putney Hill** is '60s council-built flats and houses. **Tintern Close** and **Arlesey Close** feature quite small modern town-houses, then a mix of late-Victorian/Edwardian detached and semi-detached houses. **Chepstow Close**, a good modern town-house development (flat-fronted, 3-storey with garages), backs onto tube lines. Clock House Place is a red-brick cluster of Victorian-style homes.

Kersfield Rd is mainly modern early '60s blocks of flats with some late-'30s flats (private) although **Littleton Close** is council-built. Blocks include Heath Royal, Garden Royal, Heath Rise, a series of modern-style blocks close to **Putney Hill** with well-kept gardens. Flats range from 1- to 4-bed. Council blocks in the area are of reasonable quality, built during the same period and in similar style to many of the private blocks — spot the difference. **Putney Heath Lane** has a mix of good-sized 2- and 3-storey early Edwardian semi-detached and terraced houses interspersed with modern mansion flat developments. Some houses are detached (just). **Van Dyke Close** is town-houses and flats. Behind is **Lavington Stables** — a tiny mews too small to find in the A–Z. **Rusholme Rd** has flats at the junction with **Putney Heath Lane**, thereafter late-Victorian red-brick detached and semi-detached houses, an increasing number now conversion flats. Modern flats at the junction with **Holmbush Rd** overlook an open area.

Keswick Rd runs between **Upper Richmond Rd** and **West Hill** and like **Lytton Grove** suffers badly from rat-running. Some potential buyers may also be put off by the (above ground) tube line running behind, but gardens and large grassy sidings cut noise levels. There are also some exceptional large early Victorian houses, typically 5-bed, 3-reception, with large gardens. There is an eclectic mix of houses here: big mock-Tudor mansions, hideous blocks and imitation cottages. One 3-storey house is currently being converted into 11 flats.

PAR Cavalry Gardens is a recent, sybaritic complex of houses and flats, both new and converted, with its own pool and sauna, off **Upper Richmond Rd**. **Portinscale Rd** off **Keswick Rd** features some large detached Victorian houses and '20s and '30s infill of Tudor-style herringbone brick. The road suffers some rat-running. By the junction with **West Hill** is Burntwood School and Portinscale Estate (modern houses/low-rise flats). Opposite are large '70s flats.

West Hill — a continuation of the A3 — is exceptionally busy at all times. The safest time to cross is during rush hour when the traffic is generally stationary. Close to **Tibbett's Corner** underpass is **Colebrook Close**, off **West Hill**, an extraordinary 'Spanish Hacienda' style development of houses and maisonettes built in the '30s by a film company for stars and starlets visiting Britain for filming.

Thereafter are large, mainly late-Victorian houses most, fortunately, set well back from the road with off-street parking and for the most part converted to spacious flats. At the eastern end, close to Wandsworth, further conversions are under way. Barratt have successfully converted an old college into 'Crown Mansions': flats and duplexes up to £455,000.

West Putney

This is where you live when you have made it in life and have chosen not to commute into London each day from Berkshire or Hampshire. There are some small houses, flats, even council estates. But the vast detached late-Victorian houses in wide tree-lined avenues are the Putney properties of popular imagination. They house 3-car families with daughters at Putney High or St Pauls, sons at a good boarding school and a husband with a secure seat on the Board and a useful handful of non-executive directorships. Demand for family homes in this area is so great that '60s/'70s conversions into flats are being bought for restoration into single units.

West Putney is bordered by **Upper Richmond Rd** to the N, **Putney Heath** to the S, **Putney Park Lane** and **Putney Hill**. It is a wholly residential area save for the shops and offices of the **Upper Richmond Rd** and is a conservation area.

The area is laid out on a grid pattern with four roads — **Westleigh Avenue, Chartfield Avenue, Hazlewell Rd** and **Howard's Lane** — running parallel to the **Upper Richmond Rd**. Cutting between and across are roads such as **Larpent Avenue, Castello Avenue** and **St Simon's Avenue** which run parallel to **Putney Hill**. Major building started in the 1870s and houses range from huge detached Victorian and early Edwardian through to mid-'20s architect-designed flights of fancy with some '50s and early '60s infill. The area is exceptional in the number of large detached or generous semi-detached houses on offer.

Westleigh Avenue running W from **Putney Hill** starts with low-rise council homes; then there is a mix of Victorian, Edwardian and newer detached houses all set well back from the road. From the junction with **Pullman Gardens**, council houses and small blocks of flats back onto a '50s and '60s council-built estate (the mainly low-rise flats, houses and maisonettes of **Cortis Rd, Pullman Rd** and **Heyward Gardens**). Houses on the S side of **Westleigh Avenue** between **Cotman Close** and **Pullman Gardens** back onto Elliot Secondary School in **Pullman Gardens**. By the junction with **Granard Avenue** is Granard Primary School (which produces demon 7-year-old chess players), then small council houses. Leading off **Westleigh Avenue, Genoa Avenue** is mainly late-Victorian 3-storey semi-detached with some '20s houses and small council infill. **Solna Avenue** has small modern council houses, most now owner-occupied. At the junction with **Westleigh Avenue, Granard Avenue** is small neat council houses then substantial detached — many '20s, '30s and '50s double-fronted with fine views.

Chartfield Avenue is a mixture of late-Victorian/Edwardian detached houses set back from the road with some substantial inter-war stockbroker-Tudor homes. As with **Westleigh Avenue** there are substantial amounts of council property with the Asburton Estate between **Putney Hill** and **Genoa Avenue**. Some of the largest Victorian detached double-fronted houses are now converted to vast flats; 3-bedroom, garden, 2-reception roomed ones are not unusual. Roads leading off **Chartfield Avenue** from **Putney Hill** include **Chartfield Square** and **Cherryfield Drive**, which are undistinguished modern town-houses, the former overlooked by an ugly '60s office block on **Putney Hill**. Late-'60s council flats (not high-rise) and houses opposite in **Winchelsea Close**.

Gwendolen Avenue has popular large 1880s detached and semi-detached houses. The 1980s added some large 5-bed Victorian-style semi-detached houses; **St Simons Avenue** features more very large detached houses and a church at the junction with **Hazlewell Rd. Genoa Avenue** and **Castello Avenue** are smaller (but large by any other standards) 2/3-storey semi-detached and detached red-brick houses. **Larpent Avenue** has some modern infill but generally substantial late-Victorian detached and semi-detached 2- and 3-storey houses. Some houses (the low even numbers) have extraordinary domes on the front elevations — Turkish architect perhaps? **Luttrell Avenue** has late-Victorian/early Edwardian semi- and detached houses.

Hazlewell Rd is mainly 2- and 3-storey late-Victorian and early Edwardian detached and semi-detached houses, some with 6 bedrooms. There are some smaller modern infill houses (also detached). The road suffers occasional rat-running. **St John's Avenue** runs between **Hazlewell Rd** and **Putney Hill** with very large 1880s 3-storey semi-detached and detached homes. **Ravenna Rd** and **Burston Rd**, large semi-detached and detached, are also convenient for Putney station. **Tideswell Rd** has 3-storey Edwardian semi-detacheds; **Holroyd Rd** is Edwardian 2- and 3-storey semi-detached houses. **Coalecroft Rd** (a conservation area): even numbers are very pretty flat-fronted early Victorian cottages, mainly 3-bedrooms; odd numbers are good-sized Edwardian semi-detached.

Howard's Lane is a wonderfully esoteric blend of house styles ranging from vast mid- and late-Victorian and early Edwardian to stunning early '20s architect-designed — with a few Victorian and modern terraces thrown in for good measure. The road includes one of the most desirable houses in Putney at 115 **Howard's Lane**: a detached Art Deco flight of fancy with a vast red dragon weather vane. **Howard's Lane** houses start off in the E as small (for West Putney) terraced and semi-detached mainly 4-bed houses. Nos 50–60 **Howard's Lane** is a nice-looking town-house development with integral garages, then mainly larger late-Victorian detached and semi-detached houses. A new house, a 6-bed, 5-bath, 3-storey detached affair with double garage and wine cellar, was on the market for £1.5 million last winter. **Kingslawn Close** at the junction with **Woodborough Rd** is an attractive town-house and flat development with communal gardens including tennis courts.

Leading off **Howard's Lane** to the N are **Carmalt Gardens** and **Balmuir Gardens**, turn-of-the-century, 4-bed semi-detached (just) houses. **Tideswell Rd** and **Enmore Rd** are similar but slightly larger. A new cul-de-sac, 'Eaton Mews', has been squeezed in off **Upper Richmond Rd** by St George: 14 new houses. **Parkfields** is a narrow, hidden lane concealing enchanting Georgian and early Victorian cottages and some larger Georgian houses. It is a conservation area with original, restored lamp-posts in the road. Convenient for a small parade of similar period shops in **Upper Richmond Rd**. **Dealtry Rd**, **Colinette Rd** and **Campion Rd** all have 3-storey Edwardian terraced and semi-detached homes.

The area between **Woodborough Rd**, **Malbrook Rd** and **Upper Richmond Rd** boasts some of the biggest and most popular houses in Putney. Two- and 3-storey ornate mid- and late-Victorian detached houses with 5 or 6 bedrooms (and many with more), plus drives and huge gardens. There is a small council infill block halfway up **Woodborough Rd**.

At the junction of **Woodborough Rd** and **Upper Richmond Rd** are private flats: The Briars, Somerset Lodge and also modern flats at the junction with **Briar Walk**. Pear Tree Court, which is similar, is at the junction of **Malbrooke Rd** with **Upper Richmond Rd**.

West of here is considered to be Roehampton, though the transformation is subtle. The boundary is **Putney Park Lane**, not a road but rather a woodland track marooned in suburbia, running N-S between the houses and past the bottoms of gardens.

Roehampton

Drive up the A3 **Kingston Vale** towards Putney and to your left you will see what anywhere else would be a series of luxury blocks of flats overlooking the green acres of Richmond Park. They are, in fact, the 'point' blocks of the vast Alton Estate built in the '50s and early '60s by the GLC, now owned and managed by Wandsworth Council. The views from them must be terrific — and the views of them, when seen across the park, gives an inkling of what was in the minds of tower block architects.

Roehampton is bordered by Richmond Park and Richmond Golf Course to the S and W, **Upper Richmond Rd** to the N and by enchanting rural **Putney Park Lane** to the

E. It is an area of contrasts — it is just a 5 min walk from the modern towers of the Alton Estate to the small Victorian terraces of **Medfield St** or to the top-of-the-range houses of **Roedean Crescent**.

The area bordered by Richmond Park, **Clarence Lane**, **Roehampton Lane** and the A3/**Kingston Rd** is mainly council-built properties known under the generic name of Alton but is in fact a number of different estates. Low-rise blocks and houses are increasingly owner-occupied, and tower flats with views over the park are becoming popular. **Laverstoke Gardens** and **Holybourne Avenue** back onto listed Manresa House, now the Roehampton outpost of the University of Greenwich. As usual with these big estates the planners forgot about the transport and shopping needs of inhabitants: the only shops of note are a tatty parade in **Danebury Avenue**. Heading out of Roehampton along the A3, however, there is the ASDA hypermarket.

Roehampton Village, just across **Roehampton Lane**, could not be more different. **Roehampton High St** has pretty early and mid-Victorian houses and small, bay-windowed 'village' shops. There is a 'Village Café', a 'Village Hairdresser' and even 'Pizza in the Village'. St George have just finished 'Hanover Mews', 12 2-, 3- and 4- bed houses off **Roehampton High St**: a handful left in January from £210,000 for a 2-bed. Most, but not all, of **Medfield St** overlooks Putney Heath and comprises 2- and 3-bedroom mid-Victorian terraced cottages and a row of larger red-brick terraced houses (late-Victorian) with tall chimneys, some semi-basements. The road is a bus route and suffers congested traffic during rush hours. **Ponsonby Rd**, running S off **Medfield St** back to **Roehampton Lane**, has small flat-fronted pairs of Georgian cottages overlooking the heath, then beautiful Roehampton Church and Roehampton Church School (primary). A whole row of shops and flats at the end of the village is destined for development.

On the other side of **Roehampton High St**, **Nepean St**, **Akehurst St** and **Umbria St** form a quiet enclave of semi-detached and detached houses ranging from 6-bed Edwardian semis through to early 1930s (some modern infill), many now flat conversions. They have large gardens and are generally very quiet, tree-lined roads. **Rodway Rd** however suffers occasional traffic rat-running.

From Putney Heath, **Dover House Rd** leads down to the **Upper Richmond Rd** and passes through the Dover House estate, built in the 1920s by the LCC, like the Magdalen Park estate in Earlsfield (see chapter) as a 'cottage' estate. Its borders run from **Crestway** down **Dover Park Rd** to **Upper Richmond Rd**, with **Huntingfield Rd** and **Swinburne Rd** the borders to the W and peaceful **Putney Park Lane** to the E. The houses are a mix of inter-war chalet style semi-detached and terraced with steeply inclined roofs and dormer windows, and pretty flat-fronted terraces and semis. The estate is now a conservation area but too late for some houses, where new owners have pebbledashed, rendered or fake-stone-clad. The area is now well-known to postal-zone-conscious buyers without the cash for Putney proper: 2-bed cottages from around £130,000; 3-bed around £150,000. The estate is quiet (with the exception of **Dover House Rd** which suffers some through traffic), with 'village' greens and open spaces. Among those most in demand are houses backing onto **Putney Park Lane**, an unmade-up tree-lined lane running between Putney Heath and **Upper Richmond Rd**.

Roads leading down to the estate from Putney Heath such as **Dover Park Drive** and **Longwood Drive** feature large, mainly detached family houses, most built in traditional styles in the '30s and '50s. **Coppice Drive** backs onto playing-fields behind Queen Mary's Hospital. Off **Upper Richmond Rd** are mainly late-Edwardian and early '20s homes with some modern private developments. **Putney Park Avenue** is again a private unmade-up, tree-lined road which features lethal speed humps and a mix of Edwardian and newer houses with a small modern flat development at the top of the avenue: a very quiet road. **Marrick Close** has a small development of modern town-houses. **Dungarvan Avenue** and **Langside Avenue**, with their substantial '20s semi-detached houses, could suffer rat-running. Cornerways is modern flats on the corner of **Daylesford Avenue** and **Upper Richmond Rd**. A useful small parade of shops stands on either side of the **Dover House Rd** junction.

  Roehampton Lane (A306) is at all hours of the day an exceptionally busy road, used as a route by traffic from Richmond and the South Circular to the A3 and Kingston. The best houses are set back from the road behind high walls or in private closes: some are exceptionally large. **Roehampton Close** has '20s and '30s mansion blocks set in large private grounds well away from **Roehampton Lane**, with easy access to Barnes station and the A3. **Eliot Gardens**, modern 3-storey town-houses with garages, is set back off **Roehampton Lane**. Upper numbers of **Roehampton Lane** towards Roehampton proper are mainly '30s terraced and semi-detached homes set rather close to the road and with views of the Alton Estate. On the edge of Richmond Park and bordered by playing-fields and Roehampton Golf Course, **Roedean Crescent** features large detached double-fronted houses, mainly '30s and '50s, built in traditional styles with vast gardens and most with in-and-out drives. Neighbouring **Roehampton Gate** is also quiet and has smaller, detached pre-war houses also popular, but fetching lower prices. Prices of the big 1930s detached houses in **Priory Lane** by **Roehampton Gate** tend to be lower due to traffic. At the northern (Barnes Common) end of **Priory Lane** is the 1970s brick-and-concrete Lennox council estate to the W, usually with some properties for sale, and Rosslyn Park rugby football club to the E.

Transport	Tubes: East Putney (zones 2/3, District). To Oxford Circus 25 min (1 change), City 25 min, Heathrow 50 min (1 change). Trains: Putney, Barnes to Waterloo.
Convenient for	Putney Common and Heath, Richmond Park, the Thames. Routes to the SW and W. Miles from centre: 5.
Schools	Local Authority: Burntwood (g), Elliott. Private: Ibstock Place, Putney High (g), Putney Park (g), Hurlingham, Prospect House.

SALES

Flats	S	1B	2B	3B	4B	5B
Average prices	60–85	100–135	130–250+	180–300	220–350+	—

Houses	2B	3B	4B	5B	6/7B	8B
Average prices	170–250	250–400	300–550	450–800	600–825	›1M

RENTAL

Flats	S	1B	2B	3B	4B	5B
Average prices	650–700	700–1000	1000–1200+	1200–2500	1800+	2500+

Houses	2B	3B	4B	5B	6/7B	8B
Average prices	1100–1600	1400–1900	1800–2100	2000–3000	—	—

The properties	Family houses, some large, many p/b flats and conversions, and new mews squeezed into the corners. Riverside, heath and common locations attract premiums. Smaller Victorian cottages near centre and river. Putney Hill is E-W divide: W is best.

The Market   East Putney is slightly cheaper: flats, small terraces. Then in price order come smarter cottages W of the High St, smart inter-war and modern flats on Putney Hill and spacious family homes near the Heath. Mansions with grounds, rather than mere gardens, range up to £1.5–2 million. Families tend to stay put: schools are good and gardens large. Local searches: 1 week.

Among those estate agents active in this area are:
- Allan Fuller
- Barnard Marcus
- Kinleigh Folkard & Hayward
- Woolwich
- Andrews
- Townends
- Scotts
- Winkworth*
- Douglas & Gordon
- Bairstow Eves
- Gascoigne Pees
- Allan Briegel
- Hugh Henry
- Geoffrey Jardine
- Foxtons*

* further details: see advertisers' index on p633

P

REGENT'S PARK

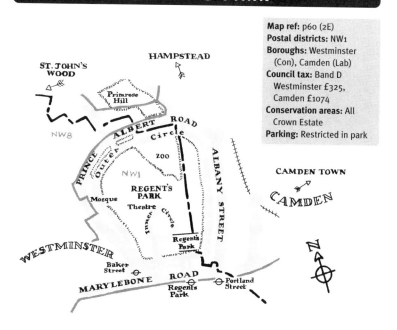

Map ref: p60 (2E)
Postal districts: NW1
Boroughs: Westminster
  (Con), Camden (Lab)
Council tax: Band D
  Westminster £325,
  Camden £1074
Conservation areas: All
  Crown Estate
Parking: Restricted in park

London, on the whole, is not a planned city. Centuries of piecemeal expansion and a strong sense of the sanctity of individuals' property have left it without the grand boulevards and squares of Continental cities. The one exception is Regent's Park. As its name implies, the graceful terraces and handful of glorious villas were planned during the Regency. Nash, with the backing of the Prince Regent, conceived the startling scheme in 1811, making each terrace of houses appear a single, Classical palace, set in a sylvan landscape – the gleaming white façades accentuating the difference between London's town streets and this idealized countryside. Regent's Park still forms part of the Crown Estate, and benefits from its careful management and long-term planning, which has led to the restoration of all the great terraces since 1945. (It survived proposals to demolish half the terraces in the brave new world of the 1950s.) A common policy has been to sell individual houses in the terraces on relatively long leases – 60 years is typical – on the condition that the leaseholder completely restores the house. The Estate stipulates the architect, has a veto over the plans and retains control over the exterior. When a lease on one of the splendid villas, St John's Lodge, came up for sale, the Estate told would-be buyers that it, the Crown, would also choose the interior decorator and the landscape designer. All the buyer had to do, of course, was to pay their fees.

The grand sweep of **Portland Place** leads triumphantly up to the park from Oxford Circus, dividing at the end into the graceful double curve of **Park Crescent** (see Marylebone chapter). The six-lane **Marylebone Rd** is decently shielded from view by the curve of its garden. North of the main road is more greenery, **Park Square**, with its two facing rows of Nash houses forming an entrance to the park. Here a number of the listed houses of **Park Square East**, together with half a dozen flats around the corner in Albany Terrace, which fronts onto **Marylebone Rd**, were sold in the early

1990s with new Crown leases following renovation. These surround the old Diorama – a Victorian precursor to the cinema, nowadays an arts centre.

Clockwise around the **Outer Circle**, terrace succeeds snow-white terrace, each with a distinguishing feature within the overall Classical style. The short **Ulster Terrace** has pairs of bow-fronted windows at either end; then come the gardens of **York Terrace East** and **West**, flanking **York Gate**: these houses face onto their own private roads, while their backs look N over the park. The East stretch is original, and is offices and apartments: it is considered the more exclusive of the two. The West terrace was rebuilt behind the façade and has good, popular flats on 75-year leases, complete with underground garage and security.

Most of the terraces have mews, some of which are still linked to the grand houses so you can buy one of each. Or you can choose a mews house on its own: a 3/4-bed one in **Park Square Mews**, tucked into the corner behind **Ulster Terrace** and **Park Square West**, was £700,000 last December.

Continuing the clockwise progress, **Cornwall Terrace** is the earliest of the park terraces, dating from 1820 and designed by Decimus Burton. Some of the 19 houses are offices. Again, there are bow windows at either end and three great, full-height porticoes with Classical columns. **Clarence Gate** leads out to the top of **Baker St**; small, elegant **Clarence Terrace**, with 2- to 4-bed flats, and studios in the basement, is next in line, backing onto busy **Park Rd**. A 2-bed, second-floor flat here was priced in December at £795,000 for a 67-year lease.

Next comes **Sussex Place**, curving round behind its own garden and served by a private road. Its astonishing row of five pairs of Saracen's helmet-shaped cupolas give it a unique, exotic air. The graceful façade is original, but behind it is a modern re-building carried out for the London Business School – whose principal has a particularly enviable private residence. The next building along, **Hanover Terrace**, is set back behind a garden, its insubstantial-looking statues still adorning its blue-painted portico. This sweep has been completely restored following the Crown's sale of 20 refurbishment leases. These enviable homes have private, west-facing gardens with their own mews houses behind.

The astonishing London Central Mosque with its gold dome stands on the western edge of the park: a splendid building whose outlines somehow marry well with Nash's Classical façades. From here on, the canal curves around the northern edge of the park. Between it and the **Outer Circle** is Hanover Lodge, the fourth of the splendid park 'villas' to revert from an institution to a privately owned home. Five new detached villas by architect Quinlan Terry have been built in the grounds. Opposite, within the park, is vast Winfield House, the American ambassadorial residence. London Zoo takes up the N corner of the park, its muted roars and trumpetings carried on the summer nights' breezes.

On the E side the terraces take up the tale once more: seven of **Gloucester Gate's** houses underwent no-expense-spared refurbishment in 1989. At that time the smallest went for a modest £1.4 million, the beautiful show house seemed cheap at £2.65 million; the largest (two houses made one) sold for £5 million. All seven boast mews houses with garages. There are also flats in the terrace: today you can pay £1,275,000 for a balconied apartment – outstanding and interior-designed but still a flat – on the top floor. You do get a 95-year lease and a garage. A second-floor maisonette on ground and lower ground level offers 2-bed for £795,000. Next in the sequence comes **St Katherine's Precinct**, with 4-storey houses, which leads to the Danish Church.

Cumberland Terrace was rebuilt behind the façade after World War II as houses and flats. The leases here can range from 25 to 50 years, with correspondingly varying prices. **Cumberland Place** boasts a lovely, large Classical villa, bow-windowed at either end. **Chester Terrace** is a long row of 42 more normal-sized houses which remain as individual homes. They were completely rebuilt behind the façade 35 years ago, so allied to their Regency proportions are such modern facilities as lifts and integral garages. The self-contained wings set forward at either end are linked to the main terrace behind them by flying buttress-like archways.

Cambridge Terrace, with its Georgian curved-top windows, nowadays contains flats, maisonettes and houses plus 30,000 sq ft of offices after a 1980s programme of modernization. The next block, **Cambridge Gate**, was built half a century later than its Regency neighbours in sandy stone, and has an ornate and overdecorated air beside their white stucco. Nos 1–9 **Cambridge Gate** are the latest Regent's Park houses to be modernized and converted. On past the uncompromising modern lines of the Royal College of Physicians, and the little Regency cul-de-sac of **St Andrew's Place**, you return to **Park Square**, overlooking its private square gardens, having completed the circuit.

Within the park, around the **Inner Circle**, are the enchanted Open Air Theatre and a handful of scattered 'villas'. Most had dwindled into institutional use, but now some, like Hanover Lodge, are becoming homes again. These glorious original mansions, where the lucky owner can easily imagine himself to be in a country house, are among London's finest. New Crown leases have been sold in the last 15 years on The Holme, Nuffield Lodge and St John's Lodge, with stringent clauses about renovation and upkeep. The Holme was the first, in a splendid position beside the lake: it has its own section of water, out to the island, roped off.

Albany St runs parallel with the E edge of the park. At the S end, **Prince Regent's Terrace**, a row of flat-fronted brick houses, was remodelled into enviable duplexes in 1988: they could be bought singly or as pairs to make a house. At the same time five mews houses were added to **Peto Place** behind. Further N, several rows of mews belonging to the park terraces open off **Albany Rd**. There is also some recent housing in brick and stucco style. On the E side is the **Cumberland Market** estate, a complex of serviceable brick buildings let by the Crown Estate as fair rent housing. The 500 flats were all renovated a decade ago.

Park Village West is an oddity, a curving lane off **Albany Rd** where the Regency style reappears laced with Gothic in a surprising collection of little Nash 'country cottages'. **Park Village East**, which lies behind, suffered when the houses on the E side were demolished to widen the Euston railway. Houses in this mock-village rarely come up for sale, but 1990 saw two unmodernized ones, with new 62-year leases, put on the market by the Crown Estate. The first, in **Park Village East**, was a large, 4,500 sq ft semi-detached listed house which sold at the time for £550,000. The second, in **Park Village West**, was £750,000. Should such houses come on the market now, the prices would be more than double. **Park Village East** and the extreme E end of **Prince Albert Rd** are very close to the rail line into Euston. This is to be upgraded with new overhead power cables – work which threatens to disturb the locals' peace. A public inquiry into the details of this scheme is due this spring.

Prince Albert Rd runs in a sweep along the N bank of the canal, its grand parade of flats, from turn-of-the-century to modern luxurious, attracting top prices with their splendid park views. It was here, in the early 1980s, that London first acquired a stock of international-standard flats – for jet-set buyers for whom 'Georgian' meant merely 'second-hand'. At the E end, by the canal, are some surviving pairs of 1850s villas. Nos 6–15, which are in pairs, were expensively reconstructed in 1989: these are vast 6-bedroomed homes, some with swimming pools, with 99-year leases: long for the Crown Estate. What is more, the normal sub-letting prohibition does not apply.

St Mark's Square has mid-19th-century houses and links with the Primrose Hill neighbourhood (see Camden Town chapter). The green sweep of the Hill rises up to the right, then the blocks of mansion flats for which **Prince Albert Rd** is famous for begin. Prince Albert Court is dark purply-grey brick, St James's Close is red-brick 1930s. Park St James, set back on **St James's Terrace**, was the first new block for some 15 years when built in 1984. Stockleigh Hall is 1920s, stucco and red-brick: a 3-bed flat here needing modernization was a mere £380,000 for a 76-year lease in December: service charge is over £4,000, however. Viceroy Court is also '20s with inset balconies and curving ends. **Bentinck Close** is more '30s; then comes 1920s Oslo Court. These blocks are a good hunting-ground for a decent-sized 3/4-bed flat. Large 3-bed flats here can be had for around £550,000, with a 5-bed flat in **Bentinck Close** commanding £1 million despite being 'in need of updating'.

Avenue Rd runs down to meet **Prince Albert Rd** from the heart of St John's Wood. On the corner, luxurious 2 **Avenue Rd** has large projecting balconies; facing it is a white stone balconied block, Imperial Court. The pair are well-established modern blocks, 20–25 years old, and flats here command premium prices. A 4-bed, 3-bath flat in Imperial Court, with a large terrace overlooking the park, was £1.3 million in January for a 990-year lease – plus service charges of £8,500 a year. Then comes Edwardian splendour: the red and white mansion blocks of Northgate which stand on the corner of **Prince Albert Rd** and **St John's Wood High St**. These are elegant, well-proportioned, well-thought-of flats. A 5-bed, 3-bath 'family apartment' was £875,000 for a 129-year lease in December. Service charges, mind you, are £6,500 a year.

Park Rd runs along the western edge of the park, a fertile ground for ever more flats schemes. Except at the extreme N end, blocks in this road lack the park views – penthouses may be an exception. The 12-year-old Beverly House is a U-shaped building on a rather cramped site, with windows eyeball to eyeball across a courtyard. The places to live here are the truly vast penthouses: 6,000 sq ft over two floors.

Crown Court (1980s) has just 23 flats of from 1 to 5 bedrooms in its seven floors. The entrance is via an enormous foyer behind an arched brick colonnade, guarded by uniformed porters. The flats each have balconies or roof gardens, reached through more arches. Abbey Lodge, '20s mansion blocks, is on the W side of the road backs onto the **Nash Terraces**, which resume with **Kent Terrace**. This, being tucked behind **Hanover Terrace**, is one of the few not to overlook the park. At the S end of **Park Rd** are some pretty early 19th-century houses, not part of the Nash ensemble.

There is scant space for new developments surrounding the park, but Barratt have discovered a plot in the old goods yard behind Marylebone Station which is 'only 250 yards' from the park. Here, off **Park Rd** and within the NW1 postcode, will be 'Prince Regent's Gate', a 400-flat complex with swimming pool and fitness suite, underground parking, electronic gates, 24hr uniformed concierge – the whole NW1 lifestyle. The layout of the stepped-roof crescent that forms the main block allows terraces for many of the 1- to 3-bedroomed flats and penthouses. Marketing began in January: no firm prices yet but count on half a million upwards, though the smallest 1-bed should start at c. £385,000. Another rumour has one 6,000 sq ft penthouse pre-sold at £4.5 million. The scheme also includes plans for 100 flats for the Acton Housing Association.

Transport	Tubes: Regent's Park (Bakerloo), Baker Street (Metropolitan, Bakerloo, Circle, Jubilee). From Regent's Park: Oxford Circus 3 min, City 20 min (1 change), Heathrow 55 min (1 change).
Convenient for	West End, City, Euston, King's Cross and St Pancras Stations. Roads to West and North. Miles from centre: 1.5.

| Schools | Local Authority: Haverstock School, Maria Fidelis Convent RC, St Marylebone C of E. Private: Cavendish School (g), Francis Holland School (g). |

SALES

Flats

	S	1B	2B	3B	4B	5B
Average prices	100–135	125–265+	220–800	300+	400+	3M

Houses

	2B	3B	4B	5B	6/7B	8B
Average prices	350–650	450–800	520–1.1M+	→2M	1.75M–6.6M	→20M

RENTAL

Flats

	S	1B	2B	3B	4B	5B
Average prices	650–1000	730–1700	1300–2400+	1800–6500	3000–13,000	5000+

Houses

	2B	3B	4B	5B	6/7B	8B
Average prices	1500–3500	2300–5500	3900–10,000	8000+	→20,000	–

| The properties | Charmed circle of top-quality homes for millionaires: no-expense-spared conversions of snowy Regency terraces into houses and apartments. Luxury 20th-century flats on Prince Albert and Park Rds, and mews behind terraces. A handful of London's finest mansions. |

| The market | Crown Estate leases are typically 40 years; strict conditions on upkeep and use: no sub-letting. Steady demand from foreign and British buyers for some of London's smartest homes. Local searches: Westminster 2 days, Camden 2 weeks. |

Among those estate agents active in this area are:
- Aston Chase
- Ancombe & Ringland *
- John D Wood
- FPDSavills
- Keith Cardale Groves
- Regents Residential
- Knight Frank
- Cluttons Daniel Smith
- Hamptons
- Kinleigh Folkard & Hayward
- Oakleys
- Regent's Park Property Services
- Winkworth *
- Goldschmidt & Howland
- Bairstow Eves
- Kay & Co Ltd*
- Foxtons*

* further details: see advertisers' index on p633

R

RICHMOND AND KEW

Map ref: p88 (5D)
Postal districts: TW9, TW10
Boroughs: Richmond
upon Thames (Lib Dem)
Council tax: Band D £762
Conservation areas: Include
Richmond town, riverside
and Green, Kew Green
Parking: Residents/meters
in centre

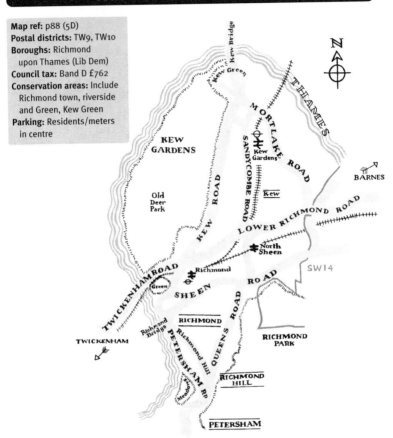

Richmond is a town. It is in no real sense a suburb of London, cut off as it is by its enormous park. The Thames and the tube link Richmond, just, to London, but the people who live here see themselves, perhaps more than any other inhabitants of areas in this book, as citizens of Richmond, Surrey rather than the wider city. And who can blame them for keeping the place to themselves? It has a river front, 2,500 acres of primeval English landscape – oaks and deer-dotted rolling grassland – in its park, and beautiful buildings. Vulgar commerce may take Richmond people by train or tube into Town, and they vehemently claim that the West End theatres are just as accessible as their own, but their heart remains in the borough.

Increasingly, people from elsewhere come to Richmond to be entertained, to eat out, to visit the pubs and bars, to stroll by the river. In the affluent reaches of South West London and Surrey, it's Kingston for shopping and Richmond for leisure.

Politically, Richmond takes in Twickenham, Kew, Petersham, Ham and a wide swathe to the W down to Hampton Court. The Thames, meandering beneath Richmond Hill and past Kew Gardens, links all these places. Here we cover Richmond and Kew; Twickenham has its own chapter. Within its boundaries Richmond has palaces, wide parks, miles of river bank and no less than 40 conservation areas. It is 9 miles SW of Central London.

Originally it was called Shene, meaning (it's alleged) 'bright and shining place'. Henry VII renamed the town after his earldom in Richmond, Yorkshire. He built a palace S of Richmond Green (the remains of which can be seen as Palace Gate), making the town a fashionable royal resort until Charles II moved to Windsor and Shene Palace fell into disrepair. Richmond continued to attract noble visitors (as is evident from the villas along **Petersham Rd**), artists and writers. The Old Deer Park (N), Richmond Park (E) and Thames-side walks still draw families and frazzled commuters who can shake off the city dust (Waterloo 20 min by express train). There is a wealth of good prep schools and church schools. The German School at Ham attracts diplomats and City people. Australian/American expatriates like the quintessential Englishness; the Japanese come for the golf courses (Old Deer Park/Fulwell/Sudbrook Park) and the reasonable proximity to the Japanese School in Acton. They all like being a fast drive away from Heathrow – and no-one seems to mind that the planes trundle over the green so low you can count the rivets. Attempts to build up a head of residents' indignation against the Terminal 5 plans at Heathrow have so far failed.

Prices are high, and stayed high when other areas slumped: this is a very popular area. It is *par excellence* a place for families. Once they get established, they stay put – to the despair of agents who are short of homes to sell.

The 1998 market was quieter than the previous two years which saw some dramatic price rises. The investors who had helped drive prices up backed away, and market dominance returned to the hands of local families steadily trading their way up. Prices stablized, and (in line with other 'prime London' areas) some reductions have been seen, particularly for flats. The best family homes, on Richmond Hill and in Petersham/Ham, still command prices around £1 million. City people and foreign businessmen drive this market. Those seeking more affordable, but still spacious, family homes look to Kew and across the river to St Margarets. Demand is fuelled by Richmond Borough's schools, which at primary level regularly top the league tables.

There is a fair supply of 1-bed flats but in prime areas near the river, hill and green, they can cost more than £150,000. A 2-bed flat may be around £250,000 if it has good views and a roof terrace. Most 3-bed flats are found in mansion blocks which may cost around £210,000 towards the **Twickenham Rd** but will start to rise to £350,000-plus approaching central Richmond.

Richmond and its satellites has a wealth of wonderful period houses. These range from Queen Anne through all stages of Georgian. When they come up for sale, which is rarely, they can cost anything up to £2 million – more for the mansions of Ham.

Richmond Town

Richmond is squeezed between the river, its park, the Old Deer Park and the open fields of Petersham. Most of it was built up in or before Victorian times: there is very little modern housing. The fact that Richmond town is a conservation area means that there are few unpleasant parts. A busy railway line passing behind **Pembroke Villas** and **Old Palace Yard** will make no difference to the price of property because the substantial houses and early 19th-century cottages have such lovely outlooks onto the green. Indeed, demand is high. Shopping is pleasant S of the green around **George St**, the town's high street. There's a full-blown department store (Dickins & Jones) and all the more tasteful high street chains, plus a Tesco Metro and Marks & Spencer. The smart shops extend S along **Hill St** towards the bridge, taking up the E side of the riverside complex (see below). Restaurants and bars are plentiful, though most are of the mid-level chain or theme sort: no-one seems to succeed with a really smart restaurant in Richmond. Alleyways lead off **George St**, with delicatessens, coffee shops, restaurants, bookshops and craft shops. **Church Walk**, one of these alleyways, opens onto Richmond Parish Church.

The green is surrounded by homes, ranging from 17th to 20th century. Most of the beautiful 18th-century houses on the SE side of the green are offices. In the SW corner is **Old Palace Terrace**, seven houses built in 1692. On the NW side are some splendid large Victorian villas; on the NE side some handsome 1970s houses.

Behind **Old Palace Yard** and **The Wardrobe**, where three surviving houses are the remains of Richmond Palace, is **Maids of Honour Row** (1724) which was built for the maids of George II's queen. One of these beauties sold for £750,000 in 1989; another for £1.5 million in 1997. Next is the Old Court House, Wentworth House, and then **Garrick Close**, which holds a collection of neo-Georgian town-houses. **Friars Lane** (where a 1-bedroomed flat is typically £180,000) runs close to **Maids of Honour Row**; it curves down to the river where it joins **Cholmondeley Walk** past Queensbury House, with its neat '30s flats, and a row of pretty Georgian houses. The restored Palladian villa, Asgill House, is at the northern end of the riverside **Cholmondeley Walk**. Here is the south façade of Trumpeter's House (now flats) with its Classical portico. Commanding spectacular views of the bridge and river is the early 19th-century **St Helena's Terrace**, a handsome row of houses built above their own boathouses.

Further S, beside the river walkway which leads to Richmond Bridge, is the £25 million Riverside complex. Designed by Quinlan Terry, and developed in the 1980s by Haslemere Estates, the scheme is one of the most argued-over pieces of architecture of recent years, pitting neo-Classicists against Modernists in a bitter professional row. Quinlan used a variety of Classical genres to produce neo-Classical façades which hide offices, shops, restaurants and a car park. Unrivalled views of the river are a plus for the studios, 1- and 2-bed flats, maisonettes and a penthouse. A 1-bed flat here was £160,000 in December.

On the other side of the town, past the station, a church in **Kew Rd** has been split into 15 flats, ranging from studios to 3-bed. Just across the road, a dozen new flats by St George all sold quickly. The roads between **Kew Rd** and the Old Deer Park are pretty if congested.

R

Richmond Hill

The main residential area of central Richmond is on the slopes of Richmond Hill, which rises S and SE of the town towards Richmond Park.

Ormond Rd has some Queen Anne houses: £700,000 was being asked for a 4-bed one in December. Favourite roads for 5-bed Victorian houses are **Mount Ararat Rd**, **Grosvenor Rd**, **Montague Rd** and **Dynevor Rd** – all E of **Richmond Hill**. However, all hill locations are desirable. **Church Rd** has big houses, some flats, but has quite a lot of traffic. **The Vineyard**, which crosses **Mount Ararat Rd**, is one of the prettiest streets of Richmond Hill. It comprises houses from late-17th to early 19th centuries, including almshouses, all clustered around St Elizabeth of Portugal RC Church. **Onslow Avenue** has Edwardian 5-bed houses: one was on the market at £560,000 in December. In general, good Hill houses go for around £750,000 and the best can top £1 million.

Further E between **Albert Rd** and **Princes Rd** is an area of tiny cottages known as **The Alberts**. These have been popular for years and they have nearly all been tidied up. Prices for 2-bed ones start at £190,000; for 3-bed £280,000 might be asked.

The top of **Richmond Hill** is lined with a mixture of prized 18th- and 19th-century houses (some split into flats) which enjoy a wonderful distant view of the Thames painted by J M Turner and Reynolds. A fourth-floor 3-bed flat here, with a raised dais so the occupants of the main bedroom could enjoy the view lying down, was £375,000 in December. A 5-storey house was £900,000. Turn E into **Queen's Rd**, which hugs Richmond Park, go past the American University buildings and on the left is a range of enormous houses, many split into flats. On the right-hand side are houses and flats of the 1970s, '80s and '90s and some side-roads which lead towards the park, **Cambrian Rd** leads to a gate into the park. West of **Queen's Rd** there are some pretty roads, such as **Park Rd,** offering a blend of early Victorian 3-storey houses and 2-bed cottages. **Marchmont Rd** and **Denbigh Gardens** have Edwardian and 1920s/'30s detached houses. **King's Rd**, with some large Victorian Gothic detached houses and a terrace of 1850s 4/5-storey ones, runs up to the prominent church at the junction with **Friars Stile Rd**, which has a clutch of smart shops and also some 5-bed period houses at around £750,000.

North of **Sheen Rd** in **Dunstable Rd**, **Sheen Park**, **Townshend Terrace** and **St Mary's Grove** there are Victorian and Regency cottages and large 3-storey houses, some of which have been converted into flats. Houses here may be cheaper than those on Richmond Hill, but the disadvantage is that some back onto the railway line. A cottage in **Townshend Terrace**, in need of total renovation, went in December for £110,000.

Between **Sheen Rd** and **Lower Mortlake Rd** is a grid of roads with 2/3-bed period cottages. Recently renovated, they fetch around £160,000. The old council depot site in **Cedar Terrace**, **Lower Mortlake Rd**, now boasts 90 new homes: 2-bed maisonettes and 2-bed terraced houses. The new depot, on **Lower Mortlake Rd**, will be mixed-use. **Sheendale Rd** has beautiful (if cramped, and gardenless) Regency cottages. **St George's Rd**, **Bardolph Rd** and **Trinity Cottages** are pretty but they face a small industrial development and are in the shadow of the old gasworks site which will become a Sainsbury's supermarket in 2000. Disgruntlement about this development – councillors and locals fear traffic chaos – is not shared by estate agents, who say house prices will go up.

Either side of the **Lower Richmond Rd** are Victorian terraced cottages which overlook a very busy road. East of **Manor Rd**, which joins **Sheen Rd** and **Lower Richmond Rd** via a constantly busy railway level crossing, there are council-built houses on **Kings Farm Avenue** and **Carrington Rd**. Roads between **Sheen Court Rd, Tangier Rd** and **Warren Rd** offer '30s-built 3/4-bed houses, which can fetch over £250,000. South of **Upper Richmond Rd** post-war houses are to be found, particularly on **Berwyn Rd**, **Orchard Rise** and **Sheen Common Drive**. Proximity to park and common raises prices here to around half a million. **Courtlands** is a large 1930s complex of mansion flats: big blocks in well-kept grounds with 'private' signs. A 3-bed flat here might cost £200,000.

Petersham and Ham Common

These villages on the borders of Richmond offer rural living to people who cannot bear to be more than half an hour by car from Hyde Park Corner. They have served this function for 300 years, as the dignified Georgian homes testify. The fast journey may only be possible at two o'clock in the morning, but Richmond does well as a substitute for the West End for most purposes, and Kingston's shopping centre is just down the road.

Petersham is surrounded on nearly every side by green spaces: deer-grazed Richmond Park to the E, the cattle-dotted water meadows by the Thames to the N, the dignified Ham House grounds to the W. Its only snag is the snarling traffic that creeps past the high brick walls that shut off the grand houses. A pretty Georgian stucco house with 7 bedrooms and lovely panelled reception rooms was £2 million last winter. However, for a taste of fine living try the flats in one of the grandest mansions. There are some smaller houses in Petersham, including a few 20th-century ones in a more suburban setting over towards Ham, but most are at least a century old. The German School – and the excellent local primary school – attract families.

Ham Common is a splendid, large triangle of manicured rural England, with the gates to ducal Ham House to add class. There are grand Georgian homes here on the Petersham scale, and a few smaller cottages. A new 'mansion' has been built on the S side in impeccable neo-Georgian: it is a clutch of new flats. Much of Ham is suburbia, including a big (mostly ex-) council estate over towards the Thames and the well-regarded '60s Parkleys estate. Towards Richmond Park, **Church Rd** has 20th-century houses, mostly big and grand. A dozen new ones sold fast last year at around £350,000 despite being next door to the (very polite) Latchmere House prison.

Kew

Kew has a village feel, with a green complete with cricket pitch – though the constant South Circular traffic, coupled with the Heathrow planes, dispels any rural illusions. It also has a village property market, with one agent finding that 75 per cent of this business is with locals moving around the area. The new estate planned on the old sewage works to the E of the area should bring in some new blood, however.

Kew is a peninsula bounded by the Thames. To the N and E, across the river, are Brentford and Chiswick, with Richmond to the S and Mortlake to the SE. The world-famous botanical gardens at Kew, together with the Old Deer Park, take up to 50 per cent of the area. Despite the green space, Kew is surrounded by main roads. Busy **Kew Rd** bears traffic SW from Kew Bridge and the M4/North Circular junction at Chiswick roundabout. From the green, **Mortlake Rd**, part of the South Circular, forks SE. Between these roads is the bulk of the area's housing. The roads on the Kew Gardens side of **Sandycombe Rd** and the railway line are most sought-after, with the eastern side (sometimes called North Sheen) increasing in desirability.

The area has firmly shrugged off its fuddy-duddy image. It was considered an old peoples' area, but the ever-

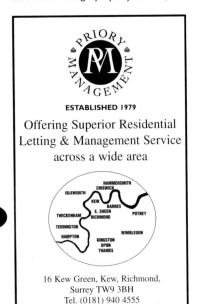

growing pressure for spacious houses near open space and good schools has seen an influx of young families. Richmond Borough's excellent schools, plus several private ones, reinforce the attraction. Such is the demand that the council are planning to expand Darell Primary School, and a new school may form part of the sewage-works scheme.

Kew Green and Gardens

The most prestigious property is found around **Kew Green**, where the best of the gracious Georgian houses and cottages, surrounded by mature trees, decked with wisteria and backing onto the river and/or facing the green can top £1 million. Few ever change hands, to the frustration of local agents. To the E of the green, in an enclave bounded by river, green and railway, **Bushwood Rd**, **Priory Rd**, and **Maze Rd** are leafy Victorian/Edwardian 3-bed terraces which can command prices of up to £500,000. Close to the bridge, **Thetis Terrace** and **Cambridge Cottages** and **Watcombe Cottages** (2-bed) fetch prices of £275,000 for their 2-bed cottages. A row of cottages (slightly sunken) overlooking the Thames and Strand-on-the-Green and fronted with green lawns can cost up to £275,000 if they face the river.

The enormous modern Public Record Office, on the riverside E of the rail bridge, is a Kew landmark. A piece of land between it and the river is destined for 207 flats if developers St George get their way: this is the fifth such scheme, four public enquiries having refused successive plans for this site since 1989. Just down river, the 24-acre sewage works is to be decommissioned (how *do* you do that?) and replaced with 400 more homes in a joint venture between Thames Water and Berkeley Homes (St George's parent company). This scheme proposes quite a bit of open land, a new path to the riverside, and low-built blocks along the present open riverside. Locals are worried about traffic: access will be off the South Circular and along **Townmead Rd**.

South into **Kew Rd** from the green, there is a clutch of interesting houses on the left-hand side, facing Kew Gardens, ranging from **Hanover Place** (early 18th century) to later styles with Regency bow windows. These give way to large Victorian villas interspersed with modern blocks of mansion flats: if high enough they can have views over Kew Gardens. Past Newens (the traditional English tea shop serving Maid of Honour tarts), **Kew Gardens Rd** dog-legs around towards **Station Approach**. Large 3-storey Victorian houses dominate; some flats, some spacious family homes.

Station Approach and **Station Parade** join at Kew Gardens station (District line and North London line). Shops and cafés cater for visitors to the gardens – a steady stream in summer – and the locals. The only other shopping area is **Sandycombe Rd** which has an odd mish-mash of useful shops, and the little shops dotted around the green. Thirlstone (Berkeley Homes again) have built 35 homes at 'Kew Place' on land N of **Station Approach**.

Popular **Lichfield Rd** and **Ennerdale Rd** join **Kew Rd** and **Sandycombe Rd**. Here the large Victorian family houses with 5 bedrooms (some converted into desirable flats) cost £850,000-plus, £1 million-plus if double-fronted. In **Sandycombe Rd** prices vary with the side of the road: the E side (odd numbers) back onto the tube line. The more favoured W side sees prices up to £285,000. **Ennerdale Rd** (transversed by **The Avenue**) stretches S down to the T-shaped **Lion Gate Gardens**, (whose large Victorian houses make for roomy flat conversions; c. £200–240,000) and on to **Stanmore Gardens** where the Victorian houses are interspersed with solid '30s styles. Turning E into **Gainsborough Rd** there is a recent development of neo-Georgian houses on the site of a school; opposite some little council houses. On **Kew Rd**, between **Lichfield Rd** and **Hatherley Rd**, are some recent blocks of studio and 1- and 2-bed flats.

To the W of **Sandycombe Rd** there are **Victoria Cottages** and **Elizabeth Cottages**, which fetch a little more (c. £190–230,000) because they do not back onto the railway.

R

Alexandra Rd and **Windsor Rd** have terraced 2-bed cottages which go for £200–270,000. East of the railway and **Sandycombe Rd**, towards **Mortlake Rd,** are **Atwood Avenue, Marksbury Avenue** and **Chelwood Gardens** where large '30s houses have been renovated to provide solid family homes. They are now commanding prices of 275–400,000 for a well-maintained 3/4-bed house. Gardens on this side of Kew are more spacious. For cheaper 3-bed houses (Victorian/Edwardian) look towards **Dancer Rd**, **Darell Rd** and **Raleigh Rds** where they can be picked up for £200,000-plus, although these roads do run down to a busy stretch of the **Lower Richmond Rd**, otherwise the A316, the direct link to the M3. This corner will be affected by the **Manor Rd** Sainsbury's. This end of Kew is within walking distance of North Sheen station, with direct trains to Waterloo.

Transport	Tubes: Kew Gardens, Richmond (zone 4, District). To Oxford Circus 35 min (1 change), City 40 min, Heathrow 45 min (1 change). M25. Trains: Richmond, North Sheen to Waterloo 20-plus min; also N London line/Silverlink from Kew Gardens.
Convenient for	Heathrow, M3/M4 for South and West, River Thames, Richmond Park, Kew Gardens. Miles from centre: 8.
Schools	Richmond Education Authority: Richmond C of E High School (formerly Christ's School), Grey Court, Shene School. Private: St Catherine's Convent School (g), St James's (b). See also Twickenham. German School (Petersham).

SALES

Flats	S	1B	2B	3B	4B	5B
Average prices	65–100	90–170+	135–300+	170–400+	250–420+	—

Houses	2B	3B	4B	5B	6/7B	8B
Average prices	160–280+	200–500	250–750+	300–900+	600–1.1M+	—

RENTAL

Flats	S	1B	2B	3B	4B	5B
Average prices	500–600	700–1200	850–1400+	1250–2000+	2000–3000+	—

Houses	2B	3B	4B	5B	6/7B	8B
Average prices	1500–3500	2300–5500+	3900–10,000+	8000+	→20,000	—

The properties	Wide range of desirable houses from early Georgian through mid-Victorian (the majority) to modern, plus mansion flats and conversions. River and parkside locations among the most charming in London. Two-bed flats are most popular; family homes always scarce. Kew offers family homes and flats at better-value prices.
The market	Demand still brisk, especially for family homes, but buyers more hesitant than in '98. Rentals increasingly popular, with movers from Chiswick, Hammersmith and Fulham. Big premiums paid for best locations on riverside and Richmond Hill. English (especially City-working) and foreign families find area gives happy mix of London and country. Local searches: 2 weeks.

R

Among those estate agents active in this area are:
- Victor Lown
- Nightingale Chancellors
- Dixon Porter
- Barnard Marcus
- Mann & Co
- Jardine & Co
- Chancellors
- G A Property
- Gascoigne Pees
- Phillip Hodges
- FPDSavills
- Hamptons
- Halifax
- Priory Management *

further details: see advertisers' index on p633

R

SHEPHERD'S BUSH

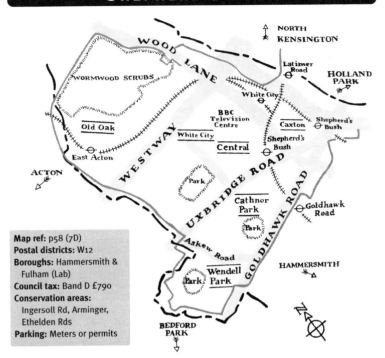

Map ref: p58 (7D)
Postal districts: W12
Boroughs: Hammersmith &
   Fulham (Lab)
Council tax: Band D £790
Conservation areas:
   Ingersoll Rd, Arminger,
   Ethelden Rds
Parking: Meters or permits

The biggest – and, due to changes in planning, perhaps the last – new shopping complex inside the M25 is about to be built next to Shepherd's Bush Green. The Bush, a now rather dowdy part of West London, is crying out for a bit of sparkle and decent shops, but how the inevitable increase in traffic will be handled remains to be seen. The area is already famous for its bottlenecks. The plus side of the White City scheme, as it is called, will be a £100 million upgrade to public transport. This is perhaps linked to the change in policy that now frowns upon such schemes. However, outline permission was granted for this one before the policy switch.

The site to be developed is the old tube depot W of the M41/railway corridor and S of **Ariel Way** and **Wood Lane**. A few streets of homes divide it from the green, but there will be access to the new mall from the E corner of the green by the Central line station. On the E side Marks & Spencer plan to build one of their biggest-ever stores. The other end of the site will have a Sainsbury's opening onto **Wood Lane**. In between will be more shops and a glass-roofed 'winter garden' with cafés and restaurants. All 4,500 parking spaces will be underground. Car access will be from a new junction halfway along the M41. Next to the existing tube a new station will serve the West London line (Willesden to Clapham Junction) and the Wood Lane (Central line) and Shepherd's Bush (Hammersmith & City line) stations will be integrated.

All this is in a plan put forward by developers Chelsfield in December 1998 for detailed permission, so the go-ahead now depends on Hammersmith and Fulham Council – not to mention the wider economy.

Until the end of the 18th century Shepherd's Bush was just another area of countryside around London. But buildings shot up during the 19th century as the capital expanded rapidly and Shepherd's Bush, well-placed on a main route from the W, soon became a centre. Its triangular green became a focus for travelling traders on their way to market.

The origins of the quirky name remain a mystery although various theories have emerged over the years. Some say the area was named after a famous landowner. Others insist that the body of a murdered shepherd was found in bushes on the green several centuries ago. But by far the most popular explanation springs from its position on a major droving route. It is likely that shepherds rested their flocks on the green before the final hike up to Smithfield Market. The only sheep there today are the ones painted on the Central line tube station.

Most houses here are of the solid 2- or 3-storey workaday terraced variety, built in the late-19th century, and Shepherd's Bush changed very little until the second half of the 20th century when council blocks, motorways and shopping precincts arrived.

Apart from the major traffic roundabout near the green, which links with the M41, the character of Shepherd's Bush has survived relatively unscathed and much of the dominant Victorian and Edwardian architecture is still intact after a century.

Much of the personality of today's Bush is derived from the heavy presence of the BBC. Its new 'super' HQ up Wood Lane now shelters nearly all the programme-making staff, with only a few bosses and accountants still enjoying the West End ambience of Broadcasting House. This has changed the area's restaurant profile. While it is certainly no Notting Hill or Soho, the area has gained a rash of up-market 'dining pubs' and other interesting eateries that are certainly kept going by the media people. The BBC tribe joins the cheerful cosmopolitan mix of Asians, Irish, West Indians, Poles, Africans and representatives of most other ethnic groups.

Shepherd's Bush is ideally situated for public transport and major routes in and out of London. It is on both the Central and Hammersmith & City tube lines and midway between the A40 **Oxford Rd** in the N and the M4 – gateway to Heathrow and the West. The Nos 12 and 88 buses take shoppers direct to the West End.

Like many other central parts of London (and despite its name), Shepherd's Bush lacks open spaces and there is a shortage of trees and greenery, and of family houses with large gardens. Shopping is humdrum and will remain so until (and if) the White City mall emerges. There is a colourful market off the **Uxbridge Rd** under the railway bridge. The Bush Theatre on the green is a well-respected fringe venue.

The boom in flat conversions, which has been checked by local planning policy after its '80s heyday, brought car parking problems to an increasing number of streets. Residents pay for a permit and towaway trucks prowl.

Shepherd's Bush has been very much a first-time buyers' market but, say agents hopefully, it is starting to attract overspill from posher and pricier Notting Hill. Many of the tall Victorian terraces were converted into 1- and 2-bedroom flats during the 1980s but the supply has slowed and some streets are seeing the bigger houses converted back into family homes. There is still a lot of rented property, and some streets remain relatively undeveloped.

Family houses are in still the minority, although they are more common near **Goldhawk Rd** on the Hammersmith borders. Shepherd's Bush does not have enclaves as recognizably self-contained as Brook Green in next-door Hammersmith, but properties of a similar type do tend to form neighbourhoods.

S

The most sought-after areas lie between the **Uxbridge** and **Goldhawk Rds**. Newer 1930s-style houses can be found near Wendell Park, and the district N of **Cobbold Rd**, really East Acton (see chapter) is a mixture of purpose-built Edwardian maisonettes and Victorian terraces.

Larger family houses lie W of **Askew Rd** around **Rylett Rd** and **Ashchurch Park Villas**, probably the lordliest road in Shepherd's Bush. You can move into a gorgeous

An essentially Victorian area, Shepherd's Bush shows every variation of the Victorian pattern-book builder's craft. Builders took house plans and details 'off the shelf', resulting in ornamentation like this bay, with its sash windows, stone, or perhaps stucco, parapet and decoration around the tops of the pillars. The house is built of London stock-brick, which when clean contrasts well with the stucco.

Victorian villa for anything between £525,000 and £800,000. Gardens here are huge and residents clearly spend a lot on upkeep. They may prefer to call this corner 'Chiswick' or 'Ravenscourt Park' despite their W12 postcode.

Moving E, Cathnor Park has a village atmosphere which disappears beyond **Boscombe Rd** – known for its 4-storey Victorian terraces, largely converted into flats. North of the **Uxbridge Rd**, properties are generally smaller, although tall houses are found between **Wood Lane** and **Loftus Rd**. West to **Wormholt Rd** is a mix of purpose-built Edwardian maisonettes and solid 2-storey Victorian terraces. Streets of larger 1930s semis border the Cleverley and Flower estates E of **Old Oak Rd**.

North of **Sawley Rd** council-built property is the norm although much of the stock E of **Bloemfontein Rd** is being sold off. Out E towards **Wood Lane** lies the sprawling White City estate with very few privately owned flats. It is not an aesthetic gem. Council-built homes, in the form of the Old Oak Estate, continues N of the **Westway** near East Acton tube station. These pleasant cottage-style homes, which are in a conservation area, often now appear for sale.

Two small but very distinct neighbourhoods complete the overall picture of Shepherd's Bush today. The first, just N of the **Westway** in **Scrubs Lane**, offers a mixture of Edwardian terraces and purpose-built maisonettes. The second is known as Caxton Village, off the green; it is a quaint network of Victorian terraces.

Wendell Park

This is the farthest W and most sylvan bit of W12. Beyond **Emlyn Rd** is the Acton border. 1914 terraced homes with an Arts and Crafts air overlook Wendell Park in tree-lined **Wendell Rd**, where 3- or 4-bed late-Victorian family homes are priced at up to £330,000. The delightful park and nearby tennis courts give this quiet, prosperous area a sense of space. **Rylett Rd, Rylett Crescent** and **Ashchurch Park Villas** to the E contain some of the most expensive properties in Shepherd's Bush. Many of the large family houses are still intact despite the '80s conversion blitz. Some are double-fronted, well-proportioned homes, others 3- or 4-storey Victorian terraces. They ooze Classic style with their ornate pillars and regal front steps. Some houses have garages. Note **Balmoral Mews** and **Cosmer Close** off **Rylett Rd**.

Roads in this district, including **Binden Rd** and **Bassein Park Rd**, are wide with plenty of trees and ornate shrubs. A 4-bed house here might cost £350–450,000. Lovely Ravenscourt Park is close by, with Stamford Brook tube a short step S along the **Goldhawk Rd**. The section of **Goldhawk Rd** that runs E-W rather than N-S is more desirable. Very pleasant 3-storey Victorian houses sell at around £300,000. Many have an attractive raised ground entrance.

Purpose-built Edwardian maisonettes can be found W of **Askew Rd** towards the **Uxbridge Rd**. The attractive red-brick Victorian houses are particularly plentiful in **Cobbold Rd**. Further N in **St Elmo Rd** Victorian terraces dominate. Many have been converted into flats but it is still possible to buy a whole house in this popular area.

Cathnor Park

Similar style continues E of **Askew Rd**. Most homes are 2-storey although elegant 3-storey versions have been converted successfully in **Westville Rd**. Wedged between two bustling districts is little Cathnor Park. **Melina Rd**, a particularly pretty corner of this villagy area, has some of the rare cottage-style houses in Shepherd's Bush. Others in the road are 3-storey terraces with basements and front door steps. Check the **Percy St** area for other pleasant cottage-style homes.

Central Shepherd's Bush

Moving E beyond **Coningham Rd** the houses are taller and mostly divided: this is the heart of flat-land. The seven or so roads W of the green are among the most popular in Shepherd's Bush. They are ideally situated for two Hammersmith & City line tube stations as well as regular buses on **Goldhawk** and **Uxbridge Rds**.

Coningham Rd is busy, though the constant stream has been slowed by traffic calming. For a quieter life try **Hetley Rd**, **St Stephens Avenue** or **Godolphin Rd**, where 1-bed flats can sell for £110,000. Many of the streets are one-way – others are closed in the middle to block off rat-runs between **Uxbridge Rd** and **Goldhawk Rd**. The flats have Classic elegance, sash windows and high ceilings. Outside the roads are relatively wide, light and tree-lined.

Moving N of the **Uxbridge Rd** divide, properties are generally smaller and the neighbourhood less well-regarded. Agents will argue the 'North's' tarnished reputation is rather unfair. W of **Wood Lane**, **Frithville** and **Stanlake Rds**, for example, have very pleasant 5-bed houses, with the best priced at around the £375,000 mark. However, nearby **Tunis Rd** has a completely different character. Its Victorian terraces have attracted conversions, and the gardens here are tiny.

Loftus Rd – an attractive tree-lined street and conservation area – has one major drawback: the stadium which is home to Queen's Park Rangers football club and Wasps rugby club. This normally quiet road turns into a sea of fans at match weekends. QPR want to move, but is short of cash which is reigning in its ambitions. This area has a mixture of flats and houses, with a 3-storey house fetching up to £300,000. A strong residents' committee looks after the neighbours' interests with respect to the presence of QPR.

West of **Loftus Rd** lies an area of Victorian terraces and purpose-built Edwardian maisonettes. **Oaklands Grove** is considered something of a gem. **Bloemfontein Rd**, where a 3-bed Victorian cottage can cost £250,000, runs straight through the neighbourhood and can be busy. Drivers are inclined to use it as a cut-through from the **Westway** in the N to the **Uxbridge Rd**.

Nearby is Hammersmith Park, all that is left of the Franco-British Exhibition of 1908, with ornamental gardens, pavilions and pools. The Janet Adegoke Leisure Centre at Wormholt Park on **Bloemfontein Rd** is also popular. West of **Wormholt Rd** to **Old Oak Rd** the houses are newer – 1930s mostly. The neighbourhood is pleasant; it borders the Cleverley and the cottagy 'Flower' council estates to the N.

The area above **Sawley Rd** to the **Westway** and E of **Old Oak Rd** to **Wood Lane** is another model village, again originally council-built and officially known as the Wormholt Estate. This is the 'Flower Estate', so-called because street names include Daffodil, Clematis and Lilac: pleasant and varied in style. Much of the stock is privately owned and the neighbourhood looks well-cared-for. **Sawley Rd** is particularly attractive: flat-fronted grey-brick homes with arched doors. Although ex-council properties are not to everyone's taste, the Flower estate is, say agents, highly saleable. Here a 2-bed house may fetch £120,000: the larger, double-fronted houses commands higher sums. The estate's cosy village atmosphere changes dramatically E of **Bloemfontein Rd**.

The White City estate, five roads arranged in a criss-cross pattern, houses council tenants in huge blocks of oppressive red-brick. **South Africa Rd** to the S runs alongside to Queen's Park Rangers FC and can be used as a cut-through to **Wood Lane** and the BBC stronghold.

North of the **Westway** is also council-built housing. Busy **Du Cane Rd** runs between **Scrubs Lane** and **Old Oak Lane** in Acton past Hammersmith Hospital and Wormwood Scrubs Prison. The area is dominated by the huge prison compound which looks out over the common towards Willesden Junction and Brent in the distance.

Old Oak

This no-man's-land area, often referred to as East Acton, is depressing and lacks identity. But a little farther down **Du Cane Rd** towards East Acton tube station is the Old Oak estate, with a strong community atmosphere. The estate is isolated from the rest of the area by the railway line. To the NE is the open space of Wormwood Scrubs, to the E the prison. West of the railway is similar estate housing, bounded to the S by the busy six lane **Western Avenue**. **Braybrook St** on the edge of Old Oak Common has attractive flat-fronted terrace brick houses with sash windows. It is surprisingly 'countrified'; 3-bed cottages sell for around £100,000. Sadly the village feel is marred by a sinister view of the imposing prison walls, bright flood lights and watch towers.

Caxton Village

Caxton Village, possibly the most convenient spot in the whole of Shepherd's Bush, will get more useful still if and when the giant White City mall is built next to it. Off the **Uxbridge Rd** on the green, this select neighbourhood of Victorian terraces is in walking distance from three tube stations, two on the Hammersmith & City line and Shepherd's Bush on the Central. The latest plan for the shopping complex buries the car parks which previously loomed over these streets.

Borders

Just N of the **Westway** is a quaint collection of roads on the Kensington and Chelsea border. The streets running off **Eynham Rd** are a mixture of purpose-built Edwardian maisonettes and tall terraces converted into flats. The roads are surprisingly quiet considering their close proximity to the Westway junction with the M41.

Over to the W, just inside the W3 postcode, is a group of streets around **Valetta Rd** that agents are trying to name 'Little Malta' (they just can't resist it, can they?). This district abuts with the Wendell Park area, and homes are similar.

S

Transport	Tubes, all zone 2: Shepherd's Bush (Central, Hammersmith & City); White City, East Acton (Central); Goldhawk Rd (Hammersmith & City). From Shepherd's Bush: Oxford Circus 15 min, City 25 min, Heathrow 1 hr.
Convenient for	BBC Centre, West End, Notting Hill, Heathrow, M4/M40 to West. Miles from centre: 4.5.

Schools Local Authority: Sacred Heart (g); London Oratory (b); Lady Margaret (g). Private: Latymer (b) (g); Godolphin (g).

SALES

Flats	S	1B	2B	3B	4B	5B
Average prices	50–80	70–125	110–180	120–220	150–250	—
Houses	2B	3B	4B	5B	6/7B	8B
Average prices	170–230	180–280	250–375	300–500	—	—

RENTAL

Flats	S	1B	2B	3B	4B	5B
Average prices	565–700	750–950	950–1300	1150–1700	1450–2000	—
Houses	2B	3B	4B	5B	6/7B	8B
Average prices	1100–1300	1200–1800	1700–2300	2400+	2800+	—

The properties Victorian terraces are the staple: smaller 2-storey ones as single homes, taller ones often converted to satisfy demand for 1/2-bed flats. Some larger family homes mainly near Hammersmith borders. Also pockets of Edwardian p/b maisonettes; some roomier inter-war houses. Cheaper: ex-council; cottages, eg 'Flower' Estate, especially popular.

The market Young buyers find the Bush convenient, with good transport to town for those who don't work for the Beeb. BBC land: the gleaming new White City headquarters set the seal on the Bush's renaissance. Singles in studios become couples in flats, but children usually presage move to more family area. Local searches: 3–4 weeks (whatever the council may say).

Among those estate agents active in this area are:
- Barnard Marcus
- Willmotts
- Sullivan Thomas
- Collingwoods
- Barber & Co
- Winkworth *
- Faron Sutaria & Co Ltd*
- Foxtons*

* further details: see advertisers' index on p633

S

SOHO AND COVENT GARDEN

Map ref: p140 (8A)
Postal districts: W1, WC2
Boroughs: Westminster (Con), Camden (Lab)
Council tax: Band D Westminster £325,
   Camden £1074
Conservation areas: Whole area
Parking: Residents/meters, clamps, tow-trucks

Soho and Covent Garden are in the very heart of London. Their streets are shaped by their Georgian past, though they are, these days, largely business and entertainment centres, attracting tourists and Londoners alike to their theatres, clubs and restaurants. They are also sought-after places to work, congenial places to employ designers from graphic to fashion, editors from film to book, creators of cartoons, web-sites and concepts of every sort. Quite a few of these creative types would like to live here too, but they face stiff competition from shops, restaurants and offices (not just their own). And from the burgeoning Chinese community based around **Gerrard St**.

The two areas are very different. Covent Garden's the more public: a meeting-place, alive with the excitement of theatre and opera, and with the equal showmanship of the market-place – one of the best places in Central London to walk and talk, to see and be seen. Soho has long been London's 'foreign' quarter, the place where daring Englishmen ventured for a little Continental naughtiness and a good meal. It's still true, though the food may be Chinese or Indonesian.

Today, Soho is perhaps the younger, and certainly the more daring, of the two, more prone to inner-city pleasures and vices of every sort. Homelessness and drugs have placed heavy burdens on both districts: they attract every lost teenager in Britain, and quite a few from further afield.

Both areas are zealously conserved, with many historic buildings under preservation orders. Consequently the pressure on space is intense. Everyone wants their office, shop, market stall or restaurant here. And both areas have been rediscovered as a place to live. Stories of cheap Soho flats above shops, or old banana warehouses in Covent Garden, are now as much wistful legends as the tales of affordable Docklands warehouses.

What homes there are in Soho and Covent Garden are not immediately apparent, often being tucked away behind the scenes in odd corners off commercial streets, or above the ground-floor shops and first-floor offices. Studios and flats dominate the lists. There are probably only a dozen houses in the whole area. The supply is growing, though (as price comparisons show) it is still not up with demand.

New developments aside, the most common sort of home is the upper floors of a shop or restaurant forming a 2/3-bedroom maisonette. There are no gardens; balconies and patios, occasionally found in new properties, add greatly to prices. They are rare in conversions. Only a handful of flats are available at any one time with brisk demand reported, even in quiet times. Many properties are purchased as pieds-à-terre by business people and can be easily let if not required all year round.

Prices vary dramatically with the size and character of the properties. This is true of sales and of lettings, which are by far the most common way to find a home here.

The obvious advantage of the area is location. It is within easy strolling distance of West End shops and theatres. The City is a 10 min tube ride away. The main demand for homes seems to come from bankers and brokers who work in the City and from people with businesses in the West End – the bachelors of both species. In Soho one finds prosperous young single people who enjoy the night life and may work in the advertising or film industries. In Covent Garden, people with a country home who want a pied-à-terre in town. Quite a few homes are owned by companies for the use of their top people. Others are held as investments and rented out to companies and visiting foreigners.

Before these folk discovered the area, people lived here. And they still do. The original population is more mixed, made up of elderly people and families who work in the traditional local industries – theatre, crafts such as leatherwork and tailoring, shops and restaurants – and who live mainly in rented homes.

Both areas are entirely jumbled: shops, offices, theatres, restaurants, bars and homes often occur in the same street. These amenities provide the plus side to living here but also cause the disadvantage of congestion, both traffic and pedestrian, noise and extreme difficulty in parking. A less tangible benefit is atmosphere.

Old-timers say Covent Garden is past its best – Peter York's 'theme park' tag is uncomfortably accurate – but Soho is if anything on the up and still manages to preserve a raffish, village feel. It's a great place to live and to work, but a wonderful one to live in if you don't have to work. Or sleep. Nowhere in London is idleness more fun.

Soho

Soho is the area S of **Oxford St**, N of **Leicester Square** and E of **Regent St**. **Charing Cross Rd** divides it from Covent Garden to the W.

In the 16th century Soho was a Royal Park where hunting took place – 'So-ho!', an ancient cry, being the presumed origin of the name. It was developed with grand houses in the 17th century and later settled by the Huguenots, giving the area its abiding Continental character. By 1711 there were 600 French householders in Soho, and 3,000 foreign lodgers, mostly French. The population increased rapidly in overcrowded houses until a serious outbreak of cholera in 1854 after which aristocratic residents moved out and prostitutes and other dubious characters moved in. At the start of the 20th century new theatres were built along **Shaftesbury Avenue** and **Charing Cross Rd**. Restaurants, invariably started by foreigners, gave the area a gastronomic reputation. One famous French restaurant was started by a French family in answer to desperate pleas by visiting compatriots for something decent to eat.

After World War II strip clubs and clip joints increased in this area and the residential population declined rapidly. This exodus of residents has now stopped and, thanks to a massive clean-up campaign mounted by Westminster City Council after pressure from the Soho Society, the number of sex clubs has been reduced from more than 100 to a couple of dozen. The area is now famous for its restaurants and cafés, specialist shops, designer workshops and smart offices. Sadly, the French connection, three centuries old, is now broken. The last truly French grocer, Roche, closed in the early '80s.

Soho is still a maze of narrow streets and alleys, and forms a conservation area. Many 18th-century and early 19th-century buildings remain, interspersed with later infill developments of varying styles. Residential Soho has seen a renaissance in recent years. Lovely old houses have been restored, new flats squeezed in, redundant commercial blocks converted. The loft apartment has made its appearance. Other homes are flats above shops or more modern, purpose-built infill developments, again usually over commercial property at ground- and possibly first-floor level.

South of **Shaftesbury Avenue**, **Wardour St**, **Gerrard St** (pedestrianized) and **Lisle St** form the core of Chinatown, a tightly knit neighbourhood characterized by many excellent restaurants, supermarkets and bakeries. Property here is largely owned by the Chinese community and the stock of homes is under great pressure: the 1997 Hong Kong handover increased the arrival rate considerably.

North of **Shaftesbury Avenue**, the area where **Brewer St**, **Berwick St**, **Wardour St** and **Old Compton St** meet is the scruffier part of Soho. But such is demand, prices here are only relatively cheaper. These streets still house the largest share of the sex industry (including **Great Windmill St**, **Archer St**, **Tisbury Court** and **Walkers Court**) and there are a few flats, mainly above shops in **Brewer St**. Typical prices start around £100,000 for a studio. In nearby **Rupert St**, Consolidated Properties created shops and 20 flats out of four houses in 1997. Consolidated are major freeholders in the Soho and Covent Garden areas.

Several renowned Italian delis and cafés are also found in these streets, and further along **Old Compton St**, now much improved due to the council clean-up, there are one or two small infill developments. **Golden Square** and the surrounding roads, **Upper** and **Lower St James St**, **John St** and **Great Pulteney St** are much more 'respectable' and quieter, but again few homes are available as this is more of a business district. However the former Ear, Nose & Throat Hospital in **Golden Square** itself recently became 14 flats. **Golden Square** is a desirable place to live – Soho's only green oasis now that **Soho Square** has become somewhat notorious (especially after dark). Prices for **Golden Square** flats can touch £500,000.

On the W fringe of Soho, towards **Regent St**, **Kingly St**, the famous

Behind the shopfronts and the neon, much of Soho is old. It was a fashionable suburb in the 17th and 18th centuries, and some houses still survive from these periods. These, in Meard St, were restored after years in disrepair. Door, elaborate doorcase and railings are all perfect examples of their period.

Carnaby St and **Fouberts Place** are largely shopping areas – rather self-conciously calling themselves 'West Soho' – and the occasional flat may come on to the market. However, close by in **Marshall St** is Marshall House, a 1989 block of 12 1-bedroom and nine 2-bedroom flats. At the other end of the street, Stirling Court is a 1970s 10-floor flat block: 1-bed flats rent for around £280 pw. **Newburgh** and **Marshall Sts** have recently been recobbled, **Fouberts Place** has been repaved as well. Sandringham Court in **Dufours Place** is a popular development, completed by Barratt in 1987; resales do come up occasionally, and the block is also popular for lettings. Flats may be had in the Georgian terraced houses of **Lexington St**.

Great Malborough St, **Noel St** and N of here is unlikely to be fruitful for homes, being more of a business/office area. **Poland St**, **Broadwick St** with its Georgian terraces and **D'Arblay St** are more popular and more expensive. **Poland St** has a modern mixed block of offices and flats. Six new flats appeared last year in this street: prices started at £235,000 for 1-bed. There are popular developments at 15 **Hollen St** and 68 **Broadwick St**: watch for the rare resales. A small block of eight flats on the corner of **Poland St/Broadwick St** produces the occasional resale. Spacious newly converted studios in **D'Arbley St** proved popular in the late '80s. They now command around £225,000 (1989: £110,000). **Berwick St**, S of **Broadwick St**, houses the well-known fruit-and-vegetable market and is therefore very noisy and delightfully messy during the day.

One-bed flats in Soho sell fast: one agent reports selling three last autumn, each in under a fortnight: £165,000 in **Old Compton St**, £155,000 in **Broadwick St**, £190,000 in **Meard St**. Meard St is unique, having a splendid terrace of early 18th-century houses (Grade II listed): a few are still in single occupation, most have been split into flats. Tenanted until 1987, the estate was then auctioned and split up. Resales are appearing. Prices tend to be high to reflect the scarcity of this kind of period house: £750,000 was being asked in the winter for a 4-bed house with that Soho rarity, a garden. The same size house rents at £750 pw. A 2-bed flat with roof terrace commands a rent of £600 pw. This is a pedestrian through-way – but beware of cycle couriers.

The next street along, **Bourchier St**, has 17 recent flats with parking spaces in a Wates-built scheme. The streets leading N from **Shaftesbury Avenue** to **Soho Square** are grander. **Dean St**, **Frith St** and **Greek St** are prestige addresses (though the hostel in **Dean St** has lowered the tone somewhat). There are several fine restaurants and famous clubs. At the northern end of these streets one or two Georgian houses may remain intact. There are some houses in **Frith St**, for instance: one has become an hotel, another has been expensively restored as a home or office. Flats in these streets will be pricey and in the square itself, the most expensive of all. Kings House, a modern block in the NE corner of the square, houses 10 flats within it. Townsend House in **Dean St** is a 1950s block. The big Mezzo restaurant nearby has some flats above it in 'Soho Lofts', a Manhattan Lofts development. These are accessed via Richmond Mews: one was on the market for £350,000 in December. Busy **Wardour St** is famous for the film industry but there is little scope for accommodation. On the edge of Soho is Centrepoint House, an 8-storey block next to the famous office tower on **St Giles High St**. The 36 refurbished 2-bed maisonettes were sold with 35-year leases in 1990 for £135,000–145,000, depending on the view. Now, they are let for £300–350 pw.

Covent Garden

The area S of **High Holborn**, E of **Kingsway** and N of **The Strand** takes its name from the development, in the early 17th century, of a former convent garden to form an Italian-style piazza laid to an Inigo Jones design. The original fashionable residents soon moved further W and by the middle of the century a fruit-and-vegetable market had started and grew rapidly. In the 18th century it became an area of seedy lodging houses and brothels. By the early 19th century the neighbourhood had been transformed by the market which had expanded and been taken over by traders in all manner of goods.

In 1830, the Duke of Bedford organized the construction of the market building in an attempt to restore order. The market remained, in greater or lesser degrees of picturesque confusion, until 1974. Londoners grew to love the fruit, vegetable and flower stalls, the ribaldry of the market traders – and the pubs which opened at four in the morning to cater for them. Covent Garden became a unique mixture of market traders and actors, banana wholesalers and ballet dancers.

When the market finally moved out, an epic row began about the area's fate. A giant scheme to knock most of it down was thwarted by an energetic local campaign and the GLC converted the central market building into a specialist shopping centre which has become a hugely successful tourist attraction. This started the transformation of the area around the market which originally comprised many fruit-and-vegetable warehouses, hardware stores and workshops of various kinds. Warehouses have been converted into flats, many small shops stayed and more have opened, and many courts and alleys have been pedestrianized.

Houses are very scarce, a few remaining around **Mercer St** and **Shorts Gardens**. Agents reckon there are only six freehold houses in Covent Garden. Most available accommodation is flats above shops and restaurants or in a selection of enviable, purpose-built developments, mainly recent, and again usually with commercial uses at ground-floor level. The eastern side of the neighbourhood has some blocks of flats belonging to housing associations and charities such as the Peabody Estate. These add to the number of residents, but not to the market for homes. A new Marks &

Spencer store in **Long Acre**, plus the existing Tesco Metro in **Garrick St**, mean that shopping is getting useful as well as pleasurable.

The borough boundary between Camden and Westminster runs along **Shelton St**. To the N lies Seven Dials, where **Monmouth St, Upper St Martin's Lane, Shorts Gardens, Earlham St** and **Mercer St** converge. 1990 saw the Seven Dials monument restored to its position at the meeting-point. The slender column of this faithful copy, adorned with its six sundials, forms the seventh itself. Seven Dials is a very popular place to live, together with **Neal St** and **Neal's Yard**, now both pedestrianized – the latter packed with wholefood cafés and organic farm produce. One particularly coveted development is **Seven Dials Court**, built around an attractive landscaped courtyard at first-floor level and approached from **Shorts Gardens** leading through to **Neal's Yard**. A 1-bed flat here was £280 pw to rent in December.

Matthews Yard off **Shorts Gardens** is a 1989 development of three houses, three 1/2-bed flats and three 4-bed maisonettes. Georgian conversions in **Monmouth St** are popular, while 15 recent flats, Fielding Court, date from 1990. A former warehouse in **Tower St** was converted into loft-style apartments in 1997. At 19 **Mercer St** is the Terry Farrell-designed development in the Comyn Ching triangle. These seven luxury flats have balconies or roof terraces. A 3-bed one, on the ground floor and with two patios, was £198,000 in 1990, an informed guess is £375,000 now. A rare house in **Mercer St**, dating from the 17th century and forming part of the Comyn Ching redevelopment, is reckoned to be worth £750,000.

Moving over to **Endell St** (still in Camden), you will find a noisier, so somewhat cheaper, corner. Conversions can be found in **Betterton St**. **Drury Lane** is again a rather busy street – especially around theatre-time – but a number of developments have been appearing. 'Garden Court', on the corner of **Drury Lane** and **Broad Court**, has 12 1-bed flats, four 2-bed and a 4th-floor penthouse with three terraces. Bruce House is a Grade II listed building owned by Westminster Council; a men's hostel has been rebuilt behind the façade as a purpose-built home for about 60 people. Over in **Macklin St**, N towards Holborn, a Victorian building has been split into six flats. Barratt are building a new block in **Newton St**, completing summer 1999: 2- and 3-bed flats from £275,000.

On the corner of **Upper St Martin's Lane** and **West St** a re-clad office tower has 12 flats in a low-rise section, Meridian Place. Very smart Art Deco style. There is a car park. Otherwise, theatres, clubs, restaurants and offices occupy this street. **Long Acre** is largely shops and offices but the quieter **Floral St** has a couple of extremely popular mid-1980s developments – about 20 flats at Nos 16 and 30, where resales have proved infrequent. Rentals are more common: a 2-bed loft-style flat was £700 pw in December.

All streets close to the Piazza are very much coveted, although most of the buildings which actually overlook the market – and the buskers performing in front of the portico of St James' Church – are in commercial use. Period conversions may be available occasionally in **King St, Henrietta St, Maiden Lane** and **New Row**. Expect to find prices of £350–500,000. A 3-bed triplex flat in **James St** with a roof terrace was £600 pw to rent in December. Off **Bedford St**, behind the Coliseum in **Bedford Court**, is a development of 10 flats with private balconies.

The Royal Opera House fronting onto **Bow St** is in the middle of a massive, expensive and controversial redevelopment scheme involving properties in **Russell St, James St** and **Long Acre**. **Hanover Place** has some converted warehouse buildings. Period conversions occasionally appear in **Russell St, Tavistock** and **Wellington Sts**.

Some council flat resales are becoming available in Covent Garden. These are likely to be up to 30 per cent cheaper than equivalent private homes if they are in municipal blocks rather than conversions: for example a 4-bed flat in **Odhams Walk** was £310,000 last winter.

Strand

Just beyond Covent Garden, between **The Strand** and **Embankment**, houses in **Craven St** have been refurbished as part of the Charing Cross Redevelopment Scheme. One or two other houses survive in this unexpected corner: a 1730 5-storey one 'ideal for entertaining on a grand scale' was to let at £1,850 pw in December. **Trafalgar Square** must be the best-known address in London: now you can live there, with 12 flats being carved out of a bank by Natwest Properties: £190–525,000. Natwest have done the same with another building in nearby **St Martin's Place**: eight flats from £250,000. A block in **King William IV St** has some very smart flats: one was on the market for £485,000 in November.

South of **The Strand** in **Buckingham St**, a handsome Georgian house has been modernized to provide six flats on the third and fourth floors. Most of the pleasant area S of **The Strand** is commercial, but other flats may be found above offices. Last year saw 66 flats converted from an office building, Little Adelphi, in **John Adam St**. These are mostly let: £550 pw is a typical rent. Sale prices are typically £225,000 for a 1-bed, £265,000 for 2-bed. And of course there are the splendid serviced apartments next to the Savoy Hotel. If you have to ask the price – you can't afford it.

Transport	Tubes, all zone 1: Leicester Square (Piccadilly, Northern), Covent Garden (Piccadilly), Oxford Circus (Victoria, Central, Piccadilly), Tottenham Court Road (Central, Northern). From Leicester Square: Oxford Circus 10 min (1 change), City 15 min (1 change), Heathrow 1 hr. Trains: Charing Cross.
Convenient for	Everywhere: West End entertainment and shopping. City.
Schools	Local Authority: Westminster City C of E (b), Grey Coat Hospital C of E (g).

SALES

Flats	S	1B	2B	3B	4B	5B
Average prices	100–225+	140–330	200–525	250–750	—	→
Houses	2B	3B	4B	5B	6/7B	8B
Average prices	350+	450+	650+	750+	—	—

RENTAL

Flats	S	1B	2B	3B	4B	5B
Average prices	800–1500	1000–2000	1300–3000+	1900–4500+	—	—
Houses	2B	3B	4B	5B	6/7B	8B
Average prices	1400–2600	2500–3000	3500–6000+	—	—	—

The properties	Pressure from commercial uses means very few buildings are homes. But these include rare, lovely pre-Victorian houses, flats above shops, conversions of warehouses, etc, and some stylish new-build aimed at company and foreign-investor markets. An exciting, historic (if noisy) place to live.

S

The market Restricted supply and growing demand as area was cleaned up raised prices in late '80s. Demand held up well through the early-'90s recession and prices held steady in late 1998 when other areas, like Clerkenwell, saw falls. Prices have doubled since 1990 — at least. Local searches: Westminster 1 week, Camden 2 weeks.

Among those estate agents active in this area are:
- Chestertons
- Weyhill
- LDG
- Winkworth*
- Simon Joseph*
- Knight Frank
- Copping Joyce
- Hurford Salvi Carr
- E A Shaw
- Foxtons*

further details: see advertisers' index on p633

S

THE SOUTH BANK

Map ref: p78 (2C)
Postal districts: SE1, SE17, SE16
Boroughs: Lambeth (Lab),
  Southwark (Lab)
Council tax: Band D Lambeth
  £647, Southwark £786
Conservation areas: Many, check
  with town halls
Parking: Varies but always scarce

The great sweep of London on the south bank of the Thames from Waterloo to Rotherhithe, opposite the West End and the City, is considered here as one unit. The Jubilee Line Extension (when it eventually opens, hopefully during 1999) will give this area a big boost. In property terms, its value is already in the prices. From Waterloo the new line runs E to Southwark, Bermondsey and Surrey Docks and on to Canary Wharf. In the other direction it offers a fast link to Westminster and the West End.

The big excitement here, in terms of new homes supply and price rises, took place in 1995–97. Things went quiet in 1998, with prices stable and few new schemes coming through. There are now ample homes to choose from, and with the transport and environment of the area still improving it could be a good place to look.

The name 'South Bank' has spread from the culture ghetto around Waterloo Bridge to take in eveything from County Hall downstream to Tower Bridge. Beyond, the Shad Thames docks and warehouses of Bermondsey are a new neighbourhood: Tower Bridge, some call it. Butler's Wharf is here. On E comes Rotherhithe and the old Surrey Docks, transformed since 1980 'as if a magic wand had been waved'. The inland sector borders on Kennington, then spreads across to the Elephant and Castle, the Borough, Walworth and the **Old Kent Rd**.

This is a very mixed area: it contains public and commercial buildings of every kind. There are theatres and railway stations, office blocks and hospitals. There is also quite a lot of council-built housing in tall and often grim blocks. Five years ago, it was hard to find anything to buy or rent in this part of London. Now, the choice is much greater. A rash of conversions of old schools, offices and factories; resale of council-built homes, new-builds in odd inland corners, riverside warehouse flats – all of a sudden there is a homes market, for both buyers and renters.

High-level rail lines and busy roads, plus the concentration of commerce and industry, have until very recently forced homes into small pockets. The area has traditionally been one of poverty and overcrowding, and some of the present-day council estates are little or no improvement on their slum predecessors. But with commercial buildings becoming homes, neighbourhoods are changing fast. Even the big estates are looking up as private buyers pick up cheap flats, and council and housing association improvements take effect.

The catalysts for change have been the City, with its earning power and need for easy access; the river; the new Jubilee line tube and the Millennium. The clean-up of the riverside is startling to anyone who has not seen it for a few years. From Westminster Bridge to Tower Bridge is a handsome and almost continuous promenade: The Queen's Walk. The new Globe Theatre is being joined by the Tate Gallery's conversion of Bankside Power Station into a gallery of modern art. A new footbridge will link Bankside to St Paul's. Restaurants, shops, bars, designer workshops, cafés abound. The only way to judge the South Bank is to go and look. Preferably on foot, or by bike. To use a local saying: 'cor, oo'd 'ave thought it!'

Waterloo, South Bank and The Borough

County Hall, giant riverside home of the now-defunct Greater London Council, is now a hotel, health club, an aquarium – and 310 flats. The South Bank cultural complex lines the river from County Hall round past Waterloo Bridge to the National Theatre, and the land to the S and E is mostly taken up by Waterloo station. Waterloo has grown to include the Eurostar terminal, Waterloo International. This has given the area a boost, though the building of the new tube line has disturbed several streets. North of the station, **Theed St**, **Whittesley St** and **Roupell St** are quiet roads of little terraced houses on a human scale which are popular buys. Off **Theed St** is the 'Royal Millenium Village' development (never use one buzzword when three will do seems to be the developer's motto). This has 2-bed, 2-bath flats at £260,000 and mews houses. South of Waterloo East station are some '30s council flats in **Wootton St**.

Coin St to the N has for a decade been the centre of a big and controversial redevelopment scheme, the row in essence pitching commercial interests against community activists supported by Lambeth Council. The activists won, and the redevelopment consequently includes homes for 1,300 people to be let. Some of the homes are in restored 1829 terraces. Private developments include the cringingly named 'Media Apartments': just seven of them, from £132,000. **Duchy St** and **Aquinas St** are part of the Duchy of Cornwall Estate (see Kennington). **Aquinas St** has 1911 cottages. Some are being sold freehold as they come vacant. A ground-floor 2-bed flat in a converted period building here was £190,000 last November.

Behind Waterloo station, **Lower Marsh** is showing signs of improvement. Some smart flats in a concierged block in nearby **Westminster Bridge Rd** have resale prices unchanged on last year at around £160,000 for 1-bed. Developers Barratt insisted on calling the neighbourhood 'South Westminster'. **Lower Marsh** is a bustling shopping street, with a market. Some flats over shops. Cobbled **Launcelot St**, off **Lower Marsh**, has a handful of cottages. East of **Baylis Rd** is a large council-built estate with some attractive homes. Resales here include 1-bed flats from £80–125,000. Further S, **Mead Row** has some flats run as a housing cooperative. **Hercules Rd** has a mix of small 19th-century cottages, some 3-storey houses (c. £275,000) and council blocks. **Lambeth Rd** is on the fringe of Kennington and has some similar early 19th-century houses.

A new source of flats is the conversion of offices. County Hall's inland blocks, just across the street from Waterloo International, have become flats. They sold briskly,

S

and resales now reach about £185,000 for 1-bed. Further tranches have been released at prices up to £430,000. The old Shell building, the downstream block next to Waterloo Bridge, became 'The White House' in 1996 amid much hype. Many of the flats in the first phases were sold to Far East buyers. Now, developer Galliard is marketing penthouses from £500,000.

To the E the borough of Southwark (not to be confused with The Borough) begins. The Oxo Tower, with its high-profile restaurant, has done a lot to smarten up the riverside. There are some flats. On the riverside, there is little housing E of the LWT tower except some council homes and expensive flats (River Court) in **Upper Ground** and some smart riverside flats in part of the King's Reach development. A converted office block in **Broadwell** off **Stamford St** has yielded 16 flats: four 2-bed duplexes were being marketed last winter at prices from £225,000. East of Blackfriars Bridge, the enormous brick-built Bankside Power Station is becoming the new Tate Gallery of Modern Art: completion 2001. Nearby, a commercial building has become loft apartments called 'The Gallery'. Close to the bridge are some riverside Southwark Council flats. **Bankside** has one of London's most desirable houses, Cardinal's Wharf. The house was already old when Christopher Wren lived there while building St Paul's. Beautifully restored, it was on the market in 1988 for £1 million. Alongside it, the late Sam Wanamaker's reconstruction of Shakespeare's Globe Theatre is a triumphant success: a magnet for the whole neighbourhood. One or two other houses survive alongside, as does the Anchor pub. There are plans for new flats close to the Globe. Inland, past the sites of the rediscovered Elizabethan theatres, the Rose and the Globe, some new homes have enviable positions. On **Southwark Bridge Rd**, a handsome Georgian terrace, Anchor Terrace, has been restored as 29 flats. It is on the site of the original Globe Theatre: the new one is a street away. A few of the 2-bed homes were still being marketed late last year between £180–300,000 with 1-bed flats from £195,000.

West of London Bridge, renovated St Mary Overie Dock is the centrepiece of a new range of riverside offices and flats. The dock contains a replica of Sir Francis Drake's 'Golden Hind'. This exceptionally successful development sweeps back to form a precinct round glorious Southwark Cathedral. Another reminder of past glories, the end wall and rose window of Winchester Palace, still stands, lending its name to **Winchester Square**. **Borough High St** meanders S from London Bridge and is the centre of the oldest part of South London. Just S of the Cathedral is Borough Market, an atmospheric survival of Victorian London much used as a film set. Progress is about to overtake it: a big railway viaduct, part of Thameslink 2000, will go through at high level if planning permission is given; a public inquiry is scheduled for this spring. And the market itself is destined to be 'London's Larder': a centre for fine foods. Taken with the Wine World wine education, sales and tasting complex under construction in **Tooley St**, this will make The Borough a gourmet's paradise.

On the other side of the **High St**, **St Thomas St**, behind London Bridge station, has some Georgian houses. **Snowfields**, behind Guys Hospital, has some good old houses, nearly all split into flats, and is a popular location: the doctors provide a ready public for these convenient homes. Local agents say they very rarely come onto the market. **Union St** has some working-men's cottages built late in the 19th century. Around here is a little neighbourhood of mostly 19th-century housing, all built by various philanthropists and public bodies. As such, they are rarely for sale.

The district between **Borough High St** and **Southwark Bridge Rd** has several streets with homes, including a new clutch of warehouse conversions. In **Borough Rd**, a new-built house has an octagonal first-floor bedroom suite: unique indeed and £330,000. More typical are the nine warehouse-conversion lofts in **Redcross Way**, £145–315,000, and the 1,200 sq ft loft in **Lant Street** for £270,000.

Williams Lynch

At Williams Lynch we pride ourselves on our professionalism and dedication to customer service - which is second to none. With over 21 years experience we also have the track record to prove it.

To find out what service really means telephone Mark Williams or Andrew Lynch who would be happy to discuss any of your property requirements.

Residential Sales and Lettings.
Specialising in Bermondsey

90 Bermondsey Street, London SE1 3UB

Tel: 0171 407 4100
Fax: 0171 407 4102

One of the new Jubilee line underground stations is on **Blackfriars Rd** just where it meets **The Cut**. The latter street is the focus of a council re-hab scheme. There are plenty of council-built properties here. **Nelson Square** and nearby streets have council flats, both low-rise and in towers. This continues down towards the S, though **Blackfriars Rd**, like all the main streets in the area, has a few surviving earlier houses, some Georgian. Most of these have, however, become offices, though the tide is on the turn with one or two becoming homes again. Off **Blackfriars Rd** there are modern houses in **Scoresby St** and a 1980s development, Bridge House Court, with 28 mews-style houses and flats built around a garden and over a car park. Indeed, some of the gardens fell into the car park, necessitating structural work. All is now well. **Southwark Bridge Rd** has some Victorian houses, now flats: £75,000 buys a 1-bed example. The residential streets S of **St George's Circus** are described under the Kennington chapter.

Walworth and The Elephant

The Elephant and Castle has suffered in the transformation from a Victorian pub at a crossroads to a modern 'complex'. Today it is far from being the busy heart of South London it once was, and that the planners intended it would continue to be. It is a vast, bleak double roundabout surrounded by unconvincing '60s buildings and mostly inhabited by pigeons. The shopping centre has failed to generate much bustle, the council housing has a sad reputation. Even cladding the shopping centre in pink (pink elephants?) has done little to help. A key building here is the former Alexander Fleming House, once HQ of the government's social security department and designed in suitably alienating concrete by Erno Goldfinger. This architect's status as a guru of Modernism led to the block being listed, despite its legendary unpleasantness as a place to work. Now it is 'Metro Central', a block of flats successfully marketed by St George as being 'at the centre of London'. The 413 flats sold out fast in 1997–98 at prices from £70,000.

From the Elephant the **Walworth Rd** runs S towards Camberwell. Once it, like other such streets, was lined with handsome houses, but few survive. **Albany Rd** runs off to the E, forming the boundary between the new Burgess Park, with its boating lake and adventure playground, to the S and the enormous Aylesbury Estate, built to house more than 8,000 people on 64 acres. Pevsner comments: 'An exploration can be recommended only for those who enjoy being stunned by the impersonal megalomaniac creations of the mid-20th century.' The triangle between **Walworth Rd**, the Elephant and the **New Kent Rd** has equally little to recommend it, though a few corners of 19th-century housing survive amid the council slabs. Some such houses occur in and around **Brandon St** and **Chatham St**. Many have been converted into flats. However, if it is a low price you seek, ex-council flats can be bought here for a tenth of the prices asked a mile to the N.

Surrey Square boasts some 1790s houses, which sell for around £250,000, and some 1970s ones which are cheaper. **East St** is another place to look, although the area is busy on days when the street market is held. Six new flats have recently been completed in **Fremantle St**, a sign of change in the area. Some purpose-built Edwardian maisonettes can be found in **Aylesbury Rd** and **Wooler St**. A few ex-council flats are beginning to come onto the market, even on these unprepossessing estates. Victorian 3-bed houses in nearby **Searles Rd** are £160,000 despite the nearby fly-over. They are being joined by six new 3-bed houses at £200,000 each.

Bermondsey

The most dramatic part of the Bermondsey, and that with most housing, is the Thames-side neighbourhood of converted warehouses and new flats developments.

These are dealt with in the Docklands chapter. Inland, the Docklands effect has been encouraging interest in the pockets of housing between the river strip and the **Old Kent Rd**. This district has a surprising number of homes, including some of the oldest in London. The Bricklayers Arms site, once a railway yard, became a vast estate of new homes as just about every big builder descended on it around 1989. Sadly, many of the homes were repossessed in the ensuing recession. Housing associations now own about half the 600 homes. A new road, **Mandela Way** (this is Southwark), leads through the site. Nearby, the Abbey development has some pleasant cottage-style 1/3-bed properties built a dozen years ago. Typical prices are unchanged over the past year at £70–90,000. To the E, the district S of **Southwark Park Rd** has some pleasant streets of Victorian terraced cottages. **Lynton Rd**, **Simms Rd**, **Esmerelda Rd** and **Strathnairn Rd** have flat-fronted cottages which are mostly well-kept and attractive. Further S, **Avondale Square** has 3-storey mid-Victorian terraced houses. To the N, **Yalding Rd** has some pretty flat-fronted houses.

To the W, the area between **Great Dover St** and the Elephant is worth a glance. **Trinity Church Square**, for example, has early 19th-century houses belonging to the Seamens' Widows' Housing Trust. Some are now being sold: houses and flats. **Trinity St** has similar houses. New 'loft-style' houses here were on the market in 1997 in a scheme called 'The Courtyard'. **Merrick Square** has 1850s houses. **Bath Terrace** has some Victorian flats in a large block. One-bed flats are to be had from £50–65,000. On the other side of **Great Dover St**, **Bermondsey Square** is in truth only a corner of handsome houses overlooking the antiques market and busy road to Tower Bridge. East of here is **Grange Rd**, the centre of some activity in recent years as houses have been renovated and buildings converted for homes.

Three houses in **Grange Walk** have medieval origins, being the last survivors of the great Bermondsey Abbey. One was sold 10 years ago when the particulars detailed some mouthwatering features including Norman cellars. There are some Victorian houses, too. A school in the street has been cleverly converted into characterful flats and galleried studio houses; further conversions and new-build are appearing in this corner. The 165-home Grange Park scheme, between **Grange Rd** and **Rouel Rd**, was completed by Laing in 1988. There are 2- and 3-bed houses and 1- and 2-bed flats. Other **Grange Rd** homes on the market last winter included the 1860s Alaska Building's 1- and 2-bed flats at between £150,000 and £190,000, and a 2000 sq ft penthouse in a converted print works at £450,000. **Leroy St** has some Victorian flats in a 4-storey terrace. **Neckinger Cottages** has neat 2-bed houses. **Bermondsey St**, which leads back up to London Bridge station, is the old village centre and has some surviving old houses. **Pages Walk** has three new 2-bed cottages. **Long Lane** has some modern terraced council-built houses.

Off **Tower Bridge Rd**, **Leathermarket St** has a big block of 1994-built flats around a courtyard. A typical price is £142,500 for 2-bed. In **Tanner St**, opposite a little park, another converted Victorian print works has a 2-bed, 2-bath flat with roof terrace at £310,000. Other, similar, schemes are mentioned in the Docklands chapter.

Rotherhithe

Most of Rotherhithe, including all the great peninsula which was once the Surrey Docks, is covered in the Docklands chapter. The old village, also described under Docklands, has a pleasant cluster of old buildings gathered peacefully around the parish church. Inland, there is quite a bit of housing, mostly council, in the area W of Southwark Park and on SE towards Deptford. Some of the council estates have their own attractions but, in residential terms, the area is very much in the shadow of the vast Surrey Docks and riverside developments. The new Bermondsey Jubilee line tube station at **Jamaica Rd** will make a lot of difference to the neighbourhood.

Transport	Tubes: Waterloo, Elephant & Castle (zones 1/2, Northern, Bakerloo); London Bridge, Borough (zone 1, Northern); Lambeth North (zone 1, Bakerloo). From Elephant & Castle: Oxford Circus 22 min (1 change), City 7 min, Heathrow 1 hr (2 changes). Trains: Waterloo, London Bridge. Jubilee Line Extension, Waterloo–Canary Wharf–Stratford, due Sept this year (but may be next . . .)
Convenient for	City, West End, South Bank, the Thames, Docklands. Miles from centre: 1.5.
Schools	Local Authority: London Nautical (b), Bacon's School C of E, Notre Dame High RC (g).

SALES

Flats	S	1B	2B	3B	4B	5B
Average prices	50–150	60–200	65–300	175–400+	→	—

Houses	2B	3B	4B	5B	6/7B	8B
Average prices	125–300	160–500+	→	→	—	—

RENTAL

Flats	S	1B	2B	3B	4B	5B
Average prices	450–1000	550–1300	650–1500	750–1800	1000 →	—

Houses	2B	3B	4B	5B	6/7B	8B
Average prices	750–1300	850–1500	1000 →	1500+ →	—	—

The properties	Big changes as lofts and office conversions, plus Docklands new-build, join ex-council homes to widen property choice. Houses scarce, flats of all sizes plentiful. Locations vary from riverside smart to very inner-city.
The market	Once a place for bargains, now becoming mainstream. Ex-council homes and resales on big developments offer lower prices. Lofts and conversions, some very smart, attract international buyers. New tube and Millennium-led schemes have raised area's profile. Local searches: Lambeth 2 weeks, Southwark 2 weeks.

Among those estate agents active in this area are:
- Alex Neil
- Cluttons Daniel Smith
- Kinleigh Folkard & Hayward
- Barnard Marcus
- Halifax
- Cityscope
- Burnet Ware & Graves
- Winkworth*
- Olivier Jacques
- Duncan Allen
- Edwards
- Williams Lynch*
- Daniel Cobb*

further details: see advertisers' index on p633

SOUTH KENSINGTON, EARL'S COURT AND WEST BROMPTON

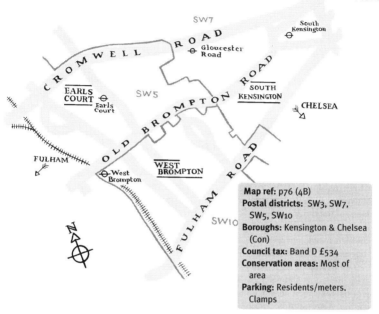

KNIGHTSBRIDGE

SW7

South Kensington

CROMWELL ROAD

Gloucester Road

SW5

EARLS COURT
Earls Court

OLD BROMPTON ROAD

SOUTH KENSINGTON

CHELSEA

FULHAM

WEST BROMPTON

West Brompton

FULHAM ROAD

SW10

N

Map ref: p76 (4B)
Postal districts: SW3, SW7, SW5, SW10
Boroughs: Kensington & Chelsea (Con)
Council tax: Band D £534
Conservation areas: Most of area
Parking: Residents/meters. Clamps

A steady revival over the past 10 years has returned these three areas to the state of bourgeois respectability intended by their 19th-century developers. The three diverse districts form a largely residential triangle between Chelsea and Kensington proper. They date from the second half of the 19th century, when there was growing demand for large family homes close to the West End.

The enormous dignified terraced houses typical of the area had a short run of luck. The demise of domestic servants made them unviable and most spent the middle half of the 20th century as hotels or cheap, if seedy, rented flats and bed-sits. But no longer. The area is still dotted with hotels, be they smart South Kensington establishments or Earl's Court B&Bs; but the rocketing values of the '80s finally made it viable to expend care and attention on the tall decaying houses. Skips, scaffolding and interior decorators moved in en masse as the classier developers set to work. Clever – indeed, state-of-the-art – conversions transformed **Evelyn Gardens**, the **Onslows**, the **Cranleys**, the **Courtfields.** Then the '90s saw conversions mop up most of the lingering South Ken hotels and spread into Earl's Court.

The area as a whole lies between **West Cromwell Rd**, **Cromwell Rd**, and **Imperial Institute Rd** to the N, **Fulham Rd** to the S, the West London railway line in the W and **Brompton Rd** and The Oratory church in the E. It contains some of the most expensive homes in London – the handsome £8-million-plus villas in **The Boltons** – and some of the most down-at-heel in Earl's Court's remaining bed-sitter land.

Two major factors influenced the development of the area, previously covered with market and nursery gardens. The first was the Great Exhibition of 1851 in Hyde

S

Park, profits from which were used to build the major museums complex on the border with Knightsbridge and the two main routes along which they stand, **Cromwell Rd** and **Exhibition Rd**. The second and most important influence was the arrival of the Metropolitan and District railways during the 1860s, which allowed speedy access to Central London. Ease of access remains one of the biggest attractions of the area.

Every neighbourhood except West Brompton has tube stations within walking distance. The Piccadilly line runs direct to Heathrow Airport: a big plus for this international area. **Cromwell Rd** also links directly with the M4 to Heathrow, drawing tourists to the hotels in the area and the transitory population which characterizes Earl's Court in particular. The area is probably the most cosmopolitan in the already various Royal Borough. Earl's Court, once known as the Polish Corridor then Kangaroo Valley after successive waves of settlers, is now home to a mini-United Nations and is also a favourite haunt of London's gay community. Some Middle Eastern families still remain in South Ken but it is no longer the 'Saudi Ken' of the 1970s. The French have colonized the area around the Lycée Français near the tube.

One thing all the neighbourhoods have in common is garden squares, although there is only one public garden – in **Redcliffe Square**, West Brompton – unless you count Brompton Cemetery, adopted as a de facto park by the locals.

The most densely populated part of the area lies to the N of **Old Brompton Rd**, where red-brick mansion blocks abound and the majority of houses have been converted to flats. The most desirable chunk lies between here and the **Fulham Rd**. Many of the terraces of big brick and stucco houses have been converted into flats but there are still enclaves of single-family houses in small-scale villagy streets, charming cobbled mews and peaceful cul-de-sacs. Shops are generally clustered around the tube stations and restricted to the main roads bounding the neighbourhoods.

Old Brompton Rd, running E-W, a busy boulevard, cuts through the middle of the area. Here the shops, pubs and big brick mansion blocks tend to congregate in groups, the shops near main junctions such as **Earl's Court Rd** and around South Ken station. A string of smart shops, restaurants, bars and antique shops stretch along most of **Fulham Rd** with a concentration of fashion stores at Brompton Cross (the junction with **Sloane Avenue**). **Cromwell Rd**, a wide noisy 6-lane highway leading to the M4, has hotels standing side-by-side with tall terraced houses divided into flats.

Wellcome Trust and Thurloe Estates

This strip between **Old Brompton Rd** to the N and **Fulham Rd** to the S, extending W to **Drayton Gardens**, is the heart of residential South Kensington. Until 1995 most of this district was owned by the Henry Smith's Charity, landowners since the 17th century. Smith's Charity sold its estate to the Wellcome Trust in 1995 in a controversial deal which hit the headlines when angry leaseholders argued they had not been given first refusal to buy the freeholds of their homes. A number of leaseholders have bought their freeholds, but they are still a minority. More people have extended their leases to 105 years. All householders, including freeholders, are still subject to strict controls on how they maintain their properties under an estate management scheme imposed by Wellcome: no pink front doors here, please. The Trust's holding is concentrated around **Onslow Gardens, Cranley Gardens, Evelyn Gardens** and the **Pelhams**. A freehold, or in the case of a flat a share of one, can boost prices: a house-sized **Cranley Gardens** flat was £1.7 million with share of freehold last winter. A degree of estate control also applies to the Thurloe Estate (lying between **Pelham St** S, **Thurloe Place** N and **Brompton Rd** E). The Thurloe Estate has sold off the freehold of a number of properties, but here too, all residents are subject to an estate management scheme.

One of the gems of the Wellcome Estate is **Pelham Crescent**. Elegant white stucco terraced houses sweep in a semi-circle around leafy private gardens, which screen the

Victorian crescent from the Brompton Cross end of **Fulham Rd**. Stretches of black iron railings, columned porches and green Victorian street lamps complete the scene. Most of the houses are still in single-family occupation: expect to pay £2–3,500,000. The white stucco continues into **Pelham Place**, which curves across **Pelham St**, a feeder road between South Kensington, Knightsbridge and the **Fulham Rd**. **Pelham Place** leads to **Thurloe Square**, one of the area's most exclusive garden squares. Here 4-storey and basement brick and stucco houses (mainly split into flats) stand on three sides of an elongated private garden. Residents in the SE corner of the square enjoy an exceptional view of the entrance to the Victoria & Albert Museum at the top of **Thurloe Place** with its imposing crown-shaped stone tower.

To the E of the square lies a group of Georgian terraced houses in **Alexander Square** and neighbouring streets. Despite its name, **Alexander Square** is a single street of early 19th-century 3/4-storey brick and stucco houses, overlooking small private gardens. These 5-bed houses command prices up to £2,500,000. The gardens act as a barrier between the houses and **Brompton Rd** as it winds from Knightsbridge to **Fulham Rd**. Just beyond here, **Brompton Rd** merges with **Fulham Rd** at fashionable Brompton Cross, with its cluster of ultra-smart shops and restaurants and the Art Nouveau Michelin Building. **Sydney Place** combines with the S leg of **Onslow Square** E to form the main through-route from South Kensington to Chelsea.

Onslow Square proper lies to the W of the main road. Immaculate terraces of 4-storey 1846 houses with columned porches overlook award-winning gardens in this choice square. The houses were split into flats during a major conversion programme in the 1960s. White stucco and brick-and-stucco terraces of varying sizes, with the same columned porches, are the dominant style in **Onslow Gardens** (tree-lined communal gardens), **Sumner Place**, **Cranley Place** and the N arms of **Cranley Gardens**. Most of these have already been converted into flats, many at top-of-the-market levels. More properties are being refurbished as single houses and go for around £1 million. The spacious, 1980s-done-up houses in **Sumner Place** have leases of 55 years. In nearby **Neville Terrace** a new-build freehold house sold in 1997 for £5.5 million, including a staff cottage. In **Onslow Mews East**, what looks like a row of cottages is in fact two handsome 3-bed 1980s-built houses, priced today at over £500,000 each. At the S end of **Cranley Gardens** and **Evelyn Gardens**, stucco gives way to Victorian red-brick flat blocks. The most attractive examples are the newly refurbished Dutch-style buildings with unusual brick and white stucco porches which line the S arm of **Evelyn Gardens**. It is a rare building round here that has not been converted and smartened up over the last 15 years.

In contrast to this densely populated area is a network of small streets just off **Fulham Rd**, N of **Elm Place**. They lie outside the Wellcome Estate. **Elm Place** (2-storey vine-clad late-Georgian

Stucco and the term cottage do not often go together but they co-exist happily in this house in Elvaston Place, called a cottage despite its Classical rusticated stucco and elegant door surround. Trees hide the lower pair of windows: there are six, set symmetrically in the façade. The six-panel door echoes the windows. These features recur on the larger homes.

cottages with tiny front gardens) and **Selwood Place** (fine Georgian terrace on the N side) are charming, leafy streets. **Selwood Place** is blocked off at its W end by the back of St Peter's Armenian Church in **Cranley Gardens**. The northern part of the Brompton Hospital, on the corner of **Foulis Terrace** and **Fulham Rd**, is now being turned into a development of 73 1- to 5-bed flats known as The Bromptons. Northacre are the developers. It will be ready in April: 70 per cent were sold by last Christmas. Prices range from £450,000 for a 1-bed flat to £3.7 million for a 5-bed family apartment. A pool, gym and underground parking are provided.

An arched brick entrance and steps on the E side of **Elm Place** leads up to **Regency Terrace**, a group of 3-storey brick and stucco terraced maisonettes above the rear of shops fronting **Fulham Rd**. As the name suggests, the houses line a Regency-style terrace at first-floor level, complete with black iron railings and street lamps. They look down on **Lecky Street**, a quiet little private cul-de-sac of white 2-storey houses with columned porches. A number of mews streets are spread throughout the area, by far the most picturesque being **Roland Way**, tucked away off **Roland Gardens**. Pretty painted cottages decorated with hanging baskets and colourful window boxes give this cobbled private street its charm. A row of 27 luxury 3/4-bedroom freehold terraced houses appeared in the late '80s in the newly named **Eagle Place** and in **Roland Way** itself. These are much in demand, with barriers at either end of the road for improved security. Prices from £600,000.

The S end of **Roland Way** leads into **Thistle Grove**, a shady pedestrian walkway lined with green Victorian lanterns and trees overhanging the rear walls of **Evelyn Gardens**. Small houses and cottages of varying styles merge with tall brick and stone mansion blocks. **Drayton Gardens**, which forms the W boundary of the area, combines a mix of styles from brick and stucco terraced houses with front gardens (NW) to Dutch-style brick and stone mansion blocks and modern flats. The most recent development here is a Fairbriar scheme for 13 2- and 3-bed flats: these were all sold to one buyer before they were complete, though some were on the market again last winter from £400,000. At the S junction with **Fulham Rd** stands the Virgin Cinema and the former South Kensington Squash Club. The squash club has been sold with permission for redevelopment as flats, but work has not yet started.

The **Fulham Rd** from here back E to Brompton Cross has many expensive shops and restaurants, belying the scruffy reputation the street held a decade or two ago. It is now far smarter (and a bit quieter) than the **King's Rd**. The **Fulham Rd** is sometimes considered to be in Chelsea, but in this stretch forms a clear boundary between the two districts. The postal district boundary puts a few homes N of the **Fulham Rd** into SW3. The traffic – and parking – in this road is especially problematic.

Museum/Lycée Area

As its name suggests, the area is dominated by the major museums standing along **Exhibition/Cromwell Rds**. The Science, Natural History, Geological and Victoria & Albert Museums were built following the Great Exhibition of 1851. The museum developments and improved transport links attracted wealthy residents to the area. Nowadays, the neighbourhood is particularly popular with the French, who have established their own colony near the Lycée Français. The school, together with the French Institute, covers a whole block stretching from **Cromwell Rd** through to **Harrington Rd**.

South Kensington underground station and a number of busy main roads have attracted a mix of shops, hotels and other uses, ranging from the College of Psychic Studies to the British Association of Cancer Research, both in **Queensberry Place**. The Aga Khan's gleaming cultural centre for Ismaili Muslims stands in **Thurloe Place** opposite the V&A Museum. Amid all the hustle and bustle, **Bute St**, with its cluster of small shops, manages to retain a delightfully village-type atmosphere. The busy junction by the tube station is dominated by the red-brick inter-war Melrose Court flats block on the S side. The council has given planning permission for complete redevelopment of the station with houses, shops and offices being built on a concrete deck over the platforms. This scheme was scuppered by the early '90s recession, and last winter its revival seemed in doubt once more.

Many of the houses around here are enormous, and they have nearly all been divided into flats at various periods and to various levels of quality. The only exceptions can be found in **Reece Mews**, a pleasant little cobbled street running N-S between **Harrington Rd** and **Old Brompton Rd**. An attractive development of new 2-storey brick mews houses fits in well with the older 3-storey painted cottages.

The NW corner of the mews lies empty, forming part of the Iranian Embassy site. The Iranian government planned to build an embassy on the site, which fronts **Queen's Gate**, in the 1970s but the idea was abandoned after the Ayatollah Khomenei's revolution. Planning consent has now expired and the site is now a car park. Standing next to the empty plot is St Augustine's Church. On the other side of the church, **Manson Place** is a wide cul-de-sac of tall brick and stucco terraces, much improved in recent years.

Courtfield

Between **Cromwell Rd** in the N and **Old Brompton Rd** in the S is a varied district which looks to Gloucester Rd rather than South Kensington tube as its transport centre. **Queen's Gate**, running N-S is a wide tree-lined boulevard – wide enough for central parking – flanked by tall brick and stucco apartment buildings and hotels (see also Kensington). Flats range in price between £200,000 and £1.2 million. To the W lies **Stanhope Gardens** with its companion mews to the W, E and S, where a number of small-scale development schemes and quality conversions have taken place. **Stanhope Gardens** itself is one of a series of garden squares in the neighbourhood. Four-storey brick and stucco terrace houses line the private gardens, the E arm forming the most attractive stretch. Developers LCR has transformed the W side of **Stanhope Gardens** into flats behind the original Victorian stucco façade. These are in two blocks known as Stanhope Court and Charlesworth House which have 83 1- to 3-bed flats, some still for sale last winter. A 2-bed flat with underground parking sold recently for £485,000 but prices range from £300,000 up to over £1 million. The mews behind contains 2/3-storey brick/painted cottages, some with roof terraces and most with their own garages.

Clareville St to the S branches off busy **Gloucester Rd**. Painted houses and cottages stand alongside a handful of offices, the Chanticleer Theatre and the Webber Douglas

Academy of Dramatic Art. The street becomes a lane as it runs S past Our Lady of Victories RC School (Fulham and South Kensington adult education institute) and wends its way towards **Old Brompton Rd**. Parallel is tree-lined **Clareville Grove**, a peaceful oasis within walking distance of both Gloucester Rd and South Ken tube stations. It is easily the most highly regarded street in the neighbourhood with its variety of attractive period houses, front gardens and hedges: houses regularly fetch £800,000-plus. The street becomes more mixed to the S with Clareville Court, a modern brick flats block near the junction with **Old Brompton Rd**. Across **Gloucester Rd**, **Hereford Square** is one of the best preserved garden squares in Kensington, its three symmetrical terraces of 3/4-storey white stucco houses built in 1848 remain unaltered, except where some parts were rebuilt following war damage. Prices for houses here rise to £1 million.

Between the square and **Bolton Gardens** to the W, the streets are dominated by concentrations of red-brick Victorian mansion flats. In **Gledhow Gardens** and **Bina Gardens** they overlook private gardens. **Wetherby Gardens**, an increasingly popular street, has a mix of styles ranging from brick and stucco paired villas to late-19th-century Dutch-style red-brick buildings. A 3-bed flat in **Wetherby Gardens** would be about £240,000. Exceptional examples of this 'South Ken Dutch' look, with its steep gables, riot of terracotta decoration and tall chimneys, are found in **Harrington Gardens** and **Collingham Gardens**. Gilbert of the Gilbert and Sullivan opera partnership lived in **Harrington Gardens**. The houses have since been converted into smaller units or for other purposes. They have rear communal gardens and properties on the E arm of the square also pleasantly overlook private gardens behind houses in **Wetherby Gardens**. Nos 48/50 **Harrington Gardens** have been converted into 19 flats.

To the N lies **Courtfield Gardens**, another garden square lined with tall Victorian brick and stucco terraces of varying quality. This square is being transformed by the conversion of hotels into smart flats: from taking up a majority of the tall houses, hotels are now down to a handful. As a result, values have risen: local agents reckon that the price of flats has gone up 10–20 per cent due to this alone. The latest scheme will see 33 flats carved out of five adjoining houses. There are still hotels in the streets between here and **Cromwell Rd**, with big hotels clustering around Gloucester Rd tube station to the E. A 12-storey block of mainly 1- and 2-bed short-let flats has been built on what was a vacant site behind the station. Dotted among the tall terraces and mansion blocks is a series of mews, mostly residential, such as **Laverton Mews** – a tiny cobbled cul-de-sac – and **Gaspar Mews** with its white-painted cottages.

Earl's Court

When Earl's Court was developed, in the second half of the 19th century, it was intended to be, and was regarded as, a select suburb. The well-to-do moved into the substantial Victorian terraced houses which sprang up alongside the original Georgian gardeners' village. The surviving gardeners, and the service workers, lived alongside in modest little cottages. Now, ironically, the situation is reversed: the workers have set up home in the big houses, long since divided into flats and bed-sits, and the prosperous pay high prices to live in the remaining cottages.

S There are clear signs of a reversion to plan here, though: hotels, bed-sits and hostels are retreating in the face of smart flat conversions. Back-packers still throng Earl's Court station, but their choice of cheapish hotels and hostels is diminishing.

The quaint colour-washed cottages lie tucked away in a triangle of streets behind busy **Cromwell Rd** and **Earl's Court Rd**, known locally as Kenway Village. Although only a few minutes' walk from the hubbub of **Earl's Court Rd**, this pocket of freehold family dwellings retains its village character, in sharp contrast to the rest of the area. Properties here are among the most sought-after in Earl's Court. The enclave, which

ESTATE AGENTS . SURVEYORS . VALUERS
44/48 Old Brompton Road, London SW7 3DY

Farley & Co established in 1900, is an independent company offering a comprehensive property service in Kensington & Chelsea, Knightsbridge and the adjoining areas.

We offer a professional and personal approach, backed up by modern computer technology, to provide a complete service in sales, lettings, management, investments and professional services.

RESIDENTIAL SALES	Patricia Farley	0171 589 1234
	Samantha Jessel	
	Ben Eastwood	
	Francis Spreyer	
	Diana Warszawski	
	Charlie Wright	
	James Rawes	
INVESTMENTS	Tim James	0171 589 1234
	Patricia Farley	
RESIDENTIAL LETTINGS	Carole Cunningham	0171 589 1244
	Niki Kenealy	
	Mandy Bissell	
	Sophie Grubb	
PROPERTY MANAGEMENT	Simon Carlon	0171 589 1246
	Jacquie Langton	
BUILDING SURVEYING & PROJECT MANAGEMENT	Michael Ashton	0171 589 1246

FAX: 0171 589 1817

formed the heart of the original village, gets its name from **Kenway Rd**, its S boundary. A 1-bed flat here can cost £170,000. Tree-lined **Wallgrave Rd** is the quietest and most popular street, pleasant and leafy with 2-storey and basement brick cottages fronted by black wrought-iron railings.

Child's Place and **Child's St** are cul-de-sacs running parallel to each other but noisier because they lie directly off **Earl's Court Rd**. The former has mainly 3-storey brick houses and the latter 2-storey cottages (c. £230,000) with small flowery front gardens. A black wrought-iron gate in **Child's St** leads into **Child's Walk**, a charming private passageway of 2-storey cottages lying no more than 10 ft apart. Tubs of flowers, window boxes and benches (complete with large snoozing cat) line the short alleyway, giving the impression of a single patio garden. **Kenway Rd** itself is a mix of 3-storey cottages and houses, rubbing shoulders with shops, restaurants and a rash of travel agents. At the top of the road, a traffic-free corner holds the entrance to 171 Cromwell Rd, a handsome, recent block of 12 flats with garaging.

North of the village at the busy junction of **Cromwell Rd** with **Earl's Court Rd**, are two 1980s apartment blocks. The flats have not worn well. Across **Cromwell Rd**, the Edwardian Moscow Mansions, now reburbished and much sought-after, has house-sized penthouses selling for up to £600,000. South of the village, **Hogarth Rd** marks the N boundary of the area's hotel land. With **Earl's Court Gardens**, it forms a buffer of Victorian terraced buildings between Kenway village and the red-brick gabled mansion blocks which dominate the rest of the area off **Earl's Court Rd**. **Barkston Gardens**, a fashionable group of red-brick buildings, overlooks a large tree-lined private garden enclosed by hedges and iron railings. Most of the N side is hotels but the rest 2/3-bed flats, with the best ones fetching up to £600,000. The **Bramham Gardens** blocks are also built around a tree-lined garden square.

Earl's Court Rd itself is dirty, noisy and battered by heavy traffic. It forms the southbound leg of the Earl's Court one-way traffic system, nicknamed locally 'Juggernaut Alley'. Several attempts to devise relief road schemes – the latest in 1989 – have all come to nothing, but a Red Route is planned.

The character of **Earl's Court Rd** has been determined largely by the transitory and tourist population which has gravitated towards the area because of its central location. Fast-food shops, restaurants, late-night supermarkets, travel agents and newsagents predominate, spreading along both sides of the road from the underground station. West of **Earl's Court Rd**, the streets of terraces lying between **Warwick Rd** W and **Penywern Rd** S make up the main chunk of hotel/bed-sitter land. **Nevern Square** with its red- and brown-brick buildings fronting private gardens is primarily residential, however, with only a few hotels sprinkled around the square. One block S at the junction of **Trebovir Rd** and **Warwick Rd** sits Kensington Mansions, a 5-storey and basement 1880s block.

Earl's Court Square is the neighbourhood's main square, lined on three sides by 4/5-storey ornate stucco-fronted houses, mostly divided into flats. The buildings look on to mature gardens surrounded by tall trees. The Chelsea Hotel is on the market with permission for conversion into 43 flats. The S arm of the square comprises 3-storey plus basement red-brick and stone gabled buildings. These set the tone for the taller red-brick gabled Wetherby Mansions on both sides of the SE arm of the square. **Warwick Rd** is lined with late-Victorian mansion blocks and undistinguished terraces.

Lying to the W is a series of crescents – **Philbeach Gardens**, **Eardley Crescent** and **Kempsford Gardens**. The condition of properties varies widely but the area is improving, as evidenced by the number of 'luxury' conversion schemes.

Tree-lined **Philbeach Gardens** enjoys the advantage of 2½ acres of exceptional landscaped gardens, forming a huge rear communal garden for the homes which sweep around the E curve of the crescent. Styles vary considerably from the heavy brown- and red-brick buildings at the N entrance of the crescent to the more desirable brick and stucco houses, with columned porches, at its mid-point.

Eardley Crescent and **Kempsford Gardens**, dubbed Brompton Village by one estate agent, have mainly 3-storey brick and stucco properties, like **Philbeach Gardens**, divided into flats. All three streets suffer from one major drawback. They are choked with traffic trying to park when shows are on at the Earl's Court Exhibition Centre immediately behind. Properties at the mid-point of the W curve of **Philbeach Gardens** also back onto the railway line: this can lower flat prices by £100,000.

West Brompton

Brompton is one of those London villages which has effectively ceased to exist. Few people, nowadays, would describe themselves as living in Brompton, and this part of SW10, bounded by **Old Brompton Rd** to the N, **Fulham Rd** to the S, and running W from **Drayton Gardens**, is known either as Chelsea or Kensington, depending on your predilictions. Or, indeed, as straightforward 'Fulham Road' – though straight may be the wrong word for the clutch of bars, restaurants and clubs between **Hollywood Rd** and **Drayton Gardens** that has given this stretch the nickname 'The Beach'.

West Brompton gains improved transport links this year when a station opens on the West London line, which links Clapham Junction with Olympia and points North.

The residential, as opposed to recreational, focal point of the neighbourhood is **The Boltons**, where handsome white stucco villas are set around an eye-shaped oval garden – unique in London. The enormous semi-detached freehold houses with their columned porches and rich ornamentation were built in the 1850–60s to attract the wealthy to the area. They still do. They were originally sold for £1,350 each. Now they fetch around £8 million. Some have staff accommodation in the grounds or are still linked to the mews houses at the rear. In the middle of the central gardens is St Mary's Church, with its angel-bedecked spire rising high above the treetops.

The Boltons also gives its name to a network of similarly salubrious streets of big stucco-fronted houses with the same 'villas-in-gardens' character. Leafy **Gilston Rd** has some fine examples with high-walled front gardens: house prices reach £900,000. **Milbourne Grove** and **Harley Gardens** are desirable small streets with a mix of paired stucco villas and brick and stucco 3/4-storey terraced houses. Houses on the E side of **Harley Gardens** overlook the walled back gardens of properties in **Gilston Rd**, as do the pastel-painted stucco terraced houses in **Priory Walk**.

Large paired brick and stucco villas predominate in **Tregunter Rd**, where properties have the advantage of forecourt parking – a feature of **The Boltons**. The **Little Boltons**, forming the W boundary of the neighbourhood, has more brick and stucco semi-detached houses but on a less grand scale. Caught up in this sea of stucco is cobbled **Cresswell Place**, a charming backwater of 2/3-storey brick cottages. It comes as an unexpected surprise as one turns the corner from **Cresswell Gardens**. No wonder that mistress of the unexpected, Dame Agatha Christie, lived here – her charming, tile-hung, dormered former home is surmounted by her 'writing room' built into the eaves. To the S lies **Cavaye Place**, a pleasant cul-de-sac of colourful cottages.

Redcliffe Rd a short distance away off **Fulham Rd** is a popular street for rented accommodation. Lined with cherry trees, it is ablaze with blossom in the spring. One street away is **Seymour Walk** – one of the earliest streets in the area, which retains its attractive period character. The oldest terrace in this exclusive cul-de-sac of 2/3-storey houses dates back to 1797. A kink in the road at the S end of the street hides it from **Fulham Rd** and a tree-lined terrace seals off its N end, creating a sense of peaceful seclusion.

Hollywood Rd to the W introduces a commercial note into this predominantly residential area. Smart restaurants, galleries, antique shops and bars creep around the corner from **Fulham Rd** into the S end of the street. A new gated mews of 18 town-houses and eight flats appeared at the start of the '90s on the W side of the street on the site of the former Unigate depot. The larger 4-storey houses with roof garden, etc, sell for £800,000, while a 4-bed period house in **Hollywood Rd** might fetch £900,000. Further N on the opposite side of the street is **Hollywood Mews**, entered through an arch. Modern 2-storey white painted cottages sit around a tiny courtyard with trees in the middle. **Hollywood Rd**, with its mix of brick and stucco homes and red-brick flats, merges with **Harcourt Terrace**, a pleasant street of terraced houses divided into flats: expect to pay at least £250,000 for a 2-bed flat here.

A surprise lies in store in **Redcliffe Mews**, lying at right angles to **Harcourt Terrace**. The mews was rebuilt in 1987 in traditional style featuring attractive 2-storey brick cottages with gaily coloured garages and entrances. Despite its proximity to noisy **Redcliffe Gardens**, the mews is surprisingly quiet thanks to a barrier of big houses separating the two and house prices are around the £600,000 mark. A short walk away lies **Redcliffe Square**, divided in half by the southbound stretch of the one-way traffic system running between Earl's Court and Chelsea. The square is lined by tall ornate brick and stucco terraced houses with French Renaissance-style dormers and polished marble porch columns. Properties on the W side of the square overlook tree-lined gardens occupied by St Luke's Church and those on the E side face the only public gardens in West Brompton. The houses have been converted into flats, as have those in **Redcliffe Gardens**.

Cathcart Rd, Fawcett St, Redcliffe Place, Redcliffe St, Westgate Terrace and **Ifield Rd** form another network of streets dominated by 3/4-storey and basement brick and stucco terraced houses split into flats. Cutting a swathe through the area is **Finborough Rd**, the northbound leg of the one-way system. A short distance from the noise and fumes of the main road lies the tranquil haven of Brompton Cemetery, which doubles as a local park.

The cemetery provides a leafy backdrop for the enclave of pretty artisan cottages in The Billings, just off **Fulham Rd**. **Billing Place, Billing St** and **Billing Rd** form a series of three private cul-de-sacs containing 2-storey and basement terraced cottages. These sell for £400–600,000.

Transport	Tubes: South Kensington, Gloucester Rd (zone 1, District, Circle, Piccadilly); Earl's Court (zone 1, District, Piccadilly); West Brompton (zone 2, District). Trains: new West Brompton station links to Clapham Junction/Willesden line. From South Kensington: Oxford Circus 12 min (1 change), City 21 min (1 change), Heathrow 41 min.
Convenient for	West End. Heathrow by tube or M4. Miles from centre: 2.
Schools	Local Authority: St Thomas More, Holland Park School. Private: Lycée Français, Falkner House (g), St James Independent Schools.

SALES

Flats	S	1B	2B	3B	4B	5B
Average prices	85–160	140–300+	200–450	375–600	400–1M	—
Houses	2B	3B	4B	5B	6/7B	8B
Average prices	85–160	140–300+	200–450	375–600	→400–1M+	→8M

RENTAL

Flats	S	1B	2B	3B	4B	5B
Average prices	700–1000	1000–1700	1200–2200	2000–3000	3000→	3200→
Houses	2B	3B	4B	5B	6/7B	8B
Average prices	2000+	2000–4000	3000–6000	5000–8000	6000+	–

The properties The peaceful, leafy streets and squares hold large brick and stucco terraces, target of much redevelopment into luxury flats. Flats, converted or p/b, reign, but there are enclaves of mewsy cottages, artists' studios and larger villas.

The market South Kensington, once a down-at-heel district, now gleams with fresh paint after 15 years of hectic refurbishment. Now the luxurious flats sell to European, American and local buyers. The huge villas of The Boltons account for the £8 million figure above. Earl's Court is catching up to its more salubrious neighbours. Local searches: 6 days.

Among those estate agents active in this area are:

- Farrar & Co
- Farley & Company*
- Cluttons Daniel Smith
- Hobart Slater
- W A Ellis*
- Russell Simpson
- Hamptons
- Druce
- Blenheim Bishop
- Faron Sutaria & Co Ltd*
- Aylesford
- Anscombe & Ringland*
- Scotts*

- Plaza
- Winkworth*
- Marsh & Parsons
- Lane Fox
- Jackson-Stops & Staff
- Beaney Pearce*
- Humberts
- Foxtons*
- De Groot Collis
- Douglas & Gordon*
- Friend & Falcke

further details: see advertisers' index on p633

SOUTHFIELDS AND EARLSFIELD

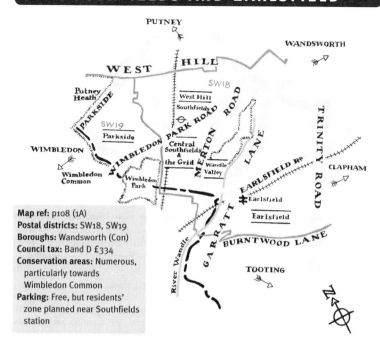

Map ref: p108 (1A)
Postal districts: SW18, SW19
Boroughs: Wandsworth (Con)
Council tax: Band D £334
Conservation areas: Numerous,
   particularly towards
   Wimbledon Common
Parking: Free, but residents'
   zone planned near Southfields
   station

The quiet streets of sober, steady houses in Earlsfield and Southfields slumbered until recently, neglected by all but very local buyers. Neighbouring Putney, Wimbledon and Wandsworth Common have more obvious charms. But since the end of the home market's long sleep from 1990–96, the ubiquitous 'young professionals' have been thronging the offices of both sales and letting agents here. They find plenty of terraced houses and flats in quiet streets, and semis – some quite large – in leafy ones. A rash of ex-council homes – some on lovely, green hillsides – and even the odd warehouse conversion have boosted the range of homes for sale and rent.

South from Wandsworth, the River Wandle must once have run through water meadows and woods. That was some centuries ago, for the river was discovered as a source of power by medieval millers, and the stream turned the wheels of some of the first factories in London, which were linked in 1803 by the Surrey Iron Railway, the first railway company in the world. Now the Wandle and its flat valley is best known as a barrier to E-W traffic rather than any kind of amenity. The valley has parks and playing-fields, depots and factories – but only two bridges linking the Victorian suburb of Earlsfield, to the E, with its slightly younger neighbour Southfields to the W. With the busy A3 and the notorious Wandsworth one-way bottleneck to the N, the area is a traffic-jam connoisseur's delight. Public transport is the key to this area: Southfields is served by the Wimbledon branch of the District line, while Earlsfield has a rail line to Clapham Junction and Waterloo.

Southfields

Southfields is a wholly residential area which blends – with surprising success – classic 1930s suburbia with older Edwardian properties. Between the District line

railway and **Merton Rd** the houses are mainly Edwardian. From **Wimbledon Park Rd** W and N to **West Hill** (the A3) and Wimbledon Common come classic 1930s semi-detached and detached houses with some older Edwardian/Victorian ones. From **Beaumont Rd** W to **Wimbledon Parkside** are many large '60s/early '70s council-built estates. The smaller blocks and houses here are largely owner-occupied: Wandsworth Council was a pioneer of Right to Buy.

The area has always been popular with families wanting good-sized houses in generally quiet roads. New arrivals to the area (notably to 'The Grid' – see below) are young couples, especially second-time buyers planning to start families, and families priced out of other areas.

Replingham Rd, near the tube station, offers the only shopping facilities of any note in Southfields, and a couple of new-style pubs; otherwise the nearest major shopping centres are in Wimbledon, Putney or Wandsworth. You'll find the occasional corner shop but there are virtually no pubs in the 'Grid' area because of covenant restrictions when the land was sold for building. The area suffers somewhat from hordes of tennis fans during Wimbledon Fortnight, but enterprising locals can let their homes out for considerable sums!

Central Southfields and The Grid

The Southfields Grid, bordered by **Astonville St**, **Elsenham Rd**, **Revelstoke Rd** and **Replingham Rd**, is named for the grid layout of the streets (which run N-S) and roads (E-W). The grid was begun with the opening of Southfields station in 1889, but was not completed until 1905. Properties are mainly spacious 3- and 4-bed Edwardian houses, although some have now been converted into flats. Typical prices for The Grid are £210–270,000 for a 3/4-bed house and £122–155,000 for a 2-bed conversion. A number of the houses in **Trentham St**, **Replingham Rd** and **Revelstoke Rd** are actually purpose-built maisonettes. The supply of newly converted flats on The Grid dried up some years back after Wandsworth Council banned any more conversions. Houses closest to Southfields station suffer some daytime parking problems: there are plans for a residents' parking zone for the streets nearest the tube, but this is not popular locally. There are some small council infill blocks in **Elsenham St** and even-numbered houses back onto the District line to Wimbledon – but have long gardens as compensation. Between **Merton Rd** and **Astonville St** are some new 2/3-bed houses in **Handford Close**. By Southfields station, **Crowthorne Close** is one of the few modern non-council developments in the area, with 2- and 3-storey blocks of flats, some backing onto the tube line. The streets between **Pirbright Rd** and **Smeaton Rd** are mainly late-Victorian/Edwardian terraces, but **Longfield St** and **Smeaton Rd** itself are smaller Victorian terraced (2-bedroom), which sell for around £140–160,000. In **Lavenham Rd** two 'Edwardian-style' 4-bed detached houses have been shoe-horned in: on the market this spring.

West of the tube line, the land rises quite steeply up towards Wimbledon Common and Putney Heath. **Gartmoor Gardens** has attractive large Edwardian houses with ornate metalwork balconies on the first floor, some now converted to flats. Proximity to Southfields station compensates for some noise from trains. Houses on the S side of **Southdean Gardens** back onto Wimbledon Park and are popular but rarely on the market. Prices last winter were around £300,000 for good 4-bed, 2-bath houses, though ones backing onto the park may fetch quite a bit more.

Further N, and E of the railway, the triangle bordered by **Granville Rd**, **Pulborough Rd** and **Merton Rd** features generally Edwardian houses in tree-lined roads slightly narrower than in The Grid. Odd-numbered houses in **Pulborough Rd** back onto the tube line but benefit from exceptionally long gardens and the large railway landholding as a buffer. From around £220,000 (3-bed terrace).

Sutherland Grove, running N from the W side of Southfields station to **West Hill**, features 1930s semi-detached mainly 3-bed houses with off-street parking. About £240,000 buys you one with a decent garden. Also a few large Edwardian houses (6-bed-plus) not all of which have been converted into popular flats.

The tube line (District) is above ground here and runs E of **Sutherland Grove**, crossing **Granville Rd** and then going into a tunnel by the junction with **Melrose Rd** and **Cromer Villas**. **Gressenhall Rd** has Edwardian-style houses and a mosque. The roads leading off **Sutherland Grove**, notably **Skeena Hill**, **Cromer Villas** and **Girdwood Rd**, are larger '30s, the majority Tudor-style, with integral garages. Internally, the houses vary enormously. Most, notably in **Coombemartin Rd**, are set well back from the road. From the junction of **Skeena Hill** and **Coombemartin Rd** there are small modern blocks of council-built flats, and the W side of **Coombemartin Rd** back onto a (low-rise) estate.

Parkside

The area bordered by **Beaumont Rd** in the E, Wimbledon Common to the W, **Queensmere Rd** (the border with Wimbledon) to the S and **West Hill** is a complex mixture of council-built estates (high- and low-rise flats, some houses) and private detached houses – some very large which fetch equally large prices. The area is quite hilly, with some splendid views eastwards towards Central London, and there are plenty of trees. Don't let the council-built housing deter you from a good look around this interesting corner.

The heaviest concentrations of council estates are between **Wimbledon Park Rd** and **Albert Drive**, **Augustus Rd** and **Whitlock Drive**. The area between **Beaumont Rd** and **Princes Way** from **Augustus Rd** to **West Hill** is almost exclusively council-built. But all the estates are well-landscaped. A lot of the flats are now owner-occupied, and there are a few small housing association schemes. Resales of council-built properties offer the cheapest homes in the area: 1-bed flats from £55,000; 3-bed houses with garage from around £130,000.

Beaumont Rd, running between **West Hill** and **Wimbledon Park Rd**, has modern council-built properties on either side and a small parade of shops by **Keevil Drive**. **Albert Drive** runs between **Augustus Rd** and **Victoria Drive**. Again there is a mix of council and private blocks and good-sized private houses (mainly detached). Between **Albert Drive** and **Wimbledon Park Rd** are mid- and late-'60s council-built blocks. On the other side of the road are some modern infill red-brick detached houses, set well back from the road, then larger detached stockbroker Tudor red-brick homes. Midway down **Albert Drive** former police flats in a 1950s block have been redeveloped as 'Southfields Village' with 2-bed flats. The same developer also undertook another similar scheme: Augustus Court off **Augustus Rd**.

Augustus Rd runs W up the hill from Southfields station to **Inner Park Rd**, and has a mix of '30s houses and older, large detached houses. The occasional late-Georgian house with 6-bed appears on the market. A number of private flat developments are grouped close to the junction with **Inner Park Rd**, including The Acorns (red-brick modern) and Dorada Court. There are also modern houses and flat developments, brick-built, mainly '60s and early '70s in style. Increasingly, from the junction with **Albert Drive**, large detached houses appear, mainly stockbroker Tudor but also older houses including the late-Georgian-style 'White House'. Some '50s infill, but all set well back from the road with large front gardens and off-street parking.

Princes Way runs roughly N-S between **West Hill** and **Wimbledon Park Rd**. From the junction with **Augustus Rd** towards **Wimbledon Park Rd** is Linden Lodge School for the Blind in large grounds, then private flats and an attractive town-house development, **King Charles Walk. Weydown Close** is modern low-rise council-built.

Off **Augustus Rd** is John Paul II Catholic Boys' Secondary School. The school buildings are followed by more mainly council-built property on either side of the road. Off **Princes Way** at the N end is the private **Fleur Gate** development of attractive brick-built Victorian-style terraced town-houses. Opposite the junction with **Castlecombe Drive** (council housing) is a small row of detached Tudor-style '30s houses.

Tree-lined **Victoria Drive** runs N-S parallel to **Princes Way** between **West Hill** and **Wimbledon Park Rd**. In character it is similar to **Princes Way** with a mix of (mainly) council-built and private property. Pines Court, a modern private block, has a selection of studio flats. **Oak Park Gardens** is a small and attractive development of town-houses followed by larger Tudor-style 1930s houses.

Inner Park Rd runs in a half-circle from Wimbledon Parkside to meet **Augustus Rd** and then back to Wimbledon Common, featuring a similar mix to the rest of **Parkside**. Close to the junction with **Parkside** stands a modern block of 16 red-brick 1- and 2-bed flats. Opposite are low-rise council flats (Windlesham Grove); thereafter private blocks of flats in older style. 'Marlborough' has some studio flats. **Pilsdon Close**, with small town-houses and flats, is set back; then comes **Holly Tree Close**, with private flats. Some exceptionally large older Victorian detached houses have mainly now been converted into flats.

Opposite the junction with **Augustus Rd** is the Argyll Estate, a mix of high- and low-rise flats. Three tall council blocks here were demolished a decade ago to be replaced with flats and houses. **Limpsfield Avenue**, with 1930s-style houses, detached and semi-detached, some mock-Tudor, backs onto a council estate. **Kingsmere Rd** has detached mainly '30s houses. A spur of **Inner Park Rd** (easy to miss), close to **Parkside** marks the entrance to **Roundacres**, a small early '60s curved, terraced house-and-flat development in communal gardens. Large, traditional-style red-brick '50s-style houses stand at the entrance.

Queensmere Rd marks the border with Merton and is very much Wimbledon rather than Southfields in feel and prices. The fairly steep tree-lined road has mainly large modern detached houses set well back from the road. **Queensmere Close** is a bungalow development. The big former college site on the corner with **Parkside** is being developed by Laing with an expensive collection of new houses and flats. (See Wimbledon chapter.)

Wimbledon Park Rd suffers traffic at rush hour, though calming measures have helped. North from the junction of **Bathgate Rd** come blocks of flats, modern council-built and older-style private. Lakeview Court flats are very comfortable and well-run, looking over Wimbledon Park and its lake. Thereafter large detached '30s- and '50s-style houses are set well back off the road up towards Southfields station, where Edwardian semi-detached and then terraced houses take over.

West Hill

The little triangle between the **West Hill** junction with **Sutherland Grove**, **West Hill Rd** and **Granville Rd** likes to considers itself West Hill (Putney) not West Hill (Southfields) and is fairly convenient for East Putney tube. It is a mix of large Edwardian semi-detached houses and 1930s semis with some modern infill and some early and mid-Victorian detached houses on **West Hill Rd**. Among the most popular roads is the 1930s **Sispara Gardens** (large semi-detached houses with integral garages) while **Cromer Villas** has a mix of '30s and Edwardian semis. **Coldstream Gardens** has '60s-style town-houses and flats, **Valonia Gardens** is neat 1930s semis with some '50s infill built '30s-style. **Melrose Rd**, at the junction with **West Hill Rd**, has large terraced and semi-detached Edwardian homes.

Merton Rd to the E is a very busy through road carrying traffic between Wimbledon and Wandsworth and is also a commuter cut-through from the A24 to the Wandsworth one-way system. Large detached and semi-detached houses (some stuccoed) appear between **West Hill Rd** and **Wimbledon Park Rd**. Thereafter, going S, the houses are semi-detached 3/4-bed late-Victorian, set well back from the road. A primary school stands at the junction with **Standen Rd**. Southfields Secondary School lies between **Burr Rd** and **Bodmin St**, with a modern town-house development opposite. Then come late-Edwardian mansion flats, originally council, now owner-occupied. At the junction of **Burr Rd** and **Kimber Rd** is Coleman Mansions, an early '30s-style block of flats with views over Kings George's Park, but industry and heavy traffic restricts prices. **Kimber Rd** is one of the few to cross the Wandle Valley and thus attracts considerable traffic. Speed humps have helped reduce rat-running.

Wandle Valley

Between **Merton Rd** and **Garratt Lane** lie a handful of early Edwardian terraces bordered by King George's Park and **Ravensbury Rd**, which are the no-man's-land between Earlsfield and Southfields. Estate agents are unable to agree on where these roads are: Wimbledon Park (bit optimistic, this), Southfields or Earlsfield.

Penwith Rd, being one of the few roads to cross the Wandle, suffers exceptionally heavy traffic which keeps prices for mainly purpose-built late-Victorian 2-bed flats lower than the rest of the area at £95–115,000 – little changed in the last year. **Acuba Rd** (Edwardian) and **Bodmin St** are quieter as is **Strathville Rd** despite a small industrial development. **Dounsforth Gardens**, a small modern town-house development off **Strathville Rd**, backs onto the River Wandle. Acuba House, an Edwardian block of flats, was council; now it's mainly owner-occupied. It borders on King George's Park playing-fields, which have a new health and fitness centre. Upper floors of **Bodmin St** have an open outlook over the park and playing-fields. The playing-fields N of **Bodmin St** have in part been replaced with homes.

Earlsfield

Earlsfield is bordered by **Allfarthing Lane**, **Garratt Lane** and **Burntwood Lane** and runs E up the hill from the Wandle Valley towards Wandsworth Common. Earlsfield, like Battersea, is trying to expand, as it becomes more fashionable, to take in areas that have been Tooting or Wandsworth since they were built. Popularity first rose in the heady days of the late '80s, but the area didn't quite make it into respectability (unlike Southfields) before the 1990 recession. Now once again an increasing number of buyers are finding themselves outpriced in Battersea, Clapham and Wandsworth

Common and are heading down **Earlsfield Rd**. They seek streets close to the station and parks, and prefer private to council-built homes – though the gap is closing.

The area between **Garratt Lane** and Wandsworth Common is essentially residential, but note the land on either side of River Wandle, between **Garratt Lane** and **Merton Rd**, is still mainly industrial. There are parks and a playing-field, and a few streets of houses, but warehouses and light industry dominate.

Between **Magdalen Rd** and **Burntwood Lane** is a large, pleasant, council-built 'cottage' estate running from **Tilehurst Rd** in the E to **Swaby Rd** in the W. The homes are a mixture of simple '20s and '30s-style terraced and semi-detached houses, most with gardens much larger than average (50–80 ft is not unusual). A double front door reveals houses that were built as two separate flats, rather than converted. This estate is now nearly totally owner-occupied. The far-sighted bought 3-bed Estate houses (freehold) for the price of a 3-bed Victorian flat – and within easy reach of Earlsfield station in **Magdalen Rd**. Traffic has been a perennial problem, but road humps etc have calmed things down.

Open View and **Field View** overlook playing-fields; **Tilehurst Rd**, marking the E end of the estate, suffers some rat-running; and **Magdalen Rd** and **Burntwood Lane** suffer serious traffic at peak hours. Some buyers are prepared to put up with the traffic to live near the junction with **Garratt Lane** for closeness to the station. The majority of the mainly '30s semis in **Burntwood Lane** have open views over the school, golf course and the grounds of Springfield University Hospital.

Swaby Rd, running N towards the station, has generally late-Victorian small terraced houses and some purpose-built Edwardian maisonettes. Running between **Tranmere Rd** (late-Victorian terraces, some maisonettes) and **Garratt Lane** are the well-regarded trio **Quinton St**, **Isis St** and **Littleton St**. There are spacious (for Earlsfield) 3-bed turn-of-century terraces increasing in popularity, especially **Littleton St** (Earlsfield third bedrooms elsewhere tend to be very small). A large Victorian primary school stands at the junction of **Tranmere Rd** and **Waynflete St**. Some houses in **Quinton St** and **Isis St** have been converted to flats. W of **Garratt Lane**, a gated development of 2- and 3-bed houses is due in **Weybourne St**. **Garratt Lane** itself has some flats, cheaper than their neighbours due to the busy road: £60,000 might buy a 1-bed.

To the N of the railway that slices diagonally through Earlsfield, properties between **Allfarthing Lane**, the N limit of the area, and **Earlsfield Rd** are generally small late-Victorian and early Edwardian terraces with some small council-built infill blocks. Traffic calming measures have improved congestion in **Earlsfield Rd**, which runs between **Garratt Lane** and **Trinity Rd**. High numbers (**Garratt Lane** end) are small late-Victorian houses set close to the road (no off-street parking and noise nuisance). Then comes modern council infill at the junction with **Inman St**. From the junction with **Dingwall St** houses are increasingly set back from the road (important given the volume of traffic) and grow from 2- to 3-storey, many now converted to flats with off-street parking.

Odd numbers of **Earlsfield Rd** back onto the railway line but generally have large gardens and the fact that the railway line is set well below garden level means noise is reduced. Houses near the **Heathfield Rd** junction enjoy a view across the railway line of Wandsworth Prison (you could always pretend it's a castle . . .). Here there are some larger, 5-bed semi-detached late-Edwardian 3-storey houses to be found. **Bassingham Rd**, **Bucharest Rd** and **Brocklebank Rd**, leading off **Earlsfield Rd** to **Swaffield Rd**, are early Edwardian/late-Victorian terraced houses, with ornate door surrounds and windows. They are mainly 3-bedroom houses, some converted into flats. At the junction of **St Ann's Hill** and **Garratt Lane** is a converted school house (early Victorian), now flats. **Swaffield Rd** and **St Ann's Hill** suffer rat-running.

Aslett St, **Treport St**, **Delia St** and **Daphne St** are all late-Victorian terraces – some maisonettes – and popular with first-time buyers. Where conversions have taken place the second bedroom tends to be fairly small. There is a development of 1-bed flats in **Aslett St**, which has a school at the **St Ann's Hill** end, and a handful of new town-houses. 'Spencer Walk' in **Aslett St** is a new clutch of 3- and 4-bed houses. This part of Earlsfield is very convenient for the shopping facilities of Wandsworth and a Sainsbury's superstore on **Garratt Lane**. **Barmouth Rd**, **Swanage Rd** and **Cader Rd** E of **St Ann's Hill** are more Wandsworth Common than Earlsfield; 3- and 4-bed late-Victorian/early Edwardian terraces with higher prices than the Earlsfield average.

Transport	Tubes: Southfields (zone 3, District). To Oxford Circus 30 min (1 change), City 30 min, Heathrow 55 min (1 change). Trains: Earlsfield to Clapham Junction and Waterloo.
Convenient for	Wimbledon Common and tennis. Tube to town via Fulham and Sloane Square, trains to Waterloo. Miles from centre: 5.
Schools	Local Authority: Southfields School, John Archer School (b), Burntwood School (g), John Paul II RC.

SALES

Flats	S	1B	2B	3B	4B	5B
Average prices	45–75	60–110	80–150	90–160	–	–
Houses	2B	3B	4B	5B	6/7B	8B
Average prices	120–200	170–250	230–300	280–350	–	–

RENTAL

Flats	S	1B	2B	3B	4B	5B
Average prices	400–600	550–800	750–1000	1000–1200	1200+	–
Houses	2B	3B	4B	5B	6/7B	8B
Average prices	800–1100	1100–1400	1400+	2000+	–	–

The properties	Edwardian terraced homes, including many p/b and converted flats, plus some larger houses towards Putney. Also (being in Wandsworth) ex-council from '20s cottages to '70s tower flats.
The market	Southfields, with its tube, is more expensive, especially for flats: 2-bed flats popular with young sharers. Earlsfield is buzzing with economic refugees priced out of Battersea and Clapham, say agents, particularly the young. Cheaper buys in ex-council cottage estates and flat blocks: can be well below averages above. Local searches: 1 week.

Among those estate agents active in this area are:
- Barnard Marcus
- Bragg & Co
- Kinleigh Folkard & Hayward
- Hamptons
- Hooper & Jackson
- Craigie & Co
- Bells
- Winkworth*
- Robert Trindle
- FPDSavills
- Woolwich
- Tower
- Rashbrooks
- Rentals & Sales
- McKenzie
- Douglas & Gordon*
- Foxtons*

further details: see advertisers' index on p633

S

SOUTHGATE AND PALMERS GREEN

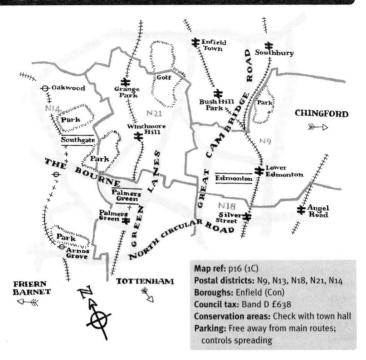

Map ref: p16 (1C)
Postal districts: N9, N13, N18, N21, N14
Boroughs: Enfield (Con)
Council tax: Band D £638
Conservation areas: Check with town hall
Parking: Free away from main routes;
 controls spreading

That part of the North Circular Rd which runs between the Lea Valley in the E and Arnos Grove tube in the W separates two remarkably different areas. Below this dividing line, the northern parts of Tottenham and Wood Green have petered out into a rather colourless hinterland, but head N and as soon as you cross the **North Circular**, the atmosphere immediately begins to change.

The large suburban tract beyond the **North Circular Rd**, which comprises Southgate (N14), Palmers Green (N13), Winchmore Hill (N21), and Upper (N18) and Lower (N9) Edmonton, is situated far enough away from the centre of London to be independent of City and West End business, but is still suitable for the commuter – inwards or outwards. While the journey to the City by train to Moorgate takes around 25–35 min from stations like Palmers Green, Lower Edmonton and WInchmore Hill, the potential for inhabitants to work elsewhere is there, thanks to the fact that the M25, M1, M11 motorways and the A10 (**Great Cambridge Rd**) are all within reach – if more often than not congested.

Edmonton, and also Palmers Green, lying closest to the **North Circular Rd**, are at first similar in style to N Tottenham and Wood Green, with rather similar shopping facilities serving similar inter-war properties; but already the *feel* of the place is different. Down the wind comes the first whiff of the Alpine North – or, at least, the fresh air from the Green Belt, blowing via a thousand Alpine-planted rock gardens. Indeed, the area changes quite dramatically the further N one travels, becoming more and more green, leafy, suburban and also prosperous: with golf clubs, parks, tree-lined streets, huge modern detached houses as well as a proliferation of 1980s and '90s developments.

The area is populated to a large extent by wealthy, middle-class families and retired (early if possible) couples who moved into the region 20–30 years ago. There is also a large Greek Cypriot community, and a smaller Asian one in Palmers Green. A decade ago there was a rush to convert large houses into flats aimed at the outwards march of the '80s yuppy, but this subsided: this is still predominantly a family area, though that encircling motorway bracket just over the horizon to the S makes it a good base for a household with one partner tied to a local, or Central London, job and the other whose work means travelling to other parts of the country. Otherwise, youth is represented by the rentals market for students from Middlesex University.

The occasional new development of flats or houses appears, but these, and more especially further conversions, are kept in check by Enfield Borough's disinclination to let on-street parking get any more congested. There are much stricter parking rules now, and rashes of speed humps.

Homes values took till last year to regain the ground lost in the early '90s recession. Prices in Southgate, Winchmore Hill and parts of Bush Hill Park rose gently before levelling out by the year's end, but on average still show good value for money compared to S of the **North Circular Rd**. A 4-bed house, Edwardian, with garden and sometimes a garage will still save you £50–80,000 or more of the price of its equivalent in Crouch End or Muswell Hill.

Southgate, Winchmore Hill, Bush Hill Park

This well-off, salubrious area, perched up between the Lea valley and Barnet, holds in the main a wealth of large semis and detached houses set in broad, tree-lined streets. The proximity to Enfield Town and the surrounding Green Belt is an added advantage. It's served by Enfield Town and Bush Hill stations to Liverpool St; Enfield Chase, Grange Park and Winchmore Hill stations to King's Cross and Moorgate; plus Oakwood and Southgate tubes (Piccadilly line to King's Cross and the West End – and on, of course, to Heathrow).

Southgate is a prosperous leafy suburb which falls into three areas: Old Southgate, New Southgate and Winchmore Hill with its village atmosphere. The tube station is Southgate's most surprising landmark: a spirited bit of '30s design, the circular building looks like a spaceship heading for Mars rather than the underground; it is in fact a listed building. It stands on **Southgate Circus**, near to a 1990 flats development of 1- and 2-bed flats whose convenience makes for price tags that start at the best part of £80,000.

The road leading down from the Southgate Circus (**High St/Cannon Hill**) is bordered by a technical college and a variety of attractive properties, including little mewsy cottages. The Southgate and District Reform Synagogue now stands on the site of the house belonging to poet Leigh Hunt.

Among the neat, untroubled streets of comfortable inter-war houses, new things are appearing – carefully. One development off **Fox Lane** is an interesting conversion of an old school house into flats (c. £80–85,000-plus), and reflects the policy of preserving the original atmosphere of the area. Churchill Court, which provides a cache of 1- and 2-bedroom retirement apartments and lies to the W of the A10 on **Church St**, is another example of the many new developments in the area, a peaceful alternative to similar schemes closer to the centre of London.

Going N along **Village Rd** towards Bush Hill Park, the roads become increasingly wider and more tree-lined, with solid 3- and 4-bedroom semis. Through the centre of the area marches **Wellington Rd**, the streets off which hold surprisingly large family houses with big gardens, and small 'courts' of neo-Georgian homes. Just off **Park Avenue**, Croft Mews' modern 2-bedroom flats and houses are positioned right next to an up-market tennis club.

Agents refer to the streets E across the tracks between the Bush Hill Park–Enfield Town railway line, **Southbury Rd** and the **Great Cambridge Rd** as 'the Triangle'. These streets, which contain the Bush Hill Park recreation ground, they reckon more desirable than comparably priced ones in Edmonton, and a good corner for home-hunters.

The large homes bordering Bush Hill Park Golf Course continue to be impressively suburban, but it is the village atmosphere of Winchmore Hill to the S, with its neat streets, quaint houses, tidy gardens and attractive pubs, that suggests the prosperity of the area. Older houses cluster picturesquely round the village green (delightful – and extremely neat); here Walton Homes are adding a small group of town-houses in Georgian style to the SW corner. **Broad Walk**, which leads off **The Green** with its antique shops, is the Beverly Hills of Southgate/Winchmore Hill. Rock stars and celebrities crop up in these vast, recently built properties which have equally vast cars parked in their driveways. £600,000 for a house in this road is around the norm: they have been known to reach the £1 million mark. **Broad Walk** leads into **The Bourne**, which borders the pleasant Grovelands Park with tennis courts, a putting green, bowling green and boating lake. **Church Hill** leads from Winchmore Hill station to leafy **Eversley Park Rd**. **Abbey Rd** is counted among the nicest roads.

Palmers Green

To the south lies Palmers Green, a quiet (away from main roads) family suburb. In its heyday it was a bastion of Edwardian respectability, whose numerous turn-of-the-century 3- and 4-bedroom houses, replete with original features, were set along leafy roads. Many of these were converted into flats – particularly in the **Ulleswater Rd**, **Derwent Rd**, **Lakeside Rd**, **Grovelands Rd** and **Old Park Rd** ladder – but the trend has now been reversed. The average prices for 3-bed Palmers Green houses are c. £160–180,000. Watch out for any whose owners resisted the lure of the double-glazing salesman and retain their original features; a good Edwardian semi-detached will start around £175,000 for 3–4 bedrooms: 5-bed ones can fetch £250,000. In the Old Lakes Estate, off **Grovelands Rd**, large Victorian houses boast original features and stained-glass windows.

Pedestrianization of part of the high street, and more parking restrictions, are in the air with a view to making the main roads more people-friendly once again. There are good shopping facilities off **Green Lanes** with a number of shops that are open late (and both Sainsbury's and Safeway have big stores in the area) but, an increase in restaurants notwithstanding, not much in the way of night life. During the day, however, and at weekends, residents relax in Broomfield Park, which adds numerous sports and leisure facilities to its tranquil lakes. Agents – and developers – look fondly on the area around the park, bounded by **Aldermans Hill** to the N, **Green Lanes** to the E, **Bowes Rd** to the S and **Wilmer Way** to the W. As well as the green open space, , this hilly corner gets some lovely views. Furlong have acquired a smallish site looking out over the park from **Aldermans Hill**, while Fairview have another on the junction of **Cranford** and **Broomfield Avenues**. Fairview have several sites in the area; Harper's Close is an electronically gated courtyard scheme, with 2-bed flats costing £120,000. Another, Chequers Green in **Chequers Way**, S of the North Circular, has over 30 houses and 100 flats. Prices for the remaining few 1-bed flats were from £59,000, the last 2-bed £75,000, last winter.

Transport in the area has happily improved. Nearest tube stations are Arnos Grove or Bounds Green and the train service into King's Cross and Moorgate is not all it could be outside of peak hours. However, there are now more buses, including the night bus from Trafalgar Square which runs up **Green Lanes**, and a good bus service into Wood Green and Enfield. Near the station there is a modern development of studios, 1- and 2-bed flats – some are galleried. A few streets away, **Windsor Rd** and **Park Avenue** sport large Edwardian houses which yield popular flat conversions. There are recent Barratt flats and houses in **Arnos Rd**, convenient for Arnos Grove tube.

Southgate's most favoured homes are the Minchenden estate: a semi-circle of closes and conifered gardens, enclosed by **Morton Way**, **Powys Lane/Cannon Hill** and **Waterfall Rd**. Prices range here from c. £240–340,000. Other favoured corners include **Meadway**, in the angle between the **High St** and **Bourne Hill**. Tucked away behind a high wall in the old part of Southgate off **Cannon Hill**, the Legal & General building, once the manor house, has been converted into exclusive, original-featured 2/3-bed apartments that cost around £200,000.

Perhaps the main point to watch in this area is the widening of the **North Circular Rd**, affecting the stretch around **Green Lanes** from Palmers Green to Edmonton. Work is nearly complete on a scheme which included the building of a fly-over and underpass, already much improving the flow through to the M11 and Essex, though there are still holdups at the big **Fore St**/Angel Eddmonton junction.

Edmonton

Upper Edmonton/Lower Edmonton is bounded by the A10 to the E, the William Girling Reservoir to the W and the **North Circular** to the S. The area is served by Silver St and Lower Edmonton rail stations and possesses one of the largest leisure centres in the S-E of England, Picketts Lock. There is also sailing on the reservoir.

Edmonton is perhaps the least 'desirable', in estate agents' terms, of the four areas – marked by a crop of huge, unsightly high-rise council blocks and a concrete shopping centre which, remarked a local, bears a marked resemblance to a German bunker. Of the two, Upper Edmonton is more 'inner city' in style, with very little green.

Small, flat-fronted 2- to 3-bed terraced houses (early 1900s) and inter-war semis, some of which have been converted into flats, are standard in this area, although styles are certainly varied, and stone cladding ubiquitous. Homes are mixed with post-war council-build and tower blocks, and with commercial or industrial corners, but also broken up by recreation grounds or the odd football pitch; some homes, too, get green, open views out towards Essex. The Huxley, Galliard, Midland, Latymer and Westerham estates offer good-value properties, with 3-bed homes starting for as little as £78,000. The area's nicer roads are **Charlton Rd**, which includes a late-'80s flats development, **Nightingale Rd** and **Oxford Rd**, leafy and neat. A new homes development in **Scotland Green Rd**, grouped round communal gardens, has sizes and prices that range from 1-bed flats, £40–45,000, to 3-bed houses for £90,000.

Near the North Circular lie Pymmes Park, complete with lake, tennis courts and bowling green. More trees generally here, in streets like **Sweet Briar Walk** which skirts the park, and around **Silver St**.

Just off **Church St** in **Lion Rd**, there is a development of 1- and 2-bed flats conveniently placed for Lower Edmonton station. Moving W along **Church St** (inter-war semis) the area becomes increasingly attractive with many playing-fields and sportsgrounds providing pleasant backdrops to the houses. Here the A10, bustling importantly off towards Cambridge, runs for a while with allotments bordering both sides of the road.

S

Transport	Tubes: Southgate, Arnos Grove, Oakwood (zone 3, Piccadilly). From Southgate: Oxford Circus 35 min (1 change), City 30 min (1 change), Heathrow 1 hr 15 min. Trains: Palmers Green, Winchmore Hill to Moorgate, King's Cross; Bush Hill Park, Lower Edmonton to Liverpool St.

Convenient for   North Circular, M25. Parks and sports/leisure. Miles
from centre: 8.

Schools   Enfield Education Authority: Latymer, Alyward, Winchmore,
Southgate, St Angela's RC (g). Private: Palmers Green High (g).

SALES

Flats	S	1B	2B	3B	4B	5B
Average prices	35–45	50–80	70–100	100–130	–	–
Houses	2B	3B	4B	5B	6/7B	8B
Average prices	90–120	110–140	150–200	250–350	–	–

RENTAL

Flats	S	1B	2B	3B	4B	5B
Average prices	400–550	600–700	650–750	800+	–	–
Houses	2B	3B	4B	5B	6/7B	8B
Average prices	700–800	750–950	1000–1400	–	–	–

The properties   Leafy, suburban homes with gardens in Southgate and
Winchmore Hill including some large expensive ones.
Lots of modern houses and flats. Palmers Green has Edwardian
3/4-bed houses, some now flats, Edmonton has smaller terraces
and inter-war homes.

The market   Commuter country, with trains to City and good access to
motorways to attract executives. For junior ranks there are
converted flats in cheaper areas; some expensive new
developments. Local searches: 1 week.

Among those estate agents active in this area are:
- Angeli
- Bairstow Eves
- Castles
- Chester Stevens
- Kinleigh Folkard Hayward
- Winkworths*
- Meadway Estates
- Adam Kennedy
- Buckinghams

further details: see advertisers' index on p633

S

ST JOHN'S WOOD

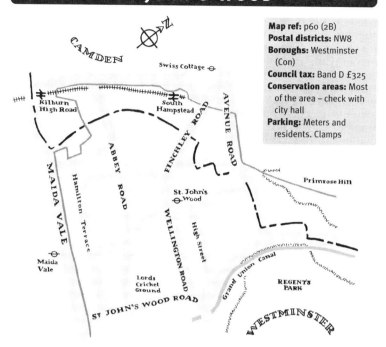

Map ref: p60 (2B)
Postal districts: NW8
Boroughs: Westminster
  (Con)
Council tax: Band D £325
Conservation areas: Most
  of the area – check with
  city hall
Parking: Meters and
  residents. Clamps

St John's Wood is London's 'first suburb' – first both in the sense of being just about the foremost and also just about the closest-in.

The green, open tracts of Primrose Hill and Regent's Park lie alongside, and yet the West End is only a mile or so away. Despite this proximity to the bustling heart of town, and despite the many modern aparment blocks which have replaced earlier mansions, the pace and the style of these select streets are set, it seems, by the lazy, summer sound of wood on willow that drifts across the high, enclosing walls of Lord's Cricket Ground.

Away from the busy artery of **Wellington Rd** and the hustle and bustle of the **High St**, The Wood's life is conducted at strolling pace – and a very pleasant place to stroll it is. The international set means a high number of renters (especially the Americans) rather than buyers – which in turn means that it's a blue-chip corner for investors. The ratio of rent:buy seems to be running at about 50:50, which invites the wry thought that one half is buying to let to the other half . . . But there is a very settled backbone, and a sense of belonging appears to develop quickly, wherever one's starting-point. An active residents' association defends the place against vulgarity, though they can do little to curb the traffic. That settled feel is one of wealth; this is not a place for violent change. Estate agents are still computing whether the admission of women members to Lord's (good grief!) will affect the market for good or ill.

Until Regency times it was still largely a wood – albeit a royal one. Hayfields, whose crops supplied City stables, abounded. The development which took place here in the early 19th century, as London spread westward, was aimed at the 'carriage people' and was brilliantly successful. Instead of the more economical terraces that

had spread across the centre of town, large and elegant Regency villas with gardens and coach houses, standing alone or in pairs, were built – and remain the hallmark of St John's Wood.

These fine houses set the tone and attracted the 'right' people – a state of affairs which has largely persisted. Its inhabitants are undeniably wealthy: well-established men and women who see a home in St John's Wood as a fair reward for their hard work; globe-trotting business people; diplomatic staff. Ambassadors find the area sympathetic. First-time buyers here are apt to be at least in their 30s, and equipped with trust fund or undiminished City bonus.

And to set the seal on things, 1998 finally saw the long-awaited opening of the Heathrow Express, which makes the airport 15 min away from Paddington station, just down the road. Other reasons for the area's appeal include proximity to good shopping along the **Finchley Rd**, the London Central Mosque, a number of synagogues, Lord's . . . and (cited by agents as paramount) the American School in **Loudoun Rd.**

During the 1990s overseas investment, particularly from Singapore and other parts of the Far East, drove the market up. New schemes such as Templar Court in **St John's Wood Rd**, a mix of flats and town-houses, were bought off-plan. Older mansion blocks saw active investment buying. The economic turmoil of the Far East since late '97 has slowed things down; prices have stabilized, but that's about all.

As various as the St John's Wood dwellers are the St John's Wood homes. Every size, from pied-à-terre flatlets to vast and splendid mansions; every period, from those Regency villas (and a few rare Regency Gothic cottages) via stock-brick terraces, high Victoriana, substantial between-the-wars mansion blocks, bomb-damage infill, '60s town-houses (garages!), small outbreaks of excellent recent houses – and flats, flats and more flats up to the super-luxury '90s models which come with share of porter and pool at the cost of the average West Country manor.

S   The earlier history of the area still has a bearing on buying homes here today. After the Priors of St John lost the land at the Reformation it was split up; a long, narrow strip (lying along the **Edgware Rd**) became, eventually, part of the Harrow School Estate. A larger section belonged to the Crown: Charles II used some of it to settle a debt. In 1720, 200 acres of this was bought (for £20,000) by Henry Eyre, a prosperous merchant, whose estate remains largely intact today and is remembered in the name of Eyre Court, a popular block on the corner of the **Finchley Rd** and **Grove End Rd**. Thus many freeholds in the area are owned by Harrow School (a typical lease is around 64 years), the Eyre Estate (shorter leases, around 50 years) and (a few) Eton College, and most property is bought leasehold. Paradoxically, some of the best houses are on these short leases. There are roads where one side has, say, 47-year leases, the other 70; which explains strange discrepancies in prices. The short leases also explain why these prestigious houses can cost no more than those in Hampstead, further away. The Leasehold Reform Acts have changed the financial equation on some of these estate houses: see the Buying and Selling chapter.

It's a neat area: its wide and leafy roads lie mainly in Westminster (which stops at the aptly named **Boundary Rd**, though a more tangible frontier is the rail tracks that separate this area from South Hampstead to the N), and encompass most of NW8. Pencil-straight **Maida Vale** (the road) rules it off to the W, with Regent's Park and Primrose Hill lapping round the eastern periphery. Its internal geography is split – neatly, of course – by the main through-route of **Wellington Rd/Finchley Rd** into two distinct halves: the Lord's side and the Park side.

The Lord's Side

The Lord's side refers, of course, to St John's Wood's most sacred shrine – the cricket ground. On this, western, side of the **Wellington Rd/Finchley Rd** divide lie most of the area's other religious institutions; churches, synagogues, etc.

The area's southernmost boundary is **St John's Wood Rd**, which cuts off Lord's and St John's Wood from Lisson Grove and Marylebone. Across the cricket ground, **Cavendish Avenue** holds some of the largest houses and gardens in St John's Wood, attracting celebrity buyers. It is also a good corner for hypochondriacs: at one end of the street is **Wellington Place**, where on the corner with **Wellington Rd** stands one of the most expensive private hospitals in London, Humana's Wellington Hospital (South). At the other end, **Circus Rd** (whose name reflects an early, but thwarted, plan to develop St John's Wood around a large circus with streets and squares containing pairs of houses) is the back of the Catholic St John and St Elizabeth Hospital.

The other source of grand mansions is **Hamilton Terrace**, which runs the length of the area: St John's Wood's premier boulevard. Wide, tree-lined, prestigious, it stretches about three-quarters of a mile. Begun in 1820, its variety of homes include semi-detached and detached mansions so large that they now provide the area's best hunting-ground for conversions (at a premium because of the preponderance of purpose-built flats). Many, though, are available only on short leases. When left intact, however, houses here range from modest to ambassador-class: at time of writing, £3,500,000 would buy you 9,100 sq ft of accommodation: 10 bedrooms, 5 reception (the right term here) rooms, garage for one, parking for 6/7 more, swimming pool . . . the lease runs out in 2084.

Flats (or apartments, maisonettes, duplexes, penthouses . . . the term escalates along with the size and price) can have great views out over greenery – the most coveted being the 22-yard strip with the Test Match being played on it. The Pavilion, a brand-new block on nine floors in **St John's Wood Rd**, launches this spring: preliminary prices for the 122 flats start from £160,000 (1-bed) to £1,950,000 (3-bed penthouse). All get a basement parking space, 24hr porterage; some a terrace and, yes, view of Lord's. In the surrounding streets, a jumble of ages and styles provide flats for all requirements: pre-war ones are in evidence in **Scott Ellis Gardens** and **Hall Rd**, while **Abbey Rd** and **Abercorn Place** have good examples of flats built just after the war. On the corner of the two, 38 **Abercorn Place** is a 1988-built block of eight smart apartments. Under its raised roof, a penthouse enjoys the entire top floor. Next door to it is a delight: a Regency artists' studio house designed by Decimus Burton.

Grove End Rd, which runs N from **St John's Wood Rd**, is a pleasant road with a mixture of flats, in blocks from mansion to modern, and large houses. Among the latter is Tadema Lodge, a magnificent house with features that include a swimming pool complex and ballroom, designed by the artist James Tissot and later owned by Sir Lawrence Alma-Tadema. The St John and St Elizabeth Hospital, founded by colleagues of Florence Nightingale, stands opposite St John's Wood United Synagogue, one of the three well-known synagogues in the area. It joins **Wellington Rd** just opposite **Acacia Rd**, on the corner of which is the St John's Wood tube station.

Running N from **Grove End Rd** is **Loudoun Rd,** where you'll find the famous American School – a magnet for US families – and, opposite it, the boys' prep school Arnold House. The street's consequent traffic problems were much improved by sleeping policemen. A 6-bed house close by was rented recently by an American on a long-term agreement before refurbishments were finished: in effect site unseen.

Parallel to **Loudoun Rd** is **Abbey Rd**, made famous by the Beatles, whose recording studios were here. It, too, has sprouted stylish new developments: the 1990 complex of eight houses and 100 apartments at No 20 was among the earliest to be marketed extensively in Hong Kong, helped by Beatles-linked promotion: a key gimmick was a pedestrian crossing mock-up on which prospective purchasers were photographed in a re-creation of the famous album cover. Recent prices for 2- and 3-bed flats in this block were c. £350–530,000: it has parking, pool and porterage, of course. Another new development is planned for the old garage site on the corner with **Abercorn Place**: no firm details yet. **Abbey Rd** is also very popular in the rentals market.

Off **Abbey Rd** is one of the prettiest corners of St John's Wood. Roads like **Blenheim Terrace, Nugent Terrace** and **Boundary Rd** have a smaller-scale village-like atmosphere. There you'll find little rows of shops and small parks like the one in **Violet Hill**. Houses round pretty **Alma Square** have access to its gardens. These 4-floor terraced homes, which date from the 1850s, have 5 or 6 bedrooms and go for prices around £1 million: two on the market last winter at £875,000 and £995,000 respectively. Some have been converted: a 2-bed, second-floor flat was a more affordable £155,000. A small new flats development appeared in the square last year.

On **Finchley Rd** the 1930s Apsley House was crowned in 1990 with six luxurious new penthouse flats. This is a popular trend for blocks in the area – Clive Court on **Maida Vale** is another example – except, of course, with the erstwhile top-floor dwellers whose penthouses are now merely penultimate.

The Park Side

East of the **Wellington Rd/Finchley Rd** divide – which connects St John's Wood with Swiss Cottage – the Park side of St John's Wood boasts not only the Hill and the Park, but the **High St**, and some peaceful corners to live. **Queen's Grove**, with its terraced houses boasting large Ionic and Corinthian columns, is a quiet, leafy road leading to Primrose Hill. **Norfolk Rd** and **Acacia Rd** are both pretty streets with stuccoed and brick houses, sought-after – even fought-over – by those who prefer older-style houses. Actress Lilly Langtry, King Edward VII's mistress, dwelt in **Acacia Rd**. Think in terms of some £1,350,000 for a 4-bed semi-detached house here.

Woronzow Rd, where learner drivers practise their three-point turns, contains the slightly less expensive terraced houses. The Woronzow in question was a Russian count who left £500 to build almshouses for the poor. The originals were built round the corner in **St John's Wood Terrace** in 1827, but were rebuilt in the 1960s.

Newer houses in St John's Wood can be seen further towards Swiss Cottage. **Queensmead** is an estate of 17 town-houses and three blocks of flats owned by the Eyre Estate, built 30 years ago. They were let until 1990, when some were refurbished and sold. They sell now for around £430–495,000 for a 3-bed flat. **The Marlowes** is another sought-after clutch of town-houses: they look, comments a local, like flats tipped on their sides, but are desirable because of their location. **St John's Wood Park** also contains other modern homes. 'The Rosetti' in **Ordnance Hill** is a 1995 scheme where 1-bed flats currently fetch £260,000 and 2-bed ones £475,000. **Ordnance Hill** houses the King's Troop Royal Horse Artillery – a splendid sight to see in the early morning when the horses are exercised: this can involve 60 horses with gun carriages.

Running between **Circus Rd** and **Prince Albert Rd** is **St John's Wood High St** with its boutiques, bistros, wine merchants and chemists. Round the corner is Panzers, St John's Wood's most up-market grocer, and the post office. Council-built flats (select ones, to match the area) lie behind the **High St**. Some in **Barrow Hill, Allitsen Rd** and **Townshend Rd** now appear for sale, having been bought by their tenants.

At the end of the **High St** is the roundabout presided over by St John's Wood Church, a large elegant building. **Prince Albert Rd** curves around the N side of the park (see Regent's Park). The Pavilions at 24–26 **Avenue Rd**, a luxurious development of six flats, a sumptuous penthouse and swimming pool, was built in 1988. **Avenue Rd** is a grand thoroughfare, highly desirable to the international set: ambassadors from all nations make their homes in the large mansions with landscaped gardens, overseas business people buy flats. A 9-bed example with only a 36-year lease still merits a £4.6 million price tag; also on the market last winter, billed as 'one of the most important houses' in the area is a 7-bed, 6-reception modern mansion with dramatic atrium within but carefully Regency-styled exterior: freehold, £7.5 million.

Eastern Borders

Across **Avenue Rd**, a small clutch of streets run eastward to the slopes of Primrose Hill. Look for flats and modern town-houses in streets such as **St Edmund's Terrace, Ormonde Terrace**. On the far side of the 200-ft high hill, the villagy streets of Primrose Hill proper are covered in the Camden chapter.

To the N of Primrose Hill's green spaces lies a group of roads with huge, handsome Edwardian red-brick villas, many still single homes. Look for them in **Harley Rd**, **Wadham Gardens** and **Elsworthy Rd**. To the S, the giant modern blocks along **Prince Albert Rd** are covered in the Regent's Park chapter.

Transport	Tubes: St John's Wood, Swiss Cottage (zone 2, Jubilee); Maida Vale (zone 2, Bakerloo). From St John's Wood: Oxford Circus 15 min (1 change), City 30 min (1 change), Heathrow 1 hr (1 change). Trains: South Hampstead (direct to Euston).
Convenient for	West End, Regent's Park, Lord's Cricket Ground. Routes to North and West. Miles from centre: 3.5.
Schools	Local Authority: Quintin Kynaston. Private: The American School.

SALES

Flats	S	1B	2B	3B	4B	5B
Average prices	75–130	115–250	180–350+	300+	400–2M+	→

Houses	2B	3B	4B	5B	6/7B	8B
Average prices	250–400+	350–800	525–1.5M	650–2M+	1M–2M+	3.5M–7.5M

RENTAL

Flats	S	1B	2B	3B	4B	5B
Average prices	700–900	1050–1500	1500–3000	2000–5000+	3500+	—

Houses	2B	3B	4B	5B	6/7B	8B
Average prices	2000+	2800–5000+	3500–8500+	6500+	—	—

S

The properties   Smart suburb with big, 19th-century villas, plus abundant mansion and modern flats. Flats become luxury-level towards Regent's Park (see chapter) and Lord's: London's highest concentration of penthouses. Some expensive new refurbishments.

The market   Cosmopolitan: diplomats, businessmen with families, celebrities all buy here for big family houses and international-standard apartments. (The latter can cost as much and more than whole houses.) Considerable overseas investment/bolt-hole buying. Far East financial turmoil slowed the market last year, and stablized prices. Local searches: 2 working days.

Among those estate agents active in this area are:
- Anscombe & Ringland*
- Bargets
- The Estate Office
- Goldschmidt & Howland
- Arlington Residential
- Foxtons*
- Keith Cardale Groves
- FPDSavills
- Knight Frank
- Winkworth*
- Behr & Butchoff
- John D Wood
- Brian Lack
- Cluttons Daniel Smith
- Hamptons

* further details: see advertisers' index on p633

S

STEPNEY AND WHITECHAPEL

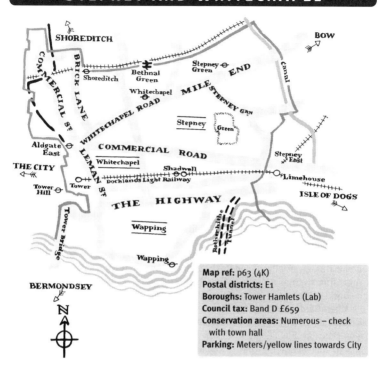

SHOREDITCH

BOW

Stepney
Green

END

Shoreditch

Bethnal
Green

Whitechapel

MILE

STEPNEY GRN

Stepney

Green

COMMERCIAL

Aldgate
East

THE CITY

COMMERCIAL ROAD

Whitechapel

Shadwell

Docklands Light Railway

Stepney
East

Limehouse

Tower
Hill

Tower

ISLE OF DOGS

THE HIGHWAY

Wapping

Wapping

BERMONDSEY

N

Map ref: p63 (4K)
Postal districts: E1
Boroughs: Tower Hamlets (Lab)
Council tax: Band D £659
Conservation areas: Numerous – check
with town hall
Parking: Meters/yellow lines towards City

Stepney, Whitechapel and Wapping are a curious mixture of some of London's best and worst housing. The area, defined quite precisely by the E1 postal district, is the heart of the old East End. War and slum clearance brought great changes, and now the ferment in its neighbouring areas brings more. The City's expansion has crossed the border into Stepney while the Docklands building boom has brought wealth to riverside Wapping (see Docklands). But some squalor remains, especially around Spitalfields – little more than a stone's throw from the thriving City.

The latest change is a vogue for living in and around the City, which until five years ago had a nocturnal population consisting of more cats than humans. The W edge of this area is Spitalfields and Aldgate, both of which are seeing big changes, which involve homes as well as offices. A linked trend is the loft movement: the City fringes and the wider area are rich in redundant buildings that can make spacious homes.

The area has three main roads running from E-W – **The Highway**, **Commercial Rd** and **Whitechapel Rd** which is a continuation of **Mile End Rd**. All three lead to the City and are, therefore, extremely busy. The Liverpool St main line cuts Stepney off from Bethnal Green to the N, while the canal devides it from Poplar to the E. The river underlines it to the S and the City lies to the W.

This part of London is packed with history, a fact reflected by no fewer than 12 conservation areas. The Tower of London falls within Stepney's boundary while Jack the Ripper once stalked the streets of Whitechapel in search of victims. Whitechapel is dominated by the world-famous London Hospital, directly opposite Whitechapel tube station and **Whitechapel Rd** market, known locally as 'The Waste'. Cultural

attractions include the Whitechapel Gallery, the first and most famous of several galleries. According to the Whitechapel, there are 7,000 artists living and working in the wider East End.

The area used to be in parts strongly Jewish, but now a Muslim flavour predominates, especially around **Brick Lane**, and the mosque in **Whitechapel High St**.

Apart from the '80s explosion of new housing developments in Wapping (described in the Docklands chapter), some of Stepney's most sought-after homes are to be found in the **Albert Gardens/Arbour Square** conservation area, which includes Arbour Square police station. Parking here is not such a problem as nearer the City and around the London Hospital. Spitalfields is on the way up, with new City-linked developments seemingly imminent. The least desirable housing is on either side of the W end of **Commercial Rd**. These areas are dominated by the East End 'rag trade' and scores of clothing manufacturers and wholesalers operate here Many of these small businesses are run by Asians. Vehicles loading and unloading in the cramped streets make driving in this area a particular problem. Spitalfields has a high crime rate but, despite its drawbacks, includes three conservation areas – **Elder St, Fournier St** and **Artillery Passage**.

Watney Market, S of **Commercial Rd**, is another far from attractive area but it has the asset of the DLR's Shadwell station. The famous Petticoat Lane market is in **Middlesex St** on Sunday mornings and there is a market throughout the week in nearby **Wentworth St**.

The old centre of Stepney was a thriving village in medieval times. All that is left is Stepney Churchyard, surrounding St Dunstan's Church, one of Stepney's most picturesque corners. Nearby, in **Stepney Way**, is Stepping Stones Farm – an unusual sight in such a highly populated area.

One-third of Stepney's homes were destroyed by wartime bombing. The council homes that replaced them are now beginning to change hands as former tenants sell and move out to Essex. Stepney is as convenient for the City as Docklands, if not so chic, and buyers are beginning to find it attractive. And unlike Docklands, Stepney's neighbourhoods have been around for some time and have more in the way of everyday amenities.

The property market woke up in 1996 and 1997 as buyers priced out of Islington, Clerkenwell and Docklands took a look at Stepney. The stigma attached to living in the East End is going fast, and the council is tidying up its housing which, with the conversion of redundant buildings to lofts, is cheering up the area.

Stepney

At the eastern end of the neighbourhood, conveniently close to Stepney Green tube, an enclave of streets is hidden between **Globe** and **Mile End Rds**. **Portelet Rd**, **Carlton Square**, **Holton St**, **Grantley St**, **Massingham St** and **Tollet St** are well-placed near the Mile End annexe of the London Hospital. These delightful 2-storey Victorian terraced houses, some with semi-basements and steps up to the front door, are also near Tower Hamlets Central Library in **Bancroft Rd** and various Queen Mary and Westfield College buildings. **Bancroft Rd's** amenities also include a music rehearsal space in the old railway arches. Residents in **Grand Walk**, at the E end of **Mile End Rd**, have new terraced houses made magic by the Grand Union Canal which facilitates the occasional houseboat and anglers. Across the canal, **Canal Rd** has disappeared in the development of Mile End Park. In **Copperfield Rd**, also by the park, Bellway are converting a canalside building into 40 flats, due this spring.

Further along **Mile End Rd**, to the S, is the sprawling, run-down Ocean council estate which includes **Beaumont Square**, **White Horse Lane**, **Ben Johnson Rd**, **Matlock St**, **Commodore St**, **Solebay St**, **Emmott St**, **Shandy St**, **Duckett St** and **Harford St** where there are gasworks. Housing associations and the Central Stepney Regeneration Project are active here building and renovating homes to rent.

White Horse Lane has 2-storey terraced houses with distinctive open porches and the green of **Beaumont Square** faces the London Independent private hospital. **Maria Terrace**, off **Beaumont Square**, has a row of 10 3-storey Victorian houses. Close by in **Louisa St**, nine 3-bed houses have been built. And in **Rectory Square**, behind **Stepney Green**, developers have converted a synagogue into flats and houses.

Stepney Green – not the open, featureless expanse between **Stepney Way**/**Redman's Rd**, but the street of the same name – is an unexpected gem. Behind the narrow strip of green, enclosed by railings, stand a row of Queen Anne/early 18th-century houses, in what is reputed to be the only blue-cobbled street left in South East England. They are supplemented by some faithful modern copies. One of these is Trinity Mews, on **Redman's Rd**, a mixed development of homes and commercial premises which includes town-houses with studio workspace. In **White Horse Lane** is 'The Rosery', an old rectory now divided into nine smart flats. Opposite are the ivy-fronted red-brick Cressy House and Dunstan House and the Stifford Estate (council) which includes **Tinsley Rd**, **Cressy Place**, **Redmans Rd**, **Jamaica St**, **Stepney Way** and **Smithy St**. On **Jamaica St** three boarded-up tower blocks loom over the Stifford Estate. One has a painted message which runs down successive stairwells: "FOR SALE, £4.99 O.N.O. ONE CARELESS OWNER HA! HA!".

Close to Whitechapel tube and in stark contrast to its busy surroundings in **Mile End Rd** is Trinity Green, a small 1961 Civic Trust Award development with beautiful gardens surrounded by railings and wall. Further E along **Mile End Rd** is **Cleveland Way**: smart new housing association flats, and Cleveland Place, a development of 10 flats: 2-bed from £110,000. **Cephas Avenue** has attractive 2- and 3-storey Victorian terraced houses, many with steps and railings and some with flat roofs, are in high demand. In **Cephas St** a church conversion has 37 new flats for sale. Nearby **Cooper's Close** has neat 4-storey modern flats.

Commercial Rd to the S, towards Wapping, lives up to its name with heavy traffic and is dotted on either side with council estates such as Pitsea, Watney Market, Exmouth and Mountmorres. The garden square of **Albert Gardens** is a peaceful haven from the noise of **Commercial Rd**. These desirable 4-storey Victorian terraced houses are part of a conservation area which also includes **Havering St** where 3-storey Victorian houses with railings lead down to a railway arch. Viewed from the rear, the roofs of **Havering St** give an unusual wave effect. To the W, St Mary and St Michael's Roman Catholic Church and Primary School are next to the Watney Market council estate which includes **Deancross St, Sidney St, Hainton Path, Hungerford St, Tarling St, Watney St, Dunch St, Bigland St, Timberland Rd** and **Burwell Close**.

From the Watney Market Estate W along **Commercial Rd** to the City, parking starts to become a problem. **Mansell St** and **Leman St,** which includes a police station, are now generally accepted as part of the City itself and are strict no-parking zones. Nearby **Prescott St** has a new development of flats with prices from £155,000. It's a conversion of a 1930s office building. **Aldgate High St**, which houses Sedgwick Sports Centre, is similarly busy. The Exmouth Estate, N of **Commercial Rd**, includes **Clark St, Musbury St, Cornwood Drive, Jubilee St, Exmouth St, Summercourt Rd, Jamaica St, Aylward St, Clovelly Way** and **Clearbrook Way**. To the E of the Estate is the **Arbour Square** conservation area where Arbour House council flats are situated alongside 3-storey Victorian terraced houses, some with front steps, facing a garden square. Houses on the S side of the square have a drawback as they back onto far less attractive 4-storey terraced houses in **Commercial Rd**. The **Arbour Square** neighbourhood also includes a police station and Tower Hamlets College.

Further E along **Commercial Rd** is **Bromley St** where railings surround delightful 2-storey Victorian terraced houses, refurbished in 1986, leading to the British Prince pub on the corner and adjoining the Mountmorres council estate. Similar homes are to be found in **Belgrave St,** which includes the Mercers Arms pub and leads down to picturesque St Dunstan's Church, much favoured for local weddings. The church is surrounded by Stepney Churchyard. Facing the churchyard is **Mercers Cottages,** four beautiful terraced homes with a communal front garden. In **Belgrave St** the Samuel Lewis Trust is building 59 homes for rent and 15 for sale (on a shared-ownership basis).

The **York Square** conservation area, to the SE of the green, is half in Stepney and half in Limehouse. The Stepney half includes **White Horse Rd** and **Barnes St.** Run-down 3- and 4-storey terraced houses in **White Horse Rd** face attractive 3-storey Victorian terraced properties with railings and hanging baskets of flowers. Similarly attractive 2-storey Victorian terraced houses in **Barnes St** which is on the opposite side of **Commercial Rd** to Limehouse rail and DLR stations. On **Cable St** Sceptre Court has underground parking. Four flats left to sell in December.

Whitechapel and Spitalfields

The world-famous London Hospital dominates the centre of Whitechapel. The front entrance of the hospital stands in **Whitechapel Rd**, directly opposite Whitechapel tube station and **Whitechapel Rd** market. Some of the Victorian terraced houses at the back of the hospital are owned by the hospital itself, for example in **Philpott St,** and used for research. Other hospital buildings are to be found in **Newark St**, part of the **Sidney Square** conservation area. The conservation area also includes part of **Cavell St, Halcrow St, Ford Square, Ashfield St, Sidney Square** and the E end of **Varden St.** **Sidney Square** is attractive with 3-storey Victorian terraced houses which have tiny wrought-iron balconies on the second floor; but parking is a big problem in this area.

The new Sainsbury's to the N of **Whitechapel Rd** has improved the area's shopping. Nearby in **Durward St** is 'Cityside', a conversion of an old school. Also situated on **Whitechapel Rd** is Albion Yard, the converted old Albion brewery.

At the junction of **Cavell St**, named after Nurse Edith Cavell, and **Varden St** is a new development of 20 luxury apartments. Six new homes in **Cleveland Way** shelter behind electronic gates. More 3- and 4-storey Victorian terraced houses, some converted into flats, are found in **Ford Square**. Many of these houses are now occupied by the local student population. The area's cramped streets also include many Asian-run garment manufacturers and wholesalers. Vans loading and unloading sometimes make access difficult. Whitechapel Bell Foundry, established in 1570, is at the junction of **Fieldgate St** and **Plumber's Row**. The Whitechapel Gallery in the **High**

St, currently being refurbished, is a world-famous art venue which balances the cultural with the practical: it's also a well-known local place to eat. The East London Mosque, on **Whitechapel Rd,** is a focal point for the Muslim community.

A big site off Gower's Walk, S of the   **Commercial Rd,** is being developed by Ballymore: among the homes here are smart warehouse conversions from £130,000 which will be ready this April. St George's 'Skyline Plaza' flats on **Commercial Rd** has 130 flats sharing a roof garden with splendid views. (For Spitalfields see City chapter.)

Transport	Tubes: Stepney Green, Whitechapel, Aldgate East (Hammersmith & City, District); Wapping (East London); Aldgate (Metropolitan, Circle); Tower Hill (Circle, District); Shadwell (East London). DLR (Docklands Light Railway). Trains: Limehouse. From Stepney Green: Oxford Circus 15 min (1 change), City 10 min (1 change), Heathrow 60 min (1 change).
Convenient for	Docklands, City. Miles from centre: 3.5.
Schools	Local Authority: Bishop Challoner RC (g), Bow (b), Central Foundation (g), Mulberry (g), Sir John Cass, Stepney Green (b), Swanlea School.

S A L E S

Flats	S	1B	2B	3B	4B	5B
Average prices	55–60	55–90	70–100	90–150	–	–
Houses	2B	3B	4B	5B	6/7B	8B
Average prices	80–115	110–150	180+	–	–	–

R E N T A L

Flats	S	1B	2B	3B	4B	5B
Average prices	500–600	600–750	650–800	750–1200	–	–
Houses	2B	3B	4B	5B	6/7B	8B
Average prices	700–1250	850–1400	1000–1800	–	–	–

The properties	Homes here range from ex-council to Grade II listed, from flats to new mews schemes, from Edwardian red-brick to Georgiana on Stepney Green. Loft conversions and new-build flats appearing as City workers discover the area.
The market	Prices reflect range, and closeness of City and Wapping. Small, everyday rows rub shoulders with large listed houses. A few 7-bed Edwardian homes: occasionally to be found undone-up. For Wapping riverside and Spitalfields see Docklands and City. Local searches: 4 weeks.

Among those estate agents active in this area are:
- Strettons
- Carrington & Partners
- Baker Allen
- Ludlow Thompson
- Docklands Estates
- Medowalls
- W J Meade
- Tower Estate Agents
- Land & Co
- Stirling Ackroyd

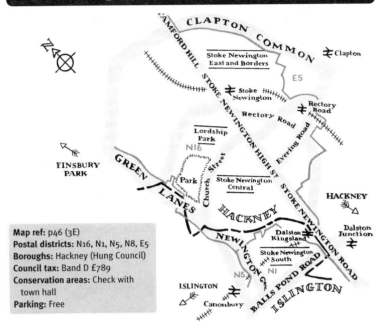

STOKE NEWINGTON

Map ref: p46 (3E)
Postal districts: N16, N1, N5, N8, E5
Boroughs: Hackney (Hung Council)
Council tax: Band D £789
Conservation areas: Check with
   town hall
Parking: Free

Go due north from London Bridge: through the City, up the Roman-straight A10. An exodus of younger (ie, poorer) media types, City workers and young families have done so in the last decade, and made a home in Stoke Newington. On the fault line between east and west (Highbury end of Islington to W, Hackney to E), new residents mingle with those three generations in. The new arrivals find they've joined a community; people know each other and get together to protect their area, support their local schools or just to hold street parties: there is a very popular midsummer festival in **Church St**.

Exciting additions are appearing: the old municipal pool is upgrading to a multi-million pound Millennium-project leisure centre, the lottery is playing fairy godmother to a watersports and recreation centre – there's even talk of a theatre, no less. But the thing that would really set the seal on this corner is a tube station. At last, even that holy grail has come one step nearer with the reopening of the East London line: this currently ends at Shoreditch, but Hackney Council are holding out hopes for a northern extension . . . they're pinning their faith on London's as yet to be elected mayor to push this through, so don't hold your breath. Meanwhile, trains to the City are good, and the trusty 73 bus goes all the way to Victoria via King's Cross, Euston and Oxford St.

Largely in N16, Stoke Newington lies N of **Balls Pond Rd**, E of **Green Lanes**, S of **Allerton Rd**, **Fairholt Rd** and **Dunsmure Rd**, and W of **Clapton Common**, with **Brooke Rd**, **Evering Rd**, **Rectory Rd** and **Shacklewell Lane** completing the circle. It is an amalgam of the ancient villages of Shacklewell and Stoke Newington itself, the northern points of Kingsland and the southern reaches of Stamford Hill. The villages are Domesday-ancient; the area was popular as a place to retreat in the 17th century, thrived in Georgian times, became built-up in Victoria's reign. Here in the 1830s Thomas Cubitt was sharpening his skills before moving on to create Belgravia and Pimlico. The area prospered until the early 20th century when the more well-to-do moved further out. Many homes became tenanted and fell into disrepair. By the last war many buildings were in poor condition, and bombs hastened their demise.

Post-war redevelopment brought ugly low-rise council-built blocks, latterly 'improved' by surface treatments such as bright paint and the landscaping of open areas. Much has been done to restore and renovate streets to a modern version of Victorian splendour – work carried out by the council, locals and the numbers of young middle-class families who have found homes here. It is an ongoing task.

Conservation areas now abound, local shopping is well-served, and restaurants – both fast-food and conventional – are numerous. Pubs have been joined by smart wine bars; arts and crafts shops and bookshops supplement the high-street basics. There's a popular jazz club here, The Vortex. All help to make the distance from Stoke Newington to the West End seem increasingly irrelevant. The Rio Cinema, which serves both West End and local tastes with its imaginative programming, reopens this July after a lottery-aided refit which will also improve access for disabled people.

Outdoors, spacious Clissold Park boasts a truly eccentric 'zoo', bowling green, tennis courts and a bandstand for summer sonatas, and has a Victorian swimming pool nearby, while Abney Park Cemetery is the resting place for many eminent Victorians, beneath wonderful Gothic tombs.

The two main thoroughfares are the A10, which in its northwards charge changes its name from **Kingsland High St** via **Stoke Newington Rd** to **Stoke Newington High St**, and the E-W **Stoke Newington Church St**. Although most of the length of the High St remains cheerfully scruffy, the area between the **Church St** and **Northwold Rd** intersections is becoming smarter. New restaurants are opening, and other long-empty premises are being renovated. There is even an example of that fashionable style of development in which a redundant Victorian school is becoming lofty 1-, 2- and 3-bed flats. The prices at 'Fleetwood' range from £110–300,000.

Church St – the high street of the original village – still boasts many buildings of 18th-century origins, and it is still the centre of Stoke Newington. The area's great mix of classes and cultures is reflected in its shops and eateries, lately joined by a rash of health-food shops, delis, exclusive second-hand book dealers and (even more tellingly) a welter of estate agents. On the Dalston borders to the S, **Ridley Rd** market sells all manner of goods at knock-down prices – and has a 24hr bagel shop.

Lordship Park

The most northerly of Stoke Newington's four neighbourhoods is Lordship Park – not a park but a road, though both Clissold Park and Abney Park Cemetery are in this leafy corner that runs N from **Stoke Newington Church St** to the reservoirs. **Lordship Park/Manor Rd**, the main thoroughfare, is an E-W bus and general traffic route. At the W end are monumental 4-storey houses, set back from the road, making them quieter than might be assumed. These give way to smaller 2-storey bay-fronted houses towards the E. Most are now flats.

North of **Lordship Park** is **Allerton Rd**, one end of which is overshadowed by a bizarre Gothic water tower – now home to Britain's premier Indoor Climbing Centre. New flats next to it are graced with the name 'Castle View' (2-bed with garden, £119,000). Homes on the N side of **Allerton Rd** have gardens backing onto the reservoir, a haven for wildlife. Happily, after a decade of rows over their future, a splendid new watersports centre is emerging on the West Reservoir (temporary facilities are already open), and the East Reservoir will be a wildlife reserve. On the W side of **Green Lanes** the former filter beds have been built on: a mix of housing association and open-market housing.

Allerton Rd leads into **Queen Elizabeth's Walk**: here you can pay £400,000 for a 4-bed house at the S end, where the houses overlook Clissold Park. The back gardens of these are in turn overlooked by council-built low-rise. Look out for the beautiful double-fronted terraces in the Walk – rare beauties. Tree-lined **Fairholt Rd** and shop-studded **Dunsmure Rd** complete Stoke Newington's northern reaches. Both roads contain generous bay-fronted family houses, some flats, some council. Look here and round about for large houses at (comparatively) lower prices. In St Andrew's Mews, off **Dunsmure Rd**, Beverley Homes is creating 1-, 2- and 3-bed apartments, due this spring.

Running S, houses tend to be less tidied, and the occasional unrenovated one is to be found. **Bethune Rd, Heathland Rd, St Andrews Grove** and busy **Lordship Rd** are all edged by large, often renovated and split up, Victorian bay-fronted houses. The E-W streets – **Paget Rd, St Kilda's Rd** and **Grangecourt Rd** – are smaller with mainly 2-storey terraces; some very pretty, notably the S side of **Grangecourt Rd** and **St Kilda's Rd** between **Bethune Rd** and **Heathland Rd**. The area has a strong Hasidic Jewish community, and homes often do not appear on the open market.

South of **Manor Rd** the streets are noticeably smarter. Most of the renovation work here has already been done, though the odd patch of run-down Victorian terrace still peeks out from between the glistening paintwork and new planting. Here **Bouverie Rd** matches **Queen Elizabeth's Walk** in desirability. Homes with even numbers back onto the cemetery and there is light industrial at the S end. Odd-numbered houses are either large, 4-storey and flat-fronted or charming 2-storey terraces. Low odd numbers have small gardens. This street, though, is used as a traffic short-cut; more peaceful are the pleasant homes in **Yoakley Rd, Grayling Rd** and **Grazebrook Rd. Yoakley Rd** has a charming Victorian terrace in the E side, broken now and then by small eccentric detached villas. Again houses here rarely come on the market – and are snapped up if they do. Much of the W side is boring council low-rise. Running E-W, **Grayling Rd** has lovely 2-storey bay-fronted houses and **Grazebrook Rd** has 3-storey terrace on the W side overlooking the edge of a largish, modern council estate. **Fleetwood St** runs N off **Church St**, a short, one-sided, Victorian terrace running up to the cemetery and local fire station. Houses in **Fleetwood St** are c. £185–220,000 for 3 bedrooms. Running parallel, **Summerhouse Rd** also has some beautiful Victorian homes.

Stoke Newington East and Borders

This neighbourhood is E of **Stoke Newington Rd, High St** and **Stamford Hill** and bordered to the N and E by the busy **Clapton Rd**. The SE border follows **Brooke Rd**, then S again down **Rectory Rd** and **Shacklewell Lane**. The S edge is marked by E-W running **Sandringham Rd**. The further N the larger the houses, interspersed by the large Stamford Hill and Broad Common estates. This big area is split by main E-W through roads: **Cazenove Rd, Northwold Rd, Evering Rd** and **Manse Rd**. Buses tend to stick to these main thoroughfares, so accessibility from some roads is poor.

At the northernmost, Stamford Hill, end, **Leweston Place** has Victorian terraces on one side of the road and '30s semis on the even side. **Darenth Rd** has large Victorian bay-fronted houses, some with basements. At its S end **Lynemouth Rd** and **Lampard Grove**, blighted by an unlovely MFI store. Moving eastwards, **Alkham Rd, Kyverdale Rd, Osbaldeston Rd, Forburg Rd** and charming **Chardmore Rd** have similar Victorian houses (also a stylish conversion of a church to flats in **Alkham Rd**). These are quiet, tree-lined streets – skip-lined, too: the houses, now much in demand, have been systematically converted and renovated. Their size (large basements) makes them popular with young families. (Stoke Newington is something of a baby boom area.)

South of **Cazenove Rd** many houses have been converted into flats and, although streets seem narrow for the size of buildings, large gardens compensate in some. E of **Fountaine Rd**, the streets become smaller again, with 2-storey and basement

Victorian terraces, bordering the Northwold council estate. **Northwold Rd** has the local shops, and southwards **Alconbury Rd, Geldeston Rd, Narford Rd** and **Reighton Rd** have mostly well-maintained medium-sized Victorian houses. From the street these houses look smaller than those further N, but they often go back a long way and contain a generous number of rooms. In the better parts of **Reighton Rd** a 5-bed unrenovated house might sell for £135,000; a renovated one was £190,000 last winter.

Moving W, **Norcott Rd, Maury Rd, Benthal Rd** and **Jenner Rd** are now well-maintained and quiet due to an eccentric traffic system. These houses enjoy more generous gardens than you might expect, and the potential of an 'end of terrace' property is exploited by the conservatories built over the porches of two at the junctions of **Norcott** and **Brooke Rds**. Odd-numbered houses in **Jenner Rd** back onto the railway (Rectory Rd station is close by), but generally these are desirable streets.

Between the **High St** and **Rectory Rd**, N of **Brooke Rd**, is the Brooke Rd Estate. The estate improves towards the E but homes at the W end are hardest to sell. It is bordered on its E side by a beautiful 4-storey flat-fronted terrace overlooking the remains of Stoke Newington Common. Running S **Darville Rd, Bayston Rd** (the better pair), **Leswin Rd** and (E-W) **Tyssen Rd** have smaller 2-storey houses, some with basements. **Tyssen Rd** is remarkably peaceful despite the proximity of the **High St**. A corner to watch. Most houses have been renovated.

South of **Evering Rd**, curving **Amhurst Rd** returns the would-be purchaser to larger houses, 3-storey with semi-basements, some still to be modernized. **Foulden St** and **Sydner Rd** are narrower and have smaller houses, some flat-fronted, some bay, and again closer to the **High St** commercial buildings impinge. The S side of **Farleigh Rd** (which has some large houses) backs onto the Somerford Estate, and the E end is overlooked by The Beckers, a bleak '60s eyesore estate. This is the least expensive part of Stoke Newington. Further S, the Somerford Estate is bordered by large areas of light industry. What housing there is is sandwiched between ugly factories and a '30s council block making this whole section less appealing than anywhere further N.

Stoke Newington's N-S spine, **Stoke Newington Rd** which becomes first the **High St** and then **Stamford Hill**, is itself a source of homes above its lining of shops. The flats are mostly tenanted, though some do come up for sale now and then. The road, it has to be said, is busy all day and most of the night. However, you can't find a location more convenient, and given that some of the buildings are quite large, flats can often be light and spacious. On the site of the old bus depot, opposite MFI on **Stamford Hill**, a planning application is in for a mixed retail and housing scheme.

Stoke Newington Central

Stoke Newington central – the old village of Shacklewell – lies S of **Church St**, W of the **High St**, and has as its southern border a stretch of **Green Lanes, Matthias Rd** and **Barrett's Grove**. It is this central area, with its mix of 2-storey terraces interspersed with streets of bigger buildings, which saw the first ungentlemanly leaps in price in the late 1980s, although the large houses to the NE of this area have been making the big jumps this time around.

The area is split in two by **Albion Rd**, a bus route and general N-S thoroughfare. Here 3-storey terraces give way to large renovated Victorian blocks. Further S, **Albion Rd** narrows and is lined by 3-storey, bay-fronted Victorian houses. These have been converted to 1- to 3-bed flats by a housing association and only very occasionally come up for sale. To the W of **Albion Rd**, running up to Clissold Park, lies that section which hopeful estate agents some years back began to dub the 'North Islington Overspill Quadrant', no less. Despite the hyperbole this patch is well worth a look. **Winston Rd** has small 2-storey houses, and off **Winston Rd** look out for **Reedholm Villas** – a wee gem of a cul-de-sac. **Springdale Rd** and **Aden Grove** have bigger homes;

Burma Rd's are 3- and 4-storey ones. **Clissold Crescent** and **Carysfort Rd** also have larger houses, many sporting original features such as decorative porch tiles or glasswork. Most gardens are tiny though.

Clissold Crescent also boasts two exciting new developments. On the E side of the road, replacing the old swimming baths, Clissold Leisure Centre is due for completion by 2000. The £13 million hi-tech building will feature swimming and diving pools, squash courts, sports hall, health suite. Opposite there are plans for a new public theatre to be built in the grounds of Stoke Newington School.

At the southern end of the crescent is a new development of housing association and private flats, part of which overlooks a car breaker's yard. In **Carysfort Rd** is a factory conversion with live/work units selling at £100–180,000.

To the E of **Albion Rd**, N of **Barbauld Rd** and **Dynevor Rd** is a maze of charming little streets, lined mainly with 2- and 3-bedroomed houses. Though occasionally turned into tiny flats, for the most part these streets remain relatively unspoilt. Some houses are bigger, having a semi-basement floor as in the N side of **Dumont Rd**; light industry behind. S of **Barbauld Rd** and the kink in **Nevill Rd** the area changes. The well-designed low-rise estate on the E side of **Nevill Rd** faces shops with flats above. From here the horizontal ladder of roads – **Beatty Rd** down to **Barrett's Grove** – hold some larger 3- and 4-storey houses. **Beatty Rd**, **Walford Rd** and **Brighton Rd** have houses with large gardens on their N sides. These streets hold many flat conversions, but watch for subsidence problems in some houses.

The further S you go, the untidier the streets become. **Palatine Rd** has smaller 2-storey houses, but the western end of the street finishes with a strange ziggurat configuration of buildings, recently renovated. **Prince George Rd** enjoys an open space halfway down, with tennis courts. **Belgrade** and **Princess May Rds** and **Barrett's Grove** are a mix of 2- and 3-storey houses, all with gardens.

North of **Allen Rd**, **Milton Grove** and **Shakspeare Walk** are 4-storey terraces, now frequently flats – narrowish streets considering the heights of the buildings but some houses have superb-sized gardens at back. **Shakspeare Walk's** (yes that *is* how it's spelt) mix of houses and flats are particularly popular. **Londesborough Rd**, **Osterley Rd** and **Clonbrook Rd** have 3-storey houses and many council flats.

South of **Allen Rd** the area gives way to a bleak '50s estate, which the council improved a great deal with bright paint, trees and turf. The streets surrounding this area hold friendly local shops with a wide and interesting range of goods.

Stoke Newington South

This area lies S of **Green Lanes**, **Matthias Rd** and **Barrett's Grove**, and N of the **Balls Pond Rd**. To the W it is bordered by **Wallace Rd** and **Petherton Rd**, and to the E by **Kingsland High St** and the S end of **Stoke Newington Rd**. At the end of **Green Lanes** lies **Newington Green**, its 'green' now a small public garden enclosed by railings and, in effect, a roundabout. Its earlier days are recalled by a small group of Georgian houses and four which, amazingly, have survived from the 1650s. At this end of **Green Lanes** the charitable Peabody Trust is building a housing complex. Completing this July, it will contain 24 shared-ownership flats and 10 private, a medical centre and restaurant. At the N end of **Petherton Rd** is a gated development of 2- and 3-bed mews houses. The 3-bed homes cost around £200–225,000.

Starting in the NW corner of the neighbourhood, **Leconfield Rd** snakes southwards and is edged with 2-storey bay-fronted Victorian houses, with semi-basements. The light industry at the N end is the downside, while large gardens are the upside. **Poet's Rd**, similar in size to the **Leconfield Rd** end, is the first in a ladder of streets: **Ferntower Rd**, **Pyrland Rd**, **Beresford Rd** and the E end of **Grosvenor Avenue**. All have large 3- and 4-storey buildings, with good-sized gardens, but the S side of **Grosvenor**

Avenue backs on to the railway, as does N side of **Northampton Grove**, where pretty 2-storey cottages are uncomfortably hemmed in by light industry. A corner to watch for conversions, however. **Northampton Park** curves S to join the **Balls Pond Rd** and is a wide tree-lined street of handsome Victorian villas interspersed with one agreeable low-rise development, and one laughable modern attempt at Victorian proportions.

Crowning this area is wide **St Paul's Place**, where the 4-storey, flat-fronted unspoilt terrace has gracious curved windows, and stucco-finished first storey painted uniformly grey. This street has an air of calm superiority unlike anything nearby. Discreet **Bingham St** is lined with lovely double-fronted but modest-sized houses. It joins **Newington Green Rd**, an extension of **Albion Rd**, which runs N-S and takes buses and through traffic. Lined with shops, pubs and restaurants, it is the place for live music and holds most of the immediate area's amenities. Some flats are available above shops, and well-maintained council-built terraces lead into a medium-sized high-rise estate, entered by **Mildmay St** and **Mildmay Avenue**. This introduces the 'Mildmay' area, where prices are high – sometimes deservedly, sometimes not. Running E-W through the middle of this corner is **Mildmay Grove**, eccentrically not one but two streets, separated along their length by the railway line. Watch out for plans for this line. The houses stand behind front gardens, and gaze at each other across the walls which separate the grand terraces from the trains. Large gardens at the rear help to hold prices. Busy **Mildmay Park** runs N-S. It is scruffy at the S end, bordered by 4-storey flat-fronted buildings, mostly flats, and some light industry.

Mildmay Rd runs E-W. There are some charming 3- and 4-storey buildings, a featureless '60s block, and homes at the eastern end overlook another bleak council high-rise. In between, wide **Wolsey Rd** and **Queen Margaret's Grove** are well worth a look, but there is a lot of council-build in the latter. **King Henry's Walk** zigzags N-S and is a hotchpotch of mostly well-kept council-built housing to the N, and Victorian buildings with shops sandwiched between less arresting structures.

Continuing the Tudor theme, **Boleyn Rd** runs N-S with a grim wasteland and run-down buildings at the N end. There have been proposals for it and **Crossway** to become a bypass for **Kingsland High St**. **Pellerin Rd** runs E and has pretty 2-storey Victorian houses on one side. The southern end of **Boleyn Rd** and the streets running off it are desolate; a place where houses once stood and others, boarded up, now stand, patiently waiting for the renovation which has taken place further north. **Bradbury St** is seeing the start of renovations in this area.

Transport	Trains: Stoke Newington, Rectory Rd to Liverpool St. See also map.
Convenient for	City. Buses to tube at Highbury & Islington (Victoria line direct to West End). Miles from centre: 4.5.
Schools	Local Authority: Our Lady's Convent RC, Skinners Senior (g), Kingsland, Stoke Newington, Clapton (g), Hackney 6th-form Centre.

S

SALES

Flats	S	1B	2B	3B	4B	5B
Average prices	40–55	50–95+	60–130	70–150	95–160+	—
Houses	2B	3B	4B	5B	6/7B	8B
Average prices	150–180	170–220	185–300+	220–320+	—	—

RENTAL

Flats	S	1B	2B	3B	4B	5B
Average prices	350–520	475–600	610–780+	650–1200	–	–
Houses	2B	3B	4B	5B	6/7B	8B
Average prices	650–1080+	820–1300	950–1500+	1200–1700	–	–

The properties Mid- to late-Victorian terraces, still gentrifying and converting, plus a few Georgian ones around Newington Green. Better houses and gardens generally to E of High St. Some p/b flats in Victorian and '30s blocks, plus council-built houses and flats. The occasional new gated development, conversion of old schools or churches, live/work scheme . . .

The market Professionals/media people/Islington refugees move here. Council now insist on one family (ie 3-bed) unit per conversion. 1/2-bed flats thus in shorter supply; 3-bed houses most plentiful. The area S of Church St is the most popular — and highly priced. Local searches: 2 weeks.

Among those estate agents active in this area are:
- Philip Phillips
- Holden Matthews
- Michael Naik & Co
- Brooks & Co
- Next Move
- Patrick Joseph
- Oakwood
- Winkworth*
- Foxtons*

further details: see advertisers' index on p633

S

STREATHAM

Map ref: p109 (5J)
Postal districts: SW16
Boroughs: Lambeth (Lab),
  Wandsworth (Con)
Council tax: Band D
  Lambeth £647,
  Wandsworth £334
Conservation areas:
  Streatham Village,
  Ullathorne/
  Abbotsleigh Rds
Parking: Free

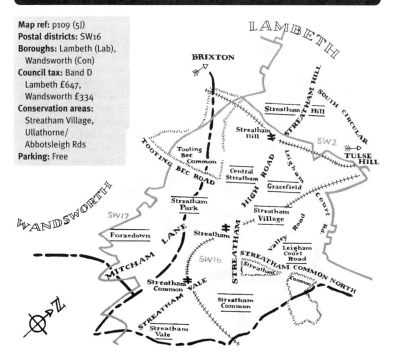

A kind of property pincer movement is closing in on Streatham. The area has long been known for cheaper prices than its neighbours Wandsworth and Clapham. Two groups are taking advantage of this, at either end of the price scale. First-time buyers find Streatham affordable on an average income, and the well-heeled can buy a big family home on the proceeds of a cramped Clapham terrace. In general, here you get more for your money: flat conversions are spacious, and there is a good selection of family houses (some very large) with gardens.

Streatham goes back a long way: the former village first became popular as a spa in the late 17th century, and growth was assured by its location on the main road to Croydon and Brighton. City merchants built magnificent estates here in the early 19th century, especially on the N side of Streatham Common. Streatham Hill station was opened in 1856 and in the 1870s–80s farmland was sold to property developers eager to capitalize on the success of the railways; as a result many estates were broken up. However, modern Streatham is divided into several neighbourhoods based to a large extent on these same estates.

The tantalizing prospect of a tube station has been raised and quashed many times. The current favourite is a southward extension of the East London line via New Cross and East Dulwich, which would give access to Docklands. This is on a 10-year timescale. Meanwhile, Streatham relies on three rail stations (Streatham, Streatham Hill, Streatham Common) and some good, reliable buses. **Streatham High Rd** is rated London's second busiest bus route: these flow faster now the Red Route is in place.

Streatham is blighted by the relentlessly busy A23, one of the main routes out of London, which does uneasy double duty as the area's main street. Several plans for relief roads have come to nothing. Lambeth Council is turning its attention to traffic calming in residential roads.

Lambeth has hired a town centre manager to boost the **High Rd's** economy, and CCTV cameras are being installed. The council is also tackling illegal dumping, tidying up the **High Rd's** central reservation with trees and new railings and improving safety for pedestrians. Streatham needs such measures: it suffered hard times in the '90s. In the '70s and most of the '80s Streatham was seen as the respectable suburban odd-man-out in Lambeth's raffish, right-on, inner-city borough. But the combination of the poll tax (particularly punitive in Lambeth) and the recession of the early '90s finally burst Streatham's bubble. The worst blow was the closure of the much-loved Pratt's department store – a branch of the John Lewis Partnership – ironically because Lambeth refused planning permission for an underground car park and rear extension in the summer of 1990. Where Pratt's led many others sadly followed, with little to replace them. Although there still remains a core to Streatham's commerce, it is much reduced and badly bruised. The emphasis is on quick-turnover leisure – a bowling alley, a skating rink, a swimming pool, two cinemas, a bingo hall and a night club. At least the last two years have seen a rash of new pubs, cafés, wine bars and restaurants – and there are shadowy plans for a big new entertainment complex. A Sainsbury's close to Streatham Common has added to local amenities.

Homes are a mix of Victorian/Edwardian and 1930s, the big old villas mostly having been demolished. A fair number of large period properties have been converted into flats over the years, and this, coupled with the relatively low prices, makes Streatham an affordable area for first- and second-time buyers. The roads between **Streatham High Rd** and the eastern edge of Tooting Bec Common contain some magnificently ostentatious houses. However, kerb-crawling is a problem here, and many roads have myriad bumps, humps and obstacles to deter a very particular kind of passing traffic.

Furzedown

Furzedown covers the area N of the Tooting–Streatham railway, W of **Mitcham Lane** and **Thrale Rd** and E of **Rectory Lane**. Two-thirds is considered part of Streatham – roughly the roads N of **Southcroft Rd** and E of **Freshwater Rd**. The rest is counted as Tooting. The whole neighbourhood is in Wandsworth Borough, not Lambeth. Furzedown is a popular family area with comfortably sized 2-, 3- and 4-bed houses. It consists mainly of Edwardian terraces, the best examples being in **Clairview Rd**, off **Thrale Rd**, with well-maintained large 6-bed properties. The rest of Furzedown has pockets of comfortable Victorian and '30s terraced houses. Catching the 'overspill' from Tooting – which has a tube – prices are relatively high: popular **Ribblesdale Rd** and **Nimrod Rd** have 3- and 4-bed houses around £190,000; 2-bed houses nearby are £130,000. Things are cheaper to the E of **Mitcham Lane** as the transport is less good. A 2-bed house on this side might be £125,000. **Rural Way**, off **Streatham Rd**, has a modern development of smart 3/4-bed houses.

Streatham Park

Streatham Park is bordered by **Tooting Bec Rd, Mitcham Lane, Thrale Rd** and the railway line to the E. This was once the 18th-century Thrale family's estate. Visits by their close friend Dr Samuel Johnson are documented in the road names: **Thrale Rd** and **Dr Johnson Avenue** (across Tooting Bec Common). The Thrale house was demolished in 1863 and the area now holds smart, well-maintained council blocks – notably the GLC-built Fayland Estate – mostly now privately owned. There are still some stately period villas from Streatham's 18th-century heyday overlooking Tooting Bec Common: pricey, if a little noisy with the main road opposite, interspersed with modern infill (flats and houses). South of the council blocks, properties are small Edwardian, grand Victorian (with some conversions) and quaint '30s whimsy. The whole area is leafy, quiet and very attractive. Streatham Park also enjoys Wandsworth Borough's favourable council tax.

The small neighbourhood to the E of Streatham Park contains real nuggets of local history. Possibly the oldest part of Streatham, it is perhaps better known because of famous resident Cynthia Payne. **Pinkerton Place**, off **Tooting Bec Gardens**, has comfortable early '80s purpose-built flats; small rooms, but well-designed. Surrounding properties are mainly stately Victorian; road names relating to the Lake District (**Thirlmere Rd**, **Rydal Rd**, etc) have large 6/7-bed period houses. Tree-lined **Riggindale Rd** has some beautiful conversions of semi-detached Victoriana. In **Thrale Rd** 1-bed flats can be found at about £60,000, while £100,000 buys a modern 2-bed flat. The parish church, St Leonards, is on the corner of **Tooting Bec Gardens**, overlooking an awesome traffic blackspot where all the main roads converge.

Central Streatham

Central Streatham comprises roads running E from **Garrad's Rd** to **Streatham High Rd**. It contains some truly splendid houses. Well-placed for shops in the **High Rd** and the rail stations of Streatham and Streatham Hill, its leafy roads are usually popular. Properties are mainly attractive '20s and '30s detached and semi-detached houses in a variety of styles – stucco and bay windows/tile-hung gables/mock-Tudor. Try Homes have just built a group of houses and flats in **Garrad's Rd**. There are large, impressive turn-of-the-century 6-bed houses in **Steep Hill**, **Becmead Avenue**, **Prentis Rd** and **Woodbourne Avenue**. Few houses in this area have been converted and there are only a couple of modern infills – very smart, but rather out of place. In **Woodbourne Avenue** a 5-bed mock-Tudor house (complete with pool) was on the market in December for £340,000; in **Kingscourt Rd** a Victorian 4-bed house was £215,000. Emsworth Court in **Ockley Rd** is flats with squash club adjoining; and **Tarrington Close** has '70s houses. One noticeable feature of 'Central' is the epidemic of doctors' and dentists' name-plates on the walls; a good plus is that most houses have off-street parking – which is needed, due to the nearby **High Rd**. The roads to the N, running up to Streatham Hill station, contain period properties in varying states of repair. A number of these large houses have been converted – particularly on the eastern side of the area near the **High Rd**. There are some spacious '30s houses in **Broadlands Avenue**.

Streatham Hill

Streatham Hill lies N of the station and **Leigham Court Rd**, E of **Rastell Avenue** and **New Park Rd**, S of **Christchurch Rd** and W of **Hillside Rd**/**Leigham Vale**. This increasingly popular area is in the SW2 postcode, which no longer has a stigma now Brixton is so fashionable. It's well-placed for transport: Brixton's Victoria line tube is a bus-ride away and Streatham Hill station is on the corner of **Sternhold Avenue**. The side W of Streatham Hill is mainly attractive period property, with purpose-built flats and some flat conversions, maisonettes and houses. **Killieser Avenue**, **Criffel Avenue** and **Kirkstall Rd** are particularly popular, with charming terraces and some larger houses. **Criffel Avenue** also has some particularly nice maisonettes. There are also '30s houses in good repair in the area. The Telford Park estate is well-regarded: a 4-bed Edwardian semi was on the market for £280,000 in December. **Telford Avenue**, **Killieser Avenue** and **Montrell Rd** hold some good conversions: a 1980s development in **Telford Avenue** has yielded six 1/2-bedroom flats, some with gardens.

The corner between the South Circular and Streatham Hill holds many conversions; Lambeth's planners eventually stepped in to curb these in streets such as **Tierney** and **Montrell Rds**, although these hold some splendid examples already. **Palace Rd**, which is closed off at its junction with the **South Circular**, has a few surviving large 19th-century houses – a 6-bed one was £440,000 in December – and an ex-GLC estate with an attractive grassy setting. **Leigham Vale** has some big (5-bed) Victorian terraces.

Nearer the station are the popular 'ABCD' streets (**Amesbury, Barcombe, Cricklade** and **Downton Avenues**) which feature late-Victorian red-brick terraced cottages and maisonettes, built by the philanthropic Artisans & General Dwellings Company in 1889–94 on the site of the old Leigham Court estate: these were the forerunners of local authority housing. There are a few conversions (flats to houses ratio is about 1:4), and attractive later terraces also in **Cricklade** and **Downton**. Look for the original stained glass in **Cricklade**, the largest gardens in popular **Downton**. (In all four, gardens get smaller towards the **High Rd**.) Beneath the 'ABCDs' are largely '20s and stately red-brick, eg the leafy **Mount Nod Rd**, but also note **Hitherfield** – its Victorian cottage terraces lining a steep hill are reminiscent of a Hovis advertisement.

The mansion flats along **Streatham Hill**, like those along **Streatham High Rd**, vary as to popularity: some are good first-time buys, some have high service charges. The Uttings estate, also known as Culverhouse, lies just beneath the Hill E of the **High Rd** and W of the railway line: a quietly respectable area, popular with local residents. It has a mix of late-Victorian and smart chalet-style '20s/'30s houses. **Pendennis** and **Pinfold Rds** have '30s semis; the former has 60-ft gardens, the latter large 5/6-bed houses. Demand exceeds supply, especially for the attractive 1930s houses.

Streatham Village

Streatham Village – a name to make the hearts of local historians beat faster – isn't as old as it sounds. The original nucleii of Streatham, around St Leonards Church and Streatham Common, date back to medieval times, whereas the 'Village' was only started in the 19th century. Houses are now very mixed in style, but rather appealing, especially the charming 2/3-bed Victorian cottages in **Sunnyhill** and **Wellfield Rds**. The bigger ones go for around £150,000, though there are some tiny cottages at £90,000-plus. There are also larger Victorian villas in red brick, and some skillful conversions are to be found. Older cottages, '30s houses and more modern 2/3-bed units will be found in **Sunnyhill Rd**. **Angles Rd** houses Peregrine Court – a courtyard development of 25 flats and houses. There is heavy demand for the cottage properties in the village, but residents are understandably reluctant to move. Well-located for transport between Streatham and Streatham Hill stations, and near to the main shopping street, it is a designated conservation area. The streets lying to the S, between **Gleneldon Rd, Valley Rd, Streatham Common North** and the **High Rd**, contain a real mix of properties from Victorian through to early 20th century and council housing, including 30 new 1/2-bed flats and houses in increasingly desirable **Valley Rd**, where a 3-bed flat might command £100,000. The 1980s purpose-built block on the corner of **Valley** and **Leigham Court Rds** is popular. Impressive red-brick homes are found in **Gleneldon Rd**. The nearby **High Rd** has flats, both above shops and in purpose-built 20th-century blocks.

Leigham Court, on its steep hill, lies between **Leigham Court Rd, Valley Rd** and **Streatham Common North Side**. Basically council-built (though now mostly privately owned) to the N, and largeish smart '30s 4-bed semis and smaller, older houses to the S. New developments keep springing up here. **Leigham Court Rd** itself was once lined with large detached Victorian mansions, standing in their own grounds – most have been turned into sought-after flats and commercial uses, though one intact house was on the market for £225,000 last autumn. The council has ambitious plans for the already pleasant Leigham Court Estate. It is now a conservation area. The **Hopton Rd/Polworth Rd** corner to the W is close to the **High Rd**, the Common and the station: a 5-bed Victorian house here was £240,000 in December.

Streatham Common

One of the original nucleii of the town was centred here, the site of the first spring that became a spa. This area, very popular with the professional classes, is filled with handsome Victorian and Edwardian houses with large gardens on the E side of the **High Rd** – pricey, highly desirable being near to the Common, with quiet leafy roads – and cheaper, if smaller and less well-maintained, houses to the W of the **High Rd**. N of the Common, **Ryecroft Rd** loops round, with detached 3-bed houses boasting large gardens. **Crown Lane** had a 4-bed town-house listed at £180,000 in December. **Ferrers** and **Natal Rds** have smaller cottages, some of which have been converted into flats and are relatively cheap. Popular roads are **Heybridge Avenue**, **Fontaine Rd**, **Copley Park** and **Braxted Park** (E of the **High Rd**). **Green Lane,** on the very southern edge of the neighbourhood, has 4-bed detached homes: one was £230,000 last winter. Traffic has increased in the area with the opening in 1997 of a large Sainsbury's/Homebase on **Streatham High Rd**, opposite the S side of the common. To the W of the area, **Lewin** and **Barrow Rds** have many popular conversions. There are more flats in **Gleneagle Rd** – just to the N of the tracks, and cheaper. **Conyer's Rd** houses a 1980s 22-home development of 1/2-bed flats and 1/3-bed houses, and another clutch of seven new 4-bed town-houses is due to be ready this May. Towards W Norwood, in SE27, Canterbury Mews is a handsome new addition to **Canterbury Grove**.

Streatham Vale

The cheapest area in Streatham, offering good value for money. Its borders run along the railway lines to the N and W, and along **Greyhound Terrace** and **Hassocks Rd**. Most of the area was built by Wates in the '20s and '30s and consists of row upon row of 2-storey terraced and semi-detached houses. It is a hunting-ground for first-time buyers and is near Streatham Common station. In a road like **Sherwood Avenue** a 3-bed house with a small garden might be £110,000. There are also a few conversions dotted around. It's an area of very intensive housing with roads packed tightly together– more like Tooting than Streatham.

Transport	Trains: Streatham Common, Streatham (London Bridge 21 min, Blackfriars 23 min); Streatham Hill (Victoria 15 min).	
Convenient for	Routes to Gatwick Airport and South Coast. Miles from centre: 5.	
Schools	Local Authority: Dunraven School (mixed, grant-maintained), Bishop Thomas Grant (mixed, RC). Private: Streatham Hill & Clapham High.	

S

SALES

Flats	S	1B	2B	3B	4B	5B
Average prices	35–40	55–70	70–95	85–100+	120+	—
Houses	2B	3B	4B	5B	6/7B	8B
Average prices	90+	95–170+	160–250+	200–500	220–500	300+

RENTAL

Flats	S	1B	2B	3B	4B	5B
Average prices	380–450	500–650	550–800	750–1000	—	—
Houses	2B	3B	4B	5B	6/7B	8B
Average prices	700–850	750–1000	1000–2000	1300–2000	1800	—

The properties   Some new developments now joining terraced Victorian/
Edwardian homes and '20s/'30s semis, plus large blocks of
1900–1940 mansion flats. Some larger houses; Victorian and
inter-war. Those overlooking the leafy common particularly
pleasant. Selling of homes by Lambeth Council has boosted
supply of converted flats.

The market   Lack of tube (though trains, buses plentiful) lowers prices
compared to neighbouring Clapham, Balham: a boon to first-time
buyers. Old-established families plus newcomers seeking larger
homes with gardens and good-value flats. Prices continued to
rise gently last year: trend is now to buy in what has been a
popular place for renting. Local searches: Lambeth 2 weeks,
Wandsworth 1 week.

Among those estate agents active in this area are:
- Halifax Property
- Winkworth*
- Townends
- Woolwich Property
- Hooper & Jackson

further details: see advertisers' index on p633

S

TOTTENHAM AND FINSBURY PARK

Map ref: p31 (4F)
Postal districts: N22, N18, N17, N15, N4
Boroughs: Haringey (Lab), Islington (Lab/Lib Dem), Hackney (Hung Council)
Council tax: Band D Haringey £856, Islington £912, Hackney £789
Conservation areas: Check with town hall
Parking: Free

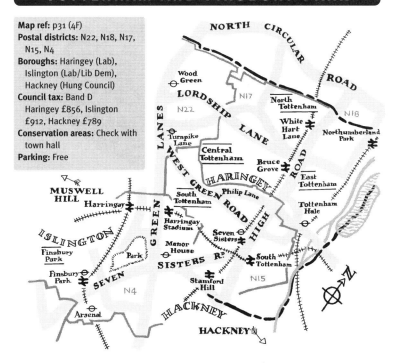

Tottenham is a good hunting-ground for first-time buyers. The area is still struggling to overcome a rather grimy past, but it has better transport links than other parts of North East London and is starting to establish itself as an affordable, identifiable place to live.

Tottenham is bounded to the N by the A406 (**North Circular Rd**), to the S by the **Seven Sisters Rd** and the Haringey/Hackney border, to the E by the Lea Valley reservoir complex and to the W by the Great Eastern Railway and the northern part of **Green Lanes** (**High Rd**).

Until the last quarter of the 19th century, Tottenham was a small village, boasting several fine houses. Today only one or two of these remain, saved by conversion into public buildings – such as Bruce Castle, which now houses the local history museum. With the advent of the railways, and especially cheap workmens' fares, street after street of small terraced houses were built. The population trebled to over 46,000 in the 20 years before 1861. Not all the terraces survived the Blitz and the council bulldozers – though in some cases the brave new tower blocks that replaced them are themselves being demolished. Expansion continued during the inter-war period, particularly in the Dowsett estate region on the E side.

A programme of council housing in the '60s resulted in further expansion in the northern area of Tottenham, including the controversial Broadwater Farm Estate – still an area to be avoided. There are some light industrial works and warehouse depots bordering Hackney Marshes, although some of these have tended to fall into disrepair. New homes are replacing industry in several places. Today the area is predominantly residential, composed mainly of 2- and 3-bed terraced houses built

1890–1920 and flat conversions. Even modernized, many of these houses have downstairs bathrooms (due to their layout), but estate agents in the area agree that around 30 per cent retain original features, such as fireplaces and cornicing and sash windows – and that these are the easiest to sell. Of course, original features are much rarer in conversions, though standards have improved greatly since the council brought in stricter controls. Most houses are small and rather ordinary: compared to areas like Crouch End, Tottenham lacks distinctive, family-sized homes.

Tottenham has excellent transport facilities, with quick access by rail and tube to the West End and the City, and by road to the North Circular, M25, M1 and M11. Such links are a major advantage of living in Tottenham. Buses are frequent, and particularly good for local travel. Transport, especially proximity to tubes, is what decides house prices here. The area is truly cosmopolitan, with a corresponding diversity in the shops and cultural activities available to residents. Shopping is good around Wood Green and Finsbury Park, but there is still a dearth of restaurants and bars in the area. You have to travel to Stoke Newington, Turnpike Lane or Finsbury Park for a good meal. However, for seekers of homes with manageable mortgages and quick access to work, it remains one of the cheapest parts of North London.

South Tottenham (N15)

The area lies S of **West Green Rd** and **Philip Lane**, N of **Seven Sisters Rd** and **Amhurst Park**, W of the **High Rd** and E of **Green Lanes**. Homes with an N15 postcode tend to be more expensive than equivalent properties in N17, because of their proximity to Stamford Hill, Stoke Newington and Turnpike Lane; the short distance from Seven Sisters tube also helps. Most homes in this neighbourhood are 2- and 3-bedroomed terraced houses, built during the later 19th and early 20th centuries. Many of the larger houses have been, or are being, converted into flats.

There are good shopping facilities on **West Green Rd**, **Philip Lane** and **Seven Sisters Rd**, including Sainsbury's on **Green Lanes**, Tesco at Seven Sisters and Safeway at Stamford Hill. There are abundant local grocers, butchers and ethnic food shops.

The W side of the **High Rd** from Seven Sisters tube to **Philip Lane** – an area that includes several small garment factories – includes (working up from the S) a row of 3-storey terraced houses, built in the 1880s, which have either been converted into flats or much modernized. On **Pelham Rd** and **Portland Rd** is an attractive, modern Barratt development, with small terraces of 2-bed properties and good parking space here for residents.

Continuing northwards, the Jewish Home and Hospital, now closed, is being converted into 80 flats to rent by the Circle 33 Housing Trust; next come the Tottenham College of Technology, the town hall (opposite **Tottenham Green**) and, off **Town Hall Rd**, the Tottenham Green Leisure Centre, with library, squash courts and swimming pool.

The triangular area bounded by **Philip Lane**, **West Green Rd** and the railway comprises a series of roughly parallel streets of 2- and 3-bed terraced houses, dating from the 1900s, broken by the popular **Clyde Circus** and **Clyde Rd**. (There are, though, larger 5/7-bedroom homes on **Bedford Rd**, some of which have escaped conversion to flats.) Similar terraces exist S of **West Green Rd** in the rectangle formed with **Green Lanes**, **St Ann's Rd** and the **High Rd**, with **Seaford Rd**, **Roslyn Rd** and **Greenfield Rd** particularly good. Houses in this corner become increasingly expensive towards **Green Lanes** and **Turnpike Lane**, with **Cranleigh Rd** and **Conway Rd** typical examples of the higher price range of 2- and 3-bed properties. The region S of **St Ann's Rd** and **Seven Sisters Rd** is bisected by **Hermitage Rd** and includes the block of neat streets made up of **Kimberley Gardens**, **Chesterfield Gardens** and **Roseberry Gardens**, which link up to **Warwick Gardens**. These streets serve motorists as short cuts between busy **St Ann's Rd** and **Grand Parade**. St Ann's General Hospital lies behind **Warwick Gardens**, with the railway running to the S of it. The Harringay Green Lanes station has trains to Gospel Oak one way and Leyton and Barking the other – and no useful tube connections in between.

On the other side of the tracks, this district includes a major development area, with Harringay Stadium now replaced by a large Sainsbury's. Next door, McAlpine's new homes scheme has now been completed: 221 homes, ranging from 1-bed flats to 4-bed houses in streets such as **Wiltshire Gardens** and **Surrey Gardens**. Prices here are comparable with the surrounding Victorian terraces in **Vale Rd**, **Eade Rd** and **Finsbury Park Avenue**, though the latter are larger.

Central Tottenham (N17)

Lying N of **West Green Rd** and **Philip Lane**, S of **Lordship Lane**, W of the **High Rd** and E of **Westbury Avenue**, this region is served by Bruce Grove rail station. Here there are mainly 2- and 3-bedroomed terraces and the Broadwater Farm Estate, a late-'60s concrete block project.

Characteristic mid-range early 20th-century 2- and 3-bed terraces (some are now flats) cluster in the eastern part of the area – **Napier Rd**, **Steele Rd**, **Chester Rd** and **Morrison Rd**. In particular, **Mount Pleasant Rd** saw extensive development in the '80s, again with houses being converted into flats. Until recently a notorious rat-run, it is now controlled by width restrictions. The constant stream of traffic might now affect neighbouring **Downhills Park Rd** and **Dongola Rd**. Green spaces come in the form of Lordship and Belmont recreation grounds and Downhills Park – house prices rise around these open spaces. Look here for larger houses in leafy roads: **Keston Rd** is one such. This neighbourhood has a quiet, settled air, and is well thought of despite being remote from a tube. To the E, roads off **Philip Lane** are also popular. The Broadwater Farm council estate still casts a shadow over nearby streets (**Higham Rd**, **The Avenue**, northern end of **Mount Pleasant Rd**), though happily some of the worst blocks are being demolished.

North Tottenham (N17)

Tottenham's northern reaches stop at a point some half-mile below the **North Circular Rd**, where N17 becomes N18 and the borough boundary also runs. The area is bounded to the S by **Lordship Lane**, on the W by the A10, and on the E by the **High Rd**. There are some inter-war semis around **Lordship Lane**. Pleasant post-war council houses lie N of **Lordship Lane** and **The Roundway**. Interesting areas include the dense grid of little streets in the Tower Gardens conservation area, enclosed by **Lordship Lane** and **The Roundway** and bisected by **Risley Avenue**. Eastwards **Church Lane** has very pleasant mews-type houses near the popular Antwerp Arms, and borders Bruce Castle Park (with the Elizabethan Bruce Castle which houses the Museum of Local History). This corner has most of Tottenham's Georgian buildings. It also has a clutch of attractive late-19th-century cottages in the **Kings Rd/Church Rd** corner. Developers Rialto have built **Somerset Gardens** here, between **Creighton Rd** and **White Hart Lane**: this has added 356 studio, 1- and 2-bed flats to the area's housing stock. They sell at good-value prices: 1-bed flats £50–55,000.

Further N is Tottenham Cemetery, White Hart Lane rail station (and football stadium – see below) and the **Great Cambridge Rd**, with purpose-built council houses leading up to the **North Circular**. The North Circular has been widened, despite local opposition. Shopping has been improved by the Sainsbury's midway up the **High Rd**.

East Tottenham (N15 and N17)

This area lies between **High Rd** to the W and Hackney Marshes to the E, bounded on the N by the **North Circular** and to the S by **Clapton Common Rd**. **Ferry Lane**, running W-E beneath Tottenham Hale tube station, marks the dividing line between N17 and N15. Part of the industry zone to the E has been redeveloped as a shopping centre.

The northerly area is characterized by the Northumberland Park estate, a development area with generally cheaper house prices because of the proximity to White Hart Lane, Tottenham Hotspur's football stadium. **Park Lane**, in particular, fails to live up to its name. Mainly 2-bedroomed terraced houses here, and some conversions into flats. South of **Lansdowne Rd** is the popular Dowsett Rd estate, with **Sherringham Rd**, **Seymour Rd** and **Thackeray Avenue** popular as they are within striking distance of the tube/rail station at Tottenham Hale.

The area enclosed by the **High Rd** and the one-way system (**Chestnut Rd/Broad Lane**) has a strange combination of older, gentrified properties and rather shabby houses. **Tynemouth Rd** is still a good first-time buyers' street, with **Talbot Rd** a slightly more up-market version. South of this area the property tends to decline, but there is room for improvement in this region. The first stage of a retail development is complete, with a series of 'shed' stores – carpets, furniture etc.

Fairview built 250 homes on **Bream Close**, S of **Ferry Lane**, in 1995. This patch of land has most of the River Lea on two sides, justifying its name: Heron Wharf. There are light, airy river views.

South of **Broad Lane** and the railway, towards Stamford Hill, is the area known as 'Tottenham Village' by residents and local estate agents. Centring on **Wargrave Avenue** and **Grovelands Rd**, prices are higher here. **Wakefield Rd**, just N of the railway, is worth a look for its larger houses. Tottenham Hale station (Victoria line tube, and trains) provides a useful alternative to Seven Sisters tube. The Stanstead Express airport service stops here.

Border Areas

To the S (in Stamford Hill) and to the W (in Harringay and Wood Green) are good home hunting-grounds, although these are also more costly. Three-bedroomed terraced houses, for example, in the section known as the Harringay Ladders (the series of parallel streets stretching from **Umfreville Rd** up to **Turnpike Lane** on the W side of **Green Lanes**) are popular, particularly in the central section (**Allison Rd, Seymour Rd**). A fair number of the Ladder's houses have been converted into 1- and 2-bed flats in streets such as **Frobisher Rd** and **Hewitt Rd**. **Green Lanes** and **Wightman Rd** – the Ladder 'uprights' – are busy traffic through-routes. Traffic calming has, however, eased problems in the Ladder's 'rungs' between the two. A Sainsbury's superstore is planned just across the tracks in **Hornsey High St** and seems likely to go ahead.

Finsbury Park

Southwards the Haringey borough boundary dips down to take in the green acres of Finsbury Park and some of its surrounding streets – **Stroud Green Rd** marks the border with Islington Borough, Seven Sisters with Hackney.

The most significant difference between Finsbury Park and the rest of the Tottenham area is in the size and quality of the houses – there is a much greater number of large, attractive 3- and 4-storey houses, built mainly around the turn of the century. There is also more variety in the style of housing, with more double-fronted, semi-detached properties.

As a result, many of the streets are more aesthetically pleasing than the streets of smaller, 2-storey terraced houses in the main Tottenham area. The larger houses – originally 5- and 6-bedroomed – are ideal for conversion into flats, something which property developers have exploited to the full. Fortunately, there are still houses available which remain as single properties, though these tend to be run-down and bought by developers.

The Finsbury Park area is characterized, naturally, by the huge park, which is bordered by **Green Lanes**, **Seven Sisters Rd**, **Endymion Rd** and the railway line running from Harringay station to Finsbury Park station.

Recreational facilities within the park include tennis courts, a cricket ground, gardens and an area set aside for rock concerts, festivals, fairs and other special events. In a region otherwise largely bereft of greenery, the park represents an important leisure area to the community. There is sometimes a problem when large music festivals are held in the park, not only because of the build-up of traffic, but also because there have in the past been outbreaks of violence. Other recreational facilities in the area include the Michael Sobel Sports Centre on **Tollington Rd**. Ten acres of old railway land has recently been transformed into 218 new houses and a garden centre. Rented homes 'at affordable prices' have been built here.

Finsbury Park is difficult to categorize in general terms because it lies in three boroughs – Haringey, Hackney and Islington. Consequently house prices and local services vary considerably within the neighbourhood. Finsbury Park's main advantage is its excellent transport facilities. The area is served by Finsbury Park tube (Piccadilly and Victoria lines) and rail station (quick and easy access to the West End and the City), by Manor House and Arsenal tubes, and a very good bus service.

The centre of Finsbury Park is marked by the X-shaped road junction formed by **Stroud Green Rd**, **Blackstock Rd** and **Seven Sisters Rd**. The section of the **Seven Sisters Rd** leading down from Manor House is bordered on its western side by the park and on its eastern side by a series of hotels, most of which serve as DHSS/temporary accommodation. Behind the hotels, in the triangle formed by **Portland Rise**, **Gloucester Drive** and **Seven Sisters Rd**, are some very attractive homes, including detached 2-storey double-fronted houses, which convert into roomy flats.

The central area of Finsbury Park is built around the tube/rail stations, which have been made part of a shopping complex. The one-way traffic system here can be confusing if you're new to the area, and it is famous for its jams. Parking is a problem in the whole area: a residents' scheme is due soon.

The rectangle formed by **Seven Sisters Rd**, **Queens Drive**, **Blackstock Rd** and **Brownswood Rd** (incorporating **Wilberforce Rd**) was a red-light district in the '40s, but the roads have been blocked off to prevent kerb-crawling, giving rise to relatively quiet, tree-lined streets – the properties are good here, fetching higher prices. **Finsbury Park Rd** is perhaps the best street: its Victorian houses have handsome porches and big windows. One-bed flats go for £90–100,000; houses needing work up to £250,000; smart ones up to £320,000. King's Crescent Estate on the S side of **Brownswood Rd** is one of the few large council estates in this area of Finsbury Park. A large tract of new homes has been built on the old filter beds behind **Queens Drive**. Alfred McAlpine Homes were marketing 4-bed houses and 1-bed flats here last winter.

The triangle formed by **Blackstock Rd**, **St Thomas's Rd** and **Gillespie Rd** houses large, attractive properties, many of which have again been converted into flats. The problem here is traffic and crowds when Arsenal Football Club are at home. Parking is restricted on match days over a wide area. The upside is 5-bed houses for around £200,000 – and the N5 (Highbury) postcode. Some new homes are appearing in hidden corners off the W side of **Blackstock Rd**.

The area to the S of **Stroud Green Rd** is made up of attractive streets such as **Charteris Rd**, **Fonthill Rd** and **Moray Rd** with many 4-storey houses converted into flats, and also includes the Finsbury Park Trading Estate. **Alexander Grove** has larger houses. Further S is a large council estate in the rectangle formed by **Durham Rd**, **Seven Sisters Rd**, **Birnham Rd/Moray Rd** and **Hornsey Rd**. SE of here is the Sobell Sports Centre, an excellent modern leisure centre. Check out the properties in the **Corbyn St** area just off **Hornsey Rd**: they were badly bombed during the war and there have been some subsidence problems.

North of **Stroud Green Rd**, some streets of Victorian 3-storey houses offer close proximity to the tube. Most are flats – very much in demand to rent – but a few houses survive. Examples are **Woodstock Rd**, **Perth Rd**, **Woods Rd**, **Ennis Rd**. Just to the N, on the Stroud Green borders, Bellway's 'Regents Quarter' in **Tollington Way** offers new flats and town-houses.

Back up in the Tottenham direction, some spacious, green streets close to Manor House tube are uneasily split between the **Woodberry Down** council-built estate and a surviving clutch of large single-occupant houses.

In general, then, Finsbury Park is an area with an increasing number of flats. There is little space for new development, but conversions are frequent. Properties in the Borough of Islington will continue to carry a slight cachet: the owner can say 'I live in Islington' rather than 'in Finsbury Park'. Nowadays, Finsbury Park's changing status is marked by the new wine bars, restaurants and refurbished pubs. But better-off drivers mean more cars: the area's hitherto unrestricted parking is going, and traffic wardens have been making forays into the area.

Transport	Tubes: Finsbury Park (zone 2, Piccadilly, Victoria); Arsenal, Manor House, Turnpike Lane, Wood Green (zones 2/3, Piccadilly); Tottenham Hale, Seven Sisters (zone 3, Victoria). From Seven Sisters: Oxford Circus 20 min, City 25 min (1 change), Heathrow 1 hr (1 change). Rail: 16 min to Liverpool St. Good buses.
Convenient for	North Circular, A10 to Cambridge, Wood Green Shopping City, Alexandra Park.
Schools	Local Authority: The Drayton, Gladesmore Community School, High Cross, Northumberland Park.

T

SALES

Flats	S	1B	2B	3B	4B	5B
Average prices	30–60	35–85	50–115	60–170	—	—
Houses	2B	3B	4B	5B	6/7B	8B
Average prices	65–90	90–160	100–200	120–200+	—	—

R ENTAL

Flats	S	1B	2B	3B	4B	5B
Average prices	400–500	480–900	600–1000	800–1100	1000–1600	–
Houses	2B	3B	4B	5B	6/7B	8B
Average prices	550–770	700–1500	800–1800	1250+	–	–

The properties Terraced houses (2/3-beds) built 1890–1920 are most common. Fair number of inter-war houses. Flat conversions and council resales mean more small houses and 1/2-bed flats.

The market Affordable prices for first-time buyers of flats and original-features terraced houses. Finsbury Park rates highest; N17 least expensive: far from tube, close to council estates and football. Local searches: Haringey 2 weeks, Islington 2 weeks, Hackney 2 weeks.

Among those estate agents active in this area are:
- Winkworth *
- Adam Kennedy
- Christopher Charles
- Bairstow Eves
- Cousins
- Blackkatz
- George Ellis & Sons
- Paul Simon
- Talbots
- Davies & Davies
- Network

* *further details: see advertisers' index on p633*

T

TOTTERIDGE AND WHETSTONE

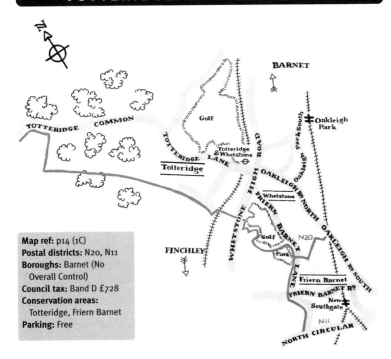

Map ref: p14 (1C)
Postal districts: N20, N11
Boroughs: Barnet (No Overall Control)
Council tax: Band D £728
Conservation areas: Totteridge, Friern Barnet
Parking: Free

Take Hampstead Garden Suburb's Bishops Avenue, move its mansions to the northern fringes of London and dot them along a meandering country lane, add ponies and paddocks – there you have Totteridge.

This foretaste of open countryside and its attendant areas of Whetstone, with its busy shopping parade and the Northern line tube, and Friern Barnet, are still London – just. To the N lies Barnet proper, out of the London postal area and suddenly, indefinably, Hertfordshire. Southwards lies Finchley, and the metropolis. A sign that these areas have joined London proper is the enhanced interest in them over the last decade by West End estate agents, as people looked further out for almost-country homes. This year sees a fertile new hunting-ground for new-build schemes: land freed by the closure of the famous Colney Hatch lunatic asylum.

Totteridge

Though it has a London postcode (N20), Totteridge is to all intents and purposes a country village – albeit one largely consisting of grand mansions. To the N of **Totteridge Common/Village/Lane** and the roads around lie the golf course and wide open spaces with the village itself as a pretty focal point. Totteridge is not a big place and neighbours tend to know each other. They have met because their children attend the village school or because they are active in the local residents' association or perhaps through one of the local sports clubs – but not, probably, over the garden fence. Houses in the area tend to be set in large, secluded plots of land. On Sundays Totteridge folk drop in to the just-refurbished Orange Tree pub for a drink, then take the dogs for a walk and head down to Laurel Farm to feed the ducks and meet their neighbours. These tend to be professionals or show-business people – a famous football star is the latest – who relish the privacy that a Totteridge home affords. This is not Hampstead (positively ostentatious by comparison) where people go to be seen; here remarkable faces go by relatively unremarked-upon.

There are few, if any, small houses in Totteridge – which is known for its 6-, 7- and 8-bedroom palaces, complete with tennis court, sauna and good security systems. **Totteridge Lane** and any of the roads that run off it are prime locations: many of the roads are private and have views over the golf course or acres of Green Belt land. Think in millions for houses in the best roads, which include, as well as **Totteridge Lane**, **Village** and **Common**, **Pine Grove**, **Grange Avenue** and properties in and around **The Green**. Another is **Northcliffe Drive** which, along with **Harmsworth Way**, recalls the great press barons who lived here. If you do not have a newspaper empire, 3-bed semis and flats can be found in roads like **Southway** and **Lynton Mead** for the relatively cheap £225–250,000. Towards the tube station, in **Coppice Walk** and **Greenway**, you can find 1930s 3-bed detached houses for £280,000-plus. By the time your budget has sailed past £650,000, heated swimming pools and electronic gates start to figure in the details . . . Some half-million-pound apartments appeared in **The Grange** a while back, but generally speaking Totteridge is not the place to look for flats and agents suggest Friern Barnet (see next page) or Woodside Park (see Finchley chapter) for luxury purpose-built blocks and new developments.

Totteridge lies in the borough of Barnet, which has one of the best local authority education records in the country – but most of Totteridge's residents prefer to send their offspring to the many private and public schools in the surrounding areas. For communications, the M1 and M25 motorways are not far away. However, for those without a chauffeur transport is a little more difficult and there is a poor bus service – though the Northern line does come out to Totteridge and Whetstone. There are no shops to speak of, but The Spires, Barnet's new shopping centre, has added major stores to the **Whetstone High Rd** selection, and a hopper bus goes to Brent Cross shopping centre. **Totteridge Lane** is a long, winding and wooded road: a daunting walk from the tube on dark evenings. Most Totteridge householders seem, however, to have enough cars to make walking a sport rather than a necessity. Several new houses have appeared in recent months: 'the Spinney' and 'the Dutch Cottage' for £2,250,000 apiece, and two more, at the entrance to Links Drive, for £1,875,000 and £1,925,000. Prices unlikely to fall until somebody torpedoes the entertainment industry.

Whetstone

Totteridge becomes Whetstone when **Totteridge Lane** reaches the tube station. The majority of properties in Whetstone are large semi- and detached houses, mostly less expensive than those in Totteridge, and there are also purpose-built flats. Off the **High Rd**, there are many favoured streets: **Chandos Avenue** and **Buckingham Avenue** have 5- and 6-bed houses. **Church Gate** is a 1980s cul-de-sac of 5-bedroomed houses behind electronic gates off **Church Crescent**. Property along the **High Rd** itself includes many fine houses and purpose-built blocks, but they do have the disadvantage of being set on a busy stretch of road. Last year saw a new block of 2- and 3-bed flats with parking: opening prices ranged from £170–200,000. Heading S along the **High Rd** past the parade of shops is the elegant corner of Oakleigh Park where roads such as **Oakleigh Park North** (especially favoured) and **Oakleigh Park South** are quiet, leafy and well-located, as are the surrounding streets. They also have the benefit of Oakleigh Park station nearby. The roads boast large houses, a mixture of mainly semi-detached homes with good gardens, and nearby at the beginning of **Oakleigh Rd North** are fine purpose-built blocks. **Oakleigh Rd North**/**Oakleigh Rd South**, similar in name, but not in stature to the 'Parks', together form the main road from Whetstone to Southgate. A new development of 4- and 5-bed houses appeared at £400,000-plus a year ago, but generally it's a mixture of small houses and shops, and prices hereabouts tend to be cheaper than elsewhere in Whetstone.

Friern Barnet

Running off **Whetstone High Rd**, **Friern Barnet Lane** leads past the North Middlesex Golf Course to Friern Barnet itself. The great landmark of Friern Barnet is the (listed) former psychiatric hospital in **Friern Barnet Rd**. The asylum itself is now 'Princess Park Manor', a luxury block of 260 1-, 2-, 3- and 4-bed flats complete with swimming pool and other leisure facilities, by Comer Homes. The first phase in the renovation was completed in late 1997 and the rest is due to be finished over the next year. The 37-acre hospital grounds have been split between a retail park and several developments of homes: firms active here include Bellway and Bryant.

The area already offers a wide range of properties: a mixture of small terraced homes, some large detached houses in **Friern Barnet Lane** and the surrounding roads, purpose-built flats, and plenty of Victorian and Edwardian properties converted into flats. Conveniently close to the **North Circular** and with a rail line into King's Cross, it is an up-and-coming area and something of a contrast to well-established Whetstone and Totteridge. A good hunting-ground for less expensive, smaller properties than those of neighbouring areas, plus some new flats, it attracts more first-time buyers.

There are some fine large semi- and detached houses in and around **Friern Barnet Lane**, probably the prime street, and its location near Friary Park makes it popular. **Friern Barnet Rd**, running towards New Southgate, has much cheaper properties with many solid houses built in the Victorian and Edwardian era. Nearby in **Woodhouse Rd** are 1930s semis and terraces.

There are many larger flats which have been converted from houses, as well as purpose-built ones, and some '80s blocks in **Colney Hatch Lane**, which runs down to the **North Circular** and **Brunswick Park Rd**.

Transport	Tubes: Totteridge & Whestone (zone 3, Northern). To Oxford Circus 35 min (1 change), City 35 min, Heathrow 1 hr 30 min (1 change).
Convenient for	North Circular, M1/M25, Brent Cross. Miles from centre: 9.
Schools	Barnet Education Authority: Ravenscroft School, Friern Barnet County School, Queen Elizabeth's (b), Queen Elizabeth High (g), Dame Alice Owen, Copthall (g). Private: Friern Barnet Grammar, Mill Hill, Haberdashers' Aske's.

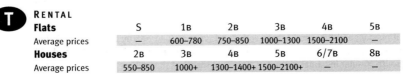

SALES

Flats	S	1B	2B	3B	4B	5B
Average prices	60–90	70–105	80–300+	175–325	–	–
Houses	2B	3B	4B	5B	6/7B	8B
Average prices	100–150	150–400	200–600	250–1M	600–1.5M	–

RENTAL

Flats	S	1B	2B	3B	4B	5B
Average prices	–	600–780	750–850	1000–1300	1500–2100	–
Houses	2B	3B	4B	5B	6/7B	8B
Average prices	550–850	1000+	1300–1400+	1500–2100+	–	–

The properties   Totteridge has grand 6/8-plus bedroom houses set in near-countryside. Whetstone has more luxury houses, slightly smaller, and smart p/b flats. Friern Barnet has a range from smaller terraced homes to large detacheds.

The market   People in Totteridge and Whetstone have arrived: show-biz, smart professionals, all with children and attendant ponies and pets. Amenities here can be anything from a swimming pool to a sunken recording studio. Friern Barnet is more urban, with scope for less prosperous buyers. Local searches: 1 week.

Among those estate agents active in this area are:
- Anscombe & Ringland *
- Blade
- Ferrier Tomlin
- Martyn Gerrard
- Henry Charles
- Joe Raymond
- Barnard Marcus
- Bairstow Eves
- Spicer McColl

* *further details: see advertisers' index on p633*

T

TWICKENHAM AND TEDDINGTON

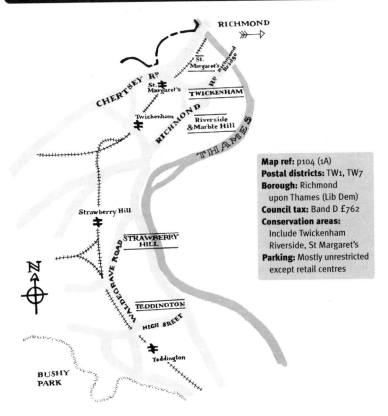

Map ref: p104 (1A)
Postal districts: TW1, TW7
Borough: Richmond
  upon Thames (Lib Dem)
Council tax: Band D £762
Conservation areas:
  Include Twickenham
  Riverside, St Margaret's
Parking: Mostly unrestricted
  except retail centres

So much of West London has the same history: from open fields through retreats for the rich to endless suburbia. Thames-side Twickenham and Teddington succumbed like the rest, but managed to keep the grand houses, and the riverside offers a sort of national gallery of the covetable homes of the 18th and 19th centuries. Marble Hill, Orleans House, York House, Strawberry Hill stand stately on or close to the river, and amid them on a lesser (and still lived-in) scale are Montpelier Row and a hundred other lovely Georgian houses. Now the area's character ranges from this semi-rural riverside grandeur to small '30s semis overlooking a dual carriageway.

Essentially these are suburbs of family homes, from cottages to mansions. Purpose-built flats make their appearance along the river and in the town centres, and there are flats converted from Victorian houses. The surviving Georgian is much in demand, as indeed are any large family homes: as elsewhere, families don't seem to be moving much.

Twickenham lacks the sophisticated charm of Richmond, though local people feel as though they have the best of both worlds. Despite recent price rises, homes cost substantially less than on the other side of the river, but residents can still enjoy Richmond's amenities – and parking is easier. Kingston, with its big shopping centre, is close by – as is Heathrow. There are pleasant Thames-side walks with views of Richmond and Petersham Meadows. Twickenham is under 10 miles from the West End and travel in is almost as quick as from Richmond. A good range of state schools (Orleans Park and Waldegrave Girls' Comprehensives and St Mary's Girls' Convent School) attracts families, as do St Paul's Girls' and St Paul's Boys' public schools in Barnes and Hammersmith, and Hampton School (boys) and Lady Eleanor Holles (girls) in nearby Hampton. Teddington shares the river and schools though it lacks the architecture, and offers somewhat cheaper prices to compensate for longer commuting times. The area's western boundary is the very busy A316, which leads to Central London in the E and the M3 in the W. To the E is the Thames. Within this tract are hardly any undesirable corners. Prices rise towards Richmond and the river, and close to stations, and fall towards the A316. The rugby stadium at Whitton (it's called Twickenham) is just N of the area: it can attract enormous crowds and the traffic jams are epic. Controversy surrounds increasing use of the massive stadium.

There is a wide range of property available. There is quite a selection of good family houses around £250–300,000 in pleasant locations. Two-bed cottages, which are dotted throughout Twickenham, can cost £140,000-plus. Flats abound in the St Margarets area (small purpose-built, small conversions and renovated mansions) and depending on the location a 1-bed flat can cost from £80–120,000. Bargain-hunters should look to the **Chertsey Rd/Staines Rd** area with its 3-bed '30s semis. Lower prices are also to be found in Whitton to the N of the A316. Renting is well-established, though students find it tough: families and professional people dominate the market.

East Twickenham/St Margarets

St Margarets, tucked into a bend of the river opposite Richmond and with its own station, used to be a good hunting-ground for value-for-money homes. It is now well-established, though still cheaper than Richmond. The last untouched terraced homes are rapidly being tidied up. Buyers are young professional first-time buyers and families, who start small and graduate to bigger local homes.

South of Richmond Bridge, **Richmond Rd** is flanked by red-brick mansion flats which overlook gardens leading down to the Thames, and by small shops which are open late and have flats above them. Left into **Cresswell Rd** semi-detached Victorian houses with huge bay windows are to be found. Neighbouring **Morley Rd** and **Denton Rd** carry on the style on a smaller scale. A 3-bed house with a garden costs £400,000.

Closer to the river is 'Richmond Bridge', a big complex of flats and town-houses. Phase II is now under way: two more blocks of flats behind the first three, and town-houses. In the winter a 1-bed flat was on the market for £205,000, a 3-bed on two floors left a few quid change from a million – with another ten grand if you want an extra parking space.

Further S, **Cambridge Park** curves around Marble Hill Park to the river. Here large double-fronted mansions (mostly flats) are mixed with small modern developments set back from the road behind mature trees. A 2-bed flat sold for £220,000 in November. Behind is **St Stephens Gardens** with a row of 3-storey semi-detached Victorian houses (mostly flats) overlooking a bowling green.

Richmond Rd swings SW towards the heart of Twickenham. To the S is Marble Hill Park, with the cool cream symmetry of the Palladian Marble Hill House, leading down to the river. **Crown Rd** has an eclectic mix of shops at its N end including smart interiors, bric-a-brac and nice cafés. **Crown Rd** and **Sandycombe Rd** stretch N to **St Margarets Rd** and offer a mix of 2-bed cottages and pleasant 3/4-bed red-brick family houses. Sandycombe Lodge, designed by J W Turner as his country retreat, is still a house. **Marble Hill Close**, situated close to the park, has neat 3-bed '30s semis priced around £200,000.

The Barons, on the opposite side of the **Crown Rd/St Margarets Rd** junction, curves down past Twickenham Film Studios into a semi-circle. Here large 3-storey houses with pillared porticoes cluster around what may once have been a private communal garden but where there is now a block of flats. To the E is **Rosslyn Rd**, with enormous double-fronted Victorian houses, now mostly flats or offices.

North of **Rosslyn Rd** is Riverdale Rd where the 1870 Gothic mansions, shaded by trees, give a touch of the Sir Walter Scotts. This is a fine example of a Victorian suburb, although the great houses are now splendid flats. Further N is **Ravensbourne Rd** with its half-timbered post-war houses and, swinging left into **Park House Gardens**, fine white-washed Art Deco semi-detached houses run down to the river. Here is **Duck's Walk**, where homes with moorings face the river. Six town-houses built two years ago as 'Richmond Bridge Moorings' sold when new for £650–750,000. Agents estimate current prices at £850,000–1 million. From this point across **The Avenue** is a cache of five roads – **St Margarets Drive, Ranelagh Drive, St Peters Rd, St Georges Rd** and **Ailsa Rd** (the latter three form an exclusive area known as 'The Trust Grounds'). Mansions either face grandly onto the road or are hidden by high walls. They all back onto secret private parkland where owner's children play contentedly and summer barbecues are held. The price of membership is high, starting around £550,000 for smaller properties, though a house in **St Peters Rd** sold in 1997 for £1.5 million.

Winchester Rd runs S from (but does not join) the roundabout at the junction of **The Avenue, Chertsey Rd** and **St Margarets Rd** and has Victorian/Edwardian flat-fronted houses and 2-bed maisonettes. Running between **Winchester Rd** and the open space of Moor Mead Ground is a grid of popular streets convenient for St Margarets station: maisonettes and terraced houses. **St Margarets Grove** and **Brook Rd** offer pretty 2-bed cottages; property here fetches around £160–250,000 (**Brook Rd** is cheaper). Some cottages in this road have gardens that back onto the River Crane.

Cole Park Rd twists up the E side of Cole Park and is lined with detached double-fronted Edwardian, '30s and modern houses. Across the tracks **Amyand Park Rd** hugs the railway from close to Twickenham station up to **St Margarets Rd**. A mixed bag of 3-storey houses with basements (now mostly flats) is to be found, though some face the rather busy railway. A 2-bed flat with garden might cost £150,000. The terraced cottages in **St Margaret's Grove** are popular: one (with downstairs bathroom) sold in November 1997 for £180,000; exactly a year later, one like it went for £235,000.

Riverside and Marble Hill

The prestige homes of Twickenham can be found S of **Richmond Rd**. **Montpelier Row** (1724) skirts the W side of Marble Hill Park: a fine example of a Georgian terrace. **Chapel Rd** with its cottages leads through to equally cottagy **Orleans Rd** where the road, shaded by huge horse chestnuts, swings around Orleans House Gallery into the pretty **Riverside** winding up to The White Swan past some spectacular late-18th-century white and pastel-washed houses. N of **Riverside** is **Lebanon Park** where you

T

can expect to pay handsomely for the 3/4-bed, red-brick Edwardian family houses. **Lebanon Park** runs parallel with **Sion Rd** where a terrace of 12 houses runs down to the river. Cross a footbridge (when it's not being mended) and Eel Pie Island has some modern houses with moorings for those who reckon boats are more important than cars. One house was for sale at £330,000 last winter.

Central Twickenham

South of **Heath Rd** is a network of roads (including **Pope's Grove**, **Upper Grotto Rd**, **Cross Deep Gardens**) which are a mix of Victorian houses with basements, harsh red-brick cottages and pleasant Edwardian family houses. Prices in the £200–300,000 range. **Cross Deep Gardens** also has houses with lawns which lead down to the river and penthouse flats; these push house prices up above half a million. Here, too, is Addison Court, a 1980s development of 21 flats: a 2-bed one goes for about £95,000. **King St** is the main street of Twickenham where the buses stop and most of the shops are. However Twickenham is crying out for more chain stores: a Marks & Spencer is top of the wish-list. There are rumours of the Volvo garage on **Heath Rd** becoming an Marks & Spencer or Tesco, but nothing firm. Plans to redevelop the site of the old swimming pool on the **Embankment** into flats, a cinema, auditorium, health club and bar/restaurant were being discussed in the autumn.

Further W **Heath Rd** feeds into **The Green**, a tree-lined triangle with large white 18th-century cottages to the S which give way to modern flat developments. There are pretty 18th-century cottages to the W. To the N, **May Rd**, **Knowle Rd** and **Colne Rd** have a mix of doll-sized cottages and modern houses. More young people are moving in here. W towards Fulwell prices drop, to rise again at Hampton Hill.

Strawberry Hill and Teddington

Horace Walpole's 18th-century Gothic mansion of Strawberry Hill is now a college, and its grounds are streets of suburban houses. This neighbourhood forms the S edge of Twickenham. Tree-lined streets like **Waldegrave Park** are lined with big detached Victorian villas, some split into flats, and batches of '50s–'70s infill: town-houses, mostly, including some of the Span ones that excite architects. There is a lot of inter-war housing around here: smart semis ranging down the scale to rather tired-looking 1920s terraces. A 4-bed house in nearby **Clifton Rd** sold for £420,000 last winter. Two new 6-bed semis have just been marketed in **Waldegrave Park** for £750,000 each.

Teddington itself has a station and a somewhat humdrum **High St** (with a few lovely Georgian homes). The best residential roads lie to the E – towards the river. Here, **Kingston Rd** runs N-S towards Hampton Wick and Kingston Bridge. Closer to the river, **Lower Teddington Rd** forms the spine of a district of moderately smart homes set in plenty of greenery – but a longish way from shops or transport. Riverside complexes of flats and town-houses line the E side, many in private estates. The most interesting houses are late-19th-century and 1930s ones in **Melbourne Rd** and **Trowlock Avenue** which lead down to the river and share a private riverside green. Beyond is a true oddity: Trowlock Island, a long thin strip of land packed with bungalows. Most started as shacks, many are now very smart; all (when and if they appear on the open market) are expensive – this is true off-shore living, mooring included, and you'll pay for the privilege. The only access is by a chain ferry with a handle you have to wind.

Broom Water and **Broom Water West** have some of Teddington's smartest homes: big houses with gardens down to a private creek. To the W of **Broom Rd** and **Lower Teddington Rd** are some 1991 flats in **Trematon Place**, plus streets, such as **Munster Rd** and **King Edward's Rd**, of tall, gabled 1890–1910 semis and 1960s town-houses.

The Lensbury Club, an enviable corporate sports and leisure complex, sits on an enviable riverside site: rumours of redevelopment, but no firm news. Then, beside the weir, comes the studios of Thames TV, lined with plaques remembering famous comedians. On the inland side is **Rivermead Close**, a big estate of '70s dark-brick houses and flats. **Ferry Rd** leads down to the footbridge over the lock, and a pair of popular pubs. It has a few Victorian homes – cottages and converted houses – and the entrance to one of the many flats blocks set beside the Teddington riverside. Further on down, Berkeley Homes are building The Moorings (not the only homes of this name along this stretch) which has 22 1- and 2-bed flats, the smaller starting at £170,000, the larger at £240,000. St George's Teddington Wharf, on the old Tough's Boat Yard, is all sold. As ever, they are 1/3-bed flats and penthouses. The roofline features striking glass conservatories. Older flats blocks along the river include '60s Fairwater House. Modern river-view 2-bed flats are priced from about £160,000, with moorings; £210,000 for 3-bed. The rest of the Teddington riverside, running along a road that changes its name from (N-S) **Strawberry Vale** to **Twickenham Rd** to **Manor Rd**, is a mix of blocks of flats from the '30s to today, Victorian and earlier villas, and inter-war suburban detached. Many have their own moorings, and all have fine views of the wooded, open Ham Lands and beyond to Richmond Park.

Going inland, there's a big tract of mixed 1880–1910 and 1930s housing, with everything from handsome Arts and Crafts detached to little terraced cottages, smartened-up council-built houses, and '70s town-houses. Similar housing appears W of the railway line, which runs behind the W side of **Waldegrave Rd**. The handsome double-fronted (though semi) Victorian houses in **Cambridge Rd** fetch around £500,000. Cheaper homes are further W: ex-council houses, Victorian cottages. If you can find a 3-bed house for under £130,000 you've got a good deal.

Transport	Trains: Twickenham, St Margarets, Teddington, to Waterloo via Richmond or Kingston. Twickenham to Waterloo 25 min.
Convenient for	Heathrow, River Thames, roads to West. Miles from centre: 9–10.
Schools	Richmond Education Authority: Rectory School, Teddington School, Waldegrave Girls' School, Whitton School, Orleans Park School. Private: Hampton School (b), Lady Eleanor Holles (g).

SALES

Flats	S	1B	2B	3B	4B	5B
Average prices	55–70	80–120	90–180	120–200+	—	—
Houses	2B	3B	4B	5B	6/7B	8B
Average prices	130–200	150–300	200–450+	250–650+	500+–1M	800+

RENTAL

Flats	S	1B	2B	3B	4B	5B
Average prices	500–700+	600–800+	700–1500	900–1600+	—	—
Houses	2B	3B	4B	5B	6/7B	8B
Average prices	600–1500	1000–2000	1450–3000	1600–3200	—	—

T **The properties** From riverside splendour – 18th-century and newer houses plus a clutch of new flats – to railway cottages, with plenty of suburbia of most vintages in between, and an increasing number of converted flats.

The market   Big premiums are paid for best riverside locations, while
mainstream family homes are cheaper than neighbouring
Richmond. Education – borough is top in UK – attracts
more and more families.

Among those estate agents active in this area are:

- Bells
- Barton & Wyatt
- Camerons Residential
- Milestone & Collis
- Mann & Co
- Jardine and Co
- Chancellors
- Churchills
- Priory Management *

- Featherstone Leigh
- Dexters
- Chase Buchanan
- Hamptons
- G A Property
- Black Horse/Gascoigne Pees
- Phillip Hodges
- Townends

* *further details: see advertisers' index on p633*

T

WANDSWORTH

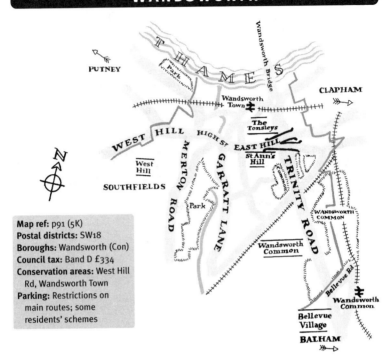

Map ref: p91 (5K)
Postal districts: SW18
Boroughs: Wandsworth (Con)
Council tax: Band D £334
Conservation areas: West Hill
  Rd, Wandsworth Town
Parking: Restrictions on
  main routes; some
  residents' schemes

Wandsworth is a classic case of name-shifting. The name of the borough, which takes in a wide swathe from Putney to Streatham, is confused with, and has in many ways replaced, the tightly knit former village where the River Wandle meets the Thames. Those who say they live in Wandsworth rarely mean the latter. This unique tribute to the town hall's persuasive powers stems from the low (even non-existent) poll tax levied back in the days of Queen Margaret. The current council tax is lower than in most boroughs, protecting the investment of the bankers and PR girls who flocked to the rather ordinary late-Victorian suburbs of Balham, Southfields, Tooting and the rest (see separate chapter).

Here we're concerned with actual Wandsworth, real existing Wandsworth, the neighbourhoods clustered around the old village centre, perhaps best-known for its one-way system in the centre of which lies the monumental town hall, protected from all but the bravest council-tax payer by the South Circular traffic.

But that is the town centre. The enclaves of desirable homes, tucked leafily away from the snarling jams, were discovered in the '80s by families who looked outward to the Home Counties countryside, and inwards (good trains, sad lack of tubes) to City or West End for jobs. And in 1997 the million-pound mark was passed for a Wandsworth mansion – and over two million demanded for another.

The busy Wandsworth town centre offers the Arndale shopping centre (Tesco, Boots, Woolworths etc) with high-rise council flats above. There is a large Sainsbury's in **Garratt Lane**. A landmark within the centre is the Victorian Ram Brewery (Young's). Leisure pursuits in King George's Park include a squash and health club and tennis courts. The 1980s saw considerable tidying-up around Wandsworth, including a much-needed facelift for Wandsworth Town station, much re-paving and, best of all, extensive work on council estates.

Along with this goes a considerable number of new development schemes, principally along the river and near the prison. Look carefully: these range from the excellent to the downright shoddy. And cast a cynical eye at the map when developers say they are selling you Wandsworth. Whatever the brochure-writers may think, Tooting doesn't cut it – even if it's in the borough.

Central and Riverside

The riverside, between Wandsworth centre and the Thames, was industrial but is now the scene of much of the development action in the area. The former industrial land between **Putney Bridge Rd** and the Thames is changing fast as developers seize on the riverside sites, made more interesting by the Wandle mouth. Some industry remains, such as the council depots at the end of otherwise pretty **Frogmore**, but every inch is under seige from developers. St George's rather stolid riverside blocks at 'Riverside West' in **Smugglers Way** are already part complete and have been selling at prices from £150–400,000. The developer's site map identifies as a neighbour the Ship Inn to the E of the site (known to every Henry in SW London for its Thames-side BBQs), but fails to mark the Solid Waste Transfer Station upwind to the W. Further W, beyond the rubbish depot and the mouth of the Wandle, is a former Shell site accessed via **Point Pleasant** and **Osiers Rd**. A public inquiry took place last year into a scheme which included 450 homes and a 17-storey office block. Following this inquiry the scene was thrown out by the Secretary of State. Further downstream, the giant site next to Wandsworth Bridge, once the Guinness-owned distillery and now known as 'Gargoyle Wharf', lies empty. Plans for a scheme with 740 homes, some in 20-storey towers, plus a hotel, have been called in by the Ministry.

Property in central Wandsworth is mainly commercial with some small industrial premises. Exceptionally beautiful Queen Anne houses (now commerce and industry) are to be found in **Wandsworth Plain**. There are four stunning Queen Anne houses on the corner of **Putney Bridge Rd** and **Armoury Way**. Thereafter are privatized blocks of modernized '30s council flats that are set well back from the road. Behind is **Frogmore** with its flat-fronted cottages and a modern, private development. **Sudlow Rd** joins **Frogmore** to **North Passage** and has mid-Victorian cottages.

The Tonsleys

Bordered by **Old York Rd**, **Trinity Rd**, **East Hill** and **Fairfield St**, this is a quiet enclave of attractive small Victorian cottages (mainly 2- and 3-bed) with some large 4- and 5-bed houses running up and across the hill which rises out of the Wandle basin.

The Tonsleys is near Wandsworth Town station (12 min to Waterloo via Clapham Junction), and was discovered by '80s yuppies. The area is popular with Fulham price refugees (easy access to parents in Parson's Green via Wandsworth Bridge) and still reverberates with the sounds of building work: at least a dozen houses in this small neighbourhood were being worked on just before Christmas.

The building of the **Swandon Way** relief road has turned **Old York Rd** from a busy, scruffy through-route into a bijou backwater, with no through traffic and new planting and paving. Mexican restaurants, a Pizza Express, bars and amusing shops burgeon. South of **Old York Rd** is **Alma Rd** with large 3-storey Victorian houses and a pub at the junction with **Fullerton Rd**. Three new 4-bed houses are under construction in **Alma Rd**, where the existing 2-bed cottages command around £210,000. In **Ebner St** (running parallel with **Alma Rd**) a church and C of E primary school have been rebuilt. The development includes an adult education centre. Especially pretty roads are **Dalby Rd** and **Bramford Rd** which run down the fairly steep hill from **Dighton Rd** to **Old**

York Rd. Tonsley Place, leading off **Fairfield St**, has modernized 2- and 3-bed cottages. Two-bed modernized ones can command £250,000-plus, 3-bed ones £280,000-plus. Mixed blocks of '30s council and private flats (Fairfield Court) front **Fairfield St** (very heavy traffic: it's part of the one-way system) along with four large, semi-detached mid-Victorian houses. Five new 2-bed flats are under construction in **Tonsley Hill**.

There are larger, 3-storey 4/5-bed houses in **Dempster Rd**, **Fullerton Rd** and **Birdhurst Rd**, N of **East Hill**. Birdhurst Rd overlooks busy **Trinity Rd**, which is in a cutting at this point, so traffic noise is no great problem. A 1990 homes development (including a shopping parade) on **East Hill** backs into **Fullerton Rd**. The 64 flats and six houses are known as 'Tonsley Heights' and are grouped round a new street called **Bloomsbury Way**. Rialto were the developers of this Victorian pastiche. A new flats complex, Almand House, has just been finished further down **East Hill**. Across **Trinity Rd**, close to **York Rd**, the old school site in **Eltringham St** now has offices and homes.

St Ann's Hill

South of **East Hill**, between **St Ann's Hill, Allfarthing Lane** and **Wandsworth Common Westside** homes are mainly well-sized, late-Victorian and Edwardian with some modern infill developments. (These include low-rise council-built flats, many of which are now privately owned.) Property prices rise approaching the Common.

Popular roads in the area include **Geraldine Rd, Melody Rd** and **Cicada Rd** (**Geraldine's** rat-running traffic is now slowed by speed humps). The architectural styles are mixed but most of the houses are large, late-Victorian 2- and 3-storey buildings. A modernized 5-bed house in **Geraldine Rd** was on the market for £595,000 last winter. There are still some unmodernized houses available and the area is a prime hunting-ground for developers and young families trading up for more space. The 3-bed/2-bath town-houses of The Washhouse are in **St Ann's Crescent**, partly overlooking the unusual, late-Georgian 'pepper pot' church. Just opposite, on the corner of **Rosehill Rd**, three terraced houses were being extensively modernized last winter to form 4/5-bed homes.

Although **St Ann's Hill** acts as the main through road from **East Hill** to **Allfarthing Lane** and **Earlsfield Rd**, it has speed humps and does not suffer too badly from traffic. Houses on and surrounding **St Ann's Hill** are mainly early Edwardian 3-bed terraces, but there are some '30s-built semi-detached houses on **St Ann's Hill**. Between **St Ann's Hill** and **Garratt Lane** there is a good supply of purpose-built late-Victorian maisonettes and flats. A council estate running along the lower end of **Allfarthing Lane** (**Iron Mill Rd, Vermont Rd**) and up to the Wandsworth end of **St Ann's Hill** means big price differentials.

Huguenot Place is at the junction of **East Hill, Wandsworth Common Northside** and **Westside**. The heavy traffic maroons the attractive 18th-century church, Book House and the Huguenot cemetery. There are some flats and houses, including Huguenot Mansions, which all suffer road noise.

West Hill

This neighbourhood is SW of Wandsworth town centre and is bounded in the N by the endlessly busy **West Hill**, which funnels traffic from the A3 into the maw of the Wandsworth one-way system. **Merton Rd** joins **West Hill** at the junction with **Wandsworth High St** and **Putney Bridge Rd** and features some good mid- and late-Victorian semi-detached and terraced houses. Many of the houses are set well back from the road with off-street parking, so are not worried by the heavy traffic. **Wimbledon Park Rd** leads down through the neighbourhood to Southfields tube station, lined with a mix of Victorian houses and low-rise council-built flats. There is a school at the junction with **Replingham Rd**. **West Hill Rd**, leading from **Merton Rd** to

W

West Hill (A3) now sees prices on a par with Putney. The houses vary in style: there are early, mid- and late-Victorian and some 1930s and '50s homes. Many of the properties are detached or semi-detached. Houses in **Sispara Gardens** and **Viewfield Rd** are set well back and have off-street parking. **Lebanon Rd**, **Amerland Rd** and **Ringford Rd** all lead off **West Hill** and are more East Putney than Wandsworth. There is a small council-built infill in **Lebanon Gardens** whose now privately owned 4-bedroomed houses occasionally come up for sale.

Further E, at the junction with **Broomhill Rd** and **Merton Rd**, is an attractive, simple development of mews-style town-houses, some with balconies and garages. Older and larger 2- and 3-storey late-Victorian houses follow from this more peaceful point on **Merton Rd** to the junction with **Buckhold Rd**.

A small council cottage-style estate off **Buckhold Rd** has mainly flat-fronted traditional-style houses. Many have been bought by tenants under 'Right to Buy' who are now selling. The large gardens of those on the eastern side of **Longstaff Crescent** back on to King George's Park.

Wandsworth Common

Wandsworth Common is quite a long way from Wandsworth Town, projecting SE as far as the borders of Balham and Tooting. This adds to the name confusion mentioned above: Wandsworth Common station, and the nearby Bellevue Village neighbourhood, are really in Balham if one is strict, but it would not be wise to say so locally. The Common is cut into chunks by roads and railways. **Wandsworth Common Westside** (the street) is at the NW corner, on the E edge of the St Ann's Hill neighbourhood. It is protected from the traffic of **Trinity Rd**, (dual-carriageway at this point) by a slice of the Common, wide at the junction with **Earlsfield Rd** and narrowing to the junction with **East Hill**. **Westside** offers large 4- and 5-bed mid-Victorian houses. Especially attractive is the row of ornate Gothic-style houses between **Quarry Rd** and **Heathfield Rd**. Further along **Heathfield Rd** just before the junction with **Earlsfield Rd** is **Heathfield Gardens**, a secret row of enchanting Regency cottages of varying sizes overlooking the common. Across **Earlsfield Rd** and further along **Heathfield Rd** is another Wandsworth landmark: Wandsworth Prison. Just opposite is Heathfields, a 'mews' development of flats and houses, with 2/4-bed houses. Across the road, **Wilde Place** has 29 well-built 2- to 4-bed town-houses. Past the prison lies the pretty early Victorian flat-fronted cottages of **Alma Terrace** facing open land Some are split into flats, and whole houses come on the market at around £220,000. Beyond are 1920s and '30s blocks of flats.

Spencer Park, overlooking the Common from the northern side, is the area's gem: it has a stunning range of large, detached and semi-detached houses built in a variety of styles as show houses for the Great Exhibition in 1851. Some have now been converted into flats or are used by institutions, but a number remain as large family homes: prices of over £2 million have been mooted. Their secret is that they back onto a large and private communal garden. Spencer Court on **Windmill Rd** is a 1930s block of flats overlooking the railway lines and the Victorian Emanuel School beyond.

Wandsworth Common Northside forms part of the traffic-plagued South Circular. Many of the houses here have been converted into flats and those on the southern side of the road are popular for their views over Wandsworth Common. Behind lie **Elsynge Rd** and **Spencer Rd**, where there is a mixture of exceptionally large, fine Victorian houses with enormous gardens, many remaining in single occupation, and smaller late-Victorian houses and double-fronted 'cottages'. Asking prices for the better houses were up to £900,000 last winter. On **Northside** itself, Fairview developers have taken six 5-floor Victorian houses back to their roots: 5-beds, an au pair flat and a garage. At least one was on the market last December at £525,000.

Approached from an easy-to-miss turning off **Trinity Rd** is Wandsworth's most spectacular building: the splendidly Gothic Royal Victoria Patriotic Building. Built to care for orphan daughters of servicemen killed in the Crimean War and later used as an interrogation centre during World War II, it now houses a theatre school, restaurant, design studios and individualistic flats (some in towers and turrets) which are popular with artistic and media types. It is set rather unfortunately between a major railway and an estate of council towers and is perhaps more fun to look at than out of. Not many came up for sale in this popular building; when they do, prices start at around £230,000.

A new bridge over the railway off **Windmill Rd** gives access to **John Archer Way** and 'Windmill Green', a Fairview development of 200 flats and 65 houses set just N of the Royal Victoria Patriotic Building. Security is a feature: railway cuttings on two sides and the Emanuel School grounds on the third. Flats are priced from £103,000, with 2-bed flats from £124,000. Houses start at £215,000, with 4-bed from £275,000.

The more traditional charms of 'The Toastrack', a grid of streets surrounded on three sides by the Common, have been attracting family buyers for a decade. This group lies off **Trinity Rd** and takes in **Dorlcote Rd**, **Nicosia Rd**, **Baskerville Rd**, **Henderson Rd** and **Patten Rd**. Here are large, detached or semi-detached 5/6-bed late-Victorian houses, some with exceptionally large gardens. It is reported that the last unreconstructed one was snapped up by a canny property person two years ago. Houses on **Dorlcote Rd** overlook the Common from the front, whilst the gardens of houses in **Routh Rd** and **Baskerville** back onto the Common. There are some flats in Greenview Court on **Baskerville Rd.**

West of **Trinity Rd** from the Toastrack are some unusually large, often double-fronted houses with good-sized gardens, which can fetch very surprising prices for exceptional properties. These are to be found in the roads adjoining **Lyford Rd**, most notably **Herondale Avenue, Loxley Rd, Frewin Rd** and **Westover Rd**. **Lyford Rd** is a no-through road running N-S between **Magdalen Rd** and **Burntwood Lane**. Houses that lie between **Routh Rd** and **Lyford Rd** back onto a wild and overgrown extension of Wandsworth Common, adding to the rural illusion beloved of many of the inhabitants. Another recent development in the **Trinity Rd** area has appeared close to **Magdalen Rd**: Trinity Grange has five 3- and 4-bedroom houses and nine flats.

Between **Routh Rd** (where Lloyd George lived) and **Burntwood Lane** are large 3-storey Edwardian and late-Edwardian houses (some semi-detached) overlooking the Common. The distinctive White House by the junction with **Frewin Rd** was designed by Voysey.

Bellevue Village

The area bordered by **Trinity Rd**, **St James's Drive** and Wandsworth Common offers pretty mid-Victorian cottages, some flat-fronted and larger than they look. The cottages were once inhabited by the working classes but are now occupied by interior designers, junior merchant bankers and divorcees whose alimony payments don't stretch to Fulham. Inhabitants tend to be seriously short-tempered owing to the fact that there is no available parking space and each house appears to have three cars. **Bellevue Rd** is lined with art galleries, chi-chi delicatessens, wine bars and restaurants which all add to the chaotic parking. This got worse after Marco Pierre White started his career here – and gets no better now he's moved on. None of this existed 15 years ago: Bellevue was a quiet suburban parade of butchers, bakers and junk shops.

St James's Drive has larger mid-Victorian terraced houses, some semi-basement and stuccoed, all suffering road noise. The former St James's Hospital site is now housing association homes. South-west of Bellevue, almost in Tooting, **Broderick Rd,**

W

Wandle Rd and **Hendham Rd** have large late-Victorian mainly 3-storey terraced and (just) semi-detached houses. **Broderick** and to a lesser extent **Wandle Rd** suffer rat-running between the ghastly traffic of **Trinity Rd** and fairly awful traffic of **Beechcroft Rd**. They are popular with families, offering easy access to Tooting Bec tube, but is really Tooting (see chapter) not Wandsworth. One advantage is Wandsworth Common station, which has a good service into Victoria via Clapham Junction.

Transport	Trains: Wandsworth Town (Waterloo 12 min), Wandsworth Common, Clapham Junction.
Convenient for	Wandsworth and Clapham Commons, Clapham Junction. Miles from centre: 4.
Schools	Local Authority: Burntwood School (g), John Archer School (b), Southfields. Private: Emanuel (b & g).

SALES

Flats	S	1B	2B	3B	4B	5B
Average prices	60–80	90–120	110–200+	150+	—	—

Houses	2B	3B	4B	5B	6/7B	8B
Average prices	140–250	210–400	250–500	400+	—	—

RENTAL

Flats	S	1B	2B	3B	4B	5B
Average prices	600–750	650–1200	900–1400	1000+	—	—

Houses	2B	3B	4B	5B	6/7B	8B
Average prices	800–1600	1200–3000+	1600–4000	3000+	—	—

The properties	Wide range, but main type is Victorian terraced in a range of locations, with cottage-style in the Tonsleys and grander ones near the Common. Despite developers' attentions, still some unmodernized houses to be had. Some '30s and '50s suburban houses in SW of area. New homes by the river and Common. Watch for resales of good ex-council flats and houses.
The market	While the town centre stays forever Wandsworth, the enclaves of fashionable homes – Tonsleys, Bellevue, 'Toastrack' (all close to stations) – are now well and truly established, and the riverside is on its way. Watch out for agents and builders selling Balham, Southfields etc as Wandsworth. Local searches: 1 week.

Among those estate agents active in this area are:
- Bells
- Realm Estates
- Barnard Marcus
- Raymond Bushell
- FPDSavills
- Friend & Falcke
- John D Wood
- Halifax Property
- Hamptons
- Douglas & Gordon
- Edwin Evans
- Robert Trindle & Co
- Vanstons
- Sullivan Thomas
- Kinleigh Folkard & Hayward
- Courteney
- Foxtons*

further details: see advertisers' index on p633

WEST HAMPSTEAD

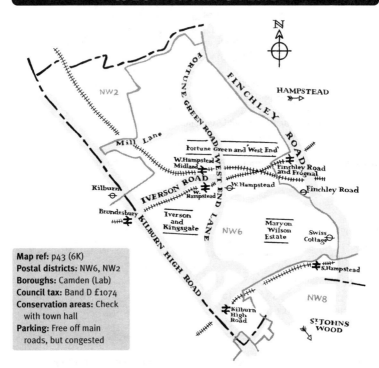

Map ref: p43 (6K)
Postal districts: NW6, NW2
Boroughs: Camden (Lab)
Council tax: Band D £1074
Conservation areas: Check
   with town hall
Parking: Free off main
   roads, but congested

West Hampstead has now got a commercial heart to go with its excellent travel links and ample supply of converted and mansion flats. The long-planned O2 complex, which opened in November, brings a giant Sainsbury's, multi-screen cinema and epic traffic jams to the heart of this quintessential flat-land area. This, plus the equally long-awaited Jubilee Line Extension which will enhance the communications, sent property prices up 15 per cent in 1998.

Victorian West Hampstead is not nearly as old, and certainly nothing like as grand, as its illustrious big sister up the hill to the E; but it has a style and location that attracts young professionals who live there until they can afford the inflated prices of Hampstead proper. The development of the area took place after the middle of the last century, much of it on the large tracts of land owned by the Maryon Wilson and Eyre estates which to this day hold the freehold of large areas of leasehold property. A few of the streets (on the E, or Hampstead side) were built with the relatively well-heeled middle classes in mind, but the bulk of the area was designed to cater for the needs of the Victorian age's growing lower-middle class. The result was large numbers of 2-storey, 2- and 3-bed terraced houses and semis. The area was also among the first to see the erection of those large blocks of purpose-built flats called mansion blocks, the word 'mansion' possibly designed to salve the blighted aspirations of those who could not afford houses. Paradoxically these flats, with their many, spacious and elegant rooms, are among the most popular properties today.

W   The change in the area over the last 30 years has been dramatic. Steeply rising prices and the spillover effect from Hampstead have proved an irresistible temptation

to the traditional inhabitants. From the 1960s on, properties were converted into flats at a brisk rate – perhaps as few as 10 per cent of the original houses remain in single occupation. That estimate maybe a bit low but nevertheless the rarest beast in West Hampstead is a 4-bedroom family house.

West Hampstead is very much a young person's area, conveniently located between the **Finchley Rd** and **Kilburn High Rd**, both good routes N and S. **West End Lane**, which runs through the centre of West Hampstead, has plenty of restaurants and bars, and the sort of shops that cater for the single and the transient – late-night grocers, futons, stripped-pine furniture. As well as the mobile young, a settled tranche of people with interesting jobs (the media, the stage, etc) give a more stable, community feel. Both groups agree that an old-fashioned, non-'theme' pub would enhance the area.

The spine of the area is **West End Lane**, which leads S into **Abbey Rd** and **St John's Wood Rd**; it has the tube and two train stations. Transport links from West Hampstead are excellent. In addition to these three stations, there are tube stations at Finchley Rd and Kilburn, and train stations at Finchley Rd, Frognal and Brondesbury nearby. There are scores of bus routes, too. Despite excellent public transport services, West Hampstead residents like to have a car. With houses converted into three or four flats (estate agents' boards abound) that means a lot of vehicles and parking in the streets is a nightmare. Being in Camden Borough, these car users face persecution: residents' parking permits are a certainty, and a clamp-down on school runs and commuting by car is threatened. The O2 centre, with its huge car park, has attracted yet more traffic, though it is hoped that the jams will ease once the initial excitement is over.

Fortune Green and 'West End'

West Hampstead is bisected diagonally by **West End Lane** leading, at the N end, into **Fortune Green Rd** which gives access to a whole group of roads rather marooned from the rest of the suburb by the Midland rail line. These include some uncharacteristically quiet and peaceful enclaves compared with the bustle and congestion of the rest of the area.

Behind the pleasant open space of Fortune Green itself is the Hampstead Cemetery, which casts a protective shadow over streets like **Gondar Gardens** and **Hillfield Rd**, one of the few corners in the area where the Victorian builders produced family houses of any size. Many have now been converted, but occasional 4- or 5-bedroom houses do still come onto the market.

W

Also interesting is the group of streets known as 'The Greeks' – not surprisingly since they include **Agamemnon Rd, Ajax Rd, Ulysses Rd** and **Achilles Rd**. These are still well supplied with modestly sized family houses, and is perhaps the best preserved corner of the entire suburb. Agents cite this as the 'best' part of West Hampstead.

Closer to **Finchley Rd** is the area once known as the West End (of Hampstead, presumably), now dominated by the large mansion blocks in **West End Lane, Mill Lane, Lyncroft Gardens, Cannon Hill** and **Honeybourne Rd**, including Buckingham Mansions, Marlborough Mansions, Cholmley Gardens, Yale Court and Harvard Court. Formerly rented accommodation, they are all now owner-occupied, and the large flats are very popular. **Cannon Hill** also has some well-regarded Edwardian blocks; flats go for upwards of £350,000 for 3/4-bedrooms.

The smartest streets in West Hampstead are E of **West End Lane: Alvanley Gardens** with its large detached houses grandly overlooking the grounds of Hampstead Cricket Club in **Lymington Rd**, and the attractive semis of **Crediton Hill**. A 3-storey Victorian house in **Kylemore Rd** was recently on the market for £420,000, while a 5-bed house in **Alvanley Gardens** was £995,000.

The biggest thing to hit West Hampstead for years is the huge new O2 scheme built on disused railway land all the way from **Finchley Rd** at the Hampstead end to **West End Lane** near West Hampstead tube station. As well as the giant Sainsbury's, car park and multiplex cinema there are offices, 10 bars and restaurants, a health club and a vast bookshop.

South of **Mill Lane** (whose wine bar, antique shops and the like reflect to some extent the inhabitants of the area) are residential streets such as **Sumatra Rd, Broomsleigh St, Solent Rd, Narcissus Rd** and **Pandora Rd** – all typical of the 2- and 3-storey terraces which West Hampstead has to offer. Most of these houses have been split into flats: it is here that first-time buyers can gain a foothold in the area with 2-bed flats starting at around £165,000. Good 3-bed ones on long leases command £220,000-plus. There is also an interesting enclave of streets, including **Menelik Rd, Somali Rd** and **Asmara Rd**, in the NW2 corner of the area, which are close to the open spaces of Fortune Green.

Iverson and Kingsgate

This is the triangle between the Midland railway line to the N, **West End Lane** and **Kilburn High Rd**. Towards the N, busy **Iverson Rd** leads past light industrial areas and large new council estates to the slightly less smart area of **Maygrove Rd, Loveridge Rd** and **Fordwych Rd**, where the large number of builders' skips which appear there regularly show that here, too, things are constantly on the move.

Further S, **Sherriff Rd** and **Hemstal Rd** lead from **West End Lane** to the densely packed streets around **Kingsgate Rd**. These are mainly 2-storey small terraced houses, and if there is a less expensive part of the area, this is it. Here the population is less affluent than elsewhere, with a number of council estates. There are, however, pleasant corners and bargains to be found, both in terms of flats and small houses, and **Lowfield, Kylemore, Gladys** and **Hilltop Rds** are well worth looking at. Homes in this corner have the advantage of useful shopping on **Kilburn High Rd**.

The southernmost strip of the area, between a railway line and **Boundary Rd**, is almost completely dominated by very large council blocks, including the Abbey Estate and the extraordinary 1,000-ft long concrete sweep of Camden's Alexandra Rd Estate in **Rowley Way**.

The Maryon Wilson estate/South Hampstead

The area bounded by **Broadhurst Gardens, Finchley Rd, Belsize Rd** and **Priory Rd** was built between 1874 and the late-1890s, and contains some of the most attractive, most popular and most expensive properties in West Hampstead (sometimes, however, this patch is called South Hampstead). They are close not only to the transport and considerable shopping facilities of **West End Lane** but also to the major shopping centre in **Finchley Rd** – with a large Waitrose supermarket and the Habitat furniture and household goods store.

Particularly attractive, in streets such as **Canfield Gardens**, **Compayne Gardens** and **Fairfield Gardens,** are the red-brick mansion blocks, often with endearing turrets on the corner properties, and large communal gardens. Some of the best of these properties are owned by the pioneering Fairhazel Housing Cooperative (the first of its kind) and are not available on the open market.

But there are other elegant roads, including **Broadhurst Gardens**, **Greencroft Gardens, Aberdare Gardens, Cleve Road** and **Goldhurst Terrace**, where there is a brisk trade in both purpose-built and converted flats, including some luxurious recent conversions. Here and there you might even find the odd large house in single occupation for sale – but you would have to move very fast (and have a capacious chequebook) in order to beat would-be developers to the purchase. There has been talk for a few years of making this tract a conservation area, but still no decision.

Transport	Tubes: West Hampstead, Kilburn (zone 2, Jubilee); Finchley Rd (zone 2, Jubilee, Metropolitan). From West Hampstead: Oxford Circus 15 min (1 change), City 30 min (1 change), Heathrow 60 min (1 change). Trains: West Hampstead (King's Cross 10 min and N London Line/Silverlink).
Convenient for	Hampstead Heath, West End, M1/A1 to the North. Miles from centre: 4.
Schools	Local Authority: St George's RC, Hampstead Comprehensive, Quintin Kynaston Comprehensive.

SALES

Flats	S	1B	2B	3B	4B	5B
Average prices	55–80	80–130	110–190	150–300	200–350+	—
Houses	2B	3B	4B	5B	6/7B	8B
Average prices	220–350	250–375	300–450	300+–500+	—	—

RENTAL

Flats	S	1B	2B	3B	4B	5B
Average prices	550–800	730–1200	850–1300+	1000–1800+	1500–2500	—
Houses	2B	3B	4B	5B	6/7B	8B
Average prices	1000–1650	1300–1800+	1600–2500	2100–3000	—	—

The properties	Victorian terraced homes, most of which now converted to flats. A few surviving family houses. Lots of big mansion flats, some almost St John's Wood-smart, some almost Kilburn-scruffy.
The market	Rapid turnover of flat-buyers, who use area as a staging-post before moving on to family homes. Conversions vary in quality. Mansion flats can be a better bet, but check service charges and leases. Local searches: 2 weeks.

Among those estate agents active in this area are:

- Kinleigh Folkard & Hayward
- Greene & Co
- Brian Lack & Co
- Bairstow Eves
- Cedar Estates
- Anscombe & Ringland *
- Harris & Co
- Parkheath Estates
- Paramount
- Foxtons *
- Goldschmidt & Howland

* *further details: see advertisers' index on p633*

WEST NORWOOD, NORBURY AND GIPSY HILL

Map ref: p110 (4C)
Postal districts: SE19, SE27
Boroughs: Croydon (Lab),
  Lambeth (Lab), Southwark
  (Lab)
Council tax: Band D Croydon
  £692, Lambeth £647,
  Southwark £786
Conservation areas: Several,
  check with town hall
Parking: Free

The South London suburbs of Norwood and Gipsy Hill lie on the slopes to the W of Crystal Palace. Clues to the area's past are found in its names: Norwood is the old North Wood, which covered the hills to the Thames basin. Tracts survive to this day, most notably the Lawns woodland area and Sydenham Hill woods. Gypsies, who gave Gipsy Hill its name, considered the woods their own until forced out by the 19th-century enclosure acts. A glance at the map shows the unusually large amount of green pockets, parks and playing-fields in this corner, even without the vast Crystal Palace Park that crowns the heights.

Ambitious plans in the early 19th century to establish a Regency-style spa town on Beulah Hill never materialized. The spa itself quickly failed thanks to a change in fashion, with the promotion of sea water as the latest remedy. Later, the arrival of the illustrious Crystal Palace gave the area a taste of prosperity. It was short-lived: 80 years on the towering edifice burnt to the ground, and locals still vividly recall the spectacle of that 1936 night. Today the impressive facilities of the National Sports Centre are the star local attraction, and a review aimed at maintaining it as a national centre for excellence and as a local amenity is under way. Plans for the palace itself – today an empty concrete plinth – to rise again as a lookalike hotel have hung fire for a decade: there's a major row in progress, detailed in the Crystal Palace chapter.

W

The area has plenty of attractions for home-buyers, with a wide range of flats and houses, and fast rail links to Central London. House-hunters spill over from pricier Dulwich and Streatham; first-time buyers are attracted by the many flat conversions in large Victorian houses. When looking for homes here, it is worth bearing in mind that, along with the choice of roads and types of property comes the choice of boroughs – Lambeth to the N or Croydon to the S, while Bromley covers a corner.

The high land affords some spectacular views of London and outlying areas – most rewarding at sunrise and dusk. Larger properties are usually found on the higher ground but there are also some sensitive council-built developments, chiefly on **Central Hill**.

The northernmost, and most inner-London, neighbourhood is West Norwood, with a shopping street running N towards Tulse Hill, a rail station and the unusual combination of church and cemetery at its urban centre. Its outer reaches, W towards neighbouring Streatham and E towards Dulwich, are more popular.

Gipsy Hill, on the W side of the commanding Crystal Palace heights, has some attractive Georgian properties and startling views of the City. Its centre, near the **South Croxted Rd** and Dulwich Wood Park roundabout, has an attractive character largely untypical of the area. It too has a rail station. The SE19 area as a whole is particularly suitable for families, with some good state schools and reasonably priced 3-bedroom houses.

Upper Norwood is in Croydon Borough: as high as its name implies. The houses slope on S and W towards Norbury, which is a southern outlier of Streatham, and Thornton Heath, like Norbury with a station, borders on Croydon.

Upper Norwood

The N end of **Beulah Hill** starts modestly with a 1930s parade of shops, then a large church and St Joseph's College. Victorian semis occupy the left side, '60s town-houses the right. As the road ascends to leafier heights, these give way to large 1930s semis and detached homes, some in mock-Tudor style. Interesting buildings make an appearance, like No 17, an 1860 villa, and there's opportunity for sweeping views. St Valery is an impressive Victorian mansion with full-height bay windows. Set away from the road on the left are walled-off '60s town-house developments. On the right, Beulah Spa pub. More large, detached '30s Tudor-timber style and Victorian properties complete the road. Some homes here (and in **Woodfield Close**) can command high prices. On **Beulah Hill** itself, Dickens Wood, eight new detached houses luxuriating in a 2.4-acre site have been selling well for developers Countryside at prices up to £550,000.

Spa Hill, running S from **Beulah Hill**, fringes The Lawns, which surviving pocket of woodland was the site of the ill-fated spa. A cottage-style lodge by Decimus Burton also survives, as does a later 1864 one. Detached inter-war houses with garages climb **Spa Hill**.

Early 19th-century All Saints, with rural churchyard, stands on the corner of **Beulah Hill** and **Church Rd**. By night the spire, which before the advent of the nearby TV masts dominated the skyline, is illuminated. **Church Rd** has some 1930s semis, council blocks, Victorian red-brick mansions and a school. Also a recent development: **Old Vicarage Gardens**, a luxury-level enclave of 1- and 2-bedroom retirement apartments in garden setting, is on the right. Some of the houses date from the early 19th century; the Victorian stucco of the 19th-century Queen's Hotel has gained a modern annexe. The road continues on past the **Westow Hill** 'Triangle' as far as Crystal Palace (see chapter for more details).

Roads off to the N of **Beulah Hill** are mainly 1930s residential. (There's an absence of shops that go to make a community.) **Hermitage Rd** has 1930s semis and council houses, also a small hospital. Larger '30s semis in **Eversley Rd** front a pleasant green. **Ryefield Rd** has recent town-houses. **Harold Rd** gives its name to a conservation area that includes many fine late-19th-century houses. This takes in **Bedwardine Rd**, part of **Central Hill, Gatestone Rd, South Vale** – whose 1860s houses are about the area's oldest – **Vermont Rd** and the recreation ground. The council (in this case Croydon) has issued guidelines for home-owners and would-be developers here: demolition of period buildings, or hiving off large gardens, will not meet with approval.

Central Hill has Norwood Park and the imposing Gothic-style Fidelis convent. Further up the hill there's a post-war council estate as well as recent terraced townhouses. Also large Victorian houses – multiple occupancy. Roads to the S such as **Essex Grove** and **Gatestone Rd** slope down attractively with Victorian semis. Victorian detached and semis overlook the vast, but carefully crafted, hillside Central Hill Estate to the N. Next to the council estate is Gipsy Hill police station.

Gipsy Hill

Proximity to the **Westow Hill** 'Triangle' with its shops and amenities (see Crystal Palace) is a bonus for **Gipsy Hill**, a popular neighbourhood that tumbles attractively down the slopes from the road of the same name. Some Georgiana survives here, and even humdrum homes are made special if they share the wonderfully long views. It borders West Dulwich to the N, and usefully its situation is in zone 3. Victorian and Edwardian properties have led the long-awaited price recovery after the early '90s recession. It is not peppered with new developments: developers have a hard time competing with the room sizes and lower service charges that period conversions offer. Conversion prices have risen more than purpose-built; 2-bed more than 1-bed. Large single homes are hunted out by professional couples, often wanting space either to work from home or to keep a nanny if they commute in to town.

There's a magnificent view of London, with City skyscrapers prominent, from **Gipsy Hill**, the road. Highlights of this busy road are the white stuccoed buildings and redbrick Victorian mansions. Roads leading off such as **Camden Hill Rd** and **Highland Rd** have period houses. Christ Church has been happily restored in the past few years. Past the station is a small green.

The Paxton pub, shops, restaurants and a wine bar make an attractive start to **Gipsy Rd**. Some renovation and dereliction characterize this gentle rising road of varied Victorian properties, which ends with council-built estates. Near Kingswood Primary School is **Salters Hill** – a road of council homes with occasional Victoriana, which overlooks Norwood Park. The large-scale Victorian villas to be found in Gipsy Hill yield some serious-sized flats: the wide-eaved, 3-storey houses in (aptly) **Victoria Crescent**, for example.

West Norwood

Between Streatham and West Dulwich, West Norwood has good bus as well as train links to Brixton (with its Victoria line tube) and the West End.

On the West Dulwich border, tree-lined **South Croxted Rd** has Victorian semis, '60s town-houses and some council estates. There's a shopping area on the junction with **Park Hall Rd**. This neighbourhood saw much change in the '80s as developers and new residents moved into the area.

At the centre of the neighbourhood, **Norwood Rd**, also called **The Broadway**, is Victorian red-brick. The road forks by St Luke's Church with its Corinthian six-column portico. There's a modern library next to the 39-acre West Norwood Cemetery of 1836.

In the cosmopolitan streets around West Norwood station (Victoria 18 min) good-quality Victorian houses can be found at reasonable prices. The E fork off **Norwood Rd** becomes **Norwood High St** which, frequently congested with traffic, has few shops

W

and is low-rise. **Dunelm Grove** is an attractive, modern cottage-style council estate. **Elder Rd**, the continuation of the **High St**, starts off with ugly grey council blocks but improves. There are 1930s semis with nicely tended gardens. **Eylewood Rd** and **Norwood Park Rd** have '30s terraces and semis respectively. There's a concentration of high-rise council blocks up by **Bentons Rise** and **Aubyn Hill**. Facing Norwood Park (tennis courts) in **Elder Rd**, what was the House of Industry for the Infant Poor is now flats. Behind this splendid piece of Georgiana Portland Homes have also added mewsy flats and houses in **Elderwood Place**. Next door is Norwood School. **Knights Hill**, which runs S from West Norwood station, is Victorian with some dilapidation. Also the modern Lambeth College and a bus garage nearby.

Popular **Lancaster Avenue**, off **Norwood Rd**, has family-owned Victorian houses with pleasant front gardens. Rosemead Mixed Preparatory School is at the West Dulwich end. **Hawkley Gardens** has town-house terraces. **Lavengrove** and **Tulsmere Rds** have turn-of-the-century bay-fronted terraces. **Chatsworth Way** is mainly Victorian and has a modern church with a needle-like spire. **Idmiston Rd** has Victorian houses with fancy wrought-iron balconies. The turreted red-brick Barston Towers graces the corner with **Barston Rd**. The road ends modestly with Victorian terraces. **Chancellor Grove** is similar. **Rosendale Rd**, with large Victorian bay-fronted semis, is broad and tree-lined S of **Thurlow Park Rd** – the South Circular. A parade of shops and an unattractive council block are other features. Continuing after **Park Hall Rd** are tall bay-fronted balconied Victorian properties, some flat conversions.

Tritton Rd has Victorian semis. On the corner with **Martell Rd** is Lambeth Industrial Enterprises. Also in **Martell Rd** is the ugly '30s white Park Hall Rd Trading Estate building. There are usually flats to be found in the larger Victorian semis. The high wall and cast-iron railings of the cemetery occupy the S of **Robson Rd** to West Norwood, but the cottage Victorian terraces on the N side are, say agents, popular.

West of **Norwood Rd**, council houses and blocks start **York Hill**. **Knollys Rd**, 1930s terraces, Victorian and recent blocks, has been the scene of much renovation. **Pyrmont Grove** and **Royal Circus** have quite pleasant Victorian terraces. The entrance to a recent new development is in **Lansdowne Hill**. **Broxholm Rd** and **Glennie Rd** are terraced – turn-of-century and '30s. Larger properties are found at the higher points of these hill roads. **Canterbury Grove** has large Victorian and turn-of-century semis; also council, 1930s, Victorian and recent terraces. Thirties semis are found in **Uffington Rd** and **Rockhampton Rd**. **Thurlestone Rd** and **Wolfington Rd** are Victorian/turn-of-the-century. **St Julian's Farm Rd** goes from 1930s semis and Victorian/turn-of-the-century to smaller properties lower down – a very popular street, due in part to its proximity to a good primary school.

Quiet pre-war suburbia includes **Lamberhurst Rd** (bay-fronted semis), **Cheviot Rd** and **Greenhurst Rd** (terraces), and **Roxburgh Rd** (semis). Near the **Knights Hill** end, **Lakeview Rd** and **Truslove Rd** are council homes.

Leigham Court Rd on the Streatham borders has 1930s mansion blocks and private blocks of flats – built high for the views, also '30s semis. Groveside Homes was responsible for the sympathetic development of luxury studio, 1-bed apartments, and 2-bed town-houses. St Julian's Primary School features, too. Victorian detached houses and imposing red-brick mansions precede Fern Lodge council estate, just improved, and a weathered '30s block before ending at **Streatham Common N**.

Norbury

The rise in prices in this neighbourhood which began in '97 has continued through '98. More families are moving into Norbury, particularly from areas like Streatham and Tooting. Norbury is seen as more up-market than Thornton Heath. Ex-council property, mainly houses, has become increasingly available around here.

London Rd's dull aspect is emphasized by the Victoriana. Shopping is unexciting, but provides most things necessary for day-to-day living. Large offices, including the headquarters of Wates, signal the approach to Croydon. Most of the area was developed between the wars, and roads such as **Ardfern Avenue, Melrose Avenue, Ederline Avenue** and **Dunbar Avenue** set the tone. Property to the E of **London Rd** is more sought-after than that in the streets towards the Mitcham border. **Gibsons Hill, Norbury Hill** and **Virginia Rd** are of the same period. That they look to the wooded areas of Beulah Hill helps to relieve the monotony. **Kensington Avenue** also has a post-war council estate. To the W of **London Rd,** the Pollards Hill area is attractive suburbia – neat greens and trimmed hedges. Detached 1930s houses encircle the small common at the summit – views of outer London, the old power station chimneys that now mark Ikea's home furnishing temple, and housing estates. 1997 saw the conversion of the area's gem: Norwood Grove Mansion stands amid parkland off **Gibsons Hill** on the site of a Charles II hunting box. Its hilltop views are shared by three apartments which reached the market at £100–145,000.

Croydon Borders: Thornton Heath

In this area W of South Norwood, first-time buyers find affordable purpose-built and conversion flats; families are attracted by a range of late-Victorian and Edwardian terraces and inter-war semis. This area has yet, however, to attract much attention from outsiders.

Suburban Thornton Heath is very much a 19th-century creation spurred on by the arrival of the railway. Good rail links to town and proximity to Croydon continue as chief attractions. The more expensive properties are found in the upper reaches towards Norbury – in roads such as **Florida, Maryland, Georgia** and **Carolina.**

Popular, too, are the 3-bed properties in and around quiet **Winterbourne Rd** – 1930s bay-fronted terraces. Closeness to local schools and shopping facilities in **London Rd** are advantages here. Larger and older properties are found in **Warwick Rd.** Flat-hunters should concentrate on **Mersham, Moffat, Hythe, St Paul's** and **Liverpool Rds** – mostly 1- or 2-beds – while families may have better luck in the area towards Mitcham. Busy **London Rd** and **Brigstock Rd** are worth investigation – especially for conversions. The Mayday Hospital dominates the lower half of **London Rd.**

The less popular roads S of the **High St** (**Ecclesbourne Rd, Kynaston Avenue, Bensham Lane**) comprise former council houses and also older-style terraces. There is a development of 1- and 2-bed retirement apartments in **Bensham Lane.**

Roads around the Crystal Palace Football Ground in **Whitehorse Lane** are best avoided – although, more usefully, there's a large Sainsbury's superstore here too. Home sales were not helped by the club's rise to the Premier Division. Fans may arrive virtually every Saturday of the football season. St Cuthberts, between **Whitehorse Lane** and **Ross Rd**, is a 1988/89 Lovell development of flats and town-houses.

Transport	Trains: West Norwood, Gipsy Hill and Norbury to Victoria; West Norwood and Gipsy Hill to London Bridge.
Convenient for	Crystal Palace Park, National Sports Centre. Routes to the South. Miles from centre: 5.5.
Schools	Local Authority: Sylvan City Technical College, Stanley Tech, Selhurst High (b), Westwood Girls High. Grant-maintained: St Joseph's College RC (b), Norbury Manor (g), Virgo Fidelis RC (g).

SALES

Flats	S	1B	2B	3B	4B	5B
Average prices	–	45–60	55–90	80–100	–	–
Houses	2B	3B	4B	5B	6/7B	8B
Average prices	85–130	90–150+	130–350	200+	→	→

RENTAL

Flats	S	1B	2B	3B	4B	5B
Average prices	400–450	450–600	600+	800–900	–	–
Houses	2B	3B	4B	5B	6/7B	8B
Average prices	700	900–1000	→1100	→1200	–	–

The properties   Popular Victorian/Edwardian homes are the staple in this area on the slopes of Crystal Palace. Its larger Victorian terraces have become flats, and there are plenty of family homes with good gardens: Victorian, semis, '60s town-houses, '30s Tudor. On Gipsy Hill, mansion and p/b flats get long views over the houses. Upper Norwood has mainly flats, while Thornton Heath/S Norwood is good hunting-ground for smaller houses at bargain prices.

The market   Renewed interest here as prices rose even more sharply last year in areas further into town. First-time buyers find relatively inexpensive flats, good rail links to town, while families come in search of more home for their money. Local searches: Croydon 2 weeks, Lambeth 2 weeks, Southwark 2 weeks.

Among those estate agents active in this area are:
- Galloways
- G A Property
- Harvey & Wheeler
- Volker & Volker
- Mann & Co
- Wates
- Firmstones
- Conrad Fox
- Foxtons*
- Halifax Property
- Winkworth*
- Cooper Giles
- Home Sellers
- Stapleton Lang
- Mitchells
- Gales
- Anscombe & Ringland*

further details: see advertisers' index on p633

W

WILLESDEN AND BRONDESBURY PARK

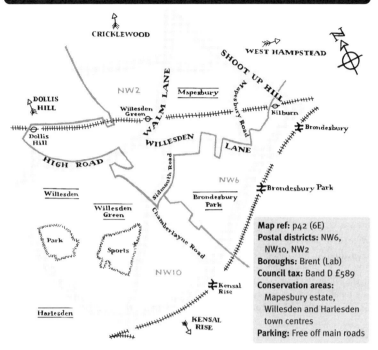

CRICKLEWOOD

WEST HAMPSTEAD

SHOOT UP HILL

NW2

WALM LANE

Mapesbury

DOLLIS HILL

Willesden Green

Kilburn

Dollis Hill

Brondesbury

WILLESDEN LANE

HIGH ROAD

Sidmouth Road

NW6

Brondesbury Park

Willesden

Brondesbury Park

Willesden Green

Chamberlayne Road

Park

Sports

NW10

Kensal Rise

Harlesden

KENSAL RISE

Map ref: p42 (6E)
Postal districts: NW6, NW10, NW2
Boroughs: Brent (Lab)
Council tax: Band D £589
Conservation areas: Mapesbury estate, Willesden and Harlesden town centres
Parking: Free off main roads

Willesden is the old lady of NW London suburbs, a faded beauty who is still recovering from the indignity suffered in 1965 when she was amalgamated with Wembley to form the Borough of Brent — notorious in the '80s for its 'loony-left' council, now in somewhat calmer waters under 'New' Labour.

However, her bone structure is good, and her horizons are broadening: the nearest major station is Paddington – from whence Heathrow is now reached in 15 min – and she's on the Jubilee line: already a good route, and soon to waft her inhabitants direct to Westminster, Canary Wharf and even The Dome. Some of the neighbours are nice, too; she's a stone's throw from West Hampstead.

Pockets of tree-lined Willesden are still elegant, and neighbouring Brondesbury Park is a *very* acceptable address: indeed a large but unreconstructed house here went at auction at the end of last year for half a million. Willesden and Brondesbury Park cover three postal districts. In order of desirability, NW6 is the most prestigious and covers Brondesbury Park; then comes NW2 and the part of Willesden towards Cricklewood and Dollis Hill; and finally NW10 where the area merges with less-classy Harlesden and Neasden. A number of railway lines carve up the area; prices can differ considerably from one end of a road to the other, from one side to the other. Grand houses stand in close contrast to council blocks; most properties are turn-of-the-century or 1930s. The Mapesbury estate and Brondesbury Park in particular attract buyers who would until recently have tried for better-established areas close by, such as West Hampstead and Maida Vale.

When it comes to amenities Willesden has plenty to offer. A huge library complex with public halls, cinema, a café-bar and a bookshop was opened in 1989 on the

W

corner of **Willesden High Rd** and **Grange Rd**; there is even talk of squeezing in the borough's local history museum. Willesden Sports Centre, fronting **All Souls Avenue**, has swimming pools, an impressive sportsground, well-maintained children's play-area and open space to wander in.

The shops, centred around **Willesden High Rd**, are good; they tend to be local, rather than of the big name variety (though there is a Somerfield supermarket) but most of them are small and specialized, where shopkeepers remember a regular face, and in many cases open late in the evening. Amid the hardware and grocers' shops are a number of restaurants catering for the younger inhabitants who dwell in the many flat conversions around Willesden Green – among them a trendy tapas bar and one of the country's first vegetarian Indian restaurants, popular with minor celebrities, the odd Hollywood star and the area's MP: will Willesden supply London's first mayor? Ken Livingstone certainly hopes so.

Willesden

Willesden was given to the Dean and Chapter of St Paul's Cathedral by King Athelstan in 938 – hence names like **Chapter Rd**. A visit to the local archive, in **Olive Rd**, will furnish more details. The area is more compact than sprawling Willesden Green; Church End is to the W; **Robson Avenue**, falling between Roundwood Park and Willesden Sports Centre, marks the E divide with Willesden Green, and the Jubilee line is at the top. Much is green, open space: Roundwood Park, schools/sports fields – and the expanse of the New and Jewish Cemeteries. The part of **Willesden High Rd** in the Willesden area is rather shabbier than the section towards Willesden Green, but the small shops are varied. Homes include the occasional small development such as the 1-bed flats of Beacon Lodge in **Beaconsfield Rd**: these sell for around £70,000.

Willesden Green and Mapesbury

Willesden Green used to be a place where well-established Jewish families lived until they moved to leafy suburbs such as Wembley and Stanmore. In recent years the ethnic and religious make-up has broadened, and parts became conversion territory in the '80s, with houses sub-divided into flats. Houses tend to be larger in Willesden Green than in Willesden, and prices have increased steadily here according to the estate agents whose boards make Willesden red, yellow and pink as well as Green. The general rule of thumb is that the closer you are to Willesden Green station (Jubilee line), the better – although the best area, the Mapesbury estate which boasts large, half a million pound-plus houses, breaks this rule.

The Mapesbury estate consists of the roads in the triangle formed by **Chichele Rd/Walm Lane**, the A5 (known at this point as **Shoot Up Hill**) and **Willesden Lane** (though note that the conservation area is slightly smaller – from **Anson Rd** to the tube line – while the active residents' association counts in roads across **Walm Lane** as far as **Riffel Rd**). This is the West Hampstead overspill, and residents would love Kilburn tube re-named – at least as North Kilburn, if not Mapesbury. **Mapesbury Rd**, **Dartmouth Rd**, **Teignmouth Rd** and **Chatsworth Rd** are names to look out for if you want a well-located conversion in a stylish Victorian property.

The '80s mania for splitting houses into flats fell out of favour with planners; the fashionable '90s equivalent, the conversion of redundant commercial or industrial buildings, is evidenced by Jubilee Heights, on **Shoot Up Hill**, at the SE border of the Mapesbury estate. Here Dari Construction last year converted Telephone House into 77 flats with all the luxurious accessories: swimming pool, gym, Jacuzzi and 24hr porterage. These ranged from 1-bed at £99,000 up to 3-bed, 2-baths apartments at £250,000; this January the remaining 2-bed were being marketed at £185,000; annual service charges run at £1,400. Behind Jubilee Heights in **Exeter Rd**, another new development is adding 30 new homes to the neighbourhood's stock: Cedar Lodge's 2-bed, 2-bath town-houses are being marketed this spring at £215–235,000. On the southern borders, in **Cavendish Rd**, Wilcon Homes are putting the finishing touches to another big scheme: four blocks of nine flats; the 1- and 2-bed flats of Chatsworth Court are £105–135,000. Cavendish runs by the tracks, but has the advantage of Brondesbury train station at the far end.

Out of the estate, on the other side of **Walm Lane**, **St Paul's Avenue** and **Blenheim Gardens** are also popular with flat-hunters thanks to adjacent Willesden Green tube. On **Walm Lane**, Rutland Park Mansions – once known as the biggest squat in London – was refurbished three years ago by Paddington Churches Housing Association as flats. On the corner of **Walm** and **Willesden Lanes**, Rialto have built Mapes Hill Place, a development of flats and town-houses which now run from £85,000 for the 1- and 2-bed flats, and from £115,000 for the 2-bed town-houses.

Other prestige roads in Willesden Green are found S of **Willesden High Rd** in the Dobree estate, built in the 1930s: **Dobree Avenue**, **Bryan Avenue**, **Rowdon Avenue**, **Alexander Avenue** and **Peter Avenue**. The estate did not, alas, prove lucky for its builders: two brothers who went bankrupt and were forced to sell off the commodious homes they had created as a job lot. It is still possible to buy undone-up homes here, and prices vary with the condition. An average 3-bed semi would cost around £200,000, while a top-of-the-range 4-bedroom detached would fetch £350,000; a 5-bedroom house with 2 bathrooms in good condition could command £450,000.

The 'royal roads', which lie N of **Willesden High Rd**, are also popular and should satisfy a tighter budget; roads like **Sandringham Rd**, **Balmoral Rd** and **Windsor Rd** fall between Dollis Hill and Willesden Green tube stations. A 3-bed semi needing work could be had here last December for £135,000. Prices vary a good deal hereabouts. A 2-bedroomed flat could cost £160,000 on the Mapesbury estate, while £70–90,000 could buy a 2-bed flat on the 'wrong side' – ie, backing onto the tracks – in **Chapter Rd**. To the N, Willesden Green becomes Cricklewood, and prices go down again.

All Souls Avenue (the Oxford college was a major landowner in the area) runs N-S through Willesden Green and has small semi-detached houses. At the N end lies Clarendon Court, a big '30s block on the corner of **Chamberlayne Rd** and **Sidmouth Rd**. A large 3-bed flat here would cost around £150,000, service charges on the high side and lease-lengths on the low side notwithstanding. **Sidmouth Rd** itself is a busy road, home of the South Hampstead club for bowls and tennis.

Spreading down towards Kensal Rise, the triangular grid of peaceful, orderly roads that fans out between **All Souls Avenue** and **Chamberlayne Rd** is disturbed by **Chelmsford Square**, a charming oval of semi-detached homes around tennis courts. More modest, pretty streets are to be found in this direction.

Willesden Lane, a main thoroughfare connecting Willesden and Kilburn, has a wide variety of purpose-built blocks, among them Marlow, Belvedere, Beechworth, Bramerton and Hadleigh Courts – the last consisting of eight flats built in 1987. Again agents warn of high service charges – c. £2,000 in some blocks – but the enticement of secure parking is irresistible to many. Down towards the **Willesden High Rd** end, Paddington Churches Housing Association have contributed Sheil Court, an attractive development of flats. The Willesdenites are spiritual people: a Hindu temple and a Jewish school are to be found on the Lane, while **Walm Lane** has a church, a synagogue and a mosque, and **Chichele Rd** an Islamic youth centre. The Willesden Registry Office is also in **Willesden Lane**: it sees a great variety of marriages.

Brondesbury Park

Brondesbury Park is more exclusive than Willesden Green. Like Willesden Green, the district used to be very Jewish; both areas have witnessed a move away. The population is now far more mixed. Houses date from the 1930s or later; the roads are wide and tree-lined, and parking is not as problematic as in West Hampstead and Swiss Cottage. Communications are good, the A5 and Kilburn tube (Jubilee line) providing access to the West End.

Manor House Drive, off **Brondesbury Park**, is a beautiful crescent, the best road in the area. Many of its detached houses are double-fronted, all have front and back gardens, many with security gates . . . a snip, say agents, at £630,000-plus. Prices here now match the '80s boom high. Six-bedroom properties complete with swimming pools along **Christchurch Avenue** and **The Avenue** can now expect to sell for at least £750,000, and a 5-bedroomed unmodernized Christchurch house with vacant possession sold for half a million at auction last November. Agents claim that these are mostly owned by foreign governments and are used by diplomats from areas as far-flung as China and Nigeria. **Christchurch Avenue**, **Cavendish Rd** and **The Avenue** also have very attractive conversions in large Victorian houses. **Aylestone Avenue** is a wide tree-lined street with both detached and semi-detached family houses. Christ Church itself became flats (and a small chapel) in the '80s in an imaginative conversion by Berkeley House: expect to pay c. £200,000 for a 2-bedroom apartment here, if one comes up for sale.

Brondesbury Park (the road) has seen changes; some of the large detached houses here have been converted into flats and purpose-built blocks have been built. One such is Elstow Grange where a 2-bed flat might cost £180,000. Also in **Brondesbury Park** is one of the most substantial developments in the area: the Honeyman Close scheme of 40-odd town-houses and a leisure complex. The 4-bedroom, 2-bathroom houses are decorated in the spirit of the Arts and Crafts designer Charles Rennie Mackintosh, and have been known to reach £350,000. At the end of the road towards **Willesden High Rd** the Heathfield Squash Club, next to a synagogue, was recently redeveloped as 1- and 2-bedroom housing association retirement homes. On the corner of **Brondesbury Park** and **Coverdale Rd**, Wates has put up Kingsbridge and Westwood Courts, two blocks of 2-bed flats. A third was completed last summer – with all the flats (c. £143,000) already sold in advance.

Parts of Brondesbury Park are very expensive, but a house with a garden may still be bought for the sort of money that buys a flat in Maida Vale.

Harlesden

Harlesden was once avoided and the Craven Park estate feared as a blight on resell. But things are gradually changing for the better. Harlesden has some lovely houses, Edwardian and Victorian, most with their original features intact. With an improved Bakerloo line service, now running every 20 min beyond Queen's Park to Harrow and Wealdstone with a full service at peak times, the area's potential is becoming evident. The town centre has been improved with funds supplied by a government regeneration fund and new people are moving in.

The better Harlesden roads are **Springwell Avenue**, **Harlesden Gardens**, **Ancona Rd** and **Cholmondeley Avenue**, and parts are described by agents as 'Kensal Rise Borders' to entice Ladbrook Grove trendies. Harlesden prices are the lowest in this area, but have risen steadily. A 2-bed purpose-built flat in **Ancona Rd**, bought for £55,000 three years ago, was worth £90,000 last year but could now ask for over £100,000. A Fairview scheme of studio and 1-bed flats in **Trenmar Gardens** that proved popular at prices of £65,000 a year ago have already risen to c. £75,000.

Brent Council hopes to attract more City workers and commuters to the area with a £2 million revamp of the run-down Willesden Junction train station, in partnership with Railtrack and Silverlink. Work will start this year, and will also improve access to the bus terminal. The council's more ambitious dreams envisage the Junction becoming a major staging-post on an outer-London rail service that would see many more trains on the route down through Olympia to Clapham Junction, and could be extended round to East London. This would be helped by a proposed new station to serve the major West London shopping centre planned near the BBC's White City HQ at Shepherd's Bush . . . Watch this space.

Transport	Tubes: Willesden Green, Kilburn, Dollis Hill (zones 2/3, Jubilee). From Willesden Green: Oxford Circus 25 min (1 change), City 35 min (1 change), Heathrow 1 hr 10 min (1 change). Trains: Brondesbury, Brondesbury Park, Kensal Rise (N London Line/Silverlink).
Convenient for	North Circular and Edgware Rds. Miles from centre: 5.
Schools	Brent Education Authority: Willesden High, Cardinal Hinsley RC (b), Convent of Jesus & Mary Language College (g), Private: N W London Jewish.

SALES

Flats	S	1B	2B	3B	4B	5B
Average prices	45–70	60–110	80–125+	90–200+	—	—
Houses	2B	3B	4B	5B	6/7B	8B
Average prices	90–110	130–240	200–500	250–500+	—	—

RENTAL

Flats	S	1B	2B	3B	4B	5B
Average prices	550–700	600–900	850–1000	1000–1500	—	—
Houses	2B	3B	4B	5B	6/7B	8B
Average prices	1000	1300–1500	1500–1700	2000	—	—

The properties	Large blocks of flats, late-Victorian villas, plus many streets of terraced homes and later semis. Some larger 20th-century homes. Brondesbury Park has some big, imposing late-Victorian houses.
The market	Willesden Green's fast tube attracts young flat-buyers. Elsewhere still a family neighbourhood – not to mention a celebrity one: £800,000-plus mansions in best roads. Developers turn redundant Telecom offices into marbled and mahoganied flats. Local searches: Camden 2 weeks, Westminster 2 days.

Among those estate agents active in this area are:
- Dunlop & Co
- Ellis & Co
- Woolwich
- Simon Lewis & Co
- Gladstones
- Chattin Estates
- Camerons Stiff
- Bairstow Eves
- Rainbow Reid
- Beavers

W

WIMBLEDON, RAYNES PARK AND MERTON PARK

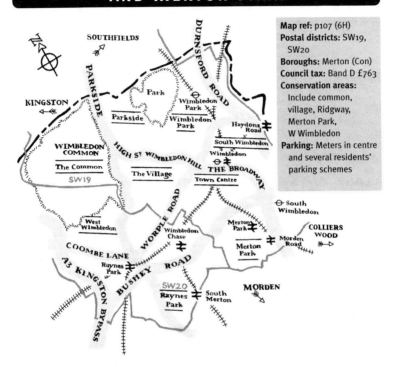

Map ref: p107 (6H)
Postal districts: SW19, SW20
Boroughs: Merton (Con)
Council tax: Band D £763
Conservation areas:
    Include common,
    village, Ridgway,
    Merton Park,
    W Wimbledon
Parking: Meters in centre
    and several residents'
    parking schemes

For 11 months of the year peaceful, leafy Wimbledon is a self-possessed, splendid, south-west London suburb, enjoying the illusion of being a country town manqué with its charming old village centre, the vast common and the busy bustle of **The Broadway** end with its main shops and station, both main line and underground – plus, by the Millennium, trams. In the twelfth month, there's tennis.

It lasts for a mere fortnight, but for the duration of the international tennis tournament, Wimbledon's fame reaches global proportions. The press, royalty and the sport's superstars arrive, police re-direct the traffic, residents as far away as neighbouring Southfields find no-parking cones outside their houses or – if in unrestricted streets – that people have parked across their entrance drives. A general state somewhere between carnival and seige prevails. But, almost as soon as the last cries of 'Henman' have died away, the town – despite the film and theatre folk who have found year-round homes here – resumes its sedate, well-heeled, well-ordered SW19 life, a place with considerably more to offer than sport.

This London suburb is only 9 miles from Charing Cross, but maintains a rural charm with its 1,100-acre common which stretches to Putney Vale. It was much loved by William Wilberforce and by William Pitt, who said it saved his sanity. For centuries the common was used for cattle grazing, duelling, archery and rifle practice. Today it is patrolled by rangers and is a haven for joggers, horse riders, ramblers, golfers, dog walkers, cyclists and nature lovers – the trees and scrub harbour more than 60 species of birds as well as squirrels, badgers, rabbits, foxes, weasels and natterjack toads. One of its noted attractions is the restored Windmill, now a museum. Not surprisingly, houses bordering this semi-wooded expanse (mainly mansions built by Victorian merchants) and luxurious modern flats with views across the common, command the area's highest – indeed, astronomical – prices. Competing with the loyal, long-time locals (the place hops with local societies and residents' associations) are international families who look here for good-sized homes.

Town Centre/South Wimbledon

There is still a great divide in property prices between 'up the hill' (common and the original village) and 'down the hill' (**The Broadway**), which takes in the main shopping centre and station serving up both trains and the District line tube. But this 'lower' area, which also includes the Wimbledon Theatre (Victorian) and the famous Polka Children's Theatre, a hotel and several restaurants, has become increasingly fashionable and far from cheap.

This 'New' Wimbledon grew up around the railway in the 1850s, when housing was built for those working for carriage-folk up the hill. Today, this part of Wimbledon is home to commuters keen to be within walking distance of the station with its fast trains to Waterloo. Its heart has been largely redeveloped as a shopping/offices centre, with everything a small town needs. The smart (and being revamped) shopping mall – called, naturally, Centre Court – runs alongside the station. This houses a variety of shops and Tesco Metro are planning to develop the Old Town Hall area of the shopping centre. On the other side of the station is Wimbledon's own department store, Ely's, a Sainsbury's and sundry car parks; across **Worple Rd** is a large 18-month-old development of 1-bed (c. £150,000) and 2-bed (c. £245,000) flats, which includes a health club.

East of the town centre, **Queens Rd** has mainly solid older-type semis, 3/4-bed, with large gardens, and joins **Haydons Rd** to South Wimbledon. Running parallel, **King's Rd** contains 4-bed double-fronted Edwardian houses, some facing South Park Gardens. (This corner is referred to as South Park.) At the junction of **Trinity Rd** and **South Park Rd**, Nairn Court is 23 flats with parking spaces in secluded courtyard. Meade Park off **Haydons Rd** offers 1- and 2-bed flats and a few houses.

The streets in this corner between **The Broadway** and **Haydons Rd** – including **Evelyn Rd** and **Ashley Rd**, which are typical – have 3-bed terraced homes with small gardens (popular with young marrieds). Roads S of the busy **Broadway** are quiet, residential and good for first-time buyers as many have scope for improvement and are handy for the station – from whence, next year they will be able to reach Ikea by the Croydon tram line . . . In **Pelham Rd**, The Pelhams (on the site of the former school playground) now holds 64 1/2-bed flats. The red-brick school building itself was converted into 28 luxury 1- and 2-bed flats and two penthouses. Prices for 2-bed run at about £127,000. Around the corner in **Gladstone Rd**, the 33 recent flats in Gladstone Court go for £125,000-plus. In a quiet cul-de-sac off **Hartfield Rd** is Hartfield Court, with two large modern 5/6-bed, 2-bath houses with garage and garden.

Across the tracks, going up **Wimbledon Hill Rd** ('The Hill') from the station, five 1990s 3-bed, 2-bath houses with integral garages and gardens appeared in a quiet cul-de-sac in **St George's Rd**. Further up the hill, The Hollies has 2-bed, 2-bath flats which fetch £300,000. The road is lined with mansion flats – some '30s, some brand-new but in retro style. Aspen Lodge has flats starting at £200,000.

Alwynne Rd and **Compton Rd**, close to the library in the town centre, hold solid '30s semis with gardens. Wimbledon Girls' High School is on the left, and to the right are terraced town-houses. Higher left is **Draxmont Approach** (luxury balconied flats); right, **Belvedere Drive**, with large houses and the 'Bluegates' estate.

Wimbledon has, with the various town-centre developments, become a major south-west London shopping and business centre – this leads to yet more traffic.

Wimbledon Village

The **High St** begins at the top of the hill and runs through the village, still Georgian in feel. Quaint Dickensian shops on either side sell high fashion, luxury gifts and home-improvements and interior-designer services. There are many restaurants, wine bars and two historic pubs – the Rose & Crown, where the poet Swinburne drank, and the Dog & Fox; the village riding school is at the rear. Many charming artisan cottages – lovingly renovated, expensive, no room to park – lie off **Church Rd**, **Belvedere Square** and **Lancaster Place**. Opposite, tucked behind new shops, is **Haygarth Place** (24 red-brick, 4-bed terraced town-houses, underground car park; plus four original cottages, modernized, with car space). The entire courtyard is paved with red-brick. At the approach to the village, off **Belvedere Grove**, are three new 3-bed mews town-houses in former car park backing onto the National Westminster Bank.

Every inch of the village has been utilized: the last major site, behind historic Eagle House (1613), provided 14 luxury private houses – three of which front onto **Marryat Rd**. The Malt House and the cottage/coach house were also converted.

The Common

At the War Memorial a left turn takes you towards **Southside Common**: here pretty Victorian villas face out over the greenery in the first of a clutch of streets that run out into this corner of the common. **West Side Common** strikes out across the grass towards the furthest-flung, **North View**, past Chester House (Georgian), some 1930s houses and a cul-de-sac of council-built homes (most now, unsurprisingly, owner-occupied). Stately Cannizaro House is now a luxury hotel; its magnificent gardens are open to the public, with an open-air theatre in the old herb garden. Two 18th-century mansions, the Keir and Stamford House – converted nowadays into flats – both gaze out across the common. **North View** and **Camp View**, surrounded by common and golf course, are distinguished by tall red-brick Victorian houses. Along **Camp Rd**, popular **Eversley Park** (Octagon Developments) is set in a landscaped garden; nearby a charming cottage, once the dairy for Camp Farm, cost £650,000 last year. **West Place** completes the square; a handsome 1850s house here was £635,000.

From **Southside Common** long tree-lined roads run down to **The Ridgway**: homes in **Lingfield Rd**, **The Grange**, **Murray Rd**, **Lauriston Rd** and **Clifton Rd** are a mixture of styles, mostly Victorian; many reverse conversions here, with houses which had been poorly split into flats from the '50s onwards reverting to single-family homes, often still harbouring many original features. On the other hand, No 11 **The Grange** has been converted into eight prestige apartments with rear parking and mature garden. In **Lingfield Rd**, which runs parallel to the **High St**, Michael Shanly homes mirrored the Victorian style with Brackenbury Lodge, a double-fronted gabled house that contains six meticulously detailed flats. At **Woodhayes Rd** is **Peregrine Way**, a modern development of detached Colonial-style 4-bed houses set among mature trees.

This corner also provides some exceptionally large mansions: in the millions, if they come up for sale. All the coveted houses and flats here are within walking distance of King's College Boys' School. Opposite, across little **Crooked Billet** green, stand the delightful old Crooked Billet and Hand in Hand pubs, surrounded by former farm labourers' cottages which nowadays change hands for well over half a million.

Parkside

Return to **Parkside**, which runs along the E side of the common and leads, eventually, to Putney. With the common on your left, on the right is the enclave of premier roads

(Marryat Rd, Peek Crescent, Parkside Avenue, Parkside Gardens, Calonne Rd, Somerset Rd, Bathgate Rd and Burghley Rd). On the corner of Somerset Rd and Parkside, an enclave of late-'80s flats boast balconies, underground car park, electronic gates. To the E of this favoured group of roads, down the hill, is the All England Tennis Club. Parkside Hospital (private) and the residence of the Apostolic Nuncio (the Papal ambassador's official London home) are also to be found along Parkside. Near the Village end is an elegant conversion of a mansion into five flats, with electronic gates and video-screened entrance. Alfreton Close is an attractive cul-de-sac of Scandinavian-style family houses in mature woodland. Opposite, in Windmill Rd on the site of the Clock House (a former embassy), are 12 ultra-luxurious flats with underground parking and resident porter. Nearby Clockhouse Close, built on common land, has six luxury detached family houses.

The Putney/Wimbledon border, leafy but dominated by council flats (see the Southfields chapter), is the scene of the largest development in the area. 'Wimbledon Parkside', by Laing, is slowly transforming the vast, pleasantly hilly site of the old Southlands College at the junction of Parkside and Queensmere Rd. This has already resulted in Southlands Drive, a rather cramped enclave of Victorian-style houses behind smart railings; a woodland path has been laid out to one side, an unfortunate water feature graces the entrance road. Things then got better: a large, good-looking flats block emerged on the hillside behind these, with its grounds running up to the council houses that run along the leafy ridge; a refurbished listed building now provides flats . . . During 1998 some handsome architectural styling began to appear on the main part of the site. By winter 2-bed, 2-bath and 3-bed, 2-bath flats in the central, 6-storey apartment blocks, with living rooms in the octagonal corner turrets, were being marketed from £295,000 and £325,000 respectively. A clutch of town-houses (4-bed, 3-bath, 3 living plus study and garage) were from £465,000.

The Parkside neighbourhood includes an exotic Buddhist Temple (Calonne Rd), said to be the finest in Europe. Most of the houses in and around Parkside are large (some vast) detached turn-of-the century family homes, secluded and expensive. These, too, have seen several instances of clumsy flat conversions being removed, and the houses returning to single-family occupation. Oaklands Park in Bethgate Rd is a recent clutch of 13 £1 million-plus 5-bed houses.

Off Somerset Rd is a modern development, Oakfield Estate; Cedar Court is high-density town-houses and flats; Burghley House and Somerset House – tower blocks, some flats with views of the Centre Court – have lift, porterage and underground car park. All these roads suffer an annual invasion (30,000 visitors daily) during the Tennis Fortnight. Off Burghley Rd is St Mary's Parish Church (mentioned in the Domesday Book) leading into Church Rd and Welford Place, an exclusive private development of terraced town-houses with children's play-area, indoor swimming complex and sauna.

West Wimbledon

The Village is linked to West Wimbledon by The Ridgway, Wimbledon's oldest road, running parallel to Worple Rd (down the Hill). Sunnyside, to the left, has a row of delightful 2-bed cottages with long front gardens but no parking. Then Ridgway Place, with a group of houses on both sides built by the Haberdashers' Company in 1860. Further along is a 'villagy' area comprising Denmark Rd, Thornton Rd and Hillside. There is a row of small shops, two pubs and livery stables here. Berkeley Place and Ridgway Gardens are cul-de-sacs with large conversion flats. Edge Hill, with its many flats, is popular with Catholics because of nearby Wimbledon College RC Boys' School and Sacred Heart Church and Marie Reparatrice (a recently built retreat). Fourteen flats and two penthouses appeared on the site of the old chapel.

The Downs has purpose-built 1930s flats either side. Lower left is **Gordon Court**, 2-bed, 2-bath, balconied apartments. Marian Lodge is a 1997 scheme of 31 flats with underground parking and gym, sold at £190–370,000. On the site of St Teresa's Hospital, **South Ridge** is an enclave of 4-bedroom town-houses. The Ursuline Convent School for Girls and Hazlehurst Girls' School are neighbours. On corner of **The Downs** and **Worple Rd** is the smartly detailed Lantern Court: 23 flats (garage, video entryphone, 2-bath, open fireplaces in sitting rooms). **Lansdowne Rd**, a cul-de-sac with purpose-built and conversion flats, leads to **Cumberland Close** and **Lansdowne Close**; family town-houses, some with roof terraces with spectacular views. In the last few years a group of town-houses has been added to this corner, opposite the new hospice. **Arterberry Rd** has the Norwegian school and older-type family houses with spacious gardens. Chimneys Court, on the corner of **The Ridgeway**, has 10 2-bed, 2-bath flats and a 3-bed penthouse, all with underground parking. These sell for £250,000 upwards.

The line of **The Ridgeway** now continues as **Copse Hill**. The lodge to the area's 18th-century Big House (all that remains of Prospect Place) is now two £600,000-plus houses behind remote-controlled gates. On the common side, **Ernle Rd**, **Wool Rd** and **Dunstall Rd** have 4- and 5-bedroom detached houses with big gardens, some backing on to the golf course or woodland. Also off **Copse Hill** to the right is **Rokeby Place**, detached 4/5-bed family houses. On the left are two recently converted Victorian mansions, Birch Lodge (10 flats) and Possil House (four maisonettes). **Cedarland Terrace** consists of five Georgian-style town-houses with wide sweeping drives. Facing the Atkinson Morley Hospital is **Thurstan Rd**, off which **Grange Park Place**, with detached family houses backing on to the golf course, is built on the site of the old Cottage Hospital. **Drax Avenue** is a leafy private road of Sussex farmhouse-style and mock-Tudor 5-bed detached houses, some with galleried reception halls and oak staircases. Leading down to **Coombe Lane**, both sides of **Copse Hill** have solid 1930s 3/4-bed semis with garages, front and rear gardens. A small scheme of 3-bed 2-bath semis with red pavers is in **Cottenham Park Rd**. From here, turn left for Raynes Park.

Raynes Park

Raynes Park lies at the bottom of the hill from Wimbledon Common; it is split in half by the railway line. Once, this was little more than an undervalued backwater of Edwardian cottages, and purpose-built flats and maisonettes in wide, well-planned tree-lined streets. Today, it still retains a small-town atmosphere and is ripe for improvement. (Note the infallible signs: estate agents now refer to the northern side of the railway as 'West Wimbledon'.)

Worple Rd, a busy main thoroughfare with blocks of new flats and small hotels, leads back to Wimbledon town centre. Elinor Court, **Worple Rd**, has four architect-designed flats and a penthouse. Roads off to the right have good small semis with price differentials dictated by the closeness of the railway: in **Southdown Rd**, the side backing on to the elevated railway is considerably cheaper than the other side. On the left are very desirable family houses in roads such as **Thornton Hill**, **Denmark Avenue** and **Spencer Hill**. These climb the hill to **Ridgeway** (by which time they have joined Wimbledon Village); the higher up, the better the views.

Hollymount School (primary, mixed) is in leafy **Cambridge Rd**, together with 3/4-bed family houses. **Amity Grove** has mainly 3-bed Edwardian bay-window cottages. South of the line, off **Kingston Rd**, are 'the apostles': 12 long parallel cul-de-sacs running down to **Bushey Rd**; an inexpensive mix of 2-bed Edwardian terraced and semi-detached, some 1930s; street parking, tiny front gardens – the glimpse of the open green space of Prince George's playing-fields at the end of each cul-de-sac adds appeal. They are never on estate agents' books for long. The 'apostles' begin at **Gore Rd** and end at **Bronson Rd**, Wimbledon Chase. Bisecting **Bushey Rd**, **Grand Drive** has inter-war 3/4-bed semi and detached family houses, many with views over Prince George's playing-fields. To the E of the fields is a big sports and leisure centre. **Cannon Close**, one of several cul-de-sacs off **Grand Drive**, has 3-bed '30s semis, with front and rear gardens, street parking and access to common.

Merton Park

Merton's main claim to residential fame is the Merton Park Estate, one of the first garden suburbs, developed in the last three decades of the 19th century. John Innes, a millionaire property developer and horticulturalist (you've used the compost), laid out the estate. The area's green appearance survives.

The earliest streets to be built, in the 1870s, were **Dorset Rd**, **Mostyn Rd** and **Kingswood Rd**. Later in the century, larger houses of the Arts and Crafts and other styles were added. The details are reminiscent of Bedford Park, but the styles are more mixed. So, too is the scale: Innes decreed that cottages as well as solid villas be built. Development continued into Edwardian times, as the houses in **Melrose Rd** and **Watery Rd** show. Building went on until the '30s, with the opening of the tube at Morden providing a renewed spur. A little developing has gone on since: off **Dorset/Erridge Rds**, in a quiet cul-de-sac, are the 14 3/4-bed detached houses and a bungalow of Hamilton Gate. Lynwood Place, four brand-new £200,000 town-houses, are off **Henfield Rd**. Next year **Dorset Rd** will find itself backing not onto railway tracks but the new tram line: will this be more peaceful?

Wimbledon Park

The rolling, leafy roads of Wimbledon Park contain some extremely large, discreet and enviable houses, in a corner that centres on the eponymous park. This, however, boasts putting, cricket, bowling and large lake, with fishing and water sports – and, of course, tennis. The All England Club is here, but except for That Fortnight the splendidly hilly roads that spread out S of the park are a peaceful and select neighbourhood. On a map the street pattern betrays the spacious layout of roads like **Home Park Rd**, **Arthur Rd**, **Leopold Rd**, and the large gardens. In this corner stood Wimbledon's original manor house and its successors – hence the park, whose layout is attributed to Capability Brown. It was indeed, as the road name betrays, the home park.

From Merton Park, take the main road to **Haydons Rd/Durnsford Rd**. First, between **Durnsford Rd** and the tracks, the roads N of Wimbledon Park station (District line) such as **Melrose Avenue**, **Braemar Avenue**, **Normanton Avenue** and **Ashen Grove** are a continuation of the Southfields 'grid' to the N (see chapter) over the borough and postcode boundaries. These are mainly long terraces of neat, solid 2/3-bed late-Victorian/Edwardian houses, with rear gardens and street parking; they are snapped up because they are relatively cheap (bordering Wandsworth), convenient (the tube) and close to the park and schools. By the tube station is a varied and useful row of shops including post office, library and late-night Co-op.

Arthur Rd winds uphill all the way from **Durnsford Rd** via the station to Wimbledon Village, becoming more and more tree-lined, with large, detached houses in secluded grounds (one might have thought the town hall could have resisted the naming of **Camelot Close**, on the left; the more so since its 4/5-bed double-fronted detacheds are in Georgian style).

Curving N from **Arthur Rd**, **Home Park Rd** houses gaze out over Wimbledon Park with its lake and the Tennis Club. In the angle of **Leopold Rd/Lake Rd** is a clutch of schools: Ricards Lodge (girls' high), and two good state schools, Park House middle school and Bishop Gilpin primary, which has a good record for its girls going on to the local high schools. **Vineyard Hill Rd**, **Dora Rd** and **Kenilworth Avenue** have terraces of 3/4-bedroomed family houses.

W

Transport Tubes: Wimbledon, Wimbledon Park (zone 3, District); South Wimbledon (zone 3, Northern). From Wimbledon: Oxford Circus 35 min (1 change), City 35 min, Heathrow 1 hr (1 change). Trains: Wimbledon to Waterloo 12 min; others see map. Tramlink from Wimbledon via Merton Park to Croydon (change for Gatwick) planned to open 2000.

Convenient for Common, Heathrow and Gatwick Airports, tennis. Miles from centre: 7.

Schools Merton Education Authority: Wimbledon College RC (b), Ursuline Convent School (g), Rutlish School (b). Private: Norwegian School, Wimbledon High (g), Hazelhurst School (g), Ricards Lodge (g), King's College School (b).

SALES

Flats	S	1B	2B	3B	4B	5B
Average prices	45–90	75–130	100–250	100–300+	–	–
Houses	2B	3B	4B	5B	6/7B	8B
Average prices	125–250	150–350+	200–500+	250–1M+	400–2M+	–

RENTAL

Flats	S	1B	2B	3B	4B	5B
Average prices	500–800	650–1000	900–1800	1200–2200	1400–3000	–
Houses	2B	3B	4B	5B	6/7B	8B
Average prices	1000–1700	1250–2600	1500–4200	1700–4400+	–	–

The properties Homes (and prices) range from 3-bed terraces near town centre ('down the Hill') via the cottages of the village to the swimming-pooled mansions near the common ('up the Hill'). Also flat conversions, Edwardian villas, '30s semis, new town-houses, flats. Further Victorian/Edwardian charm in Raynes and Merton Parks.

The market Something for everyone – at a price. Quick routes for commuters, good schools for families. Locals stay loyal and move within area: competition, therefore, for big family homes. Overseas buyers favour Wimbledon – as do investors, especially in the village and West Wimbledon. Once here, you're hooked, whether heading up to a large family house or trading down to a smart flat. Local searches: 4–6 weeks.

Among those estate agents active in this area are:
- Ellisons
- Hawes & Co
- Kinleigh Folkard & Hayward
- Lauristons
- Bairstow Eves
- Chestertons
- G A Property Services
- Hamptons
- John D Wood & Co
- Knight Frank
- Ludlow Thompson
- Robert Holmes & Co
- Quinton Scott
- Woolwich
- Foxtons*

further details: see advertisers' index on p633

W

Advertisers' Index

Index

London Property Guide – Property Information Request

To property developer or estate agent:

Name: ....
Address: ....
....
....

Phone number: ....

Please send me details of your properties.
My requirements are: ....
....
....
....
....
....
....
....
....
....
....

(Type of property required: eg detached/semi-
detached/terrace/mews/flat/purchase or to let plus other details)

Area: ....

Approximate value: ....

Please cut out and send to property developer or estate agent
(see page 633 for list of advertisers).

Notes

THE **new**
London Property Guide '99/00

The essential handbook for buying, selling, letting and renting homes in the capital

'Ridiculously useful' *The Guardian*
'Essential for homebuyers who want the inside track' Jeremy Gates, *Daily Express*

A guiding light in the bewildering property scene, this invaluable book:

- **reveals everything you need to know about today's housing market in London**
  - unique London-wide price charts – how much buys you what where
  - new rail lines, new tubes – which places gain and which lose out
  - council tax – which areas get the best deal
  - schools – which boroughs top the league tables

- **profiles 480 neighbourhoods, from Acton to Wimbledon**
  - succinct, colourful street-by-street character analysis
  - assessment of local transport and services
  - map of each area
  - property price bands

- **cuts through the jargon to explain buying, selling, renting and letting in a straightforward, accessible way**
  - how to choose the right mortgage
  - freehold, leasehold and tenancy laws explained
  - dealing with planners and surveyors
  - investing in property

ISBN 1-84000-184-4

9 781840 001846

£12.99